Lectures
in
SYSTEMATIC
THEOLOGY

Lectures
in
SYSTEMATIC
THEOLOGY

Robert L. Dabney

ZONDERVAN PUBLISHING HOUSE
OF THE ZONDERVAN CORPORATION
GRAND RAPIDS, MICHIGAN 49506

LECTURES IN SYSTEMATIC THEOLOGY

First published in 1878

Zondervan Reprint Edition © 1972 by Zondervan Publishing House, Grand Rapids, Michigan

Third printing   1976

Library of Congress Catalog Card Number 73-171200

Printed in the United States of America

CONTENTS

NOTE TO THE READER.

(Accompanying the First Edition.)

AD LECTOREM.—Our preceptor in Theology having given to the classes the course of lectures which he had delivered to previous ones, to be used by us in any manner we found most convenient for our assistance in this study, we have printed them in this form for private circulation among ourselves and our predecessors and successors in the Seminary. Our reasons for doing so are the following : We found these lectures useful, so far as we had proceeded, in assisting our comprehension of the text-books. As Dr. Dabney announced a change in the method of his instruction, in which he would cease to deliver the lectures orally, from his chair; and placed them in MS. at the disposal of the students, we desired to continue to avail ourselves of their assistance. To provide ourselves with copies, and to extend their use to subsequent fellow-students, the most convenient and obvious mode was to print them. This has been done at the expense of the students of 1878; and a small number of copies, beyond our own need, has been struck off.

A few explanations may be necessary for the understanding of the method of study, of which these notes form a part. The system consists of recitations on lessons from text-books, chiefly the Confession of Faith and Turrettin's Elenctic Theology, oral instructions and explanations of the Professor, the preparation and reading of Theses by the students upon the topics under discussion, and finally, review recitations upon the whole. The design is to combine, as far as may be, the assistance of the living teacher with the cultivation of the powers of memory, comparison, judgment, reasoning and expression, by the researches of the students themselves, and to fix the knowledge acquired by repeated views of it. When a "head" of divinity is approached, the first step which our professor takes, is to propound to us, upon the black-board, a short, comprehensive *syllabus* of its discussion, in the form of questions; the whole prefaced by a suitable lesson in the text-book. Our first business is to master and recite this lesson. Having thus gotten, from our standard author, a trustworthy outline of the discussion, we proceed next to investigate the same subject, as time allows, in other writers, both friendly and hostile, preliminary to the composition of a thesis. It is to guide this research, that the *syllabus*, with its numerous references to books, has been given us. These have been carefully selected by the Professor, so as to direct to the ablest and most thorough accessible authors, who defend and impugn the truth. The references may, in many cases, be far more numerous than any Seminary-student can possibly read, at the time, with the duties of the other departments upon his hands. To guide his selection, therefore, the most important authority is named first, under each question, [it may be from our text-book or from some other], then the next in value, and last, those others which the student may consult with profit at his greater leisure. The *syllabus* with its references we find one of the most valuable features of our course; it guides not only our first investigations, but those of subsequent years, when the exigencies of our pastoral work may require us to return and make a wider research into the same subject. It directs our inquiries intelligently, and rescues us from the drudgery of wading through masses of literary rubbish to find the opinions of the really influential minds, by giving us some of the experience of one older than ourselves, whose duty it has been to examine many books upon theology and its kindred sciences.

NOTE TO THE READER.

After the results of our own research have been presented, it has been Dr. Dabney's usage to declare his own view of the whole subject; and these lectures form the mass of what is printed below. They take the form therefore of *resumés* of the discussion already seen in the books; oftentimes, reciting in plainer or fresher shape even the arguments of the text-book itself, when the previous examination has revealed the fact that the class have had difficulty in grasping them, and often reproducing the views to which the other references of the *syllabus* had already directed us. It needs hardly to be added, that the Professor of course made no pretense of originality, save in the mode of connecting, harmonizing, or refuting some of the statements passed in review. Indeed, it seemed ever to be his aim to show us how to get for ourselves, in advance of his help, all the things to which in his final lecture he assisted us. These lectures henceforth in the hands of the classes, will take the place of a subordinate text-book, along with the others; and the time formerly devoted to their oral delivery will be applied to giving us the fruits of other researches in advance of the existing course.

It only remains that we indicate the order of subjects. This is chiefly that observed in the Confession of Faith. But the course begins with Natural Theology, which is then followed by a brief review of the doctrines of psychology and ethicks, which are most involved in the study of theology. This being done, the lectures proceed to revealed theology, assuming, as a postulate established by another department in the Seminary, the inspiration and infallibility of the Scriptures.

The form in which the lectures are presented to our comrades is dictated by the necessity of having them issued from the press weekly, in order to meet our immediate wants in the progress of the course. It need only be said in conclusion that this printing is done by Dr. Dabney's consent.   **COMMITTEE OF PRINTING.**

ADDITIONAL NOTE TO THE READER

The Committee of Publication found itself, this spring, with only one copy of Dabney's Theology on hand, and that the office copy; and this in the face of a growing demand for the book.

Knowing that questions in the syllabi at the heads of the lectures had not, in every case, been changed to correspond with changes introduced into the lectures by Dr. Dabney himself in his successive revisions, and knowing also that the book in all recent reprints had been marred by numerous typographical errors and by occasional misuse of words, the Committee asked Dr. Thos. Cary Johnson, long a user of Dr. Dabney's works, to point out such needed corrections as could be introduced into the printing plates without too much cost. This he has done with very great care and for this service we know every student of this work will be duly grateful.

It is believed that such changes as have been effected will make the book better suited as a text-book, without worsting either the vigor or the substance of the teaching.

PRESBYTERIAN COMMITTEE OF PUBLICATION.

Richmond, Va.,
    July, 1927.

PREFACE TO THE SECOND EDITION.

THE note *Ad Lectorem*, prefixed by the Students to the first edition which they printed, sufficiently explains the origin and nature of this course of Theology. The experience of several years in teaching it, has disclosed at once its utility and its defects. Much labor has been devoted to the removal of the latter, and to additional research upon every important point of discussion. The syllabus has been enriched with a great number of references. Two hundred and sixty pages of new matter have been added. The book is attended with full Table of Contents and Index; fitting it for reference. A multitude of typographical errors have been removed; and the larger type and better material, it is trusted, will concur to make the book not only more sightly, but more durable and useful.

The main design, next to the establishment of Divine Truth, has been to furnish students in divinity, pastors, and intelligent lay-Christians, a view of the whole field of Christian theology, without swelling the work to a size too unwieldy and costly for the purposes of instruction. Every head of divinity has received at least brief attention. The discussion is usually compact. The reader is requested to bear in mind, that the work is only styled "Syllabus and Notes" of a course in theology. The full expansion or exhaustive illustration of topics has not been promised. Hence unless the reader has already a knowledge of these topics derived from copious previous study, he should not expect to master these discussions by a cursory reading. He is candidly advertised that many parts will remain but partially appreciated, unless he shall find himself willing either to read enough of the authorities referred to in the Syllabus, to place him at the proper point of view; or else to ponder the outline of the arguments by the efforts of mature and vigorous thought for himself, and thus fill out the full body of discussion.

The work is now humbly offered again to the people of God, in the hope that it may assist to establish them in the old and orthodox doctrines which have been the power and glory of the Reformed Churches.

ROBERT L. DABNEY.

Union Theo. Seminary, Va., Aug. 15th, 1878.

PREFACE
TO 1972 EDITION

The Christian world will be greatly indebted to the Zondervan Publishing House for re-issuing the major work on Systematic Theology by Robert Lewis Dabney. Dabney was a Southern Presbyterian who lived during the Nineteenth Century. Archibald Alexander, the founder of Princeton Seminary, said that he was "the best teacher of theology in the United States, if not in the world." His biographer, Thomas Carey Johnson, said of him in *The Life and Letters of Robert Lewis Dabney* (1903) that he was entitled "to the first place among the theological thinkers and writers of his century." As a man who thus enjoyed such a reputation among his own contemporaries, it is no wonder that Dabney was considered the single most influential man in the Southern Presbyterian Church during the height of his ministry, 1865 through 1895.

Dabney was a native of Virginia, being born in Louisa County in 1820 of English and French Huguenot descent. He was educated at Hampden Sydney College, Virginia, the University of Virginia, and Union Theological Seminary at Hampden Sydney; he was ordained to the ministry of the Presbyterian Church in 1847. He spent his first six years of ministerial life in the historic old Tinkling Springs Church of the valley of Virginia. In 1853 he was called to the chair of Ecclesiastical History and Polity at Union Seminary. In 1859 he transferred to the Department of Systematic Theology. In 1860 he received a call to join the Princeton Theological Seminary faculty. Due to his allegiance to the South, he felt he could not go North at that time. During the War Between the States, he served briefly as a chaplain in the Confederate Army, and later as Chief of Staff to General T. J. (Stonewall) Jackson, with the rank of Major. He served under Jackson during the rigorous valley campaign of 1862. Jackson said of him that he was the most efficient officer that he knew. After Jackson's death in May, 1863, Dabney was requested by Mrs. Jackson to prepare a biography of the General. This was published in 1866 under the title *The Life and Campaigns of Lieutenant General Thomas J. Jackson (Stonewall Jackson)*. It is considered to be one of the best personal biographies of General Jackson, and remains as a major literary production of Robert L. Dabney.

Following the war, Dabney returned to Union Seminary and continued to teach in the field of Systematic Theology there until 1883. He then moved to Texas, where he became professor on the faculty of the young University of Texas in the chair of Mental and Moral Philosophy and Political Economy. He taught there from 1883 to 1894. During this same time, he together with the Reverend Robert K. Smoot established the Austin School of Theology, which was later to become Austin Presbyterian Theological Seminary. He died at Victoria, Texas, on January 3, 1898, and was buried at Hampden Sydney, Virginia.

Dabney was first of all a teacher. His principle work was in the classroom, where he set forth with intensity and vigor the principles of the Reformed faith. He was also prolific as a writer producing a number of articles in various publications. In addition to the life of Jackson, he wrote *A Defense of Virginia (and through her of the South) in the recent and pending contests against the sectional party* (1867). In 1870 he produced a book on preaching entitled *Sacred Rhetoric*. The present work was first published by Dabney's students under the title *Syllabus and Notes of the Course of Systematic and Polemic Theology taught in Union Theological Seminary,*

Virginia (1878). This work was revised by the author and reissued later in 1878. It has seen six editions, the last being 1927. He also wrote two volumes in the field of philosophy, *The Sensualistic Philosophy of the Nineteenth Century (1875)* and *Practical Philosophy (1896)*.

The present volume was first published by Dabney's students, with his permission. He later went over it and brought it into its present form. This volume reflects his rather unique way of teaching theology. Thomas Carey Johnson, his biographer, describes it thus: "Two class-meetings were devoted to each topic, separated by the interval of two days. At the close of the second meeting, the class found on the blackboard a syllabus of the topic next to be taken up. The leading points in the topic were stated in the form of questions, and authors treating that particular point. The most important reference was written first, the next most important second, etc., and the students were urged to read as many of them as they could. The textbook was Turretin in Latin. At the next meeting he held a recitation on Turretin, covering ten or twelve pages. The students were required, during the second interval of two days, to write, each one, his own thesis upon the topic. . . . The second hour of class meeting he spent in delivering to the class his own lectures on the same topic. These syllabi and lectures composed the main part of his work on theology" (p. 196).

In the original note to the readers it was indicated that the lectures assumed "as a postulate established by another department in the seminary, the inspiration and infallibility of the Scriptures." The general order of material covered is that of the *Westminster Confession of Faith*. It is regrettable that we do not have Dabney's own development of the doctrine of inspiration of Scripture. We find on page 144 his position stated without equivocation, "I hold the Scriptures to be, in all its parts, of plenary inspiration . . . this having been settled, we may proceed to assume them as inspired and infallible."

This work remained the textbook in Systematic Theology at Union Seminary in Virginia until 1930. It is a fresh and masterful exposition of the Reformed faith. The reader will not find simply the restating of old truths, but the amplification of problems that are sometimes felt concerning these truths. This work is worthy of study by all who wish to understand the Gospel and its implications more fully.

Dabney's influence was most strongly felt in the Southern Presbyterian circles. This volume, as we have already noted, became the textbook of Systematic Theology in the Southern seminaries. He was recognized by Auguste Lecerf of France in his *Introduction to Reformed Dogmatics*, and by Herman Bavinck of the Netherlands in his *Gereformeerde Dogmatiek* as being among America's outstanding theologians.

At a time when the church is certainly in need of a clear voice with regard to her theology, I can think of no finer work than that of Robert L. Dabney to be reproduced and sent forth for our generation. May it be that this republication of Dabney's *Systematic Theology* will bring fresh interest in the study and propagation of the Reformed faith.

MORTON H. SMITH
Professor of Systematic Theology
Reformed Theological Seminary
Jackson, Mississippi

July 20, 1971

Lectures
in
SYSTEMATIC
THEOLOGY

NATURAL THEOLOGY.

LECTURE I.

PREFATORY, AND EXISTENCE OF GOD.

IT is justly said: Every science should begin by defining its terms, in order to shun verbal fallacies. The word Theology,
Theology, What? ($\Theta\varepsilon o\upsilon\ \lambda o\gamma o\varsigma$), has undergone peculiar mutations in the history of science. The Greeks often used it for their theories of theogony and cosmogony. Aristotle uses it in a more general form, as equivalent to all metaphysics; dividing theoretical philosophy into physical, mathematical, and theological. Many of the early Christian fathers used it in the restricted sense of the doctrine of Christ's divinity: (SCIL. $I\omega\alpha\nu\nu\eta\varsigma\ \acute{o}\ \Theta\varepsilon o\lambda o\gamma o\varsigma$). But now it has come to be used commonly, to describe the whole science of God's being and nature, and relations to the creature. The name is appropriate: "Science of God." Th. Aquinas: *"Theologia a Deo docetur, Deum docet, ad Deum ducit,"* God its author, its subject, its end.

The distribution of Theology into didactic, polemic, and
Its Divisions. practical, is sufficiently known. Now, all didactic inculcation of truth is indirect refutation of the opposite error. Polemic Theology has been defined as direct refutation of error. The advantage of this

5

has been supposed to be, that the way for easiest and most thorough refutation is to systematize the error, with reference to its first principle, or πρῶτον ψευδος But the attempt to form a science of polemics, different from Didactic Theology fails; because error never has true method. Confusion is its characteristic. The system of discussion, formed on its false method, cannot be scientific. Hence, separate treatises on polemics have usually slidden into the methods of didactics; or they have been confused. Again: Indirect refutation is more effectual than direct. There is therefore, in this course, no separate polemic; but what is said against errors is divided between the historical and didactic.

Theology is divided into natural and revealed, according to the sources of our knowledge of it; from *Is there a Natural Theology?* natural reason; from revelation. What is *science?* Knowledge demonstrated and methodized. That there is a science of Natural Theology, of at least some certain and connected propositions, although limited, and insufficient for salvation at best, is well argued from Scripture, e. g. Ps. xix : 1–7. Acts xiv : 15; or xvii : 23. Rom. i : 19; ii : 14, &c.; and from the fact that nearly all heathens have religious ideas and rites of worship. Not that religious ideas are innate: but the capacity to establish some such ideas, from natural data, is innate. Consider further : Is not this implied in man's capacity to receive a revealed theology? Does revelation demonstrate God's existence; or assume it? Does it rest the first truths on pure dogmatism, or on evidence which man apprehends? The latter; and then man is assumed to have some natural capacity for such apprehension. But if nature reflects any light concerning God, (as Scripture asserts), then man is capable of deriving some theology from nature.

Some old divines were wont to deny that there was any science of Natural Theology, and to say *Why Denied?* that without revelation, man would not naturally learn its first truth. They attribute the grains of truth, mixed with the various polytheisms to the remnants of tradition descending from Noah's family. They urge that some secluded tribes, Hottentots, Australians, have no religious ideas; that some men are sincere atheists after reflection; and that there is the wildest variety, yea contradiction, between the different schools of heathens. These divines' seem to fear lest, by granting a Natural Theology, they should grant too much to natural reason; a fear ungrounded and extreme. They are in danger of a worse consequence; reducing man's capacity for receiving divine verities so low, that the rational sceptic will be able to turn upon them and say: "Then by so inept a creature, the guarantees of a true revelation cannot be certainly apprehended."

To reply more in detail; I grant much influence to prim-
Proofs. eval traditions, (a subject of great interest
learnedly discussed in Theo. Gale's Court
of the Gentiles). But that so inconstant a cause is able
to perpetuate in men these fixed convictions of the invisible, shows in man a natural religious capacity. That there
have been atheistic persons and tribes, is inconclusive. Some
tribes deduce no science of geometry, statics, or even numbers; but this does not prove man non-logical. Some profess to disbelieve axioms, as Hume that of causation; but this
is far from proving man incapable of a natural science of induction. Besides, the atheism of these tribes is doubtful; savages
are shrewd, suspicious, and fond of befooling inquisitive strangers by assumed stupidity. And last: the differences of Natural
theology among polytheists are a diversity in unity; all involve
the prime truths; a single first cause, responsibility, guilt, a future life, future rewards and punishments.

2. The first truth of theology is the existence of God.
Existence of God: The first question which meets us is: How
How Known? man learns the existence of God? Dr.
Charles Hodge [Systematic Theology, part
I chapter I.] states and argues that the knowledge of
it is "innate." This assertion he explains by saying that it is
"intuitive." It must be understood, however, that he also employs this term in a sense of his own. With him, any truth is
intuitive, which is immediately perceived by the mind. He dis-
sents from the customary definition of philosophers, [as Sir W.
Hamilton] which requires simplicity, or primariness, as the trait
of an intuitive judgment, He explains himself by saying, that
to Newton, all the theorems of Euclid's first book were as immediately seen as the axioms; and therefore, to him, intuitions.
We shall see, in a subsequent lecture, the dangers of this view. I
hold, with the current of philosophers, that an intuitive truth is
[a] one that is seen true without any premise, [b] so seen by all
minds which comprehend its terms, [c] necessarily seen. Strictly,
it cannot be said, that any intuitive truth is *innate*. The power
of perceiving it is innate. The explanation of the case of Newton and of similiar ones, is easy: To his vigorous mind, the
step from an intuitive premise to a near conclusion, was so prompt
and easy as to attract no attention. Yet, *the step was taken.*
When Dr. Hodge calls men's knowledge that there is a God "*innate,*" i. e., "intuitive," his mistake is in confounding a single,
short, clear step of deduction, made by common sense, with an
intuition. He, very properly, exalts the ethical evidence into
the chief place. But the amount of it is this: "The sentiment of responsibility (which is immediate) is intuitive." This
implies an Obligator. True. But what is the evolution of this
implication, save (a short, easy, and obvious step of) reasoning?

Divines and Christian philosophers, in the attempt to explain the belief in a God, which all men have, as a rational process, have resolved it into the one or the other of two modes of argument, the *a priori* and *a posteriori*. The latter infers a God by reasoning backwards from effects to cause. The former should accordingly mean reasoning downwards from cause to effect; the meaning attached to the phrase by Aristotle and his followers. But now the term *a priori* reasoning is used, in this connection, to denote a conclusion gained without the aid of experience, from the primary judgments, and especially, the attempt to infer the truth of a notion, directly from its nature or condition in the mind.

It appears to be common among recent writers (as Dick,
A Priori Argument. Chalmers' Natural Theology), to charge Dr.
What, and by Whom Samuel Clarke as the chief asserter of the
Urged?   *a priori* argument among Englishmen. This
is erroneous. It may be more correctly said to have been first intimated by Epicurus (whose atomic theory excluded the *a posteriori* argument;) as appears from a curious passage in *Cicero, de natura Deorum*, Lib. I. c. 16. It was more accurately stated by the celebrated Des Cartes in his meditations ; and naturalized to the English mind rather by Bishop Stillingfleet than by Dr. Clarke. The student may find a very distinct statement of it in the *Origines Sacræ* of the former, book III, chapter 1, § 14: while Dr. Clarke, § 8 of his Discourse, expressly says that the personal intelligence of God must be proved *a posteriori*, and not *a priori*. But Des Cartes having founded his psychology on the two positions: 1st. *Cogito; ergo sum ;* and 2nd. The *Ego* is spirit, not matter; proceeds to ask: Among all the ideas in the consciousness, how shall the true be distinguished from the false, seeing all are obviously not consistent? As to primary ideas, his answer is; by the clearness with which they commend themselves to our consciousness as immediate truths. Now, among our ideas, no other is so clear and unique as that of a first Cause, eternal and infinite. Hence we may immediately accept it as consciously true. Moreover, that we have this idea of a God, proves there must be a God ; because were there none, the rise of His idea in our thought could not be accounted for; just as the idea of triangles implies the existence of some triangle. Now the *a priori* argument of Stillingfleet is but a specific application of Des Cartes' method. We find, says he, that in thinking of a God we must think Him as eternal, self-existent, and necessarily existent. But since we indisputably do think a God, it is impossible but that God is. Since necessary existence is unavoidably involved in our idea of a God, therefore His existence must necessarily be granted.

Now surely this process is not necessarily inconclusive.
                because it is *a priori*; there are processes,
    Its Defect.   in which we validly determine the truth

of a notion by simple inspection of its contents and conditions. But the defect of Stillingfleet's reasoning is, that it does not give the correct account of our thought. If the student will inspect the two propositions, which form an enthymeme, he will see that the conclusion depends on this assumption, as its major premise: That we can have no idea in our consciousness, for which there is not an answering objective reality. (This is, obviously, the assumed major ; because without it the ethymeme can only contain the conclusion, that God, if there is one, necessarily exists.) But that major premise is, notoriously, not universally true.

Now, instead of saying that Dr. Clarke's method, in the Discourse of the Being, &c., of God, 3. Argument of Dr. S. Clarke. is the *a priori*, it is more correct to say (with Hamilton's Reid) that it is an *a posteriori* argument, or with Kant, *Cosmological*, inferring the existence of God from His effects; but disfigured at one or two points by useless Cartesian elements. His first position is: Since something now exists, something has existed from eternity. This, you will find, is the starting point of the argument, with all reasoners ; and it is solid. For, if at any time in the past eternity, there had been absolutely nothing, since nothing cannot be a cause of existence, time and space must have remained forever blank of existence. Hence, 2d., argues Dr. Clarke : there has been, from eternity, some immutable and independent Being: because an eternal succession of dependent beings, without independent first cause, is impossible. 3d. This Being, as independent eternally, must be self-existent, that is, necessarily existing. For its eternal independence shows that the spring, or causative source of its existence, could not be outside of itself; it is therefore within itself forever. But the only true idea of such self-existence is, that the idea of its non-existence would be an express contradiction. And here, Dr. Clarke very needlessly adds : our notion that the existence is necessary, proves that it cannot but exist. He reasons also : our conceptions of infinite time and infinite space are necessary: we cannot but think them. But they are not substance : they are only modes of substance. Unless some substance exists of which they are modes, they cannot exist, and so, would not be thought. Hence, there must be an infinite and eternal substance. 4th. The substance of this Being is not comprehensible by us : but this does not make the evidence of its existence less certain. For, 5th. Several of its attributes are demonstrable; as that it must be, 6th, Infinite and omnipresent; 7th, that it must be One, and 8th, that it must be intelligent and free, &c. The conclusion is, that this Being must be Creator and God, unless the universe can itself fulfil the conditions of eternity, necessary self-existence, infinitude, and intelligence and free choice. This is Pantheism: which he shows cannot be true.

On his argument as a whole, I remark, that it is in the main valid, because it is in the main *a posteriori*: it appeals to the intuitive judgment of cause, to infer from finite effects an infinite first cause. The Cartesian features attached to the 3d proposition are an excrescence; but we may remove them, and leave the chain adamantine. We will prune them away, not for the reasons urged by Dr. Chalmers, which are in several particulars as invalid as Dr. Clarke ; but for the reason already explained on pages 8 and 9.   I only add, it seems to argue that time and space can only be conceived by us as modes of substance; and therefore infinite and eternal substance must exist. The truth here is: that we cannot conceive of finite substance or events, without placing it in time and space ; a different proposition from Dr. Clarke's.

Valid, because a posteriori.

I think we have the metaphysical argument for the being of a God, stated in a method free from these objections, by the great Puritan divine, John Howe. He flourished about ·650, A. D., and prior to Dr. Clarke. See his Living Temple, chapter II. He begins thus: 1. Since we now exist, something has existed from eternity.   2. Hence, at least, some uncaused Being, for the eternal has nothing prior to it.   3. Hence some independent Being.   4. Hence that Being exists necessarily; for its independent, eternal, inward spring of existence cannot be conceived as possibly at any time inoperative.   5. This Being must be self-active; active, because, if other beings did not spring from its action, they must all be eternal, and so independent, and necessary, which things are impossible for beings variously organized and changeable ; and self-active, because in eternity nothing was before Him to prompt His action.   6. This Being is living; for self-prompted activity is our very idea of life.   7. He is of boundless intelligence, power, freedom, &c.

Howe's Demonstration.

This argument is in all parts well knit. But it is obviously *a posteriori ;* for all depends from a simple deduction, from a universe of effects, back to their cause ; and in the same way are inferred the properties of that cause. The only place where the argument needs completion, is at the fifth step. So far forth, the proof is perfect, that some eternal, uncaused, necessary Being exists. But how do we prove that this One created all other Beings? The answer is : these others must all be either eternal or temporal. May it be,all are eternal and one ? then all are uncaused, independent, self-existent, and necessary. This, we shall see, is Pantheism. If the rest are temporal, then they were all caused, but by what? Either by the one uncaused, eternal Being; or by other similar temporal beings generating them. But the latter is the theory of an infinite, independent series of finite organisms, each one dependent

What needed to complete it?

When, therefore, we shall have stopped these two breaches, by refuting Pantheism and the hypothesis of infinite series, the demonstration will be perfect.

Kant has selected this cosmological argument, as one
Cavil of Kant. of his "antinomies," illustrating the invalidity of the *a priori* reason, when applied beyond empirical things to the transcendental and absolute. His objection to its validity seems to amount to this: That the proposition "Nothing can exist without a cause out of itself," cannot be absolute: For if it were, then a cause must be assigned for the First Cause himself.

But let us give the intuition in more accurate form : "Nothing can begin to exist, without a cause out of itself." Kant's cavil has now disappeared, as a moment's consideration will show. The necessary step of the reason from the created things up to a creator, is now correctly explained. "Every effect must have a cause." True. An effect is an existence or phenomenon which has a beginning. Such, obviously, is each created thing. Hence, it must have proceeded from a cause which had no beginning, i. e., a God. Moreover: I cannot too early utter my protest against Kant's theory, that our regulative, intuitive principles of reason are merely suggestive, (while imperative,) and have no objective validity. Were this true, our whole intelligence would be a delusion. On the other hand, every law of thought is also a law of existence and of reality. Knowledge of this fact is original with every mind when it begins to think, is as intuitive as any other principle of the reason, and is an absolutely necessary condition of all other knowledge. Moreover : the whole train of man's *a posteriori* knowledge is a continual demonstration of this principle, proving its trustworthiness by the perfect correspondence between our subjective intuitions and empirical truths.

Now Platonism held that all substance is uncaused and
Platonic Scheme. eternal, as to its being. All finite, rational spirits, said this theology, are emanations of To $^{\prime\prime}ON$, the eternal intelligence ; and all matter has been from eternity, as inert, passive chaotic $^{a}Y\lambda\eta$. Platonism referred all organization, all fashioning (the only creation it admitted), all change, however either directly or indirectly, to the intelligent First Cause. This scheme does not seem very easily refuted by natural reason. Let it be urged that the very notion of the First Cause implies its singleness ; and, more solidly, that the unity of plan and working seen in nature, points to only one, single, ultimate cause ; Plato could reply that he made only one First Cause, To $^{\prime\prime}ON$, for $\dot{v}\lambda\eta$ is inert, and only the recipient of causation. Let that rule be urged, which Hamilton calls his 'law of parcimony,' that hypotheses must include nothing more than is necessary to account for effects : Plato could say : No : the reason as much demands the supposition of a material pre-existing, as of an

almighty Workman; for even omnipotence cannot work, with nothing to work on. Indeed, so far as I know, all human systems, Plato's, Epicurus,' Zeno's, Pythagoras,' the Peripatetic, had this common feature; that it is self-evident, substance cannot rise out of *nihil* into *esse;* that *ex nihilo nihil fit.* And we shall see how obstinate is the tendency of philosophy to relapse to this maxim, in the instances of Spinoza's Pantheism, and Kant's and Hamilton's theory of causation. Indeed it may be doubted whether the human mind, unaided by revelation, would ever have advanced farther than this. It was from an accurate knowledge of the history of philosophy, that the apostle declared, (Hebrews xi : 3,) the doctrine of an almighty creation out of nothing is one of pure faith.

Dr. Clarke, as you saw, does indeed attempt a rational argument that the eternity of matter is impossible. The eternal must be necessary; hence an eternal cause must necessarily be. So, that which can possibly be thought as existing and yet not necessary, cannot be eternal. Such is his logic. I think inspection will show you a double defect. The first enthymeme, as we saw (p. 8) is not conclusive; and the second, even if the first were true, would be only inferring the converse; which is not necessarily conclusive.

Can the Platonic Doctrine of the Eternity of all Substances be Refuted by Reason?

Howe states a more plausible argument, at which Dr. Clarke also glances. Were matter eternal, it must needs be necessary. But then it must be ubiquitous, homogeneous, immutable, like God's substance; because this inward eternal necessity of being cannot but act always and everywhere alike. Whereas, we see matter diverse, changing and only in parts of space. I doubt whether this is solid; or whether from the mere postulate of necessary existence, we can infer anything more than Spinoza does: that eternal matter can possibly exist in no other organisms and sequences of change, than those in which it actually exists. Our surest refutation of this feature of Platonism is God's word. This heathen theology is certainly nearest of any to the Christian, here, and less repugnant than any other to the human reason and God's honor.

Dr. R. J. Breckinridge, (vol. I, p. 56. &c,) constructs what he assures us is an argument of his own, for the being of a God. A brief inspection of it will illustrate the subject. 1. Because something now is — at least the mind that reasons—therefore something eternal is. 2. All known substance is matter or spirit. 3. Hence only three possible alternatives; either, (a.) some matter is eternal; and the source of all spirit and all other matter, Or, (b.) some being composed of matter and spirit is the eternal one, and the source of all other matter and spirit. Or, (c.) some spirit is eternal, and produced all other spirit and matter. The third hypothesis must be the true one: not the second because we are matter

4. Dr. Breckinridge.

and spirit combined, and, consciously, cannot create; and moreover the first Cause must be single. Not the first, because matter is inferior to mind; and the inferior does not produce the superior.

The objections to this structure begin at the second part,

Its defects.

where the author leaves the established forms of Howe and Clarke. First: the argument cannot apply, in the mind of a pure idealist, or of a materialist. Second: it is not rigidly demonstrated that there can be no substance but matter and spirit; all that can be done is to say, negatively, that no other is known to us Third: the three alternative propositions do not exhaust the case; the Pantheist and the Peripatetic, of eternal organization, show us that others are conceivable, as obviously does the Platonic. Fourth: that we, combined of matter and spirit, consciously cannot create, is short of proof that some higher being, thus constituted, cannot. Christ could create, if He pleased; He is thus constituted. Last: it is unfortunate that an argument, which aims to be so experimental, should have the analogy of our natural experience so much against it. For we only witness human spirits producing effects, when incorporate. As soon as they are disembodied, (at death,) they totally cease to be observed causes of any effects.

The teleological argument for the being and attributes of a

5. Teleological Argument.

God has been so well stated by Paley, in his Natural Theology, that though as old as Job and Socrates, it is usually mentioned as Paley's argument. I refer you especially to his first three chapters. Beginning from the instance of a peasant finding a watch on a common, and although not knowing how it came there, concluding that some intelligent agent constructed it; he applies the same argument, with great beauty and power, to show that man and the universe have a Maker. For we see everywhere intelligent arrangement; as the eye for seeing, the ear for hearing, &c., &c. Nor is the peasant's reasoning to a watchmaker weakened, because he never saw one at work, or even heard of one; nor because a part of the structure is not understood; nor because some of the adjustments are seen to be imperfect; nor, if you showed the peasant, in the watch, a set of wheels for reproducing its kind, would he be satisfied that there was no watchmaker: for he would see that this reproductive mechanism could not produce the intelligent arrangements. Nor would he be satisfied with a "law of nature," or a "physical principle of order," as the sole cause.

It is a fact, somewhat curious, that the metaphysical and the

Are the two, rival lines of proof?

teleological arguments have each had their exclusive advocates in modern times. The applauders of Paley join Dr. Thomas Brown in scouting the former as shadowy and inconclusive. The supporters of the metaphysical divines depreciate Paley, as leading us to nothing above a mere *Demiurgus*. In truth, both lines of reasoning are valid; and each needs the other. Dr. Brown, for instance, in carrying Paley's argument to its higher conclusions, must tacitly borrow some of the very metaphysics which he professes to disdain. Otherwise it remains incomplete, and leads to no more than a sort of *Artifex Mundi*, whose existence runs back merely to a date prior to human experience, and whose being, power and wisdom are demonstrated to extend only as far as man's inquiries have gone. But that He is eternal, immutable, independent, immense, infinite in power or wisdom; it can never assure us. True, in viewing the argument, your mind did leap to the conclusion that the artificer of nature's contrivances is the Being of "eternal power and godhead," but it was only because you passed, almost unconsciously, perhaps, through that metaphysical deduction, of which Howe gives us the exact description. Howe's is the comprehensive, Paley's the partial (but very lucid) display of the *a posteriori* argument. Paley's premise; that every contrivance must have an intelligent contriver, is but an instance under the more general one, that every effect must have a cause. The inadequacy of Paley's argument may be illustrated in this: that he seems to think the peasant's discovery of a stone, instead of a watch, could not have led his mind to the same conclusion, whereas a pebble as really, though not so impressively, suggests a cause, as an organized thing. For even the pebble should make us think either that it is such as can have the ground of its existence in its present form in itself; and so, can be eternal, self-existent, and necessary; or else, that it had a Producer, who does possess these attributes.

But, on the other hand, this argument from contrivance has

Its value.

great value, for these reasons. It is plain and popular. It enables us to evince the unity of the first cause through the unity of purpose and convergence of the consequences of creation. It aids us in showing the personality of God, as a being of intelligence and will; and it greatly strengthens the assault we shall be enabled to make on Pantheism, by showing, unless there is a personal and divine first Cause prior to the universe, this must itself be, not only uncaused, eternal, independent, necessarily existent, but endued with intelligence.

LECTURE II.

EXISTENCE OF GOD. — Continued.

SYLLABUS.

1. Show in a few instances how the Argument from Design is drawn from Animal Organisms, from Man's Mental and Emotional Structure, and from the Adaptation of Matter to our Mental Faculties.

See Paley, Nat. Theol. bk. iv, ch. iii, 16. Chalmers' Nat. Theol. bk. iv, ch. i, 2–5.

2. Can the being of God be argued from the existence of Conscience?

Turrettin, Loc. iii, Qu. 1, §14 15. Hodge, Syst. Theol. part i, ch ii, §5. Alexander's Moral Science, ch. xii. Chalmers' Nat. Theol. bk. iii. ch. 2. Charnock Attributes, Discourse i, §3. Kant, Critique of the Practical Reason. Thornwell, Lect. ii.

3. What the value of the Argument from the *Consensus Populorum*?

Turrettin, Loc. iii, Qu. i, §16–18. Dick, Lect. xvii. Cicero *de Nat. Deorum*, lib. i. Charnock, Discourse i, §1

4. Refute the evasion of Hume: That the Universe is a Singular Effect.

Alexander's Moral Science, ch. xxviii. Chalmer's Nat. Theol. bk. i, ch. 4. Watson's Theo. Institutes, pt ii, ch. i. Hodge, pt. i, ch. ii. §4. Reign of Law, Duke of Argyle, ch. iii.

5. Can the Universe be accounted for without a Creator, as an infinite series of Temporal Effects?

Alexander's Moral Science, ch. xxviii. Turrettin, as above, §6–7. Dr. S. Clarke's Discourse §2. Kant, Critique of Pure Reason, 1st Antinomy.

6. Refute the Pantheistic Scheme of the Universe.

Thornwell, Lect. ix. Alex. Moral Science, ch. xxviii. Dr. S. Clarke's Discourse, &c. § 3, 7, 9, &c. Chalmers' Nat Theol , bk i, ch v. Hodge, pt. i, ch. iii § 5, Thornwell, "Personality of God," in Works, vol. i, p. 490.

TO resume: A single instance of intelligent contrivance in the works of creation would prove an intelligent Creator. Yet, it is well to multiply these proofs,

1. Instances of Contrivance to an End.

even largely: for they give us then a wider foundation of deduction, stronger views of the extent of the creative wisdom and power; and better evidence of God's unity.

Hence, as instances, showing how the argument is constructed: If the design is to produce the physical part of the sensation of vision; the

From Organs of Animals.

eye is obviously an optical instrument, contrived with lenses to refract, expedients for obtaining an achromatic spectrum, adjustments for distance and quantity of light, and protection of the eye, by situation, bony socket, brow, lids, lubricating fluids; and in birds, the nictitating membrane. Different creatures also have eyes adapted to their lives and media of vision; as birds, cats, owls, fishes. So, the ear is an auditory apparatus, with a concha to converge the sound-waves, a tube, a tympanum to transmit vibration, the three bones (*malleus*, *stipes* and *incus*) in instable equilibrium, to convey it to the *sensorium*, &c.

The world of spirit is just as full of evident contrivances. See (e. g.) the laws of habit and im-

From Spiritual Structure of Man.

itation, exactly adjusted to educate and to form the character; and the faculties of

15

memory, association, taste, &c. The evidences of contrivance are, if possible, still more beautiful in our emotional structure; e. g. in the instincts of parental love, sympathy, resentment and its natural limits, sexual love, and its natural check, modesty; and above all, conscience, with its self-approval and remorse. All these are adjusted to obvious ends.

We see marks of more recondite design, in the natural compensation for necessary defects. The elephant's short neck is made up by a lithe proboscis. Birds' heads cannot carry teeth: but they have a gizzard. Insects with fixed heads, have a number of eyes to see around them. Brutes have less reason, but more instinct; &c., &c.

In Compensating Arrangements.

The adaptations of one department of nature to another show at once contrivance, selecting will and unity of mind. Thus, the *media* and the organs of sense are made for each other. The forms and colours of natural objects are so related to taste; the degree of fertility imparted to the earth, to man's necessity for labour; the stability of physical law, to the necessary judgments of the reason thereabout. So all nature, material and spiritual, animal, vegetable, inorganic, on our planet, in the starry skies, are full of wise contrivance.

In Adaptations.

The moral phenomena of conscience present a twofold evidence for the being of a God, worthy of fuller illustration than space allows. This faculty is a most ingenious spiritual contrivance, adjusted to a beneficent end: viz., the promotion of virtuous acts, and repression of wicked. As such, it proves a contriver, just as any organic adjustment does. But second: we shall find, later in the course, that our moral judgments are intuitive, primitive, and necessary; the most inevitable functions of the reason. Now, the idea of our acts which have rightness, is unavoidably attended with the judgment that they are obligatory. Obligation must imply an obliger. This is not always any known creature: hence, the Creator. Again, our conscience of wrong-doing unavoidably suggests fear; but fear implies an avenger. The secret sinner, the imperial sinner above all creature-power, shares this dread. Now, one may object, that this process is not valid, unless we hold God's mere will the sole source of moral distinctions: which we do not teach, since an atheist is reasonably compelled to hold them. But the objection is not just. The primitive law of the reason must be accepted as valid to us, whatever its source. For parallel: The intuitive belief in causation is found on inspection, to contain the proposition, 'There is a first Cause.' But in order for the validity of this proposition, it is not necessary for us to say that this intuition is God's arbitrary implantation It is intrinsically true to the nature of

2. Argument from Conscience.

THE EXISTENCE OF GOD

things; and the argument to a first Cause therefore only the more valid.

This moral argument to the being of a God, as it is immediate an.l strictly logical, is doubtless far the most practical. Its force is seen in this, that theoretical atheists, in danger and death, usually at the awakening of remorse, acknowledge God.

You find the argument from the Consensus Populorum, much elaborated by your authorities. I conclude that it gives a strong probable evidence for the being of a God, thus: The truth is abstract; its belief would not have been so nearly universal, nor so obviously essential to man's social existence, did not a valid ground for it exist in man's laws of thought. For it can be accounted for neither by fear, policy, nor self-interest.

3. Argument from Universal Consent.

From the affirmative argument, we return to evasions. An objection is urged, that the argument from design, if valid, proves only a creator of limited powers. For contrivance is the expedient of weakness. E. g. one constructs a derrick, because he is too weak to lift the mass as a Samson. If the Creator has eternal power and godhead, why did He not go straight to His ends, without means, as in Ps. 33 : 9? I answer, design proves a designer, though in part unintelligible. 2nd. It would not be unworthy of the Almighty to choose this manner of working, in order to leave His signature on it for man to read. 3d. Chiefly: Had God employed no means to ends, he must have remained the only agent; there would have been no organized nature; but only the one supernatural agent.

4. Objected, that Contrivance betrays Limitation.

Hume strives to undermine the argument from the creation to a Creator, by urging that, since only experience teaches us the uniformity of the tie between effect and cause, it is unwarranted to apply it farther than experience goes with us. But no one has had any experience of a world-maker, as we have of making implements in the arts. The universe, if an effect at all, is one wholly singular: the only one anybody has known, and from the earliest human experience, substantially as it is now. Hence the empirical induction to its first Cause is unauthorized.

Hume Objects that the World is a Singular Effect.

Note first: this is from the same mint with his argument against miracles. Creation is simply the first miracle; the same objection is in substance brought; viz: no testimony can be weighty enough to prove, against universal experience, that a miracle has occured. Next, Dr. Alexander, to rebut, resorts to an illustration; a country boy who had seen only ploughs and horse-carts, is shown a steam-frigate; yet he immediately infers a mechanic for it. The fact will be so; but it will not give us the whole analysis. True, the frigate is greatly larger and more complicated than a horse cart; (as the universe is than any

Dr. Alexander's Answer.

*2

human machine). But still, Hume might urge that the boy
would see a thousand empirical marks, cognizable to his experiences, (timber with marks of the plane on it, as on his
plough-beam, the cable as evidently twisted of hemp, as
his plough-lines; the huge anchor with as evident dints of
the hammer, as his plough-share,) which taught him that the
wonderful ship was also a produced mechanism. Astonishing as it is to him, compared with the plough, it is experimentally seen to be not natural, like the universe,

Chalmers, in a chapter full of contradictions, seems to
grant that experience alone teaches us the
law of causation, and asserts that still the

Chalmers' Answer.

universe is not "a singular effect." To show this, he supposes, with Paley, the peasant from a watch inferring a
watch-maker : and then by a series of abstractions, he shows
that the logical basis of the inference is not anything peculiar to that watch, as that it is a gold, or a silver, a
large, a small, or a good watch, or a machine to measure
time at all; but simply the fact that it is a manifest contrivance
for an end. The effect then, is no longer singular; yet the inference to some adequate agent holds. To this ingenious process,
Hume would object that it is experience alone which guides in
making those successive abstractions, by which we separate the
accidental from the essential effect and cause. This, Chalmers
himself admits. Hence, as we have no experience of world-making, no such abstraction is here allowable, to reduce the world
to the class of common effects. Besides; has Hume admitted
that it is an effect at all ? In fine, he might urge this difference,
that the world is native, while the watch, the plough, the ship
bears, to the most unsophisticated observer, empirical marks of
being made, and not native.

Let us not then refute Hume from his own premises;
for they are false. It is not experience
which teaches us that every effect has its
cause, but the *a priori* reason. (This Chal-

True Answer.

mers first asserts, and then unwisely surrenders.) Neither
child nor man believes that maxim to be true in the hundredth
case, because he has experienced its truth in ninty-nine ; he
instinctively believed it in the first case. It is not a true canon
of inductive logic, that the tie of cause and effect can be asserted
only so far as experience proves its presence. If it were, would
induction ever teach us anything we did not know before ? Would
there be any inductive science ? Away with the nonsense ! Grant
that the world is a "singular effect." It is a phenomenon, it
could not be without a cause of its being, either extrinsic, or intrinsic. And this we know, not by experience, but by one of
those primitive judgments of the reason, which alone make
experience intelligible and valid.

But may not this universe have the ground of its being in itself? This is another evasion of the atheists. Grant, they say, that nothing cannot produce something. Theists go outside the universe to seek its cause; and when they suppose they have found it in a God, they are unavoidably driven to represent Him as uncaused from without, eternal, self-existent, and necessary. Now it is a simpler hpyothesis, just to suppose that the universe which we see, is the uncaused, eternal, self-existent, necessary Being. Why may we not adopt it? Seeing we must run back to the mystery of some uncaused, eternal being, why may we not accept the obvious teaching of nature and experience and conclude that this is it? Since the organisms which adorn this universe are all temporal, and since the earth and other stars move in temporal cycles, we shall then have to suppose that the infinite past eternity, through which this self-existent universe has existed, was made up of an infinite succession of these organisms and cycles, each previous one producing the next: as the infinite future eternity which will be. But what is absurd in such a hypothesis?

5. Can the Present Universe be the result of an Infinite Series of Organisms?

Now I will not reply, with Dr. Clarke and others, that if the universe is eternal, it must be necessary; and this necessity must make its substance homogeneous and unchangeable throughout infinite time and space. It might be plausibly retorted, that this tendency to regular, finite organisms, which we see, was the very necessity of nature inherent in matter. Nor does it seem to me solid to say, with Robert Hall in his sermon, Turrettin, and others, that an eternal series of finite durations is impossible; because if each particular part had a beginning, while the series had none, we should have the series existing before its first member; the chain stretching farther back than its farthest link. The very supposition was, that the series had no first member. Is a past eternity any more impossible to be made up of the addition of an infinite number of finite parts, than an abstract infinite future? Surely not. Now there is to be just such an infinite future: namely, your and my immortality, which, although it may not be measured by solar days and years, will undoubtedly be composed of parts of successive time infinitely multiplied. But to this future eternity, it would be exactly parallel to object, that we make each link in it have an end, while the whole is endless; which would involve the same absurdity, of a chain extended forward after the last link was ended. The answer again is: that according to the supposition, there is no last link, the number thereof being infinite. In a word, what mathematician does not know that infinitude may be generated by the addition of finites repeated an infinite number of times?

Metaphysical Answers.

Turrettin, among many ingenious arguments, advances
another which seems more respectable. It is
in substance this: If this universe has no
Creator, then its past duration must be a proper
and absolute infinity. But created things move or succeed each
other in finite times. See, for instance, the heavenly bodies:
The sun revolves on its axis daily; around its orbit, annually.
If this state of things has been eternal, there must have been
an infinite number of days, and also an infinite number of years.
But since it requires three hundred and sixty-five days to a year,
we have here two temporal infinities, both proper and absolute,
yet one three hundred and sixty-five times as large as the other!
Now, the mathematicians tell us, that proper infinities may be
unequal; that an infinite plane, for instance, may be conceived
as constituted of infinite straight lines infinitely numerous; and an
infinite solid, of an infinite number of such planes, superposed
the one on the other. But it is at least questionable, whether
the evasion is valid against Turrettin's argument. For these
differing infinities are in different dimensions, of length, breadth
and thickness. Can there be, in the same dimension, two lines,
each infinite in length, and yet the one three hundred and sixty-
five as great as the other, in length?

Turrettin's Argument from Unequal Infinities.

Turrettin attempts to reply to the answer drawn from the
eternity *a parte post*, against the metaphysical argument. The
atheist asks us: Since (as theists say) a finite *soul* is to be
immortal, there will be a specimen of a temporal infinity formed
of finite times infinitely repeated: Why may there not have
been a similar infinite duration *a parte ante?* Because, says our
Text-book: That which was, but is past, cannot be fairly compared with a future which will never be past. Again: a thing
destined never to end may have a beginning; but it is impossible
to believe that a thing which actually has ended, never had a beginning. Because, the fact that the thing came to an end proves
that its cause was outside of itself. The last remark introduces
us to a solid argument, and it is solid, because it brings us out
of the shadowy region of infinity to the solid ground of causation. It is but another way of stating the grand, the unanswerable refutation of this atheistic theory: a series composed
only of contingent parts must be, as a whole, contingent. But
the contingent cannot be eternal, because it is not self-existent.
This argument is explicated in the following points:

(1.) Take any line of generative organisms, for instance:
(oak trees bearing acorns, and those acorns rearing oaks, e. g.)
the being of each individual in the series demands an adequate
cause. When we push the inquiry back one step, and ask the
cause of the parent which (seemingly) caused it, we find
precisely the same difficulty unanswered. Whatever distance
we run back along the line, we clearly see no approach is made
towards finding the adequate cause of the series, or of the

earliest individual considered. Hence it is wholly unreasonable to suppose that the introduction of infinitude into the series helps to give us an adequate cause. We only impose on ourselves with an undefined idea. Paley's illustration here is as just as beautiful. Two straight parallel lines pursued, ever so far, make no approximation; they will never meet, though infinitely extended.

(2.) An adequate cause existing at the time the phenomenon arises, must be assigned for every effect. For a cause not present at the rise of the effect, is no cause. Now then; when a given oak was sprouted, all the previous oaks and acorns of its line, save one or two, had perished. Was this acorn, even with its parent oak, the adequate cause of the whole structure of the young tree, including the ingenious contrivances thereof? Surely not. But the previous dead oaks and acorns are no cause; for they are not there. An absent cause is no cause. The original cause of this oak is not in the series at all.

(3.) Even if we permit ourselves to be dazzled with the notion that somehow the infinitude of the series can account for its self-productive power; this maxim is obvious: that in a series of transmitted causes, the whole power of the cause must be successively in each member of the series. For each one could only transmit what power it received from its immediate predecessor; and if at any stage, any portion of the causative power were lost, all subsequent stages must be without it. But evidently no one generation of acorns ever had power or intelligence to create the subtle contrivances of vegetable life in their progeny; and to suppose that all did, is but multiplying the absurdity.

(4) This question should be treated according to the atheist's point of view, scientifically: Science always accepts testimony in preference to hypothesis. Now there is a testimony, that of the Mosaic Scripture, as supported by universal tradition, which says that all series of organisms began in the creative act of an intelligent first Cause. The atheist may object, that men, as creatures themselves, have no right of their own knowledge, to utter such traditionary testimony; for they could not be present before the organisms existed to witness how they were brought into existence. The only pretext for such tradition would be that some prior superhuman Being, who did witness man's production, revealed to him how he was produced: but whether any such prior Being existed, is the very thing in debate, and so may not be taken for granted.

True; but the existence of the testimony must be granted; for it is a fact that it exists, and it must be accounted for. And the question is, whether the only good account is not, that the universe did have an intelligent Cause, and that this Cause taught primeval man whence he originated. Otherwise, not only is the universe left unaccounted for, but the universal tradition.

(5) Science exalts experience above hypothesis even more than testimony. Now, the whole state of the world bears the appearance of recency. The recent discovery of new continents, the great progress of new arts since the historic era began, and the partial population of the earth by man, all belie the eternity of the human race. But stronger still, geology proves the creation, in time, of race after race of animals, and the comparatively recent origin of man, by her fossil records. These show the absolute beginning of *genera*. And the attempt to account for them by the development theory (Chambers or Darwin) is utterly repudiated by even the better irreligious philosophers; for if there is anything that Natural History has established, it is that organic life is separated from inorganic forces, mechanical, chemical, electrical or other, by inexorable bounds; and that *genera* may begin or end, but never transmute themselves into other *genera*.

6. Pantheism.

As I pointed out, there are but two hypotheses by which the demonstration of an eternal, intelligent, personal first Cause can be evaded. The one has just been discussed; the other is the pantheistic. No separate first Cause of the universe need be assigned, it says, because the universe is God. The first Cause and the whole creation are supposed to be one substance, world-god, possessing all the attributes of both. As extremes often meet, pantheism leads to the same practical results with atheism. Aristotle, perhaps the most sagacious of pagan thinkers, was willing to postulate the eternity, *a parte ante*, of the series of organisms. But he, none the less, taught the existence of a God who, though in a sense an *Anima Mundi*, was yet an intelligent and active infinite Cause. Hence:

Peripatetic Pantheism.

The ancient form of pantheism, probably peripatetic in its source, admitted that matter, dead, senseless, divisible, cannot be the proper seat of intelligence and choice, which are indivisible; and that the universe is full of marks of intelligent design, so that an *Anima Mundi*, an intelligent Principle, must be admitted in the universe. Yes, I reply, it must, and that personal. Because it obviously has intelligence, choice, and will; and how can personality be better defined? Nor can it inhabit the universe as a soul its body, not being limited to it in time or space, nor bearing that relation to it. Not in time; because, being eternal, it existed a whole past eternity before it; for we have proved the latter temporal. Not in space; for we have seen this Intelligence eternal ages not holding its *ubi* in space by means of body; and there is not a single reason for supposing that it is now limited to the part of space which bodies occupy. It is not connected with matter by any tie of animality; because immensely the larger part of matter is inanimate.

Modern pantheism appears either in the hypothesis of Spinoza, the Jew, or in that of the later German idealists. Both see that even the material universe teems with intelligent contrivances: and more, that the nobler part, that known by consciousness, and so, most immediately known, is a world of thought and feeling in human breasts. Hence intelligence and will must be accounted for, as well as matter. Now, Spinoza's first position is: There can be no real substance, except it be self-existent, and so, eternal. That is: it is incredible that any true substance can pass from *nihil* into *esse*. 2d. All the self-existent must be one; this is unavoidable from the unity of its characteristic attribute. 3d. The one real substance must therefore be eternal, infinite, and necessarily existent. Hence, 4th. all other seeming beings are not real substance, but modes of existence of this sole being. . 5th. All possible attributes, however seemingly diverse, must be modes, nearer or remote, of this Being; and it is necessary therefore to get rid of the prejudice, that modes of thought and will and modes of extension cannot be referred to the same substance. Hence this is the true account of the universe. All material bodies (so called) are but different modes of extension, in which the necessary substance projects himself; and all personal spirits (so called) are but modes of thought and will, in which the same being pulsates.

Pantheism of Spinoza.

Now you see that the whole structure rests on two unproved and preposterous assumptions: that real substance cannot be except it be self-existent; and that the self-existent can be but one. The human mind is incapable of demonstrating either.

Says the modern idealist: Let the mind take nothing for granted, except the demonstrated; and it will find that it really knows nothing save its consciousnesses. Of what is it conscious? Only of its own subjective states. Men fancy that these must be referred to a subject called mind, spirit, self; as the substance of which they are states. So they fancy that they find objective sources for their sensations, and objective limits to their volitions; but if it fancies it knows either, it is only by a subjective consciousness. These, after all, are its only real possessions. Hence, it has no right to assert either substantive self or objective matter; it only knows, in fact, a series of self-consciousnesses. Hence; our thinking and willing constitute our being. Hence, too, the whole seeming objective world is only educed from a non-existence as it is thought by us. The total *residuum* then, is an impersonal power of thought, only existing as it exerts its self-consciousness in the varions beings of the universe, (if there is a universe) and in God. Its subjective consciousnesses constitute spiritual substance (so-called,) self, fellow-man, God; and its objective, the seeming objective material bodies of the universe.

Pantheism of the Modern Idealist.

Against both these forms of pantheism, I present the following outline of a refutation. (1.) If the
mind may not trust the intuition which refers
all attributes and affections to their sub-
stances, and which gives real objective sources for sensations, it
may not believe in its intuitive self-consciousness, nor in that
intuition of cause for every phenomenon, on which Spinoza
founds the belief in his One Substance. *Falsus in uno; falsus
in omnibus.* There is an end of all thinking. That the intuitions above asserted, are necessary and primary, I prove by this:
that every man, including the idealist, unavoidably makes them.

*Refutation. 1. In-
tuition must be accept-
ed as valid.*

(2.) We are each one conscious of our personality. You
cannot pronounce the words "self," *Ego*, self-
consciousness; but that you have implied it.
Hence, if we think according to our own sub-
jective law, we cannot think another intelligence and will, without imputing to it a personality. Least of all, the supreme intelligence and will. To deny this is to claim to be more perfect
than God. But worse yet; if I am not a person, my nature is a
lie, and thinking is at an end. If I am a person, and as the
pantheist says, I am God, and God is I, then he is a person; and
the pantheistic system is still self-contradicted.

*Consciousness im-
plies my Personality.*

(3.) Modes of extension and modes of thought and will
cannot be attributes of one substance. Matter is divisible: neither consciousness, nor
thought, nor feeling is; therefore the substance which thinks is indivisible. Matter is
extended; has form; has relative bulk and weight. All these
properties are impossible to be thought of any function of
spirit, as relevant to them. Who can conceive of a thought
triturated into many parts, as a stone into grains of sand; of
a resentment split into halves; of a conception which is so
many fractions of an inch longer or thicker than another; of an
emotion triangular or circular, of the top and bottom of a
volition?

*Extension and
Thought cannot be re-
ferred to a common
Substance.*

(4.) If there is but one substance Το Παν, the eternal, self-
existent, necessary; then it must be homoge-
neous and indivisible. This is at least a just
argumentum ad hominem for Spinoza. Did
he not infer the necessary unity of all real substance, from the
force of its one characteristic attribute, self and necessary existence? Now, this immanent necessity, which is so imperative
as to exclude plurality; must it not also exclude diversity; or
at least contrariety? How then can this one, unchangeable
substance exist at the same time in different and even contradictory states; motion and rest; heat and cold; attraction and
repulsion? How can it, in its modes of thought and will, at
the same time love in one man, and hate in another, the same
object? How believe and disbelieve the same thing?

*If Spinoza true, Το
Παν cannot vary.*

(5) On this scheme, there can be no responsibility, moral

No Evil nor Good. good or evil, guilt, reward, righteous penalty, or moral government of the world. All states of feeling, and all volitions are those of *To Παν*. Satan's wrong volitions are but God willing, and his transgressions, God acting. By what pretext can the Divine Will be held up as a moral standard? Anything which a creature wills, is God's will.

(6.) And this because, next, pantheism is a scheme of stark

Fatalistic. necessity. Necessity of this kind is inconsistent with responsibility. But again; it contradicts our consciousness of free-agency. We know, by our consciousness, that in many things we act freely, we do what we do, because we choose; we are conscious that our souls determine themselves. But if Pantheism were true, every volition, as well as every other event, would be ruled by an iron fate. So avowed stoicism, the pantheism of the Old World: so admits Spinoza. And consistently; for *To Παν*, impersonal, developing itself according to an immanent, eternal necessity, must inevitably pass through all those modifications of thought and extension, which this necessity dictates, and no others; and the acts of God are as fated as ours.

(7.) I retort upon the pantheist that picture which he so

God would have all much delights to unfold in fanciful and glow-
Sin and Woe. ing guise. Pantheism, says he, by deifying nature, clothes everything which is sweet or grand with the immediate glory of divinity, and ennobles us by placing us perpetually in literal contact with God. Do we look without on the beauties of the landscape? Its loveliness is but one beam of the multiform smile upon His face. The glory of the sun is the flash of His eye. The heavings of the restless sea are but the throbs of the divine bosom, and the innumerable stars are but the sparkles of His eternal brightness. And when we look within us, we recognize in every emotion which ennobles or warms our breasts, the aspirations, the loves, the gratitudes which bless our being, the pulses of God's own heart beating through us. Nay, but, say I, are the manifestations of the universal Being, all lovely and good? If pantheism is true, must we not equally regard all that is abhorrent in nature, the rending thunder, and the rushing tornado, the desolating earthquake and volcanos, the frantic sea lashing helpless navies into wreck, as the throes of disorder or ruin in God? And when we picture the scenes of sin and woe, which darken humanity, the remorse of the villain's privacy, the orgies of crime and cruelty hidden beneath the veil of night, the despairing deathbeds, the horrors of battle fields, the wails of nations growing pale before the pestilence, the din of burning and ravaged cities, and all the world of eternal despair itself, we see in the whole but the agony and crime of the divine Substance. Would it then be best called Devil or God? Since suffering and sin are

so prevalent in this world, we may call it Pan-diabolism, with more propriety than pantheism. Nor is it any relief to this abhorrent conclusion, to say that pain and evil are necessitated, and are only seeming evils. Consciousness declares them real.

LECTURE III.

THE EVOLUTION THEORY.

SYLLABUS.

I. State the Evolution Theory of man's origin, in its recent form; and show its Relation to the Argument for God's existence.

II. Show the Defects in the pretended Argument for this Descent of man by Evolution.

III. Does the Theory weaken the Teleological Argument for the Existence of a Personal God.

See "Origin of Species" and "Descent of Man," by Dr. Charles Darwin, "Lay Sermons," by Dr. Thos. Huxley, "Physical Basis of Life," by Dr. Stirling, Lectures (Posthumous) of Prof. Louis Agassiz, "What is Darwinism?" by Dr. Ch Hodge, "Reign of Law," by the Duke of Argyle.

IN the previous Lecture, I concluded the brief examination of the atheistic theory, accounting for the Universe as an eternal series, with these words: "*Genera* may begin or end, but never transmute themselves into other *genera*." We found the fatal objections to the scheme of a self-existent, infinite series uncaused from without, in these facts: That no immediate antecedent was adequate cause for its immediate successor: And that the previous links in the series could not be cause; because totally absent from the rise of the sequent effect. Thus the utter fallacy was detected, which seeks to impose on our minds by the vague infinitude of the series as a whole. We were taught that no series made up solely of effects, each contingent, can, as a whole, be self-existent. Thus perished that evasion of the atheist.

Relation of Evolution to Teleological Argument.

Obviously, if there is any expedient for resuscitating it, this must be found in the attempt to prove that the law, "Like produces Like," is not the whole explanation of the series. We have demonstrated that, by that law, it is impossible the series can be self-existent. Hence, the best hope of Atheism is, to attempt to prove that the Like does not produce merely the Like; that the series contains within itself a power of differentiating its effects, at least slightly. Thus materialists and atheists have been led in our day, either by deliberate design, or by a species of logical instinct, to attempt the construction of an "evolution theory." The examination of this attempt, thus becomes necessary in order to complete the argument for God's existence, on this, the last conceivable point of attack.

I. The evolution hypothesis is, indeed, no novelty. It is, after

No Novelty. all its pretended modern experiments, but a
revive of the "atomic theory" of the Greek
atheist, Democritus, adopted by the Epicurean school. Its application to the descent of man from some lower animal, has often been attempted, as by Lord Monboddo, who almost exactly anticipated Dr. Chas. Darwin's conclusion. In the eyes of some modern Physicists, however, it has received new plausibility from the more intelligent speculations of the Naturalist La Marck, and the "Vestiges of Creation" ascribed to Mr. Robert Chambers. But it appears in its fullest form, in the ingenious works of Dr. Chas. Darwin, "Origin of Species," and "Descent of Man." I therefore take this as the object of our inquiry.

This Naturalist thinks that he has found the law of repro-

Natural Selection   duction, in animated nature, that "Like pro-
and Survival.   duces Like," modified by the two laws of "natural selection" and a survival of the fittest."
By the former, nature herself, acting unintelligently, tends in all her reproductive processes, to select those copulations which are most adapted to each other   By the latter, she ordains, equally without intelligence, that the fittest, or ablest progeny shall survive at the expense of the inferior. These supposed laws he illustrates by the race-varieties (certainly very striking) which have been produced in *genera* and species whose original unity is admitted by all, through the art of the bird-fancier and stock-rearer, in breeding. The result of these laws, modifying the great law of reproduction, would be a slight differentiation of successors from predecessors, in any series in animated nature. This difference at one step might be almost infinitesimal. This *conatus* of Nature towards evolution, being totally blind, and moving at hap-hazard, might result in nothing through a myriad of experiments, or instances, and only evolve something in advance of the antecedents, in the ten thousandth case; yet, if we postulate a time sufficiently vast, during which the law has been thus blindly working, the result may be the evolution of man, the highest animal, from the lowest form of proto-plastic life.

The tendency of this scheme. is atheistic. Some of its

Scheme Atheistic.   advocates may disclaim the consequence, and
declare their recognition of a God and Creator, we hope, sincerely. But the undoubted tendency of the speculation, will be to lead its candid adherents, where Dr. Leopold Büchner has placed himself, to blank materialism and atheism. For the scheme is an attempt to evolve what theists call the creation without a Creator; and as we shall see, the bearing of the hypothesis is towards an utter obliteration of the teleological argument. 2nd. In assigning man a brute origin, it encourages common men to regard themselves as still brutes. Have brutes any religion? 3d. The scheme ignores all substantive distinction between spirit and matter, by evolving

the former out of the functions of mere animality. But if there be no soul in man there is, practically, no religion for him.

II. Defects in the pretended argument:

1. The favorite law of "natural selection" involves in its very name a sophistical idea. Selection is an attribute of free-agency, and implies intelligent choice. But the "Nature" of the evolutionist is unintelligent. The cause, if it be a cause, supposed by him in his natural selection, acts blindly and by hap-hazard. Now, whenever we apply the idea of selection, or any other which expresses free-agency, to such effects: we know that we are speaking inaccurately and by a mere trope. How much more sophistical is it to ascribe the force of a permanent and regular law, selecting effects, to that which is but chance? This is but giving us metaphor, in place of induction. It is farther noted by Agassiz, that the principle of life, or cause in animated nature, notoriously and frequently produces the same results under diverse conditions of action; and diverse results again, under the same conditions. These facts prove that it is not the species of variable cause painted by Darwin, and does not differentiate its effects by his supposed law of natural selection.

2. We have seen that the vastness of the time needed for the evolution of man from the lowest animated form, by these laws of natural selection, working blindly and effecting at any one movement the most minute differentiations, is not only conceded, but claimed by evolutionists. Then, since the blind cause probably has made ten thousand nugatory experiments for every one that was an advance, the fossil remains of all the experiments, of the myriads of *genera* of failures, as well as the few *genera* that were successes, should be found in more immense bulk. And especially fossil Natural History should present us with the full history of both sides of the blind process; with the remains of the degraded *genera*, as well as the "fittest" and "surviving" *genera*. The fossil-history of the former ought to be ten thousand times the fullest! But in the presence of such a history, how preposterous would a theory of evolution appear? For, the very essence of this theory is the idea of a continual advancement and improvement in nature.

3. The evolution theory is inconsistent with the wide geographical diffusion of *species*, and especially of the higher *species*. If these are the results of the "survival of the fittest," under local conditions of existence and propagation, is it not unaccountable that these, and especially man, the highest species of all, should always have been found under the most diverse and general conditions, in contrasted climates? But if we pass to the lower *species*, such as the moluscs and crustaceans, the difficulty is as great, because they have no adequate means of locomotion to migrate from the spots where the local conditions of their development existed.

But next; where improved race-varieties have actually
4. No Improvement by Selection, save under a Rational Providence. been developed, it may well be questioned whether the selections of the progenitors have ever been " natural," in the sense of the evo-
lutionist. The marked instances of which Darwin makes so much use, are the result of the breeder's art: (as the Durham cattle) that is, of a rational providence. And when we surrender any individuals of the varieties to the dominion of 'nature,' the uniform tendency is to degradation. What more miserable specimens of cattle and swine are ever seen; what individuals less calculated for " survival " in the struggle for existence, than the neglected progeny of the marvellously developed English live-stock, when left to take their chances with the indigenous stock of ill-cultivated districts? Again, many Naturalists tell us that when any incidental cause has been applied to a given species, producing variations in some individuals and their progeny, the difference is larger at first, and becomes more and more minute afterwards. The inference seems irresistible, that such variations must have fixed and narrow limits. Naturalists are familiar with the tendency of all varieties, artificially produced by the union of differing progenitors, to revert back to the type of one or other of their ancestors. Thus, all breeders of live-stock recognize the tendency of their improved breeds to "fly to pieces;" and they know that nothing but the most artful vigilance in selecting parents prevents this result. Without this watchful control, the peculiarities of one or the other original varieties would re-appear in the progeny, so exaggerated, as to break up the improved type, and give them instead, a heterogeneous crowd, the individuals varying violently from each other and from the desired type, and probably inferior to either of the original varieties compounded.

Again: is the " survival of the fittest " a " natural " fact? I
Strongest do not Naturally Survive. answer; No. The natural tendency of the violences of the strongest is, on the whole, to
increase the hardship of the conditions under which the whole species and each individual must gain subsistence. What better instance of this law needs to be sought, than in the human species; where we always see the savage anarchy, produced by the violence of the stronger, reduce the whole tribe to poverty and destitution? Why else is it, that savages are poorer and worse provided for than civilized men? Couple this law with another: that the most pampered individuals in any species, are not the most prolific; and we shall see that the natural tendency of animal life is, in the general, to the survival of the inferior. Thus the average wild Pampa horse, or "mustang" pony, is far inferior to the Andalusian steed, from which he is descended. We thus find an emphatic confirmation of the conclusion which Hugh Miller drew from the " testimony

of the rocks," that the natural tendency of the fossil *genera* has been to degradation and not to development.

Well does Dr. Sterling remark here : "Natural conjecture is always equivocal, insecure and many-sided. It may be said that ancient warfare, for instance, giving victory always to the personally ablest and bravest, must have resulted in the improvement of the race. Or, that the weakest being left at home, the improvement was balanced by deterioration. Or, that the ablest were necessarily most exposed to danger. And so——according to ingenuity *usque ad infinitnm*. Trustworthy conclusions are not possible to this method."

I have not yet seen any reason for surrendering the rule, hitherto held by Naturalists, that in the animal world, hybrids, if true hybrids, are infertile. The familiar instance is that of the mule. The *genera asinus* and *equus* can propagate an offspring, but that mule offspring can propagate nothing. If there are any exceptions to this law, they are completely consistent with the rule that hybrids cannot perpetuate their hybrid kind. If they have any progeny, it is either absolutely infertile ; or it has itself reverted back to one of the original types. It is strange that Dr. Huxley should himself appeal to this as a valid law ; when its validity is destructive of his own conclusions. In his "Lay Sermons," p. 295, when it suits his purpose to assert that natural variation has, in a given case, established a true species which is new, he appeals to the fact which is claimed : that this new species propagated its kind ; which proved it a true and permanent species. Which is to say, that hybrids cannot propagate their kind ; for it is by this law it is known that they do not form permanent species. But now, if new varieties really arose from natural selection, to the extent claimed by evolutionists, must they not fall under the hybrid class too decisively, ever to propagate their type permanently ?

5. Argument from Hybrids.

This process imagined by Dr. Darwin, if it existed, would be purely an animal one. He makes it a result of physical laws merely. Then, if there were a development by such a law, it should be the animal instincts and bodily organs, which are developed in the higher species. But it is not so. Man is the highest, and when he is compared with other *mammalia*, he is a feebler beast. The young infant has far less instinct and locomotion than the young fowl. The man has less instinct, less animal capacity, less strength, blunter senses, than the eagle, or the elephant, and less longevity than the goose. That which makes him a nobler creature is his superior intelligence with the adaptation thereto of his inferior animal instincts. He rules other animals and is "Lord of Creation" by his mind.

6. Evolution cannot account for Mind.

7. This, then, must also be explained by Dr. Darwin, as an

evolution from instinct and animal appetites ; just as he accounts for the evolution of the human hand, from the forepaw of an ape; so all the wonders of consciousness, intellect, taste, conscience, religious belief, are to be explained as the animal outgrowth of gregarious instincts, and habitudes cultivated through them. To any one who has the first correct idea of construing the facts of consciousness, this is simply monstrous. It of course denies the existence of any substance that thinks, distinct from animated matter. It ignores the distinction between the instinctive and the rational motive in human actions; thus making free-agency, moral responsibility, and ethical science impossible. The impossibility of this *genesis* is peculiarly plain in this: that it must suppose all these psychological acts and habits gradually superinduced. There is first, in some earlier generation of men, a protoplastic responsibility, free agency, reason, conscience, which are half, or one quarter animal instinct still, and the rest mental! Whereas, every man who ever nterpreted his own acts of soul to himself, knows intuitively, that this is the characteristic of them all; that they are contrasted with the merely animal acts, in all their stages and in all their degrees of weakness or strength. A feeble conscience is no nearer appetite, in its intrinsic quality, than the conscience of a Washington or a Lee.

In a word: Consciousness has her facts, as truly as physicks. These facts show that man belongs to a certain *genus* spiritually, more even than corporeally. And that *genus* is consciously separated by a great gulf, from all mere animal nature. It cannot be developed thence.

The utmost which can possibly be made of the evolution theory, is that it may be a hypothesis possibly true, even after all the arguments of its friends are granted to be valid. In fact, the scheme is far short of this. The careful reader of these works will find, amidst extensive knowledge of curious facts, and abundance of fanciful ingenuity, many yawning chasms between asserted facts and inductions; and many a substitution of the "must be" for the "may be." But when we waive this, we still find the theory unverified, and incapable of verification. One need desire no juster statement of the necessity of actual verification, in order to mature a hypothesis into a demonstration, than is given and happily illustrated by Dr. Huxley. "Lay Sermons," pp. 85-6. Until either actual experiment or actual observation has verified the expectation of the hypothesis; and verified it in such away as to make it clear to the mind, that the expected result followed the antecedent as a *propter hoc* and not a mere *post hoc*; that hypothesis, however plausible, and seemingly satisfying, is not demonstrated. But has Dr. Darwin's theory been verified in any actual case? Has any one seen the marsupial ape breed the man, in fact? The author of the scheme himself

8. Theory not proved at best.

knows that verification is, in the nature of the case, impossible.
The dates at which he supposes the evolutions took place, precede the earliest rational experience of man, according to his
own scheme, by vast ages.   The differentiations which gradually
wrought it were, according to him, too slight and gradual to be
contained in the memory of one dispensation of man's history.
The connecting links of the process are forever lost.   Hence the
utmost which these Naturalists could possibly make of their
hypothesis, were all their assumptions granted, would be the
concession that it contained a curious possibility.

These speculations are mischievous in that they present
to minds already degraded, and in love with
Dangerous to Morals. their own degradation, a pretext for their materialism, godlessness and sensuality.   The scheme can never
prevail generally among mankind.   The self-respect, the conscience, and the consciousness of men will usually present a
sufficient protest and refutation.   The world will not permaently
tolerate the libel and absurdity, that this wondrous creature,
man, "so noble in reason, so infinite in faculties, in form and
moving so express and admirable, in action so like an angel, in
apprehension so like a God," is but the descendant, at long removes, of a mollusc or a tadpole!

The worthlessness of mere plausibilities concerning the
Circumstantial evi- origin of the universe, is yet plainer when set
dence refuted by pa- in contrast with that inspired testimony upon
role.   the subject, to which Revealed Theology will
soon introduce us.   Hypothetical evidence, even at its best
estate, comes under the class of circumstantial evidence.   Judicial science, stimulated to accuracy and fidelity by the prime
interests of society in the rights and the life of its members, has
correctly ascertained the relation between circumstantial proof
and competent parole testimony.   In order to rebut the word
of such a witness, the circumstantatial evidence must be an exclusive demonstration: it must not only satisfy the reason that
the criminal act might have been committed in the supposed
way, by the supposed persons;   but that it was impossible, it
could have been committed in any other way.   In the absence
of parole testimony, every enlightened judge would instruct his
jury, that the defence is entitled to try the hypothesis of the accuser by this test: If any other hypothesis can be invented,
that is even purely imaginary, to which the facts granted in the
circumstantial evidence can be reconciled by the defence, that
is proof of invalidity in the accusing hypothesis.   Let us suppose a crime committed without known eye-witnesses.   The
prosecutors examine every attendant circumstance minutely,
and study them profoundly.   They construct of them a supposition that the crime was committed in secret by A.   They
show that this supposition of his guilt satisfies every fact, so
far as known.   They reason with such ingenuity, that every

mind tends to the conviction that A. must be verily guilty. But now there comes forward an honest man, who declares that he was eye-witness of the crime; and, that, of his certain knowledge, it was done by B., and not by A. On inquiry, it appears that B. was, at that time, naturally capable of the act. Then, unless the prosecutors can attack the credibility of this witness, before his word their case utterly breaks down. The ingenuity, the plausibility of their argument, is now naught. They had shown that, so far as known facts had gone, the act might have been done by A. But the witness proves that in fact it was done by B. The plausibility of the hypothesis and the ingenuity of the lawyers are no less: but they are utterly superseded by direct testimony of an eye-witness. I take this pains to illustrate to you this principle of evidence, because it is usually so utterly ignored by Naturalists, and so neglected even by Theologians. I assert that the analogy is perfect between the case supposed and the pretended evolution argument. Does Revelation bring in the testimony of the divine Eye-witness, because actual Agent, of the genesis of the universe? Is Revelation sustained as a credible witness by its literary, its internal, its moral, its prophetical, its miraculous evidences? Then even though the evolution hypothesis were scientifically probable, in the light of all known and physical facts and laws, it must yield before this competent witness. Does that theory claim that, naturally speaking, organisms might have been thus produced? God, the Agent, tells us that, in point of fact, they were otherwise produced. As Omnipotence is an agency confessedly competent to any effect whatsoever, if the witness is credible, the debate is ended.

III. I shall conclude this Lecture by adverting to a consequence which many of Dr. Darwin's followers draw from his scheme; which is really the most important feature connected with it. Dr. Huxley declares that the "Origin of Species" gives the death-blow to that great teleological argument for the existence of God, which has commanded the assent of all the common-sense and all the true philosophy of the human race. He quotes Prof. Kölliker, of Germany, as saying that though Darwin retains the teleological conception, it is shown by his own researches to be a mistaken one. Says the German savant, "Varieties arise irrespectively of the notion of purpose of utilty, according to the general laws of nature; and may be either useful or hurtful, or indifferent." It must be admitted these men interpret the bearings of the evolution theory aright; [and that it does bear against the impregnable evidences of design in God's creation, is a clear proof of its falsehood]. According to this scheme physical causation is blind; but it hits a lucky adaptation here and there, without knowing or meaning it, by mere chance, and in virtue of such an infinity of hap-hazard trials

Is our Teleological argument lost?

that it is impossible to miss all the time.   Such is the immediate, though blind, result of Nature's tendency to ceaseless
variations of structure.   Now, when (rarely) she happens to hit
a favorable variation, the better adaptation of that organism to
the conditions of existence enables it to survive and to propagate its type more numerously, where others perish.   Where
now is the proof of intelligence and design in such a fortuitous
adaptation?   Mr. Herbert Spencer argues that it is mere "anthropomorphism," for us to undertake to interpret nature teleo-
logically.   When we adapt anything to an end, we, of course,
design and contrive.   But when we therefore assume that the
Great Unknowable works by such thoughts, we are as absurd as
though the watch [in the well-known illustration of Dr. Paley]
becoming somewhat endowed with consciousness, should conclude that the consciousness of its Unknown Cause must consist of a set of ticking and motions of springs and cogs, because
such only are its own functions.   Some of these writers dwell
much upon the supposed error of our mixing the question of
"final causes" with that of efficient causes, in our investigation
of nature.   They claim that Lord Bacon, in his *De Augmentis*,
sustains this condemnation.   This is erroneous. He does disap-
prove the mixing of the question of final cause with the search
after the physical cause.   He points out that the former belongs to Metaphysics, the latter to Physics.   Let the question be, for instance: "Why do hairs grow around the eye-
brows?"   There are two meanings in this "Why."   If it asks
the final cause, the answer is: "For the protection of the
precious and tender organ beneath the brow."   If it asks the
physical cause, Lord Bacon's answer is: that a follicular structure of that patch of skin "breedeth a pilous growth."   He
clearly asserts, in his Metaphysic, that inquiries after the final
cause are proper; and he was emphatically a believer in the
teleological argument, as was Newton, with every other great
mind of those ages.

Let us clear the way for the exposure of the sophisms
Is our argument sus-   stated above, by looking at Spencer's ob-
picious because anthro- jection to the anthropomorphism of our Nat-
pomorphic?   ural Theology.   He would have us believe
that it is all vicious, because founded on the groundless postulate that our thought and contrivance are the model for the
mind of God.   He would illustrate this, as we saw, by supposing the watch, in Paley's illustration, "to have a consciousness,"
etc.   This simile betrays his sophism at once.   The supposition is impossible!   If the watch could have a consciousness,
it would not be a material machine, but a rational spirit: and
then there would be no absurdity whatever in its likening its own rational consciousness to that of its rational cause.
When complaint is made that all our Natural Theology is "anthropomorphic," what is this but a complaint that our knowl-

edge is human? If I am to have any knowledge, it must be my knowledge : that is, the knowledge of me, a man; and so, knowledge, according to the forms of human intelligence. All knowledge must then be anthropomorphic,in order to be human knowledge. To complain of any branch of man's knowledge on this score, is to demand that he shall know nothing! This, indeed, is verified by Mr. Herbert Spencer, who teaches, on the above ground, that God is only to be conceived of and honored as "The Unknowable ;" and who forbids us to ascribe any definite attribute, or offer any specific service to Him, lest we should insult Him by making Him altogether such an one as ourselves. I may remark, in passing, that this is equally preposterous in logic, and practically atheistic. The mind only knows substance from properties : if the *essentia* of an object of thought be absolutely unknown, its *esse* will certainly be more unknown. And how can one be more completely "without God in the world," than he who only knows of a divine Being, to whom he dares not ascribe any attribute, towards whom he dares not entertain any definite feeling, and to whom he dares not offer any service?

But why should our knowledge of a higher spiritual being be suspected, as untrustworthy, because it is anthropomorphic? It can only be, because it is suspected that this knowledge is transformed, in becoming ours. But now, let it be supposed that the great First Cause created our spirits "in his likeness, after his image," and the ground of suspicion is removed. Then it follows that in thinking "anthropomorphically," we are thinking like God : because God formed us to think like himself. Our conceptions of the divine will then be only limited, not transformed, in passing into our kindred, but finite, minds : they remain valid, as far as they reach. But it may be said : This is the very question: whether a Creator did form our spirits after the likeness of His own? The theists must not assume it at the onset as proved. Very true ; and their opponents shall not be allowed to assume the opposite as proved—they shall not "beg the question" any more than we do. But when our inquiries in Natural Theology lead us to the conclusion that in this respect "we are God's offspring," then He is no longer the "Unknown God." And especially when Revealed Theology presents us the Ἐικὼν τοῦ Θεοῦ ὁράτου in the "man Christ Jesus," the difficulty is completely solved.

To support the teleological argument farther against this philosophy of blind chance, I remark, first:
Chance cannot evolve design. that it is in no sense less unreasonable than the old pagan theory, which referred all the skillful adjustments of creation to a "fortuitious concourse of atoms." This is indeed the same wretched philosophy: re-vamped and re-furbished, which excited the sarcasm and scorn of Socrates, and was contemptuously discarded by the educated pagan mind. It is imposible to persuade the

common sense of mankind, that blind chance, whose sole attribute is chaotic disorder, is the source of the admirable order of this universal κοσμος. Something does not come out of nothing. Our opponents would ask us; since blind chance may, amidst its infinite multitudes of experiments, happen upon any result whatsoever, why may it not sometimes happen upon some results wearing the aspect of orderly adaptation? My answer is, that the question puts the case falsely. Sometimes! No! Always. The fact to be accounted for is; that Nature's results always have an orderly adaptation. I press again this crushing question: How is it that in every one of Nature's results, in every organ of every organized creature which is extant, either in living or in fossil natural History, if the structure is comprehended by us, we see some orderly adaptation? Where are Nature's failures? Where the vast remains of the infinity of her hap-hazard, orderless results? On the evolution theory, they should be a myriad times as numerous as those which possessed orderly adaptation. But in fact, none are found, save a few which are apparent exceptions, because, and only because, we have not yet knowledge enough to comprehend them. Through every grade of fossil life, if we are able at all to understand the creature whose remains we inspect, we perceive an admirable adjustment to the conditions of its existence. This is as true of the least developed, as of the most perfect. The *genus* may be now totally extinct: because the appropriate conditions of its existence have wholly passed away in the progress of changes upon the earth's surface; but while those conditions existed, they were beautifully appropriate to the *genus*. So, if there is any structure in any existing creature, whose orderly adaptation to an end is not seen, it is only because we do not yet understand enough. Such is the conclusion of true science. Anatomists before Dr. Harvey saw the valvular membranes in the arteries and veins, opening opposite ways. That great man assumed, in the spirit of true science, that they must have their orderly adaptation; and this postulate led him to the grand discovery of the circulation of the blood. Such is the postulate of true, modest science still, as to every structure: it is the pole-star of sound induction. And once more: Contrivance to an end is not limited to organic life reproducing after its kind—the department where the evolutionist finds his pretext of "natural selection." The permanent inorganic masses also disclose the teleological argument, just as clearly as the organic. Sun, moon and stars do not propagate any day! Contrivance is as obvious in the planetary motions and the tides of ocean, as in the eye of the animal. "The undevout Astronomer is mad". Commodore Maury, in his immortal works, has shown us as beautiful a system of adaptations in the wastes of the atmosphere and its currents, as the Natural Historian finds in the realms of life.

Second: I remark that if the theory of the evolutionist
were all conceded, the argument from de-
Who designed the susceptibility to evolve? signed adaptation would not be abolished,
but only removed one step backward. If
we are mistaken in believing that God made every living
creature that moveth after its kind: if the higher kinds were
in fact all developed from the lowest; then the question
recurs: Who planned and adjusted these wondrous powers
of development? Who endowed the cell-organs of the first
living protoplasm with all this fitness for evolution into
the numerous and varied wonders of animal life and function,
so diversified, yet all orderly adaptations? There is a wonder
of creative wisdom and power, at least equal to that of the
Mosaic genesis. That this point is justly taken, appears
thus: Those philosophers who concede (as I conceive, very
unphilosophically and unnecessarily) the theory of "creation by law," do not deem that they have thereby weakened
the teleological argument in the least. It appears again, in the
language of evolutionists themselves: When they unfold what
they suppose to be the results of this system, they utter the
words "beautiful contrivance of nature," "wise adjustment" and
such like, involuntarily. This is the testimony of their own reason, uttered in spite of a perverse and shallow theory.

In fine; when we examine any of these pretended results
of fortuity, we always find that the chance-accident was only
the occasion, and not the efficient cause, of that result. Says one
of the evolutionists: a hurricane may transplant a tree so as to
secure its growth. The wind may happen to drop a sapling,
which the torrent had torn up, with its roots downward, (they
forming the heavier end) into a chasm in the earth, which the
same hurricane makes by uprooting a forest tree. But I ask:
Who ordains the atmospheric laws which move hurricanes! Who
regulated the law of gravity? Who endued the roots of that
sapling, as its twigs are not endued, with the power of drawing
nutriment from the moist earth? Did the blind hurricane do all
this? Whenever they thus attempt to account for a result by
natural selection, they tacitly avail themselves of a selected
adaptation which is, in every case, *a priori* to the physical results.
Who conferred that prior adaptation and power? "If they had
not ploughed with our heifer, they had not found out our riddle."

You may be inclined to ask, why it is that I, who assuredly
believe this speculation of recent evolutionists will prove as
short-lived as it is shallow, introduce a discussion of it into this
venerable and stable science of theology? My reply is: that
"Darwinism" happens just now to be the current manifestation,
which the fashion of the day gives to the permanent anti-theistic tendency in sinful man. As long as men do not like to retain
God in their knowledge, the objection to the argument for His
existence will re-appear in some form. And the forms will all

be found cognate.   This recent evolution theory verges every
year nearer to the pagan atomic theory.   In discussing it under
its existing aspect, I seek to give you guidance which you
will find *ad rem*, in your dealing with the unbelieving minds of
our own day.   But I have also given you, in substance, principles which will be applicable to any phase of the anti-theistic
argument.

LECTURE IV.

DIVINE ATTRIBUTES.

––––

SYLLABUS.

1. How much can Reason infer of the Attributes of God? His Eternity?
How?
> Turrettin, Loc. iii, Qu. 10. Dick, Lect. 17. Dr. S. Clarke, § 1, 2, 5. Char-
> nock on Attr. Vol. 1, Discourse v.
2. His Unity? How? Turrettin, Qu. 3. Paley, Nat. Theology. Dr. Dick,
> Lect. 18. Dr. S. Clarke, §7. Maury, Physical Geography of Sea, p. 71.
3. His Spirituality and Simplicity? How? Turrettin, Qu. 7. Dick, Lect. 17.
> Dr. S. Clarke, §8. Rev. Ro. Hall, Sermon 1, Vol. 3d. Thornwell, Lect.
> 6th, pp. 162–166. Lect. 7th, pp, 186, &c.
4. His Immensity and Infinitude? How? Turrettin, Qu. 8 & 9. Dick, Lect.
> 19. Dr. S. Clarke, § 6. Charnock, Vol. 1, Discourse 7th. Thornwell,
> Lect. 8th.
5. His Immutability? Turrettin, Qu. 11. Thornwell, Lect 8, § 5. Dick, Lect.
> 20th. Dr. S. Clarke, §2. Charnock, Vol. i, Discourse 6th.

IT is exceedingly hard for us to return an exact answer to the
question, How much reason can infer of the attributes of
God?   Shall we say: "So much as the wisest
pagans, like Plato, discovered of them?"   It
still remains doubtful how much unacknowl-
edged aid he may not have received from Hebrew sources.
Many think that Plato received much through Pythagoras
and his Egyptian and Mesopotamian . researches.   Or if we
seek to find how far our own minds can go on this subject,
without drawing upon the Scriptures, we are not sure of the
answer; because when results have been given to us, it is
much easier to discover the logical tie between them and their
premises, than to detect unaided both proofs and results.   Euclid having told us that the square of the hypothenuse equals
the squares of the two remaining sides of every right angled
triangle, it becomes much easier to hunt up a synthetic argument to prove it, than it would have been to detect this great
relation by analysis.   But when we approach Natural Theology
we cannot forget the attributes which the Scriptures ascribe to
God.

*Traditionary knowl-
edge not to be separa-
ted from rational, here.*

Yet some things are as clear as God's being.   The first
and most obvious of these attributes is, that
He has no beginning, and no end.   By God's

1. God's eternity.

eternity divines also intend a third thing: His existence without succession. These three propositions express their
definition of His eternity: existence not related to time. For
the first: His being never had a beginning: for had there
ever been a time when the First Cause was not, nothing
could ever have existed. So natural reason indicates that
His being will never end, by this, that all pagans and philosophers make their gods immortal. The account of this
conclusion seems to be, that it follows from God's independence, self-existence, and necessary existence. These show that
there can be no cause to make God's being end. The immortality of the First Cause then is certain, unless we ascribe to it the
power and wish of self-annihilation. But neither of these is
possible. What should ever prompt God's will to such a volition? His simplicity of substance (to be separately proved anon)
does not permit the act; for the only kind of destruction of which
the universe has any experience, is by disintegration. The
necessity of God's existence proves it can never end. The
ground of His existence, intrinsic in Himself, is such that it
cannot but be operative; witness the fact that, had it been, at
any moment of the past infinite duration, inoperative, God and
the universe would have been, from that moment, forever
impossible.

But that God's existence is without succession, does not
seem so clear to natural reason. It is urged
Is it unsuccessive? by Turrettin that "God is immense. But
if His existence were measured by parts of duration, it
would not be incommensurable." This is illogical. Do not
the schoolmen themselves say, that *essentia* and *esse* are
not the same? To measure the continuance of God's *esse* by
successive parts of time, is not to measure His essence thereby.
A similar distinction shows the weakness of Turrettin's second
argument: "That because simple and immutable, He cannot
exist in succession, for the flux of being from past to present
and present to future would be change, and even change of
composition." I reply it is God's substance which is simple and
immutable; that its subsistence should be a continuance in sucession does not imply a change in substance. Nor is it correct
metaphysics to say that a subsistence in succession is compounded, namely of the essence and the successive *momenta* of
time through which it is transmitted. (See here, Kant.)

Nor is Dr Dick's argument even so plausible: That God's
being in a past eternity must be unsuccessive, because an infinite
past, composed of successive parts, is impossible; and whatever
God's mode of subsistence was, that it is, and will be. An infinite future made up of a succession of infinitely numerous
finite parts is possible, as Dick admits; and so an infinite past
thus constituted is equally as possible. Neither is comprehensible to our minds. If Turrettin or Charnock only meant that

God's existence is not a succession marked off by changes in
His essence or states, their reasonings would prove it.   But if it
is meant that the divine consciousness of its own existence has
no relation to successive duration, I think it unproved, and incapable of proof to us.   Is not the whole plausibility of the notion hence; that divines, following that analysis of our idea of
our own duration into the succession of our own consciousnesses,
(which Locke made so popular in his war against innate ideas,)
infer: Since all God's thoughts and acts are ever equally present
with Him, He can have no succession of His consciousnesses;
and so, no relation to successive time.   But the analysis is false
(see Lecture viii,) and would not prove the conclusion as to God, if
correct.   Though the creature's consciousnesses constituted an
unsuccessive unit act, as God's do, it would not prove that the
consciousness of the former was unrelated to duration.   But 2d.
In all the acts and changes of creatures, the relation of succession is actual and true.   Now, although God's knowledge of
these as it is subjective to Himself, is unsuccessive, yet it is
doubtless correct, i. e., true to the objective facts.   But these
have actual succession.   So that the idea of successive duration
must be in God's thinking.   Has He not all the ideas we have;
and infinitely more? But if God in thinking the objective, ever
thinks successive duration, can we be sure that His own consciousness of His own subsistence is unrelated to succession in
time? The thing is too high for us.   The attempt to debate it
will only produce one of those "antinomies" which emerge,
when we strive to comprehend the incomprehensible.

Does reason show the First Cause to be one or plural? If
one: whence the strong tendency to poly-
2. Unity of God.   theism? This may be explained in part
by the craving of the common mind for concrete ideas.   We
may add the causes stated by Turrettin : That man's sense
of weakness and exposure prompts him to lean upon superior
strength: That gratitude and admiration persuade him to
deify human heroes and benefactors at their deaths : And
that the copiousness and variety of God's agencies have
suggested to the incautious a plurality of agents.   Hodge
(Theol.   P. I. Ch. 3.) seems to regard Pantheism as the
chief source of polytheism.   He believes that pantheistic conceptions of the universe have been more persistent and prevalent
in all ages than any other.   "Polytheism has its origin in nature-
worship:......and nature worships rests on the assumption that
nature is God."

But I am persuaded a more powerful impulse to polytheism
arises from the co-action of two natural principles in the absence
of a knowledge of God in Christ.   One is the sense of weakness
and dependence, craving a superior power on whom to lean.
The other is the shrinking of conscious guilt from infinite holiness
and power.   The creature needs a God: the sinner fears a God.

The expedient which results is, the invention of intermediate and mediating divinities, more able than man to succour, yet less awful than the infinite God. Such is notably the account of the invention of saint worship, in that system of baptized polytheism known as Romanism. And here we see the divine adaptation of Christianity; in that it gives us Christ, very man, our brother: and very God, our Redeemer.

Reason does pronounce God one. But here again, I repudiate weak supports. Argues Turrettin: If there are more than one, all equal, neither is God: if unequal, only the highest is God. This idea of exclusive supremacy is doubtless essential to religious trust; Has it, thus far, been shown essential to the conception of a First Cause? Were there two or more independent eternal beings, neither of them would be an infallible object of trust. But has it been proved as yet, that we are entitled to expect such a one? Again, Dr. S. Clarke urges: The First Cause exists necessarily: but (a.) This necessity must operate forever, and everywhere alike, and, (b,) This absolute sameness must make oneness. Does not this savour of Spinozism? Search and see. As to the former proposition: all that we can infer from necessary existence is, that it cannot but be just what it is. What it is, whether singular, dual, plural; that is just the question. As to the 2d proposition, sameness of operation does not necessarily imply oneness of effect. Have two successive nails from the same machine, necessarily numerical identity? Others argue again: We must ascribe to God every conceivable perfection, because, if not, another more perfect might be conceived; and then he would be the God. I reply, yes, if he existed. It is no reasoning to make the capacity of our imaginations the test of the substantive existence of objective things. Again, it is argued more justly, that if we can show that the eternal self-existent Cause must be absolute and infinite in essence, then His exclusive unity follows, for that which is infinite is all-embracing as to that essence. Covering, so to speak, all that kind of being, it leaves no room for anything of its kind coördinate with itself. Just as after defining a universe, we cannot place any creature outside of it: so, if God is infinite, there can be but one. Whether He is infinite we shall inquire.

The valid and practical argument, however, for God's unity

Argued from Interdependence of all His Effects.

is the convergency of design and interdependency of all His works. All dualists, indeed, from Zoroaster to Manes, find their pretexts in the numerous cross-effects in nature, seeming to show cross-purposes:—e. g. one set of causes educes a fruitful crop: when it is just about to gladden the reaper, it is beaten into the mire by hail, through another set of atmospheric causes. Everywhere poisons are set against food, evil against good, death against life. Are there not two antagonist wills in Nature? Now it is a poor reply, especially to the mind aroused by the vast and solemn question of the origin of evil, or to the heart wrung by irresistible calamity, to say with Paley, that we see similarity of contrivance in all natnre. Two hostile kings may wage internecine war, by precisely the same means and appliances. The true answer is, that, question nature as we may, through all her kingdoms, animal, inorganic, celestial, from the minutest disclosures of the microscope, up to the grandest revelations of the telescope, second causes are all inter-dependent; and the designs convergent so far as comprehended, so that each effect depends, more or less directly, on all the others. Thus, in the first instance: The genial showers and suns gave, and the hail destroyed, the grain. But look deeper: They are all parts of one and the same meteorologic system. The same cause exhaled the vapour which made the genial rain and the ruthless hail. Nay, more; the pneumatic currents which precipitated the hail, were constituent parts of a system which, at the same moment, were doing somewhere a work of blessing. Nature is one machine, moved by one mind. Should you see a great mill, at one place delivering its meal to the suffering poor, and at another crushing a sportive child between its iron wheels: it would be hasty to say, "Surely, these must be deeds of opposite agents." For, on searching, you find that there is but one water-wheel, and not a single smaller part which does not inosculate, nearly or remotely, with that. This instance suggests also, that dualism is an inapplicable hypothesis. Is *Ormusd* stronger than *Ahriman*? Then he will be victor. Are both equal in power? Then the one would not allow the other to work with his machinery; and the true result, instead of being a mixture of cross-effects, would be a sort of "dead lock" of the wheels of nature.

　　　　We only know substance by its properties; but our reason intuitively compels us to refer the properties
3. God a Spirit.　　known to a *subjectum*, a *substratum* of true being, or *substantia*. We thus know, first, spiritual substance, as that which is conscious, thinks, feels, and wills; and then material substance, as that which is unconscious, thoughtless, lifeless, inert. To all the latter we are compelled to give some of the attributes of extension; to the former it is imposible to ascribe any of them. Now, therefore, if this first Cause is to be referred to any class of substance known to us, it must be to one of these two. Should it be conceived that there is a third class, unknown to us, to which the first Cause may possibly belong, it would follow, supposing we had been compelled to refer the first Cause to the class of spirits, (as we shall see anon that we must,) that to this third class must also belong all creature spirits as *species* to a *genus*. For we know the attributes, those of thought and will, common between God and them; it would be the *differentia*, which would

be unknown. Is the first Cause, then, to be referred to the class, spirits? Yes; because we find it possessed, in the highest possible degree, of every one of the attributes by which we recognize spirit. It thinks; as we know by two signs. It produced us, who think; and there cannot be more in the effect than was in the cause. It has filled the universe with contrivances, the results of thought. It chooses; for this selection of contrivances implies choice. And again, whence do creatures derive the power of choice, if not from it? It is the first Cause of life; but this is obviously an attribute of spirit, because we find full life nowhere, except we see signs of spirit along with it. The first Cause is the source of force and of motion. But matter shows us, in no form, any power to originate motion. Inertia is its normal condition. We shall find God's power and presence penetrating and inhabiting all material bodies; but matter has a displacing power, as to all other matter. That which is impenetrable obviously is not ubiquitous.

But may not God be like us, matter and spirit in one person? I answer, No. Because this would be to be organized; but organization can neither be eternal, nor immutable. Again, if He is material, why is it that He is never cognizable to any sense? We know that He is all about us always, yet never visible, audible, nor palpable. And last, He would no longer be penetrable to all other matter, nor ubiquitous.

Divines are accustomed to assert of the divine substance an absolute simplicity. If by this it is meant *Simplicity of God's substance.* that He is uncompounded, that His substance is ineffably homogeneous, that it does not exist by assemblage of atoms, and is not discerptible, it is true. For all this is clear from His true spirituality and eternity. We must conceive of spiritual substance as existing thus; because all the acts, states, and consciousnesses of spirits, demand a simple, uncompounded substance. The same view is probably drawn from His eternity and independence. For the only sort of construction or creation, of which we see anything in our experience, is that made by some aggregation of parts, or composition of substance; and the only kind of death we know is by disintegration. Hence, that which has neither beginning nor end is uncompounded.

But that God is more simple than finite spirits in this, that in Him substance and attribute are one and the same, as they are not in them, I know nothing. The argument is, that as God is immutably what He is, without succession, His essence does not like ours pass from mode to mode of being, and from act to act, but is always all modes, and exerting all acts; hence His modes and His acts are Himself. God's thought is God. He is not active, but activity. I reply, that if this means more than is true of a man's soul, viz: that its thought is no entity, save the soul thinking; that its thought, as abstracted from the soul that thinks it, is only an abstraction and not a thing; it is undoubtedly false. For then we should have reached the pantheistic notion, that God has no other being than the infinite series of His own consciousnesses and acts. Nor would we be far off from the other result of this fell theory; that all that is, is God. For he who has identified God's acts thus with His being, will next identifiy the effects thereof, the existence of the creatures therewith.

Infinitude means the absolutely limitless character of God's essence. Immensity the absolutely limitless

4. God Immense.

being of His substance. His being, as eternal, is in no sense circumscribed by time ; as immense, in no wise circumscribed by space. But let us not conceive of this as a repletion of infinite space by diffusion of particles : like, e. g., an elastic gas released *in vacuo*. The scholastic *formula* was, " The whole substance, in its whole essence, is simultaneously present in every point of infinite space, yet without multiplication of itself. This is unintelligble ; (but so is His immensity :) it may assist to exclude the idea of material extension. God's *omnipresence* is His similar presence in all the space of the universe.

Now, to me, it is no proof of His immensity to say, the necessity of His nature must operate everywhere, because absolute from all limitation. The inference does not hold. Nor to say that our minds impel us to ascribe all perfection to God; whereas exclusion from any space would be a limitation; for this is not conclusive of existences without us. Nor to say, that God must be everywhere, because His action and knowledge are everywhere, and these are but His substance acting and knowing. Were the latter true, it would only prove God's *omnipresence*. But so far as reason apprehends His immensity, it seems to my mind to be a deduction from His *omnipresence*. The latter we deduce from His simultaneous action and knowledge, everywhere and perpetually, throughout His universe. Now, let us not say that God is nothing else than His acts. Let us not rely on the dogma of the mediæval physicks: "That substance cannot act save where it is present." But God, being the first Cause, is the source of all force. He is also pure spirit. Now we may admit that the sun (by its attraction of gravitation) may act upon parts of the solar system removed from it by many millions of miles; and that, without resorting to the hypothesis of an elastic ether by which to propagate its impulse. It may be asked: if the sun's action throughout the solar system fails to prove His presence throughout it, how does God's universal action prove His *omnipresence*? The answer is in the facts above stated. There is no force originally inherent in matter. The power which is deposited in it, must come from the first Cause, and must work under His perpetual superintendence. His, not theirs, is the recollection, intelligence, and purpose which guide. Now, as we are conscious that our intel·

ligence only acts where it is present, and where it perceives, this view of Providence necessarily impels us to impute omnipresence to this universal cause. For the power of the cause must be where the effect is.

But now, having traced His being up to the extent of the universe, which is to us practically immense, why limit it there? Can the mind avoid the inference that it extends farther? If we stood on the boundary of the universe, and some angel should tell us that this was "the edge of the divine substance," would it not strike us as contradictory? Such a Spirit, already seen to be omnipresent, has no bounding outline. Again, we see God doing and regulating so many things over so vast an area, and with such absolute sovereignty, that we must believe His resources and power are absolute within the universe. But it is practically boundless to us. To succeed always inside of it, God must command such a multitude of relations, that we are practically impelled to the conclusion, that there are no relations, and nothing to be related, outside His universe. But if His power is exclusive of all other, in all infinite space, we can scarcely avoid the conclusion that His substance is in all space.

By passing from one to another of God's attributes, and
God Infinite. discovering their boundless character, we shall at last establish the infinitude of His essence or nature. It is an induction from the several parts.

5. By GOD'S IMMUTABILITY we mean that He is incapable of change. As to His attributes, His nature, his purposes, He remains the same from eternity to eternity. Creation and other acts of God in time, imply no change in Him; for the purpose to do these acts at that given time was always in Him, just as when He effected them. This attribute follows from His necessary existence; which is such that He cannot be any other than just what He is. It follows from his self-existence and independence; there being none to change Him. It follows from His simplicity: for how can change take place, when there is no composition to be changed? It follows from His perfection; for being infinite, He cannot change for the better; and will not change for the worse. Scarcely any attribute is more clearly manifested to the reason than God's immutability.

LECTURE V.

DIVINE ATTRIBUTES.—Continued.

God all Powerful. WHEN we enquire after God's power we mean here, not his *potestas*, or ἐξουσία, authority, but His *potentia* or δύναμις. When we say: He can do all things, we do not mean that He can suffer, or be changed, or be hurt; for the passive capacity of these things is not power, but weakness or defect. We ascribe to God no passive power. When we say that God's power is omnipotence, we mean that its object is only the possible, not the absolutely impossible. Here, however, we must again define, that by the absolutely impossible, we do not mean the physically impossible. For we see God do many things above nature, [φύσις ;] that is above what material, or human, or angelic nature can effect. But we mean the doing of that which implies an inevitable contradiction. Some, e. g. Lutherans of the older school, say it is a derogation from God's omnipotence, to limit it by the inevitable self-contradiction: [that He is able to confer actual ubiquity on Christ's material body.] But we object: Popularly, God's omnipotence may be defined as His ability to do all things. Now of two incompatibles, both cannot become entities together; for, by the terms of the case, the entity of the one destroys that of the other. But if they are not, and cannot be both things, the power of doing all things does not embrace the doing of incompatibles. But 2nd., more conclusively ; if even omnipotence could effect both of two contradictories, then the self-contradictory would become the true; which is impossible for man to believe. Hence, 3d., the assertion would infringe the foundation principle of all truth; that a thing cannot be thus, and not thus, in the same sense, and at the same time.

We may add, 4th, that power is that which produces an effect; and every effect is a change. Hence the absolutely changeless is not subject to power; be that power finite or infinite. Here is an application of my remark, which no reflec-

46

ting person will dispute: The event which has actually happened at some past time, is, as such, irrevocable. Even omnipotence has no relevancy towards recalling it. So, when a given effect is in place, the contradictory effect is as absolutely precluded from the same time and place. There is no room for change; and therefore, no room for power.

But between these limits, we believe God is omnipotent: That is, His power is absolute as to all being. In proof, note: He obviously has great power; He has enough to produce all the effects in the universe. Cause implies power: He is the universal first Cause. 2d. His power is at least equal to the aggregate of all the forces in the universe, of every kind; because all sprang from Him at first. A mechanic constructs a machine far stronger than himself; it is because he borrows the forces of nature. There was no source whence God could borrow. He must needs produce all those forces of nature Himself; and He sustains them. 3d. God is one, and all the rest is produced by Him; so, since all the forces that exist, except His own, depend on Him, they cannot limit His force. Hence, it is absolutely unlimited, save by its own nature. And now, the exhibition of it already made in creation is so vast and varied, embracing (probably) the very existence of matter, and certainly its whole organization, the very existence of finite spirits, and all their attributes, and the government of the whole, that this power is practically to us immense. 4th. We have found God immutable. Whatever He once did, He can do again. He is as able to go on making universes such as this indefinitely, as to make this. 5th. He does not exist by sucession; and hence He is able to make two or more at once, as well as successively. It is hard to conceive how power can be more infinite than this.

Once more, God's power must be conceived of as primarily immediate; i. e. His simple volition is its effectuation; and no means interpose between the will and the effect. Our wills operate on the whole external world through our members; and they, often, through implements, still more external. But God has no members; so that we must conceive of His will as producing its effects on the objects thereof as immediately as our wills do on our bodily members. Moreover the first exertion of God's power must have been immediate; for at first nothing existed to be means. God's immutability assures us that the power of so acting is not lost to Him. The attribution of such immediate power to God does not deny that He also acts through "second causes."

God's Power Immediate.

None who believe in God have ever denied to Him knowledge and wisdom. Wisdom is the employment of things known, with judicious reference to proper ends. Now God is Spirit: but to

2. Wisdom Distinguished from Knowledge.

think, to know, to choose are the very powers of spirits. The
universe is full of beautiful contrivances. These exhibit knowledge, wisdom, and choice, coextensive with the aggregate of
the whole.

But I had best pause and explain the usual distinctions
made in God's knowledge. His *scientia visi-*
God's Knowledge of   *onis*, or *libera*, is His knowledge of whatever
two Kinds   has existence before His view; that is, of
all that is, has been, or is decreed to be. His *scientia intelli-
gentiae,* or *simplex* (unconditioned by any volition) is His infinite conception of all the possible, which He does not purpose
to effectuate. Others add a *scientia media*, which they suppose
to be His knowledge of contingent effects including chiefly the
future free and responsible acts of free agents. They call it mediate, because they suppose God foreknows these acts only inferentially, by means of His knowledge of their characters and
circumstances. But Calvinists regard all this as God's *scientia
visionis.* Let us see whether, in all these directions, God's
knowledge is not without limit.

First, I begin from the simple fact that He is spiritual and
omnipotent First Cause. All being save His
Proved from God's   own is the offspring of His will. Grant a God,
Will.   and the doctrine of a providence is almost
self-evident to the reason. This refers not only phenomena of
specific creation, but all phenomena, to God's will. If any thing
or event has actuality, it is because He has willed it. But now,
can volition be conceived, in a rational spirit, except as conditioned on cognition *a priori* to itself? Hence, 1st, a knowledge
is implied in God, *a priori* to and coextensive with His whole
purpose. But because this purpose (that of universal almighty
First Cause) includes the whole that has been, is, and shall be;
and since volition does not obscure, but fix the cognition which
is the object thereof, God has a *scientia visionis*, embracing all
the actual. 2nd. Will implies selection: there must be more
in the *a priori* cognition than is in the volition. Hence
God's *scientia simplex* or knowledge of the possible, is wider
than his *scientia visionis.* This view will be found to have
settled the question between us and Arminians, whether God
purposes the acts of free agents because He has foreseen their
certain futurition, or whether their futurition is certain because
He has purposed them. Look and see.

But more popularly; all God's works reveal marks of His
knowledge, thought and wisdom. But these
Knowledge and wis-   works are so vast, so varied, so full of contri-
dom seen in His works. vance, they disclose to us a knowledge practically boundless. His infinite power implies omniscience, for
"knowledge is power." Certain success implies full knowledge
of means and effects. We saw God is omnipresent; but He is
spirit. Hence He knows all that is present to Him; for it is the

nature of spirit to know.   A parallel argument arises from God's providence; (which reason unavoidably infers.)   The ends which are subserved show as much knowledge and wisdom as the structure of the beings used—so that we see evidence of complete knowledge of all second causes, including reasonable agents and their acts.   For so intimate is the connection of cause with cause, that perfect knowledge of the whole alone can certify results from any.   Here also we learn, God's knowledge of past and future is as perfect as of present things; for the completion of far-reaching plans, surely evolved from their remote causes, implies the retention by God of all the past, and the clear anticipation of all the future.   Nay, what ground of certain futurition is there, save that God purposes it?   His omnipotence here shows that He has a complete foreknowledge; because that which is to be is no other than what He purposes.   God's immutability proves also His perfect knowledge of past, present, and future.   Did He discover new things, these might become bases for new purposes, or occasions of new volitions, and God would no longer be the same in will.   God's omniscience is implied also in all His moral attributes; for if He does not perform His acts understandingly, He is not praiseworthy in them.   Last, our consciences reveal an intuition of God's infinite knowledge; for our fears recognize Him as seeing our most secret, as well as our public acts.   His unfading knowledge of the past is especially pointed out by conscience ; for whenever she remembers, she takes it for granted that God does.   Thus we find God's *scientia visionis* is a perfect knowledge, past, present, and future, of all beings and all their actions, including those of moral agents.

How do we infer His knowledge of the possible? A reasonable being must first conceive, in order to produce. He cannot make, save as He first has his own idea, to make by. God then, before He began to make the universe, must have had in His mind a conception, in all its details, of whatever He was to effectuate.   Let me, in passing, call your attention to a difference between the human and the divine imagination, which is suggested here.   You are all familiar with the assertion of the psychologists, that our imaginations cannot create elements of conception, but only new combinations.   The original elements, which this faculty reconstructs into new images, must first be given to the mind from without, through sense-perception.   Thus, in human conception, the thing must be before the thought; but in God's, the thought must have been before the thing, for the obvious reason, that the thing could only come into existence by virtue of God's conception *a priori* to any objective perception.   It is thus demonstrable, that the divine mind has this power, which is impossible to the human imagination.   Such is the difference between the independent, infinite, and the depen-

Scientia Simplex Inferred.

*4

dent, finite spirit. But even in this contrast, we see that the imagination is one of man's noblest faculties, and most god-like. But, to return: All that is now in *esse*, must have been thought by God, while only in *posse*, and before it existed. How long before? As God changes not, it must have been from eternity. There then was a knowledge of the possible. But was that which is now actual, the only possible before God's thought? Sovereignty implies selection; and this, two or more things to chose among. And unless God had before Him the ideas of all possible universes, He may not have chosen the one which, had He known more, would have pleased Him best; His power was limited. In conclusion, the infaiibility of all God's knowledge is implied in His power. Ordinarily, he chooses to work only through regular second causes. But causes and effects are so linked that any uncertainty in one jeopardizes all the subsequent. But we see that God is possessed of some way of effectuating all His will. Therefore He infallibly knows all causes; but each effect is in turn a cause.

We must also believe that God knows all things intuitively
God's Knowledge all Primitive.
and not deductively. A deduction is a discovery. To discover something implies previous imperfection of knowledge. God's knowledge, moreover, is not successive as ours is, but simultaneous. Inference implies succession; for conclusion comes after premise.

God's righteousness, as discoverable by reason, means,
3. Rectitude.
generally, His rectitude, and not His distributive justice. Is He a moral being? Is His will regulated by right? Reason answers, yes; by justice, by faithfulness, by goodness, by holiness.

First, because this character is manifest in the order of nature
Rectitude of God proven by Bishop Butler.
which He has established. This argument cannot be better stated than in the method of Bishop Butler. 1. God is Governor over man; as appears from the fact that in a multitude of cases, He rewards our conduct with pleasures and pains. For the order of Nature, whether maintained by God's present providence, or impressed on it at first only, is God's doing; its rewards are His rewarding. 2. The character of proper rewards,· and especially punishments, appears clearly in these traits. They follow acts, though pleasant in the doing. They sometimes tarry long, and at last fall violently. After men have gone certain lengths, repentance and reform are vain, &c. 3. The reward and penalties of society go to confirm the conclusion, because they are of God's ordaining. Second; This God's rule is moral; because the conduct which earns well-being is virtuous; and ill-being, sinful. True remedial processes, such as repentance, reform, have their peculiar pains; but these are chargeable rather to the sin, than the remedy. True again; the

wicked sometimes prosper; but natural reason cannot but regard this as an exception, which future awards will right.   Further : Society (which is God's ordinance,) usually rewards virtue
and punishes vice.   Love of approbation is instinctive ; but
God thus teaches men most generally to approve the right.   And
last :   How clear the course of Nature makes God's approval of
the right appear, is seen in this; that all virtuous societies tend
to self-perpetuation in the long run, and all vicious ones to self-
extinction.   Third :   Life is full of instances of probation, as
seed-time for harvest, youth for old age, which indicates that
man is placed under a moral probation here.

But a most powerful argument for God's rectitude is that
presented by the existence of conscience in
God's Rectitude Ar- man.   Its teachings are universal.   Do some
gued from Conscience.
deny its intuitive authority, asserting it to be
only a result of habit or policy ?   It is found to be a universal
result; and this proves that God has laid in us some intentional
foundation for the result.   Now, whatever, the differences of
moral opinion, the peculiar trait of conscience is that it always
enjoins that which seems to the person right.   It may be disre-
garded ; but the man must think, if he thinks at all, that in doing so, he has done wrong. The act it condemns may give pleasure ; but the wickedness of the act, if felt at all, can only give
pain.   Conscience is the imperative faculty.   Now if God had
not conceived the moral distinction, He could not have imprinted it on us.   But is His will governed by it?   Does he not,
from eternity, know extension as an object of thought, an attribute of matter; and sin, as a quality of the rebel creature ?
Yet He Himself is neither extended, nor evil.   The reply is :
since God has, from eternity, had the idea of moral distinction, whence was it is derived, save from His own perfection ?
In what being illustrated, if not in Himself?   But more, conscience is God's imperative in the human soul.   This is its peculiarity among rational judgments.   But since God implanted
conscience, its imperative is the direct expression of His will,
that man shall act righteously.   But when we say, that every
known expression of a being's will is for the right, this is virtually to say that he wills always righteously.   The King's character is disclosed in the character of his edicts.

God's truth and faithfulness are evinced by the same arguments ; and by these, in addition.   The structure of our senses
and intelligence, and the adaptation of external nature thereto,
are His handiwork.   Now, when our senses and understanding
are legitimately used, their informations are always found,
so far as we have opportunity to test them, correspondent to
reality.   One sense affirms the correctness of another.   Senses
confirm reasonings, and *vice versa*.   Last, unless we can po tulate truth in God, there is no truth anywhere.   For our laws of
perception and thought being His imprint, if His truth cannot be

relied on, their truth cannot, and universal skepticism is the result. " The world is full of the goodness of the Lord." I only

4. God's Benevolence. aim to classify the evidences that God is be-nevolent. And 1st, generally: since God is the original Cause of all things, all the happiness amidst His works is of His doing; and therefore proves His benevolence. 2d, more definitely: the natures of all orders of sentient beings, if not violated, are constructed, in the main, to secure their appropriate well-being. Instance the insect, the fish, the bird, the ox, the man. 3d. Many things occur in the special providence of God which show Him benevolent; such as providing remedial medicines, &c., for pain, and special interpositions in danger. 4th. God might, compatibly with justice, have satisfied Himself with so adapting external nature to man's senses and mind as to make it minister to his being and intelligence, and thus secure the true end of his existence, without, in so doing, making it pleasant to his senses. Our food and drink might have nourished us, our senses of sight and hearing might have informed us, without making food sweet, light beautiful, and sounds melodious to us. And yet appetite might have impelled us to use our senses and take our food. Such, in a word, is God's goodness, that He turns aside to strew incidental enjoyment. The more unessential these are to His main end, the stronger the argument. 5th. God has made all the beneficent emotions, love sympathy, benevolence, forgiveness, delightful in their exercise; and all the malevolent ones, as resentment, envy, revenge, painful to their subjects; thus teaching us that He would have us propagate happiness and diminish pain. Last: Conscience, which is God's imperative, enjoins benevolence on us as one duty, whenever compatible with others. Benevolence is therefore God's will; and doubtless, He who wills us to be so, is benevolent Himself.

No Pagan theist ever has doubted God's providence. You may refer me to the noted case of the Epicureans; they were practical atheists. Their notion that it was derogatory to the blessedness and majesty of the gods to be wearied with terrestial affairs, betrays in one word a false conception of the divine perfections. Fatigue, confusion, worry, are the result of weakness and limitation. To infinite knowledge and power the fullest activities are infinitely easy, and so, pleasurable. Common sense argues from the perfection of God, that He does uphold and direct all things by His Providence. His wisdom and power enable Him to it. His goodness and justice certainly impel Him to it; for it would be neither benevolent nor just, having brought sentient beings into existence, to neglect their welfare, rights and guilt. God's wisdom will certainly prosecute those suitable ends for which He made the universe, by superintending it. To have made it without an object; or, having one, to overlook that object wholly after the world was already made,

would neither of them argue a wise being.   The manifest dependence of the creature confirms the argument.

But there stands out the great fact of the existence of much
suffering in the universe of God; and reason

Existence of Evil.
How explained.   asks: "If God is almighty, all-wise, sovereign,
why, if benevolent, did He admit any suffer-
ing in His world? Has He not chosen it because He is
pleased with it *per se ?* It is no answer to say : God makes the suffering the means of good,and so chooses it,not for its own sake,but
for its results. If He is omnipotent and all-wise,He could have produced the same *quantum* of good by other means, leaving out
the suffering. Is it replied: No, that the virtues of sympathy,
forgiveness, patience, submission, could have had no existence
unless suffering existed? I reply that then their absence would
have been no blemish or lack in the creature's character.
It is only because there is suffering, that sympathy therewith is
valuable. Suppose it be said again : "All physical evil is the
just penalty of moral evil," and so necessitated by God's justice? The great difficulty is only pushed one step farther back.
For, while it is true, sin being admitted, punishment ought to
follow, the question returns : Why did the Almighty permit sin,
unless He be defective in holiness as in benevolence? It is no *theodicee* to say that God cannot always exclude sin, without infringing free-agency; for I prove, despite all Pelagians, from Celestius downwards, that God can do it, by His pledge to render
elect angels and men indefectible for ever. Does God then choose
sin? This is the mighty question, where a *theodicee* has been so
often attempted in vain. The most plausible theory is that of
the *optimist*; that God saw this actual universe, though involving evil, is on the whole the most beneficent universe, which
was possible in the nature of things. For they argue, in support of that proposition : God being infinitely good and wise,
cannot will to bring out of *posse* into *esse*, a universe which is
on the whole, less beneficent than any possible universe. The
obvious objections to this Beltistic scheme are two. It assumes
without warrant, that the greatest natural good of creation is
God's highest end in creating and governing the universe. We
shall see, later in this course, how this assumption discloses
itself as a grave error; and in the hands of the followers of
Leibnitz and the optimists, vitiates their whole theory of morals
and their doctrine of atonement. The other objection is, that it
limits the power of God. Being infinite, He could have made
a universe including a *quantum* of happiness equal to that in
our universe, and exclusive of our evils.

But there is a more legitimate and defensible hypothesis. It
is not competent to us to say that the benefi-

Optimist Theory Mod-
ified.   cence of result is, or or ought to be, God's
chief ultimate end in creation and provi-
dence. It is one of His worthy ends ; this is all we should as-

sert.   But may we not assume that doubtless there is a set of
ends, (no man may presume to say what all the parts of that
collective end are,) which God eternally sees to be the properest ends of His creation and providence ?   I think we safely
may.   Doubtless those ends are just such as they ought to be,
with reference to all God's perfections ; and the proper inference from those perfections is, that He is producing just such a
universe, in its structure and management, as will, on the whole,
most perfectly subserve that set of ends.   In this sense, and no
other, I am an optimist.   But now, let us make this all-important
remark : When the question is raised, whether a God of infinite
power can be benevolent in permitting natural, and holy in permitting moral evil, in His universe, the burden of proving the
negative rests on the doubter.   We who hold the affirmative
are entitled to the presumption, because the contrivances of
creation and providence are beneficent so far as we comprehend
them.   Even the physical and moral evils in the universe are obviously so overruled, as to bring good out of evil.   (Here is the
proper value in the argument, of the instances urged by the optimist : that suffering makes occasion for fortitude and sympathy,
&c,, &c.; and that even man's apostasy made way for the glories
of Redemption.)   The conclusion from all these beautiful instances is, that so far as finite minds can follow them, even the
evils tend towards the good.   Hence, the presumptive probability is in favor of a solution of the mystery, consistent with
the infinite perfections of God.   To sustain that presumption
against the impugner, we have only to make the hypothesis, that
for reasons we cannot see, God saw it was not possible to separate the existing evils from that system which, as a whole, satisfied His own properest ends.   Now let the skeptic disprove that
hypothesis !   To do so, he must have omniscience.   Do you say,
I cannot demonstrate it ?   Very true; for neither am I omniscient
But I have proved that the reasonable presumption is in favor
of the hypothesis; that it may be true, although we cannot explain how it comes to be true.

   If the existence and moral perfections of God be admitted,
no one will dispute that man bears moral re-
5. Man's Duties to lations to Him.   This appears very simply
God.
from the fact that man is a moral being related
to God as his Maker and providential Ruler.   It is also inferri-
ble from the marks of a probation, and a moral rule appearing
in the course of nature.   And it is emphatically pronounced by
the native supremacy of conscience, commanding us to obey.
Rational Deists as well as Natural Theologians have attempted
to deduce the duties man owes his Creator.   They are usually
(on grounds sufficiently obvious) summed up as : 1. Love, with
reverence and gratitude ; 2. Obedience ; 3. Penitence ; 4. Worship.   The rule of obedience, is, of course, in natural religion,
the law of nature in the conscience.

LECTURE VI.

MATERIALISM.

SYLLABUS.

1. What use is attempted, of the physical doctrine of the "Correlation of Forces," by recent Materialists?

2. State and refute the theory which seeks to identify animal life with vegetable, in protoplasm.

3. Show the connection between Materialism and Atheism; and the moral results of the latter. See,

Hodge's Systematic Theology, Vol. i, pp. 246 to 299. Turrettin Locus v. Qu. 14th. Lay Sermons of Dr. Th. Huxley. Dr. Stirling on "Physical Basis of Life." Dr. Thomas Brown, Lectures, 96th.

DR. Thomas Brown, in his Lectures, very properly remarks, that the question of man's immortality is involved with that of the immateriality of his soul. There is, in-
Soul's Immateriality involves Immortality. deed, a small class of materialists, who might hold man's immortality, without contradicting themselves. It is that which, like Thomas Jefferson, believed that the soul, while distinct from the body, and an independent, personal substance and monad, is some refined species of matter. They are willing to recognize only one kind of substance. But modern materialists usually deny that there is any such separate substance as soul. They regard its functions, whether of intelligence, feeling, or volition, as all results of some organization of matter. They consequently believe, that when dissolution separates the body into its elements, what men call the soul is as absolutely obliterated, as is the colour or fragrance or form of a rose, when its substance has mouldered into dust. We utterly deny both forms of materialism. My purpose at this time is to consider a class of arguments, now again current, which may be called the physical arguments, upon the nature of life and spirit. The psychological arguments, if I may so term them, will be presented afterwards.

We have seen how evolutionists seek to identifiy human, with animal life; by supposing man to have
Does Correlation of Forces prove Soul a Force only? been slowly evolved even from the lowest form of animated creatures. If the success of this be granted, then only one more step will remain. This will be to identify animal, with vegetable life. Thus, all evidence of any separate substance of life, (*anima*) will be removed. This last step, Dr. Huxley, for instance, undertakes to supply, in his Physical Basis of Life. Before we proceed to state this theory, however, the way must be prepared, by exposing the use attempted to be made of the modern physical doctrine of the "correlation of forces."

Sound reflection would seem to indicate, that when a given physical force appears, it does not rise *ex nihilo*, and does not suffer annihilation when it seems to end. It is transmuted into

some other form of force.   Thus: in the boiler of a steam-engine, so many degrees of caloric absorbed into a given volume of
water, evolve so many pounds' weight of lifting force.   In like
manner, it is now supposed that light, heat, electricity, chemical
affinity, are all correlated.   If we knew enough of physics, it is
supposed we should find, that one of these forces might always
be measured in terms of the others.   When one of them seems
to disappear, it is because it is transmuted into some other.
The doctrine, in this sense, is held by many Christian physicists :
and in this form, Theology has nothing to do with it either for
denial or affirmation.   But recent materialists catch at it for an
anti-theological use.   They would have us infer from it, that all
physical causes are identical.   Then, say they, this analogy
should lead us to conclude the same of what have hitherto been
called vital causes; that in short, there is but one cause in Nature,
and that is of the nature of force ; while all effects are accordingly of the nature of material motion.   Thus, the converging
lines of science, say they, point to a central Force, as the only
God, which the rational man will accept.   All the universe is
the one substance (if it be a substance) matter.   And all effects
are forms of material motion, molecular or in masses.

    It is obvious that this is at best, but a vague speculation.
I deny that its basis in physical science has
been solidly settled, even could we grant that
the use made of that basis was not utterly
licentious.   Has the force of gravity been yet correlated with
heat, light and electricity? It seems fatal to such an idea, that
a mass still has the same gravity, while its calorific and electrical
conditions are most violently changed!   It may well be doubted,
whether the force of mechanical adhesion between the atoms of
homogeneous solids, is identical with chemical affinity, or with
electricity, or heat.

    The latter diminishes the atomic adhesion of solid iron, or
gold, reducing it to a liquid? But at the same time it increases
the cohesion of clay.

    Again: That this hypothesis in its extreme form, is by no
means proved, appears from the ease with which a counter-hypo-
thesis may be advanced, which physicists are not able absolutely
to exclude.   Let it be supposed that material forces are permanent properties of the different kinds of matter in which they
severally inhere.   Let it be supposed that these forces are truly
distinct from each other, and intrinsically ever present, in the
sense of being always ready to act.   Then, all that is needed to
cause the action of a given force, is to release it from the coun-
ter-action of some other force; which has hitherto counterpoised
it, thus producing for the time, a non-action which appeared to
be rest.   Then, every physical effect would be the result of a
concurrence of two or more forces; and each force would forever maintain intrinsically, its distinct integrity.   This hypoth

All forces not proved to be correlated.

esis has very plausible supports in a number of physical facts; and it is in strict accordance with the metaphysics of causation. But, not to intrude into physics: we might grant the identity of these forces of dead matter, and yet deny that they are correlated to vitality. No one has ever succeeded in transmuting any of them into vital causation, nor in measuring vitality in the terms of any of these forces. To say that all thought and volition are attended by muscular contractions, and oscillations of the nerve-matter of the brain, is very far from showing that they constitute them. Let it be proved that the nerve-force in a human muscle is electrical. Let it be observed that surprise, shame, fear, or muscular exertion, stimulate the animal heat, and that the caloric in a blush upon the cheek of youth is as literally caloric as that in the boiler of a steam-engine. To what does all this come? Who or what uses these modifications of organs? The living spirit. This muscular action is quiescent at one time, active at another, at the bidding of spirit. The eyes and ears may carry to that spirit the objective sensations which are the occasions of emotion; but the emotion is always from within. Let the state of the living spirit be changed: and the occasional cause has no more power to raise the glow of hot blood, or to nerve the arm, than in a stone. As a Christian writer has well replied: the attempt to identify vital, or spiritual causation with material forces would be exploded by this one instance. Let opprobrious words be addressed to a plain Briton in the French language: and no pulse is quickened, no nerve becomes tense. Now translate the insult into English: at once his cheek burns, and his arm is nerved to strike. Why this? The French words were as audible as the English, they vibrated to the same degree upon the auditory nerves. But to the spirit of the Briton, there was no meaning. A mere *idea* has made all this difference. The cause is solely in a mental modification, of which the material *phenomenon* was merely occasion. Tyndal himself confesses that this argument of the materialists is naught: that though they had proved all they profess to prove, there is an unbridged chasm between force and life.

For, in the next place, physical force and vital causation are heterogeneous. The former, in all its phases, is unintelligent, involuntary, measurable by weight and velocity, and quantity of matter affected, producing motion, mechanical or molecular, and tending to *equilibrium*. All animal life has some species of spontaneity. Spirit, as a cause, has the unique attribute of free-agency, the opposite of *inertia*, self-active, directive. Mind and its modifications cannot be measured in any physical terms or quantities; and *hence they cannot be correlated*. Volition controls or directs force; is not transmuted into it. If we descend to the lowest forms of animal vitality, we still find a gulf between it and dead matter, which science never has passed

Vital Cause Heterogeneous.

over. No man has ever educed life, without the use of a germ-inal vital cause. This vital cause, again, resists the material forces. When it departs, caloric and chemical affinities resume their sway over the matter of the body lately living, as over any similar matter; but as long as the vital cause is present, it is directly antagonistic to them.

2. Huxley, who himself admits that there is no *genesis* of life from dead matter, yet very inconsistently at-tempts to find a physical basis of life, common to animals and plants, in a substance whose molecules are chemically organized, which he calls *protoplasm*. He asserts that this, however varied, always exhibits a three fold unity, of *faculty*, of *form* and of *substance*. 1st. The fac ulties are alike in all; contractility, alimentation, and reproduc-tion. All vegetable things are sensitive plants, if we knew them! and the difference of these functions in the lowest plant and highest animal, is only one of degree! 2nd. Protoplasm is everywhere identical in molecular form. And, 3d. Its sub-stance is always oxygen, hydrogen, nitrogen and carbon. The fate, then, of all protoplasm is death: that is, dissolution into its four elements; and its origin is the *chemical union* of the same. Does the compound display properties very different from the elements? So has water properties very unlike the mixture of two volumes of oxygen and hydrogen gas. Yet, the electric spark flashed through them awakens the chemical affinity, which makes water. So, a little speck of pre-existing protoplasm causes these dead elements to arrange themselves into new protoplasm. There is, then, no more cause to assume in the living organism, a new and mysterious cause, above that of chemical affinity, and to name it vitality! than in the other case, an imaginary property of 'aquosity.' And, as a certain chemical aggregation of the four elements is protoplasm, the basis of all life; so the higher vital functions, including those of mind, must be explained by the same force, acting in a more complicated way.

Is there a Physical Basis of Life?

For the facts which explode this theory, we are, of course, dependent on physiologists. The most ex-perienced of them, then, declare that the most rudimental vitalized organism which the mi-croscope discloses, is not Dr. Huxley's protoplasm, but a living tissue cell, with its vital power of nutrition and reproduction. That all protoplasm, or living *protein*, is not alike in form, nor in constituent elements; and so marked is this, that microscop-ists know the different sources of these varieties of *protein*, by their appearance. That different vitalities construct different forms of *protein* out of the same elements. That some forms are utterly incapable of being nourished by some other forms; which should not be the case, were all protoplasm the same. That while vegetable vitality can assimilate dead matter, animal

No Basis of Life Ex-cept the Cell.

vitality can only assimilate matter which has been prepared for it it by vegetable (or animal) vitality. And, that all protoplasm is not endowed with contractility; so that the pretended basis for animal motion does not exist in it.

The seemingly plausible point in this chemical theory of life is the attempted parallel between the production of water and of protoplasm.

Life not Explained by Chemical Affinity.

Asks Huxley: "Why postulate an imaginary cause, 'vitality,' in this case, rather than 'aquosity,' over and above chemical affinity, in the other?" The answer is, that this analogy is false, both as to the causes and the effects, in the two cases. In the production of water from the two gases, the occasion is the electrical spark; the real, efficient cause is the affinity of the oxygen for the hydrogen. In the reproduction of living tissue, the efficient cause is a portion of preexisting living tissue, present, of the same kind. The proof is, that if this be absent, all the chemical affinities and electrical currents in the world are vain. The elements of a living tissue are held together, not by chemical affinities, but by a cause heterogeneous thereto, yea, adverse; the departure of which is the signal for those affinities to begin their action; which action is to break up the tissue. As to the effects in the two cases: In the production of water, the electric spark is the occasion for releasing the action of an affinity, which produces a compound substance. In the case of the living organism, there is an effect additional to composition: This is *life*. Here, I repeat, is an effect wholly in excess of the other case, which affinity cannot initiate. Protoplasm dead, and subject to the decomposing action of affinities (as water is of the metals) is the true analogue of water.

But this theory has another defect, the fatal nature of which Huxley himself has pointed out: the defect of actual verification. No man has ever communicated life to dead, compounded matter. Let the materialist make a living animal in his chemical laboratory; then only will his hypothesis begin to rise out of the region of mere dreams. There are, in fact, four spheres or worlds of creature existence, the inorganic, or mineral, the vegetable, the animal and the human, or spiritual. Notwithstanding analogies between them (which are just what reason expects between the different works of the same divine Architect) they are separated by inexorable bounds. No man has ever changed mineral matter into a vegetable structure, without the agency of a pre-existent living germ; nor vegetable matter into animal, without a similar animal germ; nor animal into spiritual, save by the agency of the birth of a rational soul. The scientific, as much as the theological conclusion, is: That there is in vegetable structures, a distinct, permanent cause, additional to those which combine mineral bodies; that there is another in the animal,

Has no Verification.

distinct from the mineral and vegetable; and still another in the spiritual, distinct from the other three. The inference is *a posteriori*, and bears the test of every canon of sound induction.

This suggests our next point of reply.   There is, in living tissue, a something more than the physical causes which organize it: *Design.*   We have diverse and ingenious organs, wonderfully designed for their different essential functions.   Now, design is *a thought!*   Yea, more; intentional adaptation discloses a personal volition.   Suppose that molecular and chemical affinities could make "protoplasm," can they educe design, thought, wisdom, choice?   Dr. Stirling admirably illustrates this licentious assumption of Huxley, (referring still to Paley's illustration of a newly found watch):   "Protoplasm breaks up into carbon, hydrogen, oxygen, nitrogen?   True.   The watch breaks up similarly into brass, steel, gold and glass.   The loose materials of the watch [even its chemical materials, if you will] replace its weight quite as accurately as the constituents, carbon, &c., replace the weight of the 'protoplasm.'   But neither these nor those replace the vanished idea, which was the important element.   Mr. Huxley saw no break in the series of steps in molecular complication; but, though not molecular, it is difficult to understand what more striking, what more absolute break could be desired, than the break into an idea.   It is of that break alone that we think in the watch; and it is of that break alone that we should think, in the protoplasm, which, far more cunningly, far more rationally, constructs a heart, or an eye, or an ear.   That is the break of breaks; and explain it as we may, we shall never explain it by molecules."

All Life shows Design.

Here, then, is a fatal chasm in the materialistic scheme. It not only supposes, falsely, that chemical affinities, with cohesion, can account for living substance; but that the force of this 'protoplasm,' unintelligent, blind, involuntary, has exerted thought, wisdom and rational choice in selecting ends and adapted means.   Even if the powers claimed for 'protoplasm' were granted, still a Creator, to give us the first protoplasm with which to start, would be as essential as ever.   For the scientific fact still remains, that only living structures reproduce living structures.

Last: See these words of Huxley, ("Lay Sermons" p. 38): "But I bid you beware that, in accepting these conclusions" (as to 'protaplasm') "you are placing your feet on the first rung of a ladder which, in most people's estimation, is the reverse of Jacob's, and leads to the antipodes of heaven.   It may seem a small thing to admit, that the dull, vital actions of a *fungus* or a *foraminifer* are the properties" (meaning chemical and molecular) "of their protoplasm, and are the direct results of the nature of the matter of which they are com-

Scheme Materialistic.

posed. But if, as I have endeavored to prove to you, their protoplasm is identical with, and most readily converted into, that of any animal, I can discover no logical halting place between the admission that such is the case, and the concession that all vital action may, with equal propriety, be said to be the result of the molecular forces of the protoplasm which displays it. And if so, it must be true, in the same sense, and to the same extent, that the thoughts to which I am now giving utterance, and your thoughts regarding them, are expressions of molecular in that matter of life, which is the source of other vital phenomena."

This pretended reasoning I present to you as a specimen of the absurd and licentious methods by which the attempt is made to overthrow at once the almost universal convictions of rational men, and the declarations of God's word. The conclusions I utterly deny, even if the premises were granted. If it were proved (which is not) that vegetable life was no more than the result of adhesion and chemical affinity, this would come wholly short of the identification of animal life with vegetable. If rudimental animal life were identified with chemical action, this would be utterly short of proving that mental action is identical with the other two. The chasm between animal and spiritual action, is as impassable as ever. As we have seen, the unconscious, vegetable organism contains, in its adaptation to its end, a mark of thought about it, which cannot be overlooked. But now, the intelligent being has thought in it also; making a double and an insuperable difficulty to the materialist. For thought and rational choice cannot possibly be referred to a substance extended, inert, passive and involuntary. These functions of spirit are heterogeneous with all other forces, not measured by them, and not capable of transmutation into them. But we are now upon the threshold of the psychological argument against materialism.

3. The tendency of Dr. Darwin's speculations is to obliterate the distinction between man and the brutes; thus it virtually makes man also a beast. But Huxley would have us end by reducing both beast and man to the level of the clod. Why is it that any mind possessed even of the culture necessary for the construction of these theories, does not resent the unspeakable degradation which they inflict upon mankind? Men would not thus outrage their own natures, without an interested motive. That motive probably is, to be emancipated from moral obligation to God, and to escape those immortal responsibilities which remorse foreshadows. It seems a fine thing to the sinful mind to have no omniscient Master, to be released from the stern restraints of law, to be obliged to no answer hereafter for conscious guilt. For if there is no spirit in man, there is no valid evidence to us that there is a Spirit anywhere in the universe. God and immortality are both

blotted out together. But let us see whether even the sinner has any motive of self-interest to say in his heart: "There is no God;" whether atheism is not at least as horrible as hell.

The best hope of materialism is annihilation. This is a destiny terrible to man, even as he is, con-

Has no Hope but Annihilation.

scious of guilt, and afraid of his own future. Does the materialist plead that, if this fate ends all happiness, it is at least an effectual shield against all misery? I reply first, that the destruction of man's being is a true evil to him, just to the extent that he ever experienced or hoped any good from his own existence. How strong is the love of life? Just so real and so great is the evil of extinction. Second: but for guilt and fear, a future immortality would be hailed by any living man as an infinite boon. And of this, annihilation would rob us. How base and vile is that theory of existence, which compels a rational free-agent to embrace the hope of an infinite loss, solely as a refuge from his own folly and fault? The vastness of the robbery of self can be poorly cloaked by the miserable fact, that the soul has so played the fool and traitor to its own rights, that it has compelled itself to seek the infinite loss of annihilation, rather than an alternative still worse!

But materialism and atheism do not make you sure of annihilation. A conscious identity continued

The Theory Miserable

through so many stages and changes, may continue in spite of death. Some materialists have devoutly believed in immortality. But if man is immortal, and has no God, this itself is eternal despair. Nor can any materialistic theory expel from the soul those immortal realities, sin, guilt, accountability, remorse, misery: for they are more immediately testified by our intuitions, than any physical fact possibly can be, which men attempt to employ as a *datum* for this soulless philosophy. At least, when death comes, that "most wise, mighty, and eloquent orator" dispels the vain clouds of materialism, and holds the sinner face to face with these realities, compelling him to know them as solid as his own conscious existence. But now, if his theory is true, there is no remedy for these miseries of the soul. There is no God omnipotent to cleanse and deliver. There is no Redeemer in whom dwell the divine wisdom, power, love and truth, for man's rescue. The blessed Bible, the only book which ever even professed to tell fallen man of an adequate salvation, is discredited. Providence and grace are banished out of the existence of helpless, sinful man. There is no object to whom we can address prayer in our extremity. In place of a personal God and father in Christ, the fountain and exemplar of all love and beneficence, to whom we can cry in prayer, on whom we may lean in our weakness and anguish, who is able and willing to heal depravity and wash away guilt, who is suited to be our

adequate portion through an eternal existence, we are left face
to face with this infinite nature, material, impersonal, reasonless, heartless. There is no supreme, rational or righteous
government; and when the noblest sentiments of the soul are
crushed by wrongs so intolerable, that their perpetual triumph
is felt to be an alternative as hateful as death, there is not, nor
shall there ever be, to all eternity, any appeal to compensating
justice ! But our only master and ruler is an irresistible, blind
machine, revolving forever by the law of a mechanical necessity; and the corn between its upper and nether millstones, is
this multitude of living, palpitating human hearts, instinct with
their priceless hopes, and fears, and affections, and sensibilities,
writhing and bleeding forever under the remorseless grind.
The picture is as black as hell itself! He who is "without
God in the world" is "without hope." Atheism is despair.

Materialism and atheism will never win a permanent victory over the human mind; the most they
The Scheme Short- can do is to betray a multitude of unstable
lived
souls to their own perdition, by flattering
them with future impunity in sin; and to visit upon Christendom occasional spasms of anarchy and crime. With masses
of men, the latter result will always compel these schemes to
work their own speedy cure. For, on their basis, there can be
no moral distinction, no right, no wrong, no rational, obligatory
motive, no rational end save immediate, selfish and animal
good, and no rational restraints on human wickedness. The
consistent working of materialism would turn all men into
beasts of prey, and earth into *pandemonium*. The partial
establishment of the doctrine immediately produces mischiefs
so intolerable, that human society refuses to endure them.
Besides this, the soul of man is incapable of persistent materialism and atheism, because of the inevitable action of those
original, constitutive laws of thought and feeling, which qualify
it as a rational spirit. These regulative laws of thought cannot
be abolished by any conclusions which result from themselves,
for the same reason that streams cannot change their own
fountains. The sentiment of religion is omnipotent in the end.
We may rest in assurance of its triumph, even without appealing to the work of the Holy Ghost, whom Christianity promises
as the omnipotent coadjutor of the truth. While irreligious
men explore the facts of natural history for fancied proofs of a
creation by evolution which omits a Creator, the heralds of
Christ will continue to lay their hands upon the heart-strings of
immortal men, and find there always the forces to overwhelm
unbelief. Does the materialist say that the divine deals only
with things spiritual? But spiritual consciousnesses are more
stable than all his material masses; than his primitive granite.
Centuries hence, (if man shall continue in his present state so
long) when these current theories of unbelief shall have been

consigned to that *limbus*, where Polytheism, the Ptolemaic astronomy, Alchemy and Judicial Astrology lie contemned,
Christianity will hold on its beneficent way.

There is an argument *ad hominem*, by which this discussion
might be closed with strict justice. If materialism is true, then the pretended philosopher who teaches it is a beast; and all we
are beasts. Brute animals are not amenable to moral law; and
if they were, it is no murder to kill a beast. But beasts act very
consistently upon certain instincts of self-interest. Even they
learn something by experience. But this teaches us that the
propagator of atheistic ideas is doing intolerable mischief; for
just so far as they have prevailed, they have let loose a flood of
misery. Now, then, the teacher of those ideas is venomous.
The consistent thing for the rest of us animals to do, who
are not beasts of prey, is, to kill him as soon as he shows
his head; just as the deer cut the rattlesnake in pieces whenever they see him, with the lightning thrusts of their sharp
hoofs. Why is not this conclusion perfectly just? The only
logic which restrains it, is that Christianity which says: "Thou
shalt not kill," which the atheist flouts. The only reason we do
not treat atheists thus is, that we are not like them, atheists.

*The Atheist the en-
emy of his kind.*

LECTURE VII.

IMMORTALITY OF THE SOUL, AND DEFECTS
OF NATURAL RELIGION.

SYLLABUS.

1. Show the testimony of Consciousness, Reason and Conscience to the soul's
spirituality. See
  Butler's Analogy, pt. i, ch. 1, 2. Turrettin, Locus v. Qu. 14. Hodge, Theol.
  Vol. i, ch. iii, § 4, E. Dr. S. Clarke's Disc. Vol. ii, prop. 4. Dr. Thomas
  Brown, Lec. 96, 97. Breckinridge's Theol. Vol. i, p. 58–70. Chalmers' Nat.
  Theol. bk. iii, ch. 3.
  2. Does Natural Theology show the immortality of the soul? See same
authorities.
  3. Does Reason hold out any sure prospect of the pardon of our sins?
  Butler's Analogy, pt. ii, ch. 5. University Lectures on Evidences: Dr. Van
  Zandt, pp. 43 to 51. Dr. S. Clarke as above, prop. vi.
  4. Can Natural Theology be sufficient for man's religious welfare? How much
evidence in the answer for the inspiration of the Bible?
  Turrettin, Locus i, Qu. 4. Univ. Lecture by Van Zandt. Chalmers' Nat.
  Theology, bk. v, ch. 1. Dr. S. Clarke, as above, Props. v to viii. Leland's
"Necessity of Revelation," at large.

IN advancing to the solemn question of our immortality, I
would remind you of the opening remark of the last
lecture: That practically this question is involved in that of the soul's spirituality. The
attempts made to infer that the soul is

*1. Psychological Ar-
gument for Spirit.*

ʁot a spirit, from certain physical theories, I there endeavored to overthrow. The argument from psychological facts given us in our own consciousness, now remains; and this is obviously the legitimate, the conclusive one. For, let the supposition that man has a separate, immaterial spirit, be once brought into the debate; and of course, sensuous evidences of its truth or falsehood are equally out of the question, by the very definition of spirit as substance that is simple, monadic, unextended, indivisible, devoid of all sensible attributes. The spiritual *data* of consciousness are the only ones which can possibly give conclusive evidence, for or against the proposition. When the physicist argues that " science" (meaning thereby exclusively the science of sensible phenomena) "tells him nothing of spirit," I reply: of course it does not. But if he uses that admission, to argue there is no spirit, he is precisely as preposterous, as though he should wish to decide the question whether a given crystal vase contains atmosphere, by remarking that his *eye-sight* does not detect any *colour* in the space included in the vase. Of course it does not; when the very definition of atmosphere is, of a gas absolutely transparent and colorless in limited masses. Other faculties than eye-sight must decide the question of fact. So other faculties than the senses must decide whether there is a spirit in man; when the very claim of our hypothesis is, that this spiritual substance is wholly super-sensuous. The only quarrel we have with the physicists for saying " their science tells them of no spirit," is against the apparent intimation that the science of sensible things is the only science! Let Physics observe their proper modesty, as only one branch of valid science; and let her recognize her elder sisters of the super-sensuous sphere, and we are content she shall announce that result.

The great evidence of the soul's spirituality will be found when inspected, intuitive. Man only knows by his own ideas, recognized in consciousness. The very con-

Consciousness is only of Spirit. sciousness of these implies a being, a substance which is conscious. So that man's knowledge of himself, as conscious, thinking substance is *a priori* to, though implicitly present in, all his other thinkings: That is to say; he knows his own thinking Self first, and only by knowing it, knows any other thing. In other words: Every sound mind must accept this self-evident fact; my having any idea, sensitive or other, implies the *Ego* that has it. I can only have perception of the objective, by assuming *a priori*, the reality of the subjective. I cannot construe to myself any mental state without postulating real being, a *subjectum*, to which the state may be referred. But this thinking Self is impressed from without with certain states, called sensations, which we are as inevitably impelled to refer to objective substance, to the *non Ego*. Now in comparing this conviction of the *Ego* and *non*

5*

Ego, a certain contrast between their attributes inevitably
arises.   The first conviction which arises out of a thoughtful inspection of the contents of consciousness, is the singleness of the
mind.   It learns the qualities of the objective by different sensations, but all sensations are inevitably referred to the same
knowing subject.   The Self who knows by touching, is always
identical with that which knows by tasting, smelling, seeing, and
hearing.   The Self who knows by sensations is identical with
that which reflects upon its sensations.   The Self which conceives an object of emotion, is the same that feels towards that
object.   In the midst of the conscious diversity of all these
states of mind, there remains the inexorable consciousness of the
singleness of the mind affected by them.   But the objective always exists before us in plurality.

Next, we learn from sense-perception that all the objective
is compounded.   The simplest material substance is constituted
by an aggregation of parts, and may be con-
ceived as divided.   The lightest has some

And of a Monad.

weight; the smallest has some extension; all have some figure.   But our consciousness tells us intuitively, that the thing in
us which thinks, feels, wills, is absolutely simple.   Not only
does this intution refer all our mental states and acts
to one and the same thinking subject, notwithstanding their
wide diversity.   But *we know* that they coexist in that subject,
without plurality or partition.   We are conscious that the agent
which conceives, is the same agent which, upon occasion of that
concept, is affected with passion.   That which hates one object
and loves its opposite, is the same agent, nothwithstanding the
diversity of these states.   Moreover, every affection and act of a
mind has an absolute unity.   It is impossible even to refer any
attribute of extension to it in conception.   He who endeavors
to imagine to himself a concept that is colored or ponderous (as
it is a mental act) an affection that is triangular as distinguished
from another that is circular, a judgment that has its top and its
bottom, a volition which may be divided by a knife or wedge
into halves and quarters, feels inevitably that it is unspeakable
folly.   All the attributes of extension are absolutely irrelevant
to the mind and its acts and states.   And especially is this
thought fatal to the conclusion, that mental affections may be
functions of organized bodies of matter; namely: that whereas we know all our mental affections have an absolute unity, we
are taught by our senses, that all qualities and affections of organisms are aggregates of similar affections or qualities of
parts.   The whiteness of a wall is the whiteness of a multitude
of separate points in the wall.   The magnetism of a metal rod
is the aggregate of the magnetisms of a multitude of molecules of
metal.   The properties may be literally subdivided with the
masses.   The materialistic conception receives a most complete
and exact refutation, when we recall the multitude of distinct

things in consciousness. If the soul is material, then it has some dimensions; less, at all events than the superficies of our bodies. Recall now, for instance, the countless multitude of ideas marked in our unconscious memory. How are they all distinguishably made on a surface of no more breadth? Remember, that if materialism is true, the viewing of these ideas in conception, is a sensuous perception. How many distinct lines on an inch's surface can sense perceive? That is settled with a geometrical exactness! How then are these countless marks preserved on a surface of sixty inches; or possibly, of a fraction of one inch?

Now the law of our reason compels us to refer this absolute contrast of attributes to a real difference of substance. While Contrasted attributes we name the *Ego, spirit*, we must call the imply contrasted sub- objective something else, matter. Man can-stances. not think at all, without virtually predicating his thinking on the recognition of a substance that thinks, essentially different from the objective, a spiritual *monad*. We can only know matter, by having known mind. It is impossible, my Brethren, for me to impress you too strongly with the impregnable strength of this position against the materialist. It is our 'Gibraltar.' The man who thinks consistently, must always be more certain that there is mind, than that there is matter. Because any valid act of intelligence must imply an intelligent subject. And the recognition of the *Ego* which knows, is *a priori*, and in order to perception of an object known by it. If then the existence of mind is uncertain, the existence of anything objective is inevitably more uncertain. Does sense-perception seem to the materialist to give him the most palpable knowledge of the matter external to him? But he has only been enabled to construe that perception at all, so as to make it a *datum* of valid knowledge, by first crediting the intuition of consciousness, which reveals the perceiving Agent distinct from the object revealed. How unfair, how unscientific is this attempt to use intuition in its less direct, and refuse it in its more direct, testimonies! If she is to be trusted in her interpretation of the objective sensation, she is, of course, still more to be trusted in her subjective self-consciousness.

Hence, pure idealism is less unphilosophical than materialism. That outrages one class of valid intuitions; this out-Matter only cog- rages two. The stress of the argument nized by admitting which I have just explained, is disclosed in a spirit. curious way, by the confessions of sundry of the modern materialists. Huxley, for instance, after abolishing spirit, finds himself in such difficulty, that he feels compelled to spiritualize matter! Thus his materialism is resolved into a species of idealism, which he impotently attempts to connect with the metaphysics of Des Cartes. First we are taught that there is no such substance as spirit; but its supposed functions are merely phenomena of Force, the only cause which materialism can recognize in nature. And then, to deliver us from the absurdities of this metaphysic, we are taught that there is no such substance as matter; but this is only an ideal something, possibility of force! Thus reason was destroyed, to exalt the validity of sense-perception exclusively; and now sense-perception is destroyed in turn, leaving us Nihilism.

Next, I argue, that materialism contradicts our intuition of our own free-agency. Experience shows us two rival classes of effects, the corporeal being one, thought, feel-ing and volition the other. Now it is impossible to think an effect without an adequate cause. But when the reason begins to represent to itself these causes, it perceives an inevitable difference. The corporeal effects are necessary; the spiritual are free. The one class is the result of blind force; the other is an expression of free-agency. Here are two heterogeneous causes, matter and spirit, acting the one by force, the other by free agency.

Free agency refutes Materialism.

Materialism contradicts the testimony of our moral consciousness. It teaches that matter, if a cause, is an involuntary and unintelligent cause. But we know that we are responsible; which unavoidably implies a rational spontaneity in acting. To hold a blind, material force to a moral responsibility, is preposterous. But this conviction of responsibility in conscience is universal, radical, unavoidable, and intuitive. It is impossible for a man to discharge his mind of it. He cannot think the acknowledged wrong equal to the right, and the admitted wrong-doer irresponsible for his wrong, like a rolling stone, a wave, or a flame. These facts of consciousness compel us to admit a substance heterogeneous from matter. Had man no spirit, there would be nothing to be accountable. Had he no God, there would be none to whom to be accountable. If either were true, our very nature would be a lie, and knowledge impossible.

Responsibility refutes it.

Feeble attempts are made by modern materialists to meet these arguments, by saying first: That consciousness is not to be trusted. Consciousness, say they, is incomplete. She gives no account of the subjective acts and states of infancy; and no correct account of those of the mentally diseased. She tells us nothing usually of the large latent stores of memory. She is absolutely silent as to any interaction of the nerve-system and the spirit; of which, if there is spirit, there must be a great deal.

But to what does all this amount? Consciousness does not tell us all things, and sometimes tells us wrong? If this were granted, still the stubborn proposition would remain, that if we cannot trust consciousness, we can have no ideas. The faculty which they would exalt against her, is sensation. Do the senses

Consciousness is trustworthy.

tell us all things? Are they never deceived? Does sense give any perceptions, save as it is mediated to the understanding by consciousness? Enough of such special pleadings! That consciousness reveals nothing direct of the interaction of spirit and nerve organs is precisely because spirit and matter are causes so heterogeneous—so that this fact contains one of the most conclusive proofs against materialism. If our conscious intelligence were only a function of nerve structures, then indeed it might be very natural that the function of intelligence should include, and should represent to us intellectually, every link of the action of the material nerve-force. But because conscious intelligence is not a material, organic function, but is the free action of spirit, a cause and substance wholly heterogeneous from matter, therefore it is, that just at the connecting step between nerve action in the *sensorium* and the idea in the intelligence, and between the volition in the rational agent and contraction in the voluntary nerve matter, there is naturally a chasm of mystery; a relation which the omniscient spirit was able to institute; but which sense cannot detect because the interaction is no longer merely material; which conscious intelligence does not construe to itself because it is not merely spiritual.

Again it is said: "Grant that there must be an entity within us, to be the subject of consciousness, why
Consciousness cannot be the Brain. may not that be *the Brain?*" One answer has been given above: That while the properties and functions of brain matter are material, qualified by attributes of extension; those of consciousness are spiritual, simple, monadic. Another answer is, that consciousness testifies that my own brain is, like other matter, objective to that in me which thinks. How do I know that I have a brain? By the valid analogy of the testimony of anatomists, as to the skulls of all other living men like me. But that testimony is the witnessing of a sense-perception, which that anatomist had when he opened those other skulls—of an objective knowledge. Hence I only know my brain, as objective to that which is the knowing agent. If I have any valid opinion about the brain, it is that this organ is *the instrument by which* I think, not the *Ego* who thinks. Materialists have objected that material affections have this oneness to our conception; as a musical tone, the numerous series of successive vibrations of a chord divisible into parts. I reply, that the oneness is only in the perception of it. Only as it becomes our mental affection, does it assume unity. As we trace the effect from the vibration of the chord to that of the air, the *tympanum*, the bony series, the aqueous humour, the fimbrated nerve, the series is still one of successive parts. It is only when we pass from the material organ to the mind, that the phenomenon is no longer a series of pulses, but a unified sensation. This very case proves most strongly the unifying power which belongs to the mind alone. So, when an extended object pro-

duces a sensation, though the object perceived is divisible, the perception thereof, as a mental act, is indivisible.

Now, the soul being another substance than the body, it is seen at once, that the body's dissolution does

2. The Soul Immortal. not *necessarily* imply that of the soul. Indeed, let us look beyond first impressions, and we shall see that the presumption is the other way.   The fact that we have already passed from one to another stage of existence, from *fœtus* to in. fant, to child, to man, implies that another stage may await us ; unless there be some such evidence of the soul's dependence on the body for existence (as well as for contact with the external world,) as will destroy that presumption.   But there is no such dependence ; as appears from our experience in amputations, flux of bodily particles, emaciation under disease, &c.   In none of these cases is the loss of the spirit proportioned to the bodily loss.   This independence is proved by the fact, that in sensation even, the bodily organ is merely the soul's instrument.   The eye, e. g., is but its optic glass : that in sleep the soul may be active, while the body is passive ; and chiefly, that all the higher processes of soul, memory, conception, imagination, reasoning, are wholly independent of the body.   Even if the grossest representationist scheme of perception and thought, (that, for instance, of Hartly, or of Hobbes,) were adopted, making the *phantasmata* or *species* derived through the senses, the object of perception, still the question returns, How does the soul get its conception of general notions : of time, of space, of God, of self?   Herein surely, it is independent of the body.

It has been objected to this great argument of Bp. Butler, in

Argument true, though recent days, and with great clamour, that the cerebral action attend all discoveries of modern cerebral physiology thought. discredit it. It is claimed that anatomists have now ascertained, that certain molecular actions in the brain attend what were before supposed to be abstract and independent acts of mind, (or, as the materialist would say, constitute those acts,) as regularly as other molecular actions attend the sensuous functions of the mind.   The student will see this point thoroughly anticipated, two hundred years before it was raised, by Turrettin, in the question cited in the *Syllabus*. Suppose it true, that a certain excitement of brain-matter attends the abstract processes of the mind and the acts of its original spontaneity. Is it any the less certain that in these cases, the excitement of nerve matter is consequence, and the exertion of the spirit's spontaneity is cause? Surely not. Just so surely as, in objective perception, the presentation of the new sense-idea in the intelligence follows the excitement of the nerve matter, in the order of causation ; so surely, in the case of spontaneous thought, feeling and volition, the spiritual action precedes the action of the nerve matter (if there is such action,) in the order of causation. So that, in the sense of Bp. Butler's argument, these acts of soul are independent of bodily action still. The clamour which has been made by materialists here, is a good instance of modern ignorance or oblivion of the history of opinion. Suppose the recent doctrine of the physiological " cerebration of ideas" be proved universal as to all the soul's acts, what have we, more than the hypothesis of Hartley, which made sensations " vibrations," and concepts " vibratiuncles," in a nervous substance? No competent philosopher of the past regarded that hypothesis, whether granted or refuted, as affording any sufficient account of the facts of consciousness. But the very attempt to employ the hypothesis thus has been the laughing-stock of science.

Here again, materialists have objected, that the cases of mental imbecility in infancy and dotage, and of mania or lunacy, seem to show a strict dependence of soul on body, if not an identity. In dotage, is not the mind, like the body, tottering to its extinction? If our theory of monadic spirit were true, would *mental disease* be possible? I reply, that strictly speaking, spirit is not essentially or organically diseased. It is the bodily organ of its action, which is deranged, or weakened. Bear in mind, that though there are undoubted processes of thought independent of the body, *sensations* form the larger portion of our subjects of thought and volition. Now, remember that the soul is subject to the law of *habit ;* and we shall easily see that where, through the disease of the bodily organs, the larger number of the objects of its action are distorted, the balance of its working may be disturbed, and yet the soul's substance undiseased. That this is the correct explanation is confirmed by what happens in dreams ; the mind's action is abnormal; it is because the absence of sensations has changed the balance of its working. Let the body awake, and the ordinary current of sensations flow aright, and the mind is at once itself. Again, in lunacy and dotage, ideas gained by the mind before the bodily disease or decline took place, are usually recalled and used by the mind correctly ; while more recent ones are either distorted, or wholly evanescent. Finally, while it is inconsistent to ascribe an organic disease to that which is not organized, a functional derangement does not seem wholly out of the question.

Does mental disease imply the soul's mortality.

It appears then, that the thinking monad is independent of the body for its existence. Impressive as are the changes of bodily dissolution, they contain no philosophic ground for denying the conclusion drawn from the experience of the soul's existence through so many moments and so many changes. But the phenomenon of death itself suggests a powerful analogy to show that the soul will not die. What is death? It is but separation of parts. When we examine all the seemingly destructive processes of nature, combustion, decomposition, we find no atom

Only death known is dissolution. The soul simple.

of matter annihilated; they only change their collocations.
There is no proof that God ever destroys an atom.   The soul is
a spiritual atom; why suppose it is destroyed?   The only death
is dissolution; the soul cannot dissolve.   And this is my conception of its immortality; not a *self* or *necessary* existence,
but the absence of all intrinsic ground of decay, and of all purpose in its Maker to extinguish its being.

But, objects the materialist: The same reasonings would
prove the immortality of brutes.   They
have processes of memory, association and
volition, from which the same conclusion of
the presence in them of simple, spiritual substance, would follow.
They might argue from their consciousness of mental states, the
same necessary distinction between the subject and object.
They also have a species of spontaneity.

Would not brutes be thus shown immortal?

I reply, that this is an objection *ad ignorantiam*.   Where is
the necessary absurdity, should it be that brutes have spirits?
It might contradict many prejudices; but I see not what principle of established truth.   It is no just logic to say, that our
premises may or may not contain conclusions of an unknown
nature; when the question is, whether they do not contain this
known and unavoidable conclusion, the spirituality of man.
The nature of the mental processes of the higher brutes, especially, is very mysterious.   It seems most probable that their
spirits differ from man's chiefly in these two traits: the absence
of all moral ideas and sentiments, and the inability to construe
the contents of their own consciousness rationally.   And these
two are the most essential to a rational personality.   The moral
arguments for immortality then, which are the most conclusive
in man's case, and those from the indefinite perfectibility of his
mental powers, are all lacking in the case of the brute.   What
God chooses to do with this principle in the brute, which is the
seat of instinct, appetite, perception, memory, passion, and perhaps of judgment, when the body dies, Natural Theology is
unable to tell us.   Only when we come to Revelation, do we
learn that " the spirit of the brute goeth downward, while the
spirit of man goeth upward."   Ignorance here is no argument
against the results of positive knowledge elsewhere.

The well known argument for a future existence from God's
righteousness, compared with the imperfect
distribution of awards here, need not be
elaborated.   All your books state it.   It is
conclusive.   An objection has, indeed, been urged: That if the
awards are so unequal, no evidence remains of God's perfect
rectitude; and so the former premise is lost.   I reply: The
course of temporal providence is neither the only, nor chief
proof of God's rectitude.   Conscience demonstrates that attribute, without the light of observation.   Further: while the
awards are not exact, they approximate exactness here, showing

Equal rewards require a future existence.

that it is God's nature to be, finally, strictly just, And last, the inequalities of awards are explained consistently with God's rectitude by this: that they give scope for man's fortitude and sympathy, and for God's long suffering.

Conscience, apprehending God's justice, gives us a differ-
Conscience. ent and an instinctive proof of a future existence. Remorse for sins does by no means verge towards its termination, as death approaches; but recruits its fury. If the soul could apprehend this life as its only existence, at the conscious approach of death, remorse would relax its grasp; and at the expiring breath, would release the criminal, as having paid the debt of justice. We find in the dying conscience an inevitable and universal recognition of its immortality.

The ancient, and some modern, moralists, attached much
Does hope prove it? importance to man's longing for existence, horror of extinction, and hopes in the future. I cannot but feel, with Dr. Brown, that these lack weight. Is not this horror of extinction resolvable into that love of life which we share with the animals? Hope does, indeed, ever fly before us, to the end. But is it not as much a hope of sensual or worldly good, as of spiritual? But should we infer from these premises, that a brute's or a man's animal existence will be perpetual, we should err.

I find a more solid argument in man's capacity to know
Man's spiritual capaci- ties formed for immortality. and serve God, and in his capacity of indefinite mental and moral improvement. God's motive for creating, must have been from Himself; because, when He began, nothing else existed whence to draw it. He must, therefore, have sought, in creation, to satisfy and glorify His own perfections. Natural Theology tells us of no rational creatures, save men. Should there ever be a time when there are no rational creatures in the universe, there would be no recipients of God's spiritual goodness, and none to comprehend His glory. To have no eyes to behold the light, is virtually to quench it. Can we then believe that the only creature capable of knowing and enjoying Him shall perish so soon —perish, as to the majority of our race, before they understand Him at all? But again, man, unlike all other sentient creatures, is capable of indefinite improvement. The ox, the elephant, the horse, soon reaches the narrow limits of its intelligence; and these, the same fixed by the common instincts of its race, for its progenitors. The first bee built its cells as artistically as those of this "enlightened century." But man can make almost indefinite advancements. And when he has taken all the strides between a Newton or a Washington, and a naked Australian, there is no reason, save the narrow bounds of his mortal life, to limit his farther progress. Further: it is precisely in his mental and moral powers, that the room for growth exists. His muscu-

lar strength soon reaches that standard beyond which there is
no usual increase.   His senses are educated up to a certain
penetration; there the vast and the minute arrest them.   But
memory, reason, conscience, affections, habits, may be cultivated
to indefinite grades of superiority.   Let us now view man's terrestrial pursuits, his vanity, his disappointments, his follies, and
the futilities in which the existence of most men is consumed.
How utterly trivial!   How unworthy of the grand endowment!
If this life were all, well might we exclaim, with the Hebrew
poet, "Wherefore hast Thou made all men in vain?"   *We see*
that God is unspeakably wise in all His comprehended works;
we must conclude that He has not expended so much for naught;
that these seeds of immortality will inherit their suitable growth.
I see a man setting scions in his nursery a few inches apart; but
I learn that they are trees which will require forty feet for their
ultimate growth.   If the man knows what he is about, I conclude that he intends to transplant them..

For these various reasons, then, we may look across the
gulf of death with the confident expectation
of a future spiritual existence.   I say spiritual; for the resurrection of the body is a
doctrine of pure revelation, for which natural reason presents us
only the faintest analogies, if any.   It is the glory of the Bible,
that it alone reveals the immortality of *man*, of the whole united
person, which lives, hopes, fears, sins, and dies here.   But in
proving the immortality of the soul, a sufficient basis is laid for
the larger part of the moral forces which bring our responsibility
to bear aright.   The essential point is to evince the *proper
identity* of the being who acts here, and is rewarded hereafter.
It is mental, and not bodily identity, which lays this essential
basis for responsibility.   It is the spirit which understands,
feels, and chooses, which recognizes identity in its consciousness.   Hence, it is the spirit which is responsible.

Reason divines no bodi-
ly resurrection.

Now, if existence is continued beyond the grave, there is
nothing to check the conclusion that it will
be continued forever.   Suppose a soul just
emerged from the impressive revolution of
bodily death? then it must repeat all the reasonings we have
considered, and with redoubled force, that after so many
changes are survived, *a fortiori*, all others will be.   But if man's
conscious existence is continuous and endless, few will care or
dare to deny that his moral relations to God are so, likewise.
For they proceed directly from the mere original relation of
creature to Creator.   The startling evidences that this life is
somehow a probation for that endless existence, the youth of
that immortal manhood, have been stated by Bishop Butler
with unrivalled justness.   No more is needed by the student
than to study him.

Future Existence
must be Endless, and
under Responsibility.

Conscience convinces every man that he is a sinner, and

3. Does Reason see hope of pardon? No.

that God is just. Does natural reason infer any adequate proofs that God will, on any terms, be merciful; or is His righteousness as imperative as that conscience, which is His vicegerent within us? This is the question of most vital interest to us in natural religion. We are pointed to the abounding evidences of God's benevolence, and told that mercy is but benevolence towards the guilty. But, alas! Nature is almost equally full of evidences of His severity. Again, we are pointed to that hopeful feature in the order of His providence, which is but another expression for the regular ordering of His will, where we see remedial processes offered to man, for evading the natural consequences of his errors and faults. Does man surfeit himself? Nature offers a healing medicine, and arrests the death which his intemperance has provoked. Does the prodigal incur the penalty of want? Repentance and industry may repair his broken fortunes. So, alleviations seem to be provided on every hand, to interpose mercifully between man's sins and their natural penalties. May we not accept these as showing that there is some way in which God's mercy will arrest our final retribution? This expectation may have that slight force which will prepare us to embrace with confidence the satisfaction of Christ, when it is revealed to us in the gospel. But I assert that, without revelation, all these slight hints of a possible way of mercy are too much counterbalanced by the appearances of severity, to ground any hope or comfort in the guilty breast. What is the testimony of Conscience? Does she accept any of the throes of repentance, or the natural evils inflicted on faults, as a sufficient atonement? On the contrary, after the longest series of temporal calamities, the approach of death only sharpens her lash. The last act of culminating remorse, as the trembling criminal is dismissed from his sufferings here, is to remit him to a just and more fearful doom beyond the grave. And what say conscience and experience of the atoning virtue of our repentance and reformations? They only repair the consequences of our faults in part. The sense of guilt remains : yea, it is the very nature of repentance to renew its confession of demerit with every sigh and tear of contrition. And the genuineness of the sorrow for sin has no efficacy whatever to recall the consequences of the wrong act, and make them as though they had never been. But, above all, every palliation of natural penalty, every remedial process offered to our reach by nature, or ministered by the self-sacrifice of friends, is but temporary. For, after all, death comes to every man, to the most penitent, the most genuinely reformed, the restored sinner most fenced in by the mediatorial love of his fellows, as certainly as to the most reckless profligate ; and death is the terrible sum of all natural penalties. This one, universal fact, undoes everything which more hopeful analogies had begun, and compels us to admit that the utmost reason can infer of God's mercy is, that it admits a suspension of doom.

The last question which we shall now discuss in Natural Theology, is concerning its sufficiency to lead a soul to eternal blessedness. Now, I have strenuously con-

4. Is Natural Theology sufficient? tended that there is some science of Natural Theology. We have seen that it teaches us clearly our own spirituality and future existence, the existence and several of the attributes of God, His righteousness and goodness and our responsibility to Him, His providential control over all His works, and our endless relation to the sanctions of His moral attributes. But man needs more than this for his soul's well-being; and we assert that Natural Theology is fatally defective in the essential points. We might evince this practically by pointing to the customary state of all gentile nations, to the darkness of their understanding and absurdities of their beliefs, the monstrous perversions of their religious worship, and the blackness of their general morals,their evil conscience during their lives, and their death-beds either apathetic or despairing. If it be said that I have chosen unfavourable examples, then I might argue the point practically again, by pointing to the brightest specimens of pagan philosophy. We see that with all the germs of truth mixed with their creeds, there were many errors, that their virtues lacked symmetry and completeness, and their own confessions of uncertainty and darkness were usually emphatic in proportion to their wisdom.

But to specify. One fatal defect of Natural Theology has been already illustrated. Man knows himself a sinner in the

Cannot atone, nor regenerate. hands of righteous Omnipotence, and has no assurance whatever of any plan of mercy. An equally fatal defect might be evinced, (far more clearly than divines have usually done,) in its lack of regenerating agency. If we knew nothing of the sad story of Adam's probation and fall, just reasoning would yet teach us, that man is a morally depraved being. The great fact stands out, that his will is invincibly arrayed against the mandates of his own conscience, on at least some points. Every man's will exhibits this tendency in some respects, with a certainty as infallible as any law of nature. Now such a tendency of will cannot be revolutionized by any system of moral suasion; for the conclusive reason that the efficacy of all objective things to act as inducements, depends on the state of the will, and therefore cannot revolutionize it. The effect cannot renew its own cause. But Natural Theology offers no moral force higher than moral suasion. Can then the creature who remains an everlasting sinner, possess everlasting well-being?

Another striking defect of Natural Theology is its lack of authority over the conscience. One would think that where

Lacks Authority. the inferences of natural reason appeared conclusive, bringing the knowledge of a God to

the understanding, this God would be recognized as speaking in all her distinct assertions; and the conscience and heart would bow to him as implicitly as when He is revealed in His word. But practically it is not so. Men are but too ready to hold revealed truth in unrighteousness; and Natural Theology has ever shown a still greater lack of authority, even over hearts which avowed her truth. Perhaps the reason of this is, that every mind has indistinctly and half consciously recognized this profound metaphysical defect, which underlies nearly all her reasonings. How do we first know spirit? By our own consciousness, presenting to us the thinking *Ego*. How do we know thought, volition, power? As we are first conscious of it in ourselves. What is our first cognition of the right and the wrong? It is in the mandates of our consciences. And the way we conceive of the infinite Spirit, with His thought, will, power, rectitude, is by projecting upon Him our self-derived conception of this essence and these attributes, freed from the limitations which belong to ourselves. Seeing, then, that God and His character are to so great an extent but ourselves objectified, elevated above our conscious defects, and made absolute from our conscious limits, how can we ever know that the correspondence of the objective reality, with this conception of it, is accurate? It is as though our self-consciousness were the mirror, in which alone we can see the spectrum of the great Invisible reflected. How shall we ever tell to what degree it may be magnified, distorted, coloured, by the imperfection of the reflecting surface, seeing Natural Theology can never enable us to turn around and inspect the great original, eye to eye? That something is there, a something vast, grand and real, our laws of thought forbid us to doubt; and that it has a general outline like the reflected image, we may not doubt; for else, what was it that cast the mighty spectrum upon the disc of our reason? But reason can never clear up the vagueness and uncertainty of outline and detail, nor verify His true features. Now, when Revealed Theology comes, it enables us to make this verification; and especially when we see "God manifest in the flesh," "the brightness of the Father's glory, and express image of His person."

It may be asked, if Natural Theology cannot save, why study it? I answer: 1st. It teaches some truths; and no truth is valueless. 2d. When Revelation comes, Natural Theology gives satisfaction to the mind, by showing us two independent lines of proof for sundry great propositions? 3d. It excites the craving of the soul for a Revelation. 4th. When that comes, it assists us to verify it, because it meets the very wants which Natural Theology has discovered.

Why then study Natural Theology?

Finally, if Revelation is absolutely necessary for salvation, there is the strongest probability that God has given one. This

A Revelation may be expected.

appears from God's goodness and wisdom. It is proved, second, by the admissions of the Deistical argument, which always assumes the burden of proof in the proposition: " Revelation is not necessary." It appears, third, from the general expectation and desire of a communication from the skies among Pagans. Last: when we see (as will be demonstrated at another place) that the enjoyment of infallible communications from the infinite Mind is the natural condition of life to all reasonable spirits, the argument will become conclusive, that God surely has given a message to man. Now, no other book save the Bible presents even a plausible claim to be that Revelation.

LECTURE VIII.

THE SOURCES OF OUR THINKING.

SYLLABUS.

1. Has man any " Innate Ideas " ?   See,
   Locke's Essay, bk. i, ch. 2.   Morell, Hist. Mod. Phil., pp. 76 to 95, (Carter's Ed.)   Cousin, *Du Vrai*, Leçons 1re et 2me.   Dugald Stuart on the Mind, chaps. i, iii, iv.
2. Must all thinking proceed from Intuitive Beliefs?   Why?   Why are they, if unproved, received as valid?   What the answer to the Skeptical Conclusion of Montaigne or Hume?
   Morell, pp. 252–254.   Jouffroy, Intr. to Ethics, vol. i, Lectures 8–10.   Cousin, *Du Vrai*, Leçons 3me et 4eme.
3. What are the tests of Intuitive Beliefs?   Show that our belief in our own Consciousness; In our Spiritual Existence; In our Identity; In the reality of the External World; and in Established Axioms, belong to this class.
   Cousin, as above.   Sensualistic Phil. of 19th Cent., ch. 11.   Mills' Logic, bk. ii, ch. 5th.
4. Prove, especially, that our belief in Causation and power is Intuitive.
   Same authorities.   Mill, bk. ii. ch. 5th, and bk. iii, ch. 5th and 21st.   Dr. Thomas Brown, Lect. 7th.   Morell, pp. 186, 187, 254, 382, &c.   Chalmers' Nat. Thelogy, bk. 1, ch. 4th.   Thornwell, vol. i, p. 499, &c.
Show the relation between this doctrine, and Nat. Theology and all science, ‰ 7.

M ANY think, with Locke, that the inquiry into the powers of the human mind should precede all other science, be-

Is it necessary to study the mind's powers, before all else?

cause one should know his instrument before he uses it.   But what instrument of knowing is man to employ in the examination of his own mind?   Only his own mind.   Hence, it follows, that the mind's native laws of thinking must be, to some extent at least, taken upon trust, at the outset, no matter where we begin. This is the less to be regretted, because the correct use of the mind's powers depends on nature, and not on our success in analyzing them.   Men syllogized before Aristotle, and generalized before Bacon.   I have therefore not felt obliged to begin with these inquiries into the sources of our thinking; but have given you a short sketch of Natural Theology to familiarize your minds to your work.

You may ask: Since every science must employ the mental powers, and yet the teacher of Chemistry, Mathematics, Mechanics, does not find it necessary to preface his instructions with inquiries into the laws and facts of psychology, why should the divine do it? One answer is that thoroughness in theology is much more important. Another is, experience shows that theological speculation is much more intimately concerned with a correct psychology than physical. The great English mathematicians, of the school of Newton, have usually held just views of philosophy; the French of the school of *La Place* have usually been sensualistic *idéologues* of the lowest school. In mathematics and astronomy, they have agreed well enough.; in theology, they have been as wide apart as Christianity and atheism. This is because theology and ethicks are little concerned with physical observations: much with abstract ideas and judgments. For these reasons it is necessary for the divine to attain correct views of the great facts of mental science; while yet we do not stake the validity of theological truths on the validity of any mere psychological arguments.

Why then, before Theology?

My purpose is to give by no means a complete synopsis, even, of mental science; but to settle for you correct opinions concerning those fundamental facts and laws of spirit, upon which theological questions most turn.

Of these I take up first the question: Has the mind any innate ideas? The right answer is, No; but it has innate powers, which *a priori* dictate certain laws of thought and sensibility, whenever we gain ideas by sensitive experience. Locke, famous for exploding the doctrine of innate ideas, goes too far; teaching that we derive all our ideas (he defines an idea, whatever we have in our minds as the object of thought) from sensation. This he holds is a passive process; and all that the processes of reflection (the active ones) can do, is to recall, group, compare, combine, or abstract these materials. Before sensation, the mind is a *tabula rasa*, without impress in itself, passively awaiting whatever may be projected on it from without. To show that no ideas are innate, he takes up two classes, hitherto considered most clearly such, abstract ideas of space, time, identity, and infinity, &c., and axioms; assuming that if these can be explained as derived ideas, and not innate, there are none such. He teaches, then, that we only get the idea of space, by seeing two bodies separated thereby; of time, by deriving it from the succession of mental impressions; of identity, as remembered consciousnesses. Axioms, he holds to be clearly truths of derivation, because untutored minds do not

I. Question of innate ideas.

believe them, as they would were they intuitive, until they see
them from concrete, experimental cases, by sensation.

Consider how far this kind of vicious anylysis may lead,
as in the hands of Condillac, Comte, and
Fatal consequences of Mill, to sensationalism, and last, to material-
a sensualistic psychology. ism and atheism.   If no first truth is of
higher source than an inference of experience, then none can
be safely postulated beyond experience.   Hence, the argument
for a God, the belief of all the supernatural, is invalid.   Witness Hume's evasion, that the world is a "singular effect."
How can sensation show us a God?   Another equally logical,
although a most heterogeneous consequence, is the Pyrrhonism
of Bishop Berkeley.   And another must be the adoption of
of some artificial scheme of ethicks, resolving the highest law
of conscience into a deduction of self-interest, or some such
wretched theory.   For if there is nothing in the mind, save
what comes by sense, (*Nihil in intellectu quod non prius in
sensu,*) whence the notions of right and obligation?

The great error of the analysis of Locke was in mistaking
the occasional cause, sensation, for the
True statement. efficient cause of abstract ideas, which is the
reason itself.   For example: We first develope the idea of
space, when we see bodies in space; but the idea of space is
implied *a priori*, in the very perception of that which is extended, not learned derivatively from it.   True, our most
natural conception of time is of that measured in our successive consciousnesses.   But the word, "succession" once spoken,
time is already conceived.   That is to say, the reason, on perceiving a thing extended, intuitively places it in space; and
event, in time; the sense furnishing the occasion, the reason
furnishing the abstract notion, or form, for the concrete perception.   So in the other cases.   To the attempt to derive axioms,
we answer that the sensitive experience of some instance is the
occasion, but the intuition of the reason the efficient, of these
primitive and necessary judgments.   For since our experiences
of their truth are few and partial, how can experience tell us
that they are universally true?   To the objection, that they do
not universally and necessarily command the assent of untutored minds, I fearlessly rejoin that this is only true in cases
where the language of their enunciation is not understood.
But of this, more anon.

To show the student how shallow is the analysis which
traces the whole of our thinking to sense, I
Whence new abstract ask: When the "reflective" processes of
notions? comparison, e. g., have given us perception
of a relation between two sensible objects, (as of a ratio between two dimensions,) is not this relation a new idea?
Whence is it?

In a word, you may find the simplest, and also the highest

The mind active, and endued with attributes. and most general refutation of this sensualistic philosophy in this fact. The mind is an intelligent agent. Has it any attributes? Any cognizable, permanent *essentia?* Surely. Now, then, must not those essential qualities imply powers? And will any one say that they are only passive powers, and yet the mind is an agent? Surely not. Then the mind, although not furnished with innate ideas, must have some innate powers of determining its own acts of intelligence.

It is related that when Locke's Essay on the Human Understanding was first reported to his great cotemporary, Leibnitz, some one remarked that Locke's system of psychology was built on a literal acceptation of the old scholastic maxim, *Nihil in intellectu, quod non prius in sensu.* Leibnitz answered: *Ita; Nisi Intellectus Ipse!* These words contain the key to the whole discussion.

There is a plausible temptation to deny this, and to treat all our notions and beliefs as derived. It arises from the feeling that it is more philosophical to take nothing upon trust: to require proof of everything. But does not a derived truth imply something to derive from? If therefore primitive judgments are treated as derived, the problem is only removed one step backward to this question: Whence the truths of which these are the deductions? Primary or derived? To prove every postulate is therefore impossible; because the first proof implies some premise from which to prove. Unless then, some things are seen to be true intuitively, there can be no reasoning. And these unproved truths are the foundations of all that we prove.

2. All our beliefs cannot be proved.

The question then arises, If these primary beliefs are unproved, how can we know that any of our thinking thence is true? I have now introduced you to the very centre of the skeptical objections of the school of Montaigne and Hume, against the certainty of all human knowledge. Let us also view the other, less radical grounds. They argue, then: 1st. That knowledge must be uncertain as long as it is incomplete; because the discovery of the unknown related parts may change our view of those supposed to be known. And that men in all ages have believed differently with equal confidence. 2d. That perception only shows us qualities, and not substances, so that we have only the mind's inference, unproved and undemonstrable, for the existence and essence of the latter. 3d. That our organs of sense, the instruments of all perceptions, are perpetually changing their atomic structure; that they often deceive us; that the significance which we give to sensations depends on habits, knowledge and education; and that as to memory, we must take the correctness of her reproductions wholly upon trust. 4th. That our general and abstract ideas,

Metaphysical Skepticism. Its grounds.

6*

such as those of causation, space, identity, substance, &c., have not even the uncertain evidence of sensation; but are given by the mind's own *a priori* forms of thought; so that have no proof for them, save that nature teaches us to think so. And last: The sweeping objection is, that man only knows his own subjective states; to the outside of that charmed circle he can never pass, to compare those states with objective reality. But as there is no ground for our assuming the validity of this objective perception, except that it is nature to make it, we have only to suppose a different structure given to our minds, to make all seem false, which now seems true.

Such are the sweeping objections. To the first three of the special ones, there is one general and perfectly valid answer. It is not proved that all the teachings of sensation, memory, reason, are untrustworthy, because they are sometimes misinterpreted, or because men differ about them sometimes. For the mind knows that it is furnished with *criteria* for verifying seeming perceptions, recollections, inferences, which *criteria* give certain results, when applicable, and when faithfully applied. If there are no such, how did the skeptic find out the falsehood of so many of the seeming *dicta* of these faculties? As to the 4th and 5th radical pleas, that primitive judgments must be, from their very nature, unproved, and that man can never know anything besides his own subjective states, I freely grant that a direct logical refutation is out of the question, from the very terms of it. But a valid indirect one lies in these facts: 1st. That the skeptic, just as much and as necessarily, holds these primary beliefs as we do. Being implied in the validity of all other beliefs, they must be accepted as true, or all thinking must cease; we are no longer intelligent beings. But the skeptic will think: his argument against us is thinking, (erroneous.) 2d. We cannot conceive how an intelligent being could be formed at all, against whose primary beliefs the same objections would not lie; and most against God's! 3d. The fact that primitive beliefs are unproved is the very glory of their certainty, and not their weakness. They admit no proof, only because they are so immediate. The perversity of the skeptic is just that of the man who, when in perfect contact with a tree or post, should declare it impossible to ascertain whether it was near or distant, because forsooth he was so near that no measuring rule could be introduced, to measure the distance! 4th. Chiefly we apply the *argumentum ad hominem* of Pascal. If no knowledge can be certain, then the skeptic must not affirm his unbelief; for this, if admitted, would be a true proposition. The very mental processes exhibited in these objections imply many of the primary beliefs, against the validity of which the skeptic objects. If nothing can be proved, what right has he to go about proving that nothing can be

Refutation of skepticism.

proved? Finally: Truth is intrinsic, and not a mere consequence of our mental structure.

The tests of an intuitive or primary truth established by the best writers are three. (1.) They are pri-

3. Which are primitive judgments? mary: (what Hamilton calls, ambiguously, incomprehensible, not capable of being comprehended under some more general and primary judgment, and of being explained thereby.) They are primary, because they are not derived or inferred from any other truth, prior in order of proof to them; but are seen to be true without any dependence on a premise. (2.) They are necessary—i. e., the mind not only sees they are true, but must be true; sees that the negation of them would lead to a direct contradiction. (3.) They are universal—i. e., the mind is obliged to believe them as much true in every relevant case, as in the first; and all people that are sane, when the terms of their enunciation are comprehended with entire fairness, and dispassionately considered, are absolutely certain, the world over, to accept them as true. Now, our adversaries, the sensationalists, would freely admit that if the mind has any judgments which would stand these three tests, they are indeed immediate intuitions. The most practical way, therefore, to discuss their validity, will be to do it in application to special classes of supposed intuitions.

Are the propositions called axiomatic truths, immediate

Axioms are such. intuitions; or are they derived truths? Sensationalists say, the latter; they say they are not primary truths; but deductions of our experience; for they say, as we have seen Locke write, no one has them till he learns them by experimental, sensational trial, and observation; and the announcement of them, instead of receiving from the untutored mind that immediate assent we claim, would, in many cases, excite only a vacant stare. We have already shown that the concrete case is only the occasion, not the source, of the axiomatic judgment. And as to the latter objection, the mind hitherto uninformed fails to assent to them, only because he does not understand the terms of, or comprehend the relations connected with, the proposition. Grant that the presenting of a concrete, experimental case is at first necessary to enable this mind to comprehend terms and relations; still we claim (the decisive fact) that once they are comprehended, the acceptance of the proposition is inevitable. How preposterous is this objection, that because the mind did not see, while the medium was obstructed, therefore the object is not visible? One might, with equal justice, say that my child had no faculty of immediate eye-sight, because he would not be willing to affirm which of "two pigs in a poke" was the bigger! I argue again under this head, that several axioms are incapable of being experimentally inferred; because they never can be brought under the purview of the senses; e. g. "Divergent straight lines will never meet if produced to infinity." No one will ever inspect with his sight or touch an infinite line! But, says Mill, one forms a mental diagram of an infinite pair of lines; and by inspection of them, learns the truth. On this queer subterfuge, we might remark that it is more refreshing to us than consistent for them, that sensationalists should admit that the abstract ideas of the mind can be subjects of experimental reasoning. We had been told all along that true science dealt only with *phenomena*. It is also news to us that sensationalism can grant the mind any power of conceiving infinite lines! What are those, but those naughty things, absolute ideas, with which the mind ought not to have any lawful business, because they are not given to her by sensation? But chiefly, Mill's evasion is worthless in the presence of this question: what guides and compels the mind in the formation of the infinite part of this mental diagram, so as to ensure its correspondence with the sensible part? Not sense, surely; for that is the part of the mental diagram, which no eye can ever see. It is just this *a priori* power of judgment, which Mill denies. My argument stands. Once more I argue on this head, that axioms cannot be experimentally derived; because they are universal truths: but each man's experience is partial. The first time a child ever divides an apple, he at once apprehends that the whole is larger than either of its parts. At this one illustration of it, he as much believes it of all the divided apples of the universe, as though he had spent an age in dividing millions of apples for experiment. How can a universal truth come from a single case? If experience were the source of the belief, the greatest multitude of cases one could try, would never be enough to demonstrate a universal proposition; for the proportion of similar cases possible in the universe, and still untried, would be infinitely preponderant still. Experience of the past can, of itself, never determine the future.

The sensationalist is inconsistent. He says axioms are learned from experience by sense ; and there are no primary judgments of the pure reason. Aye ! But how does the mind learn that sensational experience is true ? that perceptions have any validity ? Only by a primary judgment ! Here then is the axiomatic truth that what sense gives us experimentally is true. This, surely, is not derived! Indeed, the attempt to construct a system of cognitions with a denial of primary ideas and judgments, will be found in every case as preposterous as the attempt to hang a chain upon nothing.

When we ask whether axiomatic truths will meet the second test, that of necessity, sensationalists say: "What is a necessary truth? Does one answer, with Whewell, that it is one the negation of which is inconceivable; then this is no test of primary truths, no test of truths at all; because our capacity for con-

For axioms are necessary truths.

ceiving things to be possible or otherwise, depends on our mental habits, associations, and acquirements, notoriously: e. g. The Guinea negro king could not conceive it possible that water could be solidified by cold in the higher latitudes. This will be found to be a mere verbal sophism, deriving its whole plausibility from the unlucky use of a vague term by the friends of the true theory. A truth is not necessary, because we negatively are not able to conceive the actual existence of the opposite thereof; but a truth is necessary when we positively are able to apprehend that the negation thereof includes an inevitable contradiction. It is not that we cannot see how the opposite comes to be true, but it is that we are able to see that that the opposite cannot possibly be true. Let any man consult his consciousness: is not the proposition, "a whole is greater than its parts," seen by the reason in a light of necessity, totally different from this: "The natives of Guinea are generally black, of England generally white?" Yet the latter is as true as the former!

Last, on this head, sensationalists ring many changes on the assertion that axiomatic beliefs are not held by all men alike; that there is debate what are axioms, and the widest differences; and that some things long held to be necessary truths, (e. g. *Ex nihilo nihil fit;* nature abhors a vacuum; a body cannot act without a medium on another with which it is not present,) are now found not only to be not axioms, but not true at all. I reply, all this proves that the human mind is an imperfect instrument, as to its primary judgments; not that it has none. The same mode of objecting would prove, with equal fairness, (or unfairness,) that derived truths have no inferential validity; for the differences about them have been still wider. Man is often incautious in his thinking, unconsciously blinded by hypothesis, habit and prejudice; and thus he has sometimes (not so very often after all) failed to apply the tests of axiomatic truth carefully. Still the fact remains, that there are first truths, absolutely universal in their acceptance, on which every sane mind in the world acts, and always has acted from Adam's day, with unflinching confidence. On that fact I stand.

They are Universal.

The remarks made in introducing my discussion of the immateriality of the soul, have already indicated the grounds on which we claim our belief in our own spiritual existence as an intuition. In the proposition *Cogito, ergo sum,* Des Cartes meant to indicate what is undoubtedly true, that the very consciousness of thinking implies an intuitive perception of an existing substance that thinks. But what better definition of spirit, as a something instinctively contrasted with matter, than that it is substance which thinks?

Our own Spiritual Existence Intuitively Seen.

Locke made our very belief of our own identity, a derived

notion, the simple result of our remembered

Identity Intuitively consciousnesses. It may be very true that a
Seen.
second consciousness succeeding a first, may
be the occasion of the rise of our notion of identity. But it
cannot be the cause, for the identity of the thinking being who
has the two consciousnesses is implied *a priori* in those states.
The word self cannot be comprehended by our thought without
comprehending in it the notion of identity. And it has been
well remarked that our belief in our identity cannot be a deduction, because it must be implied beforehand, in our very capacity
to perceive any relation between premises and conclusion. If
the comprehension of the former is not felt to be the act of the
same thinking subject who comprehends the latter, then of course
there is no possibility of a logical dependence being perceived
between them.

Once more, we assert against Berkeley, and all other ideal-

Reality of the Objective ists, that our reference of our sensations to
Intuitively Seen.
an external world as their cause, and that a
world of substances to which the mind refers
the qualities which alone sensation perceives, is a valid intuition.
It is primary; witness the notable failures of all the attempts to
analyse it into something more primary, from Aristotle to Reid.
It is necessary; for the pure idealist can no more rid himself of
the practical belief that this was an objective reality, and not a
mere subjective notion of a pain, which caused him to feel that
he had butted his head against a post. And it is universal. All
minds learn it. And if we analyse the mental part of our sensation, we shall find that perception is, in its very nature, a perception of a relation between sensitive mind and outward matter. Grant to the idealist even the assertion that the mind immediately knows only its own subjective states; yet, when it is
conscious of the subjective part of what we call a perception,
it still knows by its consciousness, that there was an effect which
it did not induce upon itself. Surely this subjectivity must include a consciousness of its own volitions. So, of the absence
of a volition of its own. Then, as the mind intuitively and
necessarily knows that no effect can be without a cause, it must
refer this phenomenon, the subjective act of perception, consciously uncaused from within, to some real thing without.

But the intuition which has been most debated, and is of

4. Cause for every Ef- most fundamental importance to theologians,
fect intuitively Believed. is our notion of causation. The doctrine of
common sense here is, that when the mind
sees an effect, it intuitively refers it to some cause, as producing
its occurrence. Moreover, the antecedent something which
made it to be, is intuitively apprehended as having a *power* to
produce its occurrence; otherwise it would not have occurred.
For the mind is impelled by its own nature to think, that if
there had not been a something adequate to make the occur-

rence to be, it would not have been. Nothing can only result in nothing: and a thing cannot produce its own occurrence ; for then it must act before it is. Hence, also, this immediate deduction that this power will always produce the same result, when applied under the same circumstances. The *occasion* of the rise of this notion of power is, no doubt, as Morell has said, with many authors, our consciousness of our own volitions. Now, the sensational psychologists, at the head of whom stands Hume in this particular, deny all this; and say that our belief that similar causes will produce like effects, is only a probable induction of our experience ; (so Mill, adding that this probability rises to a practical certainty, as one induction *concurs* with another,) that the mind merely *presumes* the sequence will be repeated again, because it has been presented so often; that since the mind is entitled to no idea, save what perception gives her, and the senses perceive only the two terms of the sequence, without tie of *power* between them, the notion of this tie is baseless; and *power* in causation is naught. Dr. Thomas Brown, while he asserts the intuitive origin of our expectation, that like will produce like, and even argues it with great acuteness, still falls into the latter error, denying that the mind has any ground for a notion of *power* other than "immediate, invariable antecedence ;" for this is all perception gives us.

Now, our first remark, in defending the correct doctrine, is, that this argument is of no force to any except pure sensationalists. When perception furnishes the occasion, a sequence, the reason, by its innate power, furnishes the notion of cause in it. Perception does not show us souls, not even our own; but reason compels us to supply the notion of soul as the subject of perceptions and all other states. Perception does not show us substance in matter, but only a bundle of properties ; reason compels us to supply the notion of substance. And such an argument is peculiarly inconsistent in the mouth of Brown, who asserts that our belief in the recurrence of causative sequences is intuitive ; for it is impossible for the reason to evade the question : What except power in the antecedent can make the sequence immediate and invariable ? The something that makes it so, is just our notion of the power.

Of no Force to say : Power not Perceived.

Having thus rebutted objections to the true view, we return to show that the opposite one is unreasonable and absurd. The heterodox metaphysicians deny that we intuitively apprehend the fact, that every effect must have its proper cause, and *vice versa:* and the most plausible ground of denial is to say that this presumption grows in our minds by the operation of the associating faculty. It is a law of our minds that they are apt to repeat those sequences of thought, which they have had before in the same juxtaposition ; and hence the habit grows up, of thinking of the

The Belief not Derived from Association.

same consequent when we see the same antecedent; and we naturally learn to expect to see it. But I will show that the belief in cause is not the consequence, but the ground and origin of the association. For instance; man knows perfectly well that certain sequences which recur before him perpetually and regularly, as of light on darkness are not causative; while he believes that certain others, as of light on the sun's rising, are causative. Now if the associative habit had produced the notion of causation, it would have done it alike in both cases; for both sequences recurred with exactly the same uniformity.

I remark, farther, that no experiences of the fact that a given antecedent had produced a given consequent so far as observed, could logically produce the conviction that it would, and must do so everywhere, and in all the future, if it were not sustained by an intuitive recognition of cause and effect in the sequence. The experience of the past only proves the past; there is no logical tie which entitles us to project it on the future, if we deny the intuitive one. How many experiences of a regular sequence entitle us to carry our expectations into the future? one hundred? 500? What then is the difference between case 499th and case 500th, that the latter alone, when added to the previous past experiences, authorizes us to say that now case 501st, still in the future, must eventuate so and so? There is no reasonable answer. In truth, experience of a mere sequence, by itself, generates no confidence whatever in its future recurrence with causative certainty. You may ask, does not a mere empirical induction (*inductio simplicis enumerationis*, Bacon,) the mere recurrence of an observed sequence, beget in our minds even a probable expectation of its recurrence in the future? I answer, yes, in certain sorts of cases; but this probable expectation proceeds from this: We know intuitively that the consequent in this sequence must have some producing cause: whether we have rightly detected it among the seeming antecedents, is not yet proved; and hence two facts are inferred: this seeming, visible antecedent may be the cause, seeing it has so frequently preceded; and if it be indeed the cause, then we are certain it will always be followed by the effect. But we have not yet convinced ourselves that some unseen antecedent may not intervene in each case observed; and, therefore, our expectation that the seeming antecdent will continue to be followed by the effect, is only probable. It is, therefore, not the number of instances experienced, in which the sequence occurred, which begets our expectation that the sequence must recur in the future; but it is the probability the mind sees, that the seeming antecedent may be the true one, which begets that expectation. And if that probability rises to a certainty in one or two cases of the observed sequence, it may be as strong as after ten thousand cases.

Nor from Experience.

This was ingeniously (perhaps unintentionally) illustrated by some of the performances of the calculating machine constructed by the famous Babbage. The machinery could be so adjusted that it would exhibit a series of numbers in an aperture of the dial plate, having a given *ratio*, up to millions. And then without any new adjustment by the maker, it would change the *ratio* and begin a new series, which it would again continue with perfect regularity until the spectators were weary of watching. Now, if a regular empirical induction, however long continued, could demonstrate anything, it would have done it here. But just when the observer had convinced himself that the first *ratio* expressed the necessary law of the machine, *Presto !* a change; and a different one supersedes it, without visible cause.

Illustration of the Above.

This introduces the argument, that it is not a habit of experience which begets the belief in the regular connection of cause and effect, because, in many cases, it arises in full strength after one trial. The child thrusts his finger in flame; the result is acute pain. He is just as certain from that moment that the same act will produce the same feeling, as after ten thousand trials. It is because his mind compels him to think the primitive judgment, " effect follows cause;" and the singleness of the antecedent enables him to decide that this antecedent is the cause. Take another case : A school boy, utterly ignorant of the explosive qualities of gunpowder, shuts himself in a room with a portion for his boyish experiments. After finding it passive under many experiments, he at length applies fire, and there is an immediate explosion. But at the moment the tongs also fell on it; and hence it may not be yet patent which of the two antecedents (simultaneous) was cause. He resolves to clear up this doubt by another trial, in which the tongs shall not fall. He applies fire, excluding this time all other antecedent changes, and the explosion follows again. And now, this boy is just as certain that fire will inevitably explode any gunpowder, that is precisely like this, provided the conditions be precisely similar, as a million of experiments could make him. He has ascertained the tie of cause.

One Instance Cannot form a habit of Association.

In truth, as Dr. Chalmers well says, experience is so far from begetting this belief in the regular efficacy of causation, that its effect is, on the contrary, to limit and correct that belief. A little child strikes his spoon on the table; the effect is noise. At first he expects to be able to produce the same effect by striking it on the bed or carpet, and is vexed at the failure. Experience corrects his expectation ; not by adding anything to his intuitive judgment of like cause, like effect; but by teaching him that in this case, the cause of noise was complex, not single, as he had before supposed, being the impact of the spoon and the elasticity of the thing struck.

The subtile and yet simple reasoning, by which Kant (Crit-
ick of Pure Reason. Bk. ii, Ch. 2, § 3,) shows
the absurdity of resolving cause and effect
into mere sequence, is worthy of your attention here.   He suggests two instances : In one I look successively at the different
parts of a large house over the way.   I perceive first, for instance, its front, and then its end.   But do I ever think for
a moment that the being of the end is successive upon the being of the front ?   Never.   I know they are simultaneous.   In
another case, I see a vessel in the river just opposite to me ; and
next, I see it below me. The perceptions are no more successive
than those of the front and end of the house.   But now, can I
ever think that the being of the vessel in the two positions is co-
etaneous?   It is impossible.   Why ?   The only answer is, that
the law of the reason has, by intuition, seen effect and dependency, in the last pair of successive perceptions, which were not
in the first pair.   The same vessel has moved; motion is an effect ;
its cause must precede it.   And this suggests the other member
of his argument : In a causative sequence, the interval of time is
wholly inappreciable to the senses; the cause A and the effect B
seem to come together.   Now, why is it that the mind always
refuses to conceive the matter so as to think B leads A, and will
only think that A leads B ?   Why do you not think that the loud
sound of the blow caused the impact of the hammer, just as often as you do the impact caused the sound ?   Surely there is a
law of the reason regulating this !   Now that something which
determines the order of the sequence, is power.

Kant's Argument.

Last, it is only because our judgment of cause is *a priori*
and intuitive, that any process of induction,
practical or scientific, can be valid or demonstrative.   Bacon shows, what even J.
S. Mill admits, that a merely empirical induction can never give certain expectation of future recurrence.   To reach this, some canon of induction must be applied which will discriminate the *post hoc* from the *propter hoc.*
Does not Mill himself teach the necessity of such canons ?   Inspect any instance of their application to observed sequences, and
you will find that each step proceeds upon the intuitive law of
cause, as its postulate.   Each step is a syllogism, in which the
intuitive truth gives the major premise.

The Intuitive Belief of Cause, Necessary prior premise of all Experimental Induction.

Let us take a simple case falling under what Mill calls his
Method by Agreement.   (The student will find
my assertion true of either of the others.)   The
school boy with his parcel of gunpowder, e. g., is searching
among the antecedents for the true cause of the phenomenon of
explosion, which we will call D.   That cause is not detected at
first, because he cannot be certain that he procures its occurrence
with only a single antecedent.   First he constructs an experiment, in which he contrives to exclude all antecedents save two,

Example.

A and B. The result D follows; but it is not determined whether A or B, or the two jointly, caused it. He contrives a second experiment, in which B is excluded; but another antecedent event C happens along with A, and again D follows. Now we can get the truth. We reason thus: " In the first experiment the cause of D must have been either A or B, or the two combined." But why? Because the effect D must have had some immediate, present cause. [But we know that no other immediate antecedent effects were present, save A and B.] This is our *a priori* intuition. Well, in the second experiment, either A or C, or the two combined, must have caused D. Why? The same intuition gives the only answer. But we proved, in the first experiment, C had nothing to do with producing D ; and in the second, B, had nothing to do with producing D ; because C was absent in the first, and B in the second. Then A was the true cause all the time. Why? Why may not B have been the cause, that time when it was present? Because every effect has its own cause, which is regular, every time it is produced. The premise is still the intuition: " Like causes produce like effects."

It is thus appears, that this intuitive belief is essential beforehand, to enable us to convert an experimental induction into a demonstrated general law. Could anything more clearly prove that the original intuition itself cannot have been an experimental induction? It passes human wit to see how a logical process can prove its own premise, when the premise is what proves the process. Yet this absurdity Mill gravely attempts to explain. His solution is, that we may trust the law of cause as a general premise, because it is "an empirical law, co-extensive with all human experience." May we conclude, then, that a man is entitled to argue from the law of cause as a valid general premise, only after he has acquired "all human experience ? " This simple question dissolves the sophism into thin air. It is experimentally certain that this is not the way in which the mind comes by the belief of the law; because no man, to the day of his death, acquires all human experience, but only a part, which, relatively to the whole, is exceedingly minute ; and because every man believes the law of cause to be universal, when he begins to acquire experience. The just doctrine, therefore, is that experimental instances are only the occasions upon which the mind's own intuitive power furnishes the self-evident law.

That which is necessary prior premise cannot be deduction.

This argument, young gentlemen, has, I think, also given you an illustration of the justice of Archbishop Whateley's logical doctrine, that inductive argument is, after all, but a branch of the syllogistic. The answers made to the questions, What is inductive argument? are, as you know, confused and contra-

What is inductive proof?

dictory. Some logicians and many physicists seem to think that the colligation of similar cases of sequences in considerable numbers, is inductive demonstration. Whereas, I have cited to you Lord Bacon. declaring that if the induction proceed no farther than this, it is wholly short of a demonstration, and can but raise a presumption of the existence of a *law* of sequence, which is liable to be overthrown by contrary instances. It is this mistake, which accounts for the present loose condition of much that claims to be physical science; where an almost limitless license of framing hypotheses which have probability, prevails, claiming the precious name of " science," for what are, by Bacon's just rule, but guesses. Many other logicians, seeing the obvious defect of such a definition of inductive demonstration, and yet supposing that they are obliged to find an essential difference between inductive and syllogistic logic, invent I know not what untenable definitions of the former. It is, in fact, only that branch of syllogistic reasoning, which has the intuition, " Like causes, like effects," as its major premise, and which seeks as its conclusion the discrimination of the *post hoc* from the *propter hoc*, in seeking the true causative laws of events in nature. You may, if you please, use the word " *Inductio*," to express the colligation of similar instances of sequence. But *inductive demonstration* is another matter; a far higher matter, which must come after. It is the logical application of some established *canon*, which will infallibly detect the immediate causative antecedent of an effect, amidst the apparent antecedents. Its value is in this: that when once that discovery is clearly made, even in one instance of sequence, we have a particular *law of nature*, a principle, which is a constant and permanent guide of our knowledge and practice. But why does that discovery become the detection of a law of nature? Because we know that the great truth reigns in nature: " Like causes, like effects"—in other words, because the reason has evolved to itself the intuitive idea of *efficient power* in causes. I have shown you, that the valid application of those *canons* is, *in each step a syllogism;* a syllogism, of which the great primary law of causation is first premise.

    This exposition shows you that this great law is the very key of nature. It is, to change the meta-

Law of cause is key of nature.

phor, the corner-stone of all the sciences of nature, material and physical. Hence, if its primary and intuitive character is essential to its validity, as I have argued, in vindicating this thesis we have been defending the very being of all the natural sciences, as well as the citadel of natural theology. Hence it follows that the sensualistic school of metaphysics is as blighting to the interests of true physical science, as of the divine science. The inductive method, in the hands of physicists who grounded it substantially in the metaphysics of common sense, the metaphysics of Turrettin, of Dr. Clarke or of Reid, gave us the splendid results of the Newtonian era. That method, in the hands of Auguste Comte, J. Stuart Mill, and other sensationalists, is giving us the modern corruptions and license of Darwinism and Materialism. The unhallowed touch of this school poisons, not only theology, which they would fain poison, but the sciences of matter, which they claim as their special care.

Few words are needed to show the intimate relations be- *True doctrine of cause* tween the true doctrine of causation and *at basis of Natural The-* theology. It is on his heresy about causa- *ology.* tion, that Hume grounds his famous argu- ment against miracles. It is on the same error he grounds his objection to the teleological argument for God's existence, that the world is a "singular effect." You saw that the argu- ment just named for God's existence is founded expressly on this great law of cause.

I think we are now prepared to appreciate justly the clam- *Final Cause.* our of the sensationalists against our postu- lating final causes. I assert that *it is only by postulating them, that we can have any foundation whatever for any inductive science.* We have seen, that the sole problem of all inductive demonstration is, to discover, among the apparent antecedents in any given sequences of changes, that one, which is efficient cause.

For that being infallibly ascertained, we have a Law of *Essential to all regular* Nature. But how so ? How is it that a re- *natural law.* lation ascertained in one, or a few cases, may be assumed as a natural law ? Because our reasons tell us that we are authorized to expect that antecedent which is the true efficient in a given sequence of changes, will be, and must be efficient to produce the same sequent, every time that sequence recurs under precisely the same conditions, throughout the realm of nature, in all ages and places. [And that belief is *a priori* and intuitive ; else, as we saw, experience could never make it valid; and the demonstrations of regular law in nature would be impossible—i. e., science would be im- possible.] But on what condition can that belief be valid to the mind ? If there is nothing truly answering to the *a priori* idea of power in the antecedent; if all the mind is entitled to postu- late is mere, invariable sequence ; and if that efficient Power is to be excluded, because not given by sense perception ; is that belief valid ? Obviously not. Again: If Cause is only mate- rial necessity, only a relation in blind, senseless, unknowing, in- voluntary matter, in matter infinitely variable and mutable, is there any possible foundation for their universal and invariable relations in given sequences ? Is any intellect authorized *a pri- ori*, to expect it. Obviously not. It is only when we assume that there is a Creator to the created, that there is an intellect and will ; and that, an immutable one, establishing and governing these sequences of physical change; that the mind can find any valid basis for an expectation of law in them.   And that is to say : There is a basis of law in them because, and only because, this ruling intelligence and will has some end in view. We may not know which end ; but we know there is some end, or there would be no Law, his constancy to which is the ground, and the explanation, of the invariability.   But that is the doctrine of Final Cause ! Take it away ; and the inductive logic has no basis under it.   You will remember the line

" The undevout Astronomer is mad"—

In the same sense we may assert, that the logic of the atheistic physicist is mad.   Do we not find, in the prevalence of Positivist and Sensualistic philosophy, in our day, the natural explanation of the deplorable license which now corrupts and deforms so much of those Natural Sciences, which, in the hands of sound, theistic physicists like Newton, Davy, Brewster, have run so solendid and beneficent a course?

LECTURE IX.

SOURCES OF OUR THINKING. — Continued.

SYLLABUS.

1. Is the Intuitional Reason a different faculty from, and of higher authority than, the Logical Understanding?
    Locke's Essay, bk. iv, ch. ii, § 7.   Mosheim Eccles. Hist., Cent. 17th, Sec. 1, ¶ 24.   Morell, p. 125, pp. 161–168.
2. To ascertain the origin of moral distinctions in our minds, state and refute the Selfish System of Morals, as held by Hobbes, and others.
    Jouffroy's Introduc. to Ethicks, Lect. ii.   Dr. Thos. Brown, Lect. 78, 79. Cousin, Le Vrai, &c., Lecon 12th.   Morell, p. 71–75.
3. State and refute the utilitarian theory, (as held by Hume and Bentham.)
    "Crimes of Philanthrophy," in the Land we Love, Dec., 1866.   Jouffroy, Lect. 13, 14.   Brown, Lect. 77, 78.   Cousin, Le Vrai, &c., Lecon 13th. Morell, p. 215, &c.   Thornwell, Discourses on Truth, i, ii.   Bishop Butler's Sermons, 11th to 14th.   Jonathan Edward's Essay on the Nature of Virtue, ch. i, ii.
4. State and refute Paley's form of the Selfish System.
    Paley's Moral Phil., pp. 24–60.   (8vo. Ed.)   Jouffroy, ch. 15.   Brown, Lect. 79, 80.   Alex. Moral Science, ch. 1, 2, 3.   Cousin, Du Vrai, du Beau et du Bien, as above.
5. State and discuss the Sentimental Theory of Dr. Adam Smith.
    Jouffroy, Lect. 16–18.   Brown, Lect. 80–81.   Turrettin, Loc. xi, Qu. 1.

SEVERAL analysts of the laws of thought, such as Hobbes and Locke, set out with the fascinating idea of accepting nothing upon trust, and bringing everything to the test of experimental proof.   The miserable sensationalism and materialism to which this led in the hands of Priestly in England, and Condillac in France, taught men to reflect, that unless some primary judgments are allowed to start from, there can be no beginning

1. Transcendentalists claim primitive judgments licentiously.

at all: so that some truths must have a prior authority than that of proof. By what faculty, then, are they perceived? Transcendentalists, from Spinoza to the modern, have all answered, by the intuitive reason: whose sight is direct intellection, whose products are super - logical, and not, therefore, amenable to logical refutation. The frightful license of dogmatizing to which these schools have proceeded, shows the motive; it is to enjoy an emancipation from the logical obligations of proving dogmas. Do we say to them, Your assertions do not seem to us true, and we disprove them thus and thus: they reply, "Ah, that is by your plodding, logical understanding; intuitions of the pure reason are not amenable to it; and if you do not see that our opinion is necessarily true, in spite of objections, it is only because the reason is less developed in you." So the quarrel now stands. It seems to me obvious, therefore, that the next adjustment and improvement, which the science of mind must receive, should be an adjustment of the relations between intuitions and valid deductions.

Now, we might practically bring the transcendentalist to reason by saying, first, that they always claim the validity of the logical understanding, when they find it convenient to use it. [The very evasion above stated is a deduction, by one step, from false premises!] Hence, consistency requires them to bow to it everywhere. Second; we might apply the established tests of a true intuition to their pretended ones, primariness, necessity, and universality; and thus show that, when they profess by the pure reason to see dogmas which contradict or transcend the common sense of mankind, they are but making wild hypotheses. But third: I am convinced the radical overthrow of their system will be seen to be, at length, in this position: that the mind sees the truth of a valid deduction by the same faculty, and with equal authority, as an axiom or other first truth—i. e., when major and minor premise have a conclusive relation, and that relation is fairly comprehended, the reason sees the conclusion as immediately, as necessarily, as intuitively, as authoritatively, as when it sees a primary truth.

How resisted.

To my mind, the simple and sufficient proof of this view of the logical function is in these questions. What is the human intelligence, but a function of seeing truth? As the eye only sees by looking, and all looking is direct and immediate sense intuition, how else can the mind see, than by looking—i. e., by rational intuition? Whether the object of bodily sight be immediate or reflective, an object or its *spectrum*, it is still equally true that the eye only sees by looking—looking immediately; in the latter case the *spectrum* only is its immediate object. So the mind only sees by looking; and all its looking is intuition; if not immediate, it is not its own; it is naught. One of the

All judgments intuitive and necessary, if valid.

earliest, Locke, inconsistently concurs with one of the latest, McGuffey, of the great English-speaking psychologists, in asserting the view I adopted before consulting either. Locke's proof of it seems to me perfectly valid. He argues (*loco cita-to,*) that if the mind's perception of a valid relation between a proposition and its next premise were not immediate, then there must be, between the two, some proposition to mediate our view of it. But between a proposition and its next premise, there .can be no other interposed.

But to this view many sound philosophers, even, would probably object strenuously. That the first

Objections solved. great mark of intuitive authority, primariness, was lacking; that the position is utterly overthrown by the wide and various differences of opinion on subjects of deduction; while in first truths, there must be universal agreement; and that it is inconsistent with the fact that many derived conclusions claim no more than a probable evidence. To the first, I reply, the action of the reason in seeing a deduced truth, is not indeed a primary judgment; but the fact that the truth is seen only by relation to premises, does not make the intellection less immediate and necessary. Just so truly as the first truth is seen to be necessarily true, so the deduced truth is seen to be necessarily true, the premises being as they are. Several of our intuitions are intuitions of relations. Why should it be thought so strange that these intellections by relations should be intuitive? To the second, propositions called axioms have not always commanded universal agreement; and we are obliged to explain this fact by misapprehension of terms, or ignorance of relations included in the propositions. Well, the same explanation accounts consistently for the differences men have in their deductions; and the more numerous differences in this class of propositions are accounted for by the facts, that while the axioms are few, deductions are countless; and in any one there are more terms, because more propositions liable to misconception. But I do assert that, in a valid syllogism, if the major and minor are known to be true, and the terms are all fairly comprehended, the belief of the conclusion by the hearer is as inevitable, as necessary, as universal, as when an axiom is stated. Third; though in many deductions the evidence is but probable, the fact that there is probable evidence, may be as necessarily admitted, as in an intuitive and positive truth.

We now approach, young gentlemen, that great class of our judgments which are of supreme impor-

2. Source of our tance in theology, as in practical life—the
Moral Judgments. class known as our moral judgments. Every sane man is conscious of acts of soul, which pronounce certain rational agents right or wrong in certain acts. With these right or wrong acts our souls unavoidably conjoin certain

notions and feelings of obligation, merit, demerit, approbation or disapprobation, and desert of reward or penalty. It is this peculiar class of mental states which constitutes the subject of the science of ethicks, or morals. All questions as to the nature and validity of moral judgments run into the radical question, as to their origin. Are they the results of a fundamental and intuitive law of reason? Or are they artificial or factitious of some other natural principles developed into a form only apparently peculiar, by habit, association, or training? In answering this all-important question, I shall pursue this method, to set aside the various false analyses, until we reach the true one.

The Selfish System, presenting itself in many varied forms The Selfish System. from Hobbes (natural desire of enjoyment only motive) through Mandeville (the desire of being applauded is the moral motive) down to Paley, has always this characteristic: it resolves our idea of virtue into self-interest. Its most refined form, perhaps, is that which says, since acts of benevolence, sympathy, justice, are found to be attended with an immediate inward pleasure, (self-approbation,) that pleasure is the motive of our moral acts. We discuss several phases together.

I remark, that on the selfish system, the notion of right, Refuted. 1st. By intuitive Beliefs of Right and Free-agency. duty, obligation, free-agency, could never have arisen in the mind, and have no relevancy or meaning. Let man frame the proposition.: "That which furthers self-interest is right;" the very employment of the word right betrays the fact that the mind recognizes a standard other than that of self-interest. And any consideration of the notion shows that it is utterly violated and falsified, when made identical with self-interest. Thus, Hobbes says, each man's natural right is to pursue his own natural self-interest supremely. But according to his own showing, this "right" in A implies no corresponding duty in him, and no obligation in his neighbour, B, to respect it, and no recognition on the part of any other. Any body has a "right" to prevent A from having his "right." Queer right this!

If interest is the whole motive, then, when the question arises, whether I shall do, or omit a certain action, you cannot consistently expect me to consider anything but this: whether or not the doing of it will promote my own advantage, and that, in the form I happen to prefer. If I say, "This result will most gratify me," the argument is at an end; my proposed act is, for me, right; there is no longer any standard of uniform moral distinction. The same remark shows that the judgment of obligation to a given act is then baseless. Attempt to apply any of those arguments, by which Epicureanism attempts to interpose an "ought not" between a man and any natural in-

7*

dulgence; (as this: "This sensual pleasure will indeed promote animal, but hinder intellectual pleasure, which is higher. And since pleasure is the rational chief good, you should prefer the more to the less;") the reply is: "Animal joys are to me larger than intellectual;" and the ground of obligation is gone. If no indulgence is less or more virtuous than any other, then no possible argument of obligation can be constructed, in the face of an existing preference, for refraining from any. If the sensualistic psychology is true, from which the selfish schemes proceed, then desire for natural good, which they make the only moral motive, is a passive affection of the soul. It is no more voluntary, when the object of desire is presented, than is pain when you are struck, or a chill when you are deluged with cold water. Where, now, is that free-agency which, we intuitively feel, is rudimental to all moral action and responsibility? Man is no longer self-directed by subjective, rational motives, but drawn hither and thither like a puppet, by external forces. But if not a free, he cannot be a moral agent. Of course, also, there is no longer any basis for any judgment of merit or demerit in acts, or any moral obligation to punishment. Penalties become the mere expedients of the stronger for protecting their own selfishness. And as this is as true of the future, all religious sanctions are at an end!

This theory teaches that this selfish pleasure apprehended by the mind, in acquiring an object, must always be the motive for seeking it. The analysis is false; desire must be instinctive; otherwise man could not have his first volition till after the volition had put him on the way of experiencing the pleasant result of the fruition! Many desires are obviously instinctive; e. g., curiosity. Now, since the self-pleasing cannot be the original element of the desire, it cannot be proved that this is our element of rightness, in classifying our desires. See now, how this analysis would assign the effect as the cause of its own cause. A does a disinterested act. The conciousness of having done disinterestedly gives A an inward pleasure. This after-pleasure, proceeding from the consciousness that the act was unselfish, prompted to the act! Thus the effect caused its own cause! The absurdity of the scheme is further proved by this: If the fact that a disinterested act results in inward satisfaction to him who did it, proves that act selfish; then the fact that a selfish act usually results in inward pain to him who perpetrates it, proves that act to have been a disinterested one in motive.

If the selfish theory of action were true, the adaptation of another person's conduct to confer personal advantage on us, should be synonymous with merit in our eyes. The villain who shared with us the reward of his misdeeds, to bribe us to aid or ap-

2d. From Precedence of Instinctive Desire to Calculation.

3rd. From intuitive Difference of advantage and merit.

plaud him, would evoke the same sentiment of gratitude, as the mother who blessed us with her virtuous self-sacrifice; and there would be no generic difference between the hollow flattery of the courtier for the monster on whose bounty he fattened, and the approbation of the virtuous for patriotism or benevolence.

If our notion of good acts is nothing but a generalization 4th. From Vividness of the idea of acts promotive of our self-of Unsophisticated interest, he who has most experimental Moral Sentiments. knowledge of human affairs (i. e., he who is most hackneyed in this world's ways,) must have the clearest and strongest apprehensions of moral distinctions; because he would most clearly apprehend this tendency of actions. He who was wholly inexperienced, could have no moral distinctions. Is this so? Do we not find the most unsophisticated have the most vivid moral sympathies? The ignorant child in the nursery more than the hackneyed man of experience?

But the crowning absurdity of the theory appears here; 5th. From Conscious- that our consciousness always teaches us, that ness. No Merit where the pleasure we have in well-doing depends Self reigns. wholly upon our feeling that the virtuous act had no reference to self; and the moment we feel that self-pleasing was our prime motive, we feel that our moral pleasure therein is wholly marred. Indeed, the best and the sufficient argument against this miserable theory would, perhaps, be the instinctive loathing and denial uttered against it by every man's soul, who is rightly constituted. The honest man knows, by his immediate consciousness, that when he does right, selfishness is not his motive; and that if it were, he would be utterly self-condemned. As *Cousin* nervously remarks: Our consciousness tells us, that the approbation we feel for disinterested virtue is wholly disinterested, and it is impossible for us to feel it unless we feel that the agent for whom we feel it was disinterested in this act. Thus, a thousand things in the acts, the language, and the consciousnesses of men are utterly irreconcilable with this hateful analysis, and show it to be as unphilosophical as degrading. Our crowning objection is found in its effect on our view of the divine character. That which is man's finite virtue must be conceived infinite, as constituting the virtue of God, (if there is a God.) His holiness must be only sovereign self-interest!

In the next place, I group together three theories of the 3. Utilitarian Eth- nature of virtue, which really amount to the icks. same; that of David Hume, who taught that an act is apprehended by us as virtuous, because it is seen to be useful to mankind; that of Jeremy Bentham, who taught that whatever conduct is conducive to the greatest good of the greatest number, is right; and that of some New England divines and philosophers, who teach that

virtue consists in benevolence. The latter is practically synonymous with the two former. For the practical expression of
benevolence is beneficence. This theory of virtue is a natural
off-shoot of Jonathan Edwards' theory of virtue. This great
and good man would probably be shocked to have his speculation, as to "the nature of true virtue," classed with those of the
infidel, utilitarian school. But the historical development of it
since his death, proves the justice of the charge. It is, moreover, so interesting an exposition of the unavoidable tendencies of the "Benevolence Theory," and has so important
relations to existing errors in theology, that I must ask you to
pause a moment to consider Edwards' view.

    As is suggested by the Rev'd Ro. Hall, Edwards was
probably impelled to this piece of false anal-
Edwards' Theory of ysis, by his love of simplifying. His desire
Virtue. was to unify the ultimate principles of the
rational spirit, as much as possible. Hence, instead of regarding virtuous acts and states of soul as an ultimate and independent category, he teaches that they all most essentially
consist in "Benevolence to Being in General," meaning, of
course, rational being, or, "love to being in general." And
this love, which is the essence of all virtue, he expressly defines
as the love of benevolence only, as distinct from the love of
moral complacency. This is essential to his system ; for, as he
himself argues, the love of moral complacency must imply
moral beauty in its object. The perception of moral beauty
generates the love which is moral complacency. If the love
which constitutes moral beauty were that moral complacency,
Edwards argues that we should make a thing its own parent.
Of this, more anon. He then proceeds : "The first object of
virtuous benevolence is Being, simply considered ;" and hence :
"Being in general is its object." That to which its ultimate
propensity tends is "the highest good of being in general."
From this conclusion, Edwards draws this corollary : There
may be a benevolence towards a particular Being, which is
virtuous, because that particular Being is a part of the aggregate, general being ; but the affection is virtuous, only provided
it consists with the "highest good of being in general." Again :
That being who has the greatest *quantum* of existence must
attract the largest share of this benevolence. Hence, we must
love God more than all creatures, because He is infinite in the
dimensions of His existence ; and we ought, among creatures,
to love a great and good man proportionably more than one
less able and full of being. The grounds of proof on which
Edwards seems to rest his conclusion are these : That every
judgment of beauty, of every kind, is analysable into a perception of order and harmony ; but the most beautiful and lofty of
all rational harmonies is this *concent* or benevolence of an intelligent Being to all like Being : That the Scriptures say

"God is love;" and "Love is the fulfilling of the whole law" between man and his neighbour: And that this theory explains so well the superior claims of God to our love, over creatures' claims to our love.

The transition between this plausible, but most sophistical speculation, and the utilitarian scheme, and ethics of expediency, which underlie the New England Theology, of our day, is found in the writings of Dr. Samuel Hopkins, (and "the younger Edwards.") In their hands, "Love to Being in General," became simply the affection of benevolence; and the theory became this: That benevolence is all virtue, and all virtue is benevolence. I have already disclosed the affinity of this theory to the utilitarian, by the simple remark, that beneficence is the practical expression of benevolence. Hence, when he who has defined virtue as benevolence, comes to treat of virtue as a practical principle, he makes nothing else of it than Jeremy Bentham's "greatest good of the greatest number." We shall detect Dr. Hopkins adopting this, and even the most thoroughly selfish theory of virtue, in carryiug out his benevolence-scheme, with an amusing candour, simplicity and inconsistency.

Leads to Utilitarian Ethics.

Proceeding to the refutation of Edwards' scheme, I begin with his Scriptures. The same logic which infers it from the expression, "God is love," would infer from the text, "God is light," that He is nothing but pure intelligence; and from the text, "Our God is a consuming fire," that He is nothing but vindicatory justice. All Scriptures must be interpreted consistently. Neither can we overstrain the declarations of our Saviour and the apostle, that "love fulfils the whole law" between man and man, into the theory that benevolence is the whole essence of virtue. The proposition of the Scripture contains a beautiful practical fact: that the virtue of love (which, in Scripture nomenclature, includes far more than benevolence) prompts to all other virtues. I exclude the overstrained inference by simply referring to the other passages of Scripture, which expressly name other distinguishable virtues in addition to love. "Now abideth faith, hope, love: these three: but the greatest of these is love."— 1 Cor. xiii: 13. "Add to your faith virtue, and to virtue knowledge, and to knowledge temperance, and to temperance patience, and to patience godliness, and to godliness brotherly kindness, and to brotherly kindness love."---2 Pet. 1: 5, 6. When the Scriptures declare love to God the great Commandment, they mean a very different thing from Edwards' benevolence to Being; "a propensity to its highest good." The supreme object of holy love in the Scriptures is always God's holiness. The affection is as distinct from mere benevolence, as adoration from kindness. The love of the Scriptures, in which all man's holiness centres, is the attraction of the whole

Refuted.

soul, in all its active principles, towards all that is pure and venerable, and righteous and true, as well as good, in the divine character.

To Edwards' speculative grounds, I reply, 1st. His grounding of moral virtue in a harmony or order

Moral Beauty Unique. perceived, is utterly invalid as a support of his theory, unless he holds that æsthetic beauty, logical propriety and moral praiseworthiness, are all generically the same beauty, only differing in degree. For if not, the order and harmony whose perception gives the feeling of virtuousness, are a different kind; and Edwards, as much as I, is bound to answer the question: In what does moral beauty differ from the æsthetic and the logical? I can answer consistently: In conformity to a peculiar, original intuition, that of conscience. Indeed, the fact that every sane mind intuitively perceives that difference, is, of itself, a sufficient refutation of Edwards' and of every other false analysis of the moral sentiment.

We have seen that Edwards regards the love of benevolence, not the love of moral complacency, as

Edwards' parodox. the primary essence of virtue: and I showed you the argument which led him to this consistent conclusion. The love of complacency, then, is love to a rational agent on account of his love of benevolence; and the former is not primarily of the essence of virtue. That is: it is not virtuous to love virtue! It is true that on a subsequent page, he retracts this absurdity; availing himself virtually of a theory of sympathy between the virtuous (or benevolent) agent and the approving spectator, to argue what he had before disproved. This is but the anticipation of the vicious analysis of Adam Smith. By a parallel process, Edwards' principles should lead him to conclude that disinterested gratitude is not virtuous. Saith he, "the first benevolence cannot be gratitude." True; for this first benevolence must regard its object simply as being, not as beneficent. Hence, for me to love a being because he has been a benefactor to me, is not virtue! Edwards, in a subsequent chapter, resolves gratitude into self-love, but he is not thereby designing to depreciate the affection of gratitude, for in the same chapter he analyses the judgments and emotions of conscience into the same self-love!

We have seen that Edwards makes the essence of virtue to be "love to being in general." Another fatal

Makes an abstraction the object of virtue. objection to this is, that it assigns us as the object of every virtuous affection, a mere abstraction, a general idea. Whereas, if consciousness tells you anything clearly of your moral sentiments, it is that their objects must be personal. Only a person can oblige us to a duty. Only a person can be the object of a right. Pantheism, as we saw, abolishes morality by obliterating the personality of God. Edwards' speculation would do it as effectually, in another way. Again, says Edwards, love to a particular being is compatible with the definition of virtue as consisting in "love to being in general," provided the particular affection is consistent with the highest good of being in general. But I object again; this proviso is one which cannot be practically ascertained, by ordinary moral agents, in one of ten thousand cases in which they are called to act morally towards a particular object. The motive of the peasant-mother may be virtuous, when she forsakes the industrial avocation which she was pursuing, promotive of the public good, to nurse her own sick and dying child, provided she has successfully calculated the preponderance of the resultant general benefit of the nursing over the industry! I object farther, that this theory might lead a man to the breach of a nearer, and therefore more obligatory duty, for the sake of one remoter, and therefore less obligatory. The son would be bound to rescue a great and gifted stranger from fire or water, in preference to his own father, because the great man presented to his love a greater *quantum* of existence.

I object again; that on Edwards' theory it might be impossible to explain how it is our duty to honor a dead man for his virtues. He is beyond the reach of our benevolence; he can be neither benefited nor pleased by our plaudits. And especially is it impossible, on this theory, to include God directly in our virtuous affections. Remember, the essence of all virtue with him is that simple love of benevolence, whose propension is to promote the highest good of being in general. But God is infinitely blessed; His good cannot be promoted by creatures. Does this not obviously exempt Him from our benevolence? Edwards answers this laboriously, by pleading that our homage can promote God's declarative glory; the Scriptures exhort us to love, adore and praise Him. This is true, but the Scriptures ground these duties of love and adoration expressly upon God's moral perfections. It is these, not existence, which constitute Him the object of our moral homage This fact alone overthrows Edwards' whole speculation.

All benevolence-schemes tacitly assume the validity of the *a priori* moral intuition, with which they propose to dispense. For, suppose an advocate of the sensual selfish system to demand of their advocates: "Why is it my duty to make the greatest good of the greatest number my chief end, instead of my own personal good?" The respondent could find no answer, without resorting to the original distinction of advantage from right, and the obligation to the latter.

The moral judgment assumed.

The most mischievous part of Edwards' scheme I conceive to be, his derivation of the judgments and emotions of conscience itself, from general self-love. As that direct and simple love of benevolence, which is the pure essence of virtue, is concent and harmony with

The Belittling of Conscience.

general being, as being; so self-love, according to Edwards, is a propension towards the concent and harmony or unity of one's own being. The former principle tends to unite the individual with general Being. Hence the consciousness of an affection tending to break that benevolent unison, disunites the man's own being within itself. Self-love then produces the judgment and pain of remorse; for this pain is nothing but the sense of the breach of that self-unity, which is self-love's main object. Thus it follows that the sentiments of conscience, (like gratitude) are only of secondary rank in ethics! By this ill-starred logical jugglery is that imperial faculty degraded, whose intuitions and affections are the very spring-head of all the ethical acts of the human soul, and made an inferior consequence of the virtuous principle; a consequence of its defect, a modification of self-love. It would follow, of course, that the perfect man might be too virtuous to have any conscience at all. It is simpler reasoning still, to conclude as many of Edwards' followers have done, from his premises; that, as simple benevolence is virtue, self-love is sin. [And thus would come about that marvelous interpretation, which is one of the most recent triumphs of the New England theology; when in expounding Gen. 3: 22, it tells us that Adam and Eve acquired a knowledge of moral distinctions only by their fall. For, conscience is a development of the principle of self-love, as Edwards teaches; and self-love is the essence of sin, as the moderns say: whence it follows, that man acquires his moral nature only by his immorality.

These fatuous absurdities Edwards was too shrewd to adopt. He does not teach, as his premises should

Sin and self-love yet not identical. have taught him, that self-love is sin. Indeed, in a part of his treatise, he adopts the correct analysis of Bp. Butler, as to this affection. Inform yourselves of that analysis in his sermons, from the 11th to the 14th. He there teaches us, with his customary profound simplicity, the true testimony of our consciousness; That benevolence and self-love are in fact distinguishable, but not opposite affections of the soul (as is so often popularly assumed); That instead of being universally opposed, they often co-operate as motives to the same act; That the act thus educed may be either virtuous or vicious, according to its conditions; That both benevolence and self-love are so far in the same moral categories, that notoriously, some acts of simple self-love, (as when a man directly seeks his own calculated but lawful, or obligatory personal good) and many acts of benevolence are virtuous; and that many acts of self-love (as when a man prefers his own mischievous animal pleasure), and many acts of disinterestedness (as when a man deliberately injures himself for the sake of revenge), are vicious. From these clear statements it follows obviously, that the benevolent cannot be exalted into the universal essence of virtue, nor the selfish into that of sin.

These theories derive all the plausibility of their sophistries
What has suggested from three facts. It has been so often said,
these Benevolence that "Honesty is the best policy," that men
schemes? come to think the goodness of the policy is
what makes it honest; To promote utility, or, in other words,
to do acts of beneficence to mankind, is, in a multitude of
cases, right and praiseworthy; The duties of benevolence are
duties, and a very extensive class thereof; but not, therefore,
exhaustive of all duties. Once more, in the business of legislation, the expedient is very much the guide; and crimes are
punished chiefly in proportion to their tendency to injure the
well-doing of society. This might easily deceive one who, like
Bentham, was far more of a legislator than philosopher, to suppose that he had found, in the beneficence of acts, the essential
element of their virture. He forgets that human laws propose
as their proximate end only the protection of human well-being
in this world; and not the accurate final apportionment of
merits. This is God's function alone.

The utilitarian schemes of ethics profess to stand in
1st. It is selfish, in fact. contrast to the selfish, because they propose
not the selfish good of the agent, but the
well-being of mankind, as the element and test of virtue. But
they would really involve, as Jouffroy argues, the vice of the
selfish systems, if consistently carried out to their last result.
For when the question is raised, "Why do men come to regard
the utile as the right?" the answer must be, because well-being
(natural enjoyment) is the properest end of man. But thence
it must follow, that desire of natural good is man's properest
motive of action. Thus the moral motive is as effectually left
out of the analysis as by Hobbes himself; and the same absurd
psychology is assumed, which makes desire for natural good
the result of experienced good, whereas the desire must act
first, or the good would never have come to be experienced.
But more; if desire for natural good is man's properest motive
of action, it must follow, that his own personal good must
always be the properest end of moral action; because this
must always be the nearest, most immediate object of the
natural desire. These schemes make aggregate humanity the
supreme object of moral action; the true God. But the individual agent is a part of that aggregate; a part of his own God!
And as he is the most attainable part—the only part for whose
natural welfare he can labour effectually—I see not how the
practical conclusion is to be avoided; that he is his own properest supreme end. Thus we are led back to the vilest results
of the selfish system; and such, experience teaches us, is the
practical tendency. While the utilitarian schemes profess great
beneficence, they make their votaries supremely politic and
selfish.

But farther; the scheme does not correctly state the facts

of our consciousness. The mind does not feel that obligation to an act is always its mere utility or beneficence, nor that the merit of the agent arises out of the advantage his act effects. How often, for instance, do questions arise, as to the obligation of speaking truth ; where, if utility were the element of obligation, none would be felt ; yet the mind would feel most guilty, had falsehood been uttered in the case. Again ; were utility the element of virtue, the rightness or wrongness of an act would only be apprehended so far as experience had given us knowledge as to the beneficence or mischievousness of its effects. Is this so ? Does not the conscience lash us for secret sins which leave no loss of reputation, health, or capacity behind them ; and lash us all the more promptly and keenly, as we are inexperienced of crime and its wretched consequences? Farther ; were this theory true, all truly useful things should affect us with similar sentiments of moral approbation, a convenient bureau, or good milch cow, as truly as a faithful friend, or a benevolent rescuer. Does Hume attempt to escape by saying that it is the rational and voluntary useful act which affects us with the sentiment of approbation ? Then, we reply, he has given up the case ; for evidently the morality of the act is not in its utility, but in its rational motive. Once more ; if utility is the sole element of virtue, then the degree of utility should also be the measure of virtuous merit. We should always feel those acts to be most meritorious which were most conducive to natural good. But do we ? e. g. Which ennobles Daniel most in our eyes: the heroism which refused to bow his conscience to an impious prohibition of his king, when the penalty was the lions' den, or the diligence which dispensed order and prosperity over one hundred and twenty provinces? And the extravagant conclusions of Godwin must be accepted—that duties must be graded by us in proportion to the public importance of the person who was their object ; so that it might be the son's duty to see his own father drown, in order to save some more valuable life, who is a stranger to him.

2d. Utility not the conscious rule of obligation.

Were the utilitarian scheme true, it might be in some cases utterly impossible to convince a man that it was immoral to " do evil that good might come." If the consequences of the evil act, so far as foreseen by his mind, seemed beneficial, it would be right to do it. Nor could the claims of retributive justice in many cases be substantiated ; the criminal who gave, by his penitence, sufficient guarantee that he would offend no more, could not be made, without immorality, to pay his debt of guilt. And above all, eternal retributions would be utterly indefensible in a God of infinite wisdom and power. How can they advantage the universe, including the sufferers, as much as their pardon and thorough conversion would benefit them, without injuring the rest?

3d. If so, we might "do evil that good may come."

4. Paley's scheme. Paley's type of the Selfish System may be said to be equally perspicuous and false. That such a specimen of impotency and sophism in philosophy should come from a mind capable of so much justice and perspicuity of reasoning, as he has exhibited in the experimental field of Natural Theology, is one of the most curious facts in the history of opinion. I shall first attempt to rebut the objections which he insinuates against the originality of moral perceptions, and then criticise his own theory.

Attacks originality of moral judgments. He first proposes to test the question, whether such distinctions are originally and intuitively perceived, by supposing a case of what we call odious filial treachery, stated to a mind perfectly untutored by human associations, example, and teaching; and asking us whether he would immediately feel its vileness, with us. We answer, of course, No. But to show how absurdly preposterous the test is, we need not, with Dr. Alexander, dwell on the complexity of the moral problem involved. The simple answer is, that such a mind would not have the moral sentiment, because he would not comprehend the relations out of which the violated obligations grew, nor the very words used, to state them. In no proper sense could the untutored mind be said to see the case. Now, what a paltry trick is it, to argue that a mind has not a power of comparison, because it cannot compare objects which it does not behold at all?

Attributes them to association. Paley insinuates (none of his objections to moral intuitions are stated boldly) that our notions of the moral may all be accounted for by association and imitation. Thus, " having noticed that certain actions produced, or tended to produce, good consequences, whenever those actions are spoken of, they suggest, by the law of association, the pleasing idea of the good they are wont to produce. What association begins, imitation strengthens; this habit of connecting a feeling of pleasure with classes of acts is confirmed by similar habits of thought and feeling around us, and we dub it the sentiment of moral approbation." (Borrowed from Hume.) Now, this analysis is shown to be worthless in this one word. The law of association does not transmute, but only reproduces, the mental states connected by it. How, then, can the feeling of pleasure, which begins from a perceived tendency in a class of acts to promote natural good, be changed by association into the pleasure of moral approbation? They are distinct enough at first. Again: How, on this scheme, could men ever come to have pain of conscience at sins which are naturally pleasurable, and attended with no more direct natural ill? And how could the fact ever be explained, that we often have the sentiment of remorse for doing something in compliance with general associations and imitation?

Another class of objections is drawn from the facts that
Objects, that they man has no innate ideas of the abstract ele-
are not referable to any ment of moral right; and that moralists,
simpler type. though asserting the instinctive origin of
moral perceptions, have never been able to point to any one
type, or simple abstract element, (as veracity, &c.,) into which
all moral acts might be resolved. After our criticism of Locke,
no farther answer will be needed to the first objection. The
second, when examined, will be found to be a bald begging of
the question. The question is, whether the rightness of acts is
an original perception of the human reason. Now, if it be, it
will of course follow that it cannot be referred to some more
general type of perception. Can this general idea, truth, be
analysed? Why not? Because it is already simple and primary. Who dreams of arguing now that the human reason has
no original capacity of perceiving truth in propositions, because
it has no more general and abstract type, into which the sorts
of truth in different classes of propositions may be referred?
So, of the idea of rightness.

Paley also borrows the common argument of objectors,
from the wide variety, and even contrariety
And variable. of moral opinions in different ages and nations. In one nation, filial duty is supposed to consist in nursing
an aged parent; in another land, in eating him, &c., &c. The
answers are, that no one ever pretended any human faculty was
perfect in its actings, however original. Habit and association,
example, passion, have great influence in perverting any faculty.
Next, as justly remarked by Dr. Alexander, many of the supposed cases of contrariety of moral judgments are fully explained by the fact, that the dictate of conscience, right in the
general, is perverted by some error or ignorance of the understanding. The Christian mother feels it her duty to cherish the
life of her infant; the Hindoo to drown hers in Holy Ganges!
True. Yet both act on the dictate of conscience—that a mother
should seek the highest good of her infant. The Hindoo has
been taught by her false creed, to believe that she does this by
transferring it in childhood to heaven. Once more; it is a most
erroneous conclusion to infer that, because men perform, in some
countries, what are here regarded as odious vices, with seeming
indifference and publicity, therefore their moral sentiments
about them do not agree with ours. An educated Hindoo will
lie for a penny, and, when detected, laugh at it as smart. A Hottentot woman will seem shameless in her lewdness. Yet we are
informed that the Hindoo reverences and admires the truthfulness of a Christianized Briton; and that the poor Hottentot
scorns the unchaste European missionary, just as any female
here would. The amount of the case is, that conscience may
be greatly stupefied or drowned by evil circumstances; but her
general dictates, so far as heard, are infallibly uniform.

Paley, having succeeded, to his own satisfaction, in proving
that there is no sufficient evidence of moral
intuitions existing in the human soul, gives
his own definition. "Virtue is doing good to
mankind, according to the will of God, for the sake of everlasting happiness." And moral obligation, he defines, as nothing
else than a forcible motive arising out of a command of another.
That this scheme should ever have seemed plausible to Christians, can only be accounted for by the fact that we intuitively
feel, when God is properly apprehended, that His will is a perfect rule of right; and that it is moral to do all His commands
But when we raise the question, why? the answer is, because
His will, like His character, is holy. To do His will, then, is
not obligatory merely because an Almighty has commanded it
but He has commanded it because it is obligatory. The distinction of right and wrong is intrinsic.

Paley's definition of duty, &c.

The objections to Paley's system are patent. He himself
raises the question, wherein virtue, on his
definition, differs from a prudent self-love
in temporal things. His answer is, the latter
has regard only to this life; the former considers also future
immortal well-being. Brown well observes of this, that it is but
a more odious refinement upon the selfish system; defiling
man's very piety, by making it a selfish trafficking for personal
advantage with God, and fostering a more gigantic moral
egotism, insomuch as immortality is longer than mortal life. All
the objections leveled against the selfish system by me, apply,
therefore, justly here. This scheme of Paley is equally false to
our consciousness, which tells us that when we act, in all relative
duties, with least reference to self, then we are most praiseworthy.

Objections. The system a selfish one.

But we may add, more especially, that on Paley's scheme
of obligation, it is hard to see how he could
deny that there may be, in some cases, as
real a moral obligation to do wrong, as to do
right. A company of violent men overpower me, and command
me, on pain of instant death, to burn down my neighbor's
dwelling. Here is "a forcible motive arising from the command of another." Why does it not constitute a moral obligation to the crime? Paley would reply, because God commands
me not to burn it, on pain of eternal death; and this obligation
destroys the other, because the motive is vastly more forcible.
It seems, then, that in God's case, it is His might which makes
His right.

Force may justify sin.

Once more. On Paley's scheme, there could be no morality
nor moral obligation, where there is no revelation from God; because neither the rule,
nor motive, nor obligation of virtue exists.
They do not exist indeed, Paley might reply,

No obligation without Revelation. And no virtue in God.

in the form of a revealed theology; but they are there in the teachings and evidences of Natural Theology. " The heathen which have not the law are a law unto themselves, their consciences," &c.   But if there are no authoritative intuitions given by God to man's soul, of moral distinctions, then Natural Theology has no sufficient argument whatever to prove that God is a moral being, or that He wills us to perform moral acts. Look and see. And, in fine: What can God's morality be; since there is no will of a higher being to regulate His acts, and no being greater than He to hold out the motive of eternal rewards for obeying !

The ingenious scheme of Dr. Adam Smith, Theory of Mor.
Sents., may be seen very perspicuously
5th Dr. A. Smith's   unfolded in Jouffroy. This scheme is by no
theory.
means so mischievous and degrading as that of Hobbes, Hume or Paley. But it is incorrect. Its fundamental defect is, that in each step it assumes the prior existence of the moral sentiment, in order to account for it. For instance, it says : We feel approbation for an act, when we experience a sympathetic emotion with the sentiments in the agent which prompted it.   But sympathy only reproduces the same emotion; it does not transmute it; so that unless the producing sentiment in the agent were moral, it could not, by sympathy, generate a moral sentiment in us. It supposes conscience comes thus: We imagine an ideal man contemplating our act, conceive the kind of sentiments he feels for us, and then sympathize therewith.   But how do we determine the sentiments of this ideal man looking at our act? He is but a projection of our own moral sentiments. So, in each step, Dr. S. has to assume the phenomenon, as already produced; for the production of which he would account. Another fatal objection to Dr. Smith's scheme is, that the sympathetic affection in the beholder is always fainter than the direct sentiment in the object beheld. But conscience visits upon us stronger affections than are awakened by beholding the moral acts of another, and approving or blaming them. The sentiments of conscience should, according to Dr. Smith, be feebler; for they are the reflection of a reflection.

LECTURE X.

ETHICAL THEORIES. — Concluded.

ARE moral distinctions intrinsic; and are they intuitively perceived? We have now passed in review all the several theories which answer, no; and found them untenable. Hence, alone, we derive a strong probability that the affirmative is the true answer; e. g. All the chemists endeavour in vain to analyse a given material substance into some other known one; but fail. It is, therefore, assumed to be simple and original.

1. Moral Judgments are intuitive.

We must assume this of the moral sentiment; or else it is unintelligible how mankind ever became possessed of the moral idea. For every original and simple idea, whether sensitive or rational, with which our souls are furnished, we find an appropriate original power; and without this the idea could never have been entertained by man. Had man no eyes, he would have never had ideas of light and colours; no ear, he could never have had the idea of melody; no taste, he would forever have lacked the idea of beauty. So, if the idea of rightness in acts is not identical with that of truth, nor utility, nor benevolence, nor self-love, nor love of applause, nor sympathetic harmony, nor any other original sentiment; it must be received directly by an original moral power in the soul. To this, in the second place, consciousness testifies: the man who calmly and fully investigates his own mental processes, will perceive that his view and feeling of the rightness of some acts arise immediately in his mind; without any medium, except the comprehension of the real relations of the act; that their rise is unavoidable; and that their failure to rise would be immediately and necessarily apprehended by all, as a fundamental defect of his soul. There is, indeed, a great diversity in the estimation of the more complex details of moral questions. And man's 'tuition of those distinctions is often disturbed by three causes, well stated by Dr. Brown—complexity of elements, habits of association, and prevalent passion. But, allowing for these, there is just the universal and immediate agreement in all sane human minds, which we expect to find in the acceptance of necessary first truths. In the fundamental and simple ideas of morals, men are agreed. And in the case of any other intuitions, we have to make precisely the same allowance, and to expect the same disturbing causes. These, with the remarks I made in refutation of Paley's objections, I think suffice to sustain the true theory on that point.

I hold, then, that as there is, in some propositions, (not in all—some are truisms, many are meaningless, and some so unknown as to be neither affirmed nor denied,) the element of truth or falsehood, original, simple, incapabable of anlaysis or definition in simpler terms, and ascertainable by the mind's intellection; so there is in actions, of the class called moral, an intrinsic quality of rightness or wrongness, equally simple, original, and incapable of analysis; and, like simple truth, perceived immediately by the inspection of the reason. This quality is intrinsic; they are not right merely because God has commanded, or because He has formed souls to think so, or because He has established any relation of utility, beneficence, or self-interest therewith. But God has commanded them, and formed these relations to them, because they are right. Just as a proposition is not true because our minds are so constructed as to apprehend it such; but our minds were made by God to see it so, because it is true.

Illustrated from logical judgments.

But understand me; I do not assert that all moral distinctions in particular acts are intuitively seen, or necessarily seen. As in propositions, some have primary, and some deductive truth; some are seen to be true without premises, and some by the help of premises; so, In acts having moral qualities, the rightness or wrongness of some is seen immediately, and of some deductively. In the latter, the moral relation of the agent is not immediately seen, but the moral judgment is mediated only by the knowledge of some other truths. If these truths are not known, then the moral quality of the act is not obvious. From this simple remark it very clearly follows, that if the mind's belief touching these truths, which are premises to the moral judgment, be erroneous, the moral judgment will also err. Just as in logic, so here; false premises, legitimately used, will lead to false conclusions. And here is the explanation of the discrepancies in moral judgments, which have so confused Ethicks.

Some moral Judgments likewise deductive.

2. But there are several writers of eminence, who, while they substantially, yea nobly, uphold the originality and excel-

lence of man's moral distinctions, err, as we think, in the details of their analysis. A moment's inquiry into their several departures from my theory, will best serve to define and establish it.

(a) Seeing that the moral distinction is intrinsic; what is the faculty of the soul by which it is apprehended ? (Bear in mind a faculty is not a limb of mind, but only a name we give to one phase or sort of its processes.) Does it apprehend it by its reason; or by a distinct moral faculty? Says Dr. Hutcheson, an English writer: By a distinct, though rational perceptive faculty, which he names, the moral sense ; and describes as an internal sense- - i. e., a class of processes perceptive, and also exhibiting sensibility. Says Dr. Alexander; The perceptive part of our moral processes, is simply a judgment of the reason. It is but an intellection of the understanding, like any other judgment of relations, except that it immediately awakens a peculiar emotion, viz : the moral. Now, it might be plausibly said that the reason is concerned only with the judgment of truth; and we have strenuously repudiated the analysis which reduces the moral distinction to mere truth. But it should rather be said, that the proper field of the reason is the judgment of relations : truth existing in propositions is only one class. There seems no ground to suppose that the moral judgment, so far as merely intellective of the distinction, is other than a simple judgment of the reason; because, so far as we know, wherever reason is, there, and there only, are moral judgments. 2d. If the faculties were two, the one, we might rationally expect, might sometimes convict the other of inaccuracy, as the memory does the reason, and *vice versa*. 3d. The identity of the two processes seems strongly indicated by the fact, that if the reason is misled by any falsehood of view, the moral sentiment is infallibly perverted to just the same extent. The moral motive is always a rational one. Some rational perception of the truth of a proposition predicating relation, is necessary, as the occasion of its acting, and the object of a moral judgment. The reason why brutes have not moral ideas, is that they have not reason. In short, I see nothing gained by supposing an inward perceptive faculty called moral sense, other than the reason itself.

The Moral Distinction seen by the Reason.

(b.) Next we notice the question: at what stage of its perceptions of the relations of acts, does the reason see the moral distinction? In each separate case immediately, as soon as the soul is enough developed to apprehend the relations of the particular act? No; answers Jouffroy; but only after a final generalization is accomplished by the reason.

His theory is: 1st. That in the merely animal stage of existence, the infant acts from direct, uncalculating instinct alone. The rational idea of its own natural good is the consequence, not origin, of the

Jouffroy's Scheme.

8*

experienced pleasure following from the gratification of instinct.
2d. Thus experience presents the occasions upon which the
reason gives the general idea of personal good; and the motives
of self-calculation begin to act. But 3d. The child also observes
similar instincts, resulting in its fellow-men in natural enjoyment
to them; and as it forms the general idea of its own natural good
(satisfaction of the whole circle of instincts to greatest attainable degree) as its properest personal end, reason presents the
general truth, that a similar personal end exists for this, that
the other, and every fellow-man. Here, then, arises a still more
general idea; the greatest attainable natural good of all beings
generally; the "absolute good," or "universal order;" and as
soon as this is reached, the reason intuitively pronounces it the
moral good; to live for this, is now seen to be man's proper
end; and rightness in acts is their rational tendency to that
end. This is rather a subtle and ingenious generalization of
the result of our moral judgments, than a correct account of
their origin. This generalization, as made by the opening
mind, might suggest the notion of symmetry, or utility as belonging to the "absolute order," but surely that of obligatoriness is
an independent element of rational perception! If the idea of
rightness and obligation had never connected itself in the
opening mind with any specific act having a tendency to man's
natural good, how comes the mind to apprehend the universal
order as the obligatory moral end, when once the reason forms
that abstraction? It seems to me that the element of moral
judgment must be presupposed, to account for the result.
Again; the supposed process is inconsistent with a correct idea
of the generalizing process. The process does not transmute,
but only colligates the facts which it ranks together. The general attributes which the mind apprehends as constituting the
connotation of the general term, are precisely the attributes
which it saw to be common in all the special cases grouped
together. So that, if a moral order had not been already
apprehended by the reason in the specific acts, the mere
apprehension of the universal order would not produce the
conviction of its morality. Experience would strengthen the
moral idea. But usually the most unhackneyed have it most
vividly. But it is right to say, that Jouffroy, notwithstanding
this peculiarity of his theory, deserves the admiration of his
readers, for the beauty of his analyses, and the general elevation of his views.

(c) The ethical lectures of Dr. Thomas Brown, of Edinburgh,
are marked by great acuteness, and nobility
of general tone; and he has rendered gallant
service in refuting the more erroneous theories.
He makes moral distinctions original and authoritative; and
yet allows the reason only a secondary function in them. The
whole result of this analysis is this: when certain actions (an

Sentimental Scheme
of Dr. Thomas Brown.

action is nothing more than the agent acting) are presented, there arises immediately an emotion, called, for want of a more vivid term, moral approbation, without any previous condition of self-calculation, judgment of relation in the reason, &c. This immediate emotion constitutes our whole feeling of the rightness, obligation, meritoriousness, of the agent. As experience gathers up and recollects the successive acts which affect us with the moral emotion, reason makes the generalization of them into a class; and thus, derivatively forms the general idea of virtue. Man's moral capacity, therefore, is, strictly, not a power of intellection, but a sensibility. The reason only generalizes into a class, those acts which have the immediate power of affecting this sensibility in the same way. And Brown's system deserves yet more than Adam Smith's, which he so ably refutes, to be called the Sentimental System. The moral sentiment is with him strictly an instinctive emotion.

Now, it does not seem to me a valid objection, to say with Jouffroy, that thus, the moral emotion is made one among the set of our natural instincts: and there no longer appears any reason why it should be more dominant over the others out of its own domain, than they over it; (e. g., more than taste, or resentment, or appetite.) For the very nature of this moral instinct, Brown might reply, is, that it claims all other susceptibilities which have moral quality, are in its own domain.

The truer objections are: that this notion does not square with the analogies of the soul. In every case, our emotions arise out of an intellection. This is true, in a lower sense, even of our animal instincts. It is perception which awakens appetites. It is the conception of an intent to injure, which gives the signal to our resentment, even when it arises towards an agent nonmoral. And in all the more intellectual emotions, as of taste, love, moral complacency, the view of the understanding, and that alone, evokes the emotion in a normal way. The soul feels, because it has seen. How else could reason rule our emotions? Surely this is one of our most important distinctions from brutes, that our emotions are not mere instincts, but rational affections. Note, especially too, that if our moral sentiments had no element of judgment at their root, the fact would be inexplicable, that they never, like all other instinctive emotions, come in collision with reason. Again: Dr. B. has very properly shown, in overthrowing the selfish systems of human action, that our instincts are not prompted by self-interest. He seems, therefore, to think that when he makes the moral emotion an instinctive sensibility, he has done all that is needed to make it disinterested. But an action is not, therefore, morally disinterested, because it is not self-interested. Then would our very animal appetites, even in infancy, be vir·

Objection. 1st. Soul always sees, in order to feel. 2d. No virtue without rational, impersonal motive. 3d. There would be no uniform standard.

tues! The truth is: in instinctive volitions, the motive is personal to the agent; but not consciously so. In selfish volitions
the motive is personal to the agent; and he knows it. Only
when the motive is impersonal, and he knows it, is there disinterestedness, or virtue. Last; if Brown's theory were correct,
moral good would only be relative to each man's sensibility;
and there would be no uniform standard. An act might be
good to one, bad to another, just as it presented itself to his
sensibility; as truly as in the sense of the natural good; one
man calls oysters good; and another considers oysters bad.
Whereas the true doctrine is, that moral distinctions are as
intrinsic in certain acts, as truth is in certain propositions: and
eternal and immutable. Even God sees, and calls the right to
be right, because it so: not *vice versa*. Dr. Brown foresees
this; and attempting to rebut it, is guilty of peculiar absurdity.
Why says he, does it give any more intrinsic basis for moral
distinctions in the acts (or agents acting) themselves, to suppose
that our cognizance of them is by a rational judgment, than to
say, with him, that it is in the way they naturally affect a sensibility in us? The capacity of having the intuitive judgment is
itself but a sort of rational sensibility to be affected in a given
way; and, in either case, we have no ground for any belief of
an intrinsic permanence of the relation or quality perceived,
but that our Maker made us to be affected so! Thus, he
betrays the whole basis of morals and truth, to a sweeping
skepticism. Does not intuition compel us to believe that reason
is affected with such and such judgments, because the grounds
of them are actual and intrinsic in the objects? Dr. Brown
goes to the absurd length of saying, that the supposed relations
ascertained by reason herself, are not intrinsic; and exist
nowhere, except in the perceiving reason! e. g., the relation of
square of hypothenuse. Says he: were there nowhere a
perceiving mind comprehending this relation, the relation would
have no existence, no matter how many right-angled triangles
existed! Is not this absolute skepticism? Is it not equivalent
to saying that none of the perceptions of reason, (i. e. human
beliefs,) have any objective validity? There need be no
stronger refutation of his theory, than that he should acknowledge himself driven by it to such an admission.

The correct view, no doubt, is this: that our simplest
moral states consist of two elements: a judgment of the understanding, or rational perception of the moral quality in the act; and an
immediate, peculiar emotion, called approbation, arising thereupon, giving more or less warmth to the judgment. In our
moral estimates of more complex cases, just as in our intellectual study of derived truths, the process may be more inferential,
and more complex. It has been often, and justly remarked,
that the parallel between the rational æsthetic functions of the

The moral State com-
plex. Illustrated by
Taste.

soul, and its moral functions, is extremely instructive. Psychology teaches us that rational taste (for instance, the pleasure
of literary beauty in reading a fine passage,) consists of a
judgment, or cluster of judgments, and a peculiar emotion
immediately supervening thereon. The faculty of taste is,
then, complex, consisting of an action of the intelligence and
a motion of the sensibility. The former is cause; the latter is
consequence. After the excitement of the sensibility has
wholly waned, the judgment which aroused it remains fixed
and unchanged. Now, it is thus with our moral sentiments. A
rational judgment of the intrinsic righteousness or wrongness
of the act immediately produces an emotion of approbation,
or disapprobation, which is original and peculiar. The whole
vividness of the sentiment may pass away; but the rational
judgment will remain as permanent as any judgment of truth
in propositions. The great distinction between the æsthetic and
ethical actions of the soul, is that the latter carries the practical and sacred perception of obligation.

 Conscience, as I conceive, is but the faculty of the soul
just described, acting with reference to our
own moral acts, conceived as future, done, or
remembered as done. When we conceive
the wrongness of an act as done by ourselves, that judgment
and emotion take the form of self-blame, or remorse; wherein
the emotion is made more pungent than in other cases of
disapprobation, by our instinctive and our self-calculating self-
love, one or both. So of the contrasted case. And the merit
of an action, looked at as past, is no other than this judgment
and feeling of its rightness, which intuitively connects the idea
of title to reward with the agent. i. e. Our ideas of merit and
demerit are intuitions arising immediately upon the conception
of the rightness or wrongness of the acts; connecting natural
good or evil with moral good or evil, by an immediate tie.
Our ideas of desert of reward or punishment, therefore, are
not identical with our sentiments of the rightness or wrongness
of acts, as Dr. Brown asserts, but are intuitively consequent
theron. Dr. B. also asserts, as also Dr. Alexander, that our
notion of obligation is no other than our intuitive judgment of
rightness in acts, regarded as prospective. Therefore, it is
useless and foolish to raise the question: "Why am I obliged,
morally, to do that which is right?" it is as though one should
debate why he should believe an axiom. This is substantially
correct. But when they say: whatever is right, is obligatory,
and *vice versa*, there is evidently a partial error. For there is
a limited class of acts, of which the rightness is not proportioned to the obligation to perform them; but on the contrary,
the less obligation, the more admirable is the virtue of doing
them gratuitously. Such are some acts of generosity to
unworthy enemies: and especially God's to rebel man. That

3. Conscience, what? Obligation, what?

God was under no obligation to give His Son to die for them, is the very reason His grace in doing so is so admirable! Obligation, therefore, is not always the correlative of rightness in the act, but it is, always, the correlative of a right in the object. This is the distinction which has been overlooked—i. e., a multitude of our acts have a personal object, God, self, a man, or mankind, one or more; and the conscience in many cases apprehends, not only that the act would be right, but that such are the relations of ourselves to the object, that he has a right, a moral title to have it done, in such sense that not only the doing of the opposite to him, but the withholding of the act itself, would be wrong. In every such case, the notion of obligation arises. And that, stronger or weaker, whether the object's right be perfect or imperfect.

The most important thing, however, for us to observe, is that every sane mind intuitively recognizes this moral obligation. The judgment and emotion we call conscience, carries this peculiarity over all other states of reason or instinct; that it contains the imperative element. It utters a command, the rightness of which the understanding is necessitated to admit. Other motives, rational or instinctive, may often (alas!) overcome it in force; but none of them can dispute its authority. It is as impossible for the mind, after having given the preference to other motives, to think its choice therein right, as it is to think any other intuition untrue. Conscience is the Maker's imperative in the soul.

Imperative of Conscience is intuitive.

Hence, it must follow, that the dictate of conscience must always be obeyed; or sin ensues. But conscience is not infallible, as guided by man's fallible understanding: it is clear, from both experience and reason, that her fiat may be misdirected. In that case, is the act innocent, or wrong? If you say the latter, you seem involved in a glaring paradox; that to obey would be wrong; and yet to disobey would be wrong. How can both be true? If you say the former, other absurdities would follow. 1st. Truth would seem to be of no consequence in order to right; and the conscience might just as well be left uninformed, as informed, so far as one man is personally concerned therein. 2d. Each man's view of duty would be valid for him; so that there might be as many clashing views of duty, as men, and each valid in itself; so that we should reach such absurdities as these: A has a right to a given object, which B has an equal right to prevent his having; so that B has a moral right to do to A what is to him a moral wrong! 3d. Many of the most odious acts in the world, reprobated by all posterity, as the persecutions of a Saul, or a Dominic, would be justified, because the perpetrators believed they were doing God service.

Must conscience, misguided, be obeyed.

The solution of this seeming paradox is in this fact: that
God has not given man a conscience which
Solution.   is capable of misleading him, when lawfully
and innocently used. In other words, while lack of knowledge
necessary to perceive our whole duty may often occur, (in
which case it is always innocent to postpone acting,) positive
error of moral judgment only arises from guilty haste or heedlessness, or indolence, or from sinful passion or prejudice.
When, therefore, a man sincerely believes it right in his conscience to do what is intrinsically wrong, the wrongness is not
in the fact that he obeyed conscience, (for this abstractly is
right,) but in the fact that he had before, and at the time,
perverted conscience by sinful means.

We intuitively apprehend that all agents are not proper
subjects of moral approbation or disappro-
4. What constitutes   bation. Hence, the question must be settled:
Moral agency.   what are the elements essential to moral
responsibility! This can be settled no otherwise than by an
appeal to our intuitions. For instance: we may take an act of
the form which would have moral quality, if done by a moral
agent — e. g., inflicting causeless bodily pain; and attributing
it to successive sorts of agents, from lower to higher, ascertain
what the elements are, which confer responsibility. As we
walk through a grove, a dead branch falls on our heads; we
feel that resentment would be absurd; much more disapprobation; the thing is dead. We walk near our horse, he wantonly
kicks or bites. There is a certain type of anger; but it is not
moral disapprobation; we feel still, that this would be absurd.
Here, there is sensibility and will in the agent: but no conscience or reason. We walk with our friend; he treads on our
corns and produces intolerable pain; but it is obviously unin-
tentional. We pass through a lunatic asylum; a maniac tries
to kill us. Here is sensibility, free-will, intention; but reason
is dethroned. In neither of these cases should we have moral
disapprobation. A stronger man takes hold of our friend, and
by brute force makes him strike us; there is no anger towards
our friend; he is under co-action. We learn from these various
instances, that free-agency, intention, and rationality are all
necessary, to constitute a man a responsible moral agent.

LECTURE XI.

FREE AGENCY AND THE WILL.

BUT is man a free agent? Many have denied it. These may be ranked under two classes, Theological Fatalists and Sen-

1. Man a free-agent, denied by two parties.

sualistic Necessitarians. The former argue from the doctrine of God's foreknowledge and providence; the latter from the certainty, or, as it has unluckily been termed, necessity of the Will. Say the one party; God has foreknown and foreordained all that is done by rational man, as well as by irrational elements, and His almighty providence infallibly effectuates it all. Therefore, man's will is only seemingly free; he must be a machine; compelled by God (for if God had no efficacious means to compel, He could not certainly have foreknown) to do what God purposed from eternity: and, therefore, man never had any real choice; he is the slave of this divine fate. Say the other party, headed by Hobbes: man's volitions are all effects: following with a physical necessity upon the movement of the preponderant desires. But what are his desires? The soul intrinsically is passive; the attributes are nothing but certain susceptibilities of being affected in certain ways, by impressions from without. There is nothing, no thought, no feeling in the mind, except what sensation produced there; indeed all inward states are but modified sensations. Hence, desire is but the reflex of the perception of a desirable object; resentment but the re-action from impact. Man's emotions, then, are the physical results of outward impressions, and his volitions the necessary effects of his emotions. Man's whole volitions, therefore, are causatively determined from without. While he supposes himself free, he is the slave of circumstances: of fate, if those circumstances arise by chance.

Now, in answer to all this, it would be enough to say, that
our consciousness contradicts it. There can
Replies to them. be no higher evidence than that of consciousness. Every man feels conscious that wherever he has power
to do what he pleases, he acts freely. And the validity of this
uniform, immediate testimony of consciousness, as Cousin well
remarks, on this subject, must, in a sense, supersede all other
evidence of our free-agency; because all possible premises of
such arguments must depend on the testimony of consciousness. But still, it is correct to argue, that man must be a free
agent; because this is inevitably involved in his responsibility.
Conscience tells us we are responsible for our moral acts. Reason
pronounces, intuitively, that responsibility would be absurd were
we not free agents. It may be well added, that when you approach revealed theology, you find the Scriptures, (which so
frequently assert God's decree and providence,) assert and
imply, with equal frequency, man's free-agency. The king of
Babylon (Isaiah x :5-7) fulfills God's purpose in capturing the sinful Jews; but he also fulfills the purpose of his own heart. But
we can do more than rebut the Fatalist's views by the testimony
of our consciousness; we can expose their sophistry. God's
mode of effectuating His purposes as to the acts of free agents,
is not by compelling their acts or wills, contrary to their preferences and dispositions; either secretly or openly; but by operating through their dispositions. And as to the latter argument, from the certainty of the will; we repudiate the whole
philosophy of sensationalism, from which it arises. True, volitions are effects; but not effects of the objects upon which they
go forth. The perception of these is but the occasion of their
rise, not the cause. When desire attaches itself upon any external object, terminating in volition, the whole activity and power
are in the mind, not in the object. The true immediate cause
of volition is the mind's own previous view and feeling; and,
this, again, is the result of the mind's spontaneity, as guided by
its own prevalent attributes and habitudes.

What constitutes man a free agent? Say one party: the
self-determining power of the will; say the
2. Freedom and other: the self-determining power of the soul.
necessity defined. The one asserts that our acts of volition are
Semi-Pelangianism and uncaused phenomena, that the will remains
Calvinists.
in *equilibrio*, after all the preliminary conditions of judgment in
the understanding, and emotion of the native dispositions are
fulfilled, and that the act of choice is self-determined by the will,
and not by the preliminary states of soul tending thereto; so
that volitions are in every case, more or less contingent. The
other party repudiates, indeed, the old sensational creed, of a
physical tie between the external objects which are the occasions of our judgments and feelings; and attributes all action
of will to the soul's own spontaneity as its efficient source.

But it asserts that this spontaneity, like all other forces in the universe, acts according to law; that this law is the connection between the soul's own states and its own choices, the former being as much of its own spontaneity as the latter; that therefore volitions are not uncaused, but always follow the actual state of judgment and feeling, (single or complex,) at the time being; and that this connection is not contingent, but efficient and certain.   And this certainty is all that they mean by moral necessity.

The latter is evidently the true doctrine: because, (a) Our consciousness says so.   Every man feels that when he acts, as a thinking being, he has a motive for acting so; and that if he had not had, he would not have done it.   The man is conscious that he determines himself, else, he would not be free; but he is equally conscious that it is himself judging and desiring, which determines himself choosing: (b) Otherwise there would be no such thing as a recognition of character, or permanent principles. For there would be no efficient influence of the man's own principles over his actions; (and it is by his actions alone we would know his principles;) and his principles might be of a given character, and his actions of a different, or of no character.   (c) Consequently there would be no certain result from human influence over man's character and actions, in education and moral government.   We might educate the principles, and still fail to educate the actions and habits.   The fact which we all experience every day would be impossible, that we can cause our fellow-men to put forth certain volitions, that we can often do it with a foreseen certainty, and still we feel that those acts are free and responsible.   (d) Otherwise man might be neither a reasonable nor a moral being.   Not reasonable, because his acts might be wholly uncontrolled at last by his whole understanding; not moral, because the merit of an act depends on its motive, and his acts would be motiveless.   The self-determined volition has its freedom essentially in this, according to its advocates; that it is caused by no motive.   Hence, no acts are free and virtuous, except those which a man does without having any reason for them.   Is this good sense?   Does not the virtuousness of a man's acts depend upon the kind of reason which moved to them?   (e) In the choice of one's *summum bonum*, the will is certainly not contingent.   Can a rational being choose his own misery, apprehended as such, and eschew his own happiness, for their own sakes?   Yet that choice is free; and if certainty is compatible with free-agency in this the most important case, why not in any other?   (f) God, angels, saints in glory, and the human nature of Jesus Christ, must be certainly determined to right volitions by the holiness of their own natures, and in all but the first case by the indwelling grace and the determinate purpose of God.   So, on the other hand, devils,

3. Will determined by subjective Motive. Arguments.

lost souls, and those who on earth have sinned away their day of grace, must be certainly determined to evil, by their own decisive evil natures and habits: yet their choice is free in both cases.

(g) If the will were contingent, there could be no *scientia media;* and we should be compelled to the low and profane ground of the Socinian; that God does not certainly foreknow all things; and in the nature of things, cannot. For the definition of *scientia media* is, that it is that contingent knowledge of what free agents will do in certain foreseen circumstances, arising out of God's infinite insight into their dispositions. But if the will may decide in the teeth of that foreseen disposition, there can be no certain knowledge how it will decide. Nor is the evasion suggested by modern Arminians (*vide,* Mansel's Lim. of Relig. Thought) of any force; that it is incompetent for our finite understandings to say that God cannot have this *scientia media,* because we cannot see how He is to have it. For the thing is not merely among the incomprehensibles, but the impossibles. If a thing is certainly foreseen, it must be certain to occur, or else the foreknowledge of its certain occurrence is false. But if it is certain to occur, it must be because there will be an antecedent, certainly, or efficiently connected with the event, as cause. It is, therefore, in the knowledge of this causal connection, that God would find his *scientia media,* if this branch of His knowledge were mediate. To sum up in a word, the inutility of this evasion, this Semi-Pelagian theory begins by imputing to God an inferential knowledge of man's free acts, and then, in denying the certain influence of motives takes away the only ground of inference. (h) Last, God would have no efficient means of governing free agents; things would be perpetually emerging through their contingent acts, unforeseen by God, and across His purposes; and His government would be, like man's, one of sorry expedients to patch up His failures. Nor could He bestow any certain answer to prayer, either for our own protection against temptation and wrong choice, or the evil acts of other free agents. All the predictions of Scripture concerning events in which the free moral acts of rational agents enter as second causes, are arguments against the contingency of the will. But we see striking instances in Joseph, the Assyrians, Cyrus, and especially the Jews who rejected their Lord. From this point of view, the celebrated argument of Edwards for the certainty of the will from God's foreknowledge of creatures' free acts, is obvious. The solution of the cavils attempted against it is this position: That the principle, " No event without a cause," which is, to us, a universal and necessary first truth, is also a truth to the divine mind. When God certainly foresees an act, he foresees it as coming certainly out of its cause. Hence, I repeat, if the foresight is certain, the causation must be efficient.

I have indicated, both when speaking of fatalism and of
Certainty of the Will proved by God's sovereignty. the impossibility of a *scientia media* concerning a contingent will, the argument for the certainty of the will contained in the fact of God's sovereignty. If He is universal First Cause, then nothing is uncaused. Such is the argument; as simple as it is comprehensive. It cannot be taught that volitions are uncaused, unless you make all free agents a species of gods, independent of Jehovah's control. In other words, if His providence extends to the acts of free agents, their volitions cannot be uncaused; for providence includes control, and control implies power. The argument from God's sovereignty is, indeed, so conclusive, that the difficulty, with thinking minds, is not to admit it, but to avoid being led by it to an extreme. The difficulty rather is, to see how, in the presence of this universal, absolute sovereignty, man can retain a true spontaneity. I began by defining that, while the will of man is not self-determining, his soul is. I believe that a free, rational Person does properly originate effects; that he is a true fountain of spontaneity, determining his own powers, from within, to new effects. This is a most glorious part of that image of God, in which he is created. This is free-agency! Now, how can this fact be reconciled with what we have seen of God as absolute First Cause?

(j) The demonstration may be closed by the famous *Reductio ad absurdum*, which Edwards has borrowed from the scholastics. If the will is not determined to choice by motives, but determines itself, then the will must determine itself thereto by an act of choice; for this is the will's only function. That is, the will must choose to choose. Now, this prior choice must be held by our opponents to be self-determined. Then it must be determined by the will's act of choice—i. e., the will must choose to choose to choose. Thus we have a ridiculous and endless *regressus*.

I now return to consider the objections usually advanced against our doctrine. The most formidable is that which shall be first introduced; the supposed incompatibility of God's sovereignty as universal First Cause, with man's freedom.

The reconciliation may and does transcend our comprehension, and yet be neither unreasonable nor
Yet Man under Providence is free. incredible. The point where the little circle of creature volition inosculates with the immense circle of the divine will, is beyond human view. When we remember that the wisdom, power and resources of God are infinite, it is not hard to see that there may be a way by which our spontaneity is directed, omnipotently, and yet without infringement of its reality. The sufficient proof is, that we, finite creatures, can often efficaciously direct the free will of our fellows, without infringing it. Does any one say that still, in every such case, the agent, if free as to us, has power to do the

opposite of what we induce him to do ? True, he has physical power. But yet the causative efficacy of our means is certain; witness the fact that we were able certainly to predict our success. A perfect certainty, such as results from God's infinitely wise and powerful providence over the creature's will, is all that we mean by moral necessity. We assert no other kind of necessity over the free will. More mature reflection shows us, that so far are God's sovereignty and providence from infringing man's free-agency, they are its necessary conditions. Consider : What would the power of choice be worth to one if there were no stability in the laws of nature; or no uniformity in its powers ? No natural means of effectuating volitions would have any certainty, whence choice would be impotent, and motives would cease to have any reasonable weight. Could you intelligently elect to sow, if there were no ordinance of nature insuring seed time and harvest ? But now, what shall give that stability to nature ? A mechanical, physical necessity ? That results in naught but fatalism. The only other answer is : it must be the intelligent purpose of an almighty, personal God.

The leading objection echoed by Arminians against the certainty of the will, is, that if man is not free from all constraint, whether of motive or co-action, it is unjust in God to hold him subject to blame, or to command to those acts against which his will is certainly determined, or to punishments for failure. We reply, practically, that men are held blamable and punishable for acts to which their wills are certainly determined, both among men and before God ; and all consciences approve. This is indisputable, in the case of those who are overmastered by a malignant emotion, as in Gen. xxxvii : 4, of devils and lost souls, and of those who have sinned away their day of grace. The Arminian rejoins, (Watson, vol. 2, p. 438:) Such transgressors, notwithstanding their inability of will, are justly held responsible for all subsequent failures in duty, because they sinned away the contingency of their own wills, by their own personal, free act, after they became intelligent agents. But as man is born in this inability of will, through an arrangement with a federal head, to which he had no opportunity to dissent, it would be unjust in God to hold him responsible, unless He had restored the contingency of will to them lost in Adam, by the common sufficient grace bestowed through Christ. But the distinction is worthless : 1st, because, then, God would have been under an obligation in righteousness, to furnish a plan of redemption : but the Scriptures represent His act therein as purely gracious. 2d. Because, then, all the guilt of the subsequent sins of those who had thrown away the contingency of their own wills, would have inhered in the acts alone by which they lost it. True ; that act would have been an enormously guilty one ; the man would have therein committed moral suicide. But it would also be true that the man was thereafter morally dead, and the dead cannot work.   3d. The Arminian should, by parity of reason, conclude, that in any will certainly determined to holiness, the acts are not meritorious, unless that determination resulted from the being's own voluntary self-culture, and formation of good dispositions and habits. Therefore God's will, which has been from eternity certainly determined to good, does nothing meritorious !*

But the more analytical answer to this class of objections is: that the certainty of disobedience in the sinner's will is no excuse for him, because it proceeds from a voluntary cause—i. e., moral disposition. As the volition is only the man willing, the motive is the man feeling ; it is the man's self. There is no lack of the requisite capacities, if the man would use those capacities aright. Now, a man cannot plead the existence of an obstacle as his excuse, which consists purely in his own spontaneous emission of opposition.

Now, the objections most confidently urged, are : (a.) That

That this makes us machines.

our view makes man a machine, an intelligent one, indeed ; but a machine in which choice follows motive by a physical tie. Ans. Man is in one sense a machine, (if you will use so inappropriate an illustration); his spontaneous force of action has its regular laws. But he is not a machine, in the essential point; the motive power is not external, but is in himself.

(b) It is objected that our scheme fails to account for all

That man acts against his own judgment.

choices where the man acts against his own better judgment and prevalent feelings ; or; in other words, that while the dictate of the

---

* The antiquity of this cavil, and its proper refutation, may be seen in the *Cur Deus Homo* of Anselm, pt. ii, chap. 10, where the topic is the impeccability of Christ.

BOSO.—"I say, then, if He cannot sin, because, as you say, He cannot wish to, He obeys from necessity, whence, He is not righteous from the freedom of His will. Then, what favour will be due Him for His righteousness ? For we are wont to say, that God, therefore, made angels and men such that they could sin; since, inasmuch as they could forsake righteousness, and could keep righteousness out of the freedom of their will, they would deserve approbation and favour, which would not be due to them were they righteous from necessity."

ANSELM.—"Are the (elect) angels who now *cannot sin,* to be approved or not ? "

BOSO.—"Of course they are, because *this gift* (that they cannot sin) *they earned* in this way, viz. : by not choosing to sin when they could."

ANSELM.—"Well, what do you say about God, who is not able to sin, and yet *did not earn* that state by not choosing to sin while He had power to do it: isn't He to be praised for His righteousness ?"

BOSO.—"I wish you would answer for me there; for, if I say He is not to be praised for it, I know I am lying; but if I say He is, I am afraid I shall spoil that argument of mine about the angels."

Anselm proceeds, accepting this virtual confession of defeat, to explain : That the approvableness of the angels' conduct depends, not on the question, "*How they came by* the dispositions which prompt them to obey;" but on the question, *whether they have such dispositions, and act them out of their own accord* : That God, in creating them with free-agency, intelligence and holy dispositions, conferred His own image on them; and that their spontaneity, though conferred, is as real, and as really moral, as God's spontaneity, which was not conferred, but eternal and necessary. And that, if there were any force in Boso's cavil, that a morally necessitated righteousness would not be free and approvable in the creature, it would be far stronger against God, whose holiness is the most strictly necessitated of all, being absolutely eternal.

understanding as to the truly preferable, is one way, the will acts the other way ; e. g., the drunkard breaks his own anxiously made resolutions of temperance, and drinks. I reply, No ; still the man has chosen according to what was the prevalent view of his judgment and feelings, as a whole, at the time. That drunkard does judge sobriety the preferable part in the end, and on the whole ; but as to the question of this present glass of drink, (the only immediate object of volition,) his understanding is misinformed by strong propensity and the delusive hope of subsequent reform, combining the advantages of present indulgence with future impunity ; so that its judgment is, that the preferable good will be this one glass, rather than present, immediate self-denial,

(c)It is objected that our repentance for having chosen wrong, That repentance always implies the feeling that we might implies power of con- have chosen otherwise, had we pleased. I trary choice. reply, Yes ; but not unless that choice had been preceded at the time by a different view of the preferable. The thing for which the man blames himself is, that he had not those different feelings and views. (d.) It is objected that our theory could never account for a man's choosing between two alternative objects, equally accessible and desirable, inasmuch as the desire for either is equal, and the will has no self-determining power. The answer is, that the equality of objects by no means implies the equality of subjective desires. For the mind is never in precisely the same state of feeling to any external object or objects, for two minutes together, but ever ebbing and flowing more or less. In this case, although the objects remain equal, the mind will easily make a difference, perhaps an imaginary one. And farther : the two objects being equal, the inertia of will towards choosing a given one of them, may be infinitesimally small ; so that an infinitesimally small preponderance of subjective motive may suffice to overcome it. Remember, there is already a subjective motive in the general, to choose some one of them. A favorite instance supposed is that of a rich man, who has in his palm two or three golden guineas, telling a beggar that he may take any one. But they are exactly equal in value. Now, the beggar has a very positive motive to take some one of them, in his desire for the value to him of a guinea. The least imaginative impulse within his mind is enough to decide a supposed difference which is infinitesimal.

Most important light is thrown upon the subject, by the proper answer to the question, what is mo- Motive, what? The tive ? The will not being, as we have seen, Inducement not Motive. self-moved, what is it which precedes the volition, and is the true cause ? I reply, by distinguishing between motive and inducement. The inducement is that external object, towards which the desire tends, in rising to choice.

Thus, the gold seen by the thief is the inducement to his volition to steal. But the perception of the gold is not his motive to that volition. His motive is the cupidity of his own soul, projecting itself upon the gold. And this cupidity, (as in most instances of motive,) is a complex of certain conceptions of the intellect, and concupiscence of the heart; conceptions of various utilities of the gold, and concupiscence towards the pleasures which it could procure. The inducement is objective; the motive is subjective. The inducement is merely the occasion, the motive is the true cause of the resulting volition. The object which is the inducement projects no force into the thief's soul. On the contrary, it is the passive object of a force of soul projected upon it. The moral power is wholly from within outwards The action is wholly that of the thief's soul, the inducement is only acted on. The proof of this all important view is in this case. The same purse of gold is seen, in the same circumstances of opportunity and privacy, by two men; the second is induced by it to steal : on the first, it had no such power. Why the difference? The difference must be subjective in the two men, because objectively, the two cases are identical. Your good sense leads you to explain the different results by the differing characters of the two men. You say : " It is because the first man was honest, the second covetous." That is to say, the causative efficiency which dictated the two volitions was, in each case, from within the two men's souls, not from the gold. Besides, the objects of sense are inert, dead, senseless, and devoid of will. It is simply foolish to conceive of them as emitting a moral activity. The thief is the only agent in the case.

This plain view sheds a flood of light on the doctrine of the will. A volition has always a cause, *Sensualistic view of* which is the (subjective) motive. This cause *necessity false.* is efficient, otherwise the effect, volition, would not follow. But the motive is subjective; i. e., it is the agent judging and desiring, just as truly as the volition is the agent choosing. And this subjective desire, causative of the choice, is a function of the agent's activity, not of his passivity. The desire is as much of the agent's spontaneity (self-action) as is the choosing. Thus is corrected the monstrous view of those who deduced a doctrine of the necessity of the will from a sensualistic psychology. If volition is efficiently caused by desire, and if desire is but the passive reflex of objective perception, then, indeed, is man a mere machine. His seeming free-agency is wholly deceptive; and his choice is dictated from without. Then, indeed, the out-cry of the semi-Pelagian against such a necessity is just. But inducement is not motive; desire is an activity, and not a passivity of our souls. Our own subjective judgments and appetencies cause our volitions.

On the other hand, it is equally plain, that the adaptation

Inducement receives its influence from the subjective disposition. of any object to be an inducement to volition, depends on some subjective attribute of appetency in the agent. This state of appetency is *a priori* to the inducement, not created by it, but conferring on the object its whole fitness to be an inducement. In other words, when we seek to propagate a volition, by holding out an inducement as occasion, or means, we always presuppose in the agent whom we address, some active propensity. No one attempts to allure a hungry horse with bacon, or a hungry man with hay. Why! Common sense recognizes in each animal an *a priori* state of appetite, which has already determined to which of them the bacon shall be inducement, and to which the hay. The same thing is true of the spiritual desires, love of applause, of power, of justice, &c. Hence, it follows, that inducement has no power whatever to revolutionize the subjective states of appetency natural to an agent. The effect cannot determine its own cause.

From this point of view may also be seen the justice of that philosophy of common sense, with which we set out; when we remarked that every one regarded a man's free acts as *indices* of an abiding or permanent character. This is only because the abiding appetencies of soul decide which objects shall be, and which shall not, be inducements to choice.

The student will perceive that I have not used the phrase, "freedom of the will." I exclude it, because persuaded that it is inaccurate, and that it has occasioned much confusion and error. Freedom is properly predicated of a person, not of a faculty. This was seen by Locke, who says, B. 2, ch. 21, sec. 10, "Liberty is not an idea belonging to volition, or preferring, but to the person having the power." This is so obviously true, as to need no argument. I have preferred therefore to use the phrase, at once popular and exact: "free agency," and "free agent." Turrettin (Loc. x, Qu. 1) sees this objection to the traditionary term, "*Liberum arbitrium*," and hesitates about its use. But, after carefully defining it, he concedes to custom that it may be cautiously used, in the stipulated sense of the freedom of the Agent who wills. It would have been safer to change it.

Freedom What?

I have also preferred to state and argue the old question as to the nature of free agency, in the common form it has borne in the history of theology, before I embarrassed the student with any of the attempted modifications of the doctrine. Locke, following the sensualistic definition, says that "liberty is the idea of a power in any agent to do or forbear any particular action, according to the determination or thought of the mind." But more profound analysts, as Reid and Cousin, saw that it consists in more than the sensualist would represent: mere privilege to execute outwardly what we have willed. My consciousness insists, that I am also a free Agent in having that volition.

9*

There, is the essential feature of choice ; there, the rational preference first exhibits itself. The rational psychologists, consequently, assert the great, central truth, that the soul is self-determining. They see clearly that the soul, and not the objective inducement, is the true cause of its own acts of choice ;
and that hence man is justly responsible. But in order to sustain this central point, they vacillate towards the old semi-Pelagian absurdity, that not only the man, but the separate faculty
of will, is self-determined. They fail to grasp the real facts as
to the nature and the power of subjective motive, the exercise
of another set of faculties in the soul. Edwards saw more per-
spicaciously. Teaching that motive efficaciously determines the

Motive, What ?

will, he defined motive, as all that which, to-,
gether, moves the will to choice. It is
always a complex of some view or judgment of the understanding, and some movement of appetency or repulsion as to an
object. These two elements must be, at least virtually and implicitly, in the precedaneous state of soul ; or choice, volition,
would not result. The intelligence has seen some object in the
category of the true (or at least has thought it saw it thus), and
the appetency has moved towards it as in the category of the
desirable ; else, no deliberate, affirmative volition had occurred.
The mere presence and perception of the object is the occasion ;
the soul's own judgment and appetency form the cause of the
act of choice.

But what is appetency ? If we confound it with passion,

Desire is not Passive.

with mere impression on natural sensibilities,
we again fall into the fatal errors of the sensualist. Sir Wm. Hamilton has done yeoman's service to truth,
by illustrating the difference (while he has claimed more than
due credit for originating the distinction). He separates the
passive powers of " sensibility," from the active powers of " conation." This is but the old (and correct) Calvinistic classification of the powers of the soul under " understanding," " affections," and " will." Here, be it noted, the word "will" is taken,
as in some places of our Confession, in a much wider sense than
the specific faculty of choice. "Will" here includes all the
active powers of the soul, and is synonymous with Sir Wm.
Hamilton's "conative" powers. When we say, then, that man's
soul is self-determining, we mean that, in the specific formation
of choice, the soul choosing is determined by a complex of previous functions of the same soul seeing and desiring. In this
sense the soul is free. But, as has been stated, no cause in the
universe acts lawlessly. "Order is heaven's first law." And the

Disposition the all-
important Fact.

regulative law of souls, when causing volitions, is found in their dispositions. This all-
important fact in free-agency,is what the scho-
lastic divines called *Habitus* (not *Consuetudo*). It is the same
notion popularly expressed by the word character. We know

that man has such *habitus*, or disposition, which is more abiding than any act, or one series of acts of any one desire.   For we deem that in a knave, for instance, evil disposition is present while he is eating, or laughing, or asleep, or while thinking of anything else than his knavish plans.   If we will reflect, we shall see that we intuitively ascribe disposition, of some sort, to every rational free agent: indeed we cannot think such an object without it.   God, angel, demon, man, each is invariably conceived as having some abiding disposition, good or bad.   It is in this that we find the regulative principle of the free-agency of all volition which rises according to subjective motive.   Subjective motive arises (freely) according to ruling subjective disposition.   Disposition also is spontaneous—its very nature is to act freely.   Here then, we have the two ultimate factors of free agency; Spontaneity, Disposition,   Here we are at the end of all possible analysis.   It is as vain to ask : " Why am I disposed thus?" as to seek a prior root of my spontaneity.   The fact of my responsibility as a free agent does not turn on the answer to the question : it turns on this : that the disposition, which is actually my own, regulates the rise freely of just the subjective motives I entertain.   Let the student ponder my main argument (on pages 122 to 124) and he will see that in no other way is the free agency of either God, angel, or sinner, to be construed by us.

Dr. McCosh (Div. and Moral Gov. as cited in the syllabus,) wrests the true doctrine in some degree. He McCosh's view of the Will. calls the will the " optative faculty," correctly distinguishing desire from sensibility, (which he terms emotion.)   But he erroneously confounds appetency and volition together as the same functions of one power.   That this is not correct, is evinced by one short question : May not the soul have two competing appetencies, and choose between them ?   We must hold fast, with the great body of philosophers, to the fact, that the power of decision, or choice, is unique, and not to be confounded even with subjective desires.   It is the executive   faculty.   Dr. McCosh concedes that motive (as defined by Edwards) efficaciously decides the will ; but he then asserts, with Coleridge, that the will determines motives. Conceding this, he has virtually surrendered his doctrine to the Arminian, and gotten around to a literal self-determination of the will. He seems to have been misled by an inaccurate glimpse of the truth I stated on p. 129, that the disposition determines *a priori* which sorts of objects shall be inducements to it.   There is a two-fold confusion of this profound and important truth. Disposition is not the will ; but a regulative principle of the appetencies, or " optative " functions, through them controlling the will.   And, second, it is wholly another thing to say, that this disposition decides which objects shall be inducements, the occasions only of volitions ; and to say with Dr. McCosh, that

the will chooses among the soul's own subjective motives, **the**
veræ causæ of the very acts of choice !

Dr. Isaac Watts, as is often stated, attempted to modify
the doctrine of the will, by supposing that we
Watts' view.
had inverted the order of cause and effect.
He deemed that we do not choose an object because we have
desired it ; but that we desire it because we have chosen it.
In other words, he thought desire the result, and not the
forerunner of choice. This scheme obviously leaves the
question unanswered : How do volitions arise ? And by seeming to leave them without cause, he favors the erroneous scheme
of the Arminian. It is enough to say, that no man's consciousness, properly examined, will bear out this position. Do we
not often have desires where, in consequence of other causes in
the mind, we form no volition at all ? This question will be seen
decisive.

Dr. Albert Taylor Bledsoe, in his Reply to Edwards, Theodicy, and other essays, attempts to modify
Bledsoe's view
the Arminian theory, without surrendering it.
He is too perspicacious to say, with the crowd of semi-Pelagians,
that volitions are uncaused results in the mental world ; he
knows too well the universality of the great, necessary intuition,
ex nihilo nihil. But denying that motives, even subjective, are
cause of acts of choice, he says the mind is the immediate cause of
them. He seems here to approach very near the orthodox
view. Even Dr. Alexander could say, while denying the
self-determination of the will, that he was ready to admit the
self-determination of the mind. But this concession of Dr.
Bledsoe does not bring him to the correct ground. It leaves
the question unexplained, in what way the mind is determined
from within to choice. It refuses to accept the efficient influence of subjective motive. It still asserts that any volition may
be contingent as to its rise, thus embodying the essential
features of Arminianism. And above all : it fails to see or
admit the most fundamental fact of all ; that original disposition
which regulates each being's desires and volitions. The
applications which this author makes of his modified doctrine
betray still its essential Arminianism.

In conclusion, it is only necessary at this place to say in
one word, that the disposition which is found in every natural
man, as to God and godliness, is depravity. Hence his will,
according to the theory expounded above, is, in the Scriptural
sense, in bondage to sin, while he remains properly a free **and**
responsible agent.

LECTURE XII.

THE RESPONSIBILITY AND PROVINCE OF REASON IN RELIGION.

WIDE difference of opinion has long prevailed, as to man's responsibility for the dispositions, habits and desires tending to moral volitions. Pelagians and semi-Pelagians say, that since responsibility cannot be more extended than freedom of the will, no praise or blame can be attached to dispositions, which they hold to be involuntary. And they say that Calvinists cannot dispute the latter statement, because they make dispositions causes of volition, and thus going before. Hence, also, is the Pelagian definition of sin and holiness, as consisting only of right or wrong acts of soul. The evangelical Arminian is usually found holding the middle ground, that only those dispositions, habits and desires have a moral responsibility attached to them, which have resulted from a series of acts of free-will. But we hold that man is praise- or blame-worthy for his dispositions, principles and habits, as well as for his volitions; and that his responsibility depends on the nature, and not on the origin, of the disposition which he spontaneously and intelligently entertains.

Is concupiscence sin?

We make our appeal here to consciousness, which causes us shame and self-reproach for evil propensities not ripened into volitions, and tells us that we would feel equal resentment for evil dispositions towards us and our rights, though never formed into the overt intention of injury. 2d. Our minds intuitively judge that the moral character of an act resides in its motives. Witness the process of investigation in the charge for crime before a jury. Indeed, the act of volition, nakedly considered, is a merely natural effect, and has no more moral character than the muscular motions which follow it. For the volition which extends the hand with alms to an enemy, or with a bribe to one to commit a sin, is the same physical volition: we must go back

133

of it, to the motive by which it was caused, to settle its moral character. That element is not in the naked volition; says the Pelagian, it is not in the motives prior to volition; then it is nowhere! 3d. The notion is inconsistent with our established idea about character. Here is a man who is said to have a dishonest character. It only becomes cognizable to us by his acts. He must, then, have performed a series of acts, having the common quality of dishonesty. Now, nothing comes from nothing; there must be some cause for that sameness of character; and that cause is the prevalent disposition to steal, separate from, and prior to, each thievish act. For the bad cause cannot be in the will itself; this would be peculiarly objectionable to the Pelagian. This, then, is what is meant when this man is said to have a bad character. Has the word bad here, no proper meaning? Does the family of daughters, the separate acts, bear no relationship to their mother? 4th. On the Pelagian scheme, the wickedness of sins of omission would be inexplicable. For in them, there is often no volition at all; and therein consists their wickedness. A man passing by the water sees an innocent child drowning; the idea of rescue is suggested to his mind; but he comes to no choice, does nothing, and while he hesitates, the child sinks to rise no more. Is he innocent? Our conscience declares that he is not. Now, we can consistently explain wherein he is not, viz., in the state of his selfish and indolent feelings. But the opposite party have no explanation. There has literally been no volition; on their theory they should say, what every sound conscience rejects, that the neglect has been attended with no guilt. 5th. A similar argument is presented by instances of impulsive and unpremeditated acts, done before we have a moment for reflection. We properly approve or blame them, according as they are generous or malignant. But there has been no intelligent, deliberate choice; if we confine our view exclusively to the act of soul itself, it appears as purely irrational as the impulses of mere animal instinct. The moral quality of these acts must be found, then, in the dispositions and principles which prompted them.

Such are the reasonings, drawn from the conscience and consciousness of all men. The conclusion cannot be restricted in the way proposed by the Arminian. For, if original or congenital dispositions have no moral quality, because not created by a series of acts of intelligent free-will, then: 1st. God could never have any moral credit, His holy disposition having been not only original and eternal, but necessary. 2d. Nor could the holy man, Adam, or the holy angels have been approvable, though perfectly innocent, because their holy dispositions were infused into them by their creator. This contradicts both conscience and Scripture. 3d. When mankind see an inherited trait influencing the

Instances.

conduct, like the traditionary bravery of the Briton, or the congenital vengefulness of the American Indian, if they apprehend that the agents are not lunatic, and are exercising a sane spontaneity as qualified by these natural traits, they approve or blame them. This shows that in the judgment of common sense, the responsibility turns only on the question, what the disposition is, and not, whence it is. Last: on this view, it would be impossible that the free agent could ever construct a righteous disposition, or *habitus*, by his own free acts. For all are agreed in that rule of practical law, which judges the moral complexion of the act according to the agent's intention. But a soul as yet devoid of positively righteous principles would harbor no positively moral intentions. Hence, the first act of choice which the philosophers look to, for beginning the right moral habitude, would have no moral quality, not being dictated by a moral motive. Then it could contribute nothing to the habit as a moral one. This very plain demonstration decides the whole matter, by showing that, on either the Pelagian or Arminian scheme, a dependent being could never have a positively righteous character or action at all.

Our opponents argue that the involuntary cannot be sin, and they suppose that they have intrenched themselves in the plainest of moral intuitions. The objection is, none the less, a sophism founded in the ambiguous use of the word involuntary. Man's moral dispositions are involuntary, in the sense that they do not immediately result from volitions as their next cause. But this is not the sense in which our intuitions assert the necessity of the voluntary to our responsibility. There is an entirely different sense, in which we say an act is involuntary, when it occurs against the choice of the will. Thus, the fall of the man over the precipice was involuntary, when he was striving to cleave to the edge of the stone. This is the sense in which we say that, self-evidently, the man was not blamable for his fall. The other meaning, sophistically confounded with this, raises the question whether the state or disposition is spontaneous. If it acts spontaneously, not because a stronger agent forces the man to harbor or to indulge it against his choice, then, in the sense necessary to free agency, disposition is voluntary; that is to say, it is spontaneous; it is as truly a function of self-hood as volition itself. The evidence is very near and plain. Does any external compulsion cause us to feel our dispositions? No. From their very nature it cannot be: a compelled tendency would not be our disposition, but a violence put upon it. The main question may be submitted to a very practical test. Would a disposition to a wicked act subsist, even as not consented to or formed into a purpose, in a perfectly holy soul, like that of Gabriel, for one instant? It would die in its very incipiency. The attempt to inject concu-

But, objected "That the involuntary cannot be sin."

piscence, would be like an attempt to strike sparks from the
flint and steel, in a perfect vacuum. The fire would expire in
being born. But if the holiness of the nature thus excluded
the birth, this clearly shows that the very birth of wrong
desire or tendency is wrong.

Another objection is; that our theory of the immorality
of evil dispositions would imply that the
soul's essence is altered; or that depravity is
a change in the substance of the soul: which
would make God the author of sin, and man an unfortunate,
sentient puppet. For, say they, there is nothing but the soul
and its acts; and if you deny that all morality resides in acts,
some of it must reside in the essence of the soul itself. The
sophism of this argument would be sufficiently exposed by asking, what is a moral act. If you make it anything more than
a mere notional object of thought, an imagination about which
we think, is it any thing besides the soul acting? Well: in the
same sense, our moral dispositions are but our souls feeling. I
reply again, and yet more decisively, that immoral quality is
only negative—i. e., 'Η ἁμαρτία ἐστὶ ἡ ἀνομία. It is the lack of
conformity to God's will, which constitutes sin. The negative
absence of this principle of active conformity is all that is necessary to predicate. Thus, the idea of depravity's being a substantial change is seen to be out of the question. We might
farther reply to the challenge, whether there is anything before
us, save the soul and its acts: Yes. There is the soul's essence,
distinguishable from its substance: there is its disposition:
there are its liabilities, its affections, its desires. The terms of
the cavil are no more than a verbal quibble. What true philosopher ever questioned the existence of qualities, qualifying a
spirtual agent, yet not implying either decomposition or change
of its simple substance? Then it is possible that it may be
qualified morally.

The question whether man is responsible for his belief, is
nearly connected with the one just discussed.
Many modern writers have urged that he is
not, because belief is the necessary and involuntary result of evidence seen by the mind. Further, it is
urged; if the doctrine that man is responsible for his belief be
held, then the horrible doctrine of persecution will follow; for
erroneous beliefs being often very mischievous, if also criminal,
it would follow that they ought to be punished by society. To
the first, I reply, that while the admission of demonstrative
proofs, when weighed by the mind is necessary, and involuntary,
the voluntary powers have a great deal to do with the question
whether they shall be weighed fairly or not. Inattention, prejudice against the truth or the advocate, heedlessness, guilty and
wicked habits of perverting the soul's faculties; all these are
voluntary; and I fearlessly assert, that no erroneous belief on

any important moral question can arise in a sane mind, except through the operation of one or more of these causes. In this, then, is the guilt of false beliefs on moral subjects. To the second objection, I reply that it does not follow, because a man is responsible for his beliefs, he is responsible to his fellow-man. There are abundant reasons for denying the latter, which it would be easy to show, if I were going into the subject of freedom of thought.

On the affirmative side, I remark, first: that all the analogies of nature show us a Providence holding *Because Nature and* man responsible for his beliefs. If prejudice, *Providence rule thus.* passion, haste, inattention, prevents a man from attaching due weight to testimony or other evidence, as to the poison of a given substance, he experiences its effects just as though he had taken it of set purpose. So of all other things.

Second: Conscience clearly condemns many acts, based *Because all wrong be-* immediately on certain beliefs, which were *liefs have a criminal* sincerely held at the time of acting. Now, *cause.* if the belief had been innocent, the act necessarily dictated thereby could not have been blame-worthy. Witness Paul, confessing the sin of his persecutions. Indeed, since belief on moral subjects ought to, and must dictate conduct, if man is allowed to be a rational free agent, each man's own belief must be his own guide; and hence an act might be right to one man, and wrong to another, at the same time. A would have a right (because he believed so) to a thing which B had a right to; and so B would have a moral right to do A what would be to him a moral wrong? And farther; since whatever a man sincerely believed, would be right to him, truth would cease to be of any essential importance. This consequence is monstrous. Hence we must hold men responsible for their moral beliefs. God could not otherwise govern a world of rational free agents; for since the free dictates of each agent's soul must be, to him, the guide of his conduct, God could not justly condemn him for committing the crime which he supposed at the time to be a right act, after he had been acquitted of all responsibility for the opinion which unavoidably dictated the act. But is every one rash enough to justify all the crimes committed in this world under the influence of moral error heartily held at the time? Then the vilest crimes which have scourged the world, from the retaliatory murders of savages (dictated by stress of tribal honour) to the persecution of God's saints (by inquisitors who verily thought they were doing God service) are made perfectly innocent.

It may be well to say a few more words to relieve the seeming paradox in this truth. To this separate *Paradox resolved.* element of the act, that it was conformed to the man's opinion of the right at the time; as that element is abstracted in thought from all other features of the concrete sin; we do not suppose any criminality to attach. But we are bound to go back to the prior question : How came a being endowed with reason and conscience, actually to believe the wrong to be right ? Could this result have been innocently brought about ? To say this, would be to accuse God his Maker. I can apprehend how God's finite handiwork, a rational soul, may remain ignorant of many truths known to larger intelligences ; but I cannot admit that it can be betrayed into positive error by the normal, legitimate exercise of its powers. There is then, always a prior account of the mental perversion : The conditions of the erroneous result have been sinful indolence in looking at evidence, or unrighteous self-interest, or criminal prejudice against the truth or its advocate, or some other combination of evil affections. To these, specifically, attaches the guilt of the erroneous mental result. We see thus, that belief is not the involuntary result of evidence apprehended, in any practical moral case. The will (taking that word in its wider sense of the active, optative powers) has a great deal to do with the result, by inclining or disposing the mind to give proper heed to the attainable evidence. So much weight has this fact, that the profound *Des Cartes*, who almost deserves to be called the founder of modern philosophy, actually ranked belief as a function of will, rather than of understanding! Here then I place myself: when an action of soul is spontaneous, it may be, to that extent, justly held responsible.

The question with which we close this brief review of the nature of man's primary judgments, has ever been of fundamental importance in the Church : " What is the legitimate province of Reason, in revealed theology?" The pretended warfare between reason and faith has been waged by all those who wished to make a pretext for believing unreasonably and wickedly. On the one hand, it is possible so to exalt the authority of the Church, or of theology, (as is done by Rome,) as to violate the very capacity of reason to which religion appeals. On the other, it is exceedingly easy to give too much play to it, and admit thus the *virus* of Rationalism in some of its forms.

3. Province of Reason in Revealed Religion.

All the different forms of rationalism, which admit a revelation as true or desirable at all, may be grouped under two classes. 1st. Those who hold the PROTON PSEUDOS of the Socinians ; that man is to hold nothing credible in religion which he cannot comprehend. 2d. Those who, like the modern German rationalists, make the interpretations of Scripture square with the teachings of human philosophy, instead of making their philosophy square with the plain meaning of revelation. Under the latter class must be ranked all those who, like Hugh Miller, in his Testimony of the Rocks, hold that the interpretation of the Pentateuch, concerning cos-

Rationalism, What?

mogony, must be moulded supremely by the demands of geological theories, instead of being settled independently by its own laws of fair exegesis. Here, also, belong those who, like A. Barnes, say that the Bible must not be allowed to mean what would legitimate American slavery, because he holds that his ethical arguments prove it cannot be right : *Et id omne genus.*

The absurdity of the first class will be shown, more fully, when we come to deal with the Socinian the-ology. It is enough to say now, that reason herself repudiates such a boast as preposter-ous. She does not truly comprehend all of anything : not the whole nature and physiology of the blade of grass which man presses with his foot: nor the *modus* of that union of body and soul which consciousness compels us to admit. Every line of knowledge which we follow, leads us to the circumference of darkness, where it is lost to our comprehension ; and the more man knows, the more frequently is he compelled to stop humbly at that limit, and acknowledge his lack of comprehension. So that, the most truly wise man is he who knows and believes most things which he does not comprehend.*

Comprehension not the Measure of Truth.

That our comprehension is not the measure of truth appears, again, thus : Truth is one and immutable. But the amount of comprehension any given man has, is dependent on his cultivation and knowledge. Thirty years ago it would have been wholly incomprehensible to a " field-hand," how a message could be sent along a wire by galvanism. It was not incomprehensible to Dr. Joseph Henry, who actually instructed Morse, the nominal inventor, how it might be done. On this Socinian scheme, then, truth would be contradictory for differ-ent minds. One man's valid code of truth would properly be, to a less cultivated man, in large part falsehood and absurdity. But this is preposterous.

But does not the Protestant assert, against the Papist, that faith, in order to be of any worth, must be intelligent? Do not we scout the " implicit faith " of the Papist?

Does this counte-nance implicit Faith?

There is a distinction which fully solves this question, and which is simple and important. Every judg-ment in the form of a belief is expressed in a proposition. This, grammatically, consists of subject, predi-cate, and copula. Now, the condition of rational belief is, that the mind shall intelligently see some valid supporting evidence for the *copula*. If, without this, it announces belief, it is acting unreasonably. But it is wholly another thing to com-prehend the whole nature of the predication ; and this latter is

Answer.

* It is related that the famous Dr. Parr, upon hearing a young Socinian flippantly say, he would believe nothing he could not comprehend, answered: " Then, sir, you will have the shortest creed of any young gentleman in the kingdom."

not at all necessary to a rational faith. The farmer presents
me on the palm of his hand, a sound grain of corn, and a pebble. He says: "This is dead, but that is alive." May I not,
with him, rationally believe in the vitality of the grain? Yes:
because we have some intelligent view of the experimental evidence which supports the affirmation. But suppose
now I pass to the predication, "alive;" and demand of the
farmer that he shall give me a full definition of the nature of
vegetable vitality? The greatest physicist cannot do this.
Neither he nor I comprehend the nature of vegetable vitality.
We know by its effects, that there is such a force, but it is a
mysterious force. Let the student then hold fast to this simple
law: In order to rational belief there must be some intelligent
view of evidence sustaining the copula; but there may be no
comprehension of the nature of the predicate.

Now, if these things are just and true in all natural knowledge, how much more true in the things of the infinite God?
The attempt of the Socinian to make a god altogether comprehensible, has resulted in a plan attended inevitably with more
and worse incomprehensibilities, yes, impossibilities, than they
reject.

To the second class of rationalists, the simple answer
On Rationalist which reason gives is, that such a revelation
Scheme, no Revealed as they admit, is practically no revelation at
Rule of Faith. all. That is, it is no authoritative standard of
belief to any soul, on any point on which it may happen to
have any opinion derived from other sources than the Bible.
For each man's speculative conclusions are, to him, his philosophy; and if one man is entitled to square his Bible to his
philosophy, the other must be equally so. Further, it is well
known that the deductions of all philosophies are fallible. The
utter inconsistency of Rationalism, with any honest adoption
of a Revelation, appears thus: It is the boast of Rationalists,
that human science is progressive: that our generation is far in
advance of our fathers. May not our children be as far in
advance of us? Things now held as scientific truth, will probably be excluded; things not now dreamed of, will probably be
discovered and explained. When that time comes, it must
follow on the Rationalists' scheme, that the interpretation of
the Scriptures shall receive new modifications from these new
lights of reason. Propositions which we now hold as the
meaning of Scripture, will then be shown by the lights of
human science to be false! What is it reasonable that we
should do, at this time, with those places of Scripture? Will
any one say, "Reserve your opinion on them, until the light
comes?" Alas! there is now no means for us to know where-
abouts in the Bible they are! No; we must attempt to
construe the whole Scripture as best we may. Will any one
say that our construction is true to us, but will be false to our

more scientific children? Hardly. If, therefore, the Bible is a revelation from the infallible God, reason herself clearly asserts that where the plain teachings of Scripture clash with such deductions, the latter are to be presumed to be wrong; and unless revelation carries that amount of authority, it is practically worthless. Rationalism is the wolf of infidelity under the sheep's clothing of faith.

It follows, then, that reason is not to be the measure, nor the ground, of the beliefs of revealed theology.

But on the other hand: 1st, the laws of thought which necessarily rule in the human soul, were established by the same God who gave the Bible. Hence, if there is a revelation from Him, and if these laws of thought are legitimately used, there must be full harmony between reason and Scripture. But man knows that he is not infallible: he knows that he almost always employs his powers of thought with imperfect accuracy. On the other hand, if revelation is admitted, its very idea implies infallible truth and authority. Hence, it is clearly reasonable that opinion must always hold itself ready to stand corrected by revelation.

But Revelation does not Violate Reason.

The Scriptures always address us as rational creatures, and presuppose the authority of our native, fundamental laws of thought. If we think at all, we must do it according to those laws. Therefore, to require us to violate or ignore them fundamentally, would be to degrade us to unreasoning animals; we should then be as incapable of religion as they.

2d. Necessary laws of thought must be respected by it.

The claim which the Scriptures address to us, to be the one authentic and authoritative revelation from God, is addressed to our reason. This is clear from the simple fact, that there are presented to the human race more than one professed revelation; and that they cannot be authoritative witnesses to their own authority prior to its admission. It appears also from this, that man is required not only to obey, but to believe and love the Bible. Now he cannot do this except upon evidence. The evidences of inspiration must, therefore, present themselves to man's reason; to reason to be employed impartially, humbly, and in the fear of God. He who says he believes, when he sees no proof, is but pretending, or talking without meaning.

3rd. Authenticity of Revelation not self-evident.

Among these evidences, the reason must entertain this question: whether anything asserted in revelation is inevitably contradictory with reason or some other things asserted in revelation. For if a book clearly contained such things, it would be proof it was not from God; because God, who first created our laws of reason, will not contradict Himself by teaching incompatibles in His works and word. And again: in de

4th. Revelation cannot authorize self-contradictions. Limitations of this admission.

manding faith (always a sincere and intelligent faith,) of us in such contradictories, He would be requiring of us an impossibility. If I see that a thing is impossible to be true, it is impossible for me to believe it. Yet here, we must guard this concession against abuse; asserting first, that the reason which is entitled to this judgment of contradiction concerning the Scriptures, shall be only a right, humble, and holy reason, acting in the fear and love of God; and not a reason unsanctified, hostile, and blind. Second, that the supposed contradiction must be contained in the immediate and unquestioned language of the Scripture itself, and not merely deduced therefrom by some supposed inference. And third, that the truth supposed to be overthrown by it shall be also an express statement of God's word, or some necessary, axiomatic truth, universally held by mankind. For if one should object against the Bible, that some inference he had drawn from its words was irreconcilable with some similar inference, or some supposed deduction of his human logic, we should always be entitled to reply: that his powers of thought being confessedly inaccurate, it was always more probable he had inferred erroneously, than that Scripture had spoken inconsistently.

Reason is also to be employed to interpret and illustrate the Scriptures. To do this, the whole range of man's natural knowledge may be taxed. The interpretation is never to presume to make reason the measure of belief, but the mere handmaid of Scripture. And the mode of interpretation is to be by comparing Scripture with Scripture according to the legitimate laws of language. The Scripture must be its own canon of hermeneutics; and that, independent of all other supposed rival sciences. For otherwise, as has been shown above, it would cease to carry a practical authority over the human mind as a rule of faith. A Bible which must wait to hear what philosophy may be pleased to permit it to say, and which must change its *dicta* as often as philosophy chooses to change, would be no Bible for any sensible man.

5th Reason and human knowledge ancillary to Revelation.

Now, the prelatic system of Church-authority stands opposed to this Protestant theory of private judgment. Prelatists claim for the reasonableness of their slavish system, this analogy; that the child, in all its primary education, has to accept things on trust as he is told. Human knowledge, say they, begins in dogma, not in reasoning. So should divine. The reply is, that this is a false analogy, in two vital respects. The secular knowledge which begins absolutely in dogma, is only that of signs; not of things and ultimate truths. The child must indeed learn from dogma, that a certain rafter-shaped mark inscribed on the paper is the accepted sign of the vowel-sound A. The things of God are not mere signs, but essential truths. Second, the

Faith rests on Evidence, not Dictation.

reception of divine truth is not an infantile, but an adult work. We are required to do it in the exercise of a mature intelligence, and to be infants only in guilelessness.

Prelatists and papists are fond of charging that the theory of private judgement amounts simply to rationalism. For, say they, " to make revelation wait on reason for the recognition of credentials, virtually gives to the revealed dogma only the force of reason. ' The stream can rise no higher than its fountain.' On the Protestant scheme, revelation receives no more authority than reason may confer." The only plausibility of such objections is in the words of a false trope. Revelation it is said, ' submits its credentials to the reason,' according to us Protestants. Suppose I prefer to say (the correct trope,) we hold that revelation imposes its credentials upon the healthy reason. In fact, as when the eye looks at the sun, there are activities of the organ towards the result of vision, such as adjusting the axes of the two balls, directing them, refracting the rays, &c., and yet, the light is not from the eye, but from the sun; so in apprehending the validity of the Bible's credentials, the light is from the revelation; not from the mind. Its activities about the apprehension of the evidence, are only receptive, not productive.

Distinguish this system from Rationalism.

But the simple key to the answer is, that the question that we bring to the human reason, ' Is this book God speaking?' is one, single question, perfectly defined, and properly within the reach of reason. The other question, which the Rationalist wished to make reason answer, is : ' What are the things proper for God to say about Himself and religion ?' There is, in fact, a multitude of questions, and mostly wholly above the reach of reason. We may illustrate the difference by the case of an ambassador. The court to which he comes is competent to entertain the question of his credentials. This is implied in the expectation that this court is to treat with him. The matter of credentials is one definite question, to be settled by one or two plain *criteria*, such as a signature, and the imprint of a seal. But what may be the secret will of his sovereign, is a very different set of questions. To dictate one's surmises here, and especially to annex the sovereign's authority to them, is impertinent folly. But the messages of the plenipotentiary carry all the force of the recognized signature and seal.

Moreover, we must remember that man's state is probationary. There is an intrinsic difference between truth and error, right reasoning and sophism, and the purpose of God in revelation is (necessarily) not to supplant reason, but to put man on his probation for its right use.

Last : Let the student, from the first, discard all the false and mischievous ideas generated by the slang of the " contest between reason and faith."—

No strife of reason with Faith.

of the propriety of having "reason conquer, faith, or faith conquer reason." There is no such contest. The highest reason is
to believe implicitly what God's word says, as soon as it is clearly
ascertained to be God's word. The dictate of reason herself, is
to believe; because she sees the evidences to be reasonable.*

I need only add, that I hold the Scriptures to be, in all its
parts, of plenary inspiration; and we shall henceforward assume
this, as proved by the inquiries of another department.

LECTURE XIII.

REVEALED THEOLOGY. GOD AND HIS ATTRIBUTES.

SYLLABUS.

1. Give the Derivation and Meaning of the Names applied to God in the Scriptures.
    Turrettin, Loc. iii, Qu. 4. Breckinridge's Theology, Vol. i, p. 199. Concor-
    dances and Lexicons.
2. What is the meaning of the term, God's Attributes? And what the most
common Classifications of them?
    Turrettin, Loc. iii, Qu. 5, &c. Dick, Lect. 21. Breckinridge, Vol. i, p. 260,
    &c. Hodge, Syst. Theol. Vol. i, p. 369 to 372. Thornwell, Lect. 6, p. 162–
    166 and 167, &c.
3. What are the Scriptural evidences of God's Unity, Spirituality and Simplicity?
    Turrettin, Loc. iii, Qu. 3 and 7. Dick, Lect. 17 and 18.
4. What the Bible-proofs of God's Immensity?
    Turrettin, Loc. iii, Qu. 9. Dick, Lect. 19.
5. What the Scriptural proof of God's Eternity?
    Turrettin, Loc. iii, Qu. 10. Dick, Lect. 17.
6. Prove from Scripture that God is Immutable.
    Turrettin, Loc. iii, Qu. 11. Dick, Lect. 20. See on whole, "Charnock on
    the Attributes."

IN approaching the department of Revealed Theology, the
first question is concerning the inspiration of the Scriptures.
This having been settled, we may proceed
to assume them as inspired and infallible.
Our business now is merely to ascertain and
collect their teachings, to systematize them, and to show their
relation to each other. The task of the student of Revealed
Theology, is, therefore, in the first place, mainly exegetical.
Having discovered the teachings of revelation by sound exposition, and having arranged them, he is to add nothing, except
what follows "by good and necessary consequence." Consequently, there is no study in which the truth is more important,
that "with the lowly is wisdom."

The New Testament, and still more, the Old, presents us

Infallibility of Scrip-
tures assumed.

---

* See, for the true nature of belief, as distinguished from intuition or deduction,
'Sensualistic Phil. of the 19th Cent. Considered,' Chap. x, end.

I. God's Names re- with an interesting subject of study, in the
veal Him. names and titles of God, which they employ
to give our feeble mind a conception of His
manifold perfections. The names יְהֹוָה יָהּ אֵל אֲדֹנָי אֱלוֹהַּ
שַׁדַּי אֱלֹהִים and יְהֹוָה צְבָאוֹת in the Hebrew, and Θεός,
Κύριος, Ὕψιστος, Παντοκράτωρ, in the Greek, give, of themselves,
an extensive description of His nature. For they are all, according to the genius of the ancient languages, significant of some
quality; and are thus, when rightly interpreted, proof-texts to
sustain several divine attributes. יְהֹוָה (Jehovah) with its abre-
viation, יָהּ, (which most frequently appears in the doxology,
הַלְלוּ יָהּ) has ever been esteemed by the Church the most
distinctive and sacred, because the incommunicable name of
God. The student is familiar with the somewhat superstitious
reverence with which the later Hebrews regard it, never pronouncing it aloud, but substituting it in reading the Scriptures,
by the word אֲדֹנָי. There seems little doubt that the sacred
name presents the same radicals with יְהְיֶה, the future of the
substantive verb הָיָה. This is strikingly confirmed by Exodus
iii : 14, where God, revealing His name to Moses, says: אֶהְיֶה
אֲשֶׁר אֶהְיֶה ("I am that I am") is His name. For we have here,
in form the first person future of the substantive verb, and our
Saviour, Jno. viii : 58, claiming the incommunicable divinity,
says, imitating this place: "Before Abraham was, I AM."* In
Ex. vi : 2, 3, we learn that the characteristic name by which
God commissioned Moses was Jehovah. This is an additional
argument which shows, along with its origin, that the name
means *self-existence* and *independence*.

---

* This derivation is illustrated by a comparison, plausible and interesting, if not
demonstrative, with the Greek and Latin names of God, Ζευς and Jove. By consulting Gen. xxiv : 4, and many other places, we learn that God was known to Abraham
and his family by the name *Jehovah*. In Gen. xxvi : 28, we see that the Canaanites
under Abimelech, of Gerar, still retained the knowledge of the true God, under the
same name. The Phœnician mythology is the parent of the Grecian, as the Phœnician alphabet is of the Greek. Now the votaries of the comparative philology of
modern days, will have Ζευς derived (by a change of Z to its cognate D,) from the
sanscrit root, *Dis*, whose root-meaning was supposed to be *splendour*. To the same
source they trace θεος, *Deus, Divus*, Dies, &c. This source may plausibly answer for
the last named words. But as to Ζευς, may not another etymology be more
probable? (as is confessed by some of the best Greek scholars) that Ζευς is from Ζεω,
(the primary meaning of which is *fervere*,) and that this verb is closely cognate to
Ζαω, "I live," and Ζωη, "life." Notice, then, the strange resemblance, almost an
identity, between "Jehovah," and "Jove." The latter, with *pater*, makes the Latin
nominative Jupiter— *Jov-Pater*—father Jove. If this origin is true, then we have
the Greek name of the chief God, Ζευς, involving the same fundamental idea; "The
Living One,"—the self-existent source of life. This is much more explanatory of the
early myths touching Jove, as the "Father of Gods and men," than the primary idea
of the supposed sanscrit root.

10*

Such a meaning would, of itself, lead us to expect that this name, with its kindred derivatives, is never applied to any but the one proper God; because no other being has the attribute which it signifies. A further proof is found in the fact that it is never applied as a proper name, to any other being in Scripture. The angel who appeared to Abraham, to Moses, and to Joshua, (Gen. xviii : 1 ; Exod. iii : 2–4 ; Josh. v : 13 ; vi : 3,) was evidently Jehovah-Christ. When Moses named the altar Jehovah-nissi, (Ex. xvii : 15,) he evidently no more dreamed of calling it Jehovah, than did Abram, when he called a place, (Gen. xxii : 14,) Jehovah-jireh. And when Aaron said concerning the worship of the calf : " To-morrow is the feast of Jehovah," he evidently considered the image only as representative of the true God. But the last and crowning evidence that this name is always distinctive, is that God expressly reserves it to Himself. (See Exod. iii : 15 ; xv : 3 ; xx : 2 ; Ps. lxxxiii : 18 ; Is. xlii : 8 ; xlviii : 2 ; Amos v : 8 ; ix : 6.) The chief value of this fact is not only to vindicate to God exclusively the attribute of self-existence ; but greatly to strengthen the argument for the divinity of Christ. When we find the incommunicable name given to Him, it is the strongest proof that he is very God.

This the incommunicable Name.

אֲדֹנָי Lord, is the equivalent of the Greek Κύριος. Its meaning is possession and dominion, expressed by the Latin *Dominus*, which is its usual translation in the Vulgate, both in the Old and New Testaments, and, unfortunately, is the usual translation of Jehovah also. Hence has arisen the suppression of this name in our English version, where both are translated Lord ; and Jehovah is distinguished only by having its translation printed in capitals, (LORD.)

Other Names.

שַׁדַּי is also a *pluralis excellentiæ*, expressing omnipotence. Sometimes, as in Job v : 17, it stands by itself ; sometimes, as in Gen. xvii : 1, it is connected with אֵל (where it is rendered "God Almighty.") This seems to be the name by which He entered into special covenant with Abram. It appears in the New Testament in its Greek form of Παντοκράτωρ, Rev. i : 8.

עֶלְיוֹן is said to be a verbal form of the verb עָלָה — ' to ascend ;' and is rendered in Psalms ix : 3, and xxi : 8, " Most High." This name signifies the exaltation of God's character.

צְבָאוֹת—hosts, is frequently used as an epithet qualifying one of the other names of God, as יְהוָה צְבָאוֹת—Jehovah of hosts, (i. e., *exercituum*.) In this title, all the ranks or orders of creatures, animate and inanimate, are represented as subject to God, as the divisions of an army are to their commander.

We come now to what may be called the communicable names of God; the same words are also used to express false and imaginary Gods or mighty men, as well as the true God. It is a striking peculiarity, that these alone are subjected to inflection by taking on the construct state and the pronominal suffixes. They are אֵל expressing the idea of might, and אֱלֹהִים אֱלוֹהַּ singular and plural forms of the same root, probably derived from the verb אוּל —to be strong. The singular form appears to be used chiefly in books of poetry. The plural, (*a pluralis majestatis*) is the common term for God, Θεός, Deus, expressing the simple idea of His eternity as our Maker, the God of creation and providence.

Communicable Names.

Gathering up these names alone, and comprehending their conjoined force according to the genius of Oriental language, we find that they compose by themselves an extensive revelation of God's nature. They clearly show Him to be self-existent, independent, immutable and eternal; infinite in perfections, exalted in majesty, almighty in power, and of universal dominion. We shall find all of God implicitly, in these traits.

The Scriptures give to God a number of expressive metaphorical titles (which some very inaccurately and needlessly would classify as His Metaphorical attributes, whereas they express, not attributes, but relations,) such as " King," " Lawgiver," " Judge," " Rock," " Tower," " Deliverer," " Shepherd," " Husbandman," " Father," &c. These cannot be properly called His names.

God's attributes are those permanent, or essential, qualities of His nature, which He has made known to us in His word. When we say they are essential qualities, we do not mean that they compose His substance, as parts thereof making up a whole; still less, that they are members, attached to God, by which He acts. They are traits qualifying His nature always, and making it the nature it is. The question whether God's attributes are parts of His essence, has divided not only scholastics, Socinians and orthodox, but even Mohammedans; affecting, as it does, the proper conception of His unity and simplicity. We must repudiate the gross idea that they are parts of His substance, or members attached to it; for then He would be susceptible of division, and so of destruction. His substance is a unit, a *monad*. God's omniscience, e. g., is not something attached to His substance, whereby He knows; but only a power or quality of knowing, qualifying His infinite substance itself. To avoid this gross error, the scholastics, (including many Protestants,) used to say that God's essence, and each or

2. Attributes what? Identical with Essence?

every attribute, are identical; i. e., that His whole essence is
identical with each attribute. They were accustomed to say,
that God's knowing is God, God's willing is God, or that the
whole God is in every act; and this they supposed to be necessary to a proper conception of His simplicity. This predication
they carred so far as to say, that God's essence was simple in
such sense as to exclude, not only all distinctions of parts, or
composition, but all logical distinction of substance and essence,
entity and quiddity, and to identify the essence and each attribute absolutely and in a sense altogether different from finite
spirits.

Now, as before remarked, (Lect. IV, Nat. Theol.) if all
this means anything more than is conceded
on the last page, it is pantheism. The
charge there made is confirmed by this thought: That if the
divine essence must be thus literally identified with each attribute, then the attributes are also identified with each other.
There is no virtual, but only a nominal difference, between
God's intellect and will. Hence, it must follow, that God
effectuates all He conceives. This not only obliterates the
vital distinction between His *scientia simplex* and *scientia
visionis;* but it also robs God of His freedom as a personal
agent, and, if He is infinite by His omniscience, proves that the
creation, or His works, is infinite. Here we have two of the
very signatures of pantheism. But further: this identification
of the distinct functions of intelligence and will violates our
rational consciousness. There is a virtual difference between
intellection, conation, and sensibility. Every man knows this,
as to himself; and yet he believes in the unity of his spirit.
It is equally, or more highly, true of God, The fact that He
is an infinite spiritual unit, does not militate against this position, but rather facilitates our holding of it; inasmuch as this
infinitude accounts for the manifold powers of function exercised, better than our finite spirituality. It will be enough to
add, in conclusion, that the fundamental law of our reason forbids our really adopting this scholastic refinement. We can
only know substance by its attributes. We can only believe
an attribute to be, as we are able to refer it to its substance.
This is the only relation of thought, in which the mind can
think either. Were the reduction of substance and attribute
actually made then, in good faith, the result would be incog-
noscible to the human intellect.

God is infinite, and therefore incomprehensible, for our
minds, in His essence. (Job xi: 7–9.) Now, since our only
way of knowing His essence is as we know the attributes which
(in our poor, shortcoming phrase) compose it, each of God's attributes and acts must have an element of the incomprehensible
about it. (See Job xxvi: 14; Ps. cxxxix: 5, 6; Is. xl: 28;
Rom. xi: 33.) One of the most important attainments for you

Objections.

to make, therefore, is for you to rid your minds for once and all, of the notion, that you either do or can comprehend the whole of what is expressed of any of God's attributes. Yet there is solid truth in our apprehension of them up to our limited measure — i. e., our conception of them, if scriptural, will be not essentially false, bnt only defective. Of this, we have this twofold warrant: First, that God has told us we are, in our own rational and moral attributes, formed in His image, so that His infinite, are the *normae* of our finite, essential qualities; and second, that God has chosen such and such human words (as wisdom, rectitude, knowledge,) to express these divine attributes. The Bible does not use words dishonestly.

Another question has been raised by orthodox divines, (e. g., Breckinridge,) whether since God's essence is infinite, we must not conceive of it as having an infinite number of distinct attributes. That is, whatever may be the revelations of Himself made by God in word and works, and however numerous and glorious the essential attributes displayed therein, an infinite number of other attributes still remain, not dreamed of by His wisest creatures. The origin of this notion seems to be very clearly in *Spinozism*, which sought to identify the multifarious universe and God, by making all the kinds, however numerous and diverse, modes of His attributes. Now, if the question is asked, can a finite mind prove that this circle of attributes revealed in the Scriptures which seem to us to present a God so perfect, so *totus teres et rotundus*, are the only distinct essential attributes His essence has, I shall freely answer, no. By the very reason that the essence is infinite and incomprehensible, it must follow that a finite mind can never know whether He has exhausted the enumeration of the distinct qualities thereof or not, any more than He can fully comprehend one of them. But if it be said that the infinitude of the essence necessitates an infinite number of distinct attributes, I again say, no; for would not one infinite attribute mark the essence as infinite? Man cannot reason here. But the same attribute may exhibit numberless varied acts.

Are the Separate Attributes of Infinite Number?

In most sciences, classification of special objects of study. is of prime importance, for two reasons. The study of resemblances and diversities, on which classification proceeds, aids us in learning the individuals classified more accurately. The objects are so exceedingly numerous, that unless general classes were formed, of which general propositions could be predicated, the memory would be overwhelmed, and the task of science endless. The latter reason has very slight application, in treating God's attributes; because their known number is not great. The former reason applies very fairly. Many classifications have been proposed, of which I will state the chief.

Classification of Attributes.

(a.) The old orthodox classification was into communicable and incommunicable. Thus, omniscence

Into Communicable and Incommunicable. was called a communicable attribute; because God confers on angels and men, not identically His omniscience, or a part of it, but an attribute of knowledge having a likenesss, in its lower degree, to His. His eternity is called an incommunicable attribute, because man has, and can have nothing like it, in any finite measure even. In some of the attributes, as God's independence and self-existence, this distinction may be maintained; but in many others to which it is usually applied, it seems of little accuracy. For instance, God's eternity may be stated as His infinite relation to duration. Man's temporal life is his finite relation to duration, and I see not but the analogy is about as close between this and God's eternity, as between man's little knowledge and His omniscience.

(b.) Another distribution, proposed by others, is into abso-

Into Relative and Absolute. lute and relative. God's immensity, for instance, is His absolute attribute; His omnipresence, His corresponding relative attribute. The distinction happens to be pretty accurate in this case, but it would be impossible to carry it through the whole.

(c.) Another distribution is into natural and moral attri-

Into Natural and Moral. butes; the natural being those which qualify God's being as an infinite spirit merely—e. g., omniscience, power, ubiquity; the moral, being those which qualify Him as a moral being, viz., righteousness, truth, goodness and holiness. This distinction is just and accurate, but the terms are bungling. For God's moral attributes are as truly natural (i. e., original,) as the others.

The distribution into negative and positive, and the Cartesian, into internal (intellect and will) and external, need not be more than mentioned. Dr. Breckinridge has proposed a more numerous classification, into primary, viz: those belonging to God as simply being: essential, viz: these qualifying His being as pure spirit; natural, viz: those constituting Him a free and intelligent spirit; moral, viz: those constituting Him a righteous being; and consummate, being those perfections which belong to Him as the concurrent result of the preceding. The general objection is, that it is too artificial and complicated. It may be remarked, further, that the distinction of primary and essential attributes is unfounded. Common sense would tell us that we cannot know God as being, except as we know Him as spiritual being; and dialectics would say that the consideration of the *essentia* must precede that of the *esse*. Further, the subordinate distribution of attributes under the several heads is confused.

The distribution which I would prefer, would conform

Best Classification. most nearly to that mentioned in the third place, into moral and non-moral. The Westminster Assembly, in this case as in many others, has given us the justest and most scientific view of this arrangement, in its Catechism : " God is a spirit, infinite, eternal and unchangeable, in His being, wisdom, power, holiness, justness, goodness and truth," This recognizes a real ground of distinction, after which the other tentative arrangements I have described, are evidently groping, with a dim and partial apprehension. There is one class of attributes, (wisdom, power, purity, justice, goodness and truth,) specifically and immediately qualifying God's being. There is another class, (infinitude, eternity, immutability,) which collectively qualify all His other attributes and His being, and which may, therefore, be properly called His consummate attributes. God is, then, infinite, eternal and immutable in all His perfections. In a sense, somewhat similar, all His moral attributes may be said to be qualified by the consummate moral attribute, holiness—the crowning glory of the divine character.

3. What we conceive to be the best rational proofs of God's unity and simplicity, were presented in a previous lecture on Natural Theology ; we gave the preference to that from the convergent harmony of creation. Theologians are also accustomed to argue it from the necessity of His excellence (inconclusively,) from His infinitude (more solidly.) But our best proof is the Word, which asserts His exclusive, as well as His numerical unity. Deut. vi: 4; 1st. Kings viii: 60; Is. xliv: 6; Mark xii: 29–32; 1st. Cor. viii: 4; Eph. iv: 6; Gal. iii; 20; 1st. Tim. ii: 5 ; Deut. xxxii: 39; Is. xliii: 10–11 ; xxxvii: 16, &c.

Unity of God.

The spirituality of God we argued rationally, first, from the fact that He is an intelligent and voluntary first cause ; for our understandings are, properly speaking, unable to attribute these qualities to any other than spiritual substance. We found the same conclusion flowed necessarily from the fact, that God is the ultimate source of all force. It is implied in His immensity and omnipresence. He is Spirit, because the fountain of life. This also is confirmed by Scriptures emphatically. (See Deut. iv: 15–18; Ps. cxxxix: 7; Is. xxxi: 3; John iv: 24; 2d. Cor. iii: 17.) This evidence is greatly strengthened by the fact, that not only is the Father, but the divine nature in Christ, and the Holy Ghost, also are called again and again Spirit. (See, for the former, Rom. i: 4; Heb. ix: 14. For the latter, the title Holy Ghost, Πνεῦμα, everywhere in New Testament, and even in Old.) We may add, also, all those passages which declare God, although always most intitimately present, to be beyoud the cognizance of all our senses. (Col. i: 15; 1st. Tim. i: 17; Heb. xi: 27.)

He is a Spirit.

The simplicity of God, theologically defined, is not expressly asserted in the Bible. But it follows as a necessary inference, from His spirituality.

His Simplicity.

Our consciousness compels us to conceive of our own spirits as absolutely simple; because the consciousness is always such, and the whole conscious subject, *ego*, is in each conscious state indivisibly. The very idea of dividing a thought, an emotion, a volition, a sensation, mechanically into parts, is wholly irrelevant to our conception of them; it is impossible. Hence, as God tells us that our spirits were formed in the image of His, and as He has employed this word, Πνεῦμα, to express the nature of His substance, we feel authorized to conceive of it as also simple. But there are still stronger reasons; for (a,) Otherwise God's absolute unity would be lost. (b.) He would not be incapable of change. (c.) He might be disintegrated, and so, destroyed.

We are well aware that many representations occur in Scripture which seem to speak of God as having a material form, (e. g., in the theophanies) and parts, as hands, face, &c., &c. The latter are obviously only representations adapted to our faculties, to set before us the different modes of God's workings. The seeming forms, angelic or human, in which He appeared to the patriarchs, were but the symbols of His presence.

4. The distinction between God's immensity and omnipresence has already been stated. Both are asserted in Scriptures. The former in 1st. Kings viii : 27, and parallel in Chron.; Is. lxvi : 1. The latter in Ps. cxxxix : 7–10; Acts xvii : 27–28; Jer. xxiii : 24; Heb. i : 3. It follows, also, from what is asserted of God's works of creation and providence, and of His infinite knowledge. (See Theol. Lect. 4th.)

Immensity and Omnipresence.

5. God's eternity has already been defined, as an existence absolutely without beginning, without end, and without succession; and the rational evidences thereof have been presented. As to the question, whether God's thoughts and purposes are absolutely unconnected with all successive duration, we saw, when treating this question in Natural Theology, good reason to doubt. The grounds of doubt need not be repeated. But there is a more popular sense, in which the *punctum stans*, may be predicated of the divine existence, that past and future are as distinctly and immutably present with the Divine Mind, as the present. This is probably indicated by the striking phrase, Is. lvii : 15 and more certainly, by Exod. iii : 14, compared with John viii : 58; by Ps. xc : 4, and 2d Peter, iii : 8. That God's being has neither beginning nor end is stated in repeated places—as Gen. xxi : 33; Ps. xc : 1, 2; cii : 26–28; Is. xli : 4; 1st. Tim. i : 17; Heb .i : 12; Rev. i : 8.

Eternity.

That God is immutable in His essence, thoughts, volitions, and all His perfections, has been already argued from His perfection itself, from His in-

6. Immutability.

dependence and sovereignty, from His simplicity and from His blessedness. This unchangeableness not only means that He is devoid of all change, decay, or increase of substance : but that His knowledge, His thoughts and plans, and His moral principles and volitions remain forever the same. This immutability of His knowledge and thoughts flows from their infinitude. For, being complete from eternity, there is nothing new to be added to His knowledge. His nature remaining the same, and the objects present to His mind remaining forever unchanged, it is clear that His active principles and purposes must remain forever in the same state ; because there is nothing new to Him to awaken or provoke new feelings or purposes.

Our Confession says, that God hath neither parts nor passions. That He has something analagous to what are called in man active principles, is manifest, for He wills and acts ; therefore He must feel. But these active principles must not be conceived of as emotions, in the sense of ebbing and flowing accesses of feeling. In other words, they lack that agitation and rush, that change from cold to hot, and hot to cold, which constitute the characteristics of passion in us. They are, in God, an ineffable, fixed, peaceful, unchangeable calm, although the springs of volition. That such principles may be, although incomprehensible to us, we may learn from this fact : That in the wisest and most sanctified creatures, the active principles have least of passion and agitation, and yet they by no means become inefficacious as springs of action—e. g., moral indignation in the holy and wise parent or ruler. That the above conception of the calm immutability of God's active principles is necessary, appears from the following : The agitations of literal passions are incompatible with His blessedness. The objects of those feelings are as fully present to the Divine Mind at one time as another ; so that there is nothing to cause ebb or flow. And that ebb would constitute a change in Him. When, therefore, the Scriptures speak of God as becoming wroth, as repenting, as indulging His fury against His adversaries, in connection with some particular event occurring in time, we must understand them anthropopathically. What is meant is, that the outward manifestations of His active principles were as though these feelings then arose.

God's immutability, as thus defined, is abundantly asserted in Scriptures. (Numb. xxiii : 19 ; Ps. cii : 26 ; xxxiii : 11 ; cx : 4 ; Is. xlvi : 10 ; Mal. iii : 6 ; Jas. 1 : 17 ; Heb. vi : 17 ; xiii : 8.)

This attribute has been supposed to be inconsistent with the incarnation of the Godhead in Christ; Objections Answered. with God's work done in time, and especially His creation ; and with His reconciliation with sinners upon their repentance. To the first, it is enough to reply, that neither was God's substance changed by the incarnation ; for there was no confusion of natures in the person of Christ, nor was His

plan modified ; for He always intended and foresaw it. To the
second, the purpose to create precisely all that is created, was
from eternity to God, and to do it just at the time He did. Had
He not executed that purpose when the set time arrived, there
would have been the change. To the third, I reply, the change
is not in God : but in the sinner. For God to change His treatment as the sinner's character changes, this is precisely what His
immutability dictates.

LECTURE XIV.
DIVINE ATTRIBUTES. — Continued.

SYLLABUS.

1. What is the Scriptural account of God's knowledge and wisdom? What the
meaning of His simple, His free, His mediate knowledge? Does God's free knowledge extend to the future acts of free-agents?

Review of Breckinridge's Theology by the author. Turrettin, Loc. iii, Qu.
12, 13. Dick, Lect. 21, 22. Watson's Theo. Inst., pt. ii, ch. 4 and ch. 28, § 3.
Dr. Chr. Knapp, § xxii.

2. Do the Scriptures teach God to be a voluntary being? What limitation, if
any, on His will? Prove that He is omnipotent. Does God govern free-agents omnipotently?

Turrettin, Loc. iii, Qu. 14, 21, 22. Dick, Lect. 23. Watson, Theo. Inst. pt.
ii, ch. 28, § 3, 4. Knapp, § xxi.

3. What is the distinction between God's decretive and preceptive will? Is it
just? Between His antecedent and consequent will? Are His volitions ever conditioned on anything out of Himself?

Turrettin, Loc. iii, Qu. 15, 16, 17. Knapp, § xxv and xxvi.

4. Is God's will the sole source of moral distinctions?

Turrettin, Loc. iii, Qu. 18.

THE difference between knowledge and wisdom has been
already defined as this : knowledge is the simple cognition
of things ; wisdom is the selecting and subordinating of them to an end, as means. Not
only must there be the power of selecting and
subordinating means to an end, to constitute wisdom : but to a
worthy end. Wisdom, therefore, is a higher attribute than
knowledge, involving especially the moral perfections. For
when one proceeds to the selection of an end, there is choice ;
and the moral element is introduced. Wisdom and knowledge
are the attributes which characterize God as pure mind, as a
being of infinite and essential intelligence. That God's knowledge is vast, we argued from His spirituality, from His creation
of other minds ; (Ps. xciv: 7–10,) from His work of creation in
general, from His omnipresence ; (Ps. cxxxix: 1–12,) and from
His other perfections of power, and (especially) of goodness,
truth and righteousness, to the exercise of which knowledge is
constantly essential. Of His wisdom, the great natural proof is
the wonderful, manifold and beneficent contrivances in His

1. God's Knowledge and Wisdom.

works of creation (Ps. civ:24,) and providence. That God's knowledge is distinct, and in every case intuitive, never deductive, seems to flow from its perfection. We only know substances by their attributes; God must know them in their true substance: because it was His creative wisdom which clothed each substance with its essential qualities. We only learn many things by inference from other things; God knows all things intuitively; because there can be no succession in His knowledge, admitting of the relation of premise and conclusion.

We may show the infinite extent of God's knowledge, by viewing it under several distributions. He perfectly knows Himself. (1 Cor. ii: 11.) He has all the past perfectly before His mind, so that there is no room for any work of recollection. (Is. xli; 22; xliii: 9.) This is also shown by the doctrine of a universal judgment. (Eccl. xii: 14; Luke viii: 17; Rom. ii: 16; iii: 6; xiv: 10; Matt. xii: 36; Ps. lvi: 8; Mal. iii: 16; Rev. xx: 12; Jer. xvii: 1,)

Omniscience.

All the acts and thoughts of all His creatures, which occur in the present, are known to Him as they occur. (Gen. xvi: 13; Prov. xv: 3; Ps. cxlvii: 4 and 5; xxxiv: 15; Zech. iv: 10; Prov. v: 21; Job xxxiv: 22; Luke xii: 6; Heb. iv: 13.) Especially do the Scriptures claim for God a full and perfect knowledge of man's thoughts, feelings and purposes—however concealed in the soul. (Job xxxiv: 21; Ps. cxxxiv: 4; Jer. xvii: 10; Jno. ii: 25; Ps. xliv: 21, &c.)

God also knows, and has always known, all that shall ever occur in the future. (See Is. xiii: 9; Acts xv: 18.) Of this, all God's predictions likewise afford clear evidence. The particularity of God's foreknowledge even of the most minute things, may be seen, well defended. Turrettin, Loc. 3, Qu. 12. § 4–6.

Or, adopting another distribution, we may assert that God knows all the possible and all the actual. It is His knowledge of the former, which is called by the scholastics *scientia simplicis intelligentiæ.* Its object is not that which God has determined to effectuate, (the knowledge of which is called "free" or *scientia visionis;*) but that which His infinite intelligence sees might be effectuated, if He saw fit to will it. (The scholastics call it His knowledge of that which has *essentia,* but not *esse.*) That God has an infinite knowledge of possibles, other than those He purposes to actualize, no one can doubt, who considers the fecundity of this intelligence, as exhibited in His actual works. Can it be, that those works have exhausted all God's conceptions? Further: God's wise selection of means and ends, implies that conceptions existed in the divine mind, other than those He has embodied in creation or act, from among which He chose.

Scientia Simplex. What?

The Formalist Divines of the school of Wolff, (as represented by Stapfer, Bulfinger, &c.,) make much of this distinction between God's knowledge

Theodicea thence.

of the possible and the actual, to build a defence of God's holiness and benevolence, in the permission of evil. Say they; *Scientia simplicis intelligentiæ*, is not free in God. He is impelled by a metaphysical necessity, to conceive of the possible according to truth. It is God's conception which generates its *essentia ;* but about this, God exercises no voluntary, and therefore, no moral act of His nature. God's will is only concerned in bringing the thing out of *posse* into *esse*. But the *esse* changes nothing in the *essentia ;* determines nothing about the quality of the thing actualized. Therefore God's will is not morally responsible for any evil it produces. This pretended argument scarcely needs exposure. It is Realistic in its whole structure. The plain answer is, that the thing or event only in *posse*, is non-existent with all its evils. God's will is certainly concerned in bringing it out of *posse* into *esse*. And unless God is bound by fate, His will therein is free. It is, however, perfectly correct, to say that the object of God's *free* knowledge owes its futurition primarily to His will. Had He not purposed its production, it would never have been produced; for He is sovereign first cause. Now, if He willed it, of course He foreknew it.

This leads us to the oft mooted question: whether acts contingent, and especially those of rational free-agents, are objects of God's *scientia visionis*, or of a *scientia media*. This is said to have been first invented by the Jesuit Molina, in order to sustain their semi-Pelagian doctrine of a self-determining will, and of conditional election. By mediate foreknowledge, they mean a kind intermediate between God's knowledge of the possible (for these acts are possessed of futurition), and the *scientia visionis :* for they suppose the futurition and foreknowledge of it is not the result of God's will, but of the contingent second cause. It is called mediate again: because they suppose God arrives at it, not directly by knowing His own purpose to effect it, but indirectly; by His infinite insight into the manner in which the contingent second cause will act, under given outward circumstances, forseen or produced by God. The existence of such a species of knowledge the Calvinists deny *in toto*. To clear the way for this discussion, I remark:

God knows all acts of free agents with a scientia visionis.

First. That God has a perfect and universal foreknowledge of all the volitions of free-agents. The Scriptures expressly assert it. (Ezek. xi: 5; Is. xlviii: 8; Ps. cxxxix: 3, 4; 1 Sam. xxiii: 12; Jno. xxi: 18; 1 Jno. iii: 20; Acts xv: 18.) It is equally implied in God's attribute of heart-searching knowledge, which He claims for Himself. (Rev. ii: 23, *et passim*.) It is altogether necessary to God's knowledge and control of all the future into which any creature's volition enters as a part of the immediate or remote causation. And this department of the future is so vast, so important in God's government, that if He could not foreknow and control it, He would be one of

the most baffled, confused, and harassed of all beings; and
His government one of perpetual uncertainties, failures, and
partial expedients. Last: God's predictions of such free acts
of His creatures, and His including them in His decrees, in so
many cases, show beyond dispute that He has some certain
way to foreknow them. See every prophecy in Scripture where
human or angelic acts enter. Where the prediction is positive,
and proves true, the foreknowledge must have been certain.
For these reasons, the impiety of early Socinians in denying
God even a universal *scientia media,* is to be utterly repudiated

In discussing the question whether God's foreknowledge
of future acts of free-agents is mediate in
the sense defined, I would beg you to note,
that the theological virus of the proposition,
is in this point: That in such cases, the foreknowledge of the
act precedes the purpose of God as to it. i. e., They say God
purposes, because He forsees it, instead of saying with us, that
He only forsees because He purposes to permit it. Against this
point of the doctrine, Turrettin's argument is just and conclusive.
Of this the sum, abating His unnecessary distinctions, is: (a.)
These acts are either possible, or future, so that it is impossible
to withdraw them from one or the other of the two classes of
God's knowledge, His simple, or His actual. (b.) God cannot
certainly foreknow an act, unless its futurition is certain. If
His foreknowing it made it certain, then His knowledge
involves foreordination. If the connection with the second
cause producing it made it certain, then it does not belong at
all to the class of contingent events ! And the causative connection being certain, when God foreordained the existence of
the second cause, He equally ordained that of the effect. But
there are but the two sources, from which the certainty of its
futurition could have come. (c.) The doctrine would make
God's knowledge and power dependent on contingent acts of
His creatures; thus violating God's perfections and sovereignty.
(d.) God's election of men would have to be in every case
conditioned on His foresight of their conduct, (what semi-
Pelagians are seeking here.) But in one case at least, it is
unconditioned; that of His election of sinners to redemption.
(Rom. ix: 16, &c.)

But in a metaphysical point of view, I cannot but think
that Turrettin has made unnecessary and
erroneous concessions. The future acts of
free agents fall under the class of contingent
effects: i. e., as Turrettin concedes the definition, of effects
such that the cause being in existence, the effect may, or may
not follow.* (He adopts this, to sustain his scholastic doctrine
of immediate physical *concursus:* of which more, when we

Marginal notes: No Scientia Media. Its error.   To God nothing is contingent.

---

* For instance : the dice box being shaken and inverted, the dice may, or may
not fall with their first faces uppermost

treat the doctrine of Providence.) But let me ask : Has this distinction of contingent effects any place at all, in God's mind ? Is it not a distinction relevant only to our ignorance ? An effect is, in some cases, to us contingent ; because our partial blindness prevents our foreseeing precisely what are the present concurring causes, promoting, or preventing, or whether the things supposed to be, are real causes, under the given circumstances. I assert that wherever the causative tie exists at all, its connections with its effect is certain, (metaphysically necessary.) If not, it is no true cause at all. There is, therefore, to God, no such thing, in strictness of speech, as a contingent effect. The contingency, (in popular phrase, uncertainty,) pertains not to the question whether the adequate cause will act certainly, if present ; but whether it is certainly present. To God, therefore, whose knowledge is perfect, there is literally no such thing as a contingent effect. And this is true concerning the acts of free-agents, emphatically ; they are effects. Their second cause is the agent's own desires as acting upon the objective inducements presented by Providence ; the causative connection is certain, in many cases, to our view ; in all cases to God's. Is not this the very doctrine of Turrettin himself, concerning the will ? The acts of free agents, then, arise through second causes.

The true statement of the matter, then, should be this: The objects of God's *scientia visionis*, or free **True Distinction of** knowledge, fall into two great classes : (a.) **this knowledge.** Those which God effectuates *per se*, without any second cause. (b.) Those which He effectuates through their natural second causes. Of the latter, many are physical — e, g., the rearing of vegetables through seeds ; and to the latter belong all natural volitions of free agents, caused by the subjective dispositions of their nature, acting on the objective circumstances of their providential position. Now in all effects which God produces through second causes, His foreknowledge, involving as it does, a fore-ordination, is in a certain sense relative. That is, it embraces those second causes, as means, as well as the effects ordained through them. (And thus it is that " the liberty or contingency of second causes is not taken away, but rather established.") Further, God, purposing to produce a certain effect by means of a given second cause, must, of course, have a thorough knowledge of the nature and power of the cause. That that cause derived that nature from another part or act of God's purpose, surely is no obstacle to this. Here, then, is a proper sense, in which it may be said that God's foresight of a given effect is relative—i. e., through His knowledge of the nature and power and presence of its natural, or second cause. May not relative knowledge be intuitive and positive ? Several of our axioms are truths of relation. Yet, it by no means follows, therefore, as the semi-Pelagian would wish, that such a foreknowledge is antececdent to God's preordination concerning it. Because God, in foreordaining the presence and action of the natural cause, according to His knowledge of its nature, does also efficaciously foreordain the effect.

When, therefore, it is said that God's foreknowledge of the volitions of free-agents is relative in this sense; i. e., through His infinite insight into the way their dispositions will naturally act under given circumstances, placed around them by His intentional providence, the Calvinist should by no means flout it; but accept, under proper limitations. But the term mediate is not accurate, to express this orthodox sense; because it seems to imply derivation subsequent, in the part of God's cognition said to be mediated, from the independent will of the creature. The Calvinist is the very man to accept this view of a relative foreknowledge with consistency. For, on the theory of the semi-Pelagian, such a foreknowledge by insight is impossible; volitions being uncaused, according to them; but on our theory, it is perfectly reasonable, volitions, according to us, being certain, or necessary effects of dispositions. And I repeat, we need not feel any hyper-orthodox fear that this view will infringe the perfection of God's knowledge, or sovereignty, in His foresight of the free acts of His creatures; it is the very way to establish them, and yet leave the creature responsible. For if God is able to foresee that the causative connection, between the second cause and its effect, is certain; then, in decreeing the presence of the cause and the proper external conditions of its action, He also decrees the occurrence of the effect. And, that volitions are not contingent, but certain effects, is the very thing the Calvinist must contend for, if he would be consistent. The history of this controversy on *scientia media* presents another instance of the rule; that usually mischievous errors have in them a certain *modicum* of valuable truth. Without this, they would not have strength in them to run, and do mischief.

God's Relative Knowledge.

We should apprehend no real distinction between God's will and His power; because in our spirits, to will is identical with the putting forth of power; and because Scripture represents all God's working as being done by a simple volition. Ps. xxxiii: 9; Gen. i: 3. That God is a free and voluntary being, we inferred plainly from the selection of contrivances to produce His ends, and of ends to be produced; for these selections are acts of choice. He is Universal Cause, and Spirit. What is volition but a spirit's causation? Of His vast power, the works of creation and providence are sufficient, standing proofs. And the successive displays brought to our knowledge have been so numerous and vast, that there seems to reason herself every prob-

2. God's will and power omnipotent over free agents also.

ability His power is infinite. There must be an inexhaustible reserve, where so much is continually put forth. Finally, were He not omnipotent, He would not be very God. The being, whoever it is, which defies His power would be His rival. The Scriptures also repeatedly assert His omnipotence. See Gen. xvii: 1; Rev. i: 8; Jer. xxvii: 17; Matt. xix: 26; Luke i: 37; Rev. xix: 6; Matt. vi: 13. They say with equal emphasis, that God exercises full sovereignty over free agents, securing the performance by them, and upon them, of all that He pleases, yet consistently with their freedom and responsibility. Dan. iv: 35; Prov. xxi: 1; Ps. lxxvi: 10; Phil. ii: 13; Rom. ix: 19; Eph. i; 11, &c. The same truth is evinced by every prediction in which God has positively foretold what free agents should do; for had He not some way of securing the result, He would not have predicted it positively. Here may be cited the histories of Pharaoh. Exod. iv: 21; vi: 1; of Joseph, Gen. xlv: 7; of the Assyrian king, Is. x: 5–7; of Cyrus, Is. xiv: 1; of Judas, Acts ii: 23, &c., &c. It is objected by those of Pelagian tendencies, that some such instances of control do not prove that God has universal sovereignty over all free agents; for they may be lucky instances, in which God managed to cause them to carry out His will by some expedient. To say nothing of the texts quoted above, it may be answered, that these cases, with others that might be quoted, are too numerous, too remote, and too strong, to be thus accounted for. Further, if God could control one, He can another; there being no different powers to overcome; and there will hardly be a prouder or more stubborn case than that of Pharaoh or Nebuchadnezzar. A parallel answer may be made to the evasion from the argument for God's foreknowledge of man's volitions, from His predictions of them. Once more: if God is not sovereign over free agents, He is of course not sovereign over any events dependent on the volitions of free agents, either simultaneous or previous. But those events make up a vast multitude, and include all the affairs of God's Government which most interest us and concern His providence. If He has not this power, He is, indeed, a poor dependence for the Christian, and prayer for His protection is little worth. The familiar objection will, of course, be suggested, that if God governs men sovereignly, then they are not free agents. The discussion of it will be postponed till we treat of Providence. Enough meantime, to say, that we have indubitable evidence of both; of the one from consciousness, of the other from Scripture and reason. Yet, that these agents were responsible and guilty, see Is. x: 12; Acts i: 25. Their reconciliation may transcend, but does not violate reason—witness the fact that man may often influence his fellow-man so decisively as to be able to count on it, and yet that act be free, and responsible.

We have seen (Natural Theology) that God's omnipotence

is not to be understood, notwithstanding the
Omnipotence does not emphatic assertions of Scripture, that all
to self-contradictions. things are possible with Him, as a power to
do contradictions. It has also been usually said by Theologians that God's will is limited, not only by the necessary contradiction, but by His own perfections. The meaning is correct; the phrase is incorrect. God's will is not limited; for
those perfections as much ensure that He will never wish, as that
He will never do, those incompatible things. He does absolutely all that He wills. But thus explained, the qualification is
fully sustained by Scripture. 2 Tim. ii: 13; Tit. i: 2; Heb.
vi: 18; Jas. 1: 13.

I have argued that God's will is absolutely executed over
all free agents; and yet Scripture is full of
3. Secret and re- declarations that sinful men and devils dis-
vealed will distinguished. obey His will! There must be, therefore, a
distinction between His secret and revealed, His decretive and
preceptive will. All God's will must be, in reality, a single, eternal, immutable act. The distinction, therefore, is one necessitated by our limitation of understanding, and relates only to the
manifestation of the parts of this will to the creature. By
God's decretive will, we mean that will by which He foreordains whatever comes to pass. By His preceptive, that by
which He enjoins on creatures what is right and proper for them
to do. The decretive we also call His secret will: because it is
for the most part (except as disclosed in some predictions and
the effectuation) retained in His own breast. His preceptive we
call His revealed will, because it is published to man for his
guidance. Although this distinction is beset with plausible
quibbles, yet every man is impelled to make it; for otherwise,
either alternative is odious and absurd. Say that God has no
secret decretive will, and purposes just what He commands
and nothing more, and we represent Him as a Being whose desires
are perpetually crossed and baffled: yea, trampled on; the
most harassed, embarrassed, and impotent Being in the universe. Deny the other part of our distinction, and you represent God as acquiescing in all the iniquities done on earth and
in hell. Again, Scripture clearly establishes the distinction.
Witness all the texts already quoted to show that God's sovereignty overrules all the acts of men to His purposes. Add.
Rom. xi: 33, to end: Prov. xvi: 4. See also Deut. xxix; 29.
Special cases are also presented, (the most emphatic possible,)
in which God's decretive will differed from His preceptive
will, as to the same individuals. See Exodus iv: 21–23;
Ezekiel iii: 7, with xviii: 31. These authentic cases offer an
impregnable bulwark against Arminian objections; and prove
that it is not Calvinism, but Inspiration, which teaches the
distinction.

The objections are, that this distinction represents God as

11*

either insincere in His precepts to His crea-
Objections. tures, or else, as having His own volitions at
war among themselves : and that, by making His secret will decretive of sinful acts as well as holy, we represent Him as unholy.   The seeming inconsistency is removed by these considerations.   " God's preceptive will."   In this phrase, the word will
is used in a different sense.   For, in fact, while God wills the
utterance of the precepts, the acts enjoined are not objects of
God's volition, save in the cases where they are actually embraced in His decretive will.   All the purposes which God
carries out by permitting and overruling the evil acts of His
creatures, are infinitely holy and proper for Him to carry out.
It may be right for Him to permit what it would be wrong for
us to do, and therefore wrong for Him to command us to do.
Not only is it righteous and proper for an infinite Sovereign to
withhold from His creatures, in their folly, a part of His infinite and wise designs; but it is absolutely unavoidable; for
their minds being finite, it is impossible to make them comprehend God's infinite plan.   Seeing, then, that He could not give
them His whole immense design as the rule of their conduct,
what rule was it most worthy of His goodness and holiness to
reveal?   Evidently, the moral law, requiring of them what is
righteous and good for them.   There is no insincerity in God's
giving this law, although He may, in a part of the cases, secretly
determine not to give unmerited grace to move men to keep
it.   Remember, also, that if even in these cases men would keep
it, God would not fail to reward them according to His promise.
But God, foreknowing that they would freely choose not to keep
it, for wise reasons determines to leave them to their perverse
choice, and overrule it to His holy designs.   I freely admit that
the divine nature is inscrutable; and that mystery must always
attach to the divine purposes.   But there is a just sense in which
a wise and righteous man might say, that he sincerely wished a
given subject of his would not transgress, and yet that, foreseeing his perversity, he fully purposed to permit it, and carry out
his purposes thereby.   Shall not the same thing be possible for
God in a higher sense?

There is a sense in which some parts of God's will may be
said to be antecedent to, and some parts con-
Antecedent and Con- sequent to His foresight of man's acts—i. e.,
sequent Will. as our finite minds are compelled to conceive
them.   Thus: although God's will acts by one, eternal, comprehensive, simultaneous act, we cannot conceive of His determination to permit man's fall, except as a consequence of His
prior purpose to create man; (because if none were created,
there would be none to fall;) and of His decree to give a Redeemer, as consequent on His foresight of the fall.   But the
Arminian Scholastics have perverted this simple distinction thus,
making the antecedent act of God's will precede the view had

by God of the creature's action ; and the consequent, following upon, and produced by that foresight ; e. g., the purpose to create man was antecedent, to punish his sin consequent. I object: 1st. This notion really violates the unity and eternity of God's volition. 2d. It derogates from the independence of God's will, making it determined by, instead of determining, the creature's conduct. 3d. It overlooks the fact that all the parts of the chain, the means as well as the end, the second causes as well as consequences, are equally and as early determined by, and embraced in, God's comprehensive plan. As to a sequence and dependency between the parts of God's decree, the truth, so far as man's mind is capable of comprehending, seems to be this : That the decree is in fact one, in God's mind, and has no succession ; but we being incapable of apprehending it save by parts, are compelled to conceive God, as having regard in one part of His eternal plan to a state of facts destined by Him to proceed out of another part of it, This remark will have no little importance when we come to view supralapsarianism.

God's purposes are all independent of any condition external to Himself in this sense ; that they are not caused by anything *ab extra*. The things decreed may be conditioned on other parts of His own purpose, in that they embrace means necessary to ends. While the purposes have no cause outside of God, they doubtless all have wise and sufficient reasons, known to God.

God's will absolute.

Some, even of Calvinists, have seemed to find this question very intricate, if we may judge by their differences. Let us discriminate clearly then ; that by God's will here we mean his volition in the specific sense, and not will in the comprehensive sense of the whole conative powers. The question is perspicuously stated in this form. Are the precepts right merely because God commands, or does He command, because they are in themselves right? The latter is the true answer. Let it be understood again ; that God's precepts are, for us, an actual, a perfect, and a supreme rule of right. No Christian disputes this. For God's moral title as our Maker, Owner and Redeemer, with the perfect holiness of His nature, makes it unquestionable, that our rectitude is always in being and doing just what He requires. Let it be understoood again ; that in denying that God's volition to command is the mere and sole first source of right, we do not dream of any superior personal will, earlier than God's and more authoritative than His, instructing and compelling Him to command right. Of course, we repeat, no one holds this ; God is the first, being the eternal authority, and He is absolutely supreme. Does one ask : where, then, did this moral distinction inhere and abide, before God had given any expression to it, in time, in any legislative acts? The answer is : In the eternal principles of His

4. Is God's will the first rule of right?

moral essence, which, like His physical, is self-existent and eternally necessary.

Having cleared the ground, I support my answer thus:
Proofs. 1st. God has an eternal and inalienable moral claim over His moral creatures, not arising out of any legislative act of His, but immediately out of the relation of creature to Creator, and possession to its absolute Owner. For instance: elect angels owed love and honor to God, before He entered into any covenant of works with them. This right is as unavoidable and indestructible as the very relation of Creator and rational creature. This moral dependence is as original as the natural dependence of being. Hence, it is indisputable that there is a moral title more original than any preceptive act of God's will. 2d. We cannot but think that these axioms of ethical principle are as true of God's rectitude as of man's: (a) That God's moral volitions are not uncaused, but have their (subjective) motives. (b) That the morality of the volitions is the morality of their intentions. We must meet the question there, as to God, just as to any rational agent. What is the regulative cause of those right volitions? There is no other answer but this: God's eternally holy dispositions; His necessary moral perfections. Now, then, if a given precept of God is right, His act of will in legislating it must be right, and must have its moral quality. If this act of divine will is such, it must be because its subjective motives have right moral quality. Thus we are, per force, led to recognize moral qualities in something logically prior to the preceptive will of God, viz: in His own moral perfections. 3d. Otherwise, this result must follow, which is an outrage to the practical reason: That God's preceptive will might, conceivably, have been the reverse of what it is, and then the vilest things would have been right, and holiest things vile. 4th. There would be no ground for the distinction between the "perpetual moral" and the "temporary positive" command. All would be merely positive. But again: the practical reason cannot but see a difference between the prohibition of lying, and the prohibition of eating bacon! 5th. No argument could be constructed for the necessity of satisfaction for guilt, in order to righteous pardon; so that (as will be seen) our theory of redemption would be reduced to the level of Socinian error. And, last, God's sovereignty would not be moral. His "might would make His right."

LECTURE XV.
GOD'S MORAL ATTRIBUTES.

WE have now reached that which is the most glorious, and at the same time, the most important class of God's attributes; those which qualify Him as an infinitely perfect moral Being. These are the attributes which regulate His will, and are, therefore, so to speak, His practical perfections. Without these, His infinite presence, power, and wisdom would be rather objects of terror and fear, than of love and trust. Indeed, it is impossible to conceive how the horror of a rational being could be more thoroughly awakened, than by the idea of wicked omnipotence wielding all possible powers for the ruin or promotion of our dearest interests, yet uncontrolled alike by created force, and by moral restraints. The forlorn despair of the wretch who is left alone in the solitude of the ocean, to buffet its innumerable waves, would be a faint shadow of that which would settle over a universe in the hands of such a God. But blessed be His name, He is declared, by His works and word, to be a God of complete moral perfections. And this is the ground on which the Scriptures base their most frequent and strongest claims to the praise and love of His creatures. His power, His knowledge, His wisdom, His immutability are glorious; but the glory and loveliness of His moral attributes excelleth.

Moral attributes God's chief glory.

God's distinct moral attributes may be counted as three — His justice, His goodness, and His truth — these three concurring in His consummate moral attribute, holiness.

Enumeration.

165

God's absolute justice is technically defined by theologians as the general rectitude of character, intrinsic in His own will.   His relative justice is the acting out of that rectitude towards His creatures.   His distributive justice is the quality more precisely indicated when we call Him a just God, which prompts Him to give to every one his due.   His punitive justice is that phase of His distributive justice which prompts Him always to allot its due punishment to sin.   No Christian theologian denies to God the quality of absolute justice, nor of a relative, as far as His general dealings with His creatures go.   We have seen that even reason infers it clearly from the authority of conscience in man; from the instinctive pleasure accompanying well-doing, and pain attached to ill-doing; from the general tendency which God's providence has established, by which virtue usually promotes individual and social well-being, and vice destroys them; and from many providential retributions where crimes are made to become their own avengers.   And Scripture declares His rectitude in too many places and forms, to be disputed.   e. g., Ps. lxxi: 15; Ezra ix: 15; Ps. xix: 9; cxlv: 17; Rev. xvi: 7, &c., &c., Ps. lxxxix: 14; Hab. i: 13.

1. Justice defined.

It is upon the punitive justice of God that the difference arises.   As the establishing of this will establish *a fortiori*, the general righteousness of God's dealings, we shall continue the discussion on this point.   The Socinians deny that retributive justice is an essential or an immutable attribute of God.   They do not, indeed, deny that God punishes sin; nor that it would be right for Him to do so in all cases, if He willed it; but they deny that there is anything in His perfections to ensure His always willing it, as to every sin.   Instead of believing that God's righteous character impels Him unchangeably to show His displeasure against sin in this way, they hold that, in those cases where He wills to punish it, He does it merely for the sinner's reformation, or the good of His government.   The new school of divines also hold that while God's purpose to punish sin is uniform and unchangeable, it is only that this form of prevention against the mischiefs of sin may be diligently employed, for the good of the universe.   They hold that His law is not the expression of His essence, but the invention of His wisdom.   Both these opinions have this in common; that they resolve God's justice into benevolence, or utility.   The principle will be more thoroughly discussed by me in the Senior Course, in connection with the satisfaction of Christ.   I only remark here, that such an account of the divine attribute of justice is attended by all the absurdities which lie against the Utilitarian system of morals among men; and by others.   It is opposed to God's independence, making the creature His end, instead of Himself, and the carrying out of His own perfections.   It

Is God's punitive justice essential? Different theories.

violates our conscience, which teaches us that to inflict judicial suffering on one innocent, for the sake of utility, would be heinous wrong, and that there is in all sin an inherent desert of punishment for its own sake. It resolves righteousness into mere prudence, and right into advantage.

Now Calvinists hold that God is immutably determined by His own eternal and essential justice, to visit every sin with punishment according to its desert. Not indeed that He is constrained, or His free-agency is bound herein; for He is immutably impelled by nothing but His own perfection. Nor do they suppose that the unchangeableness is a blind physical necessity, operating under all circumstances, like gravitation, with a mechanical regularity. It is the perfectly regular operation of a rational perfection, co-existing with His other attributes of mercy, wisdom, &c., and therefore modifying itself according to its object; as much approving, yea, demanding, the pardon of the penitent and believing sinner, for whose sins penal satisfaction is made and applied, as, before, it demanded his punishment. In this sense, then: that God's retributive justice is not a mere expedient of benevolent utility, but a distinct essential attribute, I argue, by the following scriptural proofs: *Affirmative view.*

(a.) Those Scriptures where God is declared to be a just and inflexible judge. Exod. xxxiv : 7; Ps. v: 5; Gen. xviii: 25 ; Ps. xciv: 2 ; 1: 6; Is. 1: 3, 4; Ps. xcvi: 13, &c. *Proved by Scripture.*

(b.) Those Scriptures where God is declared to hate sin. e. g., Ps. vii: 11 ; Ps. v: 4, 6; xlv: 7; Deut. iv: 24; Prov. xi: 20; Jer. xliv : 4; Is. lxi: 8. If the Socinian, or the New England view were correct, God could not be said to hate sin, but only the consequences of it. Now, God has no passions. Drop the human dress, in which this principle is stated; and the least we can make of this fixed hatred of God to sin, is a fixed purpose in Him to treat it as hateful.

(c.) From God's moral law, which is the transcript of His own essential perfections. Of this law, the penal sanction is always an essential part. See Rom. x: 5; Gal. iii: 12; Rom. v: 12; Ex. xx: 7. *By the Law.*

This fixed opposition to sin is necessary to a pure Being. Moral good and evil are the two poles, to which the magnet, rectitude, acts. The same force which makes one pole attract the magnet, makes the other pole repel it. The Northern end of the needle can only seek the North pole, as it repels the Southern. Since sin and holiness in the creature are similar opposites, that moral action by which the right conscience approves the one, is the counterpart of its opposition to the other. It is as preposterous to claim that God's approval of right is essential to His perfection, but His disapproval of wrong, is not; as to tell us of a magnet which infallibly turned

its one end to the North star, but did not certainly turn its
opposite end to the Southern pole. Socinians, like all other
legalists, claim that God's approval of good works is essential
in Him. It should be added, that this essential opposition to
sin, if it exists in God, must needs show itself in regular penal
acts : because He is sovereign and almighty; and He is Supreme
Ruler. If He did not treat sin as obnoxious, His regimen
would tend to confound moral distinction. To all this corres-
ponds the usual picture of God's justice in Scripture, as Rom.
2 : 6–11 ; Prov. xvii : 15.

The ceremonial law equally proves it : for the great object
of all the bloody sacrifices was to hold forth the great theological truth that there is no pardon of the sinner, without the
punishment of the sin in a substitute, Heb. ix : 22.

(d.) The death of Christ, a sinless being who had no guilt
of His own for which to atone. We are told
By Christ's Death. that " our sins were laid upon " Christ; that
" He was made sin," that " He suffered the just for the unjust,"
" that God might be just, and yet the justifier of the ungodly ;"
that "the chastisement of our peace was upon Him," &c. Is.
liii : 5–11 ; Rom. iii : 24–26 ; Gal. iii : 13, 14 ; 1st. Pet. iii : 18,&c.
Now, if Christ only suffered to make a governmental display of
the mischievous consequences of sin, then sin itself was not
punished in Him, and all the sins of the pardoned remain forever
unpunished, in express contradiction to these Scriptures.
Moreover, the transaction at Calvary, instead of being a sub-
lime exhibition of God's righteousness, was only an immoral
farce. And last : not only is God not immutably just, but He
is capable of being positively unjust : in that the only innocent
man since Adam was made to suffer most of all men !

The particular phase of the argument from God's rectoral
justice, or moral relations to the rational
Objection, that Mag-
istrates Pardon. An-
swer. universe as its Ruler, will be considered more
appropriately when we come to the doctrine
of satisfaction; as also, Socinian objections. One of these,
however, has been raised, and is so obvious, that it must be
briefly noted here. It is that the righteousness of magistrates,
parents, masters and teachers, is not incompatible with some
relaxations of punitive justice ; why then, should that of our
Heavenly Father be so, who is infinitely benevolent ; who is
the God of love ? The answer is : that God's government
differs from theirs in three particulars. They are not the
appointed, supreme retributors of crime (Rom. xii : 19), and
their punishments, while founded on retributive justice, are not
chiefly guided by this motive, but by the policy of repressing
sin and promoting order. Second : they are not immutable,
either in fact or profession ; so that when they change their
threats into pardons without satisfaction to the threatening,
their natures are not necessarily dishonored. Third : they

are not omniscient, to know all the motives of the offender, and all the evidences of guilt in doubtful cases, so as to be able exactly to graduate the degree and certainty of guilt. These three differences being allowed for it, it would be as improper for man to pardon without satisfaction, as God.

God's goodness is, to creatures, one of His loveliest attributes; because it is from this that all the happiness which all enjoy flows, as water from a spring. Goodness is the *generic* attribute of which the love of benevolence, grace, pity, mercy, forgiveness, are but specific actings, distinguished by the attitude of their objects, rather than by the intrinsic principle. Goodness is God's infinite will to dispense well-being, in accordance with His other attributes of wisdom, righteousness, &c., and on all orders of His creatures according to their natures and rights. Love is God's active (but passionless) affection, by which He delights in His creatures, and in their well-being, and delights consequently in conferring it. It is usually distinguished into love of complacency, and love of benevolence. The former is a moral emotion, (though in God passionless), being His holy delight in holy qualities in His creatures, co-operating with His simple goodness to them as creatures. The latter is but His goodness manifesting itself, actively. The first loves the holy being on account of his excellence. The second loves the sinner in spite of his wickedness. When the student contrasts such texts as. Ps. vii: 11.; Rom. v: 8, he sees that this distinction must be made. Grace is the exercise of goodness where it is undeserved, as in bestowing assured eternal blessedness on the elect angels, and redemption on hell-deserving man. And because all spiritual and holy qualities in saints are bestowed by God, without desert on their part, they are called also, their graces, χαρίσματα. Pity, or simple compassion, is goodness going forth towards a suffering object, and prompting, of course, to the removal of suffering. Mercy is pity towards one suffering for guilt. But as all the suffering of God's rational creatures is for guilt, His compassion to them is always mercy. All mercy is also grace; but all grace is not mercy.

2. God's Benevolence, &c.

Many theologians (of the Socinian, New England and Universalists schools) overstrain God's goodness, by representing it as His one, universally prevalent moral attribute; in such sense that His justice is but a punitive policy dictated by goodness, His truth but a politic dictate of His benevolence, &c. Their chief reliance for support of this view is on the supposed contrariety of goodness and retributive justice; and on such passages as: "God is love," &c. To the last, the answer is plain: if an exclusive sense must be forced upon such a text, as makes it mean that God has no quality but benevolence, then, when Paul and Moses say: "Our God is a consuming fire," we should

Are all the moral attributes only phases of Goodness?

be taught that He has no quality but justice; and when another says: "God is light," that He is nothing but simple intelligence, without will or character. The interpretation of all must be consistent *inter se*. The supposed incompatibility of goodness and justice, we utterly deny. They are two phases, or aspects, of the same perfect character. God is not good to a certain extent, and then just, for the rest of the way, as it were by patches; but infinitely good and just at once, in all His character and in all His dealings. He would not be truly good if He were not just. The evidence is this very connection between holiness and happiness, so intimate as to give pretext for the confusion of virtue and benevolence among moralists. God's wise goodness, so ineffably harmonized by His own wisdom and holiness, would of itself prompt Him to be divinely just; and His justness, while it does not necessitate, approves His divine goodness.

The rational proofs of God's goodness have been already presented, drawn from the structure of man's sensitive, social and moral nature, and from the adaptations of the material world thereto. (See Natural Theology. Lecture 5.) To this I might add, that the very act of constructing such a creation, where sentient beings are provided, in their several orders, with their respective natural good, bespeaks God a benevolent Being. For, being sufficient unto Himself, it must have been His desire to communicate His own blessedness, which prompted Him to create these recipients of it. Does any one object, that we say He made all for His own glory; and, therefore, His motive was selfish, and not benevolent? I rejoin; What must be the attributes of that Being, who thus considers His own glory as most appropriately illustrated in bestowing enjoyment? The fact that God makes beneficence His glory, proves Him, in the most intrinsic and noble sense, benevolent.

When we approach Scripture, we find goodness, in all its several phases, profusely asserted of God. Ps. cxlv: 8, 9; 1st Jno. iv: 8; Ex. xxxiv: 6; Ps. xxxiii: 5; lii: 1; ciii: 8; xiii: 17; Ps. cxxxvi; Jas. v: 11; 2d. Peter, iii: 15, &c.

But the crowning proof which the Scriptures present of God's goodness, is the redemption of sinners. Rom. v: 8; Jno. iii: 16; 1st. Jno. iii: 1; iv: 10. The enhancements of this amazing display are, first: that man's misery was so entirely self-procured, and the sin which procured it so unspeakably abominable to God's infinite holiness; second: that the misery from which He delivers is so immense and terrible, while the blessedness He confers is so complete, exalted and everlasting; third: that ruined man was to Him so entirely unimportant and unnecessary, and moreover, so trivial and little when compared with God; fourth: that our continued attitude towards Him throughout all this plan of mercy is one of aggravating unthank-

Scriptural proofs of God's Goodness.

Crowning proof from Redemption.

fulness, enmity and rebellion, up to our conversion; fifth: that God should have given such a price for such a wretched and hateful object, as the humiliation of His own Son, and the condescending work of the Holy Ghost; and last: that He should have exerted the highest wisdom known to man in any of the divine counsels, and the noblest energies of divine power, to reconcile His truth and justice with His goodness in man's redemption. Each of these features has been justly made the subject of eloquent illustration. In this argument is the inexhaustible proof for God's goodness. The work of redemption reveals a love, compassion, condescension, so strong, that nothing short of eternity will suffice to comprehend it.

The great standing difficulty concerning the divine goodness has been already briefly considered, in Lect. v, § iv.

3. God's Truth, and Faithfulness,

God's truth may be said to be an attribute which characterizes all God's other moral attributes, and His intellectual. The word truth is so simple as to be, perhaps, undefinable. It may be said to be that which is agreeable to reality of things. God's knowledge is perfectly true; being exactly correspondent with the reality of the objects thereof. His wisdom is true; being unbiased by error of knowledge, prejudice, or passion. His justice is true; judging and acting always according to the real state of character and facts. His goodness is true; being perfectly sincere, and its outgoings exactly according to His own perfect knowledge of the real state of its objects, and His justice. But in a more special sense, God's truth is the attribute which characterizes all His communications to His creatures. When those communications are promissory, or minatory, it is called His faithfulness. This attribute has been manifested through two ways, to man; the testimony of our senses and intelligent faculties, and the testimony of Revelation. If our confidence in God's truth were undermined, the effect would be universally ruinous, Not only would Scripture with all its doctrines, promises, threatenings, precepts, and predictions, become worthless, but the basis of all confidence in our own faculties would be undermined; and universal skepticism would arrest all action. Man could neither believe his fellow-man, nor his own experience, nor senses, nor reason, nor conscience, nor consciousness, if he could not believe his God.

Evidences of it, from Reason.

The evidences of God's truth and truthfulness are two-fold. We find that He deals truly in the informations which He has ordained our own senses and faculties to give us, whenever they are legitimately used. The grounds upon which we believe them have been briefly reviewed in my remarks upon metaphysical skepticism. God has so formed our minds that we cannot but take for granted the legitimate informations of our senses, consciousness, and intuitions. But this unavoidable trust is abundantly confirmed by subsequent experiences. The testimonies of one sense, for instance, are always confirmed by those of the others, when they are applied ; e. g., when the eye tells us a given object is present, the touch, if applied, confirms it. The expectations raised by our intuitive reason, as e. g., that like causes will produce like effects, are always verified by the occurrence of the expected phenomena. Thus a continual process is going on, like the "proving" of a result in arithmetic. Either the seemingly true informations of our senses are really true, or the harmonious coherency of the set of errors which they assert is perfectly miraculous.

The second class of proofs is that of Scripture.   Truth and faithfulness are often predicated of God in the most unqualified terms.   2 Cor. i: 18 ;
From Scripture.
Rev. iii : 7; vi : 10; xv : 3 ; xvi : 7; Deut. vii : 9; Heb. x : 23; Titus i : 2.

All the statements and doctrines of Scripture, so far as they come within the scope of man's consciousness and intuitions, are seen to be infallibly true ; as, for instance, that "the carnal mind is enmity against God ;" that we "go astray as soon as we be born, speaking lies," &c., &c.   Again, Scripture presents us with a multitude of specific evidences of His truth and faithfulness, in the promises, threatenings, and predictions, which are contained there ; for all have been fulfilled, so far as ripened.

The supposed exceptions, where threats have been left unfulfilled, as that of Jonah against Nineveh, are of very easy solution.   A condition was always either implied or expressed, on which the execution of the threat was suspended.

The apparent insincerity of God's offers of mercy, and commands of obedience and penitence, held forth to those to whom He secretly intended to give no grace to comply, offers a more plausible objection.   But it has been virtually exploded by what was said upon the secret and decretive, as distinguished from the revealed and preceptive will of God.   I shall return to it again more particularly when I come to treat of effectual calling.

When places, Mount Zion, utensils, oils, meats, altars, days, &c., are called holy, the obvious meaning is, that they are consecrated—
4. God's Holiness.
i. e., set apart to the religious service of God.   This idea is also prominent, when God's priests, prophets, and professed people, are called holy.   But when applied to God, the word is most evidently not used in a ceremonial, but a spiritual sense.   Most frequently it seems to express the general idea of His moral purity, as Levit. xi : 44; Ps. cxlv : 17; 1 Pet. i : 15, 16; sometimes it seems to express rather the idea of His majesty, not exclusive of His moral perfections, but inclusive also of His power, knowledge and wisdom, as in Ps. xxii : 3; xcviii : 1 ; Is. vi : 3; Rev. iv : 8.   Holiness, therefore, is to be

regarded, not as a distinct attribute, but as the resultant of all God's moral attributes together   And as His justice, goodness, and truth are all predicated of Him as a Being of intellect and will, and would be wholly irrelevant to anything unintelligent and involuntary, so His holiness implies a reference to the same attributes.   His moral attributes are the special crown; His intelligence and will are the brow that wears it.   His holiness is the collective and consummate glory of His nature as an infinite, morally pure, active, and intelligent Spirit.

We have now gone around the august circle of the Divine attributes, so far as they are known to us.   In another sense I may say that the summation of them leads us to God's other consummate attribute—His infinitude.   This is an idea which can only be defined negatively. We mean by it that God's being and attributes are wholly without bounds.   Some divines, indeed, of modern schools, would deny that we mean anything by the term, asserting that infinitude is an idea which the human mind cannot have at all.   They employ Sir W. Hamilton's well known argument that " the finite mind cannot think the unconditioned; because to think it is to limit it."   It has always seemed to me that the plain truth on this subject is, that man's mind does apprehend the idea of infinitude, (else whence the word ?) but that it cannot comprehend it.*   It knows that there is the infinite; it cannot fully know what it is.   God is absolutely without bound, as to His substance, (immense,) as to His duration, (eternal,) as to His knowledge, (omniscience,) as to His will, (omnipotence,) as to His moral perfections, (holiness.)   It is an infinite essence.

5. God's Infinity.

One of the consequences which flows from these perfections of God in His absolute sovereignty, which in so often asserted of Him in Scripture; e. g., Dan. iv: 35; Rev. xix: 16; Rom. ix: 15–23; 1 Tim. vi: 15; Rev. iv: 11.   By this we do not mean a power to do everything, as e. g., to punish an innocent creature, contradictory to God's own perfections; but a righteous title to do everything, and control every creature, unconstrained by anything outside His own will, but always in harmony with His own voluntary perfections.   When we call it a righteous title, we mean that it is not only a *δύναμις*, but an *ἐξουσία*, not only a physical *potentia*, but a moral *potestas*.   The foundations of this righteous authority are, first, God's infinite perfections; second, His creation of all His creatures out of nothing; and third, His preservation and blessing of them.   This sovereignty, of course, carries with it the correlative duty of implicit obedience on our part.

Supremacy.

But second: Another consequence which flows from the infinite perfections of God is that He is entitled not only to dis-

* See. on this point, my work on the Sensualistic Philosophy of the 19th Century; Chap. X Schuyler'. Logic—Last Part.

pose of us and our services, for His own glory, but to receive our supreme, sincere affections. Just in degree as the hearts of His intelligent creatures are right, will they admire, revere, and love God, above all creatures, singly or collectively.

LECTURE XVI.

THE TRINITY.

SYLLABUS.

1. Explain the origin and meaning of the terms, Trinity, Essence, Substance Subsistence, Person, ὁμοούσιον.
> Turrettin, Loc, iii, Qu. 23. Hill's Divin., bk. iii. ch. 10, § 2, 3. Knapp, § 42, 3; 43, 2. Dick, Lect. 28. Dr. W. Cunningham, Hist. Theol. ch. 9, § 2.

2. Give the history of opinions touching the Trinity; and especially the Patripassian, Sabbellian and Arian.
> Knapp, § 42 and 43. Hill, bk. iii, ch. 10. Dick, Lect. 29. Hagenback, Hist. of Doc. Mosheim, Com. de Reb. ante Constantinum, Vol. i, § 68, Vol. ii § 32 and 33. Dr. W. Cunningham, Hist. Theol., ch. 9, § 1.

3. Define the doctrine of the Trinity, as held by the orthodox: and state the propositions included in it.
> Turrettin, Loc. iii, Qu. 25, 1–3, § and Qu. 27. Hill and Dick, as above. Jno. Howe, "Calm and Sober Inquiry Concerning Possibility of a Trinity."

4. What rationalistic explanations of the doctrine were attempted by the Origenists; and what by the mediæval scholastics? Are they of any value?
> Th. Aquinas, *Summa*. Hill, as above. Neander, Ch. Hist., 2 Am. Edit., Boston, Vol. ii, p. 360, &c., Vol. iv, 457, &c. Mosheim, Com., Vol. ii, § 27 and 31. Knapp, § 42. Watson, Theol. Inst., pt. ii, ch. 8, i (i.) 2.

5. Present the general Bible evidence of a Trinity, from the Old Testament and from the New.
> Turrettin, Loc. iii. Qu. 25 and 26. Dick, Lect. 28. Knapp, § 34, 35.

WHILE a part of the terms introduced by the Scholastics to define this doctrine are useful, others of them illustrate in a striking manner the disposition to sub-

1. Nomenclature.

stitute words for ideas, and to cheat themselves into the belief that they had extended the latter, by inventing the former.   The Greek Fathers, like the theologians of our country, usually make no distinction between essence, and substance, representing both by the word οὐσία, being. But the Latin Scholastics make a distinction between *essentia*, *esse*, and *substantia*.   By the first, they mean that which constitutes the substance, the kind of thing it is: or its nature, if it be a thing created.   By the second, they mean the state of being in existence.   By the third, they mean the subject itself, which exists, and to which the essence belongs.   Subsistence differs from substance, as mode differs from that of which it is the mode.   To call a thing substance only affirms that it is an existing thing.   Its subsistence marks the mode in which it exists.   e. g., matter and spirit are both substances of different kinds.   But they subsist very differently.   The infinite spirit exists as a simple, indivisible substance; but it subsists as three persons. Such is perhaps the most intelligible account of the use of these two terms; but the pupil will see, if he analyses his own ideas, that they help him to no nearer or clearer affirmative conception of the personal distinction.

The word Person, πρόσωπον *persona*, (sometimes ὑπόστασις in the later Greek), means more than the Latin idea, of a *role* sustained for the time being; but less than the popular modern sense, in which it is employed as equivalent to individual. Its meaning will be more fully defined below. ʽΟμοουσιος means of identical substance. The Greek Fathers also employed the word ἐμπεριχώρησις, intercomprehension, to signify that the personal distinction implied no separation of substance. But, on the contrary, there is the most intimate mutual embracing of each in each; what we should call, were the substance material, an interpenetration.

The subsistence of the three persons in the Godhead was the earliest subject of general schism in the primitive Church. To pass over the primitive Gnostic and Manichæan sects, three tendencies, or schools of opinion, may be marked in the earlier ages; and in all subsequent times, the Orthodox, or Trinitarian, the Monarchian, and the Arian. The first will be expounded in its place. The tendency of mind prompting both the others may be said to be the same, and indeed, the same which has prevailed ever since, viz: a desire to evade the inscrutable mystery of three in one, by so explaining the second and third persons, as to reach an absolute unity both of person and substance, for the self-existent God. (μόνη ἀρχή.) Hence, it may justly be said that Arianism, and even Socinianism, are as truly monarchian theories, as that of Noëtus, to whom the title was considered as most appropriate.

2. Three tendencies of Opinion on Trinity.

Noëtus, an obscure clergyman, (if a clergyman) of Smyrna, is said to have founded a sect on the doctrine, that there is only one substance and person in the Godhead; that the names, Father, Son, and Holy Ghost, are nothing but names for certain phases of action or *roles*, which God successively assumes. Christ was the one person, the Godhead or Father, united to a holy man, Jesus, by a proper Hypostatic union. The Holy Ghost is still this same person, the Father, acting His part as revealer and sanctifier. Hence, it is literally true, that the Father suffered, i. e., in that qualified sense in which the Godhead was concerned in the sufferings experienced by the humanity, in the Mediatorial Person. This theory, while doing violence to Scripture, and deranging our theology in many respects, is less fatal by far, than that of Arians and Socinians: because it retains the proper divinity of the Messiah and of the Holy Ghost.

Patripassian.

The Sabellian theory (broached by Sabellius, of Pentap-

Sabellian.

olis in Lybia Cyrenaica, about A. D. 268,) has been by some represented as though it were hardly distinguishable from the Patripassian; and as though he made the names, Father, Son, and Holy Ghost the mere titles of three modes of action which the one Godhead successively assumes. By others it has been represented as only a sort of high Socinianism, as though he had taught that the Holy Ghost was an influence emanating from the Godhead, and Christ was a holy man upon whom a similar influence had been projected. But Mosheim has shown, I think, in his *Com. de Rebus*, &c., that both are incorrect, and that the theory of Sabellius was even more abstruse than either of these. The term which he seems to have employed was that the Father, Son, and Holy Ghost are three forms (σχήματα) of the Godhead, which presented real portions of His substance, extended into them, as it were, by a sort of spiritual division. Thus, the Son and Holy Ghost are not parts of the Father; but all three are parts, or forms, of a more recondite godhead. According to this scheme, therefore, the Son and Holy Ghost are precisely as divine as the Father; but it will appear to the attentive student very questionable, whether the true godhead of all three be not vitiated.

Arian.

The theory of Arius is so fully stated, and well known, that though more important, it needs few words. He represents the Son, prior to His incarnation, as an infinitely exalted creature, produced (or generated) by God out of nothing, endued with the nearest possible approximation to His own perfections, adopted into sonship, clothed with a sort of deputized divinity, and employed by God as His glorious agent in all His works of creation and redemption. The Holy Ghost is merely a κτίσμα κτισμάτος produced by the Son.

Error tends either to obliterate or widen personal distinctions.

Now, it has been well stated by Dr. Hill, that there can be but three schemes in substance: the orthodox, the Patripassian, and the Subordinationist. All attempts to devise some other path, have merged themselves virtually into one or the other of these errors. Either the personal distinctions are obliterated, or they are so widened as to make the Son another and an inferior substance. Now, the refutation of the latter schemes will be sufficiently accomplished if we succeed (in the next Lecture) in establishing the proper divinity, and identity of substance of the Son.

Patripassian scheme refuted.

The refutation of the former class of theories is effected by showing that some true and definite distinction of persons is predicated in Scripture of the Father, Son and Holy Ghost. It will appear in so many places, asserted in so many forms, so intertwined with the very woof of the Scriptures, that its denial does fatal violence to the integrity of their language. (a.) I point to those numerous passages, where one Person is said to act upon, or act through, another. See, e. g., Exod. xxiii: 20; Ps. ii: 6, cx.; Is. xlii: 1; liii: 12; Jno. xv: 26; xx: 21, &c., &c., where God the Father is said to send, to enthrone, to appoint to sacerdotal office, to uphold, to reward the Son, and the Son and Father to send the Holy Ghost. (b.) Consider those, in which mutual principles of affection are said to subsist between the persons. Is. xlii: 1; Jno. x: 17, 18, &c., &c. (c) There is a multitude of other passages, where voluntary principles and volitions are said to be exercised by the several persons as such, towards inferior and external objects. Exod. xxxiii: 21. (The subject is the Messiah, as will be proved.) Eph. iv: 30, Rev. vi: 16, &c., &c. Yet, since these principles are all perfectly harmonious, as respects the three persons, there is no dissension of will, breach in unity of council, or difference of perfections. (d) There is a still larger multitude of texts, which assert of the persons as such, actions and agencies toward inferior, external objects. See, for instance, Jno. v: 19; I Cor. xii: 11, &c., &c. Now, if these personal names, of Father, Son, and Holy Ghost, meant no more than three influences or energies, or three phases of action of the same person, or three forms of one substance, is it not incredible that all these properties of personality, choosing, loving, hating, sending and being sent, understanding, acting, should be asserted of them? It would be the wildest abuse of language ever dreamed of.

The doctrine of the Trinity, as held by the Catholic Church, cannot be better defined, than in the words of our Confession. (Recite ch. II, § 3.) It embraces the following propositions:

3. Definition of Trinity.

1. The true unity, indivisibility, and simplicity of God.

2. The subsistence of a threefold personal distinction, marked by a part of the properties of separate personalities, (in some inscrutable manner, entirely compatible with true unity) as intelligence, active principles, volition, action.

3. Identity of substance, so that the whole godhead is truly in each person, without confusion or division, and all the essence belongs alike to all the persons.

4. The distinction of the three persons, each by its property, incommunicable from one person to another, and the existence consequently of eternal relations between them.

Now, that it is inscrutable how these things can be, we freely admit. Did they involve a necessary self-contradiction, we should also admit that the understanding would be incapable of receiving them all together. But we do not hold that the persons are three in the same sense in which they are one. If it be asked what is the precise meaning of the phrase, person in the

Inscrutable; but not impossible.

12*

Godhead? we very freely answer, that we know only in part.
You will observe that all the Socinian and Rationalist objections mentioned in your text-books against this doctrine, either
proceed on the misrepresentation, that we make three equal to
one, (as in the notorious Socinian formula ; let a. b. c. represent the persons, and x. the Godhead ; then a=x : b=x : c=x.
Add, and we have a+b+c=3 x=x,) in the same sense : or
they are *argumenta ad ignorantiam*. But is it not just we should
expect, that when God reveals something about the subsistence
of His being, it should be thoroughly inscrutable to us? We
must remember that the human mind has no cognizance of substance, in fact, except as the existing ground, to which our intuitions impel us to refer properties. It is only the properties
that we truly conceive. This is true of material substance ;
how much more true of spiritual substance ? And more yet of
the infinite ? God, in revealing Himself to the natural reason,
only reveals His being and properties or attributes—His substance remains as invisible as ever. Look back, I pray you, to
that whole knowledge of God which we have acquired thus far,
and you will see that it is nothing but a knowledge of attributes. Of the substance to which these properties are referred,
we have only learned that it is. What it is, remains impenetrable to us. We have named it simple spirit, But is this, after
all, more than a name, and the affirmation of an unknown fact
to our understandings ? For, when we proceed to examine our
own conception of spirit, we find that it is a negation of material attributes only. Our very attempts to conceive of it, (even
formed after we have laid down this as our prime feature of it,
that it is the antithesis of matter,) in its substance, are still obstructed by an inability to get out of a materialistic circle of
notions. We name it *Πνεῦμα, spiritus*, breath ; as though it
were only a gaseous and transparent form of matter ; and only
differed thus from the solid and opaque. This obstinate, materialistic limit of our conceptions arises, I suppose, from the fact,
that conceptions usually arise from perceptions, and these are
only of sensible, i. e., of material ideas. This obstinate incapacity of our minds may be further illustrated by asking ourselves : What is really our conception of God's immensity ?
When we attempt the answer do we not detect ourselves always
framing the notion of a transparent body extended beyond
assignable limits ? Nothing more ! Yet, reason compels us to
hold that God's substance is not extended at all, neither as a
vast solid, nor a measureless ocean of liquid, nor an immense
volume of hydrogen gas expanded beyond limit. Extension,
in all these forms, is a property wholly irrelevant to spirit.
Again : (and this is most in point,) every Socinian objection
which has any plausibility in it, involves this idea ; that a trinity
of Persons must involve a division of God's substance into
three parts. But we know that divisibility is not a property of

spirit at all—the idea is wholly irrelevant to it, belonging only to matter.

The Socinian would say here : " Precisely so ; and hence we reason against the impossibility of a trinity in unity. If divisibility is totally irrelevant to infinite Spirit, then it is indivisible, and so, can admit no trinity."

Objections all Materialistic.

Inspect this carefully, and you will find that it is merely a verbal fallacy. The Socinian cheats himself with the notion that he knows something here, of the divine substance, which he does not know. By indivisible here, he would have us understand the mechanical power of utterly resisting division, like that imputed to an atom of matter. But has Spirit this material property ? This is still to move in the charmed circle of material conceptions. The true idea is, not that the divine substance is materially *atomic ;* but that the whole idea of parts and separation is irrelevant to its substance, in both a negative and affirmative sense. To say that Spirit is indivisible, in that material sense, is as false as to say that it is divisible. Thus the stock argument of the Socinian against the possibility of a trinity is found to be a fallacy ; and it is but another instance of our incompetency to comprehend the real substance of spirit, and of the confusion which always attends our efforts to do so. We cannot disprove here, by our own reasonings, any more than we can prove ; for the subject is beyond our cognition.

I pray the student to bear in mind, that I am not here attempting to explain the Trinity, but just the contrary : I am endeavoring to convince him that it cannot be explained. (And because it cannot be explained, it cannot be rationally rebutted.) I would show him that we must reasonably expect to find the doctrine inexplicable, and to leave it so. I wish to show him that all our difficulties on this doctrine arise from the vain conceit that we comprehend something of the subsistence of God's substance, when, in fact, we only apprehend something. Could men be made to see that they comprehend nothing, all the supposed impossibilities would vanish ; there would remain a profound and majestic mystery.

The mint from which every attempted *rationale* of the Trinity has come, was the New Platonic ; and the chief *media* of their introduction to the Christian Theology, Clem. Alexandrinus and Origen. Following the trinitarian scheme which the New Platonists attributed (with insufficient grounds) to Plato, of *To Ὄν, Νοῦς* and *Ψυχή,* they usually represent God the Father as the intelligent substance, intrinsically and eternally active, the *Νοῦς,* as the idea of self, generated from eternity by God's self-intellection ; and the *Ψυχή,* as the active complacency arising upon it. The Platonizing fathers, who called themselves orthodox, were not slow to fling the charge of *monarchianism (Μονή Ἀρχή)*

4. Rational Explanation of Greek Scholastics.

against all Patripassians, which I make against the Arians also, as reaching by diverse roads, an assertion of a single divine person. The modern student will be apt to think that their rationalism betrays the very same tendency; an unwillingness to bow the intellect to the dense mystery of a real and proper three in one; and an attempt to evade it by perpetually destroying the personality of the second and third persons.

This attempted explanation appears with new completeness and fullness, after the Peripatetics had modi-

Of Aquinas.

fied the Platonic System, in the Latin Scholastics. Thomas Aquinas, for instance, states the matter about thus: Infinite activity of thought is the very essence of the Divine substance. But from eternity there was but a two-fold object of thought for this intellect to act on—God's self, and His decree. Now, as man is made intellectually in God's image, we cannot conceive of God's thinking, except by conceiving of our own acts of thought as the finite type of which His is the infinite antitype. Now, when man thinks, or conceives, it is only by means of a species of image of that which is the object of his thought, present before his mind. So, God's very act of thinking of Himself and His decree generates in the divine mind, a species of them; it generates them eternally; because God is eternally and necessarily active in thinking. This species or idea is therefore eternal as God, yet generated by God, it is of the same essence, for it is non-corporeal, spiritual entity, and God's essence is pure intellection. It is one with God; for it is God's idea of Himself, and His own eternal purpose which is Himself purposing. This is the Λόγος, the 2d Person. Again, as in our souls, so in God, the presence of a moral object in conception awakens moral sentiment, and of a plan or device, approval or disapproval; so, God's contemplation of this idea of Himself and His decree, begets a moral complacency, and a volition to effectuate (when the fullness of time shall have come) the decree. This complacency and volition are the Spirit, the 3d or practical Person of the Godhead, proceeding from the Father and the Idea, or Λόγος.

This *rationale* we cannot but regard as worthless, though ingenious. *First:* The Scriptures inform us

Objections to it.

in advance, that God is inscrutable; and that we need not expect to explain His subsistence. Job ii: 7. *Second:* According to this explanation, both the Νοῦς and the Ψυχή would be compounded, the former of the two species of God's being and of His decree; the latter of two feelings, His moral self-complacency and His volition to effectuate His decree. *Third:* Neither the 2d nor 3d persons would be substance at all, but mere idea and feeling, which have no entity whatever, except as affections of the substance of the Father. This seems to our minds an objection so obvious and conclusive, that no doubt the student is almost incredulous that acute men should have seriously advanced a theory obnoxious to it. The answer is, that the Platonic and Peripatetic metaphysics ignored, in a manner astonishing to the modern christian mind, the distinction between substance and affections. Between the two kinds of entity, they drew no generic distinction. But is this not one of the very traits of modern, transcendental Idealism, from Spinoza down? *Fourth :* On this scheme of a trinity, I see not how the conclusion could be avoided, that every intelligent free agent is as much a finite trinity in unity as God is an infinite one. Let us then attempt no explanation where explanation is impossible.

Having thus defined the doctrine, we proceed to its proof.

5. Proof of Trinity wholly of Revelation. That the evidence for the Trinity must be wholly a matter of revelation, would appear sufficiently from the weakness of the attempt made by the Scholastics, to find some proof or presumptive probability in the light of reason. The most plausible of these, perhaps, is that which Neander informs us, Raymund Lulley employed against the Unitarian Moslems of Barbary, which is not discarded even by the great Aquinas and the modern Christlieb. They say God is immutable from eternity. He exists now in a state of active benevolence. Hence, there must have always been, from eternity, some sense in which God had an object of His benevolence, in some measure extraneous; else active benevolence would have been impossible ; and the result would be, that the creation of the angels (or earliest holy creatures) would have constituted an era of change in God. The reasoning appears unsound by this simple test. God is now actively righteous and punitive, as well as good; and a parallel argument will prove, therefore, with equal conclusiveness, the eternity of a devil. The solution of the sophism is to be found in those remarks by which we defended God's immutability against the objection, that the creation of the universe constituted a change in God. It does not; because God's purpose to create, when His chosen time should have come, was unchangeably present with him from eternity. Creation makes the change in the creature; not in God. The argument would be more plausible, if left in its undeveloped form viz : That an eternal absolute solitude was incompatible with absolute blessedness and perfection. Yet the answer is, that we cannot know this to be true of any infinite essence.

The Scripture evidence for a Trinity presents itself in two forms. The most extensive and conclusive General Direct Proofs. may be called the indirect and inferential proof, which consists in these two facts when collated : 1st, That God is one. 2d, That not only the Father, but the Son and Holy Ghost, are proper God. This evidence presents itself very extensively over the Bible ; and the two propositions may be said to be intertwined with its whole woof and warp.   The other testimony is the general direct testimony, where a plurality in the one God is either stated, or involved in some direct statement.   The latter evidence is the one we present now : the former will become evident as we present the proof of the Divinity of the 2d and 3d Persons.

The text-books assigned to the students, present a collection and discussion of those passages so complete, that I shall not make an unnecessary recapitulation.   I shall only set down a list of those passages which I consider relevant ; and conclude with a few cursive remarks on the argument in a few points. The student, then, may solidly advance the following testimonies, as cited and expounded by the Books.

From the Old Testament :

Gen. i : 2, with Ps. civ : 30 : Prov. viii : 22, &c.

Gen. i : 26 : iii : 22 : xi : 7 ; Is. vi : 8,

Numb. vi : 24–26, may have some feeble weight when collated with Is. vi : 3, and 2 Cor. xiii : 14.

Hosea i : 7 ; Isaiah lxiii : 7–14, and Ps. xlv : 6.

The argument from the plural forms אֲדֹנִים, אֱלֹהִים, it seems to me ought to be surrendered after the objections of Calvin and Buxtorff.

In the New Testament a very clear argument arises from the formula of Baptism.   Matt. xxviii : 19.   The only objection of any plausibility, is that from 1 Cor. x : 2—"Baptized unto Moses."   In addition to the answers of Turrettin, it is surely sufficient to say, that this is a very different case from that where the names of the 2d. and 3d. persons are connected with that of God the Father in the same sentence and same construction.

Another indisputable argument is derived from the Apostolic benediction.   2 Cor. xiii : 14.   See also Rev. i : 4, 5 : 1 Cor. xii : 4–6.

The argument from the baptism of Christ seems to me possessed of some force, when the meaning of the Father's avowal and of the Spirit's descent are understood in the light of Scripture.

The much litigated passage in 1 John v : 7, is certainly of too doubtful genuineness to be advanced, polemically, against the adversaries of the Trinity : however, we may believe that the tenour of its teaching is agreeable to that of the Scriptures elsewhere.

LECTURE XVII.
DIVINITY OF CHRIST.

THIS may be called a prime article of revealed theolgy; affecting not only the subsistence of the Godhead, but the

A Prime Article. question whether Christ is to be trusted, obeyed and worshiped as God, the nature and efficacy of His atoning offices, the constitution of the Church, and all its rites. He who believes in the divinity of Jesus Christ is a Christian; he who does not, (whatever his profession), is a mere Deist. Without His Divinity, the Bible is, " the drama of Hamlet, with the part of Hamlet omitted."

We have already established a Trinity of persons in the

Argued Scripturally under five Heads. Godhead; and this alone, if validly proved, would show the divinity of Jesus Christ. For where else in Revelation, than in the persons of Him and the Holy Ghost, can the other persons be so naturally and plausibly found? But not to urge this: the general strain of the language of the Old and New Testaments produces an overwhelming impression, that they mean to represent the Messiah as divine. Note the contrast between their descriptions of Him and of Moses, the greatest of men; the fact that Jews have almost uniformly understood the New Testament as inculcating it, and thus rejected it as idolatrous; the laborious evasions to which Socinians are obliged to resort; and the fact that the great majority of both friends and enemies have so understood it. If the Apostles did not intend to teach this doctrine they have certainly had the remarkable ill-luck of producing the very impression which they should have avoided, especially in a Book intended to subvert idolatry.

There is, as has been intimated, a general testimony for this truth, interwoven with the whole texture of Scripture, which cannot be adequately presented in a few propositions, because of its extent.   It can only be appreciated by the extended and familiar study of the whole Bible.   But the more specific arguments for the divinity of Jesus Christ have usually been digested into the five heads: of His Pre-existence, Names, Attributes, Works and Worship.   This distribution is suffi-ciently correct.   My purpose will be, to employ the very limited space I can allot to so extensive an argument, first in giving you a syllabus of it, which shall possess some degree of com-pleteness ; and second, in illustrating some of the more important testimonies, so as to exhibit, in a few instances, the manner in which they apply, and exegetical evasions are to be met.

If Jesus Christ had an existence before he was born of the

1. Christ's pre-exis-
tence.

virgin, this at once settles the question, as Hill remarks, that He is not mere man.   And if this pre-existence was characterized by eter-nity, independence, or divine works of Creation and Providence, it further settles the question that He was not a creature.   The theophanies of a second person of the Godhead, if revealed in the Old Testament, (and if that person can be identified with Jesus Christ), as well as His works of creation, if ascribed to Him, will be parts of this argument for His pre-existence, as well as fall under other heads.

But we find a more direct testimony for His pre-existence contained in a number of passages, where Christ is said to have been " sent " to have " come from heaven," to " come into the world," to be " made flesh," &c, &c.   See John iii : 31 ; vi : 38; xvi : 28; xiii : 3 ; vi : 62 ; 1 John iv : 23; John i : 14; Heb. ii : 7. 9, 14, 16.   Of one of us, it may be popularly said that we came into existence, came into the world ; but those phrases could not be used with propriety, of one who then only began to exist.

Consult also, John i : 1–17, 15, 30; iii ; 13 : viii : 58;   xvii 5 ; 1 Cor. xv : 47 ; 2 Cor viii : 9 : Heb. i : 10, 11 ; Rev. i : 8, 17; ii : 8; iii : 14.

John i : &c.—In the passage, from John i : 1–17, only two evasions seem to have a show of plausibility : 1st, to deny the personality of the Λόγος; 2d, to deny that His pre-existence is taught in the phrase, ἐν ἀρχῇ.   But the first is refuted by show-ing that the Λόγος is the creator of all;   that in verse 4, He is identified with the Φῶς, which Φῶς again, verses 6, 7, was the object of John Baptist's preparatory ministry; which Φῶς again was rejected by the world, verses 10, 11 ; and this Φῶς, identi-cal with the Λόγος, was incarnate, (verse 14), was testified unto by John Baptist, (verse 15); and is finally identified, (verse 17), with Jesus Christ, the giver of grace and truth. That the phrase ἐν ἀρχῇ does assert His pre-existence is proved by the resem-blance of it to the Septuagint rendering of Gen. i : 1.   By the author's use of ἦν, instead of ἐγένετο, by His association with God, verse 2, showing a pre-existence similar to God's; by His creation of all things, (verse 3), and by the utter folly of the gloss which would make the Evangelist say that Jesus Christ was in existence when His ministry began. That John should have used the the peculiar philosophic titles, Λόγος and Φῶς, for Jesus Christ, is most reasonably explained by the state of opinion and theological language when He wrote His gospel. The Chaldean Paraphrase, and the Platonizing tendencies of Philo and his sect, had familiarized the speculative Jews to these terms, as expressive of the second person; and meantime, the impious speculations of Judazing Gnostics, represented by Cerinthus, had attempted to identify Jesus Christ with one of the Αειωνες of their dreams, a sort of luminous emanation of the divine intelligence. It was to vindicate the truth from this folly, that St. John adopts the words Λόγος and Φῶς in this emphatic assertion of the Messiah's proper divinity. See also 1 John i: 1; Rev. xix: 13.

That the Messiah was to be human, was so clearly revealed in the Old Testament, that no Jew misunderstood it. He was to be the Son of David according to the flesh. It may seem somewhat incompatible with a similar disclosure of His proper divinity, that the Jewish mind should have been so obstinately closed to that doctrine. But the evidences of it in the Old Testament are so strong, that we are compelled to account for the failure of the unbelieving Jews to embrace it, by the stubbornness of prejudice, and death in sin. The Messianic predictions of the Old Testament have formed the subject by themselves, of large volumes; I can, therefore, do little more than enumerate the most conclusive of them as to His divinity, giving the preference, of course, to those of them which are interpreted of, and applied to, Jesus Christ, by the infallible exposition of the New Testament. Compare, then, Num. xiv: 22, and xxi: 5, 6, and Ps. xcv: 9, with 1 Cor. x: 9. The tempting of the Lord of the Old Testament, is described by Paul as tempting Christ; in consequence of which they were destroyed of serpents. Ps. cii: 26, ascribes to God an immutable eternity; but Heb. 1: 10, 11, applies it to Jesus Christ. In Is. vi, the prophet sees a vision of Jehovah, surrounded with every circumstance of divine majesty. But Jno. xii: 41, explains: "These things said Esaias, when he saw His glory, and spake of Him." Is. xlv: 22, 23; Jehovah says: "Look unto me, and be ye saved, all ye ends of the earth; but Rom. xiv: 11, and 1 Cor. i: 30, evidently apply the context to Jesus Christ. Thus, also, compare Ps. lxviii: 18, with Eph. iv: 8, 9; Joel ii: 32, with Rom. x: 13; Is. vii: 14, with Matt. i: 22, 23; Micah. v: 2, with Matt. ii: 6, and Mal. iii: 1, with Mark i: 2, and Luke 1: 76. The last three pairs of references contain a proof

2. Divinity of Christ in Old Testament.

peculiarly striking.   In Is. vii: 14, the child born of a virgin is
to be named 'God with us.'   In Matt. i: 22, 23, a child, Jesus
Christ, is born of a virgin, and receives, by divine injunction,
through the mouth of an angel, the name 'God with us;' because
He was conceived of the Holy Ghost, and was to save His people from their sins.   In Micah. v: 2, Bethlehem is destined to
the honor of bringing forth the Ruler whose attribute was
eternity; in Matt. ii: 6, it is declared that this prediction is
fulfilled by the appearance of Jesus Christ.   In Mal. iii: 1, the
Angel of the Covenant is foretold.   He is identified with Jesus
Christ by his forerunner, John, who is expressly declared to be
the person here predicted, by Luke i: 76.   But that this Angel
is divine, is clear from his propriety in the temple (his temple)
which is God's house, and from the divine functions of Judge
and heart-Searcher, which He there exercises.   In Ps. cx: 1,
David calls the Messiah אֲדֹנִי though his descendant according to the flesh.   In Matt. xxii: 45, Christ Himself applies this
to the Messiah ("What think ye of Christ?   Whose Son is
He?") and challenges them (in substance) to account for it
without granting His divinity.   And this 110th Psalm, then
proceeds to ascribe to this Being eternity of priesthood, (v. 4,)
as expounded in Heb. vii: 3, as having "neither beginning of
days, nor end of life," supreme authority, and judgment over
mankind.   The Ps. ii, describes God as setting His King upon
His holy hill of Zion: who is declared to be His eternal Son, (v.
7,) the Ruler of the whole earth, (v. 8,) the sovereign avenger of
His opponents, (v. 9,) and the appointed object of religious
trust.   Surely these are divine attributes.   Compare Jer. xvii:
5.   But Acts iv: 25–28, attribute the whole prediction to Jesus
Christ.   So Ps. xlv: 6, calls the king God, אֱלֹהִים and attributes
to Him an everlasting throne.   But Heb. i: 8, applies these
words to the Son, afterwards defined to be Jesus Christ.   So
let the student compare for himself, (for time will fail me to go
into explanation of every text,) Zech. xii: 10, with John xix:
37, Is. lxi: 1; (Speaker calls Himself I, the LORD, v. 8,) with
Luke iv: 18–21.   Examine, also, Is. iv: 2; ix: 5, 6, 7; xi: 4,
10; Ps. lxxii: 17, 5; Dan. vii: 13, 14.   Zech. chap. xiii: 7,
compared with xi: 13; xii: 10; Jer. xxiii: 5, 6.   Ps. xcvii: 7,
with Heb. i: 6.

   But a second important class of Old Testament evidences
Argument from the   for the divinity of Christ, will appear when
theophanies and An- we inquire who was the Person who appeared
gel of Covenant.   in the theophanies granted to the Patriarchs.
A personal distinction by which God the Father might disclose
Himself to man in another person than His own, seems to be
indicated by His nature.   He is called the invisible God.   1
Tim. i: 17; Heb. xi: 27.   It is declared that no man can see
Him and live.   Exod. xxxiii: 20; and we read, in the cases of

some of the theophanies, that the persons favoured with them were amazed at their surviving the fearful privilege. Gen. xxxii: 30; Judges vi: 22, 23. But besides this concealed Person, who, though everywhere present, rarely makes Himself cognizable, and never visible to mortals, the New Testament, especially, informs us of another Person, the same in essence, whose office it has ever been, since God had a Church, to act as the mediating Messenger and Teacher of that Church, and bring man into providential and gracious relations with the inaccessible God. This function Christ has performed, both before and since His incarnation; and thus He is the Word, the Light, the visible Image to man of the invisible Godhead. See Jno. xiv: 8, 9; i: 18; 1 Jno. i: 1, 2; 2 Cor. iv: 4; Heb. i: 3.

Yet this distinction cannot be pushed so far as though the Father never communicates with men, as the 1st person. Some of the very places cited to prove the divinity of the Son, show the Father as such, testifying to the Son. Ps. ii, and cx. And in Exod. xxiii: 20; xxxii: 34, language is used by a person, concerning another person, under the title of angel, which cannot possibly be identified as a single person, yet both are divine. It would be a great error, therefore, and would throw this whole argument into confusion, to exclude Jehovah the Father wholly from these communications to Old Testament saints, and attribute all the messages to the Son immediately. It so happens that Moses received these theophanies, in which we are compelled to admit the personal presence of the 1st person *per se*, as well as the 2d. May not this be the explanation, that He was honoured to be the Μεσίτης of the Old Testament Church, in a sense in which no other mere man ever was: in that He communicated directly with the person of the Father: Exod. xxxii: 11; Numb. xii: 6–8; Deut. xxxiv: 10. Did not Jehovah Christ speak face to face to Jacob, Abraham, Manoah, &c.?

Another seeming difficulty presents itself (said to have been urged with confidence by St. Augustine and other Fathers) from Heb. i: 1, 2, and ii: 2, 3. The Apostle, it is urged, seems here to teach, that the Old Testament was distinguished from the New, by being not communicated through God, (the Son,) but through creatures, as agents. I answer, if the texts be strained into this meaning, they will then contradict the context. For the theophanies and other immediate divine communications must be imputed to a divine person, the Father, if not the Son; and then there would be no basis, on their premises, for the Apostle's argument, that the New Testament was more authoritative, because the teaching of a divine minister. The truth is, that the Apostle's contrast is only this: In the Old Testament, the Messiah did not appear as an incarnate prophet, ministering His own message ordinarily and publickly among the people. (His

Augustine's difficulty.

theophanic teachings were usually private to some one human agent.) In the New Testament, He did. Nor can it be supposed that The Angel of Jehovah, who presented these theophanies, is explained by the δἰ ἀγγέλων of Heb. ii: 2. He was wholly a different Being; their ministry was only attendant, and co-operative, at Sinai. (See Stephen, Acts vii: 53; Ps. lxviii: 17.)

The 2d person seems to be identified in the following

Instances of theoph-anies. places: Gen. xvi: 7, the Angel of Jehovah found Hagar—v. 10, He promises to exert divine power—v. 11, claims to have heard her distress; and v. 13, Hagar is surprised that she survives the Divine vision. Gen. xviii, three men visit Abraham identified, xix: 1, as angels. The chief angel of these three, in xviii: 1, 14, 17, &c., makes Himself known as Jehovah, receives Abraham's worship, &c. And in Gen. xlviii: 15, 16, this Jehovah is called by Jacob, "the Angel which redeemed me from all evil," &c., and invoked to bless Joseph's sons, a divine function. Again, in Gen. xxi: 17, The Angel of God speaks to Hagar, promising her, v. 18, a divine exertion of power. In Gen. xxii: 1, אֱלוֹהִים commands Abraham to take his son Isaac and sacrifice him. v. 11, when in the act of doing it, the Angel of Jehovah arrests, and says, v. 13, "Thou hast not withheld thy son from me;" and, v. 14, Abraham names the place Jehovah jireh. In Gen. xxxi: 11, the Angel of Jehovah appears to Jacob in a dream, identified in v. 13, with God, the God of Gen. xxviii: 11–22, the God of Bethel then declared Jehovah. In Gen. xxxii: 25, Jacob wrestles with an angel, seeks his blessing, and names the place, v. 30, *Peniel.* This Angel is in the narrative called Elohim, and Hosea xii: 4–6, describing the same transaction, Elohim, Angel and Jehovah of Hosts. In the same method compare Exod. iii: 2, with vs. 4, 6, 14–16; Exod. xiv: 19, with v. 24; Exod. xxiii: 20, with subsequent verse; Exod. xxxii: 34; v: 13 to vi: 2, with xxxiii: 3, 4, 14, 15; Numb. xxii: 22, with vs. 32–35; Josh. v. 13, to vi: 2; Judges ii: 1–4. Compare Judges vi: 11, with vs. 14, 15, 18, 21, 22, &c. Judges xiii: 3, with vs. 21, 22. And Is. lxiii: 9; Zech. i: 12–15, compare vi: 15. Compare Zech. iii: 2, with v. 1; Ps. xxxiv: 7; xxxv: 5.

Now, the amount of what has been proved in these cita-

Conclusions. tions is, that two Persons, both having unquestionable divine attributes, yet sometimes employing the incommunicable name in common, appear on the stage. They are distinguished by unquestioned personal distinctions of willing, acting, feeling, One is the Sender, the other is the Sent. (מַלְאָךְ) The one usually acts with a certain reserve and invisibility the other is called the "Angel of His countenance." Is. lxiii: 9. Compare with Col. i: 15;

Heb. i: 3. To this latter the phrase, Angel of Jehovah is so often applied, that it becomes at length a proper name. And the completing link of the evidence is given by Mal. iii: 1–3, and Isaiah xl: 3. The forerunner is predicted in the latter of these places, as a "voice of him that crieth in the wilderness, prepare ye the way of Jehovah," &c. Malachi teaches that a forerunner was to precede, when the Lord whom the Jews were expecting, even the Angel of the Covenant, would suddenly come to His temple. And this Being is clearly shown to be divine, by his proprietorship in the temple, and the sovereign judicial functions he would perform there. But now, when we look into the New Testament, we find, that the forerunner was John the Baptist, and the person introduced was our Lord Jesus Christ. See Matt. 11: 10; Mark 1: 2: Luke 1: 76, and vii: 27. Jesus Christ was, therefore, the Angel of the Covenant, the owner of the Temple, the Jehovah of Isaiah, xl: 3, 5, whose glory John was to usher in. Thus, these theophanies not only disclose a personal distinction in the Godhead, but show the pre-existence and divinity of Christ.

For objections and theories of evasion, see Hengstenberg.

The argument from the application of the divine names to Jesus Christ has been in part anticipated under the last head. To comprehend its full force, the student must recall the evidences by which we showed that Jehovah, especially, was God's incommunicable name. But in the New Testament this is not characteristically rendered, except by Κύριος, which stands also for Adonai, and Adoni, (the latter applied to human masters). Hence, it may be supposed that the Socinian evasion will be more damaging to all the argument from the cases in which the New Testament applies the terms Κύριος Θεος to Jesus Christ. That evasion, as you know, is, that the titles, God, Lord, are applied in Bible language to Magnates, Magistrates, and Angels; and, therefore, their application to Jesus Christ proves not His proper divinity, but only His dignity. But let it be borne in mind, that if the language of the New Testament is deficient in the power of distinguishing the communicable from the incommunicable titles of God, it also lacks the usage of applying His titles to exalted creatures. There is no example of such a thing in the New Testament, except those quoted from the Septuagint. Hence, when the New Testament calls Christ Lord and God, the conclusion is fair, that it attributes to Him proper divinity.

3. Names of God given to Christ.

But we argue, first, He is also called God's Son; and to show that this means more than when Angels, Church-members, &c., are called sons of God, He is called the beloved Son—God's own Son—God's only-begotten Son. See Ps. ii: 7; Matt. iii: 17; xvii: 5; Dan. iii: 25; Matt. iv: 3; xxvi: 63; xxvii: 43, 54; Luke i: 35; Jno.

Son.

iii: 18; x: 36; ix: 35 to 37; Rev. ii: 18; of v. 8.   Here He is called Son, because He can work miracles, because begotten by the Holy Ghost.   His title of Son is conceived by His enemies as a claim of proper divinity, which He dies rather than repudiate.   The attempts to evade the force of the title Only-begotten seem peculiarly impotent.   One is, that He is so called, although only a man, because conceived, without natural father, by the Holy Ghost.   Adam was still more so, having had neither natural father nor mother.   Yet he is never called only-begotten.   Another is, that Christ is Son, because of His commission and inspiration.   In this sense, Moses, Elijah, &c., were generically the same.   But see Heb. iii : 1–6.   The third is, that He is called God's only-begotten Son, because He enjoyed the privilege of a resurrection.   But the dead man of 2 Kings xiii: 21, the son of the Shunemite, and the saints who arose when Christ died, enjoyed the privilege earlier; and Enoch and Elijah enjoyed one still more glorious, a translation.

For the arguments which rebut the Socinian evasions on this head, the student must, for the rest, be referred to text Books and Comments.   The following proof-texts will be found justly applicable:

Jno. i: 1, 2; x: 30; xx : 31; Acts xx: 28; (somewhat doubtful,) Rom. ix : 5 ; 1 Tim. iii : 16; Phil. ii: 6; Heb. i: 8; 1 Jno. v: 20.

By the application of a principle of criticism asserted by Dr. Granville Sharpe and Dr. Wordsworth, Texts added by Dr. Middleton. of the English Church, and afterwards subjected to a most searching test, by Dr. Middleton on the Greek Article, this list of divine names applied to Jesus Christ, may be much enlarged.   Dr. Middleton thus states it: " When two or more attributives (i. e., adjectives, participles, descriptive substantives) joined by a copulative or copulatives, are assumed of the same person or thing, before the first attributive, the article is inserted, before the remaining ones omitted: e. g., Plutarch : Ροσκιος, ὁ ὑιος και κληρόνομος του τεθνήκοτος, where ὑιος and κληρόνομος describe the one person Roscius. (Proper nouns, abstract nouns, and simple names of substances without descriptive connotation, are exempted from this rule).   Its correctness is sustained by its consistent *rationale*, founded on the nature of the Article, by a multitude of classical examples, and by the manner in which the Greek Fathers uniformly cite the passages in question from the New Testament.   They are to be presumed to be best acquainted with their own idiom.   For instance, Eph. v : 5, we have ἐν τῇ βασιλείᾳ του Χριστου και Θεου.   Instead of rendering " Kingdom of Christ and of God," we should read, Kingdom of Him who is Christ and God.   In Titus ii : 13, του μεγάλου Θεου και Σωτῆρος ἡμῶν 'Ιησου Χριστου. is rendered " of the great God and (of) our Saviour Jesus Christ." It should be " of our great God and Saviour, Jesus Christ."

Winer, (Gram. N. T. Greek. Article § 19, 5,) impugns this conclusion, as countenanced by Tholuck and other eminent Germans. His grounds are, that in Titus ii: 13 Σωτῆρος is sufficiently defined by the possessive genitive ἡμῶν, so that, although anarthrous, it may stand for a separate object; and second, that it is inconsistent with Paul's doctrinal system to call Christ the "great God." To the last point we reply, that it is not a grammatical one, (as Winer admits); but a doctrinal hypothesis: and an erroneous one. Witness Rom. ix: 5. To advance such a surmise in exegesis of Paul is begging the question. The emptiness of the first ground is shown by a comparison of 2 Pet. i: 1. There, when the writer would separate Christ from the Father as an object of thought, he uses not only the genitive, but the article: ἐν ἐπιγνώσει τοῦ Θεοῦ καὶ Ἰησοῦ τοῦ κυρίου ἡμῶν. Compare also, Jude 4th, end.

4. Attributes. The names of God may not be incommunicable, and the application of them might possibly be ambiguous therefore; but when we see the incommunicable attributes of God given to Jesus Christ, they compose a more irresistible proof that He is very God. This is especially strong when those qualities which God reserves to Himself alone, are ascribed to Jesus Christ. We find, then:

Eternity clearly ascribed to Christ in Ps. cii: 26, as interpreted in Heb. i: 11, 12; Prov. viii: 23, &c. Is. ix: 6; Micah v: 2; Jno. i: 2; 1 Jno. i: 2; Rev. i: 7, 8, 17; iii: 14; xxii: 13; and the last three employ the very phraseology in which God asserts His eternity in Is. xiii: 10, and xliv: 6.

Immutability, the kindred attribute, and necessary corollary of eternity. Ps. cii: 26, as before; Heb. xiii: 8.

Immensity and omnipresence. Matt. xviii: 20; xxviii: 20; Jno. iii: 13: Col. i: 17.

Omniscience. Matt. xi: 27; Jno. ii: 24, 25; Heb. iv: 12, 13; Luke vi; 8; Jno. xvi; 30; xxi: 17; Rev. ii: 23, compared with 1 Kings viii: 39; Jer. xvii: 10. Here Christ knows the most inscrutable of all Beings, God Himself; and the human heart, which God claims it as His peculiar power to fathom.

Sovereignty and power. Jno. v: 17; Matt. xxviii: 18, Heb. i: 3; Rev. i: 8; xi: 15–17. And, in fine, see Col. ii: 9; i: 19. The last subdivision will suggest the next head of argument, that from His divine works. But upon the whole, it may be remarked that these ascriptions of divine attributes to Christ leave no evasion. For it is in the nature of things simply impossible that a finite nature should receive infinite endowments. Even Omnipotence cannot make a part to contain the whole.

5. Works. Divine works are ascribed to Christ. Hill, with an affectation of philosophic fairness, which he sometimes carries to an unnecessary length, seems to yield the point to the Arians, in part: that as God has

endued His different orders of creatures with degrees of power so exceedingly various, He may have given to this exalted creature powers which, to man, appear actually boundless; and that even the proposition, that God might enable him to create a world, by filling him with His mighty power, does not appear necessarily absurd. But it seems clear, that there is a limit plain and distinct between those things which finite and dependent power can, by a vast extension, be enabled to do : and those for which all measures of created power are alike incompetent. There are many things which are superhuman, which perhaps are not superangelic. Satan may perhaps have power to move an atmospheric storm, before which man and his mightiest works would be as stubble. But Satan is as unable to create a fly out of nothing, as is man. For the performance of this kind of works, by deputation, no increase of finite power can prepare a creature. Moreover, to create a world such as ours, to direct it by a controlling providence, to judge its rational inhabitants, so as to apportion to every man according to his works; all this implies the possession of omnipresence, infinite knowledge, memory, and attention, as impossible for a creature to exercise, as infinite power. But, however, this may be, Scripture always ascribes creation to God as a divine work. This is done, first, in many express passages, as Jer. x : 10–12 : Ps. xcv : civ; Rev. iv : 10, 11; and second, by all those passages, as Ps. xix : 1–7, in which we are directed to read the greatness and character of God in the works of creation. If He used some other rational agent in the work, why is Creator so emphatically His title? And why are we so often referred to His works to learn His attributes? And once more, the most noted passages, as Jno. i : 1–3, in which creation is ascribed to the Son, contain most emphatic assertions of His partaking of the divine essence; so that it is plain the divinity of the work was in the writer's mind.

The space allotted to this argument will forbid my going into the Socinian evasions of the several texts, tortuous and varied as they are. The most important of them may be seen handled with great skill by Dr. Hill, Bk. iii, ch. 3 and 4. But we clearly find the following divine works ascribed to Jesus Christ :

Creation of the world. Prov. viii : 23, 27, &c.; Jno. i : 1–3; Col. i : 15–17; Heb. i : 1, 3, 10. And along with this, may be mentioned his sustentation of all things, asserted in the same passages.

Miracles, performed, not by deputed, but by autocratic power. Jno. v; 21; vi : 40; Acts iv : 7, 10; ix : 34; cf. Jno. v : 36; Mark ii : 8–11. Jno. ii : 19; x : 18: Rom. i : 4.

Forgiving sin. Mark ii : 10.

Judging men and angels. Matt. xxv; 31, 32; 2 Cor. v : 10; Rom. xiv : 10; Acts xvii : 31; Jno. v : 22. True, it is said that the Twelve shall sit on twelve thrones, judging the twelve tribes of Israel: Matt. xiv: 28, and that the saints shall judge angels; but other Scriptures explain this, that they shall be merely assessors of Jesus Christ.

Last. The peculiar worship of God is given to Christ. See

6. Worship. Matt. xxviii: 19; Luke xxiv: 52; Jno. v: 23; Acts vii: 59, 60; Jno. xiv: 1; and Ps. 12, compared with Jer. xvii: 5; Acts x: 25, 26; 1 Cor. i: Phil. ii: 10; Heb, i: 6; Rev. i: 5, 6; vii: 10; v: 13.

In connection, weigh these passages, as showing how unlikely the Scripture would be to permit such worship, (or Christ Himself,) if He were not proper God. Is. xlii: 8; Matt. iv: 16; or Luke iv: 8; Mark xii: 29; Acts xiv: 14, 15; Rev. xix: 10; xxii: 9. Remember that the great object of Scripture is to reclaim the world from idolatry.

The Arian and Socinian evasions are well stated and refuted by Hill, Bk. iii, ch. 7, § 3.

LECTURE XVIII.

DIVINITY OF THE HOLY GHOST, AND OF THE SON.

SYLLABUS.

1. What is the doctrine of the Socinians, the Arians and the Orthodox concerning the Holy Ghost? See
   See Hagenback, Hist. of Doctr. on Arianism. Hill, bk. iii, ch. 9. Turrettin, Loc. iii, Qu. 30. Dr. Wm. Cunninghnm, Hist. Theol. ch. 9, § 4.
2. Prove the personality of the Holy Ghost.
   Turrettin, Loc. iii, Qu. 30, § 1-11. Owen on the Holy Ghost, bk. i, ch's 2, 3. Dick, Lect. 33. Hill, as above. Dwight's Theol. Sermon 70th. Knapp, § 39.
3. Prove from the Scriptures the Divinity of this Person.
   Turrettin, Loc. iii, Qu. 30, § 12, end. Dick, Hill and Dwight as above. Knapp, § 40.
4. State the controversy between the Greek and Latin Churches, on the Procession of the Holy Ghost. Which party is right? Why?
   Turrettin, Loc. iii, Qu. 31. Dick and Hill as above.
5. Show how the offices of the 2nd and 3d Persons in redemption imply the possession of proper divinity by them.
   Turrettin, Loc. iii, Qu. 24; Loc. xiii, Qu. 3. Dick, Lect. 32. Hill, bk. ii, ch. 8, end. Anselm, *Cur Deus Homo?*

THE Arian controversy was so fiercely agitated concerning the divinity of the 2d. Person that the 3d. Person was almost overlooked in it, by both

1. History of Doctrine of Holy Ghost. parties. It is stated that Arius held the Holy Ghost to be a person—but a creature —the first creature namely, which the Son brought into existence by the Father's instruction, after His own creation. He was thus, χτίσμα χτίσματος. On the other hand, few, perhaps, of the orthodox, except Athanasius, saw clearly the necessity of extending to Him likewise the same essence, (ὁμοουσίον,) with the

13*

Father; and attributing to Him in the work of Redemption, proper, divine attributes. The most of them, e. g., a great anti-Arian writer, Hilary of Poictiers, contented themselves with saying that He was a Person, and was spoken of in the Scriptures as a divine Spirit, and God's beneficent Agent in sanctification; but, farther than this, the Scriptures did not bear Him out. A little after the middle of the 4th century, Macedonius, primate of Constantinople, was led, by his semi-Arian views, to teach that the Holy Ghost was but a name for the divine power and influences, diffused from the Father through the Son. It was this error, along with others, occasioned the revisal of the Nicene Creed by the second Œcumenical Council, that of Constantinople. Yet even this, while attributing to the Holy Ghost a procession from the Father, and the same worship and glory attributed to the Father and Son, and while calling Him Life-giving Lord, still did not expressly ascribe to Him the phrase ὁμοούσιον τῳ Πατρί. The consubstantial divinity of the Holy Ghost, however, continued to be the practical doctrine of the Church Catholic. When the Socinians, in the 16th century, sought to overthrow the doctrine of the Trinity, they represented all that is said of the Holy Ghost as mere parallel locutions for the Godhead itself, or as impersonations of the power, energy, wisdom, or general influence of the Godhead on created souls. The words Holy Ghost, then, are, with them, the name, not of a Person, but of an abstraction.

Hence, the first task which we should assume, is to learn **2. His Personality.** what the Scriptures teach concerning the personality of this Being. We may premise, with Dick, that it is natural and reasonable that the Scriptures would say less to evince the personality and divinity of the Holy Ghost than of the Son; because in the order of the divine manifestation in Redemption, the Son is naturally and properly revealed first. The purchase precedes the application of Redemption. But after a plurality in unity was once established, it was easy to admit a trinity.

Now, we may freely admit that in several places, represented by Ps. cxxxix: 7, the word Spirit is a mere parallelism to express God's self. We may freely admit that were there no passages, except those in which the Holy Ghost is said to be be shed forth, as in Is. xxxii: 15, it would not be proved that it might not mean only God's influences. But there are many others which admit of no such explanation. (a) A number of personal acts are attributed to the Holy Ghost, as creation. Gen. i: 2; Ps. civ: 30, the generation of Christ's body and soul. Matt. i: 18; Luke i: 35. Teaching and revealing. John xiv: 26; xv: 25, 26; Gal. iv: 6; Rom. viii: 16; 1 Tim. iv: 1; 1 Pet. i: 11; 2 Peter i: 21; Is. xi: 2, 3. To search the decree of God, 1 Cor ii: 10. To set apart to the ministry, Is. lxi: 1; Acts xiii: 2; xx: 28. To intercede(παράκλητος) John xvi: 7; Rom. viii: 27.

To have volitions, 1 Cor. xii: 11.   To regenerate and sanctify, John iii: 6; 2 Cor. iii: 6; Eph. ii: 22, &c.   Add here, as show-ing the personal agencies of the Holy Ghost, Luke xii: 12; Acts v: 32: xv: 28; xvi: 6; xxviii: 25; Rom. xv: 16; 1 Cor. ii: 13; Heb. ii: 4; iii: 7.

(b) The Holy Ghost is said to exercise the active feelings of a person; to be tempted, Acts v: 9; to be vexed, Is. lxiii: 10; to be grieved, Eph. iv: 30.

But here we must meet the well known evasion of the Socinian, who pleads that these are but **No prosopopoeia here.** instances of the trope of Impersonation, like those of Rom. vii: 11; iii: 19; 1 Cor. xiii: 7; Gen. iv: 10; Heb. xii: 24.   We will not plead with Turrettin, that the explanation is inapplicable to the Holy Ghost; because impersonations are usually of things corporeal and inanimate, as when the blood of Abel cried, &c; for the case of 1 Cor. xiii: 7, proves that the Scripture does not limit the figure to this class of objects, but sometimes impersonates abstractions.   The true answers are, that the Socinian explanation is inapplicable, (1) because no candid writer uses an impersonation, without placing something in his context, or afterwards dropping the figure, so as to show unmistakably to the reader, that he meant only an impersonation.   The force of this is only seen when the reader gathers the multitude of places in the Scriptures, where such language prevails, speaking of the Holy Ghost as though He were a person; and when he finds the utter absence of the proper qualification.   (2) The explanation is impossible, because in a multitude of places the Holy Ghost is distinguished from the Godhead, whose impersonated attribute He would be on this supposition; e, g., when it is said, "charity suffereth long and is kind," the only possible meaning is, that the charitable man does so.   When it is said God's Spirit will guide us into all truth, if the figure of impersonation were there, the meaning would be, that God, who is spiritual, will guide us.   But in that very passage the spirit that guides is distinguished from God. "Whatsoever he shall hear, (i. e., from the Father and Son,) that shall he speak."   This leads us to argue:

(c) That the Holy Ghost must be a Person, because dis-tinguished so clearly from the Father, whose quality or influ-ence He would be, if He were an abstraction; and farther, because distinguished in some places alike from the Father and Son; e. g., He is sent by both.   John xiv: 16; xv: 26; xvi: 7. The $\pi\nu\varepsilon\tilde{\nu}\mu\alpha$, though neuter, is constructed with the masculine pronouns.   John xvi: 13; Eph. i: 13, 14.   He concurs with the Father and Son, in acts or honors which are to them undoubtedly personal: and hence, to Him likewise.   Matt. xxviii: 19; 2 Cor. xiii: 14.

(d) His presence is represented by visible symbols, a thing which is never done for a mere abstraction elsewhere in Script-

ure, and is, indeed, logically preposterous. For the propriety
of the material symbol depends wholly on some metaphorical
resemblance between the accidents of the matter, and the attributes of the Being symbolized; e. g., Shekinah represents God.
Its brightness represents His glory. Its purity—His holiness. Its
fierce heat—His jealousy, &c., &c. Now, if the dove, Matt. iii:
16, and the fiery tongue, Acts ii : 3, symbolize the Holy Ghost,
and He an abstraction, the analogy has to be sought between the
accidents or qualities of the dove and the fire, and the attributes
of an abstraction! (*Quid rides.*) But moreover, in Matt. iii : 16,
the three persons all attest their presence at once—the Father, in
His voice from heaven; the Son, in His human person; the Spirit,
in the descending dove. Here, surely, the dove does not personate an abstract attribute of the Father or Son, for this would be
to personate them as possessing that attribute. But they, at the
moment, had their distinct personal representations.

(e) The personality of the Holy Ghost is most plainly implied in the act of sinning against Him, committed by Ananias.
Acts v : 3. Israel, Is. lxiii : 10; the Pharisees, Matt. xii : 31, 32.
Some one may say: that I Tim. vi : 1, speaks of the sin of
blasphemy against God's word and doctrine. Such an explan-
ation is impossible in the above cases, and especially in Matt.
xii: 31, 32. For if the Holy Ghost only represents an attribute of
God, then to blaspheme that attribute is simply to blaspheme
God. But in this case, the acts of blaspheming the Father and
Son, are expressly distinguished from that of blaspheming the
Holy Ghost, and have different grades of guilt assigned them.

(f) It is also implied that the Holy Ghost is a Person, by
the distinction made between Him and His gifts. 1 Cor. xii:
4, 8. If the Holy Ghost were an influence, or exertion of God's
power on the creature, as He must be held to be in these places,
by Socinians, then He would be virtually here, the gift of a
gift! This leads us to notice a class of texts, in which the
Socian explanation appears supremely ridiculous; it is those in
which the Holy Ghost is distinguished from the power of God.
Now, if He be but a name of God's influences and energies
upon the souls of men, the general word power, ($\delta \acute{\nu} \nu \alpha \mu \iota \varsigma$) ought
to represent the idea of Him with substantial correctness. Then,
when Luke iv : 14 says: Christ returned from the desert to
Galilee "in the power of the Spirit," it is equivalent to: "In the
power of the power." Acts i : 8. But ye shall receive power,
after that the holy power is come unto you." 1 Cor. ii : 4.
"And my speech and my preaching were not with enticing
words of man's wisdom, but in demonstration of the power, and
of power." Also Acts x: 38; Rom. xv: 13, 19.

The Holy Ghost then, is not an abstraction, nor an influence merely, but a Person, in the full sense in which that word
is applied to the Father and Son, possessing will and active
principles, intelligence, and action.

The next step is to prove His proper divinity; and this has now become comparatively easy. We follow the familiar order, showing that He has in Scripture the names, attributes, works, and worship of God. The principles upon which the argument proceeds, are the same already unfolded in the argument for the divinity of Christ. (a) We find the name Jehovah applied to the Spirit, by comparing Exod. xvii: 7, with Heb. iii: 9; 2 Sam. xxiii: 2, Is. vi: 9, with Acts xxviii: 25; possibly Jer. xxxi: 31, compared with Heb. x: 15. The name God, is by plain implication ascribed to Him in Acts v: 3, 4, &c., and 1 Cor. iii: 16, with vi: 19. The name Highest, seems to be given Him in Luke i: 35. (b) The attributes are ascribed to Him; as omnipresence, implied by 1 Cor. iii: 16, and by the promises of the Holy Ghost to an innumerable multitude of Christians at once. Omniscience, 1 Cor. ii: 10, with v. 11; omnipresence, 1 Cor. xii: 13. The same thing appears from His agency in inspiration and prophecy. Jno. xvi: 13; 2 Pet. i: 21. Sovereignty, 1 Cor. xii: 11. (c) The works of God, as of creation, Gen. i: 2. Preservation, Ps. civ: 30. Miracles, Matt. xii: 28; 1 Cor. xii: 4. Regeneration and sanctification, Jno. iii: 5; 1 Cor. vi: 11; 2 Thess. ii: 13; 1 Pet. i: 2. Resurrection of the dead, Rom. viii: 11. (d) The worship of God is also attributed to Him, in the formula of Baptism, the Apostolic benediction, and the prayer of Rev. i: 4. Other passages cited seem to me of very questionable application.

3. This Person is Divine.

Against the Spirit's personality, it has been urged, that it is preposterous to speak of a Person as shed forth, poured out; as constituting the material of an anointing, as in 1 Jno. ii: 27; whereas, if the Holy Ghost is understood as only a name for God's influences, the figure is proper. The answer is, that the Holy Spirit's gifts are meant, when the giver is named, a most common and natural metonymy. The expressions are surely no harder to reconcile, than those of "putting on Christ," to be "baptized into Christ." Eph. v: 30; Rom. xiii: 14; Gal. iii: 27.

Objections answered.

To the proper divinity of the Holy Ghost it has been objected, that He is evidently subordinate, inasmuch as He is sent by the Father and the Son, and is limited in His messages by what they commit to Him. John xvi : 7, 13. The obvious answer is, that this subordination is only economical, relating to the official work to which the Divine Spirit condescends for man's redemption, and it no more proves His inferiority, than the humiliation of the Son, His.

The Nicene Creed, as settled A. D. 381, by the Council of Constantinople, had stated that the Holy Ghost proceedeth from the Father, saying nothing of any procession from the Son. But the Western Doctors, especially Augustine, leaned more

4. History of Question of Procession.

and more towards the view, that His personal relation connected
Him in the same inscrutable way, with the Father and the Son.
As the Arian Christians of the Gothic nations, who had occupied the Western provinces of the empire, began to come into
the Orthodox Catholic Church, it was judged more important,
to assert the procession of the Holy Ghost from the Son
equally with the Father, in order to eradicate any lingering ideas
of a subordination of substance in the Son, which converts
from Arianism might be supposed to feel.   Hence, we are told,
a provincial council in Toledo, A. D. 589, first enacted that the
Latin form of the creed should receive the addition of the
words, *filioque*.   But this, although popular in Spain and
France, was not adopted in Rome, even so late as A. D. 809,
when Charlemagne endeavored in vain to secure its adoption
by the Bishop of Rome.   But the Latin Christians were continually using it more extensively, to the indignation of the
Greeks.   This addition, as yet unwarranted, was the bone of
contention (along with others,) throughout the 9th and subsequent centuries.   The Latin Primate seems to have sanctioned
the addition to the creed, about the 11th century, proceeding
upon that general doctrinal consent, which the Latin Church had,
for so many centuries, held to be the voice of inspiration, according to the maxim of Vincentius of Lerins.   In the great Council
of Lyons, A. D. 1274, the Greeks, eager for a compromise, on
account of the pressure of the Mohammedans, submitted to the
Latin doctrine.   But they soon returned to their old views with
new violence.   Again, in 1439, the kingdom of Constantinople,
then tottering to its fall, submitted to a partial compromise, in
order to secure Western support; and it was agreed in the
Council of Ferrara-Florence, 1438-9,   that it should be said:
the Holy Ghost proceedeth from the Father through the Son.
But even this, the Greeks soon repudiated; and both parties
have returned, ever since, to their opposition.

To the dispassionate mind, the dispute cannot but appear
of small importance, and the grounds of both
parties uncertain.   The basis on which the
idea itself of an eternal and necessary rela-
tion of procession rests, seems to me scarcely sufficiently solid
without the analogy of the Son.   It is composed of the facts
that the Holy Ghost is called the Spirit, ($\pi\nu\varepsilon\tilde{\upsilon}\mu\alpha$,) of the
Father, (from $\pi\nu\varepsilon\omega$,) and that in one solitary passage, (John xv:
26,) it is said, He "proceedeth from the Father."   All parties
admit, that if there is such an eternal relation as procession, it
is inscrutable.   On the one hand, the Greeks rely on the fact
that He is never said to proceed from the Son; and on the
ancient view of the Greek scholastic fathers, that the Father
alone is the $A\rho\chi\eta$, or $\pi\eta\gamma\eta$ '$\Theta\varepsilon ov$.   On the other hand, the Latins
urge, that the Holy Ghost is stated to be related to the Son, in
the Scriptures, in every way, except procession, just as He is

Argument Inconclu-
sive.

to the Father.   He is the "Spirit of the Son," as well as the
Spirit of the Father, (and they suppose the very name, Spirit,
expresses His eternal relation as much as the word procession.)
He is sent by the Son, and He is sent by the Father; He
shows the things of the Son as much as those of the Father;
for Christ says, (John xvi: 15,) "All things that the Father hath
are mine."   But as Dick well observes: unless it can be proved
that spiration, mission, and speaking the things of Christ,
exhaust the whole meaning of procession, the demonstration is
not complete.   And since the whole meaning of procession is
not intelligible to human minds, that quality of meaning cannot
be known, except by an express assertion of God Himself.
Such an express word we lack; and hence, it appears to me,
that this is a subject on which we should not dogmatize.   Should
it be that the Son does not share with the Father the eternal
spiration of the Spirit, this would no more imply an essential
inferiority of the second Person, than does his filiation.   The
essence is common to the three Persons; the relations incommunicable.   Enough for us to know the blessed truth, that
under the Covenant of Grace, the Divine Spirit condescends
economically to commit the dispensation of His saving influences to the Son as our king, and to come at His bidding,
according to the agreement, to subdue, sanctify, and save us.
It may be said, that, as there is a peculiar point of view from
which the grace, condescension and majesty of both the other
persons are especially displayed, calling for our gratitude and
reverence, so the same thing is true of the Holy Ghost.   The
Father condescends, in giving his Son.   The Son, in assuming
our nature and guilt; and the Spirit, in making His immediate
abiding place in our guilty breasts, and there purging out the
depravity, which His majesty and justice, as very God, would
rather prompt Him to avenge.

The nature of the offices performed by the 2d and 3d
persons in redemption, implies and demands a
proper divinity.   This argument will require
us to anticipate some truths concerning the
mediatorial offices, and the doctrines of
redemption; but I trust that sufficient general knowledge
exists in all well-informed young Christians, to make the discussion intelligible to them.   This argument is peculiarly
important and interesting, although too little urged by theologians, ancient or modern.   It shows that this high mystery of
the Trinity has a most extensive practical aspect; and that the
scheme of the Socinian not only impugns a mystery, but makes
havoc of the Christian's most practical hopes.

Christ performs the work of our redemption in three
offices, as prophet, priest, and king.   The offices of the Holy
Ghost, in applying redemption, connect themselves with the
first in enlightening and guiding us, and with the third in con-

5. Divinity of 2nd and 3d persons prov- ed by offices in re- demption.

verting us. I shall, therefore, couple the evidence of His divinity from those two offices, with what I have to say of the Son's under the same heads.

1st. Christ and His Spirit cannot be the sufficient guides of an immortal spirit, unless they have a truly infinite understanding. If our view be limited only to the preparation of a Bible for us, and all the constant, varied, endless, inward guidance be left out of view, then the wonder would be, how one moderate volume could be made to contain principles sufficient for an infinite diversity of applications. No human book does this. To draw up, select topics for, digest such a code, required omniscience.

Christ and Holy Ghost, as Guides, must be Divine.

But this is not all. We have daily inward guidance, by the Holy Ghost and providences applying the word. Now, so endlessly diversified and novel are the exigencies of any one soul, and so eternal and infinite the consequence connected, it may be, with any one act, that it requires an infinite understanding to lead one soul, infallibly, through its mortal life, in such a way as to insure safe consequences to all eternity. How much more to lead all Christians at once?

But this is not all. Saints will be under duty in heaven. They will have approached towards moral stability and wisdom to an indefinite degree, by means of their ages of holy action and strengthening habits. But they will still not be omniscient nor absolutely immutable. These perfections belong to God only. To a fallible creature, every precept and duty implies a possible error and transgression, just as a right branch in a highway implies a left. But as the saint's existence is protracted to immortality, the number and variety of these moral exigencies become literally infinite. Hence, had he only a finite wisdom and holiness to guide him through them, the possibility of error, sin and fall at some one of these tests, would become a probability, and would grow ever towards a violent one, approaching a certainty. The gospel promises that the saint's glorified state shall be everlasting and infallible. This can only be accomplished by his having the guidance of infinite perfections. But since we are assured that "the Lamb is their light," we see at once, that his light is none other than that of omniscience.

2d. None but a properly divine being could undertake Christ's priestly work. Had he been the noblest creature in heaven, his life and powers would have been the property of God, our offended Judge; and our Advocate could not have claimed, as He does, John x: 18, that He had ἐξουσίαν to lay down His life and to take it again. Then: unless above law, He could have no imputable, active obedience. Third: unless sustained by omnipotence, unless sustained by inward omnipotence, He

Christ as a Priest, must be divine.

could never have endured the wrath of the Almighty for the
sins of the world; it would have sunk Him into perdition.
Fourth: had there not been a divine nature to reflect an infinite dignity upon His person, His suffering the curse of sin for
a few years, would not have been a satisfaction sufficient to
propitiate God for the sins of a world.   After the sacrifice,
comes intercession.   His petitioners and their wants are so
numerous, that unless He were endowed with sleepless attention, an omnipotence which can never tire, an infinite understanding, omnipresence, and exhaustless kindness, He could
not wisely and graciously attend to so many and multifarious
calls.   Here we see how worthless are Popish intercessors, who
are only creatures.

  3rd.   Christ, through His Holy Ghost, begins His kingly
work with us, by "subduing us unto Him-
self."   This is effected in the work of regeneration.   Now we shall see, when we discuss

Our king must be di-
vine.

effectual calling, that this is a directly almighty work.   Our
sanctification also demands omniscience.   For he who would
cure the ulcer, must probe it; but the heart is deceitful beyond
all created ken.   If the Holy Ghost, who is the practical,
indwelling agent of these works, is a creature, then we have
but a creature redemption, no matter how divine the Persons
that send Him.   For the channel of communication to our
souls being finite, the communications would be limited.   If
you have the whole Atlantic Ocean connected with your reser-
voir by an inch pipe, you can draw but an inch of water at
once.   The vastness of the source does you no good, beyond
the calibre of the connecting pipe.

  Moreover, Christ has all power committed to His hand,
for the Church's good.   It requires omniscience to comprehend
this, and omnipotence to wield it, especially when we recall the
power of our enemies.   See Rom. viii: 38, 39; Eph. vi: 12.

  In fine, all is enhanced, when we remember that our stake
is the soul, our all, whose loss is irreparable.   There is no comfort unless we have an infallible dependence.

LECTURE XIX.
PERSONAL DISTINCTIONS IN THE TRINITY.

———

SYLLABUS.

1. What can we know about the Personal Distinctions in the Godhead? Personal Properties, etc.?

2. What were the opinions of the ante-Nicene Fathers, concerning the subordination, of the 2nd and 3rd Persons, the three-fold generation of the Son, and the distinction of *Λόγος ενδιαθετος* and *Λόγος Προφορικος?*

Turrettin, Loc. iii, Qu. 27 and 29. Hill's Divinity, bk. iii, ch. 10. Dr. S. Hopkins' System, Vol. i, p. 362, &c. Dick, Lect. 29 Cunningham's Hist. Theol., ch. 9, § 3. Knapp, § 42. Alexander Campbell, "Christian System," ch. 4. Neander, Ch. Hist., Vol. i, p. 585.

3. State the opinions of Socinians, Arians and Orthodox, concerning the generation and filiation of the Son.

The same citations. Knapp, Lect. 43.

4. Prove the eternal generation of the Son, refute the common objections, and overthrow the Socinian and Arian explanations thereof.

Same citations. "Letters on the Eternal Sonship of Christ," by Dr. Samuel Miller, iii, iv. Watson's Theol. pt. ii, ch. 12, § 5.

5. What is the difference between the generation of the Son, and the Procession of the Spirit? Can the latter be proved eternal?

Same citations.

I. THE discussions and definitions of the more formal and scholastic Theologians, concerning the personal distinctions in the Godhead, have always seemed to me to present a striking instance of the reluctance of the human mind to confess its own weakness. For, let any read them with the closest attention, and he will perceive that he has acquired little more than a set of terms, whose abstruseness serves to conceal from him their practical lack of meaning. It is debated whether the personal distinction is real, or formal, or virtual, or personal, or modal. Turrettin decides that it may best be called modal — i. e., as a distinction in the *modus subsistendi.* But what those modes of subsistence are, remains none the less inscrutable; and the chief reason why the term modal is least objectionable, seems to be that it is most general. After all, the mind must be content with these facts, the truth of which it may apprehend, although their full meaning cannot be comprehended by us; that there is an eternal and necessary distinction between the essence and the persons, the former being absolute, and the latter relative; that the whole essence is truly in each person, with all its attributes; that yet the essence is not divided or distributed between them, but single and indivisible; that the distinction of persons is one truly subsisting, subsisting eternally by the very necessity of the divine nature, and not merely relative to our apprehensions of it; and that the persons are not convertible the one into the other, nor the properties of the one predicable of another.

Each Person has its peculiar property, which is not indeed constitutive of, but distinctive of it. The

Personal Properties.

property of the Father is to be unbegotten:

of the Son, generation; and of the Spirit, procession.   Hence, three characteristic relations — in the Father, paternity; in the Son, filiation; and in the Holy Ghost, spiration.   That there are such properties and relations, we know; what they are, we do not know.

2. Order of the Persons. We find ourselves speaking almost inevitably of 1st, 2d, and 3d persons; thus implying some order in the persons.   No orthodox Christian, of course, understands this order as relating to a priority of time, or of essential dignity.   To what, then, does it relate?   And is there any substantial reason for assigning such an order at all?   We reply: There must be; when we find that where the three persons are mentioned by Scripture, in connection, as in Matt. xxviii: 19, &c., &c., they are usually mentioned as Father, Son, and Holy Ghost, and not in reversed order; that in all allusions to the properties and relations of the three, the Father is always spoken of (e. g. the word Father) by some term or trait implying primary rank, and the other two, by some implying secondariness; as Christ is His Son, the Holy Ghost His Spirit; they are sent, He the Sender; and in their working, there is always a sort of reference to the Father's primariness, (if I may coin a word,) directing their operation.   See also Jno. v; 26; x: 38; xiv: 11; xvii: 21; Heb. i: 3.

View of Greek Fathers thereon. But if it be asked, what is the primariness, the answer is not so easy.   It was the usual answer of the ante-Nicene, and especially the Greek Fathers, that it indicated the order of derivation, that the personality of the Son is from that of the Father, not the Father's from the Son; and so of the Holy Ghost.   (And so far, it must be allowed, the fair force of the Scripture facts just stated, carries them properly enough.)   The Father they regarded as ἀναίτιος, as πήγη Θεοῦ, or Ἀρχή Θεοῦ, the Son and Holy Ghost as αἰτιατοι, as Θεοι εχ Θεοῦ, and as deriving their personal subsistence from the eternal act of the Father in communicating the divine essence to them in those modes of subsistence.   And this view was embodied in both forms of the Nicene Creed, of A. D. 325 and 381, where the Son is called, "God of God, Light of Light, and very God of very God;" language never applied to the Father as to the Son.   Their idea is, that the Father, the original Godhead, eternally generates the person, not the substance of the Son, and produces by procession the person, not the substance of the Holy Ghost, by inscrutably communicating the whole indivisible divine substance, essentially identical with Himself in these two modes of subsistence; thus eternally causing the two persons, by causing the two additional modes of subsistence.   This statement, they suppose, was virtually implied in the very relation of terms, Father and His Son, Father and His πνεῦμα, by the primariness of order always assigned to the Father, and by the distinction in the order of working.   And they relied upon this view to vindicate the doctrine of the Trinity from the charge of tritheism.   You will probably think, with me, that its value for this last purpose is questionable, for this reason : that the modes of subsistence of the persons being wholly inscrutable, the true answer to the charge of tritheism is to be found for our minds, in that fact, coupled with the Scriptural affirmation, that God is one as truly as the persons are three.   Hence no explanation of the derivation of one subsistence from another really brings us any nearer to the secret, how it is one and three.   But the answers, which the advocates of this Patristic view presented to objections, seem to my mind much more consistent than Dick would intimate.   Was it objected, that they represented the 2d and 3d persons as beginning to exist, and thus robbed them of a true self-existence and eternity?   These Fathers could answer with justice : No; the processes of personal derivation were eternal, immanent processes, and the Father has a personal priority, not in time, but only in causation ; e. g.. the sun's rays have existed precisely as long as he has ; yet the rays are from the sun and not the sun from the rays. And the 2d. person may be derived as to His personality, θεός ἐκ θεοῦ, and yet self-existent God; because His essence is the one self-existent essence, and it is only His personality which is derived.   They regard self-existence as an attribute of essence, not of person.   Was it objected that these derived personalities were unequal to the 1st. person?   They answer : No ; because the Father put His whole essence in the two other modes of subsistence.   Was it said, that then the personal subsistence of the 2d. and 3d. was dependent on the good pleasure of the 1st. ; and, therefore, revocable at His pleasure? They answered, that the generation and procession were not free, contingent acts, but necessary and essential acts, free indeed, yet necessitated by the very perfection of the eternal substance.   You will perceive that I have not used the word subordination, but derivation, to express this personal relation. If you ask me whether I adopt the Patristic view, thus cleared, as my own, I reply, that there seems to me nothing in it inconsistent with revealed truth; yet it seems to me rather a rational explanation of revealed facts, than a revealed fact itself. On such a subject, therefore, none should dogmatize.

It may be well to explain, also, how the Rationalizing Λόγος ἐνδιάθετος, &c.   Fathers connected their theory of the Trinity with this generation of the Son.   Attempting to comprehend the Divine essence through the analogy of the human spirit, and according to the Platonic metaphysics, they said that the Son or Λόγος, is God's Reason or intellective action ; and the Holy Ghost His ψυχή, or emotive and vital activity.   In the ages of eternity the Son was the Λόγος ἐνδιάθετος, or

Ratio insita, God's reason acting only by self-comprehension, according to Prov. viii : 22 : John i : 2. When, in time, God began to effectuate His decree in works of creation and providence, He became the Λόγος προφορικός, or *ratio prolata*. When at length He was born of the flesh for man's redemption, He became the Λόγος ενσαρκικός, incarnate. Hence, the Father may be said to have made three productions of the Son—one from eternity, one when, in time, the Son was sent out as Agent of God's working, one when He was born of the Virgin.

This is the transition point, to enable us to comprehend the views of the Arians concerning Christ's generation. These heretics usually admitted the justice of the metaphysical explanation of God's immanent acts. But, said they, as the human mind has not one, but a numerous series of acts of intellection, νοήματα, so *à fortiori*, the infinite mind of God. There is, of course, some primary νόημα, and this is the eternal, immanent Λόγος of John i : 2. There are other νοήματα in the divine mind, and some one of these is the one embodied, in time, in the creation of the Son, " by whom He made the worlds." Thus they endeavoured to reconcile the creation of the Son out of nothing, with the eternity of a Λόγος. How worthless all this is, I need not say.

3. False Views of Christ's Origin.

The Arians, like all others, heterodox and orthodox, find in the Scriptures ascriptions of a peculiar Sonship of Christ, needing some explanation. And we might as well array the more general of these Scripture representations here, as at a later stage of the discussion. I shall then pursue the method of bringing the several explanations of the Arian, Socinian, and orthodox, to the test of these Scriptures. The Messiah is called the Son of God, directly or indirectly, once in the Old Testament, and about one hundred and sixteen times in the New Testament, and the Father receives that title two hundred and twenty times ; while no creature is ever called the Son of God, in the singular number, except Adam. Luke iii : 38. And there the peculiarity is accounted for by the fact that it was the Evangelist's purpose to show that Adam, like Christ, had no human father. Christ is God's beloved Son. Matt. iii : 17 ; xvii : 5 ; Mark i : 11, &c. He is the Son who alone knoweth the Father. Luke x : 22 ; Jno. x : 15 ; and who reveals Him. He claims God as " His own Father," in such a sense as to make the Jews believe that He made Himself equal with God. Jno. v : 17–19. He is a Son to be honoured as the Father is. Jno. v : 23. He doeth whatever He seeth the Father do. Jno. v : 19. He is one with the Father. Jno. x : 30. He is in the bosom of the Father, though incarnate. Jno. i : 18 ; and is the only-begotten of the Father. Jno. i : 14 ; and πρωτότοκος πάσης κτίσεως. Col. i : 15. Here, surely, is evidence of some peculiar relation other

Scripture language thereon.

than that borne by God's rational, or even His holy creatures generally.

Now, says the Arian, this Divine Creature is called the Son, and only-begotten, because He is the first Creature the Father ever produced out of nothing, and the only one whom He produced immediately, by His own agency; all subsequent productions, including those of the Holy Ghost, being through the agency of this Son. He is called Son, moreover, because He has received a peculiar adoption, is deputized God to other creatures, and a splendid creature-image of the divine glory. He is also called Son, as being born by miraculous power of a virgin, and being constituted God's Messenger to fallen man. And last: He is Son, as being the Heir, by adoption, of God's throne and glory.

Arian Exposition.

The Socinian makes Jesus Christ only a holy man: and in his eyes His peculiar Sonship means nothing more than that He was born of a virgin without human father, that He was adopted by God, and endued with most eminent spiritual endowments, that He was sent forth as God's chosen mouth-piece to call a fallen race to repentance and obedience; and that He received the privilege of an immediate glorification, including His resurrection, ascension, and exaltation to God's throne.

Socinian explanation.

But among Trinitarians themselves there are some, who give to Christ's Sonship a merely temporal meaning. They believe that the 2d and the 3d persons are as truly divine as we do; they believe with us, that there is a personal distinction, which has been eternal; but they do not believe that the terms generation and procession were ever intended by Scripture to express that eternal relation. On the contrary, they suppose that they merely denote the temporal functions which the persons assume for man's redemption. Such appears to have been the view of the Hollander Roell, of Dr. Ridgeley, in Eng; of Emmons and Moses Stuart, of New Eng.; and of the notorious Alex. Campbell.

A peculiar view of some Trinitarians.

Now, to begin with the lowest scheme, the Socinian: it utterly fails at the first blush of the contest. It does not explain why Christ is called the Son, while all other creatures are called sons in the plural only. It does not explain why He was the beloved Son, why He comprehended and revealed the Father, why He was of equal honour, and identical substance, rather than other holy creatures. It utterly fails to explain why He is only-begotten; for Adam was begotten by God's direct power, not only without father, but without mother. His endowments and His mission only differed, according to Socinians, in degree from those of other prophets, who were, therefore, in this sense, as truly sons as He. And last: His resur-

Socinian Explanation fails.

rection and glorification leave Him behind Enoch and Elijah, who were translated.

The Arian scheme also fails to explain how His Sonship made Him one with the Father, and of equal

Arian explanation fails. honour; how it capacitates Him to be the revealer and image of the Father's person and glory in a manner generically different from all other creatures; and how it proves Him only-begotten. It leaves unsatisfied the declaration, that while they were κτίσις, He was πρωτότοκος: and begotten before every creature; so that He would be produced in a totally different way from, and produced before, the whole creature class to which, on their scheme, He belongs! And last, like the Socinian scheme, it leaves wholly unexplained how a creature (therefore finite) could be competent to the exercise of all the works he seeth the Father do, and to a divine glorification.

Against the third view I would urge the general force of the passages I collected above. It may at

4. Only an eternal Generation meets the texts. least be said, that if it were not intended to teach that the permanent personal distinction was that of filiation, the Scriptures have been singularly unfortunate. But I shall proceed to cite other authorities, which are more decisive of the point. In doing this I shall be also adding to the overthrow of the Arian and Socinian views by an *a fortiori* argument. For if a scheme of temporal filiation, coupled with the admission of a true and eternal, though unnamed, personal distinction, will not satisfy the meaning of the texts; still less will the scheme of a temporal filiation which denies the eternity and divinity of the 2d person.

(a) In a number of passages it is said, that God "sent," "gave," &c., His Son: e. g., Rom. viii: 3. "God

Because Christ is Son, when sent. sending his own Son, in the likeness of sinful flesh," &c. So, Jno. iii : 16; Jno. iii : 8; iv: 9; Gal. iv: 4; Acts iii: 26. Now, who would dream that when God says, "He sends the Son in the flesh," He was not His Son before, but was made such by the sending? See also 1 Tim. iii: 16; 1 Jno. iii: 8.

(b) The three Old Testament passages, Ps. ii: Prov. viii: 7; 22, 23; Micah v: 2, are advanced with great

Son, when pre-existent. subtlety and force by Turrettin. He favours, for the first, the interpretation of the "to-day" ("have I begotten thee,") as the *punctum stans*, or eternal now, of the divine decree. The great objection is, that the idiom and usage of the Psalms do not sustain it. It is better, with Calvin and Hengstenberg, to understand the verb, "have begotten," according to a frequent Hebrew usage, as equivalent to the manifestation, or declaration, of His generation. This took place when Christ was revealed to His Church. The passage then does not prove, but neither does it disprove, the

eternity of His generation. In this text, as well as Prov. viii:
22, 23, Turrettin argues the identity of the subject with Jesus
Christ, with great force. In Micah v: 2, the application to
Jesus Christ is indisputable, being fixed by Matt. ii: 6. The
relevancy of the text to His eternal generation depends on two
points — whether the phrase "going forth," מוֹצָאֹת means generation or production, or only manifestation in action; and
whether the phrase "from of old, from days of forever" means
eternity, or only antiquity. As to the former question, we are
shut up to the first meaning of generation, by the usage.
(Gesenius giving only "origin, descent,") and by the consideration that Christ's manifestation in action has not been eternal.
As to the second question, the sense of proper eternity is certainly the most natural. The only plausible rendering besides
the one given by Turrettin is the one hinted by Gesenius:
("whose descent is from antiquity;" referring to the antiquity
of Christ's human lineage.) And manifestly this gives to the
noun the perverted sense of channels of descent instead of act
of production, its proper meaning.

(c) We find another argument for the eternal generation
of the Son, in a number of passages, as the
Father is eternally Baptismal formula; the Apostolic benedic-
Father. tion; Matt. xi: 27; Luke x: 22; Jno. v: 22;
x: 33–37; Rom. viii: 32; &c., &c. In all these cases the word
Son is used in immediate connection with the word Father, so
that it is impossible to avoid the conclusion that the one is
reciprocal to the other. The Son is evidently Son in a sense
answering to that in which the Father is Father. But do these
passages permit us to believe that the first Person here receives
that term, only because He has produced a human nature in
which to clothe the Son, when the two first passages give an
enumeration of the three divine Persons as making up the
Godhead, presented in its most distinctive divine attitude,
receiving the highest acts of worship, and all the others bring
to view acts in which the Father and Son mutually share
essentially divine acts or honours? It is plain that the paternity here means something characteristic and permanent; so,
then, does the filiation.

(d) In Rom. i: 3, 4; we read that the "Son of God was
made of the seed of David according to the
Rom. i: 3, 4. flesh, declared with power ὁρισθέντος to be
the Son of God according to the Spirit of Holiness," &c.
Here we not only find the evidence of head (a) that the Son
was made flesh, and so was Son before; but the evident antithesis between the flesh and the Spirit of holiness, His divine
nature, compels us to read that His resurrection forcibly manifested Him to be God's Son as to His divine nature, even as He
was David's as to His human. But if His filiation to God

respects His divine nature, as contrasted with His human, the question is settled.

(e) I may group together two very similar passages, Col. i: 14–17; and Heb. i: 3–6. The Sonship is surely not merely the incarnation, when it is stated to be a begetting before every creature! The Son as Son, and not as incarnate only, is represented in both passages as performing divine functions, as representing the Father's nature and glory; whence we must infer that His Sonship is something belonging to His divinity, not His humanity merely. And in Heb. v: 5, 6, the Apostle seems to aim explicitly to separate His Sonship from that of all others as divine and peculiar. Consider thus: Heb. i: 2; iii: 5, 6; vii: 3, and vii: 28. In a word, the generation of the Son, and procession of the Spirit, however mysterious, are unavoidable corollaries from two facts. The essence of the Godhead is one; the persons are three. If these are both true, there must be some way, in which the Godhead multiplies its personal modes of subsistence, without multiplying or dividing its substance. The Scriptures call one of these modes a $\gamma\acute{\epsilon}\nu\epsilon\sigma\iota\varsigma$ and the other an $\epsilon\kappa\pi\acute{o}\rho\epsilon\upsilon\sigma\iota\varsigma$. We thus learn two truths. The 2d and 3d substances are eternally propagated in dissimilar modes. The inscrutable mode of the 2d substance bears some mysterious analogy to the generation of human sons.

Christ is Son when creating.

It has been supposed that the following texts were repugnant to our view, by showing that the filiation had a temporal origin in Christ's incarnation and exaltation as a mediatorial Person: Matt: xvi: 16; Luke i: 35; Jno. i: 49; seem, it is said, to imply that His Sonship is nothing else than His Messiahship, and in Jno. x: 35, 36; it is said, He states Himself to be Son because sanctified and sent into the world by the Father. The answer is, that this argument confounds the traits which define Him as Son with those which constitute Him the Son. To say that the Messiah, the Sent, is the one who is Son, is far short of saying that these offices make Him the Son. It is said that Acts xiii: 33, and Col. i: 18 refer the Sonship to his resurrection, the former of these passages especially, citing Ps. ii: 7 in support of that view. I reply, that it is only a mistranslation which seems to make Acts xiii: 33 relate to Christ's resurrection at all. We should read, in that God hath set up (as Messiah) Jesus: as it is written in the 2nd Ps.: "Thou art my Son: this day have I begotten Thee." Here we see a striking confirmation of the sense given above to this Ps. viz: that Christ's Sonship was declaratively manifested by His installment as Messiah. In the Col. i: 18; Christ is said to be the $\pi\rho\omega\tau\acute{o}\tau o\kappa o\varsigma$ $\grave{\epsilon}\kappa$ $\tau\tilde{\omega}\nu$ $\nu\epsilon\kappa\rho\tilde{\omega}\nu$. But evidently the concluding words should explain the meaning: "That in all things He might have the pre-eminence," in the resurrection of New Testament saints, as well as in an eternal generation.

Objections.

14*

Once more, it is claimed that Luke i: 35; plainly defines the incarnation as the ground of the Sonship. The simplest reply is, that the divine nature (compare Rom. i : 4;) was never born of the virgin, but only the humanity. This nature, thus united in the mediatorial Person, was called God's Son, because of its miraculous generation, so that the whole mediatorial person, in both natures, might be Son of God ; that which is eternal, eternally Son, and that which is temporal, temporally Son. If the adverse rendering is to hold, then, (a) the Holy Ghost, and not the First Person, is the Father of Christ, and (b) His Sonship would be only equal to Adam's.

In fine, there is a general argument for the eternal generation of the Son, in the simple fact the Scripture has chosen this most simple and important pair of words to express a relation between the first and second Persons. There must have been a reason for the choice, there must be something corresponding to the well-known meaning of this pair of words, else eternal truth would not have employed them. That meaning must of course be compatible with God's immateriality and eternity, and must be stripped of all the elements arising from man's corporeal and finite nature and temporal existence. It is not corporeal generation, nor generation in time ; but after stripping it of all this, do we not inevitably get this, as the *residuum* of meaning, that the personal subsistence of the Son is derivative, though eternal, and constitutes His nature the same with the Father's?

General force of Words: Father—Son.

It is a remarkable fact, that while so many terms and traits belonging to generation are given to the 2d Person, not one of them is ever given in Scripture to the 3d. He is indeed "sent" as the Son is "sent;" but this is in both cases, not the modal, but merely the official term. The nature of the 3d personality is always represented by the word "breath," and his production is only called a "proceeding out" The inference seems fair, that the mode of personal subsistence, and the personal relation is therefore different from that of the Son. But as both are inscrutable, we cannot tell in what they differ. See Turrettin, Locus 3, Qu. 31, § 3.

5. Personal Relation of Holy Ghost.

The evidence for the eternity of this personal relation between the Spirit and the other two Persons, is much more scanty than that for the eternity of the Son's filiation. In only one place, Jno. xv: 26, is the Holy Ghost said to proceed from the Father. If that place stood alone, it could never be determined from it whether it was intended by our Saviour to define the mode of the eternal subsistence of the 3d person, or only to denote his official function in time. But beside the analogy of the Son's relation, we may infer with reasonable certainty that it intends an

Is it Eternal?

eternal relation. As his generation is not a mere commissioning in time, so the Spirit's procession is not a mere sending or an office in time. Otherwise the symmetry of the doctrine of the Trinity would be fatally broken; while the Scriptures hold out three co-ordinate Persons, eternally subsisting and related as Persons, *inter se*, we should be guilty of representing the 3d as bearing no permanent relation to the others.

LECTURE XX.
DECREES OF GOD

SYLLABUS.

1. How do Theologians classify the acts of God?
Turrettin, Loc. iv, Qu. 1. Dick, Lect. 34.
2. What is God's Decree? Wherein different from **Fate**? What is the distinction between permissive and efficacious?
Conf. of Faith, ch. 3. Turrettin, *ubi supra,* and Loc. vi, Qu. 2. Dick, *ubi supra*. Calv. Inst., bk. iii, ch. 21.
3. Establish the following properties of the decree, (a) Unity, (b) Eternity, (c) Universality, embracing especially the future acts of free agents, (d) Efficiency, (e) Absoluteness from conditions, (f) Freedom, and (g) Wisdom.
Turrettin, Loc. iv, Qu. 2, 3 and 4. Hill, bk. iv, ch. 7, § 1-3. Dick, *ubi supra*. Watson's Theol. Inst., ch. 26, § 1. Knapp, § 32. Witsius on Cov., bk, iii, ch. 4. Dr. S. Hopkins' System, Vol. i, p. 136-153.
4. How may the objections be answered; (a) That the Decree destroys free agency and responsibility; (b) Supersedes the use of means; (c) Makes God the author of Sin.
Turrettin, as above. Dick, Lects. 34 and 36.

OUR study now leads us from the consideration of God's nature to His acts. Theologians have usually classified them

1. God's acts classified. under three sorts. The 1st are God's immanent eternal acts, which are wholly subjective. These are the generation of the Son, and procession of the Holy Ghost. 2d, are God's immanent and eternal acts having reference to objects out of Himself. This class includes His decree; an unchangeable and eternal act of God never passing over so as to cease to be His act, yet being relative to His creatures. 3d, are God's transient acts towards the universe external to Himself, including all His works of creation and providence done in time.

"The decrees of God are His eternal purpose according to

2. Decree proved by God's intelligence. the counsel of His will, whereby, for His own glory, He hath foreordained whatsoever comes to pass."

Nature and Revelation concur to teach us that God is a Being of infinite intelligence, and of will. The eternal object of His cognition, as we saw, when investigating His omniscience, is nothing less than the whole of the possible; for the wisdom and selection displayed in the creation of the actual, show that

there was more before the Divine Mind, than what was effectuated. But when we inquire for the ground of the difference
between God's natural and His voluntary knowledge, we find no
other than His volition. That is, the only way in which any
object can by any possibility have passed from God's vision of
the possible into His foreknowledge of the actual, is by His
purposing to effectuate it Himself, or intentionally and purposely to permit its effectuation by some other agent whom
He expressly purposed to bring into existence. This is clear
from this fact. An effect conceived in *posse* only rises into actuality by virtue of an efficient cause or causes. When God was
looking forward from the point of view of His original infinite
prescience, there was but one cause, Himself. If any other
cause or agent is ever to arise, it must be by God's agency. If
effects are embraced in God's infinite prescience, which these
other agents are to produce, still, in willing these other agents
into existence, with infinite prescience, God did virtually will
into existence, or purpose, all the effects of which they were to
be efficients. That this prescience is all-embracing, the Scriptures assert in too many places. (Acts xv: 18; Is. 42: 9; xlvi:
10; Ps. cxlvii: 5; Jno. xxi: 17. Hence His purpose must extend
to all that is, or is to be effectuated.

The same conclusion follows by a more popular reasoning
By His Power. from God's power; that power extends to all
beings and events, and is the source of all
existence. Now it is impossible for us to conceive how an
intelligent Being can set about producing anything, save as He
has the conception of the thing to be produced in His mind, and
the intention to produce it in His will. Least of all can we
attribute an unintelligent and aimless working to God. But if
He is concerned in the production of all things, and had an intelligent purpose with reference to all which He produced, there
is His decree; and His perfections, as we shall see, forbid our
imputing any beginning to it. So, the sovereignty of God,
which regulates all the universe, the doctrine of His providence,
so fully asserted in Scripture, and His concurring perfections of
knowledge and wisdom, show that He must have a purpose as
to all things. See Eph: i: 11; Ps. xxxiii: 11. Other passages,
extending this purpose specifically to various departments of
events, and especially to those concerning which the decree is
most contested, will be cited in other connections. These also
are appropriate here.

The question whether God's decrees abide in Him essen-
Is the Decree in God tially or accidentally, is but the same with
Essentially? that which we saw raised concerning the simplicity of the divine essence. The scholastic
divines, in order to defend their metaphysical notion of this,
said that God knows, feels, wills, &c., by His essence, or that
God's knowledge is but His essence knowing, &c. As we then

concluded concerning His knowledge, so I now say concerning His purpose. If it is meant that God's purpose is but God purposing, and as abstracted from Him, is but an abstraction, and not an existent thing, I fully concur. But in the same sense, the purpose of a human soul is but that soul purposing. The difference of the two cases is, that God's purpose is immanent and immutable, the man's evanescent and mutable. To make the decree of God's essence in any other sense, is to give it essence; to make it a mode of the divine subsistence. And this trenches hard by the awful verge of pantheism. For if the decree is but a mode of the divine subsistence, then its effectuation in the creature's existence must still have the same essence, and all creatures are but modes of God, and their acts of God's acts. The decrees are not accidents with God, in the sense that, being the result of God's immutable perfections, they cannot change nor fail, but are as permanent as God's essence.

The doctrine of God's decree has been often impugned as no better than the Stoic's Fate. The modern, Fate, What? and indeed, the ancient interpreters of their doctrine, differ as to their meaning. Some, as Seneca, seem to represent fate as no other than the intelligent, eternal purpose of the Almighty. But others describe it as a physical necessity, self-existent and immanent in the links of causation themselves, by which effect is evolved out of cause according to a law eternally and necessarily existent in the Universe and all its parts. To this necessity Gods are as much subject as men. This definition is more probably the true one, because it agrees with a pantheistic system, and such Stoicism was. Now it is obvious, that this fate necessitates God as much as man, and that not by the influence of His own intelligence and perfections, but by an influence physical and despotic. Whereas our view of God's purpose makes it His most free, sovereign, wise and holy act of choice. This fate is a blind necessity; God's decree is intelligent, just, wise and benevolent. Fate was a necessity, destroying man's spontaneity. God's decree, in purposing to make and keep man a free agent, first produced and then protects the exercise of it.

God's decree "foreordains whatsoever comes to pass;" there was no event in the womb of the future, the God's decree effec- futurition of which was not made certain to tive or permissive. God by it. But we believe that this certainty is effectuated in different ways, according to the different natures of God's creatures. One class of effects God produces by His own immediate agency, (as creations, regenerations, inspirations,) and by physical causes, which are continually and immediately energized by His power. This latter subdivision is covered by what we call the laws of material nature. As to these, God's purpose is called effective, because He Himself effects the results, without the agency of other intelligent agents. The

other class of effects is, the spontaneous acts of rational free
agents other than God. The being and powers of these are
derived from and dependent on God. But yet He has been
pleased to bestow on them a rational spontaneity of choice,
which makes them as truly agents, sources of self-determined
agency, in their little, dependent sphere of action, as though
there were no sovereign over them. In my theory of the will,
I admitted and claimed as a great truth of our consciousness,
that man's action is spontaneous, that the soul is self-determined (though not the faculty of willing) in all its free acts, that
the fountain of the volition is in the soul itself; and that the
external object of the action is but the occasional cause of volition. Yet these spontaneous acts God has some way of directing, (only partially known to us) and these are the objects of His
permissive decree. By calling it permissive, we do not mean
that their futurition is not certain to God; or that He has not
made it certain; we mean that they are such acts as He efficiently brings about by simply leaving the spontaneity of other
free agents, as upheld by His providence, to work of itself, under
incitements, occasions, bounds and limitations, which His wisdom
and power throw around. To this class may be attributed all
the acts of rational free agents, except such as are evoked by
God's own grace, and especially, all their sinful acts.

The properties of God's decree are, (a) Unity. It is one
act of the divine mind; and not many. This
view is at least suggested by Scripture, which
speaks of it usually as a πρόθεσις, a "purpose," a "counsel." It follows from the nature of God. As
His natural knowledge is all immediate and cotemporaneous,
not successive, like ours, and His comprehension of it all
infinitely complete always, His purpose founded thereon, must
be a single, all-comprehensive and simultaneous act. Besides,
the whole decree is eternal and immutable. All therefore must
co-exist together always in God's miud. Last, God's plan is
shown, in its effectuation, to be one; cause is linked with effect,
and what was effect becomes cause; and influences of events
on events interlace with each other, and descend in widening
streams to subsequent events; so that the whole complex result
is interconnected through every part. As astronomers suppose
that the removal of one planet from our system would modify
more or less the balance and orbits of all the rest, so the failure
of one event in this plan would derange the whole, directly or
indirectly. God's plan is, never to effectuate a result apart
from, but always by, its own cause. As the plan is thus a unit
in its effectuation, so it must have been in its conception. Most
of the errors, which have arisen in the doctrine, have come
from the mistake of imputing to God that apprehension of His
purpose in successive parts, to which the limitations of our minds
confine us, in conceiving of it.

3. Properties — The
decree a unit.

(b) The decree is eternal.   One may object : that God must
exist before His decree, the subject before
its act.   I reply, He exists before it only in
the order of production, not in time.   For
intellection is His essential state, and His comprehension of His
purpose may be as eternal as Himself.   The sun's rays are from
the sun, but measuring by duration, there were rays as early as
there was a sun.   It has been objected that some parts of the
decree are consequent on other parts, and cannot therefore be
equally early.   I reply, the real sequence is only in the events
as effectuated, not in the decree of them.   The latter is a co-
existent unit with God, and there is no sequence of parts in it,
except in our feeble minds.   It is said the comprehension of the
possible must have gone before in the divine mind, in order that
the determination to effectuate that part which commended itself
to the divine wisdom, might follow.   I reply : God does not
need to learn things deductively, or to view them piecemeal and
successively ; but His infinite mind sees all by immediate intuition and together ; and in seeing, concludes.   The most plausible objection is, that many of God's purposes must have been
formed in time, because suspended on the acts of other free
agents to be done in time ; e. g., Deut. xxviii : 2, 15 ; Jer. xviii :
10.   The answer is, that all these acts, though contingent to
man, were certainly foreknown to God.

The decree eternal— objections.

Having thus cleared away objections, we might argue very
simply : If God had an intention to act, before
each act, when was that intention born ?   No
answer will be found tenable till we run back
to eternity.   For, God's knowledge was always perfect, so that
He finds out nothing new, to become the occasion of a new
plan.   His wisdom was always perfect, to give Him the same
guidance in selecting means and ends.   His power was always
infinite, to prevent any failure, or successful resistance, which
would cause Him to resort to new expedients.   His character is
immutable ; so that He will not causelessly change His own
mind.   There is therefore nothing to account for any addition
to His original plan.   But we may reason more comprehensively.
It is, as we saw, only God's purpose, which causes a part of the
possible to become the actual.   As the whole of God's *scientia
simplicis intelligentiæ* was present to Him from eternity, a reason
is utterly wanting in Him, why any part of the decree should be
formed later than any other part.

Its Eternity Argued from God's perfections and Scripture.

And to this agree the Scriptures : Is. xlvi : 10 ; Matt. xxv :
34 ; 1 Cor. ii : 7 ; Eph. i : 4 ; 2 Thess. ii : 13 ; 2 Tim. i : 9 ; 1
Pet. i : 20.   On these, two remarks should be made.   Although
they do not expressly assert the eternity of all God's decrees,
several of them do assert the eternity of the very ones most
impugned, His decrees concerning events dependent on free
agent.   In the language of Scripture, to say a thing was done

"before the formation of the world," is to say it is from eternity, because with the creation of the universe began successive duration. All before this is the measureless eternity. In conclusion, I add the express assertion of Acts xv: 18.

(c) The decree is universal, embracing absolutely all creatures, and all their actions. No nominal Christians contest this, except as to the acts of free agents, which the Arminians, but especially the Socinians, exempted from God's sovereign decree, and the latter heretics from His foreknowledge. We have seen that God's foreknowledge is founded on His foreordination. If then we prove that God has a perfect foreknowledge of all future events, we shall have virtually proved that He has foreordained them. The Socinians are more consistent than the Arminians here, in that they deny both to God. They define God's omniscience as His knowledge of all the cognizable. All the future acts of free-agents, say they, cannot be foreknown, because a multitude of them are purely contingent; the volitions springing from a will in *equilibrio*. It is therefore no derogation to God's understanding, that He does not foreknow all of them, any more than it would be to the goodness of an eye, that it does not see what as yet does not exist. When free agents perform acts unforeseen to God, His wisdom, say they, provides Him with a multitude of resources, by which He overrules the result, and still makes thcm concur substantially (not absolutely) with His wise and good plans.

The decree universal.

Now, in opposition to all this, we have shown that the future volitions of free agents are none of them among the unknowable; because none contingent to God. We argue farther that God must have foreordained, and so foreknown all events, including these volitions: (a.) Because, else, His providence would not be sovereign, and His independence and omnipotence would be impugned. We have seen that the course of events is a chain, in which every link has a direct or remote connection with every other. Into a multitude of physical events, the volitions of free agents enter as part causes; and if God has not a control over all these, He could not have over the dependent results. His government would be a capricious patchwork of new expedients. Beeause He could not control everything, He would not be absolutely sure of controlling anything, for all are interdependent. (b.) God's knowledge would receive continual accretions, and hence His feelings and plans would change with them; His immutability would be gone. (c.) Prophecy concerning the acts of free agents would have been impossible. For unless all the collateral links of causation are under God's control, it may be that He will be unable to control a single result. But a multitude of the acts of the proudest, most arrogant and rebellious men were exactly and confidently predicted,

Includes the volitions of free agents.

of your Nebuchadnezzars, Pharaohs, Cyrus, &c., &c. To this last agree the Scriptures: Eph. i: 10, 11; Rom. xi: 33; Heb. iv: 13; Rom. ix: 15, 18; Acts xv: 18; xvii: 26; Job xiv: 5; Is. xlvi: 10. Men's volitions, especially including the evil. Eph. ii: 10; Acts ii: 23; iv: 27, 28; Ps. lxxvi: 10; Prov. xvi: 4, 33; Dan. iv: 34, 35; Gen. xlv: 5; Is. x: 5, 15; Josh. xi: 20; Prov. xx: 24; Is. xlv: 7; Amos iii: 6; Ps. cvii: 17; 1 Sam. ii: 25; 2 Sam. xvi: 10; 1 Kgs. xii: 15, 24; 2 Kgs. xxvi: 2, 3, 20. Add all those texts where the universality of God's providential control is asserted: for Providence is but the execution of the decree.

(d) Nearly akin to this is the remark that the decree is efficient. By this I mean that God's purpose is in every case absolutely sure to be effectuated. Nearly all the arguments adduced under the last head apply here: God's sovereignty, God's wisdom, His independence, and the dependence of all other things on Him, the "immutability of His counsel," and of His knowledge and other attributes, the certainty of His predictions, all demand that "His counsel shall stand, and He shall do all His pleasure." See Matt. xxvi: 54; Luke xxii: 22; Acts iv: 28; Prov. xvi: 33; Matt. x: 29, 30. Here we see that things most minute, most contingent in our view of them, and most voluntary, are yet efficaciously produced by God.

The decree efficient.

The Arminians have too much reverence for God's perfections to limit His knowledge as to the actions of free agents. But they endeavor to evade the inevitable conclusion of the decree, and to save their favorite doctrine of conditional purposes, by limiting His concern with the acts, and especially sins, of free agents, to a mere foreknowledge, permission, and intention to make the permitted act a condition of some part of the decree I urge that they who concede so much, cannot consistently stop there. If the sinful act (to make the least possible concession to the Calvinist,) of the free agent has been from eternity certainly forseen by God, then its occurrence must be certain. But in this universe, nothing comes without a cause; there must therefore be some ground for the certainty of its occurrence. And it is upon that ground that God's foreknowledge of it rests. Do you ask what that ground is? I reply by asking: How does God's knowledge of the possible pass into His knowledge of the actual? Only by His determining to secure the occurrence of all the latter. Conceive of God as just now about to create a free agent, according to His plan, and launch him out on his path of freedom. If God foreknows all that the free agent will choose to do, if created; does He not purpose the doing of all this, when He creates him? To deny this is a contradiction. We may not be able to see fully how God certainly procures the doing of such acts

Over free agents also.

by free agents, still leaving them to act purely from their own
spontaneity; but we cannot deny that He does, without over-
throwing His sovereignty and foreknowledge. Such events
may be wholly contingent to man; but to God none of them
can be contingent; else all the parts of His decree, connected as
effects with them as causes, would be in the same degree contingent. For instance: if Christ be not "taken, and by wicked
hands crucified and slain," then, unless God is to proceed by
rupturing the natural ties of cause and effect, all the natural
and historical consequences of Christ's sacrifice must also fail,
down to the end of time and through eternity. If God is to
be able to prevent all that failure, we must ascribe to Him
power to make sure by His determinate counsel and foreknowledge that the wicked hands shall not fail to take and slay the
victim. The same argument may be extended to every sinful
act, from which the adorable wisdom of God has evolved good
consequences. When we remind ourselves how moral causes
interlace and spread, as time flows on, we see that, unless the
decree extends to sinful acts, making them also certain, God
will be robbed, by our day, of nearly all His providential
power over free agents, and His foreknowledge of their doings.
As this branch of the decree is most impugned (by Arminians
and Cumberland Presbyterians) let it be fortified by these
additional Scriptures. 1st. They assert that God's purpose is
concerned in such sins as those of Eli's sons. 1 Sam. ii: 25,
of Shimei, 2 Sam. xvi: 10, 11, of Ahithophel, 2 Sam. xvii: 14,
of the Chaldeans, 2 Kings, xxvi: 2, 3, 20, of Jeroboam, 1 Kings,
xii: 15, 24, of Amaziah, 2 Chron. xxv: 20, of Nebuchadnezzar,
Jer. xxv: 9: li: 20, of Pilate and Herod, Acts iii: 17, 18. 2d.
The Scriptures say that God, in some way, moves men to
actions, such as Hadad, the Edomite, and Rezon, the son of
Eliada, against Solomon, 1 Kings xi: 14, 23. David to number Israel, 2 Sam. xxiv: 1. Pul and Tiglath-pileser, 1. Chron. v:
26. The Medes against them, Isaiah xiii: 17. The Egyptians,
Ps. cv: 25. The secular Popish princes, Rev. xvii: 17. 3d.
The Bible represents God as being concerned, by His purpose
and providence, in men's self-deceptions. Job xii: 16; Ezek.
xiv: 9; 2 Thess. ii: 11, 12. 4th. God is described as "hardening"
sinners' hearts, in order to effectuate some righteous purpose.
Isaiah vi: 9, 10; xxix: 10; Rom. xi: 7, 8; Exod. iv: 21, *et
passim.* Rom. 9: 18. How can all those declarations be
explained away? We do not, of course, advance them as
shewing God to be the author of sin, but they can mean no
less than that His purpose determines, and His providence sup-
erintends the occurrence of sins, for His own holy ends.

(e) We are now prepared to approach the proposition, that
God's act in forming His decree is unconditioned on anything to be done by His
creatures. In another sense, a multitude of

The decree not
conditional.

the things decreed are conditional; God's whole plan is a wise
unit, linking means with ends, and causes with effects. In
regard to each of these effects, the occurrence of it is conditional on the presence of its cause, and is made so dependent
by God's decree itself. But while the events decreed are conditional, God's act in forming the decree is not conditional, on
anything which is to occur in time; because in the case of each
dependent event, His decree as much determined the occurrence of the cause, as of its effect. And this is true equally of
those events in His plan dependent on the free acts of free
agents. No better illustration can be given, of the mode in
which God decrees dependent or conditioned events, absolutely,
by equally decreeing the conditions through which they are to
be brought about, than Acts xxvii: 22 with 31. The Arminian admits that all such intermediate acts of men were eternally
foreseen of God, and thus embraced in His plan as conditions:
but not foreordained. We reply: if they were certainly foreseen, their occurrence was certain; if this was certain, then
there must have been something to determine that certainty;
and that something was either God's wise foreordination, or a
blind physical fate. Let the Arminian choose.

Here enters the theory of *scientia media* in God; and here
Scientia Media. we detect one of the objects for which it is
invented. The student is referred to the
demonstration (on p. 157-9,) of its falsehood. Were the free
acts of moral agents contingent to God, the conclusion of the
Socinian would be true, that they are not certainly cognizable,
even to an infinite mind. Arminians, who recoil from this
irreverent position, refer us to the infinitude of God's mind to
account for His having certain prescience of all these contingent
acts, inconceivable as it is to us. But I reply: it is worse than
inconceivable, absolutely contradictory. What does the Arminian propose as the medium, or middle premise, of this inferential knowledge in God? His insight into the dispositions of all
creatures enables Him, they suppose, to infer how they will act
in the presence of the conditions which His omniscience foresees, will surround them at any given time. But it is obvious,
this supposes such an efficient and causative connection between
disposition and volition, as the Calvinist asserts, and the Arminian denies. So that, if volitions are contingent, the middle
term is annihilated. We ask then, does mental perfection
prompt a rational being to draw a certain inference after the
sole and essential premise thereof is gone? Does infinitude
help any mind to this baseless logic? Is this a compliment, or
an insult to the divine intelligence? To every plain mind it is
clear, that whether an intellect be greater or smaller, it would
be its imperfection and not its glory. to infer without a ground
of inference.

Hence, it follows, that the eternity of the decree, already

proved, offers us a demonstration against a conditional decree in God. For, *scientia media* of a contingent act of the creature being impossible, whenever an event decreed was conditioned on such contingent, creature act, as second cause, it might have been, that God would be obliged to wait until the creature acted, before He could form a positive purpose as to the event. Therefore we must hold, this creature act never was contingent to God, since His purpose about it was eternal; and the effect was foreordained in foreordaining the condition of its production.

The immutability of God's decree argues the same, and in the same way. If the condition on which His results hung were truly contingent, then it might turn out in one or another of several different ways. Hence it would always be possible that God might have to change His plans.

It is equally plain that His sovereignty would no longer be entire: but God would be dependent on His creatures for ability to effectuate many of His plans; and some might fail in spite of all He could do. I have already indicated that God's foreknowledge of the conditions, and of all dependent on them, could not possibly be certain. For if a thing is not certain to occur, a certain expectation that it will occur, is an erroneous one. Hence, the Arminian should be driven by consistency to the conclusion of the Socinian. limiting God's knowledge.

But Arminians are exceedingly fond of saying, that the dream of absolute decrees is a metaphysical invention not sustained by Scripture, and only demanded by consistency with other unhallowed, human speculation. Hence I shall take pains, as on other points, to show that it is expressly the doctrine of Scripture. Here may be cited all the proofs by which I showed that the decree is universal and efficacious. For the very conception of the matter which I have inculcated is, that events are conditioned on events, but that the decree is not; because it embraces the conditions as efficaciously as the results. See also Is. xlvi: 10, 11: Rom. ix: 11; Matt. xi: 25, 26; Eph. i: 5 and 11; Is. xl: 13; Rom. ix: 15–18; Acts ii: 23; iii: 18; Gen. l: 20.

His decree includes means and conditions. 2 Thess. ii: 13; 1 Pet. i: 2; Phil. ii: 13; Eph. ii: 8; 2 Tim. ii: 25.

But against this view objections are urged with great clamour and confidence. They may be summed up into two: -that absolute decrees make God the author of sin; and that the Scriptures contradict our view by displaying many conditional threats and promises of God, e. g., Ezek, xviii: 21; Ps. lxxxi: 13, 14; &c., &c., and some cases in which decrees were actually revoked and changed in consequence of men's conduct, as 1 Sam. xiii: 13; Luke vii: 30.

Does this make God the author of sin?

That God is not, and cannot be the author of sin, is plain

from express Scripture, Jas. i: 13, 7; 1 Jno. i: 5; Eccl. vii: 29; Ps. xcii: 15; from God's law, which prohibits all sin; from the holiness of His nature, which is incapable of it; and from the nature of sin itself, which must be man's own free activity, or else is not responsible and guilty. But I remark, 1st, that so far as the great mystery of God's permission of sin enters into this objection, our minds are incapable of a complete explantion. But this incapacity is precisely the same, whatever scheme we adopt for accounting for it, unless we deny to God complete foreknowledge and power. 2. The simple fact that God clearly foresaw every sin the creature would commit, and yet created him, is attended with all the difficulty which attaches to our view. But that foresight the Arminian admits. By determining to create the creature, foreknowing that he would sin, God obviously determined the occurrence of the sin, through the creature's free agency; for at least He could have refrained from creating him. But this is just as strong as our view of the case involves. The Arminian pleads: Yea, but God determined to create a creature who, He foresaw, would sin, not for the sake of sin, but for the sake of the good and holy ends connected therewith. I reply, 3d. Well, the very same plea avails for us. We can say just as consistently: God purposed to produce these free agents, to sustain their free agency untrammeled, to surround them with outward cir- cumstances of a given kind, to permit that free agency, moved by those circumstances as occcasional causes, to exert itself in a multitude of acts, some sinful, not for the sake of the sin, but for the sake of some good and holy results which His infinite wisdom has seen best to connect therewith. Last, in the sinful act, the agency and choice is the sinner's alone; because the inscrutable modes God has for effectuating the certain occurrence of His volitions never cramp or control the creature's spontaneity: as consciousness testifies.

The second class of objections Arminians also advance *Objected that God's threats and promises are conditional.* with great confidence; saying that unless we are willing to charge God with insincerity, His conditional promise or threat must be received by us as an exact disclosure of His real purpose. Let us test this in any case, such as our adversaries usually select: e. g., Is. i: 19; "If ye be willing and obedient, ye shall eat the good of the land." Did not God know, at the time He uttered these words, that they would not be willing and obedient? See ch. vi: 10–12. Was it not His fixed intention, at that very moment to deprive them of the good of the land, in consequence of their clearly foreseen disobedience? Here then is the very same ground for the pretended charge of insincerity in God. The truth is, that God's preceptive threats and promises are not a disclosure of His secret purpose. But the distinction between His secret and revealed will is one which is

inevitably made by every thinking mind, and is absolutely unavoidable, unless man's mind can become as capacious as God's.
And see Deut. xxix : 29. Nor does this impugn God's sincerity.
The sophism of the Arminian is just that, in this case, already
pointed out; confounding conditionality of events decreed,
with conditionality of God's decree. God purposed, in this
case, that the event, Israel's punishment, should be conditioned
on the other event, their disobedience. So that his conditional
promise was perfectly truthful. But He also purposed, secretly,
to withhold that undeserved constraining grace, which might
have prevented Israel's disobedience, so that the condition, and
the thing conditioned on it should both come to pass. Again,
the idea that God has revocable decrees, is as utterly incompatible with the foreknowledge of man's free acts, as with their
foreordination. When it is said that the Pharisees rejected the
counsel of God concerning themselves, the word counsel means
but precept. cf. Ps. cvii : 11 ; Prov. i : 25, 30 ; Rev. iii : 18.

(f) The freedom of God's decree follows from what has
been already argued. If it was eternal, then,
The decree free.
when it was formed, there was no Being out-
side of Himself to constrain or be the inducement to it. If absolute, then God was induced to it by no act of other agents, but
only by His own perfections. And this leads us to remark,
that when we say the decree is free, we do not mean God acts
in forming it, in disregard of His own perfections, but under
the guidance of His own perfections alone. Eph. i : 5. Rom.
xi : 34.

(g) The wisdom of God's decree is manifest from the wisdom of that part of His plan which has been unfolded.
Although much there is inscrutable to us, we see enough to
convince us that all is wise. Rom. xi : 33, 34.

Of the general objections against the decree of God, to
which I called your attention, two remain to
4. Does the decree su-
persede means?
be noticed. One is, that if it were true, it
would supersede the use of all means. " If
what is to be will be, why trouble ourselves with the useless and
vain attempt either to procure or prevent it ?"

This popular objection is exceedingly shallow. The answer
is, that the use of the means, where free agents are concerned,
is just as much included in the decree, as the result. God's
purpose to institute and sustain the laws of causation in nature,
is the very thing which gives efficacy to means, instead of taking
it away. Further, both Scripture aud consciousness tell us, that
in using man's acts as means, God's infinite skill does it always
without marring his freedom in the least.

But it is objected, second, that if there were an absolute
decree, man could not be free; and so, could
Is it inconsistent with
free agency?
not be responsible. But consciousness and
God's word assure us we are free. I reply,

the facts cannot be incompatible because Scripture most undoubtedly asserts both, and both together. See Is. x: 5 to 15;
Acts ii: 23. Second, feeble man procures free acts from his
fellow-man, by availing himself of the power of circumstances
as inducements to his known dispositions, and yet he regards
the agent as free and responsible, and the agent so regards
himself. If man can do this sometimes, why may not an
infinite God do it all the time? Third, If there is anything
about absolute decrees to impinge upon man's freedom of
choice, it must be in their mode of execution, for God's merely
having such a purpose in His secret breast could affect man in
no way. But Scripture and consciousness assure us that God
executes this purpose as to man's acts, not against, but through
and with man's own free will. In producing spiritually good
acts, He "worketh in man to will and to do;" and determines
that he "shall be willing in the day of His power." And in
bringing about bad acts, He simply leaves the sinner in circumstances such that he does, of himself only, yet certainly, choose
the wrong. Last: This objection implies that man's acts of
choice could not be free, unless contingent and uncaused. But
we have seen that this theory of the will is false, foolish, and
especially destructive to rational liberty.

LECTURE XXI.

PREDESTINATION.

SYLLABUS.

1. Wherein are the terms Predestination and Election distinguished from God's
Decree? What the usage and meaning of the original words, Προγνωσις, εκλογη and
cognates?
   Turrettin, Loc. iv. Qu. 7. Dick, Lect. 35. Conf. of F., ch. 3.
2. Prove that there is a definite election of individual men to salvation, whose
number can neither be increased nor diminished.
   Turrettin, Loc. iv, Qu. 12, 16. Conf. of F., ch. 3. Calv. Inst., bk. iii, chs.
   21, 22. Witsius, bk. iii, ch. 4. Dick, Lect 35. Hill's Div., bk. iv. ch. 7.
   Burnet on 39 Articles, Art. xvii. Knapp, ¿ xxxii. Watson's Theol. Inst., ch.
   26, ¿ 1, 2.
3. Has the decree of predestination the qualities predicated of the whole decree?
   Dick, Lect. 35.
4. Does predestination embrace angels as well as men; and with the same kind
of decree?
   Turrettin, Loc. iv, Qu. 8.
5. State the differences between the *Sublapsarian* and *Supralapsarian* schemes.
Which is correct?
   Dick, Lect. 35. Turrettin, Loc. iv, Qu. 9, 14 and 18, ¿ 1-5. Burnet, as above.

WHILE God's decree is His purpose as to all things, His
predestination may be defined to be His purpose concerning the everlasting destiny of His rational
1. Definitions.   creatures. His election is His purpose of

saving eternally some men and angels. Election and reprobation are both included in predestination. The word προόρισ-
μος, the proper original for predestination, does not occur in this
connection in the New Testament; but the kindred verb and
participle are found in the following passages, describing God's
foreordination of the religious state or acts of persons; Acts
iv: 28; Rom. viii: 29, 30; Eph. i: 5; Luke xxii: 22. That
this predetermination of men's privileges and destinies by God
includes the reprobation of the wicked, as well as the election
of the saints, will be established more fully in the next lecture.

    The words πρόγνωσις προγινώσκω, as applied to this subject
mean more than a simple, inactive cognition of the future state
of men by God, a positive or active selection. This is proved
by the Hebraistic usage of this class of words: as in 1 Thess.
v: 12; Jno. x: 14; Ps. i: 6; 2 Tim. ii: 19, and by the following passages, where the latter meaning is indisputable: Rom.
xi: 2; 1 Peter i: 20. This will appear extremely reasonable,
when we remember that according to the order of God's acts,
His foreknowledge is the effect of His foreordination.

    ᾽Εκλογή, ἐκλέγω are used for various kinds of selection to
office, &c., and once by metonymy, for the body of Elect, Rom.
xi: 7. When applied to God's call to religious privilege or to
salvation, it is sometimes inclusive of effectual calling; as Jno.
xv: 16, 19. Some would make this all of election: but that it
means a prior and different selection is plain in Matt. xxii: 14; 2
Thess. ii: 13. The words πρόθεσις, Rom. viii: 28; ix: 11;
Eph. i: 11, and τάσσω, Acts xiii: 48, very clearly express a
foreordination of God as to man's religious state.

    " By the decree of God, for the manifestation of His
own glory, some men and angels are predestinated unto everlasting life, and others foreordained to everlasting death."

  2. Propositions.

    " These angels and men, thus predestinated and foreor-
dained, are particularly and unchangeably designed; and their
number is so certain and definite, that it cannot be either :n-
creased or diminished."

    To discuss this thesis, first, as to men. I would argue 1st:
From the general doctrine of the decree. The
decree is universal, If God has anything to
do with the sinner's redemption, it must be

Predestination of men
proved. From decree.

embraced in that decree. But salvation is everywhere attributed to God, as His work. He calls. He justifies. He regenerates. He keeps us by faith unto salvation. He sanctifies. All
the arguments drawn from God's attributes of wisdom, infinite
knowledge, omnipotence, and immutability, in support of His
eternal decree, show that His agency in saving the sinners who
are saved, is a purposed one, and that this purpose is eternal.
Ps. xxxiii: 11; Numb. xxiii: 19; Mal. iii: 6; Jas. i: 17;
Heb. vi: 17.

2d. The same thing follows from what Scripture and observation

From original sin. teach us of the heart of all men. We are by nature ungodly, hostile to God, and His law, blind in mind, and certainly determined to worldliness in preference to godliness, by a native disposition. Hence, no man cometh to Christ, except the Father who hath sent Him draw him. Unless some power above man made the difference between the believer and unbeliever, it would never vitally appear. But if God makes it, He does it of purpose, and that purpose must be eternal. Hence, no intelligent mind which admits original sin, denies election. The two doctrines stand or fall together.

3d. A number of passages of Scripture assert God's election

From Scripture testimonies. of individuals, in language too clear to be evaded: Matt. xxiv: 24; Jno. xv: 16; Acts xiii: 48; Rom. viii; 29, 30; ix: 11, 16, 22, 24; xi: 5, 7; Eph. i: 4, 11; Phil. iv: 3; 2 Tim. i: 9; 2 Tim. ii: 19. The most of these you will find commented on in your text books, in such a manner as effectually to clear them of the evasions of adversaries. 4th. The saints have their names "written in the book of life," or in "the Lamb's book," or "in Heaven." See Phil. iv: 3; Heb. xii: 23; Rev. xiii: 8. The book of life mentioned in Scripture is of three kinds: 1st, of natural life, Exodus xxxii: 32; when Moses, interceding for Israel prays God, that he may be removed from this life, rather than see the destruction of his brethren: 2d, of federal, visible, church life: as in Ezek. xiii: 9; lying prophets "shall not be written in the writing of the house of Israel": 3d, of eternal life, as in the places first cited. This is the catalogue of the elect.

This class of passages is peculiarly convincing: and especi-

Predestination more than selection of a character to be favored. ally against that phase of error, which makes God's election nothing else than a determination that whosoever believes and repents shall be saved, or in other words, a selection of a certain quality or trait, as the one which procures for its possessors the favour of God. This feeble notion may be farther refuted by remarking that all the language employed about predestination is personal, and the pronouns and other adjuncts indicate persons and not classes. It is "whom (masculine) He foreknew, them He also did predestinate." It is "As many as were ordained to eternal life, believed," (masc.) Acts xiii: 48. The verb προορίζω means a definite decision. See e. g., Acts xvii: 31, or x: 42. Christ tells His disciples that their names are written in heaven; not merely the general conditions of their salvation. Luke x: 2c; In Phil. iv: 3, Clement and his comrades' names are written in the book of life. The condition is one; but in the book are multitudes of names written. Again: a mere determination to bestow favour on the possessors of certain qualities, would be

15*

inert and passive as to the propagation of those qualities;
whereas God's election propagates the very qualities.   See Rom.
ix: 11, 18, 22, 23; Eph. i: 4, 5; 2 Thess. ii: 13.   "He hath
chosen us to salvation through, &c."   And once more : were
this determination to bestow favour on faith and penitence the
whole of election, no one would ever possess those qualities;
for, as we have seen, all men's hearts are fully set in them to do
evil, and would certainly continue impenitent did not God, out
of His gracious purpose, efficaciously persuade some to come to
Him.   These qualities which are thus supposed to be elected,
are themselves the consequences of election.

    5th. A most convincing proof, of a very practical nature, may
be derived from the observed course of God's
Predestination proved by Providence. providence.   That providence determines
sovereignly the metes and bounds of each
man's outward privileges, of his life and opportunities.   It
determines whether he shall be born and live in a Pagan, or a
Christian country, how long he shall enjoy means of grace, and
of what efficacy, and when and where he shall die.   Now in deciding these things sovereignly, the salvation or loss of the man's
soul is practically decided, for without time, means, and opportunity, he will not be saved,   This is peculiarly strong as to two
classes, Pagans and infants.   Arminians admit a sovereign election of nations in the aggregate to religious privileges, or rejection therefrom.   But it is indisputable that in fixing their outward
condition, the religious fate is virtually fixed forever.   What
chance has that man practically, for reaching Heaven, whom
God caused to be born, to live, to die, in Tahiti in the sixteenth
century ?   Did not the casting of his lot there virtually fix his
lot for eternity ?   In short, the sovereign election of aggregate
nations to privileges necessarily implies, with such a mind as
God's, the intelligent and intentional decision of the fate of
individuals, practically fixed thereby.   Is not God's mind infinite ?   Are not His perceptions perfect?   Does He, like a feeble
mortal, "shoot at the covey, without perceiving the individual
birds ?"   As to infants, Arminians believe that all such, which
die in infancy, are redeemed.   When, therefore, God's providence determines that a given human being shall die an infant,
He infallibly determines its redemption, and in this case, at least,
the decision cannot have been by foresight of faith, repentance,
or good works; because the little soul has none, until after its
redemption.   This point is especially conclusive against the
Arminians because they are so positive that all who die in infancy
are saved.

    6th. The declarations of the Holy Ghost in Rom. ix and xi are
so decisive in our favour, that they must needs
Evasions of Rom. ix considered. end the debate, with all who revere the Divine
authority, but for an evasion.   The escape
usually sought by Arminians (as by Watson, Inst.) is : That the

Apostle in these places, teaches, not a personal election to salvation, but a national or aggregate election to privileges. My first
and main objection to this is, that it is utterly irreconcilable
with the scope of St. Paul in the passage. What is that scope?
Obviously to defend his great proposition of "Justification by
free grace through faith," common to Jew and Gentile, from a
cavil which, from pharisaic view, was unanswerable, viz: "That
if Paul's doctrine were true, then the covenant of election with
Abraham was falsified." How does the Apostle answer? Obviously (and irresistibly) that this covenant was never meant to
embrace all his lineage as an aggregate, Rom. ix: 6. "Not as
though the word (covenant) of God had taken none effect."
"For they are not all Israel, which are of Israel," &c. This
decisive fact he then proves, by reminding the Jews that, at the
very first descent, one of Abraham's sons was excluded. and the
other chosen; and at the next descent, where not only the
father, but the mother was the same, and the children were even
twins of one birth, (to make the most absolute possible identity
of lineage) one was again sovereignly excluded. So, all down
the line, some Hebrews of regular lineage were excluded, and
some chosen. Thus, the Apostle's scope requires the disintegrating of the supposed aggregates; the very line of his argument compels us to deal with individuals, instead of masses.
But according to Watson, the Apostle, in speaking of the rejection of Esau, and the selection of Jacob, and of the remaining
selections of Rom. ix and xi, only employs the names of the
two Patriarchs, to impersonate the two nations of Israel and
Edom. He quotes in confirmation, Mal. i: 2; 3; Gen. xxv:
23. But as Calvin well remarks, the primogeniture typified the
blessing of true redemption; so that Jacob's election to the
former represented that to the latter. Let the personal histories
of the two men decide this. Did not the mean, supplanting
Jacob become the humble, penitent saint; while the generous,
dashing Esau degenerated into the reckless, Pagan, Nomad
chief? The selection of the two posterities, the one for Church
privileges, and the other for Pagan defection, was the consequence of the personal election and rejection of the two progenitors. The Arminian gloss violates every law of Hebrew
thought and religious usage. According to these, the posterity
follow the *status* of their progenitor. According to the Arminians, the progenitors would follow the *status* of their posterity.
Farther, the whole discussion of these chapters is personal, it is
individuals with whom God deals here. The election cannot be
of masses to privilege, because the elect are explicitly excepted
out of the masses to which they belonged ecclesiastically. See
ch. ix: vs. 6, 7, 15, 16, 23, 24; ch. xi; vs. 2, 4, 5, 7. "The election hath obtained it and the rest were blinded." The discussion ranges, also, over others than Hebrews and Edomites, to
Pharaoh, an individual unbeliever, &c. Last, the blessings

given in this election are personal. See Rom. viii : 29 ; Eph.
i : 5 ; 2 Thess. ii : 13.

God's decree we found possessed of the properties of
unity, universality, eternity, efficiency and
immutability, sovereignty, absoluteness and
wisdom, Inasmuch as predestination is but
a part, to our apprehension, of this decree, it partakes of all
those properties, as a part of the whole. And the general
evidence would be the same presented on the general subject
of the decree. The part of course is not universal as was the
whole. But we shall find just what the general argument would
have led us to expect: that the decree of predestination is :

*3. Predestination eter-
nal, efficacious, un-
changeable, &c.*

(a) Eternal. Eph. i: 4. " He **hath** chosen us in Christ
before the foundation of the world. " 2 Thess. ii : 13. " From
the beginning." 2 Tim. i: 9. " Before the world began. " (See
last Lect.)

(b) Immutably efficacious. There is no reason why this
part of the decree should not be as much so as all the rest : for
God's foreknowledge and control of the acts of all His creatures
have been already established. He has no more difficulty in
securing the certain occurrence of all those acts of volition,
from man and devils, which are necessary to the certain
redemption of the elect, than in any other department of His
almighty providencc. Why then, should this part of the decree
be exempted from those emphatic assertions of its universal
and absolute efficacy? Numb. xxiii: 19; Ps. xxxiii: 11. Is.
xlvi: 10. But farther, unless God's purpose of saving each
elect sinner were immutable and efficacious, Christ would have
no certain warrant that He would ever see of the travail of His
soul at all. For the same causes that seduce one might
seduce another. Again : no sinner is saved without special
and Almighty grace; for his depravity is total, and his heart
wholly averse from God; so that if God has not provided, in
His eternal plan, resources of gracious power, adequate to subdue unto Himself, and to sustain in grace, every sinner He
attempts to save, I see no probability that any will be saved at
all. For, the proneness to apostacy is such in all, that if God
did not take efficacious care of them, the best would backslide
and fail of Heaven. The efficacy of the decree of election is
also proved by the fact, that God has pre-arranged all the
means for its effectuation. See. Rom. viii: 29, 30. And in fine,
a multitude of Scripture confirms this precious truth: Matt.
xxiv: 24; John x: 28–30; xvii : 6, 12; Heb. vi : 17; 2d.
Tim. ii : 19.

Objections against this gracious truth are almost countless,
as though, instead of being one of the most
precious in Scripture, it were oppressive and
cruel. It is said that the infallibility of the
elect, and their security in Christ, Matt, xxiv: 24; John x : 28,

*Objections to efficient
predestination.*

only guarantee them against such assaults as their free will may
refuse to assent to; and imply nothing as to the purpose of God
to permit or prevent the object of His favour from going
astray of his own accord.   Not to tarry on more minute
answers, the simple reply to this is : that then, there would be
no guarantees at all; and these gracious Scriptures are mere
mockeries of our hope ; for it is notorious that the only way
the spiritual safety of a believer can be injured is by the assent
of his own free will; because it is only then that there is responsibility or guilt.

It is objected that this election cannot be immutably
Objected that the efficacious, because we read in Scripture
Saints warned against of saints who are warned against forfeiting
falling.   it ; of others who felt a wholesome fear of
doing so; and of God's threats that He would on occasion of
certain sins,blot their names from His book of life, &c. Rom. xiv:
15 ; 1 Cor. ix : 27; Ps. lxix : 28; Rev. xxii : 19; 2 Pet. i: 10.
As to the last passage, to make sure βεβαίαν ποιεῖσθαι, our
election, is most manifestly spoken only with reference to the
believer's own apprehension of it, and comfort from it ; not as
to the reality of God's secret purpose.   This is fully borne out
by the means indicated—diligence in holy living.   Such fruits
being the consequence, and not the cause of God's grace to us,
it would simply be preposterous to propose to ensure or
strengthen His secret purpose of grace, by their productions.
All they can do is to strengthen our own apprehension that
such a purpose exists.   When the persecuted Psalmi t prays,
Ps. lxix: 28, that God would " blot his enemies out of the book
of the living," it by no means seems clear that anything more
is imprecated than their removal from this life.   But grant the
other meaning, as we do, in Rev. xxii: 19, the obvious explanation is that God speaks of them according to their seeming
and profession.   The language is adapted *ad hominem*.   It is
not intended to decide whether God has a secret immutable
purpose of love or not, as to them, whether they were ever
elected and effectually called indeed, and may yet be lost ; but
it only states the practical truth, that wickedness would forfeit
that position in God's grace, which they professed to have.
Several of the other passages are in part explained by the fact
that the Christians addressed had not yet attained a comforta-
ble assurance that they were elected.   Hence they might most
consistently feel all these wholesome fears, lest the partial and
uncertain hope they entertained might turn out spurious.   But
the most general and thorough answer which covers all these
cases is this : Granting that God has a secret purpose infallibly
to save a given soul, that purpose embraces means as fully as
ends ; and those means are such as suit a rational free agent, including all reasonable appeals to hope and fear, prospect of
danger, and such like reasonable motives.   Now, that an elect

man may fall totally, is naturally possible, considering him in his own powers; hence, when God plies this soul with fears of falling it is by no means any proof that God intends to permit him to fall, in His secret purpose. Those fears may be the very means designed by God to keep him from it.

God's predestination is wise. It is not grounded on the foreseen excellence of the elect, but it is doubtles grounded on good reasons, worthy of the divine wisdom. See Rom. xi:–end, words spoken by Paul with especial reference to this part of the decree. The sovereignty and unconditional nature of God's predestination will be postponed till we come to discuss the Arminian view.

Selection not a caprice.

There is undoubtedly a predestination of angels. They are a part of God's creation and government, and if what we have asserted of the universality of His purpose is true, it must fix their destiny and foresee all their acts, just as men's. His sovereignty, wisdom, infinite foreknowledge, and power necessitate the supposition. The Scriptures confirm it, telling us of elect angels, 1 Tim. v: 21; of "holy angels," Matt. xxv : 31, *et passim*, as contrasted with wicked angels; that "God spared not the angels that sinned, but cast them down to hell, and delivered them into chains of darkness, to be reserved unto judgment," 2 Pet. ii : 4. Of the "everlasting fire prepared for the devil and his angels," Matt. xxv : 41. Of the "angels which kept not their first estate, but left their own habitation, whom God hath reserved under darkness, in everlasting chains unto the judgment of the great day," Jude. 6 : and of Michael and his angels, and the Dragon and his angels," Rev. xii : 7. Collating these passages, I think we clearly learn, that there are two kinds of spirits of that order; holy and sinful angels, servants of Christ and servants of Satan; that they were all created in an estate of holiness and happiness, and abode in the region called Heaven; (God's holiness and goodness are sufficient proof that He would never have created them otherwise), that the evil angels voluntarily forfeited their estate by sinning, and were then excluded forever from Heaven and holiness; that those who maintained their estate were elected thereto by God, and that their estate of holiness and blessedness is now forever assured. Now the most natural inference from these Bible facts is, that a covenant of works was the dispensation under which God's predestination of angels was effectuated. The fact that those who sinned, fell thereby into a state of irreparable condemnation is most naturally explained by such a covenant. The fact that the elect angels received the adoption of life by maintaining their holiness for a time, seems almost to necessitate that supposition. That the probation under that covenant was temporary, is implied in the fact that some are already separated,

4. Angels are predestinated.

and known as elect, while others are condemned.   The former
must be finally justified and confirmed; the latter finally
reprobated.

1st. Now it is manifest, that these gracious and righteous
dealings of God with His angels in time,
were all foreordained by Him from eternity.
Those who fell, He must have permissively
ordained to fall, and those who are confirmed, He must have
selected from eternity to be confirmed.   But in two respects,
this election of angels differs from that of men.   God's predestination apprehended men, as all lying alike in a mass of total
depravity and condemnation, and the difference He has made
was in pure mercy, unprompted by any thing of good foreseen
in the saints.   But God's predestination apprehended angels as
standing alike in innocency at first, and as left to the determination of a will which, as yet, had full ability to keep the law
perfectly.   In the election of men, while the decree is unconditional, its effectuation is dependent on the elect man's
believing and repenting.   So, in the case of angels, while the
decree was unconditional, the effectuation of it seems to have
been conditioned on the elect angel's keeping the law perfectly
for a given time.   Now here is the difference of the two cases;
in the elect man the ability of will to perform that condition of
his salvation is inwrought in him by God's power, executing
His efficacious decree, (see last Lect.) by His sovereign and
almighty regeneration of the dead soul.   In the case of the
elect angel, the condition of his salvation was fulfilled in his
own natural strength; and was ordained by God no otherwise
than by His permissive decree.   So also, the effectuating of
the reprobation of the non-elect angels was dependent on their
voluntary disobedience, and this too was only determined by
God's permissive decree.   It has been asked if all the angels
were alike innocent and peccable, with full ability of will to
keep the law perfectly, and yet with freedom of will to sin;
how came it that the experiment did not result alike for all,
that all did not fall or stand, that like causes did not produce
like effects?   Must there not have been a cause for the different results?   And must not this cause be sought outside the
angels' wills, in God's agency?   The answer may be, that the
outward relations of no two beings to circumstances and beings
other than themselves can ever be identical.   In those different
circumstances, were presented occasional causes for volitions,
sufficient to account for different volitions from wills that were
at first in similar moral states.   And it was by His providential
ordering of those outward relations and circumstances, that
God was able permissively to determine the results.   Yet the
acts of the two classes of angels, good and bad, were wholly
their own.

The second difference between their election and man's,

Predestination of an-
gels differs from men's.

2d difference.   is that the angels were not chosen in a mediator. They needed none, because they
were not chosen out of a state of guilt, and had not arrayed
God's moral attributes against them. Some have supposed
that their confirming grace was and is mediated to them by
Jesus Christ, quoting Col. ii: 10; 1 Pet. i: 12; Heb. i: 6; Phil.
2: 10; 1 Pet. iii: 22; Eph. i: 10; Col. i: 14, 15, 20.

These passages doubtless teach that the Son was, in the
beginning, the immediate agent of creation for these, as for all
other beings; and that the God-man now includes angels in
His mediatorial kingdom, in the same sense in which He
includes the rest of the universe, besides the saints. But that
He is not a mediator for angels is clear, from the fact that,
while He is never called such, He is so emphatically called "the
Mediator between God and man," 1 Tim. ii: 5. Second. He
has assumed no community of nature with angels. Last. It
is expressly denied in Heb. ii: 16, 17. (Greek.)

5. All who call themselves Calvinists admit that God's
decree is, in His mind, a cotemporaneous unit. Yet the attempt
to assign an order to its relative parts, has led to three different
schemes of predestination: that of the *Supralapsarian*, of the
Sublapsarian, and of the *Hypothetic Universalist*.

The first suppose that in a rational mind, that which is
Supralapsarian scheme. ultimate as end, is first in design; and that,
in the process of planning, the mind passes
from the end to the means, traveling as it were backwards.
Hence, God first designed His own glory by the salvation of a
definite number of men conceived as yet only as *in posse*, and
the reprobation of another definite number; that then He purposed their creation, then the permission of their fall, and then
the other parts of the plan of redemption for the elect. I do
not mean to represent that they impute to God an actual succession of time as to the rise of the parts of the decree in His
eternal mind, but that these divines represent God as planning
man's creation and fall, as a means for carrying out His predestination, instead of planning his election as a means for repairing his fall.

The Sublapsarian assigns the opposite order; that God
Sublapsarian scheme. determined to create man in His own image,
to place him under a covenant of works,
to permit his fall, and with reference to the fallen and guilty
state thus produced, to elect in sovereign mercy some to be
saved, passing by the rest in righteous judgment upon their
sins, and that He further decreed to send Jesus Christ to redeem
the elect. This milder scheme the Supralapsarians assert to be
attended with the vice of the Arminian, in making the decree
conditional; in that God's decree of predestination is made
dependent on man's use of his free will under the covenant of
works. They also assert that their scheme is the symmetrical

one, in that it assigns the rational order which exists between ultimate end and intermediate means.

In my opinion this is a question which never ought to have been raised.   Both schemes are illogical and **Both erroneous.** contradictory to the true state of facts.   But the Sublapsarian is far more Scriptural in its tendencies, and its general spirit far more honourable to God.   The Supralapsarian, under a pretense of greater symmetry, is in reality the more illogical of the two, and misrepresents the divine character and the facts of Scripture in a repulsive manner.   The view from which it starts, that the ultimate end must be first in design, and then the intermediate means, is of force only with reference to a finite mind.   God's decree has no succession; and to Him no successive order of parts; because it is a cotemporaneous unit, comprehended altogether, by one infinite intuition.   In this thing, the statements of both parties are untrue to God's thought.   The true statement of the matter is, that in this co-etaneous, unit plan, one part of the plan is devised by God with reference to a state of facts which He intended to result from another part of the plan; but all parts equally present, and all equally primary to His mind.   As to the decree to create man, to permit his fall, to elect some to life; neither part preceded any other part with God; but His purpose to elect had reference to a state of facts which was to result from His purpose to create, and permit the fall.   It does not seem to me that the Sublapsarian scheme makes the decree conditional. True, one result decreed is dependent on another result decreed; but this is totally another thing.   No scheme can avoid this, not even the Supralapsarian, unless it does away with all agency except God's, and makes Him the direct author of sin.

Objections to the Supralapsarian. But we object more particularly to the Supralapsarian scheme.

(a) That it is erroneous in representing God as having before His mind, as the objects of predestination, men conceived *in posse* only; and in making creation a means of their salvation or damnation.   Whereas, an object must be conceived as existing, in order to have its destiny given to it.   And creation can with no propriety be called a means for effectuating a decree of predestination as to creatures.   It is rather a prerequisite of such decree.

(b.) It contradicts Scripture, which teaches us that God chose His elect "out of the world," Jno. xv : 19, and out of the "same lump" with the vessels of dishonour, Rom. ix : 21. They were then regarded as being, along with the non-elect, in the common state of sin and misery.

(c.) Our election is in Christ our Redeemer, Eph. i : 4; iii : 11, which clearly shows that we are conceived as being fallen, and in need of a Redeemer, in this act.   And, moreover, our election is an election to the exercise of saving graces to be wrought in us by Christ, 1 Pet. i : 2; 2 Thess. ii : 13.

(d.) Election is declared to be an act of mercy: Rom. ix : 15, 16; xi : 5, 6, and preterition is an act of justice, Rom. ix : 22. Now as mercy and goodness imply an apprehension of guilt and misery in their object, so justice implies ill-desert. This shows that man is predestinated as fallen; and is not permitted to fall because predestinated. I will conclude this part, by repeating the language of Turrettin, Loc. 4, Qu. 18, §5.

1. "By this hypothesis, the first act of God's will towards some of His creatures is conceived to be an act of hatred, in so far as He willed to demonstrate His righteousness in their damnation, and indeed before they were considered as in sin, and consequently before they were deserving of hatred; nay, while they were conceived as still innocent, and so rather the objects of love. This does not seem compatible with God's ineffable goodness.

2. "It is likewise harsh that, according to this scheme, God is supposed to have imparted to them far the greatest effects of love, out of a principle of hatred, in that He determines to create them in a state of integrity to this end, that He may illustrate His righteousness in their damnation. This seems to express Him neither as supremely good nor as supremely wise and just.

3. "It is erroneously supposed that God exercised an act of mercy and justice towards His creatures in His foreordination of their salvation and destruction, in that they are conceived as neither wretched, nor even existing as yet. But since those virtues (mercy and justice) are relative, they pre-suppose their object, do not make it.

4. "It is also asserted without warrant, that creation and the fall are means of election and reprobation, since they are antecedent to them: else sin would be on account of damnation, whereas damnation is on account of sin; and God would be said to have created men that He might destroy them."

LECTURE XXII.

PREDESTINATION. — Concluded.

SOME French Presbyterian Divines of Saumur about 1630–50, devised still another scheme of relations between the parts of the decree, representing God as first (in order, not in time) purposing to create man; second, to place him under a covenant of works, and to permit his fall; third, to send Christ to provide and offer satisfaction for all, out of His general compassion for all the fallen; but fourth, foreseeing that all would surely reject it because of their total depravity, to select out of the rebellious mass, some, in His sovereign mercy, to whom He would give effectual calling. They supposed that this theory would remove the difficulties concerning the extent of the sacrifice of Christ, and also reconcile the passages of Scripture which declare God's universal compassion for sinners, with His reprobation of the non-elect.

1. Hypothetic scheme.

This scheme is free from many of the objections which lie against the Arminian; it holds fast to the truth of original sin, and it avoids the absurdity of conditioning God's decree of election on a foresight of the saints' faith and repentance. But in two respects it is untenable. If the idea of a real succession in time between the parts of the divine decree be relinquished, as it must be; then this scheme is perfectly illusory, in representing God as decreeing to send Christ to provide a redemption to be offered to all, on condition of faith, and this out of His general compassion. For if He foresees the certain rejection of all at the time, and at the same time purposes sovereignly to withhold the grace which would work faith in the soul, from some, this scheme of

Wherein untenable.

235

election really makes Christ to be related, in God's purpose, to the non-elect, no more closely nor beneficially than the stricter Calvinistic scheme. But second and chiefly, it represents Christ as not purchasing for His people the grace of effectual calling, by which they are persuaded and enabled to embrace redemption. But God's purpose to confer this is represented as disconnected with Christ and His purchase, and subsequent, in order, to His work, and the foresight of its rejection by sinners. Whereas Scripture represents that this gift, along with all other graces of redemption, is given us in Christ, having been purchased for His people by Him. Eph. i: 3; Phil. i: 29: Heb. xii: 2.

I have postponed to the last, the fourth scheme for arranging the order of the parts of the decree, which is the Arminian. Unwilling to rob God openly of His infinite perfection, as is done by the Socinians, they admit that He has some means of foreseeing the contingent acts of free-agents, although He neither can nor does, consistently with their free-agency, exercise any direct foreordination over those acts. Such contingent acts, they say, would be unknowable to a finite mind, but this does not prove that God may not have some mode of certainly foreknowing them, which implies no foreordination, and which is inscrutable to us. This foresight combines with His eternal purpose in the following order. 1st. God decreed to create man holy and happy, and to place him under a covenant of works. 2nd. God foreseeing man's fall into a state of total depravity and condemnation, decreed to send Jesus Christ to provide redemption for all. (This redemption included the purchase of common, sufficient grace for all sinners.) And God also, in this connection, determined the general principle that faith should be the condition of an actual interest in this redemption. 3d. Next He foresaw that some would so improve their common grace as to come to Christ, turn from sin and persevere in holiness to the end of life. These He eternally purposed to save. Others, He foresaw, would neglect their privileges, so as to reject, or after embracing, to forsake Christ; and these He eternally purposed to leave in their guilt and ruin. Thus His purpose as to individuals, while eternal, is conditioned wholly on the conduct foreseen in them.

2. Arminian scheme.

This plausible scheme seems to be, at the first glance, attended with several advantages for reconciling God's goodness and sincerity with the sinner's damnation. But the advantages are only seeming For 1. The scheme is overthrown by all the reasons which showed generally that God's decrees cannot be conditional; (see p. 218, &c.) and especially by these. (a.) That every one of the creature acts is also foreordained, on which a part of the decree is supposed to be conditioned. (b.) That all the future events into which these contingent acts enter,

Objections. 1st. That the decree cannot be conditional.

directly or indirectly, as causes, must be also contingent; which would cast a quality of uncertainty and possible failure over God's whole plan of redemption and moral government, and much of His other providence. (c.) And that God would no longer be absolute sovereign; for, instead of the creatures depending on Him alone, He would depend on the creature.

One can scarcely believe that Paul would have answered the objections usually raised against God's sovereign decree, as He does in Rom. ix, had He inculcated this Arminian view of it. In verses 14 and 19, he anticipates those objections; 1st that God would be unjust; 2d that He would destroy man's free agency, and He deigns no other answer than to reaffirm the absolute sovereignty of God in the matter, and to repudiate the objections as sinful cavils. How different this from the answer of the Arminian to these cavils. He always politely evades them by saying that all God's dealings with men are suspended on the improvement they choose to make of His common mercy offered to them. This contrast leads us to believe that St. Paul was not an Arminian.

2nd. That Paul does not reply thus to cavils.

The believer's faith, penitence, and perseverance in holiness could never be so foreseen by God, as to be the condition moving Him to determine to bestow salvation on him, because no child of Adam ever has any true faith, &c., except as fruits of God's grace bestowed in election. This is evinced in manifold ways throughout Scripture. (a.) Man is too depraved ever to exercise these graces, except as moved thereto by God, Rom. viii: 7; 2 Cor. iii: 5; Rom. vii: 18; Gen. vi: 5. (b.) The elect are declared to be chosen to the enjoyment of these graces, not on account of the exercise of them, Rom. viii: 29; 2 Thess. ii: 13, 14; Eph. i: 4; ii: 10. (c.) The very faith, penitence and perseverance in holiness which Arminians represent as conditions moving God to elect man, the Scripture represents as gifts of God's grace inwrought by Him in the elect, as consequences of His election, Eph. ii: 8; Acts v: 31; 2 Tim. ii: 25; Phil. i: 6; 2 Pet. i: 3. (d.) All the elect believe on Christ, Jno. x: 16, 27 to 29; vi: 37, 39; xvii: 2, 9, 24, and none others do, Jno. x: 26: Acts xiii: 48; ii: 47. Couple these two facts together, and they furnish a strong evidence that faith is the consequence (therefore not the cause) of election.

3rd. Faith, &c., consequences of electing grace.

The Scriptures in the most express and emphatic terms declare that it was no goodness in the elect which caused God to choose them; that His electing love found them lying in the same mass of corruption and wrath with the reprobate, every way deserving the same fate, and chose them out of it for reasons commending themselves to His own good pleasure, and in sovereign benevolence.

4th. Express texts.

This was seen in Jacob and Esau, Rom. ix: 11–13, as to Israel; Ezek. xvi: 3–6.   As to all sinners, Rom. ix: 15, 16, 18, 21; Rom. xi: 4–7; viii: 28.   (Here the Arminians claim that God's foreknowledge precedes and prompts His foreordination.   But we have shown that this foreknowledge implies selection.)   2 Tim. i: 9; Matt. xi: 26; Jno. xv: 16–19.

5th.   From the Arminian doctrine of conditional election, must flow this distinction, admitted by many Wesleyans.   Those who God foresaw would believe and repent, He thereupon elected to adoption.   But all Arminians believe that an adopted believer may "fall from grace."   Hence, the smaller number, who God foresaw would persevere in gospel grace, unto death, He thereupon elected to eternal life.   And the persons elected to eternal life on foresight of their perseverance, are not identical with those elected to adoption on foresight of their faith. But now, if the former are, in the omniscience of God, elected to eternal life on foresight of their perseverance, then they must be certain to persevere.   We have here, therefore, the doctrine of the perseverance of this class of the elect.   The inference is unavoidable.   On this result we remark first: It is generally conceded by both Calvinists and Arminians, that the doctrine of perseverance is consistent only with that of unconditional election, and refutes the opposite.   Second: In every instance of the perseverance of those elected unto eternal life (on certain foresight of their perseverance) we have a case of volitions free and responsible, and yet certainly occurring.   But this, the Arminians hold, infringes man's freedom.   Third: No effect is without a cause.   Hence, there must be some efficient cause for this certain perseverance.   Where shall it be sought?   In a contingent will? or in efficacious grace?   These are the only known sources.   It cannot be found in a contingent source; for this is a contradiction.   It must then be sought in efficacious grace.   But this, if dispensed by omniscience, can be no other than a proof and result of electing grace.

The word reprobate ($\dot{\alpha}\delta\dot{o}\varkappa\iota\mu o\varsigma$) is not, so far as I know, applied in the Scriptures to the subject of predestination.   Its etymology and usage

3. Preterition.

would suggest the meaning of something rejected upon undergoing a test or trial, and hence, something condemned or rejected.   Thus Rom. i: 28, $\dot{\alpha}\delta\dot{o}\varkappa\iota\mu o\nu$ $\nu o\tilde{\nu}\nu$, a mind given over to condemnation and desertion, in consequence of great sin, 2 Tim. iii: 8.   Sectaries, $\dot{\alpha}\delta\dot{o}\varkappa\iota\mu o\iota$ $\pi\varepsilon\rho\dot{\iota}$ $\tau\dot{\eta}\nu$ $\pi\dot{\iota}\sigma\tau\iota\nu$, finally condemned and given over to apostasy concerning the Christian system.   1 Cor. ix: 27, "Lest after I have preached to others, I myself should be $\dot{\alpha}\delta\dot{o}\varkappa\iota\mu o\varsigma$," rejected at the final test, i. e., Judgment Day.   Hence the more general sense of "worthless," Tit. i: 16; Heb. vi: 8.

The application of this word to the negative part of the decree of predestination has doubtless prej-

The word ill-chosen.

udiced our cause.   It is calculated to mis-

represent and mislead, because it suggests too much the idea
of a comparative judicial result. For then, the query arises,
if the non-elect and elect have been tested as to their deserts,
in the divine mind, how comes it that the elect are acquitted
when they are as guilty, and the non-elect condemned when
they are no worse? Is not this partiality? But the fact is,
that in election, God acted as a sovereign, as well as a judge;
and that the elect are not taken because they are less guilty
upon trial, but because God had other secret, though sufficient
reasons. If the negative part of the decree of predestination
then must be spoken of as a decree of reprobation, it must be
understood in a modified sense.

The theologians, while admitting the strict unity of God's
decree, divide reprobation into two elements,
as apprehended by us, preterition and pre-
damnation. These Calvinists, were they con-
sistent, would apply a similar analysis to the decree of election,
and divide it into a selection and a prejustification. Thus we
should have the doctrine of an eternal justification, which they
properly reject as erroneous. Hence, the distinction should
be consistently dropped in explaining God's negative predestination.

*Does it include pre-
terition and predam-
nation.*

I would rather say, that it consists simply of a sovereign,
yet righteous purpose to leave out the non-elect, which preterition was foreseen and intended to result in their final righteous
condemnation. The decree of reprobation is then, in its
essence, a simple preterition. It is indeed intelligent and
intentional in God. He leaves them out of His efficacious
plan and purpose of mercy, not out of a general inattention or
overlooking of them, but knowingly and sovereignly. Yet
objectively this act is only negative, because God does nothing
to those thus passed by, to make their case any worse, or to
give any additional *momentum* to their downward course. He
leaves them as they are. Yea, incidentally, He does them
many kindnesses, extends to multitudes of them the calls of
His word, and even the remonstrances of His Spirit, preventing
them from becoming as wicked as they would otherwise have
been. But the practical or efficacious part of His decree is,
simply that He will not " make them willing in the day of His
power."

When we thus explain it, there is abundant evidence of a
decree of preterition. It is inevitably implied
in the decree of election, coupled with the
fact that all are neither elected nor saved. If salvation is of
God; if God is a Being of infinite intelligence, and if He has
eternally purposed to save some; then He has *ipso facto*
equally purposed from eternity to leave the others in their ruin.
And to this agree the Scriptures, Rom. ix : 13, 17, 18, 21 and 22;
Matt. xi : 25; Rom. xi : 7; 2 Tim. ii : 20; Jude. 4; 1 Pet. ii : 8.

Preterition proved.

This is a part of God's word which has ever been assailed with the fiercest cavils. It has been repre-

Objections. Answers. sented as picturing a God, who created a number of unfortunate immortals, and endued them with capacities for sinning and suffering, only in order that He might damn them forever; and to this wretched fate they are inexorably shut up, by the iron decree, no matter what penitent efforts or what cries for mercy and escape they may put forth; while the equally or more guilty objects of the divine caprice and favouritism are admitted to a Heaven which they cannot forfeit, no matter how vilely they behave. There is no wonder that a Wesley should denounce the doctrine thus misrepresented, as worthy only of Satan. There is, indeed, enough in the truth of this subject, to fill every thoughtful mind with solemn awe and holy fear of that God, who holds the issues of our redemption in His sovereign hand. But how differently does His dealing appear, when we remember that He created all His creatures at first in holiness and happiness; that He gave them an adequate opportunity to stand; that He has done nothing to make the case of the non-elect worse than their own choice makes it, but on the contrary, sincerely and mercifully warns them by conscience and His word against that wicked choice; that it is all a monstrous dream to fancy one of these non-elect seeking Heaven by true penitence, and excluded by the inexorable decree, because they all surely yet voluntarily prefer their impenitence, so that God is but leaving them to their preferred ways; and that the only way He ensures the elect from the destruction due their sins, is by ensuring their repentance, faith, and diligent strivings to the end in a holy life.

Yet it must be confessed that some of the odiousness of

Is preterition grounded on the sin of those passed by. the doctrine is in part due to the unwise views of it presented by the Orthodox sometimes, going beyond all that God's majesty, sovereignty and word require, out of a love of hypothesis. Thus, it is disputed what is the ground of this righteous preterition of the non-elect. The honest reader of his Bible would suppose that it was, of course, their guilt and wickedness foreseen by God, and, for wise reasons, permissively decreed by Him. This, we saw, all but the supralapsarian admitted in substance. God's election is everywhere represented in Scripture, as an act of mercy, and His preterition as an act of righteous anger against sin. The elect are vessels of mercy, the non-elect of wrath. (God does not show anger at anything but sin) as in Rom. ix : 22. Everywhere it is sin which excludes from His favour, and sin alone.

But it is urged, with an affected over-refinement, the sin of the non-elect cannot be the ground of God's preterition, because all Adam's seed being viewed as equally depraved, had this been the ground, all would have been passed by. I reply,

yes; if this had been the only consideration, *pro* or *con*, present
in God's mind.   The ill-desert of all was in itself a sufficient
ground for God to pass by all.   But when His sovereign wisdom
suggested some reason, unconnected with the relative desert or
ill-desert of sinners, which was a good and sufficient ground for
God's choosing a part; this only left the same original ground,
ill-desert, operating on His mind as to the remainder.   It is
perfectly true that God's sovereignty concerns itself with the
preterition as well as the election; for the separate reason
which grounded the latter is sovereign.   But with what propriety can it be said that this secret sovereign reason is the
ground of his preterition, when the very point of the case was
that it was a reason which did not apply to the non-elect, but
only to the elect?   As to the elect, it overruled the ground for
their preterition, which would otherwise have been found, in
their common ill-desert.   As to the non-elect, it did not apply,
and thus left the original ground, their ill-deserts, in full force.
If all sinning men had been subjects of a decree of preterition, nobody would have questioned, but that God's ground
for passing them by was simply their ill-desert.   Now, then, if
a secret, sovereign motive, counterpoising that presented by the
ill-desert, led to the election of some; how does this alter the
ground for God's preterition of the rest?   Three traitors are
justly condemned to death for capital crimes confessed.   The
king ascertains that two of them are sons of a noble citizen, who
had died for the commonwealth; and the supreme judge is
moved by this consideration to spare the lives of these men.
For what is the third criminal hung?   No one has any doubt
in answering: " For his treason."   The original cause of death
remains in operation against him, because no contravening fact
existed in his case.

But it is said again: that if we make the sin of the non-
elect the ground of their rejection, then by parity of reasoning,
we must make the foreseen piety of the elect the ground of
their election; and thus return to the error of conditional
decrees.   This perversely overlooks the fact, that, while the
elect have no piety of their own originating to be foreseen, the
others have an impiety of their own.   Reviewing the arguments
against conditional election, the student will see that this is the
key to all: It cannot be, because no men will have any piety to
foresee, save as it is the result of God's grace bestowed from
election.   But is it so with men's sin?   Just the opposite.   Sin is
the very condition in which God foresees all men as standing, for
all except supralapsarians admit that God in predestination
regards man as fallen.   Man's foreseen sin may be the ground
of God's preterition, because it is not the effect of that preterition, but of another part of His eternal purpose, viz: that to
permit the fall.   And, as again and again taught, while the decree
is absolute, the results decreed are conditioned; and we cannot

16*

but conceive God as predicating one part of His eternal purpose on a state of facts which was destined to proceed out of another part thereof.

Again: it is said, Scriptures teach, that the sin of the non-elect was not the ground of their preterition. "In John x: 26, continued unbelief is the consequence, and therefore not the ground of the Pharisees' preterition." Matt. xi: 25; Rom. ix: 11, 18. "God's will," they say, "and not the non-elect's sin, is the ground of His purpose to harden." And "Esau was rejected as much without regard to his evil, as Jacob was elected without regard to his good deeds." To the first of these points I reply, that the withholding of God's grace is but the negative occasion of a sinner's unbelief, just as the absence of the physician from a sick man is the occasion, and not the cause, of His death. Men say that "he died because he failed to receive medical help," when speaking popularly. But they know that the disease, and not the physician, killed him. So, our Saviour teaches, in Jno. x: 26; that the stubborn unbe-lief of the Pharisees was occasioned by God's refraining from the bestowal of renewing grace. But He does not deny that that this unbelief was caused by their own depravity, as left uninfluenced by the Spirit. Turrettin (Loc. iv: Qu. 15,) although inconsistently asserting on this point the supralapsarian extreme, says, (Sec. 3,) that we must distinguish between the non-elect man's original unbelief, and his acquired: and that it is the latter only, which he denies to be a ground of preterition, because it is a result thereof. He admits that the original unbelief may be a ground of preterition. This virtually con-cedes the point. To the second argument, we reply, that God's decree of preterition is, like all others, guided by His εὐδοκία. But is this sovereign good pleasure motiveless? Is it irrational caprice? Surely not. It is the purpose of a sovereign; but of one who is as rational, just, holy and good, as He is absolute. Such a being would not pass by, in righteous displeasure, His creature in whom He saw no desert of displeasure. The third point is made from the oft-cited case of the twins, Esau and Jacob. Let the supralapsarian strain the passage to mean that Esau's preterition was no more grounded in his ill-desert, than Jacob's election in his merit, because "the children had not done good nor evil;" and he will only reach a result obnoxious to his own view as to mine. He will make the Apostle teach that these children had no original sin, and that they stood before the divine prescience in that impossible state of moral neutrality, of which Pelagians prate. We are shut up to inter-pret the passage, just as Turrettin does elsewhere, that it is only a relative guilt and innocence between Esau and Jacob, which the Apostle asserts. In fact, both "were by nature children of wrath, even as others."

When it is said that God hardens the non-elect, it is not,

G o d ' s hardening, what?

and cannot be intended, that He exerts positive influence upon them to make them worse. The proof of this was given under the question, whether God can be the author of sin. See especially Jas. i: 13. God is only the negative cause of hardening—the positive depravation comes only from the sinner's own voluntary feelings and acts. And the mode in which God gives place to, or permits this self-inflicted work, is by righteously withholding His restraining word and Spirit; and second, by surrounding the sinner (through His permissive providence) with such occasions and opportunities as the guilty man's perverse heart will voluntarily abuse to increase his guilt and obduracy. This dealing, though wrong in men, is righteous in God. Even when God's decree and providence concerning sins are thus explained, our opponents cavil at the facts. They say that the rule of holiness enjoined on us is, not only to do no sin, but to prevent all the sin in others we righteously can. They say that the same rule obliges God. They say we represent Him as like a man who, witnessing the perpetration of a crime, and having both the right and power to prevent it, stands idly by: and they refer us to such Scriptures as Prov. xxiv: 11, 12. And when we remind them, that God permissively ordains those sins, not for the sake of their evil, but for the sake of the excellent and holy ends He will bring out, they retort, that we represent Him as " doing evil that good may come." These objections derive all their plausibility from forgetting that we are creatures and bondsmen of God, while He is supreme judge. The judicial retribution of sin is not our function: He claims it as His own. Rom. xii: 19. It is a recognized principle of His rule, to make permitted sins the punishment of sins. Hence, we deny that it follows, the same rules oblige Him, which bind us. It does not follow, that the sovereign proprietor can righteously deal towards His possessions, only in the modes in which fellow servants can properly treat each other. Hence such dealing, making guilty souls the executors, in part, of their own righteous punishment, as would be an intrusion for us, is righteous and holy for Him.

4. Is predestination unjustly partial?

To notice briefly the standing objections: The doctrine of predestination as we have defined it, is not inconsistent with the justice and impartiality of God. His agency in the fall of angels and men was only permissive—the act and choice were theirs. They having broken God's laws and depraved themselves, it would have been just in God to leave them all under condemnation. How then can it be more than just when He punishes only a part? The charge of partiality has been absurdly brought here, as though there could be partiality where there are no rights at all, in any creature, on the mercy of God; and Acts x: 34; Levit. xix: 15; Deut. i: 17; 2 Sam. xiv: 14; Rom.

ii: 11, have been quoted against us. As Calvin very acutely remarks on the first of these, one's *persona*, πρόσωπον, in the sense of these passages, means, not the moral character, as judicially well or ill-deserving, but his accidental position in society, as Jew or Gentile, rich or poor, plebeian or nobleman. And in this sense it is literally true of election, that in it God respects no man's *persona*, but takes him irrespective of all these factitious advantages and disadvantages. To this foolish charge, Matt. xx: 15, is a sufficient answer. God's sovereignty ought undoubtedly to come in as a reply. Within the bounds of His other perfections of righteousness, truth and benevolence, God is entitled to make what disposal of His own He is pleased, and men are His property—Rom. ix: 20, 21. Paul does not imply here that God is capable of doing injustice to an innocent creature, in order to illustrate His sovereignty; but that in such a case as this of predestination, where the condemnation of all would have been no more than they deserved, He can exercise His sovereignty, in sparing and punishing just such as He pleases, without a particle of injustice.

2. It is objected, that God's holiness would forbid such a predestination. How, it is said, can it be

Is it unholy?

compatible with the fact that God hates sin, for Him to construct an arrangement, He having full power to effectuate a different one, by which He voluntarily and intentionally leaves multitudes of His creatures in increasing and everlasting wickedness? And the same objection is raised against it from His benevolence. The answer is, that this is but the same difficulty presented by the origin of evil; and it presses on the Calvinist with no more force than on the Arminian, or even on the Socinian. Allow to God a universal, perfect foreknowledge, as the Arminian does, and the very same difficulty is presented, how an almighty God should have knowingly adopted a system for the universe, which would embody such results. For even if the grossest Pelagian view be adopted, that God is literally unable certainly to prevent the wicked acts of man's free will, and yet leave him a free agent, it would doubtless have been in His power to let alone creating those who, He foresaw, would make a miserable immortality for themselves, in spite of His grace. The Arminian is obliged to say: "There are doubtless inscrutable reasons, unknown to us, but seen by God to be sufficient, why He should permit it?" The same appeal to our ignorance is just as available for the Calvinist. And if the lowest Socinian ground is taken, which denies to God a universal foreknowledge of the volitions of free agents, still we must suppose one of two things. He must either have less wisdom than many of His creatures, or else, He made these men and angels, knowing in the general, that large immortal misery would result. So that there is no evasion of this difficulty, except by so robbing God of His perfections as practically to dethrone Him. It is not Calvinism which creates it; but the simple existence of sin and misery, destined never to be wholly extinguished, in the government of an almighty and omniscient God. He who thinks he can master it by his theory, only displays his folly.

3. It is objected that God's goodness and sincerity in the offer of the Gospel to all is inconsistent with predestination. It is urged: God says He "hath no pleasure in the death of him that dieth;" that He would have all men to be saved; and that Christ declared His wish to save reprobate Jerusalem. Now, how can these things, and His universal offer: "Whosoever will, let him come," consist with the fixed determination that the non-elect shall never be saved? I reply, that this difficulty (which cannot be wholly solved) is not generated by predestination, but lies equally against any other theory which leaves God His divine attributes. Let one take this set of facts. Here is a company of sinners; God could convert all by the same powers by which He converts one. He offers His salvation to all, and assures them of His general benevolence. He knows perfectly that some will neglect the offer; and yet, so knowing, He intentionally refrains from exerting those powers, to overrule their reluctance, which He is able to exert if He chose. This is but a statement of stubborn facts; it cannot be evaded without impugning the omniscience, or omnipotence of God, or both. Yet, see if the whole difficulty is not involved in it. Every evangelical Christian, therefore, is just as much interested in seeking the solution of this difficulty as the Calvinist. And it is to be sought in the following brief suggestions. God's concern in the transgression and impenitence of those whom He suffers to neglect His warnings and invitations, is only permissive. He merely leaves men to their own sinful choice. His invitations are always impliedly, or explicitly conditional; suspended on the sinner's turning. He has never said that He desires the salvation of a sinner as impenitent; He only says, if the sinner will turn, he is welcome to salvation. And this is always literally true; were it in the line of possibilities that one non-elect should turn, he would find it true in his case. All, therefore, that we have to reconcile is these three facts; that God should see a reason why it is not proper, in certain cases, to put forth His almighty grace to overcome a sinner's reluctance; and yet that He should be able to do it if He chose; and yet should be benevolent and pitiful towards all His creatures. Now God says in His Word that He does compassionate lost sinners. He says that He could save if He pleased. His word and providence both show us that some are permitted to be lost. In a wise and good man, we can easily understand how a power to pardon, a sincere compassion for a guilty criminal, and yet a fixed purpose to punish, could co-

How reconciled with Gospel offers to all?

exist; the power and compassion being overruled by His wisdom. Why may not something analogous take place in God, according to His immutable nature? Is it said: such an explanation implies a struggle in the breast between competing considerations, inconsistent with God's calm blessedness? I reply, God's revelations of His wrath, love, pity, repentance, &c., are all anthropopathic, and the difficulty is no greater here, than in all these cases. Or is it said, that there can be nothing except a lack of will, or a lack of power to make the sinner both holy and happy? I answer: it is exceeding presumption to suppose that, because we do not see such a cause, none can be known to God !

"The doctrine of this high mystery of predestination is to be handled with special prudence and care."

5. How to be taught, and its results. In preaching it, that proportion should be observed, which obtains in the Bible ; and no polemical zeal against the impugners of the doctrine ought to tempt the minister to obtrude it more often. To press it prominently on anxious inquirers, or on those already confused by cavils of heretics or Satanic suggestions, or to urge it upon one inclined to skepticism, or one devoid of sufficient Christian knowledge, experience and humility, is unsuitable and imprudent. And when taught, it should be in the mode which usually prevails in Scripture, viz: *a posteriori*, as inferred from its result, effectual calling.

But when thus taught, the doctrine of predestination is full of edification. It gives ground for humility, because it leaves man no ground for claiming any of the credit of either originating or carrying on his salvation. It lays a foundation for confident hope ; because it shows that "the gifts and calling of God are without repentance." It should open the fountains of love and gratitude, because it shows the undeserved and eternal love of God for the undeserving. See here an eloquent passage in Witsius, b. 3, chap. 4, § 30. We should learn to teach and to view the doctrine, not from an exclusive, but from an inclusive point of view. It is sin which shuts out from the favour of God, and which ruins. It is God's decree which calls back, and repairs and saves all who are saved. Whatever of sin, of guilt, of misery, of despair the universe exhibits, arises wholly out of man's and Satan's transgression. Whatever of redemption, of hope, of comfort, of holiness and of bliss alleviates this sad panorama, all this proceeds from the decree of God. The decree is the fountain of universal benevolence ; voluntary sin is the fountain of woe. Shall the fountain of mercy be maligned because, although it emits all the happiness in the universe, it has a limit to its streams?

LECTURE XXIII.

CREATION.

THE words rendered to create, cannot be considered, in their etymology and usage, very distinctive of the nature of the act. The authorities make בָּרָא

1. Terms defined.

mean "to cut or carve," primarily, (from the idea of splitting off parts, or separation) hence "to fashion," then to "create;" and thence the more derivative sense of producing or generating, regenerating the heart, &c. The verb עָשָׂה carries, according to the authorities, more of the sense of the Greek verb ποιέω—"to do or to make," and is used for fashioning, manufacturing, doing (as a function or business), acquiring property, &c. The verb יָצַר seems to me to carry more distinctively the idea of fashioning out of pre-existent materials, as a potter (יוֹצֵר) out of clay, &c. And it will be observed that wherever it is applied to making man or animals in Gen., the material out of which, is mentioned or implied, as ii : 7. God fashioned man (וַיִּיצֶר) out of the dust of the earth. The word usually employed from Greek in Septuagint and New Testament to express the idea of creating, as distinguished from begetting or generating is κτίζω. This, authorities say, means primarily to "found," or "build," and hence, "to make," "create."

It will be clearly seen hence, that the nature of the creative

2. Creation was out of nothing.

act is but faintly defined by the mere force of the words. Yet Scripture does not lack passages, which explicitly teach, that God produced the whole Universe out of nothing by His almighty power; i. e., that His first work of creation did not consist merely of fashioning materials already existent, but of bringing all substance, except His own, out of non-existence into existence. How impossible this seemed to the ancient mind appears from this fact, that the opposite was regarded as an axiom (*ex nihilo nihil fit*) and lay as such at the basis of every system of human device. So that it was from an accurate knowledge, that the author of Hebrews says (xi : 3,) that the true doctrine of creation was purely one of faith. And this is our most emphatic proof text. We may add to it Rom. iv : 17; perhaps 1 Cor. i : 28; 2 Cor. iv : 6; Acts xvii : 28; Col. i : 17. The same meaning may be fairly argued for the word בָּרָא, Gen. i : 1, from the fact that its sense there is absolutely unqualified or limited by any previous proposition, or reference to any material, and also from the second verse. The work of the first verse expressed by בָּרָא, left the earth a chaos.

Therefore it cannot contain the idea of fashioning, so that if you refuse to it the sense of an absolute production out of nothing, you seem to leave it no meaning whatever. This truth also appears very strongly, from the contrast which is so often run by Scripture between God's eternity and the temporal nature of the creation. See Ps. xc : 2; Matt. xxv : 34; 2 Tim. i : 9; and especially Prov. viii : 23-26, "nor the highest part of the dust of the world." It is hard to see how it could be more strongly asserted, that not only was the organization, but the very material of the world as yet all non-existent.

This inscrutable, but not impossible.

How almighty power brings substance into existence from absolute non-entity, our minds may not be able to conceive. Like so many other questions of ontology, it is too impalpable for the grasp of our understandings. As we have seen, the mind neither sees nor conceives substance, not even material; but only its attributes; only, it is intuitively impelled to refer those attributes (of which alone it has perception), to some *substratum* as the substance in which they inhere. The entity itself being mysterious, it need not surprise us to find that its rise out of non-entity is so. It is objected that a creation out of nothing is a contradiction, because it makes nothing a material to act on, and thus, an existence. We reply that this is a mere play upon the meaning of a preposition; We do not mean that "nothing" is a material out of which existences are fashioned; but the term from which an existence absolutely begins. God created a world where nothing was before. Is it objected that, in all our experiental knowledge of causation, the object to receive, is as necessary as the agent to emit, power? True; but our knowledge of power is not an experimental idea, but an intuitive, rational notion; and in the most ordinary effect which we witness, is as really inscrutable to our perception and imagination, as the causation of a totally new existence. The latter is beyond our finite powers; we are certainly incompetent to say that it is beyond the reach of infinite power. So, all the transcendental difficulties which Pantheists make against a creation *ex nihilo*, have this common vice: They are attempts to bring down to our conceptual forms of thought the relations of the infinite, which inevitably transcend them.

   3. There are three other schemes which offer us an alternative to this of an absolute creation; that of the atomic philosophers, that of the Platonists, and that of the Pantheists.

   The Atomic theory of the Universe, advanced by Demo-
Atomic theory. Ref-   critus and Leucippus, adopted by Epicurus,
utation.   and greatly opposed by Socrates and the
Platonists, might be so stated, if freed from the mechanical technicalities of the Greeks, as to embrace as few absurdities as perhaps any possible anti-Christian system. That is, it has the merit of atheism, of making two or three gigantic falsehoods, assumed at the outset, supersede a whole train of minor absurdities. Grant, say the atomists, the eternal existence of matter, in the state of ultimate atoms, endued by the necessity of nature, with these three eternal attributes, motion, a perpetual appetency to aggregation, and diversity of ultimate form, and you have all that is necessary, to account for universal organization. Now, without dwelling on the metaphysical objection (whose soundness is questionable) that necessary existence is inconsistent with diversity of form, these obvious reasons show that the postulates are not only unproved (proof I have never seen attempted) but impossible. First: motion is not a necessary attribute of matter: but on the contrary, it is indifferent to a state of rest or motion, requiring power to cause it to pass out of either state into the opposite. Second: Intelligent contrivance could never be generated by mere necessary, mechanical aggregations of material atoms; but remains still an effect without a cause. Third: the materialistic account of human and other spirits, which this theory gives, is impossible.

   The Pantheistic theory has been already refuted, as space
Platonic Scheme.   would allow, in Lect. ii, which see. The
Refutation.   Platonic is certainly attended with fewest
absurdities, and best satisfied the demands of thinking minds not possessed of Revelation. Starting with the maxim *ex nihilo nihil fit*, it supposes two eternal substances, the sources of all that exists; the spiritual God, and chaotic matter; the spirits of demi-gods, and men

being emanations of the former, and the material universe having been fashioned out of the latter, in time, through the agency of the Νοῦς or Δημιουργὸς. The usual arguments against the eterntiy of the unorganized matter of the universe, have been weighed in the Second Lecture, and many of them found wanting, (which see). I now aim only to add to what is there said, such considerations as human reason seems able to advance solidly against this doctrine. You will remember that I there argued, 1st: From the testimony of the human race itself, and 2d, from the recency of population, history, traditions, arts, &c., on the earth, against the eternity of its organized state. To this we may add: 3d. If matter unorganized was eternal, it must have been self-existent, and hence, whatever attributes it had from eternity must have been absolutely necessary. Hence there was a necessary limitation on the power of God, in working with such a material; and it may be that He did not make what He would have preferred to make, but only did the best He could under the circumstances. (Indeed, the Platonist, knowing nothing of the doctrine of a fall in Adam, accounted for all the disorders and defects in the world, by the refractory nature of eternal matter. The creator excuses himself as a smith does, who, though thoroughly skillful, produces an imperfect edge-tool, because he had nothing but bad steel). But, if this is so, then: (a) God as Creator is not infinite; there are limitations upon His powers, as necessary and eternal as His own attributes. And these limits obstruct His providential action as they did His creative. Hence, He is no longer an object of religious trust, and perfect confidence. He is only an able artificer. (b) Then, also, God's knowledge of this self-existent matter, external to Himself, was experimentally gained; and the doctrine of His omniscience is fatally vitiated. 4th. The elementary properties of matter, which on this theory, must have been eternal and necessary, have an adaptation to God's purposes in creation, that displays intelligent contrivance, just as clearly as any organized thing can. But matter is unintelligent; this design must have had a cause. 5th. The production of spiritual substance out of nothing is, we presume, just as hard to account for as material substance. Hence, if an instance of the former is presented, the doctrine of the eternity of the Universe may as well be surrendered. But our souls each present such an instance. No particle of evidence exists from consciousness or recollection, that they pre-existed, and everything is against the notion that they are scintillations of God' substance. They began to exist: at least man has no knowledge whatever of any other origin: and by the rule: *De ignotis idem quasi de non existentibus,* any other origin is out of the debate. They were produced out of nothing. In conclusion, it may be said that, if the idea of the production of something out of nothing is found to be not impossible, as we think, when we have supposed an Almighty Creator, we have cause enough to account for everything, and it is unnecessary to suppose another.

The question whether a creature can receive, if God choose, delegated power to create, has been agitated between the Orthodox and some of the Romanists, (who would fain introduce a plea for the making of a Saviour by the priest, in the pretended miracle of the mass) and the old Arians and Socinians, who would thus evade the argument for Christ's proper divinity, from the evident ascription to Him of works of creation.   We believe not only that the noblest of finite creatures is incapable of exercising creative power proper, of his own motion; but of receiving it by delegation from God, so that the latter is one of those natural impossibles which it would argue imperfection in omnipotence to be capable of doing.

4. No creature can be enabled to create.

(a) God, in a multitude of places, claims creation as His characteristic work, by which His Godhead is manifested, and His superiority shown to all false gods and idols; Is. xliv; 7, 24; xl: 12, 13, 18, 28; Job ix: 8; Jer. x: 11, 12; Is. xxxvii: 16; Ps. xcvi: 5.   Thus Creator comes to be one of God's names.

(b) To bring anything, however small, out of non-existence is so far above man's capabilities, that he cannot even conceive how it can be done.   In order that a work may be conceivable or feasible for us, it must have subject and agent.   Man has no faculty which can be directed upon non-entity, in any way, to bring anything out of it.   Indeed, however small the thing thus produced out of nothing, there is an exertion of infinite power. The distance to be passed over between the two is a fathomless gulf to every finite mind.

(c.) To make one thing, however limited, might require infinite powers of understanding.   For however simple, a number of the laws of nature would be involved in its structure; and the successful construction would demand a perfect acquaintance with those laws, at least, in their infinite particularity, and in all their possible combinations, and with the substance as well as attributes.   Consider any of the constructions of man's shaping and joining materials God has given him, and this will be found true.   The working of miracles by prophets, apostles, &c., offers no instance to the contrary, because it is really God who works the miracle, and the human agent only announces, and appeals to the interposition of divine power.   See Acts iii: 12.

If we suppose that Gen. i: 1, describes a previous production in a time left indefinite, of the heavens and the matter of the earth, then the work of the first of the six days will be the production of light.   It may seem unreasonable at the first glance, that light should be created, and should make three days before the sun, its great fountain at present, was formed.   But all the researches of

5. The Creative Week.

modern optics go more and more to overthrow the belief that light is a substantive emanation from the sun. What it is, whether a substance, or an affection of other substance, is still unknown. Hence it cannot be held unreasonable, that it should have existed before the sun ; nor that God should have regulated it in alternations of day and night. On the second day the atmosphere seems to have been created, (the expanse) or else disengaged from chaos, and assigned its place around the surface of the earth. This, by sustaining the clouds, separated the waters from the waters. The work of the third day was to separate the terrestrial waters from the dry ground, to assign each their bounds, and to stock the vegetable kingdom with its *genera* of trees and plants. The fourth day was occupied with the creation, or else the assignment to their present functions, of sun, moon and stars. And henceforth these became the chief depositories, or else propagators, of natural light. The fifth day witnessed the creation of all oviparous animals, including the three classes of fishes, reptiles and birds. The sixth day God created the terrestrial animals of the higher order, now known as mammalia, and man, His crowning work.

In our age, as you are aware, modern geologists teach, with great unanimity, that the state of the structures which compose the earth's crust shows it to be vastly more than 6,000 years old. To explain this supposed evidence to you, I may take for granted your acquaintance with the classes into which they distribute the rocks and soils that form the earth, so far as man has pierced it. Lowest in order, and earliest in age, are the *azoic* rocks, many of them crystalline in texture, and all devoid of fossils. Above them are rocks, by the older geologists termed secondary and tertiary, but now termed *palaeozoic, mesozoic,* and *cainozoic.* Above them are alluvia, the more recent of which contain remains of existing *genera.* Only the barest outline of their classification is necessary for our purpose. Now, the theory of the geologists is, that the materials of the stratified rocks were derived, by disintegration, from masses older than themselves ; and that all this material has been re-arranged by natural processes of deposition, since the creation of our globe. And hence, that creation must have been thousands of ages before Adam. (a.) Because the crystalline rocks, which are supposed to have furnished the material for all the later, seemed to have resulted from a gradual cooling, and are very hard, disintegrating very slowly. (b.) The made-rocks and earths are very abundant, giving an average thickness of from six to ten miles. Hence a very great time was requisite to disintegrate so much hard material. (c.) The position of these made *strata* or layers, indicates long series of changes, since they were deposited, as upheavals, dislocations, depressions, subsequent re-dissolvings.

(d.) They contain 30,000 species and more, of fossil remains

6. The view of modern geology explained.

of animal life, besides vegetable; of which, not only are whole *genera* now extinct, but were wholly extinct ages before another cluster of *genera* were first created; which are now extinct also. And the vast quantities of these fossils, as shells in some lime-stone, remains of vegetation in vast coal beds, &c., &c., point to a long time, for their gradual accumulation.

(f.) There are no human fossils found with these remains of earlier life, whence they were pre-Adamite.

Last. Since the last great geologic changes in the strata of the made rocks, changes have been produced in them by natural and gradual causes, which could not have been made in 6,000 years, as whole *deltas* of alluvial mud deposited, e. g.. Louisiana, deep channels dug out by rivers, as Niagara from Lake Ontario to the falls, water worn caves in the coast lines, and former coast lines of countries, e. g., Great Britain, which are rock-bound.

Modern divines, usually yield this as a demonstration: and offer one of two solutions to rescue Moses from the appearance of mistake. First, Drs. Pye Smith, Chalmers, Hitchcock, Hodge, &c., suppose Gen. i: 1 and 2, 1st clause, to describe God's primeval, creative act; which may have been separated by thousands of ages from Adam's day; and in that vast interval, occurred all those successive changes, which geologists describe as pre-Adamite, and then lived and died all those extinct *genera* of animals and vegetables. The scene had been closed, per-haps ages before, by changes which left the earth's surface void, for..less and dark. But all this Moses passes over with only one word; because the objects of a religious revelation to man were not concerned with it. The second verse only describes how God took the earth in hand, at this stage, and in six days gave it the order, the *genera* of plants and animals, and last, the human race, which now possesses it.

Attempts to recon-cile this with Moses. 1st. Scheme.

The geological objections which Hugh Miller, its ablest Christian assailant, brings, may be all summed up in this: That the fossils show there was not such a clean cutting off of all the *genera* of plants and animals at the close of the pre-Adamite period, and re-stocking of the earth with the existing *genera ;* because many of the existing co-exist with the prevalent *pleio-cene genera*, in the tertiary rocks, and many of those again, with the older *genera*, in the palaeozoic rocks. This does not seem at all conclusive, because it may have suited God, at the close of the pre-Adamite period, to suffer the extinction of all, and then to create, along with the totally different new *genera*, some bearing so close a likeness to some extinct *genera*, as to be indistinguishable by their fossils.

The exegetical objections are chiefly these. 1. That the sun, moon and light were only created at the Adamic period. Without these there

Exegetical difficulties.

could have been neither vegetable nor animal life before. 2. We seem to learn from Gen. i: 31; iii: 17–19; Rom. v: 12; viii: 19–22, that all animal suffering and death came upon our earth as a punishment for man's sin; which our conceptions of the justice and benevolence of God seem to confirm. To the 1st the common answer is, that the chaotic condition into which the earth had fallen just before the Adamic period, had probably shut out all influences of the heavenly bodies; and that the making of sun, moon, &c., and ordaining them for lights, &c., probably only means their apparent creation, i. e., their reintroduction to the earth. To the 2d it is replied, that the proper application of the texts attributing all terrestrial disorder and suffering to man's fall, is only to the earth as cotemporary with man; and that we are too ignorant of God's plan, and of what sin of rational free agents may, or may not have occurred on the pre-Adamite earth, to dogmatize about it. These replies seem plausible, and may be tenable. This mode of reconciling geology to Moses, is certainly the least objectionable, and most respectable.

The second mode of reconciliation, now made most fashionable by H. Miller, Tayler Lewis, &c., sup-

The theory of six symbolic days.

poses that the word יוֹם day, in the account of creation, does not mean a natural day of 24 hours, but is symbolical of a vast period; during which God was, by natural laws, carrying on changes in the earth's surface and its inhabitants. And they regard the passage as an account of a sort of symbolic vision, in which God gave Moses a picture, in six *tableaux*, of these six vast series of geologic and creative changes: so that the language is, to use Dr. Kurtz' (of Dorpat,) fantastic idea, a sort of prophecy of the past, and is to be understood according to the laws of prophetic symbols. This they confirm by saying that Moses makes three days before he has any sun or moon to make them: that in Gen. ii: 4, the word is used for something other than a natural day; and that it is often used in Hebrew as a general and undefined term for season or period. Miller also argues, that geology reveals the same succession of fossils which Moses describes; first plants, then monstrous fishes and reptiles and birds, (all oviparous), then quadrupeds and mammalia, and last, man.

The following objections lie against this scheme. Geologists are not agreed that the succession of fossils is that which its advocates assert.

Objections.

Some of the weightest authorities declare that plants (assigned by this scheme to the third day, and to the earliest production of organic things) are not the earliest fossils. Crustaceous, and even vertebrate animals precede the plants. Second. The narrative seems historical, and not symbolical; and hence the strong initial presumption is, that all its parts are to be taken in their obvious sénse. The advocates of the symbolic days (as Dr. G. Molloy) attach much importance to their claim that theirs is not an afterthought, suggested by geologic difficulties, but that the exposition was advanced by many of the ' Fathers '. After listening to their citations, we are constrained to reply that the vague suggestions of the different Fathers do not yield them any support, because they do not adopt their theory of explanation. Third. The sacred writer seems to shut us up to the literal interpretation, by describing the day as composed of its natural parts, " morning and evening." Is the attempt made to break the force of this, by reminding us, that the "evening and the morning" do not make up the whole of the civic day of twenty-four hours ; and that the words are different from those just before, and commonly afterwards employed to denote the " day " and the " night," which together make up the natural day? We reply : it is true, morning and evening do not literally fill the twenty-four hours. But these epochs mark the beginnings of the two seasons, day and night, which do fill the twenty-four hours. And it is hard to see what a writer can mean, by naming evening and morning as making a first, or a second "day"; except that he meant us to understand that time which includes just one of each of these successive epochs : — one beginning of night, and one beginning of day. These gentlemen cannot construe the expression at all. The plain reader has no trouble with it. When we have had one evening and one morning, we know we have just one civic day ; for the intervening hours have made just that time. Fourth. In Gen. ii : 2, 3 ; Exod. xx : 11, God's creating the world and its creatures in six days, and resting the seventh, is given as the ground of His sanctifying the Sabbath day. The latter is the natural day ; why not the former ? The evasions from this seem peculiarly weak. Fifth. It is freely admitted that the word day is often used in the Greek Scriptures as well as the Hebrew (as in our commmon speech) for an epoch, a season, a time. But yet, this use is confessedly derivative. The natural day is its literal and primary meaning. Now, it is apprehended that in construing any document, while we are ready to adopt, at the demand of the context, the derived or tropical meaning, we revert to the primary one, when no such demand exists in the context. Last. The attributing of the changes ascribed to each day by Moses, to the slow operation of natural causes, as Miller's theory does, tramples upon the proper scope of the passage, and the meaning of the word " create ; " which teach us this very truth especially ; that these things were not brought about by natural law at all, but by a supernatural divine exertion, directly opposed thereto See Gen. ii : 5. If Moses does not here mean to teach us that in the time named by the six " days " (whatever it may be), God was employed in miraculously creating and not naturally " growing " a world, I see not how language can be construed. This decisive difficulty is wholly separate from the questions about the much debated word, " day," in this passage.

APPENDIX.

Without presuming to teach technical geology (for which I profess no qualification ; and which lies, as I conceive, wholly outside the functions of the Church teacher), I wish, in dismissing this subject, to give you some cautions and instructions touching its relations with our revealed science.

There must always be a legitimate reason for Church teachers adverting to this subject ; because geology, as often asserted, is virtually a theory of *cosmogony*, and cosmogony is but the doctrine of creation, which is one of the modes by which God reveals Himself to man, and one of the prime articles of every revealed theology. Were not all the ancient cosmogonies but natural theologies ? Not a few modern geologists resent the animadversions of theologians, as of an incompetent class, impertinent and ignorant. Now I very freely grant that it is a very naughty thing for a parson, or a geologist, to profess to know what he does not know. But all logic is but logic ; and after the experts in a special science have explained their premises in their chosen way, it is simply absurd to forbid any other class of educated men to understand and judge their deductions. What else was the object of their publications ? Or, do they intend to practice that simple dogmatism, which in us religious teachers, they would so spurn ? Surely when geologists currently teach their systems to boys in colleges, it is too late for them to refuse the inspection of an educated class of men ! When Mr. Hugh Miller undertook, by one night's lecture, to convince a crowd of London mechanics of his pet theory of the seven geologic ages, it is too late to refuse the criticism of theologians trained in philosophy ?

1. This subject must concern Theologians.

I would beg you to notice how distinctly either of the current theories contradicts the standards of our Church. See Conf. of Faith, ch. iv, §1. Larger Cat., que. 15, 120. Our Confession is not inspired ; and if untrue, it should be refuted. But if your minds are made up to adopt either of these theories, then it seems to me that common honesty requires of you two things ; to advertise your Presbyteries, when you apply for license and ordination, of your disbelief of these articles; that they may judge whether they are essential to our system of doctrine ; and second; to use your legitimate influences as soon as you become church rulers, to have these articles expunged from our standards as false.

2. Westminster Confession inconsistent with it

Let me urge upon you a wiser attitude and temper towards the new science, than many have shown, among the ministry. Some have shown a jealousy and uneasiness, unworthy of the stable dignity of the cause of inspiration. These apparent difficulties of geology are just such as science has often paraded against the Bible; but God's word has stood firm, and every true advance of science has only redounded to its honour. Christians, therefore, can afford to bear these seeming assaults with exceeding coolness. Other pretended theologians have been seen advancing, and then as easily retracting, novel schemes of exegesis, to suit new geologic hypotheses. The Bible has often had cause here to cry, "Save me from my friends." Scarcely has the theologian announced himself as sure of his discovery that this is the correct way to adjust Revelation to the prevalent hypotheses of the geologists, when these mutable gentlemen change their hypothesis. The obsequious divine exclaims: "Well, I was in error then; but now I have certainly the right exposition to reconcile Moses to the geologists." And again the fickle science changes its ground. What can be more degrading to the authority of Revelation! As remarked in a previous lecture, unless the Bible has its own ascertainable and certain law of exposition, it cannot be a rule of faith; our religion is but rationalism. I repeat, if any part of the Bible must wait to have its real meaning imposed upon it by another, and a human science, that part is at least meaningless and worthless to our souls. It must expound itself independently; making other sciences ancillary, and not dominant over it.

3. Deliberation enjoined.

It should be freely conceded that it was not God's purpose, in giving the Bible, to foreshadow the scientific *rationale* of natural phenomena. Its object is theological. And the Bible is, in this respect, a strictly practical book. Hence, it properly speaks of those phenomena as they appear, and uses the popular phrases, "sun rises," "sun sets," "sun stood still," etc., just as any other than a pedantic astronomer would, when not expressly teaching astronomy. Hence, we admit, that the attempt made by Rome and the Reformers to array the Bible against the Copernican System was simply foolish. The Bible only professed to speak of the apparent phase of the facts; the theory of the astronomer professed to give the non-apparent, scientific mechanism of the facts. So far as geology does the analogous thing, we should have no quarrel with it. But how far does this concession go? When Moses seems to say that God created the world and its inhabitants out of nothing, are we at liberty to treat him as we do Joshua, when he speaks of the sun as standing still? I think not. First: Moses' reference to the facts of creation is not, like Joshua's reference to the

4. Popular terms to be expected; in Bible, Reasons. But not applicable to cosmogony.

17*

astronomical event, merely incidental to a narrative of human history, but is a statement of what is as much a theological doctrine as a natural fact, introduced by him for its own theological purpose. Second: Joshua's language is defended, as being true to the apparent phase of the event. But creation had no apparent phase; for the simple reason that it had no human spectators. There is no popular language about world-making, conformed to the seeming phenomenon, as we have about the moving and setting suns which we daily seem to behold; for none of us, of any generation, have witnessed the exterior appearances of world-making. Hence, I must believe that we are not authorized to class the declarations of Moses here, with those of these oft-cited passages.

It is an all-important point that, if debate arises between a geologic hypothesis and the fair and natural meaning of the Bible touching cosmogony, the geologist must bear the burden of proof. We are entitled to claim this, because the inspiration of the Scriptures is in prior possession of the field, in virtue of its own independent, historical, prophetic, internal and spiritual evidences, and of the immense and irreparable stake which every awakened soul has in its truth. Hence, the geologist does not dislodge the Bible, until he has constructed his own independent, and exclusive, and demonstrative evidence that his hypothesis must be the true one, and the only true one. Has the science ever done this? This logical obligation geologists perpetually forget. They perpetually substitute a "may be" for a "must be." As soon as they hit upon a hypothesis which, it appears, may satisfy the known facts, they leap to the conclusion that it is the obviously, the only true one. But now, our position is not approached until such a complete, and exclusive demonstration is made. We are under no obligation, in order to defend ourselves, to substantiate another hypothesis by geologic reasoning; our defence is complete, when we show by such argument that their hypothesis comes short of an exclusive and perfect demonstration. It requires, as yet, little knowledge to show this; when the leading geologists are still differing between themselves, touching the igneous, the aqueous, the gradual and the sudden systems; when effects are so hastily and confidently ascribed to one species of natural agency, which may, very possibly, have been effected by it, or by one of several other possible agencies; when we see the greatest names assuming as premises for important deductions, statements which are corrected by the practical observation of plain men; from the oversight of important questions as to the consistency and feasibility of their theories of cosmogony, with observed facts; and last, from the truth that the most truly scientific are most cautious in asserting any such scheme with confidence.

5. Burden of proof rests on Geologists.

I have reserved the most vital point to the last. It is this:

6. Usual inference of cause from observed resemblances. The structures of nature around us cannot present by their traits of naturalness, a universally demonstrative proof of a natural, as against a supernatural origin, upon any sound, theistic theory. Because, supposing a Creator, originating any structures or creatures supernaturally, He must also have conferred on His first things traits of naturalness. Hence, should it be found that the Creator has uttered His testimony to the supernatural origin of any observed things, that testimony cuts across and supersedes all the arguments *a posteriori*, from natural analogies to a natural origin. Thus, many geologists, seeing that sedimentary action by water now produces some stratified rocks, claim that they are entitled, by the similarity of effects, to ascribe all stratified rocks to sedimentary action. This, they say, is but a fair application of the axiom, that "like causes produce like effects," which is the very corner-stone of all inductive science. But the real proposition they employ is the converse of this: that like effects imply like causes. Now, first: it is trite as true, that the proof of a proposition does not prove its converse. Second: the theist has expressly admitted another cause, namely, an infinite, personal Creator, confessedly competent to any effect He may choose to create. Hence, all theists are compelled to admit that the natural, *a posteriori* argument cannot universally hold, as to the origin of beings. Once admit a Creator, and that argument remains, in every case where the Creator's absence is not proved by some positive evidence other than physical, the invalid species of induction, which Bacon exploded under the name of *inductio enumerationis simplicis*. Nov. Organum, Lib. 1, § 105. "*Inductio enim, quæ procedit per enumerationem simplicem, res puerilis est, et precario concludit, et periculo exponitur ab instantia contradictoria,*" &c. In the case under discussion, any natural structure originated by the Creator, would be such a contradictory instance. Unless then the divine cause is excluded by some other than physical evidence, such induction can never be universally valid. Third: A wise God always has some "final cause," guiding His action. We may not be presumptuous in surmising, in every case, what His final cause was; but when His own subsequent action has disclosed it, we are on safe ground; we may assuredly conclude that the use to which He has actually put a given thing is the use for which He designed it. When, therefore, we see Him subjecting all structures to natural law, we know that those which He himself created, He designed to subject to such law. Then, He must have created them as natural as though their origin also had been from nature. Fourth: To the theist, this argument is especially clear as to living, organized creatures. Supposing a Creator, the first of each species must have received from the supernatural, creative hand, every trait of naturalness; else it could not have fulfilled

the end for which it was made; to be the parent of a species. What are the attributes connoted by the name of any species? Natural History answers: they are precisely those regularly transmitted by natural generation.   Then, in order to be the parent of a natural species, the first thing, while supernatural in origin, must have been thoroughly natural in all essential traits. Fifth: If we deny this, we must assign a natural parent before the first-created parent of each species of generated organisms. Thus we should be involved in a multitude of infinite series, without cause external to themselves; a result which science herself has repudiated, as an impossible absurdity.   Suppose then, that by some chance, a physicist should examine the very remains of one of those organisms which God creatively pro- duced, as a bone of Adam's body; he would, of course, find in it the usual traits of naturalness.   Yet he could not thence infer for this thing a natural origin; since, according to the sup- posed case, it was a first thing.   Hence, it is concluded with mathematical rigidity, that when we grant an omnipotent Crea- tor anywhere in the past, the argument from naturalness of traits to a natural origin ceases to be universally conclusive.

This case is exactly illustrated by what lawyers term "circumstantial evidence" in a court of jus-

Illustrated by Cir- tice.   The science of law, charged with the
cumstantial Evidence.
solemn issues of life and death, has exactly defined the proper rules for this species of evidence.   Before a man can be convicted upon circumstantial evidence, the prose- cution must show that their hypothesis of his guilt not only may satisfy all the circumstances known, but that it is the only possible hypothesis.   And the enlightened judge will rule, that the defence are entitled to test that fact even by their imagina- tions.   If they can suppose or invent another hypothesis, unsupported by a single positive proof, that demonstrates the fact, that the hypothesis of guilt is not the only possible one, the accused must be discharged.   But let us suppose that, just when the circumstantial evidence of guilt seemed com- plete, an eye-witness is adduced, who swears that he saw the crime perpetrated by another.   Let us suppose that other agent was naturally competent to the act.   Then the judge will rule, that the whole farther discussion must turn on the consistency and credibility of that witness.   He will say to the accusers: that if they have any valid way to impugn the wit- ness' competency, or credibility, they may do so; otherwise, in presence of his positive evidence, their circumstantial proof, in spite of all its ingenuity and plausibility, is utterly broken down.   Now the *a posteriori* argument of the geologists is such a circumstantial proof.   The Bible is the parole-witness; if its competency and trustworthiness stand, their case has collapsed before it.

Again : why should the Theistic philosopher desire to push

back the creative act of God to the remotest possible age, and reduce His agency to the least possible *minimum*, as is continually done in these speculations? What is gained by it? Instead of granting that God created a χόσμος, a world, some strive continually to show that He created only the rude germs of a world, ascribing as little as possible to God, and as much as possible to natural law. *Cui bono;* if you are not hankering after Atheism? Is a completed result any harder for infinite powers than a germinal one? What is natural law; and what its source? It originated in the creative power, and is maintained, energized, and regulated by the perpetual providence of God. Do you crave to push God away, as far as possible? It does not help you to say, natural law directed the formation of this mass of marble, instead of supernatural creation; for God is as near and as infinite in His common, natural, as in His first, supernatural working.

But if you must persist in recognizing nothing but natural forces, wherever you see a natural analogy, I *Illustrated by Nebu-* will show you that it will land you, if you are *lar Hypothesis.* consistent, no where short of absolute atheism. Suppose that nebular theory of the origin of the solar system were true, which the anti-Christian, La Place, is said to have suggested as possible, and which so many of our nominal Christians have adopted, without proof, as certain. An observer from some other system, fully imbued with the principles of modern science, comes to inspect, at the stage that he finds only a vast mass of incandescent vapor, rotating from west to east around an axis of motion. If he uses the confident logic of our geologists, he must reason thus: " Matter is naturally inert; *momentum* must come from impact; therefore, this rotary motion which I now behold, must be the result of some prior force, either mechanical, electrical, or some other. And again, I see only vapor. Vapor implies evaporation; and sensible heat suggests latent heat, rendered sensible either by electrical or chemical action, or compression. There must, therefore, have been a previous, different, and natural condition of this matter now volatilized, heated, and rotating. The geologists of the 19th century, therefore, will be mistaken in calling this the primitive condition of the system." Before each first, then, there must still be another first. This is, therefore, the eternity of Naturalism—it is Atheism.

This argument is usually dismissed by geologists with a *Argument just, as* sort of summary contempt, or with a grand out-*against exclusion of* cry of opposition. It does indeed cut deep *Creator.* into the seductive pride of their science, sweeping off at one blow that most fascinating region, the infinite past. It is urged, for instance, that my argument would subvert the foundations of all natural science. They exclaim, that to concede this would be to surrender the whole *organon* of scientific discovery. I answer, no. Within the domain of time, the known past of human history, where its testimony proves the absence of the supernatural, the analogical induction is perfectly valid. And there is the proper domain of natural science. In that field, their method of reasoning is a useful *organon*, and a legitimate; let them use it there, to the full, for the good of man. But in the unknown eternity of the past, prior to human history, it has no place; it is like the mariner's compass carried into the stellar spaces. That compass has a known attraction for the poles of this globe; and therefore on this globe, it is a valued guide. But away in the region of *Sirius*, where we know not whether the spheres have poles, or whether they are magnetic, it is naught. He who should follow it would be a madman.

Another objection, supposed to be very strong, is drawn
Objection from Fos-
sils answered. from the fossil remains of life. The geologists say triumphantly, that however one might admit my view as to the mere *strata*, it would be preposterous when applied to the remains of plants and animals buried in these *strata*, evidently alive thousands of ages ago. They assert roundly that, in order to make any application of this argument, anywhere, I shall have to hold the preposterous assertion, that all the fossil remains of vegetable and animal life, which lived during the vast, pre-Adamite ages, are mere stones, never alive: or that, in other words, we must refuse the evidence of our own senses, and suppose the Creator imposed this cheat on them. This supposed consequence we expressly repudiate. And it is very easy to show that it does not follow. In attempting to fix the relative age and order of *strata* and fossils, geology reasons in a circle. Sir Chas. Lyell states that a stratigraphical order has been inferred from three classes of data. 1. The observed order of *strata* where actually found in juxtaposition. 2. The kinds of organic life contained in the different *strata*. 3. The material and structure of the *strata* themselves. Evidently such inferences are invalid, from two grounds. First: they have not proved that the *azoic* stratified rocks, a large class by their own showing, may not have had an immediate, supernatural origin: for I have evinced that their naturalness of structure alone is no proof against this. If then, these stratified rocks are really as old as the igneous, here is a huge chasm in their system. Second: They reason in a circle, in that they argue the relative oldness of certain fossils from the *strata* in which they are found; and then argue the oldness of the *strata* from the assumed age of the fossils. For instance: they conclude that the non-fossiliferous clay-slate is a very old stratified rock, because without fossils. Again, they have concluded that some given species of fossil life is very old, because found in a *stratum* very near that very old slate. Then they infer that some other *stratum* is very old,

because this fossil is found in it!   Third: Concede once (I care not where in the unknown past) an almighty Creator of infinite understanding, (as you must, if you are not an atheist,) arid then both power and motive for the production of these living structures at and after a supernatural creation, become infinitely possible.   It would be an insane pride of mind, which should conclude that, because it could not comprehend the motive for the production, death, and entombment of all these creatures under such circumstances, therefore it cannot be reasonable for the Infinite Mind to see such a motive.   So that my same formula applies here also.   Once concede an Infinite Creator, and all inferences as to the necessarily natural origin of all the structures seen, are fatally sundered.

In fine, if that account of the origin of the universe, which theology gives us, is to be heeded at all, the *Creation had a moral end.* following appears the most philosophical conception of a creation: That God, in producing a world which His purposes required to pass under the immediate domain of natural laws, would produce it with just the properties which those laws perpetuate and develope.   And here appears a consideration which brings theology and cosmogony into unison.   What was God's true end in the creation of a material world?   Reason and Scripture answer: To furnish a stage for the existence and action of a moral and rational creature.   The earth was made for man to inhabit.   As the light would be but darkness, were there no eye to see, so the moral design of the world would be futile without a human mind to comprehend it, and praise its Maker.   Now, such being God's end in creation, it seems much more reasonable to suppose that He would produce at once the world which He needed for His purpose, rather than spend hundreds of thousands of years in growing it.

LECTURE XXIV.

ANGELS.

Against ancient Sadducees, who taught neither resurrection, angel, nor spirit, (Acts xxiii: 8) and made the angels only good thoughts and motions visiting human breasts; and our modern Sadducees, among Rationalists, Socinians and Universalists, who teach that they are impersonations of divine energies, or of good and bad principles, or of diseases and natural influences; we prove the real, personal existence of angels thus: The Scriptures speak of them as having all the acts and properties, which can characterize real persons. They were created, by God, through the agency of the Son. Col. i: 16; Gen. ii: 1; Exod. xx: 11. Have a nature, for Christ did not assume it, Heb. ii: 16. Are holy or unholy, Rev. xiv: 10. Love and rejoice, Luke xv: 10. Desire, 1 Pet. i: 12. Contend, Rev. xii: 7. Worship, Heb. i: 6. Go and come, Gen. xix: 1; Luke ix: 26. Talk, Zech. i: 9; Luke i: 13. Have knowledge and wisdom, (finite) 2 Sam. xiv: 20; Matt. xxiv: 36. Minister in various acts, Matt. xiii: 29, 49; Luke xvi: 22; Acts v: 19. Dwell with saints, who resemble them, in heaven, Matt. xxii: 30, &c. If all this language was not intended to assure us of their personal existence, then there is no dependence to be placed on the word of God, or the laws of its interpretation.

1. Personality of Angels.

The name angel (messenger) is indeed applied to ordinary messengers, Job i: 14; Luke vii: 24; to prophets, Is. xlii: 19: Mal. iii: 1; to priests, Mal. ii: 7; to ministers of the Church, Rev. i: 20, and to the Messiah, Mal. iii: 1; Is. lxiii: 9, &c., &c. But the other sense of personal and spiritual existences, is none the less perspicuous. They are called angels generally, because they fulfill missions for God.

The invisible and spiritual nature of these beings does not make their existence less credible, to any, except atheists and materialists. True, we have no sensible experience of their exist-ence. Neither have we, directly, of our own souls, nor of God. If the existence of pure, finite spirits is impossible, then man cannot be immortal; but the death of the body is the death of the being. Indeed, analogy would rather lead us to infer the ex-istence of angels, from the almost numberless gradations of beings below man. Is all the vast gap between him and God a blank?

Spiritual creatures possible.

To fix the date of the creation of angels is more difficult. The old opinion of the orthodox Reformers was, that their creation was a part of the first day's work. (a.) Because they, being inhabitants, or hosts (see Ps. ciii: 21; cxlviii: 2) of heaven, were created when the heavens were. But see Gen. i: 1; ii: 1; Exod. xx: 11. (b.) Because Scripture seems to speak of all the past eternity "before the foundation of the world" as an unbroken infinity, in which nothing existed except the uncreated; so that to speak of a being as existing before that, is in their language, to rep-resent him as uncreated. See Prov. viii: 22; Ps. xc: 2; Jno. i: 1. Now I concede that the including of the angels with the heavens, under the term hosts of them, is correct. But first, the angels were certainly already in existence when this earth was begun. See Job xxxviii: 7. Second: the "beginning" in which God made the heavens and the earth, Gen. i: 1, is by no means necessarily the first of the six creative days. Nor does Gen. ii: 1, ("Thus were finished," is an unnecessarily strong rendering of וַיְכֻלּוּ) prove it. Hence, third, it may be granted that the beginning of the creation of God's created universe may mark the dividing point between unsuccessive eternity, and successive time, and between the existence of the uncreated alone, and of the creature; and yet it does not follow that this point was the first of the Mosaic days. Hence, it is best to say, with Calvin, that the age of the angels is unrevealed, except that they are older than the world and man.

Date unknown.

The angels are exceedingly numerous. Gen. xxxii: 2; Dan. vii: 10; Luke ii: 13; viii: 30; Matt. xxvi: 53; Heb. xii: 22. Their nature is undoubtedly spiritual, belonging generally to that class of substances to which man's

2. Qualities of the Angels; Incorporeal? Whence the forms of their apparitions?

rational soul belongs, They are called Πνεύματα. Heb. i : 13, 14, 7 ; Luke xx : 36 ; xxiv : 39 ; Col. i : 16. This also follows from what we learn of their traits, as intelligent and voluntary beings, as invisible, except when they assume bodies temporarily, as inexpressibly quick in motion; and as penetrable, so that they occupy the same space with matter, without displacing or being displaced by it. Several supposed objections to their mere spirituality have been mooted. One is, that they have, as we shall see, so much physical power. The answer is, that the ultimate source of all force is in spirits; our limbs only have it, as moved by our spirit's volitions. Another is, that if pure spirits, they would be ubiquitous, because to suppose any substance possessed of locality must imply that it is defined by extension and local limits. But extension cannot be an attribute of spirit. I reply, that it must be possible for a spirit to have locality "definitely," though not "circumscriptively," because our consciousness assures us that our spirits are within the superficies of our body, in some true sense in which they are not elsewhere; yet it is equally impossible for us to attribute dimension, either to our spirits or their thoughts. And just as really as our spirits pass through space, when our bodies move, so really angels change their locality, though far more swiftly, by an actual motion, through extension; though not implying extension in the thing moved. Again, it is objected: angels are spoken of as having wings, figure, and often, human shape, in which they were sometimes, not merely visible, b' tangible, and performed the characteristic material acts of ea - ing and drinking. See Gen. xviii : 2, 5, 8 ; xix : 10, 16. On th ; it may be remarked that Scripture expressly assigns wings to n orders but cherubim and seraphim. We see Dan. ix : 21, and Rev. xiv : 6, speaking of angels, not cherubim and seraphim, as "flying." But this may be in the general sense of rapid motion; not motion with wings. The purpose of these appearances is obvious, to bring the presence and functions of the angelic visitant under the scope of the senses of God's servants, for some particular purpose of mercy. Angelic apparitions seem to have appeared under three circumstances—in dreams—in states of inspired ecstacy, and when the observer was in the usual exercise of his senses. Only the latter need any explanation; for the former cases are accounted for by the ideal impression made on the conception of the dreaming or ecstatic mind by God. But in such cases as that of Gen. xviii and xix, we are bound to believe that these heavenly spirits occupied for the time, real, material bodies. Any other opinion does violence at once to the laws of exegesis of Scripture language, and to the validity of our senses as inlets of certain and truthful perceptions. Whence then, those bodies? Say some, they were the actual bodies of living men, which the angels occupied, suppressing, for the nonce, the consciousness and personality of the human

soul to which the body belonged. Some, that they are material, but glorified substances, kept in heaven, ready for the occasional occupancy of angels on their missions; as we keep a Sun-
day-coat in our wardrobes. Some, that they were aerial bodies,
composed of compacted atmosphere, formed thus for their temporary occupancy, by divine power, and then dissolved into air
again. And still others, that they were created by God for
them, out of matter, as Adam's body was, and then laid aside.
Where God has not seen fit to inform us, I think it best to have
no opinion on this mysterious subject. The Scriptures plainly
show us, that this incorporation is temporary.

The angels are intelligent and voluntary beings, as is most
manifest, from their functions of praising,
The Angels intelli- worshipping, teaching the prophets, and min-
gent agents.
istering to saints, and from their very spirit-
uality ; for thought is the characteristic attribute of spirit. We
naturally infer that as angels are incorporeal, they have neither
senses, nor sensation, nor literal language. Since our senses are
the inlets of all our objective knowledge, and the occasional
causes of all mental action, we have no experience nor conception of a knowledge without senses. But it does not seem
unreasonable to believe that our bodies obstruct the cognitions
of our souls, somewhat as imprisoning one within solid walls does
his communication with others; that our five senses are the win-
dows, pierced through this barrier, to let in partial perceptions;
and that consequently, the disembodied soul perceives and
knows somehow, with vastly greater freedom and fulness, by
direct spiritual apprehension. Yet all of the knowledge of
angels is not direct intuition. No doubt much of it is mediate
and deductive, as is so much of ours ; for the opposite form of
cognition can only be universal, in an infinite understanding. It
is very clear also, that the knowledge of angels is finite and susceptible of increase. Mark. xiii : 32 ; Eph. iii : 10 ; 1 Pet.
i : 12 ; Dan. viii : 16. Turrettin's four classes of angelic knowledge—natural, experimental, supernatural, and revealed—
might, I think, be better arranged as their concreated, their
acquired, and their revealed knowledge. It is, in fine, clear that
their knowledge and wisdom are great. They appear, Dan.
and Rev., as man's teachers, they are glorious and splendid
creatures, and they enjoy more favour and communion from
God. See also, 2. Sam. xiv : 20.

They are also beings of great power; passing over vast
spaces with almost incredible speed, Dan.
Powerful.   ix : 23 ; exercising portentous physical powers, 2 Kings xix ; 35 ; Zech. xii : 8 ; Acts xii : 7, 10 ; Matt.
xxviii : 2, and they are often spoken of as mighty beings Ps.
ciii : 20 ; Rev. x : 1 ; v : 2, and are spoken of as δυναμεις, prin-
cipalities, &c., Eph. vi : 12 ; 2 Thess. i : 7. This power is undoubtedly always within God's control, and never truly super-

natural, although superhuman. It seems to have extended at times, by God's permission, to men's bodies, to diseases, to the atmosphere, and other elements.

The romantic distribution of the angels into a hierarchy of three classes and nine orders, borrowed by the Pseudo Dionysius from the Platonizing Jews, need not be refuted here. It is supposed by many Protestants, that there are differences of grade among angels, (though what, we know not,) from the fact—(a) That Paul uses several terms to describe them, Col. i : 16; (b) That there is at least one superior angel among the evil angels; (c) That we hear of an archangel, Michael; (d) That God's terrestrial works exhibit every where, gradations.

Their Orders.

If, as some suppose, Michael is identical with the Angel of the Covenant, the third of these considerations is removed. Their reasons are, that he is called the Archangel, and is the only one to whom the title is given; that he is called the Prince, and great Prince, who stood for Israel, (Dan. x : 21; xii : 1,) and that he is seen, (Rev. xii : 7,) heading the heavenly war against Satan and his kingdom; a function suited to none so well as to the Messiah. But it is objected, with entire justice, that his name (Who is as God?) is not any more significant of the Messiah than that of Michaiah, and is several times the name of a man— that he is one, "one of the chief princes." Dan. x : 13. That in Jude, he was under authority in his dispute over Moses' body, and that he is plainly distinguished from Christ, (1 Thess. iv : 16,) where Christ descends from heaven with the voice of the archangel, and trump of God.

Michael not Angel of Covenant.

A more difficult question is, what were the cherubim mentioned, Gen. iii : 24; Exod. xxv : 18; 1 Kings vi : 23; Ps. xviii : 10; Ezek. x : 5, 7, &c., and most probably, under the name of seraphim, in Is. vi : 2. It is very evident, also, that the "living creatures, described in Ezekiel's vision, ch. i : 5, as accompanying the wheels, and sustaining the divine throne, were the same. Dr. Fairbairn, the most quoted of modern interpreters of types and symbols, teaches that the cherubim are not existences at all, but mere ideal symbols, representing humanity redeemed and glorified. His chief argument, omitting many fanciful ones drawn from the fourfold nature, and their wings, &c., is: that they are manifestly identical with the $Z\tilde{\omega}\alpha$ of Rev. iv : 6–8, which evidently symbolize, ch. v : 8–10, somehow, the ransomed Church. The great objections are, that the identification is not certain, inasmuch as John's $Z\tilde{\omega}\alpha$ had but one face each; that there is no propriety in founding God's heavenly throne and providence on glorified humanity, as His immediate attendants; but chiefly, that while it might consist with prophetic vision to make them ideal symbols, it utterly outrages the plain narrative

Cherubim. What?

of Gen. iii : 24. And the duty of the cherubim, there described, obstructing sinful man's approach to the tree of life, with a flaming sword, the symbol of justice, is one utterly unfitted to redeemed and glorified humanity. Hence, I believe, with the current of older divines, that the cherubim are not identical with John's "living creatures," but are angels, like all the others, real, spiritual, intelligent beings; and that when God was pleased to appear to Isaiah and Ezekiel in prophetic vision, they received temporarily these mixed forms, to be symbolical of certain traits of obedience, intelligence, strength, and swiftness, which they show as ministers of God's providence and worshippers of His upper sanctuary. (The etymology of the word is utterly obscure.)

That all these spiritual beings were created holy and 3. The Angels' first happy, is evident from God's character, estate, their probation, which is incapable of producing sin or misand issue thereof. ery; see Gen. i : 31 ; from the frequent use of the term holy angels, and from all that is revealed of their occupations and affections, which are pure, blessed and happy. The same truth is implied, in what is said, 2 Pet. ii : 4, of "angels that sinned," and so were not spared, but cast down to hell, and Jude 6, of "angels that kept not their first estate." This first estate was, no doubt, in all, an estate of holiness and happiness. As to the change which has taken place in it, we are indeed left mainly to inference, by God's word; but it is inference so well supported by His attributes, and the analogy of man's case, that I feel a good degree of confidence in drawing it. A holy, intelligent creature, would owe service to God, with love and worship, by its natural relation to Him. And while God would be under no obligations to such a creature, to preserve its being, or bestow a happy immortality, yet His own righteousness and benevolence would forbid His visiting external suffering on that creature, while holy. The natural relation then, between such a creature and God, would be this: God would bestow perfect happiness, just so long as the creature continued to render perfect obedience, and no longer. For both the natural and legal consequence of sin would be spiritual death. But it would seem that some of the angels are elect, and these are now confirmed in a state of everlasting holiness and bliss. For holiness is their peculiarity, their blessedness seems complete, and they are mentioned as sharing with man the heavenly mansions, whence we know glorified saints will never fall. On the other hand, another class of the angels have finally and irrevocably fallen into spiritual death. The inference from these facts would seem to be, that the angels, like the human race, have passed under the probation of a covenant of works. The elect kept it, the non-elect broke it; the difference between them being made, so far as God was the author of it, not by His efficacious active decree and grace.

but by His permissive decree, in which both classes were wholly left to the freedom of their wills. God only determin-- ing by His Providence the circumstances surrounding them, which became the occasional causes of their different choices, and limiting their conduct. On those who kept their proba- tion, through the efficacy of this permissive decree, God graciously bestowed confirmation in holiness, adoption, and inheritance in life everlasting. This, being more than a tempo- rary obedience could earn, was of pure grace; yet not through a Mediator; because the angels, being innocent, needed none. When this probation began, what was its particular condition, and when it ended, we know not; except that the fall of Satan, and most probably that of his angels, preceded Adam's. Nor is the nature of the sin known. Some, from Mark iii : 29, sup- pose it was blasphemy against the Holy Ghost. Others, from I Tim. iii : 6, suppose it was pride; neither conclusively. Guess- ing is vain, where there is no key to a solution. It may very possibly be that pride was the sin, for it is one to which Satan's spiritual nature and exalted state might be liable. The great difficulty is how, in a will prevalently holy, and not even swayed by innocent bodily wants and appetites, and where there was not in the whole universe a single creature to entice to sin, the first wrong volition could have place. At the proper time I will attempt to throw on this what light is in my power.

The good angels are engaged, first, in the worship and adoration of God. Matt. xviii : 10; Rev.

4. Occupations of good angels.

v : 11. Second, God employs them in ad- ministering His gracious and providential government over the world. Under this head we may notice : (a) That they aided in the giving of Revelation, as the Law. Acts vii : 53; Gal, iii : 19, and many prophetic messages and disclosures, as Dan. x. (b) They seem to have some concern in social and national events, procuring the execution of God's purposes. Dan. x : 13. (c) They are employed to punish His enemies, as instruments of His righteous vengeance. 2 Kings xix : 35; Acts xii : 23; I Chron. xxi : 16. (d) They are sent forth to minister to those who shall be heirs of salvation. Heb. i : 14; Acts xii : 7; Ps. xci : 10–12. (e) They guide the departing souls of Christians home to their mansions in heaven. Luke xvi : 22. Last. They are Christ's agents in the general judgment and resurrection. Matt. xiii : 39; xxiv : 31; I Thess. iv : 17, 18.

As to the exact nature of the agencies exerted for the saints by the ministering angels, Christians

How exercised?

are perhaps not very well instructed, nor agreed. A generation ago, it was currently believed that they communicated to their minds instructions important to their duty or welfare, by dreams, presentiments, or impressions. Of these, many Christians are now skeptical. It seems more certain that they exert an invisible superintendence over our welfare, in and under the laws of nature. Whether they influence our waking minds unconsciously by suggesting thoughts and feelings through our law of associated ideas, is much debated. I see in it nothing incredible. The pleasing and fanciful idea of guardian angels is grounded on the following scriptures: Dan. x : 13, 20; Matt. xviii : 10; Acts xii : 15. The most that these passages can prove is, that provinces and countries may have their affairs committed in some degree to the special care of some of the higher ranks of angels; and that superstitious Jews supposed that Peter had his own guardian angel, who might borrow Peter's body for the purpose of an apparition. The idea has more support in New Platonism than in Scripture.

5. Satan a Person. The personality of Satan and his angels is to be established by an argument exactly similar to that employed for the good angels. Almost every possible act and attribute of personality is ascribed to them; so that we may say, the Scripture contains scarcely more proof of the existence of a personal God, than of a Devil. He speaks, goes, comes, reasons, hates, is judged, and is punished. See for instance, such passages as Matt. iv : 1–11; Jno. viii : 44; Job i : 6 to ii : 7.

Scriptures induce over whole Bible History the form of the two rival Kingdoms. There is no subject on which we may more properly remember that " There are more things in heaven and earth than are dreamed of in our philosophy."

It is evidently the design of the Scriptures to make much of Satan and his work. From first to last, the favorite representation of the world's history is, that it is the arena for a struggle between two kingdoms—Christ's and Satan's. Christ leads the kingdom of the good, Satan that of the evil; though with different authorities and powers. The headship of Satan over his dæmons is implied where they are called " his angels." He is also called Prince of Devils. Eph. ii : 2; Matt. xxv : 41; ix : 34. Prince of the powers of the air, and Prince of darkness. Eph. vi : 12. This pre-eminence he doubtless acquired partly by seducing them at first, and probably confirmed by his superior powers. His dominion is compacted by fear and hatred of God, and common purposes of malice. It is by their concert of action that they seem to approach so near to ubiquity in their influences. That Satan is also the tyrant and head of sinful men is equally plain. This prevalent Bible picture of the two kingdoms may be seen carried out in these particulars. (a) Satan originated sin. Gen. iii : 1; Rev. xii : 9, 10; xx : 2, 10; 1 Jno. iii : 8; Jno. viii : 44; 2 Cor. xi : 3. (b) Satan remains the leader of the human and angelic hosts which he seduced into hostility, and employs them in desperate resistance to Christ and His Father. He is the " God of this world." 2 Cor. iv : 4. "The Spirit that worketh in the children of this world." Eph. ii : 2. Wicked men are his captives. See above, and 2 Tim. ii : 26. He is "the Adversary" (Satan,) "the Accuser," (Διαβόλος,) "the Destroyer," ('Απολλύων). (c) The progress of Christ to the final overthrow of this kingdom is the one great business of all time; the history of the conflict is the history of man and redemption. Gen. iii : 15; Jno. xii : 31; 1 Jno. iii : 8–10; 1 Pet. v : 8; Eph. vi : 11; Jno. viii : 44; Mark. iii : 23–27; Rom. xvi : 20; Acts xxvi : 18; Luke x : 18. The single fact that ungodly men, until the end of the world, compose Satan's kingdom, proves that he has, and will have some power or influence over their souls.

The powers of Satan and his angels are (a) always, and in all forms, strictly under the control of God and His permissive decree and providence. (b) They are often, perhaps, super-human, but never supernatural. If they do what man cannot, it is not by possession of omniscience or omnipotence, but by natural law : as a son of Anak could lift more than a common man, or a Davy or Brewster could control more of the powers of nature than a peasant.

6. Powers of bad Angels.

There is a supposition, which seems to have plausible grounds, that as the plan of redemption advances, the scope of Satan's operations is progressively narrowed; just as the general who is defeated, is cut off from one and another of his resources, and hemmed in to a narrower theatre of war, until his final capture. It may be, then, that his power of afflicting human bodies, of moving the material elements, of communicating with wizzards, of producing mania by his possessions, has been, or will be successively retrenched; until at last the millennium shall take away his remaining power of ordinary temptation. See Luke x : 18: Mark iii : 27; Rev. xx : 3. But

(1) Over Nature.

Satan once had, and for anything that can be proved, may now have extensive powers over the atmosphere and elements. The first is proved by Job, ch. 1 and 2. From this would naturally follow influence over the bodily health of men. No one can prove that some pestilences and droughts, tempests and earthquakes are not his work now.

(2) Over human minds.

He once had at least an occasional power of direct injection of conceptions and emotions, both independent of the man's senses and suggestions. See Matt. iv : 3, &c. This is the counterpart of the power of good angels, seen in Dan. ix : 22; Matt. ii : 13. It this power which makes the crime of witchcraft possible. The wizzard was a man, and the witch a woman, who was supposed to communicate with an evil angel, and receive from him, at the cost of some profane and damnable price, power to do superhuman things, or to reveal secrets beyond human ken. Its criminality was in its profanity, in the alliance with God's enemy, and its malignity in employing the arch-murderer, and always for wicked or malicious ends against oth-

Witchcraft.   ers. In Exod. xxii : 18, witchcraft is made
a capital sin; and in Gal. v : 20, it is still mentioned as a "work of the flesh." Yet some suppose that the sin never could be really committed. They account for Moses' statute by supposing that the class actually existed as impostors, and God justly punished them for their *animus*. This, I think, is hardly tenable. Others suppose the sin was anciently actual; but that now, according to the supposition of a gradual restriction, God no longer permits it; so that all modern wizzards are impostors. Doubtless there was, at all times, a large infusion of imposture. Others suppose that God still occasionally permits the sin, relaxing His curb on Satan in judicial anger against men, as in the age of Moses. There is nothing unscriptural in this. I do not admit the reality of any modern case of witchcraft, only because I have seen no evidence that stands a judicial examination.

Evil spirits had power over men's bodies and souls, by
(3) Possession.   usurping a violent control over their sug-
gestions, emotions and volitions, and thus violating their rational personality, and making the human members, for the time, their implements. This, no doubt, was attended with unutterable horror and agitation of consciousness,

These real.   in the victim. This has been a favourite
topic of neologic skepticism. They urge that the Evangelists did not really mean to teach actual posses-sion; but their object being theological, and not medical or psychological, they used the customary language of their day, not meaning thereby to endorse it, as scientific or accurate; because any other language would have been pedantic and use-less. They refer to Josh. x : 12. In Matt. iv : 24, lunatics (σεληνιαζομένοι) are named; but we do not suppose the author meant to assert they were moonstruck. They remind us of similar cases of mania now cured by opiates or blisters. They remind us that "possessions," like other superstitions, are limited to the dark ages. They argue that dæmons are said, Jude 6th, to be in chains, &c.

In this case the theory is incompatible with the candour of the sacred writers. For : 1st. They distinguish between "pos-sessions" and diseases of a physiological source, by mentioning both separately. See Mark i : 32; Luke vi : 17, 18; Matt. iv : 24, &c. 2d. The dæmons, as distinct from the possessed man, speak, and are spoken to, are addressed, commanded and re-buked by our Saviour, and deprecate His wrath. Mark i : 25, 34; ix : 25; Matt. viii : 32; xvii : 18. 3d. They have person-

18*

ality after they go out of men; whereas the disease has no entity apart from the body of which it was an affection. See Luke viii: 32. 4th. A definite number of dæmons possessed one man, Mark v: 9, and one woman, Mark xvi: 9. 5th. Their moral quality is assigned. 6th. The victories of Christ and His Apostles over them, announced the triumph of a spiritual kingdom over Satan's. Mark iii: 27; Luke xi: 20.

Do "possessions" now exist? Many reply, No; some, on the supposition of a progressive restriction of Satan's license; others, supposing that in the age of miracles, Providence made special allowance of this malice, in order to give Christ and His missionaries sp cial opportunity to evince the power of His kingdom, and show earnests of its overthrow. The latter is one object of Christ's victories over these "possessions." See Mark iii: 27: Luke xi: 20: x: 17–20, (where we have a separate proof of the spiritual nature of these possessions, as above shown). Whether "possessions" occur now, I do not feel qualified to affirm or deny.

The fourth power of Satan and dæmons is doubtless ordinary, and will be until the millennium; that (4) Temptations. of tempting to sin. This they may still carry on by direct injection of conceptions, or affections of the sensibility, without using the natural laws of sensibility or suggestion; and which they certainly do practice through the natural co-operation of those laws. Thus: A given mental state has a natural power to suggest any other with which it is associated. So that of several associated states, either one might naturally arise in the mind by the next suggestion. Now, these evil spirits seem to have the power of giving a prevalent vividness (and thus power over the attention and emotions) to that one of the associated states which best suits their malignant purposes. Thus: shall the sight of the wine-cup suggest most vividly, the jollity and pleasure of the past, or the nausea and remorse that followed it? If the latter, the mind will tend to sobriety; but if the former, it is tempted to sin. Here is the subtlety, and hence the danger of these practices, that they are not distinguished in our consciousness from natural suggestions, because the Satanic agency is strictly through the natural channels.

The mutual influence of the physiological states of the nerves and acts of organs of sense, over the May operate through mind, and *vice versa*, is a very obscure subbody. ject. We know, at least, that there is a mass of important truth there, as yet partially explored. Many believe that a concept, for instance, actually colours the retina of the eye, as though the visual *spectrum* of the object was formed on it. All have experienced the influence of emotions over our sense-perceptions. Animal influences on the organs of sense and nerves influence both concepts and percepts. Now, if evil spirits can produce an animal effect on our functions of nervous sensibility, they have a mysterious mode of affecting our souls.

We must also consider the regular psychological law, that vivid suggestions recurring too often always evoke a morbid action of the soul. The same subject of anxiety, for instance, too frequently recalled, begets an exaggerated anxiety. The "One-idea-man" is a monomaniac. It thus becomes obvious, how Satan may now cause various grades of lunacy, and often does. (This is not to be confounded with actual "possessions.") Hence, in part, religious melancholies, the most frightful of mental diseases. The maniac even, has recessions of disease; or he has seasons of glee, which, if maniacal, are actual joy to his present consciousness. But the victim of religious melancholy has no respite; he is crushed by a perpetual *incubus*. You can see how Satan (especially if bodily disease co-operates) can help to propagate it by securing the too constant recurrence of subjects of spiritual doubt or anxiety. You will see also, that the only successful mode to deal with the victims of these attacks is by producing diversion of the habitual trains of thought and feeling.

Recurring sugges-tions unwholesome.

7. How powerful is the motive to prayer, and gratitude for exemption from these calamitous spiritual assaults, for which we have no adequate defence in ourselves? The duty of watchfulness against temptations and their occasions, is plain. It becomes an obvious Christian duty to attempt to preserve the health of the nervous system, refraining from habits and stimulants which may have, we know not what influence on our nervous idiosyncrasy. It is also the duty of all to avoid overcoming and inordinate emotions about any object; and to abstain from a too constant pursuit of any carnal object, lest Satan should get his advantage of us thereby.

This discussion shows us how beneficent is the interruption of secular cares by the Sabbath's break.

LECTURE XXV.

PROVIDENCE.

SYLLABUS.

1. Define God's Providence. State the other theories of His practical relation to the universe. What concern has Providence in physical causes and laws?
Conf. of Faith, ch. 5. Turrettin, Loc. vi, Qu. 1, 2, 4. Dick, Lect. 41, 42. Calvin's Inst., bk. i, ch. 16 to 18. "Reign of Law," by Duke of Argyll. Southern Presbyterian Review, Jan., 1870, Art. i. Knapp, Chr. Theol., Art. viii. McCosh, Div. Gov., bk. ii, ch. 1.

2. Argue the doctrine of a special, from that of a general Providence.
Turrettin, Loc. vi, Qu. 3. Dick and Calvin as above.

3. Prove the doctrine of Providence; (a) from God's perfections; (b) from man's moral intuition; (c) from the observed course of nature and human history; (d) from the dependence of creatures.
Turrettin, Loc. vi, Qu. 1. Calvin and Dick as above. Knapp, Art. viii, § 68.

4. Present the Scriptural argument; (a) from prophecies; (b) from express testimonies. Answer objections.
Same authorities, and Dick, Lect. 43.

5. Does God's Providence extend to all acts of rational free-agents? What is His concern in the gracious acts of saints? What, in the evil acts of sinners? Discuss the doctrine of an immediate *concursus* in the latter.
Turrettin, Loc. vi, Qu. 4–8. Calvin, Inst., bk. i, ch. 18. Witsius, *de Oec Fed,* bk. i, ch. 8, § 13–29. Dick, Lect. 42, 43. Hill's Div., bk. iv, ch. 9, § 3. Knapp, Art. viii, § 70–72, Hodge's Outlines, ch. 13. Hodge, Syst. Theol.. Vol. i, ch. 11, § 1, 3, 4.

PROVIDENTIA, Greek, πρόνοια, is the execution in succes-sive time, of God's eternal, unsuccessive purpose, or πρόθεσις.

1 & 2. Definitions, and other theories. We believe the Scriptures to teach, not only that God originated the whole universe, but that He bears a perpetual, active relation to it; and that these works of providence are "His most holy, wise, and powerful preserving and governing all His creatures, and all their actions." It may be said that there are, besides this, three other theories concerning God's relation to the Universe; that of the Epicurean, who, though admitting an intelligent deity, supposed it inconsistent with His blessedness and perfections, to have any likings or anger, care or concern in the multiform events of the worlds; that of the Rational Deists, Socinians, and many rationalists, that God's concern with the Universe is not universal, special and perpetual, but only gene-ral, viz: by first endowing it with general laws of action, to the operation of which each individual being is then wholly left, God only exercising a general oversight of the laws, and not of specific agents; and that of the Pantheists, who identify all seeming substances with God, by making them mere modes of His self-development; so that there is no providential relation, but an actual identity; and all the events and acts of the Uni-verse are simply God acting.

The first theory is, as we shall see, practical atheism, and

General Providence unreasonable without special. is contradicted by a proper view of God's attributes. The third has been already refuted, as time and ability allowed. Against the second, or Deistical, I object: 1st. The seeming analogy by which it is suggested is a false one. That analogy is doubtless of human rulers—e. g., a commander of an army, who regulates general rules and important events, without being himself cognizant of special details; and of machinists, who construct a machine and start its motion, so that it performs a multitude of special evolutions, not individually directed by the maker. The vital difference is, that the human ruler employs a multitude of intelligent subordinates, independent of him for being, whose intention specifically embraces the details; whereas God directs inanimate nature, according to deists, without such intervention. The Platonist conception of a providence administered over particulars by dæmons is more consistent with this analogy. And the machinist does but adjust some motive power which God's providence supplies (water on his wheel, the elasticity of a spring, &c.,) to move his machine in his absence; whereas God's providence itself must be the motive power of His universal machine. 2d. On this deistical scheme of providence, results must either be fortuitous to God, (and then He is no longer Sovereign nor Almighty, and we reach practical atheism,) or else their occurrence is determined by Him through the medium of causations possessed of a physical necessity, (and we are thus landed in stoical fate!) 3d. It is a mere illusion to talk of a certain direction of the general, which does not embrace the particulars; for a general class is nothing, when separated from the particulars which compose it, but an abstraction of the mind. Practically, the general is only produced by producing all the specials which compose it. If the agents or instruments by which a general superintendence is exercised, be contingent and fallible, the providence must be such also. God's providence is efficient and almighty: it must then be special, or all its instruments Gods. 4th. God's providence evolves all events by using second causes according to their natures. But all events are interconnected, nearly or remotely, as causes and effects. And the most minute events often bear the connection with the grandest; e. g., the burning of a city from a vagrant spark; the change of King Ahab's dynasty by an errant arrow. Hence, according to this mode of providence, which we see God usually employs, unless His care extended to every event specially, it could not effectuate any, certainly. To exercise a general providence without a special, is as though a man should form a chain without forming its links.

The definition of Providence, which we adopted from the Catechism, divides it into two works—sustentation and government.

According to the Augustinian scholastics, the Cartesians, and many of the stricter Calvinistic Reformers, this sustentation of creatures in being is effected by a perpetual, active efflux or concursus of divine power at every successive instant, identical with that act of will and power by which they were brought out of *nihil* into *esse*; and they conceive that on the cessation of this act of God, for one instant, towards any creature whatsoever, it would return incontinently to non-existence. So that it is no figure of speech with them to say, " Sustentation is a perpetual re-creation." Their arguments are: (a) That God alone is self-existent; hence those things which have a dependent existence cannot have the ground of the continuance of their existence in themselves. (b) That all creatures exist in successive time: but the instants of successive time have no substantive tie between them by which one produces the next; but they only follow each other, whence it results that successive existence is momentarily returning to *nihil*, and is only kept out of it by a perpetual re-creation. And (c) They quote Scriptures, as Neh. ix : 6; Job. x : 12; Ps. civ : 27–30; Acts xvii : 28 ; Heb. i : 3 ; Col. i : 17; Isa. x : 15.

Scholastic conception of Sustentation.

This speculation has always seemed to me without basis, and its demonstration, to say the least, impossible for the human understanding. But let me distinctly premise, that both the existence and essence, or the being and properties of every created thing, originated out of nothing, in the mere will and power of God ; that they are absolutely subject, at every instant of their successive existence, to His sovereign power ; that their action is all regulated by His special providence, and that He could reduce them to nothing as easily as He created them. Yet, when I am required to believe that their sustentation is a literal, continuous re-production by God's special act out of *nihil*, I cannot but remember that, after all, the human mind has no cognition of substance itself, except as the unknown *substratum* of properties, and no insight into the manner in which it subsists. Hence we are not qualified to judge, whether its subsistence is maintained in this way. The arguments seem to me invalid.

This not proved.

If man's reason has any necessary ontological judgment whatever, it is this : That substance involves reality, continuity of existence, and permanency. Such is, in short, substantially the description which the best mental science now gives of that thing, so essential to our perception. When we deny self-existence to creatures, we deny that the cause which originates their existence can be in them; but this is far from proving that God, in originating their existence, may not have conferred it as a permanent gift, continuing itself so long as He permits it. e. g., Motion is never assumed by matter of itself; but when impressed from without, it is never self-arrested. To say that

finite creatures exist in successive time, or have their existence
measured by it, is wholly another thing from showing that this
succession constitutes their existence.   What is time, but an
abstract idea of our minds, which we project upon the finite
existence which we think of or observe ?   Let any man analyse
his own conception, and he will find that the existence is conceived of as possessing a true continuity; it is the time by
which his mind measures it, that lacks the continuity.   Last.
These general statements of Scripture only assert the practical
and entire dependence of creatures; no doubt their authors
would be very much surprised to hear them interpreted into
these metaphysical subtilties.

You will observe that the class of ideas which leads to this
Monads not de- doctrine of a perpetual efflux of divine power,
pendent in same way in recreation, are usually borrowed from
as organisms.   organized, material bodies.   Men forget that
the existence of organisms may be, and probably is, dependent,
in a very different sense, from that of simple existence, such as
a material ultimate atom, or a pure spirit.   For the existence of
an organized body is nothing but the continuance of its organization, i. e., of the aggregation of its parts in certain modes.
This, in turn, is the effect of natural causes ; but these causes
operate under the perpetual, active superintendence of God.
So that it is literally true, the existence of a compounded organism, like the human body, is the result of God's perpetual,
providential activity; and the mere cessation of this would be
the end of the organism.   But the same fact is not proved of
simple, monadic substances.

But what are natural causes and laws ?   This question
What is second enters intimately into our views of provi-
cause?   dence, inasmuch as they are the means with
                               which providence works.   The much-abused
phrase, law of nature, has been vaguely used in various senses.
The Duke of Argyle says he finds the word " Law," used in
five senses.   1. For an observed order of facts.   2. The unknown force implied therein.   3. The ascertained limit of a
force.   4. Combinations of force for a ' final cause.'   5. The
order of thought which the reason supplies for explanation of
observed effects, as in Mechanics, the ' first law of motion.'
The list might be larger, but properly it means that it is the
observed regular mode or rule, according to which a given
cause, or class of causes operates under given conditions.
This definition of itself will show us the absurdity of offering a
law of nature to account for the existence of anything.   For
nature is but an abstraction, and the law is but the regular mode
of acting of a cause ; so that instead of accounting for, it needs
to be accounted for itself.   The fact that a phenomenon is produced again and again regularly, does not account for its production!   The true question which lies at the root of the

matter is, concerning the real power which is present in natural causes. We say that they are those things which, under certain conditions, have power to produce certain effects. What, then, is the power? It is answered that the power resides in some property of the thing we call cause, when that property is brought into certain relations with the properties of some other thing. But still the question recurs: Is the power, the activity, a true property of the thing which acts as cause, or is the power truly God's force, and the occurrence of the relation between the properties of cause and effect, merely the appointed occasion of its exertion? This is the question. Let me premise, before stating the answers given, that the question should be limited to the laws of material nature, and to physical causes. All sound philosophy now regards intelligent spirits as themselves proper fountains of causation, because possessed of a true spontaneity and self-determination, not indeed emancipated from God's sovereign control, yet real and intrinsically active, as permitted and regulated by Him.

But, as to physical causes, orthodox divines and philosophers give different answers. Say the one class, as Dick, matter is only passive. The coming of the properties of the cause into the suitable relation to the effect, is only the occasion; the true agency is but God's immediately. All physical power is God directly exerting Himself through passive matter; and the law of the cause is but the regular mode which He proposes to Himself for such exertions of His power. Hence, the true difference between natural power and miraculous, would only be, that the former is customary under certain conditions, the latter, under those conditions, unusual. When a man feels his weary limbs drawn towards the earth, by what men call gravity, it is in fact as really God drawing them, as when, against gravity, the body of Elijah or Christ was miraculously borne on high. And the reason they assign is: that matter is negative and inert; and can only be the recipient of power: and that it is incapable of that intelligence, recollection, and volition, implied in obedience to a regular law.

Some admit no natural force but God.

Others, as McCosh, Hodge, &c., would say, that to deny all properties of action to material things, is to reduce them to practical nonentity; leaving God the only agent and the only true existence, in the material universe. Their view is that God, in creating and organizing material bodies, endued them with certain properties. These properties He sustains in them by that perpetual support and superintendence He exerts. And these properties are specific powers of acting or being acted on, when brought into suitable relations with the properties of other bodies. Hence, while power is really in the physical cause, it originated in, and is sustained by, God's power. The question

Theory of McCosh Defective.

then arises: If this be so, if the power is intrinsically in the physical cause, wherein does God exert any special providence in each case of causation? Is not His providential control banished from the domain of these natural laws, and limited to His act of creation, which endued physical causes with their power? The answer which McCosh makes to this question is: that nothing is a cause by itself; nor does a mere capacity for producing a given effect make a thing a cause; unless it be placed in a given relation with a suitable property of some other thing. And here, says he, is God's special, present providence; in constituting those suitable relations for inter-action, by His superintendence. The obvious objection to this answer seems to have been overlooked; that these juxta-positions, or relations, are themselves always brought about by God (except where free agents are employed) by natural causes. Hence, the view of God's providence that would result, would be nothing more than the pre-established harmony of Leibnitz, from whom, indeed, his views seem derived. This would, indeed, give the highest conception of the wisdom, power, and sovereignty exercised in establishing the amazing plan; but it would leave God no actual providential functions to perform in time, except the doubtful one of the mere sustentation of simple being. For, you must note : since the continued aggregation of the parts of an organism results from the operation of natural laws between its elementary parts, His concern in the sustentation of compounded bodies would be no other than in the working of natural laws. The explanation is therefore obviously defective.

Let us see to what extent the defect can be supplied. The problem which the Rationalist supposes
How amended ?   to be involved is this: How God's effective providence can intervene consistently with the uniformity of natural laws. Now, the laws of nature are invariable, only in the sense defined above. When a given law is the expression of the mode in which a real, natural cause acts; then it is invariable in this sense, that granting the same conditions in every respect, the same power will produce the same effect. But it must be noted, that in nature, effects are never the sole results of a single power. Combination of natural powers is the condition of all effects. Our description of God's providence over nature must be, in a good sense, "anthropopathic." How then, does man's personal will use the powers of nature? He is not able, and does not aim, to change the invariability of either of the powers which he borrows. But, knowing the invariable law of one cause, he combines with this some other power, or powers, which are also used in strict accordance with their laws, so as to control the conditions under which they together act. Thus, he modifies the effects, without infringing at all the regularity of the natural laws. And this is rational con-

trivance for an end.   Thus, even in man's hands, while the law of each power is invariable, by combination of a rational providence, the uses are widely flexible.   Must not this be much more possible in God's hands?   Thus, for instance, man constructs a clock, for the purpose of keeping time.   He avails himself of one law, the gravitation of a mass of metal suspended, which is absolutely unchangeable.   He combines with this, by a set of wheels, and an "escapement," the action of another law; the regular beat of a pendulum thirty-nine inches long.   This is also invariable.   But by this combination, the mechanic has made a clock, which he can cause to keep siderial or solar time, to run faster or slower.   It is not by interrupting the regularity of two forces, but by virtue of that regularity, that he is enabled to produce these varied effects.   By a rational providence, these invariable forces are made to perform a new function.

Now, man's agency here is *supra material*, namely, personal, intelligent and voluntary.   Is then, all God's working in special providence supernatural?   The answer is, it is *supra physical* being personal; but not in the proper sense supernatural, any more than man's similar agency.   For that which Personal Will effectuates through the regular laws of second causes, is properly natural.   The supernatural is that which God effectuates by power above those causes.

Is Providence, then, supernatural.

It may be objected, that, as we observe the clock maker shaping and adjusting the parts of machinery, by which he combines two or more invariable powers for a varying function, so, we should have experimental knowledge of God's processes in His providence. We reply: Is the machinist's result any the less natural, because he chose to work only in secret?   The answer contained in this question has its force greatly enhanced by remarking that the Agent of providence is an invisible Spirit.   It is also certainly a part of His purpose that His hand shall be invisible, in His ordinary working.   This His objects require.   Hence, we are to reconcile our minds to this fact, that while the reality of a special providence, and its possibility, are rationally demonstrable, man is not to find its method explicable.   Here faith must perform her humble office.   But when the possibility of its execution by infinite power and wisdom are shown, all is done that is needed to silence rationalism.

Objection.

The speculations of the Duke of Argyle have been mentioned above, with approbation.   This imposes a necessity of dissenting from his opinion as to the miracle.   Desiring, apparently, to conciliate the rationalistic cavil, that the "invariability of the laws of nature," renders a miracle absolutely impossible and incredible, he advances this definition; Let a miracle be called an

Is a miracle the result of an inner Law.

effect which, while above and beside all laws of nature explored by man, will yet be found (in the light of heaven perhaps,) to be but an expression of some higher and more recondite law. From this view I wholly dissent. It is inconsistent with the prime end for which God has introduced miracles, to be attestations to man of God's messages. For, we have only to suppose human physical science carried to higher stages, and the events which were miraculous to a ruder age, would become natural. All miracles would cease to be σημεῖα just so soon as they were comprehended; but it is the glory of the true miracle, that the more fully it is comprehended, the more certainly it would be a σημεῖον. On this plan the effects of the electric telegraph, to us merely human, would have been veritable miracles to Peter and Paul, and would now be, to the Hottentot christians. This definition then, virtually destroys the christian miracles. We must hold fast to the old doctrine; that a miracle is a phenomenal effect above all the powers of nature; properly the result of supernatural power: i. e., of God's immediate power which He has not regularly put into any second causes, lower or higher. The advocates of the new definition may retort, that in denying miracles to be expressions of some higher, recondite law, I assign them a lawless character. Should we not, they ask, claim for them, as for all God's acts, a lucid method, a rational order? I reply: By all means, yes. Miracles are not anarchical infractions of nature's order. But they confound the law of the divine purpose, which is but the infinite thought regulating God's own will and acts, with some recondite natural law. Every miracle was wrought in strict conformity with God's decree. But this is in God: the natural law is impressed on the nature of second causes.

We see, then, that all general providence is special. And the special is as truly natural as the general.

The natural arose out of the supernatural, and in that sense, reposes upon it at all times. The Divine will is perpetually present, underlying all the natural. Else God is shut back to the beginning of the universe, and has no present action nor administration in His empire. Reason: Because, if you allow Him any occasional, or special present interventions, at decisive crises, or as to cardinal events, those interventions are found to be, as events, no less natural than all other events. They also come through natural law.

A providence is proved: (a.) From God's perfections. His infinite essence, immensity, omniscience, and omnipotence enable Him to sustain such functions to His universe, if He pleases. And we believe it is His will to do so; first, because His wisdom would not have permitted Him to make a universe without an object; and when made, the same wisdom will undoubtedly employ due means to attain that end. Second. His good-

3. Providence proved, 1st, from God's perfections.

ness would not permit Him to desert the well being of the various orders of sentient beings He has created and endued with capacities for suffering. Third. His righteousness ensures that after having brought moral relations into existence between Himself and His moral creatures, by the very act of creating them, He cannot desert and neglect those relations.

(b.) Man's moral intuitions impel him to believe that God is just, good, true and holy; and that the natural connection which generally prevails in the course of this life, between man's exercise of these virtues, and well-being, is intentional and retributive. If so, then God's providence is concerned in all that course of nature. So we argue from the instinct of prayer. (c.) The intelligent order which we see in the working of material nature splendidly displays a Providence. A multitude of elements and bodies are here seen connected by most multifarious influences, and yet the complex machine moves on, and never goes wrong. There is a guiding hand! The same fact is revealed by the steadiness of all the laws of reproduction in nature, especially in the vegetable and animal world, and in man's and animal's sensitive, and man's emotional and intellectual nature. Like does not fail to beget like. Why? It is strikingly seen in the ratio of the sexes among human births, and the diversity of human countenances. And the revelation of wise designs made at least occasionally in human history (e. g., in the formation of Washington's character, prevalence of the Greek language at the Christian era,) shows that it moves on under the constant superintendence of God.

2d, From Man's Moral Intuitions. 3d, From Nature's Order.

Man's conscious dependence teaches him the same truth. He has no control over a single one of the laws of nature, such as enables him to educe anything necessary to his well-being from them, with any certainty. If there is no controlling mind to govern them for him, he is the child of a mechanical fate, or of capricious chance.

(d.) From man's dependence.

Scriptures prove a Providence. A preliminary doctrinal argument may be found in God's decree. If its existence is proved, then a providence is proved: for the one is complementary to the other, (a.) By its predictions, promises, and threats, many of which have been explicit and detailed, and long afterwards have been accurately accomplished. e. g., Ex. xii: 46, with Jno. xix: 36; Ps. xxii: 18, with Jno. xix: 24; 1 Kings xx: 13, with xx: 34, 35–38; Micah. v: 2, with Matt. ii: 5; Is. xiv: 23; Jer. i: 23 to end; Jer. xlix: 17, &c.; Ezek. xxvi: 4, 5. Without a control that was efficacious, over particular events, God could not thus positively speak. Ps. xci.

4. From Scriptures.

(b.) The duty and privilege of prayer, as exercised by inspired saints, and enjoined in precepts, implies a providence for else, God has no sure way to answer. No Providence is practical atheism.

(c.) A multitude of express Scriptures assert God's providence to be universal. e. g.. Ps. ciii: 17–19; Dan. iv: 34, 35; Ps. xxii: 28, 29; Job xii: 10, and Chaps. xxxviii–xli; Col. i: 17; Heb. i: 3; Acts xvii: 28.

Efficacious and Sovereign.—Job xxiii: 13, Ps. xxxiii: 11; cxxxv: 6; 2d Sam. xvii: 14.

The evolution of His eternal purpose.—Ps. civ: 24; Is. xxviii: 29; Acts xv: 18: Eph. i: 11.

Special and particular.—Matt. x: 29-31; Luke xii: 6, 7; Nehemiah ix: 6; Matt. xi: 26; Ps. xxxvi: 6; cxlv: 15, 16; Gen. xxii: 13, 14; Jonah iv: 6, 7, 8.

Over the material world.—Job, Chaps. xxxviii–xli; Ps. civ: 14; cxxxv; 5–7: cxlvii: 8–18; cxlviii: 7, 8; Acts xiv: 17; Matt. vi: 30; vi: 26.

Over acts to us fortuitous, i. e. those of which the natural causes are unassignable by us, either because undiscovered, as yet, or so subtile, or complex. Gen. xxiv: 12, 13, &c.; Exod. xxi: 12, 13; Deut. xix: 4; Ps. lxxv: 6, 7; Job v: 6; Prov. xvi: 33; xxi: 31.

Last: over the good and bad acts of free agents. Reason shows this; for otherwise God could not govern any of the physical events into which human volitions enter as modifying causes, either immediately or remotely. Prophecy, threats, promises, and the duty of prayer prove it, (see on Decrees,) and Scripture expressly asserts it. Prov. xvi: 9; xx: 24; xxi: 1; Jer. x: 23; Ps. xxxiii: 14, 15; Gen. xlviii: 8, &c.; Exod. xii: 36; Ps. xxv: 9–15; Phil. ii: 13; Acts ii: 23; 2 Sam. xvi: 10; xxiv: 1; lxxvi: 10; Rom. xi: 36; Acts iv: 28; Rom. ix: 18; 2 Sam. xii: 11; 1 Kings xxii: 23; Ps. cv: 25.

The objections against the Bible doctrines may all be reduced to these heads:

Objections.

1. Epicurean; that God would be fatigued from so many cares.

2. That it is derogatory to His dignity to be concerned with trivialities.

3. The disorders existing in material nature, and in the course of human affairs, would be inconsistent with His benevolence and righteousness.

4. The doctrine infringes the efficacy of second causes, and the free-agency of intelligent creatures.

5. Last: It makes God the author of sin.

For answers, see discussions above and below: and Dick. Lect. 43.

5. In proceeding to speak of the control of Providence over the acts of intelligent free agents, we must bear in mind the essential difference between them and physical bodies. A

body is not intrinsically a cause. Causation only takes place when a certain relation between given properties of two bodies, is established by God's providence. (See § 1.) But a soul is a fountain of spontaneity; it is capable of will, in itself, and is self-determined to will, by its own prevalent dispositions. Soul is a cause.

Now, the Bible attributes all the spiritually good acts of man to God. Rom. vii: 18; Phil. ii: 13; iv: 13; 2 Cor. xii: 9, 10; Eph. ii: 10; Gal. v: 22–25. God's concern in such acts may be explained as composed of three elements. (a.) He perpetually protects and preserves the human person with the capacities which He gave to it naturally. (b.) He graciously renews the dispositions by His immediate, almighty will, so as to incline them, and keep them inclined by the Holy Ghost, to the spiritually good. (c.) He providentially disposes the objects and truths before the soul thus renewed, so that they become the occasional causes of holy volitions freely put forth by the sanctified will. Thus God is, in an efficient sense, the intentional author of the holy acts, and of the holiness of the acts, of His saints.

But, the question of His concern in the evil acts of free agents (and the naturally indifferent,) is more difficult. The Dominican Scholastics, or Thomists, followed by some Calvinistic Reformers, felt themselves constrained, in order to uphold the efficiency and certainty of God's control over the evil acts of His creatures, to teach their doctrine of the physical *concursus* of God in all such acts, (as well as in all good acts, and physical causes). This is not merely God's sustentation of the being and capacities of creatures; not merely a moral influence by truths or motives providentially set before them; not merely an infusion of a general power of acting to which the creature gives the specific direction, by his choice alone, in each individual act; but in addition to all this, a direct, immediate physical energizing of the active power of the creature, disposing and predetermining it efficaciously to the specific act, and also enabling it thereto, and so passing over with the agency of the creature, into the action. Thus, it is an immediate, physical, predisposing, specific and concurrent influence to act. Their various arguments may be summed up in these three: that the Scripture, e. g., Gen. xlv: 7; Is. x: 15, &c.; Acts xvii: 28; Phil. ii: 13; Col. i: 13, demand the *concursus* of God to satisfy their full meaning: That as man's *esse* is dependent on the perpetual, recreative efflux of God's power, so his acting must perpetually depend on God's *concursus*, because the creature must act according to his being. Under this head, for instance, Witsius may be seen, following Aquinas, arguing thus: Nothing but a first cause can act without the aid and influence of a prior

God's Agency in man's spiritual acts.

God's agency in Man's sins. Is there a concursus?

cause.   Hence, if the human will were able to produce any
action of which God was not the efficient, the creature's will
would hold the state of a First Cause.   Again: All action proceeds from powers: but the creature's powers emanate from his
essence.   Hence if the essence is derived, the action must also
be derived.   They argue, in the third place, that without the
concursus they describe, God's providence over human acts
could not be efficient and sovereign, as the Scripture teaches,
and as we must infer from the doctrine of the decree, and
from the certain fulfilment of prophecy.

Turrettin obviously implies, in his argument, that the
rational creature's will, like a second cause in matter, is indeter-
terminate to any specific effect.   For he argues that a cause
thus indeterminate or indifferent must receive its determination
to a specific effect, from some cause out of, and above itself,
which must be active, and determinating to the specific effect.
(Qu. 5, § 8, &c.)

Now, on this I remark, see here the great importance of
the distinction I made (in last lecture, and on the difference of
permissive and efficacious decrees) and between material and
rational second causes.

Again: Consider if Turrettin does not here surrender a
vital point of his own doctrine concerning the will.   That point
is, that the rational will is not *in equilibro;* that volitions are
not contingent phenomena, but regular effects.   Effects of
what?   Sound metaphysics says, of subjective motive.   The
soul (not the faculty of choice itself,) is self-determining — i. e.,
spontaneous.   But this according to a law, its subjective law.

Now, to this I reply farther, (a) The doctrine that God's
sustentation is by a perpetual active efflux
of creative power, we found to be unproved
as to spirits, which unlike bodies, possess the
properties of true being, absolute unity and simplicity.   That
doctrine is only true, in any sense, of organized bodies; which
are not proper beings, but rather organized collections of a
multitude of separate beings, or atoms.   My consciousness
tells me that I have a power of acting (according to the laws
of my nature) dependent indeed, and controlled always by
God, yet which is personally my own.   It originates in the spring
of my own spontaneity.   As to the relation between personal
power in us, and the power of the first cause, we know nothing; for neither He, nor consciousness, tells us anything.

(b) Surely the meaning of all such Scriptures as those
referred to, is sufficiently satisfied, as well as
the demands of God's attributes and government, by securing these two points.   First,
God is not the author of sin; Second, His control over all the
acts of all His creatures is certain, sovereign and efficacious;
and such as to have been determined from eternity.   If a way

It is not revealed by consciousness.

Not required by God's Sovereignty.

can be shown, in which God thus controls these sinful acts, without this physical *concursus*, the force of the other arguments for it is all removed.* May not this mode be found in this direction? Thus:

God's eternal purpose as to evil acts of free agents is more than barely permissive; His prescience of it H o w, t h e n, a r e is more than a *scientia media* of what is, to Men's E v i l A c t s Brought About? Him, contingent. It is a determinate purpose effectuated in providence by means efficient, and to Him, certain in their influence on free agents. What are those means? Volitions are caused. The efficient causes of volitions are the soul's own dispositions; the occasional causes are the objects providentially presented to those dispositions. Even we may, in many cases, so know dispositions as efficiently to procure, and certainly to predict, given volitions, through the presentation of objective causes thereof. An infinite understanding may so completely know all dispositions and all their complex workings, as to foretell and produce volitions thus in every case, as we are able to do in many cases. Add to this, omnipotent, providential power, which is able to surround any soul with circumstances so adapted to his known dispositions, as infallibly to prove the occasions of given desired volitions. And the presentation of the objective inducement to do wrong is also wrought, after the manner of God's permissive decree, by the free actions of other sinners permissively ordained. Thus: The offer of the Ishmaelitish merchants (Gen. xxxvii: 25,) to buy Joseph, was the sufficient inducement to his brethren's spite and cupidity. It was these subjective emotions in them, which constituted the efficient motive of the crime of selling their brother. God did not himself present that inducement by His own immediate act or influence; but He permissively ordained its presentation by the merchants. Here you have means enough to enable God to purpose and efficiently produce a given act of a free agent, without any other special *concursus*, in the act itself, than the providential power by which He sustains the being and capacities of that soul, whatever that power is. This, then, is my picture of the providential evolution of God's purpose as to sinful acts; so to arrange and group events and objects around free agents by His manifold wisdom and power, as to place each soul, at every step, in the presence of those circumstances, which, He knows, will be a sufficient objective inducement to it to do, of its own native, free activity, just the thing called for by God's plan. Thus the act is man's alone, though its occurrence is efficaciously secured by God. And the sin is man's only. God's concern in it is holy, first, because all His personal agency in arranging to

---

* If a soul is not spontaneous cause, it is not responsible. If its spontaneity is **above** providence, it is a God!

secure its occurrence was holy; and second, His ends or purposes are holy. God does not will the sin of the act, for the
sake of its sinfulness; but only wills the result to which the act
is a means, and that result is always worthy of His holiness.
E. g.: A righteous king, besieged by wicked rebels, may
arrange a sally, with a view to their righteous defeat, and the
glorious deliverance of the good citizens, in which he knows
the rebels will slay some of his soldiers. This slaying is sin;
the good king determines efficaciously to permit it; not for the
sake of the slaying, but for the sake of the righteous triumph
of which it is part means. The death of these good soldiers is
the sin of the rebels; the righteousness of the end in view, is
the king's.

It may be said, that this scheme represents God, after all,
as governing free agents by a sort of *scientia*
Is God's intelligence *media*. I reply: Let us not be scared by
herein Scientia Media? unpopular names. It is a knowledge conditioned on His own almighty purpose, and His own infallible
knowledge of the dispositions of creatures; and it is, in this
sense, relative. But this is not a dangerous sense. For only
lay down the true doctrine, that volitions are efficiently determined by dispositions, and there is, to God, no shadow of contingency remaining about such foreknowledge. (That was the
ugly trait.) As I showed you, when explaining this *scientia
media*, in the hands of him who holds the contingency of the
will, it is illogical; in the hands of the Calvinist, it becomes
consistent.

(c) This doctrine of physical *concursus* neglects the proper
distinction between the power of causation
Such concursus would in physical bodies and in free agents. It
be physical. also commits a fatal error in making God's
agency in bad acts, about as immediate and efficacious
as in good acts; and indeed very much the same. It represents the soul, like a physical cause, as undetermined to action
or non-action, till God's *præcursus* decides it to act. Of course,
then, an unholy will might be equally decided by it to a holy or
an unholy act! Thus hyper-Calvinism actually betrays its own
cause to the opposite party, who teach the *equilibrium* of the
will; and contradicts Scripture, which always claims more
credit and agency for God (and an essentially different agency)
in the good acts, than in the evil acts, of the creature.

(d) This doctrine leads us too near to the awful verge of
Pantheism. See how readily it can be made
Its tendency Panthe- to tend towards one of the very types of
istic. Idealistic Pantheism, lately prevalent in parts
of Europe. If God's efficient *præcursus* is essential to all the
creature's acts, then, of course, it is essential to his acts of perception. But now, if it is not the objective world, which is the
efficient cause of sensations in our minds, but God: why

19*

should we predicate any objective world at all? The real evidence of its existence is lacking, and if this doctrine is true, the supposition of an objective world should be excluded by the "law of parcimony." And since the mind is not, according to this doctrine, the efficient of its own acts, why should we predicate its personality either? But, more simply stated, the road towards Pantheism is this: If there is such a universal *præcursus*, God is the only true agent in the universe. Turrettin himself admits, that according to this scheme, God's *concursus* is the efficient cause of every act, and the creature's volition only the formal cause. How easy the step from this to making the creature's being a mere efflux of God's being? Do not these writers claim that the mode of the action must agree to that of the *esse?* Thus we have another illustration of the justice of the charge that Scholastic Realism prepared the way for modern Pantheism.

(e) Last. Like all Pantheism, it comes too near making God the author of sin; for it makes God an immediate, intentional efficient of acts which are sinful. The scholastics endeavour to evade this, by distinguishing between the physical entity of the act and its moral relation. God, say they, is an efficient of the entity, not of the moral evil which qualifies it. Thus: when a musician strikes an untuned harp, the sound is from him, the discord of the sound is from the disorder of the strings. When a partial paralytic essays to move his limbs, motion is from his volition; the halting or jerking is from the disease. The illustrations are false; for the musician's intention is to produce, not only sound, but harmonious sound,— the paralytic's, not only motion, but correct motion. God's intention embraces not only the physical entity of the act, but its moral quality. It is not only the act as an act, but the act as sinful, which He intends to permit. For how often are the holy ends He has in view connected with the sinfulness of the act? That the distinction is incorrect may be practically evinced thus: The same distinction would serve as well to justify the Jesuit doctrine of intention. Search and see. I see no way to escape the horrid consequence of making God the author of sin, except by making sinful acts immediately the acts of the sinner alone; and this is certainly the testimony of his own consciousness. He feels that he is wholly self-moved thereto; and hence his sense of guilt therefor.

The inadequacy of this evasion appears in that Turrettin (Qu. 5, § 17,) admits himself to be constrained by it to hold the deplorable dogma, that no moral act has intrinsic moral quality *per se.* He even quibbles, that the hatred of God felt by a sinner is not evil by its intrinsic nature as a simple act of will; but only by its adjuncts. Ans. The act, apart from its adjuncts, is either no act at all, or a different act intrinsically. There is false analysis here. Turrettin (again) is misled by instances such as these admitted ones. All killing is not murder. All smiting is not malice. All taking is not theft, &c., &c. The sophism is, that these are outward acts: effectuated through bodily members. As to the mere physical phenomenon of volitions moving bodily members, we admitted, and argued that, abstracted from its psychical antecedents and adjuncts, it has no moral quality. Proof is easy. But, in strictness of speech, the physical execution of the volition in the act of striking, &c., is not the act of soul — only the outward result thereof. The act of soul is the intent of will. In this, the right or wrong moral relation is intrinsic. Now, would not Turrettin say, that the *concursus* he teaches incites and directs the act of soul, and not that of the body merely? Certainly. Thus it appears that his distinction and evasion are inadequate.

Or thus: No Calvinist will deny that the morality of an act is determined by its intention. But intention is action of soul, as truly as volition. And if a physical *concursus* is necessary to all action, it is so to intention. Thus God's action would be determinative of the morality of the act. In a word, these Calvinists here betray, in their zeal for this *præcursus*, that doctrine of the essential originality of the moral distinction, which they had already established; (see Lec. xiv, § 4, and Loc. iii, Qu. 18th,) and which we shall find essential in defend ing against Socinians, the necessity of satisfaction for guilt.

LECTURE XXVI.

MAN'S ESTATE OF HOLINESS, AND THE COVENANT OF WORKS.

SYLLABUS:

1. Was man's person constituted of matter and spirit? Wherein consisted the " image of God " in which man was created? Wherein consisted his original righteousness? See

Turrettin, Loc. v, Qu. 10. Dick, Lect. 40. Witsius, *Œcon Fæd*, bk. i, ch. 2. Watson's Theo. Inst., ch. 18. Knapp, Chr. Theol., ₰ 51–53.

2. Was Adam's original righteousness con-created, or acquired by acting? State the answers of Calvinists and Pelagians, and establish the true one.

Turrettin, Loc. v, Qu. 9, 11; Loc. viii, Qu. 1, 2; Loc. ix, Qu. 2. Hill, bk. iv, ch. 1, ₰ 2. Dick, Lect. 40. Watson, ch. 18, ₰ 1 (2). Knapp, ₰ 54. Thornwell, Lect. 14, pp. 394–end.

3. What was Adam's natural relation to God's law?

Turrettin, Loc. v, Qu. 12. Thornwell, Lect. 11 and 12. Witsius, bk. i, ch. 5, ₰ 22, and bk. i, ch. 4, ₰ 1–5. Dick, Lect. 44. Watson, ch. 18, ₰ 1.

4. Did God place man under a Covenant of Works? And did Adam therein represent his posterity?

Turrettin, Loc. viii, Qu. 3, 6. Witsius, bk. i, ch. 2, ₰ 14, &c., ch. 8, ₰ 31, &c. Hill, bk. iv, ch. 1, ₰ 1, 2. Dick, Lect. 44, 45. Watson, ch. 18, ₰ 3. Thornwell, Lect. 12, p. 284, &c.

5. What was the condition, and what the seal of that Covenant?

Turrettin, Loc. viii, Qu. 4, 5, 7. Witsius, bk. i, ch. 3. Dick and Hill as above.

THE first three chapters of Genesis supply a *desideratum* wholly unsupplied by any human writing, in a simple, natu-

1. Man's origin from One Pair. ral, and yet authentic account of man's origin. The statement that his body was created out of pre-existent mattter, and his soul communicated to that body by God, solves a thousand inquiries, which mythology and philosophy are alike incompetent to meet. And from this first father, together with the helpmeet formed for him, of the opposite sex, from his side, have proceeded the whole human race, by successive generation. The unity of race in the human family has been much mooted by half-scholars in natural science of our day, and triumphantly defended. I must remit you wholly for the discussion to the books written by Christian scholars on that subject, of which I may mention, as accessible and popular, Cabell, the University Lectures, and the work of Dr. Bachman, of Charleston. I would merely point out, in passing, the theological importance of this natural fact. If there are men on earth not descended from Adam's race, then their federal connection with him is broken. But more, their inheritance in the *protevangelium*, that the "seed of the woman shall bruise the serpent's head," is also interrupted. The warrant of the Church to carry the Gospel to that people is lacking; and indeed all the relations of man to man are interrupted as to them. Lastly, the integrity of the Bible as the Word of God is fatally affected ; for the unity of

292

the race is implied in all its system, in the whole account of God's dealings with it, in all its histories, and asserted in express terms. Acts xvii : 26. See Breckinridge's Theol., vol. I, ch. 3, i. For additional Scriptures, Gen. iii : 20 ; vii : 23 ; ix : 1, 19 ; x : 32. Unity of race is necessary to relation to the Redeemer.

But a yet more precious part of this passage of Scripture is the explanation it gives of the state of universal sin, self-condemnation, and vanity, in which we now find man ; which is so hard to reconcile with God's attributes. The simple, but far reaching solution is, that man is not in the state in which he was made by his Creator. The record tells us that God "formed man of the dust of the ground, and breathed into his nostrils the breath of life, and man became a living soul." Here, in the simple language of a primeval people, the two-fold nature of man, as matter and spirit, is asserted. As the popular terms

Man, Body and Spirit.

of every people have selected breath, רוּחַ, πνεῦμα, spiritus, to signify this inscrutable substance, thinking spirit, the narrative describes the communication of the soul to the body by the act of breathing. And, it may be added, the view to which reason led us, as to the spirituality of man's thinking part, is confirmed by all Scripture. Here, Gen. ii : 7. The body is first formed from one source, and then the spirit is communicated to it from a different one. God is thus the Father of our spirits. Heb. xii : 9. At death, the two substances separate, and meet different fates. Eccl. xii : 7 ; 2 Cor. v : 1–8 ; Phil. i : 22, 23. The body and soul are in many ways distinguished as different substances, and capable of existing separately. Matt. x : 28 ; Luke viii : 55. The terms body, soul and spirit, are twice used as exhaustive enumerations of the whole man. 1 Thess. v : 23 ; Heb. iv : 12.

Next : we learn that man, unlike all lower creatures, was formed in the "image of God" — "after His likeness." The general idea here is obviously, that there is a resemblance of man to God. It is not in sameness of essence, for God's is incommunicable; nor likeness of corporeal shape, for of this God has none; being immense. This image has been lost, in the fall, and regained, in redemption. Hence, it could not have consisted in anything absolutely essential to man's essence, because the loss of such an attribute would have destroyed man's nature. The likeness which was lost and restored must consist, then, in some *accidens*. The old Pelagians and Socinians represented the image as grounded in man's rationality, and consisting especially in His dominion over the animals and the world. The Reformed divines represent it as grounded upon man's rationality and immortality, which make him an humble representation of God's

Image of God what ?

spiritual essence ; but as consisting especially in the righteousness and true holiness, in which Adam was created.   The
dominion bestowed upon man is the appropriate result of his
moral likeness to his Maker.   Thus Witsius — The image consisted *antecedenter*, in man's spiritual and immortal nature :
formaliter, in His holiness ; *consequenter*, in His dominion.
The first was the precious tablet; the second was the image
drawn on it ; the third was the ray shining from it.   But we
substantiate the definition of God's image; as to its first particular, by Gen. ix : 6, where we learn that the crime of murder
owes its enormity chiefly to this, that it destroys God's image.
See also, Jas. iii : 9.   But since the fall, man has lost his original righteousness, and his likeness to God consists only in his
possession of an intelligent spiritual nature.   Dominion over the
earth and its animals was plainly conferred, Gen. i : 26, 27 ; Ps. viii,
and it is implied that this feature made man, in an humble
sen e, a representative of God on the earth, in Gen. i : 26, 27,
from the connection in which the two things are mentioned, and
in 1 Cor. xi : 7, from the idea there implied, that the authority
given him by God over the other sex makes him God's representative.   But the likeness consists chiefly in man's original moral
perfection, the intelligence and rectitude of his conscience.
This is argued from the fact that the first man, like all the other
works of creation, was " very good."   Gen. i : 31.   This " goodness " must, in fairness, be understood thus, that each created
thing had in perfection those properties which adapted it to its
designed relations.   Man is an intelligent being, and was created to know, enjoy and glorify God as such; hence his moral
state must have been perfect.   See also, Eccl. vii : 29.   And
that this was the most important feature of God's likeness, is
evident ; because it is that likeness which man regains by the
new creation.   See Rom. xii : 2 ; Col. iii : 10 : Eph. iv : 24.
This also, is the likeness which saints aspire after, which they
hope to attain when they regain Adam's original perfection.
Ps. xvii : 15 ; 1 Jno. iii : 2.

This all-important likeness of man to his God justifies that
trait of all our natural theology, which is
Hence, our theology now made ground of cavil by many, that it is
Anthropomorphic. necessarily anthropomorphic.   In the seventh
lecture, this trait is admitted, and the insufficiency which it
causes in any theology merely natural, as a means of sanctification and redemption, is disclosed.   But our opponents would
use this concession to destroy both natural theology and revealed.
Our rational self-consciousness is the medium by which we conceive God and His attributes.   We know power and causation
first in our own conscious volitions: and thus we step to a First
Cause.   We know spirit, as contrasted with matter, first, as the
subject of the functions of consciousness: and thus we know
that God, the cause of all intelligence, and the omniscient,

must also be spirit.   We conceive His knowledge and wisdom, as revealed in His works, after the mode of our thinking to our final causes, but without the limitations of our thoughts. Our conscience is the revelation to us of God's rectitude.   It was only by the method of our control over natural powers, that we could construe God's providence.   And thus came all our natural knowledge of God.

It is from this feature that worthlessness has been charged upon it all.   But this is simply preposterous.

But not therefore untrue. Let it be considered whether it is not the inevitable condition of knowledge to man that it shall be anthropomorphic?   What is this, but to say, that man's knowledge must be human, in order to be his? For if he is to have any cognition, it must be according to the forms of his intelligence.   This unreasonable cavil is evidently grounded in this illusion; that a symmorphism of the divine science to our forms of thought must be a transformation: that the propositions of this science must be so changed, in order to translate them into our modes of cognition, as to be invalid. Now, if we knew that the human intelligence was wholly heterogeneous from the divine, there would be some ground for this suspicion.   But suppose it should turn out that the human intelligence is, in its lower sphere, homogeneous with the divine, then the symmorphism of knowledge implies no corruption of its truth.   Does the opponent exclaim, that we must not 'beg the question,' by assuming that homogeneity? We reply; Neither shall he beg the question in denying it.   But when the inspired witness, the Bible, comes to us, with attestation, (by miracles, prophecies, &c.,) exactly suited to the forms of the human understanding, and assures us that our spirits are made in the likeness of God's, all fear of our theology, as made invalid by anthropomorphism, is removed.   And especially when we are shown the Messiah, as the image of the invisible God, and hear Him reason, we have a complete verification.   It would appear that this simple, primeval narrative was so framed, as to give the answer to a subtile modern cavil, and to satisfy this fundamental difficulty.*

If we attempt to define the original righteousness of man's nature, we must say that, first, it implies the

Adam's Natural righteousness defined. possession of those capacities of understanding and conscience, and that knowledge, which were necessary for the correct comprehension of all his own moral relations.   This equally excludes the extravagant notion, that he was endued by nature with all the knowledge ever acquired by all his descendants; and its opposite, that his soul commenced its existence in an infantile state. Second: Man's righteousness consisted in the perfectly harmo-

---

* See a similar view, in the recently published Lectures of Dr. Thornwell. Vol. I pp. 112-113.

nious concurrence of all the dispositions of his soul, and, consequently, of all his volitions prompted thereby, with the decis-
ions of his conscience, which in its turn was correctly directed
by God's holy will. His righteousness, was then, a natural and
entire conformity, in principle and volition, with God's law.
Adam was doubtless possessed of free will, (Confession, ch. iv,
§ 2; ix, § 2,) in the sense which, we saw, was alone appropriate
to any rational free agent; that in all his responsible, moral acts,
his soul was self-determined in its volitions—i. e., he chose
according to his own understanding and dispositions, free from
co-action. But his will was no more self-determining, or in
equilibrio, than man's will now. (We saw that such a state would
be neither free, rational, nor moral). Just as man's dispositions
now decisively incline his will, in a state of nature, to ungodliness, so they then inclined it to holiness. This inclination was
prevalent and complete for the time, yet not immutable, as the
event proved. But this mutability of will did not imply any
infirmity of moral nature peculiar to man, as compared with
angels. The fate of the non-elect angels shows that it is the
inevitable result of man's being finite. Impeccability is the
property of none but the Infinite, and those to whom He communicates it by His indwelling wisdom and grace. How a
creature soul could be prevalently and completely holy in its
dispositions, and yet mutable, is a most abstruse problem, to
which we will return in due place.

Was Adam's righteousness, in his estate of blessedness,
native or acquired? The Calvinist answers,
it was native; it was conferred upon him as
the original *habitus* of his will, by the creative act which made him an intelligent creature. And the
exercise of holy volitions was the natural effect of the principles which God gave him. This is the obvious and simple
meaning of our doctrine; not that righteousness was so an
essential attribute of man's nature, that the loss of it would
make him no longer a human being proper.

2. Adam's righteous-
ness concreated.

The Pelagians of the 5th century, followed by modern
Socinians, and many of the New England
school, assert that Adam could only have
received from his Maker a negative inno-
cency; and that a positive righteousness could only be the
result of his own voluntary acts of choice. Their fundamental
dogma is, that nothing has moral quality except that which is
voluntary (meaning by this, the result of an act of choosing).
Hence, they infer, nothing is sin, or holiness, but acts of volition. Hence, a con-created rectitude of will would be no
righteousness, and have no merit, because not the result of the
person's own act of choice. Hence, also, they say *a priori*
dispositions have no moral quality, except where they are
acquired habitudes of disposition resulting from voluntary acts.

Views of Pelagians
and Socinians.

Of this kind was Adam's holy character, they say.   And so, in the work of conversion, it is irrational to talk of being made righteous, or of receiving a holy heart; man must act righteousness, and make by choosing a holy heart.

This is the most important point in the whole subject of man's original state and relation to God's law.

Intermediate Romish ground.   Before proceeding, however, to its discussion, it may be well to state the evasive ground assumed by the Romish Church, between the two.   In order to gain a semi-Pelagian position, without avowing the above odious principles, they teach that the first man was holy, *ab initio ;* but that original righteousness was not a natural *habitus* of his own will, but a supernatural grace, communicated to him temporarily by God.   According to Rome, concupiscence is not sin, and it existed in holy Adam; but it has a perpetual tendency to override the limits of conscience, and thus become sin.   So long as the supernatural grace of original righteousness was communicated to Adam, he stood; the moment God saw fit to withdraw it, natural concupiscence became inordinate, sin was born, and man fell.   The refutation of this view of man's original rectitude will be found below, in the proof that concupiscence is sin, and that man was made by nature holy.   We understand that it is implied, if man had not sinned, he would have transmitted that holy nature to his posterity ; surely supernatural grace does not " run in the blood"?   The idea is also derogatory to God's wisdom and holiness, that He should make a creature and endue it with such a nature as was of itself inadequate to fulfil the end of its existence as a moral being, and so construct its propensities, that sin would be the normal, certain and immediate result of their unrestricted action !   It represents God as creating imperfections.

(a) We assert against the Pelagians, that man was positively holy by nature, as he came from God's hand;

Proof of our view. because the plea that nothing can have moral

Pelagian argument ambiguous. quality which is involuntary, is ambiguous and sophistical.   That which occurs or exists against a man's positive volition can be to him neither praise nor blame.   This is the proposition to which common sense testifies.   It is a very different proposition to say that there cannot be moral desert, because no positive volition was exercised about it.   (The Pelagian's proposition.)   For then there could be no sins of omission, where the ill-desert depended on the very fact that the man wholly failed to choose, when he should have chosen.   The truth is, man's original dispositions are spontaneous; they subsist and operate in him freely ; without co-action ; and only because of their own motion.   This is enough to show them responsible, and blame- or praiseworthy.   A man always feels good or ill desert according as his spontaneous feelings are in a right or wrong state, not according to the mode or process by

which they came into that state. Men strangely forget that
their free-agency may as spontaneously prefer, and thus make
them responsible for, a state which was original, as though this
preference of theirs had originated it. Here is a man who was
born with carroty hair : he is absurdly proud of its supposed
beauty, and prefers it to any other. Every one decides that he
thereby exhibits precisely the same bad taste, as though, having
been gifted by nature with the finest brown hair, he had produced the unsightly color with a hair-dye. So, he who, naturally having a perverse disposition, delights in, prefers, and
fosters it, is as truly spontaneous and responsible therein, as
though he had himself acquired it in the impossible way the
Pelagians imagine.

   Dr. Thornwell (Lecture xix. p. 395,) seems to teach, that
the inability of the will, if truly natural, in the sense of being
a part of man's original nature, would destroy his responsibility.
He defends the proposition that the sinner is now responsible,
notwithstanding his thorough inability of will, on the exclusive
ground that it is self-procured by man. This statement must
be regarded as incautious. It is very true, that a holy God is
incapable of creating any rational creature with a wrong disposition. But to fallen man his evil *habitus*, or inability of will, is
now natural : it is connate, and is the regular incident of man's
nature. In what sense can it be said of an individual man now,
that his inability of will is self-procured? Only as he fell in
Adam. And it is hard to see how Dr. T. can save his own true
position that the sinner is responsible, notwithstanding his total
inability of will, without implying a personal unity of each sinner and Adam. His statement is unhappy, again : because it
jeopardizes the clearness of the all-important distinction (see
Confession, Chap. ix.) between the destruction of man's *essentia*,
by the loss of any constitutive faculty (which would end his
responsibility,) and that total " aversion" from the right, which
results in an entire inability, and yet leaves to the sinning agent
his inalienable spontaneity.

   (b.) We have already seen, from Gen. i: 26, 27; i : 31 ;
Eccles. vii : 29, that man was made in the
Scripture teaches our view. image of God, and that this image was most
essentially his original righteousness. God's
word, therefore, sustains our view. The same thing is seen in
the language of Scripture concerning the new creation, regeneration. This, the Bible expressly affirms, is a " creation unto
righteousness." Eph. iv : 24; ii : 10 ; Rom. viii : 29 : Eph. i : 4.
It is a supernatural change of disposition, wrought not merely
through motive, but by almighty power. Eph. i: 19, 20;
ii : 1-5. It determines not only the acts, but the will. Ps.
cx : 3; Phil. ii : 13. And God has Himself suggested the
analogy on which our argument proceeds, by choosing the term
" new creation," to describe it. Hence, as the new-born soul

is made holy, and does not merely act a holiness, the first man was made righteous. Let me remark here, that ancient and modern Pelagians virtually admit the justice of this, by denying the possibilty of such a regeneration by grace; and on the same grounds; that a state of holiness not primarily chosen by the will, could not be meritorious. On their theory the human soul of Christ would not have had a positive righteousness by nature. But see Luke i : 35.

(c.) Their theory is contradicted by common sense in this: that a moral neutrality, in a being who had the rational faculties and the data for comprehending the moral relations in a given case, is impossible; and if possible, would be criminal. It is the very nature of conscience, that when the moral relations of a given case are comprehended, her *dictum* is immediate, inevitable and categorical. The dispositions also must either be disposed actively, one way or the other, or they are not dispositions at all. They cannot be in *equilibrio*, any more than motion can be quiescent. And does not every sane conscience decide that if Adam, on comprehending his moral relations to his infinitely good, kind, glorious and holy Father, had simply failed to choose His love and service instantly; if he had been capable of hesitation for one moment, that would itself have constituted a moral defect, a sin?

No natural Neutrality Possible.

(d.) Had Adam's will been in the state of *equilibrium* described, and his moral character initially negative, then there would have been in him nothing to prompt a holy choice; and the choice which he might have made for that which is formally right would have had nothing in it morally good. For the intention determining the volition gives all its moral quality. Thus he could never have chosen or acted a righteousness, nor initiated a moral habitude, his initial motive being nonmoral.

No Principle of right choice would have been present.

(e.) These false principles must lead, as Pelagians freely avow, to the denial of original depravity in infants. That which does not result from an act of intelligent choice, say they, cannot have moral quality; so, there can be no sin of nature, any more than a natural righteousness. But that man has a sin of nature, is proved by common experience, asserted by Scripture, and demonstrated by the fact that all are " by nature the children of wrath," and even from infancy suffer and die under God's hand.

Corruption of Infants refutes Pelagianism.

(f.) If the doctrine be held that a being cannot be created righteous without choice, then those that die in infancy cannot be redeemed. For they cannot exercise as yet intelligent acts of moral choice, and thus convert themselves by choosing God's service. The Pelagian does indeed virtually represent the infant as needing no redemption, having no sin of nature. But the Bible and experience prove that he does need redemption: whence, on Pelagian principles, the damnation of all who die in infancy is inevitable.

Last, the theory of the Pelagian is utterly unphilosophical in this, that it has no experimental basis. It is a mere hypothesis. No human being has ever existed consciously in the state of moral indifference which they assume; or been conscious of that initial act of choice, which generated his moral character. Surely all scientific propositions ought to have some basis of experimental proof! Ethics should be an inductive science.

Their Theory Has No Facts.

Any intelligent moral creature of God is naturally bound to love Him with all his heart, and serve Him with all his strength. i. e., this obligation is not created by positive precept only, but arises out of the very perfections of God, and the relations of the creature, as His property, and deriving all his being and capacities from God's hands. Doubtless Adam's holy soul recognized joyfully this obligation. And doubtless his understanding was endowed with the sufficient knowledge of so much of God's will as related to his duties at that time. It may be very hard for us to say how much this was. Now, it is common for divines to say, that a creature cannot merit anything of God. This has struck many minds as doubtful and unfair, whence it is important that we should properly distinguish. In denying that a creature of God can merit anything, it is by no means meant that the holy obedience of a creature is before God devoid of good moral character. It possesses praiseworthiness, if holy, and undoubtedly receives that credit at God's hands. The fact that it is naturally due to God does not at all deprive it of its good quality. But the question remains: What is that quality? Obviously, it is that the natural connection between holiness and happiness shall not be severed, as long as the holiness continues; that, as the obedience rendered is that evoked by the natural relation to the Creator's will; so the desert acquired is of that natural well-being appropriate to the creature's capacities. The guarantee to the creature for this, in the absence of any positive covenant from God, is simply the divine goodness and righteousness, which render God incapable of treating a holy being worse than this. The creature is God's property.

3. Natural Relation of Creature to God's Will.

But it is equally obvious that such obedience on the creature's part cannot bring God in his debt, to condescend to him in any way, to communicate Himself as a source of supernatural blessedness, or stability in holiness, or to secure his natural well-being longer than his voluntary and mutable obedience is continued. And the reasons are, simply that none of the crea-

The Creature Cannot Merit.

ture's obedience can be supererogatory, he owing his utmost at any rate; and that all his being and capacities were given by God, and are His property. I cannot bring my benefactor in my debt by giving him something which he himself lent to me; I am but restoring his own. This is what is intended by the Confession of Faith, ch. vii, § 1. The Scriptures clearly support it. Ps. xvi : 2 ; Job, xxxv : 7, 8; Acts. xvii : 24, 25; Ps. l : 9–12; Luke xvii : 7–10.

But it is equally clear that mortality and the connected ills
of life could not have been the natural lot of man, irrespective of his sin and fall, as the Pelagians and Socinians pretend. Their motive in assuming this repulsive tenet, is, to get rid of the argument for original sin, presented by the sufferings and death of infants who have committed no overt sin. They say that dissolution, to an organized animal body, is as natural and unavoidable as the fall of the leaves from the trees. They claim, that only the monadic and indiscerptible can be exempt from that fate; and that it is the natural counterpart of generation, and of animal nutrition. I reply, First: If they only used these arguments to prove that animal bodies are not self-existent, they would have reason. But we must remember that the human person, whose dissolution is now in question, is a responsible agent, not a vegetable, whose destiny in this particular a righteous God has to decide judicially. From this point of view, it is too plain to need argument, that the providence of that same almighty power which framed Adam's body at first, was abundantly able to continue its organic existence indefinitely. It is not necessary to speculate as to the mode; but we have only to suppose God suspending the molecular forces which now war against the vital force; and the holy man's body might have all the permanency of a diamond, or lump of gold. But the main point is : that to a moral person, dissolution is not a mere chemical result, but a penal misery. Does this befall a responsible agent absolutely guiltless? The assertion is abhorrent to the justice and goodness of God. Physical evil is the appointed consequence of moral evil, and the sanction threatened for the breach of God's will. To suppose it appointed to an obedient moral being, irrespective of any guilt, overthrows either God's moral attributes or His providence, and confounds heaven with earth. Second: It is inconsistent with that image of God and that natural perfection, in which man was created. The workmanship was declared to be very good: and this doubtless excluded the seeds of its own destruction. It was in the image of God; and this included immortality. But last, the Scriptures imply that man would neither have suffered nor died if he had not sinned, by appointing death as the threat against transgression. And this, while it meant more than bodily death, certainly included this, as is

But, Death would not have Entered without Sin.

evident from Gen. iii : 17–19.   See, then, Gen. ii : 17 ; Rom.
v : 12 ; vi : 23 ; Matt. xix : 17 ; Gal. iii : 12.   These last evidently have reference to the covenant of works made with
Adam : and they explicitly say, that if a perfect obedience
were possible, (as it was with Adam before he fell), it would
secure eternal life.

God's act in entering into a covenant with Adam, if it be
substantiated, will be found to be one of pure
grace and condescension.   He might justly
have held him always under his natural relationship ; and Adam's obedience, however long continued,
would not have brought God into his debt for the future.
Thus, his holiness being mutable, his blessedness would always
have hung in suspense.   God, therefore, moved by pure grace,
condescended to establish a covenant with His holy creature,
in virtue of which a temporary obedience might be graciously
accepted as a ground for God's communicating Himself to him,
and assuring him ever after of holiness, happiness, and communion with God.   Here then is the point of osculation between the covenant of works, and the covenant of grace, the
law and the Gospel.   Both offer a plan of free justification, by
which a righteousness should be accepted, in covenant, to
acquire for the creature more than he could strictly claim of
God ; and thus gain him everlasting life.   In the covenant of
grace, all is "ordained in the hand of a mediator," because
man's sin had else excluded him from access to God's holiness.
In the covenant of works, no mediator was required, because
man was innocent, and God's purity did not forbid him to condescend to him.   But in both, there was free grace ; in both a
justification unto life ; in both, a gracious bestowal of more than
man had earned.

Under the natural relation of man to law, there was room
neither for mercy in case of transgression, nor for assured
blessedness.   This relation was modified by the Covenant of
works, in three respects.   First, a temporal probation was
accepted, in place of an everlasting exposure to a fall under
the perpetual legal demand.   Second : The principle of representation was introduced by which the risques of the probation
were limited to one man, acting for all instead of being indefinitely repeated, forever, in the conduct of each individual.
Third, a reward for the probationary obedience was promised,
which, while a reward for right works, was far more liberal
than the works entitled to ; and this was an adoption of life,
transferring man from the position of a servant to that of a
son, and surrounding him forever with the safeguards of the
divine wisdom and faithfulness, making his holiness indefectible.
Thus, the motive of God in this covenant was the same infinite
and gratuitous goodness, which prompted him to the covenant
of grace.

Covenant of Works Gracious.

The evidences that God placed Adam under a Covenant of
4. Covenant of Works, Works are well stated by the standard
What? Proof of its In- authors. A covenant, in its more technical
stitution. cal sense, according to Turrettin, implies: 1.
Two equal parties. 2. Liberty to do or not do the covenanted
things before the covenant is formed. In this sense there could
be no covenant between God and man. But in the more general sense of a conditional promise, such a transaction was evidently effected between God and Adam, and is recorded in
Gen. ii: 16, 17. There are: (1st) The two parties: God proposing a certain blessing and penalty on certain conditions, and
man coming under those conditions. It has been objected that
it was no covenant, because man's accession to it was not
optional with him: God's terms were not a proposal made him,
but a command laid upon him. I reply, if he did not have an
option to accede or not, he was yet voluntary in doing so; for
no doubt his holy will joyfully concurred in the gracious plan.
And such compacts between governors and governed are by no
means unusual or unnatural. Witness all rewards promised by
masters and teachers, for the performance of tasks, on certain
conditions. (2d) There was a condition: the keeping of God's
command. (3rd) There was a conditional promise and threat:
life for obedience, and death for disobedience. That the promise of life was clearly implied is shown: (a) By the fact itself, that
life is the correlative of death, which was threatened in the
covenant. For the soul not to live, is to die; not to die, is to
live. It is shown: (b) From the natural law of conscience, which
expects life for obedience, as death for transgression. Did this
fatherly dispensation to Adam suspend the favorable part of
this universal law, and thus place him in a worse, instead of a
more hopeful condition? Heb. xi: 6, tells us " he that cometh
unto God must believe that He is, and that He is the rewarder
of them that diligently seek Him." Here we have a general
principle of service: surely Adam's introduction into Paradise
did not revoke it. (c) During his rectitude, Adam evidently enjoyed the use of the " Tree of Life," which was a
sacramental pledge to him of the promised result. And when
the covenant was broken, his partaking of this seal was forbidden, as utterly inconsistent with the new state of things. Unless
Adam had had before him the promise of life for obedience,
this would have been idle. (d) That the correlative promise
of life was given, appears from the relation of Adam and
Christ, the second Adam. Both were representative heads.
The covenant which fell through in Adam's inept hands, was
successfully accomplished in Christ's. But the result through
Him was a " justification of life." And in the frequent contrasts which the Epistles of Paul draw between the justification
of works and of faith, it is never hinted that the impossibility
of the former now arises from anything in the covenant of

works, but only from man's sin and lost estate. See Rom. viii : 3, 4. And (e) the Scriptures in expounding the nature of the Covenant of Works, expressly say that life would have been the result of perfect obedience. Let the student consult Levit. xviii: 5; Deut. xxx : 15; Ezek. xx : 11 ; Matt. xix: 17; Rom. ii : 6, 7: vii : 10; x: 5; Gal. iii: 12. The fact that in some of these places the offer of life through the covenant of works was only made in order to apply an argument *ad hominem* to the self-righteous Jews, does not weaken this evidence. For the reason that life cannot, in fact, be gained through that covenant, is not that it was not truly promised to man in it, and in good faith ; but that man has now become through the fall, morally incapable of fulfilling the conditions. Nor is the argument in favor of our position weakened surely by the other fact ; that the Apostle's reference to this covenant of works promising life for obedience, was designed to shut up sinners who have broken it, under condemnation.

In this transaction Adam represented his posterity as well as himself. This appears from 1. The parallel which is drawn between Christ and Adam. Rom. v ; 12–19 ; 1 Cor. xv : 22, 47. In almost every thing they are contrasted, yet Christ is the second Adam. The only parallelism is in the fact that they were both representative persons. 2. The fact proves it, that the penalty denounced on Adam has actually taken effect on every one of his posterity. See Gen. v: 3. 3. The Bible declares that sin, death, and all penal evil came into the world through Adam. Rom. v: 12; 1 Cor. xv: 22. 4. Although the various other communications of the first three chapters of Genesis are apparently addressed to Adam singly, we know that they applied equally to his posterity, as the permission to eat of all the fruits of the earth ; the command to multiply and replenish the earth ; the threatened pains of child-bearing ; the curse of the ground, and the doom of labor, &c.

Adam a Representative.

Every one is familiar with the Bible account of the condition of this covenant : the eating or not eating of the fruit of a tree called the "tree of knowledge of good and evil." This prohibition was, obviously, a "positive command." Our divines are accustomed to argue, very reasonably, that when God's design was to apply a naked test of the principle, obedience, a positive command is better adapted to the end than a perpetual moral one. For the latter class have usually rational grounds in the interests and affections of men ; but the ground of the positive precept is only the rightful authority of God. A more difficult point is : Whether this single, positive precept substituted, during Adam's probation, all the moral law. In other words : Was this the only command Adam now had to observe : the only one by the breach of which he could fall? Presbyterians answer this in

5. Condition and seal of the covenant.

the negative. We regard all the moral law known to Adam is represented in this command, as the crucial test of his obedience to all. The condition of his covenant was perfect compliance, in heart and act, with all God's revealed law. This is manifest from the unreasonableness of any moral creature's exemption from the law of God, which is immutable. It appears also, from all the representations of the covenant of works, quoted in a previous paragraph; where the obedience required is to the whole law. It appears, finally, from this obvious view: that a consistent sense of moral obligation was the only thing which could have given to Adam's compliance with the positive prohibition, any moral significance or worth.

The seal of the covenant is usually understood to be the tree of life, whose excellent fruit did not, indeed, medically work immortality in Adam's frame, but was appointed as a symbol and pledge, or seal of it. Hence, when he had forfeited the promise, he was debarred from the sign. The words of Gen. iii : 22 are to be understood sacramentally.

Why is it supposed that an obedience for a limited time would have concluded the Covenant trans-
The Probation Temporary.   action ? The answer is, that such a covenant, with an indefinite probation, would have been no covenant of life at all. The creature's estate would have been still forever mutable, and in no respect different from that in which creation itself placed him, under the first natural obligation to his Maker. Nay, in that case man's estate would be rightly called desperate; because, he being mutable and finite, and still held forever under the curse of a law, which he was, any day, liable to break, the probability that he would some day break it would in the infinite future mount up to a moral certainty. The Redeemer clearly implies that the probation was to be temporary, in saying to the young Ruler: "If thou wilt enter into life, keep the commandments." If the probation had no limits, his keeping them could never make him enter in. Here again, Adam's representative character unavoidably implies that the probation was temporary. His personal action under the trial was to decide whether his posterity were to be born heirs of wrath, or adopted sons of God. Had his probation been endless, their state would have been wholly unsettled. Only a moments' reflection is needed, to show the preposterous confusion which would arise from that state of facts. Adam's trial still continuing thousands of years after Seth's birth, for instance, and after his glorification, if the father then fell, the son's glorification must have been revoked.

LECTURE XXVII.

THE FALL, AND ORIGINAL SIN.

SYLLABUS.

1. What is sin? Is guilt its essence, or adjunct?
Conf. of Faith, ch. 6. Cat. Qu. 14. Turrettin, Loc. ix, Qu. 1, 3. Knapp, § 73. Muller, "Christian Doctrine of Sin," ch. 2, 3. Bp. Butler's Sermons, 11–14. Thornwell, Lect. 14, pp. 347, 389. Dr. Wm. Cunningham, Historical Theol., ch. 19, § 5.

2. What was Adam's first sin? How did it affect his own moral state and relations to God? How could a will prevalently unholy form its first unholy volition?
Turrettin, Loc. xi, Qu. 6, 7, 8. Hill, bk. iv, ch. 1. Dick, Lect. 47. Knapp, § 85. Watson, ch. 18, § 11. Witsius, bk. i, ch. 8, § 1, 13. Thornwell, Lect. 10, pp. 240–247. Butler's Analogy. Muller, Chr. Doc. of Sin, bk. ii.

3. Who was the tempter? What the sentence on him?
Turrettin, Loc. ix, Qu. 7, § 9, &c. Dick, Lect. 44. Hill and Watson as above.

4. What were the effects of Adam's fall on his posterity, (a) according to the Pelagian theory; (b) the lower Arminian theory; (c) the Wesleyan; and (d) the Calvinistic theory?
Augustine, Vol. ii, Ep. 899, c., Vol. viii. *De Natura et Gratia*, and *Libri Duo adv. Pelagius et Cœlestius*. Hill as above. Turrettin, Loc. ix, Qu. 9, 10. Dick, Lect. 46, 47. Cunningham, Hist. Theol., ch. 10, §, 12, and ch. 19, § 3. Thornwell, Lect. 13. Whitby's Five Points. Knapp, § 79, 10. Watson's Theol. Inst., ch. 18, § 3, 4. Wesley on Original Sin.

5. Are the souls of Adam's posterity directly created or generated? And how is depravity propagated in them?
Turrettin, Loc. ix, Qu. 12, and Loc. v, Qu. 13. Baird's Elohim Revealed, ch. 11. Sampson on Hebrews, ch. 12, v. 9. Literary and Evangel. Magazine, of Dr. Jno. H. Rice, vol. iv. p. 285, &c. Watson, ch. 18, § 4. Augustine, *De Origine Animarum*.

WE have now reached, in our inquiries, the disastrous place, where sin first entered our race. Let us therefore pause, and ascertain clearly what is its nature.

The most characteristic Hebrew word for it is חַטָּאָה,

Sin what? which has the rudimental idea of missing the aim. The Greek, ἁμαρτία is strikingly similar, expressing nearly the same idea, of failure of designed conjunction. The Latin, *peccatum* is supposed by some to be a modification of *pecuatum*, brutishness, and by others, of *pellicatus,* moral adultery. These words suggest, what will be found true upon analysis, that the common abstract element of all sins is a privative one, lack of conformity to a standard. If this is so, then farther, sin can only be understood, when viewed as the antithesis to that standard, a law of right, and to the righteousness which is conformed thereto. The student may be reminded here, in passing, of that speculation which some of the Reformed divines borrowed from the Latin Scholastics, by which they made sin out a negation. Their reason seemed to be mainly this: That God, as universal First Cause, must be the agent of all that has entity; and so, all entities must be *per se* good. Hence sin, which is evil, must be no entity, a

306

negation. This doctrine received such applications as this: That even in adultery or murder, the action *per se*, so far as it is action only, is good; the negative moral quality is the evil. We see here, the mint, from which was coined that dangerous distinction, by which the same divines sought to defend God's efficacious *præcursus* in sinful acts of creatures. (See Lect. xxv, end.) To a plain mind, the escape from this confusion is easy. Sins are, indeed, not entities, save as they are acts or states of creatures, who are personal entities. When we speak of sins in the abstract, if we mean anything, we speak of the quality common to the concrete acts, which we literally call sins: the quality of sinfulness. What now, is a quality, abstracted from all the entities which it qualifies? Not necessarily a negation, but a mere abstraction. As to the quibble, that God is the agent of all that has entity; we reply: Predicate the real free-agency of the sinning creature; and we shall have no philosophic trouble about that truth of common sense, that the actor is the agent of his own sinful act; and not God.

Some have supposed that the just distinction between "sins of commission and omission" must overthrow the definition of sinfulness as always a privative quality. This, say they, may be true of sins of omission; but then it cannot be true of sins of commission, which are positive. This is invalid, for the basis of that distinction is different. Both classes of sins are equally privative, and equally real. The difference is, that sins of commission are breaches of prohibitory commands, and sins of omission of affirmative precepts. In either case, the sinfulness arises out of evil motive, and this is, in either case, positive; while its common quality is discrepancy from the standard of right. And now, if any other proof of our definition is needed, than its consistency, we find it in 1 Jno. iii : 4, where the Apostle gives this as his exact definition of sin; arguing against a possible Antinomian tendency to excuse sins in believers, as venial, that all sin is lawless; *Ἡ ἁμαρτία ἐστὶν ἡ ἀνομία*—"The sin is the discrepancy from law." (Scil. *νόμος Θεοῦ.*)

Dr. Julius Müller, in his important work, "The Christian Doctrine of Sin," revives, in a new form, the erroneous doctrine of Jon. Edwards, resolving sin into selfishness. Seizing upon the declaration of our Savior, that love to God is the first and great command, on which the whole law depends, he resorts to the admitted fact, that sin must be the antithesis of righteousness; and concludes that the former must therefore be love of self. Why may we not conclude, from the same process, that since all duty is included in the love of God, all sin will be included in hatred of God? (instead of love of self.) This gives us a more plausibly exact antithesis.

But more seriously, the student is referred to the remarks in Lecture ix, upon Edwards' theory, and to Bp. Butler's Sermons. We now add, with especial reference to Müller's spec-

ulation, these points of objection. If all sin is resolved into
self-love as its essence, then is not all self-love sinful? If he
answers, No, then I reply: So there is a sinful, and a righteous
self-love? He must say, Yes. Then, I demand that he shall
give me the differentiating element in the sinful self-love, which
makes it, unlike the other self-love, morally evil. Will he give
me self-love for this differentiating element? This is but moving in a circle. Again: it would follow, that if some self-love
is lawful, and yet self-love is the essence of all sin, it must
become sin, by becoming too great; and thus sin and holiness
would differ only in degree! Once more, if this theory is to
be carried out with any consistency, it must teach, that the act
which is intended by me to promote my own well-being, can
only be virtuous provided I sincerely aim at that well-being
(which happens to be my own) from motives purely impersonal
and disinterested. In other words, to do any act aright, promotive of my own welfare, I must do it, not at all for the sake
of myself, but exclusively for the sake of God and my fellows,
as they are interested in my welfare. We will not dwell on the
question, whether any man ever seeks his own good from so
sublimated a motive; we only point to this resultant absurdity;
all one's fellows, acting in this style of pure disinterestedness,
are directly seeking his welfare; and in this is their virtue.
How can it be then, that it is always sinful for him to seek that
same end?

Does anyone ask, into what common type all sin may be
resolved? We answer: Into that of sin. We have no other
definition than this: Sin is sin. Or sin is the opposite of holiness; sin is discrepancy from an absolutely holy law. If this
is so, and if the idea of moral good is one of ultimate simplicity, and so, incapable of definition in simpler terms, we are
to accept the same view as to sin. All attempts to reduce it to
some simpler element, as they have been prompted either by
an affectation of over-profundity, or by an over-weening desire
to unify the functions of man's soul, have also resulted in
confusion and error.

The next question concerning the nature of sin would be,
whether it is limited to acts of will, or includes also states of
moral propensity and habit. The answer given by the Calvinist is familiar to you. "Sin is not being, or not doing what
God requires." Not only, then, are intentional acts of will contrary to law, sinful; but also the native disposition to these
acts, and the desires to commit them not yet formed into volitions. This raises the oft mooted question, whether "concupiscence is sin?" This question has been already debated
from a rational point of view, in Lect. xii, § 1, and the cognate
one, in the xxvi, § 2. It is only necessary now, to add a summary of the Scriptural argument. The Bible, in many places
applies moral terms to the abiding habitudes of the soul, both

acquired and native. See Ps. li : 5; lviii : 3; Matt. xii: 35, or 33; vii : 17. James i : 15 says: "Then when concupiscence hath conceived, it bringeth forth sin." Rome, indeed, quotes this text as implying that concupiscence is not itself sin; for it must "conceive," must be developed into another form, in order to become sin. But James here evidently uses the word sin in the sense of sins of act. So he uses "death," the mature result of "sin when it is finished," in the sense of the final spiritual death, or the second death; for many other Scriptures assure us that a state of sin is a state of death. He would rather teach us, in this text, that concupiscence and actual sin, being mother and daughter, are too closely related not to have the same moral nature. But the most conclusive text is the 10th Commandment. See this expounded by Paul, Rom. vii : 7. He had not known coveting, except the law had said, "Thou shalt not covet." And it was by this law, that he was made to know sin. How could he more expressly name concupiscence as sin?

There is, however, a distinction, which is needed here, for the consistent establishment of this doctrine. coveting is often defined as "desiring the possession of another." Now, it is clear, that there are such desires, and such thoughts, which are not the sin of concupiscence. The intellectual apprehension of natural good, not possessed by me, but attainable, cannot be sinful always; for if so, I could never put forth a normal and rational effort for any good. So a certain desire for such good must also be innocent; else I could never have a lawful motive for effort, tending to the advancement of my own welfare. A very practical instance may evince this. A godly minister needs a useful horse. He sees his neighbour possessing the horse which suits his purposes. He righteously offers, and endeavors, to buy him. But, as a reasonable free agent, he could not have proposed to part with a valuable consideration for this horse, unless he had had, first, an intellectual judgment of the animal's fitness for his uses; and second, a desire to enjoy its utility. But he had these sentiments while the horse was still another man's? Is it, then neccessary for one to break the 10th Commandent in order to effect an equitable horse-trade? The answer is: These sentiments in the good man are not of the nature of evil concupiscence. This sinful affection then, is not merely desire for attainable good; but desire for an attainment conditioned wrongfully; desire still harboured — though not matured into a purpose of will — while seen in the conscience to be thus unlawfully conditioned. Thus, for instance, the moment this good man's desire to possess the useful animal verged into a craving to gain it unfairly, as by payment in spurious money, or untruthful depreciation of its market value, that moment concupiscence was born. This distinction removes all just objections to the

Scripture teaching. It is useful also, in explaining how an impeccable Redeemer could be "tempted of the devil," and yet wholly without sin. Had this holy soul been absolutely impervious to even the intellectual apprehension of attainable good, and to the natural sentiment arising on that apprehension, he would not have been susceptible of temptation. But he had these normal traits. Hence, he could be tempted, and yet feel not the first pulse of evil concupiscence..

What Turrettin calls potential guilt is the intrinsic moral ill-desert of an act or state. This is of the essence of the sin: it is indeed an inseparable part of its sinfulness. Actual guilt is obligation to punishment. This is the established technical sense of the word among theologians. Guilt, thus defined, is obviously not of the essence of sin; but is a relation, viz., to the penal sanction of law. For if we suppose no penal sanction attached to the disregard of moral relations, guilt would not exist, though there were sin. This distinction will be found important.

Guilt, what?

The first sin of our first father is found described in Gen. iii : 1—7, in words which are familiar to every one. This narrative has evidently some of that picturesque character appropriate to the primeval age, and caused by the scarcity of abstract and definite terms in their language. But it is an obvious abuse to treat it as a mere allegory, representing under a figure man's self-depravation and gradual change: for the passages preceeding and following it are evidently plain narrative, as is proved by a hundred references. Moreover, the transactions of this very passage are twice referred to as literal (2 Cor. xi : 3; 1 Tim. ii : 14), and the events are given as the explanation of the peculiar chastisement allotted to the daughters of Eve.

2. Man's First Sin.

The sin of Adam consisted essentially, not in his bodily act, of course; but in his intentions. Popish theologians usually say that the first element of the sin of his heart was pride, as being awakened by the taunting reference of the Serpent to his dependence and subjection, and as being not unnatural in so exalted a being. The Protestants, with Turrettin, usually say it was unbelief; because pride could not be naturally suggested to the creature's soul, unless unbelief had gone before to obliterate his recollection of his proper relations to an infinite God; because belief of the mind usually dictates feeling and action in the will; because the temptation seems first aimed (Gen. iii : 1) to produce unbelief, through the creature's heedlessness; and because the initial element of error must have been in the understanding, the will being hitherto holy.

Unbelief its First Element.

How a holy will could come to have an unholy volition at first, is a most difficult inquiry. And it is much harder as to the first sin of Satan, than

If Volitions are certainly Determined,

How could a Holy of Adam, because the angel, hitherto per-
Being have his First fect, had no tempter to mislead him, and had
Wrong Volition?
not even the bodily appetites for natural
good which in Adam were so easily perverted into concupiscence. Concupiscence cannot be supposed to have been the
cause, pre-existing before sin; because concupiscence is sin,
and needs itself to be accounted for in a holy heart. Man's, or
Satan's, mutability cannot be the efficient cause, being only a
condition *sine qua non*. Nor is it any solution to say with Turrettin, the proper cause was a free will perverted voluntarily.
Truly; but how came a right will to pervert itself while yet right?
And here, let me say, is far the most plausible objection
against the certainty of the will, which Arminians, &c., might
urge far more cunningly than (to my surprise) they do. If the
evil dispositions of a fallen sinner so determine his volitions as
to ensure that he will not choose spiritual good, why did not
the holy dispositions of Adam and Satan ensure that they
would never have a volition spiritually evil? And if they
somehow chose sin, contrary to their prevalent bent, why may
not depraved man sometime choose good?

The mystery cannot be fully solved how the first evil
choice could voluntarily arise in a holy soul;
Answer.   but we can clearly prove that it is no sound
reasoning from the certainty of a depraved will to that of a holy
finite will. First: a finite creature can only be indefectible
through the perpetual indwelling and superintendence of infinite wisdom and grace, guarding the finite and fallible attention
of the soul against sin. This was righteously withheld from
Satan and Adam. Second: while righteousness is a positive
attribute, incipient sin is a privative trait of human conduct.
The mere absence of an element of active regard for God's
will, constitutes a disposition or volition wrong. Now, while
the positive requires a positive cause, it is not therefore inferri-
ble that the negative equally demands a positive cause. To
make a candle burn, it must be lighted; to make it go out, it
need only be let alone. The most probable account of the
way sin entered a holy breast first, is this: An object was
apprehended as in its mere nature desirable; not yet as unlawful. So far there is no sin. But as the soul, finite and fallible
in its attention, permitted an overweening apprehension and
desire of its natural adaptation to confer pleasure, to override
the feeling of its unlawfulness, concupiscence was developed.
And the element which first caused the mere innocent sense of
the natural goodness of the object to pass into evil concupiscence, was privative, viz., the failure to consider and prefer
God's will as the superior good to mere natural good. Thus natural desire passed into sinful selfishness, which is the root of all
evil. So that we have only the privative element to account
for. When we assert the certainty of ungodly choice in an

evil will, we only assert that a state of volition whose moral quality is a defect, a negation, cannot become the cause of a positive righteousness. When we assert the mutability of a holy will in a finite creature, we only say that the positive element of righteousness of disposition may, in the shape of defect, admit the negative, not being infinite. So that the cases are not parallel: and the result, though mysterious, is not impossible. To make a candle positively give light, it must be lighted; to cause it to sink into darkness, it is only necessary to let it alone: its length being limited, it burns out.

Adam's fall resulted in two changes, moral and physical. Effects of Sin in Adam—Self-Deprava-tion. The latter was brought on him by God's providence, cursing the earth for his sake, and thus entailing on him a life of toil and infirmities, ending in bodily death. The former was more immediately the natural and necessary result of his own conduct; because we can conceive of God as interposing actively to punish sin, but we cannot conceive of Him as interposing to produce it. It has been supposed very unreasonable that one act, momentary, the breach of an unimportant, positive precept, should thus revolutionize a man's moral habitudes and principles, destroying his original righteousness, and making him a depraved being. One act, they say, cannot form a habit. We will not answer this, by saying, with Turrettin, that the act virtually broke each precept of the decalogue; or that it was a "universal sin;" nor even by pleading that it was an aggravated and great sin. Doubtless it was a great sin; because it violated the divine authority most distinctly and pointedly declared; because it did it for small temptation; because it was a sin against great motives, privileges, and restraints. There is also much justice in Turrettin's other remarks, that by this clear, fully declared sin, the chief end of the creature was changed from God to self; and the chief end controls the whole stream of moral action directed to it; that the authority on which all godliness reposes, was broken in breaking this one command; that shame and remorse were inevitably born in the soul; that communion with God was severed. But this terrible fact, that any sin is mortal to the spiritual life of the soul, may profitably be farther illustrated.

Note, that God's perfections necessitate that He shall be How Accounted for by One Sin? the righteous enemy and punisher of transgression. Man, as a moral and intelligent being, must have conscience and moral emotions. One inevitable effect of the first sin, then, must be that God is made righteously angry, and will feel the prompting to just punishment. (Else not a holy ruler!) Hence, He must at once withdraw His favour and communion (there being no Mediator to satisfy His justice.) Another inevitable effect must be, the birth of remorse in the creature. The hitherto healthy action of conscience must ensure this. This remorse must be attended with an apprehension of God's anger, and fear of His punishment. But human nature always reciprocates, by a sort of sympathy, the hostility of which it knows itself the object. How many a man has learned to hate an inoffensive neighbour, because he knows that he has given that neighbour good cause to hate him? But this hostility is hostility to God for doing what He ought; it is hostility to righteousness! So that, in the first clearly pronounced sin, these elements of corruption and separation from God are necessarily contained in germ. But God is the model of excellence, and fountain of grace. See how fully these results are illustrated in Adam and Eve. Gen. iii: 8, &c. Next; every moral act has some tendency to foster the propensity which it indulges. Do you say it must be a very slight strength produced by one act; a very light bond of habit, consisting of one strand! Not always. But the scale, if slightly turned, is turned: the downhill career is begun, by at least one step, and the increase of momentum will surely occur, though gradually. Inordinate self-love has now become a principle of action, and it it will go on to assert its dominion. Last, we must consider the effects of physical evil on a heart thus in incipient perversion; for God's justice must prompt Him to inflict the bodily evils due to the sin. Desire of happiness is instinctive; when the joys of innocence are lost, an indemnification and substitute will be sought in carnal pleasures. Misery developes the malignant passions of envy, petulance, impatience, selfishness, revenge. And nothing is more depraving than despair. See Jer. ii: 25; xviii: 12.

What a terrible evil, then, is Sin! Thus the sentence, " In the day thou eatest thereof, thou shalt surely die," carried its own execution. Sin, of itself, kills the spiritual life of the soul.

The true tempter of Adam and Eve was undoubtedly the evil angel Satan, although it is not expressly said so in the narrative. A serpent has no speech, still less has it understanding to comprehend man's moral relations and interests, and that refined spiritual malice which would plan the ruin of the soul. It is said, " the serpent was more subtle than any beast of the field," as though this natural superiority of animal instincts were what enabled it to do the work. A moment's thought, however, must convince us that there is a deeper meaning. Moses, speaking for the time as the mere historian, describes events as they appeared to Eve. The well known cunning of the serpent adapted it better for Satan's use, and enabled him to conceal himself under it with less chance of detection. The grounds for regarding Satan as the true agent are the obvious allusions of Scripture. See Jno. viii: 44; 2 Cor. xi: 3; 1 Thess. iii: 5; 1 Jno. iii: 8; Rev. xii: 9, and xx: 2. The doom of the serpent is also allusively applied to Christ's triumph over Satan. Col. ii: 15; Rom. xvi: 20;

3. Satan the Tempter.

Heb. ii: 14; Is. lxv: 25. It is also stated in confirmation, by
Dr. Hill, that this was the traditionary interpretration of the
Jews, as is indicated, for instance, in Wis. ii: 23, 24; Ecclus.
xxv: 24, and the Chaldee paraphrast on Job xx: 4, 6. Turrettin supposes that God's providence permitted the employment
of an animal as the instrument of Satan's temptation, in order
that mankind might have before them a visible commemoration
of their sin and fall.

I propose to state the Pelagian theory with some degree of
4. Effect of Adam's fulness, and more methodically than it would
Sin on His Posterity— perhaps be found stated in the writings of its
Pelagian Theory.   own early advocates, in order to unfold to
the student the *nexus* between original sin and the whole plan
of redemption. The Pelagian believes that Adam's fall did not
directly affect his posterity at all. Infants are born in the same
state in which Adam was created, one of innocence, but not of
positive righteousness. There was no federal transaction, and
no imputation, which is, in every case, incompatible with justice.
There is no propagation of hereditary depravity, which would
imply the generation of souls *ex traduce*, which they reject.
Man's will is not only free from coaction, but from moral certainty, i. e., his volitions are not only free, but not decisively
caused, otherwise he would not be a free agent.

(b.) If this is so, whence the universal actual transgression
of adult man? Pelagianism answers, from concupiscence, which
exists in all, as in Adam before his sin, and is not sin of itself,
and from general evil example.

(c.) If man has no moral character, and no guilt prior to
intelligent choice, whence death and suffering among those who
have not sinned? They are obliged to answer: These natural
evils are not penal, and would have befallen Adam had he not
sinned. They are the natural limitations of humanity, just as
irrationality is of beasts, and no more imply guilt as their necessary cause.

(d.) Those, then, who die in infancy, have nothing from
which they need to be redeemed. Why then baptized? Pelagianism answered, those who die in infancy are redeemed from
nothing. If they die unbaptized, they would go to a state
called Paradise, the state of natural good, proceeding from
natural innocence, to which innocent Pagans go. But baptism
would interest them in Christ's gracious purchase, and thus they
would inherit, should they die in infancy, a more positive and
assured state of blessedness, called the Kingdom of Heaven.

(e.) All men being born innocent, and with equilibrium of
will, it is both physically and morally possible that any man
might act a holy character, and attain Paradise, or " eternal
life," without any gospel grace whatever. The chances may be
bad, on account of unfavourable example, and temptation,
amidst which the experiment has to be made. But there have

been cases, both under the revealed law, as Enoch, Job, Abel, Noah (who had no *protevangelium*); and among Pagans, as Numa, Aristides, Socrates; and there may be such cases again. Nor would God be just to punish man for coming short of perfection unless this were so.

(f.) Now, as to the theory of redemption: As there can be no imputation of Adam's guilt to his people, so neither could there be of Christ's people's guilt to Him, or of His righteousness to them. But sins are forgiven by the mercy of God in Christ (without penal satisfaction for them), on the condition of trust, repentance, and reformation. The title of the believer to a complete justification must then be his own obedience, and that a sinless one. But this is not so exalted an attainment as Calvinists now regard it. Concupiscence is not sin. Moral quality attaches only to actual volitions, not to states of feeling prompting thereto; and hence, if an act be formally right, it is wholly right; nor does a mixture of selfish and unselfish motives in it make it imperfectly moral; for volition is necessarily a thing, one decisive and entire. Hence, a prevalent, uniform obedience is a perfect one; and none less will justify, because justification is by works, and the law is perfect. But as equilibrium of will is essential to responsibility, any shortcoming which is morally necessitated, by infirmity of nature, or ignorance, thoughtlessness, or overwhelming gust of temptation, contrary to the soul's prevalent bent, is no sin at all. See here, the germ of the Wesleyan's doctrine of sinless perfection, and of the Jesuit theory of morals.

Since a concreated righteousness would be no righteousness, not being chosen at first, so neither would a righteousness wrought by a supernatural regeneration. The only gracious influences possible are those of co-operative grace, or moral suasion. Man's regeneration is simply his own change of purpose, as to sin and holiness, influenced by motives. Hence, faith and repentance are both natural exercises.

(g.) The continuance of a soul in a state of justification is of course contingent. A grace which would morally necessitate the will to continued holy choices, would deprive it of its free agency.

(h.) God's purpose of election, therefore, while from eternity, as is shown by His infinite and immutable wisdom, knowledge and power, is conditioned on His foresight of the way men would improve their free will. He elected those He foresaw would persevere in good.

The whole is a consistent and well-knit system of error, proceeding from its πρῶτον ψεῦδος.

Among those who pass under the general term, Arminians, two different schemes have been advanced; one represented by Whitby, the other by Wesley and his Church. The former admit

Arminian Theories.
1. Lower.

that Adam and his race were both much injured by the fall. He has not indeed lost his equilibrium of will for spiritual good, but he has become greatly alienated from God, has fallen under the penal curse of physical evil and death, has become more animal, so that concupiscence is greatly exasperated, and is more prone to break out into actual transgression. This is greatly increased by the miseries, fear, remorse, and vexation of his mortal state, which tend to drive him away from God, and to whet the envious, sensual and discontented emotions. These influences, together with constant evil example, are the solution of the fact, that all men become practically sinners. This is the state to which Adam reduced himself; and his posterity share it, not in virtue of any federal relation, or imputation of Adam's guilt, but of that universal, physical law, that like must generate like. In that sense, man is born a ruined creature.

The Wesleyans, however, begin by admitting all that a

2. Wesleyan. Moderate Calvinist would ask, as to Adam's loss of original righteousness in the Fall, bondage under evil desires, and total depravity. While they misinterpret, and then reject the question between mediate and immediate imputation, they retain the orthodox idea of imputation, admitting that the legal consequences of Adam's act are visited upon his descendants along with himself. But then, they say, the objections of severity and unrighteousness urged against this plan could not be met, unless it be considered as one whole, embracing man's gracious connection with the second Adam. By the Covenant of grace in Him, the self-determining power of the will, and ability of will are purchased back for every member of the human family, and actually communicated, by common sufficient grace, to all, so far repairing the effects of the fall, that man has moral ability for spiritual good, if he chooses to employ it. Thus, while they give us the true doctrine with one hand, they take it back with the other, and reach a semi-Pelagian result. The obvious objection to this scheme is, that if the effects of Adam's fall on his posterity are such, that they would have been unjust, if not repaired by a redeeming plan which was to follow it, as a part of the same system, then God's act in giving a Redeemer was not one of pure grace (as Scripture everywhere says), but He was under obligations to do some such thing.

The view of the Calvinists I purpose now to state in that

Calvinistic theory. comprehensive and natural mode, in which all sound Calvinists would concur. Looking into the Bible and the actual world, we find that, whereas Adam was created righteous, and with full ability of will for all good, and was in a state of actual blessedness; ever since his fall, his posterity begin their existence in a far different state. They all show, universal ungodliness, clearly proving a native, prevalent, and universal tendency thereto. They are borr spiritually dead, as Adam made himself. And they are obviously, natural heirs of the physical evils and death pronounced on him for his sin. Such are the grand facts. Now Calvinists consider that it is no unauthorized hypothesis, but merely a connected statement, and inevitable interpretation of the facts, to say: that we see in them this arrangement; God was pleased, for wise, gracious, and righteous reasons, to connect the destiny of Adam's posterity with his probationary acts, so making him their representative, that whatever moral, and whatever legal condition he procured for himself by his conduct under probation; in that same moral and that same legal condition his posterity should begin to exist. And this, we say, is no more than the explanation necessarily implied in the facts themselves.

But before we proceed to the detailed discussion of this, an inquiry, a subject of the greatest intricacy

5. Origin of Souls. History of opinions.

and interest, arises as a preliminary: How is this connection transmitted; what is the actual tie of nature between parents and children, as to their more essential part, the soul? Are human souls generated by their parents naturally? Or are they created directly by God, and sent into connection with the young body at the time it acquires its separate vitality? The former has been called the theory of Traducianism; (*ex traduce,*) the latter, of creation. After Origen's doctrine of pre-existent human souls had been generally surrendered as heretical (from the times of Chrysostom, say 403,) the question was studied with much interest in the early Church. Tertullian, who seems first to have formally stated Adam's federal headship, was also the advocate of the *ex traduce* theory. But it found few advocates among the Fathers, and was especially opposed, by those who had strong tendencies to what was afterwards called Pelagianism, as favouring original sin. Gregory of Nyssa seems to have been almost alone among the prominent Greek Fathers who held it. So perhaps did Ambrose among the Latins; but when Jerome asserts that the *ex traduce* view prevailed generally among the Western Christians, he was probably in error. Augustine, the great establisher of Original Sin, professed himself undecided about it, to the end. It may be said however, in general, that in history, the *ex traduce* theory has been thought more favourable to original sin, and has been usually connected with it, till modern times; while Creationism was strenuously advocated by Pelagians. If the Traducian theory can be substantiated, it most obviously presents the best explanation of the propagation of sin.

I shall state the usual arguments, *pro* and *con*, indicating as I go along my judgment of their force.

1. The Traducianists assert that by some inexplicable law

Arguments of Traducianists — F r o m Scripture.

of generation, though a true and proper one, parents propagate souls, as truly as bodies; and are thus the proper parents of the whole

persons of their children. They argue, from Scripture, that
Gen. ii : 2 states, " on the seventh day God ended the work
which He had made, and He rested on the seventh day from
all His work," &c. Hence, they infer, God performs since, no
proper work of immediate creation in this earth. This seems
hardly valid; for the sense of the the text might seem satisfied
by the idea, that God now creates nothing new as to species.
With a great deal more force, it is argued that in Gen. i : 25–
28, God creates man in His own image, after His own likeness,
which image is proved to be not corporeal at all, but in man's
spirituality, intelligence, immortality, and righteousness.   In
Gen. v : 3, "Adam begat a son in his own likeness, after his
image." How could this be, if Adam's parental agency did
not produce the soul, in which alone this image inheres?
Surely the image and likeness is in the same aspects.   See also
Ps. li : 5 ; Job. xiv : 4 ; Jno. iii : 6, &c. The purity or impurity
spoken of in all these passages is of the soul, and they must
therefore imply the propagation of souls, when so expressly
stating the propagation of impurity of soul.

They also argue that popular opinion and common sense
clearly regard the parents as parents of the
From   Experience whole person. The same thing is shown by
and from Imputation. the inheritance of mental peculiarities and
family traits, which are often as marked as bodily. And this
cannot be accounted for by education, because often seen where
the parents did not live to rear the child; nor by the fact that
the body with its animal appetites, in which the soul is encased,
may be the true cause of the apparent hereditary likeness of
souls; for the just theory is, that souls influence bodies in these
things, not bodies souls; and besides, the traits of resemblance
are often not only passional, but intellectual.   Instances of congenital lunacy suggest the same argument. Lunacy is plausibly explained as a loss of balance of soul, through the undue
predominance of some one trait. Now, these cases of congenital lunacy are most frequently found in the offspring of cous-
ins.   The resemblance of traits in the parents being already
great, '' breeding in and in '' makes the family trait too strong,
and hence derangement. But the chief arguments from reason
are : if God creates souls, as immediately as He created Adam's
or Gabriel, then they must have come from His hand morally
pure, for God cannot create wickedness. How, then, can depravity be propagated? The Bible would be contradicted, which
so clearly speaks of it as propagated ; and reason, which says that
the attachment of a holy soul to a body cannot defile it, because
a mere body has no moral character. Creationists answer : the
federal relation instituted between Adam and the race, justifies
God in ordaining it so that the connection of the young, immortal spirit with the body, and thus with a depraved race,
shall be the occasion for its depravation, in consequence of

imputed sin. But the reply is, first, it is impossible to explain the federal relation, if the soul of each child (the soul alone is the true moral agent), had an antecedent holy existence, independent of a human father. Why is not that soul as independent of Adam's fall, thus far, as Gabriel was; and why is not the arrangement, which implicates him in it, just as arbitary as though Gabriel were tied to Adam's fate? Moreover, if God's act in plunging this pure spirit into an impure body is the immediate occasion of its becoming depraved, it comes very near to making God the author of its fall. Last: a mere body has no moral character, and to suppose it taints the soul is mere Gnosticism. Hence, it must be that the souls of children are the offsprings of their parents. The mode of that propagation is inscrutable; but this constitutes no disproof, because a hundred other indisputable operations of natural law are equally inscrutable; and especially in this case of spirits, where the nature of the substance is inscrutable, we should expect the manner of its production to be so.

2. On the other hand, the advocates of creation of souls argue from such texts as Eccl. xii : 7; Is. lvii : 16 ; Zech. xii : 1 ; Heb. xii : 9, where our souls are spoken of as the special work of God. It is replied, and the reply seems to me sufficient, that the language of these passages is sufficiently met, by recognizing the fact that God's power at first produced man's soul immediately out of nothing, and in His own image; that the continued propagation of these souls is under laws which His Providence sustains and directs; and that this agency of God is claimed as an especial honour, (e. g. in Is. lvii : 16,) because human souls are the most noble part of God's earthly kingdom, being intelligent, moral, and capable of apprehending His glory. That this is the true sense of Eccl. xii : 7, and that it should not be strained any higher, appears thus: if the language proves that the soul of a man of our generation came immediately from God's hand, like Adam's, the antithesis would equally prove that our bodies came equally from the dust, as immediately as Adam's. To all such passages as Is. lvii : 16; Zech. xii : 1, the above general considerations apply, and in addition, these facts : Our parents are often spoken of in Scripture as authors of our existence likewise; and that in general terms, inclusive of the spirit. Gen. xlvi : 26, 27; Prov. xvii : 21; xxiii : 24; Is. xlv: 10. Surely, if one of these classes of texts may be so strained, the other may equally, and then we have texts directly contradicting texts. Again, God is called the Creator of the animals, Ps. civ : 30, and the adorner of the lilies, Matt. vi : 30; which are notoriously produced by propagation. In Heb. xii : 9, the pronoun in "Father of our spirits," is unauthorized. The meaning is simply the contrast between the general ideas of "earthly fathers," and "heavenly father."

Arguments of Creationists.

For if you make the latter clause, "Father of spirits" mean Creator of our souls, then, by antithesis, the former should be read, fathers of our bodies; but this neither the apostle's scope permits, nor the word σάρξ which does not usually mean, in his language, our bodies as opposed to our souls; but our natural, as opposed to our gracious condition of soul.

Again : Turrettin objects, that if Adam's soul was created, and our's propagated, we do not properly bear his image, 1 Cor. xv : 49, nor are of his species. The obvious answer is, that by the same argument we could not be of the same corporeal species at all! Further, the very idea of species is a propagated identity of nature. But the strongest rational objections are, that a generative process implies the separation of parts of the parent substances, and their aggregation into a new organism; whereas the souls of the parents, and that of the offspring are alike monads, indiscerptible, and uncompounded. Traducianism is therefore vehemently accused of materialist tendencies. It seems to me that all this is but an *argumentum ad ignorantiam.* Of course, spirits cannot be generated by separation of substance and new compoundings. But whether processes of propagation may not be possible for spiritual substance which involve none of this, is the very question, which can be neither proved nor disproved by us, because we do not comprehend the true substance of spirit.

The opponents might have advanced a more formidable objection against Traducianism: and this is the true difficulty of the theory. In every case of the generation of organisms, there is no production of any really new substance by the creature-parents, but only a reorganizing of pre-existent particles. But we believe a soul is a spiritual atom, and is brought into existence out of non-existence. Have human parents this highest creative power? With such difficulties besetting both sides, it will be best perhaps, to leave the subject as an insoluble mystery. What an *opprobrium* to the pride of human philosophy, that it should be unable to answer the very first and nearest question as to its own origin!

The humble mind may perhaps find its satisfaction in this Bible truth: That whatever may be the adjustment adopted for the respective shares of agency which the First Cause and second causes have in the origin of an immortal, human soul; this fact is certain (however unexplained) that parents and children are somehow united into one federal body by a true tie of race: that the tie does include the spiritual as well as the bodily substances: that it is *bona fide*, and not fictitious or supposititious. See Confession of Faith, ch. vi, § 3. "Root of all mankind." Now, since we have no real cognition by perception, of spiritual substance, but only know its acts and effects, we should not be surprised at our ignorance of the precise agency of its production, and the way that agency acts. It may not be explained; and yet it may be true, that divine power, (in bringing substance out of *nihil* into *esse*) and human causation may both act, in originating the being and properties of the infant's soul!

May not this insoluble question again teach us to apprehend a great truth, which we are incompetent to comprehend; that there is such a reality as spiritual generation, instanced in the eternal generation of the Word, in the infinite Spirit, and in the generation of human souls from the finite? The analogy must, indeed be partial, the lower instance being beneath the higher, as the heavens are lower than the earth. In the eternal generation, the generative spirit was sole; in the human, the parents are dual. In the former, the subsistence produced was not an individual numerically distinct from the producer, as in the latter. But it may be added, that familiar and fundamental as is our notion of our race unity, we know only in part what is connoted in it. It is possible that when "we know even as also we are known," we shall find, that Adam's creation "in the image and likeness" of God has still another meaning, not apprehended before; in that omnipotence endued man with a lower, though inscrutable form of that power by which the eternal Father forever generates the eternal Son.

LECTURE XXVIII.

ORIGINAL SIN. — Continued.

SYLLABUS.

6. What is Original Sin? What is meant by total depravity? And does it affect the whole man, in all faculties and capacities?
Conf. of Faith, ch. 6, § 3. Cat. Qu. 18. Turrettin, Loc. ix, Qu. 8, 10, 11, Dick, Lect. 46, 47. Hill, bk. iv, ch. 1. Watson, Theo. Inst., ch. 18. Thornwell, Lect. 17.

7. How is the existence of this total depravity proved, (a) from facts; (b) from Scripture? Are any of the secular virtues of the unrenewed genuine?
Turrettin, Qu. 10. Dick and Hill as above. Edwards on Original Sin, pt. i, ch. 1, 2, pt. ii, ch. 2, 3, pt. iii, ch. 1, 2. Muller, Chr. Doc. of Sin, bk. iv, ch. 1, 2. Dorner's History of Protestant Theology, Vol. i, § 2, ch. 1.

8. Define and prove the imputation of the guilt of Adam's first sin to his posterity.
Turrettin, Qu. 9, 12, 15. Dick and Hill as above. Edwards on Orig. Sin., pt. ii, ch. 1, 4, pt. iii, ch. 1, 3. Wines' "Adam and Christ." Dr. Wm. Cunningham's Hist. Theol., ch. 19, § 2. Knapp, § 76. Watson as above. Calvin and Hodge on Rom. 5th.

6. "THE sinfulness of that estate whereinto man fell, consists of the guilt of Adam's first sin, the want of original righteousness, and the corruption of his whole nature, which is commonly called original sin; together with all actual transgressions which proceed from it."

21*

Here, as in the Larger Catechism, Original Sin (so called because native, and because the fountain of all other sin) is the general term, expressing both elements, of imputed guilt and total depravity. By many theologians it is often used for the latter specially. I discuss the latter first.

Turrettin asserts that this total depravity is not merely or negatively a *carentia justitiæ originalis* but positively, an active principle of evil. But this does not contradict the definition which represented the essence of sin as discrepancy from law. The essential nature of virtue is, that it positively or affirmatively requires something; or makes a given state or act positively obligatory on the human heart. It admits no moral neutrality; so that the simply not being, or not doing what God requires, is Sin. But the soul is essentially active. Hence, it follows, that in a sinful state or act, the action or positivity of the sin is from the essential nature of the soul, its wrongness is from the mere absence of conformity to law. Depravity, as Pres. Edwards says, is a defective or privative quality; yet it assumes a positive form. I would prefer to say that depravity is active as opposed to simple negation. That it is active, is proved by Turrettin from those texts which attribute effects to it, as binding, deceiving, and slaying &c. Yet it is also important to distinguish that it is, in its origin, privative, and not the infusion of some positive quality of evil into the soul; in order to acquit God of the charge of being author of sin. The Bible term, ἁμαρτία, suggests the arrow swerving from its proper target. The swerving is privative. But this arrow does not stand still, or lie in the quiver; it flies, and perhaps with as much momentum and velocity, as the arrow which hits the mark.

Original Sin a positive bent to wrong.

The same reason compels us to believe that native depravity is not a substantial corruption of the soul; i. e., does not change or destroy any part of its substance. For souls are, as to their substance, what God made them; and His perfections ensure His not making anything that was not good. Nor is there any loss of any of the capacities or faculties, which make up the *essentia* of the soul. Man is, in these respects, essentially what his Creator made him. Hence depravity is, in the language of metaphysics, not an attribute, but *accidens* of the human soul now. This is further proved by the fact that Jesus Christ assumed our very nature, at His incarnation, without which He would not be our Mediator. But surely, He did not assume moral corruption! Last: Scripture clearly distinguishes between sin and the soul, when they speak of it as defiling the soul, as easily besetting; Heb. xii : 1, 2, &c. If it be asked, what then, is native depravity: if it be neither a faculty, nor the privation of one, nor of the man's essence, nor a change of substance? I reply, it is a vicious *habitus* which qualifies man's

But not a corruption of the Soul's substance.

active powers, i. e., his capacities of feeling and will. Although we may not be able to fully describe, yet we all know this idea of bents which naturally qualify the powers of action in all things.

The Confession states that the first man " became wholly defiled, in all the faculties and parts of soul and body." The seat of this vicious moral *habitus* is, of course, strictly speaking, in the moral propensities. But since these give active direction to all the faculties and parts of soul and body, in actions that have any moral quality, it may be said that, by accommodation of language, they are all morally defiled. The conscience (the highest department of rational intuitions) is not indeed destroyed; but its accuracy of verdict is greatly disturbed by evil desire, and the instinctive moral emotions which should accompany those verdicts, are so seared by neglect, as to seem practically feeble, or dead, for the time. The views of the understanding concerning all moral subjects are perverted by the wrong propensions of the heart, so as to call good evil, and evil good. Thus "blindness of mind" on all moral subjects results. The memory becomes a store of corrupt images and recollections, and thus furnishes material for the imagination; defiling both. The corporeal appetites, being stimulated by the lusts of the soul, by a defiled memory and imagination, and by unbridled indulgence, become tyrannical and inordinate. And the bodily limbs and organs of sense are made servants of unrighteousness. Thus, what cannot be literally unholy is put to unholy uses. But when we thus discriminate the faculties, we must not forget the unity and simplicity of the spirit of man. It is a monad. And, as we do not conceive of it as regenerated or sanctified by patches; so neither do we regard it as depraved by patches. Original corruption is not, specifically, the perversion of a faculty in the soul, but of the soul itself.

By saying that man's native depravity is total, we do not by any means intend that conscience is destroyed, for the man's guilt is evinced by this very thing, that his heart prefers what conscience condemns. Nor do we mean that all men are alike bad, and all as bad as they can be. Nor do we mean to impugn the genuineness and disinterestedness of the social virtues and charities in the ungodly. Far be it from us to assert that all the civic rectitude of an Aristides or Fabricius, all the charities of domestic love, all the nobleness of disinterested friendship among the worldly, are selfishness in disguise. But if it be allowed that many of these acts are of the true nature of virtue, how can man be called totally depraved? We mean, first, that as to the chief responsibility of the soul, to love God, every soul is totally recreant. No natural man has any true love for God as a spiritual, holy, true, good, and righteous Sovereign. But this being the pre-eminent duty over all others in the aggregate, utter dereliction here, throws all smaller, partial virtues wholly into the shade. Second: while there is something of true virtue in many secular acts and feelings of the unrenewed, which deserves the sincere approval and gratitude of fellowmen to them, as between man and man, there is in those same acts and feelings a fatal defect as to God, which places them on the wrong side of the moral dividing line. That defect is, that they are not prompted by any moral regard for God's will requiring them. "God is not in all their thoughts." Ps. x : 4. Let any worldly man analyze his motives, and he will find that this is true of his best secular acts. But the supreme regard ought to be, in every act, the desire to please God. Hence, although, these secular virtues are much less wrong than their opposite vices, they are still, in God's sight, short of right, and that in the most important particular. The deficiency of this carnal and social virtue receives a very practical illustration thus: The sphere of relation, in which the secular virtues of the unbelievers are practiced, is merely temporary. As children, husbands or wives, parents, neighbours, business men, they perform many disinterested acts of moral form; being prompted thereto by natural, social principles. In the other world, all these relations are abolished. Where then will be the rectitude of persons, who, with all their social excellencies, had no godliness, when God is the only good, and the immediate object of duty and intercourse?

But third, native depravity is total, in this sense; that it is, so far as man's self-recuperation is concerned, decisive and final. Original sin institutes a direct tendency to progressive, and at last, to utter depravity. In a word: it is spiritual death. Corporeal death may leave its victim more or less ghastly. A corpse may be little emaciated, still warm, still supple; it may still have a tinge of colour in the cheek and a smile on its lips: it may be still precious and beautiful in the eyes of those that loved it. But it is dead, and a loathsome putrefaction approaches, sooner or later. It is only a question of time.

7. The proofs of a native and total depravity toward God, are unfortunately, so numerous, that little more can be attempted in one Lecture, than a statement of their heads. They may be grouped under the two heads of experience, and Scripture statements and facts.

Adam's sin reduced him to a total depravity, as has been shown in a previous Lecture. But the great

Depravity of the Race proved, 1st, by law of reproduction.

law, which seems to reign throughout the vegetable and sentient universe, wherever a law of reproduction reigns, is that like shall beget like. And this appears to be confirmed by Gen. v : 3; Job xiv: 4. Whence Adam's ruin would be *a priori*, a ground for expecting his posterity to be born depraved. There are indeed some, (as Dr.

Thornwell, Review of Breckinridge, January, 1858,) who deny
that this law would naturally apply here, and attribute the result
of Adam's producing a sinful posterity, exclusively to the positive, federal connection appointed for them.   They urge, that
the thing propagated by this natural law is the attributes of the
species, not its accidents ; that by this cause any other progenitor between us and our first father would be as much the source
of our depravity as he; and that if the accident of Adam's fall
is propagated, so ought to be the regenerate nature produced in
him, and in other progenitors, by grace.   This is clearly against
the Confession, ch. 6, § 3, and, it seems to me, against the texts
quoted.   It confounds accidents in the popular sense with *accidens*, in the sense of the Logician.   Very true : a man who loses
an arm by accident, does not propagate one-armed children.
But in the other sense of the word, it will hardly be asserted
that the red colour of Devon cattle is an attribute, and not
accidents of horned cattle, and the more refractory and savage
temper of the wild boar an attribute of the species swine; yet
both are propagated by this law of generation, As I have
before said, the properties which define a species, whether
attributes or accidents, are just those which are propagated in
it; this is the very idea of species.   And we may at least claim,
that our progenitors, since Adam, have certainly been channels
of transmission of depravity to us.   Their agency herein was
the same as Adam's toward Seth.   Regenerate character does
not define the species man, as a species ; and hence, is not
propagated, especially as it is a character only incipient in the
parents in this life.   Chiefly, regenerate character is not propagated by parents, because it is now not a natural, but a supernatural property.

  We argue native depravity from the universal sinfulness of
man, as exhibited in fact.   Premise, that the
2nd. By Universal Sin. strength of this argument ought to be judged
according to the tendencies which this prevalent ungodliness
would exert, not as it is in fact, but as it would be, if unrestrained by the grace and providence of God.   What then is
the fact ? We see all men, under all circumstances, do much
that is wrong.   We see the world full of wickedness, much of
it enormous.   We behold parents, masters, magistrates and
teachers busy with multitudes of rules and laws, and a vast apparatus of prisons, police, armies, and penalties, striving with
very indifferent success, to repress wickedness.   It is no allevi-
ation to this picture to say, that there are also many virtues in
the world, and more correct people who leave no history, because
they quietly pursue a virtuous life, than of those who make a
noise in the world by sin.   For the majority of men are relatively wicked, taking the world over; and a truly honourable
secular character, even, is the exception.   Again : as we have
seen, all these virtues contain a fatal defect, that of not being

performed for God's honour and pleasure; a defect so vital, that it throws any element of goodness as to man wholly into the shade. Take the standard: "Thou shalt love the Lord thy God with all thy heart," and it will be seen that the best natural man in the world never comes up to it in any one act. How then can he claim any good acts to balance against his bad ones, when there are none at all wholly in the right scale? None that are in the right scale as to the most weighty particular.

Again: the universal result of the growth of human beings
3d. By early apostacy is, that as soon as they are old enough to
of children from the exhibit any moral qualities in intelligent
right. action, they exhibit some wrong ones. And thenceforward, their doing some wrong things is a constant occurrence, not an occasional accident. Yea, more: infants, before they are old enough to understand their own evil tempers, show wicked tempers, selfishness, anger, spite, revenge. So testifies Scripture. Ps. lviii: 3; Gen. viii: 21; Ps. li: 5.

Once more, we find universally, a most obdurate blindness,
4th. By opposition to stupidity, and opposition concerning the
God and Redemption. things of God. Rom. viii: 7. So averse
are men to the spiritual service of God, that they all, if left to themselves, postpone and refuse it, against the dictates of reason and conscience, which they partially obey in other things, against inducements absolutely infinite; and, such is the portentous power of this opposition, it overrides these motives and influences, usually, without a seeming struggle. This universal prevalence of sin has appeared in man's history, in spite of great means for its prevention: not only by the legislation, &c., mentioned: but by chastisements, the Flood, religious dispensations, miracles, theophanies, prophecies, and the incarnation of Christ Himself.

Such is a fair and moderate picture of human experience.
5th. By Scripture. Scripture confirms it, asserting the universal
and prevalent sinfulness of man. Gen. vi: 5; 1 Kings viii: 46; Eccl. vii: 20: Ps. cxilii: 2; Gal. iii: 22; Rom. iii: 10–18; Jas: iii: 1, 2; Eccl. ix: 3, &c., &c.: Ps. xiv: 2, 3; Jer. xvii: 9.

Now an effect requires a cause. Here is an effect, occur-
Universal effects re- ring under every variety of outward condi-
quire a cause. tion and influences, universal, constantly re-
curring, appearing immediately the time arrives in the human being's life which permits it. There must be a universal cause, and that, within the human being himself. We may not be able to comprehend exactly how a moral *habitus* subsists in an undeveloped reason and conscience; but we are just as sure, that there is an innate germinal cause, in the human being's moral nature, for all these moral results, as we are that there is, in young apes, an innate cause why no nurture or outward circumstances will ever by any possibility

develope one of them into a Newton. This intuition is confirmed by Scripture. Luke vi: 43–45, &c.: Ps. lviii: 3, with verse 4.

The universal prevalence of bodily death, with its premonitory ills, of bodily infirmity, a cursed ground, toil and hardship, show that man's depravity is total and native. These ills are a part of the great threatening made against Adam, and when inflicted on him, it was in immediate connection with spiritual death. Why suppose them severed, in any other case? It is vain to say that these things are not now the curse of sin, but a wholesome chastisement and restraint, and thus a blessing in disguise; for if man were not depraved, he would not need such a lesson. Why does not God see that Paradise is still man's most wholesome state, as it was Adam's? But from Gen. ii: 17, onward, death is always spoken of as a punishment for sin. Then, where death goes, sin must have gone. Rom. v: 12; 1 Cor. xv; 22. Especially the death of infants proves it; because they cannot understand the disciplinary effects of suffering and death. See especially the cases of the infants of Sodom, of Canaan, of Jerusalem, in Ezek. ix: 6. Nor can it be said that infants die only by the imputed guilt of Adam's sin; for imputed guilt and actual depravity are never found separated in the natural man.

6th. Argument from prevalence of the curse.

The fact that all need, and some of all classes are interested in the redemption of Jesus Christ, proves that all have a sin of nature. For if they were not sinners, they would not be susceptible of redemption. Among the Redeemed are "elect infants dying in infancy," as is proved by Luke xviii: 16; Matt. xxi: 16. But infants have no actual transgressions to be redeemed from! Socinians and Pelagians talk of a redemption in their case, which consists neither in an actual regeneration nor forgiveness, but in their resurrection, and their being endued with a gracious and assured blessedness. But this is a mere abuse of Scripture to speak of such a process as the redeeming work of Christ for any human being. For His very name and mission were from the fact that He was to save His people from their sins. Matt. i: 21; 1 Tim. i: 15; Mark ii: 17; Gal. ii: 21; iii: 21. Christ was sent to save men from perishing. Jno. iii: 16. His redemption is always by blood, because this typifies the atonement for sin. Sin is therefore co-extensive with redemption.

7th. From need of Redemption.

Again; the application of this redemption in effectual calling is evidence of native depravity. In order that Christ may become ours, it is most repeatedly declared that we must be born again. This regeneration is a radical and moral change, being not merely a change of purpose of life made by a volition, but a revolution

8th. From Regeneration.

of the propensities which prompt our purposes. This is proved by the names used to describe the change, a new birth, a new creation, a quickening from death, a resurrection, and from the Agent, which is not the truth, or motive, but almighty God. See Jno. iii : 5 ; Eph. i : 19 to ii : 10. Now, if man needs this moral renovation of nature, he must be naturally sinful. We find our Saviour Himself, Jno. iii : 5, 6, stating this very argument. The context shows that Christ assigns the sixth verse as a ground or reason for the fifth, and not as an explanation of the difficulty suggested by Nicodemus in the fourth. Moreover, the word σάρξ means, by established Scripture usage, not the body, nor the natural human constitution considered merely as a nature, but man's nature as depraved morally. Compare Rom. vii : 14, 18 ; viii : 4, 7, 8, 9 ; Col. ii : 18 ; Gal. v : 16–24 ; Gen. vi : 3.

To this we may add, one of the meanings of circumcision and baptism was to symbolize this regeneration, (another, to represent cleansing from guilt by atonement.) Hence, sin is recognized in all to whom these sacraments are applied by divine command. And as both were given to infants, who had no intelligent acts of sin, it can only be explained by their having a sin of nature.

We have seen how the Bible asserts a universal sinfulness in practice, and how it sustained us in tracing that universal sin up to its source in a sin of nature. We close with a few specimens of other texts, which expressly assert original sin. Job xiv : 4 ; xv : 14–16 ; Prov. xxii : 15 ; Ps. li : 5 ; Eph. ii : 3.

9th. Scripture proofs.

The evasions to which the deniers of Original Sin are forced to resort, to escape these categorical assertions, are too numerous and contradictory to be recited or answered here. Let these texts be carefully studied in their scope and connection.

One of these I will notice : It has been objected that the innocence of children seems to be asserted in such places as Ps. cvi : 38 ; Jonah iv : 11 ; Jno. ix : 3 ; Rom. ix : 11. I explain, that this is only a relative innocence. The sacred writers here recognize their freedom from the guilt of all actual transgression, and their harmlessness towards their fellow men during this helpless age. This, together with their engaging simplicity, dependence, and infantile graces, has made them types of innocence in all languages. And this is all the Scriptures mean.

The Hebrew word חָשַׁב and the Greek, λογίζομαι both mean primarily to think, then to deem or judge, then to impute or attribute. In this sense the former occurs in Ps. xxxii : 2, and the latter in Rom. iv : 6–8, as its translation. See also 2 Sam.

8. Imputation defined.

xix : 19; 2 Cor. v : 19; Gal. iii : 6; Jas. ii : 23. Without going at this time into the vexed question, whether anything is ever said in Scripture to be imputed to any other than its own agent, I would define, that it is not Adam's sin which is imputed to us, but the guilt (obligation to punishment) of his first sin. This much misunderstood doctrine does not teach that Adam's act was actually made ours. This consciousness repudiates. We know that we personally did not will it. Nor does it mean that we are to feel personally defiled and blameworthy, with the vileness and demerit of Adam's sin. For us to undertake to repent of it in this sense, would be as preposterous as for us to feel self-complacency for the excellence of Christ's right-eousness imputed to us. But we are so associated with Adam in the legal consequences of the sin which closed his probation, and ours in his, that we are treated as he is, on account of his act. The grounds of this legal union we hold to be two; 1st the natural union with him as the root of all mankind; 2d the federal relation instituted in him, by God's covenant with him. Now, we do not say that the Scriptures anywhere use the par-ticular phrase, the guilt of Adam's sin was imputed to us; but we claim that the truth is clearly implied in the transactions as they actually occurred, and is substantially taught in other parts of Scripture.

If Adam came under the covenant of works as a public I. Imputation person, and acted there, not for himself proved. alone, but for his posterity federally, this implies the imputation of the legal consequences of his act to them. The proof that Adam was a federal head, in all these acts, is clear as can be, from so compendious a narrative. See Gen. i : 22, 28; iii : 15 to 19; ix : 3. In the dominion assigned man over the beasts, in the injunction to multiply, in the privil-ege of eating the fruits of the earth, in the hallowing of the Sabbath, God spoke seemingly only to the first pair; but His words indisputably applied as well to their posterity. So we infer, they are included in the threat of death for disobedience, and the implied promise of Ch. ii : 17. To see the force of this inference, remember that it is the established style of Genesis. See ix : 25 to 27; xv : 7; xvi : 12; xvii : 20; in each case the patriarch stands for himself and his posterity, in the meaning of the promise. But this is more manifest in Gen. iii : 15–19 where God proceeds to pass sentence according to the threat of the broken Covenant. The serpent is to be at war with the woman's seed. The ground is cursed for Adam's sin. Does not this curse affect his posterity, just as it did him? See Gen. v : 29. He is to eat his bread in the sweat of his face. Does not this pass over to his posterity? The woman has her pecul-iar punishment, shared equally by all her daughters. And in the closing sentence, death to death, we all read the doom of our mortality. So plain is all this, that even Pelagians have allowed that God acted here judicially. But Adam's posterity is included in the judgment. No better description of imputation need be required.

A presumption in favour of this solution is raised by a number of facts in God's providence. He usually connects the people and their head, the children and parents, in the consequences of the representative's conduct. Wherever there is such a political union, this follows. Nor is the consent of the persons represented always obtained, to justify the proceeding. Instances may be found in the decalogue, Exod. xx : 5, the deliverance of Rahab's house by her faith, Josh. vi : 25; the destruction of Achan's by his sin, Josh. vii : 24, 25; of the posterity of Amalek for the sins of their forefathers, 1 Sam. xv : 2; of Saul's descendants for his breach of covenant with the Gibeonites, 2 Sam. xxi : 1–9; of the house of Jeroboam, 1 Kings xiv: 9, 10; and of the generation of Jews cotemporary with Christ, Matt. xxiii : 35. So, nations are chastised with their rulers, children with their parents. It is not asserted that the case of Adam and his posterity is exactly similar; but cases bearing some resemblance to its principles show that it is not unreasonable; and since God actually orders a multitude of such cases, and yet cannot do wrong, they cannot contain the natural injustice which has been charged upon Adam's case.

II. Imputation confirmed by Experience.

The explanation presented by the doctrine of imputation is demanded by the mere facts of the case, as they are admitted by all except Pelagians and Socinians. Man's is a spiritually dead and a condemned race. See Eph. ii : 1–5, *et passim*. He is obviously under a curse for something, from the beginning of his life. Witness the native depravity of infants, and their inheritance of woe and death. Now, either man was tried and fell in Adam, or he has been condemned without a trial. He is either under the curse (as it rests on him at the beginning of his existence) for Adam's guilt, or for no guilt at all. Judge which is most honorable to God, a doctrine which, although a profound mystery, represents Him as giving man an equitable and most favoured probation in His federal head; or that which makes God condemn him untried, and even before he exists.

III. Imputation implied in man's estate.

Note here, that the lower Arminian view, in making man's fallen state by nature a mere result of the law: "Like must beget like," does not relieve the case. For who ordained that law? Who placed the human race under it, as to their spirits as well as their body? Was not God able to endue a race with a law of generation which should be different in this particular, or to continue the race of man by some other plan, as successive creations? The very act of God, in ordaining this law for man

IV. Not to be accounted for by mere law of reproduction.

whom He purposed to permit to fall, was virtually to ordain a
federal connection between Adam and his race, and to decide
beforehand the virtual imputation of his guilt to them.   For
man is not a vegetable, nor a mere animal; but a rational,
responsible person.   The results of this law of reproduction
prove to be, in the case of Adam and his posterity, just such
as, when applied to rational agents, are penal.   Now, the question is: Why does God subject souls, which have a personal
liberty and destiny, to the dominion of a law which we see, in
its other instances, merely vegetative and animal?   This is the
moral problem.   It is no solution to say, that the case is such.
To say this is only to obtrude the difficulty as the solution.   If
then, this extension of the law of reproduction was not a
righteous, judicial one and based on the guilt of Adam, it was an
arbitrary one, having no foundation in justice.

But the great Bible argument for the imputation of
V. Argument of   Adam's sin, is the parallel drawn between
Rom. 5th and 1 Cor.   Adam and Christ, in 1 Cor. xv : 21, 22, 45–
15th.   49, and Rom. v : 12–19.   The latter of these
passages, especially has been the peculiar subject of exegetical
tortures.   See, for scheme of immediate imputationists, Hodge
on Rom.; of moderate Calvinists, Baird, Elohim Rev., Chap.
xiv., and Calvin *in loco*.   I shall not go over the expository
arguments, for time forbids; and they are rather the appropriate business of another department; but shall content myself
with stating the doctrinal results, which, as I conceive, are
clearly established.   In 1 Cor. xv : Adam and Christ are compared, as the first and the second Adam.   In almost every thing
they are contrasted; the one earthy, the other heavenly; the
one source of death, the other of life; yet they have something in common.   What can this be, except their representative characters?   In verse 22, Adam is somehow connected
with the death of his confederated body; and Christ is similarly (ὥσπερ ... οὕτω) connected with the life of his.   But Christ
redeems His people by the imputation to them of His righteousness.   Must not Adam have ruined his, by the imputation
to them of his guilt?

In Rom. v : 12–19, it is agreed by all Calvinistic interpreters that the thing illustrated is justification
Exposition of Rom.   through faith, which is the great doctrine of
5th.   the Epistle to Romans, denied at that time
by Jews.   The thing used for illustration is Adam's federal
headship and our sin and death in him, more generally admitted by Jews.   The passage is founded on the idea of verse 14,
that Adam is the figure (τύπος) of Christ.   And obviously, a
comparison is begun in verse 12, which is suspended by paren-
thetic matter until verse 18, and there resumed and completed.
The amount of this comparison is indisputably this: that like
as we fell in Adam, we are justified in Christ.   Hence our gen-

eral argument for imputation of Adam's sin; because justification is notoriously by imputation.

2. It is asserted verse 12, and proved vs. 13, 14, that all
men sinned and were condemned in Adam; death, the established penalty of sin, passing upon them through his sin, as is
proved, verse 14, by the death of those who had no actual
transgression of their own.

3. The very exceptions of vs. 15–17, where the points are
stated in which the resemblance does not hold, show that
Adam's sin is imputed. Our federal union with Adam, says
the Apostle, resulted in condemnation and death with Christ in
abounding grace. In the former case, one sin condemned all;
in the latter, one man's righteousness justifies all. The very
exceptions show that men are condemned for Adam's sin.

4. In vs. 18, 19, the comparison is resumed and completed;
and it is most emphatically stated that, as in Christ many are
constituted righteous, so in Adam many were constituted sinners. Scriptural usage of the phrase καθιστηναι δικαιοι, and
what is taught of the nature of our justification in Christ,
together with the usage of the phrase δικαίωσιν ζωῆς, verse 18,
by which it is defined, prove that it is a forensic change which
is implied. Then it follows that likewise our legal relations
were determined by Adam. This is imputation.

LECTURE XXIX.

ORIGINAL SIN. — Concluded.

SYLLABUS.

9. Refute the evasions of the Pelagians and others from the argument for
native depravity.

Turrettin, Loc. ix, Qu. 10. Edwards on Orig. Sin, pt. i, ch. 1, § 9.

10. Answer the objections to imputation, (a) from the Scriptures, as Deut.
xxiv : 16, and Ezek. xviii : 20; (b) from the absence of consent by us to
Adam's representation; (c) from God's goodness; (d) from its supposed injustice.

Turrettin, Qu. 9. Edwards, pt. iv. Stapfer, Pol. Theol., Vol. iv, ch. 17, § 78.
Thornwell, Lect. 13. Knapp, § 76. Hodge, Theol., pt. ii, ch. 8, § 13.

11. Explain the theories of Mediate and Immediate Imputation and show the
correct view.

Turrettin, Qu. 9. Edwards, pt. iv, ch. 3. Stapfer, Pol. Theol., Vol. i, ch. 3,
§ 856–7; Vol. iv. ch. 16, and as above. South. Presb. Rev., April, 1873, Art.
i, and April, 1875, Art. 6. Breckinridge's Theol., Vol. i, ch. 32. Review of
Dr. Thornwell's Collected Works, Vol. i, p. 445, &c. Hodge, pt. ii, ch. 8.
Baird's Elohim Revealed, ch. 14. Calv. Inst., bk. i, ch. 2, and Com. on Rom.
v. Chalmers' Theo. Institutes. Princeton Review, 1830, pp. 481–503.

12. What the importance of the doctrine of Original Sin, from its connections
with the other doctrines of Redemption?

9. WE now group together the usual objections advanced
by opponents against our argument for native depravity.

It is urged, if the sinning of men now proves they have
native depravity, Adam's sinning would prove
that he had; since the generality of an effect
does not alter its nature.   I reply, the sophism is in veiling Adam's continued and hab-
itual sinning, after he fell, with the first sin, by which he fell.
Did we only observe Adam's habit of sinning, without having
known him from his origin, the natural and reasonable induction, so far as human reason could go, would be, that he was
originally depraved.   But the proof would be incomplete,
because our observation did not trace this habit up, as we do in
the case of infants, to the origin of his existence.   It is revelation which informs us how Adam became a habitual sinner,
not inference.   But if Adam's first sin be compared with his
descendant's perpetual sins, the difference is, that an occaional
effect requires an occasional cause; but a constant effect
requires a constant cause.

Objections. Adam sinned; but was not originally corrupt.

Some Pelagians say, a self-determined, contingent will, is
enough to account for all men's sinning.   We reply: how comes
a contingent force to produce always uniform effects?   If a die,
when thrown, falls in various ways, its falling is contingent.   But
if it always fall the same way, every gambler knows it is loaded.

Pelagians offer the general power of an evil example, as
the sufficient explanation why all men grow
up sinners.   Calvinists answer. (a). How
comes it that the example is universally evil?
This itself is the effect to be accounted for. (b). If there were no
innate tendency to evil, a bad example would usually repel and
disgust the holy soul.   (c). All young immortals have not been
subjected to an equally bad example ; witness the godly families of Adam, Seth, Noah, Abraham, and the pious now, and
above all, the spotless example of Jesus Christ.   If the power
of example were the decisive cause, these good examples (not
perfect, but,) approximating thereto, would sometimes have
produced an efficient upward tendency in some families.

Example. May it account for it?

Some say: Sense developes before reason; and thus
the child is betrayed under the power of appetite, before its moral faculties are strong
enough to guide him.   I answer, mere ani-
mal appetite, without moral element, has no moral quality;
it is the heart which gives the evil element to bodily appetite,
not *vice versa*.   But chiefly; we show that the result is uniform
and certain: whence it would be the efficient result of God's
natural law; which makes it more obnoxious to the charge of
making God the author of sin, than the Calvinistic theory.

May influence of sense account for sin!

Against the other element of original sin, the imputed
guilt of Adam's first sin, it is also objected,
that it cannot be true: for then God will
appear to have acted with equal severity

10.   Objections to Imputation.

against poor helpless babes, who, on the Calvinist's theory, have no guilt except total depravity never yet expressed in a single overt act against His law; and against Adam, the voluntary sinner: and Satan and his angels. We reply, No. All infinites are not equal. Paschal and Sir Isaac Newton have shown, that of two true infinites one may be infinitely larger than another. If the infant, Adam, and Satan, be all punished eternally, they will not be punished equally. Further; has it been proved that any infants who die in infancy, (without overt sin), are eternally lost? The question however is: are infants depraved by nature? And is this tendency of will to evil, morally evil? Then God is entitled to punish it as it deserves.

A Scriptural objection is raised, from such passages as Deut. xxiv : 16. It is urged with great con-
Objections f r o m fidence, that here, the principle on which
Scripture. Calvinists represent God as acting, (God the pure and good Father in Heaven,) is seen to be so utterly wicked, that imperfect human magistrates are forbidden to practice on it. I reply; it is by no means true that an act would be wicked in God, because it would be wicked in man. e. g. Man may not kill; God righteously kills millions every year. But second: the object of civil government is very different from that of God's government. The civil magistrate does not punish sin in order to requite absolutely its ill-desert, (this is the function of God alone,) but to preserve the public order and well-being, by making an example of criminals. Now, of that element of guilt against society, the children of the murderer or thief are clear; for the magistrate to shed their blood for this, would be to shed innocent blood: i. e., innocent as to that element of guilt which it is the civil magistrate's business to punish. Here, let it be noted, the punishment of Achan's, Saul's, &c., children, for their fathers, was the act of God, not the magistrate. The cases were exceptional.

Again: it is urged with much clamour, that in Ezek. xviii :
Objections f r o m 1–23, God expressly repudiates the scheme
Ezek. xviii : 1–23 an- of imputation of fathers' sins to their poster-
swered. ity, for Himself, as well as for magistrates; and declares this as the great law of His kingdom: " The soul that sinneth, it shall die." We reply: He does not mean to disclaim the imputation of Adam's sin to the human race. For first: He does not mean here, to disclaim all principles of imputation in His Providence even as to parents and posterity subsequent to Adam. If you force this sense on His words, all you get by it is an irreconcilable collision between this passage and Exod. xx : 5, and obvious facts in His providence. Second, if it were true universally of human parents subsequent to Adam, it would not follow as to Adam's first sin. For there is a clear distinction between that act of Adam,

and all the sins of other parents.   He alone was a federal head
in a Covenant of works.   The moment he fell, by that act, the
race fell in him, and its apostasy was effected; the thing was
done; and could not be done over.   From that hour, a Covenant of works became inapplicable to man, and neither parents
nor children, for themselves, nor for each other, have had any
probation under it.   So that the case is widely different,
between Adam in his first sin, and all other parents in their
sin.   Third : the Covenant to which this whole passage has reference was, not the old Covenant of works, whose probation
was forever past, but the political, theocratic Covenant between
God and Israel.   Israel, as a commonwealth, was now suffering
under providential penalties, for the breach of that political
covenant exactly according to the terms of the threatenings.
(See Deut. xxviii).   But although that was indisputable, the
banished Jews still consoled their pride by saying, that it was
their fathers' breach of the national Covenant for which they
were suffering.   In this plea God meets them: and tells them
it was false : for the terms of the theocracy were such that the
covenant-breaking of the father would never be visited under
it on the son who thoroughly disapproved of it, and acted in
the opposite way.   How far is this from touching the subject of
Original Sin ?   But last: we might grant that the passage did
refer to original sin: and still refute the objector thus : God
says the son who truly disapproves of and reverses his father's
practices, shall live.   Show us now, a child of Adam who fulfills this condition, in his own strength; and we will allow that
the guilt of Adam's sin has not affected him.

In defending the federal relationship instituted between
Adam's Representa- Adam and his posterity against the charge of
tion a humane arrange- cruelty, let it be distinctly understood, that
ment. we do not aim to justify the equity of the
arrangement merely by the plea that it was a benevolent one,
and calculated to promote the creature's advantage.   For if it
were an arrangement intrinsically unrighteous, it would be no
sufficient answer to say, that it was politic and kindly.   God
does not " do evil, that good may come ; " nor hold that " the
end sanctifies the means."   But still, we claim that, as the separate charge of cruelty, or harshness, is urged against this federal arrangement, we can triumphantly meet it, and show that
the arrangement was eminently benevolent ; thus reconciling it
to the divine attribute of goodness, so far as that is concerned
in it.   And further : while the benevolence of an arrangement
may not be a sufficient justification of its righteousness, yet it
evidently helps to palliate the charge of injustice, and to raise a
presumption in favor of the equity of the preceeding.   If there
were injustice in such a transaction, one element of it must be
that it was mischievous to the happiness of the parties.

The federal relation, then, was consistent with God's good-

Its benevolence ness. Let the student remember what was
proved by Compari- established concerning the natural rights and
son. relations of a holy creature towards his Creator. The former could never earn a claim, by natural justice,
to any more than this : to be well treated to the extent of his
natural well-being merely, as long as he behaves himself perfectly, or until God should see fit to annihilate him. If God
condescended to any fuller communications of happiness, or to
give any promise of eternal life, it must be by an act of free
grace. And the covenant of works was such an act of grace.
Now, a race of men being created, holy and happy, there were,
as far as the human mind can imagine, but four plans possible
for them. One was, to be left under their natural relation to
God forever. The second was, to have the gracious offer of a
covenant of works, under which each one should stand for
himself, and a successful probation of some limited period,
(suppose 70 years,) be kindly accepted by God for his justification, and adoption into eternal life. The third was, for God
to enter into such a covenant of works, for a limited period,
with the head of the race federally, for himself and his race, so
that if he stood the limited probation, justification and adoption
should be graciously bestowed on him, and in him, on all the
race ; and if he failed, all should be condemned in him. The
last was the plan actually chosen : Let us compare them, and
see if it is not far the most benevolent of the three.

The first plan, I assert, would have resulted, sooner or
later, in the sin and fall of every member of the race, and that,
with a moral certainty. (This may be the reason that God has
condescended to a Covenant with each order of rational
creatures after creating them). For creatures, no matter how
holy, are finite, in all their faculties and habitudes. But, in
an existence under law, i. e., under duty, requiring perpetual
and perfect obedience, and protracted to immortality, the number and variety of exegencies or moral trials, would become
infinite ; and therefore the chance of error, in the passage of a
finite holiness through them, would become ultimately a most
violent probability, mounting nearer and nearer to a moral certainty. Whenever sin occurred, the mere natural relation of the
soul to God would require Him to avenge it. Thus one after
another would stumble, till ultimately all were lost. Were innocent creatures thus required to sustain and guide themselves,
as they moved in their exact orbits around the throne of God :
one after another would, in the lapse of an eternity, forsake the
path, increase his centrifugal force, and fly off into outer darkness ; leaving God at last, a sun without a planet. This plan
would have been least benevolent.

But suppose each man allowed the privilege of a Covenant
of works, for some limited time, to win the grace of adoption
unto life by a perfect obedience for, say, 70 years, and begin-

ning his probation with a perfectly innocent nature. How would that work? Why: have we not here, the very state of the case which Socinians and Pelagians say, actually prevails? Let man's experience then, even as interpreted by these heretics, give the answer how it works. Do they not admit that, by virtue of evil example, nearly all fall? Can they deny that the earth is full of misery and wickedness; and that none remain absolutely innocent? If then, our present state were consistently interpreted as a probation under a Covenant of works, in which any sin forfeits the prize; if Pelagians would be consistent, and not introduce the preposterous idea of pardon under such a plan, where it has no place; even they would be compelled to admit that this second scheme does actually result in a total failure. Under it, all are destroyed. It too, then has as little beneficence as the first. This, I grant, is an *argumentum ad hominem;* but it is a just one. But we might leave the Pelagian's premises, and still reason, that the second scheme would only result in death. The actual failure of the first man's probation settles the question as to him. The next would have had the same chances of fall, aggravated by the evil example and enticements of the first; and soon, the current of evil would have become so general that all would go with it.

Let us come to the third plan. Is it said, that practically, Advantage of Covenant of Works, with a Representative. all have died under that also, so that it is just on a par with the other two? I answer, no; because the probabilities of a favourable issue were as great as could well be imagined, compatibly with leaving the creature mutable at all. For, instead of having a risque repeated millions of times, under circumstances increasingly untoward, only one risque was permitted. And this was under the most favourable possible conditions. The probationer had no human bad company; he was in the maturity of his powers and knowledge; whereas his posterity would have had to begin their trial in their inexperienced boyhood. He had the noblest motives to stand, imaginable. Had the probation resulted favourably, so that we had all entered existence assured against sin and misery, and the adopted heirs of eternal life, how should we have magnified the goodness of God in the dispensation? The grace bestowed through the first Adam, would have been only second in its glory, to that we now adore in the second! Now, the failure was not God's fault; His goodness is just the same in the plan, as though it had eventuated well. It is no objection to say, that God foreknew, all the while, how unfortunately it would eventuate, and even determined to permit it. For this objection is no other than the one against the permission of evil; which no one can solve. It is but to restate the question: Why did not God just communicate Himself at once to every reasonable creature, so as absolutely to confirm His will against sin, without proposing any covenant, or proba-

22*

tion at all ? There is no answer, but Matt. xi : 26. This plan, the fourth and only other, being excluded, as stubborn fact proves it was, the federal arrangement made with Adam for his posterity, was the most liberal one.

But the grand objection of all Pelagians and skeptics, is still repeated : How can it be justice, for me, who gave no consent to the federal arrangement, for me, who was not present when Adam sinned, and took no share in it, save in a sense purely fictitious and imaginary, to be so terribly punished for another man's deed. This is nothing else than the intrinsic injustice of punishing an innocent man for the fault of the guilty. As well might God have gotten up a legal fiction of a federal relation between Gabriel and Satan, and when the latter sinned, dragged Gabriel down, innocent, and even ignorant of any crime, to hell. Against such a plan, the moral instincts of man rebel. It is simply impossible that they should accept it as righteous.

Objection against justice of imputation.

I have thus stated this objection in its full force. So far as I am aware, there have been five several expedients proposed for meeting it. 1. The Wesleyan says : the injustice would appear, if it were not remedied in the second Adam, in whom the imputation of Adam's guilt and original sin are so far repaired, as to give common sufficient grace to every child of Adam. So that the two dispensations ought to be viewed together ; and what is harsh in one will be compensated in the other. This is inadmissible for many reasons; chiefly because there is no common sufficient grace ; and because if this solution be adopted, then the gospel will be of debt, and not of grace.

The several answers.
1. The Wesleyan is inadequate.

We find President Edwards endeavoring to evade the objection, by asserting that our federal oneness with Adam is no more arbitrary, in that it was constituted by God's *fiat*, than our own personal identity : for that also is constituted only by God's institution. If it be asked why it is just that I should be punished to-day, for a sin committed last year, our moral instincts answer : Because I am the same person who sinned. But the Pelagian objection urges that we are not one with Adam in any real sense, and therefore cannot be justly made guilty for Adam's sin. But, says Edwards : "What is personal identity ; and is it any less arbitrary than our federal identity with Adam ?" He answers : In no wise. Because our existence is dependent and successive. Its sustentation is a perpetual recreation. Its succession is a series of moments, of which one moment's existence does not cause or produce a succeeding moment's, not being coexistent with it, as cause and effect must always be. Hence, our continued identity is nothing else than a result of the will of God, sovereignly ordaining to restore our existence out of *nihil*, by a perpetual recreation, at the begin-

2. President Edwards' also inadequate.

ning of each new moment, and to cause in us a consciousness which seems to give sameness. I will venture the opinion that no man, not Edwards himself, ever satisfied himself, by this argument, that his being had not a true, intrinsic continuity, and a real, necessary identity, in itself. And it may usually be concluded, that when any scientific hypothesis conflicts thus with universal common sense, it is sophistical. In this case, a more correct Metaphysics has justified common sense. Our belief in our own identity is not derived from our remembered consciousness, but implied in it. Belief in identity is an *a priori*, and necessary conception. If it be not accepted as valid, there is no valid law of thought at all. When I speak of the I, a true and intrinsic continuity of being is necessarily implied. Nor is it true that because the moments of successive time are not connected, therefore the existence which we necessarily conceive of as flowing on in time, is disconnected in its *momenta*. We have seen that the notion of a perpetual recreation in the providential support of dependent being is unproved. Hence we repudiate this Edwardean speculation as worthless, and contradicted by our own intuitions.

Another attempt is made to establish a real identity of Adam's posterity with him, so as to lay a seeming basis for the imputation, by a class of theologians represented by Dr. S. J. Baird's "Elohim Revealed," who claim St. Augustine as of their party. They say, we are made guilty of Adam's sin, because "we sinned in him and fell with him," not merely in a putative and federal sense, but really and truly. Thus we are involved in a true and proper responsibility for the sin of Adam, because we were actually in him seminally, as our root. They teach that we become sinners in him, because the Nature sinned in him, and became guilty in him, as well as depraved; and this nature we have. Our nature they define to be that aggregate of forces, or attributes which constitute the human race what it is ; and this, they hold, is not an abstraction when regarded distinctly from all individual men, but an objective reality, not indeed a substance, yet an entity. This nature, which thus sinned, and became guilty and depraved in Adam's act, is transferred as a real germ, to every human being from him ; and hence depravity and guilt go along. This theory, while not exactly mediæval Realism, is certainly something near akin to it ; and the objections are of the same kind. That the phrase, human nature, expresses anything more than a complex conception of our thought, when abstracted from any one and every one human person, is untrue. This nature, they say, is the aggregate of all the forces which characterize man as man. But have those forces, each one, separate existence, as abstracted from all the individual men whom they characterize ? Has the attribute of risibility, e. g. separate existence from each and every risible

3. Dr. S. J. Baird's unsound.

being? Obviously not. How then can the aggregate of these attributes? Again: we cannot attach the idea of sin, morality, responsibility, and guilt to anything but a personal being. If the nature, along with which the depravity and responsibility are transmitted, has not personality, the theory does not help us at all. But if you give it personality, have you not gotten back to the common soul of Averroes, the half-way house of Pantheism? Third: if the imputation of Adam's guilt is grounded solely on the fact that the nature we bear sinned and was corrupted in him, must it not follow that Christ's human nature is also corrupt, inasmuch as it was made guilty? And indeed is not our obeying and atoning in Him, through the community of the nature that obeyed and atoned, precisely as real and intrinsic, as our sinning and corrupting ourselves in Adam? For these reasons, we must reject this explanation as untrue, if anything more be meant by it, than a strong way of stating the vital truth, that imputation is partly grounded on the fact Adam was the natural head of the race.

The fourth solution attempted for the great objection, brings us to the 11th question: the scheme of mediate imputation. The author and history of this are sufficiently stated by Turrettin. Placæus said that the imputation of Adam's sin was only mediate, and consequent upon our participation in total native depravity, which we derive by the great law, that like begets like. We, being thus depraved by nature, and, so to speak, endorsing his sin, by exhibiting the same spirit and committing similar acts, it is just in God to implicate us in the same punishments.

11. Mediate Imputation.

Let it be remarked, first, that the charge made in the National Synod of Charenton, was, that Placæus had denied all imputation of Adam's guilt, and had made original sin consist exclusively in subjective depravity. This is precisely what the Synod condemned. It was to evade this censure, that he invented the distinction between an "antecedent and immediate imputation" of Adam's guilt, which he denied, and a "mediate and subsequent imputation," which he professed to hold. It appears then, that this invention was no part of the theology, of the Reformed churches, and had never been heard of before. So thought Dr. A. Alexander, (Princeton Review, Oct. 1839.) The distinction seems to have been a ruse designed to shelter himself from censure, and to lay a snare for his accusers. It was unfortunate that they, like his chief opponent, Andrew Rivet, fell into it, by advocating the "antecedent and immediate imputation," as the only true view. It does not appear to me that those who, with Rivet, have laboured to show that this is the doctrine of the Reformed Symbols, have at all proved their point. The distinction is, like that of the Supralapsarian and Infralapsarian, an attempted over-refine-

ment, which should never have been made, which explained
nothing, and whose corollaries increased the difficulties of the
subject.

Turrettin, and those who assert the "antecedent immediate imputation," charge that the scheme of Placæus is only
Arminianism in disguise, and that it really leaves no imputation of Adam's guilt at all; inasmuch as they say it leaves the
personal guilt of the child's own subjective corruption, as the
real ground of all the penal infliction incurred by original sin.
While these objections seem just in part, I would add two
others: First. Placæus, like the lower Arminian, seems to
offer the fact that God should have extended the law "like begets
like," to man's moral nature, as an explanation of original sin.
This, as I urged before, is only obtruding the fact itself as
an explanation of the fact. To extend this law of nature to
responsible persons, is an ordination of God. The question is:
on what judicial basis does this ordination rest? Second:
Placæus' scheme is false to the facts of the case, in that it represents Adam's posterity as having, in God's view, an actual,
antecedent, depraved existence, at least for a moment, before
they passed therefor under condemnation; whereas the Scriptures represent them as beginning their existence condemned,
as well as depraved. See Eph. 2 : 3.

In opposition to this scheme, Turrettin states the view of
immediate imputation, which has since been
Immediate Imputa-   defined and asserted in its most rigid sharp-
tion.
ness by the Princeton school. It boldly
repudiates every sense in which we really or actually sinned in
Adam, and admits no other than merely the representative
sense of a positive covenant. It says that the guilt of Adam's
first sin, which was personally nobody's but Adam's own, is
sovereignly imputed to his posterity. Depravity of nature is a
part of the penalty of death, due to Adam's sin, and is visited
on Adam's children purely as the penal consequence of the
putative guilt they bear. For sin may be the punishment of
sin. Very true, after depravity of nature thus becomes personally theirs, it also brings an addition of personal guilt, for which
they are thenceforward punished, as well as for actual transgressions. The grounds for this statement are chiefly these
two: 1. That Rom. v : 12–20 asserts an exact parallel between
our federal relation to Adam and to Christ, so that, as the
imputation of Christ's righteousness to us, conceived as personally unrighteous, goes before procuring our justification,
and then all sanctifying grace is bestowed working personal
sanctification, as purchased by Christ's righteousness for us;
so, we must conceive Adam's guilt imputed to us, we being
conceived as, in the first instance, personally guiltless, but for
that guilt; and then depravity given us, working personal sin
and guilt, as the mischievous purchase of Adam's federal act

for us. And, as the parallel must be exact, if this view of original sin be rejected, then the view of justification must be modified " to suit;" making it consist first in an infusion of personal righteousness in the believer, and then the consequent accounting to us of Christ's righteousness. But that is precisely the Romish justification. 2. The connection between the second Adam and His believing people, in the covenant of grace, includes an imputation which is the exact counterpart of that of the first Adam's guilt. This is the two-fold imputation of our sins to Christ, and of His righteousness to us. But the former of these is strictly an imputation of *peccatum alienum* to Christ; and the latter is an immediate imputation of His righteousness to us. Hence, if we deny this scheme of antecedent, immediate imputation, we must give up salvation by imputed righteousness, and there remains no way of escape for sinners.

I propose to dwell upon this question a little more than its intrinsic importance deserves. Having pronounced it a useless and erroneous distinction, I might be expected to dismiss it with scant notice. But it receives an incidental importance from the important truths connected with it. These are, most prominently, the difficulties concerning the righteousness of the imputation of Adam's guilt, and also, the nature of imputation in general, justification, union to Christ, God's providence in visiting the sins of parents on children, (Ex. xx : 5,) and the manner in which the ethical reason should be treated, when it advances objections against revealed truth.

I sustain my position, then, that this distinction between " mediate," and "immediate" imputation should never have been made, by showing that it causelessly aggravates the difficulties of the awful doctrine of original sin, exaggerating needlessly the angles of a subject which is, at best, sufficiently mysterious; that the arguments by which the immediate imputation must be sustained misrepresent the doctrines of the spiritual union and justification; and especially, that it is false to the facts of the case, in a mode the counterpart of Placæus'. It represents the child of Adam as having a separate, undepraved, personal existence, at least for an instant; until from innocent, it becomes depraved by God's act, as a penal consequence of Adam's guilt imputed as *peccatum alienum* solely. *
But in fact, man now never has any personal existence at all, save a depraved existence. As he enters being condemned, so he enters it depraved. This over-refinement thus leads us to an error in the statement of fact, which matches that resulting from the opposite scheme. Does not this show very clearly, that the distinction should never have been made? And can those who advocate the "immediate, precedaneous imputation,"

---

* That the drift of the scheme makes the infant soul initially pure, may be seen from Hodge on Rom. v : 13. Theol. vol. 2, pp. 210, 203. Thornwell, vol. 1, pp. 346, 347, 349. Chalmers' Theo. Institutes, vol. 1, pp. 485 and 497.

after applauding the refutation of Placæus' scheme by the parallel argument, justly recoil from its application to themselves?

But it is argued, that since the imputation of our guilt to Christ is an immediate imputation of *peccatum alienum*, grounded in His community of nature with His people, the parallelism of the two doctrines shuts us up to a similar imputation of Adam's guilt to us. I reply: the cases indisputably differ in two vital respects. It may be asked if both covenants do not rest on the principle of imputation? The answer is, of course, yes; both covenants involve the principle, that God may justly transfer guilt from one moral agent to another, under certain conditions. But it does not follow, that He will do this under any conditions whatever.* Does any one suppose, for instance, that God would have condemned holy Gabriel for Satan's sin, without any assent, complicity or knowledge, on the part of the former? But we shall find that the cases of Adam and Christ are conditioned differently in two important respects. First: Christ's bearing our imputed guilt was conditioned on His own previous, voluntary consent. See Jno. x : 18. All theologians, so far as I know, regard this as essential to a just imputation of *peccatum alienum* directly to Him. See, for instance, Dr. Thornwell's Mission Sermon of 1856. "It" (Christ's covenant with the Father), "binds not by virtue of a right to command, but by virtue of a consent to obey." Butler's Analogy, pt. II, chap. 5, § 7. Owen on Justif. p. 194. Chalmers' Theol. Inst., vol. I, p. 498.) If a man were to hold that the Father would have made this imputation of another's guilt upon His Son, in spite of the Son's exercising His legitimate autocracy to refuse and decline it, I should consider that man past reasoning with. But Adam's infant children receive the imputation, when they are incapable of a rational option or assent about it. The other difference in the two cases, (which it seems amazing any one can overlook,) is the one pointed out in Rom. v : 16–19, and vi : 23. For the judgment was by one to condemnation; but the free gift (verse 15, "gift by grace") is of many offences unto justification." The imputation of Adam's sin was a transaction of strict, judicial righteousness; the other transaction was one of glorious, free grace. Now, can any righteous judge be imagined, who would allow himself equal latitude in his judicial convictions, which he claims in his acts of voluntary beneficence? Would not the righteous magistrate answer, that in condeming, he felt himself restricted by the exact merits of the parties; but that in giving, he felt himself free to transcend their merits, and bestow what his generous impulses prompted? It may be praiseworthy to dispense blessings above the deserts of the beneficiaries; it cannot be other than injustice to dis

---

* See Hodge's Theol. vol. 2, p. 196. Turrettin, Loc. ix, Qu. 9.

pense penalties beyond the deserts of the culprits. We thus find that the imputation to us from Adam, and from us to Christ, are unavoidably conditioned in different ways in part; in other respects they are analogous.

Our next point is founded on the admission, in which we are all agreed, that the imputation of Adam's guilt to us, is in part grounded, essentially, in the community of nature. But with which nature of Adam, are we united by the tie of race; the fallen, or the unfallen? Adam had no offspring until after he became a sinner. Then he begat even Seth, the father of the holy seed, "in his own likeness, after his image." (Gen. v : 3.) The Scriptures, from Job to Christ, assure us, that the thing which is born of the flesh is flesh. The race union obviously unites us with Adam fallen, in his corrupted nature. Hence we argue, that if this race union is one of the essential grounds of the imputation, it cannot be antecedent to that subjective corruption of nature, on which it is partly grounded. This reasoning has been felt as so forcible, that the advocates of immediate imputation have found it necessary to study evasions. One is, to argue that our federal union was with the nature of Adam unfallen, because the moment he fell, the covenant of works was abrogated. I reply: Not so; for if that covenant was then abrogated, it is strange that we are still suffering the penalty of its breach! The true statement is, that the broken covenant still remains in force, against all not in the second Adam, as a rule of condemnation; its breach by our representative only made it ineffectual as a rule of life. Another evasion is, to say, that our Nature had its representation and probation in Adam, before any of us had a personal existence, and while the nature in him was unfallen. I reply by asking: What sense do the words, "our Nature," have in this statement? Is it of the imputation of Adam's guilt to the Nature, that we are debating? or of its imputation to persons? Now, it is only a metaphor to speak of beings as bearing a relation to each other, while one of them, (Adam's descendant) is non-existent as yet. Only existing beings sustain actual relations. The only other sense, in which the relation between me and Adam had an actual being before I existed, was as it stood in God's decree. This may be illustrated by the counterpart doctrine of justification. The Conf. chap 11, § 4, says: "God did from all eternity decree to justify all the elect. * * * nevertheless they are not justified until the Holy Spirit doth, in due time, actually apply Christ unto them." By parity of reasoning I hold, that God did, from all eternity, decree to condemn all men federally connected with Adam in his fall; nevertheless, they are not condemned actually, until they actually begin to exist in natural and federal union with their fallen head. But this is almost a truism.

Hence we pass to a corresponding argument from the de-

pendence of the actual imputation of Christ's righteousness
to us upon a certain union between Him and us. All again
admit this. What species of union is it? The spiritual union.
This question and answer, like the touch-stone, reveal the
unsoundness of the opposing logic. The student will remember how it argues: That inasmuch as we must make an exact
parallel between the imputation of Adam's guilt and Christ's
righteousness, we must hold that the imputing of the guilt of
Adam's first sin precedaneously and immediately as solely
peccatum alienum must go before, upon the offspring conceived
as so far personally innocent: and then, we must consider his
subjective depravity as following that putative sentence, and as
the penal result thereof. Else, the symmetry of the two cases
will lead us from Placæus' ground, to conceive of justification
thus: that God finds in the sinner an inherent righteousness,
which mediates the imputation to him of the subsequent righteousness of Christ for his full acceptance. But this is virtually
the vicious, Popish view of justification. True, I reply: this
explodes Placæus: but it also explodes their own scheme.
For if we make justification correspond, by an exact symmetry, to the scheme of their "immediate, antecedent imputation," then we must get this doctrine of justification: viz.
The sinner, while still in his depravity, get's Christ's righteousness directly, gratuitously and antecedently, imputed to him;
and then, as part of the consequent reward of that imputed
merit, has regeneration wrought, infusing the sanctified nature
of his redeeming Head into his soul. But as faith is in order
to justification, this speculation must lead us to the following
order. First, the convicted sinner, while unrenewed, exercises
the initial saving faith. Second, he is thereupon justified.
Third, he then procures, as one of the fruits of the reconciliation, a holy heart, like his Saviour's. Now, a moderate tinc-
ture of theology will teach any one that this is precisely the
Arminian Theory of justification. And a little reflection will
show, that he who makes faith precede regeneration in the
order of causation, must, if consistent, be a synergist. Thus it
appears that this scheme cuts off the Calvinistic doctrine of
justification as rigidly as it does Placæus. That doctrine, as
none have stated more clearly than Dr. Hodge, [as Theol. vol.
2, p. 195,] distinguishes between inherent and legal righteousness. The latter no justified sinner has of his own, either at
the moment he is justified, or ever after. The former, every
believer partakes, through the grace of effectual calling, in
order to the faith by which he receives justification. All intelligent Calvinists, so far as I know, teach that the application of
redemption begins with effectual calling. The order they give
is this: First, regeneration, implanting Christ's spiritual life, by
which the sinner is enabled to believe: Second, faith, and
then justification. In short, the believer is not first justified in

order to become a partaker of Christ's nature. He is made a partaker of that nature, in order to be justified. The vital union is both legal and spiritual: community in Christ's righteousness is one fruit; holy living is the other.

Once more: All Calvinists will concur with Dr. Hodge in stating, [Theol. vol. 2, pp. 196, 211], that since the ground of the imputation of Adam's guilt to us is the union of nature, the consequences of the fall come on us in the same order as on Adam. But now, I ask, was Adam's depravity solely a penal consequence of his first transgression? Surely not; for unless a depraved motive had prompted his act, it would not have carried guilt. The intention of the crime is what qualifies the act as criminal. In Adam's case, the subjective depravation (self-induced) and the guilt, were simultaneous and mutually involved. Then, according to the concession made, the scheme of immediate, precedaneous imputation is surrendered. We return, then, to the consistent statement with which the discussion of original sin began: That the federal and representative union between Adam and his offspring, in the covenant of works, was designed to result thus: whatever legal *status*, and whatever moral character Adam should win for himself under his probation, that *status*, and that character each of his children by nature should inherit, on entering his existence.

I have not appealed to the illustrative cases in which God visits the iniquities of parents on their children; because I do not regard them as strictly parallel to our federal union with Adam. Our parents now are not acting for us under a covenant of works. In this sense they are not our federal representatives, as Adam was. But as the attempt has been made to wield these cases against me, I willingly meet them. It has been said, for instance, that Achan's infant children, incapable of the sin of political treason and sacrilege, were put to death for their father's guilt. Does any one suppose, that they would have died by God's order, if they had been as pure before Him, as the humanity of the infant Jesus? Hardly! The doctrine as taught by God, (Deut. v : 9 ; Matt. xxiii : 32–35) is, that He now visits the guilt of sinful parents on sinful children. The Pharisees' filling up, by their own sins, the measure of their fathers, was the condition of their inheriting the penalty of all the righteous blood shed from Abel to Zacharias. This Turrettin teaches, Loc. ix : Qu, 9, against the interest of his own erroneous logic. Thus, we find, in this extensive class of providential dealings, cases of what Dr. Hodge correctly deems, true imputation. But the conditions are not identical with those which he claims for Adam's case.

I have said that the attempts made by Rivet and other later divines, to prove that their doctrine of immediate, precedaneous imputation is that of the Reformed Churches and symbols, are vain. My conviction is, that this scheme, like the supralapsarian, is a novelty and an over-refinement, alien to the true current of the earlier Reformed theology, and some of Placæus' day were betrayed into the exaggeration by the snare set for them by his astuteness, and their own over-zeal to expose him. I beg leave to advance one or two witnesses in support. Stapfer, who has been erroneously quoted, as on Placæus' side, says: (Vol. iv; ch. xvii: § 78. Note.) "The whole controversy they" (impugners of the justice of imputation,) "have with us about this matter, evidently arises from this: that they suppose the mediate and the immediate imputation are distinguished one from the other, not only in the manner of conception, but in reality. And so indeed, they consider imputation only as immediate, and abstractedly from the mediate, when yet our divines suppose that neither ought to be considered separately from the other. Therefore I choose not to use any such distinction. * * * While I have been writing this note, I have consulted all the systems of divinity which I have by me, that I might see what was the true and genuine opinion of our chief divines in this affair, and I found they were of the same mind with me." Markius, in DeMoor, says: If Placæus meant nothing more by mediate imputation, than that "*hominum natorum actualem punitionem ulteriorem non fieri nudo intuitu Adamicæ transgressionis, absque interveniente etiam propria corruptione, et fluentibus hinc sceleribus variis, neminem orthodoxonem posset habere obloquentem.*" DeMoor quotes Vogelsang, (Com. vol. iii: p. 275,) as saying: "*Certe neminem sempiterna subire supplicia propter inobedientia protoplasti, nisi mediante cognata perversitate.*" Calvin in his Inst. but more distinctly in his exposition of Rom. v: 12–19, teaches just the view I have given. This much belaboured passage has been often claimed, as clearly teaching the immediate, antecedent imputation. Thus Dr. Hodge assumes. He claims that the correct interpretation of this passage, demands his view of the exact identity of the two imputations, in the Covenant of works, and of grace. He then, reasoning in a circle, defends his interpretation chiefly from the assumed premise of that identtiy. The details of his exposition seem to be more akin to those of the Socinian expositors, and of Whitby, than of the old Reformed. To me it appears, that Calvin shows a truer insight into the scope of the Apostle's discourse, and gives more satisfactory meanings of the particular phrases. The question is urged: Since Paul illustrates justification by original sin, must we not suppose an exact parallel between the illustration and the thing illustrated? I reply: We must suppose so real a resemblance as to make the illustration a fair one; but this does not include an exact parallel. Few scriptural illustrations present an exact one. I have showed that Dr. Hodge's effort here to maintain one, is deceptive; and that if it were faithfully carried out, it would land us all in Arminianism, (where Whitby stood). The

Apostle himself, in verse 13–17, makes exceptions to the exactness of his own parallel! In view of these facts, and of the silence of our Confession touching the exaggerated scheme, we treat the charge that we are making a defection from Calvinism by preferring the old, Calvinistic doctrine to the new one of Princeton, with the entire indifference it deserves.

But it is time to return to the rationalistic objection against the justice of imputation, which has been the occasion of the speculations reviewed. (See p. 338,). Dr. Hodge seems to dispose of this objection, by simply disregarding it. The amount of satisfaction he offers to the recalcitrant reason, is: God makes this immediate imputation, and therefore it must be right, whatever reason says. Whether this is wise, or prudent, or just logic, we shall see. All the other writers I have read, who incline to the extreme view, betray a profound sense of this difficulty, by their resort to uneasy expedients to evade it. (We have seen those of Wesley and of Edwards: who belong to different schools of opinion from Turrettin, and from each other). But these evasions, if they satisfy themselves, do not satisfy each other. That adopted by Dr. Hodge, from Turrettin, (Loc. ix : Qu. 9 : § 14 ; Theology, Vol. ii : p. 211), is, that the penalty we incur from Adam's imputed guilt is, (a) privative, and (b), positive. The former, involving simply the lack of original righteousness, is visited on us by the immediate, precedaneous imputation. The latter, carrying spiritual death and all positive miseries, is imputed mediately. Though the second inseparably follows the first, yet they are to be thus distinguished. Dr. Thornwell effectually explodes this evasion for us. (Works, Vol. 1 : p. 333). He asks : if the child of Adam is initially pure, is there any less difficulty in a just and Holy God's treating him as a sinner, than in His causing him to be a sinner? And if this penal treatment (on imputation of *peccatum alienum*) does cause him to be a sinner, have we not both the difficulties on our hands? For, second: the distinction between a privative, and a positive depravation is, for a Calvinist, utterly inconsistent. Turrettin, when arguing against Pelagians and Papists, has himself proved that the privative state of a lack of original righteousness is, *ipso facto*, positive depravity. So says common sense. That a rational creature of God, knowing His perfections, and His own accountability, should fail to love and reverence Him, is itself to be in a positively unholy state. I add, third, that even if the distinction were allowed, yet if from the privative, the positive depravation unavoidably and naturally follows, then the same judicial act which inflicts the one has also inflicted the other. The executioner, who swings off the felon to be hanged, from the platform of the gibbet, does thereby choke him to death.

Dr. Thornwell, in turn, after looking the doctrine of immediate precedaneous imputation steadily in the face, finds himself constrained to seek a palliation for its difficulty, in the same direction from which he had sought to recall Dr. S. J. Baird a few years before. On pp. 349, 350, of his Lectures, he says: "On these grounds I am free to confess, that I cannot escape from the doctrine, however mysterious, of a generic unity in man, as the true basis of the representative economy in the covenant of works. The human race is not an aggregate of independent atoms, but constitutes an organic whole, with a common life springing from a common ground. * * * There is in man what we may call a common nature. That common nature is not a mere generalization of logic, but a substantive reality." Thus, the stress of the rationalistic objection appears to him so heavy, that it drives him to the solution he had before refuted. For the reasons stated on p. 339, this resort appears to me invalid. It is true, Adam was "the root of all mankind." This race unity is, as our Confession states, an all-important condition of the federal union. But apart from each human person, we see in this race-unity no moral, and still less any personal entity, to be the subject of responsibility.

The difficulty then recurs: Is the doctrine of original sin founded on that which seems to the natural conscience an intrinsic injustice, punishing innocent persons, without their consent, for another man's sin? Let the student bear in mind, that we have no intention of denying the mysteriousness of the divine dispensation of the fall of our race in their first father. It is an inscrutable providence. But while the view I sustain, leaves it enveloped in a mystery which the wisest and best of us most clearly see will never be solved in this world; the advantage I claim is, that it leaves the doctrine in a state where no man can convict it of injustice. This advantage appears in two ways. First: man reasons chiefly by parallel instances; his reasoning is comparison. Consequently, in a case wholly unique, where there is no parallel, while he may not comprehend, he cannot convict of injustice. The case is above his grasp; he has no experimental scales in which to weigh it. Second: our fall in Adam, as properly stated, lacks the essential point wherein the caviller finds, in the instance of his pretended parallel, the intrinsic injustice. But it is evident, on consideration, that, upon the theory of immediate imputation, that essential point is yielded to the caviller. It is, that the innocent is punished, without his consent, for the guilty. Let us suppose the case usually cited for illustration, the peaceful citizen charged, under human laws, with the putative guilt of a murder to which he had not consented. This injustice is indisputable. But let us see what is involved in the fact of personal innocency in this case; for there lies the basis of our moral judgment about it. It means that this peaceful citizen has complied with the prohibitory laws of his country, in refraining from all injury to others' lives. But a law, sustained by sanction, is of the nature of a covenant with the citizens. The man who has actually kept the law has thereby earned his covenanted title to immunity. This is what this man means, by claiming his innocency. He has been invested by the covenant of the law itself, with this title to immunity, before the putative murder was committed, and he can now be righteously divested of this title only by his own transgression. To impute to this man now, the guilt of *peccatum alienum*, divests him of this pre-existent righteous title to immunity. There is the impregnable ground upon which he will resist the charge.

Now, let us represent imputation as the Scriptures do, and the sinner fallen in Adam has no such argument to use. He does not approach the judicial issue clothed with a pre-existing, personal title to favour, derived from a previous, personal rectitude under a covenant of works. For, previous to his condemnation in Adam, he has no personal, innocent existence, not for one moment, not even in any correct order of thought; for he has had no actual existence at all. He enters existence depraved, as he enters it guilty; he enters it guilty as he enters it depraved. This is the amount of his federal union with Adam; that the offspring shall have, *ab initio*, the same legal *status* and moral nature, which his head determined for himself, by his acts while under probation. This statement is strictly correspondent to the facts revealed and experienced. And it has this great advantage, that it leaves the sinner, fallen in Adam, no pretext to complain that he has been stripped of any just personal title to immunity, by thus bringing him under putative guilt. For he had no such personal title to be stripped of, seeing he had no personal existence at all, prior to the depravity and guilt. This dispensation of God, then, remains unique, without any parallel in any human jurisprudence. It is solemn, mysterious, awful; but it is placed where it is impossible to convict it of injustice on God's part. That His exercise of His sovereignty in this strange dispensation is holy, righteous, benevolent, and wise, we have this sufficient proof; that He has given His own Son, in free grace, to repair the mischiefs which human sin causes under the case. Let us remember, that the covenant of paradise was liberal, equitable, and splendidly beneficent in its own character. Its failure was exclusively man's and Satan's fault. God has not been the efficient of any man's sin or depravation, but only the permissive Disposer: the only efficients of both evils have been men and their spiritual seducers. In the great, gospel Remedy, God is real Efficient.

12. That one's view of original sin will be decisive of his whole system of theology, is obvious from the familiar truth; that the remedy is determined by the disease. As is the *diagnosis*, so will be the medical treatment. If the Pelagian view of human nature prevails, the corresponding view of its regen-

eration must prevail. Thus, faith, repentance, and the other essential graces of the new life, will be traced to the human will as their source. Then, the office-work of the Spirit will be degraded; and the Socinian result, which denies His personality will be natural. The analysis of Nestorianism will show us also, how the same view of human nature and of free-agency, will modify the doctrine of the Hypostatic Union, preparing the way for a belief in a merely human Christ.

But if the scriptural doctrines of native depravity and federal representation be firmly held, then there will follow, as reasonable corollaries, all the points of the Calvinistic, or Augustinian scheme, supernatural regeneration, unconditional election, perseverance in grace, divinity of Christ, and personality and divinity of the Holy Ghost.

LECTURE XXX.

LAW.

SYLLABUS.

1. In what senses is the word Law used in Scripture?
See Concordances and Lexicons.
2. Is the law of God written on the natural conscience intuitively? What the authority of this natural law? Is the Decalogue of Moral or of Positive obligation?
See Turrettin, Loc. ix, Qu. 1, 2. Sensualistic Philosophy of 19th Cent., ch. 12. Dick, Lect. 102.
3. If the Covenant of Works is now inapplicable for us, what uses has the law in a plan of salvation by grace?
Turrettin, Qu. 22, 25. Calvin, bk. ii, ch. 7. Ridgely, Qu. 94–97.
4. Recite the origin of the Decalogue. How is it divided? What are the principles on which it is to be interpreted?
Calvin, bk. ii, ch. 8. Turrettin, Qu, 5, 6. Dick, Lect. 102, 103. Ridgeley, Qu. 98, 99.
5. Is the Decalogue a perfect rule of life? Did Christ abrogate or amend any part of it?
Turrettin, Qu. 3, 4. Dick as above. Dr. Ashbel Green's Lect. 34–36, on Shorter Catechism.

THE word "Law," (תּוֹרָה, νόμος) is employed in the Scripture with a certain latitude of meaning, but always carrying the force of meaning contained in the general idea of a regulative principle. First, it sometimes expresses the whole of Revelation, as in Ps. i : 2. Second, the whole Old Testament, as in Jno. x : 34. Third, frequently the Pentateuch, as in Luke xxiv : 44. Fourth, the preceptive moral law (Prov. xxviii : 4; Rom. ii : 14. Fifth, the ceremonial code, as in Heb. x : 1. Sixth, the decalogue, Matt. xxii : 36–40. Seventh, a ruling power in our nature, as in Rom. vii : 23. Eighth, the covenant of works, Rom. vi : 14. By the Law, in the following discussions, we intend the preceptive moral law, as epitomized in the decalogue.

1. Definitions.

The student will be prepared to expect my answer to the second point, from what has been taught of the eternity of moral distinctions. These are intrinsic in that class of acts. They are not instituted solely by the positive will of God, but are enjoined by that will because His infinite mind saw them to be intrinsic and eternal. In a word: Duties are not obligatory and right solely because God has commanded them; but He has commanded them because they are right. Hence, we confidently expect to find the natural powers of reason and conscience in man impressed with the moral distinction, and pronouncing it intuitively.

2. Moral Distinction Intrinsic.

(a.) From the fact that the Scriptures represent God Himself, at least in one particular, as bound by this distinction of right and wrong, "God cannot lie;" that is, the eternal perfections of His own mind so regulate His own volitions that His will certainly, yet freely, refuses all error. See also 2 Tim. ii : 13.

(b.) The very nature of a creature implies rightful subjection to a Creator; its denial would be utter contradiction. Thus the law of our reason teaches us, that the creature existing, these moral relations cannot but exist, whether God has published them in express precepts, or not.

(c.) If these moral distinctions owed their origin solely to God's positive will, no distinction could be drawn between moral and positive precepts. The prohibition, " Thou shall not bear false witness," would be exactly like this : " Thou shalt not seethe a kid in its mother's milk." But there is a distinction between the two classes, recognized by God and our reason. 'Judgment, mercy, and truth,' are pronounced ' weightier matters of the law,' compared with tithing mint, anise, and cummin.

(d.) If there were no cause, save God's mere will, why moral distinctions were drawn as they are, He might have made treachery a virtue, and truth a crime, &c. Against this every moral intuition revolts. Why might not God have done this ? The only answer is, that His own unchangeable moral perfections made it impossible. Just so; it is admitted that the basis of the moral distinction is a *priori* to all volition of God; which is substantially my proposition. And last, (e) and most conclusively : If God's mere positive volition made an act of the creature morally right, then of course God must be morally right in entertaining that volition. For the moral character of volitions depends wholly on that of the principles which prompt them. So that, we see, if there were no moral distinction *a priori* to God's mere will, God could have no moral character in acts of His will.

The moral distinction being then intrinsic and eternal, it follows that the intuition and feeling of its obligation must be one of the natural endow-

Consequences.

ments of the rational creature made in God's image. This obligation must be recognized by man's conscience as natural and moral, and not merely positive. To this agree the Scriptures, Rom. i : 19–21 ; ii : 14, 15 ; Acts xiv : 17. And these declarations are confirmed by the *consensus populi* upon the existence of a moral obligation, and its main outlines, by a multitude of the facts of our consciousness, by the admissions of Pagans. But here, the distinction so clearly made between moral *principia* and *conclusiones*, must be noted. In some cases of moral obligation, the perception and verdict of conscience are immediate. In other cases, they are deductive. Should a creature obey its Creator? To this the sane reason answers intuitively, Yes. Should the borrower pay any hire for the use of money? To this the mind can only answer deductively ; certain premises must be known to the understanding, from which the moral answer must be by deduction drawn.

If the moral distinction is thus intrinsic in acts, unchangeable in God, and natural in man, the preceptive law receives a new dignity, immutability, and sacredness. Then it follows, also, that the natural conscience is God's viceregent in man ; and its dictates must be obeyed, or guilt arises. But when we remember that the light in man's conscience is imperfect, we see that it is not true that this faculty is a sufficient rule of duty. That rule is found in God's precepts alone. The seeming paradox arising out of the dictate of an ill-informed conscience has been already considered, in lecture X.

It has beeen asked, if the Law can no longer be a covenant of life to fallen sinners, what place and use can it properly have in a plan of salvation by grace? You are aware that there have been, in the Church, errorists called Antinomians, who, in fact, sought to exclude the law from their system, asserting that since it is no longer a term of life, since it has been fully satisfied both in its preceptive and penal demands by the believer's divine Substitute, it can have no binding force upon, and no application to him. But the view I have given of the Law, as the necessary and unchanging expression of God's rectitude, shows that its authority over moral creatures is unavoidable. If God reveals Himself to them, He cannot but reveal Himself as He is. Just these precepts are the inevitable expression of a will guided by immutable perfections. It is therefore simply impossible that any dispensation, of whatever mercy or grace, could have the effect of abrogating righteous obligation over God's saints. God's mercy through a Redeemer satisfying justice, may lift off the curse of the law for transgression ; but it is impossible that it should abrogate rightful authority. First, the Law must remain, under every dispensation, the authoritative declaration of God's character.

3. Uses of Law under Covenant of Grace—The Law Immutable.

23*

A second essential use of the Law under the New Covenant, is that which Gal. iii : 24 states : " The
Law was our schoolmaster to bring us unto
Christ." By showing us our penal debt, and
the high terms of the covenant of works, now impossible for
the sinner to fulfill, it prepares his soul to submit to the righteousness of the Redeemer. A third, and equally essential use
appears to the believer, after his adoption. He is " chosen in
Christ that he should be holy " ; "redeemed from all iniquity to
be Christ's peculiar people, zealous of good works." This
great end, the believer's sanctification, can only be attained in
practice, by giving him a holy rule of conduct. Such a rule is
the Law. It is to be as assiduously observed, as the guide to
that holiness which is the fruit of adoption, as though its
observance could earn adoption. A fourth important purpose
of the publication of the Law in the Church, appears in this ;
that its precepts restrain the aboundings of sin. They partially
instruct the consciences even of the unrenewed. They guide
secular laws, and thus lay a foundation for a wholesome civil
society. And last : the publication of the Law is preparatory
for that use which God will make of it in the Judgment Day,
for the conviction of His enemies. He is now, in every such
message, preparing to close the mouths of the disobedient in
that day.

For these reasons, the preaching and expounding of
the Law is to be kept up diligently, in every gospel
Church

The whole decalogue is found written out in full, in two
places of the Bible ; besides a number of
other places, where one or more of the precepts is cited. These places are Exodus
xx : 2 to 17, and Deut. v : 6 to 21. It is the doctrine of the Cate
chism, that these " Ten Words " were intended to be a summary
of man's whole duty. Why, it may be asked, is so much made
of them ? Why not make equal account of some few verses
taken from the Proverbs, or the Sermon on the Mount? We
reply : the manner of their publication plainly showed that
God intended to give them the peculiar importance we assign
them. They were uttered by Him, to His Church, in an audible voice, εἰς διαταγὰς ἀγγέλων, (Acts vii : 53), with the terrible
adjuncts of clouds, and thunders, and lightnings, and the sound
of a trumpet. They were the only parts of Revelation thus
spoken. " These words Jehovah spake unto all your assembly
in the mount, out of the midst of the fire, of the cloud, and
the thick darkness ; with a great voice ; and He added no
more," Deut. v : 22. None of the ceremonial nor civic rules
were thus distinguished. These ten precepts were then graven
by God Himself on two tables of stone ; the imperishable
material signifying the perpetuity of the laws—and these tab-

Marginalia:

The Law convicts of our need of Christ, &c.

4. Decalogue God's Summary of Duty.

les were to be kept among the most sacred things of their religion. Christ, in giving that summary of man's duty into the two precepts of love to God, and love to man, is evidently abridging the Decalogue. He says that on these two abridged commands, hang all the law and the prophets. Therefore all the Old Testament hangs on the Decalogue, of which these two are the epitome. These are the grounds, together with the obvious comprehensiveness and perfection of the ten precepts, (which will be evinced in their exposition) on which the Jewish and Christian Churches have always held this Decalogue to be designed as the epitome of the whole Law.

Expositors have not been entirely agreed in the division of **How Divided ?** the Decalogue. Some would have it, that five precepts belonged to the first table, and five to the second. This opinion seems to be dictated only by a fondness for mechanical symmetry. It is now generally held, that four precepts composed the first table, and six the second. This is the natural division. Of the duties enjoined in the first four, God is the direct object : of those inculcated in the last six, man is the direct object. Thus we conform our division to our Saviour's summary, love to God and love to man. Some have supposed that they found an evidence of this division in the words of the Apostle Paul, when he calls the fifth the "first commandment with promise." It is observed that this is not the first containing a promise, if the first table be included; whence they suppose that the Apostle calls it first, with reference to the second table, at the head of which it stood.

It remains that we settle the principles upon which the **Rules of Interpreta-** decalogue is to be interpreted and applied. **tion—The Precepts are** If it is an epitome of duty, it contains of **Spiritual.** course more than the formal propositions in which it is verbally expressed : 1st. The most important of those principles is that announced by St. Paul in the 7th of Romans : 'The Law is spiritual.' It claims to regulate, not only the acts, but the desires and thoughts, the inner as well as the outer man. For farther proof, note that Christ, in His exposition (Matt. v,) expressly extends the prohibitions to the secret motions of the heart towards sin. Causeless anger is declared to be the soul's sin of murder; lust is the soul's adultery; coveting, as Paul indicates, is the soul's theft. I prove the same rule from this : that Christ resolves all duties into love, which is an inward state of affection. And last, the same rule must follow from the spiritual nature of the God whose law it is. He claims to be the 'Searcher of Hearts.' He judgeth not by the outward appearance. 'He requireth truth in the inward parts.' The law of such a being must apply chiefly to the inward affections, as our reason approves.

2d. In each precept, the chief duty or sin is taken as

The Sin or Duty Named is Representative. representative of the various lesser duties or sins of that class; and the overt act is taken as representative of all related affections, and under it they are all enjoined or forbidden. Thus, our Saviour teaches us that under the head of murder, angry thoughts and abusive words are also forbidden. We are authorized by such examples to conclude that under the one precept, 'Thou shalt not kill,' all offences against our fellow-men's lives, safety, and personal welfare, are forbidden. So of the other commandments. This follows from the fact that the decalogue is a summary.

3rd. To command a given class of duties plainly implies a prohibition of the opposite class of sins, and *vice versa*. Thus: Injuries against the life and person of fellows are forbidden; this implies the obligation of active efforts to protect them, as we have opportunity. This follows from the practical scope of the law. What is the design or intent of the sixth commandment? Obviously to secure our fellows the enjoyment of life and safety. If, then, the obligation is adequate to the practical end, it must include active efforts to promote, as well as refraining from injuring, that end. This is confirmed by our Saviour's summation: "Thou shalt love thy neighbour as thyself." Hence, while the 6th commandment says, "Thou shalt not kill;" it also means, "Thou shalt save thy fellow from killing."

Commandment Implied in Prohibition, &c.

4th. When anything is commanded or forbidden, the regular and necessary means and incitements thereto are also commanded or forbidden. And when any duty of one party towards another is enjoined, the relative state or duty thereto is also enjoined on the second party towards the first.

Means Included in Duties.

5th. The precepts of the first table, containing duties towards God, are superior in obligation to the second table, towards man. See Luke xiv : 26; Matt. v : 37; Acts iv : 19; Eph. vi : 1. Whenever the authority of man clashes with that of God, the former must therefore give way. But moral duties, though they be duties of the second table, are superior to mere positive or ceremonial duties of the first table. See Matt. xii : 7; Prov. xxi : 3.

God before Man: Moral Precepts before Positive.

6th. The prohibitory precepts bind us equally at all times; the mandatory, only when the proper objects of the duty are present. The precept "Thou shalt not kill," binds at every moment; the command, "Honour thy father and mother," only binds when we bear suitable relations to some superior.

Prohibitions Perpetual, &c.

Many Socinians and Abolitionists, and some Papists, in order to support favourite prejudices, strenuously assert that the moral law, as given to the Jews, was an imperfect rule, and was completed and perfected by Jesus Christ. We

5. The Law Perfect—Christ made no Changes of Substance, because Immutable.

grant, indeed, that Christ freed this law from the corrupt glosses
of tradition, and that He showed the true extent of its application. But we deny that He made any change or substantial
addition. We admit that He carried it farther in the way of
detail, but we deny that He corrected anything of its principle.
These errorists pretend to claim this as an honour to Christ
and His mission, and as evincing His superiority over Moses.
First: They hereby do Him dishonour. For the decalogue
is as much Christ's law as the Sermon on the Mount. He was
the authoritative agent for giving both. For it was "with the
Angel which spake unto him in Mount Sinai," (Christ, Acts vii:
38) that Moses "received these lively oracles to give unto us."
Second: It would be dishonorable to a perfect God to suppose
that He would reveal to His chosen people, as a rule of righteousness, a law which allowed some sin. Then, all the holiness
produced under that law was spurious. Third: God forbade that
the law should receive addition. Deut. iv : 2; xii: 32. Fourth:
Christ honoured this law, declared it everlasting and unchangeable, and said that He came not to destroy, but to fulfil it.
Fifth: Christ says that on His abridgments of this law hang all
the law and the prophets. And last: St. Paul, having resolved
the precepts of this decalogue into the one principle of love
(Rom. xiii : 9), verse 10th says: "Love is fulfilling of the law."
This is said by this minister of the new dispensation. And
both the Old and New Testaments assert the perfection of this
Old Testament law. See Ps. xix: 7; Rom. vii: 12; Ps. cxix: 96.

In further support of this view, I remark that the very particulars in which it is pretended Jesus amend-
ed, softened, and completed the moral law,
are stated just as distinctly, although perhaps
not as forcibly in all cases, by Moses and the prophets, in their
expositions of the decalogue. E. g., the love of enemies, in
Matt. v : 44; see it in Exod. xxiii : 4, 5, Levit. xix : 18. The
great laws of love of Matt. xxii : 37, &c.; see Deut. vi : 4, 5,
Levit. xix : 18. The command of benevolence to strangers in
Luke x : 36, 37: see it in Levit. xxiv : 22, xxv : 35, Deut. x :
19. The spiritual interpretation of the law, as embracing not
only outward acts, but the thoughts and desires of the heart;
see Levit. xix : 17, 18, Deut. xi : 13, Ps. xxiv : 4, li : 6. Christ's
new commandment (Jno. xiii : 34) was only "the old command
renewed," only a re-enactment with an additional motive:
Christ's love for us. Christ, in His Sermon on the Mount, then,
and other places, rebukes and corrects, not the law itself, nor
the Old Testament interpretations of the law, but the erroneous
and wicked corruptions foisted upon it by traditions and Pharisaic glosses. The moral law could not be completed, because
it is as perfect as God, of whose character it is the impress
and transcript. It cannot be abrogated or relaxed, because
it is as immutable as He.

*Precepts of New Tes-
tament also in Old.*

LECTURE XXXI.
THE FIRST TABLE. (COMMANDMENTS
1st, 2nd, 3d.)

IN the exposition of the precepts, I do not propose to detain you with those ordinary particulars which you may find in your catechisms and text-books. I would, once for all, refer you to those authorities, especially for answers to the question, what each commandment especially enjoins and prohibits. My chief aim, in the few, disjointed discussions which time will allow, is to enter into a few of the more disputed and more important questions of morals and ecclesiastical usage, which now agitate society and the Church.

1. The affirmative and negative obligations of the 1st

    Scope of the 1st Commandment.

Commandment all depend upon the great truth of God's exclusive unity, which we have proved from reason and Scripture. The duty of "having Him for our God" may be said to be the summary of almost all the commands of love, reverence and obedience, which so abound in the Scriptures. But we may say that it includes especially, under the general idea of rendering Him all the affection and service which our nature, His character, and our relations to Him require; the following: The duty, (a) of loving Him supremely. (See Matt. xxii : 37). (b) Of regulating all our moral acts by His revealed will. Matt. xxviii : 20. (c) Of owning and acknowledging Him publicly. Josh. xxiv : 22. (d) Of promoting His cause and glory in all suitable ways. 1 Cor. x : 31. (e) Of rendering to Him such acts of religious worship as He may see fit to demand. Ps. xxix : 2. (f) Of thanking Him for His benefits. Ps. cvi : 1. (g) Of trusting to His promises. Is. xxvi : 4. (h) Of submitting to His chastisements. 1 Pet. v : 6. (i) Fearing His anger. Ps. lxxxvi : 11. (j) Repenting of having sinned against Him, Acts xvii : 30, and in short, (k) Choosing Him as the portion and eternal inheritance of our souls. Ps. lxxiiii : 25 ; xvii : 15.

    The most current breach of this commandment in nomi-

358

Sin of Idolatrous Affections. nally Christian communities, is doubtless the sin of inordinate affections. Scripture brands these as idolatry, or the worshipping of another than the true God, especially in the case of covetousness; (Eph. v : 5; Col. iii : 5; Job xxxi : 24–28.) and parity of reasoning extends the teaching to all other inordinate desires. We conceive formal idolatry, as that of the Hindoo, a very foolish and flagrant thing; we palliate this spiritual idolatry of passions. God classes them together, in order to show us the enormity of the latter. What then is it, that constitutes the "having of God for our God?" It includes, (a) Love for Him stronger than all other affections. (b) Trusting Him, as our highest portion aud source of happiness. (c) Obeying and serving Him supremely. (d) Worshipping Him as He requires. Now that thing to which we render these regards and services, is our God, whether it be gold, fame, power, pleasure, or friends.

2. Romish Idolatry. Founded on Creature Mediation. Rome's worship of saints and angels is founded on her assertion of their heavenly mediation for us, which she asserts, against 1 Tim. ii : 5. You will find this error discussed and refuted in your Senior year, when we come to treat and defend the sole mediation of the Lord Jesus Christ. I shall now anticipate that conclusion, as one basis of my denial of the worship of creatures; only adding that, if you feel curiosity concerning Rome's defence of it, you may find her arguments in the places cited from the documents of the Council of Trent.

Arguments against Saint Worship. But as there is no heavenly mediation of angels or saints, we argue the more, that no intelligent worship can be paid them, without idolatry. (a) Because there are no examples nor precepts foɪ it in the Bible. The honour due superiors is social and political; between which and religious worship, there is a fundamental difference. In all the cases cited by Rome, of the worshipping of creature-angels, there was only a hospitable and deferential obeisance to persons supposed to be dignified strangers and human beings. Where there was worship proper, it was always the Angel of the Covenant, the Son of God, who was worshipped. Compare Gen. xviii : 2, and xix : 1, with Gen. xviii : 22, 23, we learn that of the persons to whom Abraham did social obeisance as respectable guests and human beings, the one to whom Abraham actually prayed, was the Jëhovah-Christ; and the others were creature-angels in human form. But the student is referred to the argument on the pre-existence of Christ, Lect. xvii; where it is proved that all these cases of worship of the "angel," were cases of homage offered to Christ.

(b) Inspired saints and creature-angels are represented in every case, as repudiating proper religious worship, when attempted towards them, with holy abhorrence. See Matt. iv : 10; Acts xiv : 13–15; Rev. xix : 10; xxii : 9.

Rome herself acknowledges, (Cat. Rom. Pt. III, Ch. 2, Qu.

Δουλέια also Idola- 4, or Pt. IV, Ch. 6, Qu. 3), it would be idolatrous. try to worship creatures with the same sort
of worship paid to God. Here then, their
doctors bring in their distinction of λατρεία and δουλεία to justify themselves. This distinction is utterly vain and empty.
Because first, the usage neither of classic nor biblical Greek
justifies it; nor that of the primitive Fathers. The one word,
as much as the other, is used of the worship peculiar to God
Himself. See Matt. vi : 24; 1 Thess. i : 9, &c. The Galatians
are rebuked for having served those who by nature are no
Gods. (Ch. iv : 8), ἐδουλεύσατε. If then the δουλεία of the New
Testament is that of Rome, the case is decided. But let us see
how they distinguish their δουλεία. Here we say, second : that
it is religious worship. This is proved by its being rendered in
Church (God's house), at the altar, in the midst of their liturgies, on God's holy day, and mixed with God's own worship.
This confusion at least is unpardonable. Third : in practice
they do not limit themselves to δουλεία but ask of the saints,
and especially of Mary, gifts most essentially divine; not intercession merely, but protection, pardon, sanctification, victory
over death. Here see Romish Breviaries, *passim;* and the
Stabat Mater. Daniel's Thesaurus Hymnolog, vol. 2, p. 133.
Streitwolff, *Libri. Symbolici*, vol. 2, p. 343, &c. Fourth, even
if only intercession were asked, the δουλεία would still imply in
the saints omnipresence, omniscience, infinite goodness, and
such-like divine attributes. To evade this crushing objection,
some Romish doctors have advanced their figment of the
Speculum Trinitatis. They imagine that the saints, blessed
with the beatific vision of God, see reflected in His omniscience
whatever He sees, at least of the wants and petitions of the
Church. But besides the fatal lack of Scriptural warrant, this
figment is absurd. For to see an overwhelming multitude of
objects at once, in a mirror, reflected, will confound a finite
mind as much as to see them directly. And besides, the figment
contradicts Scripture, Matt. xxiv : 36; John xv : 15 ; 1 Cor. ii : 11.

(c) Rome's saint- and angel-worship is but baptized paganism,

Moral effects of and like all other, it tends to degrade the
Creature-Worship. worshipers. Hence, the importance of the
prohibition of idolatry. Nothing but infinite
perfection should be the object of religious worship. The reverence and admiration which worship implies invest every
quality of the object worshiped with sanctity. Blemishes are
always reproduced in the votaries. The worship of an imperfect object is therefore the deification of defects. Rom. i : 25,
26; Ps. cxv : 8. But the more the worshiper is corrupted, the
more degraded will be the divinities which he will construct for
himself out of his defiled heart, until the vile descent is realized
which St. Paul describes in Rom. i : 22, 23.

As the first commandment fixes the object, so the second fixes the mode of religious worship. Under that most extreme corruption of mode which consists in image-worship, all erroneous modes of homage to the true God even, are prohibited. It may be said in general, that this commandment requires those acts and modes of worship for the true God which He hath required of us in His word, and prohibits all others. What Protestants call will-worship is forbidden, on these obvious grounds: God is infinite, and, in large part, inscrutable to creature minds. It is His prerogative to reveal Himself to us, as He has done. If we form surmises how He is to be honoured, they will be partially erroneous; for error belongs to man. Hence (as experience too fully confirms), the offering of worship of human invention to God has always dishonoured Him, and corrupted the worshipers. Our Saviour, therefore, expressly condemns it. Matt. xv : 9.

3. Scope of Second Commandment.

The doctrine of Rome concerning the use of images in worship, with its defence, may be seen in the Rom. Cat., Pt. III, Ch. 2, Qu. 9–14 inclusive. 1st. You will there remark the curious arrangement which makes our second commandment a part of, or appendix to the first, and usually prints it with small type. While this claims some little patristic countenance, its object is undoubtedly to depreciate this command. As the number of ten precepts is too well fixed to be called in question, Rome attempts to make it up by dividing the 10th, without shadow of valid reason, as we shall see.

4. Image Worship.

Rome grants (Qu. 12) that the Deity should not be represented by any shape, because immense and inconceivable. To concede thus much, indeed, was unavoidable; the prohibitions are so plain. But to excuse her image-worship, Qu. 13th teaches that the making of images of persons of the Trinity is no wrong, for this, when correctly understood, is no attempt to represent the Divine essence; it only expresses the property and actions which the Scriptures give the Persons. Thus, the Father is represented, in supposed imitation of Daniel vii : 9, as a hoary old man; the Son in a human figure; and the Holy Ghost, after Matt. iii: 16, as a dove. The idea of trinity in unity is usually represented as a luminous triangle.

Romish Excuses.

To this evasion I reply, are not the Persons very God? Is not their essence one, and properly divine? How, then, can it be right to picture them, and wrong to picture Deity? If we may use the image of the Person, because it is designed to represent some act or property of it, why not of the Deity? Indeed, the luminous triangle is an attempt to represent the latter.

2d. Rome urges also that to figure or picture objects of wor-

ship cannot be wrong, because God has done
God's Example no it. He appears as a man in Gen. xviii, and
Rule to Us.
in Gen. xxxii : 24; as an angel in Exod. iii :
2; as a shekinah, 2 Chron. vii : 1. The Holy Ghost appears
as a dove, Matt. iii : 16. God also commanded the cherubim
to be placed in the most sacred part of the oracle, at the very
part towards which the High Priest directed his worship. God
also directed Moses to make a brazen serpent and elevate it
upon a pole. Numb. xxi : 8.

Now, the general and sufficient answer to this is, that
God's doing a thing Himself is no warrant whatever for us to
presume on imitating Him. May we kill people at will, because
He slays some thirty millions annually? His precepts are our
rule, not the acts of His own sovereignty, which His incommunicable attributes properly render unique and inimitable.
The representations which God has seen fit to make of Himself to one and another prophet were temporary, not permanent, occasional — yea, rare — presented only to the prophet's
own private eye, not to the Church customarily; and they
were, after all, phantasmata, impressed on the prophet's imagination in esctatic vision — not actual, material constructions,
like the idols of men. Chiefly, as visions, they were true, for
they were to the prophets symbols of some special presence of
God, and God was in some way specially present then and
there. But these figures, when used by Papists, are symbols
of no such truth; for God has not authorized them to expect
any special presence where they exhibit the images. They are
therefore false, while God's visions were true.

The carved Cherubim over the mercy-seat were not idols
at all, but merely architectural ornaments,
No Image-Worship having, indeed a symbolical fitness, but no
in Scripture.
more objects of worship than the knops and
lilies of the carving. The brazen serpent too, was a type, and
not an object of worship. As well might the Papist bring as a
plea, the fact that God has represented Christ by bread and
wine. See Jno. iii : 14. Especially since the coming of the
antitype, has this case not a shadow of force to excuse idolatry.
That its worship was never permitted is clearly shown by 2d
Kings xviii : 4; where we read that the good King Hezekiah,
detecting the Jews in this error, had the identical serpent
crushed, saying "it is brazen." ("It is but brass.") As to
the picturing and worshipping of the man Jesus, the delineation
of His human person has more shadow of reason, because He
is incarnate. But there is no portrait or description of Christ,
which is authentic. If there was, He is now, when glorified,
wholly unlike it. Chiefly; an image could only represent His
humanity, as distinguished from His divinity; and the former,
thus abstracted, is no proper object of worship. The use of
the crucifix in worship, therefore, tendeth to evil.

3d. The Council of Trent urges that the image is not itself regarded as divine; but only as a visible representation, to assist the unlearned especially, in conceiving the real presence of the invisible. To this I reply: it is just the distinction which all the pagans make, except the most besotted. Does any one suppose that the acute Hindoo is so stupid as to mistake the lump of clay or wood, which yesterday was a clod or a stick, and which he saw helpless in the hands of the mechanic, for a true God? If charged with such folly, he makes precisely the Papist's reply: that he worships the invisible God through the help of the visible representation of Him. So answered the ancient idolaters to the primitive Christians. By adopting it, the Papist puts himself, where he properly belongs, in the pagan category. And this is the very sin which the Scriptures intend to prohibit. An examination of the sin with Aaron's calf, Exod. xxxii, of Micah's idolatry, Judges xvii : 3-13, and of the sin of Jeroboam, 1 Kings xii : 28, &c., will show that in each case the criminal attempt was to worship the true Jehovah, unmistakeably recognized by His incommunicable name, or as He who brought Israel out of Egypt, through an image supposed appropriate.

All Idolaters profess to look above the idol.

4th. To worship the true God by an image is, then, the very thing forbidden, because such a representation is necessarily false. For, God being a spiritual, immense, and invisible Being, to represent Him as a limited material form, is a falsehood. To clothe Him with the form of any of His creatures, angelic, human, or animal, is the most heinous insult to His majesty. God is a Spirit, cognizable by no sense. To represent Him by a material, visible and palpable image or picture is a false representation. He is omnipresent. To draw or carve Him as bounded by an outline, and contained in a local form, belies this attribute. He is self-existent, and has no beginning. To represent Him by what His puny creature made, and what yesterday was not, belies His self-existence and eternity. He declares Himself utterly unlike all creatures, and incomprehensible by them. To liken Him to any of them is both a misrepresentation and insult. Hence, a material image of the Godhead, or of any Person thereof, is an utter falsehood. Papists used to be fond of saying: "Images are the books of the unlearned." We reply: they are books then, which teach lies only. The crowning argument against them, is that the Scriptures expressly forbid them; and equally plainly, base their prohibition on the fact that no image can correctly represent God. Deut. iv : 15, 16; Is. xl : 12-18; Acts xvii : 29. "Take ye therefore good heed unto yourselves, (for ye saw no manner of similitude on the day that the Lord spake unto you in Horeb, out of the midst of the fire), lest you

This the very Definition of Idolatry in Scripture Cases. God inimitable.

corrupt yourselves, and make you a graven image," &c.

You are familiar with the answer to our last head of inquiry, which says the third Commandment requireth the holy and reverent use of God's name, titles attributes, ordinances, word, and works; "and forbiddeth all profaning or abusing of anything whereby God maketh Himself known." The scope of this precept is to secure a reverential treatment of God and all that suggests Him, in our speech and other *media* of communication, with each other. Its practical importance is justified by what the Apostle James teaches us of the responsibility and influence of our faculty of speech. When you read his statements, and consider how fully experience justifies them; when you consider the large place which this power of communicating ideas fills in society, you will see why God has elevated the sanctification of the tongue into a place among the "ten words."

5. Scope of Third Commandment.

Every Christian is familiar with the idea that this precept is meant to prohibit sins of profane cursing and swearing in all their forms. Among these abuses may also be classed all irreverent uses of Sacred Scripture; all heartless and formal worship, whether by praying or singing; all irreverence and levity in the house of God during the celebration of His worship or sacraments; all heedejaculations of His name and attributes; and most flagrantly, perjury. This, the crowning crime of this class, is a breach both of the third and ninth Commandments. It violates the obligations of truth; and also violates those of reverence in the most flagrant manner. An oath is an appeal to God for the sanction of the asseveration then made. It invokes all His attributes in the most formal manner, to act as umpires between the parties, and if the asseveration is falsified, to witness and avenge it. Where an oath is falsely taken, it is a heaven-daring attempt to enlist the Almighty in the sanction of the creature's lie; and is thus, either the most outrageous levity, or the most outrageous impiety, of which he can be guilty.

Sins forbidden in it.

But we do not hold that the reverential occasional use of religious vows, or the serious taking of the oath from the civil magistrate, is a breach of this commandment. You are aware that the Quakers, and some other Christians hold all oaths unlawful. We base our view on the following reasons:

Lawful Oaths and Vows not Forbidden.

Moses expressly commands the people to swear by the name of Jehovah, whenever they did swear. Deut. vi : 13. This surely implies that there is a right and proper time to swear. The Israelites were carefully instructed how to swear. Levit. xix : 12. Oaths were appointed to be administered by Divine authority, in certain cases. Exod. xxii : 11; Numb. v : 19. Surely God would not require His people to sin! We find that God sware; and "because He could swear by no greater, He sware by Himself." His example is worthy of mention here, although we do not presume a right to make it our rule in every case. We find that the apostles also, and especially Paul, frequently appealed to God in oaths. Rom. i : 9; 2 Cor. i : 23; Gal. i : 20. These expressions involve all the essentials of an oath. But we have a more indisputable example. Jesus Christ took an oath, when it was tendered to Him by Caiaphas the High Priest, acting as an authorized (though a wicked) magistrate of his people. Matt. xxvi : 63, 64. When the Chief Priest said: "I adjure Thee (I swear Thee) by the living God," Christ, who had before refused to respond, immediately gave an affirmative answer, thereby taking the oath tendered Him. Let it be noticed, also, that in this He was acting in His human capacity. These New Testament examples also effectually estop the plea, untenable in all cases, that legislation given by Moses was corrected by Christ, so that the latter made things sins, which Moses made right. For all this was under the new dispensation, or at least after the utterance of the commands by Christ which furnish the argument of the Quakers.

Those commands are found in Matt. v : 34 and 37; Jas. v : 12. Their claim is, that these prohibitions **Supposed Prohibition in New Testament.** are meant to forbid oaths under all possible circumstances; that the language is absolute, and we have no right to limit it. I reply, that if this view be pressed, all that is gained will be to represent Christ and Paul as expressly violating the new law. An understanding of the circumstances relieves the case. The Jewish elders had corrupted the third commandment by teaching that a man might interlard his common conversation with oaths, provided he did not swear falsely. They also taught that one might swear by anything else than the name of God, as his own head, or Jerusalem. Against these corruptions our Saviour's precept is aimed. In our common intercourse we are not to swear at all, because the suitable and solemn juncture is lacking. When that juncture is present, what more reasonable than the appeal to God; that God who is, by His omniscience and providence, the actual witness and umpire of all such declarations. But, in conclusion, it is a great abuse for the magistrate to multiply oaths on frivolous occasions.

LECTURE XXXII.

FIRST TABLE. (4th COMMANDMENT.)

THERE is, perhaps, no subject of Christian practice on which there is, among sincere Christians, more practical diversity and laxity of conscience than the duty of Sabbath observance. We find that, in theory, almost all Protestants now profess the views once peculiar to Presbyterians and other Puritans; but, in actual life, there is, among good people, a variety of usages, from a laxity which would almost have satisfied the party of Archbishop Laud, up to the sacred strictness of the "Sabbatarians" whom he and his adherents reviled and persecuted. It is a curious question : how it has come about that the consciences of devout and sincere persons have allowed them such license of disobedience to a duty acknowledged and important ; while on other points of obligation equally undisputed, the Christian world endeavors, at least, to maintain the appearance of uniform obedience. The solution is probably to be found, in part, in the historical fact, of which many intelligent Christians are not aware—that the communions founded at the Reformation, were widely and avowedly divided in opinion as to the perpetuity of the Sabbath obligation. A number of the Reformation churches, including some of the purest, professed that they saw no obligation in the Scriptures to any peculiar Sabbath observance; and the neglect of everything except attendance on the public exercise of Christianity, and that cessation of secular labor required by secular statutes was, in them, at least consistent. Now the descendants of these communions, in this mixed country, live dispersed among the descendants of Presbyterians and Puritans ; and while they no longer defend

3. Diversity Accounted For.

366

the looser theory of their forefathers, they retain the tradition-ary practices and customs in their use of the sacred day. Thus, by example and the general intermingling of religions, a remiss usage is propagated, which is far beneath the present professed theory of Protestant Christendom. And hence, we conceive that it will be interesting and profitable to give a history of opinions on this subject, before we proceed to that full discus-sion of the whole grounds of our belief and practice which we shall attempt.

It may be stated then, in general terms, that since the primitive times of Christianity, two diverse opinions have prevailed in the Christian world. The first is that adopted by the Romish, Lu-theran, and most of the continental communions in Europe, in-cluding, it must be confessed, those founded by Calvin. This theory teaches that the proper sanctification of one day from every seven was a ceremonial, typical, and Jewish custom, established when the Levitical institutions were introduced; and, of course, abrogated by the better dispensation, along with the rest of the typical shadows. The Lord's day is, indeed, worthy of observance as a Christian festival, because it is the weekly memorial of the blessed resurrection, and the example of the primitive Church commends it; not because its obli-gation is now *jure divino*. The cessation of our worldly labors is a beneficent and commendable civil institution; and while the magistrates enjoin it, is, for this reason, of course to be prac-tised by all good citizens. Public and associated worship is also a duty of Christians; and, in order that it may be associated, it must be upon a stated day and hour; and what day so appro-priate as this, already famous for the great event of the new dispensation, and set apart by civil laws from the purposes of business. But this is all. To observe the whole day as a reli-gious rest, under the supposition of a religious obligation, would be to Judaize, to remand ourselves to the bondage of the old and darker dispensation.

The second opinion is that embodied in the Westminster symbols, and, to the honour of Presbyterianism be it said, first avowed in modern times, even among Protestants, by that party in England. This is, that the setting apart of some stated por-tion of our time to the special and exclusive worship of God, is a duty of perpetual and moral obligation (as distinguished from postive or ceremonial), and that our Maker has, from the cre-ation, and again on Sinai, appointed for all races and ages, that this portion shall be one day out of seven. But when the cere-monial dispensation of Levi was superadded to this and the other institutions of the original, patriarchal religion, the seventh day did) in addition, become a type and a Levitical holy-day; and the theory admits that this feature has passed away with the Jewish ceremonial. After the resurrection of Christ, the per-

Two opinions prev-alent.

petual Divine obligation of a religious rest was transferred to
the first day of the week, and thence to the end of the world,
the Lord's day is the Christian's Sabbath, by Divine and apostolic appointment, and is to be observed with the same religious
spirit enjoined upon the patriarchs, and the Israelites, abating
those features which proceeded from its ceremonial use among
the latter, and from their theocratic government.

Among the advocates of the first opinion is to be adduced
Papal Opinion. first the Roman Catholic communion. This
statement must, however, be made with qualification; for the "Romish Catechism" of Pope Pius V., embodying the opinions of the Council of Trent (P. iii, ch. iv),
treats of the Lord's day more scripturally, in some respects,
than many Protestants. But this correctness of opinion is grievously marred by the doctrine, that the other Church holidays
are sustained by equal authority with the Lord's day—the
authoritative tradition of the Church. Bellarmine also argues
that it must be allowable to the true Church to make the observance of sacred days of human appointment binding on the
conscience, because otherwise the Church would have no sacred
days at all, since none whatever are enjoined in the New Testament. This reasoning obviously proceeds upon the assumption
that there is no other sort of obligation for the Lord's day than
for a Church festival. The well-known practice of Romish
Christians, prevalent in all Popish countries, and unrebuked by
the priesthood, sustains exactly that theory of Sabbath observance which we first described. After the duties of confession
and hearing mass are performed in the morning, the rest of the
holy-day is unhesitatingly devoted to idleness, amusements, or
actual vice.

The Lutheran communion, as ordered by Luther, Melanc-
Lutheran Opinion. thon, and their coadjutors, held that it was
lawful and proper for Church authorities to
ordain days, and rites not contrary to the letter or spirit of
Scripture, but additional to those appointed therein. It was,
indeed, one of the most constant and noble parts of their
testimony against Rome, that it was spiritual tyranny for any
Church authority, however legitimate, to ordain anything contrary to the letter or spirit of Scripture, or to enforce any ordinance of human authority, however innocent, as binding on the
Christian conscience, or as necessary to acceptance with God.
But they taught that the rulers of the Church might lawfully
institute rites, ordinances and holy-days, consonant to the Word
of God, though additional to those set down in it; and that
they might lawfully change such ordinances, from time to time,
as convenience and propriety required. But they could only
invite, they could not compel the compliance of their brethren;
and this compliance was to be rendered, not of necessity, but
from considerations of Christian comity, peace and conveni-

THE FIRST TABLE (COMMANDMENT 4)

ence.   When days or ordinances additional to Scripture were thus enjoined, and thus observed, it was held proper, lawful and praiseworthy, in both rulers and ruled.   And the Lutheran symbols expressly assert that it was by this kind of Church authority, and not *jure divino*, that the observance of the Lord's day obtained among Christians; and that it could not be scripturally made binding on the conscience of Christians any more than the observance of Easter or Christmas, or of any other day newly instituted by a Church court, in accordance with Christian convenience and edification.   They also teach that the Sabbath, with its strict and enforced observances, was purely a Levitical institution.   In the 28th article of the Augsburg Confession, which treats of "the power of the bishops or clergy," we find the following [We will take the liberty of italicising those phrases which we wish to be particularly weighed]: "What, then, should be held concerning *Sunday and other similar Church ordinances* and ceremonies?"   To this our party make the following reply: That *the bishops or pastors may make regulations, in order that things may be carried on orderly in the Church, not in order to obtain the grace of God, nor yet in order to atone for sins, or to bind the consciences of men with them, to hold them as necessary services of God, and to regard them as if they commit sin, if they break them without offence to others.   Thust St. Paul, in the Corinthians, ordains that the women in the congregation should cover their heads; 1 Cor. xi: 5.   *   *   *   *   "*In like manner is the regulation concerning Sunday, concerning Easter, concerning Pentecost*, and the like holy-days and rites.   Those, then, who are of opinion that the regulation of Sunday instead of the Sabbath, was established as a thing necessary, err very much.   For the *Holy Scripture has abolished the Sabbath*, and it teaches that all ceremonies of the old law, since the revelation of the Gospel, may be discontinued.   And yet, as it was of need to ordain a certain day, so that the people might know when they should assemble, *the Christian Church ordained Sunday* for that very purpose, and possessed rather more inclination and willingness for this alteration, in order that the people might have an example of Christian liberty, that they might know that neither the observance of the Sabbath, nor of any other day, is indispensable."   Melancthon, in the 8th article of his "apology," ("*Of human ordinances in the Church,*") briefly asserts the same view.   "Further, the most ancient ordinances however in the Church, *as the three chief festivals, Sundays, and the like*, which were established for the sake of order, union and tranquility, we observe with willingness.   And with regard to these, our teachers preach to the people in the most commendatory manner; in the meantime, however, holding forth the view, that they do not justify before God."

The evangelical Christians of Germany seem now to appre-

24*

hend the prime necessity of a stricter Sabbath-observance for the interests of piety; and have recently combined to promote it. But it will be vain for them to attempt to engraft such a reform on this doctrinal theory of Lutheranism. No plausible tampering with a doctrine so fundamentally erroneous will suffice. The connection between a false theory and a vicious practice is too inevitable. If the reform is to be established successfully, its foundation must be laid in the retraction of these opinions, and the explicit adoption of the Presbyterian theory of the Lord's day.

It may here be added, that the Mennonite Church, both in Europe and America, holds substantially the Lutheran ideas of the Sabbath, and that their practice is influenced by them in a similar way. When this communion, led by Menno Simonis, set about ridding themselves of the reproach of fanatical Anabaptism, they were careful to assume so much of the prevalent religion as they could consistently with their essential peculiarities, in order to substantiate their plea that they were no longer a radical, political sect, but a proper, evangelical denomination. The prevalent Protestantism of those countries was Lutheran; and hence the theology of the Mennonites, and their ideas of Sabbath observance, are largely Lutheran. The articles of their most current confession are silent concerning the observance of the Lord's day.

Next in order should be mentioned the opinions of the Socinian sect. The Racovian Catechism, the recognized Confession of this body, in the 16th century, states their erroneous belief with unmistakable precision and brevity. Under the fourth commandment are the following questions and answers:

Socinian Opinion.

"What is the fourth commandment?"

"Remember the Sabbath day to keep it holy."

"What dost thou believe concerning this commandment?"

"I believe that it is removed under the new covenant, in the way in which other ceremonies, as they are called, are taken away."

"Why, then, was it inserted in the decalogue?"

"Thus that it might be manifest the most absolute part of the Mosaic law was not perfect, and that some indication might exist of this fact, that a law was to succeed the Mosaic law, by far more perfect, the law, namely, of our Lord Jesus Christ."

"Did, or did not, Christ ordain that we should observe the day which they call Lord's day, in place of the Sabbath?"

"Not at all; since the religion of Christ entirely removes the distinction of days, just as it does the other ceremonies, as they are called; as the Apostle clearly writes in Col. ii : 16. But since we see that the Lord's day has been celebrated from of old time by Christians, we permit the same liberty to all Christians."

A day of religious rest, then, according to Socinians is utterly abolished by Christ, just as the other Levitical ceremonies.

As to the ground held by the Anglican Church, concerning the authority of the Lord's day, its standards are indecisive. It holds the same opinion with the Augsburg Confession, concerning the power of the Church to ordain rites, ceremonies, and holydays, additional, but not contrary to the Scriptures; but it has not observed the scriptural modesty of the Lutherans, in enforcing the uniform observance of these human appointments. While its theory on this point is not greatly more exaggerated in words than that of the Augsburg Confession, its practice has been unspeakably more tyrannical. The twentieth of the "Thirty-nine Articles," ("Of the authority of the Church,") says: "The Church hath power to decree rites or ceremonies, and authority in controversies of faith; and yet it is not lawful for the Church to ordain anything that is contrary to God's Word written, &c." The thirty-fourth says: "Whosoever, through his private judgment, willingly and purposely doth openly break the traditions and ceremonies of the Church, which be not repugnant to the Word of God, and be ordained and approved by common authority, ought to be rebuked openly, (that other may fear to do the like,) as he that offended against the common order of the Church, and hurteth the authority of the magistrate, and woundeth the consciences of the weak brethren." The articles contain no nearer reference to the Lord's day. Our purpose in quoting these words will be seen in connection with the following from the thirteenth of the ecclesiastical canons and constitutions:

All manner of persons within the Church of England, shall from henceforth celebrate and keep the Lord's day, commonly called Sunday, and other holy days, according to God's holy will and pleasure, and the orders of the Church of England prescribed in that behalf," &c.

The Church of England, then, is not, by her standards, definitely committed to that loose theory which we have unfolded; but the association of Sundays and holy-days, as equal in their claims, and the nature of their authority, is significant. The Church, according to these articles, has power to ordain days, additional to those appointed in Scripture, provided they are not condemned in Scripture; and to enforce their observance by censures. And it is plainly implied that the obligation to keep a Sunday is only of the same character with the obligation to keep an Epiphany or Good Friday. Both are alike according to God's holy will; but it is God's will, not pronounced in Scripture, but through the authoritative decree of the Church. It was the primitive Church which introduced the festivals of Epiphany and others ; and it was the same authority which introduced Sunday. As the thirty-fourth article claims that the same church authority which made, can unmake or alter these appointments, it would seem that even the Lord's day might be liable to change by human authority.

We proceed now to state the opinions of Calvin, and some of the Reformed Churches. By consulting Calvin's Institutes, (B. 2, chap. 8), it will be seen that his views of Sabbath-observance are substantially those of Luther. He states that, among the Israelites, there were three grounds for the observance of the seventh day : first, that it might be a type of that cessation of the works of self-righteousness which true believers practice ; second, that there might be a stated day for public worship ; and third, that domestic animals and servants might enjoy a merciful rest from bodily labor. Only the last two of these grounds exist, according to Calvin, under the New Testament. Hence he says (ch. 8, § 33) : " We celebrate it not with scrupulous rigor, as a ceremony which we conceive to be a figure of some spiritual mystery, but only use it as a remedy necessary to the preservation of order in the Church." In the previous section he says : " Though the Sabbath is abrogated, yet it is still customary among us to assemble on stated days, for hearing the Word, for breaking the mystic bread, and for public prayers ; and also to allow servants and laborers a remission from their labor." And in section 34 : " Thus vanish all the dreams of false prophets, who in past ages have infected the people with a Jewish notion, affirming that nothing but the ceremonial part of this commandment, which, according to them, is the appointment of the seventh day, has been abrogated ; but that the moral part of it, that is, the observance of one day in seven, still remains. But this is only changing the day in contempt of the Jews, while they retain the same opinion of the holiness of a day ; for, on this principle, the same mysterious signification would be attributed to particular days, which formerlly obtained among the Jews," And in the same tenour, he remarks upon Col. ii ; 16 : (" Let no man, therefore, judge you in meat or in drink, or in respect of a holy-day, or of the new moon, or of the Sabbath-days " " Such a distinction (of days) suited the Jews, to observe sacredly the appointed days, by separating them from other days. Among Christians, such a distinction hath ceased. But, somebody will say that we still retain some observance of days. I answer, that we by no means observe them, as if there were any religion in holy-days, or as if it were not right to labor then ; but the regard is paid to polity and good order, not to the days."

To those who are aware of the close relationship between Socinianism and Arminianism, it will not be surprising that the latter sect, at its birth,

Opinion of Calvin, [marginal note]

Arminian Opinion. [marginal note]

adopted an idea of the Lord's day only less relaxed than that
of the former. It is unnecessary to multiply citations; a single
passage from Limborch, one of the distinguished heads of their
seminary in Amsterdam, in his commentary on Romans xiv : 5,
will be both sufficiently distinct and authoritative :

Romans xiv : 5. "Another esteemeth every day alike,"
viz : (explains Limborch) "The converts to Christ from among
the Gentiles, on whom the burden of the ritual law was never
imposed, did not recognize this distinction of days, but esteemed
all days equal, and one no more noble than another. It is
true, indeed, that the apostles and primitive Church were
already accustomed to assemble in sacred meetings the first
day of the week; but not because they believed that day more
eminent than any other, nor because they believed the rest of
that day to be a part of Divine worship, as the rest of the
seventh day had been under the law; nor that it must be
observed with rigor, as formerly, under the law. By no means :
but because it was convenient to designate some time for
sacred exercises : and that a man might the better be at leisure
for them, rest also from daily labor was required. The first day
of the week, on which the Lord rose from the dead, (which is
thus called the Lord's day, Rev. i : 10), seemed most meet to
be destined to these services; but not because it was judged
more holy, or because a rigid rest and cessation of all work
in observing that day was a part of Divine worship. For thus,
it would have been not a taking off of the yoke, but a shifting
of it."

On the whole, it may be said that the Protestant Churches
of continental Europe have all occupied this
Continental Usage. ground, concerning the sanctification of the
Lord's day. These Churches, properly speaking, have never
had the Sabbath; for it has only been to them a holy-day,
ranking no higher than Christmas or Easter, or a season set
apart by civil enactment, or a convenient arrangement for concert in public worship; and not a sacred day of Divine appointment. The manner in which it is desecrated, commonly, throughout the Protestant States of the continent is shocking to the feelings and usages of strict, American Protestants; and seems to
them to approximate only too much to the license of Popery.
But we have now seen that this desecration is not an accidental
irregularity : it is the natural and proper result of the theory in
which these Churches have been educated since the Reformation. That the greatest and best of the Reformers should have
failed to embrace the truth concerning the Lord's day, is indeed
no subject of surprise. That men emerging at a bound from
the meridian darkness of Popery into Gospel light should see
all things correctly at first, was not to be expected. That they
saw so many things "eye to eye," and erred in so few, is a
wonder, only to be explained by the presence of the Spirit of

all truth.   It is wholesome to become acquainted with their few errors, and to explode them; for it will tend to correct that overweening spirit of party which ever prompts Christians to call themselves by the name of men, like those who said; "I am of Paul, and I of Apollos, and I of Cephas." But it may well be inquired also, whether a part of the spiritual decline which has almost extinguished the true light in the ancient seats of Luther, Calvin, Witsius and De Moor, is not due to this misconception of Sabbath obligation, and its consequent neglect.   The sacred observance of one day in seven is God's appointed means for the cultivation of piety: when piety vanishes, orthodoxy necessarily follows it in due time.

As has been already indicated, the first successful attempt to establish the theory of a Christian Sabbath, since the Reformation, was made among the English Puritans.   About the year 1595, a dissenting minister of Suffolk, Dr. Nicholas Bound, published a book entitled "*Sabbatum Veteris et Novi Testamenti,* or The True Doctrine of the Sabbath," in which he advocated the view afterwards adopted by the Westminister Assembly.   This treatise had great currency among the devout dissenters and evangelical churchmen, and was the beginning of a discussion which continued, under repeated attempts for its suppression by high church authorities, until the doctrines of the Puritans became those of the bulk of sincere Christians throughout Great Britain and the American colonies.   Archbishop Whitgift condemned Dr. Bound's book to suppression.   James I., published his Declaration of Sports, encouraging the people to dancing, trials of archery, erecting May-poles, and other amusements, at any hours of the Lord's day not occupied by public worship. The flood of immoralities introduced by this measure became so odious, that the secular magistrates, at the urgent instance of the people themselves, suppressed the Sunday sports. Under Charles I., Laud invoked the aid of his clergy to reestablish them; and the strange spectacle was seen of the laity petitioning against the profane desecration of the sacred· day, and their spiritual guides compelling them to perpetrate it! (Neal, Hist. of the Puritans, vol. 1, ch. viii; vol. 2, ch. 2–5.

The first great Synod which ever propounded, in modern ages, the true doctrine of the Lord's day, was the Westminster Assembly.   Their Confession of Faith, which is now the standard of the Scotch, Irish and American Presbyterian, and of many independent Churches, states the truth so luminously, (ch. xxi : § 7–8), that we shall repeat their words here, though familiar, as the best statement of the proposition and text of our subsequent discussion.

"Sec. 7. As it is of the law of nature that, in general, a due proportion of time be set apart for the worship of God ; so

in His word, by a positive, moral, and perpetual commandment,
binding all men, in all ages, He hath particularly appointed one
day in seven for a Sabbath, to be kept holy unto Him ; which
from the beginning of the world to the resurrection of Christ,
was the last day of the week; and, from the resurrection of
Christ, was changed into the first day of the week, which in
Scripture is called the Lord's day, and is to be continued to the
end of the world as the Christian Sabbath."

"Sec. 8. This Sabbath is then kept holy unto the Lord,
when men after a due preparing of their hearts, and ordering
of their common affairs beforehand, do not only observe an
holy rest all the day from their own works, words, and thoughts,
about their worldly employments and recreations; but also are
taken up the whole time in the public and private exercises of
His worship, and in the duties of necessity and mercy."

As the doctrinal articles of the Westminster Assembly
were generally adopted by the Calvinistic dissenters of England
and America, they also embraced these views of the Sabbath.
The reader will now easily comprehend, from this historical review, what would naturally be the views of these several denominations concerning Sabbath-observance, and what is the legitimate source of that diversity, vagueness and license, which are
exhibited in this country, in our Sabbath usages. To partic-
ularize further would be unnecessary, and might be supposed
invidious.

We proceed now to the attempt to give a full but summary
statement of the grounds upon which Pres-
4. (a) Sabbath byterians assert the doctrine of a Christian
Command moral.
Sabbath as it is set forth in their Confession.
And first : it is most obvious, that if the Sabbath-law contained in
the decalogue is " a positive, moral and perpetual commandment, binding all men, in all ages," and not ceremonial and positive, like the Jewish laws of meats, new moons and sacrifices,
it cannot have passed away along with the other temporary
shadows of Judaism. If it was not introduced by the Levitical economy for the first time, but was in force before, and if
it was binding not on Jews only, but on all men, then the abrogation of that economy cannot have abrogated that which it
did not institute. The Apostle Paul justifies us here, by using
an argument exactly parallel in a similar case. " The covenant
that was confirmed before of God in Christ, the law which was
four hundred and thirty years after cannot disannul." Gal. iii :
17. Upon the question whether the fourth commandment was
of Mosaic origin, or earlier, the fathers were divided : and this
fact is another among the many proofs of their slender acquaintance with the Hebrew literature and antiquities.

That it is a positive, moral, and perpetual command, we
argue from the facts that there is a reason in the nature of
things, making such an institution necessary to man's religious

interests; and that this necessity is substantially the same in all ages and nations. That it is man's duty to worship God, none will dispute. Nor will it be denied that this worship should be in part social; because man is a being of social affections, and subject to social obligations; and because one of the great ends of worship is the display of the Divine glory before our fellow-creatures. Social worship cannot be conducted without the appointment of a stated day; and what more reasonable than that the Divine authority, who is the object of this worship, should meet this necessity, by Himself fixing the day for all mankind? And even for the cultivation of our individual devotion, a periodical season is absolutely necessary to creatures of habit and of finite capacities, like us. What is not regularly done will soon be omitted; for periodical recurrence is the very foundation of habit. Unless these spiritual thoughts and exercises were attached to some certain season, they would inevitably be pushed out of the minds of carnal and sensuous beings like man, by the cares of this world. Now, when it is our duty to perform a certain work, it is also our duty to employ all the necessary means for it. The question, whether the Sabbath command is moral or positive, seems, therefore, to admit of a very simple solution. Whether one day in six, or one in eight, might not have seemed to the Divine wisdom admissible for this purpose; or which day of the seven, the first or last, should be consecrated to it, or what should be the particular external ceremonies for its observance; all these things, we freely admit, are of merely positive institution, and may be changed by the Divine Legislator. But that man shall observe some stated, recurring period of religious worship, is as much a dictate of the natural reason and conscience, as immediate a result of the natural relations of man to God, as that man shall worship his God at all. And no reason can be shown why this original moral obligation was more or less stringent upon the Israelites of the Mosaic period, than on men before or since them. If the ground of the Sabbath institution, in the moral relations existing by nature, is universal and perpetual, is it not reasonable to expect the precept to be so also?

We argue further, that the enactment of the Sabbath-law (b) Sabbath Command Primeval. does not date from Moses, but was coeval with the human race. It is one of the two first institutions of paradise. The sanctification of the seventh day took place from the very end of the week of creation. (Gen. ii : 3.) For whose observance was the day, then, consecrated or set apart, if not for man's? Not for God's; because the glorious paradox is forever true of Him, that His ineffable quiet is as perpetual as His ever-active providence. Not surely for the angels', but for Adam's. Doubtless, Eden witnessed the sacred rest of him and his consort from

> " The toil
> Of their sweet gardening labor, which sufficed
> To recommend cool zephyr, and made ease
> More easy, wholesome thirst and appetite
> More grateful."

And from that time downward, we have indications, brief indeed, but as numerous as we should expect in the brief record of Genesis and Exodus, and sufficient to show that the Sabbath continued to be an institution of the patriarchal religion. A slight probable evidence of this may even be found in the fact, that seven has ever been a sacred and symbolical number, among Patriarchs, Israelites, and Pagans. In Genesis we read of the "seven clean beasts," the "seven well-favoured," and "seven lean kine," the "seven ears of corn, rank and good." Now there is no natural phenomenon to suggest the number: for no noted heavenly body, or natural element, revolves precisely in seven hours, days, weeks, or months. Whence the peculiar idea everywhere attached to the number, if not from the institution of a week for our first parents? But to proceed to more solid facts: It is at least probable that the "end of days," (Gen. iv : 3), rendered in our version, "process of time," at which Cain and Abel offered their sacrifices, was the end of the week, the seventh, or Sabbath-day. In Gen. vii : 10, we find God Himself observing the weekly interval in the preparations for the flood. We find another clear hint of the observance of the weekly division of time by Noah and his family in their floating prison. (Gen. viii : 10–12.) The patriarch twice waited a period of seven days to send out his dove. From Gen. xxix : 27, we learn that it was customary among the patriarchs of Mesopotamia, in the days of Laban, to continue a wedding festival a week; and the very term of service rendered by Jacob for his two wives, shows the use made of the number seven as the customary duration of a contract for domestic servitude. Gen. l : 10, shows us that at the time of Jacob's death, a week was also the length of the most honourable funeral exercises. In Exod. xii : 3–20, we find the first institution of the passover, when as yet there were no Mosaic institutions. This feast was also appointed to last a week. In Exodus xvi : 22–30, where we read the first account of the manna, we find the Sabbath institution already in force; and no candid mind will say that this is the history of its first enactment. It is spoken of as a rest with which the people ought to have been familiar. But the people had not yet come to Sinai, and none of its institutions had been given. Here, then, we have the Sabbath's rest enforced on Israel, before the ceremonial law was set up, and two weekly variations wrought in the standing miracle of the manna, in order to facilitate it. And when at length we come to the formal command of the decalogue, it is expressed in terms which clearly indicate that the Sabbath was an institution already known, of which the obligation was now only re-affirmed.

The very fact that this precept found a place in the awful "ten words," is of itself strong evidence that it is not a positive and ceremonial, but a moral and perpetual statute. Confessedly, there is nothing else ceremonial here. An eminent distinction was given as we saw, Lect. 30th, to the subjects of these ten commands, by the mode in which God delivered them. How can it be believed that this one ceremonial precept has been thrust in here, where all else is of obligation as old, and as universal as the race? This is strengthened also by the reflection that the ground first assigned in Genesis, and here repeated for its enactment, is in no sense Jewish or national. God's work of creation in six days, and His rest on the seventh, have just as much relation to one tribe of Adam's descendants as to another. Note the contrast: that, in many cases, when ceremonial and Jewish commands are given, like the passover, a national or Jewish event is assigned as its ground, like the exodus from Egypt.

This proved by Decalogue.

The assertion that the Sabbath was coeval with the human race, and was intended for the observation of all, receives collateral confirmation also from the early traditions concerning it, which pervade the first Pagan literature. It can hardly be supposed that Homer and Hesiod borrowed from the books of Moses, sabbatical allusions which would have been to their hearers unintelligible. They must be the remnants of those primeval traditions of patriarchal religion, which had been transferred by the descendants of Japheth, to the isles of Chittim. The early allusions to a sacred seventh day may be sufficiently exhibited by citing a collection of them from Eusebius' *Preparatio Evangelica* (L. xiii, § 13), which he quotes from the Stromata of Clement of Alexandria. The latter father is represented as saying: "That the seventh day is sacred, not the Hebrews only, but the Gentiles also acknowledge, according to which the whole universe of animals and vegetables revolves." Hesiod, for instance, thus says concerning it:

Proved by Tradition.

"The first, the fourth also, and the seventh is a sacred day." ('Ιεσον 'Ημαρ.) Dierum, line 6.

And again: "The seventh day once more, the splendid dawn of the sun."

And Homer: "The seventh day then arrived, the sacred day."

Again: "The seventh was sacred."

"The seventh dawn was at hand, and with this all the series is completed."

And once more: "On the seventh day, we left the stream of Acheron."

And thus also writes Callimachus the poet: "It was now the Sabbath day: and with this all was accomplished."

Again: "The seventh day is among the fortunate; yea, the seventh is the parent-day."

Again: "The seventh day is first, and the seventh day is the complement."

And: "All things in the starry sky are found in sevens; and shine in their ordained cycles."

"And this day, the elegies of Solon also proclaim as more sacred, in a wonderful mode."

Thus far Clement and Eusebius. Josephus, in his last book against Apion, affirms that "there could be found no city, either of the Grecians or Barbarians, who owned not a seventh day's rest from labour." This of course is exaggerated. Philo, cotemporary with Josephus, calls the Sabbath ἑορτή πάνδημος.

We argue once more, that the Sabbath never was a Levitical institution, because God commanded its observance both by Jews and Gentiles, in the very laws of Moses. "In it thou shalt not do any work, thou, nor thy son, nor thy daughter, thy man-servant, nor thy maid-servant, nor thy cattle, nor thy stranger that is within thy gates." To see the force of the argument from this fact, the reader must contrast the jealous care with which "the stranger," the pagan foreigner residing in an Israelitish community, was prohibited from all share in their ritual services. No foreigner could partake of the passover—it was sacrilege. He was even forbidden to enter the court of the temple where the sacrifices were offered, at the peril of his life. Now, when the foreigner is commanded to share the Sabbath-rest, along with the Israelite, does not this prove that rest to be no ceremonial, no type, like the passover and the altar, but a universal moral institution, designed for Jew and Gentile alike?

Because enforced on foreigners.

We have thus established this assertion on an impregnable basis, because the argument from it is direct and conclusive. If the Sabbath command was in full force before Moses, the passing away of Moses' law does not remove it. If it always was binding, on grounds as general as the human race, on all tribes of mankind, the dissolution of God's special covenant with the family of Jacob did not repeal it. If its nature is moral and practical, the substitution of the substance for the types does not supplant it. The reason that the cermonial laws were temporary was that the necessity for them was temporary. They were abrogated because they were no longer needed. But the practical need for a Sabbath is the same in all ages. When it is made to appear that this day is the bulwark of practical religion in the world, that its proper observance everywhere goes hand in hand with piety and the true worship of God; that where there is no Sabbath there is no Christianity, it becomes an impossible supposi-

Conclusion.

tion that God would make the institution temporary. The
necessity for the Sabbath has not ceased, therefore it is not
abrogated. In its nature, as well as its necessity, it is a permanent, moral command. All such laws are as incapable of
change as the God in whose character they are founded. Unlike mere positive or ceremonial ordinances, the authority of
which ceases as soon as God sees fit to repeal the command for
them, moral precepts can never be repealed; because the purpose to repeal them would imply a change in the unchangeable,
and a depravation in the perfect character of God.

We will now proceed, in the second place, to consider
the passages of the New Testament from
(c) New Testament which the abrogation of the Sabbath obliga-
does not Abrogate. tions has been argued, together with some
considerations growing out of them. In atempting to refute the
exposition and arguments of those who advocate the repeal of
those obligations, we shall not pause to attribute each gloss
which we reject to its special author, or load our page with citations of learned names. It may be remarked once for all in
the outset, that the erroneous expositions of Calvin are far the
least objectionable, and at the same time, the most subtle and
acute; and that those of Neander are in full contrast with his
in both these respects.

The first passage is that contained, with some variation, in
Matt. xii : 1-8; Mark ii : 23-28; Luke vi :
Matt. xii : 1-8; Mark   1-5. The reader, on examining these places
ii: 23-28; Luke vi: 1-5.   in connection, and supplying from the second
or third evangelist what is omitted by the first, will find that our
Lord advances five ideas distinguishable from each other. His
hungry and wearied disciples, passing with Him through the
fields of ripe corn, had availed themselves of the permission of
Deut. xxiii : 25, to pluck, rub out, and eat some grains of wheat,
as a slight refreshment. The Pharisees seize the occasion to
cavil that He had thus permitted them to break the Sabbath-
law, by engaging in the preparation of their food in sacred
time; objecting thus against the trivial task of rubbing out, and
winnowing from the chaff a few heads of wheat as they walked
along. Our Saviour defends them and himself by saying, in
the first place, that the necessity created by their hunger justified the departure from the letter of the law, as did David's
necessity, when, fleeing for his life, he employed the shew-bread
(and innocently) to relieve his hunger; second, that the example
of the priests, who performed necessary manual labour without
blame about the temple on the Sabbath, justified what His disciples had done; third, that God preferred the compliance with
the spirit of His law, which enjoins humanity and mercy, over a
mere compliance with its outward rites; for, in the fourth
place God's design in instituting the Sabbath had been partly
a humane one, seeing He had intended it, not as a burdensome

ceremonial to gall the necks of men to no benevolent purpose, but as a means of promoting the true welfare of the human race; and last, that He Himself, as the Messiah, was the Divine and Supreme authority in maintaining the Sabbath law, as well as all others—so that it was enough for Him to pronounce that His disciples had made no infraction of it.

The first general view presented hereupon by the anti-Sabbatarians is, that Christ here, for the first time, introduces the freer, more lenient law of the new dispensation, by His Messianic authority, as a substitute for the stricter Mosaic law. The simple and short answer is, that it is the Sabbath as it ought to be observed by Jews, under the Mosaic laws, which our Saviour is here expounding. The new dispensation had not yet come; and was not to begin till Pentecost. After all this discussion, Christ complied with all the requisitions of the Levitical institutions up to His death. If then, any thing is relaxed, it is the Mosaic Sabbath, as Jews should keep it, which is the subject of the alteration. But we wish the reader to bear in mind, as a point important here and hereafter, that our Saviour does not claim any relaxation at all for His disciples. The whole drift of His argument is to show that when the Mosaic law of the Sabbath is properly understood, (as Jews should practice it,) His disciples have not broken it at all. They have complied with it; and need no lowering of its sense in order to escape its condemnation. Bearing this in mind, we proceed to the second erroneous inference. This is, that our Saviour illustrates and expounds the Sabbath law, by two cases of other laws merely ceremonial, the disposition of the old shew-bread and the Sabbath sacrifices. Hence, the inference, that the Sabbath also is but a ceremonial law. But to those who will notice how entirely the Jewish Scriptures neglect, in their practical recitals and discussions of religious duties, the distinction which we make between the "moral" and the "positive," this inference will be seen to be utterly worthless. The Jewish mind never paused to express the distinction, in its practical views of duty. See how Moses mixes, in Exodus, prohibitions against idolatry, and hewing the stones of which the altar was made: against eating flesh torn of beasts in the field, and bearing false witness. See how Ezek. (ch. xviii,) conjoins eating upon the mountains and taking usury on a loan, with idolatry and oppression, in his description of the sins of his cotemporaries. But again: It has been admitted that the external and formal details of Sabbath observance may be of only positive obligation, while the obligation to keep religiously a stated season is moral. It does not, then, at all imply that the substantial observance of such a stated day is not of moral and perpetual obligation, because any of those details concerning the labours of necessity or mercy which are wholly compatible with such observance, are

Marginal note: Our Saviour here defines Jewish Sabbath.

illustrated by comparison with other ceremonial precepts.   It is argued again, that " our Saviour, in His third point, implies that Sabbath observance is but ceremonial, while the duty of mercy is of moral obligation, when He indicates   that if   the   two clash, the Sabbath observance is to give way.   " The positive gives way to the moral."   The force of this is entirely removed by recalling the fact that it is not a failure of Sabbath observ- ance, which He excuses by the argument that the positive should give place to the moral; but it is an incidental labour of necessity wholly compatible with Sabbath observance.   There had been no failure.   Nor is it true that when we are com- manded to let one given duty give place to the higher demands of another, the former is, therefore, only positive, while the latter is moral.   There is a natural, moral, and perpetual obli- gation to worship God; and yet it might be our duty to sus- pend any acts of worship, to almost any number, in order to meet the demands of urgent cases of necessity calling for our compassion.   The wise man expresses precisely the sense of our Saviour's argument when he says: " To do justice and judgment is more acceptable to the Lord than sacrifice." (Prov. xxi : 3.)   And the meaning is, that the formal acts of religious worship, though in general demanded by nature and reason, are less important in God's eyes than the direct acts which express the true spirit of holiness in which religion consists.   " Sacri- fice," both here, and in our Saviour's citation from Samuel, represents the whole general idea of outward religious worship. It is not because " sacrifice" is merely ceremonial, that it is postponed in importance, to mercy and justice, but because it is external, and may be merely formal.   Religious worship, here intended by the more special term " sacrifice," is surely not a duty merely ceremonial and positive in its obligations, though external.   Our Saviour, then, does not imply that the Sabbath is an institution merely ceremonial, by comparing it to sacrifice.

The perverted gloss of the fourth idea : " The Sabbath is made for man," is almost too shallow to need exposure.   It has been used as though it sanctioned the notion, that man was not intended to be cramped by the Sabbath, but, on the contrary, it was intended to yield to his convenience and gratification. But since the object of the Sabbath is here stated to be a humane one, namely, the promotion of man's true welfare, it must be settled what that true welfare is, and how it may be best promoted, before we are authorized to conclude that we may do what we please with the holy-day.   If it should appear that man's true welfare imperatively demands a Sabbath-day, strictly observed and fenced in with Divine authority, the humanity of the Divine motive in giving a Sabbath would argue any thing else than the license inferred from it.

The concluding words of the passage, in Matthew, have

Christ does not Remit. suggested an argument which is at least more plausible. Calvin paraphrases them thus: "The Son of man, agreeably to His authority, is able to relax the Sabbath-day just as the other legal ceremonies." And just before: "Here He saith that power is given to Him to release His people from the necessity of observing the Sabbath." The inference is obvious, that if this is His scope in these words, then the Sabbath must be admitted by us to be only a ceremonial institution; for we have ourselves argued that moral laws are founded on the unchangeable nature of God Himself, and will never be changed, because God cannot change. But this is clearly a mistaken exposition. It may be noted that the conjunction which is rendered by Calvin and the English version, "the Son of man is Lord even (or also) of the Sabbath-day," is unanimously rejected by modern editors of the text. Calvin, of course, makes this conjunction regard the ceremonials just mentioned: "The Son of Man is Lord of the Sabbath also," (as well as of matters of shew-bread and sacrifice). But we should almost certainly read the clause without the conjunction: "If ye had known what this means, 'I prefer mercy rather than sacrifice,' ye would not have condemned the innocent. For the Son of Man is Lord of the Sabbath." What force shall we assign to the illative "for," wholly neglected by Calvin? There is no reasonable explanation of it, but that which makes it introduce the ground on which the innocence of the disciples is asserted. "These men, blamed by you, are innocent; it is enough that I defend them: *for* I am Lord of the Sabbath. This law is my law. Mine is the authority which enacts it, and if I am satisfied, that itself is innocence in my subjects." But this is comparatively unimportant. The evident reason which shows Calvin's paraphrase to be entirely a misconception, is this: As we have said, the whole drift of our Saviour's argument is not to excuse His disciples, but to defend them. He does not claim that the Sabbath law, as enacted for Jews, must needs be relaxed, in order to admit the conduct of the disciples; but that this law justified their conduct. He concludes His defence by telling their accusers, "you have condemned the innocent." Now, to represent Him as shielding them by asserting a right in Himself to relax the Sabbath law for them, makes Him adopt in the end a ground of defence contradictory to the former. The last argument would stultify all the previous ones. And, as a question of fact, is it true, that Christ did, at this time, exercise His divine authority to relax any Mosaic institution in favour of His disciples? Is it not notorious, on the contrary, that He taught them to give an exemplary compliance in every respect, until the time was fully come after His resurrection?

But to conclude. It is most obvious that, whatever is our exposition of the particular parts, our Saviour's drift is to unfold the true nature of the Mosaic Sabbath, as then obligatory on Jews still obedient to the ceremonial law, as He admitted Himself and His disciples to be; and not the nature of the Christian Sabbath. The latter was not to be introduced until many months after, as our opponents themselves admit. And this short view is a sufficient refutation in itself.

It may be as well to notice here a supposed difficulty attending our argument. It is said: "If you **Is Jewish Strictness still Required?** deny that Christ promises any relaxation of the stringency of the Levitical Sabbath, as of a ceremonial yoke, then you ought in consistency to exact of Christians now as punctilious an observance as was demanded of the old Jews, in every respect. You should refuse to make a fire in your dwellings on the Sabbath. You should seek to re-enact the terrible law of Numb. xv : 35, which punished a wretch with death for gathering a few sticks."

This is only skillful sophistry. We have not asserted that all the details of the Sabbath laws, in the books of Moses, were of perpetual moral obligation. We have not denied that some of them were ceremonial. The two instances mentioned, which are the only plausible ones which can be presented against us, are not taken from the decalogue, but from subsequent parts of the ceremonial books. We expressly contrasted the Sabbath precept as it stands in the "ten words" with all the rest, with reference to its perpetual, moral nature. The precept there contains only two points—rest from secular labour, and the sanctification of the day, which means in our view its appropriation to sacred services. The matter which is of perpetual moral obligation in the Sabbath law, is only this, that a finite, sensuous, and social being like man, shall have some periodical season statedly consecrated to religious services, (such season as God shall see fit to appoint). And all matters of detail and form which do not clash with this great end, are matters of mere positive enactment, which may be changed or repealed by Him who enacted them. But we can present several very consistent and sufficient reasons why the ceremonial details, added to the great moral law of the decalogue by the subsequent and ritual part of the Levitical legislation, should be more stringent, and enforced by heavier penalties, than among us. First: the Sabbath became to the Israelite not only a religious institution of moral obligation, but a type. It took rank with his new-moon, and his passover. Of this, more hereafter. But the very nature and design of a symbolical ritual demand that it shall be observed with technical accuracy. Next, the government was a theocracy, and no line whatever separated the secular and sacred statutes from each other. Hence, it is natural that offences should deserve very different penalties under such a government, and especially an offence aimed so especially against the Divine Chief Magistrate, as Sabbath labour. Third:

The Hebrews' houses had no hearths, nor chimneys, except for cooking; so that in that warm climate a prohibition to light fire on the Sabbath is exactly equivalent to a prohibition to cook food on the holy-day. Even if this prohibition were a part of the decalogue, it would be a ridiculous sacrifice of its spirit to its letter, to compel us, in our wintry climate, to forego the fire which is hourly necessary to health and comfort. But as the prohibition signifies in its spirit, we freely admit that with us, as with the Jews, all culinary labours should be intermitted, except such as are demanded by necessity and mercy, or by the different nature of a part of the food on which civilized nations now subsist. For us to allow ourselves further license would be to palter with that which we have so carefully pointed out as the essential and perpetual substance of the Sabbath law—the cessation of labour, and the appropriation to religious pursuits of one day (not one fragment of a day) in seven. When the Confession of Faith says that we are commanded to rest "all the day" from our own employments and amusements, and to "take up the whole time" in religious exercises, it only assumes that "a day" means, in the decalogue, a day.

The second group of passages which are used against our theory of Sabbath obligation are, Rom. xiv; 5-6; Gal. iv: 9-11; Col. ii: 16, 17. To save the reader trouble, we will copy them.

"One man esteemeth one day above another; another esteemeth every day alike. Let every man be fully persuaded in his own mind. He that regardeth the day, regardeth it unto the Lord; and he that regardeth not the day, to the Lord he doth not regard it. He that eateth, eateth to the Lord, for he giveth God thanks; and he that eateth not, to the Lord he eateth not, and giveth God thanks."

Rom. xiv; 5-6; Gal. iv: 9-11; Col, ii: 16, 17.

"But now, after that ye have known God, or rather are known of God, how turn ye again to the weak and beggarly elements, whereunto ye desire again to be in bondage? Ye observe days, and months, and times, and years. I am afraid of you, lest I have bestowed upon you labour in vain."

"Let no man therefore judge you in meat, or in drink, or in respect of an holy-day, or of the new-moon, or of the Sabbath-days: Which are a shadow of things to come; but the body is of Christ."

The facts in which all are agreed, which explain the Apostle's meaning in these passages, are these: After the establishment of the new dispensation, the Christians converted from among the Jews had generally combined the practice of Judaism with the forms of Christianity. They observed the Lord's day, baptism, and the Lord's supper; but they also continued to keep the seventh day, the passover, and circumcision. At first it was proposed by them to enforce this double system on all

25*

Gentile Christians; but this project was rebuked by the meeting of apostles and elders at Jerusalem, recorded in Acts xv. A large part, however, of the Jewish Christians, out of whom ultimately grew the Ebionite sect, continued to observe the forms of both dispensations; and restless spirits among the mixed churches of Jewish and Gentile converts planted by Paul, continued to attempt their enforcement on Gentiles also; some of them conjoining with this Ebionite theory the graver heresy of a justification by ritual observances. Thus, at this day, this spectacle was exhibited. In the mixed churches of Asia Minor and the West, some brethren went to the synagogue on Saturday, and to the church-meeting on Sunday, keeping both days religiously; while some kept only Sunday. Some felt bound to keep all the Jewish festivals and fasts, while others paid them no regard. And those who had not Christian light to apprehend these Jewish observances as non-essentials, found their consciences grievously burdened or offended by the diversity. It was to quiet this trouble that the apostle wrote these passages. Thus far we agree.

We, however, further assert, that by the beggarly elements of "days," "months," "times," "years," "holy-days," "new-moons," "Sabbath-days," the apostle means Jewish festivals, and those alone. The Christian's festival, Sunday, is not here in question; because about the observance of this there was no dispute nor diversity in the Christian churches. Jewish and Gentile Christians alike consented universally in :ts sanctification. When Paul asserts that the regarding of a day, or the not regarding it, is a non-essential, like the eating or not eating of meats, the natural and fair interpretation is, that he means those days which were in debate, and no others. When he implies that some innocently "regarded every day alike," we should understand, every one of those days which were subjects of diversity—not the Christians' Sunday, about which there was no dispute.

But the other party give to Paul's words a far more sweeping sense. They suppose him to assert ' that the new dispensation has detached the service of God from all connections with stated seasons whatever; so that in its view, all days, Sabbath or Sunday, Passover or Easter, should be alike to the Christian spirit. He who ceased to observe the Jewish days, in order to transfer his sabbatical observances, his stated devotions and special religious rest to the Christian days, was still in substance a Judaizer. He was retaining the Jewish bondage of spirit under a new form. The true liberty which Paul would teach was this: To regard no day whatever as more related to the Christian consciousness than any other day, and to make every day a rest from sin, pervading all with a sacred spirit by performing all its labours to the glory of God. This is the true, thorough, and high ground, which the apostle called them to occupy with him. But opposition to Judaism, and reverence for Christ in His resurrection had led the Christians to hold their public meetings on Sunday instead of Saturday ; and some little allowance of set days (including Easter and Whitsuntide) had been granted to the weakness of the Christian life, which, in the common average of Christians, had not yet risen to that level which would enable them, like Paul, to make every day equally a Lords' day. This concession had been possibly established with Paul's connivance, certainly very early in the history of the Church ; and, on the whole, was a very convenient and useful human appointment.' See this view in Neander, Hist., vol. i, § 3, vol. 2, § 3 ; and Planting and Training vol. i : bk. 3, ch. v, § 2. The chief argument by which he supports his view is a perversion of the figurative and glowing language found in the few and not very perspicuous writings of the Christians immediately next to the apostles, where they speak affectionately of the Christian's whole life as belonging to God by the purchase of redemption, and of the duties of every day as an oblation to His honour. The thankful spirit of the new dispensation, urges Neander, unlike the Jewish, felt itself constrained by gratitude for redemption to consecrate its whole life to God. Whatever the Christian's occupation, whether secular or religious, all was alike done to the glory of God. Hence, all was consecrated; every day was a holy day, for the whole life was holy; every Christian was a perpetual priest. Hence, there was no room for the idea of a Sabbath at all. Strange that the learned and amiable antiquary should have forgotten, that all this was just as true of pious Hebrews before, as of Christians after Christ—of Isaiah as of Paul. Isaiah, if redeemed at all, was redeemed by the same blood with Paul, owed substantially the same debt of gratitude, and would feel, as a true saint, the same self-consecration. The spirit of the precept, " Do all to the glory of God," actuates the pious Israelite exactly as it did the pious Christian. Let the reader compare Deut. vi : 4, 5, with Matt. xxii : 37. So, this argument proves that there ought to be no room for a sabbatical distinction of days under the old dispensation, just as under the new. Unluckily, the explicit language of the books of Moses is rather damaging to the validity of the inference.

Neander concedes that Paul's ground was too high for many ; and hence an observance of some days, not *jure divino*, was allowed them. On this I remark, first, that it is a low view of the apostle's inspiration, which makes him set up a standard so impractical, that the teaching needed amendment by a human expedient; and second, that this admitted fact goes far to prove that a Sabbath is grounded, as a permanent and moral precept, in man's wants and nature. Third, this plea leaves the Lord's day in the attitude of a piece of will-worship.

In our remaining discussion of the passages cited from the
epistles. we may confine our remarks to Col.
ii : 16, 17. For it contains all the apparent
difficulties for the Sabbatarian, and all the
supposed arguments for his opponent, in the strongest form.
The point made by Calvin upon the words, " Sabbath-days,
. . . . are a shadow of things to come, but the body is of
Christ," is far the most plausible, and indeed the only one of
serious difficulty. It is in substance this : That if it be admitted that the Lord's day was never included by the earlier
Christians in the term Sabbata—and the apostle is here condemning the Jewish holy-days only—still the fact will remain that the
Jewish Sabbath was a shadow. That is, it was a typical, and
not a perpetual moral institution, so that it must pass away
along with all the other types, after the substance comes, unless
some positive New Testament precept re-enact it. But there is
no such precept. To this we answer, that the Sabbath was to
the Jews both a perpetual, moral institution, and a type. That
it was the former, we have proved in the first general branch of
our discussion. It was as old as the race of man, was given to
all the race, was given upon an assigned motive of universal
application, and to satisfy a necessity common to the whole race,
was founded on man's natural relations to his Maker, was observed before the typical dispensation came among all tribes,
was re-enacted in the decalogue where all the precepts are perpetual. and was enjoined on foreigners as well as Jews in the
Holy Land : while from all types foreigners were expressly
excluded. That it was to the Jews also a type, we admit.
Like the new-moons, it was marked by an additional number
of sacrifices. It was to the Israelites a memorial of their exodus from Egypt, and their covenant of obedience to God.
Deut. v : 15, Exod. xxxi : 13; Ezek. xx : 12. It was for a
time, at least, a foreshadowing of the rest of Canaan. Heb. iv :
4–11. It was to them, as it is to us, a shadow of the rest in
heaven. Heb. iv : 9. Calvin adds, (Institutes, Bk. 2, ch. 8,
§ 29) that its most important typical use was to represent the
cessation of the efforts of self-righteousness in us, that we may
repose in the justifying and sanctifying grace of Christ. For
this his proofs seem to us very slender. When the Epistle to
the Colossians says that Sabbaths, along with holy days and
new-moons, are a shadow, it seems to us much the most simple
explanation to say that it is the sacrificial aspect of those days,
or (to employ other words) their use as special days of sacrifice, in which they together constituted a shadow. They were
a shadow in this : that the sacrifices, which constituted so
prominent a part of their Levitical observance, pointed to
Christ the body. This is exactly accordant with the whole
tenor of the Epistles.

The seventh day had been, then, to the Jews, both a moral

Is the Sabbath a Type.

institution and a ritual type. In its latter use, the coming of
Christ had of course abrogated it. In its former use, its whole
duties and obligations had lately been transferred to the Lord's
day. So that the seventh day, as distinguished from Sunday,
along with the new-moons, was now nothing but a type, and
that an effete one. In this aspect, the apostle might well argue
that its observance then indicated a Judaizing tendency.

We fortify our position farther by re-asserting that the fair
exposition of all these passages should lead
us to understand by the phrases, "days,"
"times," "holy-days," only those days or
times which were then subjects of diversity among the Christians to whom the apostle was writing. When he implies that
some innocently "regarded every day alike," we ought in fairness to understand by "every day," each of those days which
were then in dispute. But we know historically that there was
no diversity among these Christians concerning the observance
of the Lord's day. All practised it. If we uncritically persist
in taking the phrase "every day" in a sense absolutely universal, we shall place the teachings and usages of the apostle
in a self-contradictory light. We make him tell his converts
that the Lord's day may be regarded as just like any other day;
when we know that, in fact, neither the apostle nor any of his
converts regarded it so. They all observed it as a religious festival, and, as we shall show, with the clear sanction of inspired
example. Again: it must be distinctly remembered that the
word Sabbath was never applied, in New Testament language,
to the Lord's day, but was always used for the seventh day, and
other Jewish festivals, as distinguised from the Christian Sunday. We have the authority of Suidas, Theophylact and
Cæsarius, and Levit. xxiii : 24, that the "Jews called any of
their stated religious festivals $\Sigma \alpha \beta \beta \alpha \tau \alpha$. We might then argue,
perhaps, that there is no evidence that the seventh day is
intended in this place of Colossians at all; but only the Jewish
feasts. But we waive this, as too near to special pleading.
With far more confidence we argue, that since all parties have
claimed the parellelism of three passages in Romans, Galatians
and Colossians, as to their occasion and doctrine, we are entitled to assume that the passage in Colossians, the most
explicit of the three, is to be taken as explicative of the other
two. And we assert that, according to well known usage of
the word $\Sigma \alpha \beta \beta \alpha \tau \alpha$ at that time, the Sundays were definitely
excluded from the apostle's assertion. When he says here,
"holy-days, new-moons, and Sabbath-days, he intentionally
excludes the Lord's days. We are entitled to assume, therefore, that they are excluded when he says in the parallel passage of Romans, "every day," and in Galatians, "days, and
months, and times, and years." That the Lord's days were
sacred was not in debate; this is set aside as a matter known to

The "Days" ex-
cluded are Jewish.

all, consented unto by all.   It is the Jewish holy-days from the observance of which the Christian conscience is exempted.

Let us recur to that view of the necessity of a Sabbatical institution in some form.   It is not a tempo-

rary or ceremonial need, but one founded on man's very nature and relations to his God. If there is no stated sacred day, there will be no religion.   Now shall we so interpret the apostle's words as to leave the New Testament Church no Sabbath at all in any shape?   After the experience of all ages had shown that a Sabbath rest was the natural and necessary means essential to religious welfare, was the New Testament Church stripped more bare, left more poor than all preceding dispensations?   Paradise had enjoyed its Sabbath, though needing it less.   The patriarchal saints enjoyed it.   Abraham enjoyed it.   Israel, under the burdensome tutelage of the law, enjoyed it.   But now that the last, the fullest, the most gracious and blessed dispensation of all has come, this one of the two institutions of Eden is taken away !   We cannot accept such an exposition of the apostle's meaning.

We shall now, in the third branch of our discussion, attempt to show the ground on which we

(d)   Lord's day is Christian Sabbath.

assert that the Sabbath, " from the resurrection of Christ, was changed into the first day of the week, which in Scripture is called the Lord's day, and is to be continued to the end of the world as the Christian Sabbath."   This proof is chiefly historical, and divides itself into two branches; first, that drawn from the inspired history of the New Testament; and second, that found in the authentic but uninspired testimony of primitive Christians.   The latter, which might have been thought to demand a place in our review of the history of Sabbath opinions has been reserved for this place, because it forms an interesting part of our ground of argument.   But let us here say, once for all, that we invoke this patristic testimony, in no popish or prelatic spirit of dependence on it.   In our view, all the uninspired church testimony in the world, however venerable, would never make it our duty to keep Sunday as a Sabbath.   We use these fathers simply as historical witnesses; and their evidence derives its whole value in our eyes from its relevancy to this point; whether or not the apostles left a custom of observing Sunday, instead of the Sabbaths, established by their example in the Churches.

Our first, or preliminary argument for the observance of Sunday as the Sabbath, is that implied in the

Inferred from Abrogation of Seventh Day.

second Scripture reference subjoined by our Confession to the sentence we have just quoted from it.   If we have been successful in proving that the Sabbath is a perpetual institution, the evidence will appear perfect.   The perpetual law of the decalogue has commanded all men, in all time, to keep a Sabbath-day; and " till heaven and earth pass, one jot or tittle shall not pass from the law of God till all be fulfilled." The Apostle, in Col. ii : 16, 17, clearly tells us that the seventh day is no longer our Sabbath. What day, then, is it? Some day must have been substituted; and what one so likely to be the true substitue as the Lord's day? The law is not repealed; it cannot be. But Paul has shown that it is changed. To what day is the Sabbath changed, if not to the first? No other day in the week has a shadow of a claim. It must be this, or none; but it cannot be none: therefore it must be this.

The other main argument consists in the fact that disciples, inspired apostles, and their Christian associates, did observe the Lord's day as a religious festival. And this fact must be viewed, to see its full force, in connection with the first argument. When we find them at once beginning, and uniformly continuing, the observance of the Lord's day, while they avow that they are no longer bound to observe the seventh day, and when we couple with this the knowledge of the truth that they, like all the rest of the world, were still commanded by God to keep His Sabbath, we see that the inference is overwhelming, that the authority by which they observed the Lord's day was from God, although they did not say so. That which is inferred from Scripture, " by good and necessary consequence," is valid; as well as that which is set down expressly in it." Examination shows us, then, that the disciples commenced the observance of the Lord's day by social worship the very next week after the resurrection. From John xx : 19, we learn that the very day of the resurrection, at evening, the disciples were assembled with closed doors, with the exception of Thomas Didymus. Can we doubt that they had met for worship? In verse 26 we learn: " And after eight days again His disciples were within, and Thomas with them: then came Jesus, the doors being shut, and stood in the midst, and said, ' Peace be unto you.' " None will doubt but that this was also a meeting for worship, and the phraseology implies that it was their second meeting. In Jewish language, and estimates of time, the days at which the counts begin and end are always included in the counts; so that " after eight days," here indisputably means just a full week.

By consulting Leviticus xxiii : 15, 16; Deut. xvi : 9, we find that the day of Pentecost was fixed in this way. On the morrow after that Sabbath (seventh day) which was included within the passover week, a sheaf of the earliest ripe corn was cut, brought fresh into the sanctuary, and presented as a thank-offering to God. The day of this ceremonial was always the first day of the week, or our Sunday, which was, to the Israelites, a working day. From this day they were to count seven weeks complete and the fiftieth day was Pentecost day, or the feast of ingathering.

Thus we reach the interesting fact that the day selected by God for the pentecostal outpouring, and the inauguration of the Gospel dispensation, was the Lord's day—a significant and splendid testimony to the importance and honour it was intended to have in the Christian world. But we read in Acts i : 14, and ii : 1, that this day also was observed by the disciples as a day for social worship. Thus the first day of the week received a second, sacred and august witness, as the weekly solemnity of our religion, not only in its observance by the whole body of the new Church, but by the baptism of fire, and the Holy Ghost—a witness only second to that of Christ's victory over death and hell. Then the first public proclamation of the Gospel under the new dispensation began; and surely, when every step, every act of the Divine Providence was formative and fundamental, it was not without meaning that God selected the first day of the week as the chosen day.

It is most evident from the New Testament history, that the Apostles and early Church uniformly
Acts 20 : 7. Lord's celebrated their worship on the first day of
Day at Troas.   the week. The hints are not numerous; but they are sufficiently distinct. The next clear instance is in Acts xx : 7. The Apostle was now returning from his famous mission to Macedonia and Achaia, in full prospect of captivity at Jerusalem. He stops at the little church at Troas, to spend a season with his converts there: "And upon the first day of the week when the disciples came together to break bread, Paul preached unto them, (ready to depart on the morrow,) and continued his speech until midnight." Here we have a double evidence of our point. First, Paul preached unto the disciples on this day, while we see from the sixth verse, that he was a whole week in Troas, including the Jewish Sabbath. Why does he wait nearly a whole week to give these his more solemn and public instructions, unless there had been some usage? Again: the words, "when the disciples came together to break bread," clearly indicate that the first day of the week was their habitual day for celebrating the Lord's Supper. So that it is clear, this Church of Troas, planted and trained by Paul, was in the habit of consecrating the first day of the week to public worship; and the inspired man here concurs in the habit. Neander does, indeed, suggest an evasion, in order to substantiate his assertion that there is no evidence the Lord's day was specially sanctified during the life-time of Paul. He says that it is so very probable this day was selected by the brethren, because Paul could not wait any longer, (ready to depart on the morrow,) that no safe inference can be drawn for a habitual observance of the day by them or Paul! But verse 6, tells us that Paul had been already waiting a whole week,

and might have had choice of all the days of the week for his meeting! No other word is needed to explode this suggestion.

The next clear instance is in 1 Cor. xvi : 1, 2. "Now con-
1 Cor. 16th : 1 and 2. cerning the collection for the saints; as I have given order to the Churches of Galatia, even so do ye. Upon the first day of the week let every one of you lay by him in store as God hath prospered him, that there be no gatherings when I come." The points here indicated are two — that the weekly oblation of alms-giving was fixed for the Lord's day — and that this rule was enacted for the Church of Corinth, and all those of Galatia. The inference is overwhelming, that the Apostle made the usage ultimately uniform in all the churches of his training. Neander again attempts to destroy this evidence for the sancti- fication of Sunday, by saying that this does not prove there was any church meeting, or public worship on this day. The sum of alms was, most probably, simply laid aside at home, in an individual, private manner; and this is made more probable by the Apostle's own words : "let every one of you lay by him in store." But suppose this understanding of the passage is granted, against the uniform custom and tradition of the earliest Christians, which testifies with one voice, that the weekly alms- giving took place in the church meeting; Neander's point is not yet gained. This alms-giving was, in the New Testa- ment meaning, an act of worship. See Phil. iv : 18. And the early tradition unanimously represents the first Christians as so regarding it. Hence, whether this alms-giving were in public or private, we have here an indisputable instance, that an act of worship was appointed, by apostolic authority, to be statedly performed on the Lord's day, throughout the churches. This is evidence enough that the first day of the week was the day already known and selected for those forms of worship which were rather weekly than diurnal.

Only one other remains to be cited : that in Rev. i : 10.
John observes the first day in Patmos. John the Apostle introduces the visions of Patmos, by saying, "I was in the spirit on the Lord's day." This is the only instance of the application of this title to the first day of the week in the sacred writings. But all expositors, ancient and modern, say unhesitatingly that Sunday is designated by it. On this point the Church has had but one understanding, from the first century down. The Apostle evidently means to inform us that on Sunday he was engaged in a spiritual frame of mind and feelings. The application of the name, Lord's day, to Sunday, by inspired authority, of itself contains almost enough of sig- nificance to establish its claims to sanctification, without another text or example. What fair sense can it bear, except that it is a day consecrated to the Lord? Compare Isaiah lviii : 15, when God calls the Sabbath "my holy-day." If the Sabbath

is God's day, the Lord's day should mean a Christian Sabbath.
And the occupation of the Apostle this day, with peculiar spiritual exercises, gives additional probability to the belief that it
was observed by the New Testament Christians as a day of
devotion.

We come now to the second branch of the historical argument
—the testimony of the early, but uninspired
Christian writers. The earliest of all cannot
be called Christian. In the celebrated letter
of inquiry written by Pliny the younger to the Emperor Trajan,
on the treatment of persons accused of Christianity, this pagan
governor says, that it was the custom of these Christians, " to
meet, *stato die*, before light, to sing a hymn to Christ as God,
and bind each other in an oath, (not to some crime but) to refrain from theft, robbery and adultery, not to break faith, and
not to betray trusts." This letter was written a few years after
the death of the Apostle John. We cannot doubt that this
stated day, discovered by Pliny was the Lord's day. Ignatius,
the celebrated martyr-bishop of Antioch, says, in his epistle to
the Magnesians, written about A. D. 107 or 116, that this is
"the Lord's day, the day, the day consecrated to the resurrection, the queen and chief of all the days."

Justin Martyr, who died about A. D. 160, says that the
Christians " neither celebrated the Jewish festivals, nor observed
their Sabbaths, nor practised circumcision." (Dialogue with
Trypho, p. 34). In another place, he says, that " they, both
those who lived in the city and those who lived in the country,
were all accustomed to meet on the day which is denominated
Sunday, for the reading of the Scriptures, prayer, exhortation
and communion. The assembly met on Sunday, because this
is the first day on which God, having changed the darkness and
the elements, created the world ; and because Jesus our Lord
on this day rose from the dead."

The epistle attributed to Barnabas, though not written by
this apostolic man, is undoubtedly of early origin. This unknown writer introduces the Lord, as saying : " The Sabbaths
which you now keep are not acceptable to me ; but those which
I have made when resting from all things, I shall begin the
eighth day, that is the beginning of the other world." " For
which cause, we (Christians) observe the eighth day with glad-
ness, in which Jesus rose from the dead," &c.   Eph. ch. xv.

Tertullian, at the close of the second century, says : " We
celebrate Sunday as a joyful day.   On the Lord's day we think
it wrong to fast, or to kneel in prayer."

Clement of Alexandria, cotemporary with Tertullian, says :
"A true Christian, according to the commands of the Gospel,
observes the Lord's day by casting out all bad thoughts, and
cherishing all goodness, honouring the resurrection of the Lord,
which took place on that day."

Tradition of Lord's Day.

But, perhaps the most important, because the most learned, and, at the same time, the most explicit witness, is Eusebius, the celebrated bishop of Cæsarea, who was in his literary prime about the era of the Council of Nice, A. D. 325. In his Commentary on the xcii Psalm, which the reader will remember, is entitled " a psalm or song for the Sabbath-day," he says : " The Worb, (Christ), by the new covenant, translated and transferred the feast of the Sabbath to the morning light, and gave us the symbol of true rest, the saving Lord's day, the first (day) of light, in which the Saviour gained the victory over death, &c. On this day, which is the first of the Light, and the true Sun, we assemble after the interval of six days, and celebrate holy and spiritual Sabbath; even all nations redeemed by Him throughout the world assemble, and do those things according to the spiritual law, which were decreed for the priests to do on the Sabbath. All things which it was duty to do on the Sabbath, these we have transferred to the Lord's day as more appropriately belonging to it, because it has the precedence, and is first in rank, and more honourable than the Jewish Sabbath. It is delivered to us ($\pi\alpha\rho\alpha\delta\acute{\epsilon}\delta\sigma\tau\alpha\iota$) that we should meet together on this day, and it is evidence that we should do these things announced in the psalm."

The first Church council which formally enjoined cessation of labour upon the Lord's day was the provincial synod of Laodicea, held a little after the middle of the fourth century. The twenty-ninth canon of this body commanded that none but necessary secular labours should be carried on upon Sunday. But Constantine the Great, when he adopted the Christian as the religion of the State, had already enacted that all the labours of courts of justice, civil and military functionaries, and handicraft trades, should be suspended on the Lord's day, and that it should be devoted to prayer and public worship. This suspension of labour was not, however, extended to agriculturists, because it was supposed they must needs avail themselves of the propitious season to gather their harvests, or sow their seed, without regard to sacred days. But the Emperor Leo (who came to the throne A. D. 457) ultimately extended the law to all classes of persons.

The Christians did not for several hundred years apply the word Sabbath to the first day of the week, but always used it distinctly to indicate the Jewish seventh day. Their own sacred day, the first day, was called by them the Lord's day ($\mathring{\eta}\mu\epsilon\rho\alpha$ $\varkappa\upsilon\rho\iota\acute{\alpha}\varkappa\eta$), as they said, because it was dedicated to the honour of Christ, and because it was the head, crown, and chief of all the days. They also called it Sunday (*Dies solis*, a phrase frequently found among the Latin Christians), because, according to their interpretation of Gen. i : 3, the sun was created on the first day of the week; but still more, because on that day the brighter

Christian Nomenclature.

Sun of Righteousness arose from the dead, with healing in His beams. The objection often made by persons over-puritanical, that it smacks of Pagan or Scandinavian profanity to say Sunday, because the word indicates a heathenish consecration of the day to the sun, is therefore more Quakerish than sensible. We are willing to confess that we always loved the good old name Sunday—name worthy of that day which should ever seem the brightest in the Christian's conceptions, of all the week, when the glorious works of the natural creation first began to display the honours of the great Creator, and when that new and more divine creation of redeeming grace was perfected by the resurrection of Jesus Christ. But, in the application of the phrase " Christian Sabbath" to the first day, the Westminster Assembly had a definite and truthful design, although the early Church had not given it this name. It was their intention to express thus that vital head of their theory; that the Old Testament institute called Sabbath, which was coeval with man, and was destined to coexist with all dispensations, was not abrogated; that it still existed substantially, and that Christians were now to find it in the Lord's day. To the Christian the Lord's day is the Sabbath. (Such is the significance of the name) possessing the Divine authority, and demanding in the main the sanctification which was formerly attached to the seventh day.

Another head of the Sabbath argument remains: from its practical necessity, as a means of securing 5. Practical Argument. man's corporeal and mental health, his morality, his temporal success in life, and his religious interests. This is the department of the discussion which has been more particularly unfolded in the " Permanent Sabbath Documents," published under the auspices of Dr. Justin Edwards, and more recently in the remarkable essays on the Sabbath, produced by workingmen in Great Britain. It is now by so much the best understood part of the Sabbath discussion that we should not have introduced it at all except that it was one of the stones in the arch of our attempted demonstration, that there is a natural necessity in man for a Sabbath rest. The Creator, who appointed the Sabbath, formed man's frame ; and all intelligent observers are now agreed that the latter was adapted to the former. Either body or mind can do more work by resting one day in seven, than by labouring all the seven days. And neither mind nor body can enjoy health and continued activity without its appointed rest. Even the structure of the brutes exhibits the same law. Again : As a moral and social institution, a weekly rest is invaluable. It is a quiet domestic reunion for the bustling sons of toil. It ensures the necessary vacation in those earthly and turbulent anxieties and affections, which would otherwise become inordinate and morbid. It brings around a season of periodical neatness and decency, when the soil of weekly labour is laid aside, and men meet each other amidst the decencies of the sanctuary, and renew their social affections. But above all, a Sabbath is necessary for man's moral and religious interests. Even in Paradise, and in man's state of innocence, it was true that a stated season, resolutely appropriated to religious exercises, was necessary to his welfare as a religious being. A creature subject to the law of habit, of finite faculties, and required by the conditions of his existence to distribute his attention and labours between things secular and things sacred, cannot successfully accomplish this destiny without a regular distribution of his time between the two great departments. This is literally a physical necessity. And when we add the consideration that man is now a being of depraved, earthly affections, prone to avert his eyes from heaven to the earth, the necessity is still more obvious. Man does nothing regularly for which he has not a regular time. The absolute necessity of the Sabbath, as a season for the public preaching of religion and morality, as a leisure time for the domestic religious instruction of the young, as a time for private self-examination and devotion, is most clear to all who admit the importance of these duties. And now, it is most obvious to practical good sense, that if such a stated season is necessary, then it is proper that it should be ordained and marked off by Divine authority, and not by a sort of convention on man's part. To neglect the stated observance of a religious rest, is to neglect religion. And when there is so much of mundane and carnal affection—so much of craving, eager worldly bustle—to entice us to an infringement of this sacred rest, it is certain that it will be neglected, unless it be defended by the highest sanction of God's own authority. Nay, do we not see that this sanction is insufficient, even among some who admit its validity? Again: If such a stated rest is necessary, then it is also necessary that its metes and bounds be defined by the same authority which enjoins the rest itself. Otherwise, the license which men will allow themselves in interpreting the duration of the season, and in deciding how much constitutes the observance of it, or how little, will effectually abrogate the rest itself. If, then, the necessities of human nature require a Sabbath, it does not appear how God could ordain less than we suppose He has done, in requiring the whole of a definite length of time to be faithfully devoted to religious exercises, and in making this command explicit and absolute.

LECTURE XXXIII.

SECOND TABLE. (5th and 6th COMMANDMENTS.)

WE enter now upon the consideration of the Second Table. The immediate objects of the duties of this table are our fellow-men. But still, the breach of one of them is a sin against God also, because it is He who has enjoined them, and has placed us in those relations in which the duties arise.

As the first table began with that which is fundamental to **1. Scope of the Fifth Commandment. Parents represent all Superiors.** all religion, the pointing out of the only proper Object of religious service; so the second table begins with that duty which is fundamental to all social duties, and the most important of all; subjection to domestic authority. I must here again remind you of the rule of interpretation laid down at the outset, that a whole class of duties is enjoined, and of sins forbidden, under one prominent specimen. So, we understand that here, under the example of filial duties, all the relative duties between superiors and inferiors, in the Family, the Church, and the Commonwealth, are included. Not only the duties of children to parents, but of servants to masters, pupils to teachers, and people to rulers in Church and State, are here implied. If these, most important classes of social duties are not intended to be included in this precept, then they are nowhere in the decalogue: for there is no other precept where they can be fairly embraced. Can we believe that the summary so omits what the subsequent Scriptures so often enforce in detail? The including of all these duties under the fifth commandment will seem far more natural, if we remember that the original forms of government in the old world were all patriarchal; in which the father was the head, priest, and prince of all his descendants and servants. The family was no doubt the germ out of which civil institutions and the organized Church grew. The Jewish nation was just now passing,

398

in part, out of this patriarchal form; and many of its features were retained in the Mosaic government. How natural then, to an ancient Israelite, to represent the general idea of civil and ecclesiastical superiors under the term Parents? Servants (who were usually slaves) were on much the same footing in ancient society with children. Kings were called Fathers, 1 Sam. xxiv : 11. Prophets were generally addressed as Fathers, by the young men entrusted to their religious instruction, who, in turn, were called "sons of the prophets," 2 Kings ii : 3 and 12.

Many duties are of a reciprocal nature. Obligation on one side implies a correlative obligation on the other. Thus the duties of inferiors imply the reciprocal duties of superiors. Under this commandment then, are included the duties of parents towards their children, masters towards servants, rulers towards subjects, church-teachers towards their charges. Thus, we find that St. Paul, in the former part of the sixth chapter of Ephesians, (which may fairly be taken as his exposition of the fifth commandment), begins with the duties of children towards parents, but follows it up immediately with the duties of parents towards their children; and after instructing servants, proceeds immediately to instruct their masters. We feel therefore fully justified in giving the fifth commandment the general scope assigned to it in the Catechism. "The general scope of the fifth commandment is the performance of those duties which we mutually owe in our several relations, as superiors, inferiors, or equals."

2. It is under this head of the decalogue, that the important Scripture doctrine of the civil magistrate, and duty of citizens, should fall, which is the subject of the 23d chapter of our Confession. But this is a subject of so much importance, that I reserve it for separate discussion in the Senior course. The details of the other duties of inferiors and superiors may be seen so fully stated in your catechisms, that it would be mere repetition to recite them here.

The fifth commandment is peculiar in closing with a promise to encourage to its observance: "That thy days may be long upon the land which the Lord thy God giveth thee." The first recipient of the promise was the Nation; and it may be national permanency which is pledged. But the Apostle applies it (Eph. vi : 2), to Christian children, after Israel was cast out. This authorizes us to give it a personal application. As a long life spent in adversity would be no boon, this promise is obviously understood as one of "long life and prosperity." We understand it to give us that encouragement which is also presented by the established connection of causes and effects in God's providence, where the faithful and general performance of the duties of inferiors and superiors, and especially of parents and children, ensures, as far as any earthly means can, general health, peace, prosperity and temporal welfare; whereas the anarchical neglect of those duties, and especially of the parental and filial, plunges every society into violence, disease, disorder, misery, and premature death. We do not understand God's promise in this commandment as absolute and universal. To claim this would be to claim that God should work for dutiful sons a continual miracle, in suspending the mutual influences of men on each other's welfare, by which the virtuous, especially when few, share the calamities procured by the more prevalent crimes of the wicked. The first promise is given to a society (as to Israel) in the aggregate. The general performance of the duty is necessary to ensure the happy result. If there is a general neglect of the duties, as in our day, it must result in calamities; and some of the most dutiful of our sons may fall, as many a virtuous Confederate soldier fell, in the prime of his days, in the general disorder.

The sixth commandment is in these terse words: "Thou shalt not kill." Its obvious scope is the preservation of life. It forbids all that unrighteously assails our own and others' lives, and enjoins all suitable means for the preservation of both. This command is based upon these two great truths: that life is God's gift, and therefore to be abridged or taken away only at His command; and that life is of supreme value to every man. In robbing a man of life, you would virtually rob him of every valuable thing which life includes. It is committing against a fellow-man every species of robbery in one. The Scriptures also ground the prohibition of taking man's life on his likeness to God. Gen. ix : 6. "For in the image of God made He man. James iii : 9; also founds the lesser sin of slander and reviling partly on the same fact. Man's rational, moral and immortal nature is the chief glory of his being; it reflects the glory of God's. Hence, to invade this being is at once the most enormous wrong against the creature, and an act of impiety against God.

4. Scope of Sixth Commandment. .

We have here then, another instance of the profoundly logical arrangement which infinite wisdom has given to the decalogue. The second table, after fixing those relative duties out of which society itself emerges, then proceeds to protect, first, that value which is transcendent with every man—his temporal existence. It then secures that which is next in order of essential importance—man's chastity, including the purity of the marital relation, the foundation of the domestic; and postpones to the last those duties of commutative righteousness, and of truth, which are the outer bonds of society.

But when God says, "Thou shalt not kill," what are the things whose slaying is thus inhibited? There is a small class of fanatics in Christian

5. Animal Life may be Taken.

lands, larger in some Pagan ones, who answer, that we may kill nothing that has animal life.   Hence the use of the flesh of quad-rupeds, birds, and fishes, for food, is of course inhibited by them. This party is known in America as Grahamites.   Their tendency is infidel; for the Bible speaks too plainly on this subject to be questioned by any devout believer.   We read that God gave to Adam and his family only the vegetable world for food, assigning him the use of the animals as his servants.   (Hence, the skins in which God clothed Adam and Eve after their fall, must have come either from the religious sacrifices which He taught them to offer, the more probable surmise; or from beasts which died by the vio-lence of their own kind, or by disease).   But after the flood, the fruitfulness of the earth having been probably impaired for all subsequent time, God expressly gave Noah and his family the privilege of eating the flesh of animals, only reserving the blood, with which they should " make atonement for their souls upon the altar."   This permission is doubtless now valid.   It was expressly continued to the Hebrews, in the distinction of the clean beasts.   It is equally certain that it was not abro-gated after Christ came; for we find Him, even after His resur-rection (Luke xxiv : 43 ; Jno. xxi : 9), eating the flesh of fishes, and encouraging His followers to do so.   See also Rom. xiv : 3, and 1 Cor. x : 25.

Reason approves this.   The sanctity of human life is placed, where inspiration places it (in Gen. ix : 6), in man's rational responsibility and immortality.   The life of the beast, "whose spirit goeth downward," is no such inviolable boon to him.   And while we admit that the duty of benevolence extends to the brutes, as does God's benevolence, we argue that the employment of animals for food has, on the whole, greatly promoted their animal well-being.   For man thus has a sufficient motive for their careful nurture, whereas otherwise he would regard them as nuisances.

Still another, and a larger class of fanatics, hold that there **6. Capital Punish-** are no circumstances under which human life **ments and Defensive** can be taken lawfully by man.   Claiming the **War, &c., Not Forbid-** admission which we have made, that life is to **den.** man God's loan, they urge that no creature can under any circumstances assume authority to take it away from his fellow man.   Hence it must follow that personal self-defence against unrighteous aggression, that the defensive wars of commonwealths, and the infliction of capital punishments upon the most enormous criminals even, are all unlawful. Here is the theory of the "non-resistance" and the "peace parties."

I may make the same remark of these, that they are virtu-**Arguments—Magis-** ally infidel parties.   If the authority of the **trate Slays by Dele-** Scriptures is admitted, their conclusions are **gated Authority.** obviously false.   They are obviously illogi-

26*

cal. It is true that human life is God's loan to His creatures.
No one may take it away without the authority of the Divine
Giver. It is therefore simply a question of revealed testimony,
whether God has, in any cases, deputized to man, or to society,
the authority to take life. If He has, then it is God's authority which, in the appropriate case, takes away the boon; and
the human agent is merely God's executioner. It is, then,
simply a question of fact as to the Scriptural teachings.

If life is thus sacred, as God's boon, and is man's one possession of transcendent value, then to take
it away without right is an enormous outrage.
Suppose this outrage is obviously about to
be perpetrated by an aggressor upon an innocent person. Suppose, also, that the protection of the law is absent, and cannot be successfully invoked? What shall the defendant do?
Is it his duty to be passive and yield up his life; or to take the
defensive, and protect it by force, even to the extent of taking
the assailant's life if necessary? Human laws and conscience
concur in the latter answer. Remember that the aggressor
unrighteously creates the dilemma, making it necessary that
at least one life must go. Whose had best go? Obviously the
life of the criminal, rather than that of the innocent man.
Again: If law subsequently has its just course, the murderer,
after his guilty success, will have to die for it. The case is then
still stronger: that the passive theory sacrifices two lives, one
innocent; whereas the theory of self-defence saves the righteous
life, and only sacrifices the guilty one. Our conclusion is also
confirmed by the existence in us of the emotion of lawful
resentment, the righteousness of which, within its proper
bounds, the Saviour allows (Matt. v : 22; Eph. iv : 26). For
if there is no forcible self-defence against wrong, there is no
reasonable scope for this emotion.

The Scriptures expressly confirm us. The right of slaying
the house-breaker clearly implies a right of self-defence.
Exod. xxii : 2. The law of the cities of refuge contains the
same right. Numb. xxxv : 22. The effect of this permission
is evaded, indeed, by the pretence that Moses' legislation was
imperfect and barbarous, and is corrected by the milder instructions of our Saviour. Matt. v : 39. But I have taught you the
falsehoood of this notion, and showed you that the Old Testament teaches precisely the same morality with the New.

As to the delegation of the right of capital punishment
for flagrant crimes, the feeble attempt has
been made to represent the injunction of
Gen. ix : 6 as not a precept, but a prediction;
not as God's instruction what ought to be done to the murderer, but His prophecy of what human vindictiveness would
do. The context refutes this. This command for the capital punishment of the murderer, having been given to Noah,

*Self-Defence Law-
ful.*

*Capital Punishment
in Scripture.*

the second father of mankind, and before there was a chose people, is of course, universal. Look also at the expres. injunction of capital punishments for several crimes in the Pentateuch: for murder, Num. xxxv : 31 ; for striking a parent, Exod. xxi : 15 : for adultery, Levit. xx : 10; for religious imposture, Deut. xiii : 5, &c. In Numb. xxxv : 33, a reason is given which, on general principles, necessitates the capital punishment of murder : " For blood, it defileth a land, and the land cannot be cleansed of the blood that is shed therein, but by the blood of him that shed it." Capital punishments are also authorized in the New Testament. Rom. xiii assures us that the magistrate " beareth not the sword in vain," but in bearing it he is God's minister to execute wrath upon the evildoer.

Unprovoked war is the most monstrous secular crime that can be committed: it is at once the greatest of evils, and includes the worst forms of robbery and murder. Wherever war is prompted by mere pique. or lust of aggrandizement, or ambition for fame and power, it deserves all that can be said of its mischiefs and criminality by the most zealous advocates of peace And nothing can rescue a people waging war, from this guilt, except the fact that their appeal to arms is necessary for the defence of just and vital rights. But while the Scriptures teach this, they give no countenance to the weak fanaticism, which commands governments to practice a passive non-resistance, in such a world as this. Nations are usually unjust and unscrupulous. The very fact that they are politically sovereign implies that there is no umpire between them, except Divine Providence. A passive attitude would usually only provoke, instead of disarming attack. Hence its only effect would be to bring all the horrors and desolations of invasion upon the innocent people, while the guilty went free. God has therefore both permitted and instructed rulers, when thus unjustly assailed, to retort these miseries upon the assailants who introduce them. The very fact that all war is so terrific a scourge, and that aggressive war is such an enormous crime, only makes it more clear that the injured party are entitled to their redress, and are justified in inflicting on the injurers such chastisement as will compel their return to justice, even including the death and ruin which they were preparing against their inoffensive neighbors.

7. Defensive War Lawful.

It is perfectly clear that Sacred Scripture legalizes such defensive war. Abram, Moses, Joshua, Samuel, David, Josiah, the Maccabees, were such warriors : and they were God's chosen saints. It was " through faith they waxed valiant in fight, turned to flight the armies of the aliens." Heb. xi : 34. God fought for and with them by giving, in their battles, answers to their prayers, and miraculous assistance to their anns. Under the New Testament, when Christ's forerunner was preaching the baptism of repentance, he did not enjoin on soldiers the surrender of their profession as sinful, but only the restricting of themselves to its lawful duties. The New Testament tells us of a Centurion, affectionately commended by our Redeemer as possessed of "great faith;" and of a Cornelius, who was "accepted with God, as fearing Him and working righteousness." Luke iii : 14; vii : 9; Acts x : 35. The Apostle Paul, Rom. xiii : 4, tells us that the magistrate "beareth not the sword in vain; for he is the minister of God, a revenger to execute wrath upon him that doeth evil." It would be strange indeed, if the ruler who is armed by God with the power of capital punishment against the domestic murderer, could not justly inflict the same doom on the foreign criminal, who invades our soil unprovoked, for the purpose of shedding blood. The security of life and property which the magistrate is intended to provide by his power of punishing, would be illusory indeed, if it could only be used against individual criminals, while the more mischievous and widespread crimes of organized multitudes must go unpunished. Aggressive war is wholesale murder; and when the government sends out its army to repel and chastise the invader, it does but inflict summary execution on the murderer caught in the act.

8. Dueling Murder. The modern duel is a very peculiar usage, which has descended to us from a perversion of an institution of chivalry; the ordeal by battle. This was a means adopted by the ignorance of the middle ages, to appeal to God's judgment where the question of right was too obscure to be unravelled by their rude courts. It was founded on an abuse of the doctrine of Providence. Because the Scriptures teach that this providence is concerned in all events, the Middle Ages jumped to the conclusion, that this providence would so decide the issue, as to vindicate justice. It needs no argument to show you the fallacy. Since the intelligence of modern days has exploded the idea of the divine ordeal, the duel remains a barbarous remnant of the middle ages, without even the shadow of an argument in its favor.

Arguments for it Futile. In refuting the arguments by which the duel is defended, I shall not take the ground that the sentiment of personal honour is irrational or unchristian; I shall not assume that it is no real injury to wound it. My position is, that the duel is no proper remedy for that injury. And, first: the only lawful object, when one is wounded in his honour, is self-defence, and not revenge. The latter is expressly forbidden in every case. Now, for the defence of one's honour and good name, a duel is naught. Perhaps where malignant passions are not harboured, the challenger to a duel is most frequently actuated by this feeling; that his passive endurance of an insult will cause his fellow-men to think him a coward; and that therefore he must expose himself to the dangers of combat, in order to evince that he is not a coward; and thus retrieve his credit. Now dueling does not prove courage; for notoriously, if some brave men have fought, so have many cowards. It only proves a species of moral cowardice, which shrinks from the path of rectitude, and cowers before the finger of scorn. It is yet more obvious that the issue of the duel will prove nothing as to the truth or falsehood of the charge which constituted the insult. If one calls me a liar, and I kill him therefor, this shows nothing whatever as to my truth or falsehood. The proper and reasonable remedy here, is to require the accuser to substantiate his charge, or else confess its injustice. His refusal to do either would place him so effectually in the wrong, that no other reparation would be needed.

Another objection to the duel is, that it usually prevents, and that in the most deadly manner, that very fairness and equality which it boasts of securing. The plea is, that it puts the weak man equal to the strong one, by appealing from mere, brute muscle, to arms and skill. But according to its laws, the duel authorizes an inequality of skill far more deadly. I am ignorant of the use of the pistol. A violent and malignant man who knows himself a dead shot, so outrages me that I am impelled under the code of honour, to challenge him. He, exercising the right of the challenged, chooses pistols. Thus he has me more completety at a disadvantage than if he were a pugilist of the first fame, and I an infant; and the result is not a parcel of bruises, but my death. The system is, when tried by its own pretences, flagrantly unfair.

Duels Unfair.

It is also absurdly unequal in this: that if its proceedings have any justice, then it puts the righteous man and the culprit on the same footing. Unless the challenger is committing a monstrous wrong, he must hold that the challenged is a capital criminal: for does he not claim that it is right to subject him to the liability of a capital punishment? Why then should the innocent man, already so grievously wronged, when he proceeds to inflict the righteous penalty, give the culprit equal chances to inflict the same penalty on him? Shall the magistrate, in putting a condemned felon to death, courteously invite him to take his equal chances to put the magistrate to death? What more absurd? If the assailant really deserves to die, and this is duly ascertained (if it is not, the challenger is guilty of murder in seeking to slay an innocent man) then by all means, let him be killed, without giving him opportunity to perpetrate another unprovoked crime. When one has to kill a mad dog, he does not feel bound to give the dog a chance to bite him!

Jeopardizing of the Injured Unjust.

Last, the dueling code is a monstrous one, because it
makes the man who supposes himself
wronged, accuser, judge, and executioner in
his own cause. It is righteously then, that
the statute laws of the Commonwealth treat the duelist who
has slain his adversary, as a murderer with prepense malice.

The Interested made Judge, &c.

One plea for dueling is, that it is the necessary chastisement for classes of sins, (as against one's
good name, against the chastity of one's
family) for which the laws afford either no remedy, or such a
one as no man of delicacy can seek. The answer is: that if
the facts are true, they are arguments for perfecting the penal
laws, not for the iniquities of dueling. Another argument is,
that nothing but the code of honour will secure chivalrous manners; which it boasts of doing through the influence of the
knowledge that the man who departs from that style of manners is in danger of a challenge. The answers are two. Surely
that courtesy has little claim to be chivalrous, which is only
coerced by fear? And facts show that the influence of the
code is not what is claimed; for the societies where it has
fullest sway, are sometimes the rudest and most debauched.

Pleas Refuted.

LECTURE XXXIV.

SECOND TABLE. (7th and 8th COMMANDMENTS.)

SYLLABUS.

1. What are the scope and extent of the 7th Commandment, and what sins are
forbidden under it?
2. What the degree of guilt in adultery, and what its grounds?
3. Was polygamy ever lawful? Explain Moses' law of divorce. Is celibacy
meritorious?
  Turrettin, Loc. xi, Qu. 18. Hodge's Theology, pt. iii, ch. 19, § 11. Dr. C.
  C. Jones' History of Israelitish Nation. Michaelis' Com. on Laws of Moses.
4. Ought this precept to be publicly preached?
5. What is the scope of the 8th Commandment, and what the particular duties
and sins embraced under it?
6. What is the origin of the Right of Private Property?
7. Is usury lawful?
8. What rule should govern the Christian as to making gain of his neighbor's
necessities?
  Turrettin, Loc. xi, Qu. 19. Hodge as above, § 12. See, on whole, Larger
  Catechism, Qu. 137-142. Calvin's Inst. bk. ii, ch. 8, § 41-46. Ridgeley's
  Div., Qu. 137-142. Bp. Hopkins on 7th and 8th Commandments. Green's
  Lect. 51-53.

A S has been already observed, the scope of the seventh
commandment is to regulate the relations between the
sexes, with all the virtues of purity connected
therewith. These virtues are the basis of
the domestic relations. And as the family is

1. Scope of Seventh Commandment.

the foundation of human society, the importance of the class of duties involved is second only to those which preserve man's existence itself. It should be added also, that the sins against personal purity are peculiarly flagrant, because they involve in sensual bestiality the body which is the habitation of the rational, responsible soul, and the temple of the Holy Ghost. See 1 Cor. vi : 15, &c. Experience also shows that sins of unchastity have a peculiarly imbruting and degrading effect on both sexes, but especially on that which should be the purer, seducing them to hypocrisy, lying, treachery, cruelty, drunkenness, gluttony, and shamelessness. For the usual details of the sins embraced under the capital instance, adultery, I refer you to your catechisms.

Adultery, in strictness of speech, is the sin of illicit cohabitation by a married person. Its eminence in criminality is due to these traits; that in addition to the uncleanness, it involves the breach of the marriage contract, and the treachery contained therein; and that by corrupting the descent of families, it uproots the whole foundation of domestic society. Adultery and causeless divorce are directly antagonistic thereto. They are therefore deadly stabs against all home affections, against all training of children, against every rudiment of social order. Were all to take the license of the adulterer, men would in due time be reduced precisely to the degradation of wild beasts. The sin of the adulterer therefore, is scarcely less enormous than that of the murderer. The latter destroys man's temporal existence; the former destroys all that makes existence a boon. Let the crime of the adulterer be tried by its effects upon the family it invades. We must either suppose that the husband and wife have, or have not, the sentiments of modesty, natural jealousy, purity, and shame, usually imputed to virtuous persons. If they have not, then the lack of them implies a degradation which can only make them the parents of reprobates; and the general prevalence of such a type of character would dissolve domestic society into ultimate putrescence. If the parents have those sentiments, then the success of the seducer plunges the husband into agonies of revenge, despair and wounded affection, the guilty wife into a shame and remorse deeper than the grave, the children into privation of a mother, and all the parties into a bereavement at least as irreparable as that of a death, and far more bitter. It would have been, in some aspects, a less crime to murder the mother while innocent.

The laws of Moses, therefore, very properly made adultery a capital crime; nor does our Saviour, in the incident of the woman taken in adultery, repeal that statute, or disallow its justice. The legislation of modern, nominally Christian nations, is drawn rather from the grossness of Pagan sources than from Bible

2. Criminality of adultery.

Proper Punishment of it.

principles. The common law of England, and the statutes and usages which our Commonwealth has drawn thence, present a most inconsistent state. There is no statute whatever for punishing adultery as a crime! And yet a usage, which is as fully recognized both in England and Virginia as any common law, entitles juries to acquit the injured husband of murder who slays the violator of his bed in heat of blood. This seems to be a recognition of the capital guilt of the crime of adultery, and at the same time an allowance, in this case, of the barbarous principle of 'goelism,' which the law, in all other cases, has so stringently prohibited. But here is the monstrous inconsistency, that if the crime of the adulterer be of long standing, and gradually discovered, no matter how certain the guilt, the husband, because no longer punishing in heat of blood, is debarred from inflicting the just punishment. The only other remedy that remains at the law is an action of damages against the seducer, in which the injured husband is constrained to degrade all his wrongs to the sordid, pecuniary plea of the loss of his wife's services, as a domestic, by this interference. And juries are instructed, after ascertaining that there has been an unjust interruption of the wife's domestic services, to appraise the compensation, not at its commercial, but at any imaginary value, which the seducer's wealth may enable him to pay. Such is the wretched fiction which the law offers to the outraged spouse as the satisfaction for his wrongs.

It has always seemed to me that much causeless doubt and debate exist among expositors, and that many gratuitous admissions have been made by the most of them, touching the true status of polygamy and divorce in the Old Testament. But so much misapprehension exists about the two cases, that the general interests of truth prompt a little farther separate discussion of each. The two enactments touching divorce which present the supposed contradiction in the strongest form, are those of Moses in Deut. xxiv : 1 to 4, and Matt. xix : 3 to 9. These the reader is requested to have under his eye. The form of the Pharisees' question to Christ, " Is it lawful for a man to put away his wife for every cause?" concurs with the testimony of Josephus, in teaching us that a monstrous perversion of Moses' statute then prevailed. The licentious, and yet self-righteous Pharisee claimed, as one of his most unquestioned privileges, the right to repudiate a wife, after the lapse of years, and birth of children, for any caprice whatsoever. The trap which they now laid for Christ was designed to compel him either to incur the odium of attacking this usage, guarded by a jealous anger, or to connive at their interpretation of the statute. Manifestly Christ does not concede that they interpreted Moses rightly; but indignantly clears the legislation of that holy man from their licentious perversions, and then, because of their abuse of

3. Divorce and Polygamy in Pentateuch.

it, repeals it by His plenary authority. He refers to that constitution of the marriage tie which was original, which preceded Moses, and was therefore binding when Moses wrote, to show that it was impossible he could have enacted what they claimed. What, then, did Moses enact? Let us explain it. In the ancient society of the East, females being reared in comparative seclusion, and marriages negotiated by intermediaries, the bridegroom had little opportunity for a familiar acquaintance even with the person of the bride. When she was brought to him at the nuptials, if he found her disfigured with some personal deformity or disease (the undoubted meaning of the phrase " some uncleanness "), which effectually changed desire into disgust, he was likely to regard himself as swindled in the treaty, and to send the rejected bride back with indignity to her father's house. There she was reluctantly received, and in the anomalous position of one in name a wife, yet without a husband, she dragged out a wretched existence, incapable of marriage, and regarded by her parents and brothers as a disgraceful incumbrance. It was to relieve the wretched fate of such a woman that Moses' law was framed. She was empowered to exact of her proposed husband a formal annulment of the unconsummated contract, and to resume the status of a single woman, eligible for another marriage. It is plain that Moses' law contemplates the case, only, in which no consummation of marriage takes place. She finds no favour in the eyes " of the bridegroom." He is so indignant and disgusted that desire is put to flight by repugnance. The same fact appears from the condition of the law, that she shall in no case return to this man, "after she is defiled," i. e., after actual cohabitation with another man had made her unapproachable (without moral defilement) by the first. Such was the narrow extent of this law. The act for which it provided was divorce only in name, where that *consensus, qui matrimonium facit*, in the words of the law maxim, had never been perfected. The state of social usages among the Hebrews, with parental and fraternal severity towards the unfortunate daughter and sister, rendered the legislation of Moses necessary and righteous at the time; but "a greater than Moses" was now here; and He, after defending the inspired law-giver from their vile misrepresentation, proceeded to repeal the law, because it had been so perverted, and because the social changes of the age had removed its righteous grounds.

Under the New Testament, divorce proper can take place only on two grounds, adultery and permanent desertion, See Matt. xix : 9; v : 32; 1 Cor. vii : 15. A careful examination of these passages will lead us to these truths: That marriage is a permanent and exclusive union of one woman to one man; and so, can only be innocently dissolved by death: But that extreme criminality and breach of contract by one party annihilates the bond so that the criminal is as though he were dead to the other: That the only sins against the bond, which have this effect, are those which are absolutely incompatible with the relation, adultery, and wilful, final desertion.   In these cases, the bond having been destroyed for the innocent party, he is as completely a single man, as though the other were dead.   Some commonwealths have added many other trivial causes of divorce; thus sinning grievously against God and the purity of the people.   The Church may not recognize by her officers or acts, any of these unscriptural grounds, or the pretended divorces founded on them.

The case of the polygamist is still clearer; for we assert that the whole legislation of the Pentateuch and of all the Old Testament is only adverse to polygamy.   As some Christian divines have taught otherwise, we must ask the reader's attention and patience for a brief statement.   Polygamy is recorded of Abraham, Jacob, Gideon, Elkanah, David, Solomon; but so are other sins of several of these ; and, as every intelligent reader knows, the truthful narrative of holy writ as often discloses the sins of good men for our warning, as their virtues for our imitation.   And he who notes how, in every Bible instance, polygamy appears as the cause of domestic feuds, sin, and disaster, will have little doubt that the Holy Spirit tacitly holds all these cases up for our caution, and not our approval.   But, then, God made Adam one wife only, and taught him the great law of the perpetual unity of the twain, just as it is now expounded by Jesus Christ. (Genesis ii : 23, 24, with Matthew xix : 4 to 6). God preserved but one wife each to Noah and his sons.   In every statute and preceptive word of the Holy Spirit, it is always wife, and not wives.   The prophets everywhere teach how to treat a wife, and not wives.   Moses, Leviticus xviii : 18, in the code regulating marriage, expressly prohibits the marriage of a second wife in the life of the first, thus enjoining monogamy in terms as clear as Christ's.   Our English version hath it: "Neither shalt thou take a wife to her sister, to vex her, to uncover her nakedness, besides the other, in her lifetime."   Many insist on taking the word sister here in its literal sense, and thus force on the law the meaning that the man desiring to practice polygamy may do so, provided he does not marry two daughters of the same parents ; for if he did this, the two sisters sharing his bed would, like Rachel and Leah, quarrel more fiercely than two strangers.   But the word "sister" must undoubtedly be taken in the sense of mates, fellows, (which it bears in a number of places, e. g., Exod. xxvi 3, 5, 6, 17 ; Ezek. i : 9 and iii : 13), and this for two controlling reasons.   The other sense makes Moses talk nonsense and folly, in the supposed reason for his prohibition; in that it makes him argue that two sisters sharing one man's bed will quarrel, but two women having no kindred blood will not.   It is false to fact and to nature. Did Leah and Rachel show more jealousy than Sarah and Hagar, Hannah and Peninnah? But when we understand the law in its obvious sense, that the husband shall not divide his bed with a second mate, the first still living, because such a wrong ever harrows and outrages the great instincts placed in a woman's heart by her Creator, we make Moses talk truth and logic worthy of a profound legislator. The other reason for this construction is, that the other sense places the 18th verse in irreconcilable contradiction to the 16th verse. This forbids the marriage of a woman to the husband of her deceased sister; while the 18th verse, with this false reading, would authorize it.

Once more: Malachi (chap. ii : 14, 15), rebuking the various corruptions of the Jews, evidently includes polygamy; for he argues in favour of monogamy (and also against causeless divorce) from the fact that God, "who had the residue of the Spirit," and could as easily have created a thousand women for each man as a single one, made the numbers of the sexes equal from the beginning. He states this as the motive, "that He might seek a godly seed;" that is to say, that the object of God in the marriage relation was the right rearing of children, which polygamy notoriously hinders. Now the commission of an Old Testament prophet was not to legislate a new dispensation, for the laws of Moses were in full force; the prophets' business was to expound them. Hence, we infer that the laws of the Mosaic dispensation on the subject of polygamy had always been such as Malachi declared them. He was but applying Moses' principles.

To the assertion that the law of the Old Testament discountenanced polygamy as really as the New Testament, it has been objected that the practice was maintained by men too pious towards God to be capable of continuing in it against express precept; as, for instance, by the "king after God's own heart," David. Did not he also commit murder and adultery? Surely there is no question whether Moses forbids these! The history of good men, alas! shows us too plainly the power of general evil example, custom, temptation, and self-love, in blinding the honest conscience. It has been objected that polygamy was so universally practised, and so prized, that Moses would never have dared to attempt its extinction. When will men learn that the author of the Old Testament law was not Moses, but God? Is God timid? Does He fear to deal firmly with His creatures? But it is denied that there is any evidence that polygamy was greatly prevalent among the Hebrews. And nothing is easier than to show that, if it had been, Moses was a legislator bold enough to grapple with it. What more hardy than his dealing with the sabbatical year, with idolatry? It is objected that the marriage of the widow who was childless to the brother of the deceased, to raise up

seed to the dead, presents a case of polygamy actually commanded.   We reply, no one can show that the next of kin was
permitted or required to form such marriage when he already
had a wife.   The celebrated J. D. Michaelis, a witness learned
and not too favourable, says, in his Commentaries on the Laws
of Moses, of this law, "Nor did it affect a brother having
already a wife of his own."   Book iii, ch. vi. § 98.

It is objected that polygamy is recognized as a permitted
relation in Deut. xxi : 15–17, where the husband of a polygam-
ous marriage is forbidden to transfer the brirthright from the
eldest son to a younger, the child of a more favoured wife ; and
in Exod. xxi : 9, 10, where the husband is forbidden to deprive
a less favoured wife of her marital rights and maintenance.
Both these cases are explained by the admitted principle, that
there may be relations which it was sin to form, and which yet
it is sinful to break when formed.   No one doubts whether the
New Testament makes polygamy unlawful ; yet it seems probable that the apostles gave the same instructions to the husbands of a plurality of wives entering the Christian Church.
There appears, then, no evidence that polygamy was allowed in
the laws of Moses.

The light of nature, as revealed in the sentiments of nearly
all mankind, teaches that there are degrees of relationship,
between which marriage would be unnatural and monstrous.
Thus, most commonwealths make incest penal.   The only
place in the Scriptures, where these degrees are laid down, is
Levit. xviii.   Concerning this place two important questions
arise :   1. Is this law still binding ?   2. How is it to be expounded ?   We hold that this law, although found in the
Hebrew code, has not passed away ; because neither ceremonial nor typical, and because founded in traits of man and
society common to all races and ages.   We argue also, presumptively, that if this law is a dead one, then the Scriptures contain nowhere a distinct legislation against this great crime of
incest.   But we have more positive proof.   In the law itself it
is extended to foreigners dwelling in Israel.   (Levit. xviii : 26)
and to all pagan nations, equally with the Hebrew, (verses 24
to 27).   In the New Testament, we find the same law enforced
by the Apostle Paul.   1 Cor. v : 1.   For this incestuous member evidently took his step-mother as his wife.   Unless this
Levitical law is the one on which this man is condemned, there
is no other.   The permanent, rational grounds, for prohibiting
marriage within these degrees, seem to be the following :   The
marital affection is unique, and such that it cannot righteously
obtain towards more than one object.   But the virtuous social
affections, which should obtain towards near relatives, embrace
all such with similar sentiments, though varying in degree.   The
one affection is incompatible with the other.   The fraternal, for
instance, excludes marital.   Second, if the more intimate rela

tions were legitimately in prospect, between persons who must before live in the daily intimacy of the same home, temptation presented by this privacy and opportunity would corrupt the family and reduce it to a bestial grossness. And third : man's animal nature now utters its protest, by the deterioration and congenital infirmities, which it visits usually on the unfortunate children of these marriages within lawful degrees. Naturalists now teach, that among the lower animals, the deterioration of offspring from " breeding in " depends on the question, whether the blood of the parents is purely of one variety. They say that if it is, no depreciation appears. But if the parents are of a mixed stock, " breeding in " results in a rapid decline of the progeny.

This curious fact may perhaps throw some light on the difficult question : whence Adam's sons drew their wives without incest. We, who hold to the unity of the race, must answer that they married their own sisters. Must we admit then, that an act which is now monstrous, was then legitimate ? Does not this admission tend to place the law against incest among the merely positive and temporary precepts ? The only reply is : that the trite saw, " Circumstances alter cases," has some proper applications even to problems essentially moral. The peculiar condition of the human family may have rendered that proper at first, which, under changed conditions became morally wrong. Among these circumstances, was the purity or homogeneity of the blood. There was absolutely but the one variety of the human race ; so that deterioration of the progeny by physical law could not follow. But now, in consequence of the dispersions and immigrations of the race, the blood of every tribe is mixed, and breeding in becomes a crime against the offspring. But we know too little of the scanty history of the first men, to speculate with safety here. The command to replenish the earth was given to Adam and Eve in their pure estate, in which, had it continued, incest, like every other sin, would have been impossible. Who can deny, but that the marriages contracted between the sons and daughters of the first parents, after the fall, were sinful in God's eyes? It is not unreasonable to suppose that, thus, the very propagation of the degraded race, to which its present earthly existence under the mercy of God is due, began in sin and shame ; that its very perpetuation is the tolerated consequence of a flagrant crime !

Every Christian Church and commonwealth has acted on the belief, that this Levitical law fixes, for all subsequent time, the degrees within which marriage is lawful. The second question is touching its interpretation. We must either assume that every degree within which God designed to prohibit marriage is expressly mentioned in the law : or that the prohibitions mentioned are representatives of classes. The former construction is excluded by this thought; that it would have permitted cases of incest precisely as unnatural and monstrous as those so sternly forbidden. Why should it be a crime for a man to marry the widow of his deceased brother; and legitimate for a woman to marry the husband of a deceased sister? Hence, all sound expositors are agreed in this view. That when marriage within a given relationship is forbidden, this excludes the connection between other corresponding degrees of the same nearness. The law in some cases, as in verse 10, extends itself on this principle, and thus confirms our construction.

Rome and many other corrupt Churches, while allowing marriage to be lawful for laymen, yet exalt celibacy as a state of superior purity and excellence. She seeks to find ground for this, in such passages as Matt. xix ; 11–13 ; 1 Cor. vii : 34. We set her plea aside, by showing that the New Testament only advises celibacy as a matter of prudence, (not of sanctity) in times of persecution and uncertainty. Rome's doctrine finds its real origin in the philosophy of the Gnostics and Manichæans, who regarded the flesh as the source of all evil, and hence its propagation as unholy. The same error led them to deny Christ's corporeal humanity, and the resurrection of the body. It needs no refutation here. That "marriage is honourable in all," we argue from man's very nature, as male and female : from the fact that God instituted it for man in Paradise : from the example of the holiest prophets : from the fact that it is the chosen type of Christ's union to his Church : and from its necessity to the existence of man's most holy social affections, as the maternal.

A supposed obligation of propriety and delicacy has usually kept our pulpits silent concerning the sins of unchastity; and hence, no doubt, in large part, the shocking callousness and unsoundness of public opinion concerning the sins of its breach. It is my opinion that this omission should be corrected by the pastors. When I say this, I would not by any means be understood as encouraging ministers to disregard any sentiment of delicacy or propriety which may exist. On the contrary, all such sentiments, where not positively false, are to be honoured by him; and he should be, in all his intercourse, the model of delicacy. But there is a guarded and holy way of discussing such subjects, which clearly reveals chastity and not pruriency as its temper, and purity as its object. This is the style in which the pastor should speak on these difficult subjects.

Sins against Seventh Commandment to be Rebuked with Sanctity.

In discussing the eighth commandment, we proceed from the duties of chastity to those of commutative justice. The scope of the command is to protect the rights of property. Under the simple head of "stealing" it "forbids whatsoever doth or may unjustly hinder our own, or our neighbour's wealth and

5. Scope of Eighth Commandment.

outward estate;" and "requireth the lawful procuring and furtherance of the wealth of ourselves and others." This exposition implies that there is a sense in which a man may steal from himself. While there is a sense in which our property belongs to us, and not to our neighbour, and his to him, and not to us; yet we are all stewards of God, and in the higher sense, all property belongs to Him. Obviously then, God's property right may be as much outraged by our misuse of what is lawfully in our stewardship, as by interfering with another's trust. The forms in which the worldly estate of our neighbour may be wronged, are innumerable. The essence of theft is in the violation of the Golden Rule as to our neighbour's property. The essence of stealing is the obtaining our neighbour's goods without his intentional consent and without fair market value returned. However it may be done, whenever we get from our neighbour something for nothing, without his consent, there is theft.

This commandment requires us, as to our own wordly estate, to practice such industry as will provide for ourselves and those dependent on us a decent subsistence—to eschew idleness, which is a species of robbery practiced on the common hive by the drone; to avoid prodigality; and to appropriate our own goods in due proportion to their proper uses. The commandment, as it applies to our neighbour's wealth, forbids robbery, or forcible taking, theft, or taking by stealth, all swindling and getting of property by false pretences; forestalling and regrating in times of scarcity; wastefulness, tending to the greed for other's wealth, extortion, embezzlement of public wealth, false measures and weights, contracting debts beyond the known ability to pay, eating usury, gambling, infidelity in working for wages, or in the quality of things manufactured for sale, availing oneself of legal advantages for evading obligations morally binding, &c., &c.

Special Sins and Duties under it.

But what is the origin of the moral rights of possession? The sense of *meum* and *tuum* is one of the earliest rational ideas developed, and continues to be one of the strongest. But its ethical origin has been much debated. Some have reasoned that in a state of nature, it arose out of first possession. But is not priority in finding and possessing a natural object, a mere accident? And if men are naturally equal in rights, as these persons always assume, can it be that a mere accident determines the moral right? Some, therefore, desert this theory, and suppose that the right of possession in a state of nature, arises out of the expenditure of some labour on the object possessed. This theory, again, fails to account for many cases, where no labour is bestowed, and yet the right is perfect; and it is moreover, unreasonable. Jurists incline much to make

6. Right of Possession Whence.

property the mere creature of civil law. This is evidently erroneous. For the right of property must precede civil society,
being one of the foundations on which it is built. These futile
surmises illustrate the folly and defect of a philosophy which
insists on proceeding upon mere naturalistic grounds. These
men leave out God, the most essential, and in a true sense, the
most 'natural' member of the theorem; and they assume a
'state of nature,' in which no creature ever rightfully existed.
No wonder, therefore, that their solution is abortive. Now, the
truth is, that there is but one perfect source for a right of property, creation out of nothing; and consequently, but one natural proprietor, God the Maker. The only rational solution of
the existence of a right of property in man is also the scriptural one, that contained in the second and ninth chapters of
Genesis, God's gift of the world and its contents to man, as His
tenant. Our individual interests in the gift are, then, based on
the golden Rule, and properly regulated in detail by the laws of
civil society. This position is vital to our security. For on
any lower theory of right, an invasion of property may be
plausibly justified whenever the majority persuade themselves
that it is most politic.

The question whether all usury, or hire for the use of
money, is not unrighteous, was much de-
7. Usury, not Un-
lawful, if Moderate.   bated by mediaeval moralists. The usual
argument against it was, that money coin,
had in it no power of increase. A box of coin, said these
Scholastics, is not like a measure of corn, capable of germination and increase; it is as barren, if left to itself, as the gravel
of the Sahara. It is labour only (or nature) which multiplies
values. Hence to exact hire for money is taking something for
nothing—essential theft. And the legislation of Moses, which
prohibited the taking of any usury from brother Hebrews, was
misunderstood, and then cited to confirm their conclusion.

If their premises were true, their conclusion would be
valid. Money is not, in fact, fruitless, and utterly devoid of a
power of reproduction. It is a mere illusion to compare the
box of coin to a box of barren gravel. For money is the representative of values; it is its purchasing power, and not its
metallic constitution as simple matter, which makes it money.
Now values are reproductive. Capital has a true power of
increase. The multiplication of values is by the combination
of capital and labour. If labour fecundates capital, it is
equally true that capital arms labour for success. Hence, it is
just as fair that capital lent should receive its just hire, as that
labour should.

It is interesting to notice that the Bible never commits
itself to any erroneous philosophy, no matter how current
among men. The Hebrew laws, properly understood, do not
condemn all usury as sinful. They permit taking reasonable

usury from Gentiles, forbid it from their brethren. Nor was this permission as to Gentiles an expression of hostility towards them.   The system of Moses harboured no such spirit; but taught the Hebrews to regard Gentiles (except the Amorites, &c.) as neighbours. On the contrary, the taking of a fair hire for money lent, lawful and reasonable in itself, was only forbidden as to their Hebrew brethren, as one instance of that special fraternity and mutual help, which God enjoined on them as pensioners upon His land. The case stands on the same footing with the prohibition to glean the fields, to beat the olive groves, or to take up the sheaf casually dropped on the road.   These things were exacted, as special contributions to their more needy brethren. The law of the case may be seen in Exod. xxii : 25 ; Levit. xxv : 36, 37 ; Deut. xxiii : 19, 20 ; Nehem. v : 7 and 8, &c. ; Matt. xxv : 27.

When we take advantage of the urgent necessities of our neighbour, in buying or selling, we sin against both honesty and charity.   If our neighbour is compelled by his wants to sell some commodity, for whatever he can get, that fact does not make that commodity worth less than the market price to you who buy it.   If he is compelled to have some commodity instantly, whatever it may cost him, that fact does not make it worth more than the market price to you who sell it to him.   If therefore, you take advantage of his necessity, to force him to sell you his goods for a less price than you yourself would give, if you could not take this advantage, you rob him of the difference.   And it is fraud committed under peculiarly base circumstaeces. For his necessity, instead of arousing your cupidity, ought to excite compassion.   Instead of taking advantage of his necessities, you should charitably aid in relieving them. Such measures are excused, I know, by saying that he makes the bargain voluntarily, or that his necessity makes the price which you give him, actually worth to him individually, in his circumstances, what he gave in exchange for it.   To these heartless excuses there is one answer, which at a touch, exposes their worthlessness, "Do unto others as ye would they should do unto you."   How would you like to have your necessity thus abused? And yet, how many men are there who watch, like harpies, for these opportunities to make what they call a good bargain.

8. Buying and Selling under the Law of Charity.

It is much to be feared that one chief trait of modern civilization is its fertility in expedients by which theft may be committed without incurring its social and legal penalties.   The Wise Man has said, that "money answereth all things."   Its purchasing power commands all material, and many intellectual values.   Hence the desire for money, or avarice, is the protean and all-including affection.   Money gratifies ambition, pride, all sensual appetites, in a word, all the appetencies which make

27*

up the "carnal mind." Hence the eighth commandment, is, in a peculiar sense, the perpetual object of invasion and assault in the daily lives of worldly men. With the multiplication of the expedients and combinations for creating wealth, opportunities by which astute men can abstract their fellows' possessions without just equivalent, are enormously multiplied. The intricacies of finance, the power of boards of directors sitting in secret to enhance or depreciate the values entrusted to them, the vastness and complication of the business and obligations of the great corporations who are debtors to multitudes of private persons, rendering the credit of the former a question utterly unfathomable to their creditors ; the unscrupulous means for blighting the credit of securities ; and a thousand other arts of like character, enable the adepts to filch from their neighbours vast aggregates of wealth. All these measures are but disguised thefts. And alas ! they constitute a large part of modern methods of business. The sudden accumulation of a large speculative fortune can rarely be innocent, and ought not to be the object of any Christian's desire. So, the concealment from the vendor of a recent increase in the value of what he sells, in order to buy it for less than its worth, is an injustice exactly parallel to the concealment of a defect in the thing sold for the purpose of getting more than its worth. Those who plead for this, urge that their special knowledge is their private property, which they have a right to use for their own profit. The answer is, that knowledge affecting a joint transaction, like bargain and sale, where two parties' rights are equitably involved, is not private property, and cannot be monopolized without violating the law of love. It should be admitted, that when merchants employ their means and industry to collect useful commercial intelligence, a fair compensation for that use of capital and labour should be a part of the lawful profits of traffic. But when this power of knowledge is pressed beyond that limit, it becomes a breach of the precept. It is to be feared, that the chief practical obstacle to the proper exposition of it is the consciousness, that it would ' cut too deep,' and condemn inexorably the larger part of what nominal Christians practice.

LECTURE XXXV.

SECOND TABLE. (9th and 10th COMMANDMENTS.)

SYLLABUS.

1. What is the general scope of the 9th Commandment, and what the duties required, and sins forbidden under it? See
   Thornwell on Truth.   Pascal's Provincial Letters.
2. On what is the duty of speaking truth grounded, and how does its practical importance appear?
3. Define the sin of speaking evil of ones' neighbor, and argue.
4. Is it ever lawful to deceive?
5. What the scope and meaning of the 10th Commandment, and what are the duties required and sins forbidden under it?
6. What evidence of the divine mission of Moses in the character of the Decalogue?
7. What doth every sin deserve at God's hands? See
   Anselm, *Cur Deus Homo*, pt. i, ch. 21. See, on the whole, Larger Cat., Qu. 143-152. Ridgeley (same Qu). Turrettin, Loc. xi, Qu. 20-23, and Qu. 26. Green's Lect., 54-58. Calvin's Inst., bk. ii, ch. 8, § 47-51. Hodges' Theol., pt. iii, ch. 19, § 13, 14. Bp. Hopkins on the 9th and 10th Commandments.

WE hold that the general scope of the Ninth Commandment is to enjoin the virtue of Truth, as represented, according to the usual method of the Decalogue, under the capital duty of fidelity in public witness-bearing. This precept " requireth the maintaining and promoting of truth between man and man, and of our own and our neighbour's good name, especially in witness-bearing." It " forbiddeth whatsoever is prejudicial to truth, or injurious to our own or our neighbour's good name."

1. Scope of Ninth Commandment.

The duty of veracity is founded on the nature and importance of God's will enjoining truth. Truth may be said to be the using of signs by which we express or assert anything, conformably to our belief of the real state of the thing spoken of. All the practical concerns of man's life are with the real state of things. Fictitious informations are, to us, naught, or worse than naught. They may fatally betray us into mistake ; they cannot be the grounds of any beneficial or successful action. On the real state of the markets depends the merchant's profits. On the real power of the medicine depend the physician's success and the sick man's restoration. On the real nature of vegetable laws depends the reward of the farmer's toil. In every conceivable concern of man it is truth, the communication which is in accordance with reality, that is useful. Accordingly our Maker has endued us with a mental appetite of which truth is the natural food. The statement on which we cannot rely gives no pleasure. True, another faculty than the

2. Grounds of Duty of Veracity.

Only Real Communications Useful.

419

understanding, the fancy, finds its appropriate pleasure in fiction. But here also a tribute is paid to the truth; for in order that the fictitious may give any pleasure to the fancy, even, it must be truth-like.

Now veracity is the observance of truth in our communications. Its importance appears from the fact
that almost all man knows is derived from communication. The whole value of the state-
ments we receive is in their truth. If they are false they are naught, or worse than naught. The usefulness of communi-cated knowledge to us, depends, therefore, wholly on our confi-dence in its truth. Every lie helps to destroy that confidence. Just so far as we perceive lies prevail, so far the value of com-municated knowledge to us is destroyed. Should we reach that state when no trust could be put in the veracity of any fellow-man, all such knowledge would, to us, virtually, cease to exist. But to what a state would this reduce us? We proudly call the brutes dumb; indicating that it is man's gift of speech mainly, which separates us from beasts. It is this which enables us to receive facts and ideas besides our own. The wise teach the ignorant. The skill of each generation does not die with it; but it is communicated to the next. Knowledge is handed down, until our generation finds itself endowed with the accu-mulated experience of all previous ones. It is this which makes our civilization. But if all reliance upon communicated knowledge is destroyed, we are reduced to a state of savage ignorance, but little above that of the higher animals. We should know nothing but what we had ourselves seen and expe-rienced; because we could trust nothing else. Education would be impossible; for how can knowledge be communicated when truth is banished? We must continue to exist in that in-fantile ignorance in which the child begins life, except so far as our own unaided efforts might instruct us, at the cost of suffer-ing and perhaps of destruction. The advance which each indi-vidual made in such a condition, would wholly die with him; his son must begin life as he did, an ignorant savage, and run the same contracted round of puny, misdirected progress, and in his turn die, carrying all his knowledge to the grave with him. The latest generation would live in the same savage igno-rance with the earliest. Religion would be as impossible as education; and all its blessings and consolations equally un-known; for religion cannot exist without trust. Each one of you would be an insulated, helpless, wretch, more completely deprived of society than the gregarious herds. He who deals in falsehood does what in him lies to bring his race to this degraded and miserable state. If all men should be false like him, and in all their communications, this state would be actu-ally reached.

It may be shown in another light that the liar is the enemy

Knowledge chiefly Derived.

Lies Destroy Confidence.

of God and man, by considering the effect of his vice on our mutual confidence. The intercourse of human business is but a countless series of implied engagements. Unless we can trust the fidelity of those whom we must employ, co-operation is at an end. If you cannot trust the postman who contracts to carry your letters, the conductor who guides the vehicle in which you ride, the pilot who steers your ship, the agent who transacts your business, the cook who engages to dress your food, you can neither write, nor ride, nor sail, nor eat, nor conduct any trade. Government would be at an end, because the ruler could not trust his agents and officers, and his power would be limited to his own presence. In short, if confidence is destroyed then all the bands which unite man with his fellow are loosed : each man must struggle on unaided by his fellows, as though he were the sole forlorn remnant of a perishing race. Confidence is as essential also, to all the social affections which shed happiness on the heart, as to the utilities of our outer life. It is the basis of friendship and love. To mistrust is to despise. To trust, to be trusted with unshaken faith, is the charm of domestic love.

Falsehood upturns Affection.

Were there no truth then, every fellow-man would be your enemy; you would be insulated from your kind; every social affection would take its flight from the earth. Man would be reduced to a solitary miserable savage, "whose hand would be against every man and every man's hand against him." Even the animals must, in a certain sense, keep faith with each other, in order to make their gregariousness possible. Even savages must cultivate fidelity to truth within some narrow limits; or else the extermination of their scanty existence would speedily follow.

Indeed the conditions of savage society are sufficient illustrations of my conclusions; for when you examine into the causes of its barbarism, when you detect why savages are, compared with civilized men, few, poor, wretched, insecure and unfurnished with all the blessings which ameliorate life; you perceive that it is because falsehood and unrighteousness have made trust, mutual aid, and instruction almost impossible among them. They remain such, only because they cannot trust each other. Savagery is simply sin; and most notably the sin of lying.

Truth in Order to all Morality.

Not only is veracity a virtue, but truth is, in a certain sense, the condition of all other virtues. Hence it is that in many places of the Bible, truth is almost synonymous with righteousness. The "man that doeth truth" is the man that does his duty. The godly man is "he that speaketh the truth in his heart." To "execute the judgment of truth" is to execute righteous judgment. This language is profoundly accurate. The motive of every act which has moral quality must be a reasonable one; and truth, as we know, is the appointed light of the understanding. I mean that no man does a truly virtuous act unless he has an intelligent reason for doing it. But how can the mind see a reason unless it finds it in some truth? Consider, farther, that all the inducements to right actions are in the truth; but all the inducements to wrong acts are false. Error and sin are kindred evils, as truth and holiness are handmaid and mistress. Truth is the instrument by which the Holy Ghost sanctifies the soul. John xvii : 17. Thus we find its most exalted value in this, that it is the means of redemption for a ruined world. It is as beneficent as falsehood is mischievous. The one is our guide to heaven; the other leads to hell.

There is a world just such as the liar would make this: where falsehood reigns and where confidence is unknown. There, in its fiery lake, all liars have their part. The ruler of this world is he who "was a liar from the beginning and the Father of it." There, to deceive and be deceived is the universal rule, and therefore mistrust sits brooding over every heart, and scowls in every look. Each one beholds in every other an object of fear and scorn, and feels an equal scorn for himself, because he knows himself as false as they. In the midst of myriads each suffering heart is alone, for it finds no other breast on which it can repose. Hostility and solitude separate each wretch from his fellows, and the only society is the reciprocations of reproaches and injuries. Hell is but the complete and universal reign of falsehood, and the tendency of every lie is to reduce our world to it.

If we weigh these things we shall see the grounds of that practical truth, that the virtue of veracity is the foundation of all right character. Says the French proverb. *Qui dit menteur dit aussi larron.* And a more infallible proverb asserts that "If any man offend not in word, the same is a perfect man." (Jas. iii : 2). Hence a sacred regard for truth should be inculcated on the young especially; and they should be taught to regard lying as the inlet of all vice and corruption.

In thus illustrating the usefulness and importance of the practice of veracity, I do not intend to rest its obligation on that ground. These facts are merely subordinate to the argument. They illustrate, but do not constitute, the obligation. And even for this use, their chief value is, that they are instances under a general truth, leading us to it. That proposition is, that truth is natural to man's soul. It is the appointed *pabulum animæ.* As the eye craves light, so the mind loves the truth. It is the natural instinct of the mind, undebauched by a sinful experience, to credit what is told it by any rational fellow-creature; and it requires the bitter experience of deceptions often repeated to curb this tendency. While we are limited to the sphere of philosophy and natural theology then, we find the obligation to truth in these fundamental facts, which reveal the will of the Creator as it is impressed on the constitution of the soul. " To those therefore, who would ask: Why am I bound to speak the truth ? I would briefly answer: Because it is the law of our nature: it is the fundamental *datum* of conscience, a command of God impressed upon the moral structure of the soul." It follows hence that the obligation is universal, and is not conditioned, as Paley intimates, on any implied promise given by the speaker. When we pass from philosophy to revelation, we find a still broader and deeper foundation for the obligation to truth, in the nature of that God " who cannot lie," who is the " God of truth," His precepts are the sure and sufficient rule of our duty. He has told us that " every liar is abomination in His sight," and has required us to speak truth one to another.

Every right habit of action (*consuetudo*) implies a right disposition (*habitus*) of will. This general law should be enough to convince us of another great fact, which is too often overlooked in ethical discussions of this duty: that there is a virtue of truthfulness, back of the practice of veracity, and the source of it, which we are bound to possess. This is the love of truth for its own sake. The virtue in its last analysis is not a habit qualifying the actions and words, but an active principle qualifying the will itself. Just as in any other class of moral acts, the act is moral simply because of the active principle which is regulative thereof. No more is needed than to state the truth. And this truth dissolves, at a touch, the vain assertion that the intelligence acts by its necessary logical laws and therefore irresponsibly to the conscience. On the contrary, the intelligence acts always under strict responsibility to the conscience ; and man is responsible for his mental beliefs.

The sin of slander, or backbiting, where the assertions of evil in our neighbour are false, is understood.

3. Evil Speaking, What ? Its malignity is great, as it assails him in a point very dear to him—his good name—and is usually attended with vile adjuncts of secrecy and treachery. Jas. iii : 6, 7. But it is not so well understood that it is often a sin of evil speaking to repeat true accusations against our neighbour. There are times when the cause of virtue demands that ill-conduct shall be denounced. And when such occasions arise, the virtuous man will not be afraid to speak out. But it is a sin against our erring neighbour to give unnecessary currency to his faults. " Charity rejoiceth not in iniquity." The fact that our neighbour has truly sinned does not place him outside the pale of charity, nor does it entitle us to inflict on him any unnecessary injury or pain. Moreover, the recital of evil, true or false, has a natural tendency to familiarize the soul with it, to defile the memory and imagination, and to habituate the mind and conscience to wrong. It is, especially to the young,

a real misfortune to have to hear of that which is morally foul. This mischief should never be causelessly wrought by detailing sins, no matter how true, without necessity.

Many Christian moralists have held that there are inten-
4. Are all Decep- tional deceptions which are not breaches of
tions Lies ? Negative the ninth commandment, and are innocent
Argument. in God's sight. They describe these, as the cases where the person deceived had no right to know ; and where the result of the deception was righteous and beneficial; as when a robber or murderer is misled away from his victim by an innocent deception ; or where a defensive army deceives an invader by strategems. Their arguments are chiefly these ; that the parties deceived, in such cases, being engaged in a wicked design, have no right to the benefits of veracity as between man and man : That the best men, as Joshua, Washington, &c., when commanders of armies, made adroit use of stratagems; and the common conscience of mankind approves, and would count it morbid conscience and insane quixotry, to refuse such means of defence: That many instances are recorded, of Bible saints as Abraham, Moses, Joshua, &c., who prosperously employed concealment and stratagems, (see for instance, Joshua viii : 3, &c.,) and that there are even cases in which God or Christ seems to do the same, as in the assumption of a human body, Gen. xviii : 2. in the walk to Emmaus, Luke xxiv : 28. They add, also, that the consistent enforcement of the opposite doctrine would many times be suicidal and preposterous.

There are however, those who hold that absolutely "no lie
is of the truth." They admit indeed, that it
Affirmative Argu- is a man's privilege, where no right exists to
ment demand information of him, to keep silence, or use concealment. But they assert that, if he employs any signs by which it is usually understood information is conveyed, he must employ them absolutely according to reality; and that in no case can he intentionally produce a deception, without the sin of lying. They argue in general, that the opposite license proceeds upon a utilitarian theory of obligation. But this theory is false, and as no finite mind can correctly judge the whole utility or hurtfulness of a given declaration in its ulterior consequences, no practical basis or rule of obligation would be left at all   To the instances of deception in war, by great patriots, and their approval by the world, they reply, that good men are imperfect, and commit errors ; and that the public conscience is unhealthy. To the instances of Bible-saints, they say with justice, that often the errors of good men are recorded for our instruction, when they are by no means sanctioned. As to the instances claimed, from the acts of the Messiah, concealment is not deception ; His appearance in human form, without at first disclosing His divinity, was not a *suggestio*

falsi, but only a concealment of His nature until the suitable time.   So, His seeming to design a journey farther than Emmaus was a mere question propounded to the disciples. As to the inconveniences of absolute truth, sometimes extreme, they point to the obligations laid upon the martyrs, and remind us, that it is no rare thing for Christ to require of us obedience rather than life.   In fine, they urge that on any other ground than theirs, no tenable or consistent rule remains; and we have a mere ' point of honour' requiring us to speak truth under certain contingencies, instead of a fixed rule of moral obligation.

It must be confessed, that the reasons of the latter party
Solution. are more honourable to the divine authority, and more elevating and safe, than those of the former.   The replies given to a part of their arguments are also valid.   I would add that it is of perilous tendency and obviously erroneous, to represent one's obligation to speak truth as only correlated to the hearer's right to receive a true communication.   Man could never be safely trusted to judge for himself when his fellow man had that right.   Indeed, on that basis, human declarations would be practically worthless; for the hearer must always remember that the speaker's word can only be accepted as conveying truth, provided he secretly judges the hearer to be entitled to it; and of this proviso there can be no assurance not encumbered with the same fatal condition. Again, it is very far from being a general truth, that our duties are only corelated to the rights of their objects.   Thus, I may be under a high obligation (to God) to bestow alms on my undeserving enemy.   And this suggests the still stronger answer; that God, and not the hearer, is the true object on whom any duty of veracity terminates.   God always has a right to expect truth of me, however unworthy the person to whom I speak.

Yet the sober mind cannot but feel that there is an extreme, to which the higher view cannot be pushed.   I presume that no man would feel himself guilty for deceiving a mad dog in order to destroy him, or for misleading an assassin from his victim, when helpless otherwise, to prevent murder.   But it is more important to say, that, in at least a few cases, as in Joshua viii : 2, God Himself authorized a designed deception for the purpose of punishing the guilty.   As His authorizing Joshua to exterminate the Amorites proves that all killing is not murder, so, does not His authorizing him to deceive them prove that all deception is not lying?   Hence, I would offer, with diffidence, another statement of the matter, which may be found to contain the reconciliation of the difficulty.   Under what circumstances is killing by man no murder?   Is not human life sacred, and the property of the Maker alone?   The law answers: Man may kill, when the guilty life is forfeited to God, and He authorizes man to destroy it, as His agent.   So, I conceive, extreme purposes of aggression, unjust and malignant, and aiming at our very existence, constitute a forfeiture of rights for the guilty assailant. During the dominancy of his active malice, they dehumanize him as to his intended victim: his life is forfeited to the superior right of self-defence. That right emerges, and the man attacked innocently slays the assailant. By the rule that the greater includes the less, may he not also deceive him for a righteous purpose? One advantage of this view is, that it gives this right of deception only in the extreme case, where life is maliciously assailed. And the argument is not the same we discarded, which made the duty of veracity correlative only to the hearer's right to truth. For my plea is; this assailant not only has no right to it, he is out of the category of beings to whom truth is relevant, for the time. He is not a rational man, but a brute. It may be asked with much force: has this outlaw for the time being, a right to truth, after he has forfeited the right to existence? Does not the greater forfeiture include the less? Is he not, *pro tempore*, in the category of a beast of prey? But the moment he is disabled from aggression, or turns to a better mind, his rights to truth revive, as do his claims on our charity and forbearance. Hence, while the good man will righteously deceive his invading enemy with stratagems, the moment a flag of truce appears, or his enemy is disabled and captured, he is bound to act with as perfect sincerity as towards his bosom friend. I would add, in guarding this concession, that if an innocent man makes a vow, promise, or engagement to his unrighteous assailant, under whatever violent threat, or other inducement, he is bound to the faithful performance of that engagement, unless the thing promised is sin *per se*. For the engagement was voluntary; he had the option of choosing to make it or endure the threatened evil. The good man is one who "sweareth to his own hurt, and changeth not." Ps. xv : 4.

Rome, as we saw, having suppressed the 2nd Commandment, divides the 10th in order to make out the requisite number. Her 9th Commandment is, "Thou shalt not covet thy neighbor's house;" and her 10th, "Neither shalt thou desire his wife," &c. Her plea is, that houses are typical of property; and wives of those things which excite sensual desire. The 9th Commandment, therefore forbids covetousness; the 10th, lust and appetite. But unfortunately, the "ox and ass," obvious "property" are in the latter part; and in Deut. v : 21, where Moses recites the Decalogue literally, he puts the wife first, and the property second. There is no basis for the distinction. For what is property craved by sinners? Only for its instrumentality to satisfy some appetite or sensual desire. The general unity of the subject, besides, proves that it was one command.

5. Popish Division of 10th Commandment.

It may be said, in brief, that this command finds the key-note of its exposition in the text: "Keep thy heart with all diligence; for out of it are the issues of life." The five commands of the second table cut off the streams of transgression; this deals with the fountain head. The others forbid wrong volitions; this forbids concupiscence, as tending thereto. In the 10th Commandment, then, we have the crowning spirituality of the Law; thus making it complete, and every way worthy of God, and adapted to man as a rational free agent.

Its Scope.

In closing this subject I would offer two remarks. The first is upon the admirable comprehension, wisdom, and method of the Decalogue. We have here ten simple and brief precepts, each one commending itself to the natural conscience of the most unlearned, simple in word, few in number, unostentatious in arrangement. When we first look at them, we are inclined to think that, while they are very true and good, there is nothing very wonderful; that they are obvious things which any good man might utter, aud to a much greater number than ten. But when we examine them in detail, we find that they are the heads of all the branches of man's duty, arranged with the most logical order, presenting nothing superfluous, and yet, with all their brevity, omitting nothing of all the vast circle of human duty! How clear their purity and justice! How amazing their comprehension! What completeness! Let human ingenuity hunt out some branch of human duty which is omitted. It cannot. In these ten words, we have a system of morality more wise and complete than human wisdom ever devised. Now, we ask, whence did Moses get these ten words? A man of an unlearned and pastoral race, educated in the learned follies of Egypt, whose theology and morals, as they are revealed to us by Herodotus and the modern decypherers of their monuments, show an impurity and puerility utterly opposite to the Bible, goes into a waste desert, and after forty years, comes forth with this strangely wise and perfect law! Whence did he get it? There is but one rational account—that given by the Bible—that it was written for him by the finger of God. Unless Moses was an inspired man, then he has produced a miracle of wisdom more incredible than all the difficulties of inspiration.

6. Decalogue only from God.

Our Catechism, while recognizing the greater gravity of some sins than others, by reason of their aggravations, teaches us that, "Every sin deserveth God's wrath and curse, both in this life and that which is to come." The exceeding demerit of sin, and its desert of eternal and grievous punishment is a doctrine which meets with obstinate resistance from sinners. It is urged that to make the desert of any sin such is to revive the old

7. What does every Sin Deserve.

Stoic absurdity, of the equality of all sins; for if the lesser sin
is punished eternally, and so infinitely, the greater cannot be
punished more. The answer is, that infinities are by no means
all equal; as we have shown.

To clear this awful truth of the desert of sin, from the
cavils of unbelief, I would observe, first, that sinful men are in
a most unlikely attitude to judge correctly between themselves
and God, in this matter. They naturally desire to break the
law. Our emotions always blind the judgment to the objects
which are opposed to their current. They are condemned by
the law of God, which fact produces a natural jealousy of it.
They have their moral judgments brutified by the universal
habitude and example of sinning, amidst which they live. It
would be almost a miracle, if there were not, under these circumstances, a perversion of the moral judgments here.

But affirmatively the ill-desert of sin is infinite, because of
the excellence, universality, and practical
Grounds.   value of the law broken by it. Because of
the natural mischievousness of sin to the sinner himself; as was
illustrated when I spoke of Adam's first transgression. Because
of the Majesty and perfections of the Law-giver assailed by
transgression. Because sin is committed against mercies and
blessings so great. Because it violates so perfect a title to our
services, that of creation out of nothing. And last, because it
is so continually multiplied by transgressions.

Men deny the demerit and guilt of sin, because they are so
in the habit of attempting to measure transgression as the civil
magistrate does, insulated from all its attendants and sequels.
Does the court, for instance, indict a man for murder? The
act is considered by itself, and the court does not concern itself
with antecedent character, or with results, save as they throw
light on the intention or evidence. Now men mislead themselves by these examples, as though an omniscient God could,
or would judge sins against himself in this partial, fragmentary
way. In denying the gravity of sin against God, they seem to
have before them some such case as this: Here is one actual sin
committed by a man, which God is to judge, as expressive of
no moral state preëxisting in the man; as destined to breed no
repetitions, as exercising no influence to form a vicious habit in
the agent's soul, and as carrying no consequence into his own
immortal character or those of his fellows. The caviller seems
to think the question is: Has God declared a single act, thus
insulated, by itself worthy of eternal penalty? I reply, that
neither the caviller nor I know anything of that question. For
in fact, God can never have such a case to judge, because it
can never arise. Every case which He has to judge is that of
a sinner, not of a sin: and in weighing any one act, the omniscient mind will, of course, look at it as it really occurs, with all
its antecedents, connections, and consequences. Is it an oath?

God sees in it, first, a specific breach of the 3d Commandment; then, an expression of pre-existent sentiments of wilfulness, irreverence, levity or malice, in the profane man: then thirdly, an evil influence on spectators, to be propagated, unless grace intervene, forever: fourth, a confirming influence, intensifying the wicked temper and habit; and last, a natural tendency involving a series of increasing profanities forever. In a word, God, as final and omniscient judge, has to judge each sinner as a concrete whole, and each transgression as index, part, and cause, as well as fruit, of a disease of sin, a deadly, spiritual eating cancer, whose tendency is to involve an immense evil, eternal death. Thus judged, sin is an infinite evil, and deserves an eternal penalty. One reason why God punishes forever is, that the culprit sins forever. God's point of view is, that this everlasting series of sins is the fruit of the first rebellion.

LECTURE XXXVI.
THE COVENANT OF GRACE.

SYLLABUS.

1. What the Scriptural uses of the terms בְּרִית and διαθήκη? What the theological uses of the terms, 'Covenant of . ? Redemption,' 'Covenant of Grace'? See

Conf. of Faith, ch. 7. Sh. Cat., Qu. 20. Larger Cat., Qu., 31. Lexicons, *sub vocibus.* Sampson on Heb., ix : 16. Southern Presb. Rev., Jan., 1876. Hodge's Theol., Vol. ii, ch. 2 of pt. ii. Hill's Div., bk. v, ch. 5, § 1. Turrettin, Loc. xii, Qu. 1. Dick. Lect. 48.

2. Prove the existence of a Covenant of Redemption. How related to the Covenant of Grace, and the Διαθῆκαι? See

Turrettin, Loc. xii, Qu. 2. Dick, Lect. 48. Hodge as above. Witsius, bk. ii, ch. 2.

3. Who are the original parties to the Covenant of Redemption? Their motives? See same authorities.

4. What is the date and duration of the Covenant? Explain, then, the terms "new" and "old" in Heb. viii : 8, or xii : 24.

Turrettin and Dick as above. Hodge, Com. on 1 Cor. xv : 24-28. See, on the whole. Witsius, bk. ii, ch. 2, 3.

5. What the conditions stipulated between the Parties? Is any condition required of the believer? What? Faith? or also repentance?

Dick, Lect. 48, 49. Hodge as above. Turrettin, Qu. 3 and 2.

6. Are Terms proposed between God and the Believer in the Covenant of Grace?

G OD having created man upright, and he having sought out many inventions, and thus fallen into sin; our next inquiry must be into the remedy which God's love and mercy found for this fall. This remedy, in its exhibition, was of course subsequent to the ruin; but when we consider it in its inception in the Divine mind, we must go back into the recesses of a past eternity. God ever foreknew all things; and all His works, unto the end, are according to His original, eternal plan. Conceiving of God's eternal decree then in parts, (the only mode

1. Covenant of Grace
God's Remedy.

of conception of it competent to our finite minds,) we must consider that part of His plan formed from eternity, which was implied in that other part of the same plan whereby He purposed to permit man's fall and ruin. This remedial part of God's decree is the thing which the more recent Calvinistic divines term the COVENANT OF GRACE—e. g., Dick.

When it is thus considered, as a part of the Decree, we are enabled to condense much of the discus-

Identical with Decree. sion and proof concerning it, given by the theologians; and to say in brief: that being such, the Covenant of Grace must of course possess those general properties which we asserted of the Decree; and for the same reasons, viz., eternity, immutability, wisdom, freeness, absoluteness, graciousness.

When we come to the Scriptures, we find a frequent use of the words rendered in our English version, 'Covenant,' 'Testament,' applied to transactions of God with men, through their Surety, Jesus Christ. Before we can proceed farther in the connected evolution of the subject, the proper meaning of these terms must be examined; בְּרִית, διαθήκη. The former of these words, both by its etymology and usage, is shown to mean 'covenant,' or 'agreement;' being often used to express theologically, God's covenants with man, and naturally, compacts between individuals. There are also cases in which it means an arrangement or disposition of matters determined on. Exod. xxxiv : 28 ; Jer. xxxiii : 20. It must be remarked, that the word currently used by the Sept. to render this, is διαθήκη. This fact would naturally lead us to attribute to it in the New Testament, the same meaning of disposition or covenant. It is admitted that the meaning so often given to it by our English version of 'testament,' (will,) is the primary etymological meaning in classic Greek. But there is only one case, (Heb. ix : 16,) where that meaning is supportable. Thus, when Christ is said by the English version to be "a surety of a better testament," (Heb. vii : 22,) there is an obvious incongruity between the office and the document. Wills do not have sureties. When the same version says, (1 Cor. xi : 25,) "This is my blood of the New Testament," the words, καινῆς διαθήκης, imply the Old, to which the character of a testament is inappropriate. But in Heb. ix : 16, 17, the meaning of "Testament" is to be retained, (against McKnight, Hill and others.) For, if their rendering be attempted, making the passage allusive to a covenant ratified by an animal sacrifice, three insuperable critical difficulties arise, that if διαθήκη means covenant, διαθέμενον should mean the "covenanter," i. e., God the Father, (Christ being the ratifying sacrifice.) But the Father did not die ; that νεκρος cannot be properly used to describe dead animals sacrificed : and that the passage would then be made to assert too much : for it is not universally true, that compacts were only of force anciently, after the death of a sacrifice to solemnize them. (See Sampson's Com. *in loco*.) Hence we assert that the statement of our Confession of Faith is substantially correct, that the Scripture does set forth the dispensation of God's grace to man under the idea of " a testament ; " though perhaps not " often," as is said there. Their assertion refers to the English version.

The terms are used then, in their general or theological sense. 1st, by Theologians, and probably by Scripture, (Hos. vi : 7,) for the Covenant of works with Adam. 2nd, for the Abrahamic dispensation. 3rd, for the Mosaic dispensation. 4th, for the new or Christian dispensation. (Not covenants, but dispensations; for we shall show that there is only one covenant, besides that of works.)

If there is any gospel remedy for sin, then there must have been, from eternity, such a remedial plan in the Divine mind. But the question is, was this part of the eternal decree, in any proper sense a covenant ? Has it properly the form of an eternal compact between persons of the Trinity? This is purely a question of Revelation, to be decided not so much by finding the words, covenant, compact, agreement, applied to it in Scripture, as the substance of the thing asserted. Calvinists hold that in the one, eternal decree of the Trinity, which is one in essence and attributes, and harmonious in will and thought, this remedial purpose (or part of the plan) has from eternity held the form of a concert or agreement between the Father and the Son, for the redemption of believers. But here we must carefully avoid confusing the subject, by giving to this immanent transaction of the Trinity all the technical features of a " covenant." Thus some divines have erred, especially of the Cocceian school. Obviously, we must not conceive of it, as though the one party produced in the other a willingness to do what he had not previously purposed, by exhibiting a certain reward or compensation, not before exhibited. Nor must we conceive that the second party produces, by his fulfilment of the conditions, a fixed purpose to bestow the given compensation, the purpose to do so having been hitherto uncertain. Nor, in a word, that there is any contingency on either hand, holding the purposes of either party suspended in doubt on the promisings or doings of the other party. But it has always been certain from eternity, that the conditions would be performed ; and the consequent reward would be bestowed, because there has always been an ineffable and perfect accord in the persons of the Trinity, on those points : an accord possessing all the absoluteness of the other parts of the decree. Our limited understandings, of course, cannot fully understand the actings of the divine, triune spirit ; seeing its constitution

2. In what respects a Covenant ?

is inscrutable to us. This is perhaps as near as we, can come to the conception designed to be given us.

The Scriptural proof of such an immanent, eternal trans-

Scriptural Proofs of action between the Father and Son, is the
a Covenant of Re- following: First. Inferentially, Eternal life
demption. was not only purposed to be bestowed, but, "promised, before the world began"—Tit. i : 2. To whom? for man did not yet exist? To Christ, for believers. Compare Eph. i : 4. Again: Christ is clearly implied to bear a federal relationship; as in 1 Cor. xv : 22, 47, 45 ; Rom. v : 17, 18. Our first federal head entered into covenant on our behalf; we infer that our second has ; He would else not fulfill the idea of a federal person at all. Again: Christ is expressly called the Surety of a διαθήκη. Heb. vii ; 22. But a surety is one who voluntarily enters under the obligations of a compact on behalf of another. Many other passages would ground a similar inference ; the student has now had sufficient examples how to use them. Note all conditional promises: To believers, to Christ. These are of nature of covenants.

Second. Many express passages describe (not always in the use of word covenant et similia, but in substance) such an eternal agreement. See Is. xlii : 6, xlix : 8 ; Mal. iii : 1 ; especially Ps. xl : 7, 8, as quoted by Heb, x ; 5. This covenant of Christ is unfolded by other Scriptures under the specific heads of His three offices—e. g., Prophetic. Is. lxi : 1, 2. Priestly. Isaiah, liii : 10, 11 ; Ps. cx : 4 ; John, x : 17, 18. Kingly. Ps. ii : 7, 8, cx : 6 ; Luke, xxii : 29, &c. Zech. vi : 13. Witsius somewhat fancifully argues also, that Christ's partaking of the Sacraments of the Old Testament could only have been to seal His covenant of redemption with His Father.

I hold that this subject cannot be treated intelligibly without distinguishing the covenant existing from eternity between the Father and Son, from that Gospel promise of salvation on terms of true faith offered to sinners through Christ. Many of our divines have agreed to retain this distinction, and to name the former covenant, for convenience' sake, the "Covenant of Redemption," while they call the Gospel promise to believers, "Covenant of Grace." To these I heartily accede. The Covenant of Redemption between the Father and Son, I hold to be the real covenant transaction, being a free and optional compact between two equals, containing a stipulation which turns on a proper, causative condition, and bearing no relation to time, as it includes no mutable contingency or condition dependent on the uncertain will of creatures. The Covenant of Grace (so called) is a dispensation of promise to man, arising out of and dependent on the Covenant of Redemption. Dr. John Dick seems to use the phrase Covenant of Grace, in a sense comprehensive of both transactions, and to assert that there is no use for the distinction. Turrettin, Witsius, and our

Confession employ the same phrase in the sense of the Gospel promise to believing sinners, made through Christ as surety. See Confession ch. vii : § 3 ; Shorter Catechism qu. 20. It is true that the Larger Catechism, qn. 31, verges nearer to the distinction and the recognition of a prior Covenant of Redemption with Christ saying : " This Covenant of Grace was made with Christ as the second Adam, and in Him, &c."

Now, I repeat, the distinction which Dick repudiates, and which so many others obscure, is essential. It is true that the covenant with believing men is the consequence and sequel of that eternally made with Christ; and that the promises published in the former are the fruit of Christ's action in fulfilling the latter. In that sense the transactions are intimately connected. But the value and necessity of the distinction are easily evinced, against Dr. Dick, by such questions as these : Is Christ a party to the Covenant of Grace? Or is man the party of the second part ? Here Dr. Dick must be fatally embarrassed. In the Covenant of Grace with man, Christ is not party, but surety — True : But unless there is some party to the transaction less mutable, feeble and guilty than believing sinners, man's prospect of deliverance is gloomy indeed ! Yet it seems inconsistent to make the same Person both principal party and surety in the same transaction ! I can give the solution, which Dick could not : In the eternal Covenant of Redemption Christ is principal party : in the Covenant of Grace, He is surety. Again : Is the Covenant conditioned or unconditioned ? Here also, Dick is fatally entangled. Will he say it is conditioned, and thus ascribe to the sinner's faith an efficient merit ? Or will he say it is unconditioned : and thus defraud us of hope with an unbought redemption? I can answer: The Covenant of Redemption was conditioned, on Christ's meritorious woik. The Covenant of Grace is unconditioned : its benefits are offered to believers without price.

To my view Turrettin has given his virtual support, though in a rather inconsistent fashion. After beginning with the one definition, of a Covenant of Grace, eternal and yet made with man in a surety, in Qu. ii § 12, he raises the question whether this Covenant of Grace was made by the Father with Christ as the other contracting party (for man's benefit); or whether it is made with the body of believers as the second party, in Christ as a " *Pars Media.*" His answer is, that " the debate is superfluous : because the thing comes to the same." But he adds, just after ; " *Certum est duplex hic pactum necessario attendendum esse vel unius ejusdemque pacti duas partes et gradus. Prius pactum est quod inter Patrem et Filium intercedit ad opus redemptionis exequendum. Posterius est, quod Deus cum electis in Christo contrahit.* Witsius is more lucid, and so more consistent. After stating that God's Covenant of Grace with man is the remedy for the broken Covenant

28*

of Works, he pauses, and begins his 2nd chapter. " *De pacto Dei Patris et Filii.*"

Ut Fœderis Gratiæ natuta penitius perspecta sit, duo imprimis distincte consideranda sunt. I. Pactum, quod inter Deum Patrem et Mediatorem Christum intercedit. II. Testamentaria illa Dispositio qua Deus salutem æternam electis, et omnia eo pertinentia immutabili fœdere addicit. Prior Conventio Dei cum Mediatore est. Posterior Dei cum Electis. Haec illam supponit, et in illa fundatur."

The original parties to the Covenant of Redemption are the Father and the Son. It is plausibly urged by Dick, that in this transaction, the Father acted not only for Himself, as one person of the Trinity, but for the whole Godhead, as representative of the offended majesty of the three persons equally. His reason is, that all the persons being similar in attributes and dignity, must be conceived of as all alike offended by man's sin and guilt; and alike demanding the reconciling intervention of a Daysman; the Holy Ghost as much as the Father. It must be confessed that Dick cannot present any scriptural, direct proof of this view; but it seems reasonable. The Father on the one part, then, acts as the representative of the Godhead; Christ as the representative of the elect. The question is raised by Dick: Is Christ surety for man to God only, or for God also to believers? He answers, not for God to believers; because this is derogatory to God, as implying that His fidelity and mercy need or admit of any higher warrant than His own word. (But see Turretin, Loc. cit. § 16.) Does not God make known His fidelity as a promiser of pardon and life, and His mercy, precisely through this surety, as the prophet of the Covenant? Would man be any otherwise warranted to hope for any mercy? Further, the fact that God's goodness to us needs and admits of any certifying by a surety, results from nothing discreditable to God, but from something discreditable to us—our guilty mistrust. That God, who deserves to be trusted on His mere word, should condescend to give us warranty of His fidelity in the messsage, death and sacraments of His Son; this is His amazing grace and goodness. (See I Tim. i : 16.) And are not the sacraments seals? Does not Christ in them act as surety for God to us?

3. Original Parties to the Covenant.

To the question whether believers are also parties in the Covenant of Grace, no better answer can be given than that of Turrettin, § 12. In the eternal sense of the Covenant, they were not parties; in the sense of its exhibitions in time, they are parties; i. e., in their surety.

The Covenant of Redemption being, as regards the Father and the Son, but a part of the single Decree, must be as eternal as that Decree. It began in the counsels of a past eternity : and in

4. The Covenant Eternal.

one sense, its administration will extend (if not in the mediatorial offices of the Surety, at least in the communications of
grace,) to a future eternity. In proof of its eternity, see Heb.
xiii : 20; 1 Pet. i : 20. Hence the Covenant can only be one ;
and therefore it can only be spoken of as " first," " second "
(e. g., Heb. viii : 7,) or " old," " new," (as Heb. viii : 8 ; xii : 24,)
with reference to its forms of manifestation.

    Having considered the Godhead (represented in the Father,)
and Christ, as the original parties to this
covenant, the question naturally arises :
What motive prompted them to this dispensation of amazing love and mercy ? The
only consistent answer is : their own will, moved by their own
intrinsic benevolence, compassion and other attributes. To
this agree all the passages of Scripture which describe God's
electing love as free and unprocured by anything in man ;
(Rom. ix : 11, 16,) because our election is but the embracing of
us in the Covenant of Redemption. Eph. i :4. This is equally substantiated by the argument that God could not be moved by
foreseen good in us, to embrace us in this covenant; because
the only foreseen good in us was that which was to result from
the administration of the grace of that very covenant. It cannot be said that man's misery was more than the occasion of
God's purpose in forming this Covenant of Grace; for if we
supposed it the procuring, or efficient cause, the misery of
non-elect men and angels ought equally to have procured a
Covenant of Grace towards them also.

Motives of God to the Covenant. The Father not persuaded by the Son to it.

    Some have misrepresented the truth hereupon by teaching
that Christ's undertaking to satisfy the law in man's stead is the
procuring cause of God's purpose of mercy towards man. The
error of this view is evident from this consideration, that, then,
Christ would be originally more benevolent and merciful than
the Father. But they are equal and harmonious originally, in
this, as in all other excellencies. The true statement is, that
Christ's promise of a vicarious righteousness was necessary to
enable the Father's purpose of mercy to be effectuated consistently with other attributes—that purpose being precisely as
original and uncaused in the Father as in the Son.

    Dick (Lec. 49,) has very happily simplified the question,
"What were the conditions agreed upon by
the Son to the Godhead, on behalf of His
people ?" by considering Him as placed precisely in His people's room and stead. He
bargained to do precisely what they should have done, to supply
precisely " their lack of service." The intrinsic righteousness of
the rules imposed on man in the Covenant of Works, as being
precisely what they ought to have been ; and the immutability
of God's nature, show that whoever came forward to be their
surety, must expect to have to undertake precisely what was

5. Conditions pledged by Christ— just what man owed. 1st. Obedience.

incumbent on them in that covenant. The first part of this obligation was to a life of perfect obedience. This life Christ rendered. (See, e. g., Matt. xvii : 5). A class of theologians has rejected the idea that Christ's active obedience was vicarious, and is imputed to His people. While this question will come up more naturally when we discuss the subjects of Satisfaction and Justification, we may briefly remark of it now, that the consideration above offered is obviously in favour of the Calvinistic view. Besides; when the Messiah is represented as saying, "A body hast thou prepared me," &c., (Ps. xl : 6, 8, quoted; Heb. x : 5, 10,) it is surely a very contracted and perverse interpretation, to suppose that He was clothed with humanity only with reference to one and the last act of His humanity; and that the general phrase, " I come to do Thy will," is to be understood only of the single act of offering His flesh. (See also Gal. iv : 4 and 5).

But man, while still bound to perpetual obedience, has already come under penalty, by failing to render it. Hence, our Surety bargained to bear that penalty in His people's stead. This cannot be more clearly stated than in the language of Is. liii : 5, 6; 2 Cor. v : 21. Some have supposed that there is an incompatibility between the first and second condition : that if the penalty for a neglected obedience is paid, law has no longer any claim for that obedience. This represents the relation between the law and penalty, erroneously. God does not accept the penalty as an equivalent for obedience, in the sense that either the one or the other satisfies the demands of the Law and of His nature, alike well. His relation to His rational creatures demands of them, by an inevitable and perpetual demand, perfect obedience : and if that fails, penalty also. But waiving this, does not the believer (having paid for his past delinquency by his surety,) owe a perpetual and perfect obedience for the future ? And can he render it in the flesh ? Hence his surety must render it for him, as well as pay the penalty.

2nd. Penalty.

In the third place, we may say scripturally, that Christ bargained, among all other compliances with His Father's will, to do as Mediator, all those things pertaining to His prophetic and kingly offices, necessary on His part, to the salvation of the elect. He undertook their instruction, guidance, protection and conquest to Himself. Weigh John xvii : 12–14, for instance, where our Saviour speaks of His agency in instructing and guiding His disciples as of a fulfilled compact. (See also, Ps. xxii : 22).

3d. The Offices of Mediator.

Passing now to the other side of the compact, we may say that the Godhead, represented in the Father, engaged on His side, to the Son, to clothe Him with humanity for the fulfilment of His task, (Ps. xl : 6,) and to endue Christ plenteously with gifts and

Conditions pledged by the Father.

graces therefor, (Is. xlix : 2 ; lxi : 1, 2,) to uphold Him under His heavy task, (Is. xlii : 1–7,) to give Him an elect seed as the sure reward of His labours, (Is. xlix : 6 ; liii : 10,) and to bestow His royal exaltation, with all its features of glory. (Ps. ii : 6 : Phil. ii :9, 10). As there is a secondary sense, in which God, in unfolding His eternal Covenant of Redemption, engages with man, so there is a sense in which there are terms proposed between God and believers also. It may be remarked in general, that there is a sense in which a part of the benefits promised to Christ are promised through Him also to His people; and a part of the blessings covenanted to them, are honours and rewards to Him. Thus His mediatorial graces are their gain ; and their redemption is His glory. Hence, this division between benefits covenanted to His people, and those covenanted to Christ, cannot be sharply carried out.

When we consider the covenant between God and
6. The Covenant of believers, however, it is evident that there
Grace; Condition Re- are terms bargained between them. These
quired of Men.
may be found briefly expressed in the words so often repeated, and obviously intended to be so significant in Scriptures ; Gen. xvii : 7 ; Jer. xxxi : 33 ; Rev. xxi : 3 ; " I will be their God, and they shall be My people." In this covenant God briefly bargains, on His part, to be reconciled to believers, and to communicate Himself to them as their guide, light, consolation, and chief good. They, on their part, are held bound to the correlative reconciliation, grounding their weapons of rebellion and exercising the spirit of adoption, to a life of self-consecration and obedience, to separation from the world of His enemies, and conformity of heart and life to God's will. It is true, that the transaction of Gen. 17th is rather ecclesiastical than spiritual ; but the spiritual is always included and represented in the outward.

The full and blessed significance of this formula will not be apprehended, unless we consider that it is not used in Scripture once, but as often as the covenant of grace proposed or renewed. Compare not only Gen. xvii : 7, 8, but Exod. xx : 2 ; xxix: 45 ; Deut. v : 2, 3, 6; Jer. xxiv : 7 ; xxx : 22 ; xxxi: 33 ; Ezek. xi : 20 ; Zech. xiii : 9. And in the New Testament, 2 Cor. vi : 16 ; Heb. 8, 10, and Rev. xxi : 3. We thus see from this emphatic repetition, that these words are the summary of all the blessings and duties arising out of the gospel relation They are common to both dispensations. They re-appear as a grand " refrain," whenever the prophets sing most triumphantly the blessings of the covenant: until we hear them for the last time as the song of the ransomed and glorified Church. This relation thus expressed is to be understood then; not as the general one of Creator and creature, sovereign proprietor and servant ; but as the special and gracious relation established in the Mediator by the Gospel. In it God promises to be to believers all that is implied in their redemption and eternal adoption; while the believer is held bound to all that is implied in faith and repentance.

The question then arises, whether all the graces and duties of the Christian life may be accounted as conditions of the Covenant of Grace. If so, is it not reduced again to another Covenant of Works? The answer is, that it is only in a very slight, and improper sense, the Christian's holy life can be called a condition of his share in grace—only as in the order of sequence it is true that a holy life on earth must precede a complete redemption in heaven. So far is it from being true that this holy life is in any sense a meritorious condition of receiving grace, or a procuring cause; it is itself the fruit and result of grace. But when we examine more minutely the account of that gracious transaction in the Scriptures shadowed forth in the ecclesiastical transaction of Gen. 17th, and stated first more simply in Gen. 15th, we find that Abraham's faith only was imputed to him for righteousness. Gen. xv : 6; Rom. iv : 9, 10, &c. This effectually explains the matter. The argument in favour of the position we have assumed, is sufficiently strengthened by adding that all graces and holy living are everywhere spoken of by God, and sought by Bible saints in prayer, as God's gifts bestowed as the fruit of the Covenant of Grace. Citations are needless.

Faith the only Condition.

The question has been keenly agitated between Calvinists, whether Faith itself should be spoken of as a condition of the covenant. One party has denied it, because they supposed that the language which represented man as performing a condition of his own salvation would make an inlet for human merit. But it is most manifest that there is a sense in which Faith is the condition, in all such passages as John iii : 16; Acts viii : 37; John xi : 26; Mark xvi : 16. No human wit can evade the fact, that here God proposes to man a something for him to do, which, if done, will secure redemption; if neglected, will ensure damnation—and that something is in one sense a condition. But of what kind? Paul everywhere contrasts the condition of works, and the condition of faith. This contrast will be sufficiently established, and all danger of human merits being intruded will be obviated, if it be observed that Faith is only the appointed instrument for receiving free grace purchased by our Surety. It owes its organic virtue as such, to God's mere appointment, not to the virtue of its own nature. In the Covenant of Works, the fulfilment of the condition on man's part earned the result, justification by its proper moral merit. In the Covenant of Grace, the condition has no moral merit to earn the promised grace, being merely an act of receptivity. In the Covenant of Works, man was required to fulfil the condition in

May Faith be properly called a condition.

his own strength. In the Covenant of Grace, strength is given
to him to believe, from God.

The question now remains, whether, in this instrumental
sense, any thing else besides faith is a condition of the Covenant of Grace. (See Cat.
Ques. 33). " Received by faith alone." There
are two evasions : one, that which makes Repentance a condition along with faith,   Luke xiii : 3 ; Acts ii : 38, &c.   Contrast
with Jno. iii : 16–18 ; Acts xvi : 30, 31.   The other is the one
common to Papists, (*meritum condignum* of *fides formata*,) some
classes of New England Divines (justification by faith apprehended as the generative principle of holiness, and inclusive
thereof,) and the Campbellites, (justification by the " obedience
of faith," viz: immersion).   Here is a subtile inlet for works.
These perversions have all this common mark, that they desert
the scriptural doctrine, which makes faith the instrument of
justification solely through its receptive agency, and they claim
for faith a purchasing power, or merit of the result.   Recurring
to the former evasion, which makes repentance a cc-condition
of the covenant, along with faith, we shall do no more in this
place than refer the student to the discriminating statements of
Turrettin. Ques. 3, § 15, 16, 17.   When we come to justification, we shall resume it.

*No other Condition.
Evasions.*

LECTURE XXXVII.

COVENANT OF GRACE. — Continued.

INASMUCH as the plan of our Seminary directs the teacher of Systematic Theology to give special prominence to the successive developments of revealed truth,

Development of Grace to be traced. found as we proceed, from the Patriarchal to the Mosaic, and thence to the Christian ages, we devote other exercises to the subject above announced. In discussing it briefly, the order of topics indicated in the syllabus of questions will be pursued.

Has God ever had more than one Covenant of Grace with

1. The Covenant one in all ages. Opposing views. man since the fall? And is the covenant made with the Patriarchs and with Israel substantially the same spiritual covenant with that of the New Testament? The Socinians and Anabaptists give a negative answer to this question, relying on the passages of Scripture represented by Jno. i : 17. They say that the covenant with Abraham and Israel was only national and temporal; that it promised only material good; that those of the Old Testament who were saved, were saved without a revealed promise, in virtue of that common natural religion, known, as they suppose, to good Pagans alike; by which men are taught to hope in the mercy and benevolence of a universal Father. To these views the European Arminians partly assented, teaching that the Gospel through the mediator is only involved implicitly and generally in the Old Testament, and that no special promise through a Christ is there.

The motive of the Socinians is two fold; that they may

440

Motive of the Socinians. Of the Anabaptists.

escape this insuperable difficulty; if Christ's redeeming work (in the New Testament) is only what they teach, that of a prophet and exemplar, and not vicarious, there is no sense in which He can have redeemed Old Testament saints, and 2nd, that by making the difference of light and grace between the Old Testament and the New, as wide as possible, they may plausibly represent Christ as having something to do in the New Testament, *dignum vindice nodum*, without any atoning work. The Anabaptists, whose Socinian affinities were originally strong, take the same view of the Old Testament, in order to get rid of the doctrine that a gospel Church, substantially identical with that of the New Testament, existed in the Old Testament with its infant church members.

This discussion will be found to have an equal importance, when we come to the Popish theory of sacramental grace. Rome claims for her sacraments under the New Testament an *opus operatum* power. She does not claim it for the sacraments of the Old Testament: for the reason that the Apostle Paul, among other inspired men, by implication contradicts it, as Rom. ii: 25–29, and I Cor. x : I–5. Now, if we identify the substance of the Covenant of Grace under both Testaments, we found at least a very strong probable argument for concluding that the sacraments of the two Testaments were means of grace of the same kind. Then all the explicit denials of efficiency *ex opere operato* uttered in Scripture as to the Old Testament sacraments, become conclusive as to the sacraments of the Christian Church.

As to the unity of the Covenant, we may argue thus : If man's fall laid him necessarily obnoxious

Unity of this Covenant appears *a priori*.

to certain immutable attributes of God, if man's sin necessarily and everywhere raises a certain definite difficulty between him and communion with God in consequence of those inevitable attributes of God, we may fairly conclude, that whatever plan (if there can be any) is adopted by God to reconcile a sinner, that same plan substantially must be adopted to reconcile all other sinners of Adam's race, everywhere and always. To the Socinian indeed, this *a priori* consideration carries no weight ; because he does not believe in God's essential, retributive justice, &c. Let us then see from the more sure word of Scripture, whether the covenant of grace set forth in the Old Testament is not substantially identical with that in the New, in the things promised, the parties, the conditions, and the mediator ; while a difference of clearness and mode is admitted.

Unity of the Covenant argued Scripturally.

This Scriptural argument cannot be better collected than under the heads given by Turrettin, (Ques. v, § 7–23).

The identity of the Covenant is substantially asserted in
general terms—e. g., in Luke i : 68–73 ; Acts
ii : 16, with vs 38, 39 ; iii : 25 ; John viii : 56;
Rom. iv : 16 ; Gal. iii : 8, 16, 17 ; especially
the last.   Remark here, that the very words in which the Covenant was formed with the seed of Abraham, Gen. xvii : 7 ; and
which are so formally repeated in subsequent parts of the Old
Testament are the very terms of the compact in the new dispensation, repeated as such with emphasis.   See Jer. xxxi :
33 ; 2 Cor. vi : 16 ; Rev. xxi : 3.

(a) From direct testi-mony.

The Mediator is the same.   1 Tim. ii : 5, 6 ; Gal. iii : 16 ;
Mal. iii : 1 ; Acts iv : 12, x : 43, xv : 10, 11 ;
Luke xxiv : 27 ; 1 Pet. i : 9–12 ; Rom. iii :
25 ;   Heb. ix : 15 ;   with many passages
already cited.   We need not depend on such passages as Heb.
xiii : 8 ; Rev. xiii : 8 ; for although their application to prove
the mediatorial office of Christ under the Old Testament is
probably just, plausible evasions exist.

(b) From sameness of Mediator.

The condition assigned to man is the same in both—e. g.,
faith.   And it is useless for the Socinians,
&c., to say, that the faith of the Old Testament was not the specific faith in the Son,
the Messiah, set forth in the New, but only a general trust in
God as the Universal Father.   For their assertion is not true ;
and if true, it would still remain, that the faith of the Old Testament and that of the New, include the same substantial features.   Look at the fact that Heb. xi goes for its illustrations of
faith, (surely it was inculcating the Christian faith,) exclusively
to the Old Testament!   See, also, Gen. xv : 6, with Rom. iv :
3 : Ps. ii : 12.   (Is not this specifically faith in the Son ?)   Acts
x : 43 ; Ps. xxxii : 10, *et passim.*

(c) From its condi-tion.

In the fourth place, it may be asserted that to this faith of
the Old Testament saints, redemption in the
true New Testament sense was held forth,
with all its several parts ; of justification, Ps. xxxii ; Is. i : 18 ;
Regeneration, Deut. xxx : 6 ; Ps. li : 10 : Spiritual gifts—
passim—e. g., Joel ii : 28, 32, as expounded by Peter, Acts ii :
Isaiah xl : 31 ; eternal life : (as we shall more fully argue under
a subsequent head, now only noticing,) Heb. iv : 9, xi : 10 ;
Exod. iii : 6, as expounded by Christ ; Matt. xxii : 31, 32, and
this eternal life, including even the resurrection of the body.
Ps. xvi : 10, 11, applied in Acts xiii : 34 : Job xix : 25 ; Dan.
xii : 1, 2.   In view of this array of proofs, how weak appears
the idea, that nothing more than the Land of Canaan and its
material joys was proposed to Israel's faith?   But of this more
anon.

(d) From its promise.

An argument for our proposition may be constructed out
of all those types under the old dispensation,
which can be proved to have had an evan-

(e.) From the Types.

gelical meaning. The promised land itself, the deliverance from Egypt, with its significant incidents ; circumcision and the passover, (" seals of the righteousness of faith,") with the whole tabernacle ritual, are proved by several parts of the New Testament to have had this evangelical meaning. The argument is too wide to be briefly stated; but every intelligent Bible reader is familiar with its materials. In its very wideness is its strength. As one specimen of it, take the Epistle of Hebrews itself. The Apostle, in interpeting the Levitical ritual, there shows that all prefigured the gospel, and the New Testament, Messiah and redemption. During the Old Testament times, therefore, it was but a dispensation of this same Covenant of Grace.

And in general, all the gospel features sown so thickly over the Old Testament, especially over the books of Psalms and Isaiah, prove our point,

Of such passages as Rom. xvi : 25 ; Gal. iv : 24; 1 Pet. i : 12, &c., we are well aware. We shall show their compatibility with the proposition above demonstrated, when we come to unfold the resemblances and differences of the two dispensations.

We conceive the familiar and established division to be correct, which makes two dispensations only, the Old Testament and the New. There seems no adaquate reason for regarding the patriarchal age, from Adam to Moses, as essentially a different dispensation from that of Moses. Certainly that representation is incorrect which makes the former a free and gracious dispensation, while the latter only was burdened with the condemning weight of the moral and ritual law. For the moral law as to its substance, was already in force from Adam to Moses. Sacrifices already smoked on altars, and the knife descended in symbol of wrath, on innocent victims. And gracious promises on the other hand, are, at least, as thickly strown over the Scriptures of the Mosaic period, as of the patriarchal. We hardly need cite cases. There are passages, such as Gal. iii : 17 to 19th ; Deut. v : 2, 3, which speak of a ritual burden, and law which could minister only condemnation, as superadded at the Mosaic era. But we shall find that the elements of a moral law impossible for the depraved to fulfil, and of a ritual which typified only wrath to him who persisted in ignoring the Mediator and the Covenant of Grace, were also present in the patriarchal religion. The history of Cain too clearly establishes these traits of the patriarchal age. These elements were only re-affirmed by Moses. If it be said that they were then brought forward with far greater prominence and distinctness, I answer, so were the gospel elements brought forward, to true believers, at the same time, with increased distinctness. When the Apostles bring out so prominently this condemning burden

2. T w o Dispensations only. Objection answered.

of the Mosaic law, they are dealing, for the time, with only one
side of the subject. Because, they are dealing with Jews who
persisted in looking for justification to this law, which apart from
Christ, is only a ministry of condemnation; who persisted in
stickling for Moses, Moses, as their authority for their self-
righteous perversions of the law and gospel. In dealing with
this subject, theologians perpetually forget how necessarily the
Apostles had to use the *argumentum ad hominem* against these
Jews. That the patriarchial and Mosaic form properly but one
dispensation appears from this. Both exhibit the great, prevalent characteristic of types: both were prefigurative instead of
being, like the New Testament, commemorative; both had sacrifice, circumcision, priests. The difference between them is
only one of degree, and not of contrast. But when we come
to the New Testament, there is a real contrast. Human priests,
sacrifices and circumcision end. Types give place to antitypes;
prefiguring to commemorative ordinances.

To the question why God has administered the Covenant
of Grace under two different dispensations,
Why two Dispensa-
tions of the same Cov-   no complete answer can be rendered, except
enant? Ans.   that of Matt. xi : 26. The true difficulty of
the question lies chiefly back, in this prior question : Why did
God see fit to postpone the incarnation of the mediator so long
after the fall? For, supposing this question settled, we can see
some reasons why, if the effectuating of the terms of the Covenant of Grace, was to be postponed thus, its declarations to
man must be by a different dispensation before and after the
surety came. Before, all was prospective. Every promise
must, in the nature of things, be a prediction also ; and prediction, prior to its fulfilment, must needs be, to finite minds,
less plain than experience and history after the occurrence.
Many symbolical ordinances (both dispensations for good reasons have such) are types foreshadowing things in an ulterior
and higher development of the same religion. May it not
be, that the greater variety and number of the symbolical ordinances under the Old Testament were due to the very fact that
they must needs be less distinct? God sought to make up in
number what was lacking in distinctness. But to the question :
why the mission of Christ was postponed nearly 4000 years,
there is no adequate answer. The circumstances which made
that era " the fullness of time " have been pointed out by the
Church Historians. But the relations of influence and causation in human affairs are too intricate and numerous for man to
speculate here.

The causes assigned by Turrettin(Que. 7, § 2–6) do indeed
indicate the existence of an analogy with God's other working
herein. God performs all His grand results by gradations.
Childhood and pupilage go before manhood and independence.
So majestic a luminary as the Sun of Righteousness may be

expected to rise gradually, and send His twilight before Him! True; but these are only palliations, not answers to the difficulty.

To appreciate correctly the amount of Gospel light pos-

3. The Gospel was preached to Adam.

sessed in the patriarchal, and even in the Mosaic ages, we must bear in mind a thing often overlooked, that the human race had just enjoyed, in Adam, personal communication with God, in fullest theophanies, which Adam, by the faculties of his perfect manhood, and other patriarchs, through their longevity, were admirably qualified to transmit well. Adam was cotemporary with Methuselah 243 years, Methuselah with Noah 600 years (dying the year of the flood) and Noah with Abram 58 years. Thus Abraham received the revelations of paradise through only two transmissions! We must not suppose that this traditionary knowledge of God was scanty, because the hints of it given in earlier revelations are scanty; for the purposes of the revelation to us through Moses did not require that God should give us full information as to the religious knowledge of the Antediluvians. The Bible is always a practical book, and does not wander from its aim: it concedes nothing to a merely useless curiosity. Now, the object of God in giving to the Church of later ages this brief history of primeval man was to furnish us only with the great facts, which are necessary to enable us understandingly to connect the Covenants of Works and Grace, and to construe the spiritual history of our race. We have seen how briefly and sufficiently the book of Genesis gave us the cardinal facts of man's creation in holiness, his home in paradise, his Sabbath, the institution of his family, the unity of the race, the federal constitution by which God has been pleased from the first to deal with it, the Covenant of Works, its breach, and the far-reaching consequences. So, God next gives us the main facts concerning the changes in His religion, which were necessary to adapt it, as a religion for sinners. These main features are all that were needed for God's purposes: and they contain the whole substance of the Covenant of Grace.

Man's theological relation is founded primarily on the nature of God and His creature; and is essentially permanent. Hence, the theistic worship of paradise, with the Sabbath rest, its necessary means, remained as before. So, the constitution of human society, under a family government founded in monogamy, remained unchanged, with the whole code of ethical duty. But man's sin and depravity had changed his attitude towards God in vital respects. Duty having been violated, the new and hitherto inoperative obligation of repentance has emerged. God teaches man this great doctrine of the religion of sinners, by converting his life from one of ease and bliss, to one of sorrow and discipline. His home is changed from a paradise to a prison. Again; guilt having been contracted, there emerges, out of the moral attributes of God, a necessity of satisfaction for it, in order to the pardon of the sinner. This, the central truth of the religion of sinners, which points also to the central promise of the covenant of grace, had unhappily become the very truth, to which man, by reason of his corruption, would be most obtuse. His selfish depravity would incline him ever to forget the right of God's attributes in the question of a reconciliation; and his selfish fears would prompt him to crave impunity, instead of righteous justification. Hence, in the wisdom of God, the most notable and impressive addition made by Him to the *cultus*, was the one which was devised to teach the great doctrine of the necessity of propitiation, and to hold out its promise. This, indeed, is the only ritual fact which needed recording. God appointed bloody sacrifice, and required it to be the perpetual attendant of the worship of sinners. Thus He taught them, in the most impressive possible way, at once the great need, and the great promise of the Covenant of Grace!

That bloody animal sacrifice was of divine appointment at this time, we argue, first, presumptively from the fact that natural reason would not have suggested it, as a suitable offering to God. The doctrine of substitution, however honourable to God when revealed, is not, and cannot be, a deduction of the natural reason. Whether the Sovereign Creditor will be pleased to accept a substitutionary payment of penal debt, is a question which He only may answer. Again: doubtless the natural reason of Adam and his family saw the obvious truth, which is stated as self-evident, in the Epistle to the Hebrews, that "the blood of bulls and goats cannot take away sins." The mere animal has neither the dignity, nor community of nature, which would suggest even the possibility of its life's being an equivalent for an immortal soul. Hence, we do not believe that the human reason, left to itself, would ever have devised such a mode of appeasing God. This is illustrated by the rationalistic will-worship of Cain. Not having suitable conviction of guilt, regard for God's rights as requiring satisfaction in order to pardon, nor faith in the future, undescribed sacrifice of the "Woman's Seed," he did what all other will-worshippers since have done: he exercised his own rationalistic ideas of the suitable, and his own æsthetic sentiments, in devising another oblation. He probably thought the bleeding and burning flesh unsuitable, because it was abhorrent to natural sensibility, and even to the instincts, and the senses of sight and smell. Does God find pleasure in the death-pangs of an innocent, sentient creature? How much more appropriate the inanimate fruits of His bounty, for an oblation: the brilliant flowers, the blushing fruits, the nodding sheaf, all redolent of peace, abundance and fragrance. But it was precisely this rationalism, which, we are told in Genesis, caused the rejection of his offering. Here we find a strong proof that Abel's was not will-worship, but the fulfilment of a divine ordinance.

This is strongly confirmed by the language of Heb. xi : 4, which tells us, that the preferableness of Abel's offering arose from this : that he " offered it by faith." Now faith implies a revealed warrant; without this it is presumption. This text virtually tells us that animal sacrifice was by divine appointment. This conclusion is also strengthened by the truth, clearly implied in Gen. ix : 3, 4, that, until after the flood, animals were not killed for food by God's people. Yet in Gen. iii : 21, Adam and Eve are, by God, clad in the skins of animals, in lieu of the frail coverings of fig leaves, which they had devised for themselves, to conceal their shame. Whence came those skins ? They might possibly be stripped from the corpses of those that died natural deaths, or were slain by beasts of prey. But it is much more probable, that they were the skins of the sacrifices Adam was then and there taught to offer. Man's superiority to the need of raiment in Paradise was doubtless an emblem of his present holiness and guiltlessness: as his newly born shame was an emblem of his guilt and corruption. How natural then, is the conclusion, that this first effectual clothing of man the sinner was the immediate result of sacrifice, that it was sacrificial raiment he wore ; and thus we have here the natural introduction of the great idea of כָּפַר, "covering," " propitiation," so fully expanded afterwards. Once more, when Noah's family was at length authorized to eat animal food, the blood was expressly excepted, because, as God teaches, He had reserved it to make atonement for their souls. Does not this imply that the reservation was, from the first, God's express ordinance ? Animal sacrifice was then, God's appointment ; and it found its aim in its signification of the need of satisfaction for guilt, and the promise and foreshadowing of a worthy substitute, to be afterwards provided by God. Thus we see, that the maintenance of bloody sacrifice among the Pagans to our day, is a ritual perversion precisely parallel to that we see made, by nominal Christians, of the New Testament sacraments, a reliance on the efficacy, *ex opere operato*, of the symbol, instead of the divine grace symbolized. Trent herself could not define her doctrine of the *opus operatum* more expressly than it was held by the Maori of New Zealand and the classic Pagans, as to their bloody rites.

The third essential truth of the Covenant of Grace taught primeval man, (and the only remaining one,) was that set forth in the *protevangel* of Gen. iii : 15. By becoming an apostate from God, he had become the subject of Satan, who is represented by the serpent. (See Lect. xxvii : Qu. 3). The race was now become his kingdom, instead of the " kingdom of heaven." Already a sad experience was teaching them, that sin was now become a ruling principle, and not a mere incident : as their outward misery was now ordained to be a permanent state of chastisement. Doubtless the great question with the sinners was : " Is this final ?" " Or is there to be a deliverance?" The covenant of Grace answers : " Yes, there shall be a deliverance." Satan's conquest was to be reversed, destructively for Satan, by the " Seed of the Woman." The promise is brief, but wonderfully instructive. Let only faith read it consistently ; and it pointed to a Mediator, a Deliverer, human, yet more than human, miraculously reared up, who was to be the antitype to the bleeding lamb even now exhibited, who should experience, in prosecuting the work of delivery, a blood-shedding at the hands of the adversary, like that of the suffering lamb, yet not destructive ; inasmuch as He should survive to crush the evil angel, and to deliver the captives.

That this promise is a *protevangel* is argued first, presumptively, from the triviality of the alternative meaning. Did God go out of His way, on this momentous occasion, to describe merely the animal instinct, which prompts the peasant to kill a snake? Second, the "woman's seed," properly weighed, must be seen to promise something supernatural ; because in Hebrew language, the seed is always elsewhere ascribed to the male, (which is physiologically accurate). Compare Gen. xxi : 13, where Ishmael is carefully distinguished as Abraham's " seed," while " son " " of the bond-woman." Eve knew that *she* could only have a " seed" supernaturally. Third : the Deliverer must, from the very nature of the promised victory, be superior to Satan, who was superior to Adam. Fourth : subsequent Scriptures, when using language evidently allusive to this promise, represent this warfare as being between Satan and the Messiah. Thus, Jno. xii : " Now shall the prince of this world be cast out." Luke x : 17–19. Christ's comment on the success of His Apostles in subduing " devils" is : " I beheld Satan as lightning fall from heaven," and He then promises them farther victory over " serpents and scorpions" and " over all the power of the enemy." Here we have the old warfare of Gen. iii : 15 ; and it is between Messiah and Satan and his angels, not only symbolized by " scorpions and serpents," but expressly named. This onset of the incoming kingdom of heaven was seen by Christ to give Satan such a blow, that he appears like one dashed violently from his seat, and falling, thunder-smitten and blighted, to the earth. In Rom. xvi : 20, Paul promises God " shall bruise Satan under your feet shortly." The allusion is beyond mistake. In Heb. ii : 14, the woman's seed, " through death destroys him that had the power of death, that is, the devil ;" where we see an exact reproduction of the bruised heel and crushed head. In Rev. xii : 9, and xx : 2, we have the final victory of Messiah, in the chaining and imprisonment of Satan the dragon.

The short record of Genesis gives us other evidences of a gospel dispensation, in the existence of the two classes, ' sons of God,' and ' sons of men'. Gen. vi : 2. So, the preaching of repentance by Enoch and Noah, and the strivings of the Holy Ghost with carnal minds, Gen. vi : 3, all imply a covenant of Grace. In conclusion, we know that the patriarchs before the flood had a gospel promise, because we are assured by Hebrews, chap. xi, that they had faith.

The second dividing epoch of the old dispensation was the calling of Abraham, the history of which may be seen in Gen. chap. xii to xvii. There was now an important development. All that had been given to believers remained in force, the " Church in the house," the Sabbath, the sacrifices, the moral law, and the promise. The most notable additions made upon the calling of Abraham were, first, the separation of the " sons of God " from the mass of the world, as a peculiar people, and the organization of a visible church-state in the tribe of Abraham ; and next, the institution of a sealing ordinance, circumcision, as a badge of membership, and " seal of the righteousness of faith." The repeated tendency of the race, in spite of admonitions and judgments, towards apostasy and idolatry, had at length made the necessity of the visible Church separation obvious : it remained the only human means to preserve a seed to serve God. In that age of the world, every organized society unavoidably took the patriarchal form ; hence the family, or clan of Abraham, became the visible Church : and the race-limit tended approximately to be the boundary between Church and world. Abraham and his seed did indeed receive a promise of the temporal possession of Canaan : as in Gen. xv : 18; xvii : 7. But the spiritual and gospel feature implied is clear in some of the promises themselves, and is made plainer by subsequent Scriptures. The best exposition of the Abrahamic covenant is that given by Rom. chaps. iii and iv, and Gal. iii. We are there expressly taught, that the seed in whom the promise was made was Christ : that the central benefit received by Abraham, was gospel salvation through faith : that the sacrament was a gospel one, a seal of the righteousnesss of faith : that the promise of Canaan was typical of that of heaven ; that Abraham is the exemplar and head of all gospel-believers : and that the society founded in his family was, and is, the visible Church of Christ, reformed and enlarged at the new dispensation.

The original meaning of the bleeding lamb was strikingly illustrated to Abraham by the proposed sacrifice of Isaac. This taught, first, that the lamb was insufficient: a more precious substitute must be found. Just at the crisis, when the patriarch was about to offer his only son, a rational victim, God arrests his hand, and substitutes the ram (again a mere type,) which He had provided. Abraham named the place, יְרְאֶה

29*

יְהוָֹה "Jehovah hath chosen," thus acknowledging that when he answered Isaac's question, in Gen, xxii : 8, אֱלֹהִים יִרְאֶה, "God will provide Himself a lamb," he had (possibly unwittingly) uttered a great, gospel-truth; that the sinner's real substitute was to be one in the unknown future, which God was to provide, and not the believer. Thus, salvation is to be gratuitous, though only through a divinely constituted substitute, and man's part is to embrace it by faith.

Last, the compact with Abraham was summed up in the words : " I will be a God unto thee and to thy seed after thee." We have seen that this was the formula of the Covenant of Grace. Such then, was God's compact with the Father of the faithful.

And here we must pause a moment, to consider the question famously debated in the negative, for instance, by Warburton's Divine Legat. of Moses: "Whether the patriarchal ages had any revealed promise of future eternal life ? " I would premise that the scantiness of the teachings on this point will not surprise us, if we remember that this fundamental truth is rather assumed than taught. It has been well remarked, that the Bible no where sets itself deliberately to teach the existence of God! We may well suppose the traditionary religion received from Adam made the immortality of the soul and future rewards, so clear that little was then needed to be said about it. The being of a God and the immortality of the soul are the two postulates essential to all religion. We assert then that the natural and proper way for inspiration to proceed, in revealing a religion, is to postulate these two truths, and not to waste time in proving them. The soul's immortality is as essential to the being of a religion as the existence of God. I might prove this experimentally by the fact, that materialists are always virtually without a religion. It follows logically; for experience concurs with revelation in showing, that in this life, " the wicked flourish like the bay tree; " so that, if the future life be denied, there will remain, for the denier, no room whatever for the sanctions of any religion. But let us see if this doctrine was not made sufficiently clear to the patriarchs. (It may be found acutely argued in Calv. Inst. bk. ii : ch. 10, which we mainly follow).

Eternal Life was revealed to the Patriarchs.

(a.) They had promises: The New Testament expressly declares these promises were the gospel. See Luke i : 69–73, x : 24 ; Rom. iv : 13, &c.

(b.) The patriarchs embraced the promises they had (be they what they may) with a religious faith. Who can dispute this? It is too expressly declared in Heb. ch. xi. But both Testaments tell us, that faith is a principle of eternal life. Habak. ii : 4 : Heb. x : 38.

(c.) The Covenant made with Abraham in Gen. xvii : 7, to be a God to him and his seed, implies the continued existence of the patriarch. All this promise of a prosperous seed and of their continued relation to God as their patron, could have had no interest to Abraham, and could have been no boon to him, if he was doomed to extinction. Besides, as this promise is expounded in the Pentateuch itself, and more fully in subsequent Scriptures, it is the eternity of God, which makes the covenant so great a privilege. See Deut. xxxiii : 27, and Ps. xvi : 5 and end, and xlviii : 14. What interest would a party doomed to early extinction have in the eternity of his benefactor?

(d.) Our Saviour's argument, in Matt. xxii : 32–34, is founded on Exod. iii : 6. " God is not the God of the dead, but of the living." The peculiar appropriateness of this refuta-- tion of Sadduceeism is seen in this : That they are said to have admitted only the inspiration of the Pentateuch: and hence Christ goes for His proof-text to that code and not to any later revelation. Materialists as they were, they gloried professedly in the national covenant with God, (as ensuring earthly privilege). Christ therefore cites them to the familiar terms of that covenant, as of itself containing enough to show, that the doctrine of immortality is its very foundation. It is as though He said to them, that it was unnecessary to contend about the authority of the later prophets, who confessedly say so much about immortality. He can find abundant refutation in that most familiar formula, which was in everybody's mouth. The subsistence in Moses' day of a covenant relation with Abraham, Isaac, and Jacob, implies the continued existence of those parties. And as the parties were not ghosts, but incarnate men, when the everlasting God bargained with them ; it is implied that His power, of which the Sadducees had no proper idea, would restore them by a bodily resurrection to that state.

(e.) If the promise to the patriarchs were only of temporal good, it was never fulfilled ; for they were strangers and pilgrims in the very land promised them.

(f.) Their dying exercises pointed to an immortality. Heb. xi : 16 tells us that they sought a better country, even a heavenly. This is borne out as a fact, by such passages as Gen. xlix : 18, and 33, and Numb. xxiii : 10.

When we resort to the New Testament we find many evidences, that its writers regarded the Old Testament as containing the Covenant of Grace, and the doctrine of immortality, in all its parts. Two passages may be cited, as specimens. In Jno. v : 39, our Lord says to the Jews, " Search the Scriptures " (the Old Testament), " for in them ye think ye have eternal life, and they are they which testify of me." In Acts xxiv : 14, 15. Paul, when pleading before Felix, declared that he believed " all things which are written in the law and in the prophets, and had hope towards God, which they themselves also allow, that there shall be a resurrection of the dead."

LECTURE XXXVIII.
COVENANT OF GRACE. — Concluded.

SYLLABUS.

5. What farther developments of the Covenant of Grace were made by the Mosaic Economy?

Turrettin, Loc. xii, Qu. 7, § 24-26. Witsius, bk. iii, ch. 3; bk. iv, ch. 4. Ridgeley, Qu. 33, 34, § 1. Knapp, § 90, 91.

6. What was the true nature of the Covenant made by God with Israel at Sinai, through Moses?

Turrettin, Qu. 12. Calvin, bk. ii, ch. 7, 10. Witsius as above, and bk. iv, ch. 10. Ridgeley, Qu. 34, 35.

7. How do the Old and New Dispensations differ *inter se?*

Turrettin, Qu. 7, § 27 to end, and Qu. 28. Calvin, bk. ii, ch. 10, 11. Witsius, bk. iv, ch. 12, 13. Ridgeley, Qu. 34, 35.

8. Do the Scriptures teach a *Limbus Patrum?* And were Old Testament believers glorified at their death or not?

Turrettin, Qu. 10, 11; Qu. 9, § 1-11. Knapp, § 150. Catech. Rom., pt. i, ch. 6, Qu. 1-6. Knapp, § 96. Witsius, bk. iv, ch. 12. On the whole Fairbairn's Typology.

COMING now to the last stage of the old dispensation, the Covenant of Sinai, we find several marked and impressive additions to the former revelations. But **5. Additions at Sinai.** they will all be found rather developments of existing features of the gospel, than new elements. These traits were, chiefly the republication of the moral Law with every adjunct of majesty and authority, the establishment of a Theocratic State-Church, in place of simpler patriarchal forms, with fully detailed civic institutions, the Passover, a new sacrament; and the great development of the sacrificial ritual.

The Covenant of Sinai has seemed to many to wear such **The Covenant of Sinai not a Covenant of Works.** an aspect of legality, that they have supposed themselves constrained to regard it as a species of Covenant of Works; and, therefore a recession from the Abrahamic Covenant, which, we are expressly told, (John viii : 56 ; Gal. iii : 8,) contained the gospel. Now, it is one objection, that this view, making two distinct dispensations between Adam and Christ, and the first a dispensation of the Covenant of Grace, and the one which came after, of the Covenant of Works, is *a priori*, unreasonable. For, it is unreasonable in this : that it is a recession, instead of a progress; whereas every consistent idea of the plan of Revelation makes it progressive. It is unreasonable ; because both the Old and New Testaments represent the Sinai Covenant as a signal honour and privilege to Israel. But they also represent the Covenant of Works as inevitably a covenant of death to man

after the Fall; so that had the transactions of Sinai been a
regression from the " Gospel preached before unto Abraham,"
to a Covenant of Works, it would have been a most signal curse
poured out on the chosen people.   The attempt is made to
evade this, by saying that, while eternal life to the Hebrews
was now suspended on a covenant of works, they were ritual
works only, in which an exact formal compliance was all that
was required.   This is untenable ; because it is inconsistent
with God's spiritual and unchangeable character, and with His
honour ; and because the Mosaic Scriptures are as plain as the
New Testament in disclaiming the sufficiency of an exact ritual
righteousness, as the term of eternal life, and in requiring a perfect, spiritual obedience.   If a ritual obedience was accepted
instead of a spiritual one, that was an act of grace—a remission of the claims of laws—so that the Mosaic turns out a dispensation of grace, after all.   But grace was preached to Abel,
Noah, Abraham, in a prior dispensation, through a Mediator to
come.   Now, through what medium was this gracious remission
of law given to Israel, at Sinai?   The answer we give is so
consistent, that it appears self-evident, almost: That it was
through the same Christ to come, already preached to the Patriarchs, and now typified in the Levitical sacrifices.   So that the
theory I combat resolves itself, in spite of itself, as it were, into
the correct theory, viz: That the promise contained in the Covenant of Sinai was through the Mediator, typified in the Levitical sacrifices; and that the term for enjoying that promise was
not legal, not an exact ritual obedience, but gospel faith in the
antitype.

The French divines, Camero and Amyraut, proposed an
ingenious modification of the legal theory of Moses' covenant:
That in it a certain kind of life was proposed (as in the Covenant of Works,) as a reward for an exact obedience : But that
the life was temporal, in a prosperous Canaan, and the obedience was ritual.   This is true, so far as a visible church-standing
turned on a ritual obedience.   But to the Hebrew, that temporal life in happy Canaan was a type of heaven ; which was not
promised to an exact moral obedience, but to faith.   Were this
theory modified, so as to represent this dependence of the Hebrew's church-standing on his ritual obedience, as a mere type
and emblem of the law's spiritual work as a " schoolmaster to
lead us to Christ," it might stand.

But let us proceed to a more exact examination.   We find
that the transactions at Sinai included the
Additions at Sinai.   following : (a) A republication of the Moral
Law, with greatest majesty and authority.   (b) An expansion
of the Ritual of the typical service, with the addition of a
second sacrament, the passover.   (c) The change of the visible
Church instituted in Gen. 17th, into a theocratic Commonwealth-
Church—both in one.   (d) The legal conditions of outward

good-standing were made more burdensome and exacting than they had been before. This last feature was not a novelty, (See Gen. xvii : 14,) but it was made more stringent.

Can the designs of these modifications be explained con-

Their Designs.   sistently with our view? Yes. As to the theocratic state, this was necessitated by the numbers of the Church, which had outgrown the family state — and needed temporal institutions capable of still larger growth, even into a grand nation. The amplified ritual was designed to foreshadow the approaching Christ, and the promises of the Covenant more fully. Next: The legal conditions for retaining outward ecclesiastical privileges were made more stringent, in order to enable the Law to fulfil more energetically the purpose for which St. Paul says it was added, to be a pædagogue to lead to Christ. (See Gal. iii ; 19, 22). For this stringency was designed to be, to the Israelite, a perpetual reminder of the law which was to Adam, the condition of life, now broken, and its wrath already incurred, thus to hedge up the awakened conscience to Christ. This greater urgency was made necessary by the sinfulness of the Church and its tendencies to apostacy, with the seductions of Paganism now general in the rest of mankind.

The passover, a peculiarly gospel sacrament, was added, to illustrate the way of salvation by faith, upon occasion of the exodus and deliverance of the first-born. The captivity in Egypt was an emblem of man's bondage under the curse ; and the dreadful death of the first-born, of the infliction of the sentence. The Hebrews escape that doom, by substituting a sacrifice; which is a type of Christ. (See Jno. i : 36 ; 1 Cor. v : 7). But the saved family then eat that victim, thus signifying the appropriating act of faith, very much as is done in the commemorative sacrament of the Supper now.

The followers of Cocceius and his school have texts which,

6. Moses' Dispen- we admit, bear plausibly against our identifi-
sation same in sub- cation of the Mosaic and Abrahamic dispen-
stance as Abraham's. sations. They point us, not only to the numerous places in the Pentateuch which seem to say, like Levit. xviii : 5, " Do, and live ;" but to such passages as Jer. xxxi : 32, which seems to say that the Covenant of Grace is " not according to the covenant made the fathers in the day God took them by the hand to bring them out of the land of Egypt." So, they urge Jno. i : 17 : Gal. iii : 12 ; Rom. x : 5 ; Gal. iv : 25 ; Heb. viii : 7–13 ; ix : 8 ; ii : 3. (The new covenant " began to be spoken by the Lord," and so, must not antedate the Christian era), vii : 18, and such like passages.

But, notwithstanding this array, there are irresistible arguments for the other side. And first, we urge the general consideration that the Bible never speaks of more than two kinds of Covenants with man: that of the Law, or Works, and that of Grace. The dispensations also are but two, " the first and the second ;" the " new and the old." But if Moses' dispensation was a legal one in essence, then we must have three ; for Abraham's was doubtless a gracious one. We add, that there are but two imaginable ways ; and but two known to Scripture ; "grace" and "works," by which a soul can win adoption of life. The latter, the Scriptures declare to be utterly impracticable after man's fall. Since the Israelites were fallen men, if their covenant was not gracious, it was only a condemning one. Its result was only their destruction. But, second, the latter conclusion is utterly inconsistent with the fact that God covenanted with them at Sinai, in mercy, and not in judicial wrath : as their redeemer and deliverer, and not as their destroyer. This transaction, whatever it was, was proposed and accepted as a privilege, not a curse. Exod. xix : 5 ; xx : 2 ; xxxiv : 6, 7 ; Ps. lxxviii : 35. For, third, the compact of Sinai included all the essential parties and features, and adopted the very formula, which we have seen were characteristic of the Covenant of Grace. On the one side was God, transacting with them, not as Proprietor and Judge, but, as beneficent Father. On the other side was the people, a mass chosen in their sin and unworthiness. See Ezek. xvi : 3–6 ; Ps. cix : 21 ; Is. xxxvii : 35. Between these parties was Moses, as a Mediator, the most eminent type of Christ in the whole history. And the compact is ratified in the very terms of the covenant of Grace. " I will be your God, and ye shall be my people." (See Levit. xxvi : 12 ; Jer. xi : 4 ; xxx : 22). Fourth : I borrow the argument of the Apostle from Gal. iii : 17 ; fidelity to the bond already contracted with Abraham and his seed, forbade the after formation of a different compact with them. The last testament is valid in law against the previous ones, but the first bond excludes subsequent contracts of an inconsistent tenour. This is powerfully confirmed by the fact, that Moses, in confirming the Sinai-Covenant with Israel, tells them more than once, that they enter it as Abraham's seed. Deut. vii : 8, 9, 12 ; Exod. iii : 6, 7. Compare Ps. cv : 6 ; Isaiah xli : 8. This shows that, whatever the covenant with Abraham was, that with Israel was a renewal of it. Fifth : The very "book of the testimony," and all the utensils of the sanctuary were purified with blood ; as we are taught in Heb. ix : 18–23. Why all this ? The Apostle says it was to foreshadow the truth, that Christ's blood must be the real propitiation carried, for sinners, into the upper sanctuary. Our opponents would agree with us, that the sacrifices of the altar were the most notable features of the Levitical dispensation. But we are taught that these all pointed to Christ, the true priest and victim. Heb. ix : 23, &c., tells us that this great feature, that "without the shedding of blood was no remission," was to hold up the grand truth of the necessity of satisfaction for guilt by Christ's blood. Thus, the more Levitical sacrifices we find, the

more Gospel do we find.   Sixth : Men feel driven to the conclusion we combat, they say, by the re-enactment of the law.
But the law, both moral and ritual, was in force under Abraham.   See Rom. v : 13, 14 ; Gen. xvii : 14.

Seventh : Both the moral, and a (less burdensome) ritual
law are still binding, in the same sense, under the New Testament dispensation,   (See Matt. v : 17; Jno. iii : 5; Mark xvi :
16.)   Surely the New Testament is not therefore a Covenant of
Works !   Last, Christ expressly says, that Moses taught of
Him.   Luke xxiv : 27; Jno. v : 46.   Moses must then, have
taught the Gospel.   And in Rom. x : 6, the inspired expositor,
when he would state the plan of salvation by grace through
faith, in express contrast to the Covenant of Works (as stated
iu Levit. xviii : 5, for instance) borrows the very words of
Moses' Covenant with Israel from Deut. xxx : 11.   Does he
abuse the sense ?

To remove the cavil founded on each text quoted against
us, by a detailed exposition, would consume too much space.
It is not necessary.   By discussing one of the strongest of them,
we shall sufficiently suggest the clue to all.   The most plausible objection is that drawn from Jer. xxxi : 32, where the
prophet seems to assert an express opposition between the
new covenant, which Heb. vii, indisputably explains as the Covenant of Grace, and that made with Israel at the Exodus.
There is unquestionably, a difference asserted here ; and it is
the difference between law and grace.   But it is the Covenant
of Sinai viewed in one of its limited aspects only, which is here
set in antithesis to the Covenant of Grace : It is the secular
theocratic covenant, in which political and temporal prosperity
in Canaan was promised, and calamity threatened, on the conditions of theocratic obedience or rebellion.   The justice and
relevancy of the prophet Jeremiah's, and of the apostle's logic,
in selecting this aspect of the Sinai Covenant to display, by
contrast, the grace of the new covenant, are seen in this : that
self-righteous Jews, throwing away all the gracious features of
their national compact, and thus perverting its real nature,
were founding all their pride and hopes on this secular feature.
The prophet points out to them that the fate of the nation,
under that theocratic bond, had been disaster and ruin ; and
this, because the people had ever been too perverse to comply
with its legal terms, especially, inasmuch as God had left them to
their own strength.   But the spiritual covenant was to differ (as
it always had), in this vital respect : that God, while covenanting with His people for their obedience, would make it His part
to write His law in their hearts.   Thus He would Himself
graciously ensure their continuance in faith and obedience.
Witsius happily confirms this view, by remarking that, in all the
places where the secular, theocratic compact is stated, as a Covenant of Works, we see no pledge on God's part, that He

"will circumcise their hearts," as in Deut. xxx : 6. There, the
ensuing compact is interpreted by St. Paul (Rom. x : 6,) as the
Covenant of Grace. So, in Jer. xxxi: 33, 34. God engages
graciously to work in His elect people the holy affections and
principles, which will embrace, and cleave to the promise.
But in all such places as Levit. xviii : 5 ; Jer. xxxi : 29; Ezek.
xviii, the duties required are secular, and the good gained or
forfeited is national. In truth, the transaction of God with
Israel was two-fold: it had its shell, and its kernel; its body,
and its spirit; its type, and its antitype. The corporate, theocratic, political nation was the shell: the elect seed were the
kernel. See Rom. chaps. x and xi. The secular promise was
the type : the spiritual promise of redemption through Christ
was the antitype. The law was added as "a schoolmaster," to
bring God's true people, the spiritual seed mixed in the outward body, to Christ. This law the carnal abused, as they do
now, by the attempt to establish their own righteousness under it.

A correct view of the nature of that display made of the
7. Differences of Covenant of Grace in the Old Dispensation,
Old Dispensation from will be gained by comparing it with the New.
New. All orthodox writers agree that there is both
law and gospel in the Old Testament Scriptures. If, by the
Old Testament Covenant, is understood only that legal covenant
of moral and ceremonial works, then there will indeed be
ground for all the strong contrast, when it is compared with the
Gospel in the New Testament, which some writers draw between
the severity and terror of the one, and the grace of the other.
But in our comparison, we shall be understood as comparing
the Old Dispensation with the New, taken with all their features, as two wholes. We find Turrettin (Ques. 8, § 18, 25),
makes them differ in their date or time, in their clearness, in
their facility of observance, in their mildness, in their perfection, in their liberty, in their amplitude, and in their perpetuity.
Calvin (B. 2, ch. 11,) finds five differences: that the Old Testament promises eternal life typically under figures of Canaan,
that the Old Testament is mainly typical, that it is literal (while
the New Testament is spiritual) that it gendered to bondage,
and that it limited its benefits to one nation.

I am persuaded that the strong representations which these
The Old too much writers (and most others following them,) and,
Depreciated. yet more, the Cocceian school, give of the
bondage, terror, literalness, and intolerable
weight of the institutions under which Old Testament saints
lived, will strike the attentive reader as incorrect. The experience, as recorded of those saints, does not answer to this
theory ; but shows them in the enjoyment of a dispensation
free, spiritual, gracious, consoling. I ask emphatically: does
not the New Testament Christian of all ages, go to the
recorded experiences of those very Old Testament saints, for

the most happy and glowing expressions in which to utter his
hope, gratitude, spiritual joy? Is it said that these are the
experiences of eminent saints, who had this full joy (even as
compared to New Testament saints) not because the published
truth was equal to that now given: but because they had higher
spiritual discernment? I reply: By nature they were just like
"us, sinners of the gentiles;" so that if they had more spiritual
discernment, it must be because there was a freer and fuller dispensation of the Holy Ghost to them than to us. (Much fuller!
to repair all defect of means, and more than bring them to a
level.) But this overthrows Calvin's idea of the dispensation as
a less liberal one. Or, is it pleaded that these are only the
inspired, and therefore exceptional cases of the Old Testament
Church? I answer: Did not God give the inspired experiences as appropriate models for those of their brethren? These
distorted representations have been produced by the seeming
force of such passages as Jno. i : 17; 2 Cor. iii : 6, 7; Gal. iii :
19, 23; iv : 1, 4 and 24–26; Heb. viii : 8; Acts xv : 10. But
the scope and circumstances of the Apostles, in making
such statements, are greatly overlooked. They were arguing,
for the gospel plan, against self-righteous Jews, who had perversely cast away the gospel significance out of the Mosaic
institutions to which they clung, and who retained only the
condemning features of those institutions; vainly hoping to
make a righteousness out of compliance with a law, whose very
intent was to remind men that they could make no righteousness for themselves. Hence we must always remember that
the Apostles are using, to a certain extent, an *argumentum aa'
hominem*: they are speaking of the Mosaic institutions under
the Jewish view of them. They are treating of that side
or aspect, which alone the perverse Jew retained of them.
Here is the key.

The truth is, both dispensations are precisely alike, in having two sides to them: a law which condemns
those who will persist in self-righteous plans;
and a gospel which rescues the humble
believer from that condemnation. The obligation of Works, (which was reënacted in the
Decalogue,) is perpetual, being founded on the
very relations between man and God, on all except those who
are exempted from it by the substitutionary righteouness of the
Mediator. It is of force now, on all others. It thunders just as
it did in Eden and on Sinai. Nor, I beg you to note, is the
Old Testament singular, in enjoining a ritual law, which is also
"the letter that killeth," a "carnal ordinance," a "ministration
of death," to those who perversely refuse to be pointed by it to
the Messiah, and who try to make a self-righteouness out of it.
The New Testament also has its sacraments; all are commanded to partake, yet he that eateth and drinketh, not dis-

*The New Testament
Language as to it Ex-
plained. New Testa-
ment also a Dispensa-
tion of Bondage to
Ritualist.*

cerning the Lord's body, "eateth and drinketh damnation to himself;" and he that takes the water of Baptism self-righteously, only sees therein a terrible symbol of his need of a cleansing which he does not receive. Let an evangelical Christian imagine himself instructing and refuting a modern Ritualist of the school of Rome or the Tractarians. He would find himself necessarily employing an *argumentum ad hominem* precisely like that of Paul against the Pharisees. The evangelical believer would be forced to distinguish between the legal or condemning, and the gospel side of our own sacraments; and he would proceed to show, that by attempting to make a self-righteousness out of those sacraments, the modern Pharisee was going back under a dispensation of condemnation and bondage; that he was throwing away 'the spirit which giveth life,' and retaining only the 'letter that killeth.'

The New Testament has also its sacrifice; the one sacrifice of Christ; and to him who rejects the pardon which it purchased, it is a ministry of damnation, more emphatic than all the blood of beasts could utter. Both dispensations have their "letter that killeth," as well as their "spirit that giveth life," their Sinai as well as their Zion. And in the very place alluded to, it is the killing letter of the New Testament of which Paul speaks, 2 Cor. ii: 15, 16. Besides in the Old Testament no part of the ritual could be more crushing than the moral commandment "exceeding broad," is to the unrenewed. But see Matt. v: 17-20.

Again, the Old Testament distinguished both as to its word, and its ordinances, between this letter that killeth and this spirit that giveth life. Deut. x: 12; Ps. l: 16, 17, 22 and 23; Prov. xxi: 3; i Samuel xv: 22; Ps. li: 16, 17; Isa. i: 13-20 &c.

Now just as the Christian minister would argue with a nominal Christian who persisted in making a righteousness out of the sacraments, so the Apostles argued with the Jews, who persisted in making a righteousness out of their ritual. Thus abused, the ritual of the Old Testament and of the New loses its gracious side, and only retains its condemning. Peter says, Acts xv: 10, the ritual was a yoke which neither Jews nor their fathers were able to bear. Did God signalize His favour to His chosen people by imposing an intolerable ritual? Is it true that well disposed Jews could not bear it? See Luke i: 6; Phil. iii: 6. No: Peter has in view the ritual used in that self-righteous sense, in which the Judaizing Christians regarded it while desiring to impose it on Gentiles. As a rule of justification it would be intolerable. The decalogue (2 Cor. iii: 7) would be a ministration of death to him who persisted to use it as these Jews did. But Moses gave it as only one side, one member of his dispensation, "to be a schoolmaster to lead us to Christ." Gal. iii: 16 speaks of a law given 430 years after the Convenant of Grace, and seeming to be contrasted. But it "could not disannul it." Did not Abraham's Covenant of Grace survive this law, as much in the ante-Christian, as in the post-Christian times?

Calvin says, as I conceive, perverting the sense of Gal. 4th, that the time of bondage, in which "the heir differed nothing from the slave," was the time of the Jewish dispensation, while the time of liberation was the time of the Christian dispensation. Not so. As to the visible Church collectively, and its outward or ecclesiastical privilege, this was true; but not as to individual believers in the Church. And this distinction satisfies the Apostle's scope in Gal. 3d and 4th, and Heb. viii: 7, 8, and reconciles with passages about to be quoted. [cf. Turrettin on Heb. ix: 8, Que. 11, § 14.] Was David still in bondage, "differing nothing from that of a slave," when he sung Ps. xxxii: i, 2, cxvi: 16? The time of tutelage was, to each soul, the time of his self-righteous, unbelieving, convicted, but unhumbled struggles. The time of the liberty is, when he has flown to Christ. This, whether he was Israelite or Christian. Isaac, says another, symbolized the gospel believer, Ishmael, the Hebrew. Were not Isaac and Ishmael cotemporary? Interpret the allegory consistently. And was it not Isaac, who was, not allegorically, but literally and actually, the Hebrew, the subject of an Old Testament dispensation, a ritual dispensation, a typical one, only differing from the Mosaic in details? This would be to represent the Apostle as making a bungling allegory, indeed, to choose the man who was actually under the dispensation of bondage, as the type of the liberty, had St. Paul intended to prove that the Old Dispensation was a bondage. And it would be bungling logic, again, to represent the spiritual liberty to which he wished to lead his hearers, by sonship to Abraham, if Abraham were the very head, with whom the dispensation of bondage was formed! St. Paul warns the foolish Galatians who "desired to be under the law." "Do ye not hear the law?" (Gal. iv: 21.) The thing which the law says to such self-righteous fools, is read in Gal. iii: 10. "As many as are of the works of the law are under the curse," &c. St. Paul's allegory says that Ishmael's mother (the type of the soul in bondage) represents Sinai, and Sinai again, "The Jerusalem which now is." Sarah, then, represents what? "The Jerusalem which is above, and is free." Which of these answereth to King David's Zion' "the city of the great King, in whose palaces God is known as a Refuge"? (Ps. xlviii: 3, 4.) Obviously, Sarah and her children. But the Pharisees of the Apostle's day claimed to be the heirs of that very Zion, and did literally and geographically inhabit it! How is this? They were in form the free-woman's heirs—in fact, bastards. And they had disinherited themselves, by casting away the gospel, and selecting the legal significance of the transactions of Sinai. The Sinai

Gal. 3d and 4th Explained.

which now anwsereth to the bond-woman is not the Sinai of Moses, of Jehovah, and of Abraham; but the Sinai of the legalist,
the Sinai which the Pharisee insisted on having.

You will not understand me as asserting that the Old Testament dispensation was as well adapted to
the pursposes of redemption as the New.
This would be in the teeth of Heb. viii:
7, &c. The inferior clearness, fullness, and liberality result
necessarily from the fact that it preceded Christ's coming in the flesh. The visible Church, in its collective capacity,
was as to its outward means and privileges, in a state of minority
and pupilage. But every true believer in it looked forward by
faith, through that very condition of inferiority, to the blessings
covenanted to him in the coming Messiah; so that his soul,
individually, was not in a state of minority or bondage; but in
a state of full adoption and freedom. This state of the visible
Church, however, as contrasted with that which the Church
now enjoys, is illustrative of the contrast between the spiritual
state of the elect soul, before conversion, while convicted and
self-righteous, and after conversion while rejoicing in hope.
This remark may serve to explain the language of Galatians
3d and 4th.

Yet the Old Neces-
sarily Inferior.

I would discard, then, those representations of the intolerable harshness, bondage, literalness, absence
of spiritual blessing, in the old dispensation,
and give the following modified statement.

Real Points of Dif-
ference.

(a.) The old dispensation preceded the actual transacting
of Christ's vicarious work. The new dispensation succeeds it.

(b.) Hence, the ritual teachings, (not all the teachings) of
the old dispensation were typical; those of the New Testament
are commemorative symbols. A type is a symbolic prediction;
and for the same reason that prophecy is less intelligible before
the event, than history of it afterwards, there was less clearness and fullness of disclosure. (See i Pet. i: 12.) Again,
because under the Old Testament the Divine sacrifice by which
guilt was to be removed, was still to be made; the sacrificial
types, (those very types which foreshadowed the pardoning
grace as well as the condemning justice,) presented a more
prominent and repeated exhibition of guilt than now, under
the gospel; when the sacrifice is completed; (Heb. x: 3,)
because it was harder to look to the true propitiation in the
future, than it is now in the past; the voice of the law, the
pædagogue who directed men's eyes to Christ, was graciously
rendered louder and more frequent than it is now.

(c) Perspicuity in commemorating being easier than in
predicting, the ritual teachings of the previous dispensation
were more numerous, varied and laborious.

(d) God, in His inscrutable wisdom, saw fit to limit the old
dispensation to one nation, so far at least, as to require that any

sinner embracing it should become an Israelite; and to make the necessary ritual territorial and local.   Under the New Testament all nations are received alike.

(e) The previous dispensation was temporary, the New Testament will last till the consummation of all things.

With reference to the state of the Old Testament saints in the other world, we discard the whole fable 8. Old Testament of the Papists concerning a *limbus patrum*, Saints Redeemed at and the postponement of the application of Death. redemption to them till Christ's death.   Christ's suretyship is such that His undertaking the believer's work, releases the believer as soon as the condition is fulfilled.   He is not merely *Fidejussor,* but *expromissor* (Turrettin), Christ being an immutable, almighty and faithful surety, when He undertook to make satisfaction to the law, it was, in the eye of that God to whom a thousand years are but as one day, as good as done.   (Here, by the way, is some evidence that the chief necessity of atonement was not to make a governmental display, but to satisfy God's own attributes).   See Rom. iii : 25 ; Heb. ix : 15 ; Ps. xxxii : 1, 2 ; li : 2 ; 10–13 ; ciii : 12 ; Is. xliv : 22 ; Luke xvi : 22, 23 ; with Matt. viii : 11 ; Luke ix : 31 ; Ps. lxxiii : 24 ; 1 Pet. iii : 19 ; Heb. xi : 16 ; xii : 23.

These texts seems to me to prove, beyond all doubt, that Christ's sacrifice was for the guilt of Old Testament believers, as well as those under the New Testament; that the anticipative satisfaction was imputed to the ancient saints when they believed, and that at their death, they went to the place of glory in God's presence.   What else can we make of the translations of Enoch and Elijah, and the appearance of Moses in glory, before Christ's death?

The strength of the Papists' scriptural argument is in the last two of the texts cited by me.   I may No *Limbus Patrum.* add, also, Rev. xiv : 13, which the Papists would have us understand, as though the *terminus a quo* of the blessedness of the believing dead were from the date of that oracle ; implying that hitherto those dying in the Lord had not been immediately blessed.   It is a flagrant objection to this exposition, that the Apocalypse was a whole generation after Christ's resurrection, when, according to Papists, the dying saints began to go to heaven.   The terminus is, evidently, the date of each saint's death.   The testimony from Heb. ix : 8, you have seen answered, by your text-book, Turrettin.   The Apostle's scope here shows that his words are not to be wrested to prove that there was no application of redemption until after Christ died.   The author is attempting to show that the Levitical temple and ritual were designed to be superseded.   This he argues, with admirable address, from the nature of the services themselves: The priests offered continually, and the High Priest every year, by the direction of the Holy Ghost; by

THE COVENANT OF GRACE

which God showed that that ritual was not to be permanent;
for if it had been adequate, it would have done its work and
ceased.   Its repetition showed that the work of redemption was
not done ; and never would be, until another dispensation came,
more efficacious than it.   Such is the scope.   Now, the words,
"the way into the sanctuary was not yet manifested," in such a
connection, are far short of an assertion, that no believing soul
could, at death, be admitted to heaven.   Is not the meaning
rather, that until Christ finished His sacrifice, the human priest
still stood between men and the mercy-seat?

But the *locus palmarius* of the Papists for a *Limbus Pa-*
trum, is 1 Pet. iii : 19, &c.   On this obscure
text you may consult, besides commentaries,
(among whom see Calvin *in loco*,) Knapp,
Chr. Theol., § 96 ; Turrettin, Loc. xii, Que. 11, § 15 ; Loc. xiii,
Que. 15, § 12.   Here, again, our safest guide is the Apostle's
scope, which is this: Christ is our Exemplar in submitting
patiently to undeserved suffering.   For Him his own people
slew: the very Saviour who, so far from deserving ill at their
hands, had in all ages been offering gospel mercy to them and
their fathers, even to those most reprobate of all, the Antediluvians.   But the same Divine Nature in which Christ had been
so mercifully carrying a slighted gospel to that ancient generation, (now, for their unbelief, shut up in the prison of hell,)
gloriously raised Him from the dead, after their equally reprobate posterity had unjustly slain Him.   Here is our encouragement while we suffer innocently after the example of our Head.
For this resurrection, which glorified Him over all His ancient
and recent enemies, will save us.   Then we, redeemed by that
grace which was symbolized to the ancient believers by the
type of the ark, and to modern, by the sacrament of baptism,
will emerge triumphantly from an opposing and persecuting
world ; as Christ's little Church. (consisting then of a number
contemptible in unbelievers' eyes,) in Noah's day, came out
from the world of unbelievers.

With this simple and consistent view of the Apostle's drift,
the whole dream of a descent into Hades, and a release of the
souls of the patriarchs from their *limbus*, is superfluous, and
therefore unreasonable.

Especially, not in 1.
Pet. i : 19, &c.

LECTURE XXXIX.

MEDIATOR OF THE COVENANT OF GRACE.

1. Mediator what? THE word mediator is in the New Testament $M\epsilon\sigma\iota\tau\eta\varsigma$ middle man. The phrase does not occur in the Old Testament, except in the Sept. translation of Job ix : 33. (Engl. v : "days-man,") and then with the sense of umpire, not of mediator. Its idea in the New Testament is evidently of one who intervenes to act between parties, who cannot, for some reason, act with each other directly. Thus, Moses was (Gal. iii : 19) the mediator of the Theocratic covenant. But in this, he was no more than *internuncius*. Christ's mediation included far more, as will appear when we prove His three offices of prophet, priest and king; which are here assumed.

Why Needed in Covenant of Grace? No mediator was necessary in the Covenant of Works between God and angels, or God and Adam; because, in unfallen creatures, there was nothing to bar direct intercourse between them and God. Hence the Scripture presents no evidence of Christ's performing any mediatorial function for them. On the contrary the Bible implies always, that Christ's offices were undertaken, because men were sinners. Matt. i : 21 ; Is. liii ; Jno. iii : 16. But, man being fallen, the necessity of Christ's mediation appears from all the moral attributes of God's nature; His truth, (pledged to punish sin,) His justice, (righteously and necessarily bound to requite it,) His goodness, (concerned in the wholesome order of His kingdom,) and His holiness, (in-

464

trinsically repellent of sinners). So also, man's enmity, evil conscience and guilty fear, awakened by sin, call, though not so necessarily, for a mediator.

It has been objected that this argument represents God's will as under a constraint; for else what hindered His saving man by His mere will? And that it dishonours His wisdom by making Him go a roundabout way to His end, subjecting His Son to many humiliations and pangs. The answer is: the necessity was a moral one, proceeding out of God's own voluntary perfections. Note. To sustain our argument we must assert that God's mere will is not the sole origin of moral distinctions. See Lect. x : on that point.

Against the Jews we assert that Jesus of Nazareth is the 2. Jesus the Mediator of the Old Testament. Messiah and Mediator of this Covenant. Of an argument so comprehensive, and containing so many details, only the general structure can be indicated. In this argument the standard of authoritative reference assumed is the Old Testament, which the orthodox Jew admits to be inspired. (As for the Rationalistic, they must first be dealt with as other skeptics.) Second. In this argument no other authority is claimed for the New Testament in advance, than that it is an authentic narrative. As such, it is substantiated by the profane and Jewish history. We then make two heads :

The promised Mediator of the Old Testament must have (a) Because the Time is Passed. already come. For the time has passed. (See Gen. xlix : 10 ; Dan. ix : 24–27). He was to come while the second temple was standing. (Hag. ii : 6–9 ; Mal. iii : 1–3). He was to come while the Jewish polity subsisted; (Gen. xlix : 10,) and while Jerusalem was still the capital of that theocracy. (Hag. ii : 6–9 ; Is. ii : 3 ; lxii : 1, &c.) This polity and city have now been overwhelmed for nearly 1,800 years : so that the very ability to give genealogical evidence of the birth of Christ from David's stock is now utterly gone! The Messiah's coming was to be signalized by the cessation of types. (Dan. ix : 27). Last : the Messiah's coming was to be marked by the accession of multitudes of Gentiles to the religion of the Old Testament. (See Is. ii : 3 ; xlii : 1–6; xlix : 6 ; lx : 3, &c.)

Jesus of Nazareth is the Person; because all the qualities (b.) Because He has the appointed Traits. and incidents foretold in the Old Testament, wonderfully tally with Him and His life. (See Acts iii : 18.) The strength of the argument is in the completeness of this correspondence. In fairly estimating this proof, reference must be made to the doctrine of probabilities. The occurrence of one predicted trait in a person would prove nothing. The concurrence of two would not be a demonstration; because that concurrence might be fortuitous. But, when three independent and predicted traits

30*

concurred, the proof would greatly strengthen; because the
likelihood that chance could account for all three, is diminished,
in a multiplying ratio. So, as the number of coincident, predicted traits increases, the evidence mounts up, by a multiplying
ratio, towards absolute certainty. Jesus, then, answers the prophetic description in the time of His birth. (See above.) In
the place; Micah. v : 2. In His nativity of a virgin; Is. vii :
14. In His forerunner; Mal. iii : 1, &c. In His lineage; Gen.
iii : 15, xviii : 18, xlix : 10; Is. xi : 1 ; Ps. cxxxii : 11 ; Is. ix : 7,
&c. In His preaching; Is. lxi : 1–3. In His miracles ; Is.
xxxv : 5–6. In His tenderness and meekness; Is. xlii : 3. In
the circumstances of His end, viz., His entry into Jerusalem;
Zech. ix : 9. Betrayal; Zech. xi : 12, 13. Rejection and contempt ; Is. liii : 3. Death; liii : 8. Mockings therein ; Ps.
xxii : 8. Vinegar; Ps. lxix : 21. Piercing; Zech. xii : 10.
Yet no bones broken ; Ps. xxxiv : 20. Death with malefactors;
Is. liii : 9. Honourable burial; Is. liii : 9. Resurrection; Ps.
xvi : 9, 10; lxviii 18. Spiritual effusions, Joel. ii : 28. Again:
the Messiah of the Old Testament was to have a wondrous
union of natures, offices and destinies, which was mysterious to
the Old Testament saints, and absurd to modern Jews; yet was
wonderfully realized in Jesus. He was to be God, (Ps. ii : 7;
Is. ix : 6); yet man, (Is. ix : 6.) The history of Jesus, taken
with His words, shows Him both human and divine. The Messiah was to be both priest and victim. (Ps. cx; Is. liii.) He
was to be an outcast, (Is. liii,) and a king, (Ps. ii.) So wa
Jesus. He was to conquer all people, (Ps. xlv and lxxii : 110);
yet, without violence. (Is. xlii : 3; Ps. xlv : 4.) He was to
combine the greatest contrasts of humiliation and glory. These
contrasts are so hard to satisfy in one Person (to all unbelieving
Israel it seems impossible,) that when we find them meeting in
Jesus, it causes a very strong evidence to arise, that He is the
Mediator.

The doctrine of the constitution of Christ's person, is
3. Hypostatic Union. purely one of Revelation, and involves a
mystery (1 Tim. iii : 16,) as great, perhaps, as
that of the Trinity itself. But though inexplicable, it is not
incredible. The nature of the scriptural argument by which
this twofold nature in one person is established, is analogous to
that establishing a Trinity in unity. The text nowhere defines
the doctrine in one passage, as fully as we assert it. But our
doctrine is a necessary deduction from three sets of Scriptural
assertions. First. Jesus Christ was properly and literally a
man. (See, e. g., Jno. i : 14; Gal. iv : 4; Jno. i : 51; Is. ix : 6;
Heb. ii : 17; Matt. iv : 2; Luke ii : 40, 52; Matt. viii : 24;
Mark xiii : 32; Jno. xi : 35; Matt. xxvi : 37, &c.) Second.
Christ is also literally and properly divine. (See, e. g., Jno. i : 1 ;
Rom. ix : v 1 John v : 20; Is. ix : 6; Phil. ii : 6; Col. ii : 9;
Heb. i : 3; 1 Tim. iii : 16, &c.) Yet this Man-God is one and

the same ; in proof of which we need only allude to the fact, that in every text speaking of Him, oneness of person, and personal attributes, are either asserted or implied of Him. In many passages the same proposition asserts both natures in one person, (e. g., Jno. iii : 13 ; 1 Tim. iii : 16.)

To Socinians, and other errorists, these passages seem contradictory, because being unwilling to admit the "incarnate mystery," they insist on explaining away one class of them. The true explanation is, that both are true, because of the hypostatic union. By these means such seeming paradoxes are to be explained, as those in Mark xiii : 32, compared with John v : 20 ; Matt. xi : 27, &c. The first of these verses asserts that even the Son does not know the day and hour when the earth and heavens shall pass away. The others ascribe omniscience to Him. The explanation (and the only one) is that Christ in His human nature has a limited knowledge, and in His divine nature, an infinite knowledge.

The opinions of Gnostics are sufficiently narrated by Hill, (*loc cit.*) As they have no currency in Gnostic Theory of Christ's Person. modern times, I will content myself with briefly reminding you of the distinction between the other Gnostics and those called Docetai. Both parties concurred in regarding matter as the source of all moral evil. Hence, they could not consistently admit the resurrection and glorification, either of the saints or of Jesus' body. The Docetai, therefore, taught that Christ never had a literal human body ; but only a phantasm of one, on which the malice of His persecutors was spent in vain. The others taught that the Aion, who they supposed constituted Christ's superior nature, only inhabited temporarily in the man Jesus, a holy Jew constituted precisely as other human beings are ; and that, at the crucifixion, this Aion flew away to heaven, leaving the man Jesus to suffer alone.

The historical events attending the Nestorian controversy, and the personal merits of Nestorius, I shall The Nestorian view. not discuss. The system afterwards known as Nestorianism was apprehended by the Catholic Christians, as by no means a trivial one, or a mere logomachy about the θεοτοχος. The true teacher of the doctrinal system was rather Theodore of Mopuestia, (a teacher of Nestorius) than the latter prelate. In his hands, it appears to be a development of Pelagianism, which it succeeded in date, and an application to the constitution of Christ's person of the erroneous doctrines of man's native innocence. Theodore set out from opposition to Apollinaris, who taught that the divine Reason in Christ substituted a rational human nature, leaving Christ only a material and animal nature on the human side. According to Theodore, Christ is a sort of impersonated symbol of mankind, first as striving successfully against trial, and second, as rewarded with

glory for this struggle. He supposed Christ the Man to exercise a self-determining power of will, which, he taught, is necessary to moral merit in any man.   Christ, the man, then, began
His human career, with the Word associated and strengthening
His human nature.   As Christ the man resisted trial and exhibited His devotion to duty in the exercise of His self-
determination, He was rewarded by more full and intimate
communications of divine indwelling, until His final act of
devotion was rewarded with an ascension, and full communication of the Godhead.   The process in each gracious soul offers
an humble parallel.   The indwelling of God the Word in Jesus,
is not generically unlike that of the Holy Ghost in a saint : but
only closer and stronger in degree.   There are, indeed, three
grades of this one kind of union, first, that of the Holy Ghost,
in sanctification ; second, that of the same person, in inspiration ; third, that of the Word in Christ.   And the Nestorians
preferred rather to speak of the last, as a *συνάφεια* than a
ἕνωσις, the preferred term of Cyril.

This view seemed to involve two Pelagian errors ; first, that
grace is bestowed as the reward of man's
right exercise of moral powers, (in his own
self-determined will,) instead of being the
gratuitous cause thereof ; and second, that inasmuch as the
human purity of the man Jesus went before, and procured the
divine indwelling, it is naturally possible for any other man to
be perfect, in advance of grace.   Again, from the separation of
the nexus between the two natures in Christ, there seemed to
the Catholics to be a necessary obscuring of the communication of attributes ; so that Christ's sacrifice would no longer be
divine and meritorious enough to cover infinite guilt.   And
thus would be lost the fundamental ground of His substitution
for us.   The whole scheme goes rather to make Christ incarnate
rather a symbolical exemplar of the work of God in a believer,
than the proper redeeming purchase and Agent thereof.   Its
tendencies, then, are Socinian.

Doct trinal Conse-
quences.

The Alexandrine theologians generally leaned the other
way.   Cyril was fond of quoting from the
great Athanasius ; that while "he allowed
Christ was the Son of God, and God, according to the spirit,
but son of man, according to the flesh ; but not two natures
and one son ; the one to be worshipped and the other not ; but
one nature of God the Word incarnated, and to be worshipped
by single worship along with His flesh."   They loved to assert
the *ἕνωσις* (unification) of the natures, rather than the *συνάφεια*
(or conjunction,) of Theodore.   They preferred to conceive of
Christ as so clothing Himself with human nature, as to assimilate it, by a species of subsumption, with His divinity.
Hence the error of Eutyches was prepared ; that while the
mediatorial person was constituted from two natures, it existed

Eutychian View.

only in one, the divine. This error is as fatal to a proper conception of Christ's mediatorial work, as the Nestorian. By really destroying the humanity in Christ, from the moment of His birth, it gives us a Redeemer who has no true community of nature with us; and so, does not render a human obedience, nor pay the human penalty in our room and stead. The creed of Chalcedon, intermediate between these two extremes, is undoubtedly the scriptural one, as it has been adopted by all orthodox churches, ancient and modern, and is the basis of the propositions of the Westminster Assembly on this point. You have these symbols within your reach; and I shall not here repeat them.

For Orthodox creed of Chalcedon, see Mosheim, vol. i, p.
Orthodox Views. . 366. For our own, see Confession of Faith, ch. 8, § 2. This doctrine, however inexplicable, is not incredible; because it is no more mysterious than the union of two substances, spirit and body, into one human person, in ourselves. Yet, who is not conscious of his own personality? That the infinite Creator should assume a particular relation to one special part of His creation, the man Jesus, is not impossible, seeing He bears intimate relations (e. g., as providential upholder,) to all the rest. That an infinite spirit should enter into personal union with a man, is surely less mysterious than that a finite spirit should constitute a personal union with a body; because the infinite and almighty possesses, so to speak, more flexibility to enter into such union; and because the intimate union of spirit to spirit, is less mysterious than that of spirit with body. (A perfect analogy is not asserted.)

This Hypostatic union is the cornerstone of our redemption. The whole adaptation of the Media-
Hypostatic Union ground of the Efficacy of Christ's work. Socinian objection quashed. torial person to its work depends on it, as will be shown in the discussion of heads 5th, 6th. The general result of the Hypostatic union is stated well in the Confession of Faith, Ch. 8, § 7, last part. This is that κοινωνία ἰδιωμάτων which we hold, in common with the early Fathers, repudiating the Lutheran idea of the attributes of Divinity being literally conferred on the humanity; which is absurd and impossible. Apt instances of this κοινωνία may be seen in John iii : 13; Acts xiii : 15, xx : 28, xvii : 31 ; Mark ii : 10; Gal. iv : 4; and Rom. i : 17, or iii : 21 ; 1 Cor. ii : 8. Hence, it is, that Mediatorial acts performed in virtue of either nature, have all the dignity or worth belonging to the Mediatorial person as made up of both natures. Socinians do, indeed, object : that inasmuch as only the creature could, in the nature of things, be subjected to the law, and to penalty, the active and passive obedience of Christ have, after all, only a creature worth; and it is a mere legal fiction, to consider them as possessed of the infinite worth of a divine nature, since the divine nature did not especially render

them.   The answer is: The person possessed of a divine nature, rendered them.   If the Socinian would honestly admit the personal union as a thing which (though inscrutable) is real and literal, his objection would be relinquished.   For then, many analogies of human persons (not perfect indeed, applicable fairly) would show that this κοινωνια is not unnatural even. We shall see that the common sense and conscience of men always estimate the acts and sufferings of a united person (constituted of two natures) according to the dignity of the higher nature, to whichever of them those acts or sufferings may specially belong; e. g.   There are many bodily affections, as appetite, pain, which we characterize as distinctively corporeal; and yet, had not our bodies souls in them, these affections could have no place.   Why then is it incredible, that the divine substance in the Medatorial person should be the ground of a peculiar value in the human sufferings of that person; though in strictness of speech, the divine could not be the seat of the suffering?   Again, corporeal sufferings of martyrs have a moral value, which can only be attributed to the fact that those suffering men were not brutes, but spiritual and moral beings; while yet the soul may have been unconscious of the pangs, through spiritual joy, or other cause.   I argue, also, from the fact, that moral character is given to merely physical acts of men, because of the character of the volition prompting those acts.   Now, I pray, did not the will of the Λογος prompt all the acts of active and passive obedience performed by the human nature?   If when my bones and muscles in my arm gι through identically the same functions, with the same stick, to beat a dangerous dog, and to beat my friend, one physical act has the spiritual character of lawfulness and the other physically identical act has the spiritual character of sinfulness, because of the concern of my volition in them, why should it be thought a thing incredible, that the human sufferings of Christ should have a divine character, when prompted by the volition of the divine nature in His person?   And is not the bodily pain of a man more important than that of a dog?   It is enough, however, to show that the infinite dignity of Christ's divine nature is, in Scripture, given as ground of the infinite value of that work.   See Heb. ix : 13, 14, vii : 16, 24; John iii : 16; 1 Pet. i: 18, 19; Ps. xl : 6; Heb. x : 5—14.

4. The old doctrine of the Reformed Churches asserted not only the actual sinlessness, which none but violent infidels impugn, but the impeccability of our Redeemer.   In recent days, some of whom better things should have been expected, deny the latter.   They concede to the God-man the *posse non peccare*: but deny to Him, or at least to the humanity, the *non posse peccare*.   Their plea is in substance, that a being must be peccable in order to experience temptation, to be meritorious for resisting it, and to be an exemplar and encouragement

to us, who are tempted. Thus argue Ullman, Farrar, the author
of " Ecce Deus," Dr. Schaff, and even Dr. Hodge; while Dr.
Dorner, in his "History of Protestant Theol.," revives the
Nestorian and Pelagian doctrine, of a meritorious growth or
progress of Christ's humanity from peccability to impeccability, by virtue of the holy use of His initial contingency and
selfdetermination of will.

Now, none will say that the second Person, as eternal
Word, was, or is peccable. It would seem then, that the trait
can only be asserted of the humanity. But, 1st, It is the unan-
imous testimony of the Apostles, as it is the creed of the
Church, that the human nature never had its separate personality. It never existed, and never will exist for an instant, save
in personal union with the Word. Hence, (a.) Since only a
Person can sin, the question is irrelevant; and (b.) Since the
humanity never was, in fact, alone, the question whether, if
alone, it would not have been peccable, like Adam, is idle.
Second: It is impossible that the person constituted in union
with the eternal and immutable Word, can sin; for this union is
an absolute shield to the lower nature, against error. In the
God-man "dwells the fullness of the God-head bodily." Col.
ii : 9; So. i : 19. Third, this lower nature, upon its union with
the Word, was imbued with the full influences of the Holy
Ghost. Ps. xlv : 7; Isaiah xi : 2, 3; lxi : 1, 3; Luke iv : 21;
and iv : 1; Jno. i : 32; iii : 34. Fourth, Christ seems to assert
his own impeccability. Jno. xiv : 30. "Satan cometh and
hath nothing in me." So Paul, 2 Cor. v : 21, Christ "knew
no sin;" and in Heb. xiii : 8. "Jesus Christ is the same yesterday, to-day and forever." Jno. x : 36. "The Father hath
sanctified and sent Him in the world." Fifth: If this endowment of Christ's person rose no higher than a *posse non peccare*,
it seems obvious that there was a possibility of the failure of
God's whole counsel of redemption. For, as all agree, a sinning sacrifice and intercessor could redeem no one. There
must have been then, at least a decretive necessity, that all his
actions should be infallibly holy.

The pretext for imputing peccability to the Redeemer has
been explained: it only remains to prove it groundless. He
was certainly subjected to temptation, and was, in a sense, thus
qualified to be a perfect example to and sympathizer with us,
in our militant state. But this consists with his impeccability.
These writers seem to think that if, in the hitherto sinless will
of Jesus, there had been no contingency and no possibility of self-
determination to evil when He came to be tempted, He could have
had no actual realization of spiritual assaults, and no victory. Does
not this amount to teaching that a rudiment at least of "concupiscence" in Him was necessary to this victory and merit. Then it
would follow that we shall hold, with Pelagius, that concupiscence
is not sin *per se;* for that cannot be sin *per se,* which is essential to

right action, under a given condition assigned the responsible
agent by God's own providence.

In fact, the supposed stress of our opponents' plea is dissolved, when we make the obvious distinction between the act
of intellection of the natural desirableness seen in an object,
and a spontaneous appetency for it apprehended as unlawful. It
is the latter which is the sin of concupiscence. The former is
likely to take place in any intellect, simply as a function of intelligence, just in proportion to the extent of its cognitive
power, and is most certain to take place, as a simple function of
intelligence, as to all possible objects, in the infinite mind of
the holy God ! So far as intellectual conception goes, none
conceive so accurately as God, just how "the pleasures of sin
which are but for a season," appear to a fallible creature's mind.
To say that God feels the sin of "concupiscence" would be
blasphemy. This distinction shows us how an impeccable being
may be tempted. While the human will of Jesus was rendered
absolutely incapable of concupiscence by the indwelling of the
Godhead and its own native endowment; He could doubtless
represent to Himself mentally precisely how a sinful object
affects both mind and heart of His imperfect people. Does not
this fit Him to feel for and to succor them ? And is His victory
over temptation the less meritorious, because it is complete?
Let me explain. We will suppose that the idea of a forbidden
object is suggested (possibly by an evil spirit,) before the intellect of a Christian. One of two things may happen. By the
force of indwelling sin the presence of that idea in conception
may result in some conscious glow of appetency towards the
object; but the sanctified conscience is watchful and strong
enough to quench this heat before it flames up into a wrong
volition. This perhaps is the usual case with Christians. And
there, our opponents would exclaim, is the wholesome self-dis-
cipline ! There is the creditable and ennobling warfare against
sin ! Let us now suppose the other result; which, in the hap-
pier hours of eminent saints, doubtless follows sometimes : that
when the tempting idea is presented in suggestion, the conscience is so prompt, and holy desires so pre-occupy the mind,
that the thought is ejected before it even strikes the first spark
of concupiscence; that the entire and immediate answer of the
heart to it is negative. Is not this still more creditable than the
former case? Surely ! If we approved the man in the former
case because the state of his soul's moral atmosphere was such,
that the evil spark went out before it set fire to the stream of
action; we should still more approve, in the latter case, where
the atmosphere of the soul was such that the spark of evil was
not lighted at all. Will any one say, that here, there was no
temptation. This is as though one should say, there was no
battle, because the victory was complete and the victor un-
scathed.

Those who make this difficulty about Christ's impeccability seem to discard another truth, which is a corner-stone of our system. This is the consistency of a real free agency with an entire certainty of the will. They argue that unless Jesus were free in his rejection of temptation, He would have wrought no moral victory. This is true. But they wish us to infer therefrom, that because His will was free, it must have been mutable. This deduction would be consistent only in a Pelagian. Every Calvinist knows that a holy will may be perfectly free, and yet determined with absolute certainty, to the right. Such is God's will. "He cannot lie." Yet He speaks truth freely. The sinner presents the counterpart case, when "his eyes are full of adultery, and he cannot cease from sin." Yet is this sinner free in continuing his course of sin and rejecting the monitions of duty. This case sufficiently explains, by contrast, the impeccability of Jesus. He has every natural faculty which, in Adam's case, was abused to the perpetration of his first sin. But they were infallibly regulated by, what Adam had not, a certain, yet most free, determination of His dispositions to holiness alone. It is useless to argue, whether Jesus could have sinned if He had chosen. It was infallibly certain that He would not choose to sin. This was the impeccability we hold.

The question, whether Christ performs the functions of

5. Does Christ mediate in both Natures ?

Mediator in both natures is fundamental. Romanists limit them to the human nature, in order to make more plausible room for human mediators. They plead such passages as Phil. ii : 7, 8 ; I Tim. ii : 5, and the dialectical argument, that the divinity being the offended party, it is absurd to conceive of it as mediating between the offender and itself.

Now, it must be distinguished, that ever since the incarnation, the *Logos* may perform functions of incommunicable divinity, inalienable to Him as immutable; such as sitting on the throne of the universe and possessing incommunicable attributes; in which the humanity can no more have part than in that creative work, which Christ performed before His incarnation. So, likewise, the humanity performed functions, in which it is not necessary to suppose the *Logos* had any other concern than a general providential one ; such as eating, sleeping, drinking. But these were not a part of the Mediatorship. We assert that, in all the Mediatorial acts proper, both natures Τὸ πρόσωπον θεανθρωπον act concurrently, according to their peculiar properties. This we prove, 1st, by the fact, that in Christ's priestly work, the divine nature operated and still operates, as well as the human. See I Cor. ii : 8 ; Heb. ix : 14 ; John x : 18. Even in this work of suffering and dying, see how essential the concurrent actions of the divine nature were! Else, there would have been none of the autocracy as to His own life, necessary for His vicarious work ; nor would there have been strength to bear an infinite penalty in one day. Only the Omniscient can intercede for all. Hence, we argue *a fortiori*, that if His divinity concurred in His priestly work, the part usually supposed most irrelevant to deity, much more does it concur in His prophetic and kingly. See Matt. xi : 27, xxviii : 18. 2d. If Christ does not perform His Mediatorial work in His divine nature as well as His human, He could not have been in any sense the Mediator of Old Testament saints; because their redemption was completed before He was incarnate. Did Romanists attend to the fact, that it is the very design and result of the Covenant of Grace, that the persons of the Trinity should act " economically," in their several offices of redemption, they would not have raised the inconsistent objection about the Godhead's propitiating the Godhead. The Son, having become man's Surety, now acts economically and officially for him, in his stead propitiating the Father, who officially represents the majesty of the offended Trinity. Besides, unless the Romanists will assert not only two wills, but these two in opposition, in the Mediatorial person, the divine will of God the Son must, on their scheme, have concerned itself with propitiating God; the same difficulty !

One remark applies to all His mediatorial functions also; that the will of both natures concurred in them.

The demands of Christ's mediatorial work required that Christ should be proper and very man. Mankind had fallen, and was conscience-struck, hostile, and fearful towards God. Hence it was desirable that the Daysman should appear in his nature as his brother in order to encourage confidence, to allure to a familiar approach, and quiet guilty fears. To such a being as sinful man, personal intercourse with God would have been intolerably dreadful; (Gen. iii : 8 ; Ex. xx : 19,) and even an angel would have appeared too terrible to his fears.

Why must the Mediator be Man?

Again. The Bible assures us that one object gained by the incarnation of Christ, was fuller assurance of His sympathy, by His experimental acquaintance with all the woes of our fallen condition. (Heb. ii : 17, 18 ; iv : 15 to v : 2.) The experience of every Christian under trial of affliction, testifies to the strength of this reasoning by the consolation which Christ's true humanity gives Him. It is very true that the Son, as omniscient God, can and does figure to Himself conceptions of all possible human trials, just as accurate as experience itself; but His having experienced them in human nature enables our weak faith to grasp the consolation better.

Another purpose of God, in clothing our Redeemer with human nature, was to leave us a perfect human example. The importance and efficacy of teaching by example, need not be unfolded here. (See 1 Pet. ii : 21 ; Heb. xii : 2, &c.)

In the fourth place, Christ's incarnation was necessary, in

order to establish a proper basis for that legal union between Him and His elect, which should make Him bearer of their imputed guilt, and them partakers of His imputed righteousness and of His exaltation. (See 1 Cor. xv : 21.) It was necessary that man's sin should be punished in the nature of man, in order to render the substitution more natural and proper. (Rom. viii : 3.) Had the deity been united with some angelic, or other creature, the imputation of man's sin to that Person, and its punishment in that foreign nature would have appeared less reasonable. (See Heb. ii : 14–16.) So, likewise, the obedience rendered in another nature than man's, would not have been so reasonable a ground for raising man's race to a share in the Mediator's blessedness.

And this leads us to add, last, that a created nature was absolutely essential to the Mediator's two works, of obeying in man's stead, and suffering for his guilt. For the obedience, no other nature would have been so appropriate as man's. And no person without a creature nature could come under law, assume a subject position, and work out an imputable righteousness. God is above law, being Himself the great law-giver. For the other vicarious work, suffering a death penalty, not only a created, but a corporeal nature is necessary. Angels cannot feel bodily death, and brutes could not experience spiritual; but both are parts of the penalty of sin. The divine nature is impassible, and unchangeable in its blessedness. Hence, Heb. x : 5 ; ix : 22, &c.

It is of the highest importance to prove that the mediatorial offices could not be performed without the divine nature. (See Is. xlv : 22 ; Jer. xvii : 5–7, xxiii : 6.) Because this is one of the most overwhelming arguments against Arians and Socinians. We assert that a purpose to save elect men by a mediatorial plan, being supposed in God, the very necessities of the case required that this mediator should be very and proper God. But as this was substantially argued in Lect. xviii, when proving the divinity of the Holy Ghost and the Son, the student is referred to that place.

Why the Mediator must be God.

But the sixth question of our Syllabus raises a point in this direction, which requires fuller explanation. The scope of the Socinian system is to find a common religion, including the fewest possible essential elements. Hence, they like to represent, that virtuous Pagans may belong to this common religion, holding the doctrines of Natural Theology. The consequence is, that the Socinians, while speaking many handsome things of Jesus Christ as a messenger from God, still concur with other Deists and infidels, in depreciating the necessity of Revelation. They say that the Scriptures are valuable, but not essential. We are thus led again to the old question of the necessity of revelation.

6. Is Christ's Prophetic work essential, or, as Socinians say, only useful ?

Let us not assert this on the usual partial grounds. The

Partial grounds of argument corrected.

case is too often put by our friends as though the fall alone necessitated a revelation; the effects of sin in blinding the mind and con-science are too exclusively mentioned. Thus, there is an im-plied admission that a revelation is, in man's case, an exceptional expedient, caused by the failure of God's general plan. Thus, the objection is suggested, which Socinians and other enemies of inspiration have not failed to put in form; and which many of us are inclined perhaps to feel, as though the idea of a reve-lation were unnatural, and hence not probable. The cavil is, that the analogy of all creation discloses this plan: Our wise and good God, in creating each order of sentient beings, sur-rounded them with all the appointed conditions for their well-being, by the established course of nature. Having made fishes for the water, He made water for the fishes; the grass is for oxen, and the oxen for grass; the birds for the air, and the air for the birds. Every order, by living within the natural conditions provided for it, secures its appropriate end. But according to the orthodox, man, the noblest, the rational crea-ture, cannot fulfil the ends of his being, immortal blessedness, by his natural means. A supernatural expedient must be found, against the general analogy; or else man's existence is a fright-ful failure. This, they urge, is unnatural, discreditable to God, and improbable.

Now I meet it by asserting that, to make a rational crea-

Revelation necessary to Holy Creatures.

ture dependent on a revelation of God for His spiritual welfare, is not unnatural, or extraordinary: but is, for all spiritual crea-tures, the universal and strictly natural condition. It does not arise out of man's sin only; the truth holds as well of angels, and all other rational creatures, if there are others. We must remember that none originally had God in their debt, to assure their holiness and bliss; but were naturally under this relation, bound to obey Him perpetually; free from evil as long as they did so: but subject to His wrath whenever they sinned. Now holy creatures were not infallible, nor omniscient. Their wills were right and free, but not indefectible. Bound to an unend-ing career of perfect obedience, they would have been to all eternity liable to mistake, and sin and death. Now, when a finite wisdom and rectitude are matched against an infinite series of duties to be done, of choices to be made, each natur-ally implying some possibility of a wrong choice, that possi-bility finally mounts up from a probability to a moral certainty, that all would some day fail. How, then, could an angel, or holy Adam, inherit immutable blessedness forever? Only by drawing direct guidance from the infallible, infinite Mind. Thus we see that the enjoyment of its appropriate revelation by each order, is the necessary condition of its well-being; a condition as natural, original, and universal as its own moral nature and obligations. If Gabriel had not his revelation he would not be an 'elect angel.' Do I mean a written document? Do I speak of parchment and ink? No; but of that which is the essence of a Revelation, a direct communication from the infinite Mind, to instruct the finite.

Thus we may, if we choose, admit the analogy which the Socinian claims, and find it wholly against him. Our Bible is not an exceptional providence; it is in strict accordance with God's method towards all reasonable creatures. If our race had none, this would be the fatal anomaly against us.

Revelation not Anomalous.

LECTURE XL.

THE MEDIATOR. — Continued.

SYLLABUS.

7. Is there any other mediator between God and man, than Jesus Christ? (Against Papists).

For Popish view, see Council of Trent. Session xxv. Cat. Rom. pt. iii, ch. 2, Qu. 4–7, pt. iv, ch. 6. Bellarmine's Controversies. Dens' Theol. Daniel's Thesaurus Hymn, Vol. 1, p. 241, Vol. 2, p. 133. *Missale Romanum passim.* Turrettin Loc. xiv, Qu. 4. Ridgley Qu. 36. Essay (15th) on Romanism, Presb. Bd. Dick Lect. 59.

8. How was Christ inducted into His office?

Dick, Lect. 54. Turrettin, Loc. xiv, Qu. 6, and Loc. xiii, Qu. 12. Ridgley, Qu. 41, 42.

9. How many offices does Christ fulfil as Mediator; and why these?

Turrettin, Loc. xiv, Qu. 5. Dick, Lect. 54. Calv. Inst. bk. ii, ch. 15. Ridgley, Qu. 43. Conf. of Faith, ch. 8.

10. Prove that Christ is Prophet. Under how many Periods and Modes did He fulfil this office?

Turrettin, Loc. xiv, Qu. 7. Dick, Lect. 54, 55. Ridgley, Qu. 43.

THE Apostle Paul teaches us, (1 Tim. ii : 5,) that as there is but one God, there is only "one mediator between God and man, the man Christ Jesus." Rome seeks to evade this and similar testimonies, by speaking of a primary and a secondary mediation, reserving the first exclusively to Christ. The activity of angels and dead saints as secondary mediators, Rome argues, first, from the benevolence and affection of these pure spirits. This kindness we daily experience at the hands of the saints while alive; and the Saviour (Luke xv : 7,) seems to ascribe similar feelings to the angels. The Church believes that the dead saints retain a local interest in the places and people which they loved while living; and she thinks that Dan. x : 13, teaches the angels, as ministers of God's providence, have their districts,

7. Christ only Mediator. Rome's Argument for Contrary.

and even their individuals, (Matt. xviii : 10,) whom they serve and watch.   Second.   Rome urges that numerous cases exist in which the mediatorial intervention of one saint for another occurs, in the Bible.   Of this the most obvious instance is the requesting of the brethren's prayers (e. g., 1 Thess. v : 25 ; 2d Thess. iii : 1,) and this case alone, Rome thinks, would be enough to rebut the Protestant objections that such intercession interferes with the mediatorial honours of Christ.   But, say they, there are numerous instances of more definite intervention, where the merit of a saint availed for other men expressly ; or where, (better still,) the pardon of men was suspended on the efforts of some eminently meritorious saint in their behalf.   (See Gen. xx : 7 ; xxvi : 5 ; 1 Kgs. xi : 12, *et passim* ; Job. xlii : 8 ; Luke vii : 3–6.   And they assert the actual intercession of angels in heaven is taught.   (Gen. xlviii : 16 ; Rev. v : 8, or viii : 3.)

Third.   Rome argues reciprocally, that the worship of saints and angels implies their mediation ; because the only thing for which we can petition them, consistently with theism, is their intercession.   Hence all the rational and scriptural arguments in favor of saint-worship, are by inference, arguments in favor of their mediation.   See, then, such considerations and such texts as these : God commands an appropriate reverence of teachers, magistrates, parents, kings.   Can we believe that He intends no proportionable honor of these more beneficent and majestic beings ?   Can it be wrong to ask their aid with Christ, when we should esteem it pious to ask the aid of Christian friends on earth ?   Surely these glorified creatures have not become less benevolent toward us, or less acceptable to Christ, by reaching heaven.   Then see scriptural instances (Gen. xviii : 2–23 ; xix : 1 ; xxxii : 26 ; Josh. v : 14.

The closing argument of Rome is from tradition, and the Apocrypha.

One valid reply, though the least one, is, that all such appeals to the mediation of the saints or angels in heaven, are superstitions.   As to dead saints, the Scripture representation is, that they are effectually severed from all earthly relations, and are done with all earthly interests. Rev. xiv : 13.   They " rest from their labors."   1 Tim. vi : 7.   "For we brought nothing into this world, and it is certain we can carry nothing out."   Isa. lvii : 2.   " He shall enter into peace ; they shall rest in their beds."   Eccles. ix : 6.   " Neither have they any more a portion forever in anything that is done under the sun."   Job. iii : 17.   "There the weary be at rest."   xiv : 21. " His sons come to honour, and he knoweth it not ; and they are brought low, but he perceiveth it not of them."   The simple idea of asking a share in the prayers of dead friends, if it were all of the Romish doctrine, would be thus shown to be only foolish and superstitious ; for since we know we have no

Replies.

access to them, our words are thrown away. It may be urged,
that though this be true as to the dead saints, it may not hold
as to the angels, who do have intercourse with earth, as they
are "sent forth to minister to them who shall be heirs of salvation." Our answer is, that the Scriptures only teach an intercourse on one side; they may know some of our acts and
needs; we know nothing of their nearness or absence. So that,
as to the angels likewise, this attempted intercourse is wholly
unwarranted by Scripture, and therefore superstitious. But:

Second. In our ignorance of their nearness or absence, we
can never know that they hear our plea for their intercession, without imputing to them divine attributes. This fact
was briefly stated in our 31st Lecture. Thus the doctrine of
their intercession is idolatrous in its tendencies, and a robbery
of God. Especially is this true of the more popular gods and
goddesses of the Romish pantheon, the Virgin, Peter, Gabriel;
to whom Romanists the world over are generally praying. They
must have omnipresence to be with their votaries in various lands at the same time; omniscience, to discriminate,
understand and judge wisely of their varied requests; omnipotence, to bear the burden of care laid upon them; infinite benevolence, to make them willing to bear so much care and take so
much trouble for others; and immutability, to be a secure reliance for the wants of a priceless soul. The poor subterfuge of
the hypothesis of the saints' beholding all earthly affairs *in speculo
Trinitatis*, has been exposed; it only pretends to meet one of
the points we have here made.

Third. Were the design of papists merely to seek a communion in the prayers of dead saints and angels, it would only
be superstitious and idolatrous. But this does not at all satisfy them. The essential peculiarity of their doctrine is, that
the mediatory access of these holy creatures is founded on
their merits with God. This their divines expressly teach; and
the hymns to which we cited the student, expressly assert this
element of doctrine. But it is expressly injurious to Christ,
utterly false, and indeed impious. No one who comprehended
the rudiments of either the Covenant of Works, or of that of
Grace, would ever dream of making the supererogatory merit of
an unfallen, much less of a fallen creature, a basis for an
imputed righteousness. In that sense the creature cannot
merit. Take the case of Abraham, Gen. xx: 7. The Romish
argument is ruined by the fact that Abraham was himself "justified by faith." If he was himself a sinner, accepted in the
righteousness of another, how could he have supererogatory
merit to spare for a fellow-sinner? Job is mentioned, xlii: 8,
as sacrificing for his erring friends; Because he was righteous.
But see the 6th verse, where Job avows his utter sinfulness.
Surely, then he was not righteous in such a sense as to be a
meritorious mediator. Job was directed to sacrifice for his

friends.   What?   Himself?   No; but bullocks and rams, tpyical of the "Lamb of God that taketh away the sin of the world."   This tells the whole story: that his intervention was ministerial, and not mediatorial.   As to King David, 1 Kings xi : 12, compare David's own language, Ps. xxxii: 1, 2.   It is God's regard for His own gracious covenant with David, and His own fidelity, which leads Him to favour Solomon.   David himself, although comparatively a faithful ruler, was indebted to God's mercy both in his personal and official capacities, for escaping condemnation.   If Christ made full expiation for our sins, how can other intercessors be intruded without an insult to the sufficiency of His sacrifice and intercession?   Is the plea this: that He intercedes with the Father; while the lower mediators intercede with Him?   I reply: Why may we not directly obey His gracious command: "Come unto Me, all ye that labour?"   Does the same argument which persuades us to go to the Virgin to ask her Son to ask His Father to save us, also require us to seek another intermediary between us and Mary?   If the Papist says "yes," to this question, then by the same argument we shall need still a second intermediary between us and the one who is to commend us to Mary; and we have a ridiculous regressus, which may be endless; we have to go all around the world, in order to reach Christ.   But if a negative answer be given, then the Papist must answer this question: Why does Mary need an intermediary between us and her, less than Jesus does?   This implies that she is more benevolent and placable than Christ!   "But greater love hath no man than this that he lay down his life for his friends."

The student should know, that this theory of creature-mediation is not only condemned by the utter silence of the word and the express and implied assertion of truths incompatible with it: but that it has been articulately examined and rejected in the Scriptures.   That inspired refutation, as it is seen in the Epistle to the Colossians, furnishes us the best possible argument.   It is substantially our third argument.   The Judaizing Gnostics were infesting the Colossian church with this very theory: that the saving work of Christ must be supplemented by the intercession of some super-angelic beings; (See Ch. ii : 18,) and by the practice of asceticism. (ii : 21).   The first of these innovations the Apostle meets, with admirable sagacity, by laying down a few indisputable, gospel-statements. Christ, the eternal Son of God, hath already made for us a sacrifice in His blood, so complete as to secure to believers a full justification and an actual translation into God's family, (i : 13, 15, 22).   This our Priest is the Image of God, eternal, the creator and actual ruler of all creatures, including these very thrones and dominions proposed as angelic intercessors, (verse 16, 17,) so that instead of their guiding Him, He governs them : and they themselves derive their heavenly adoption (not indeed

from His sacrifice,) but from His ministerial providence, (verse
20). This Divine Christ is also human, (ii : 3–10,) so that He is
as near akin to us as any advocate can be : just as truly our
kinsman, as near by blood, as approachable, as tender, as it is
possible for Peter or Paul, or Mary to be. Whatever love and
beneficence these have, they received from Him. Thus He has
in Himself all possible qualifications for the intercessory work;
all the higher (verses 3 and 9,) and all the softer and gentler.
Hence, (verse 10,) the believer is " complete in Him." Christ so
completely satisfies the demands of an intercessory work, that
no room is left for any other intercessor; even as His righteousness so satisfies the claims of law, that there is no room for any
ritual or ascetic righteousness to procure fuller adoption. This,
in a word, is the Apostle's argument. That Christ's priestly
work is such, it is not possible that any other intercessory
agency can be needed, or be added. The plea, that the
Apostle discards the intercession of the Gnostic *æons*, because
they are imaginary beings, is of no avail; because his argument is evidently construed designedly, (see Ch. i : 16,) so as to
hold, equally, whether the creatures invoked might be real, or
not. In conclusion of this head, it should be noted, that the
vital point in the popish theory is, that these creature-mediators
have an imputable merit of their own, to plead for us. Hence
the cases they cite, where Christians ask an interest in each
others' prayers, are wholly inapplicable, and their citation is
indeed, uncandid.

Fourth. Their doctrine of angelic mediation is easily met.
The only instances in which an angel is worshipped, are those of the worship of the Angel
of the Covenant, the eternal Word. Let the
student examine all the cases of angel-worshp claimed by the
Romanists, and he will find that each one is a worship of that
Divine Person. We are referred to Rev. v : 8, and viii : 3, for
instances of angelic mediation. In the first, the odours presented by the four living creatures, and the four and twenty
elders, are their own. They both, beyond doubt, symbolize the
ransomed Church : (see verse 9,) and the prayers they present
are simply their own. In Rev. viii ; 3, we assert that the great
Angel, who takes the golden censer, and offers the incense, is
Christ; the Angel of the Covenant again. It is objected that
the Redeemer has already appeared in the scene, as "the
Lamb in the midst of the throne." This is no valid objection
to our exposition. The natures and functions of Christ are so
glorious and full, that one symbol fails to exhaust them. Hence
the multiplication of symbols for the same Divine Figure, even
in the same scene, is not unusual in the prophets. The symbol
of the Lamb represents Christ's humanity, the victim of justice,
while that of the Angel conveys to us Christ the prophet, and
intercessor, and king ; a priest upon his throne. There is, then,

No Created Angel Mediated.

31*

no exegetical difficulty in receiving this angel as a symbol of Christ; and the coherency of this view, with the whole passage, and the whole Scripture, every way recommends it.

In conclusion, the powerful demonstration which the Scripture gives us against creature worship, is the strongest proof against creature mediation; for if they mediated, they must be worshipped.

The Scripture testimony must hold the fifth, and crowning place. We have heard the Apostle assert, (1 Tim. ii : 5,) that as there is one God, there is one Mediator, between God and men; and that this is the Being who gave himself a ransom for all. As the words, " one God," doubtless express the exclusive unity of God, so we are bound to construe the connterpart words, "one Mediator," in the same way. And it is implied that He who mediates must have given the adequate ransom, on which to found His plea. So, our Saviour declares, (Jno. xiv : 6,) "No man cometh to the Father but by me," and Peter, (Acts iv : 12,) " There is none other name under heaven, given among men, whereby ye must be saved." So, the words of Christ, (Jno. vi : 37,) "Him that cometh to me, I will in no wise cast out," at least prove that any other intercessor is superfluous. It is said, that affirmations do not prove the counterpart negative. But when we find the Scriptures full of such passages as Rom. viii : 34; Heb. viii : 25; 1 Jno. ii : 1, 2, which all assert with emphasis that the Lord Jesus Christ is our Mediator; and that there is an absolute silence throughout the Bible as to any other, even this proof is complete.

Feeble efforts are made to break the force of this testimony. To show that saints do make imputable merit for their brethren, Papists point us to Col. i : 24, where Paul claims that " he is filling up that which is behind of the sufferings of Christ, for his body's sake, which is the church." We reply that this construction makes the Apostle here teach precisely what he repudiates in 1 Cor. i : 13, " Was Paul crucified for you ?" The scope of his argument requires us to construe this question: Was Paul a propitiation for you? Has Christ any rival to divide his credit or claim as the sole propitiation? No. Paul was afterwads beheaded and Peter crucified. Shall we give so preposterous a sense to the argument that the opponent could, after these events, meet the apostolic negative with a flippant 'Yes' and say: " Yes, both Paul and Peter have died for the Church, and so, Christ is now divided, and the threefold faction is legitimate." It is only the ministerial and exemplary features of Christ's sufferings, in which the Apostle claims a share in Colossians. In that sense, every true labourer and martyr is still furthering the work which Christ began. But His sufferings alone could be vicarious.

The attempt is made to escape the force of the places which assert the oneness of Christ's intercession, by saying that

He is the only Mediator of Redemption; saints and angels are Mediators of Intercession.   On this subterfuge I remark: (a) 1 Tim. ii : 5, asserts the singleness of Christ's intercessory work first, and at least as pointedly as of His ransoming work.   (b) Since intercession is grounded only in redemption by satisfaction, the two kinds of mediators must be one.   (c) Romanists themselves undermine their own distinction by impiously ascribing to their creature-intercessors an imputable merit as the necessary ground of their influence with Christ.

Sixth. Rome's use of this doctrinal error yields the strongest practical argument against it.   It has been the means of thrusting Christ aside, out of the thoughts and affections of Papists, until Mary and the saints attract a larger share of worship than the Son of God.   As the idea of creature-Mediators is virtually pagan, it has thrown an almost pagan aspect over the Romish countries.

The words Messiah, Christ, mean "Anointed," in allusion to the spiritual unction bestowed on Christ.
8. Christ's Anointing. When. This was appropriate to all His offices; witness the anointing of Aaron, Saul, David, Solomon, Elisha. The thing typified by the oil, was spiritual endowment; and this was bestowed without measure on Christ. (See Ps. xlv : 2; Is. xi : 2; xlii : 1; lxi : 1, &c; Matt. iii : 16; Jno. iii : 34; Acts x : 38, &c.) The seasons of this anointing were, not a journey into heaven during the forty days' temptation—a notion unknown to Scripture, and moreover refuted by Luke ii : 46, 47,—but His birth and baptism especially.   The immediate seat of these spiritual influences was His humanity. His divinity was already infinite, perfect and immutable.   He is Himself a source of the Holy Ghost, as God.   The consequence was, to make Him, not infinite as to His humanity, nor incapable of progress, but perfectly holy, and wise, pure, zealous, faithful, &c., above all others.   All forms of grace appropriate to a perfect man acted in Him, in such manners as were suitable to His Person.

That Christ fulfils, as Mediator, the three offices of Prophet, Priest and King, is proved by this
9. Christ's Offices Three, and Why? argument.   We find these three offices predicated of Him in Scripture in a specific and pointed manner, while all other terms of function or service applied to Him as " Servant," " Elect," " Messenger," &c., are rather to be regarded as general appellatives.   For the prophetic office, see Heb. i : 1; Is. xi : 2, xlii : 1, 2, lxi : 1; Deut. xviii : 15, with Acts iii : 22-26; Is. xlix : 6; John iv : 25.   For the priestly, see Ps. cx : 4; Heb. viii : 1, &c., *passim*; 1 John ii : 1.   Kingly, Ps. ii : 6; Is. ix : 6, 7; Ps. cx : 1; Zech. vi : 12-14, &c., 1 Cor. i : 30, displays all three offices.

That the offices of Christ are these three, we prove again by showing in detail, that all His mediatorial works can be

referred to one or more of these three classes. All is either
instructing, or atoning, or interceding, or conquering and ruling
or several of them together. The necessity for these offices,
(which we show) also proves it. Man lay under three evils—
ignorance, guilt, rebellion. And redemption consists of three
parts—announcing, purchasing and applying salvation.

The proof has already been presented, that Christ performs the office of a Prophet.

The Prophet is God's Spokesman, נָבִיא either to enforce,

10. Christ's Prophetic Work. Its three stages. reveal or predict. Christ, in the highest sense,
did all. For definition of His prophetic
work, see Cat., Que. 24. The work of our
Savior had three different stages. 1st, from the fall to His baptism by John; 2d, during His personal ministry until His ascension ; 3d, thence to the final consummation. During all these
stages, He has carried on His prophetic work, by these agencies
common to the three: His Revelation given to us by the hand
of Prophets and Apostles: His Spirit applying that revelation,
and giving understanding and love ; His providence, directing
our conduct and the events happening us, including a constant,
universal and particular control of our mental laws and states,
as well as physical. (This trenches on His kingly powers).
But, during the first stage, Christ acted as Prophet, in addition,
by His theophanies, for which see Hengstenberg's Christol, vol.
i, pp. 164–170, and His Prophets, see 1 Pet. i : 10, 11.

During the second stage, Christ literally fulfilled the work
of a Prophet in His own person, by inculcating truths known,
revealing truths, and predicting future events. During the last
stage, He gave His Holy Ghost to Apostles and Evangelists,
thus enduing their teachings with His own authority. See John
xvi : 12–15; Acts i : 8; xv : 28; ii : 4; 1 Thess. i : 5.

Wherein Superior to Human Prophets. Dick contrasts Christ's prophetic work with that of all
other Prophets, in its fullness, its perspicuity,
(arising from His fuller endowments and
knowledge, as well as from a clearer dispen-
sation), its giving realities instead of types, its authority, arising
from His divinity, and its efficacy, arising from His divine power
to send forth spiritual influences along with His word. But
when we say Christ was fuller as a revealer, let us not fall into
the Socinian's error, who, to make a *nodus vindice dignus*, while
they deny Christ's vicarious work, teach that Christ not only
developed, but made substantial additions to, and alterations in,
the Old Testament. A perfect and holy God could not reveal
a faulty code. See also Matt. v : 17; Mark xii : 31 ; Rom. xiii :
9. And if the pretended cases of alteration be examined, they
will be found supported by the teachings of the Old Testament.

LECTURE XLI.

THE MEDIATOR. — Concluded.

SYLLABUS.

11. Prove that Christ is truly a Priest. What the several Parts of a Priest's Functions ? What the Peculiarities of Christ's priesthood ?

Turrettin, Loc. xiv, Qu. 8, 9. Dick, Lect. 56. Anselm, *Cur Deus Homo*, pt. i, ch. 12, and 13. Ridgley, Qu. 44, § 1, 2. "The Atonement," by Rev. Hugh Martin, ch. 3. Hodge's Theo., vol. ii, pt. iii, ch. 6.

12. Prove against Socinians, &c., the Necessity of Satisfaction, in order to Remission of Sin.

Turrettin, Loc. xiv, Qu. 10, with Loc. iii, Qu. 19. Thornwell, Vol. ii, Art. 5. Dick, Lect. 56. Hill, bk. iv, ch. 3, § 1. Hodge's Theo., pt. iii (Vol. ii), ch. 7. Ridgley, Qu. 44, § 3. "Magee on Atonement.' A. A. Hodge on Atonement, chs. 5, 6. Watson's Theo. Inst. ch. 19, bk. ii, ch. 8.

THE proof that Christ is a true and real Priest, would begin with texts such as Ps. cx : 4; Heb. v : 5; viii : 1, *et passim*. Were there no Socinian evasion, these would end the debate. But their plea is that Peter (Epistle 1, Ch. ii : 9), and John (Rev. i : 6, call Christians generally Priests. But since the name is thus applied to persons who only render to God the oblation of their thankful service and devotion, its application to Christ does not prove any more. Hence, they assert, it is vain for Calvinists to quote texts which call Christ a Priest, as proof that he was properly so, in the strict sense of the Hebrew כֹּהֵן or Greek Ἱερεύς

11. Christ the True Priest.

And they attempt to further their evasion by saying that Christ is a Priest only in heaven, where He performs the intercessory function. If they can gain assent to this, since there is no suffering in heaven, they effectually exclude Christ's proper sacrifice and expiatory work. To meet these cunning subterfuges then, we must proceed farther, and show that Christ is called Priest in wholly another sense from believers, and that He literally performs the two peculiar functions of that office—sacrifice and intercession.

This argument leads us to anticipate the evidences by which Christ's sufferings are shown to be truly vicarious. The points will therefore be briefly stated here. In Heb. v : 1, we have an exact definition of a priest, as a person "ordained for men, from among whom he is taken, in things pertaining to God, that He may offer both gifts and sacrifices for sins." Such, we may add, is precisely the meaning attached to the word by all men, including pagans. The priestly office is a mediatorial one. Its necessity arises out of man's sin and guilt, which exclude him from immediate access to a holy God. The priest is the intermediary who goes for him. Hence, he must have a sacrifice with which to expiate sin and propitiate God ; and he must found his plea for his clients on this as the ransom price. No Jew, Pagan, or Christian (not perverted by Socinian views) ever conceived of a priest as anything else than this. But it is far more conclusive to say, that the Epistle, after this definition of a priest, immediately asserts that Christ was made our high priest. The subsequent chapters assert that He was formally and solemnly ordained to the office ; that He acted for others, and not for Himself in that office ; that He transacted for us with God ; and that He offered a vicarious sacrifice. These traits are conclusive of His real priesthood. He was appointed priest (Heb. vii : 20) with peculiar emphasis. He made His soul a sacrifice for sin by dying ; while Christians, when described as metaphorical priests, only make their services a thank-offering by living. See Rom. xii : 1. That the Christian's oblation is only metaphorical, the apostle expresses by a beautiful paradox ; He is a " living sacrifice." But a sacrifice proper is a thing that dies ! It is a very strong evidence that, while the official name, priest, was so familiar to Jews, it is never once applied to gospel-ministers in the New Testament. They are " teachers," " presbyters," " ministers," " angels of the Churches," " ambassadors," " servants," but never 'Ιερεῖς ! Finally, Christ is the antitype to a long line of typical priests. See Heb. viii : 4, 5 ; ix : 11. That these Levitical officers represented in type, the very idea of the priesthood proper, is demonstrated by every feature of their service. The animals they slew died vicariously. Every act was mediatorial, and their whole function began and was continued with expiation. Now, by the rule that the body must be more substantial than the shadow which it casts before, Christ's work, as antitype, must at least be as priestly as that of the prefiguring emblems.

The peculiarities of Christ's priesthood are : 1. The dignity of His person. 2. The solemnity of His appointment, by an oath. 3. His combining royalty and priesthood like Melchisedec. 4. His having, like him, neither predecessor nor successor ; because, 5. His oblation had such infinite value and complete efficacy, that, 6. It grounded at once an everlasting and all prevalent intercession ; and that, 7. Not only for one man, or race, but for all the Elect.

The argument for the necessity of an atonement proceeds chiefly on the question, whether distributive justice is an essential moral attribute of God ; or whether, as Socinians assert, there is nothing in His nature which renders it less natural and proper for Him to remit guilt without satisfaction, than to create, or leave uncreated, a given thing. The Socinians, as we have seen, in order to evade the doctrine of a vicarious atonement, deny both the necessity of it, and the essential justice of God.

12. Necessity of Satisfaction in order to pardon : (1) Question stated.

Bear in mind, then, that in this whole argument we attribute to God all the perfections which make Him an immutable and infinite Being. We shall not pause to argue these against Socinians, but refer you to your previous course of theology.

But the necessity which we assert for God's punishing guilt is only moral. It is not a physical necessity like that which ensures that fire will burn, supposing the presence of fuel, and that water will wet, supposing its application. Here, then, falls the cavil of Socinus, that if retributive justice be made an essential attribute of God, its exercise must be conceived of as inevitable in every case, because of God's immutability, (as we call it,) so that mercy in every case would be impossible. Divine immutability does not imply that God must ever act in modes mechanically identical; but that His acting must always be consistent with the same set of essential attributes. As circumstances change, His very immutability requires a change of outward actings. Again; for God to effectuate a given part of His decrees of mercy, when, in time, the conditions of that execution are first in existence, is no change of purpose in Him. When God passes from wrath to reconciliation, as to a given sinner, it is no change in Him. The change is in the sinner. The same attributes which demanded wrath before, now demand peace; because the sinner's guilt is gone. The proper view of God's immutable perfections, therefore, leads us to conclude, that without an atonement they would render pardon of sin absolutely and universally impossible: but that, an atonement being provided, they offer no obstacle to pardon.

The Necessity not Physical.

Again, it is another perversion to carry the idea of pecuniary debt so far, in our conceptions of guilt, as to conceive of a vicarious atonement as legal tender. When a security comes forward, and offers to pay the whole debt of the poor insolvent in jail, with principal and interest, cost and charges, the creditor must accept this legal tender; if he does not, he cannot claim payment afterwards. And the insolvent demands his release as of right. Now, guilt is not a mere debt, in this sense. It is a personal obligation to penalty; because the responsibility violated was strictly personal; and strict justice would entitle the ruler to hold the guilty party to endure that penalty in himself. Therefore, when the personal relation to law is waived by the ruler, and a substitute accepted, there is an act of grace, of mercy. This is the answer to the objection, that "if the necessity of the atonement be asserted, God the Father performs no act of grace, and deserves no thanks for letting the transgressor go free. He has exacted the last penny, and the release is a mere act of justice." To our Surety it is; but not to us. Besides, was there no grace in giving us the surety to pay for us?

Satisfaction does not Compel God.

Socinians clamorously object, that we who teach the neces-

Socinian Objections.
Ans. by 4 Distinctions.

sity of an atonement, strip God of those qualities which in all others would be most noble, generous and admirable; a willingness to overlook His own resentment, and magnanimously forgive without payment of the injury, where penitence was expressed. That we represent God as an odious and cruel being, who would rather see His erring creatures damned, no matter how penitent, than sacrifice His own pique; and who is determined to pour out His revenge somewhere, if not on the sinner, on his substitute, before He will be satisfied. These cavils are already answered by the above view. For a private man to act thus would be unamiable; he is himself a sinner. God has told him, "Vengeance is Mine;" and the supreme rule of the man's life is, that he shall do everything, forgiving injuries among the rest, for God's pleasure and honour. But God is Himself the supreme End of all His doings, as well as Chief Magistrate of the Universe. Turrettin, Hill, &c., also appeal to other distinctions, to rebut these objections. Four things may be considered in a transgression, viewed as against a human ruler. The debt contracted thereby, the wrath or indignation excited, the moral defilement contracted by the transgressor in the eyes of the injured party, and the guilt, or obligation to legal penalty, incurred. Now, the plausibility of the Socinian cavil arises wholly from regarding the first three elements of sin, and studiously averting the eyes from the fourth. So far as the injury done me, as a magistrate, was a personal debt of wrong, humanity might prompt me to release it without satisfaction rendered; for that element of debt being personal, I have a personal right to surrender it if I choose. So far as I have had a personal sense of indignation and resentment excited by the wrong, that also it might be generous and right in me to smother, without satisfaction, in compassion to the wrong doer. I conceive that a certain element of moral defilement has come on him by his evil act, which constitutes a reason for punishing. If he amends that moral defilement by sincere penitence and reform, that obstacle to an unbought pardon is also removed. But it is far otherwise with the debt of guilt to law, of which I am the guardian. That is not a debt personal to me; and therefore I, as lawgiver, may not remit it without satisfaction. If I do, I violate my trust as guardian of the laws. Such is their arguing, and it is just. But it applies to God, as against sinning creatures, far more than to human lawgivers. And the same reasonings which show that the human ruler ought to surmount the first, second, and third elements of offence in order to pardon, do not apply to God. The human lawgiver is but a man, and the transgressor is also a man, his brother, and nearly his equal in God's eye. In the other case, the offended party is infinite, and the offender His puny, absolute property, whom God may and ought to dispose of for the sovereign gratification of His own admirable and excellent perfections.

We shall not say, as Hill incautiouly does in one place,
that the fact that God is a Lawgiver is the
first principle on which the doctrine of satisfaction rests; although we shall, in its proper
place, assign it due importance. The importance of God's
jnstice being protected, does not arise only or chiefly from the
fact that the order of His universal empire is concerned therein.
God Himself, and not His creature's well-being, is the proper
ultimate end of His own actings, as well as of our deeds of
piety; a doctrine repugnant indeed to all Socinian and rationalistic views, but founded in reason and Scripture. If the perfections and rights of God are such that it is proper all other
beings should love and serve Him supremely, by what argument can it be proved that He should not do so likewise?
Again: He being before all things, and having all the motives
and purposes for making all things from eternity, while as yet
nothing was, must have found those motives only in Himself.
He being the only Thing existent, there was no where else to
find them.   Third: If creatures ought to render the supreme
homage of their powers and being to God, ought not He to
receive it?   1 Cor. x : 31.   Last, to make any thing else the
ultimate End of the universe, deposes God, and exalts that
something to the true post of deity; to which God is made to
play the part of an almighty convenience. Let human pride
be pulled down. As for Scriptures, see Prov. xvi : 4 ; Is. lxi :
3 ; Rom. xi : 36.

God's Glory His owu properest End.

God ought, therefore, to regard transgression, which outrages His holy attributes and excites His
wrath, in a very different way from that proper
for us creatures, sinners ourselves, when our
fellow-sinners offend us. It may be very true that it is good,
magnanimous, for one of us to forgive injury without satisfaction, and to extirpate our indignation for the sake of rescuing
our fellow-creature from suffering the punishment; but the
reasoning does not hold, when applied to the Supreme. The
executing of His good pleasure, the illustration of His perfections are, for Him, more proper ends than the continued well-
being of any or all sinful worlds, bestowed at the expense of
His attributes. It is a more proper and noble thing that God
should please Himself in the acting out of His own infinitely
holy and excellent attributes, than that He should please His
whole creation by bestowing impunity on guilty creatures. And,
therefore, not only do reasons which arise out of God's moral
relations to His creatures as their Ruler, but yet more reasons
arising directly out of His own supremacy and righteousness,
require Him to punish guilt without fail.

Satisfying His own Justice therefore His chief Motive.

Necessity for Satisfaction in order to pardon: (2) argued.

(a) The Scriptures ascribe to God holiness, righteousness, and justice, in a sense which shows them to be essential attributes. See Is vi : 3 ; Ps. lxxxix : 14 ; v : 4 ; Gen. xviii : 25 ; Exod. xxxiv : 7 ; Hab. i : 13 : Rom. i : 18–32 ; ii : 6–11 ; iii : 6, &c., &c. Some of these passages bring to view His *justitia universalis,* or the general rectitude of His nature ; and some His administrative justice, as dealing with His moral creatures. Now, we argue from the former, that since God is immutable, and this perfection is essential, He will not, and by a moral necessity cannot, be affected by moral evil as He is by good. It is impossible that His feeling and will can confound the two, can fail to be opposed to sin, and favourable to rectitude. But God, while His will is governed by His own perfections, is absolutely free ; so that no doubt His conduct will follow His will. God's distributive justice we naturally conceive as prompting Him to give every one His due. As naturally as well being is the just equivalent of obedience, just so naturally is suffering the equivalent of sin ; and justice as much requires the punishment of sin, as the reward of merit. To fail in apportioning its desert to either, is real injustice. Now, does not God assert that His ways are equal ? Shall not the like rule guide Him which He imposes on us ? See, then, Prov. xvii : 15 ; Rom. ii : 6–11.

Holiness, Justice, and Truth.

Again God has pledged His Truth to the execution of penal sanctions. He has threatened. See Numbers xxiii : 19. The argument is enhanced by the repetitions, energy, and oaths, with which He has said and sworn, the wicked shall not enter into His rest. Hence His essential attribute of truth is engaged to require satisfaction for guilt.

(b) The argument from God's moral perfections is confirmed by observing His administration towards man. In the first revelation made to man, that of paradise, justice was declared as clearly as grace. Was goodness displayed in the bounties to man, and was the adoption of life offered to Him on easy terms ? Yet justice added the threat, " In the day thou eatest thereof, thou shalt surely die." As soon as innocent man fell, and a religion for sinners was to be revealed, the foremost point of this creed was the necessity that sin must be punished, for the satisfaction of divine justice, truth and holiness. The chief aim of God, in every institution of the Old Testament religion was obviously, to make this prime truth stand out to the apprehension of sinners. What was the prominent addition made to the worship of paradise ? Bloody sacrifice ; and that, undoubtedly, ordained by God ; as we have seen. And this remained the grand characteristic of the religion for sinners, until the " Lamb of God " came to meet the great demand of satisfaction. Wherever the Patriarchs approached the throne of grace, there the altar must

His Actual Government.

Perpetual Sacrifice Designed to Teach this.

be raised, from the day Abel worshipped before the gates of the lost Eden, until Christ rent the veil of the sanctuary. The orisons of faith and penitence must be accompanied with the streaming blood of the victim and the avenging fire of the altar. Prayer could only rise to heaven, as the way was opened for it by the smoke of the sacrifice. God was thus teaching all ages, this foundation-truth of the theology of redemption that, " with out the shedding of blood, there was no remission." Thus impressively are we introduced to the Levitical argument.

The necessity of atonement is taught in all the Old Testament sacrifices (as the Gentile sacrifices are the testimony of man's conscience to the same truth). The Apostle Paul, as already intimated, makes a grand induction of the ritual facts of the Old Testament, in Heb. ix : 22. "And without shedding of blood was no remission." It is literally true, that the ceremonial law remitted no trespass, sin, or uncleanness, without a substitutionary animal death; save in the exception for the very poor, of Levit. v : 11. Search and see. The theological principle thus set forth is just my thesis ; the necessity of satisfaction in order to pardon. Now, there is no idea which is inculcated, in the whole of Revelation, so constantly, so early, so carefully. It was the first truth, in the religion of redemption, taught to Adam's family. The awful, bloody symbol of it was ever present in all the worship of the Old Testament Church. With God's mind, it is ever the first and strongest thought. With man's unbelieving mind, it is the last and least. Indeed, the contrast here is amazing ; and the stupidity of the human mind in apprehending this first rudiment, is one of the strongest proofs of its natural deadness in sin. God's example, in perpetually obtruding on sinners the impressive sacrificial symbol of this truth, should be instructive to pastors. They must constantly urge the necessity of satisfaction.

Argument from Sacrifices.

This obstinate obtuseness is manifested at once by the crude notions of the people and the refined speculations of the scholar. Even the convicted sinner is stubbornly oblivious of the claims of God upon his sins, and assigns anything rather than the true ground, his repentance, his reformation, his anxieties, for the title to his pardon. When these " refuges of lies" are swept away, and the soul is left desperate and cowering before its righteous doom, the pastor may hold up the gospel doctrine of satisfaction, and the convicted man will turn from it stolid and blind, until God shines into his heart. Carnal philosophy is equally prejudiced. It proposes any inconsequent scheme rather than the true one, to account for the punishment of sin, and the call for a sacrifice from Christ. One tells us, that suffering has no penal significance, but is the regular and unavoidable effect of natural law upon creatures organized and finite,

Obstinate Errors of Sinners.

as though that law were anything else than the expression of God's moral will: and as though He had not told us, "death came by sin." Another tells us, that punitive justice is nothing but "benevolence guided by wisdom," that as Love is God's only moral attribute, the only ends of penalty must be philanthropic, that it is but a prudent expedient to protect men from the miseries involved in sin. So, when they come to explain the sacrifice of Calvary, they give any other than the true account of it. Says one: It was designed to attest the divine mercy offered us in the gospel promises. Another: It was to set us a splendid example of long-suffering. Another: It was to break our hearts by the spectacle of dying love. And others: It was to make a wholesome exhibition of the evil of sin. The Scripture saith it was all this: but because it was more, because it was primarily designed to make satisfaction for our guilt.

(c) Many minds, like the great jurist Grotius', have deluded themselves by likening God's penal adminis-
False Theories of Penalty Refuted. tration to that of the civil magistrate; which is, in a large degree, an expedient to repress the mischiefs of transgression. They suppose no higher aim is to be imputed to God's justice. But the comparison is partial. God has reserved to Himself the supreme function of retribution, delegating to earthly rulers only the temporary and lower purposes of law. Yea, even if the magistrate loses sight of the true ground of his penalties in the evil desert of the crimes he punishes, they at once sink from the rank of a righteous expediency, to that of an odious and unprincipled artifice.

That the benefit of the culprit is not the true end of penalty may be very quickly decided by the fact, that many of God's most notable penalties summarily destroyed their objects; as the Flood, doom of Sodom, and the retributions of hell. Of course God has done in these cases, what He meant to do. But they say: God, having seen that the amendment of these sinners was hopeless, and that they were infallibly drawing on themselves the worst mischiefs of sin, made examples of these for the good of others. So His only motive is still benevolence, seeking thus to overrule the unavoidable calamities of the few, to the "greatest good of the greatest number." Having thus placed a fragment of truth in the place of the whole, they sometimes turn on us, with an arrogant contrast between the boasted mildness of their scheme, and what they call the vengeful severity of ours. Our God, say they, is the God of love. Yours is the theology of ancient barbarians, who sanctified their vindictive malice under the name of vindicatory justice, and imagined a God like themselves, pleased with the fumes of His enemies' blood. They say ours is "the theology of the shambles."

But let us see how this declamation will stand the test of

reason and Scripture. Is God any better pleased with a holy creature than with a transgressor? Of course, yes. But for what is He better pleased with the holy? For his righteousness. It is right then in God to love righteousness? Of course, yes: Did He not, He would be Himself unrighteous. But righteousness and sin are the opposite poles of character. Just as the attraction of the one end of the magnet to the North pole is the repulsion of the other end towards the South; so to love holiness is to hate sin. The perfection, then, which prompts God to the amiable work of rewarding good desert, is the same perfection which consistently prompts to punish ill desert. Hear Anselm of Canterbury, reasoning with his imaginary opponent, Boso.

"To remit sin" (without satisfaction) "is nothing else than not to punish it. And since nothing else than punishment is the right adjustment of the sin that has not been satisfied for, if it is not punished, it is left unadjusted."—Boso. "What you say is reasonable."—Anselm. "But it is not becoming for God to leave anything in His kingdom unadjusted."—Boso. "If I wish to assert otherwise, I fear to sin."—Anselm. "So then it does not become God to leave sin thus unpunished."—Boso. "So it follows."—Anselm. "And there is another thing that follows; that if sin is thus left unpunished, it will be just the same with God whether one sins or does not sin; and that does not befit God."—Boso. "I cannot deny it."—Anselm. "Look at this too. Nobody is ignorant, that the righteousness of men is under the law; so that the measure of its recompense is dispensed by God according to its quantity."—Boso. "So we believe."—Anselm. "But if sin is neither paid for nor punished, it is subject to no law."—Boso. "I cannot understand it otherwise,"—Anselm. "Then, unrighteousness, if it be remitted by mere mercy, is freer than righteousness? And that seems extremely unsuitable. This absurdity also is attached to it: that it makes unrighteousness like God, in that, just as God is subject to no law, so unrighteous is not."

This pretended resolution of punitive justice into benevolent expediency is, in its result, impious towards God, and practically identical with the selfish system of morals. We have seen above, that "man's chief end is to glorify God, and enjoy him forever." This humanitarian scheme says that this would make God the supreme egotist. It proposes as a more suitable supreme end, not self, but mankind: the advantage of the greatest number. This they claim, is true disinterestedness. But is not that which is made our highest ultimate end thereby made our God? It is nothing to the purpose that names and titles are decently exchanged, and man still called the creature, and Jehovah the God. Virtually, the aggregate of humanity is made our deity, by being made our moral End; and Jehovah is only retained, if retained at all, as a species of omnipotent conveniency and Servitor to this creature-God. Further: inasmuch as the benevolent man is himself a part of this aggregate humanity, which is his moral End, he himself is, at least in part, his own supreme end! Here the supreme selfishness of this scheme of pretended disinterestedness begins to crop out. In this aggregate humanity I am an integer, "by nature equal" to any other. What then so reasonable, as that I should deem the humanity embodied in myself, as my own nearest and most attainable moral End? Does not the natural instinct of self-love point to this conclusion; as well as the facts that I cannot, with my limited nature benefit all, that I am more nearly responsible for my own welfare, and that I have more means to promote it with certainty than any other man's? Hence, the properest mode to promote "the greatest good of the greatest number," will be for each one to make his own personal advantage his supreme end! Here the abominable process from these utilitarian premises, is completed. Dr. Samuel Hopkins, the great American inventor of this scheme, has himself carried his system to this result, with a candour which is amusing for its simplicty: Says he: vol. I : p. 475.

"As every person is nearest to himself, and is most in his own view, has opportunities to be better acquainted with his own circumstances, and to know his own wants, his mercies and enjoyments, &c: and has a more particular care of his own interest, than of that of others: is under greater advantage to promote his own happiness than others; his disinterested universal benevolence will attend more to his own interest, and he will have more and stronger exercises of it respecting his own circumstances and happiness than those of others, all things being equal: not because it is his own interest, but for the reason just given." That is to say; his virtue will be to practice supreme selfishness, provided he is not selfish in doing so! Thus this boasted scheme resolves itself into one of selfish expediency.

This theory of penalty receives the following refutation. If it is only a benevolent expedient for reforming sinners and repressing sin, then the expedient which is most effectual is most just. If a case arises in which the criminal and those like him will be more deterred by punishing the innocent than the guilty, it will be more just to do so. The instance may easily arise in actual life. Here, for example, is an outlaw, hardened in crime, desperate, callous to shame, weary of his life, whom it is proposed to curb by punishments. But none of them reach him. Shame has for him no deeper gulfs. The prison is less a hardship than his vagrant and starving life. Corporal pains have little terror for one familiar with misery. Death is rather a welcome refuge than a dread. The expediency fails. But now

The Effective Expedient would be Just.

there steps forth a policeman, who says that there is yet one green spot in this seared and arid heart; that this desperado has an only child, an innocent and tender daughter, whose purity has shielded her from all taint. Punish her with stripes. Let him stand and see her tender flesh torn with the scourge, and hear her screams; and his rugged heart will relent. He will promise anything to save his beloved child. Does not the success of this experiment justify its righteousness? Every right heart answers, with abhorrence, No. Such a punishment of the guiltless would be a monstrous crime. Then we must reject that theory of penalty.

But further: Expedients are the resort of the weak. Omnipotence has no need of them for it can Inconsistent with Omnipotence. march straight to its ends. Now, if love is God's whole moral rectitude, as an infinite being, He must be infinitely benevolent. Why then has He not adopted the other plan, to which His omnipotence is certainly competent, of effectually excluding the mischiefs of sin by making and keeping all His creatures holy? Why does He not convert Satan, instead of damning him? Thus a large aggregate of happiness would have resulted; all that, namely, arising out of Satan's innocency minus the penal pangs. Moreover, penalty has turned out but an imperfect and partial preventive, after all, for in spite of it earth and hell are full of sin, and God must have foreseen this failure of the repressive policy. Benevolence must, then, on these principles, have led Him to adopt a system of universal efficacious grace, instead of a policy of penal sanctions.

But especially is it impossible, on this theory of expediency, to account for everlasting punishments Eternal punishments inexplicable. under an Almighty God. Here the remedial theory is out of the question; for the culprit is to sin and suffer forever. Nor will the other plea avail; that the penalties in this case are for the benefit of others. For this infliction is to continue everlasting ages after all the penitent shall have been perfected, and the perfect securely enclosed within the protecting walls of heaven. There, endowed as they are, with perfect love and holiness, they need no threatening example, to keep them from sin. He who holds this theory of punishment, must, if he is consistent, go on to modern Universalism, or else he must deny God's omnipotence over free agents.

(d)   Resuming the affirmative argument, I make my first appeal to conscience. Every man who believes in Affirmative Arguments from the Teaching of Conscience. a God, believes His justice the same in essence with that imprinted on his own conscience. For two reasons, we must believe this: That we are made in God's rational image. And that Governor and governed must live by the same code of justice in order to understand each other.   Let any man, then, ask himself impartially, why he approves of a just punishment. The answer of his rea- son will be simply: because the sin deserves it.   Our judgment of right and wrong is intuitively accompanied with the convic- tion of good and ill desert. But, desert of what?   Reason answers, of reward or penalty, of well being or suffering.   The title to the one is a counterpart to the title to the other.   That this judgment is intuitive, is disclosed by the following instan- ces: If any reverent or fair mind is asked how the presence of so much suffering in the world can consist with God's benevo- lence, the reason turns instinctively to the solution: Because so much sin is here.   The presence of the sin justifies the pres- ence of the suffering.   Second.   Every sane human being who is in his sin, dreads to meet God. Why?   Witness the moral fear of death, and the certainty with which the most reckless men apprehend their doom and its justice, when the solemn hour has dissipated vain illusions and recalled the soul from the chase of vanities.   The same conviction is familiarly but justly argued from the conscious guilt of pagans, and their desire for expiatory sacrifice.   Said Ovid: *Timor fecit Deos.*   To this shallow solution Edmund Burke answered: *Quis fecit timorem?* The belief in God and conviction of His punitive justice must be *a priori* to the fear of them. Third.   When any right- minded man witnesses the escape of a flagrant criminal from justice, he is indignant. He says: " The gallows is cheated;" and this expression conveys a certain just complaint and sense of moral grievance.   Should the escaped man charge this as a malicious thirsting for his destruction, the spectator would indignantly deny this construction. He would say : " My sen- timents are not cruelty, but justice."   And he would declare that they were compatible with sincere pain at the anguish of a justly punished culprit.

We have seen that the title of the guilty to penalty is the

Title to Penalty Cor-
relative to Title to Re-
ward.

correlative to the title of the righteous to reward.   If a benevolent policy may properly suspend the former, why not also the latter? But we presume that if the consciously righteous man were robbed of his immunity, *pro bono publico,* against his own consent, no picture of the beneficent results would reconcile his soul to the intrinsic injustice.   Let the stu- dent ponder, in this connection, Prov. xvii: 15 ; Rom. ii: 9–11. 2 Thess. i: 6.   This loose view of punishment thus appears peculiarly foolish and suicidal in those who hold it, in that they, with their Socinian tendencies, rely more or less on their own merits for their acceptance.   But if sin carries the same merit of penalty that righteousness does of reward, and if they will have God sever the former tie at the dictate of expediency, they must be prepared to find the latter uncertain also.

The moral law is the transcript of God's own essential perfections. This teaches us to expect that permanency in it, which our Saviour, in Matt. v : 18, claims for it. But is not the penal sanction a substantive part of the statute? The common sense of mankind would certainly answer, yes. What is the object of a penal sanction? To support the law. If then the law is to be immutable, the penal sanction which supports it must be so. There is a curious evidence of the judgment of human legislators on the question, whether the penal sanction is a substantive part of the law; that in their prohibitory statutes, it is the only part they usually publish at all! Now then if the law is irrevocable, the penalty is also inevitable.

The Law Immutable.

The whole of the above argument may be put in a very practical light—thus: Is not judicial impartiality with God "a matter of principle?" The upright human judge who was entreated by the convicted man, or by his counsel, to act as the Socinian expects God to act in pardoning, would be insulted! Now, how does God require us to act, in matters of principle? He literally requires us to die rather than compromit our principles. He requires us to meet martyrdom, rather than yield them. Now does God first command us to seek our complete rectitude in the imitation of Himself, and then act oppositely to His injunction to us? Surely not. In representing the necessity of satisfaction as so high, as to call for the infinite satisfaction of Christ's death in order to make sin pardonable, we conform precisely to the system of morals which the Scriptures commend to us for ourselves. The tendency of Calvinism is wholesome herein.

Else God's Requirement of us Unfair.

On the other hand, the looser doctrine is as corrupting to man as it is dishonouring to God. Its advocates flout the obligation to penalty in every sin. They say Calvinism deifies revenge. They declare substitution and imputation immoral fictions. The student may be forewarned that, when he hears one of these "advanced thinkers" thus teaching, if he be not idly babbling, he had best be shunned as a man not to be trusted. It is a confession of indifference to moral obligation. He who is ready so flippantly to strip his God of His judicial rights, will probably not stickle to plunder his fellow of his rights. In this theory of guilt and penalty, he has adopted the creed of expediency. Will he not act on it, when tempted by his own interests? Worse than all, he has fashioned to himself a God of expediency. Saith the Psalmist, (cxv : 8), "They that make them are like unto them; so is every one that trusteth in them." As man never comes up to his model, a corrupt idol always sinks the votary to a lower degradation than its own. Nor could God repair this consequence by any preceptive stringency. Shall He

Other Doctrine is Corrupting.

32*

forbid us to sacrifice principle to expediency, even to save life
itself? Shall He exact of us martyrdom itself, rather than we shall
tamper with right and truth; and all this under the penalty of
His eternal wrath? Shall He charge us, also, that our holiness
is to consist in imitation of Him? And shall He then adopt a
standard of expediency forHimself,which He has so sternly inhibited to us? The only effect would be to make men hypocrites.

(e) Moreover; does not God bear moral relations to His
creatures, as well as they to Him? Gen.
Argument from God's Rectoral Justice. xviii : 25. Surely. As Ruler, and especially
as Almighty Ruler, with nothing to hinder
Him from doing His will, He is bound to His own perfections to
rule them aright, as truly as they are bound to Him to serve
aright. This being so, retributive justice will be seen to flow
as a necessity from the holiness and righteousness of God. By
these attributes God necessarily and intrinsically approves and
delights in all right things. Wrong is the antithesis of right.
A moral *tertium quid* is an impossibilty, as the mere absence of
light is darkness. There is no moral neutrality. Hence, it
results, that God must hate the wrong by the very reason He
approves the right; e. g., if a man feels moral complacency at
a filial affection, will he not, *ipso facto*, be certain to feel repugnance at ingratitude? I see not how God would be holy at all,
unless His justice were necessary.

Again; were it not so, God would be unjust to His innocent creatures. Sin is injurious; to all but infallible Being con-
tagious, and universally mischievous. God has been pleased to
adopt a plan of moral sanctions, to protect the universe from
sin. Those beings who kept their covenant with God, have a
right on Him, which He, in infinite condescension, gave them,
to be protected efficiently. Hence, His righteousness must
lead Him to inflict penal sanctions with exactness, for it is well
known that uncertainty in this encourages transgressions, confounds moral distinctions, and relaxes government. Should
God do thus, He would be sacrificing the well-being and rights
of those who deserved well at His hands, to a weak compassion
for those who deserved nothing. God's essential justice is the
foundation of the rights and order of the universe. Unless its
actings are certain and regular, we are all at the mercy of an
unprincipled Omnipotence. Even the damned have no interest
in making God's justice uncertain; because it is the only guarantee that they shall not be punished more than they deserve.
And the wider God's dominions, the greater strength have all
these arguments, forcible as they are even in the narrow domain
of the family, school or state.

The parallel drawn from acts of pardon without satisfaction, safely and beneficially indulged in by
Pardons by Magis- trates no Precedents. human rulers, is deceptive, because they have
not the divine perfections of omnipotence,

unchangeableness and omniscience. It might be no dishonour to a human magistrate to modify his purposes; he never professed to be either perfectly wise or immutable. Cases may arise of conviction, where the evidence of guilt is uncertain, or the criminal intention doubtful. In these cases, and these alone, the pardoning power may find a wholesome exercise. Such cases have no existence in the administration of an omniscient God. Once more; the power and authority of human rulers are limited. They must govern as they can, sometimes not as they would. God can do all things.

In a word, God's moral government, in its ultimate conclusion, must be as absolute and perfect as His own nature. For, being supreme and almighty, He is irresponsible save to His own perfections. Therefore, if He is a Being of infinite perfections, His government must be one of absolutely righteous, final results. It will be an exact representation of Himself, for He makes it just what He pleases. If there is moral defect in the final adjustment, it can only be accounted for by defect in God. It must be an absolute result, because the free act of an infinite Being.

(f) The death of Christ argues the necessity of satisfaction. For Socinus admits that He was an innocent Man, God's adopted Son. Surely God would not have made Him suffer under imputed guilt, (He had none of His own), unless it had been morally necessary. In this view, we see that the atonement, instead of obscuring, greatly exalts God's love and mercy; that though He knew the price of pardon must be the blood of His own Son, His pity did not fail.

(g) Last; it is tacitly implied in the admissions of Socinians themselves, that God could not consistently pardon without the repentance and reform of the sinner. For this gives up the point that, in some sort, a satisfaction to the divine honour must be exacted. But, repentance and reform are not satisfactions. Second, we shall prove that repentance is the consequence and result of pardon, so that it cannot be its procuring cause. An injured man, we admitted, might regard repentance as obviating the third element of transgression, the subjective moral turpitude But, in God's case, it may not, because God must bestow the repentance as truly as the pardon, and as a consequence of the pardon. See Acts v : 31 ; Jer. xxxi : 18, 19.

Tacit Admission of Adversaries.

(h) We will close with these general Bible testimonies to the necessity of satisfaction: Heb. vii: 27; viii: 3; ix: 7, 12, 22, 23, 28; x: 9, 10, 26, 27 to 29; ii: 10, 14, 17.

LECTURE XLII.

NATURE OF CHRIST'S SACRIFICE.

TO the question, How shall man be just with God, natural theology gives no certain answer. It seems, if we do not

1. Redemption Foreshadowed in Providence.

deceive ourselves by attributing to its light discoveries really borrowed from inspiration, to inform us very clearly that God is just, and man therefore condemned. Having thus shut us up under wrath, its light deserts us, leaving only an uncertain twilight shining towards the gate of mercy and hope. When reason looks into the analogies presented by that course of nature, as unbelief terms it, which is, in reality, nothing else than the course of Providence, she sees that there are certain evils consequent upon certain faults—e. g., sickness on intemperance, want on idleness, bodily death on reckless imprudence ; but she also sees that there are certain remedial provisions made in nature, by availing themselves of which men may sever the connection between the fault and the natural penalty. This fact would seem to hint that in God's eternal government there may be a way of mercy provided. But then, the analogical evidence is made very faint by this fact : that these natural reliefs for the natural evils incurred here by our misconduct, are rather postponements than acquittals. After all, inexorable death comes to sinful man, in spite of all expedients.

500

But the most interesting fact to be noticed in this feeble analogy is, that these partial releases from the natural consequences of our faults, are most often received through a mediatorial agency, and that this agency is usually exerted for us by our friends at some cost to themselves, often at the cost of suffering the whole or a part of the very evils our faults naturally incurred. A man is guilty of intemperance ; its natural consequence is sickness and death, and without mediatorial intervention this consequence would become certain, for the foolish wretch is too sick to minister to himself. But Providence permits a faithful wife, or parent, or friend, to intervene with those remedies and cares which save his life. Now, at what cost does this friendly mediator save it? Obviously, at the cost of many of the very pains which the sick man had brought upon himself—the confinement, the watching, the loss of time, the anxieties of the sick room. Or, a prodigal wastes his substance, and the result is want ; a result, so far as his means are concerned, inevitable. But his friend steps in with his wealth, pays his debts and relieves his necessities. Yet the cost at which he does it is in part the very same incurred by the guilty man's prodigality : decrease of his substance and consequent want. We may say, yet more generally, that the larger part of all the reliefs which Providence administers to the miseries of man's sinful condition, from the cradle to the grave, from the maternal love which shields and blesses his infancy, down to the friendship which receives his dying sighs, are administered through others, and that at the cost of sacrifice or effort on their part for him. Here, then, we have a general analogy pointing to a vicarious method of rescuing man from his guilt, and to sacrifice by a Mediator for him. We have called the evils adverted to in our illustrations, natural consequences of our faults; but they are not therefore any the less ordained of God, and penal; for what is the course of nature, but God ordering? and does not our natural conscience show that suffering can only occur under the almighty providence of a just and good God as the penal consequences of ill-desert?

The revealed idea of a satisfaction for sin, or vicarious arrangement to deliver man from guilt, has been made the butt of rationalistic objections. The value of this analogy is to silence these objections, by showing that the idea, however mysterious, is not unnatural.

It has been objected by rationalists, that vicarious punishments are not admitted in the penal legislation of just and civilized men ; and if introduced, would strike our moral judgments as wrong and unreasonable. It may be remarked, that among the ancients these arrangements frequently appeared, in the cases of hostages, and αντιψυχοι. In modern legislation they appear at least in the case of suretyships for debt. But there are four very good reasons which distinguish between human governments and God's.

1st. It is in my view, unreasonable and mischievous, to reply to objections against the morality of a substitution (Christ's or Adam's) by such a reference to God's sovereignty, as should represent it as irresponsible, not only to man's imperfect conceptions of rectitude, but to the intrinsic principles thereof. What is this but saying that because God is omnipotent Owner, therefore He may properly be unjust. Does might make right?

Because God is a Sovereign Legislator.

But it is a very different (and proper) thing to say that, while God as Sovereign, regulates His every act by the same general principles of rectitude, which He enjoins on His creatures, yet He very justly exercises a width of discretion, for Himself, in His application of those principles, which He does not allow to human magistrates, in delegating them a little portion of His power. Deut. xxiv : 16. This is made proper by His sovereignty. (I may righteously do with my horse, what would be cruel in him to whom I had hired him, for a day's ordinary journey—e. g., ride him to extremity, or even to death, to rescue the life of my child.) And by God's infinite knowledge and wisdom, judging the whole results of a substitution as a creature cannot. Hence, the impropriety of vicarious arrangements among men may be compatible with their admission between God and man ; and yet no contrariety of moral principles in the two governments is involved ; e. g. I delegate to a teacher, at a distance, a portion of my parental power over my child. I tell him he is to consider himself, as to this extent, *in loco parentis,* and govern my boy on strictly parental principles ; yet he would be very unreasonable if he assumed power to exercise every kind of discretion as to him, which I might properly exercise.

2d. When men inflict penalties less than capital, one object of the infliction is the reform of the offender ; for which a personal endurance of the pain is necessary. But when God inflicts the eternal penalty of sin, He has no intention of reforming the sufferer thereby.

His Object in Punishing Vindicatory.

3d. In those cases where human tribunals punish by the loss of life or liberty, the vicarious arrangement cannot be adopted, because no one can be found who is owner of his own life and well-being. But he cannot pay away, in ransom of another, what he has no right to part with.

No Substitute Among Men, sui juris.

4th. We found that one of the elements of offence contracted by wrong-doing was the moral turpitude ; that and the removal of this by genuine repentance is one of the necessary conditions for pardoning the wrong-doer. Now, a vicarious satisfaction is

Civil Magistrate cannot Sanctify.

inapplicable in human governments, because the human magistrate would have no means to work genuine repentance in the criminal, though an atonement were offered. But without such repentance, guilt could not be properly pardoned, by God or man, however adequate the satisfaction to justice. Now, God can work and insure genuine repentance in His pardoned criminals, through the Holy Ghost. See Acts v : 31. Hence, He can properly avail Himself of the principle of vicarious penalty. Even supposing a man could be found who had autocracy of his own life, time, and social relations, and who was willing to die for a murderer, when slain, he could not rise again; he would be a final loss to society, and society would gain, in exchange, the life of the murderer, now penitent and reformed, (supposing the magistrate, like God, had regenerating power over him). So, all the result would be, that society would lose a citizen who always had been good, and gain one who was about to become good. The magistrate would not feel himself justified in admitting the substitution, for such results, however it might be generous in the friend to propose it.

Word atonement is used often in the Old Testament, once in the New, Rom. v : 11. The Hebrew is

2. Definitions. usually כִּפֶּר literally, " covering," because that which atones is conceived as covering guilt from the eye of justice. The Greek is καταλλαγή—reconciliation, as it and its cognates are elsewhere translated. It is plausibly supposed that "atonement" is "at-one-ment,"—i. e., reconciliation. These words, then, are generic, and not specific of the particular means of reconciliation, according to etymology. The word which I should prefer to use, is one sanctioned by the constant usage of the Reformed theologians, " satisfaction." This expresses truly and specifically what Christ did for believers. It points explicitly to the divine law and perfections, whose demand for satisfaction constitute the great obstacles to pardon. It inincludes, also, Christ's preceptive, as well as His penal, compensation for our debt. We shall see that both Christ's obedience to the preceptive law and His voluntary endurance of the penal sanction enter into His satisfaction, paid as our substitute. The established word, which has been deliberately attested and approved by the Church, is by all means to be retained. Atonement, or reconciliation is related to satisfaction, as effect to cause.

The Reformed divines are also accustomed to make a distinction between penal and moral satisfaction,

Satisfaction not Commercial. on the one hand, and pecuniary payment, on the other. In a mere pecuniary debt, the claim is on the money owed, not on the person owing. The amount is numerically estimated. Hence, the surety, in making vicarious payment, must pay the exact number of coins due.

And when he has done that, he has, *ipso facto*, satisfied the debt. His offer of such payment in full is a legal tender which leaves the creditor no discretion of assent or refusal. If he refuses, his claim is cancelled for once and all. But the legal claim on us for obedience and penalty is personal. It regards not only the *quid solvatur*, but the *quis solvat*. The satisfaction of Christ is not *idem facere;* to do the identical thing required of the sinner, but *satis facere;* to do enough to be a just moral equivalent for what is due from the sinner. Hence, two consequences: Christ's satisfaction cannot be forced on the divine Creditor as a legal tender; it does not free us *ipso facto*. And God, the Creditor, has an optional discretion to decline the proffer, if He chooses (before He is bound by His own covenant), or to accept it. Hence, the extent to which, and the terms on which, Christ's vicarious actions shall actually satisfy the law, depend simply on the stipulations made between Father and Son, in the covenant of redemption.

Yet, we shall by no means agree, with the Scotists, and the early Remonstrants, that Christ did not make a real, and equivalent satisfaction for sinners' debts. They say, that His sacrifice was not such, because He did not suffer really what sinners owed. He did not feel remorse, nor absolute despair; He did not suffer eternally; only His humanity suffered. But they suppose that the inadequate sufferings were taken as a ransom-price, *per acceptilationem:* by a gracious waiver of God's real claims of right. And they hold that any sacrifice, which God may please thus to receive, would be thereby made adequate. The difference between their view and the Reformed may be roughly, but fairly defined, by an illustration drawn from pecuniary obligations: A mechanic is justly indebted to a land-owner in the sum of one hundred pounds; and has no money wherewith to pay. Now, should a rich brother offer the landlord the full hundred pounds, in coin of the realm, this would be a legal tender; it would, *ipso facto*, cancel the debt, even though the creditor captiously rejected it. Christ's satisfaction is not *ipso facto* in this commercial sense. There is a second supposition: that the kind brother is not rich, but is himself an able mechanic; and seeing that the landlord is engaged in building, he proposes that he will work as a builder for him two hundred days, at ten shillings *per diem* (which is a fair price), to cancel his poor brother's debt. This proposal, on the one hand, is not a "legal tender," and does not compel the creditor. He may say that he has already enough mechanics, who are paid in advance; so that he cannot take the proposal. But, if he judges it convenient to accept it, although he does not get the coin, he gets an actual equivalent for his claim, and a fair one. This is *satisfactio*. The debtor may thus get a valid release on the terms freely covenanted between the surety and creditor. But there is a

Yet not per acceptilationem.

third plan : The kind brother has some " script " of the capital stock of some company, which, "by its face " amounts nominally, to one hundred pounds, but all know that it is worth but little. Yet he goes to the creditor, saying: "My brother and I have a pride about bearing the name of full payment of our debt. We propose that you take this ' script' as one hundred pounds (which is its nominal amount), and give us a discharge, which shall state that you have payment in full." Now, if the creditor assents, this is payment *per acceptilationem.* Does Christ's satisfaction amount to no more than this ? We answer emphatically, it does amount to more. This disparaging conception is refuted by many scriptures, such as Isa. xlii : 21 ; liii : 6. It is dishonourable to God, representing Him as conniving at a "legal fiction," and surrendering all standard of truth and justice to confusion. On this low scheme, it is impossible to see how any real necessity for satisfaction could exist.

The Reformed assert then, that Christ made penal satisfaction, by suffering the very penalty demanded by the law of sinners. In this sense, we say even *idem fecit.* The identity we assert is, of course, not a numerical one, but a generic one. If we are asked, how this could be, when Christ was not holden forever of death, and experienced none of the remorse, wicked despair, and subjective pollution, attending a lost sinner's second death ? We reply: the same penalty, when poured out on Him, could not work all the detailed results, because of His divine nature and immutable holiness. A stick of wood, and an ingot of gold are subjected to the same fire. The wood is permanently consumed : the gold is only melted, because it is a precious metal, incapable of natural oxidation, and it is gathered, undiminished, from the ashes of the furnace. But the fire was the same ! And then, the infinite dignity of Christ's person gives to His temporal sufferings a moral value equal to the weight of all the guilt of the world.

Christ Suffered the very Penalty.

Christ, or His work, is also called $\lambda \dot{\upsilon} \tau \rho o \nu$, ransom-price; and the transaction an $\dot{\alpha} \pi o \lambda \dot{\upsilon} \tau \rho \omega \sigma \iota \varsigma$ or redeeming. The obvious idea here, is that of purchase, by a price, or equivalent, out of bondage. He is also our $\dot{\iota} \lambda \alpha \sigma \mu \dot{o} \varsigma$, or $\dot{\epsilon} \xi \iota \lambda \dot{\alpha} \sigma \mu o \varsigma$, making for us propitiation, $\dot{\iota} \lambda \alpha \sigma \tau \dot{\eta} \rho \iota o \nu$. Expiation is the sacrificial and satisfactory action, making the offended Judge propitious to the transgressor. These terms applied to Christ's suffering work, justify us in describing His sacrifice, as His vicarious suffering of the penalties due our sins, to satisfy God's justice and thus reconcile Him to us.

Other terms.

Before proceeding to refute the Socinian theory of the atonement, let us briefly re-state it. The sufferings of Jesus, they suppose, were not penal; but only natural, such as would have

3. Socinian Theory stated.

been incurred by Adam in Paradise, had he not fallen. Yet God permitted and ordained them, 1st. As an example to teach us patience, fortitude, and submission. 2d. As an attestation of the honesty and truth of His teachings concerning the way of life through imitation of Him. 3d. To make Him a compassionate Teacher, Friend, and Patron to His brethren. 4th. To make way for His resurrection ; which was the all-important evidence and warrant to us that eternal life may be hoped for, through repentance and reform. Thus, He died, suffered for us — i. e., *pro bono nostrum* — in a general sense. Thus, He is the Saviour and Redeemer of men — i. e., the Agent of their salvation in a sense. But He made no penal satisfaction for sin.

Now, an overwhelming indirect refutation of this theory has already been given, in our argument for the necessity of a proper vicarious penalty. Another will be presented under the succeeding head, when we prove that Christ's sufferings were vicarious. But for direct refutation, note :

There can be little reasonable encouragement in the example of one who suffered so bitterly without deserving anything. Such a spectacle, instead of shedding light, hope and patience on the sorrows of believers, could only deepen the darkness and anguish ; for it could only suggest difficulties concerning the justice and benevolence of God, and raise the torturing doubt, " Can any one be secure of blessedness, any angel or saint in heaven, or is there any justice and benevolence in God, in which I may hope for release from present sufferings ; seeing a creature so holy as Jesus suffered thus ? He was enabled to triumph over them at last ? Yea, but why did God make Him suffer at all, when He was entirely innocent ? I, who am not innocent, may not be thus released after suffering ! "

Theory Inconsistent.
1st. Because a Guiltless Sufferer Suggests an Unjust God.

To represent His death as of such importance as the attestation of the truthfulness of His teachings, contradicts good sense and Scripture. All that the death of a martyr can prove is, that he sincerely believes the creed for which he dies. False creeds have had their martyrs. The Scriptures nowhere refer to Christ's death as the evidence of His truth ; but uniformly to His works. See John xiv : 11 ; v : 36 ; x : 25–38 ; xv : 24, &c.

2nd. Martytdom only Demonstrates Martyr's Sincerity.

The Socinian scheme gives the chief importance to Christ's resurrection, rather than His death, as the means whereby " life and immortality were brought to light." His death was then rather the necessary preliminary step, to make His resurrection possible ; that the latter might be, to our faith, the splendid and crowning evidence of a future life for us. Did God, then, kill Jesus, to have the opportunity of raising Him ? Since a resurrection is but the repairing of a death, it seems to me that the

3rd. Christ's Death Purchases Salvation, not His Resurrection.

whole transaction inspires at least as much terror as hope. He ordained the death of Him who deserved to live ; so there is an instance of severity, if not injustice, fully counterpoising the instance of goodness in raising Him. Again ; the Scriptures do not agree to the Socinian view; for they everywhere represent the benefit we derive from Christ as chiefly flowing from Christ's death. Heb. ii : 14. His resurrection was indeed a glorious attestation ; but it was an attestation of the sufficiency of that death, as a satisfaction to law, and an adequate purchase of our relief.

Again ; the whole plausibility of the Socinian's account of Christ's death and resurrection is ruined by the fact of His pre-existence. For a mere man to rise again after dying, like Lazarus, is an encouraging instance ; but the rising again of a Being who possessed a previous and glorious life besides that of His humanity, presents on the Socinian view no analogy to encourage mortal man to hope for a resurrection. The answer is too obvious : that the strange anomaly of a resurrection in Jesus' case was most probably the result of His glorious, pre-existent nature. Man has no such nature, and therefore should not expect, from such an instance, to imitate Him. As well might a log of wood infer that, because a living creature is seen to rise erect when laid on its back, therefore logs of wood may hope to rise, when laid on their backs. 4th. The Socinian scheme utterly fails to account for Christ's royal exaltation. We do not allude now to the fact that those regal functions (Matt. xxviii : 18 ; xxv : 31, 32 ; Eph. i : 22) could only be fulfilled by proper divinity. On the Socinian scheme, He ought not to have any regal functions. He has not earned them. He does not need them. Sinners regenerate themselves ; and their own repentance and reform are their righteousness ; so that the tasks of the royal priest, interceding and ruling on His throne, are useless and groundless.

He pre-existent.

Last ; on the Socinian theory, Christ could not have been in any sense the Mediator or Redeemer of Old Testament saints. Their sins could not have been remitted on the ground of Christ's prospective satisfaction for sin ; for, according to Socinians, there was none in prospect. Those saints could not have profited by Christ's example, teachings, and resurrection ; because they were in heaven long before Christ existed. But see Heb. ix : 15 ; Rom. iii : 25 ; Jno. viii : 56, &c.

5th. Christ, on this Scheme, did not Redeem Old Testament Saints.

Against the scheme of Dr. Price, called by Hill the Mid-Scheme, (see Hill, p. 422,) these objections obviously lie : that it represents Christ as acquiring His title to forgive sin only by His death. But Matt. ix : 6, says that the Son of Man had power on earth to forgive sins before. It speaks splendidly of Christ's suffering in order

The Middle Scheme.

to acquire this title to pardon; but it gives no intelligible account of how these sufferings acquired that title. It is, in this, as vague as Socinianism.

The scheme of atonement with which we have now most concern, as defenders of truth, is that usually known as the governmental scheme—i. e. that which resolves the sufferings and death of Christ into a mere moral expedient of God, to connect such a display of His justice and hatred of sin, with His acts of pardon, as will prevent bad effects from the failure to punish strictly according to law. This view proceeds from that theory of ethics which resolves all virtue into benevolence, teaching that an act is right or virtuous only because it tends on the whole most to promote the welfare of Beings; (and the contrary). (We cannot pause here to debate this theory, but only note how intimately ethics and metaphysics affect Theology). Hence, these divines hold, God has no intrinsic, essential justice, other than His benevolence—i. e., that the whole amount of His motive for punishing sin is, to preserve His moral empire from the mischiefs which sin unchecked would produce. Hence, the only necessity for an atonement which they recognize, is the necessity of repairing that defence against disorder in God's government, which the dispensing with the penalty would break down. They, consequently, deny that Christ was properly substituted under the believer's guilt, that He bore any imputation, that He made a real satisfaction to God's justice, and that the justifying virtue of His righteousness is imputed to men. The author of this system in New England seems to have been the younger Pres. Edwards, son of Jonathan, and its great propagator, Dr. Taylor, of New Haven. This is the system known as the New School, in the North, and advocated by Barnes and Beman on the atonement. It is a striking matter of history, that nearly all the arguments by which Edwards, Jr., sought to remove the old Calvinistic theory, to substitute his, were unconsciously Socinian.

Governmental Influence Scheme.

If the necessity of satisfaction is proved from God's essential justice, as we have attempted, this view of the atonement is proved false. Again: if we shall succeed in proving that Christ's was a proper, vicarious sacrifice, this, also, overthrows it. Third: we have seen that this New England plan rests on this proposition; that a governmental policy of repressing sin, is the only ground of God's justice; resolving all right into mere utility. The abominable consequences of this ethical principle have been shown; they are such that the principle cannot be true. We might add that man's intuitive moral judgments pronounce that sin is wrong, not merely because it tends to injure well-being, but wrong in itself; and that the very wording of such a statement, implies a standard of wrong and right other than that of mere utility.

Refutation.

This ethical principle being untrue, the plan falls with it.

But further, for direct refutations: This plan of atonement leaves us practically on Socinian ground, as to man's justifying righteousness. If imputation is denied, and if Christ wrought out no proper satisfaction to justice for the believer's sin, to be set over to the believer's account for his justification, there is no alternative left; the advocates of this plan are shut up to the Arminian definition of justification, as an imputing of the believer's own faith (along with the repentance and holy living flowing therefrom) as the ground of the sinner's justification, as his righteousness. Accordingly Messrs. Barnes, &c., do explicitly accept this. But we shall show, in the proper place, that such a justification is unscriptural. Justification is no longer properly through Christ, saving faith would no longer be such a coming to Christ directly, as the Scriptures describe it; and the whole tenour of Bible language concerning His divine righteousness, concerning His being the immediate object of faith, &c., &c., would be violated.

It gives us no Righteousness Imputed.

Last: the overwhelming objection to this plan is, that according to its definition, the sufferings of Christ would be no governmental display whatever of the evils of sin, or of God's determination to punish. These divines avow that Christ is a Person possessed of a pre-existent, divine, holy and supreme nature, not only guiltless, but above law; and of a pure and sinless humanity, the voluntary assumption of which only placed Him, by His own consent, under law, for a particular atoning purpose. His mediatorial person stood forth as the exemplar of sinless purity and perfection, to all creatures, in both its natures; and in every relation; attested by holy writ, by the voice of God speaking His divine approval from heaven in tones of thunder, by the reluctant tribute of His enemies, by the haughty Pagan who condemned Him, by the very traitor who betrayed Him, as he appears scathed with the fires of his own remorse, before his plunge into hell, and confesses that he had "betrayed the innocent blood." All heaven and all earth testified to the Son of Man, that He was "holy, harmless, undefiled, and separate from sinners;" testified to the universe. And yet, the universe is invited to come and behold this Being, the only innocent Man who had appeared since Adam, delivered to torments more cruel than any of Adam's guilty sons had ever endured, "delivered by the determinate counsel" of His Father, while without guilt, either personal or imputed! Is this a glorious display of justice? Does this illustrate the evil of sin, and the inexorable connection which God's benevolence requires Him to maintain between sin and punishment? Does it not rather confound all moral distinctions, and illustrate the evils of holiness, the cruelty and injustice of the Hand that

It is False on its own Showing.

rules the world? There is no explanation of Christ's suffering innocence, which does not involve an insuperable contradiction, except the orthodox; and that, we admit, involves a great mystery.

Each of the false schemes attempts to express what is true. But ours really includes all that theirs claim, while it embraces the vital element which they omit, vicarious penal satisfaction.

Orthodox View includes All the others.

And note: It is only by predicating the latter, that the moral influences claimed by the inadequate schemes really have place. Says the Socinian, Christ's suffering work is not vicarious, but only exemplary, instructive, and confirmatory. Says the modern "Liberal Christian;" it was intended only for that, and to present a spectacle of infinite tenderness and mercy, to melt the hearts of transgressors. Says the New Haven doctor: It was intended for those ends, and also to make a dramatic display of God's opposition to sin, and of its evils. But we reply: If it was not a vicarious satisfaction for imputed guilt, then it was not consistently either of the others. But if it is vicarious satisfaction for guilt, then it also subserves, and admirably subserves, all these minor ends.

4. Bible proofs of true Theory. We now proceed to the centre of the subject to establish what has been several times anticipated—Christ's proper vicarious suffering for imputed guilt.

1st. From various sets of Bible phrases, exceedingly numerous and varied, of which we only present specimens. Thus:

He is said to have suffered and died "for us," "for the ungodly." Rom. v: 6, 8; and "for our sins." 1 Pet. iii: 18. περὶ ἁμαρτιῶν. Socinians say: "True, He died in a general sense for us, inasmuch as His death is a part of the agency for our rescue: He did die to do us good, not for Himself only." The answer is, that in nearly every case, the context proves it a vicarious dying, for our guilt. Rom. v: "We are justified by His blood." 1 Pet.iii: 18. "The just for the unjust." (ὑπὲρ ἀδίκων.) Then, also, He is said to be a λύτρον ἀντὶ πολλῶν. Matt. xx: 28. This proposition properly signifies substitution. See Matt. ii: 22 for instance.

Christ died for us, &c.

Again: He is said to bear our sins, and equivalent expressions. 1 Pet. ii: 24; Heb. ix: 28; Is. liii: 6. And these words are abundantly defined in our sense by Old Testament usage. (cf.) Num. ix: 13. An evasion is again attempted, by pointing to Matt. viii: 17, and saying that there, this bearing of man's sorrows was not an enduring of them in His person, but a bearing of them away, a removal of them. We reply, the Evangelist refers to Is. liii: 4, not to liii: 6. And Peter says: "He bore our sins in His body on the tree." The language is unique.

Christ bore our sins, &c.

Another unmistakable class of texts, is those in which He

is said to be made sin for us; while we are
made righteousness in Him. See 1 Cor. i :
30 ; 2 Cor. v : 21. A still more indisputable place is where He
is said to be made a curse for us. Gal. iii : 13. The orthodox
meaning, considering the context, is unavoidable.

Christ made Sin for us.

Again : He is said in many places to be our Redeemer—
i. e., Ransomer—and His death, or He, is our
Ransom, Matt. xx : 28 ; 1 Pet. i : 19 ; 1 Tim.
ii : 6 ; 1 Cor. vi : 20. It is vain to reply that God is said to
redeem His people in many places, when the only meaning is,
that He delivered them; and that Moses is called the redeemer
of Israel out of Egypt, who certainly did not do this by a vicarious penalty: Christ's death is a proper ransom, because the
very price is mentioned.

Christ our Ransom.

Christ's work is shown to be properly vicarious, from His
personal innocence. This argument has
been anticipated. We shall, therefore, only
tarry to clear it from the Pelagian evasion,
and to carry it further. Pelagians, seeing that Christ, an innocent being, must have suffered vicarious punishment, if He suffered any punishment, deny that the providential evils of life
are penal at all; and assert that they are only natural, so
that Adam would have borne them in Paradise; the innocent
Christ bore them as a natural matter of course. But what is
the course of nature, except the will of God? Reason says
that if God is good and just, He will only impose suffering
where there is guilt. And this is the scriptural account, " death
by sin."

*2nd. Christ Bore Impu-
ted Guilt because Per-
sonally Innocent.*

Further, Christ suffered far otherwise than is natural to
good men. We do not allude so much to the peculiar severity
of that combination of poverty, malice, treachery, destitution,
slander, reproach and murder, visited on Christ; but to the
sense of spiritual death, the horror, the fear, the pressure of
God's wrath and desertion, and the satanic buffetings let loose
against Him. (Luke xxii : 53 ; Matt. xxvi : 38 ; xxvii : 46). See
how manfully Christ approaches His martyrdom; and how
sadly He sinks under it when it comes! Had He borne nothing more than natural evil, He would have been inferior to
other merely human heroes; and instead of recognizing the
exclamation of Rousseau as just: " Socrates died like a philosopher; but Jesus Christ as a God," we must give the palm of
superior fortitude to the Grecian sage. Christ's crushing agonies must be accounted for by His bearing the wrath of God
for the sins of the world.

Another just argument for Christ's proper vicarious sacrifice is brought from the acknowledged belief
of the whole Pagan world, at the Christian
era especially, concerning the meaning and
intent of their bloody sacrifices. No one doubts that, however

*3d. Christ a Sacrifice.
Pagan Sense of Word.*

mistaken the Pagans are, they have always regarded their bloody sacrifices as proper offerings for guilt. Now, we use this fact in two ways. First. Here is the great testimony of man's universal conscience to the necessity of satisfaction for human guilt. Second. The sacred writers knew that this was what the whole world understood by "sacrifice." Why, then, did they call Jesus Christ, in so many phrases, a sacrifice? Did they wish to deceive?

We find another powerful Bible proof, in the import of the
4th. Jewish Sense.   Levitical sacrifices. This argument is contained in two propositions. First. The theological idea designed to be symbolized in the Levitical sacrifices, was a substitution of a victim, and the vicarious suffering of it in the room of the offerer, for his guilt. (See Levit. xvii : 11 ; Levit. i : 4, *et passim;* xvi : 21). Second. Christ is the antitype, of which all these ceremonies were shadows. (See Jno. i : 29; 1 Cor. xv : 3; 2 Cor. v : 21; Heb. viii : 3; ix : 11–14, &c., &c.) Now, surely the great idea and meaning of the types is not lacking in the antitype! Surely the body is not more unsubstantial than the shadow! This important argument may be seen elaborated with great learning and justice, in the standard works on Theology, as Dick or Ridgley, in works on Atonement, such, especially, as Magee ; and in works on the sacred archeology of the Hebrews, such as Outram, Fairbairn, &c. Hence few words about it.

The value of Christ's work may be said to depend on the
5. Conditions of following circumstances :
Efficacy of Christian   The infinite dignity of His person. (See
Atonement.   Lect. xxxix.

The possession of the nature of His redeemed people.

His freedom from all prior personal obligation to obey and suffer.

His authority over His own life, to lay it down as He pleased.

His voluntariness in undertaking the task.

His explicit acceptance by the Father as our Priest.

[These have been already expounded].

His union with His people.

LECTURE XLIII.

NATURE OF CHRIST'S SACRIFICE. — Continued.

OBJECTIONS to our view of vicarious Atonement are chiefly of Socinian and Pelagian origin. (1) It is objected that we represent the Father in an odious light, as refusing to remit anything till His vindictiveness is satiated, and that to suppose full satisfaction made to the penal demands of law, leaves no grace in the remission of sin. It is not of grace, but of debt.

6. Objections.

The answer to the former part of this objection is suggested in the lecture on Necessity of Atonement. Add, that Christ's atoning work did not dispose the Father to be merciful; but the Father sent Him to make it, because He was eternally disposed to be merciful. The objection is Tritheistic. There is no mercifulness in the Son that was not equally in the Father.

Satisfaction Consistent with Grace in Remission.

To the latter part of the objection the answer is plain: Satisfaction to Law is not incompatible with gracious remission; unless the same person pays the debt who receives the grace. Does the Socinian rejoin: that still, the debt is paid, (we Calvinists say, fully,) and no matter by whom paid, it can not be remitted? The answer is three-fold: (a) There is grace on the Father's part, because He mercifully sent His Son to make the Satisfaction. (b) The distinctions made in the last lecture, in defining Satisfaction, answer the whole cavil. As Satisfaction does not release *ipso facto*, the creditor's grace appears also, in his optional assent.

In fine: The Father's grace on our scheme is infinitely

33*   513

higher than on Socinian or semi-Pelagian. According to them, redemption only opens the door for the sinner to work out his own salvation. He may thank God and Christ somewhat, for being so kind as to open the door ; and himself more for doing the work ! But on our scheme, God, moved *a priori* by His own infinite mercy, gives us Christ, to reconcile vicariously the divine attributes with our pardon ; and gives us in Him, a complete justification, new heart, sanctification, perseverance, resurrection, and eternal life.

The Socinians object, that on our scheme, since Christ fully pays the Father, and He remits nothing, the redeemed have only Christ to thank. The answer to this is contained in the preceding.

(2). Father's Grace to be Praised.

It is a favourite objection of the Socinians, that if Christ is God, we Calvinists represent Him as placating Himself, by His own vicarious offering; which involves the absurdity of supposing Him so angry as to demand penalty, and so merciful as to pay it, all in one breath. The answer is : (a) This difficulty concerning God's wrath only exists, when we view it *anthropopathically*. (b) Such a state of mind, though contradictory in a private person, who had nothing but personal considerations to govern him, is not inconsistent in a public Person. who has government interests to reconcile in pardoning. (c) It is His humanity which suffers the penal satisfaction, His divinity which demands it. (d) The objection is an argument *ab ignorantia*. We do not know all the mystery of the persons in the Trinity, but have good reason to believe that the Son acts economically in the Covenant of Grace, as man's representative, and the Father as that of all three persons.

(3). Does Christ placate Himself?

(4) Socinians object, that since an infinite number of sins are to be atoned, Christ must have paid an infinite penalty ; and therefore you must either make His humanity suffer forever, or else make His proper divinity suffer. If the latter alternative is taken, there are two absurdities. God is impassible. But 2d, if He can suffer at all, one single pang of pain was of infinite value (according to Calvinistic principles), and hence all the rest was superfluous cruelty in God.

The answers are : First. Infinite guilt demands an infinite punishment, but not therefore an everlasting one ; provided the sufferer could suffer an infinite one in a limited time. We do not view the atoning value of Christ's sacrifice, as a quantity, to be divided out by pound's weight, like some material commodity. We do not hold that there must be an arithmetical relation between the quantity of sacrifice, and the number and size of the sins to be satisfied for ; nor do we admit that, had the sins of the whole body of elect believers been greater, the suffer-

How Could Temporal Suffering Satisfy for Infinite Guilt.

ings of the substitute must also have been increased; as when the merchant buys more pounds of the commodity, he must pay more money for his purchase. The compensation made to justice is not commercial, but moral. A piece of money in the hand of a king is worth no more than in the hands of a servant; but the penal sufferings of a king are. One king captive would exchange for many captive soldiers. Hence, Christ paid, not the very total of sufferings we owed, but like sufferings, not of infinite amount, but of infinite dignity.

Christ's sufferings were vast; and the capacity for feeling and enduring conferred on His humanity by the united divinity, enabled Him to bear, in one life-time, great wrath. Second. It is the great doctrine of hypostatical union, according to Heb. ix : 14, which grounds the infinite value of Christ's sufferings. (See that doctrine, Lect. 39th.) As the infinite nature of the God, against whom sin is committed, makes it an infinite evil, although the act of finite creature, so the acts of Christ's human nature in suffering, have infinite value, because of the dignity of His person. As to the latter part of the Socinian objection, the answer is, that one pang, or one drop of blood, would not suffice; because the law demanded a penalty of similar kind to that incurred by man; a bodily death and a spiritual death.

(5) The 5th, and most radical objection is, that imputation is at best a legal fiction; and vicarious punishment intrinsically immoral. They say, God has pronounced it so; (Deut. xxiv : 16; Ezek. xviii : 4, 20,) and the moral sense of civilized commonwealths, banishing laws about hostages and αντιφυχοι. They argue that the immorality of the act is nothing but that of the agent; that desert of punishment is nothing but this intuitive judgment of immorality in the agent, when brought into relation with law; and therefore when penalty is separated from personal immorality, it loses its moral propriety wholly. Hence guilt must be as untransferable as immorality.

Imputation not Unjust.

To the scriptural arguments, we answer: God forbids imputation of capital guilt by human magistrates; or on special occasion, (Ezek. 18th.) foregoes the exercise of it for a time Himself; but that He customarily claims the exercise of it in His own government, See in Josh. vii : 15; Matt. xxiii : 35, The differences between God's government and man's, fully explain this. Human magistrates are themselves under law, in common with those they rule; God above law, and His will is law. They shortsighted; He infinitely wise. They cannot find one who is entitled to offer his life for his neighbor, it is not his property; God's substitute could dispose of His own life. (Jno. x : 18.) They, if the αντιφυχος were found, could not ensure the repentance and reform of the released criminal; without which his enlarge-

God not to be Measured here by Men.

ment is improper; God does. (Acts v: 31.) The human ἀντίψυχος, having sacrificed his life, could never resume it, and his loss to the community would be irreparable; so that the transaction would give to society an injurious member, at the expense of taking from it a righteous and useful one. But Christ resumes the life laid down, and His useful position in the universe. For such reasons as these, it may be improper to have substitutes for capital guilt in man's government; and yet very proper in God's.

This, of course, implies that it is only made with the free consent of the substitute. This Christ gave.

To the rational argument I reply:

If the objection be True, then Pardon is Immoral. (a.) It proves too much, viz: that there can be no remission in God's government at all. For, when pardon is asserted on the general plan of the Socinian and rationalist, the elements of guilt and immorality are distinguished and separated. i. e., the guilt is alienated from the sinning agent, while the bad character remains his, so far as the pardoning act is concerned. Is not his own compunction the same as before? Hence his repentance; and the human reason apprehends that no state of soul is so appropriate to the pardoned man, as one that abounds in the heartfelt confessions of his ill desert. But we have proved irrefragably that God's rectoral justice includes the disposition to give appropriate penalty to sin, as truly, and in the same way, as His disposition to bestow appropriate reward on obedience. The two are correlative. If the one sort of legal sanction is not righteously separable from the personal attribute of the agent, even with his own consent, then the other sort (the penal) is not. But when God treats the holy Surety as guilty, (not immoral,) He makes the same separation of elements, which is made, if He should, (without vicarious satisfaction, as the rationalists say He does,) treat the guilty sinner as guiltless (not holy) by remitting a penalty of which he continues to confess himself personally deserving, (as God knows very well he is.)

(b.) If imputation of guilt (without personal immorality) to Christ is unjust, even with His own consent; then *a fortiori*, laying of sufferings upon Him without even imputed guilt, is still more unjust. This for the Socinian.

(c.) Penal Consequences Transferred by Providence and Society. God, in His providential rule over mankind, often makes this separation between the personal bad character and penal consequences; for the punishments incurred in the course of nature by vice, descend to posterity; while so far is He from imputing the personal unworthiness always along with the penalty, the patient and holy enduring of it is counted by Him an excellent virtue. So, too, the whole law of sympathy (Rom. xii: 15; Gal. vi: 2,) makes the sympathizer suffer

the penalty along with the sufferer, and yet, so far from treating
him as personally defiled with him, regards it as an excellent
virtue.

(d.) Man's own practical judgment habitually makes the
separation of elements, which the rationalistic objection
declares impossible, and we feel that the separation is right.
Thus, when the voluntary security relieves the bankrupt debtor,
it is only at the cost of what is to him a true mulct (precisely the
penalty of the debtor's prodigality), and we feel the security is
rightly made to pay ; but so far is this from being due to his
personal demerit in the transaction, we feel that he is acting gen-
erously and nobly.   So, we feel that we justly insist on maintaining certain social disabilities against children, incurred by
parents' crimes, at the very time we approve the former, as personally, deserving people.

Thus, by indirect refutation, we prove that the objection of
the rationalist to imputation, and the analysis on which he
founds it, cannot be true, whether we are able to specify its
error or not.

But I think we can specify it. It is in ignoring the broad distinction which divines make between poten-
(e.)   Potential and   tial and actual guilt—i. e., between the qual-
Actual Guilt.   ity of ill-desert, and the obligation to punish-
met.   Consider the objector's process (fairly stated above), and
it will be seen that it is this :   Because the judgment we have of
the ill-desert of the bad agent is nothing else than the judgment
we had of his badness, viewed in its relation to law, therefore
his guilt (obligation to penalty) is as personal and inseparable to
him, as his quality of badness.   This is sophism.   The true
analysis is this.

The badness of the act is nothing else than the badness of
the agent; and is his personal quality or attribute.   The judgment of ill-desert arises immediately therefrom, when his quality
is viewed in relation to law.   True.   But what is law?   Religion's law is nothing else than God's will, which is its source and
measure.   So that, as our judgment of the attribute of badness
takes the form of a judgment of ill-desert, it passes into a judgment of relation—i. e., between two persons, the sinner and God.
So that even potential guilt is rather a relation than an attribute.   But when we pass to actual guilt (which is merely obligation to penalty, a moral obligation, as I grant, and not
one of force only), this is not the sinner's attribute at all ; but
purely a relation.   And although its rise was mediated by the
personal attribute of badness, expressed in the guilty acts, it is
not a relation of that attribute, abstracted, to something else,
but of his person to the will of God—i. e., to God willing.   And
in this obligation to penalty, this sovereign will is obligator.   It
is God's sovereignty, which, though moral, is absolute, that
imposes it.   Now, without teaching that God's will is the sole

source of moral distinctions, or retracting anything that I have said against that error, I remark, that far too little weight is attached, in the objection, to this great fact that this obligation to penalty, which we denominate guilt, is one imposed by the sovereign and omnipotent will of our Maker and Proprietor. Let the mind take in this fact properly, and it will appear how rash is the assertion that even He may not, without immorality, separate from the person qualified by the attribute of badness, this relation to penalty, which His own holy will imposes, even though the party to whom the guilt is transferred freely assents; and the divine ends in the transaction are those of holiness.

But to return: It appears that the agent's badness is his attribute, his guilt is his relation; and that, a relation to another Person and will. The two elements belong to different categories in logic! But did any sound mind ever admit this as a universal and necessary law of logic (which it must be, to make the objection conclusive): that relations are as untransferable as attributes; as inseparable from the things related? Is it so in geometry? But it is better to show, in analogous cases, that it is not so in metaphysics; e. g., A. expresses, by acts of beneficence towards me, his quality of benevolence, which institutes between us, as persons, the relation of an obligation to gratitude from me to him. A. is succeeded by his son; and this obligation, in some degree, transfers itself and attaches itself to that son, irrespective of, and in advance of, his exhibiting the quality of benevolence for me, in his own personal acts. I present another illustration which is also an argument, because it presents an exact analogy—the obligation to recompense—resting on me by reason of A's benefactions to me. I say we have here a true, complete analogy; because this title to recompense from the object of beneficent acts is a fair counterpart to the obligation to bear a penalty from the ruler, who is the object (or injured party) of the bad act. Now, I ask—e, g.: In 2 Sam. xix; 31–38, was it incompetent for Barzillai, the Gileadite, to ask the transfer of King David's obligation to recompense to his son Chimham, on the ground of his own loyalty? Did not David's conscience recognize his moral right to make the transfer? But it is made irrespective of the transfer of Barzillai's attribute of loyalty to his son, which, indeed, was out of the question. Here, then, is the very separation which I claim, as made, in the case of imputation, between the sinner's personal attribute (badness), and his personal relation to God's sovereign will, arising upon his badness (guilt).

This discussion is of fundamental importance also in the doctrines of original sin and justification.

The question of the "extent of the atonement," as it has
7. The Design of been awkwardly called, is one of the most
God in Christ's difficult in the whole range of Calvinistic
Death: Different
Theories. Theology. That man who should profess to

see no force in the objections to our views, would only betray the shallowness of his mind and knowledge. There are three grades of opinion on this subject.

The theory of the Semi-Pelagian denies any proper impu-
1st. Semi-Pelagian. Refuted. tation of any one's sins to Christ, makes His suffering a mere general exhibition of God's wrath against sin, having no relation to one person's sin in particular; and of course it consistently makes the atonement perfectly general and indefinite.

The refutation of this view is found in the facts already argued; that there was a substitution, a vicarious suffering of penalty, and a purchasing of the gracious gifts for the redeemed which make up the application of redemption.

The Wesleyan view is, that there was a substitution and
2nd. Wesleyan. an imputation; and that Christ provided a penal satisfaction for every individual of the human race, making His sins remissible, provided he believes in Christ; and that He also purchased for every man the remission of original sin, and the gift of common grace, which confers a self-determing power of will, and enables any one to believe and repent, provided he chooses to use the free-will thus graciously repaired aright; God's purpose of election being conditioned on His foresight of how each sinner would improve it.

The fatal objections to this scheme are, particularly, that it is utterly overthrown by unconditional election, which we have proved, and that the Scriptures and experience both contradict this common grace. But of this, more hereafter.

The view of the Hypothetical Universalists was professedly
3d. Amyraut's. Calvinistic, and was doubtless, and is, sincerely held in substance by many honest and intelligent Calvinists, (e. g., Richard Baxter, R. Hall, Bellamy) although Turrettin and Dr. Hodge condemn it as little better than Arminianism in disguise. It presents the divine plan in redemption thus: God decreed from eternity, to create the human race, to permit the fall; then in His infinite compassion, to send Christ to atone for every human being's sins, (conditioned on his believing); but also foreseeing that all, in consequence of total depravity and the bondage of their will, would inevitably reject this mercy if left to themselves, He selected out of the whole a definite number of elect, to whom He also gave, in His sovereign love, grace to "make them willing in the day of His power." The non-elect, never enjoying this persuasive grace, infallibly choose to reject the provided atonement; and so, as its application is suspended on faith, they fail to receive the benefit of it, and perish.

This theory, if amended so as to say that God sent His
Refuted. Son to provide a vicarious satisfaction for the sin of all whom His Providence intended to

place under the Gospel offers, would be liable to less objection than the others. But several objections lie against it. In the first place, the advantage proposed to be gained by it appears illusory. It was hoped that this view would meet the cavils urged by Arminians against the seeming lack of candour in offering Christ's sacrifice for reconciliation, to those for whom God never designed it. But I submit that this cavil is not in the least dissolved by saying, that God designed Christ's sacrifice to provide satisfaction for every non-elect man's guilt, which would avail for his atonement only on condition of his true faith, while the omniscience of God showed him that this sinner would certainly refuse this faith, in consequence of his total depravity, and God's purpose was distinctly formed not to remove that depravity by His effectual grace. To say that God purposed, even conditionally, the reconciliation of that sinner by Christ's sacrifice, while also distinctly proposing to do nothing effectual to bring about the fulfillment of the condition He knew the man would surely refuse, is contradictory. It is hard to see how, on this scheme, the sacrifice is related more beneficially to the non-elect sinner, than on the strict Calvinist's plan. Second : The statement of Amyraut involves the same vice of arrangement pointed out in the supralapsarian and sublapsarian plans : it tends towards assigning a sequence to the parts of the decree, as it subsists in God's mind. He thinks and purposes it as one cotemporaneous, mutually connected whole. The student is referred to the remarks already made upon this error. Third, and chiefly, Armyraut has to represent the graces which work effectual calling, while free and unmerited, indeed, as yet the free gift of the Father's electing love, irrespective of Christ's purchase, (for that is represented as made in common for all) and not mediated to the elect sinner through Christ's sacrifice. Since Christ's intercession is expressly grounded in His sacrifice, we shall have to conceive of the benefit of effectual calling as also not mediated to the sinner by Christ's intercession. But this is all contrary to Scripture ; which represents Christ as the channel, through which all saving benefits come, and the very graces which fulfil the instrumental conditions of salvation as a part of His purchase for His people. See, for instance, Acts v : 31 ; Rom, viii : 32; Eph. i : 3, 4 ; 2 Tim. i : 9; Titus. ii : 14; 2 Pet. i : 2, 3.

The view of the strict Calvinist is as follows: God decreed to create the race, to permit the fall, 4. Strict Calvinistic. and then, in His infinite compassion, He elected out of the fallen an innumerable multitude, chosen in Christ, to be delivered from this ruin ; and for them Christ was sent, to make full penal satisfaction for their unrighteousness, and purchase for them all graces of effectual calling and spiritual life and bodily resurrection, which make up a complete redemption, by His righteousness and intercession founded thereon.

It represents the Atonement as limited only by the secret intention of God as to its application, and not in its own sufficiency for, or adaptation to all. Symmetrical theory, but attended with some difficulties.

In proof of the general correctness of this theory of the extent of the Atonement, we should attach but partial force to some of the arguments advanced by Symington and others, or even by Turrettin. e. g. That Christ says, He died " for His sheep," for " His Church," for " His friends," &c., is not of itself conclusive. The proof of a proposition does not disprove its converse. All the force which we could properly attach to this class of passages is the probability arising from the frequent and emphatic repetition of this affirmative statement as to a definite object. Nor would we attach any force to the argument, that if Christ made penal satisfaction for the sins of all, justice would forbid any to be punished. To urge this argument surrenders virtually the very ground on which the first Socinian objection was refuted, and is incompatible with the facts that God chastises justified believers, and holds elect unbelievers subject to wrath till they believe. Christ's satisfaction is not a pecuniary equivalent; but only such a one as enables the Father, consistently with His attributes, to pardon, if in His mercy He sees fit. The whole avails of the satisfaction to a given man is suspended on His belief. There would be no injustice to the man, if he remaining an unbeliever, his guilt were punished twice over, first in his Saviour, and then in Him. See Hodge on Atonement, page 369.

Inconclusive Proofs.

But the irrefragable grounds on which we prove that the redemption is particular are these:

Real Proofs of Calvinistic Theory.

(a) From the doctrines of unconditional election, and the Covenant of Redemption. (Argument is one, for Covenant of Redemption is but one aspect of election). The Scriptures tell us that those who are to be saved in Christ are a number definitely elected and given to Him from eternity, to be redeemed by His mediation. How can anything be plainer from this than that there was a purpose in God's atonement, as to them, other than that it had as to the rest of mankind? See Scriptures.

From Decree.

(b) The immutability of God's purposes. (Is. xlvi : 10; 2 Tim. ii : 19). If God ever intended to save any soul in Christ, [and He has a definite intention to save or not to save towards every soul], that soul will certainly be saved. Jno. x : 27, 28; vi : 37–40. Hence, all whom God ever intended to save in Christ will be saved. But some souls will never be saved; therefore some souls God never intended to be saved by Christ's atonement. The strength of this argument can scarcely be overrated. Here it is seen that a limit as to the intention of the

From God's Immutability and Power.

atonement must be asserted to rescue God's power, purpose and wisdom.

(c) The same fact is proved by this, that Christ's intercession is limited. (See Jno. xvii : 9, 20). We know that Christ's intercession is always prevalent. (Rom. viii : 34 ; Jno. xi : 42). If He interceded for all, all would be saved. But all will not be saved. Hence there are some for whom He does not plead the merit of His atonement. But He is the " same yesterday, to-day and forever." Hence there were some for whom, when He made atonement, He did not intend to plead it.

Christ's Intercession Limited.

(d) Some sinners (i. e., elect), receive from God gifts of conviction, regeneration, faith, persuading and enabling them to embrace Christ, and thus make His atonement effectual to themselves ; while other sinners do not. But these graces are a part of the purchased redemption,and bestowed through Christ. Hence His redemption was intended to affect some as it did not others. (See above).

From Facts.

(e) Experience proves the same. A large part of the human race were already in hell before the atonement was made. Another large part never hear of it. But "faith cometh by hearing." (Rom. x), and faith is the condition of its application. Since their condition is determined intentionally by God's providence, it could not be His intention that the atonement should avail for them equally with those who hear and believe. This view is destructive, particularly, of the Arminian scheme.

(f) " Greater love hath no man than this, that a man lay down his life for his friends." But the greater includes the less ; whence it follows, that if God the Father and Christ cherished for a given soul the definite electing love which was strong enough to pay for him the sacrifice of Calvary, it is not credible that this love would then refuse the less costly gifts of effectual calling and sustaining grace. This is the very argument of Rom. v : 10, and viii : 31–end. This inference would not be conclusive, if drawn merely from the benevolence of God's nature, sometimes called in Scripture, " his love ; " but in every case of his definite electing love, it is demonstrative.

From Greatness of Christ's Love.

Hence, it is absolutely impossible for us to retain the dogma, that Christ, in design, died equally for all. We are compelled to hold that He died for Peter and Paul in some sense in which He did not for Judas. No consistent mind can hold the Calvinistic creed, as to man's total depravity towards God, his inability of will, God's decree, God's immutable attributes of sovereignty and omnipotence over free agents, omniscience and wisdom, and stop short of this conclusion. So much every intelligent opponent admits, and in disputing particular redemption to this extent, at least, he always attacks these connected truths as falling along with the other.

In a word, Christ's work for the elect does not merely put them in a salvable state; but purchases for them a complete and assured salvation. To him who knows the depravity and bondage of his own heart, any less redemption than this would bring no comfort.

But the difficulties which beset the subject are great; and unless you differ from me, you will feel that the manner in which they are dealt with by some Calvinistic writers, is unsatisfactory. The objections are of two classes: From the universal offer of atonement through Christ, and from Scripture. The fact that God makes this offer literally universal, cannot be doubted, nor must we venture to insinuate that He is not sincere therein. (Matt. xxviii: 19; Mark xvi: 15, 16). The usual answer given by Calvinists of the rigid school to this objection is, that God may sincerely offer this salvation to every creature, because, although not designed for all, it is in its nature sufficient for, and adapted to all. They say that since Christ's sacrifice is of infinite value, and as adequate for covering all the sins of every sinner in the universe, as of one; and since Christ bears the common nature of all sinners, and God's revealed, and not His secret, decretive, will is the proper rule of man's conduct, this satisfaction may be candidly offered to all. Arminians rejoin, that this implies an adoption of their conception of the nature of the atonement, as a general satisfaction for human guilt as a mass and whole; that the punishment of gospel-hardened sinners for unbelief (which we admit will occur), would be unjust on our scheme, since by it they would be punished for not believing what would not be true, if they had believed it; and that since, on our scheme the believing of a non-elect sinner is not naturally, but only morally impossible, it is a supposable case for argument's sake, and this case supposed, God could not be sincere, unless such a sinner should be saved in Christ, supposing he came. The honest mind will feel these objections to be attended with real difficulty. Thus, in defining the nature of Christ vicarious work, Calvinists assert a proper substitution and imputation of individuals' guilt. On the strict view, the sins of the non-elect were never imputed to Christ. The fact, then, that an infinite satisfaction was made for imputed guilt, does not seem to be a sufficient ground for offering the benefits thereof to those whose sins were never imputed.

The student should understand fully the ingenious pertinacity, with which this line of objection is urged, and re-inforced; from the command which makes it all sinners' duty to believe on Christ for their own salvation; from the alleged impossibility of their reaching any appropriating faith by the Calvin-

But the Subject Difficult. (a) From Universal Offer of Atonement.

istic view, and from the various warnings of Scripture, which clearly contemplate the possible destruction of one for whom Christ died. Our opponents proceed thus. God commands every man to believe on Christ. But since only an appropriating faith saves, and since God of course calls for a saving faith, and not the faith of Devils: God commands every man to appropriate Christ by his faith. But the man for whom Christ did not die has no right to appropriate Him: it would be erroneous presumption, and not faith. Again: both Romanists and Arminians object, that the strict Calvinistic scheme would make it necessary, for a man's mind to pass through and accept a paralogism, in order to believe unto salvation. This point may be found, stated with the utmost adroitness, in the works of Bellamy, (*loco citato*). He argues: if I know that Christ died only for the elect, then I must know whether I am elect, in order to be sure that He died for me. But God's election is secret, and it is mere fanaticism to pretend that I know my own election by direct revelation. My name is nowhere set down specifically in the Bible. That book directs me to find out my election *a posteriori*, by finding in my own graces the results of the secret decree towards me. Thus I am shut up to this sophism, in order to obey God's command to believe: I must assume, in advance of proof, that I am elected, in order to attain through faith the Christian traits, by which alone I can infer that I am elected. The third argument is that founded on the warnings against apostasy. In Rom. xiv : 15, for instance, the Apostle cautions strong Christians "not to destroy, with their meat, those for whom Christ died." Hebrews x : 29, the apostate " counts the blood of the covenant wherewith he was sanctified, an unholy thing." 2 Peter ii : 1, heretics " even deny the Lord that bought them." Here, it is urged, Calvinists must either hold that some of the elect perish, or that Christ died for others than the elect.

The other class of objections is from the Scriptures; e. g.: [b] From Texts Those which speak of Christ as having com-Teaching a Seeming passion for, or dying for, " the whole world," Universality. " all," " all men," " every man," &c. Jno. i : 29 ; Jno. iii : 16 ; iv : 42 ; vi : 51 ; 2 Cor. v : 19 ; 1 Jno. ii : 1, 2 ; Jno. xii : 32 ; 1 Cor. xv : 22 ; 2 Cor. v : 14, 15 ; 1 Tim. ii : 6 ; 1 Tim. iv : 10 ; Heb. ii : 9, &c. The usual explanation, offered by the strict Calvinists, of these texts is this : that terms seemingly universal often have to be limited to a universality within certain bounds by the context, as in Matt. iii : 5 ; that in New Testament times, especially when the gospel was receiving its grand extension from one little nation to all nations, it is reasonable to expect that strong affirmatives would be used as to its extent, which yet should be strained to mean nothing more than this : that persons of every nation in the world were given to Christ. Hence, " the world," " all the world," should be taken to mean no more than people of every nation in the world, without distinction, &c. There is a certain amount of justice in these views; and many of these passages, as 1 Cor. xv : 22 ; Jno. i : 29, and xii : 32, may be adequately explained by them. The explanation is also greatly strengthened by this fact, too little pressed by Calvinists, that ultimately, the vast majority of the whole mass of humanity, including all generations, will be actually redeemed by Christ. There is to be a time, blessed be God, when literally all the then world will be saved by Christ, when the world will be finally, completely, and wholly lifted by Christ out of the gulf, and sink no more. So that there is a sense, most legitimate, in which Christ is the prospective Saviour of the world.

But there are others of these passages, to which I think, the candid mind will admit, this sort of explanation is inapplicable. In Jno. iii ; 16, make "the world" which Christ loved, to mean "the elect world ;" and we reach the absurdity, that some of the elect may not believe, and perish. In 2 Cor. v : 15, if we make the all for whom Christ died, mean only the all who live unto Him—i. e., the elect—it would seem to be implied that of those elect for whom Christ died, only a part will live to Christ. In 1 Jno. ii : 2, it is at least doubtful whether the express phrase, "whole world," can be restrained to the world of elect as including other than Jews. For it is indisputable, that the Apostle extends the propitiation of Christ beyond those whom he speaks of as "we," in verse first. The interpretation described obviously proceeds on the assumption that these are only Jewish believers. Can this be substantiated ? Is this catholic epistle addressed only to Jews ? This is more than doubtful. It would seem then, that the Apostle's scope is, to console and encourage sinning believers with the thought, that since Christ made expiation for every man, there is no danger that He will not be found a propitiation for them who, having already believed, now sincerely turn to him from recent sins.

Having made these candid admissions, I now return to test

Answers.

the opposing points above recited. I take them in reversed order. The language of Peter, and that of Hebrews x : 29, may receive an entirely adequate solution, without teaching that Christ actually "bought," or "sanctified" any apostate, by saying that the Apostles speak there "ad hominem." The crime of the apostate is justly enhanced by the fact, that the Christ, whose truth he is now outraging, is claimed by him as gracious Redeemer. It is always fair to hold a man to the results of his own assertions. This heretic says Christ has laid him under this vast debt of gratitude : so much the worse then, that he should injure his asserted benefactor. But there is another view : The addressing of hypothetical warnings of apostasy or destruction to believers is wholly compatible with the efficacy of Christ's work, and the immutability of God's counsel for them. For that counsel is executed in them, by moral and rational means, among which the force of truth holds the prime place. And among these truths, the fact that if they are not watchful and obedient, professed believers may fall, is most reasonably calculated to produce watchfulness. But naturally speaking, they may fall; for the impossibility of destroying the elect is only moral, proceeding from the secret purpose of God. This important view will be farther illustrated and defended when we argue the perseverance of the saints: where it will be found to have a similar application.

The second and first objections really receive the same solution. That the process described by Dr. Bellamy is a paralogism, we freely admit. But Calvinists do not consider it as a fair statement of the mode in which the mind of a believer moves. Turrettin (Loc. xiv :   Qu. 14, § 45, &c.) has given an exhaustive analysis of this difficulty, as well as of its kindred one. He had distinguished the reflex, from the direct actings of faith. He now reminds the objector, that the assurance of our own individual interest in God's purposes of mercy is reached only *a posteriori*, and by this reflex element of faith. The reflex element cannot logically arise, until the direct has scriptural place in the soul. What then is the objective proposition, on which every sinner is commanded to believe ?   It is not, that "Christ designed His death expressly for me." But it is, "whosoever believeth shall be saved." This warrant is both general and specific enough to authorize any man to venture on Christ. The very act of venturing on Him brings that soul within the whosoever. It is only voluntary unbelief which can ground an exclusion of any man from that invitation, so that it is impossible that any man, who wishes to come to Christ, can be embarrassed by any lack of warrant to come. But now, the soul, having believingly seen the warrant, "whosoever believeth shall be saved," and becoming conscious of its own hearty faith, draws, by a reflex act, the legitimate deduction ; "Since I believe, I am saved." Unless he has first trusted in the general invitation, we deny that he has any right, or that God makes it his duty, to draw that inference. Hence, we deny that God commands the sinner to believe himself elected, or to believe himself saved, by the primary act of his faith. The Arminian asks: Does not God, in requiring him to believe, require him to exercise all the parts of a saving faith? I reply: He does ; but not out of their proper order. He requires the lost sinner first to accept the general warrant, "whosoever will," in order that he may, thereby, proceed to the deduction; "Since I have accepted it I am saved." Thus it appears, that in order for the sinner to see his warrant for coming to Christ, it is not necessary for him presumptuously to assume his own election; but after he embraces Christ, he learns his election, in the scriptural way pointed out by Peter, from his calling.

This seems, then, to be the candid conclusion: that there is no pasaage in the Bible which asserts an intention to apply redemption to any others than the elect, on the part of God and Christ; but that there are passages which imply that Christ died for all sinners in some sense, as Dr. Ch. Hodge has so expressly admitted. Certainly the expiation made by Christ is so related to all, irrespective of election, that God can sincerely invite all to enjoy its benefits, that every soul in the world who desires salvation is warranted to appropriate it; and that even a Judas, had he come in earnest, would not have been cast out.

Conclusion.

But the arguments which we adduced on the affirmative side of the question demonstrate that Christ's redeeming work was limited in intention to the elect. The Arminian dogma that He did the same redeeming work in every respect for all, is preposterous and unscriptural. But at the same time, if the Calvinistic scheme be strained as high as some are inclined, a certain amount of justice will be found against them in the Arminian objections. Therefore, *In mediis tutissime ibis.* The well known Calvinistic formula, that "Christ died sufficiently for all, efficaciously for the Elect," must be taken in a sense consistent with all the passages of Scripture which are cited above.

8. The relation of limited redemption to the Universal call.

I will endeavor to contribute what I can to the adjustment of this intricate subject in the form of a series of remarks.

The difficulty which besets this solemn subject is no doubt in part insuperable for finite minds. Indeed, it is the same difficulty which besets the relation of God's election to man's free agency, (and not a new one), re-appearing in a new phase; for redemption is limited precisely by the decree, and by nothing else. We shall approximate a solution as nearly as is perhaps practicable for man, by considering the same truths to which we resort in the seeming paradox arrising from election. There are in the Bible two classes of truths; those which are the practical rule of exertion for man in his own free agency; and those which are the recondite and non-practical explanations of God's action towards us; e. g., in Jno. v : 40 is the one; in Jno. vi : 44 is the other. In Jno. 3: 36 is one; in 2 Thess. ii : 13 is the other. In Rev. xxii : 17 is one; in Rom. ix : 16 is the other. These classes of truths, when drawn face to face, often seem paradoxical; but when we remember that God's sovereignty is no revealed rule for our action, and that our inability to do our duty without sovereign grace arises only from our voluntary depravity, we see that there is no real collision.

(1.) The Difficulty the Same as in the Decree, to be Resolved in the Same Way.

Now Christ is a true substitute. His sufferings were penal

(2). Christ's Satis- and vicarious, and made a true satisfaction
faction not Commer- for all those who actually embrace them by
cial.   faith.   But the conception charged on us
seems to be, as though Christ's expiation were a web of the
garment of righteousness, to be cut into definite pieces, and distributed out, so much to each person of the elect; whence, of
course, it must have a definite aggregate length, and had God
seen fit to add any to the number of elect, He must have had an
additional extent of web woven. This is all incorrect. Satisfaction
was Christ's indivisible act, and inseparable vicarious merit,
infinite in moral value, the whole in its unity and completeness,
imputed to every believing elect man, without numerical division, substraction or exhaustion.   Had there been but one elect
man, his vicarious satisfaction had been just what it is in its
essential nature. Had God elected all sinners, there would have
been no necessity to make Christ's atoning sufferings essentially
different.   Remember, the limitation is precisely in the decree,
and no where else.   It seems plain that the vagueness and
ambiguity of the modern term "atonement," has very much
complicated the debate.   This word, not classical in the
Reformed theology, is used sometimes for satisfaction for guilt,
sometimes for the reconciliation ensuing thereon; until men on
both sides of the debate have forgotten the distinction.   The
one is cause; the other effect.   The only NewTestament sense
the word atonement has is that of *καταλλαγή*, reconciliation.   But
expiation is another idea. *Καταλλαγή* is personal. *Εξιλασμος* is
impersonal.   *Καταλλαγή* is multiplied, being repeated as often as
a sinner comes to the expiatory blood: *εξιλασμος* is single.
unique, complete; and, in itself considered, has no more relation to one man's sins than another.   As it is applied in effectual calling, it becomes personal, and receives a limitation.   But
in itself, limitation is irrelevant to it.   Hence, when men use the
word atonement, as they so often do, in the sense of expiation,
the phrases, "limited atonement," "particular atonement," have
no meaning.   Redemption is limited, i. e., to true believers, and
is particular.   Expiation is not limited.

There is no safer clue for the student through this per-
plexed subject, than to take this proposition;
(3). God's Design which, to every Cavanist, is nearly as indis-
and Result Exactly
Co-extensive.   putable as a truism; Christ's design in His
vicarious work was to effectuate exactly
what it does effectuate, and all that it effectuates, in its subsequent proclamation. This is but saying that Christ's purpose
is unchangeable and omnipotent. Now, what does it actually
effectuate?   "We know only in part;" but so much is certain:

(a.)   The purchase of the full and assured redemption of
all the elect, or of all believers.

(b.)   A reprieve of doom for every sinner of Adam's race
who does not die at his birth. (For these we believe it has pur-

chased heaven).   And this reprieve gains for all, many substantial, though temporal benefits, such as unbelievers, of all men, will be the last to account no benefits.   Among these are postponement of death and perdition, secular well-being, and the bounties of life.

(c.) A manifestation of God's mercy to many of the non-elect, to all those, namely, who live under the Gospel, in sincere offers of a salvation on terms of faith.   And a sincere offer is a real and not a delusive benefaction; because it is only the recipient's contumacy which disappoints it.

(d.) A justly enhanced condemnation of those who reject the Gospel, and thereby a clearer display of God's righteousness and reasonableness in condemning, to all the worlds.

(e.) A disclosure of the infinite tenderness and glory of God's compassion, with purity, truth and justice, to all rational creatures.

Had there been no mediation of Christ, we have not a particle of reason to suppose that the doom of our sinning race would have been delayed one hour longer than that of the fallen angels.   Hence, it follows, that it is Christ who procures for non-elect sinners all that they temporarily enjoy, which is more than their personal deserts, including the sincere offer of mercy.   In view of this fact, the scorn which Dr. William Cunningham heaps on the distinction of a special, and general design in Christ's satisfaction, is thoroughly short-sighted.   All wise beings (unless God be the exception), at times frame their plans so as to secure a combination of results from the same means.   This is the very way they display their ability and wisdom.   Why should God be supposed incapable of this wise and fruitful acting ? I repeat ; the design of Christ's sacrifice must have been to effectuate just what it does effectuate.   And we see, that, along with the actual redemption of the elect, it works out several other subordinate ends.   There is then a sense, in which Christ " died for " all those ends, and for the persons affected by them.

The manner in which a volition which dates from eternity, subsists in the Infinite mind, is doubt-(4). God's Voli-less, in many respects, inscrutable to us. But tions Arise out of a Complex of Motive. since God has told us that we are made in His image, we may safely follow the Scriptural representations, which describe God's volitions as having their rational relation to subjective motive ; somewhat as in man, when he wills aright.   For, a motiveless volition cannot but appear to us as devoid both of character and of wisdom.   We add, that while God " has no parts nor passions," He has told us that He has active principles, which, while free from all agitation, ebb and flow, and mutation, are related in their superior measure to man's rational affections.   These active principles in God, or passionless affections, are all absolutely holy and

34*

good. Last: God's will is also regulated by infinite wisdom. Now, in man, every rational volition is prompted by a motive, which is in every case, complex to this degree, at least that it involves some active appetency of the will and some prevalent judgment of the intelligence. And every wise volition is the result of virtual or formal deliberation, in which one element of motive is weighed in relation to another, and the elements which appear superior in the judgment of the intelligence, preponderate and regulate the volition. Hence, the wise man's volition is often far from being the expression of every conception and affection present in his consciousness at the time; but it is often reached by holding one of these elements of possible motive in check, at the dictate of a more controlling one. For instance a philanthropic man meets a distressed and destitute person. The good man is distinctly conscious in himself of a movement of sympathy tending towards a volition to give the sufferer money. But he remembers that he has expressly promised all the money now in his possession, to be paid this very day to a just creditor. The good man bethinks himself, that he "ought to be just before he is generous," and conscience and wisdom counterpoise the impulse of sympathy; so that it does not form the deliberate volition to give alms. But the sympathy exists, and it is not inconsistent to give other expression to it. We must not ascribe to that God whose omniscience is, from eternity, one infinite, all-embracing intuition, and whose volition is as eternal as His being, any expenditure of time in any process of deliberation, nor any temporary hesitancy or uncertainty, nor any agitating struggle of feeling against feeling. But there must be a *residuum* of meaning in the Scripture representations of His affections, after we have guarded ourselves duly against the anthropopathic forms of their expression. Hence, we ought to believe, that in some ineffable way, God's volitions, seeing they are supremely wise, and profound, and right, do have that relation to all His subjective motives, digested by wisdom and holiness into the consistent combination, the finite counterpart of which constitutes the rightness and wisdom of human volitions. I claim, while exercising the diffidence proper to so sacred a matter, that this conclusion bears us out at least so far: That, as in a wise man, so much more in a wise God, His volition, or express purpose, is the result of a digest, not of one, but of all the principles and considerations bearing on the case. Hence it follows, that there may be in God an active principle felt by Him, and yet not expressed in His executive volition in a given case, because counterpoised by other elements of motive, which His holy omniscence judges ought to be prevalent. Now, I urge the practical question: Why may not God consistently give some other expression to this active principle, really and sincerely felt towards the object, though His sovereign wisdom judges it not proper to express it in volition? To return to the instance from which we set out: I assert that it is entirely natural and reasonable for the benevolent man to say to the destitute person: "I am sorry for you, though I give you no alms." The ready objection will be: "that my parallel does not hold, because the kind man is not omnipotent, while God is. God could not consistently speak thus, while withholding alms, because he could create the additional money at will." This is more ready than solid. It assumes that God's omniscience cannot see any ground, save the lack of physical ability or power, why it may not be best to refrain from creating the additional money. Let the student search and see; he will find that this preposterous and presumptuous assumption is the implied premise of the objection. In fact, my parallel is a fair one in the main point. This benevolent man is not prevented from giving the alms, by any physical compulsion. If he diverts a part of the money in hand from the creditor, to the destitute man, the creditor will visit no penalty on him. He simply feels bound by his conscience. That is, the superior principles of reason and morality are regulative of his action, counterpoising the amiable but less imperative principle of sympathy, in this case. Yet the verbal expression of sympathy in this case may be natural, sincere, and proper. God is not restrained by lack of physical omnipotence from creating on the spot the additional money for the alms; but He may be actually restrained by some consideration known to His omniscience, which shows that it is not on the whole best to resort to the expedient of creating the money for the alms, and that rational consideration may be just as decisive in an all-wise mind, and properly as decisive, as a conscious impotency to create money in a man's.

This view is so important here, and will be found so valuable in another place, that I beg leave to give it farther illustration. It is related that the great Washington, when he signed the death-warrant of the amiable but misguided Andre, declared his profound grief and sympathy. Let us suppose a captious invader present, and criticising Washington's declaration thus: "You are by law of the rebel congress, commander-in-chief. You have absolute power here. If you felt any of the generous sorrow you pretend, you would have thrown that pen into the fire, instead of using it to write the fatal words. The fact you do the latter proves that you have not a shade of sympathy, and those declarations are sheer hypocrisy." It is easy to see how impudent and absurd this charge would be. Physically, Washington had full license, and muscular power, to throw the pen into the fire. But he was rationally restrained from doing so, by motives of righteousness and patriotism, which were properly as decisive as any physical cause. Now, will the objector still urge, that with God it would have been different,

The Motive not Executed may be Expressed.

in this case ; because His omnipotence might have enabled Him
to overrule, in all souls, British and Americans, all inconvenient results that could flow from the impunity of a spy caught
in flagrante delicto ; and that so, God could not give any
expression to the infinite benevolence of His nature, and yet
sign the death-warrant, without hypocrisy ? The audacity of
this sophism is little less than the other. How obvious is the
reply : That as in the one case, though Washington was in possession of the muscular ability, and also of an absolute license,
to burn the death-warrant, if he chose ; and yet his wisdom and
virtue showed him decisive motives which rationally restrained
him from it ; so God may have full sovereignty and omnipotence to change the heart of the sinner whose ruin He compas-
sionates, and yet be rationally restrained from doing it, by
some decisive motives seen in His omniscience. What is it,
but logical arrogance run mad, for a puny creature to assume
to say, that the infinite intelligence of God may not see, amidst
the innumerable affairs and relations of a universal government
stretching from creation to eternity, such decisive considerations ?

  The great advantage of this view is, that it enables us to
receive, in their obvious sense, those precious
declarations of Scripture, which declare the
pity of God towards even lost sinners. The
glory of these representations is, that they show us God's
benevolence as an infinite attribute, like all His other perfections. Even where it is rationally restrained, it exists. The
fact that there is a lost order of angels, and that there are persons in our guilty race, who are objects of God's decree of preterition, does not arise from any stint or failure of this infinite
benevolence. It is as infinite, viewed as it qualifies God's
nature only, as though He had given expression to it in the salvation of all the devils and lost men. We can now receive,
without any abatement, such blessed declarations as Ps. lxxxi :
13 ; Ezek. xviii : 32 ; Luke xix : 41, 42. We have no occasion
for such questionable, and even perilous exegesis, as even Calvin and Turrettin feel themselves constrained to apply to
the last. Afraid lest God's principle of compassion (not purpose of rescue), towards sinners non-elect, should find any
expression, and thus mar the symmetry of their logic, they say
that it was not Messiah the God-man and Mediator, who wept
over reprobate Jerusalem ; but only the humanity of Jesus, our
pattern. I ask : Is it competent to a mere humanity to say :
" How often would I have gathered your children ? " And to
pronounce a final doom, " Your house is left unto you deso-
late ? " The Calvinist should have paused, when he found himself wresting these Scriptures from the same point of view
adopted by the ultra-Arminian. But this is not the first time
we have seen " extremes meet." Thus argues the Arminian :

Marginal note: Scriptures Ascribe to God Pity Towards Lost.

" Since God is sovereign and omnipotent, if He has a propension, He indulges it, of course, in volition and action.
Therefore, as He declares He had a propension of pity
towards contumacious Israel, I conclude that He also had a
volition to redeem them, and that He did whatever omnipotence could do, against the obstinate contingency of their
wills. Here then, I find the bulwark of my doctrine, that
even omnipotence cannot certainly determine a free will."
And thus argues the ultra-Calvinist: "Since God is sovereign and omnipotent, if He has any propension, He indulges it, of course, in volition and action. But if He had
willed to convert reprobate Israel, He would infallibly have succeeded. Therefore He never had any propension of pity at all
towards them." And so this reasoner sets himself to explain
away, by unscrupulous exegesis, the most precious revelations
of God's nature! Should not this fact, that two opposite conclusions are thus drawn from the same premises, have suggested
error in the premises? And the error of both extremists is
just here. It is not true that if God has an active principle
looking towards a given object, He will always express it in
volition and action. This, as I have shown, is no more true of
God, than of a righteous and wise man. And as the good
man, who was touched with a case of destitution, and yet determined that it was his duty not to use the money he had in giving alms, might consistently express what he truly felt of pity,
by a kind word; so God consistently reveals the principle of
compassion as to those whom, for wise reasons, He is determined not to save. We know that God's omnipotence surely
accomplishes every purpose of His grace. Hence, we know
that He did not purposely design Christ's sacrifice to effect the
redemption of any others than the elect. But we hold it perfectly consistent with this truth, that the expiation of Christ for
sin—expiation of infinite value and universal fitness—should be
held forth to the whole world, elect and non-elect, as a manifestation of the benevolence of God's nature. God here exhibits a provision, which is so related to the sin of the race,
that by it, all those obstacles to every sinner's return to his
love, which his guilt and the law presents, are ready to be taken
out of the way. But in every sinner, another class of obstacles exists; those, namely, arising out of the sinner's own
depraved will. As to the elect, God takes these obstacles also
out of the way, by His omnipotent calling, in pursuancc of the
covenant of redemption made with, and fulfilled for them by,
their Mediator. As to the non-elect, God has judged it best not
to take this class of obstacles out of the way; the men therefore
go on to indulge their own will in neglecting or rejecting Christ.

But it will be objected: If God foreknew that non-elect
Objections Solved.   men would do this; and also knew that
                     their neglect of gospel-mercy would infal-

libly aggravate their doom in the end, (all of which I admit), then that gospel was no expression of benevolence to them at all.   I reply, first; the offer was a blessing in itself; these sinners felt it so in their serious moments; and surely its nature as a kindness is not reversed by the circumstance that they pervert it; though that be foreseen.   Second; God accompanies the offer with hearty entreaties to them not thus to abuse it.   Third; His benevolence is cleared in the view of all other beings, though the perverse objects do rob themselves of the permanent benefit.   And this introduces the other cavil: That such a dispensation towards non-elect sinners is utterly futile, and so, unworthy of God's wisdom.   I reply: It is not futile; because it secures actual results both to non-elect men, to God and to the saved.   To the first, it secures many temporal restraints and blessings in this life, the secular ones of which, at least, the sinner esteems as very solid benefits; and also a sincere offer of eternal life, which he, and not God, disappoints. To God, this dispensation secures great revenue of glory, both for His kindness towards contumacious enemies, and His clear justice in the final punishment.   To other holy creatures it brings not only this new revelation of God's glory, but a new apprehension of the obstinacy and malignity of sin as a spiritual evil.

Some seem to recoil from the natural view which presents God, like other wise Agents, as planning to gain several ends, one primary and others subordinate, by the same set of actions.   They fear that if they admit this, they will be entrapped into an ascription of uncertainty, vacillation and change to God's purpose.   This consequence does not at all follow, as to Him.   It might follow as to a finite man pursuing alternative purposes.   For instance, a general might order his subordinate to make a seeming attack in force on a given point of his enemy's position.   The general might say to himself: " I will make this attack either a feint, (while I make my real attack elsewhere), or, if the enemy seem weak there, my real, main attack."   This, of course, implies some uncertainty in his foreknowledge; and if the feint is turned into his main attack, the last purpose must date in his mind from some moment after the feint began.   Such doubt and mutation must not be imputed to God.   Hence I do not employ the phrase " alternative objects " of His planning; as it might be misunderstood.   We "cannot find out the Almighty unto perfection."   But it is certain, that He, when acting on finite creatures, and for the instruction of finite minds, may and does pursue, in one train of His dealings, a plurality of ends, of which one is subordinated to another.   Thus God consistently makes the same dispensation first a manifestation of the glory of His goodness, and then, when the sinner has perverted it, of the glory of His justice.   He is not disappointed. nor does He change His secret purpose.   The mutation is in the relation of the creature to His providence. His glory is, that seeing the end from the beginning, He brings good even out of the perverse sinner's evil.

There is, perhaps, no Scripture which gives so thorough and comprehensive an explanation of the design and results of Christ's sacrifice, as Jno. iii : 16–19. It may receive important illustration from Matt. xxii : 4. In this last parable, the king sends this message to invited guests who, he foresees, would reject and never partake the feast. " My oxen and my fatlings are killed : come, for all things are now ready." They alone were unready. I have already stated one ground for rejecting that interpretation of Jno. iii : 16, which makes "the world" which God so loved, the elect world, I would now, in conclusion, simply indicate, in the form of a free paraphrase, the line of thought developed by our Redeemer, trusting that the ideas already expounded will suffice, with the coherency and consistency of the exposition, to prove its correctness.

This Christ's own Explanation.

Verse 16 : Christ's mission to make expiation for sin is a manifestation of unspeakable benevolence to the whole world, to man as man and a sinner, yet designed specifically to result in the actual salvation of believers. Does not this imply that this very mission, rejected by others, will become the occasion (not cause) of perishing even more surely to them ? It does. Yet, (verse 17,) it is denied that this vindicatory result was the primary design of Christ's mission : and the initial assertion is again repeated, that this primary design was to manifest God, in Christ's sacrifice, as compassionate to all. How then is the seeming paradox to be reconciled ? Not by retracting either statement. The solution, (verse 18,) is in the fact, that men, in the exercise of their free agency, give opposite receptions to this mission. To those who accept it as it is offered, it brings life. To those who choose to reject it, it is the occasion (not cause) of condemnation. For, (verse 19,) the true cause of this perverted result is the evil choice of the unbelievers, who reject the provision offered in the divine benevolence, from a wicked motive ; unwillingness to confess and forsake their sins. The sum of the matter is then : That Christ's mission is, to the whole race, a manifestation of God's mercy. To believers it is means of salvation, by reason of that effectual calling which Christ had expounded in the previous verses. To unbelievers it becomes a subsequent and secondary occasion of aggravated doom. This melancholy perversion, while embraced in God's permissive decree, is caused by their own contumacy. The efficient in the happy result is effectual calling : the efficient in the unhappy result is man's own evil will. Yet God's benevolence is cleared, in both results. Both were, of course, foreseen by Him, and included in His purpose.

LECTURE XLIV.

RESULTS OF CHRIST'S SACRIFICE, AS TO GOD'S GLORY AND OTHER WORLDS.

SYLLABUS.

1. What results flow from Christ's sacrifice, as to God's glory, and other Worlds?
Turrettin, Loc. xiv, Qu. 3, and 4. Symington on the Atonement, § 4. Hill, bk. iv, ch. 6. Hodge on Atonement, pt. ii.

2. Is Christ's Satisfaction for Believers so complete as to leave no room for Penance and Purgatory? State the Romish doctrines, with their Arguments and Replies. Turrettin, Loc. xiv, Qu. 12. Calvin, Inst. bk. iii, ch. 5. Council of Trent. Session xxv. Bellarmine, Controversia, Vol. ii, p. 285. &c. Peter Dens, Moral Theo., Berg's Abridg., p. 502. Dick, Lect. 81. "Essays on Romanism," Presbyn. Bd., Phila. 19. Mosheim, Com. de Reb. Chr. ante Constantinum, Vol. ii, p, 38. Neander, Ch. Hist. Vol. i, p. 217, &c., ii, p. 675, Torrey.

BEFORE I proceed to that which is to be the chief topic of this lecture, the exclusion of the whole doctrine of penance and purgatory by the completeness of Christ's satisfaction, let us advert for a moment to the point raised at the close of the last lecture. This was concerning the effects of the atonement on the glory of God, and creatures other than the elect.

1. Results of Redemption to others.

The Scriptures tell us that Christ "took not on Him the nature of angels." This, with kindred declarations. assures us that He is not the Mediator of angels; as they need no express mediation. Yet many passages show that they have a certain interest in the work of Christ. Examine 1 Pet. i : 12 ; Eph. i : 10 ; Col. i : 20 ; Eph. iii : 10 ; Phil. ii : 10 ; Heb. i : 6. Now, we should greatly err, if, for instance, we understood such a passage as Col. i : 20, as teaching that the Messiah has " reconciled " any angels to God, by suffering penal satisfaction and making intercession for them. For the elect angels never had any sins to suffer for ; and we are assured that Satan and his angels will never be reconciled to God. What, then, is the concern of the heavenly orders, with Christ's mediatorial work ?

Angels not Redeemed by Christ, but Instructed and Cheered.

1st. The Scriptures abundantly teach us that this work enhances the declarative glory of God. The Mediator is proposed to us and to all creatures likewise, as "the image of the invisible God," "the brightness of His glory and the express image of His person." But Christ's mission and character are those of ineffable benevolence, pity, love, and tenderness; as well as of purity, devotion, magnanimity, and righteousness. Hence, all creatures receive, in His incarnation and work, a revelation of God's character peculiarly dear to them; to the holy, as truly as the unholy. The holy angels now know, love, trust, and serve their Jehovah, as they would not have done, had they

God's Condescension Seen and Felt by Angels.

not learned better these lovely perfections, in the person and work of Christ. God, in taking on Him the nature of one creature, man, has come nearer to all creatures, and opened up new channels of communion with them. All the creatures had important things in common, a dependent nature, intellect, conscience and will, responsibility, and an immortal destiny to win or lose. God, in uniting Himself to one nature, has, in a certain sense, united Himself to the whole class; the condescension does not avail man alone, but brings God nearer to all orders. Thus, humanity appears to be a kind of *nexus*, or point of contact between God and all the holy creatures. And thus, it appears that the extent and grandeur of the beneficent results of the incarnation are not to be measured by the comparative smallness of the earth and man amidst the other parts of creation. It appears how it may be most worthy of God, to have selected the most insignificant of His rational creatures, as well as the ones who were guilty, for this hypostatic union with Himself; because thereby the designed condescension to, and unification of all creatures, in heavenly communion and love, would be more complete and glorious. The lowest nature best answered the purposes. When Mrs. Elizabeth Fry was moved by God's grace to manifest the beauty of Christian philanthropy, she went to the female felons in Newgate. By going to the very bottom of the scale of moral degradation she displayed a love marked by perfect and entire beauty and condescension. Her love was shown to be the highest, because its objects were the lowest. This view of our Redeemer's choice of objects also gives the best answer to the cavil discussed in Dr. Chalmers' "Astronomical Discourses." It had been objected, that the Christian scheme could only seem probable in connection with the old Ptolemaic astronomy, which made the earth the centre of the whole heavens. For, when once it was found that this earth was a very small planet in our system, it would appear very absurd, that the Lord of all this host of worlds should die for a little speck among them. The point of Dr. Chalmers' reply was to show, that to God's immensity, no world is really great, and all are infinitesimally small. The more complete answer is that which I have suggested above.

2d. It is also the doctrine of Christ's sacrifice, coupled with His proper divinity, which enables us to complete our "theodicy" of the permission of evil. In the end of Lect. v: the dimensions of this fearful question: Why a holy, sovereign, omnipotent and benevolent God should permit the natural and moral evil, repugnant to His pure and good nature, to enter His dominions, were intimated, and also the insufficiency of the Pelagian, and the optimistic replies. It is the sacrifice of Christ which gives the humble believer, not a solution, but a satisfying reply. There must have been a reason, and a good one, and it must have been one implying no stint or defect of God's holiness or benevolence. For had there been in God the least defect of either, he certainly would never have found it in His heart to send His infinite Son, more great and important than all worlds, to redeem any one. Note, that the Unitarian, who makes Christ a creature, cannot use this theodicy! The same argument shows, that the secret reason for Esau's preterition must have been both right and benevolent: because Christ's sacrifice for sinful Jacob alone demonstrates a nature of infinite goodness.

3d. But God not only enhances the manifestation of His attribute of benevolence, by the incarnation of the Son. All His other moral perfections and His wisdom are equally exalted. His justice, impartiality, holiness, and determination to punish guilt, appear far more in Christ's penal sufferings, than in the damnation of Satan and of wicked men. For they being His mere creatures, easily replaced by His creative power, insignificant to His well being, and personally injurious to His rights and character, it was easy and natural to punish them as they deserve. Cavilling spirits might say, with a show of plausibility, that resentment alone, rather than pure justice and holiness, may have prompted Him to their doom. But when the Father proceeds, with equal inflexibility, to exact the penalty of His own Son, a being infinitely glorious, united by identity of nature and eternal love to the Judge, characterized personally by infinite moral loveliness, only the more lovely by this act of splendid devotion, and only concerned by voluntary substitution with the guilt of sinners; there is an exhibition of unquestionable and pure justice, impossible to be carried further. So the faithfulness of God to His covenants is displayed in the most wondrous and exalted degree. When God's truth finds such a manifestation in His threats, it appears as the equally infallible ground of our trust in His promises. Now, as these qualities are the basis of the hope of the ransomed sinners, so they are the source of the trust and confidence of all the heavenly orders. Their bliss is not purchased by the Cross; but it reposes on the divine perfections which are displayed on the Cross.

God Glorified in all His Attributes.

The general idea of a Purgatory, that is, of temporary penal and purging pains beyond the grave, to be followed by eternal blessedness, is the common characteristic of all false religions. It seems to be adopted in some form, by all minds not corrected by revelation; by Pythagoreans, Platonists, the Jewish Mishnical doctors,(ii Mac. xii: 43-45; Josephus and Philo), by the Latins from the Greeks, (Virgil, Æneid 6th. *Ergo exercentur pœnis veterumque malorum supplicia expendunt*) by the Mohammedans, the Brahmins, &c. There are two very strong and natural sources for this tendency: first the prompting of our

2. Purgatorial Ideas Common to all False Religions.

affections to follow our dead friends with labours for their benefit and hope; and second, the obstinate reluctance of a heart at once guilty and in love with sin, to be shut up between the sharp alternatives of present repentance, or final damnation. The idea of a purgatory offers a third alternative by which the deceitful heart may for a time solace itself in sin.

The idea came early into the Christian Church, through two channels; a Jewish, through their per-version of the doctrine of Hades, and a Platonic, through Origen's restorationism.

How Introduced Into the Early Church.

The extension of a final restoration to all the wicked, and even to Satan, was, however, regarded by the bulk of the Church as an extravagance of Origen. Thus, we are told, prayers for the dead appear in the earliest liturgies, as Basil's, and in the current of the Fathers, from the "Apostolic constitutions," so called, and the Pseudo Dyonisius, downward. When the priestly conception of the Christian ministry was intruded (which may be traced as early as A. D. 200), the sacrament of the mass began to be regarded as a sacrifice, which is evinced by their giving it to infants; and soon the idea was borrowed, that it availed for the dead. Thus, says Calvin, in his Institutes, the custom of praying for the dead had prevailed almost universally in the Latin Church for 1300 years before his time. Augustine, even, tolerated it. Aerius, the so-called heretic, seems to have been the only noted disentient in the early ages. But prayers for the dead imply that their state is not yet fixed, nor yet perfectly blessed, and that it may be amended. The fully developed doctrine was embodied in the Romish creed, by the Councils of Lyons 2nd and Florence.

The student may find a very express and full statement of the Roman doctrine, in the 25th Session of the Council of Trent. To understand it, and the distinction of the *Reatus pœnæ*, and *Reatus Culpæ*, on which it is founded, its development out of the simple usages of the primitive Church about penitents must be explained. When a Church-member had scandalized the Church, especially if it was by idolatry, he was required, after his repentance, to undergo a strict penance. This was considered as satisfaction made to the wounded credit of the Brotherhood. Out of this simple idea grew the distinction between penitential, and theological, temporal, and spiritual guilt. The latter, they suppose, is expiated by Christ's divine blood. For the former, the believer must make satisfaction himself, partly in the sacrament of penance and self-mortifications, the remainder in purgatory. The two classes of punishment are, therefore, complementary to each other: the more of one is paid, the less of the other remains to be demanded. Venial sins incur only the *temporal;* mortal sins carry both forms of guilt. Baptism, the Church holds, removes all

Doctrine Stated, Purgatory the Complement of Penance.

previous guilt—original and actual; so that were the infant to die immediately after its baptism, it would incur neither hell nor purgatory. All other believers, including even the highest clergy, even Popes, except the Christian martyrs, must go to purgatory, for a time longer or shorter, to pay the *reatum pœnæ* of their sins after baptism. The baptism of fire, which the martyr receives is, in his case, a sufficient purgation, and substitutes the purgatorial sufferings.

The arguments of Rome on this subject may be found so fully and learnedly stated by Cardinal Bellar-

Bellarmine's Arguments. mine, (*Controversia* vol. ii, bk. i, *de Purgatorio* p. 285, &c.,) that nothing can be added after him. He ranks his arguments under three heads— from Scriptures, from the Fathers, from Reason.

From the Apocrypha is quoted 2 Mac. xii : 43-45, which states that Judas Mac. sent to Jerusalem 2,000

From Apocrypha and Old Testament. drachmae, to be expended in sacrifices for the dead, and adds the sentiment: "Therefore it is holy and wholesome to pray for the dead, that they may be loosed from their sins." The answer is: the book is not canonical; nor is the rendering clear. The same answer may be made to the citation from Tobit iv, which recommends the giving of a sepulchral feast to the pious poor, in order that they may pray for the souls of the departed. From the Scriptures, Malachi iii : 2, 3, is also quoted, and applied to Christ's second coming instead of His first. At the final day, they say, a purgatorial influence will be very briefly exerted by the final conflagration, on the souls of those then living. There, they claim, the principle of a purgatory is granted. The answer is, that the New Testament proves that this and similar passages relate to Christ's first coming. (John i : 23; Luke i : 17; iii : 4, or iii : 16). And the trying fire is the searching and judgment of God's convincing Spirit, then peculiarly poured out. To see how hardly bestead they are for Scriptural proof, you may note how they quote 1 Sam. xxxi : 13; 2 Sam. i : 12; iii : 35; Gen. i : 25; Ps. lxvi : 12; Isa. iv : 4; ix : 18; Micah. vii : 8; Zech. ix : 11. It is only by some preposterous application of the Fathers, or mistranslation of the Vulgate, that these passages seem to have any reference to purgatory.

From the New Testament are quoted the following: Matt. xii : 31, 32, where, it is claimed, there is a

Texts From the Gospels. plain implication that some sins are forgiven in the other world. But first, the assertion of a proposition does not prove its converse. Second, if the passage implies that any sins are pardonable after death, it implies that they are such as blasphemy against the Father and the Son. But Rome herself makes these mortal sins. Third, our Saviour's words are simply an amplification of the idea that such sin "hath never forgiveness;" as in fact He expresses it in

Mark iii : 12, the parallel passage. Last, the phrase αἰών μελλων, never means anything else than either the Christian dispensation as contrasted with the Mosaic or else the time after the judgment.

Bellarmine also cites 1 Cor. iii : 10–15, saying, "the foundation is Christ, the founders are the apostles, the good builders are Catholic clergy, their successors; the 'gold, silver, and precious stones, are true Catholic doctrine; the 'wood, hay, and stubble,' are erroneous, but not damnably heretical doctrines· and the inference is, that these heedless Catholic teachers shall be punished in purgatory for their careless teaching." But if clergymen need a purgatory, the principle is established. Others reach the same conclusion more directly. Now, the true exposition of this passage, very strangely overlooked by the most of the Protestants, makes the 'gold, silver, and precious stones,' true converts or genuine Christians united to the Church, which Christ has founded; while the 'wood, hay, and stubble,' are spurious professors. The proof is in the coherency of this sense with the whole passage; in the context, v. 16, and in Is. xxviii : 16; 1 Pet. ii : 4–6. Next, "the day" which shall try every man's work, what sort it is, is evidently the judgment day. Compare 1 Cor. iv : 3, where man's judgment is, literally, "man's day." But the judgment day is subsequent to all purgatory, according to Rome herself. The fire which is to try each man's work is figurative, the divine judgment and Spirit. Compare Heb. xii : 29. And to suppose that the fire in v. 15 is purgatorial fire implies a change of sense; for the trial is not by literal fire, as the Romanists make purgatory to be, but figuratively; οὕτως ὡς.

I Cor. iii : 10, &c., Expounded.

From Matt. v : 25, 26, it is inferred that the debtor may pay divine justice the last farthing, and "come out." This is not implied: if the debt is 10,000 talents, and he has nothing to pay, he will never come out. See Matt. xviii : 24, 25. Matt. v : 22, is also quoted, as implying different degrees of punishment; but if all are sent together to an eternal hell, no difference can be made. We reply, this does not follow, for all infinites are not equal. Their citations of 1 Cor. xv : 29, and Phil. ii : 10, need scarcely be argued.

Other Texts.

The opinions of the Fathers we easily set aside by denying the Church's infallibility.

Bellarmine's arguments from reason are four. First: Some sins are venial, and since they do not deserve infinite punishment, a just God must punish them temporally. The answer is, that the Bible knows no venial sins. Some are, undoubtedly, less guilty than others. But God will know how to apportion their just penalties, without a purgatory.

Argument from Venial Sins.

Second: This acute polemic argues, that the satisfaction
of Christ does not take off believers all
forms of the guilt and consequences of sin:
for God chastises all of them by bodily
death, and by more or less of affliction. Nor
is it worth while for the Protestants to endeavor to evade this,
by saying that these chastisements are merely disciplinary.
For they are of the nature of other penal evils; they are a
part of the curse; they are notoriously the consequences
of sins; the paternal love of God would never lead Him
to use such means for promoting the glorification of sinless creatures. And that they are actually penal is proved by two
cases—that of David, 2 Sam. xii : 14, where God thus explains
David's bereavement of his child by Bathsheba ; and that of the
baptized, elect infant, suffering and dying in "infancy." For
there is an heir of redemption ; yet it suffers the curse ; and
the Protestant cannot explain it as merely disciplinary, because
the infantile sufferer cannot understand, and, therefore, cannot
profit by its own pangs. And indeed, suggests Bellarmine,
here is seen the folly of Protestants, in dragging those texts
into this question, which they say, teach that Christ's atonement
is an absolute satisfaction for all guilt, such as Rom. x : 4: viii :
1; Ps. ciii : 12–14; Heb. vii : 25; x : 14. For if these texts
be taken in the Protestant sense, then they are incompatible
with the chastisements and deaths of justified persons, which
are such stubborn facts. How does the Protestant reconcile
them? Why, he has to resort to that definition of vicarious
satisfaction, which all sound Christians advance; (as, for
instance, to solve Socinian objections,) that satisfaction is not
a legal tender, but an optional, moral equivalent for the sinner's
own punishment. Hence, as the Protestant himself teaches,
the offering of even an adequate equivalent by Christ does not
compel the Father to release the debtor, the condemned sinner,
absolutely; as in pecuniary debts, the offer of the legal tender
compels the creditor to accept it and release his debtor, or else
lose his whole claim forever. The Father's sovereign option is
still necessary to make the transaction valid ; He might withhold
it if He chose. Hence, Protestants themselves infer the extent
to which, and the terms on which, the vicarious satisfaction shall
avail for the sinner, depend on the actual option which God the
Father sees fit to exercise. Therefore, it is all folly for Protestants to argue, that because Christ gives us a perfect vicarious
righteousness, therefore, God cannot exact from the believing
sinner any penal debt whatever; it is not theoretically true; it
is not true in fact. How much of the penal debt God remits,
and how much He still requires of the believing sinner, must
be a question of revealed testimony purely. And farther:
Suppose a true believer, dying before he has gotten his fair
share of penance and chastisements. He cannot go to hell ; he

*Argument from
Nature of Christ's
Satisfaction, and Chris-
tians' Afflictions.*

is justified.   Must there not be a purgatory, where his unpaid
debt of penitential guilt can be paid?   Else, when his case is
compared with that of the aged and ripened saint, who, with fewer
venial sins, has paid a larger amount of penances and afflictions,
there is flagrant partiality.

In refuting this adroit argument, I would expressly admit

Refutation.

that view of vicarious satisfaction advanced,
as the true one.   I would expressly accept
the appeal to the revealed testimony.   And now, setting aside
the apocrypha, and the Fathers, as of no authority, I plant
myself on this fact : that the Scriptures are absolutely silent, as
to any penitential guilt remaining after the *reatus culpæ* is
removed, and as to any purgatorial punishment.   Search and
see.   This is the view which decided Luther, against all the
prejudices of his education.   Next, the chastisements of the
justified are represented by God as only disciplinary, and not
punitive.   Heb. xii : 6–10.   "Whom the Lord loveth"   *   *
*   "But He for our profit."   Nor can the case of David, or of
the dying elect infant, rebut this blessed truth.   All that is
said by Nathan is, that one reason of God in sending the chas
tisement of the infant's death was, that its manner of birth had
given the wicked great occasion to blaspheme.   Well, this end
of the bereavement is after all, disciplinary, and not vindicatory!
The case of the dying infant, plausible at the first blush, is a
complete sophism.   Its whole plausibility is in the false dogma
of baptismal regeneration.   To make Bellarmine's argument
hold, he must be able to say that this suffering infant is not only
elect, but already justified.   This, he supposes, is effected in
baptismal regeneration.   Now, we know that this is a figment.
It is not a baptism previous, which redeems this infant, but the
blood and Spirit of Christ applied only when he dies.   So that
during the time of his infantile sufferings, he is yet unjustified,
is still under wrath, and is suffering for his birth-guilt.

Again, I say : let the statement of vicarious satisfaction as

**Argument from
Perfect Sanctification
of Believers at Death.**

not a legal tender, be accepted.   Let us to
the law and the testimony, to learn whether
God, in His sovereign acceptance of Christ's
equivalent righteousness, reserved any form of guilt to be
exacted of the justified.   Let it be a question of fact.   Now, I
argue, that no cleansing sufferings can be exacted of believers
after death, because God says that they are then pure, and have
no taint of sin to purge away.   See Shorter Catechism, que. 37.
If God teaches that "the souls of believers are at their death
made perfect in holiness," then, according to the Papist's own
showing, there is no room for purgatorial cleansing.   This,
then, is the cardinal question.   1 John iii : 2.   We are like
Christ when we see Him as He is.   Eph. v : 27.   See also
2 Cor. v : 1–8, and Phil. i : 21–23, compared with Rev. xxi : 27,
or Heb. xii : 14.   See also Rev. xiv : 13; Is. lvii : 1, 2; 2 Kings

xxii : 20. And now, I return, and from this point of view claim all those precious texts which declare the completeness of Christ's justifying righteousness, as applicable. When God, after teaching us this fact of perfect sanctification of the believer at death, adds that there is no condemnation to the man in Christ, (Rom. viii : 1), that His blood cleanseth from all sin, (1 John i : 7), that "by one offering He hath perfected (them) forever," (Heb. x : 14), that "He will cast all their sins into the depths of the sea, (Micah vii : 19), the testimony is applicable, and conclusive.

Before proceeding, however, with this affirmative argument, let us notice Bellarmine's 3d and 4th points. One is to argue the principle of a purgatory, as we do the existence of God, from the *consensus populorum*. The answer is, that the universal testimony for the existence of a God is given against the leanings of a guilty conscience and self-interest; and is, therefore, valuable, because disinterested. But the popularity of a purgatory among sinners is no argument in its favour, because the invention is prompted by the leanings of a guilty heart. The Romanist's fourth argument is, that there certainly is a purgatory, because several Popish Ghosts have come thence, and stated the fact! This, of course, is unanswerable!

Romish Argument from Popular Consent, &c.

In pursuance of the argument, I cite the case of the penitent thief, (Luke xxiii : 43), so well argued by Turrettin. I only add, that surely, if there ever was a justified believer who needed purgatory, this man, just plucked, at his dying hour, out of the foulest sins, was the one. The Romish evasion is to say, Martyrs are exempt from purgatory. Now, first, the thief was no martyr; he did not die for the truth; but died for a robbery. Second, the exemption of martyrs is unreasonable and unscriptural. Their dying pangs are often fewer and shorter than of many saints who have died in their beds; and their devotion less meritorious. Here, also, we may quote the act of Stephen, who, speaking by immediate revelation, commended his soul to Christ in glory. So St. Paul, who, according to the Romish doctrine, had every reason at the time of his speaking to suppose himself a candidate for purgatory, evidently believed the opposite; for he held that being absent from the body was to be present with the Lord.

Refutation from Bible Instances.

Next: the whole idea of "satisfaction" to divine justice by temporary sufferings is unscriptural. So, the idea that penal sufferings have in themselves any sanctifying virtue, is equally unreasonable.

Once more: the soul in purgatory being, according to the Popish theory, still imperfect, would be still sinning; and thus, new guilt would be accruing, while it was paying for the old. It could

The Soul Would Contract Debt in Purgatory.

never get out; purgatory would be merged into an endless hell. To avoid this conclusion, which Bellarmine expressly admits would otherwise follow, the Papists lay it down as a principle, that souls after death can neither merit reward nor penalty. The only show of proof for this is the perversion of such passages of Scriptures as say that, at death, man's probationary state ends; as, e. g., Eccles. ix : 10; Jno. ix : 4, &c. But the statement that probation ends at death, is better satisfied by our theory, that there is no purgatory. Hence, this reasoning is a vicious circle. The idea that souls after death cease to merit, is, moreover, absurd and unscriptural. Angels can, and did, and do merit although mere spirits. Responsibility is directly founded on the natural relation of Creator and rational creature; it cannot end, save by the change of the creature's nature, or of God's. Hence, the passage of the creature under a penal, or rewarding dispensation, has no effect to suspend his responsibility. It is not true, that obligation rests on covenant alone, as Papists and Arminians say; so that when covenant is broken by sin, obligation is suspended. It rests on God's intrinsic rights and the creature's nature. The opposite view leads to the absurdity of letting the sinner gain by his sin.

The cunning of Rome is illustrated by this dogma. She may well say, "By this craft we have our wealth." It prolongs indefinitely the hold of priestcraft over the guilty fears and hopes of men, which otherwise must have terminated at death. Men would not pay money to evade a misery which was admitted to be inevitable; the expenditure would appear useless. The cruelty of priestcraft, in thus making traffic of the remorse of immortal souls, and the dearest affections of the bereaved for their departed friends, is as impious as unfeeling.

On the other hand, how blessed is the creed of the Bible touching the believer's death? With the end of that struggle, all our trials end, and our everlasting rest begins. With the grave, and all its horrid adjuncts, the Christian really has no concern; for when the senseless body is consigned to its darkness, the soul, the true *Ego*, the only being which fears, and hopes, and rejoices and suffers, has already soared away to the bosom of its Redeemer, and the general assembly of the glorified.

LECTURE XLV.

CHRIST'S HUMILIATION AND EXALTATION.

I. WHEREIN did Christ's humiliation consist? See Cate-chism, Qu. 27. That Christ should fulfil the work of a Redeemer in both estates, was necessary for the purchase and the application of sal-vation. There is seeming Bible authority for the clause of the Creed, (inserted later than the body,) which says that "He went into hell." See Ps. xvi : 10, as quoted by Peter and Paul. Acts ii and xiii. The Hades into which Christ is there said to have gone, receives four explana-tions. 1. The grave. But it was not the grave into which His "soul" went. 2. The *limbus patrum*, the Popish. They quote, also, 1 Pet. iii : 19, and explain it of the Old Testament saints; and thus explain Matt. xxvii : 53. But we have shown that there is no *limbus patrum*. 3. Some earlier Lutherans understood Ps. xvi : 10; 1 Pet. iii : 19, that Christ went into the hell of the damned, to show them His triumph over death, and seal their fate. Thus it was a part of His exaltation. Both this and the previous notion are contradicted by Luke xxiii : 43. 4. Protestants, by *hades* of Ps. xvi : 10, now understand simply the invisible or spirit world, to which Christ's soul went while disembodied. Calvin understands the creed to mean, by Christ's descent into hell, the torments of spiritual death, which He suffered in dying, not after. His idea is, that the creed meant simply to asseverate, by the words, " descended into hell," the fact that Christ actually tasted the pangs of spiritual

Christ's Humiliation. Did He Descend into Hell? Calvin's View.

546

death, in addition to bodily, and in this sense endured hell-torments for sinners, so far as they can be felt without sin. But Calvin expressly says that the whole of that torment was tasted before the Redeemer's soul left the body. For thence it went to rest in the bosom of the Father. He even raises and answers this question: If this is the meaning of the Creed, why is the descent into hell mentioned after the death and burial; if the thing it means really occurred before? The answer is unsatisfactory; but this at least shows that I have not misunderstood Calvin in his peculiar view. And this is all the ground which exists for the charge so often made by persons who professed much more acquaintance with Calvin than they possessed, that he held to Christ's actual descent into the world of damned spirits!

For Christ's exaltation, see Cat., Qu. 28 ; Phil. ii : 6–11 ;

2. Exaltation.

Is. liii : 10–12 ; Ps. xxii, &c. In what sense was the exaltation of a divine Saviour possible? (a) By removing the veil thrown over His glory by incarnation. (b) By economical reward to Mediatorial person, for humiliation. See Phil. ii : 10, &c. (c) By exaltation of His human nature. Matt. xvii : 2 ; Rev. i : 12–16. This exaltation now, doubtless, takes place, as to Christ's humanity, in a place, called the third heaven, to which He went by literal local motion, from our earth. Sitting at God's right hand means nothing more than the post of honour and power. God has no hand, literally, being immense spirit. The Lutheran argument for ubiquity of Christ's humanity, drawn hence, is foolish ; for in the sense in which the humanity sits at the right hand, that hand is not ubiquitous. It is sophism by conversion of terms. Of this exaltation, the Kingship is the more permanent feature.

Christ's resurrection is every where spoken of in Scrip-

3. Resurrection of Christ Proved. Its Importance.

ture as a hinging point of the believer's salvation and hope. See Rom. iv : 25, and i : 4 ; Jno. xiv : 19 : 1 Cor. xv : 14, 17, 20, &c.; Acts i : 21, 22 ; 1 Pet. i : 3, &c. The Apostles everywhere put it forth as the prime article of their system, and main point of their testimony. Whence this importance? Before we answer this question, it may be well to advert to the evidences upon which we are assured, that this event, equally cardinal and wonderful, really occurred. If you are required to show that the fact is authentic, you may prove it.

(a) From Old Testament predictions, such as Ps. xvi : 10. This event is one of the *criteria* predicted for the Messiah. Then, if you have proved that Jesus of Nazareth is the Messiah; you may claim that a resurrection is to be expected for Him.

(b) Christ expressly predicted His own resurrection. Matt. xx : 19, and xxvii : 63 ; John x : 18. If He is not a monstrous impostor, which His lovely character disproves, we must expect to find it true.

(c) We have the testimony of many witnesses who saw Him after His rising; of the eleven, of above 500 brethren, and last of Paul; witnesses, competent, honest, and credible. They knew Christ by sight; yet they were at first incredulous. They had everything to lose, and nothing to gain, by bearing false testimony here. On this point the convincing arguments of the Christian writers are familiar to your reading.

(d) The miracles wrought in confirmation of the fact prove it. See Heb. ii : 4. The Apostles, we read, in the act of invoking God's miraculous aid, appealed to it as proof that their testimony was true. See Acts iii :15-16. Now, to suppose that God sanctioned such an appeal, by putting forth His own power then, would make Him an accomplice to the deception. So the spiritual effusion of Pentecost, especially, and all the subsequent, are proofs; for they are fruits of His ascension. See Acts ii : 33 ; v : 32.

(e) The change of the Sabbath is a perpetual monumental evidence of the resurrection. For 4,000 years it had been observed on the 7th day of the week. It is now universally observed on the 1st day by Christians. Whence the change? The Church has constantly asserted that it was made to commemorate the rise of its Redeemer from the dead. Now a public, monumental observance cannot be propagated among men to commemorate an imaginary event. The introduction of the observance would inevitably challenge remark, and the imposture would have been instantly exposed. Americans celebrate the 4th of July. They say, it is to commemorate American independence. Had there been no such event as the publishing of the Declaration, July 4th, 1776, the commemoration could not have been successfully introduced to the universal observance of Americans, afterwards. The false reason assigned must have provoked exposure. Multitudes of the best informed would have said : " But, historically, there has been no such event to remember !" This must have arrested the proposal. Rome has, indeed, introduced memorials of legendary, and probably imaginary, Saints. But this could only be done, (a) through the prevalence of great superstition and ignorance : (b) many centuries after the pretended events : (c) and only to a partial extent, among local votaries, who make money by the deception.

Let us now resume and answer the questions. What the importance of this cardinal fact, in the doctrine of our redemption ? 1. Because it was necessary to clear His memory of the charge of religious imposture, under which He died, and to vindicate His character as God's well-approved Son. See Rom. i : 4. 2. Because it evinced the adequacy of His satisfaction for man's guilt. When our Surety comes triumphing out of prison, we know our whole debt is settled. 3. It was necessary to demonstrate His power, as the Captain of our salvation, to conquer our most dreaded enemies. Heb. ii : 14, 15. 4. The resurrection was necessary to enable Christ to be our Sanctifier, Advocate, and King. See Jno. xvi : 7 ; Rom. viii : 11 ; 1 Cor. vi : 15 ; 1 Thess. iv : 14. 5. The resurrection of Christ is the earnest and proof of ours. 1 Cor. xv : 20, 24 ; Phil. iii : 21, &c.

The ground of Christ's intercession is His vicarious righteousness, which He pleads before the Father. Is. liii : 12. The mode of His intercession is by petition; e. g., Jno. xvii.

4. Christ's Intercession. Its Ground, &c. When Does it End?

Some have supposed that this suppliant attitude implies an inferiority incompatible with the proper divinity of the Son. To mediate does imply a certain economical inferiority of attitude ; but no more. Some find, in Jno. xvii : 24, "Father, I will," &c., evidence of a more authoritative intervention. It is overstraining the verb, $\vartheta\epsilon\lambda\omega$. But compare Jno. v : 6, *et passim.* Yet it is certain that Christ's petitions have a more authoritative basis than ours, being urged on the ground of His covenant and perfect purchase. 1 Jno. ii : 1. A more plausible difficulty is this : " If all power is given into Christ's hands, (Matt. xxviii : 18 ; Eph. i : 22 ; Col. ii : 9, 10,) why need He intercede at all? Why not do, of Himself, without interceding, all that His people need ?" The answer is, that Christ is a royal Priest, (Zech. vi : 13,) not Aaronic, but Melchisedekan : and His intercession is rather a perpetual holding up of His own righteousness on behalf of His people, by a perpetual pleading, in order that He may, on that ground, have this viceroyal power of succouring all their wants. And as a royal Priest, He holds up His righteousness to the Father, as a plea for admitting each one of the elect into that body, His kingdom, to which the Father has authorized Him to dispense His fulness.

The objects of Christ's intercession are the elect particularly. See Jno. xvii : 9. Also, His official intercession is always prevalent ; if He prayed for all, all would be saved : but all are not saved.

Its Objects.

Hence, His prayer for the pardon of His murderers, Luke xxiii : 34, must be explained, as being limited by its terms to those of His persecutors who sinned in ignorance. And we conclude that every one of these was among the "great company of the priests, Acts vi : 7, who became "obedient to the faith." There is an alternative solution, which is less satisfactory : That this prayer was not Messianic and officially Mediatorial ; but only the expression of Christian meekness by our pattern, the man Jesus. This attempt to discriminate between the agency of the divine and human wills in Christ, where the act is ethical and spiritual, is perilous.

He must have also interceded officially for the Old Testament saints, for three reasons : 1st. The theophanies are believed to have been interventions of the Son. This implies that He

had already sought and obtained leave to bless His people.
2d. If they had no intercessor, how could a holy and righteous
God give His favour to sinners? 3d. We have a case: Zech.
iii : 1–6. But while Christ's mediation is limited to the elect,
there is a sense in which He intervenes for the whole race.
Doubtless, it is His work for man, which prevented the doom
from following the fall, as promptly as Satan's, and which procures for the world all the instances of God's long-suffering.

    The duration of Christ's intercession seems different to dif-
ferent minds. Some suppose that He will
plead forever; and that His pleading will
secure an everlasting suspension of wrath, and bestowal of ever-
renewed graces and gifts. They quote Heb. vii : 25. Others
suppose that this is only relatively endless, compared with the
brief ministry of an Aaronic priest; and that having thoroughly reconciled the whole Church to God, and re-instated
them in holiness as well as favour, no farther need of His intercession will exist; but God can dispense His blessings unasked
by an advocate, as on the holy angels. I lean to the former
part. Add: that His priesthood is spoken of as everlasting.
Ps. cx; Heb. vii : 3, 24. His sacrifice is ended, "once for all."
If His intercession is not eternal, in what sense does His priesthood continue? Further: He seems still to be the Medium,
after the full glorification of the church, through which they
receive the blessings of redemption. Rev. vii : 17, &c. And
this is much the most consistent and pleasing view of the relation of the glorified Church to God.

    See Cat. question 26. As eternal Son, the 2d person
doubtless shares forever, the natural and infinite dominion of the Godhead. But this
Mediatorial kingdom is conferred and economical, exercised
not merely in His divine nature, but by Him as Θεάνθρωπος
The Person receives this exaltation. The extent of His kingdom is universal. See texts above, and Phil. ii : 10, 11. The
Church is His immediate domain: its members are His citizens; and for their benefit His powers are all wielded. But
His power extends over all the human race, the angelic ranks,
good and bad, and the powers of nature. This exaltation,
therefore, shows our Saviour as clearly divine, for no finite wisdom or powers are at all adequate to its task. The nature of
this benign kingdom is very clearly set forth in Ps. ii, xlv, cx,
and lxxii; in Is. ix, &c., &c., and in the passages above quoted.
The phrase, "Kingdom of God," of "Heaven," &c., is used in
the New Testament in somewhat varying senses; but they all
signify the different aspects of that one spiritual reign, called
"the kingdom of Christ." (a) True religion, or the reign of
Christ in the heart. Luke xii : 31; xvii : 21; Mark x : 15;
iv : 26. (b) The visible Church under the new dispensation.
Mat. xiii : 40, 41; iv : 17; Mark i : 15. (c) The perfected

Its Duration.

5. Christ's King-
dom.

Church in glory. Luke xiii : 29 ; 2 Pet. i : 11. It is a purely spiritual kingdom, as is proved by our Saviour's words, (Jno. xviii : 36), by the nature of its objects ; the redemption of souls ; by the nature of its agencies, viz., truth and mercy and holiness, (see Ps. xlv : 3, 4), by the conduct of Christ and His Apostles while on earth, in paying tribute, living subordinate to magistrates, &c. This respects its terrestrial modes of administration : for as to its secret and superhuman modes, they are properly almighty, and both physical and spiritual.

Orthodox divines are not agreed as to the duration of this **6. Duration of** kingdom. If we would fix the date of its **Christ's Kingdom. Be-** beginning, we must make it, in some respects, **ginning.** co-eval with Christ's intercession—i. e., with the protevangelium proclaimed to man. For it is plain, that saints before the incarnation had all the same necessities for a divine King to conquer, protect, and rule them, which we experience now ; and lay under the same obstacles as to receiving these blessings from a holy God directly, who was bound by His justice and truth to punish and destroy sinners. Again ; we have seen instances, the various theophanies, in which the Son, under the person of the Angel of the Covenant, busied Himself for the protection of His people. Again, Ps. ii speaks of Christ's kingdom, not only as promised, but as having an institution co-eval with the declaration to man of His Sonship. See best interpretation of v. 7. But yet the God-man was only inducted into His peculiar and delegated viceroyalty, after, and as a reward of, His sufferings. See Phil. ii. And the "kingdom of God" is often spoken of at the time of Christ's coming, as being then at hand, or as a thing then coming. We must, therefore, conclude, that while the Son was permitted to intercede and rule before His incarnation, on the ground of His work to be rendered to the Father, His kingdom received a still more explicit establishment after His resurrection.

When we come to consider the other terminus, we are met **Termination?** by a still more serious difference of opinion. Some, with Turrettin, suppose that the delegated mediatorial kingdom over the Church will undergo a change in the mode of its administration at the final consummation, its relation to its enemies, as well as the nature of its own wants, being greatly modified ; but that in other respects it will continue : in that the $\Theta\varepsilon\acute{\alpha}\nu\vartheta\rho\omega\pi\sigma\varsigma$ will be the direct medium for the saints' guidance and government still ; and this forever and ever. The arguments are, that perpetual and everlasting duration are promised to it ; e. g., Ps. lxxii : 17 ; Is. ix : 7 ; Dan. vii : 14 ; Dan. ii : 44. Second. His people will need protection and guidance, just as they will need teaching and intercession, forever. For their glorification will not render them naturally impeccable or infallible. Yea, as we have seen, when speaking of Socinianism, they must have this ruling and teach-

ing, or some day in futurity they will go astray again. But it
seems far more natural to suppose that these blessings will still
be given through Christ their Head, to whom they were spiritually united at their conversion. The personal union of the
divine and human will continue. But for what purpose, if the
mediatorial connection is terminated? Moreover, the Revelation seems to decide the question, showing us the Lamb, (ch.
v : 6), receiving the homage of the glorified Church, (ch. vii :
17), leading and feeding it still, and (ch. xxi : 22, 23), acting,
after the final consummation, as the light of heaven. Third.
In Rev. xix : 7, 8, the marriage of the Church to the Lamb is
spoken of as then consummated, amidst the glories of the final
consummation. All that was previous was but the wooing, as
it were ; and it seems very unnatural to conceive of the peculiar connexion as terminating with the marriage. Then it only
begins properly.

Others, as Dick, seem to attach so much importance and
force to 1 Cor. xv : 24-28, as to suppose that
it necessitates another supposition ; that
Christ having reinstated the Church in holi-
ness and the favour of God, and subdued all its enemies, there
will no longer be any necessity for the peculiar mediatorial
plan ; but God will rule directly over saints as over the rest of
His holy universe before man fell ; and Christ will have no
other kingdom than that which He naturally holds as of the
Godhead. In answer to Turrettin's first argument, they would
say that the everlasting duration promised to Christ's kingdom,
is only relative to the evanescent generations of men : and
means no more than that it shall outlast all generations of earth.
This, they say, is even indicated in the Ps. lxxii ; 17, where the
" forever" is defined to mean as long as the Sun. But " the sun
shall be turned into darkness before the great and terrible day
of the Lord." As to the second argument, it is admitted that
the saints in heaven will always need teaching and ruling ; but
it is supposed that they being thoroughly justified and sanctified, God may bestow these graces on them directly, as the
elect angels, without a mediatorial intervention. These views
appear plausible ; but they come short of a full clearing up of
the subject. They leave unbroken the force of the passages
cited from Revelation. The whole tenour of the Scripture
seems to imply that the peculiar relationship, not only of gratitude and affection, but also of spiritual union, formed between
Christ and His people, is to be everlasting. He is their *"alpha
and their omega."* His life is the spring and warrant of their
life. It is their union to Him which ensures the resurrection of
their bodies, and the eternal life of both body and spirit. See
Jno. xiv : 19. The change made in the method of God's governing the universe, by means of the incarnation, will continue,
in some respects to all eternity, as a standing monument of

1 Cor. xv: 24 Ex-plained.

Jesus Christ's victory and grace.   Nor does the passage from
I Cor. xv : 24, seem insuperable.   That a striking change will then
take place in the method of the mediatorial kingdom, cannot
be doubted.   Perhaps it will consist largely in this, that Christ's
power over the universe (external to His body, the Church),
will be returned to the Godhead.   But the restoration of the
Church to the Father, as an accomplished enterprise, is to be
received, not as implying a severance of Christ's headship, but
as a surrendering of Himself along with it, body and head, as an
aggregate.   Let I Cor. iii : 23, be compared.   It need not follow,
that, because the dominion of the God-man over wicked men
and angels and inanimate nature, is restored to the Godhead, so
that it may again be " all in all," Christ's redeeming headship to
His people must be severed.   The Viceroy may bring back the
province once in insurrection, under His Father's authority, so
that it shall be paramount and universal; and yet, the Son's most
appropriate reward may be, that He shall continue the immediate Ruler and Benefactor of the restored subjects.   This, on the
whole, seems to be the Bible teaching.   It is at once most consoling to believers and most honorable to Christ.

LECTURE XLVI.
EFFECTUAL CALLING.

SYLLABUS.

1. How are we made partakers of the Redemption purchased by Christ? See.
Conf. of Faith, ch. 9, Cat. Qu. 29.
2. Whence the Necessity of a Call to man ?
Dick, Lect . 65.   Hill, bk. v, ch. 1.
3. How many calls does God give to men ?   And what is the difference between
Common and Effectual Calling ?
Shorter Cat. Qu. 31.   Larger Cat. Qu. 68.   Turrettin, Loc. xv, Qu. 1, 4.
Hill, bk. v, ch. 1.   Ridgley, Qu. 67.   Knapp. § 129.
4. What then can be God's true Design in the " Common Call " of non-elect
Men ;   and how may His Sincerity therein be cleared ?
Turrettin,, Loc. xv, Qu. 2.   Howe's Works, " Reconcilableness of God's
prescience, &c., with the Wisdom and Sincerity of His Counsels."   Works of
Andrew Fuller.   Gospel Worthy of all acceptation, pt. iii.   Arminian and
Socinian *Polemics*.   *Passim*.   Hodge's Theol. pt. iii, ch. 14.

" WE are made partakers of the redemption purchased by
Christ, by the effectual application of it to us by
1. Application of   Christ's Holy Ghost."   We now come to the
Redemption by Holy   great branch of Theology—The Application
Ghost.   of Redemption—in which the kingdom
founded by Jesus Christ's humiliation is set up and carried on.
In this work, His priestly office is only exercised in heaven, by
His intercession.   It is His prophetic and kingly which He
exercises on earth.   And the person of the Trinity now

brought into discussion is the Holy Ghost, which proceedeth from the Father through the Son. As the doctrines of Creation, Providence, the Law, chiefly concerned the Father; that of atonement and priesthood chiefly concerned the Son; so this brings into view chiefly the Holy Ghost. This would, therefore, be the most natural place to bring into view the doctrine of the Spirit's personality, nature, and agency; but as you have already attended to these, I proceed.

The great necessity for the effectual calling of man is in his original sin. Were he not by nature depraved, and his disposition wholly inclined to ungodliness, the mere mention of a plan, by which deliverance from guilt and unholiness was assured, would be enough; all would flock to embrace it. But such is man's depravity, that a redemption must not only be provided, but he must be effectually persuaded to embrace it. Now since our effectual calling is the remedy for our original sin; as is our conception of the disease, such will be our conception of the remedy. Hence, in fact, all men's theology is determind hereupon, by their views of original sin. We, who believe the unconverted will to be certainly determined to ungodliness, by ungodly dispositions, therefore believe in an effectual and supernatural call. Jno. iii : 5 and 6.

2. Sin Necessitates the Call.

Calvinists admit only two kinds of call from the gospel to man—the common and the effectual. They deny that there is any natural call uttered by the voice of nature and Natural Theology; for the simple reason that whatever information it might give of the being and government of God, of His righteousness, and of His punishments for sin, it holds out no certain warrant that He will be merciful to sinners, nor of the terms whereon He can be so. Where there is no revealed gospel, there is no gospel call. And this is only to say, that Natural Theology is insufficient to salvation.

3. Call Either Common or Effectual.

The common call consists of the preached word, addressed to men's ears and souls, together with (in most, at least), the common convincing operations of the Holy Ghost. This call is made generally to the whole human race in Scripture, and specifically to each adult to whom the gospel comes. The effectual call, we hold, consists of these elements, and also of a work of the Holy Ghost, "whereby convincing us of our sin and misery, enlightening our minds in the knowledge of Christ, and renewing our wills, He doth persuade and enable us to embrace Jesus Christ freely offered to us in the gospel." Arminians, indeed, assert that the call is one and the same, so far as God's dispensation towards men is concerned, to all under the gospel; and that it only differs by its results in different cases, which difference is made only by man's free will. This we shall more fully disprove when we come to show the nature of regeneration ; but it may now be disproved briefly by these thoughts : (a). That a difference is asserted between the nature of God's calls ; in Scripture, Matt. xxii : 14 ; Jno. vi : 44, 45. (b). That the effectual calling is a result of election ; but the event proves that all are not elect. See Rom. viii : 28 ; xi : 29 ; viii : 30 ; Acts xiii : 48. (c). If the call only differed in the answer made to it by man's free will : 1 Cor. iv : 7, would not remain true ; nor Rom. ix : 16.

God's design in the common call of the unconverted may 4. Designs of God in Common Call. To Gather Elect. be said to be threefold. First, it is His appointed and proper means for saving from among them, the elect. And He either must have adopted this generality in the outward call ; or else He must have adopted one of two expedients. He must have actually saved all, or He must have separated the non-elect wholly from the participation of the common call. Had He adopted the latter plan, surely those who now complain of partiality would then have complained far more loudly. Had He adopted the former, where would have been His manifestation of His sovereignty ; and where that evidence of regular customary connection between means· and ends, conduct and destiny, on which He has seen fit to found His government ?

God's second design in making the common call universal, To Express His Benevolence. was the exercise of the general holiness, goodness, and compassion of His nature, (which generally regard all His creatures), in dissuading all from sin and self-destruction. God's holiness, which is universally opposed to sin, makes it proper that He shall dissuade from sin, every where, and in all sinners. God's mercy and goodness, being made possible towards the human race by their being under a gospel dispensation, make it proper that He shall dissuade all from self-destruction. And this benevolence not only offers a benefit to sinners generally, but actually confers one—i. e., a temporary enjoyment of a dispensation of mercy, and a suspension of wrath, with all the accompanying mercies, and the offer itself of salvation. This offer is itself a benefit : only man's perverseness turns it into a curse. Blessed be God, His word assures us that this common call is an expression of sincere benevolence towards all sinners, elect and non-elect, (a compasssion whose efficient outgoing is, however, conditioned, as to all, on faith and penitence in them). Ezek. xxxiii : 11 ; Ps. lxxxi : 13 ; 1 Tim. ii : 4.

God's third design in making the common call universal is, To Clear Himself. that when men ruin themselves, as He foresaw they would, His holiness, goodness, compassion and truth may be entirely cleared, in their fate, before heaven and earth. It was a part of His eternal plan, to magnify His own goodness, by offering to human sinners a provision for salvation so complete, as to remove every obstacle arising out of His justice and law; so that in their final damnation, all the universe may see how lovely God is; and how desperate an evil sin is. And this is properly God's highest end.

It has been often charged that, if God makes an internal dif-
Is the Common Call Insincere. ference in sinners' hearts, between the common call and the effectual, His wisdom, or His sincerity, in extending that common call to all, is tarnished.

In defending God's sincerity and wisdom in this matter, let us make this preliminary remark: That we have discarded the Thomist proposition, which asserts God's efficient *præcursus* in the sinful acts of men. The student may recall our grounds, in the twenty-fifth Lecture, for disencumbering God's providence of that dogma. Hence, we have not to account here for any *præcursus* of God's, in those unbelieving acts of the sinner under the gospel, by which he resists its gracious invitations and commands. All we have to account for is God's prescience and permission of the unbelief and disobedience. So that the problem we have to discuss is exactly this. Is God both wise and sincere, in invititing and commanding to gospel duty, such sinners as He foresees will neglect it; while His own purpose is distinctly formed, not to put forth His omnipotent Spirit, to cause them to submit? That He is wise in doing so, follows without difficuty, from the positions already laid down assigning the several consistent ends God has in view in His dealings with unbelievers. If that part of these ends, which does not include their own redemption is wise, then the providence is wise.

In reply we assert, First: The Scriptures explicitly direct
Scripture Orders It. the common call to be extended to all; e. g., Mark xvi : 15. They assert that God does efficaciously persuade some, and not others, to embrace it: Rom. ix : 16 ; xi : 7. And they also say that God is both wise and sincere in His offers and dealings, Ezek. xxxiii : 11 ; Luke xix :42; 1 Tim. ii : 4. Now, in any other science than theology, when facts are ascertained on valid evidence, they are all admitted, whether they can be reconciled or not. I remark farther: that to deny the doctrine of effectual calling does not much relieve the subject; for God's prescience of the actual results of His universal call, involve very much the same difficulties as to His wisdom and sincerity.

Second: The objector says that God cannot have done the
Scriptures Assert the Very Cases. thing Calvinists represent Him as doing, because incompatible with His sincerity. But what if we find Him saying that He does this very thing? This is precisely the case. In His Scriptures He represents Himself as giving unquestionable admonitions and invitations to men whom, He expressly declares at the time, He intends to permit to destroy themselves. Compare, for in-

stance, Exod. v : i, with vii : 3, 4. In the one text God says to
Pharaoh : " Let my people go," while in the other, He informs
Moses : " He will not hearken, that I may lay my hand upon
Egypt." In Isaiah vi : 9, Jehovah commissions Isaiah to preach
to Judea : and the tenour of his preaching may be seen in
Chap. i : 18 ; which is a gracious offer of cleansing. But in Ch.
vi : 11, Isaiah is informed that his preaching is destined to
harden his countrymen to their almost universal destruction.
Ezek. iii : 7, 11, presents the very same case. One is presented
in Matt. xxiii : 33–35, with 37, which is, if possible, still stronger.
These cases end the debate, so far as the question of fact goes.
My point is, that God here avows the doing of the very thing
the Arminians say He must not do. This is a perfect proof, at
least, that their difficulty has not arisen from any Calvinistic
misstatement of God's plan. We might then, dismiss the
debate, and leave them to settle their controversy with God, as
best they may.

Third: The course of God's providence in natural things,
is liable to the same difficulty. He spares
Providence Involves the Same Question. sinners. " He sends His rain on the just and
unjust ; and causeth His sun to rise on the
good and evil." See Acts xiv : 17. Now Peter (2 Peter iii : 15)
tells us that the "long suffering of our God is salvation." If
His admitting sinners to the gospel call, whom He yet foresees
to be bent on their own destruction, is insincere ; and the
reality of His benefit therein is doubted, because He never efficaciously purposed to make them repent, His providential goodness also is no true goodness. But what sinner believes this ?
We have here every feature, in which, Arminians say, their difficulty inheres. These earthly blessings are overtures of mercy,
and are intended as such. God foresees their neglect, and the
continued impenitence of the recipients. Physically, He is able
to add to these suasives the other means, and the efficacious
grace, which would certainly bring the recipients to repentance.
But He does not see fit to add them.

In the fourth place, we find the explanation of the common
God's Infinite Good- call, in the views expounded in the remarks
ness Regulated by Wis- upon the design of the sacrifice of Christ.
dom. The student was there advertised, that we
should find another application for those important ideas. That
subject, and the one now in hand, are obviously cognate : the
purpose of God in Christ's sacrifice, and in His offer of its benefits, must be guided by the same attributes of wisdom, benevolence and righteousness. We there saw, that the executive
volition which is wise and good, is prompted in God, (as in a
lower manner in any righteous creature,) by comprehensive
deliberation ; and is not the result of an insulated principle, but
of all the right principles of the Agent's nature harmonized
under His best wisdom. We saw how a good man may have

sympathy with a calamity, which he may yet, for wise reasons, freely determine not to relieve. And we raised the question: Since he really has that sympathy, why may he not give candid expression to it in other forms than acts of rescue? Thus, the good and consistent human magistrate makes overtures of mercy to a criminal on given terms: and yet he is well aware that the criminal's malice and contumacy are such, that the terms will be refused; and he is equally fixed in his mind not to degrade the majesty of the law, by pardoning on any lower terms. No one charges this ruler with insincerity or folly. Why may not our God do the parallel thing? We have seen how the extremists, Arminian and ultra-Calvinist, meet in a common ground of cavil: that the difference is; God is able to renew the criminal's heart, so as to ensure his complying with the requisite terms: the human magistrate is not. I reply, that while God has the δυναμις, the spiritual might, adequate to renew Satan or Judas, He has not the sanction of His own comprehensive wisdom for doing it. I ask with emphasis: May not God see, amidst the multifarious relations of His vast kingdom, many a valid reason which we have not surmised, for determining that it is not best for Him to do a certain act, to which He feels His power competent? To deny this is insane arrogance. The Calvinist need not fear, lest the Arminian here triumph in representing God's desires as crossed by the invincibility of the creature's perverse free will. My view represents His desires and actions as regulated only by His own perfections: but by all His perfections harmoniously combined. It may perhaps be objected farther, that such a picture of the co-action of God's active principles, and of the rise of His volitions, cannot be correct; because it would represent His purposes as emerging out of a state of internal struggle, during which God would be drawn different ways by competing motives, like a poor mortal. Such a picture, they exclaim, is unworthy both of the majesty and blessedness, and the immutability of God. The sufficient answer is contained in the remark already made in the previous lecture: That God's active principles are not passions. They are principles of action; but they exist in Him in their unchangeable vigour, without agitation, and without passionate access or recess. Hence their co-action in the deliberations of the infinite Mind are without struggle. That this may be so, may be illustrated in some small degree, even to our feeble apprehension. We have adduced the example of the great Washington, contemplating the fate of Andre with profound compassion, and yet with a firm and wise determination to give justice its awful dues. This implied of course, some struggle in Washington's heart. But it is equally obvious, that had it been the lower and feeble nature of a Gates or a Schuyler, (both also sincere and honest patriots) which was called to this solemn task, he would have performed it at the cost of much greater disturbance to his equanimity. Why would this have occurred? Not because their natures were, really, more compassionate than Washington's: but because his, while capable of a more profound compassion than theirs, was cast in a grander mould, and regulated by a higher virtue and wisdom. It is strength which gives equanimity. Take this instance, which is infinitesimally humble, beside God's majesty: and it will assist us to apprehend how His infinite wisdom may regulate the several infinite activities of His nature, absolutely without a struggle. And let the student bear in mind, that my attempt is not to bring down the actions of the divine Spirit to man's comprehension: they are ineffable: but to prevent other men from cramping, within the trammels of their human logic, the incomprehensible, but blessed, workings of infinite goodness.

Fifth: When we assert this sincere compassion of God in His common calls to the non-elect, we do not attribute to Him anything futile, or insincere; because, in the expressions of this compassion, He always makes an implied or expressed condition: that they shall turn. He does not say anywhere, that He has any desire to see any one saved while continuing a rebel. Nor does He say anywhere, that it is His unconditioned purpose to compel all to turn. But He says, He would like to see all saved provided they all turned. So that His will in the universal call is not out of harmony with His prescience. And last: God's invitations and warnings to those who, He foresees, will reject them, are the necessary expressions of His perfections. The circumstance that a given sin is foreseen, does not rob it of its moral character; and hence should constitute no reason why a righteous God shall forbear to prohibit and warn against it. That God shall yet permit creatures to commit this sin against His invitations, is therefore just the old question about the permission of evil. Not a new one.

Common Call Always Conditioned.

LECTURE XLVII.

EFFECTUAL CALLING. — Continued.

———

THE Scriptures always speak of the Holy Ghost as the efficacious Agent of effectual calling. "Except a man be
born of water and of the Spirit." Jno. iii :

5. Agent and Instru-
ment of Regeneration. 5. "It is the Spirit that quickeneth." vi : 63.
See, also, 2 Cor. iii : 17 ; Eph. iv : 30. But
this proposition will be supported by the whole subsequent
argument. It is also very important that we assert, against
Mystics and Fanatics, the counterpart truth : that His customary instrument (in all cases except the redemption of infants
and idiots) is the Word. If we allow any other standard or
instrumentality of regeneration than the Word, there will be no
barrier to the confounding of every crude impulse of nature
and Satan, with those of the Holy Ghost. The work of grace
is the work of the divine Spirit. The Word is also His ; and
He always works His works in accordance with, and through
His word, because He is a wise and unchangeable Agent.
Such is the uniform teaching of Scripture, confirmed by experience. Christians are "born again, not of the corruptible
seed : but of incorruptible, by the word of God, which liveth
and abideth forever." 1 Pet i : 23. The Holy Ghost renovates
the mental vision ; the word of God alone furnishes the luminous medium through which the renovated vision sees. Here
is the only safe middle ground between Rationalism on the one
hand, and Fanaticism on the other. To give up the first truth
is to surrender the whole doctrines of grace. To forsake the
second is to open the floodgates to every wild delusion.

There are two grades of Pelagian view, as to the nature

6. Pelagian and
semi-Pelagian View of
Regeneration. and agency of regeneration. Both regard it
as only a change of purpose in the sinner's
mind : whereas Calvinism regards it as a rev-

560

olution of the moral dispositions which determine the purpose of the mind; accompanied with an enlightening of the understanding in spiritual things. The ancient, thorough Pelagian taught a regeneration produced, in the baldest sense, by mere moral suasion—i. e., by the mere force of moral inducements, operating according to the laws of mind. In his mouth, converting grace meant nothing more than God's goodness in revealing the moral inducements of the Scriptures; in endowing man with reason and conscience, and in providentially bringing those revealed encouragements into contact with his sane understanding. See Histories of Doctrines. But the New England Pelagian attributes to the Holy Ghost some indirect agency in presenting moral truths with increased energy to the soul. Still, he denies a proper supernatural agency therein; teaches that the office of the Holy Ghost is only suasive through the truth, and not renovating; and makes His work the same generically, only vastly stronger in degree, with that of the minister who holds forth the gospel to his fellow-men. It was said, for instance, that Dr. Duffield said: " The only reason I cannot convert a sinner with gospel truth, like the Holy Ghost, is that I am not as eloquent as He is." !*

Now, if we disprove this higher theory, the lower is of
Regeneration Properly Defined. course disproved along with it. But we prove that regeneration is not a mere change of the human purpose, occurring in view of motive; but a supernatural renovation of the dispositions which determine the moral purpose, and of the understanding in the apprehension of moral and spiritual truth; the whole resulting in a permanent and fundamental conversion in the actings of the whole man as to sin and holiness—the flesh and God. To such a change the human will is utterly inadequate and irrelevant; because the change goes back of the will. It is therefore a divine and almighty work of the Father and Son through the Holy Ghost, as Their Agent. And this conception of regeneration is in strict conformity with that view of the nature of the will, which we saw a correct psychology dictate. It distinguishes properly between motive and inducement, the former being subjective, the latter objective; the former being the efficient, the latter only the occasion, of rational volitions. So, our view recognizes the practical truth, that the subjective dis-

---

*You will, some of you, recall the queer statement of Woods, in his "Old and New Theology," of the geometrical illustration of conversion, given by a famous theologian of the semi-Pelagian school. The cross is the centre of attraction. The sinner is moving around it in a semi-circle, during the process of conversion, under the suasive influence of gospel truth. This finds him, at first, proceeding along the downward limb of the curve, directly towards hell. But the inducement deflects the sinner more and more, until at that point where the first quadrant ends, the downward motion ceases, and an upward tendency is about to begin. This point marks the stage of regeneration. As gospel inducement still continues to draw, the sinner pursues more and more of an upward course. This quadrant represents the progress of sanctification, at the end of which, the sinner flies off at a tangent to heaven!

36*

position is decisive of all rational volitions—i. e., that the free agent chooses according to his moral nature, because his own moral nature decides how he shall view inducements.   And we also concur with that practical view, which regards subjective character as a permanent and uniform cause, communicating regularly its own quality to the series of moral volition.   This character is, in the sinner, carnal.   To make the conduct spiritual, the character must be renewed.

(a) Our view is probably proved by the fact that, while man shows so much efficiency in all his physical exploits, especially where combined power is applied, his moral enterprises are so feeble and futile.   He can bridge mighty floods, navigate the trackless seas, school the elements, renovate the surface of the globe ; but how little can he do to ameliorate moral evils by all his plans !   Where are all his reformed drunkards, savages civilized, races elevated, without divine grace ?   If his external works of moral renovation are so scanty, we may expect his internal to be so.

Proved. 1st. By Man's Failures in Moral Revolutions.

Every instance of the permanent change of a hardened sinner to godliness, bears, to the experienced eye, the appearance of a power above man's ; because we see so few men make otherwise a radical change of habits and principles, after these are fully formed.   The wise observer of the world will tell you that few men, except under this peculiar power of Christianity, change their course after they pass the age of thirty years.   Those who are indolent then, do not become systematically industrious.   Those who are then intemperate, rarely become sober.   The radically dishonest never become trustworthy.   It is also happily true, that good principles and habits then well established, usually prove permanent to the end of life.   But, as it is easier for feeble man to degenerate than to improve, the few instances in which this rule does not hold, are cases of changes from the better to the worse. When, therefore, I see, under the gospel, a permanent change of a hardened sinner for the better, my experience inclines me to believe that he has felt some power above that of mere nature.

(b) I argue that the new birth is the exceeding greatness of God's power, because of the different effects which accompany the preaching of the gospel to different men, and to the same men at different times.   Were the power only the natural influence of the truth, these diverse effects could not be explained consistently with the maxim that "like causes produce like effects."   The same gospel-inducements are offered to a congregation of sinners, and "some believe the things which are spoken and some believe not."   It is not always the most docile, amiable, or serious mind that yields ; such unbelievers

2nd. By Different Effects of Truth in Same Subjects.

often remain callous to its appeals, while some ignorant, stubborn and hardened sinner is subdued. How is this? If the whole influence were in the truths preached, should not the effects show some regular relation to the cause? Should not the truth prevail where the natural obstacles are least, if it prevailed at all? Why do we see cases in which it fails before the weaker, and triumphs over the stronger resistance? It is because, in one case, "the exceeding greatness of God's power" is behind that truth, and in the other case, is absent.

But if you deny the sovereign agency of the Holy Ghost in the new birth, you have a more impracticable case to explain. It is the case of him who had resisted this gospel for twenty, thirty, or fifty years, and has yet been subdued by it at last. If the truth had natural power within itself to persuade this soul, why did it not effect it at first? If it lacked that power, how does it come to effect the work at last, after so many failures? This mystery is enhanced by two great facts. The one is, that the futile presentation of this gospel-truth for so many years must, in accordance with the well-known law of habit, have blunted the sensibilities of the soul, and rendered the story of redemption trite and stale. If you know anything of human nature, you cannot but admit this result. Repetition must make any neglected story dull. That which at first somewhat excited the attention and sensibilities, urged so often in vain, must become as

> "Irksome as a twice told tale,
> Vexing the dull ear of a drowsy man."

Familiarity and inattention must blunt the feelings toward such a story. The man who first approaches Niagara has his whole ear filled with that mighty, sullen roar of the waters, which shakes the very ground beneath his feet. The dwellers at the spot are so habituated to it by use, that they forget to hear it at all! The ingenuous boy almost shudders at the first sight of blood, though it be only that of the bird he has brought down in his sport. See that person, when hardened by frequent scenes of carnage and death into the rugged soldier, insensible to the fall of the comrade by his side, and planting his foot with a jest upon human corpses, as he mounts to the "imminent, deadly breach."

The other fact that you must take into the account is, that while the sinner is growing more callous to sacred truth by its neglect, every active principle of ungodliness within him must be growing by its indulgence. Is any one ignorant of this law, that a propensity indulged is thereby strengthened? Need I bring instances to prove or illustrate it? How else does any man grow from bad to worse ; how does the temperate drinker grow into a drunkard, the card-player into a gambler, save by the force of this law? It must be then, that while the sinner is neglecting the gospel, at the bidding of ungodliness, the love of the world, avarice, sensual lusts, self-will, pride, ambition, false shame, with every evil outward habit are growing into giant strength.

This, then, is the case which you have to solve. Here is an influence, the natural force of sacred truth, which was 'fully plied to overcome the unbelief of the young heart, with every advantage of fresh interest, the tenderness of maternal love, the gentle and venerable authority of a father amidst the sweet sanctities of home ; plied when the soul was still unformed, and in the plastic gristle of its childhood. But even in this tender heart, the inborn power of ungodliness was too strong; the application utterly failed. But now, after this truth has been exhausted of its power by twenty, thirty, or it may be, fifty years of useless presentation ; and after this native ungodliness, too strong in its infancy, has been hardened by as many years of sin into the rugged bone of manhood, lo! the powerless truth suddenly becomes powerful! The stubborn sinner listens, feels, and submits! Natural agencies cannot account for this. The finger of God is there. Let me suppose a parallel case. Years ago, suppose, when the trees which embower this Seminary, were lithe saplings, and I in the vigor of my first prime, you saw me lay hold of one of them with my hands, and attempt to tear it from its seat. But, though a sapling, it was too strong for me. Now years have rolled around, that tree has grown to a giant of the forest ; and I return, no longer in the pride of youth, but a worn and tottering old man; and you, the same spectators, are here again. You see me go to that very tree, and attempt to wrench it from its place. You laugh scornfully; you say: "Does the old fool think he can pull up that sturdy oak? He was unable to do it before, when it was a sapling, and he was strong." Yes, but suppose the tree came up in his feeble hand? You would not laugh then! You would stand awe-struck, and say : "Something greater than nature is here."

And so say I, when I see the sturdy old sinner, hardened by half a century of sins and struggles against the truth, bow before the same old gospel story, which he had so often spurned. When I see the soul which was by nature dead in trespasses and sins, and which has been stiffening and growing more chill, under the appliances of human instruction and persuasion, at the last, when the zeal and hope and strength of man are almost spent, suddenly quickened under our hands, I know that it is "the exceeding greatness of God's power (not ours) according to the working of His mighty power which He wrought in Christ when He raised Him from the dead."

Does any one attempt to escape this conclusion by saying that the new efficacy of the truth may have been derived from the superior force or eloquence of the orator who preached it on this occasion, or from the advantage of some such circumstance?

I have two answers. One is, that there are no circumstances so auspicious, and no eloquence so persuasive as those which this soul has already resisted as an impenitent child. What eloquence is equal to that of the Christian mother, as she draws her beloved son to her knee, and tells him the history of Jesus' love, in accents tremulous with unutterable tenderness? The other answer is, that the plain facts and persuasives of the gospel are, in themselves too infinite to receive any appreciable weight from the trivial incidents of a perspicuous statement and an eloquent tongue. In the simple story of the cross, with divine love there dying a shameful and bitter death for its guilty enemies; in the offer of a heaven of everlasting and unspeakable bliss, and the threat of an eternal and remediless hell; even if they be but intelligibly lisped in the feeble voice of a child, there should be a weight so immense, that beside it, all the enlargements of human rhetoric would be as naught

Man's skill of speech does not weigh where Christ and eternity prove too light. It is as though a great mountain had been put in the balance against the mightier strength of ungodliness, but could not counterpoise it. And then I come and with my puny hand, cast one little stone at the mountain's base and say: "There; I have added to its weight; it will no longer prove too light." Such folly is it to expect that man can convert. Where the story of the cross has been resisted, naught can do it, " save the exceeding greatness of His power."

But (c): when we consider what the change in the new birth is, and what the heart to be changed is, 3d. Nature Cannot Revolutionize Itself. we plainly see that the work is above nature. The soul of a man has its natural laws, as truly as the world of matter. In both worlds, we learn these laws by the uniformity of our experience. Because all men have ever seen water run down hill, therefore, we say that this is the law of its gravitation. And, therefore, when the waters of Jordan stood on a heap while the ark of God and Israel passed through its channel, men knew it was a miracle. The sun and the moon have always proceeded regularly from their rising to their setting. Hence, when their motion ceased at the word of Joshua, it was plainly a miracle.

Now universal observation proves that ungodliness is the natural law of man's soul, as the Scriptures declare. This heart is, in different degrees and phases, universal among natural men, in all races and ages, under all religions and forms of civilization; whatever religious instincts men may have, and to whatever pious observances they may be driven by remorse, or self-righteousness, or spiritual pride. We percieve that this disposition of soul begins to reveal itself in all children as early as any intelligent moral purpose is disclosed. We observe that while it is sometimes concealed, or turned into new directions by the force of circumstances, it is always latent, and is a uni-

versal and controlling principle of conduct towards God. We
find that it holds its evil sway in spite of all light, and rational
conviction in men's own minds, and of inducements drawn from
conscience and heaven and hell, which ought to be omnipotent.
Such is every man's inward history, until grace reverses his
career.

Now I claim that these facts of experience authorize me in
regarding this ungodly disposition in man as natural and fundamental.   How do we learn more certainly that any other native
trait or affection belongs to the constitution of his soul?   It is
plain that since Adam's fall, ungodliness is as radically a native
disposition of man's soul, as the desire of happiness, or the fear
of pain. (John iii : 6.)

But here I remind you, that no man ever reverses or totally
eradicates, or revolutionizes any material or fundamental disposition of soul, by his own purpose or choice ; nor can any
mere inducement persuade him to do so.   Look and see.
These principles may be bent, they may be concealed, they
may be turned into new channels by self-interest, or by education, or by restraint.   The same selfishness which in the season
of heady youth prompted to prodigality, may in thrifty age
inspire avarice ; but it is never eradicated by natural means.
Hunger is a natural appetite.   Should a physician tell you that
he had a patient with a morbid appetite, but that by his eloquent pictures of the dangers of relapse and death from the
imprudent indulgence in food, he had actually caused the man
no longer to be hungry ; you would tell him, " Sir, you deceived
yourself; you have only persuaded him to curb his hunger; he
feels it just as before."   Suppose this physician told you, that
he had plied his patient's mind with such arguments for the
utility of a certain nauseous drug, that it had actually become
sweet to his palate ?   Your good sense would answer: "No,
sir; it is in itself bitter to him as before; you have only induced
him by the fear of death—a more bitter thing—to swallow it in
spite of its odiousness ? "

Try my assertion again, by some of the instinctive propensities of the mind, instead of these animal appetites, and
you will find it equally true.   The distinction of *meum* and
tuum is universal in human minds, and the love of one's own
possessions is instinctive in men's hearts.   Can you then argue
or persuade a man into a genuine and absolute indifference to
his own ?   This was one of the things which monasticism professed to do : monks were required to take the three vows of
" obedience, chastity and poverty."   Many devout and superstitious persons, upon entering monasteries, reduced themselves
to absolute and perpetual poverty, by giving their goods to the
Church or the poor, and foreswore forever the pursuits by
which money is acquired.   But was the natural love of possession really eradicated ?   The notorious answer was, No.   Every

one of these monks was as ready as any other man to contest the posession of his own cell, his own pallet, his own gown and cowl, his own meager food. And for the common wealth of their monastery and order, they uniformly contended with a cunning and greediness which surpassed all others; until they engrossed to themselves half the wealth of Europe.

The love of applause is native to man. Can reasoning or persuasion truly extinguish it? These may correct, direct, or conceal this passsion; they can do no more. The hermit professed to have extinguished it. He hid himself in deserts and mountains from the society of men, and pretended that he was dead to their praise and their attractions, dead to all but heaven. But he who sought out this hermit and conversed with him, soon detected in him an arrogance and spiritual pride above those of all others: and the chief reason why he was content to dwell in savage solitudes, was that the voice of fancy brought to his soul across the wastes which sundered him from the haunts of men, their applause for his sanctity, in strains sweeter to his pride than the blare of bugles and the shouts of the multitude.

I return, then, to my point. There is, there can be, no case, in which mere inducements work in man a permanent purpose, contrary to the natural dispositions of his soul. But ungodliness is a native, a universal, a radical propensity. Hence, when we see such a revolution in this as the Gospel requires in the new birth, we must believe that it is above nature. This great change not only reforms particular vices, but revolutionizes their original source, ungodliness. It not only causes the renewed sinner to submit to obedience, as the bitter, yet necessary medicine of an endangered soul; it makes him prefer it for itself, as his daily bread. It not only refrains from sin which is still craved; as the dyspeptic refuses to himself the dainties for which he longs, lest his indulgence should be punished with the agonies of sickness; it hates sin for its own sake. The holy and thorough submission to God's will, which the convert before dreaded and resisted, he now loves and approves. Nothing less than this is a saving change. For God's command is: "My son, give me thine heart." He requireth truth in the inward parts, and in the hidden parts He shall make us to know wisdom. Saith the Saviour; "Either make the tree good and his fruit good, or else make the tree corrupt and his fruit corrupt." Such is the change which makes the real Christian.

This is also more than an argument of experience. By all sound mental science, man's moral spontaneity, while real, puts itself forth according to a law. That law is found in the natural state of his dispositions: i. e., the dispositions direct the will. Man is free. His soul is (wherever responsible) self-

By Consistent View of the Will.

determined, but it is the dispositions which determine the will. Now, it is preposterous to expect the will to renovate the original dispositions; the effect to determine its own cause.   Nor can the presentation of inducement alone change those dispositions, because the influence, which external objects shall have as inducements, is itself dependent on the state of the dispositions.   For illustration: What would be thought of an attempt to revolutionize the tastes of the palate for the sweet, by presenting the bitter as attractive ?   It is the state of that palate by nature which determines the attraction to be in the sweet, and only repulsion in the bitter.   A direct physiological agent must be applied.

(d.)   We argue this truth from the tenour of Scripture.
First: man's natural condition is said to be
By Scripture Fig- one of blindness, of deadness, of impotency,
ures. of bondage, of stony-heartedness.   Rev. iii:
17; Eph. ii: 1; Rom. v: 6; Acts viii: 23; Ezek. xi: 19. Now, these are figures ; but if there is any accuracy or justice in the Bible use of figures, they must be incompatible with the idea that light alone causes vision in the blind eye, or truth and inducement alone, motion in the dead, bound, helpless soul. Next: the proper, supernatural character of regeneration is proved by the Bible accounts of the work itself.   It is a new creation. Ps. li: 10; Eph. ii: 10.   A new birth.   Jno. iii: 5; Titus iii : 5. A resurrection from death. Eph. ii: 1–4, 5. A giving of a fleshly in place of a stony heart.   Ezek. xxxvi: 26. An opening of blind eyes.   2 Cor. iv: 6.   Here again the creature cannot create itself, the child beget itself, the dead body re-animate itself, the stony heart change itself, the darkness illuminate itself at the prompting of inducements.   An external and almighty power is requisite.   Again do we urge that if these tropes are not false rhetoric (which none can charge on the Holy Ghost without profanity) they cannot convey less meaning than this: that in this change an external power is exerted on the soul, which the latter can have no share in originating, even as the material, however susceptible of becoming an organism, cannot, as material, participate in the initial, fashioning act.   We find a third and large class of Scriptures, which speak of the renewing grace as in order to the characteristic acts of conversion.   Such are Ps. cxix: 18.   Prov. xvi: 1.   Jer. xxxi: 19; xxxii: 40.   Ezek. xxxvi: 27.   Acts xiii: 48; xvi: 14.   Jno. vi: 44, 45.   Phil. ii: 13.   According to the first of these texts, the opening of the eyes is in order to vision. Then the light, which enters by vision, cannot be the original, opening agent.   Again, we have a number of Scriptures, in which the power of the Holy Ghost working in us is distinguished from the Word.   See 1 Cor. ii: 4, 5.   1 Thess. i: 5, 6.   1 Cor. iii: 6, 9.   Last: The immediate operation of God is asserted in sundry places, in the most discriminating forms of

speech possible. Such are Jno. i: 12, 13. Eph. i: 19, 20, and ii: 10. Further Scriptural and logical proofs will appear under the next head; which will reinforce the present argument, while bearing especially upon their own proposition.

(e.)If regeneration were by moral suasion, man would be his own saviour in a sense, excluded by the Scriptures: as in 1 Cor. iv: 7. If it were by moral suasion, of course regenerating grace would always be vincible; and, consequently, believers would have no sufficient warrant to pray to God for salvation. There would be only a probability at best, that God could save them; and to the mind taking an impartial survey of the relative numbers who have ever resisted the Gospel, that probability would not appear strong. If the change were by moral suasion only, we should have no difference of kind, between this divine work and the human work of the teacher in training his pupils to right habits, and the temperance lecturer in persuading people away from drunkenness. Can any one believe that the Scriptures mean no more than this by all their strong assertions of the divine power in effectual calling? But worse than this, we should leave no generic difference between the renewing work of God and the seductive work of the devil. He decoys men to their ruin, by the suasive influence of objective inducements. God allures them to salvation by the suasive influence of an opposite sort of inducements. Thus we should degrade God's almighty work of grace, into an equal contention between Him and His doomed rebel slave, Satan, in which the latter succeeds at least as often as God!

By Absurd Consequences.

7. There is a sense in which the Holy Ghost is said to operate regeneration only mediately, through the truth, which is held not by Pelagians, but by Calvinists.

Is the Operation of the Spirit Mediate? Dick's View.

But that we may do no injustice, let us distinguish. Among those who explain depravity and regeneration by Gospel light, there appear to be four grades of opinion. The lowest is that of the Pelagian, who denies all evil *habitus* of will, regards regeneration as a mere self-determination to a new purpose of living, and holds that it is wrought simply by the moral suasion of the truth. This virtually leaves out the Holy Ghost. The second is that of the semi-Pelagian, who holds that the will is not indeed dead in sin, but that it is greatly corrupted by evil desires, cares of this world, bad example, and evil habits (*consuetudines* not *habitus*). Hence, Gospel truth never engages the soul's attention strongly enough to exert an efficacious moral suasion, until the Holy Ghost calms and fixes the mind upon it by His gracious, suasive influence. The truth, thus gaining access to the soul, regenerates it. The third class, disclaiming all semi-Pelagianism, hold that the truth ought to, and would control the will, if clearly and fully seen; but that in virtue of

the natural blindness of the understanding (which they regard
as the source of depravity) the truth cannot be thus seen, until
the mind is divinely illuminated; and this illumination, a true,
gracious, spiritual and efficacious work, is regeneration. As soon
as that is done, the truth spiritually seen, revolutionizes the will
by its natural power; for the will must always follow the prevalent dictate of the understanding.   Such was most probably
the scheme of Claude Pajon.   The fourth class is that of Dr.
Alexander, Dr. Dick, and we presume, of Dr. Hodge.   Holding
that the rudiments of our depravity are in the blinded understanding primarily, and in the perverted will derivatively, they
also hold that illumination is regeneration; but they add that,
in order for this illumination, a supernatural operation on the
mind itself is necessary.   And that operation is the causative
source of conversion.   This distinguishes their scheme from
that of Pajon.   This also saves their orthodoxy; yet, we repeat,
it seems to us an inconsistent orthodoxy in one particular.   We
ask them: Is that immediate operation of the Holy Ghost—
that prerequisite of illumination—the sovereign and immediate
revolution in the *habitus* of the will?   And they answer, No;
for that would imply the view which we hold, and they disclaim
it, as to the radical source of moral quality in the soul.   What
then is the operation?   They reply: We do not know; it is
inscrutable, being back of consciousness.   But to us it appears,
that if illumination of the understanding is the whole direct efficiency of the Holy Ghost in regeneration, it is more natural
and consistent to stop where Pajon stops, with a mediate conversion through the truth.

Another consequence of this view must be to modify the
definition of saving faith.   If blindness of
mind is the ultimate element of spiritual
death, and illumination the primary element in regeneration,
then faith ought to be defined, as Dr. Alexander does (Relig.
Exp.) as being simply, a hearty mental conviction of truth.
A third result must be to decide the order in which repentance
and faith are related in their genesis.   From the same premises it must follow, that faith is in order to repentance, instead
of repentance being implicit in the first movement of faith and
motive thereto, as Scripture seems to teach.   This question,
then, is by no means a mere logomachy, or a psychological curiosity.   It carries grave results.   These divines would by no
means teach that regeneration is not a divine, supernatural and
invincible work of grace.   But they suppose that the essential
change is in the illumination of the understanding, which God's
Spirit indeed almightily effects; but, to effect which, nothing
more is needed than to secure for the truth a true spiritual
apprehension by the understanding.   The truth being truly
apprehended, they suppose the renovation of the will follows as
a   necessary   result,   without   further   supernatural   agency;

Consequences.

because, according to our Calvinistic psychology, the soul's emotions are governed by its views of the objects thereof; and the will always follows the latest and most decisive conviction of the understanding. They claim the order of phrases in the Catechism, question 31. They sometimes describe the alternative doctrine, as teaching that depravity is in the feelings as distinguished from the intelligence; that the only inability of the sinner is his disinclination to good, that the understanding follows the will instead of the will's following the understanding, that regeneration is only a change in the feelings; and that it affects only a part (the emotive) and not the whole of the soul. Much stress is iaid by them on the fact, that the soul is a *monad*, and its faculties not divisible parts, but only modes of function in the monadic spirit; that both depravity and regeneration are not by patches, but of the soul as a soul.

But we beg leave to re-state our view in our own way. The soul is a unit, a monad, not constituted, as material things are, of parts, or members; but endowed with faculties which are distinct modes of its indivisible activity. These, according to the psychology of the Bible and of common sense, fall into the three divisions of intelligence, will, and sensibility—the latter class being passive powers. By the word "will," in this discussion, we mean, not the specific power of volition, but that which the Reformed divines and our Confession mean by it, the whole active power of man's spontaneity; what Sir William Hamilton terms "the conative powers;" i. e. the whole faculty of active desire and purpose. While the soul is simply passive only in its sensibilities, and its functions of intelligence are its own self-directed functions, yet it is by its will, or conative powers, that it is an agent, or puts forth its spontaneity. Now, the soul is depraved as a soul; and is regenerated as a soul; not by patches or parts, seeing it has no parts. But we conceive that this obvious fact is entirely consistent with the proposition, that sin (or holiness) affects the soul as to one of its faculties more primarily than the others. And let us remark here once for all, that it is entirely inconsistent in Dr. Hodge, to object the simplicity of the soul to those who think with us, that sin affects the soul rudimentally in the faculty of will, and consequentially in those of understanding and sensibility; when he himself teaches, *vice versa*, that sin affects it rudimentally in the faculty of intelligence, and consequentially in those of will and sensibility. For, if the fact that the soul is a unit refutes us, it equally refutes him. Both opinions would in that case be out of the question equally, and the debate impossible. Again: Dr. Hodge, and those who think with him, dwell much on the complexity of the soul's acts, as involving at once two or more of its faculties or modes of function. They tell us that an act of understanding accompanies every act of desire or choice.

Definition of Doctrine.

True. But they themselves go on to assert a relation of causation between the intellective element and the conative element, as to the production, or rise of the concrete act of soul. Why, then, may not we assign a causative relation to the one or the other of these two elements, as to the moral quality of that concrete act of soul? We shall find the divines we indicate, (as Chalmers, A. Alexander, and Hodge,) when hardly bestead to sustain their peculiar views on this point, resorting very freely to the statements, that the soul is a unit; that it is depraved or regenerated as a unit; that it acts as a unit; that it performs one concrete function often through two or more faculties, which act not separately as members, but only distinguishably as modes of function. We repeat, all this is granted; but it is irrelevant. For it would, if it proved anything in the case, as much preclude the one causative order as the other. It would be as unreasonable to say "the understanding guides the will," as to say "the will sways the understanding." Let this be remembered.

We have thus disencumbered the issue which we wish to examine. It is this: In defining depravity, are we to place the rudimentary element of the sinful nature, in the blinded understanding, misleading the spontaneity, and thus qualifying the soul as a whole morally evil? Such is the view of the divines named. Or, are we to find it rudimentally in the perverted *habitus* of the will, causatively corrupting and blinding the understanding, and thus qualifying the soul as a whole morally evil? Such is our understanding of the Scriptures, and the Reformed theology.

In support of this, we advance this simple argument. By its function of intelligence the soul sees; by Argument.   its will it acts. Now, does not common sense teach us, that moral responsibility attaches to those acts and states of soul which it puts forth from itself, by its spontaneity, more primarily than to those with which it is affected by causes out of itself? Witness the fact, that multitudes of percepts and concepts affect our minds, without any movement of desire or volition whatever; the former from objective sources, the latter from the instinctive law of suggestion. This is the decisive feature which, according to common sense, forbids our regarding the cognitive acts of the soul as those by which it is primarily qualified with moral character.

It is true, that conscience is the faculty, which is our moral guide; but then our moral quality as persons is in our conformity or enmity to that guidance. What is it, in us, that is conformed or opposed to that guidance? Primarily, the will. And this brings our debate, it appears to us, up to that scriptural test, which is the decisive one. It so happens that the Holy Ghost has given us an exact definition of the idea of sin. Ἡ ἁμαρτία ἐστὶν ἡ ἀνομία, (1 John iii : 4,) which our Catechism imitates. The νόμος, the standard is, first, the law of our moral nature written on our hearts by our Creator; and, secondly, His revealed precepts taught to our intellects. The sin consists, according to St. John, in lack of conformity to that standard. We repeat the question: What is it in sinful man which is not conformed to that standard? Every sinner's consciousness answers; partially the reason, but chiefly and primarily the will; and thence, consequentially, the animal appetites and bodily members. This scriptural view is confirmed by one remark: Let any one collect as many as he can, of those acts of men, to which the Scriptures and theologians appeal, as *a posteriori* proofs of native depravity, and he will find that they all fall under this common predication—that in them the will opposes itself obstinately to the soul's own moral judgments. This, in fine, is the analytic statement of that universal fact, in which the moral disorder and ruin of man's soul manifests itself.

The reasonings which we have attempted to answer seem to us to involve this illusion; that because man is a reasonable agent, his spontaneity is but a modification of his reason. But is this so? Is not this sufficiently refuted, by the fact which Dr. Hodge cites against us; that other creatures have a spontaneity, which have no reason? In truth, spontaneity is an ultimate fact of human consciousness, and an ultimate power of the soul, as much so as reason. It is co-ordinate in primariness and simplicity with the power of reason. It has its own original *habitus*, its "disposition," which re-acts on the reason as truly as it is acted on. Against this view some may cry out: "Then the action of a man's spontaneity might be no more a rational action, than the pulsation of his heart!" We reply: The instance is unfair; because the will is not a separate member like that muscle called "heart" in the body; but it is a mode of function of the soul, a spiritual unit. And that soul which wills is a rational unit. So that all action of will is the action of a rational agent. But we concede that spontaneity is sometimes unconsciously irrational; and that is lunacy. Oftentimes it is contra rational; and that is sinfulness. Sometimes, by God's grace, we find it truly conformed to reason; and that is holiness.

But the favorite plea of the fathers who differ with us, is that it is the recognized doctrine of all sound philosophers, that the will follows the prevalent judgment of the intellect. They say: "Man feels as his mind sees; the view of the mind therefore must direct or govern the feeling; and the prevalent last judgment must decide the will." It is from this statement Dr. Hodge infers that depravity and holiness must be ultimately traced to the intellect; Dr. Dick infers that the revolution of the will, in effectual calling, is the natural effect of true illumination; and Dr. Alexander infers that a faith which is simply

How Moral Opinions Arise.

full conviction of the truth, is all we need to make the soul embrace salvation and duty. This psychological law we fully admit; it is what defines man as a reasonable agent. That is, granted that the prevalent judgment of the intellect be of a given nature on a specific subject, then the feeling and choice of the soul on that subject will of course correspond. But the analysis stops one step too short. Whence the kind of view and judgment which the intellect is found to have on that given subject? Is it always of a purely intellectual origin? This is tacitly assumed, but erroneously. Let the subject be one of a moral nature, involving an object of choice or desire, and it will be found that there, the heart has taught the head; the opinion is the echo of the disposition; the power of spontaneity, co-ordinate with that of intelligence, has announced its own original *habitus*. Let us explain: A child tastes experimentally, candies, sweetmeats, honey, sugar. In each case his palate is gratified. On this similarity of power to gratify the palate, his mind constructs a generalization, forms the class of "sweet things," and concludes the general judgment; "Sweet things are good." Now, this general judgment may be as truly and purely accounted an intellectual process, as the arithmetical one that a larger subtrahend must make a smaller remainder. And it may be said that, in every subsequent desire and purpose to seek the "sweet things," the child's will follows this intellectual judgment. Very true. And yet it is none the less true, that the judgment is itself a generalization of a series of acts of appetency; the mere echo of the instinctive verdict of an animal appetite. So that in its last analysis, the causation of the choice is traced up, through the intellect, to a law of the spontaneity.

We shall be reminded that the instance we have chosen gives us only an animal appetite, a phenome-

Moral Opinions Follow the Heart.

non of animal spontaneity; whereas the thing in debate is moral emotion and choice, which is always rational emotion and choice. This we fully admit, and we advance the instance only for an illustration. Perhaps it is a clumsy one. But has not the will as real, and as original, appetencies, as the palate? When we call the former rational, moral desires, what do we mean? That disposition is nothing but a modification of thought? We apprehend that our meaning is this: the intellect is the faculty by which we conceive the object of the moral appetency; as, in the case of the animal appetite, the nerves of sensation are the medium by which we perceive the sweet object. Yet in the moral phenomenon, there is an original disposition of will, which is as truly a spiritual appetency, as the bodily appetite is an animal appetency. If we are correct in this, we shall find that the judgments generalized in the mind, as to the desirableness of moral good or evil, however purely intellectual, when abstracted from their source,

are yet but the echoes of the original, or regenerated appetencies of the will. Let us now apply this analysis to the sinner's
conversion. Why does the renewed sinner embrace Christ as a
Saviour from sin, by his faith; and new obedience instead of
sin, by his repentance? Because his understanding illuminated
by grace, now judges clearly that salvation and new obedience
are not only the obligatory, but the preferable good. Such is
our brethrens' answer; and we fully assent. Were it not so, the
new choice would not be rational, and so, not spiritual. But
now, one question more; How came this illuminated intellect to
judge the salvation from sin, and the new obedience, the preferable good; when the original, native disposition of the will was
to prefer the sin, and dislike the obedience? It was only because
the Holy Ghost sovereignly revolutionized the disposition of
will. This was the primary cause; illumination the immediate
consequence; and faith and repentance the practical result.
Thus the profound Paschal, (*Pensees*, 1re Partie. § 3); "God
alone can put divine truths into the soul; and by the mode
which pleases Him. I know He hath willed them to enter from
the heart into the mind, and not from the mind into the heart,
in order to humble the proud power of reasoning, which presumes to be judge of the things the will chooses, and in order
to heal this infirm will, which has wholly corrupted itself by its
unworthy attachments. And hence it results, that while in
speaking of human affairs, men say: One must know in order
to love, which hath passed into a proverb; the saints on the
contrary say, in speaking of divine things: " One must love in
order to know."

But the decisive appeal should be, not to philosophy, but
to the Scriptures. These would seem to sus-
Argument from tain our view in a multitude of places; where
Scripture.
sin and depravity are traced to an "evil heart,"
a " hardened heart;" and holiness to a " pure heart;" or where
regeneration is a cleansing of the heart, a giving of a fleshly
heart.

But there are Scriptures which not only do this, but do also
assign an order; and with reference to moral objects, the order
of relation is from the heart to the head. Here we claim all
the texts already cited touching the relation of repentance to
faith. We claim also, Mark iii : 5, where Jesus disapproved the
Pharisees' theory of Sabbath observance; and this because He
was "grieved at the hardness of their heart." So, in Eph. iv :
18, Gentiles "have the understanding ($\delta\iota\acute{a}\nu o\iota\alpha$) darkened, being
alienated from the life of God through the ignorance that is in
them, because of the blindness (or hardness, $\pi\acute{\omega}\rho\omega\sigma\iota\varsigma$), of their
heart." Here the Apostle distinctly traces sinful ignorance to
the heart for its source. Nor can this be evaded by saying that
heart here means " soul," " mind." For this would.be flagrantly
violent exegesis : When the Apostle has designedly introduced

a distinct reference to the state of the cognitive faculty, by his own, most discriminative word, διάνοια : and then, evidently, designs to refer to the conative faculties of the soul, by the recognized word for them, καρδία ; will any one say he shall not teach what he aims to teach? Had he still meant "understanding," we presume He would have still said "διάνοια," in the last member of the verse. Permit such interpretation, and next, we shall meet this fate, viz: That when we are trying our best to say, that in spiritual things, "the heart leads the head ;" we shall be told : "No, you do not mean that; you use the word 'heart' in the comprehensive sense of 'soul;'" you mean that the head leads the head !"

We are also referred to many passages, where, as our brethren understand them, regeneration is Other Scriptures Reconciled. described as illumination, and depravity as blindness. "To turn them from darkness to light." "God," says Paul, "was pleased to reveal His Son in me." "The eyes of the understanding being enlightened." "Sanctify them through thy truth." "Renewed in knowledge after the image," etc. "God hath shined in our hearts, to give the light of the knowledge of the glory of God, in the face of Jesus Christ." We reply that regeneration doubtless includes illumination, as an essential and glorious part thereof. But it is a different thing to say that regeneration is only illumination. Should we force the Scriptures to assert the latter, we should only make the Bible contradict itself, when it describes a quickening or revolutionizing work of divine grace, which is in order to illumination, and therefore prior in causation.

We are thus led back to that application of our theory, which is at once its best illustration and most This Psychology applied to the Question. important use ; its bearing upon the doctrine that the Holy Ghost in regeneration operates, not only mediately through the Word, but also immediately and supernaturally.

(a.) Because the Scriptures often speak of a spiritual power precedaneous to the truth, on the operation of which power, the saving apprehension of truth is conditioned. See Ps. cxix: 18. The opening is the precedent cause ; the beholding of wonderful things out of the law, the consequence. As the eye closed by cataract cannot be restored to vision by any pouring of beams of light on it, however pure and condensed, so the soul does not acquire spiritual vision by bringing the truth alone in any degree of spiritual contact. The surgeon's knife goes before, removing the obstruction; then, on the presentation of light, vision results. Both must concur. Let the student examine, in the same way, Luke xxiv : 45 ; Eph. i : 17, 18 ; Acts xvi : 14 ; 1 Cor. iii : 6, 7, 9 ; Jer. xxxi : 33.

(b.) We argue, secondly, against this conception of depravity and regeneration, and in favor of the immediate agency of the Holy Ghost, that were the former scheme true (even as set forth by Dr. Dick), faith would be in order to the regeneration of the will. However he might eliminate any sequence of time, if "this gracious knowledge necessarily leads the will from the world to God," it remains clear, that faith as cause must precede this first renewal of the will. But the Scriptures make faith the fruit of renewal. The other view is Arminian.

(c.) The analytical exposure of the absurdity of the Pelagian scheme, regeneration by moral suasion, results ultimately in this, namely; that the state of disposition determines *a priori* whether any given object presented to the soul shall be of the nature of objective inducement or not. Moral suasion is that influence over the will, which objects of natural or moral excellence, presented from without, are supposed to have as inducements to right feeling and choice. Now, any object whatsoever is not inducement to any being whatsoever. One cannot attract a hungry horse with bacon; nor a hungry man with hay. Whether the object shall be inducement, depends upon its relation to the existing appetency of the being to be influenced. And that state of appetency is obviously related, as cause, to the influence of the inducement as occasion. Hence, if the sinner's will is naturally indisposed and disabled to all spiritual good, that good cannot exert moral suasion over that will; for the simple reason that the effect cannot reverse its own cause. Such is the argument; and it is exhaustive. But now, who does not see that this analysis proceeds upon our theory; that the will has its own disposition, original, characteristic? If the *habitus* of the will is nothing else than a modification of the intelligence; and the sinner's intellect is adequate to the more intellectual apprehension of moral truth (as it is), we see no reason why moral suasion might not be expected to "lead the will necessarily from the world to God."

(d.) Dr. Hodge expounds, with peculiar force and fullness, the solemn fact, that there is a "common grace" of the Holy Ghost (which is not "common sufficient grace") convincing men of sin and misery up to a certain grade; but not renewing them. Now, this partial, spiritual light in unrenewed minds must be correct light as far as it goes; for it is the Spirit's. Yet it does not even partially subdue the enmity of those minds to God and duty. The usual effect is to inflame it. See Rom. vii : 8, 9. It appears, then, that light, without immediate grace revolutionizing the will, does not effect the work. Nor is the evasion just, that this conviction of duty inflames the carnal enmity, only because depravity has made it a distorted and erroneous view of duty. We assert that convicted, but unrenewed souls fight against God and duty, not because He is misconceived, but because He begins to be rightly conceived. There is, of course, distortion of mental view concerning him as long as sin reigns; but He is now feared and hated, not only because

37*

of that error of view; rather is He the more feared and hated, because the sinful soul now begins to see Him with less error, as a sovereign, holy, just, pure Being.

(e) We infer the same view of sin and new birth, from the regeneration of infants. They cannot be renewed by illumination, because their intellects are undeveloped. Yet they are renewed. Now, we grant that there is a wide difference in the circumstances and means of their redemption, and that of adults. Yet are they delivered from a state of original sin generically the same with ours; and delivered by the same Redeemer and Sanctifier. Must not the method of the renewing power be the same intrinsically? Luke xviii : 17.

(f.) This view gives us a consistent *rationale* of that impotency of the natural man to receive the things

Doctrine True, because it Explains carnal blindness.

of the Spirit of God, which are foolishness unto him, described in 1 Cor. ii : 14, and elsewhere. This impotency too plainly exists. Dr. Dick cannot define wherein it consists. See his 66th Lecture. Does it consist in the absence of any substantive revelation, which the believer gains? No; this would be perilous fanaticism. Does it consist in the hiding of any esoteric sense of the Word to which the believer has the key? No; this would be Origenism. Does it consist in the loss of a cognitive faculty by the fall? No; that would suspend his responsibility. Whence this impotency? They have no answer.

But we have one. The will has its own *habitus*, regulative of all its fundamental acts, which is not a mere modification of the intelligence, but its own co-ordinate, original character; a simple, ultimate fact of the moral constitution. Hence an interaction of will and intellect. On moral and spiritual subjects the practical generalisations of the intellect are founded on the dictates of the disposition of the will. But now, these practical judgments of the sinner's understanding, prompted by the carnal disposition, contradict certain propositions which are premises to the most important gospel conclusions and precepts. No wonder, then, that such a mind cannot apprehend them as reasonable! For example: The sinner's real opinion, taught by a carnal heart, is, that sin in itself, apart from its penalty which self-love apprehends as an evil, would be the preferred good. A gospel is now explained to him, proposing deliverance from this sin, through the instrumentality of faith. But the plan postulates the belief that the sin is *per se* so great an evil, that deliverance from it is a good greatly to be desired! No wonder, then, that, as this postulate breaks upon the understanding of the sinner, he is obfuscated, stumbled, dumb-founded! He is required to act on a belief which his carnal heart will not let him believe. His action, to be reasonable, must assume sin to be hateful. But he loves it! He feels that he naturally loves it, and only hates its consequences. "He cannot know the truth, for it is spiritually discerned." Were a sprightly child allured to approach the reader by the promise of "something good," and told that he should have it upon holding out his hand for it; and were he to perceive, just then, that the thing you held out was a nauseous medicine, of whose utility to himself he was ignorant, he would be struck with a similar "inability." There would be a sense in which he would become unable to hold out his hand even: he would not know how to do it. He would stand confused. Now, this child is not becoming idiotic, but his native appetencies repel that which you propose as an attraction; and, hence, his obstinate apprehension of the unreasonableness of your proposal.

Thus, as it appears to us, the simple psychology, which is assumed in the Bible, is found to be the truest philosophy, and throws a flood of light upon the doctrines held in common by us and by all Calvinists.

LECTURE XLVIII.

ARMINIAN THEORY OF REDEMPTION.

SYLLABUS.

I. Give a connected view of the Arminian Five Points.
 Art. of Synod of Dort. Whitby's Five Points. Hill's Divinity, bk. iv, ch. 8. Stapfer's Pol. Theol., Vol. iv., ch. 17, § 12-35.
II. Disprove the doctrine of Common Sufficient Grace.
 Turrettin, Loc. xv, Qu. 3. Hill, bk. iv, ch. 9, § 1. Ridgley, Qu. 44. Watson's Theol. Inst., ch. 24, 25.
III. Is the grace of God in regeneration invincible? And is the will of man in regeneration, active or passive?
 Turrettin, Loc. xv, Qu. 5, 6. Hill, bk. iv, ch. 9. Knapp, § 130, 132.
IV. Can any Pagans be saved, without the instrumentality of the Scriptures?
 Turrettin, Loc. i, Qu. 4, and Loc. x, Qu. 5. Ridgley, Qu. 60. Annual Sermon for Presb. Board For. Miss., June, 1858.

THE subjects which are now brought under discussion introduce us to the very centre of the points which are debated between us and Arminians. I propose, therefore, for their farther illustration, and because no better occasion offers, to consider here their scheme.

Sources of the Arminian Theology.

The sources of Arminian Theology would be best found in the apology of Episcopius, Limborch's Christian Theology, and Knapp's Christian Theology. Among the English may be consulted, as a low Arminian, Daniel Whitby's Five Points; as high Arminians, Wesley's Doctrinal Tracts, and Watson's Theological Institutes. For refutation of Arminianism, see Stapfer, Vol. 4; Turrettin; Hill, bk. 4, ch. 9.

I. A connected view of the Arminian tenets:

The five points handed in by the Arminians to the States General of Holland, in their celebrated Remonstrance, were so covertly worded as scarcely to disclose their true sentiments. The assertions concerning original Sin and Free will, were seemingly such as Calvinists could accept. The doctrine of common grace was but obscurely hinted; and the perseverance of Saints was only doubted. But their system soon developed itself into semi-Pelagianism, well polished and knit together. Discarding the order of the five points, I will exhibit the theory in its logical connection.

Five Points of Remonstrants Ambiguous.

1. Its starting point is the doctrine of indifference of the will, and a denial of total depravity, as held by Calvinists. According to the universal consent of Pelagians and Socinians, this self-determination of the will is held necessary to proper free agency and responsibility. Take Whitby as a type of the grosser Arminians. He thinks Adam was created liable, but not subject, to bodily death, and his immunity in Paradise was secured by his access to the Tree of Life. His sin made death and its attendant pains inevitable; and this his posterity inherit, according to the natural law, that like begets like. This has produced a set of circumstances, making all men so liable to sin, that, practically, none escape. But this results from no moral necessity or certainty of the will. Man has natural desires for natural good, but this *concupiscentia* is not sin till formed into a positive volition. But the sense of guilt and fear drives man from God, the pressure of earthly ills tends to earthly mindedness; man's pains make him querulous, envious, inordinate in desire; and above all, a general evil example misleads. So that all are, in fact, precipitated into sin, in virtue of untoward circumstances inherited from Adam. This is the only sense in which Adam is our federal head. This relation is not only illustrated by, but similar to that which exists between a bad parent and an unfortunate offspring now—in instance of the same natural law.

Logical Source in Doctrine of Indifferency of the Will. View of Original Sin.

But Wesley and Watson repudiate this, as too low; and teach a fall in Adam, prior to its reparation by common grace, going as far as moderate Calvinists. Watson, for instance, (Vol. ii, p. 53, &c.,) says that imputation is considered by theologians as mediate and immediate. Mediate imputation he says, is " our mortality of body and corruption of moral nature in virtue of our derivation from Adam." Immediate means "that Adam's sin is accounted ours in the sight of God, by virtue of our federal relation." This, the student will perceive, is a very different distinction from that drawn by the Reformed divines. Watson then repudiates the first statement as defective: and the latter as extreme. Here he evidently misunderstands us:

Wesleyan View of Original Sin.

for he proceeds to say, with Dr. Watts, that Adam did act as a public person; our federal head, and that the penal consequences of our sin (not the sin itself), are accounted to us, consisting of bodily ills and death, privation of God's indwelling, (which results in positive depravity) and eternal death. In this sense, says he,"we may safely contend for the imputation of Adam's sin."

But in defending against Pelagians, &c., the justice of this arrangement of God, he says it must be viewed in connection with that purpose of redemption towards the human race, which co-existed in the divine mind, by which God purposed to purchase and bestow common sufficient grace on every fallen man, thus repairing his loss in Adam. (The fatal objection to such a justification is, that then God would have been under obligations to provide man a Saviour: and Christ's mission would not have been of pure grace).

2. This leads us to their next point: God having intended all along to repair the fall, and having immediately thereafter given a promise to our first parents, has ever since communicated to all mankind a common precedaneous sufficient grace, purchased for all by Christ's work. This is not sufficient to effect a complete redemption, but to enable, both naturally and morally, to fulfil the conditions for securing redeeming grace. This common grace consists in the indifferency of man's will remaining, notwithstanding his fall, the lights of natural conscience, good impulses enabling unregenerate men to do works of social virtue, the outward call of mercy made, as some Arminians suppose, even to heathens through reason, and some lower forms of universal spiritual influence. The essential idea and argument of the Arminian is, that God could not punish man justly for unbelief, unless He conferred on him both natural and moral ability to believe or not. They quote such Scripture as Ps. lxxxi : 13 ; Is. v : 4 ; Luke xix : 42 ; Rev. iii : 20 ; Rom. ii : 14 ; John i : 9. So here we have, by a different track, the old conclusion of the semi-Pelagian. Man, then, decides the whole remaining difference, as to believing or not believing, by his use of this precedent grace, according to his own free will. God's purpose to produce different results in different men is wholly conditioned on the use which, He foresees, they will make of their common grace. To those who improve it, God stands pledged to give the crowning graces of regeneration, justification, sanctification, and glorification. To the heathen, even, who use their light aright, (unfavourable circumstances may make such instances rare), Christ will give gospel light and redeeming grace, in some inscrutable way.

3. Hence, the operations of grace are at every stage vincible by man's will ; to be otherwise, they must violate the conditions of moral agency.

Common Sufficient Grace.

Grace in Regeneration Vincible.

Even after regeneration, grace may be so resisted by free will, as to be dethroned from the soul, which then again becomes unrenewed.

4. The redeeming work of Christ was equally for all and every man of the human race, to make his sins pardonable on the condition of faith, to purchase a common sufficient grace actually enjoyed by all, and the efficient graces of a complete redemption suspended on the proper improvement of common grace by free will. Christ's intention and provision are, therefore, the same to all. But as justice requires that the pardoned rebel shall believe and repent, to those who, of their own choice, refuse this, the provision remains forever ineffective.

Redemption General.

5. In the doctrine of justification, again, the lower and higher Arminians differ somewhat. Both define justification as consisting simply of pardon. According to the lower, this justification is only purchased by Christ in this, that He procured from God the admission of a lower Covenant, admitting faith and the Evangelical obedience flowing out of it, as a righteousness, in place of the perfect obedience of the Covenant of works. According to the higher, our faith (without the works its fruits) is imputed to us for righteousness, according, as they suppose, to Rom. iv : 5. Both deny the proper imputation of Christ's active (as distinguished from His passive) obedience, and deny any imputation, except of the believer's own faith ; although the higher Arminians, in making this denial, seem to misunderstand imputation as a transference of moral character.

Justification.

Hence, it will be easily seen, that their conception of election must be the following: The only absolute and unconditional decree which God has made from eternity, concerning man's salvation, is His resolve that unbelievers shall perish. This is not a predestinating of individuals, but the fixing of a General Principle. God does, indeed, (as they explain Rom. ix–xi chapters), providentially and sovereignly elect races to the enjoyment of certain privileges; but this is not an election to salvation; for free-will may in any or each man of the race, abuse the privileges, and be lost. So far as God has an external purpose toward individuals, it is founded on His foresight, which He had from eternity, of the use they would make of their common grace. Some, He foresaw, would believe and repent, and therefore elected them to justification. Others, He foresaw, would not only believe and repent, but also persevere to the end ; and these He elected to salvation.

6. Personal Election Conditional.

A thoroughly-knit system, if its premises are granted.

II. The refutation of the Arminian theory must be deferred, on some points, till we pass to other heads of divinity, as Justification and Final Perseverance. On the extent of the atonement enough has already been said. On the remaining points we shall now attempt to treat.

In opposition to the assertion of a common sufficient grace, we remark, 1. That there is no suf-

Common Sufficient Grace Refuted. ficient evidence of it in Scripture. The passages quoted above do, indeed, prove that God has done for all men under the gospel all that is needed to effect their salvation, if their own wills are not depraved. But they only express the fact that God's general benevolence would save all to whom the gospel comes, if they would repent; and that the obstacles to that salvation are now only in the sinners. But whether it is God's secret purpose to overcome that internal obstacle, in their own perverse wills, these texts do not say, It will be found, on examination, that they all refer merely to the external call, which we have proved, comes short of the effectual call: or that they are addressed to persons who, though shortcoming, or even backsliding, are regarded as God's children already. Look and see.

The doctrine is false in fact; for how can grace be suffi-

2. Doctrine False, in Fact. cient, where the essential outward call, even, is lacking? Rom. x : 14. God declares, in Scripture, He has given up many to evil. Acts xiv : 16; Rom. 1 : 21, 28; ix : 18. Again: the doctrine is contradicted by the whole doctrine of God, concerning the final desertion of those who have grieved away the Holy Ghost. See Hos. iv : 17; Gen. vi : 3; Heb. vi : 1–6. Here is a class so deserted of grace, that their damnation becomes a certainty. Are they, therefore, no longer free, responsible and blameable?

3. If we take the Arminian description of common sufficient grace, then many who have its elements most largely, an enlightened conscience, frequent compunctions, competent religious knowledge, amiability, and natural virtues, good impulses and resolutions, are lost; and some, who seem before to have very little of these, are saved. How is this? Again: the doctrine does not commend itself to experience; for this tells us that, among men, good intentions are more rare than good opportunities. We see that some men have vastly more opportunity vouchsafed them by God's providence than others. It would be strange if, contrary to the fact just stated, all those who have less opportunity should have better intentions than opportunities.

We have sometimes illustrated the Wesleyan doctrine of common sufficient grace thus: "All men lie

4. Common Grace, if Sufficient, Saves. in the 'slough of despond' in consequence of the fall. There is a platform, say Arminians, elevated an inch or two above the surface of this slough, but yet firm, to which men must struggle in the exercise of their common sufficient grace alone, the platform of repentance

and faith.   Now, it is true, that from this platform man could
no more climb to heaven without divine grace, than his feet
could scale the moon.   But God's grace is pledged to lift up to
heaven all those who will so employ their free-agency, as to
climb to that platform, and stay there."   Now, we say, with the
Arminian, that a common sufficient grace, which does not work
faith and repentance, is in no sense sufficient; for until these
graces are exercised, nothing is done.   Heb. xi : 6 ; Jno. iii : 36.
But he who has these graces, we farther assert, has made the
whole passage from death to life.   That platform is the platform of eternal life.   The whole difference between elect and
non-elect is already constituted.   See John iii : 36 ; 1 John v :
1 ; Acts xiii : 48 ; 2 Cor. v : 17, with Eph. iii : 17.   If then there
is sufficient grace, it is none other than the grace which effectuates redemption; and the Arminian should say, if consistent
with his false premises, not that God by it puts it in every man's
free will to fulfill the conditions on which further saving communications depend; but that He puts it in every man's free
will to save himself.

      If the doctrine is true, it is every man's own uninfluenced
5. Or else, it is either choice, and not the purpose of God, which
not Common, or not determines his eternal destiny.   Either the
Sufficient.   common grace effects its saving work in those
who truly believe, in virtue of some essential addition made to
its influences by God, or it does not.   If the former, then it was
not "common," nor "sufficient," in those who failed to receive
that addition.   If the latter, then the whole difference in its success must have been made by the man's own free will resisting
less—i. e., the essential opposition to grace in some souls, differs from that in others.   But see Rom. iii : 12, 27 ; Eccl. viii :
11 ; Eph. ii : 8, 9 ; 1 Cor. iv : 7 ; Rom. ix : 16 ; and the whole
tenour of that multitude of texts, in which believers ascribe
their redemption, not to their own superior docility or penitence, but to distinguishing grace.

      To attain the proper point of view for the rational refuta-
tion of the doctrine of "common" sufficient grace, it is only
necessary to ask this question: What is the nature of the
obstacle grace is needed to remove?   Scripture answers in
substance, that it is inability of will, which has its rudiments
in an ungodly *habitus* of soul.   That is to say : the thing
grace has to remove is the soul's own evil disposition.
Now, the idea that any cause, natural or supernatural, half
rectifies this, so as to bring this disposition to an equipoise,
is absurd.   It is the nature of disposition to be disposed :
this is almost a truism.   It is impossible to think a moral
agent devoid of any and all disposition.   If God did produce in a sinful soul, for one instant, the state which common sufficient grace is supposed to realize, it would be an
absurd *tertium quid*, in a state of moral neutrality.   As we

argued against the Pelagian, that state, if possible, would be immoral, in that it implied an indifferent equipoise as to positive obligations. And the initial volitions arising out of that state would not be morally right, because they would not spring out of positive right motives; and such acts, being worthless, could not foster any holy principles or habits. The dream of common grace is suggested obviously, by the Pelagian confusion of inability of will with compulsion. The inventor has his mind full of some evil necessity which places an external obstruction between the sinner and salvation; hence this dream of an aid, sufficient but not efficacious, which lifts away the obstruction, and yet leaves the sinner undetermined, though free, to embrace Christ. Remember that the obstruction is in the will; and the dream perishes. The aid which removes it can be nothing short of that, which determines the will to Christ. The peculiar inconsistency of the Wesleyan is seen in this: that, when the Pelagian advances this idea of Adam's creation in a state of moral neutrality, the Wesleyan (see Wesley's Orig. sin. or Watson, ch. 18th), refutes it by the same irrefragible logic with the Calvinists. He proves the very state of soul to be preposterous and impossible. Yet, when he comes to effectual calling, he imagines a common grace, which results, at least for a time, in the same impossible state of the soul! It is a reversion to Pelagius.

III. The views of regeneration which Calvinists present, in calling the grace of **God therein** invincible, and in denying the synergism (συνεργεια) of man's will therein, necessarily flow from their view of original sin. We do not deny that the common call is successfully resisted by all non-elect gospel sinners; it is because God never communicates renewing grace, as He never intended in His secret purpose. Nor do we deny that the elect, while under preliminary conviction, struggle against grace, with as much obstinacy as they dare; this is ensured by their depraved nature. But on all those whom God purposes to save, He exerts a power, renewing and persuading the will, so as infallibly to ensure their final and voluntary submission to Christ. Hence we prefer the word invincible to irresistible. This doctrine we prove, by all those texts which speak of God's power in regeneration as a new creation, birth, resurrection; for the idea of successful resistance to these processes, on the part of the dead matter, or corpse, or *fœtus*, is preposterous. Conviction may be resisted; regeneration is invincible. We prove it again from all those passages which exalt the divine and mighty power exerted in the work. See Eph. i : 19, 20; Ps. cx : 3. Another emphatic proof is found in this, that otherwise, God could not be sure of the conversion of all those He purposed to convert; yea, not of a single one of them; and Christ would have no assurance that He should ever " see of the travail of

Grace in Regeneration Invincible.

His soul" in a single case! For, in order for God to be sure of
the result, He must put forth power adequate to overcome all
opposing resistances. But see all those passages, in which the
security and immutability of God's purposes of grace are asserted. Rom. ix : 21, 23 ; Eph. i : 4; John xv ; 16, &c., &c.
Eph. ii : 10.

Here, the Arminian rejoins, that God's *scientia media,* or
foreknowledge of the contingent acts of free
agents (arising not from His purpose of control over those acts, but from His infinite in-
sight into their character, and the way it will act under foreseen
circumstances), enables Him to foreknow certainly who will improve their common grace, and that some will. His eternal
purposes are not crossed, therefore, they say, because He only
purposed from eternity to save those latter. The fatal answer
is, that if the acts of free agents are certainly foreseen, even
with this *scientia media,* they are no longer contingent, but certain ; and worse than this : Man's will being in bondage, all the
foreknowledge which God has, from His infinite insight into human character, will be only a foreknowledge of obdurate acts
of resistance on man's part, as long as that will is unsubdued.
God's foreknowledge, in that case, would have been a foreknowledge that every son of Adam would resist and be lost.
The only foreknowledge God could have, of any cases of submission, was one founded on His own decisive purpose to make
some submit, by invincible grace.

Mere Foreknowledge Inadequate.

The Arminian objects again, that our doctrine represents
man as dragged reluctating into a state of
grace, like an angry wild beast into a cage ;
whereas, freedom of will, and hearty concur-
rence are essential elements of all service acceptable to God.
The answer is, that the sinner's will is the very subject of this
invincible grace. God so renews it that it neither can resist,
nor longer wishes to resist. But this objection virtually reap-
pears in the next part of the question.

Grace does not De- stroy Free Agency.

Calvinists are accustomed also to say, in opposition to all
synergistic views, that the will of man is not
active, but only passive in regeneration. In
this proposition, it is only meant that man's
will is the subject, and not the agent, nor one of the agents of
the distinctive change. In that renovating touch, which revolutionizes the active powers of the soul, it is acted on and not
agent. Yet, activity is the inalienable atttribute of an intelligent
being; and in the process of conversion, which begins instan-
taneously with regeneration, the soul is active in all its exercises
towards sin, holiness, God, its Saviour, the law, &c., &c.

The Soul Passive in its Quickening. Proof.

This doctrine is proved by the natural condition of the active
powers of the soul. Man's propensities are wholly and certainly directed to some form of ungodliness, and to impeniten-

cy.   How, then, can the will, prompted by these propensities, persuade itself to anything spiritually good and penitent? It is expecting a cause to operate in a direction just the opposite to its nature—as well expect gravity to raise masses flung into the air, when its nature is to bring them down.   And this is agreeable to the whole Bible representation.   Does the *fœtus* procure its own birth? the dead body its own resurrection? the matter of creation its own organization?   See, especially, John i : 13.   Yet this will, thus renewed, chooses God, and acts holiness, freely, just as Lazarus, when resuscitated, put forth the activities of a living man.

The objections of the Arminian may all be summed up in this : that sinners are commanded, not only to put forth all the actings of the renewed nature, such as believing, turning from sin, loving God, &c., but are commanded to perform the very act of giving their hearts to God, which seems to contain the very article of regeneration.   See Prov. xxiii : 26 ; Is. i : 16 ; Ezek. xviii : 31 ; Deut. x : 16.

The answer is, 1st.   That God's precepts are no test of the extent of our ability of will, but only of our duty.   When our Creator has given to us capacities to know and love Him, and the thing which prevents is our depraved wills, this is no reason why He should or ought to cease demanding that which is His due.   If the moral opposition of nature into which God's creatures may sink themselves by their own fault, were a reason why He should cease to urge His natural rights on them, He would soon have no right left. Again : the will of man, when renovated by grace, needs a rule by which to put forth its renewed activity, just as the eye, relieved of its darkness by the surgeon needs light to see.   Hence, we provide light for the renovated eye; not that light alone could make the blind eye see.   And hence, God applies His precepts to the renovated will, in order that it may have a law by which to act out its newly bestowed, spiritual free-agency. But 3d, and chiefly: These objections are all removed, by making a sound distinction between regeneration and conversion. In the latter the soul is active; and the acts required by all the above passages, are the soul's (now regenerate) turning to God.

Objection Answered.

IV. The salvability of any heathen without the gospel is introduced here, because the question illustrates these views concerning the extent of the grace of redemption, and the discussions between us and the Arminians.   We must hold that Revelation gives us no evidence that Pagans can find salvation, without Scriptural means.   They are sinners.   The means in their reach appear to contain no salvation. a.) One argument is this : All of them are self-convicted of some sin (against the light of nature). "Without the shedding of blood is no remission."   But the gospel is the only proposal of atonement to man.   b.) Paganism

Bible Promises No Salvation to Heathen.

provides nothing to meet the other great want of human nature, an agency for moral renovation. Is any man more spiritually minded than decent children of the Church are, because he is a Pagan? Do they need the new birth less than our own beloved offspring? Then it must be at least as true of the heathen, that except they be born again, they shall not see the kingdom. But their religions present no agencies for regeneration. They do not even know the Word. So far are their theologies from any sanctifying influence, their morals are immoral, their deities criminals, and the heaven to which they aspire a pandemonium of sensual sin immortalized.

Now, the Arminians reject this conclusion, thinking God

God no more Unjust to them than to Non-Elect under the Gospel.

cannot justly condemn any man, who is not furnished with such means of knowing and loving Him, as put his destiny in every sense within his own choice. These means the heathen do not fully possess, where their ignorance is invincible. The principle asserted is, that God cannot justly hold any man responsible, who is not blessed with both "natural and moral ability." I answer, that our doctrine concerning the heathen puts them in the same condition with those unhappy men in Christian lands, who have the outward word, but experience no effectual calling of the Spirit. God requires the latter to obey that Law and Gospel, of which they enjoy the clearer lights; and the obstacle which ensures their failure to obey is, indeed, not any physical constraint, but an inability of will. Of the heathen, God would require no more than perfect obedience to the light of nature; and it is the same inability of will which ensures their failure to do this. Hence, as you see, the doctrine of a common sufficient grace, and of the salvability of the heathens, are parts of the same system. So, the consistent Calvinist is able to justify God in the condemnation of adult heathens, according to the principles of Paul. Rom. ii : 12. On the awful question, whether all heathens, except those to whom the Church carries the gospel, are certainly lost, it does not become us to speak. One thing is certain : that "there is none other Name under heaven given among men, whereby we must be saved." Acts iv : 12. Guilt must be expiated; and depravity must be cleansed, before the Pagan (or the nominal Christian) can see God. Whether God makes Christ savingly known to some, by means unknown to the Church, we need not determine. We are sure that the soul which "feels after Him if haply he may find Him," will not be cast off of God, because it happens to be outside of Christendom. But are there such? This question it is not ours to answer. We only know, that God in the Scriptures always enjoins on His Church that energy and effort in spreading the gospel, which would be appropriate, were there no other instrumentality but ours. Here is the measure of our duty concerning foreign missions.

LECTURE XLIX.

ARMINIAN THEORY OF REDEMPTION. —
Concluded.

SYLLABUS.

1. Are God's decrees of personal election conditional or unconditional ?
Turretin, Loc. iv, Qu. 3, § 1-7. Qu. 11. § 10-24. Loc. xv, Qu. 2, 3. Hill,
bk, iv, ch. 7, 10. Dick, Lect. 35. Knapp, Chr. Theol., § 32. and Note.
Watson's Theol. Inst., ch. 26.

2. Show the relations between the orthodox views of effectual calling and election, and the true theory of the will and free-agency. (a). That the natural will is
certainly determined to carnality, and yet free-agency exists therein. (b). That the
renewed will, after it is sovereignly renewed to godliness, and efficaciously preserved
therein, is yet more free : And therefore, responsibility exists in both states.
See Lect. 11, above on the Will. Turrettin, Loc. x, Qu. 4. Southern Presbn. Rev.,
Oct. 1876, July and Oct., 1877. Articles on Theory of Volition. Alexander's
"Moral Science," chs. 16 to 18. Hill, bk. iv. ch. 9, § 3. Edwards on the
Will, pt. i, ch. 3, and pt. iii. Watson's Theol. Inst., ch. 28, § 3. Anselm. *Cur*
Deus Homo., pt. i, ch. 24.

THE favourite Arminian dogma, that God's will concerning
the salvation of individuals is conditioned on His simple
foresight of their improvement of their common grace, in genuine faith, repentance, and
holy obedience, is necessary to the coherency
of their system. If grace is invincible, and all true faith,
&c., are its fruits, then God's purpose as to working them
must be absolute in this sense. If grace is only synergistic,
and the sinner's free will alone decides the question of resisting
it, or co-operating with it, then, of course, the sovereignty of
decision, in this matter, is in the creature, and not in God ; and
He must be guided in His purpose by what it is foreseen the
creature will choose to do. Thus we reach, by a corollary from
the Arminian doctrine of " Calling," that which in time is first,
the nature of the Divine purpose about it. The student is here
referred to the Lecture on the Decree. But as the subject is so illustrative of the two theories of redemption, the
Arminian and the orthodox, I shall not hesitate to discuss
the same thing again, and to reproduce some of the
same ideas.

And let me begin by reminding you of that plain distinction, by the neglect of which, Arminians get
all the plausibility of their view. It is one
thing to say that, in the Divine will, the
result purposed is conditioned on the presence of its means ;
another thing to say that, God's purpose about it is also conditioned or dependent on the presence of its means. The
former is true, the latter false. And this, because the presence
of the means is itself efficaciously included in this same Divine
purpose. Thus, a believer's salvation is doubtless dependent

1. Conditional De-crees are Implied in Synergism.

The Result May be Conditioned, and not the Decree.

589

on his repentance ; in the sense that, if he does not repent, he will not be saved.   But God's purpose to save him is not dependent on his choosing to repent ; for one of the things which God's purpose efficaciously determines is, that this believer shall have grace to repent.   Remember, also, that when we say God's election is not dependent on the believer's foreseen faith, &c., we do not represent the Divine purpose as a motiveless caprice.   It is a resolve founded most rationally, doubtless, on the best of reasons—only, the superior faith and penitence of that man were not, *a priori* among them ; because had not God already determined, from some better reasons unknown to us, that man would never have had any faith or repentance to foresee.   And this is a perfect demonstration, as well as a Scriptural one.   The Arminian opinion makes an effect the cause of its own cause.   And that our faith, &c., are effects of our calling and election, see Rom. viii : 29 ; Eph. i : 4, 5 ; 2 Thes. ii : 13 ; I Cor. iv : 7 ; Jno. xv : 16.

(b). But to this I may add the same idea in substance, which I used against Common Sufficient Grace : That, in fact, differences are made, in the temperaments and characters, opportunities and privileges of individuals and nations, which practically result in the death of some in sin.   Thus : what practical opportunity, humanly speaking, had the man born in Tahiti, in the 18th century, for redemption through Christ?   Now the Arminian himself admits an election of races or nations to such privilege, which is sovereign.   Does not this imply a similar disposal of the fate of individuals ?   Can an infinite understanding fail to comprehend the individuals, in disposing of the destiny of the mass?   But, under this head especially, I remark : the time of every man's death is decided by a sovereign Providence.   But by determining this sovereignly, God very often practically decides the man's eternal destiny.   Much more obvious is this, in the case of infants.   According to Arminians, all that die in infancy are saved.   So, then, God's purpose to end their mortal life in infancy is His purpose to save them.   But this purpose cannot be formed from any foresight of their faith or repentance ; because they have none to foresee, being saved without them.

Providence Makes Sovereign Distinctions in Men's Outward Opportunities. Especially of Infants.

(c). God's foresight of believers' faith and repentance implies the certainty, or " moral necessity " of these acts, just as much as a sovereign decree.   For that which is certainly foreseen must be certain.   The only evasion from this is the absurdity of Adam Clarke, that God chooses not to foreknow certain things, or the impiety of the Socinians, that He cannot foreknow some things.   On both, we may remark, that if this faith and repentance are not actually foreknown, they cannot be the bases of any resolve on God's part.

If Foreseen, Faith Must be Certain.

(d) That any purposes of God should depend on the acts of a
creature having an indeterminate, contingent
will, such as the Arminian describes, is
incompatible with their immutability and
eternity.   But all His decrees are such.   See
Ps. xxxiii: 11; 2 Tim. ii: 19; Eph. i: 4: Is. xlvi: 10.   In a
word, this doctrine places the sovereignty in the creature,
instead of God, and makes Him wait on His own servant.   It is
disparaging to God.

Immutable Decree Cannot be Conditioned on a Mutable Cause. Scripture.

Last: This very purpose of individual election to salvation is often declared to be uncaused by any foreseen good in
us.   See Matt. xi: 26: Rom. ix: 11–16: xi: 5, 6, etc.

But Arminians cite many passages, in which they assert,
God's resolve as to what He shall do to men
is conditioned on their good or bad conduct.
They are such as 1 Sam. xiii: 13; Ps. lxxxi:
13, 14: Luke vii: 30; Ezek. xviii: 21, etc.; Luke xix: 42.   Our
opponents here make an obvious confusion of things, which
should be distinguished.   When God preceptively reveals a
connection between two alternative lines of conduct, and their
respective results, as established by His law or promise, he does
not at all reveal anything thereby, as to what He purposes with
reference to permitting or procuring the exercise of that conduct
by man.   Of course, it does not imply that His purpose on
this point is contingent to Him, or that the consequent results
were uncertain to Him.   We have seen that many of the
results decreed by God were dependent on means which man
employed; but that God's resolve was not dependent, because
it secretly embraced their performance of those instrumental
acts also.   But the proof that the Arminians misconstrue those
Scripture instances, is this: That the Bible itself contains many
instances of these conditional threats and promises, and
expressions of compassion, where yet the result of them is
expressly foretold.   If expressly predicted, they must have been
predetermined.   See, then, Is. i: 19, 20, compared with vii:
17–20.   And, more striking yet, Acts xxvii: 23–25, with 31.

Texts Seeming to Express a Conditioned Purpose.

Rom. ix: 11–18, is absolutely conclusive against conditional election.   The only evasion by which
the Arminian can escape its force, is, that this
passage teaches only a national election of
Israel and Edom, represented in their patriarchs, Jacob and
Esau, to the outward privileges of the Gospel.   We reply, as
before, that Jacob and Esau certainly represented themselves
also, so that here are two cases of unconditional predestination.
But Paul's scope shows that the idea is false: for that scope is
to explain, how, on his doctrine of justification by grace, many
members of Israel were lost, notwithstanding equal outward
privileges.   And in answering this question, the Apostle evidently dismisses the corporate or collective, in order to consider

Evasion Attempted from Rom. ch. ix: 11.

the individual relation to God's plan and purpose. See the
verses 8, 15, 24. That the election was not merely to privilege,
is clearly proved by the allusion of verse 8, compared with
verses 4, 21, 24.

2. I am now to show that the Calvinistic scheme is consistent, and the Arminian inconsistent, with
the philosophical theory of the will and free-
agency. Let me here refer you to Lecture
xi, where the true doctrine of the will is
stated and defended, and request you, if your mastery of the
views there given is not perfect, to return and make it so,
before proceeding. While I shall not repeat the arguments,
the definition of the true doctrine is so important (and has so
often been imperfectly made by Calvinists), that I shall take the
liberty to restate it.

*Calvinistic   View
Agreeable to the True
Nature of the Will.*

The Arminian says that free-agency consists in the self-
determining power of the will, as a distinct
faculty in the soul. The Calvinist says, it
consists in the self-determining power of the
soul. An Arminian says an agent is only free, when he has
power to choose as the will may determine itself either way,
irrespective of the stronger motive. The Calvinist says that an
agent is free, when he has power to act as his own will chooses.
The Arminian says that in order to be free, the agent must be
exempt from the efficient influence of his own motives; the
Calvinist, that he must be exempt from co-action, or external
constraint; The Arminian says, that in order to be free, the
agent must always be capable of having a volition uncaused.
The Calvinist says that if an agent has a volition uncaused, he
cannot possibly be free therein, because that volition would be
wholly irrational ; the agent would therein be simply a brute.
Every free, rational, responsible volition is such, precisely
because it is caused i. e. by the agent's own motives; the
rational agent is morally judged for his volitions according to
their motives, or causes.

*True Theory of the
Will Stated.*

But when we ask : What is the motive of a rational volition, we must make that distinction which all
Arminians, and many Calvinists heedlessly
overlook between motive and inducement. The object offered
to the soul as an inducement to choose is not the cause, the
motive of the choice ; but only the occasion. The true efficient cause is something of the soul's own, something subjective ;
namely, the soul's own appetency according to his prevalent,
subjective disposition. The volition is not efficaciously caused
by the inducement or object which appeals, but by the disposition which is appealed to. Thus, the causative spring of a
free agent's action is within, not without him ; according to the
testimony of our consciousness. (The theory which makes the
objective inducement the true cause of volition, is from that old,

Motive What?

mischievous, sensualistic psychology, which has always been such a curse to theology). But then, this inward or subjective spring of action is not lawless; it is not indeterminate; if it were, the agent would have neither rationality nor character; and its action would be absolutely blind and brutish. This subjective spring has a law of its own activity—that is to say, its self-action is of a determinate character (of one sort or another). And that character is what is meant by the radical *habitus*, or natural disposition of the agent. And this subjective disposition is what gives uniform quality to that series of acts, by which common sense estimates the character of an agent. (And this, as we saw, was a sufficient proof of our doctrine; that otherwise, the exhibition of determinate character by a free agent, would be impossible). God is an excellent Agent, because He has holy original disposition. Satan is a wicked agent, because he has an unholy disposition, etc.

Now, this *habitus* or disposition of soul is not by any
Disposition What? means always absolutely simple; it is a complex of certain active principles, with mental habitudes proceeding therefrom, and modified by outward circumstances. With reference to some sorts of outward inducements, these active principles may act with less uniformity and determinateness; with reference to others, with more. Here, modifying outward influences may change the direction of the principles. The avaricious man is sometimes prompted to generous volitions, for instance. But our common sense recognizes this truth: that the more, original and primary of those active principles constituting a being's disposition or *habitus*, are perfectly determinate and uniform in their action. For instance: no being, when happiness and suffering are the alternatives, is ever prompted by his own disposition, to choose the suffering for its own sake; no being is ever prompted, applause or reproach being equally in its reach, to prefer the reproach to the applause for its own sake. And last: this disposition, while never the effect of specific acts of volition (being always *a priori* thereto, and cause of them) is spontaneous; that is, in exercising the disposition, both in consideration and choice, the being is self-prompted. When arguing against the Pelagian sophism, that man could not be responsible for his disposition, because it is "involuntary," I showed you the ambiguity wrapped up in that word. Of course, anything which, like disposition, precedes volition, cannot be voluntary in the sense of proceeding out of a volition; what goes before of course does not follow after the same thing. But the question is, " whether disposition is self-prompted." There is a true sense in which we intuitively know that a man ought not to be made responsible for what is "involuntary," viz.: for what happens against his will. But does any man's own disposition subsist against his will? If it did it would not be his own. There is here a fact of com-
38*

mon sense, which is very strangely overlooked ; that a man may most freely prefer what is natural to him, and in that sense his prior to his volition choosing it. Let a simple instance serve. Here is a young gentleman to whom nature has given beautiful and silky black hair. He, himself, thinks it very pretty, and altogether prefers it. Does he not thereby give us as clear, and as free an expression of his taste in hair, as though he had selected a black wig? So, were he to purchase hair dye to change his comely locks to a " carroty red,," we should regard him as evincing very bad taste. But I ask, if we saw another whom nature had endowed with " carroty red hair," glorying in it with pride and preference, we should doubtless esteem him guilty of precisely the same bad taste, and precisely as free therein as the other. But the colour of his hair was determined by nature, not by his original selection. Now, my question is : must we not judge the moral preference just as free in the parallel case, as the aesthetic ? I presume that every reflecting mind will give an affirmative answer. If, for instance, a wicked man made you the victim of his extortion, or his malice, you would not think it any palliation to be told by him that he was naturally covetous or malignant, nor would you be satisfied by the plea, that this evil disposition was not at first introduced into his soul by his personal act of soul; while yet he confessed that he was entirely content with it and cherished it with a thorough preference. In fine : whether the moral agent is free in entertaining his connate disposition, may be determined by a very plain test. Does any other agent compel him to feel it, or does he feel it of himself? The obvious answer discloses this fact; that disposition is the most intimate function of our self-hood, and this, whether connate or self-induced.

Is not this now the psychology of common sense and consciousness? Its mere statement is sufficiently evincive of its truth. But you have seen a number of arguments by which it is demonstrated, and the rival theory reduced to absurdity. Now, our assertion is, that the Calvinistic doctrine of effectual calling is agreeable to these facts of our free-agency, and the Arminian inconsistent with them.

This Theory Obvious. Calvinism in Harmony with it.

(a.) First, the equilibrium of will, to which Arminians suppose the gospel restores all sinners, through common sufficient grace, would be an unnatural and absurd state of soul, if it existed. You will remember that the Wesleyans (the Arminian school which we meet) admit that man lost equilibrium of will in the fall; but say that it is restored through Christ; and that this state is necessary to make man truly free and responsible in choosing the Saviour. But we have shown that such a state is impossible for an active agent, and irrational. So far as it existed, it would only show the creature's

Grace Cannot Produce an Equilibrium between Holiness and Sin.

action irrational, like that of the beasts.   Hence, the evangelical choice arising in such a state would be as motiveless, as
reasonless, and therefore, as devoid of right moral character, as
the act of a man walking in his sleep.   And, to retort the Arminian's favourite conclusion, all the so-called gracious states of
penitence, &c., growing out of that choice, must be devoid of
right moral quality,   how can those exercises of soul have that
quality?   Only as they are voluntary, and prompted by right
moral motives.   But as we have seen, motive is subjective; so
that the action of soul cannot acquire right moral quality
until it is prompted by right moral disposition.   Hence, if
that common sufficient grace were anything at all, it would
be the grace of moral renovation; all who had it would be
regenerate.

(b.) Second: We have seen that the notion of a moral agent
The Natural Will without determinate, subjective moral char-
Decisively Bent to acter, of some sort, is absurd.   The radical,
Carnality.   ruling *habitus* has some decisive bent of its
own, some way or other.   Is not this simply to say that disposition is disposed?   The question of fact then arises, which is
the bent or determinate direction, which man's natural disposition has, touching spiritual things?   Is it for, or against?   Or,
as a question of fact, is the disposition of mankind naturally,
and uniformly either way?   Or, are some men one way disposed by nature, and some the other, as to this object?   The
answer is, that they are all naturally disposed, in the main, the
same way, and that, against the spiritual claims of Christ and
God.   What are these claims?   That the sinner shall choose
the holy will of God over his own, and His favour over sensual,
earthly, and sinful joys in all their forms.   Nothing less than
this is evangelical repentance and obedience.   Now note, we
do not say that no men ever choose any formal act of obedience by nature.   Nor, that no man ever desires (what he conceives to be) future blessedness by nature.   Nor, that every
natural man is as much bent on all forms of rebellion, as every
other.   But we assert, as a matter of fact, that all naturally prefer self-will to God's holy will, and earthly, sensual, and sinful
joys (in some forms) to God's favour and communion; that this
is the original, fundamental, spontaneous disposition of all; and
that in all essential alternatives between self and God, the disposition is, in the natural man, absolutely determinate and certain.   If this is true, then the unconverted man without sovereign grace is equally certain to choose carnally, and equally
a free agent in choosing so.

But that such is the determinate disposition of every nat-
Proved by Con- ural man, is obvious both from experience
sciousness and Exper- and from Scripture.   Every renewed man,
ience.   in reviewing his own purposes, is conscious
that, before regeneration, self-will was, as against God, abso-

lutely dominant in all his feelings and purposes; of which no
stronger test can be imagined than this conscious fact; that the
very best religious impulses to which his soul could be spurred
by remorse or alarm, were but modifications of self-will, (self-
righteousness.) Every true Christian looks back to the time
when he was absolutely incompetent to find, or even to imagine, any spontaneous good or joy in anything except carnality;
and the only apprehension it was possible for him to have of
God's service, in looking forward to the time when, he supposed, the fear of hell would compel him to undertake it, was of
a constraint and a sacrifice. So, when we look without, while
we see a good many in the state of nature, partially practising
many secular virtues, and even rendering to God some self-
righteous regards, we see none preferring God's will and favour
to self-will and earth. All regard such a choice as an evil
per se; all shrink from it obstinately ; all do so under inducements to embrace it which reasonably ought to be immense and
overwhelming. The experimental evidence, that this carnality
is the original and determinate law of their disposition, is as
complete as that which shows the desire of happiness is a law of
their disposition. And all this remains true of sinners under
the gospel, of sinners enlightened, of sinners convicted and
awakened by the Holy Ghost in His common operations ;
which is a complete, practical proof that there is not any such
sufficient grace, common to all, as brings their wills into equilibrium about evangelical good. For those are just the elements which the Arminians name, as making up that grace:
and we see that where they are, still there is no equilibrium, but the old, spontaneous, native bent, obstinately dominant still.

The decisiveness of that disposition is also asserted in
Scripture in the strongest possible terms.
Proved by Scripture. All men are the " servants of sin," Jno. viii :
34 ; Rom. vi : 20 ; 2 Pet. ii : 19. They are " sold under sin."
Rom. vii : 14. They are " in the bond of iniquity." Acts viii :
23. They are " dead in sins." Eph. ii : 1. They are " blind ;"
yea, " blindness" itself. Eph. iv : 18. Their " hearts are
stony." Ezek. xxxvi : 26. They are " impotent " for evangelical good. 2 Cor. iii : 5 ; Jno. xv : 5 ; Rom. v : 6 ; Matt.
vii : 18 ; xii : 34 ; Jno. vi : 44. " The carnal mind is enmity,
and cannot be subject to the law of God." Rom. viii : 7.
Surely these, with the multitude of similar testimonies, are
enough to prove against all ingenious glosses, that our view of
man's disposition is true. But if man's free-agency is misdirected by such active principles as these, original, uniform,
absolutely decisive, it is folly to suppose that the mighty revolution to holiness can originate in that free-agency; it must
originate without, in almighty grace.

Nor is it hard for the mind which has comprehended this

Inability does not Supersede Responsibility. philosophy of common sense and experience, to solve the current Arminian objection; that the man in such a state of will cannot be responsible or blameworthy for his continued impenitency. This "inability of will" does not supersede either free-agency or responsibility.

Inability Defined. There is here an obvious distinction from that external coaction, which the reason and conscience of every man recognizes as a different state, which would supersede responsibility. The Calvinists of the school of Jonathan Edwards make frequent use of the terms, "moral inability," "natural inability," to express that plain, old distinction. Turrettin teaches us that they are not new. In his Locus, x, que. 4, § 39, 40, you will find some very sensible remarks, which show that this pair of terms is utterly ambiguous and inappropriate, however good the meaning of the Calvinists who used them. I never employ them. That state which they attempt to describe as "moral inability," our Confession more accurately calls, loss of all "ability of will." (Ch. ix : § 3). It should be remarked here, that in this phrase, and in many similar ones of our Confession, the word "will" is used in a sense more comprehensive than the specific faculty of choosing. It means the "conative powers," (so called by Hamilton,) including with that specific function, the whole active power of soul. The "inability," then, which we impute to the natural man, and which does not supersede responsibility, while it does make his voluntary continuance in impenitence absolutely certain, and his turning of himself to true holiness impossible, is a very distinct thing from that physical coaction, and that natural lack of essential faculties, either of which would be inconsistent with moral obligation. It is thus defined in Hodge's outlines: "Ability consists in the power of the agent to change his own subjective state, to make himself prefer what he does not prefer, and to act in a given case in opposition to the co-existent desires and preferences of the agent's own heart." I will close with a statement of the distinction, which I uttered under very responsible circumstances. "All intelligent Calvinists understand very well, that "inability" consists not in the extinction of any of the powers which constituted man the creature he was before Adam's fall, and which made his essence as a religious being; but in the thorough moral perversion of them all. The soul's essence is not destroyed by the fall; if it were, in any part, man's responsibility would be to that extent modified. But all his faculties and susceptibilities now have a decisive and uniform, a native and universal, a perpetual and total moral perversion, by reason of the utter revolt of his will from God and holiness, to self-will and sin; such that it is impossible for him, in his own free will, to choose spiritual good for its own sake."

(c) Regeneration, correspondingly, does not constrain a
Regeneration does man to will against his dispositions; but it
not Violate, but Per- renews the dispositions themselves. It re-
fects Free-agency. verses the morbid and perverse bias of the
will. It rectifies the action of all faculties and affections,
previously perverted by that bias. God's people are "willing in
the day of His power." Ps. cx : 3. "He worketh in them
both to will and to do of His good pleasure." Phil. ii : 13.   In
that believers now form holy volitions at the prompting of their
own subjective principles, unconstrained by force, they are precisely as free as when, before, they spontaneously formed sinful
volitions at the prompting of their opposite evil principles. But
in that the action of intellect and desire and conscience is now
rectified, purified, ennobled, by the divine renovation, the believer is more free than he was before.   "He cannot sin, because
the living and incorruptible seed" of which he is born again
"liveth and abideth in him." Thus, regeneration, though
almighty, does not infringe free-agency, but perfects it.

The standing Arminian objection is, that man cannot be
praise- or blame-worthy, for what does not
Objection Solved. proceed from his own free-will.   Hence, if he
does not primarily choose a new heart, but it is wrought in him
by another, he has no more moral credit, either for the change
or its consequences, than for the native colour of his hair. This
objection is, as you have seen, of a Pelagian source. By the
same argument Adam could have had no concreated righteousness; but we saw that the denial of it to him was absurd. By
the same reasoning God Himself could have no moral credit
for His holy volitions; for He never chose a righteousness,
having been eternally and necessarily righteous. We might
reply, also, that the new and holy state is chosen by the regenerate man, for his will is as free and self-moved, when renovated,
in preferring his own renovation, as it ever was in sinners.

To sum up, then : The quickening touch of the Holy
Ghost operates, not to contravene any of the
This Because the
Spirit Moulds Disposi- free actings of the will; but to mould dispo-
tion *a priori* to the sitions which lie back of it.   Second : all the
Will. subsequent right volitions of the regenerate
soul are in view of inducements rationally presented to it. The
Spirit acts, not across man's nature, but according to its better
law. Third : the propensities by which the renewed volitions
are determined are now noble, not ignoble, harmonious, not
confused and hostile; and rational, not unreasonable. Man is
most truly free when he has his soul most freely subjected to
God's holy will. See those illustrious passages in John viii :
36; 2 Cor. iii: 17.   Since this blessed work is like the ability
for the good which it reinstates, one wholly unique among
the actions of God, and essentially different from all
physical effects, it cannot receive any adequate illustration.

Any parallel attempted, from either material or animal causes, would be incomplete. If, for instance, I were to say that the carnal man " in the bonds of iniquity," is like a wretch, who is hindered from walking in the paths of his duty and safety by some *incubus* that crushes his strength, I should use a false analogy: for the *incubus* is external: carnality is internal: an evil state qualifying the will itself. But this erroneous parallel may serve us so far; the fortunate subject of effectual calling has no more occasion to complain of violence done to his free-agency, than that wretch would, when a deliverer came and rolled the abhorred load off his body, restoring his limbs to the blessed freedom of motion, which might carry him away from the death that threatened him. You must learn to think of the almighty grace put forth in effectual calling, as reparative only; not violative. Augustine calls it a *Delectatio victrix*. It is a secret, omnipotent, silent, beneficent work of God, as gentle, yet powerful, as that which restored the vital spark to the corpse of Lazarus. Such are all God's beneficent actions, from the launching of the worlds in their orbits, to the germination of the seed in the soil.

LECTURE L.
FAITH.

AFTER noting those cases, as 1 Tim. i : 19, where Faith is evidently used for its object, we may say that the Scrip-

1. Faith of Four Kinds. Temporary Faith not of the Kind of Saving. tures mention four kinds—historical, temporary, saving and miraculous. As the only difference among theologians in this list respects the question, whether temporary and saving faith are generically different, we shall only enlarge on this. Arminians regard them as the same, in all except their issue. This we deny. Because: (a) The efficient cause of saving faith is effectual calling, proceeding from God's immutable election. Titus i : 1 ; Acts xiii : 48 : that of temporary faith is the common call. (b) The subject of saving faith is a "good heart ; " a regenerate soul: that of temporary faith is a stony soul. See Matt. xiii : 5, 6, with 8 ; John iii : 36, or 1 John v : 1, with Acts viii : 13 and 23. (c) The firmness and substance of the two differ essentially. Matt. xiii : 21 ; 1 Pet. i : 23. (d) Their objects are different: saving faith embracing Christ as He is offered in the gospel, a Saviour from sin to holiness: and temporary faith embracing only the impunity and enjoyments of the Christian. (e) Their results are different: the one

600

bearing all the fruits of sanctification, comfort and persever
ance; the other bearing no fruit unto perfection. See the par
able of the sower again.

The special object of saving faith is Christ the Redeemer,
2. Christ the Special Object of Faith. and the promises of grace in Him. By this,
we do not mean that any true believer will
willfully and knowingly reject any of the
other propositions of God's word. For the same habit of faith,
or disposition of holy assent and obedience to God's authority,
which causes the embracing of gospel propositions, will cause
the embracing of all others, as fast as their evidence becomes
known. But we mean that, in justifying faith, Christ and His
grace are the object immediately before the believer's mind; and
that if he have a saving knowledge of this, but be ignorant of
all the rest of the gospel, he may still be saved by believing
this. The evidences are, that the gospel is so often spoken of
as the object of faith; [but this is about Christ]; e. g. Mark
xvi : 15, 16; Eph. i : 13; Mark i : 15; Rom. i : 16, 17; *et passim.* That believing on Christ is so often mentioned as the
sole condition, and that, to men who must probably have been
ignorant of many heads of divinity; e. g., Acts xvi : 31; Jno.
iii : 18 ; vi : 40 ; Rom. x : 9, &c. The same thing may be
argued from the experiences of Bible saints, who represent
themselves as fixing their eyes specially on Christ. 1 Tim. i :
15, &c., and from the two sacraments of faith, which point
immediately to Jesus Christ. Still, this special faith is, in its
habitus, a principle of hearty consent to all God's holy truth, as
fast as it is apprehened as His. Faith embraces Christ substantially in all His offices. This must be urged, as of prime practical importance. Dr. Owen has in one place very incautiously
said, that saving faith in its first movement embraces Christ
only in His priestly, or propitiatory work. This teaching is far
too common, at least by implication, in our pulpits. Its result
is "temporary" faith, which embraces Christ for impunity only,
instead of deliverance from sin. Our Catechism defines faith,
as embracing Christ "as He is offered to us in the gospel."
Our Confession (chap. xiv, § 2), says: "the principle acts of
saving faith are accepting, receiving, and resting upon Christ
alone for justification, sanctification and eternal life." How
Christ is offered to us in the gospel, may be seen in Matt. i : 21;
1 Cor. i : 30; Eph. v : 25--27; Titus. ii : 14. The tendency of
human selfishness is ever to degrade Christ's sacrifice into a
mere expedient for bestowing impunity. The pastor can never
be too explicit in teaching that this is a travesty of the gospel;
and that no one rises above the faith of the stony-ground-
hearer, until he desires and embraces Christ as a deliverer from
depravity and sin, as well as hell.

The papists represent faith as an implicit exercise of the

3. Faith Must be Explicit. mind, in which the believer accepts the doctrines, not because of his own clear understanding of their evidence, but because of the pious and submissive temper of mind towards the Church ; her authority being, to Romanists, the ground of faith. Faith accordingly may be compatible with ignorance, both of the other evidence, (besides the Church's assertion), and of the very propositions themselves ; so that a man may embrace with his faith, doctrines, when he not only does not see evidence for them, but does not know what they are! Indeed, says Aquinas: Since ἀγάπη is the formative principle of faith, the less a man's acceptance of the Catholic doctrine proceeds from intelligence, and the more from the impulse of right dispositions, the more praiseworthy it is. This description of faith is evidently the only one consistent with a denial of private judgment.

Proofs of Romanists Invalid. Protestants, on the other hand, hold that faith must be explicit and intelligent; or it cannot be proper faith—that the propositions embraced must be known; and the evidence therefor comprehended intelligently. They grant to Aquinas, that faith derives its moral quality from the holiness of principles and voluntary moral dispositions actuating the exercise; but his conclusion in favour of an unintelligent faith is absurd, because voluntary moral dispositions can only act legitimately, through an intelligent knowledge of their objects. The right intelligence is in order to the right feeling. Protestants, again distinguish between a comprehension of the evidence, and a full comprehension of the proposition. The former is the rational ground of belief, not the latter. The affirmations of many propositions, not only in theology, but in other sciences, are rationally believed, because their evidences are intelligently seen, when the predications themselves are not fully or even at all comprehended. This distinction answers at once all the objections made by Papists to an explicit faith, from the case of the Patriarch, who believed a gospel promise only vaguely stated and of us, who believe mysteries we cannot explain. Nor is it of any force to say, many Protestants could not give an intelligent view of any one sufficient argument for a given point in their creed. We grant that many professed Protestants have only a spurious faith. Again: an humble mind cannot always state in language intelligently, what he understands intelligently.

Affirmative Arguments. For an explicit faith, thus defined, we argue: 1. That it is the only sort possible, according to the laws of the mind. A man cannot believe, except by seeing evidence. As well talk of perception of objects of sight occurring in one, without using one's own eyes. But, say Papists: the Catholic's implicit faith is not thus

totally blind, but rests on the testimony of the Church. His
mind, influenced by ἀγάπη, has intelligently embraced this as
plenary and infallible. Now, may not a man have a conviction
in such case, implicit even of unknown propositions? e. g., you
Protestants have your authoritative rule of faith, your Scripture. Once adopt this, and you accept its unknown contents
as true; of which there are to you some, until your study of
Scripture-exegesis is exhaustive. Ans. Very true. But the
Romanist has no right to resort to this case as a parallel;
because he does not permit private judgment to exercise itself
in rationally weighing the proofs of the Church's authority, any
more than of the Bible's authority. He cannot; because then,
the individual must exercise his private judgment upon the
Scripture; the argument for the Church's authority being
dependent thereon, in essential branches. 2. The Bible agrees
to this, by directing us to read and understand in order to
believe; to search the Scriptures. See Jno. v : 39; Rom. x :
17; Ps. cxix : 34; Prov. xvi : 22; Acts xxviii : 27; Jno. xvii : 3;
1 Cor. xi : 29; Jno. vi : 45. 3. We are commanded to be " able
to give to every man that asketh of us, a reason of the hope
that is in us." 1 Pet. iii : 15. And faith is everywhere spoken
of as an intelligent exercise; while religious ignorance is
rebuked as sin.

But we now approach an inquiry concerning faith, on which
our own divines are more divided. Is faith
4. Is Faith Simple or Complex? a perfectly simple exercise of the soul, by its
single faculty of intellect; or is it a complex
act of both intellect and active moral powers, when stripped of
all antecedent or consequent elements, which do not properly
belong to it? The older divines, with the confession, evidently
make it a complex act of soul, consisting of an intellectual,
and a voluntary element. Turrettin, indeed, discriminates
seven elements in the direct and reflex actings of faith: 1.
Cognition; 2. Intellectual assent; 3. Trust; 4. Fleeing for refuge; 5. Embracing; and (reflex) 6. Self-consciousness of true
actings of faith, with 7. Consolation and assurance of hope.
The two latter should rather be named the ulterior consequences of saving faith, than a substantive part thereof. The
first is rather a previous condition of faith, and the third, fourth
and fifth seem to me either identical, or, at most, phases of the
different actings of the will toward gospel truth. Of the old,
established definition, I have seen no sounder exponent than A.
Fuller. Now, Drs. A. Alexander and Chalmers, among others,
teach that saving faith is nothing but a simple belief of propositions; and they seem to regard it as necessary to suppose the
act as capable of being analysed into a perfectly simple one,
because it is everywhere spoken of in Scripture as a single
one. Dr. Alexander also argues, with great acuteness and
beauty of analysis, that since the soul is an absolute unit

always, and its faculties are not departments of it, but only different modes it has of acting, the enlightening of the mind in
regeneration and the moral renovation of will, must be one simple act of the Holy Ghost and one effect, not two.   And
hence, there is no ground to suppose that faith, which is the
first characteristic acting of the new born, and result of new
birth, is complex.   Moreover, he argues, since the will always
follows the latest dictate of the understanding, it is unnecessary to attribute to faith any other character than a conviction
of truth in the intellect, to explain its practical effects in turning the soul from sin to Christ.

Now, in examining this subject, let us remember that the resort must be to the Bible alone, to learn what

The Question to be   it means by πίστις. And this Bible was not
settled by Scripture.   written for metaphysicians, but for the popular mind ; and its statements about exercises of the soul are not
intended to be analytical, but practical.   This being admitted,
and Dr. Alexander's definition of the soul and its faculties being adopted as evidently the true one, it appears to me that, the
fact that the Scriptures every where enjoin faith as a single act of
the soul (by the doing of which one exercise, without any other,
the soul is brought into Christ), does not at all prove it may not
be a complex act, performed by the soul through two of its
modes of action.   Dr. Chalmers, Dr. Alexander, and every
other divine often speak of acts as single, which they would
yet analyse into two elements, and those not of the same faculties ; e. g., the exercise of repentance or moral approval
by the soul, consisting (in some order) of a judgment and an
emotion.

In explaining the defect of the other argument of Dr. Alex-

The Heart Guides   ander, I would remind the student of the dis-
the Head in Moral   tinctions made in defending the doctrine of
Choice.   the immediate agency of the Spirit of regeneration.   True, the regenerating touch which enlightens the understanding and renews the will, is one, and not two, separate,
or successive exertions of power.   True, the will does follow
the last dictate of the understanding, on all subjects.   But let
us go one step farther back : How comes the understanding by
its notions, in those cases where the subjects thereof are the objects of its natural active propensities ?   As we showed, in all
these cases, the notion or opinion of the understanding is but
the echo and the result of the taste or preference of the propensity.   Therefore, the change of opinion can only be brought
about by changing the taste or preference.   Now, inasmuch as
all the leading gospel truths are objects of native and immediate moral propensity, the renovation of those propensities
procures the enlightening of the understanding, rather than
the contrary.   So in faith, the distinctive exercise of the
renewed soul (renewed as a soul, and not only as one faculty

thereof,) it is more correct to regard the element of active moral propensity (now towards Christ and away from sin) as source, and the new state of opinion concerning gospel truth, as result. But now, the understanding apprehends these objects of natural moral propensity, according to truth, because of the correct actings of the propensity towards them; and according to the soul's customary law, this apprehension according to truth, is followed by right volitions: the first of which, the embracing of Christ for salvation, is in the Scriptural, practical account of faith, included as a part of the complete act. If that which the Bible represents as a single, may yet be a complex act of the soul, exerting itself in two capacities (which I have proved), then it is no argument to say the embracing of Christ by the will is no part of saving faith proper, but only a consequence; because it is a natural consequence of the law that the will follows the last dictate of the mind. Grant it. Yet why may not that very act of will, thus produced, be the very thing the Bible means by saving faith? (According to the Confession.) Then, to settle this, let us resort to the Bible itself. Be it remembered that, having distinguished the two elements of belief and embracing, it is simply a question of fact, whether the Scriptures mean to include the latter as a part of that exercise, by which the sinner is justified; or a result of it. Then,

1. The very object proposed to faith implies that it must be an act as well as a notion: for that object is not merely truth but good, both natural and moral good. We often determine the character of the soul's actings by that of their object. Now, the exercise provoked or occasioned by an object of appetency, must be active. Here, we may remark, there is strong evidence for our view in this, that the Scriptures often speak of faith as trust. See Ps. ii : 12; xvii : 7; *et passim*; Matt. xii: 21; Eph. i : 12, &c. Chalmers most strangely remarks, that still faith does not seem to be anything more than simple belief; because when we analyse trust in a promise, we find it to consist of a belief in a proposition accompanied by appetency for the good propounded; and the belief is but belief. I reply yes; but the trust is not mere belief only. Our argument is in the fact that the Scriptures say faith is trust, and trust is faith. Chalmers' is a strangely bald sophism.

The Object of Faith not an Opinion, but a Good.

2. The Scriptures describe faith by almost every imaginable active figure. It is a "looking," (Is. xlv : 22,) a "receiving," (Jno. i : 12, 13,) an "eating" of Him, (Jno. vi : 54,) a "coming," (Jno. v : 40,) an "embracing," (Heb. xi : 13,) a "fleeing unto, and laying hold of," (Heb. vi : 18,) &c. Here it may be added, that every one of the illustrations of faith in Heb. xi (whose first verse some quote as against me) come up to the Apostle's

Faith always Active in Scripture.

description in the 13th verse, containing an active element of trust and choice, as well as the mental one of belief.

3. The manner in which faith and repentance are coupled together in Scripture plainly shows that, as faith is implicitly present in repentance, so repentance is implicitly in faith. But if so, this gives to faith an active character. Mark i: 15; 2 Tim. ii: 25.

4. The Scriptures represent faith, not only as a privilege, but a duty, and unbelief as a sin. I Jno. iii: 23; Jno. xvi: 9. Now, it seems clear that nothing is a sin, in which there is no voluntary element. The mere notion of the understanding arises upon the sight of evidence involuntary; and there is no moral desert or ill-desert about it, any more than in being hurt when hit. And the reason why we are responsible for our belief on moral subjects is, that there is always an active, or voluntary element, about such belief. The nature thereof is explained by what has been said above on the order of causation between our disposition or propensities, and our opinions concerning their objects.

Unbelief a Sin.

5. If we make faith nothing but simple belief, we are unable to give a satisfactory account of the difference between historical and saving faith. Chalmers, in the summary of his 6th chapter, as good as acknowledges this. But surely that must be a defective theory, which makes it impossible to see a difference, where yet, it admits, a substantial difference exists! Some would get out of the difficulty by denying that, in strictness of speech, there is any historical faith where there is not saving faith—i. e., by denying that such persons truly believe, even with the understanding. Many candid sinners will declare that their consciousness contradicts this. Says Dr. Alexander, the historical faith does not differ in that it believes different propositions; but in that it believes them with a different and inferior grasp of conviction, I would ask, first, whether this statement does not give countenance to that radical Arminian error, which makes saving differ from temporary faith, only in degree, and not in kind? And I would remark, next: This is a singular desertion of a part of the strength of his own position, (although we believe that position includes only a part of the truth.)

Historical Faith Differs How?

It is certainly true that historical faith does not believe all the propositions embraced by saving faith, nor the most important of them. Cat. que. 86. It believes, in a sense, that Christ is a Saviour, but does it believe that all its best works are sins; that it is a helpless captive to ungodliness; that sin is, at this time, a thing utterly undesirable in itself for that person; and that it is, at this moment, a thing altogether to be preferred, to be subdued unto holiness and obedience in Jesus Christ? No, indeed; the true creed of historical faith is: that " I am a great sinner,

It does not Accept the same Propositions.

but not utter; that I shall initiate a rebellion against ungodliness successfully some day, when the 'convenient season' comes, and I get my own consent. That the Christian's impunity and inheritance will be a capital thing, when I come to die; but that at present, some form of sin and worldliness is the sweeter, and the Christian's peculiar sanctity the more repulsive, thing for me." Now, the only way to revolutionize these opinions, is to revolutionize the active, spiritual tastes, of whose verdicts they are the echo—to produce, in a word, spiritual tastes equally active in the opposite direction. We have thus shown that historical faith does not embrace the same propositions as saving; and that the difference is not merely one of stronger mental conviction. But we have shown that the difference is one of contrasted moral activities, dictating opposite opinions as to present spiritual good; and thus procuring action of the will to embrace that good in Christ. See also, 2 Thess. ii : 10; Rom. x : 9 and 10.

It is very clear, that if this account of faith is correct, it Faith the Fruit of Regeneration. can only be an exercise of a regenerate heart. The moral affections which dictate the opinions as to moral good and evil, according to truth, and thus procure action, are spiritual affections. To this agree the Scriptures, See Rom. viii : 7; 1 Cor. ii : 14; Eph. i : 19, 20; ii : 8; Ezek. xxxvi : 26, 27; Phil. i : 29; Gal. v : 22; Tit. i : 1; Heb. xii : 2. To this representation there are three objections urged:

1. "That of the Sandemanian, that by giving faith an Objections. active and holy character, we virtually bring back justification by human merit."

2. "That by supposing regeneration (the very germ of redemption) bestowed on the sinner before justification, we make God reconciled to him before He is reconciled."

3. "That we tell the sinner to go to Christ by faith in order to be made holy, while yet he must be made holy in order to go."

The answer to the 1st, is that we define faith as a holy Answers. exercise of the soul; but we do not attribute its instrumentality to justify, to its holiness, but to the fact that it embraces Christ's justifying righteousness. It is neither strange nor unreasonable, that a thing should have two or more attributes, and yet be adapted by one special attribute among them, to a given instrumentality. The diamond is transparent, but it is its hardness which fits it for cutting glass. True faith is obediential: it involves the will: it has moral quality: but its receptive nature is what fits it to be the organ of our justification. Hence it does not follow that we introduce justification by our own moral merit.

To the 2d, I answer, it owes its whole plausibility to assuming that we make a difference in the order of time between regeneration and justification by faith. But we do not. In this sense, the sinner is justified when he is regenerated, and regenerated when justified. Again, God has purposes of mercy towards His elect considered as unregenerate. For were they not elected as such? In the Covenant of Redemption, Christ's vicarious engagement for them did not persuade the Father to be merciful to them. On the contrary, it only enabled His original mercy, from which the gift of Christ Himself proceeded, to go forth compatibly with His holiness. Hence, at the application of Redemption, God justifies in the righteousness of Another, in order that He may consistently bless, with regeneration and all other graces; and He regenerates, in order that the sinner may be enabled to embrace that righteousness. In time they are simultaneous; in source, both are gracious; but in the order of production, the sinner is enabled to believe by being regenerated, not *vice versa*.

To the 3d, I reply, that this is but to re-affirm the sinner's inability; which is real, and not God's fault,
Sinner Dependent on Grace. but his own. True; in the essential revolution from death to life, and curse to blessing, the sinner is dependent on Sovereign grace; (it is the virulence of sin that make him so;) and there is no use in trying to blink the fact. It is every way best for the sinner to find it out: for thus the thoroughness of legal conviction is completed, and self-dependence is slain. Let not the guide of souls try to palliate the inexorable fact, by telling him that he cannot regenerate himself and so adapt himself to believe; but that he can use means, &c., &c. For if the awakened sinner is perspicacious, he will answer, (logically), "Yes; and all my using means and instrumentalities, you tell me, will be adding sin to sin; for I shall use them with wholly carnal motives." If not perspicacious, he will thrust these means between himself and Christ; and be in imminent risk of damnation by endeavouring to make a Saviour of them. No, let the pastor only reply to the anxious soul in the words of Paul, (Acts xvi : 31) "Believe on the Lord Jesus Christ and thou shalt be saved," while he also refuses to retract the truth, that "no man cometh unto Christ, except the Father draw him." The healing of the withered arm is here a parallel. Matt. xii : 10–13. Had that afflicted man possessed the spirit of this cavil, he would have objected to the command, "Stretch forth thy hand;" that it must first be miraculously healed. But he had, instead, the spirit of faith: and He who gave the command, gave also the strength to obey. In the act of obeying he was miraculously enabled.

If the sinner recalcitrate against the gospel paradox, the triumphant answer will be: that the root of the reason why he cannot embrace Christ in his own strength is, that his own spontaneous preference is for self-will and ungodliness. So that if he fails in coming to Christ, why does he murmur? He has followed precisely his own secret preference, in staying away If the minister feels responsible and anxious for the successful issue of the case entrusted thus to his tuition, let him remember: (a) That after all, it is sovereign grace that must regenerate, and not the separate efficiency of any views of truth, however correct; and that he is not responsible to God for persuading the sinner to Christ, which is God's own work; and (b) That God does in fact make the "sinner's extremity His own opportunity;" and where we see Him thus slaying carnal self by this thorough law-work, it is because He intends thereby to prepare the way for His sovereign regenerating work. Let not the minister, therefore, become disbelieving, and resort to foolish, carnal expedients; let him simply repeat the gospel condition; and then "stand still and see the salvation of God."

This difficulty is presented in its most interesting form, by the question, whether an anxious sinner conscious of an unrenewed state, may begin to pray with an expectation of answer. Some professed Calvinists have been so embarrassed, as to give a very unscriptural answer. They have argued that "without faith it is impossible to please God;" and as faith is a result of regeneration, it is the unrenewed sinner's duty to abstain from praying, until conscious of the saving change. But Scripture commands sinners to pray. See Acts viii : 22 ; Rom. x : 13. Man's logic is vain, against God's express word. Again: it is wrong to command any one to abstain from prayer (or any other duty) because he is in a state of unbelief, because it is wrong for him to be in that state. It is preposterous reasoning, which makes a man's own sin an exemption for him. Do we then, in commanding the unbeliever to begin praying, tell him to offer an unbelieving prayer? By no means. We intend that he shall so begin, that by God's grace that prayer, begun in the impotency of nature, shall instantly transform itself into the first breathing of a living faith. We say to him; Begin praying; "and be no more faithless, but believing." It is most instructive to notice how Christ Himself encourages the anxious sinner to pretermit the obstacle of this seeming paradox. The parables by which He inculcates prayer are evidently constructed with a view to encourage the awakened soul to waive the question whether it is renewed or not. In Matt. vii : 11, the tenderness of parents for their hungry children is the example by which He emboldens us. But in applying it, He actually breaks the symmetry of His own comparison, in order to widen the promise for the encouragement of sinners. We at first expect Him to conclude thus : "If ye then, though evil, know how to give good things to your children : how much more shall your Father in heaven give His Holy Spirit to His children." But no: He concludes: "to them that ask Him;" thus graciously authorizing us to waive the question whether we have become

39*

His children.   So, in Luke xviii : 14, the parable of the publi-
can shows us a man who ventured to pray in the profound and
humble conviction of his unrenewed state; and he obtained
justification, while the confident professor of godliness was
rejected.   These instructions authorize the pastor to invite
every sinner to the mercy-seat, provided only he is hearty in
his petition; and to direct him to the free mercy which comes " to
seek and save that which is lost."   Yet it is certainly true, that
the prayer of abiding unbelief will not be accepted.   But
Prayer is God's own appointed means for giving expression to
the implanted faith, and thus passing out of the unbelieving
into the believing state.

Rome teaches that historical faith is the substance of saving; (*fides informis*;) which becomes true
faith by receiving its form, love. (Thus *fides
formata*.)   Her doctrine of Justification is
accordant, viz: a change of moral, as well as legal state, consisting not only in pardon and acceptance of person, but in the
inworking of holy love in the character.   Now, in this error, as
in most mischievous ones, we find a certain perverted element
of truth, (without which errors would not usually have life
enough to be current.)   For faith, as an act of the soul, has
moral character; and that character, holy.   But the sophism
of Rome is two-fold: (a.)   Her *fides informis*, or historical
faith, is not generically the same act of the soul at all as saving
faith; being an embracing of different propositions, or at least
of far different apprehensions of the gospel propositions, being
the acts of different faculties of the soul; (historical faith, characteristically of the head ; saving faith, essentially of the heart.
Rom. x : 10;) and being prompted by different motives, so far
as the former has motive.   For the former is prompted by self-
love, the latter by love of holiness and hatred of sin.   (b.)
Faith does not justify in virtue of its rightness, but in virtue of
its receptivity.   Whatever right moral quality it has, has no
relevancy whatever to be, of itself, a justifying righteousness;
and is excluded from the justifying instrumentality of faith ;
Rom. iv : 4, 5 ; xi : 6.   But faith justifies by its instrumentality
of laying hold of Christ's righteousness, in which aspect it does
not contribute, but receives, the moral merit.   (c.)   Love cannot be the " Form of faith," because they are co-ordinate graces.
See I Cor. xiii : 13.   Rome virtually concedes this fatal point,
by pleading that love may be metaphorically the form of faith.
To the modern mind a conclusive general objection remains:
this Peripatetic mode of conception and definition, by matter
and form, is wholly irrelevant to a spiritual exercise or function :
it is only accurate when applied to concrete objects.

The solution of Rome's favourite proof-texts is easy; e. g.,
in I Cor. xiii : 2, the faith is that of miracles.   In Gal. v : 6,
faith is the instrument energizing love, and not *vice versa*.   In

5. *Fides Formata.*
Distinction.

Jas. ii : 26, works (loving ones of course), are not the causes, but after-signs of faith's vitality, as breath is of the body's. 1 Cor. vi : 11 ; Titus iii : 5 ; Eph. i : 13 ; Luk. xv : 22. &c., refer to the sanctification following upon justification.

By assurance of faith, we mean the certain and undoubting conviction that Christ is all He professes to be, and will do all He promises. It is of the essence of saving faith, as all agree. See Heb. x : 22, xi : 6; Jas. i : 6, 7; 1 Tim. ii : 8; Jer. xxix : 13. And it is evident that nothing less than full conviction of the trustworthiness of the gospel would give ground to that entire trust, or envoke the hearty pursuit of Christ, which are requi site for salvation. The assurance of grace and salvation is the assured conviction (with the peace and joy proceeding therefrom) that the individual believer has had his sins pardoned, and his soul saved. Rome stoutly denies that this is a part of faith, or a legitimate reflex act, or consequence thereof, (except in the case of revealed assurance.) Her motive is, to retain anxious souls under the clutch of her priest-craft and tyranny. The Reformers generally seem to have been driven by their hatred of this odious doctrine, to the other extreme, and make assurance of hope of the essence of faith. Thus, Calvin says, in substance : " My faith is a divine and spiritual belief that God has pardoned and accepted me." The sober view of the moderns (see Conf., ch. 18) is, that this assurance is the natural and proper reflex act, or consequence of true faith, and should usually follow, through self-examination and experience ; but that it is not of the essence of faith. 1st. Because, then, another proposition would be the object of faith. Not whosoever believeth shall be saved ; but " I am saved." The latter is a deduction, in which the former is major premise. 2d. The humble and modest soul would be inextricably embarrassed in coming to Christ. It would say : " I must believe that I am saved, in order to be saved. But I feel myself a lost sinner, in need of salvation. 3rd. God could not justly punish the nonelect for not believing what would not have been true if they had believed it. 4th. The experience of God's people in all ages contradicts it. Ps. lxxiii : 13 ; xxxi : 22 ; lxxvii ; 2, 9, 10. 5th. The command to go on to the attainment of assurance, as a higher grace, addressed to believers, shows that a true believer may lack it.

6. Asurance Distinguished.

God has chosen faith for the peculiar, organic function of instrumentally uniting the soul to Christ, so as to partake of His righteousness and spiritual life. Why ? This question should be answered with modesty. One reason, we may suppose, is, that human glorying may be extinguished by attaching man's whole salvation instrumentally to an act of the soul, whose organic aspect is merely receptive, and has no procur-

7. Faith Suitable Organ of Justification.

ing righteousness whatever. Rom. iii : 27. Another reason is, that belief is, throughout all the acts of the soul, the preliminary and condition of acting. See 1 Jno. v : 4, 5. Everything man does is because he believes something. Faith, in its widest sense, is the mainspring of man's whole activity. Every volition arises from a belief, and none can arise without it. Hence, in selecting faith, instead of some other gracious exercise, which may be the fruit of regeneration, as the organic instrument of justification, God has proceeded on a profound knowledge of man's nature, and in strict conformity thereto. A third reason may perhaps be found in the fact that faith works by love : that it purifies the soul; and is the victory which overcomes worldliness. See Confesson of Faith, ch. xiv : § ii, especially its first propositions. Since faith is the principle of sanctification, in a sinner's heart, it was eminently worthy of a God of holiness, to select it as a term of justification.

LECTURE LI.
UNION TO CHRIST.

SYLLABUS.

1. By what similitudes is the union of Christ with His people set forth in the Scripture ?
2. What are the several results to believers, of this union?
3. What is the essential, and what the instrumental bond of this union ?
4. Show the resemblances and differences between this union and that of the Father and the Son; between this and that of Christ's divinity and humanity; between this and that of a leader and his followers ?
5. Does this union imply a literal conjunction of the substance of Christ with that of the believer's soul ?
6. How does the indwelling of the Holy Ghost in this union, differ from that by which it is everywhere present ?
7. Is this union indissoluble ?
  See on whole, Dick, Lect. 67. Ridgley, Vol. iii, Qu. 66. Calvin's Inst., bk. iii, ch. 1. Hill, bk. v, ch. 5, § 1. Conf. of Faith, ch. 26. Hodge, Theol. Vol. iii, pp. 650–661.

IT is through this union to Christ that the whole application of redemption is effectuated on the sinner's soul. Although all the fullness of the Godhead dwelleth bodily in Him since His glorification, yet until the union of Christ is effected, the believer partakes of none to its completeness. When made one with His Redeeming Head, then all the communicable graces of that Head begin to transfer themselves to him. Thus we find that each kind of benefit which makes up redemption is, in different parts of the Scripture, deduced from this union as their source; justification, spiritual strength, life, resurrection of the body, good works, prayer and praise, sanctifi-

1. Union to Christ Effectuates Salvation.

cation, perseverance, &c., &c.   Eph. 1: 4, 6, 11, 13; Col. i : 24;
Rom. vi : 3, 4, 5, 6, 8 ; Col. ii : 10; Gal. ii : 20; Phil. iii : 9; Jno.
xv : 1-5.

The nature of this union is to be deduced from a full comparison of all the similitudes by which the
Word illustrates it.   In one place it is
described by the union of a vine with its
branches; and in another, of the stock of an olive tree with its
limbs.   Jno. xv : 1-5; Rom. xi : 16-24.   The stock is Christ,
diffusing life and fructifying sap through all the branches.
Second ; Our Saviour briefly likens this union to that between
Himself and His Father.   Jno. xvii : 20, 21.   Grace will bring
the whole body of the elect into a sweet accord with Christ
and each other, and harmony of interest and volition, bearing
some small relation to that of the Father and the Son.   Third :
We find the union compared by Paul to that between the head
and the members in the body ; the head, Christ, being the seat
and source of vitality and volition, as well as of sense and intelligence ; the members being united to it by a common set of
nerves, and community of feeling, and life, and motion.   Eph.
iv : 15, 16.   Fourth : We find the union likened to that between
husband and wife: where by the indissoluble and sacred tie,
they are constituted one legal person, the husband being the
ruler, but both united by a tender affection and complete community of interest, and of legal obligations.   Eph. v : 31, 32;
Ps. xlv : 9.   Fifth : It is illustrated by the union of the stones
in a house to their foundation corner-stone, where the latter
sustains all the rest, and they are cemented to it and to each
other, forming one whole.   But stones are inanimate ; and
therefore the sacred writer indicates that the simile is, in its
nature, inadequate to express the whole truth, by describing the
corner-stone as a living thing, and the other stones as living
things together composing a spiritual temple.   See 1 Cor.
iii : 11-16; 1 Pet. ii : 4-6.

Described by Im-ages.

Now, these are all professed similes or metaphors; yet
they must indicate, when reduced to literal language, an
exceedingly close and important union.   It is hard to see how
human language could be more completely exhausted, to express this idea, without running it into identity of substance
or person.   Its nature may be best unfolded by looking successively at its results, conditions, &c.   Let it be again noted,
that our union to Christ bears to all the several benefits which
effectuate our redemption, the relation of whole to its parts.

The results of this union may be said to be threefold ; or,
in different language, it may be said that the
union exists in three forms.   1st. A Legal
union, in virtue of which Christ's righteousness is made ours, and we " are accepted in the beloved."
See Rom. viii : 1; Phil. iii : 9.   This is justification.   2d. A

2. Why Called Mys-tical ? Three Results.

Spiritual, or mystical union, by which we participate in spiritual influences and qualities of our Head Jesus Christ; and have wrought in us, by the indwelling of the Holy Ghost, which was given to Him without measure, spiritual life, with all its resultant qualities and actings. See Jno. v : 25, 26; xv : 2–5 ; Eph. ii : 5 ; Rom. vi : 11 ; 2 Cor. v : 17 ; Gal. ii : 20. This union the orthodox divines have called mystical, (μνστικα), borrowing the expression, most likely, from Eph. v : 32. They did not mean thereby, that in their views of this union spiritual, they adopted the views held by the ancient and mediæval Mystics, who taught an essential oneness of the human intelligence with the substance of the Λόγος to be developed by quietism and asceticism. Orthodox divines have rather meant thereby, what is the proper, scriptural idea of the word μνστήριον from μνω, something hidden and secret : not something incomprehensible and incapable of being intelligibly stated. The spiritual union is indeed mysterious in that sense ; but not otherwise than regeneration is mysterious. The incomprehensible feature is not only similar, but identical ; it is one and the same mystery. But the tie is called mystical, because it is invisible to human eyes ; it is not identical with that outward or professed union, instituted by the sacraments ; it is a secret kept between the soul and its Redeemer, save as it is manifested by its fruits. The third result of the union, is the communion of saints. As the stones of the wall, overlapping the corner-stone, also overlap each other, and are cemented all into one mass, so, every soul that is united truly to Christ, is united to His brethren. Hence, follows an identity of spirit and principle, a community of aims, and a oneness of affection and sympathy.

The essential bond of this union is the indwelling influence of the Holy Ghost. This Spirit is indeed immense and omnipresent; nor is His providential agency dead or inoperative in any creature of God. But in the souls of believers, He puts forth a different agency, viz.: the same which He exerts in the man Jesus Christ, by which He fills Him with all the fullness of the Godhead. Thus the bond of union is formed. The vegetative influences of the sun are on the whole surface of the earth. In many plants those influences produce a growth, wild or useless, or noxious ; but in every cultivated field, they exhibit themselves in the vegetation of the sweet and wholesome corn which is planted there. In proof of this bond, see 1 Cor. iii : 16; vi : 17 : xii : 13 ; 1 Jno. iii : 24 : iv : 13. To return to the Bible figure of a vine or tree, the sap which is in the branches was first in the stock, and proceeded thence to the branches. It has in them the same chemical and vital characters ; and produces everywhere the same fruit. The sense and feeling of every limb are the common sense and feeling of the head. Hence we are entitled to take this pleasing view of all genuine, spiritual affections

3. Its Instrumental and Essential Bond.

in the members of Christ; each one is in its humble measure,
the counterpart of similar spiritual affections in Christ. There
are indeed some affections, e. g., those of penitence, which
Christ cannot explicitly share, because He is sinless; but even
here the tide of holy affection, of enmity to all moral impurity,
and love for holiness, wells from the Saviour's bosom; in passing through the believer's sinful bosom it assumes the form of
penitence, because modified by his personal sense of sin. Each
gracious affection is a feeble reflex of the same affection, existing, in its glorious perfection, in our Redeemer's heart. As
when we see a mimic sun in the pool of water on the earth's
surface, we know that it is only there because the sun shineth
in his strength in the heavens. How inexpressible the comfort and encouragement arising from this identity of affection and principle! Especially is it consoling in the assurance which it gives us of the answer to all our prayers which
are conceived in the Holy Ghost. Does the believer have, for
instance, a genuine and spiritual aspiration for the growth of
Zion? Let him take courage; that desire was only born in his
breast because it before existed in the breast of His head, that
Mediator whom the Father heareth always.

The instrumental bond of the union is evidently faith—i. e.,
when the believer exercises faith, the union begins; and by the
exercise of faith it is on his part perpetuated. See Eph. iii:
7; Jno. xiv; 23, Gal. iii: 26, 27, 28. First: God embraces
us with His electing and renewing love; and we then embrace
Him by the actings of our faith, so that the union is consummated on both sides. One of the results, or, if you please,
forms, of the union is justification. Of this, faith is the instrument; for, "being justified by faith, we have peace with God."
The other form is sanctification. Faith has the instrumental relation to this also; for He "purifieth our hearts by faith;" "faith
worketh by love;" and it is the victory which overcometh the
world.

Christ compares the spiritual union of His people to Him
self, with that of Himself to His Father. The
4. The Union Illus-   resemblance must be in the community of
trated.   graces, of affections, and of volitions; and
not in the identity of substance and nature. Our consciousness assures us that our personality and separate free-agency
are as complete after as before the union; and that our being is
no how merged in the substance of Christ. To this agree all
the texts which address the believer as still a separate person, a
responsible free agent, and a man, not a God. The idea of a
personal or substantial union would imply the deification of man,
which is profane and unmeaning. But when we consider
Christ's relation as Mediatorial person (and not merely as
Λογος) to God the Father, we have a more apt representation of
His union to His people. For this union is maintained by a

spiritual indwelling in Him.   The union between Christ's divinity and humanity, as conceived by the Nestorians (see lecture xxxix.) would afford also a more apt representation of the believer's union.   The Nestorians represented it as a συναφεια, not a ένωσις, and expressly asserted it to be generically the same with, and only higher in degree than, the mystical union of the Godhead with believers.   But then, they were understood as making of Christ two persons,   We, who hold with the Council of Chalcedon, cannot use the union of the two natures of the person of Christ, to illustrate the believer's union to Him; because we have shown that it does not result in a proper oneness of person.   The Church with its Head is only a spiritual corporation, and not a literal person.

But on the other hand, to represent Christ's union as only that of a mere Leader and His followers a union of sentiment, interests and affections, would be entirely too feeble.   In the case of the Leader admired and devotedly followed, there is only an emission of moral suasion and example, producing these results.   In the case of Christ and His people, there is far more; there is the emission of a Divine and vital Substance, the Holy Ghost, who literally unites Christ and His people, by dwelling and operating identically (though far differently in degree) in both; and who establishes and maintains in the creature by supernatural power, the same peculiar condition, called spiritual life ,which exists in the Head.   In a word, there is truly a sap, a cement which unites the two, that is a thing, and not merely an influence, a divine, living, and Almighty Person, viz.: Holy Ghost.

Not that of Mere Leader.

Yet, while we thus assert a proper and true indwelling of the Holy Ghost, with the believer's soul (and thus mediately of the soul and Christ), we see nothing in the Bible to warrant the belief of a literal conjunction of the substance of the Godhead in Christ, with the substance of the believer's soul; much less of a literal, local conjunction of the whole mediatorial person, including the humanity, with the soul. " Christ does dwell in our hearts by faith."   " It is He that liveth in us," but it is in a multitude of other places explained to mean the indwelling of His Holy Ghost.

5. Not a Partaking of the Substance of the Godhead.

Now, I cannot but believe that the gross and extreme views of a real presence and *opus operatum*, in the Lord's supper, which prevailed in the Church from the patristic ages throughout the mediæval, and which infect the minds of many Protestants now, arise from an erroneous aud overstrained view of the mystical union.   This union effectuates redemption.   We all agree that the sacraments are its signs and seals.   (See 1 Cor, xii : 13: 1 Cor. x: 17, *et passim*).   Now, the Fathers seem to have

Determines our View of Lord's Supper.

imagined that spiritual life must result from a literal and substantive intromission of Christ's person into our souls, just as corporeal nutrition can only result when the food is taken substantially into the stomach, and assimilated with our corporeal substance. In this sense they seem to have understood the eating of Jno. vi: 51, etc. (which was currently misapplied to the Lord's supper). Hence, how natural that in the Lord's supper, the sacramental sign and seal of the vitalizing union, they should imagine a real presence, not only of the God-head naturally, and of the Holy Spirit in His sanctifying influences, but of the whole Mediatorial person, and a literal feeding thereon. Hence, afterward, transubstantiation and consubstantiation, and the more refined, though equally impossible theory of Calvin, of a literal, and yet only spiritual feeding on the whole person.

The same general law of thought appears in what may be called the Pan-Christism of the "Mercersburg School," of modern semi-Pantheism. These divines having revived the old mystical idea of the substantive oneness of the human and divine spirit, through the medium of the incarnation, consistently assert a species of real-presence of the mediatorial person in the Supper. The connection is conclusive.

Let us disembarrass our views of the mystical union; and these unscriptural perversions of the sacraments will fall away of themselves. We shall make them what the Word makes them—commemorative signs, and divinely appointed seals of covenant blessings; all of which blessings are summed up in our legal and spiritual union to Jesus Christ; and this union constituted solely by the blessed and ineffable indwelling of Christ's Holy Spirit in our souls, as a principle of faith and sanctification. There is, then, no other feeding on Christ's person but the actings of the soul's faith responsive to the vital motion of the Holy Ghost, embracing the benefits of Christ's redeeming work.

To one who apprehends the dignity and intimacy of this
7. The Union In- union aright, there will appear a strong *a*
dissoluble. *priori* probability that it will be indissoluble.
The efficient parties to it are Christ and the Holy Ghost; parties divine, omniscient, immutable. The immediate effect on man's soul is the entrance of supernatural life, and the beginning of the exercises of new and characteristic and spiritual acts. One would hardly expect to find that these Divine and Almighty Agents intended any such child's play, as the production of a temporary faith and grace, in such transactions! When we discuss the doctrine of the perseverance of the saints, we shall find this *a priori* evidence confirmed. Our purpose now is not to anticipate that argument; but to suggest at this place, the presumption.

LECTURE LII.

JUSTIFICATION.

IT is obvious to the first glance, that it is a question of the first importance to sinners, "How shall man be just with
1. Its Importance.   God ?" The doctrine of justification was the radical principle, as we have seen, out of which grew the Reformation from Popery. It was by adopting this, that the Reformers were led out of darkness into light. Indeed, when we consider how many of the fundamental points of theology are connected with justification, we can hardly assign it too important a place. Our view of this doctrine must determine, or be determined by, our view of Christ's satisfaction ; and this, again, carries along with it the whole doctrine concerning the natures and person of Christ. And if the proper deity of Him be denied, that of the Holy Ghost will very certainly fall along with it ; so that the very doctrine of the Trinity is destroyed by extreme views concerning justification. Again : "It is God that justifieth." How evident, then, that our views of justification will involve those of God's law and moral attributes ? The doctrine of original sin is also brought in question, when we assert the impossibility of man's so keeping the law of God, as to justify himself. It is a more familiar remark, that the introduction of the true doctrine of justification excludes that whole brood of Popish inventions, purgatory and penance, works of supererogation, indulgences.

sacrifice of the mass, and merit of congruity acquired by alms and mortifications.

Not to go again into these subjects at large, which are illustrated in your history of the Reforma-

Justification as its Ground. tion, it may be briefly repeated, that as is our conception of the immediate ground of justification, such will be our conception of its nature. This proposition will be found necessarily decisive of every man's scheme of justification, be it what it may. If its ground is absolute, complete and infinite, the righteousness of Jesus Christ, it also will be an act complete, final and absolute, equal in all justified persons, admitting no increment, and leaving neither need nor room for any sacramental merit or penitential atonement. Once more : The blessed doctrine of an assurance of hope is intimately dependent on justification. If the latter is grounded on infused grace, and admits of loss and increment, the Christian's opinion concerning the certainty of his own justification can never become an assurance, this side the grave; for the very sufficient reason, that the fact itself is still suspended. If he were assured of it, he would believe an untruth; for the thing itself is not yet sure. Hence, the propriety of Luther's decision, when, taught by his personal, as well as his theological, experience, he declared justification to be the cardinal doctrine of the Church's creed.

The question concerning the true nature of justification should be strictly one of exegesis. All are

2. Etymology of Term. agreed that it is God's act. Hence, the opinions of men, or the human meanings of words by which men have expressed God's descriptions of it in Scripture, are not worth one particle, in determining its nature. It may, however, be remarked, that all English theologians have adopted the Latin word justify (*justifico*) from the *Vetus Itala*, Latin Fathers and Latin Vulgate, an unclassical word, which would mean, etymologically, to make righteous. I may also remind you, that Augustine, and a few of the other fathers, misled by this etymology, and their ignorance of Greek, conceived and spoke of justification as a change of moral state, as well as of legal condition. Here is the poisonous germ of the erroneous doctrine of the Scholastics and of Trent concerning it; a striking illustration of the high necessity of Hebrew and Greek literature, in the teachers of the Church.

When we pass to the original Scriptures, we find the act of justification described by a Hebrew and

Bible Terms. Romish Definition. Our Definition Greek verb, הִצְדִּיק, (hiphil) and δικαιόω, with their derivatives. Now, the Romish Church asserts, that the Scriptural idea of the act is not only God's accounting, but also making the sinner righteous, by both infusing the divine righteousness, and declaring it acceptable, in the sinner. We believe that the true meaning is not to make righteous in that sense, but only to declare righteous or make righteous in the forensic sense; and that the act of justification does not change the moral state, but only declares, in the forum of heaven, the legal state of the sinner. The soundest reasons for this, we shall give, without any claim whatever to originality, merely aiming to present them in a brief, lucid, and logical order. The Holy Ghost, then, by justification, intends a forensic act, and not a moral change.

(a) Because, in a number of cases, He expresses a justification of objects incapable of being made righteous by a moral change, by the justifying agents, in the given cases. Thus, Wisdom: Matt. xi : 19. God: Ps. li : 4; Job xxxii : 2; Luke vii : 29.

Proofs.

(b) Because, in a multitude of cases, to justify is the contrast of condemning; e. g., Job. ix : 20; Deut. xxv : 1; Rom. viii : 33, 34, &c. Now, to condemn does not change, but only declares the culprit's moral condition; it merely fixes or apportions the legal consequence of his faults. Therefore, to justify does not make holy, but only announces and determines the legal relation.

(c) In some places, the act of a magistrate in justifying the wicked is pronounced very sinful. Prov. xvii : 15; Is. v : 23. Now, if to justify were to make righteous, to justify the wicked would be a most praiseworthy and benevolent act on the magistrate s part. From this very argument, indeed, some have raised a captious objection; saying, if it is so iniquitous in the human magistrate to pronounce righteous him who is personally unrighteous, it must be wrong for God to justify in this (Calvinistic) sense, the sinner. The answer is, that God, unlike the magistrate, is able to impute to the justified ungodly, a vicarious satisfaction for his guilt, and to accompany this justification with sanctifying grace, ensuring his future obedience.

(d) The adjuncts of the act of justification are all such as would indicate a forensic character for it. Rom. iii : 19, 20 : the objects of the act are men who are ὑπόδικοι. See also Job ix : 2, 3; Ps. cxliii : 2. There is a bar at which the act is performed. Luke xvi : 15; Rom. iv : 2; Is. xliii : 26. There is an advocate, pleading our cause. 1 Jno. ii : 1.

e.) Finally, the equivalent expressions all point to a forensic act. Thus, in Rom. iv : 4–6, justification is explained by the forgiveness of iniquity, and covering of sin. In Rom. v : 9, we are justified by His blood and saved from wrath through Him; and v : 10, it is farther explained by reconciliation. In Jno. iii : 18; v : 24, &c., it is being not condemned, and passing from death to life. In a word, the only sense of the word which makes Paul's argument in Romans, chs. ii-v, intelligible, is the forensic sense; for the whole question there is concerning the way of acquittal for a sinner before God.

Papists, therefore, admit that the original words often carry
a forensic sense, even an exclusive one; and

Popish Objections. that in the justification of the sinner the forensic idea is also present; but they claim that, in addition, a
production of inherent righteousness in the justified person is
intended by the word; so that the believer is accounted, because made personally righteous in justification. And in support of this, they quote Is. liii : 11 ; Dan. xii : 3, from the Old
Testament, and in the New, Rom. iii : 24; iv : 22; vi : 4, 5;
viii : 10, 30; 1 Cor. vi : 11 ; Heb. xi : 4; Titus iii : 5–7; Rev.
xxii : 11. Of the first two texts it is enough to say, that the
forensic sense of the verb is perfectly tenable, when we assign
only an instrumental agency to the gospel, or minister mentioned ; and that sort of agency the Papist himself is compelled
to give them. Of 1 Cor. vi : 11, it should be said that it is a
case of introverted parallelism, in which the " washing " is general; and the sanctifying and justifying the two branches
thereof. Can they be identical : tautological ? " Ye are sanctified by the Spirit of our God, and justified in the name of
Christ." Rev. xxii : 11, only has a seeming relation to the subject, in consequence of the Vulgate's mistranslation from an
erroneous reading. · The other passages scarcely require notice.

The Protestant view of justification as to
3. Protestant Defini- its nature, and meritorious cause may be seen
tion. in Shorter Catechism, que 33.

The doctrine of Rome is a masterpiece of cunning and
plausible error. According to this doctrine,

Justification Accord- justification is rather to be conceived of as a
ing to Rome. process, than an absolute and complete· act.
The initiation of this process is due to the gracious operation of
the Holy Ghost, (bestowed first in Baptism,) infusing and inworking a *fides formata* in the soul. Free will is by itself inadequate for such an exercise, but yet neither doth the Holy
Ghost produce it, without the concurrence of the contingent
will of the believer. So that Rome's doctrine herein is synergistic. Moreover, the meritorious cause which purchases for
the believer, this grace of a *fides formata*, is Christ's righteousness and intercession. But now, the ἀγάπη, with resultant good
works, thus inwrought by grace, is the righteousness which is
imputed to the believer, for his justification—i. e., to entitle him
to life and adoption ; so that the work of justification not only
accounts, but makes the sinner personally righteous. It will be
seen how cunningly this doctrine, by mixing justification with
sanctification, avails itself of the seeming support of such passages as Rom. iv : 22, 24; x : 10; Acts x : 35 ;Gal. v : 6; Jas. ii :
26, how plausibly it evades those peculiar texts, as Rom. i : 17 ;
Phil. iii : 9, which say that the righteousness which justifies us
is God's ; and how " it keeps the word of promise to the ear,
and breaks it to the sense," in seeming to ascribe something

to the merit of Christ, while yet it is practically justification by
works.

According to the Council of Trent then, the final cause of
justification is (correctly), God's glory in the
bestowal of eternal life. The efficient cause,
God's grace ; the meritorious cause, the righteousness of Jesus Christ; (i. e., of His passion); the instrumental cause, baptism ; the formal cause, the infused righteousness
of God, dwelling in the believer. Justification will consequently
be imperfect in all, different in degree in different ones, capable of increment and diminution, and liable to entire loss,
in case of backsliding ; nor can its continuance unto glory be
certainly ascertained by the believer (except in case of inspiration), inasmuch as its continuance is not itself certain.

*Causes of Justifica-
tion according to Rome.*

Now all sound Protestants assert, on the contrary, that
there is no other justification than pardon
and acceptance as righteous in God's sight,
which is a complete and absolute act; done
for the believer once for all, perfect and complete in all, needing
and admitting no increment ; and above all, that God is not
moved in any sort, to bestow this grace of justification by the
condign merit of our inwrought holiness ; but that this latter
is, on the contrary, one of the fruits of our justification. We utterly exclude our own inherent holiness.

*Justification not by
Inherent Grace and its
Works.*

(a.) Because, however gracious, it is always imperfect. But
the Law of God (Gal. iii : 10; Jas. ii : 10,)
can accept nothing but a perfect righteous-
ness. Nor is it worth the Papist's while to say, that the believer's holiness is perfect *in habitu*, but imperfect *in actu*. They
also plead, since conversion is God's work, the godliness infused
must be perfect in principle, because "the work of our Rock
is perfect." Deut. xxxii : 4. I reply, His own works are, of
course, perfect ; but it may be far otherwise with those in which
imperfect man is recipient, and his feeble faculties means. I
urge, farther, that it is a fiction to represent that godliness as
perfect in disposition and principle, which is imperfect in act.
For the act expresses the principle. Said our Saviour : " Make
the tree good, and the fruit good." It is a favorite claim of unbelievers and Socinians, to say that their intentions and hearts
are better than their conduct : whereas, Bible-saints always confess the human heart worse than its outward developments.
And last : the plea would not avail the Papist, if granted ; because God says that when man is judged on his merits, it is the
overt act by which he is especially tried. Matt. xii : 37.

Arguments.

(b.) The Apostle sternly excludes works from the ground of
justification. Rom. iii : 20, 28, &c., &c. And
it is no adequate answer to say: he means
only to exclude ceremonial works. For be-
sides that, it is improbable the Apostle would ever have thought

*Evasion of Rom. iii :
20, &c.*

it worth his while to argue against a justification by ceremonial works alone, inasmuch as we have no proof any Jew of that day held such a theory; we know that the Hebrew mind was not accustomed to make the distinction between ceremonial and moral, positive and natural precepts. Moreover, the law whose works are excluded is, evidently from the context, the law whose works might prompt boasting, the law which was over Jew and Gentile alike, the law which was the term of the Covenant of works, and from whose curse Christ delivers us.

Another evasion is attempted, by saying the Apostle only

Another Evasion.
excludes the works of the unrenewed heart. We reply: Was it worth his while to argue their exclusion, when nobody was so impudent as to assert their value? Again, his language is general. He excludes all works which stand opposed to faith; but there is as much contrast between working and believing, after, as before conversion. Then, the illustrations which the Apostle uses, are David and Abraham, all of whose works he excludes from their justification. Surely the Hebrew would not naturally refer to their good works, as those of an unsanctified man! In fine, the manner in which, in Rom. vi, the Apostle answers the charge of " making void the law through faith," proves that he meant to exclude all works.

(c.) Our justification is asserted, in many forms, to be all of grace, to exclude boasting, to be by Christ's righteousness, as contrasted with ours. We assert that the freedom of grace, and the honour of Christ in our salvation are grievously marred by the Popish doctrine. Human merit is foisted in.

(d.) No holy exercises, nor gracious acts, whatever their source, have any relevancy to atone for past guilt. But remission of this is the more essential part of the justification, if either is.

(e.) When once the righteousness of Christ, which the Council of Trent allows to be the meritorious cause for initiating a justified state, is applied, we assert that the whole change of legal attitude is effected; and nothing remains that can be done more. The man " is passed from death unto life," and hath eternal life," Jno. v : 24; iii : 36. There is no condemnation to him. Rom. viii : 1. He " hath peace " with God. Rom. v : 1. He " is reconciled," v ; 10, and has acquired a vicarious merit, which *a fortiori* assures all subsequent gifts of grace without any additional purchase. He is adopted. Jno. i : 12. In a word, the righteousness imputed being infinite, the justification grounded on it is at once complete, if it exists at all.

(f.) The Popish idea that justification can be matured and carried on by inherent grace is inconsistent with God's nature and law. Suppose the believer reinstated in acceptance, and left to continue and complete it by his imperfect graces; why should not his first shortcoming hurl him down into a state of condemnation and spiritual death, just as Adam's first did him? Then his justification would have to be initiated over again. The only thing which prevents this, is the perpetual presentation of Christ's merit on the believer's behalf. So that there is no room for the deservings of inherent grace.

The Catechism defines justification as a pardoning of all our sins, and an acceptance of us as righteous in God's sight. It is more than remission, bestowing also a title to God's favour, and adoption to that grace and glory which would have been won had we perfectly kept the Covenant of Works. On the contrary, the Arminian declares justification to be nothing but simple forgiveness, asserting that, as absence of life is death, cessation of motion is rest, so absence of guilt is justification. The Scriptural ground on which they rely is that class of passages represented by Rom. iv : 4–8, where Paul defines, for instance, justification as that pardon of iniquities and covering of sin which David sung in Ps. xxxii. See also Acts v : 31 ; Eph. i : 7 ; Rom. v : 16, &c. We reply: We admit that forgiveness is the first element, and a very important element of justification ; and that wherever bestowed, it always infallibly draws after it the whole act and grace. In passages where it was not the immediate scope of the sacred writer, therefore, to define the whole extent of justification, what more natural than that it should be denominated by this characteristic element, in which a guilty conscience will naturally feel itself more immediately interested? Surely, if in other places we find the act described as containing more, we should complete our definition of it, by taking in all the elements which are embraced in all the places. We argue, then:

4. (1) Justification is both Pardon and Adoption.

(a) That the use of the words and their meaning would indicate that remission is not the whole idea of justification. Surely, to declare righteous is another thing than a mere declaration of exemption from penalty, even as righteousness is another state, than that of mere exemption from suffering. This leads us to remark:

(b) That the law contains a two-fold sanction. If its terms be perfectly kept, the reward will be eternal life ; if they be broken in any respect, the punishment will be death. Pardon alone would release from the punishment of its breach, but would not entitle to the reward of its performance. In other words, he who broke it, and has suffered the penalty, therefore does not stand on the same platform with him who has kept it. Suppose, for instance, I promise to my servants a reward for keeping my commands, and threaten punishment for breaking them. At the end of the appointed time, one of them has kept them, and receives the reward. A second one has broken them, and is chastised. Suppose this second should then arise and claim

Righteousness more than Guiltlessness.

his reward also, on the ground that suffering the full penalty of the breach was an entire equivalent for perfect obedience? Common sense would pronounce it absurd. Hence, the Arminian logic, that remission is justification, is seen to be erroneous. Since Christ steps into the sinner's stead, to fulfil in his place the whole Covenant of Works, He must, in order to procure to us full salvation, both purchase pardon for guilt, and a positive title to favour and life. The sinner needs both. Arminians have sometimes argued that the one necessarily implies the latter; because a moral *tertium quid* is inconceivable; there is no place between heaven and hell to which this person, guiltless and yet not righteous, could be consigned. We reply, the two elements are indeed practically inseparable; but yet they are distinguishable. And, while there can be no moral neutrality, yet, in the sense of this argument, guiltlessness is not equal to righteousness; e. g., Adam, the moment he entered into the Covenant of Works, was guiltless, (and in one sense righteous). God could not justly have visited him with inflictions, nor taken away from his present natural happiness. But did Adam, therefore, have a title to that assured eternal life, including all the blessings of perseverance, infallible rectitude, and sustaining grace, which was held out in the Covenant, as the reward to be earned by obedience? Surely not. Now this is what the sinner needs to make a complete justification— what Christ gives therein. The Arminian's error is betrayed by another of his own positions. He insists that the believer's faith is imputed to him for righteousness: i. e., as a putative righteousness graciously accepted for his justification. But he will not deny that pardon is for the merit of Christ's sacrifice. For what justification then is this imputation of faith made? His own dogma is only rescued from absurdity, by having in the mind that very element of justification which he denies: an acceptance or adoption into life which is more than mere pardon.

(c) To this agree the Scriptures. Zech. iii : 4, 5, justification is not only the stripping off of the filthy garment, but the putting on of the fair

Scriptures.

mitre and clean robe. Acts xxvi : 18, faith obtains forgiveness of sins, and inheritance among the saints. Rom. v : 1, 2, justification by faith brings us not only peace with God, but access to a state of grace, and joy and glory. Gal. iv : 5, Christ's coming under the curse for us, results in a redemption, which includes adoption. Jno. i : 12, believing is the immediate instrument of adoption, &c., &c.

Second: Those who admit this definition of justification, will, of course, admit that the righteousness by which the sinner is justified must include a full obedience to the preceptive, as well as the penal part of the law. And as that righteousness. (to an-

4. (2) Christ's Active Obedience Imputed.

40*

ticipate a point of future discussion) is Christ's, hence, the merit of His obedience to the precepts, as well as of His atoning sufferings, must be imputed to us for justification. [It is common for theologians to say : "both His active and passive obedience" are imputed. The phrase is clumsy. In truth, Christ's sufferings contained an active obedience; and it is this which made them a righteousness : for mere pain, irrespective of the motive of voluntary endurance, is not meritorious. And Christ's obedience to precepts was accompanied with endurance.]

(a) All the arguments then, by which the last head was **Arguments.** supported, also go to prove that both parts of Christ's righteousness are imputed for justification, (if either is). He undertook to stand in our law-stead; and do for us, what the Covenant of Works demanded of us for our eternal life. We have seen that after we sinned, it required an obedience penal and preceptive.

(b) It is most scriptural to suppose that all Christ did as a mediatorial person, was for us, and in our stead. Did Christ then, obey the preceptive law, as one of His official functions? The answer is, there was no other reason why He should do it —of which more anon. See Matt. iii : 15 ; v : 17.

(c) In many places, Christ's bearing the preceptive law is clearly implied to be for our redemption. See for instance, Gal. iv : 4. By what fair interpretration can it be shown that the iaw under which He was made, to redeem us, included nothing but the penal threatenings? "To redeem us who were under the law." Were we under no part of it but the threats? See, also, Rom. v : 18, 19, "By the obedience of Christ, many are made righteous." The antithesis and whole context show that obedience to precepts is meant. Rom. viii : 3, 4. What the law failed to do, through our moral impotency, that Christ has done for us. What was that? Rather our obedience than our suffering. See, also, Heb. x : 5–7.

In the days of the Reformation, Andr. Osiander vitiated **Osiander's View.** the doctrine of justification by urging, that if Christ was under a moral obligation to keep the preceptive law, (as who can doubt?) then He owed all the obedience of which He was capable on His own account, and therefore could not render it as our surety. Hence, he supposed that the righteousness imputed to us is not that of the God-man on earth, but the inherent or natural righteousness of ihe Deity. The Socinians and others have adopted this cavil, making it the staple of one of their objections to imputation. The answer is threefold. 1st. Christ did, indeed, owe complete obedience to law, after assuming His vicarious task. But for what purpose was the obligation assumed? For what purpose was the very humanity assumed, by which He came under the obligation? To redeem man. The argument is, therefore, as preposterous as though, when a surety comes forward, and gives his own bond, to release his bankrupt friend, the creditor should refuse to cancel the bankrupt man's bond, saying to the surety: "Now, you owe me the money for yourself, for I hold your bond!" The security would speedily raise the question: "What was the value received, for which I, who otherwise owed nothing, gave this bond? It was nothing else than the promised release of this bankrupt's bond." Thus every lawyer would scout the argument of the Socinian, as profligate trifling. See Witsius, bk. ii : chap. 3, § 14, &c. But second : Christ, as God-man, was not obliged to render any obedience to the law, to secure the justification of His own mediatorial person: because He was personally accepted and justified from the beginning. See Matt. iii : 17 ; Heb. i : 6. For whom, then, was this obedience rendered, if not for His people? And third : The obedience, though rendered in the human nature, was the obedience of the divine person. That person, as divine, could not be subject, on His own personal behalf, to law, being the sovereign. Hence, it must be vicarious obedience, and being of infinite dignity, is sufficient to justify not one believer only, but all.

Adoption cannot be said to be a different act or grace from justification. Turrettin devotes only a brief 5. Adoption. separate discussion to it, and introduces it What? in the thesis in which he proves that justification is both pardon and acceptance. Owen says that adoption is but a presentation of the blessings bestowed in justification in new phases and relations. And this is evidently correct; because adoption performs the same act for us, in Bible representations, which justification does: translates us from under God's curse into His fatherly favour. Because its instrument is the same : faith. Gal. iii : 26, with iv : 6, 7 ; Titus iii : 7 ; Heb. xi : 7 ; Jno. i : 12. And because the meritorious ground of adoption is the same with that of justification, viz : the righteousness of Christ. See Heb. xi : 7 ; Eph. i : 6 ; and texts above. The chief doctrinal importance of this idea then is, that we have here, the strongest proof of the correctness of our definition of justification, and of the imputed righteousness upon which it is based, in the fact that it is both a pardon and an adoption.

The representation of our adoption given in Scripture, with its glorious privileges, is full of consoling and encouraging practical instructions. The student may see these well set forth in Dick's 73d Lecture.

LECTURE LIII.

JUSTIFICATION. — Continued.

———

THE particular phase in which the Romish Church foists the merit of works into justification, has been considered

6. Justification not by Works. Evasions of Scripture. in discussing its nature. But now that we approach the subject of its grounds, it is necessary that we study the general reasons for the exclusion of works, in more comprehensive views. We find the Apostle, Rom. iii : 20, declaring : " Therefore, by the deeds of the law, there shall no flesh be justified in His sight ; for by the law is the knowledge of sin."

(1) To this agree the views expressed by all the sacred writers of the Old and New Testaments. See Ps. cxxx : 3, 4 ; lxxi : 16 ; cxliii : 2 ; Dan. ix : 18 ; Job xl : 4. These instances are peculiarly instructive, as showing that Paul broaches no new doctrine ; and especially as excluding the Romish pretext, that only works of the carnal nature are excluded ; because the Psalmist and Job are the very men who, in other places, make most earnest protestations of their sincerity and piety. Then our Saviour teaches the same doctrine. Luke xvii : 10 ; xviii : 14. And the Epistles likewise. Rom. iii : 28 ; iv : 6 ; xi . 6 ; Gal. iii : 11 ; Eph. ii : 8, 9, &c., &c.

(2) Justification cannot be by the law, " because by the law is

Because the Law Convicts. the knowledge of sin." That law which has already condemned cannot be the means of our acquittal. See Eph. ii : 3. The battle is already hopelessly lost, the die cast, and cast against us on this

628

scheme. If it is to be retrieved, some other method must be found for doing it.

(3) The law of God is absolute; as the transcript of God's moral perfections, and the rule of a perfectly holy God, who cannot favour any sin, it requires a perfect, universal, and perpetual obedience during the time of the probation. See Matt. xxii : 37, 38, &c.; James ii : 10; Gal. iii : 10. Every precept applicable to our condition must be kept; they must be kept all the time; and must all be always kept with perfectly proper motives or intentions! There is not a man upon the earth who, when his conscience is convinced of sin by the Holy Ghost, and enlightened to apprehend the majesty and purity of his Judge, would be willing to risk his acquittal on the best act he ever performed in his life. But see 1 Jno. iii : 20.

Because the Law is Absolute.

(4) While sincerely good works are an all-important part of our salvation, they cannot be the ground of our justification, because they are a result thereof. It is by coming into a state of favour with God, that we acquire from His grace spiritual strength to do anything truly good. See Jno. xv : 1–5; Rom. v : 1–2; vi : 3, 4, 6; Gal. ii : 20. All other works which man does are carnal, selfish, or slavish, and wholly unmeritorious before a perfect God. Hence, it is preposterous to attribute to our works any procuring influence as to our justification.

Because our Only Works Fruits of Justification.

Indeed, the exclusion of works by Paul is so emphatic, that there must be some evasion adopted, to limit his meaning in order to leave a loophole for doubt. Those evasions we have discussed in detail. We would remark generally, in closing this topic, that the fair way to judge what Paul meant by "works of law," is to find out what an intelligent Pharisee (he was reared one, and was now debating with them), would mean by "the Law," when named without qualification. The answer is plain, the Torah, the whole Law of the Pentateuch, moral, civic and ceremonial. And this law was conceived of, not merely as a set of carnal ordinances, or dry forms, but as a rule spiritually holy and good. See Ps. xix : 7; i : 2. Nor are we to conceive that the intelligent Jews thought of an obedience to this law merely unspiritual, slavish and carnal. They comprehended such precepts as Deut. vi : 4, 5; Ps. li : 6, to be an important part of the Law: and the evidence is, in such passages as Mark xii : 28–33; x : 19, 20. This certainly is the sense in which St. Paul employed the phrase, "works of the law," when he excludes them from justification, in his epistles. See Rom. iii : 20, with vii : 1–12 : viii : 3, 4: ix : 31; x : 3.

Fair View From Apostle's Point.

The Scripture which has been supposed to offer the greatest difficulty against Paul's view, is Jas. ii : 12 to end. On this it may be remarked, for

7. James ii : 12–26.

introduction : that if there is a real contradiction, both Epistles cannot be regarded as canonical; our alternative is to reject Paul or James, or else to show their difference only seeming. Further: when one writer treats a given topic formally and professedly, (as Paul obviously does justification in Rom.), and another only incidentally, it is out of all reason to force the seeming sense of the latter on the former.

It is well remarked by Owen, that James' scope is totally different from Paul's. James' is, to defend justification by faith from an Antinomian preversion. (See ver. 14.) Paul's is, to prove, against Legalists, what is the meritorious ground of justification. Rom. i : 17. Again: the faith of which James speaks, is a dead faith: such a faith as Paul himself would judge non-justifying; that of which Paul speaks, when he makes it the sole instrument of justification, is a living faith, infallibly productive of good works. See Rom. vi. And third: the justification of which James speaks, presents a different phase from Paul's, namely : not God's secret and sovereign judicial act, transferring the sinner from a state of condemnation at the time of his conversion, but that act declaratively manifested at any and every subsequent time, especially at the day of judgment. That this is James' meaning, is argued by Owen irrefragably from vv. 21–23. The apostle says, Abraham's justification by works, when he proposed to sacrifice Isaac, was a fulfilling of that Scripture, (Gen. xv : 6), which says: "He believed God, and it was imputed to him for righteousness." Now, that justification by faith was notoriously some thirty years before the offering of Isaac. The latter transaction must therefore be the fulfilling of the former stamement, in the sense that Abraham's justification was then not originated, but evinced. See close of ver. 23. These three remarks do sufficiently show, that James ought not to be held as contradicting Paul, when their scope and use of terms are so very different.

But a juster view of the matter will be gained by connecting our view of James ii : 14–26, with the other passages, where a similar, seeming difference is presented—e. g., Ps. xv : 1, 2 ; xxiv : 3, 4 ; Matt. xxv : 34, 35, 41, 42 ; Jno. xv : 8, 14 ; Acts x : 35 ; 1 Jno. iii : 7. The amount of all these texts is, that a just life is the test of a justified state ; and the general remark is obviously true, that this is a very different thing from asserting that the former is the procuring cause of the latter. Fruit is the test of healthy life in a fruit tree : not therefore the cause of that life. These simple ideas go far to explain the seeming contrariety of these texts to former citations. But perhaps the application of such an explanation to Jas. ii : 14–26, will be attended in the student's mind, with some difficulty, just here. Are we dealing fairly with the text, to suppose that

James' Scope and Terminology Different.

Work Essential as Sign of Justification, Worthless as Cause.

James does indeed use the word justify, a word of meaning so exact, definite and thoroughly established in Bible usage, in a new sense, without giving us any notice thereof? The exegetical evidence that he does, is well stated by Owen, (above). And the view is greatly strengthened by observing that the difference of meaning is in fact not so great. What is the transaction described, for instance, in Matt. xxv : 34, 35, and how does it differ from the act described in Rom. iii : 28? The latter describes the sinner's justification to God; the former the sinner's justification to God's intelligent creatures, (a more correct statement than Owen's, that it describes his justification by man). Each is a declaratory and forensic act; but the one is secret as yet to God and the justified soul; the other is a proclamation of the same declaration to other fellow-creatures. And it is most proper that the latter should be based on the personal possession of a righteous character : in order that the universe may see and applaud the correspondence between God's justifying grace and His sanctifying grace; and thus the divine holiness may be duly magnified.

A scheme of justification has been advanced by many of the lower Arminians, which is, in its practical results, not far removed from the Popish. It represents that the purpose of Christ's work for man was not to procure a righteousness to be imputed to any individual believers ; but to offer to God such a mediatorial work, as would procure for believers in general the repeal of the old, absolute and unbending law as a rule of justification, and the substitution of a milder law, one which demands only sincere evangelical obedience. The thing then, which is imputed for the sinner's justification, is the whole merit of his sincere faith, humble penitence, and strivings to do his duty, which God is pleased, for Christ's sake, to accept in lieu of a perfect righteousness. These theologians would say, with the Romanists, and higher Arminians, that our "faith is accounted as our righteousness;" but they would define justifying faith as a seminal principle of good works, and inclusive of all the obedience which was to flow from it. The point of inosculation of this, and the Popish theory, (determining them to be the same in essential character) is here. They both conceive Christ as having procured for man (in general) a new probation, evangelical indeed, instead of absolute; but in which the sinner still has his own proximate merit of justification to work out, by something he does. Whereas, the Bible conception is, that the Second Adam perfected, for His people, the line of probation dropped by Adam, by purchasing for them a title to eternal life, and covering also all guilt of the breaches of the first covenant. The student cannot discriminate these two conceptions too carefully. The former is "another gospel." It robs us of the very essence of

8. Christ did n o t Lower the Law.

a salvation by grace. It violates that fundamental principle laid down by the Apostle, Rom. xi : 6 : that the two plans of adoption unto life, the legal and gospel plans, cannot be combined. The attempt to do so confounds both. In one word : since man's will, in its best estate is, *per se*, fallible, if the plan of our salvation is that of a new probation by obedience, and if God's grace in regeneration and sanctification is only synergistic, then no believer is ever sure of his redemption. Our view of Christ's substitution under the Covenant of Paradise determines our view of justification. Thus : Adam by nature was righteous, innocent and guiltless ; but not yet adopted. The first covenant was given him, that he might by it earn his adoption of life, his elevation from the state of a (holy) servant, to that of a son. He failed in the undertaking, and fell, with his race, into the state of an enemy, both corrupted and guilty. The second Adam steps into the place vacated by the fall of the first, takes up the work where he dropped it ; and, while He makes expiation for the guilt, original   and   actual   purchases for all believers a perfect title, not to restoration to that mutable state from which Adam fell, but to that state of adoption, to which he had aspired. My desire is, that the student adopt this view as the touchstone of his doctrine.

I would remark, at the outset, that it comes with a very poor grace from these men to object to the imputation of Christ's righteousness to us, because it was not literally and personally wrought by us. It seems they consider that it is more consistent in God to account a believer's righteousness to him as that which it is not, thus basing his justification on a falsehood, than to account the legal benefits of Christ's righteousness to him for what it truly is—i. e., a perfect righteousness !

I refer here to the favourite cavil against imputation ; that it dishonours God, by representing Him as basing His judgment on a legal fiction. But I retort with the question : Which is more a legal fiction ; the Arminian scheme, which makes God adjudge a partial righteousness a complete one, *per acceptilationem ;* or ours, which represents Him as admitting an appropriate substitution, by which a perfect righteousness is rendered in the sinner's stead, and the law gloriously satisfied? There is, in fact, no legal fiction in this whatever ; unless men mean to denounce the Scriptural doctrine of substitution. God's judgment does not assert the perfect righteousness as done by the believer ; which it was not ; but as done for the believer ; which it was. I explained the true nature of " satisfaction," by the parable of the landlord and his bankrupt tenant. The bankrupt's brother, who is his surety, is a competent and faithful carpenter. As the landlord is building extensively, the surety proposes to pay the whole debt in faithful labour, at so much *per diem*, the fair market price of such labour. When that labour is all rendered, where is the legal fiction in the creditor's giving receipt in full? But had the surety proposed that he should receive receipt in full for some half-worthless script belonging to his bankrupt brother, this would have been a legal fiction indeed!

Against this form of the Arminian scheme, I present the following:

1. The source and basis of God's moral law is His own moral character; which is necessary and immutable. Supposing creatures to exist, there are certain relations between them and God, which cannot be other than they are, God continuing what He is. Among these must obviously be the essential moral relations of the law. These flow, not from any positive institution of God alone, but also from the very relations of creatures and the attributes of God. And if any moral relations are necessary, the requirement of a universal obedience is clearly so; because our Saviour represents the obligation to love God with all the mind, soul, heart, and strength, and our neighbor as ourself, as the very essence of that law. Hence, the idea that God can substitute an imperfect law for one perfect, is a derogation to His perfection. Either the former standard required more than was right, or the new one requires less than is right; and in either case God would be unrighteous. That Christ should perform all His work as an inducement to His father to perpetrate such unrighteousness, would be derogatory to Him. Hence, we find that He expressly repudiates such a design. Matt. v : 17. And here we may add, that the Bible nowhere indicates such a relaxation of the believer's law of living. David, a justified person, represents the rule by which he regulated himself, as " perfect," " pure," and " right," and " very righteous." Ps. xix : 7, 8 ; cxix : 140; Jas. i : 25 ; ii : 10. Everywhere, the law which we are still required to obey, is the same law which, by its perfectness, condemned us. Practically, the allowance of an imperfect standard of obedience would be ruinous; because man ever falls below his standard.

Proofs. 1. The Law Unchangeable as God.

It is objected again: God has changed His law, substituting certain simpler and easier precepts, in place of old ones; as in abrogating the burdensome ritual of Moses, and giving in its place the easy yoke of the New Testament ceremonial. We reply: those were only positive, not eternal and natural precepts of morality; the obligation to keep them only arose from God's command to do so; and hence, when the command was retracted, there was no longer any sin in their omission. To retract such commands is far different from making that no longer sin, which is in its nature sin. Again, it has been objected, that God's permission has been given, in some cases,

Asserted Changes of Law Explained.

to do what, without such permission, would have been, in its nature sin; as when Abraham was directed to slay Isaac, and and Israel the Canaanites. It seems to me surprising that these cases should be advanced with any confidence in this argument, or that they should be supposed by any to prove that the intrinsic relations of morality are alterable by God's mere positive precepts; or that so acute a writer as Mansel, in his "Limits of Religious Thought," should feel occasion to take refuge from the exigencies of the case, in the inability of human reason to conceive the infinite and absolute Being fully. The truth is, that in those cases there is no alteration whatever of any principle of natural morality, by which God has ever regulated Himself, or His human subjects. It always has been right for God to slay any of His rebel creatures, whom He pleases; He kills some thirty millions of them each year, by various means. And whenever God appoints man to slay it is no sin for him to do so, be it in the case of magistrates, self-defence, or defensive war. So that God's appointment of a man to take a given life renders it perfectly moral to take it. An instance of such an appointment is therefore no instance at all, of a conversion of what is naturally sinful into right. As fairly might one say, that when the master tells his servants that the unauthorized use of his substance is theft, and afterwards directs one of them to take and consume some fruit of his field, he has undertaken to alter the fundamental relations of morality! We repeat: there is, and can be no case, in which God has made that which is naturally wrong to be right.

2. Scripture represents the Bible saints as repudiating all their own works, even while they protest their affectionate sincerity in them. See Job xl : 4, &c. Moreover, their consciences rebuke them for every shortcoming from perfect love and holiness. Surely that which cannot justify us to our own consciences, will hardly answer with God! We appeal to each man's conscience : when it is enlightened by the Holy Ghost, does not it bear out this experience of Bible saints ?

Saints Strive to Keep the Perfect Law.

3. By such a scheme of justification Christ's work, instead of resulting in a complete harmonizing of God's absolute holiness and perfect Law, in the sinner's acceptance, would leave the law forever ruptured and dislocated. We are taught in Scripture that Christ was to " magnify the Law, and make it honourable ; " "that mercy and truth were to meet together, and righteousness and peace kiss each other " ; that He " came not to destroy the Law, but to fulfill." Now, if He has procured the abrogation of that perfect law, during each believer's Christian life, there is a demand of the law which remains unmet; and that forever. The doctrine makes a piece of patchwork: men do not sew new cloth on an old garment.

The Law Would Not be Magnified.

We conclude then, that the two methods of obtaining an adoption of life cannot be compounded; that, namely, by a probation of works; and that by gospel grace. The adoption of the one must exclude the other. This conclusion raises at once the question; Has not the Covenant of Works, then, been abrogated? To this many of the Reformed reply: Yes: and they refer us, for proof, to such passages as Heb. viii : 13. Arminius also asserted an abrogation of the legal covenant with Adam, but it was in a far different sense, and for a different scope from those of the Reformed. Hence has arisen confusion and intermingling of views, which calls for careful disentanglement. Arminius claims that the legal covenant was wholly abrogated at Adam's fall; because first, the promise of life through that covenant was then revoked, and vhere there is no compact there can be no obligation; because second, man could not be justly bound to obedience in a state of orphanage where God neither promised nor bestowed the gracious help essential to enable him to a true and hearty service; and because, third: it would be derogatory to God's wisdom, holiness and majesty, to practice such a farce as calling the depraved creature to a service of holy and entire love; the only one a spiritual God can condescend to accept. The use which his party designed to make of their conclusion, was this : In order that fallen man may be justly brought again under obligation to obey, the law of a new covenant must be enacted for him, to which his impaired powers may be adequate, and the imposition of which must be accompanied by the enabling helps of common grace. Thus he sought to prepare the way for the theory of justification which we have been discussing under our eighth head.

Now, the Reformed divines of Holland easily refuted this kind of abrogation of the legal covenant by such facts as these. Man's obligation to obey never was founded merely in covenant between him and his Maker. It is founded immutably in the nature of God, and of His rational creature, and in their natural relation as Master and servant. The covenant only added a reinforcement to that original obligation. Supposing the covenant completely abrogated, the original bond of duty would remain. Second: The inability of will, into which the race has fallen, is self-induced, and is itself criminal. Hence it does not at all relieve man of his just obligation. Third: It is one thing to say, it would be derogatory to God to allow Himself to be cheated by a heartless and hostile service from corrupt man; but wholly another thing to say, as Arminius does, that man's criminal and voluntary hostility has stripped God of the proper right to demand of him the hearty and loving service naturally due. And the whole argument of Arminius is shown to be preposterous, by this result: That it makes the sinner gain emancipation from righteous obligation, by sinning. There is no principle of law clearer than this; that no man is entitled to plead his own wrong-doing. Posit the conclusion of Arminius; and it will be only necessary for every creature in the universe to make himself vile, in order to strip God of His whole right of rule. That is, the servant's wrong may dethrone his rightful Lord! Once more: "where there is no law, there is no transgression." After obligation has ceased, of course, there is no more sin or guilt, and ought to be no more punishment. Thus we should reach this amazing result: Only let the creature make Himself wicked enough; and God will no longer have a right to punish him for his new wickedness.

The abrogation of the legal covenant in that sense, then, is absurd and unscriptural; and the student is placed at the proper point of view for appreciating the arguments by which we have above refuted that scheme of justification.

To what extent, then, does the consistent Reformed theologian hold the old covenant to be abrogated? The answer may be given by a series of propositions, which will commend themselves to belief by their mere statement: (1) The Ruler's claims to obedience are not abrogated by the subjects' falling by transgression, under penal relations to Him: So, all moralists and jurists hold, of all governments. (2) God's law being the immutable expression of His own perfections, and the creature's obligation to obey being grounded in his nature and relation to God, it is impossible that any change of the legal status under any covenant imaginable, legal or gracious, should abrogate the authority of the law as a rule of acting for us. (3) It remains true, under all dispensations, that the "wages of sin is death." (4) It remains forever true, that a perfect obedience is requisite to purchase eternal life. And such a compliance is rendered to the covenant of works for our justification, namely, by our Surety. Let us then beware how we speak of the covenant of works as in every sense abrogated; for it is under that very covenant that the second Adam has acted, in purchasing our redemption. That is the covenant which He actually fulfills, for us. Again, it is that covenant under which the sinner out of Christ now dies, just as the first sinner was condemned under it. The law is still in force, then, in three respects: as the dispensation under which our Substitute acts for us: as the rule of our own obedience; and as the rule by which transgressors dying out of Christ are condemned. Some, even, of the Reformed, have been so incautious as to conclude, that by the rule that "a compact broken on one side, is broken for both sides," transgression abrogates the legal covenant wholly, as soon as it is committed. One plain question exposes this: By what authority, then, does the Ruler punish the transgressor after the law is broken? If, for instance, a murder abrogated the legal covenant between the murderer and the commonwealth, from the hour it was committed, I presume that he would be exceedingly mystified to know under what law he was going to be hung! The obvious statement is this: The transgression has indeed terminated the sinner's right to the sanction of reward; but it has not terminated his obligation to obey, nor to the penal sanction.

This last remark shows us, in what sense the covenant of works was abrogated when Adam fell—and this is obviously the sense of Paul. The proposal of life by the law is at an end for the fallen; they have forever disabled themselves for acquiring, under that law, the sanction of reward, by their own works. Hence, God, in His mercy, withdraws that covenant so far as it is a dispensation for that result; and He substitutes for all who are in Christ, the covenant of grace. Compare Gal. v : 3; iii : 10; Matt. v : 18; Rom. vi : 14, 15.

The Wesleyan divines, while they disclaim and argue
9. Wesleyan View. against the imputation of Christ's righteousness, also discard the scheme we have just considered. They say that faith is imputed as the believer's justifying righteousness. Justification is, with them, simply pardon. They define faith properly as a simply receiving and resting upon Christ for salvation, and they earnestly disclaim the Socinian confusion adopted by so many of the Continental Arminians, which includes in the justifying power of faith the evangelical obedience of which it is operative. If asked whether Christ has not made satisfaction for sin, they fully assent, and they say in many forms, that pardon is "through His blood," "in His name" and "for His sake alone." If we ask, "How is it then, that an act whose organic virtue in the matter of our justification is a simple receptivity, an act which brings nothing to satisfy the claims of law, but only receives, can be accounted to us as a substitute for a whole and complete righteousness?" They reply that this is the gracious effect of Christ's sacrifice; this is what His precious blood procures for us; and this is the sense in which pardon is of free grace. Thus they suppose they escape the "absurdities of imputation," and still exalt the absolute freeness of Gospel redemption.

In this view, the doctrine is open to all the objections
Makes Faith a urged against the one just refuted above, and
Work. in greater force; for it represents God's imputation as a most glaring violation of truth, in accounting not the imperfect duties of a Christian life, but one imperfect act as a complete obedience! And while it seems to repudiate works, and establish faith, it really foists in again the doctrine of human merit and works; for faith is also an act, an act of obedience to law. (Jno. vi : 29; 1 Jno. iii : 23), and if rendered as a matter of righteousness before God, or, indeed, for anything except the mere instrument of accepting Christ, it is a work. But faith and work should be opposed.

Again: the idea that faith is accounted to us as our justifying righteousness, contradicts, in two ways,
that nature which Scripture attributes to it.

Faith only Re-
ceives.

It is said in many places, that righteousness
is by faith, (Rom. i: 17, etc., etc). Now, then, it cannot be
identical with it. Moreover, faith is defined as an act purely
receptive, and receptive of Christ our righteousness. Jno. i:
12. Now, that it should be a righteousness when its very nature
is to embrace a righteousness, is as contradictory, as that the
beggar's confessions of destitution can constitute a price to purchase relief.

And last: the whole question is decisively settled against
this theory, as well as against the Popish,
and all other false ones, which make the
procuring cause of our justification to be,
either in whole or in part, anything wrought by us, or wrought
in us, in all those passages which declare that we are justified on account of God's righteousness, and sometimes it is God's
righteousness as contrasted with ours. See Rom. i: 17; iii:
22; Phil. iii: 9. How can these expressions be evaded? The
righteousness by which we are justified is not ours, but God's
—therefore not constituted of any acts or graces of ours.

The Righteousness Im-
puted is God's.

But, says the Arminian, it is vain to speculate against the
express words of Scripture; and here we have
it, four times over, Gen. xv: 6; Rom. iv.; 3,
5, 22, 24. We reply that they clearly over-
strain and force the text. It is true, that in Gen. xv: 6, the
construction is, "His faith was accounted righteousness (no
preposition). Now, suppose that in the other three cases in the
New Testament, the construction were even as difficult as they
suppose in this: would not a fair criticism say, that these somewhat peculiar statements should not be strained into a sense
contradictory to the current of plainer expressions elsewhere,
which always say we obtain righteousness by our faith! And
as Calvin well argues, on Gen. xv: 6, when the very context
clearly shows that the whole amount of Abraham's faith in this
case was to embrace a set of promises tendered to him, since
it did not bring anything on its own part to the transaction, but
merely received what God brought, in His promise; the sense
must not and cannot be strained to make the receptive act the
meritorious cause of the bestowal which itself merely accepted.
There is obviously just such an embracing of the result in the
instrument, as occurs in Jno. xii: 50; xvii: 3. But our case is
far stronger than even this. The Septuagint and Paul, an
inspired interpreter, uniformly give the sense, πίστις λογίζεται
εἰς δικαιοσύνην. This all these Arminian interpreters, with a
perverse inattention or ignorance, persist in translating "faith is
accounted as righteousness;" the English ones being probably
misled by the occasional use of our preposition, "for" in the

Wesleyan Proof-
texts Considered.

sense of our "as" (e. g., " I reckon him for a valuable citizen)."
But the Greek preposition, εις, with the accusative, rarely carries
that sense. See one instance, Rom. ix : 8; and its obvious
force in this passage is, that of designed results. " His faith
is imputed in order to the attaining of righteousness "—i. e.,
Christ's. This gives faith its proper instrumental office. Compare Rom. x : 10. Πιστεύεται εἰς δικαιοσύνην. Consult Harrison's
Greek Prep., and cases, p. 226. Our argument for the Apostle's construction is greatly strengthened by observing that the
Hebrew Syntax (see Nordheimer), expressly recognizes the
construction of a noun objective after a verb, to express this very
sense of intended result.

In conclusion of this head, the Scriptures clearly assign
that office, on the whole, to faith. This
appears, first, from its nature, as receptive of
a promise. The matter embraced must of
course be contributed by the promiser. The act of the receiver
is not procuring, but only instrumental. Second: all the locutions in which faith is connected with justification express the
instrumental idea by their fair grammatical force. Thus, the
current expressions are justified πίστει (Ablative), δια πίστεως,
ἐκ πίστεως. Never once are we said to be justified δια πίστιν ;
the construction which is commonly used to express the relation of Christ's righteousness, or blood, to our justification.

All Locutions of Scripture Prove Faith Instrumental.

We have now passed in review all the prominent theories
which deny the truth. By precluding one,
and then another, we have shut the inquirer
up to the Bible doctrine, that the sinner is
justified " only for the righteousness of Christ imputed to us."
The remaining affirmative argument for this proposition is therefore very short and simple ; it will consist in a grouping
together of the Bible statements ; so classified as to exhibit the
multitude of proof-texts by a few representatives :

10. Proof of the Doctrine from Scrip- ture.

1. Our justification is gratuitous. Rom iii : 24; Eph. ii : 5 ;
Tit. iii : 7.

2. Christ is our Surety. Heb. vii : 22 : and our sins are
imputed to Him, that His righteousness may be imputed to us.
Is. liii : 6 and 11 ; 2 Cor. v : 21 ; 1 Pet. ii : 24.

3. He is our propitiation. Rom. iii : 25 ; 1 Jno. ii : 2.

4. We are justified through Christ, or for His name, or His
sake, or by His blood. Acts x : 43 ; xiii : 38, 39 ; Eph. i : 7 :
iv : 32 ; Rom. v : 9 ; 1 Jno. ii : 12.

5. Christ is called "our righteousness." Jer. xxxiii : 6 ;
1 Cor. i : 30 ; Rom. x : 4.

6. We are justified by His obedience, or righteousness.
Rom. v : 18, 19.

7. The righteousness that justifies us is God's and Christ's,
as opposed to ours. Rom. i : 17 ; iii : 22 ; Phil. iii : 9.

Let the student weigh these and such like texts, and he will see accumulative proof of the proposition. In fine; no other construction of the facts coheres with the doctrine of Christ's substitution. Let but the simple ideas, in which all evangelical Christians concur, be weighed; that Christ acted as our surety; that His mediatorial actions were vicarious; that we are justified in Him and for their sake; and we shall see that the doctrine of our catechism is the fair and obvious result. What do men mean by a substitute or vicar? That the acts which he does as such are accounted, as to their legal effect, as the acts of his principal.

LECTURE LIV.

JUSTIFICATION. — Concluded.

SYLLABUS.

11. Define and prove the Imputation of Christ's righteousness, and answer objections. Compare Adam's case, Rom. v.
> See Turrettin. Loc. xvi, Qu. 3. Owen on Justif., chs. 7, 8. 10. Dick, Lect. 70. Dr. A. Alexander, Tract. Dr. Wm. Cunningham, Hist. Theol. ch. 21, § 3. Watson's Theol, Inst., ch. 23.

12. Is Justification a single, complete, and absolute Act? How related to after sins, and to the general Judgment?
> Turrettin, Qu. 9, 10. Owen, ch. 6. Hill, bk. v, ch. 2. Knapp, § 113. Dr. Cunningham, as above, § 90. Turrettin, Qu, 5.

13. Is Faith the sole instrumental condition of Justification, or also Repentance?
> Turrettin, Qu. 7, 8. Owen, ch. 2, 3. Breckinridge, Theol. Subjective, bk. i, ch. 4. Thornwell's Collected Works, Vol. ii, pp. 37-40. Dick, Lect., 71.

14. How are Justification and Sanctification distinguished! Are they inseparable? Why then discriminate? (For discussion, see p. 663 et seq.)
> Turrettin, Loc. xvii, Qu. 1. Dick, Lect., 71. Hill, bk. v, ch. 3.

15. What the proper Place and Importance of Good Works, in the Believer's Salvation?
> Turrettin, Loc. xvii. Qu. 3. Dick, Lect. 71. Hill, as above. Knapp, § 116, 117.

16. "May we then sin, because we are not under the Law, but under Grace?"
> Dr. Jno. Witherspoon on Justification. Southern Review, (edited by Bledsoe) Art. 1, April, 1874. Owen, ch. 19. Turrettin, Loc. xvii, Qu. 1. Dick, Lect. 72. Watson, ch. 23. § 3.

OUR last attempt was to prove that the meritorious cause of the believer's justification is the righteousness of Christ. But how comes it that this righteousness

11. Imputation. avails for us, or that its justifying efficacy is made ours? The answer to this question leads us to the doctrine of imputation. The Catechism says that Christ's righteousness is imputed to us. This Latin word, to reckon or account to any one, is sometimes employed in the English Scriptures as the translation of חָשַׁב, λογίζομαι, ἐλλογέω, and correctly. Of the former we have instances in Gen. xv : 6; xxxviii : 15; 2 Sam. xix : 19; of the next in Mark xv : 28; Rom. ii : 26; iv : 5, &c.; Gal. iii : 6, &c.; and of the last, in Rom. v : 13; Philem. 18.

It is evident that sometimes the thing imputed is what is actually done by, or belongs personally to, the person to whom it is reckoned, or set over. (This is what Turrettin calls imputation loosely so called). Sometimes the thing imputed belonged to, or was done by another, as in Philem. 18; Rom. iv : 6. This is the imputation which takes place in the sinner's justification. It may be said, without affecting excessive subtlety of definition, that by imputation of Christ's righteousness, we only mean that Christ's righteousness is so accounted to the sinner, as that he receives thereupon the legal consequences to which it entitles. In accordance with 2 Cor. v : 21, as well as with the dictates of sound reason, we regard it as the exact counterpart of the imputation of our sins to Christ. Owen does, indeed, deny this: asserting that the latter only produced a temporary change in Christ's legal state, and that He was able speedily to extinguish the claims of law against our guilt, and return to His glory; while the former so imputes His very righteousness as to make a final and everlasting change in our legal relations. We reply: the difference is not in the kind of imputation, but in the persons. The mediatorial Person was so divine and infinite, that temporary sufferings and obedience met and extinguished all the legal claims upon Him. Again: Owen pleads that we must suppose Christ's righteous obedience, imputed to us, in another sense than our sins are to Him; because, to talk of imputing to us the legal consequences of His righteousness, such as pardon, &c., is nonsensical, pardon being the result of the imputation. But would not the same reasoning prove as well, that not only our guilt, but our very sinfulness must have been imputed to Christ; because it is nonsensical to talk of imputing condemnation! The truth is, the thing set over to our account, in the former case, is in strictness of speech, the title to the consequences of pardon and acceptance, founded on Christ's righteousness, as in the latter case it was the guilt of our sins—i. e., the obligation to punishment founded on our sinfulness. All are agreed that, when the Bible says, " the iniquity of us all was laid on Christ," or that " He bare our sins," or " was made sin for us," it is only our guilt and not our moral attribute of sinfulness which was imputed. So it seems to me far more reasonable and scriptural to suppose that, in the imputation of Christ's righteousness, it is not the attribute of righteousness in Christ which is imputed, but that which is the exact counterpart of guilt — the title to acquittal. Owen, in proceeding to argue against objections, strongly states that imputation does not make the sinner personally and actually righteous with Christ's righteousness as a quality. We should like, then, to know what he means, when saying that this righteousness is really and truly imputed to us in a more literal sense than our sins were to Christ. A middle ground is to me invisible.

Defined. Owen Criticised.

41*

The basis on which this imputation proceeds, is our union
to Christ. There is, first, our natural union

Basis of Justifica-
tion.
constituting Him a member of our race; a
man as truly as we are men. But this,
though an essential prerequisite, is not by itself enough; for if
so, mere humanity would constitute every sinner a sharer in
His righteousness. There must be added our mystical union,
in which a legal and spiritual connection are established by
God's sovereign dispensation, making Him our legal and our
spiritual Head. Thus imputation becomes proper.

When we attempt to prove this imputation, we are met
with the assertion, by Arminians and theo-

Is the Idea in Scrip-
ture?
logians of the New England School, that
there is no instance in the whole Bible of
anything imputed, except that which the man personally does
or possesses himself; so that there is no Scriptural warrant for
this idea of transference of righteousness as to its legal consequences. We point, in reply, to Philem. 18, and to Rom.
iv : 6. If God imputeth to a man righteousness without works,
and his faith cannot literally be this imputed righteousness, as
we have abundantly proved, we should like to know where that
imputed righteousness comes from. Certainly it cannot come
personally from the sinner who is without works. The whole
context shows that it is Christ's. But how sorry an artifice is it
to seize on the circumstances that the word λογιζεσθαι happens
not to be immediately connected with Christ's name in the same
sentence, when the idea is set forth in so many phrases? Moreover, as Turrettin remarks, every case of pardoned guilt is a
case (see 2 Sam. xix : 19), of this kind of imputation : for something is reckoned to the sinner — i. e., legal innocency, or title
to immunity, which is not personally his own.

The direct arguments for the imputation of Christ's righteousness are : 1st. The counterpart imputa-

Proofs, Farther.
tion of our guilt to Him. (Proved by Is.
liii : 5, 6, 12 ; Heb. ix : 28 ; 1 Pet. ii : 24, &c). For the principles involved are so obviously the same, and the one transaction
so obviously the procurer of the other, that none who admit a
proper imputation of human guilt to Christ, will readily deny
an imputation of His righteousness to man. Indeed both are
conclusively stated in 2 Cor. v : 21. The old Reformed exposition of this important passage, by some of our divines, was to
read, " Christ was made a sin-offering for us." The objection
is : that by this view no counterpart is presented in the counterpart proposition : "we are made the righteousness of God in
Him." It is obvious that St. Paul uses the abstract for the concrete. Christ was made a sinner for us, that we might be made
righteous persons in Him. The senses of the two members of
the parallelism must correspond. There is no other tenable
sense than this obvious one — that our guilt (obligation to pen-

alty) was imputed to Christ, that His righteousness (title to reward) might be imputed to us. 2d. Christ is said to be our righteousness. Jer. xxiii : 6 ; 1 Cor. i : 30, &c., expressions which can only be honestly received, by admitting the idea of imputation. 3d. By "His obedience many are constituted righteous ; " (κατασταθήσονται). Here is imputation. So we might go through most of the passages cited to prove that we are justified on account of Christ's righteousness, and show that they all involve the idea of imputation. Indeed, how else can the legal consequences of His righteousness become ours ? To see the force of all these, we have only to remember that all who deny imputation, also deny that Christ's righteousness is the sole meritorious ground, thus plainly implying that the latter necessarily involves the former. 4th. Imputation of Christ's righteousness to us is argued by Paul in Rom v, from imputation of Adam's sin to us.

Objections have been strenuously urged against this doctrine, of which the most grave is that it encourages licentiousness of living. This will be separatly considered under § xv. It has again been urged that it is impious, in representing Christ as personally the worst Being in the universe as bearing all the sins of all believers; and false to fact, in representing His act in assuming our law place as the act which drew down God's wrath on Him; whereas it was an act of lovely benevolence, according to the Calvinistic view of it; and also false, as representing the sinner as personally holy at the very time his contrition avows him to be vilest. The answer is, that all these objections mistake the nature of imputation, which is not a transfer of moral character, but of legal relation. And Christ's act in taking our law place was a lovely act. In strictness of speech, it was not this act which drew down His Father's wrath, (but His love—Jno. x : 17), but the guilt so assumed. For the discussion of more subtile objection, that guilt must be as untransferable as personal demerit, because it is the consequence of demerit alone,—see Lect. xliii, pages 517-18.

Objections Solved.

The important principle has already been stated, that justification must be as complete as its meritorious ground. Since faith is only the instrument of its reception, the comparative weakness or strength of faith will not determine any degrees of justification in different Christians. Feeble faith which is living truly leads to Christ, and Christ is our righteousness alone. Our justifying righteousness is in Christ. The office of faith, is simply to be the instrument for instituting the union of the believing soul to Him ; so that it may "receive of His fullness grace for grace." Suppose in men's bodies a mortal disease, of which the perfect cure was a shock of electricity, received from some exhaustless "receiver," by contact. One man discover-

12. Justification Complete.

ing his mortal taint, but yet a little enfeebled, rushes to the electrical receiver and claps his hand swiftly upon it, with all the force of a violent blow.   He receives his shock, and is saved. Another, almost fainting, can only creep along the floor with the greatest difficulty, and has barely strength to raise his languid hand and lay it on the "receiver."   He also derives the same shock, and the same healing.   The power is in the electricity, not in the impact of the two hands.   Hence, also, it will follow that justification is an instantaneous act, making at once a complete change of legal condition.   See Rom. iii : 22 ; Jno. iii : 36; v : 24; Rom. viii : 1, 32 and 34; Col. ii : 9, 10; Heb. x : 14; Micah. vii : 19; Jer. i : 20; Ps. ciii : 12, &c.   And this legal completeness, it is too evident to need proof, begins when the sinner believes, and at no other time.

But here two distinctions must be taken—one between the completeness of title, and completeness of possession as to the benefits of our justification ; the other between our justification in God's breast, and our own sense and consciousness thereof. On the latter distinction, we may remark : as our faith strengthens, so will the strength of our apprehension of a justified state grow with it.   The former also may, to some extent, be affected by the increase of our faith.   God may make that increase the occasion of manifesting to the soul larger measures of favour and grace.   But the soul is not one whit more God's accepted child then, than when it first believed.   We have seen that the thing which, strictly speaking, is imputed, is the title to all the legal consequences of Christ's righteousness—i. e , title to pardon and everlasting adoption, with all the included graces.   Now, the acknowledged and legitimate son of a king is a prince, though an infant.   His status and inheritance are royal, and sure ; though he be for a time under tutors and governors, and though he may gradually be put into possession of one and another, of his privileges, till his complete majority. So the gradual possession of the benefits of justification does not imply that our acquisition of the title is gradual.

But Sense and Fruits of it may Grow.

These views may assist us in the intricate subject of the relation which justification bears to the believer's future sins.   On the one hand these things are evident; that there is not a man on the earth who does not offend, (Jas. iii : 2), that sin must always be sin in its nature, and as such, abhorrent to God, by whomsoever committed; and even more abhorrent in a believer, because committed against greater obligations and vows; and that sins committed after justification need expiation, just as truly as those before.   On the other hand, the proofs above given clearly show, that the justified believer does not pass again under condemnation when betrayed into sin.   Faith is the instrument for continuing, as it was for originating our justified

Does Justification Remit Sins in Future?

state. This is clear from Rom. xi : 20; Heb. x : 38, as well as from the experience of all believers, who universally apply afresh to Christ for cleansing, when their consciences are oppressed with new sin. In strictness of speech, a man's sin must be forgiven after it is committed. Nothing can have a relation before it has existence, so that it is illogical to speak of sin as pardoned before it is committed. How, then, stands the sinning believer, between the time of a new sin and his new application to Christ's cleansing blood? We reply: Justification is the act of an immutable God, determining not to impute sin, through the believer's faith. This faith, though not in instant exercise at every moment, is an undying principle in the believer's heart, being rendered indefectible only by God's purpose of grace, and the indwelling of the Holy Ghost. So God determines, when the believer sins, not to impute guilt for Christ's sake, which determination also implies this other, to secure in the believer's heart, the unfailing actings of faith and repentance, as to all known sin. So that his justification from future sins is not so much a pardoning of them before they are committed, as an unfailing provision by God both of the meritorious and instrumental causes of their pardon, as they are committed.

There are two qualified senses, in which we are said to be justified at the judgment-day. See Acts iii : 19–21; Matt. xii : 36, 37. Indeed, a forensic act is implied somehow in the very notion of a judgment-day. First: Then, at length, the benefits of the believer's justification in Christ will be fully conferred, and he will, by the resurrection, be put into possession of the last of them, the redemption of his body. Second: There will be a declaration of the sentence of justification passed when each believer believed, which God will publish to His assembled creatures, for His declarative glory, and for their instruction. See Malachi iii : 17, 18. This last declarative justification will be conditioned on believers' works, (Matt. xxv), and not on their faith, necessarily; because it will be addressed to the fellow-creatures of the saints, who cannot read the heart, and can only know the existence of faith by the fruits.

How Related to Judgment-day?

That faith alone is the instrument of justification, is asserted by the Catechism, que. 33. The proof is two-fold: First. That this is the only act of the soul which, in its character, is receptive of Christ's righteousness. Repentance and other graces are essential, and have their all important relations to other parts of our salvation; but faith alone is the embracing act, and this alone is the act which contributes nothing, which looks wholly out of self for its object and its efficacy, and thus is compatible with a righteousness without works. Second. All the benefits we receive in Christ are suspended on our union with Him. It is because we are united, and when we

13. Faith Only Instrument.

are united to Him, that we become interested in His blood and righteousness, and in His sanctifying Spirit. But, as we have seen, faith is the instrumental bond of that union. Hence it follows, that our standards are right in saying that justifying righteousness is received by faith alone. Third. It is said in so many forms, that righteousness is by faith; and especially is this said most frequently where the technical act of justification is formally discussed, as separated from the other parts of our salvation. Fourth, there are passages in which this is held up singly, in answer to direct inquiries, as the sole instrumental act; which do not leave us at liberty to suppose that any other one would have been omitted, if there had been one; e. g., Jno. vi : 29; Acts xvi : 31.

Yet, it is strenuously objected by some, (even of sound divines), that in many places repentance is spoken of, along with faith, as a term of gospel salvation, and in some cases, even to the exclusion of faith. Mark i : 15; Luke xiii : 3; Acts xx : 21; and especially, Acts ii : 38; iii : 19. The chief force is in the last two. As to the previous ones, it is very obvious that to make repentance necessary to salvation, does not prove that it performs this particular work in our salvation, the instrumental acceptance of a justifying righteousness. We might even say that repentance is a necessary condition of final acceptance, and yet not make it the instrument; for there is a sense in which perseverance is such a condition. Heb. x : 38. But to make it the instrument is absurd; for then no one would be justified till death. But it may be urged, in Acts ii : 38, and iii : 19, repentance is explicitly proposed as in order to remission, which is an element of justification itself. We reply: this is not to be pressed; for thus we should equally prove, Acts ii : 38, that baptism is an instrument of justification; and, Rom. x : 9, 10, that profession is, equally with living faith, an instrument of justification. These passages are to be reconciled to our affirmative proof-texts, by remembering that repentance is used in Scripture much more comprehensively than saving faith. It is the whole conversion of the soul to God, the general acting in which faith is implicitly involved. When the Apostle calls for repentance, he virtually calls for faith; for as the actings of faith imply a penitent frame, so the exercise of repentance includes faith. It is therefore proper, that when a comprehensive answer is demanded to the question, " What must we do ? " that answer should be generally, " Repent," and that when the instrument of justification is inquired after specially, the answer should be, " Believe."

Connection of Repentance Explained.

The question once debated : whether faith or good works be most important to a believer? is as foolish as though one should debate, whether roots or fruits were most essential to a fruit-

14. Works do not justify, yet Necessary.

tree. If either be lacking, there is no fruit-tree at all. Good works, when comprehensively understood for all holy actings of heart and life, hold the place of supreme importance in our redemption, as the ulterior end, not indeed in any sense the procuring cause, but yet the grand object and purpose. And the dignity of the end is, in one sense, higher than that of the means.

The final cause of God, or ultimate highest end in His view Because they most in our justification, is His own glory. The Essential to God's Ulti- chief means or next medium thereto, is our mate End. sanctification and good works; for God's nature is holy, and cannot be glorified by sin, except indirectly in its punishment. If we look, then, at His immutable will and glory, we find an imperative demand for holiness and works. If we look next at the interests of God's kingdom as affected by us, we find an equal necessity for our good works : for it is sin which originates all mischief and danger, and disorder to the subjects of God's government. And if we look, third, at our own personal interests and well-being, as promoted by our redemption, we see good works to be equally essential; because to be sinful is to be miserable ; and true holiness alone is true happiness.

Hence, we find that God in many places mentions redemp- Because all the Plan tion from corruption, rather than redemption of Redemption Incites from guilt, as His prominent object in the Them. Covenant of Grace. See Titus ii : 14 ; Eph. i : 4 ; v : 25–27 ; I Thess. iv : 3 ; I Jno. iii : 8 ; Matt. i : 21. And all the features of this plan of redemption, in its execution, show that God's prime object is the production of holiness— yea, of holiness in preference to present happiness, in His people. The first benefit bestowed, in our union to Christ, is a holy heart. The most constant and prominent gifts, ministered through Christ, are those of sanctification and spiritual strength to do good works. The designs of God's providence constantly postpone the believer's comfort to his sanctification by the means of afflictions. When the question is, to make one of God's children holier, at the expense of his present happiness, God never hesitates. Again, the whole gospel system is so constructed as to be not merely an expedient for introducing justification, but a system of moral motives for producing sanctification, and that of wondrous power. Let the student look up its elements. And last. This very gospel teems with most urgent injunctions on believers already justified to keep this law, in all its original strictness and spirituality. See, especially, Matt. v : 17–20 ; Gal. v : 13 ; Rom. vi : 6 ; vii : 6 ; Jno. xiii : 34 ; I Pet. i : 15, 16, &c.

The law is no longer our rule of justification, but it is still our rule of living.

We have reserved to the close the discussion of the objec-

15. Is Justification oy Grace Licentious in Tendency? tion, that this doctrine of justification, by faith on Christ's righteousness, tends to loosen the bonds of the moral law.   There are two parties who suggest this idea—the legalists, who urge it as an unavoidable objection to our doctrine ; and the Antinomians, who accept it as a just consequence of the doctrine. Both classes may be dealt with together, except as to one point growing out of the assertion that Christ fulfilled the preceptive, as well as bore the penal law in our stead.   If this be so, says the Antinomian, how can God exact obedience of the believer, as an essential of the Christian state, without committing the unrighteousness of demanding payment of the same debt twice over ?   I reply, that it is not a pecuniary, but a moral debt.   In explaining the doctrine of substitution, I showed that God's acceptance of our Surety's work in our room was wholly an optional and gracious act with Him, because Christ's vicarious work, however well adapted to satisfy the law in oui stead, did not necessarily and naturally extinguish the claims of the law on us; was not a " legal tender," in such sense that God was obliged either to take that, or lose all claims.   Now, as God's accepting the substitutionary righteousness at all was an act of mere grace, the extent to which He shall accept it depends on His mere will.   And it can release us no farther than He graciously pleases to allow.   Hence, if He tells us, as He does, that He does not so accept it, as to release us from the law as a rule of living, there is no injustice.

We preface further, that the objection of the legalist proceeds upon the supposition, that if the motives of fear and self-interest for obeying God be removed, none will be left.   But are these the only motives ?   God forbid.

Indeed, we assert that the plan of justification by faith **No, but Sanctifying.** leaves all the motives of self-interest and fear, which could legitimately and usefully operate on a soul under the Covenant of Works, in full force ; and adds others, of vast superiority.   Rom. iii : 31.

The motives of self-interest and fear remain, so far as they **1. All Legitimate Self-Interest Remains.** properly ought to operate on a renewed soul. (a) While "eternal life is the gift of God," the measure of its glories is our works.   See Luke xix : 17–19 ; Matt. x : 42 ; 2 Cor. ix : 6.   Here is a motive to do as many good works as possible.   (b) Works remain, although deposed from the meritorious place as our justification, of supreme importance as the object and end.   Hence, (c) they are the only adequate test of a justified state, as proved above.   Thus, the conscience of the backslider should be as much stimulated by the necessity of having them, as though they were to be his righteousness.   It is as important to the gratuitous heir of an inheritance to preserve his evidence of title, as it was to the purchaser, to be furnished with money enough to pay for the estate.

2. The gospel shows its superior efficiency over a system of legality, in producing holy living, in this respect; that its instrument in justification is a living faith. A dead faith does not justify. Now, it is the nature of a justifying faith to give an active response to the vitalizing energy of God's truth. It is granted that the truth, which is the immediate object of its actings unto justification, is Christ's redemption ; but its nature ensures that it shall be vitally sensitive to all God's truth, as fast as apprehended. Now, the precepts are as really divine truth, the proper object of this vital action of a living faith, as the promises. Such is the teaching of our Confession in that instructive passage, ch. xiv, § 2. " By this faith a Christian believeth to be true whatsoever is revealed in the word, for the authority of God Himself speaking therein, and acteth differently, upon that which each passage thereof containeth ; yielding obedience to the commands, trembling at the threatenings, and embracing the promises of God for this life, and that which is to come. But the principal acts of saving faith are accepting, receiving, and resting upon Christ alone for justification, sanctification, and eternal life, by virtue of the Covenant of Grace." The soul is not made alive in patches. It is alive all over. That principle of faith, therefore, which actively responds to the promise, responds just so, likewise, to the precepts : especially as precepts and promises are so intertwined, See Ps. xxxii : 1, 2 ; Rom. viii : 1.

> **Faith Purifies.**

(b). The gospel is efficient in producing holy living, because it gives the strongest possible picture of the evil of sin, of God's inflexible requisition of a perfect righteousness, and of His holiness.

> **Gospel Appeals to Love.**

(c). Above all, it generates a noble, pure and powerful motive for obedience, love begotten by God's goodness in redemption. And here, the peculiar glory of the gospel, as a religion for sinners, appears. I believe that the justified believer should have motives to holy living, which if their whole just force were felt, would be more operative than those which Adam in innocence could have felt under the Covenant of Works. See above. But when we consider that man is no longer innocent, but naturally condemned and depraved, under wrath, and fundamentally hostile to God, we see that a Covenant of Works would now be, for him, infinitely inferior in its sanctifying influences. For the only obedience it could evoke from such a heart, would be one slavish, selfish, and calculated — i. e., no true heart obedience at all — but a mere trafficking with God for self-interest. Now, contrast with this an obedience of love, and of gratitude, which expects to purchase nothing thereby from God, because all is already given, freely, graciously ; and therefore obeys with ingenuous love and thankfulness. How much more pleasing to God ! And last ; Love is a principle of action as permanent and energetic, as it is pure. Witness even the human examples of it. When we look to those social affections, which have retained their disinterestedness (towards man) through the corruptions of our fall, we see there the most influential, as well as the purest principles of human action, the springs of all that is most energetic, and persevering, as well as most generous.

We sometimes hear the legalists, of various schools, say :

Love, the Most Operative. "A correct knowledge of human nature will warn us, that if the principles of fear and self-interest are removed from man's religious obedience, he will render none ; for these are the main springs of human action." We do not represent the gospel scheme as rejecting the legitimate action of those springs. But their view of human nature is false; fear and self-interest are not its most energetic principles. Many a virtuous son and daughter render to an infirm parent, who has no ability or will to punish, and no means of rewarding save with his blessing, a service more devoted, painful, and continued, than the rod ever exacted from a slave. Indeed, slavery itself showed, by the occasional instances of tyranny, which occurred, that fear was an inadequate principle ; the rod by itself never secured industry and prosperity on a plantation; but the best examples of success were always those, where kindnesss was chiefly relied on, (with a just and firm authority), to awaken in the slaves affection and cheerful devotion. The sick husband receives from his wife, without wages, nursing more assiduous than any hire can extort from the mercenary professional nurse. And above all, does the infant helpless to reward or punish, exact from the mother's love and pity, a service more punctilious and toilsome, than was ever rendered to an eastern sultan by the slave with the scimetar over his head?

Suppose, then, that the all-powerful Spirit of God, employing the delightful truths of gospel grace as His instrument, produces in believers a love and gratitude as genuine as these instinctive affections, and more sacred and strong, as directed towards a nobler object ; has He not here a spring of obedience as much more efficacious, as it is more generous, than the legalists ?

> " Talk they of morals ? O Thou bleeding Love,
> The great morality is love to Thee !"

When, therefore, these heretics object, that justification by free grace will have licentious results; God's answer is; that He will provide against that, by making the faith which justifies also a principle of life, which " works by love."

LECTURE LV.

REPENTANCE.

I. "REPENTANCE unto Life is an evangelical grace, the doctrine whereof is to be preached by every minister of the gospel, as well as that of faith in Christ." Conf. xv, 1. The brevity, and in some cases neglect, with which this prominent subject is treated by many systems, is surprising and reprehensible.

In the New Testament there are two classes of words, used for two exercises, both of which, in the English version are called "repentance," "repent." One class is μεταμέλομαι μεταμέλεια, the other, μετανοέω μετάνοια. The one means, etymologically, after regret, a merely natural feeling ; the other, change of mind after conduct. And the two classes are used in the New Testament with general, or, as I would assert, universal discrimination. The only alleged cases of confusion are Matt. xxi : 32 ; Luke xvii : 3, 4 ; Heb. xii ; 17. In the first, the verb is μετεμελήθητε with accurate and proper reference to the relation between carnal conviction and sorrow, and turning to Christ, as a preparation for the result. Those expositors who will have it to be used here for evangelical repentance, urge, that this alone is vitally connected with saving faith. The chief priests " repented not that they might believe." But give the verb its ordinary meaning : Christ charges on them such obduracy, and self-sufficiency, that they felt not even that carnal sorrow, which is the preliminary step towards true repentance, faith, and conversion. Thus, so far is the ordinary sense from being difficult here, it adds great force to our Saviour's meaning. So in the next case. Luke xvii : 3, 4. In this μετάνοια is used for the professed repentance of an erring, and even a very unstable brother, to show that his profession, so long as it is not absolutely discredited by his bad conduct, is to be taken by the judgment of charity, (1 Cor. xiii : 7), as evidence of genuine, Christian sorrow, so far as to secure forgiveness. A profession of mere carnal sorrow would not entitle to it. In the third, the best commentators are agreed that Τόπον μετανοίας refers to a change in Isaac, which the historian indicates, must have been (whatever profane Esau may have hoped) Christian conviction of and sorrow for error ; (otherwise He would not have changed His prophecy). Now, when we see that μετανοέω is used in the New Testament 34, and μετάνοια 24 times=58, and μεταμέλομαι and family 7 times, the demarcation made by the sacred writers is very broad.

See this distinction carried out with instructive accuracy in 2 Cor. vii : 8–10, (original). In verse 8th the Apostle says that he had regretted, but now no longer regretted (μετεμελόμην) the writing of the 1st Epistle. He is too accurate to speak of repenting the peformance of a duty, though painful. Verse 9, Now He is glad that the Corinthians sorrowed unto μετάνοιαν. See how accurately he distinguishes sorrow (λύπη) from gracious repentance. Verse 10 tells us that gracious sorrow worketh "repentance unto salvation," which is not to be " regretted " (ἀμεταμέλητον). Paul is too discriminating to intimate, as the English version does; that true repentance can ever, by any possibility, be subject of repentance — No : folly might perchance deem it subject of regret ; but, to repent truly of true repentance, would be a contradiction too glaring even for the sinner to entertain.

In the Old Testament two families of words are used for those acts promiscuously expressed in our English version by *repent ;* שׁוּב and its derivatives, and נָחַם with its derivatives. The latter is used to express both regret and repentance proper, (variously translated by Sept.) ; the former I believe, in its theological uses, always expresses true repentance. *

The Latin Vulgate has lent us a mischievous legacy, in giving us the word "repent" as the rendering of Μετάνοειν. " Repentance " is from *pœnitet, pœna* ; and that from the Greek word ποινή. Its English progeny is seen in the word pain ; and its original idea is penalty. See the use of ποινη ; *Iphigenia in Aulide,* for expiatory penalty. No wonder the Latin Church, in the dark ages, slid into the error of regarding penance, as a satisfaction for the guilt of sin ; when it had been taught to call μετάνοιαν by such a misnomer as *pœnitentia. Lactantius,* (the most elegant in his Latinity, of the Christian fathers), proposes to render it by *Resipiscentia,* (from resapio). " *Ideoque Græci*

---

*Thus Augustine : *Pœnitentiam nomen habere a punitione, ut sit quasi punitentia, dum ipsum homo punit pœnitendo, quod male admisit.*

melius et significantius μετάνοιαν *dicunt, quam nos possumus resipiscentiam dicere."*

I wish that the English tongue had enabled our version to distinguish the two exercises uniformly by two distinct words.

Μεταμέλεια is the natural pain consequent on sin, arising in the carnal mind, either with or without the common, convincing influences of the Holy Ghost, and contains three elements, fear and dread of the danger incurred, shame, and remorse or involuntary self-condemnation of conscience denouncing the sin. It is a purely selfish emotion ; but it is still the emotion of a moral nature, and implies a conscience ; though compatible with an entire preference of will for sin.

For μετάνοια, (See Shorter Cat., qu. 87. Conf., xv, § 2). It involves the two elements of the former ; but it includes chiefly another ; viz : "a sight and sense of the filthiness and odiousness of his sins, as contrary to the holy nature, and righteous law of God." There is not only that painful sense of wrong doing inflicted by conscience on the sinner ; conscience, which a depraved will, although fully set on transgression, cannot corrupt nor wholly silence. But there is the pain arising from a true hatred of sin, now existing in the will, as a moral disposition and principle, and from the preference for, and love of conformity to God, arising out of a thorough approval of and complacency in His moral perfection. Of course, this hatred of sinfulness and appetency of holiness, are not two principles, but one, expressing its spontaneous nature as to two opposite objects—sin and righteousness. And last, that view of the odiousness of sin, and attractiveness of godliness, proceeds chiefly in the believer's experiences, from the Cross ; from the exhibitions of mercy, purity, goodness, and hope there made. True repentance may be defined as the moral emotion and act of the regenerate nature towards its personal sinfulness, and towards godliness, especially as the two are exhibited in the Cross.

The terms Legal and Evangelical Repentance have been used by divines with a mischievous uncertainty. By some, legal repentance is defined as though identical with μεταμέλεια. If this were really the distinction, the terms would be unnecessary. Paul gives us better ones in 2 Cor. vii : 10 : The "sorrow of the world," and "and godly sorrow." But other divines, perceiving a truer and more accurate distinction in the actings of godly sorrow itself, have employed the phrases in a useful sense. These, by legal repentance, mean a genuine sorrow for sin, including both fear of its dangers, and conscience of its wrongness, and also loathing of its odiousness, with a thorough justifying and approving of God's holy law ; a sorrow wrought by the Holy Ghost, but wrought by Him only through the instrumentality of the convincing Law, and unaccompanied

2. Legal Repentance What ?

with conscious hopes of mercy in Christ. By Evangelical Repentance they mean that godly sorrow for sin, which is wrought by the renewing Spirit, including the above actings, but also, and chiefly, the tender sorrow combined with hopes of mercy proceeding from appropriating faith, when the believer "looks on Him whom he hath pierced," and sees there at once a blessed way of deliverance, and a new illustration of God's love, and his own aggravated vileness. This, in a word, is the repentance of the Catechism, Qu. 87.

In completing our view of the nature of repentance, the question presents itself: Of what should man repent? The general answer, of course, must be: Of all sin. Is it man's duty, then, to repent of original sin? If we say, no, the Arminian will press us with this consequence: "If it is not your personal duty to repent of it, you imply that you are not in earnest in saying that it is truly and properly sin." Yet, how can a man feel personally blameworthy (an essential element of repentance) for an act committed by another, without his consent, and before he was born! We reply: "The sinfulness of that estate into which man fell, consists in the guilt of Adam's first sin, the want of original righteousness, and the corruption of his whole nature, which is commonly called original sin." The Christian will, of course, regret the guilt of Adam's first sin, but not repent of it. But of the corruption of nature, of the concupiscence and inordinate desire of our hearts, it is our duty to repent, to feel blameworthy for them, to sorrow for, and to strive against them, just as of actual transgression; for this is not only our guilt, (imputed), but our proper sin.

Do we Repent of Original Sin?

Again, Conf., xv: § 5, men ought not only to repent of their sinfulness, both of heart and life, as a general quality, but also of particular sins, so far as they are known, with a particular repentance. Repentance is the medium of sanctification, and sin is only conquered by us in detail. There is no other way for a finite creature to fight the good fight of faith. Hence, it is obvious, every conscious, and especially every known recent transgression should be made the subject of particular repentance. The impenitent man cannot be forgiven. What, then, shall we answer concerning those unconscious and forgotten transgressions (probably the "secret sins" of Ps. xix: 12), to which the attention and recollection of even the honest penitent never advert, in consequence of the limitation of his faculties and powers? We answer, that each Christian is aware of his guilt of these forgotten faults, and grieves over the general fact that he has them. And this general repentance is accepted; so that the atonement of Christ blots them out of God's book of remembrance.

Of Particular Sins.

After this definition of repentance, it need hardly be added. that it is not only an act, to be performed at the beginning of conversion, and then to be dismissed as complete, but also a life-long work, proceeding from an abiding temper of soul. The saint is a penitent, until he reaches heaven.

If we confound worldy with godly sorrow, or if we take a Pelagian view of human nature, we may indeed ascribe true repentance to the unaided workings of the natural heart. But if repentance is understood as above, we shall see that while it is a duty for man to exercise, it is still one to which he must be moved by the supernatural grace of God. Hence, the Scriptures always represent it as God's gift or work. See New Testament first, as plainest: Acts v: 31: xi: 18; 2 Tim. ii: 25. In Old Testament: Ps. lxxx: 3, 7, 19; lxxxv: 4; Jer. xxxi: 18; Ezek. xi: 19. Nor can these texts be evaded by saying, that God is the Author of repentance only mediately, by teaching that Gospel which inculcates and prompts repentance. In several of them, those who are already possessed of the Gospel means, pray to God to work repentance in them; and in 2 Tim. ii: 25, there is a "peradventure" whether God will give a heart to repent, to those to whom Timothy was to give the light; showing that the grace of repentance is a separate and divine gift.

3. Repentance Fruit of New Birth.

But let any one look at the Scriptural definition of Repentance, and he will be convinced that none but a regenerate heart is competent to the exercise. The true penitent not only feels the danger of his sins, and the involuntary sting of a conscience, which he would disarm if he could ,but an ingenuous sorrow for the sinfulness of his sin, and a sincere desire for godliness. Can any one feel this but a regenerate soul? Can he who hates God thus grieve for having wounded His holy law; can he who loves sin as the native food of his soul, thus loathe it for its own sake! No one feels godly sorrow, but he who is passed from death unto life.

But the Arminians, while avowing that repentance is the work of the Holy Ghost, assert that it must be held to begin before regeneration in the order of production, as they also hold concerning faith and justification. Their reasons are two. First: we are taught (e. g., Ps. li: 10), to pray for regeneration. But prayer, to be acceptable, must be sincere; and a sincere request for a holy heart implies, or presupposes, repentance for ungodliness. And second: repentance must be presupposed in faith, because to fly to Christ as a refuge from sin presupposes a sense of sin. But justification, secured by faith, must precede regeneration; because God cannot be supposed to bestow the beginning of communion in the Holy Ghost, and what is substantially eternal life, on a rebel before he is reconciled to Him. Thus, they suppose Rom. vii, to describe repentance; Rom. vii: 24, 25, the dawnings of saving faith; Rom. viii: 1, first clause, the justification consequent thereon; and viii: 1, last clause,

Arminian Objections to this. Answer.

the beginning of spiritual life.   Now, to both objections, we
reply that their plausibility is chiefly due to the oversight of
this fact, that the priority of one over another of these severa!
steps, is only one of production, or causation, and not of time.
Practically, every one who is regenerate is then, in principle,
penitent, and believing, and justified.   And since all parts are
of God's grace, is it not foolish to say that His righteousness or
His wrath forbids Him to bestow this before that, seeing His
grace permits neither to precede in time, and none to be lacking?   But on the first objection we remark, farther, if we must
need rationalize about it, it is at least as great an anomaly, that
a man should feel a sincere desire for godliness, while his nature
remained prevalently ungodly, as it is that an ungodly prayer
for a new heart should be answered by the heart-searching God.
The objection derives its seeming force from a synergistic theory of regeneration.   But, in truth, no true spiritual desire can
exist till God has actually renewed the will.   God must do the
work, not man.   And God must savingly begin it, unasked by
man.   This is sovereign grace.   That a man should hold this
theory, and yet pray for a new heart, is no greater paradox than
that the hope our sins are pardoned should encourage us to
pray for pardon.   The truth is, the instincts of a pre-existent
spiritual life find their natural expression in a breathing after
spiritual life.   To the second objection we reply: if it seems
anomalous that God should anticipate His reconciliation to the
condemned sinner, by bestowing that gift of a new heart, which
virtually constitutes eternal life, it would be equally anomalous
that He should anticipate the bestowal of peace, by bestowing
those essential gifts of faith and repentance, to which eternal
blessedness is inevitably tied by the Gospel.   Must not the
Arminian, just as much as the Calvinist, fall back, for his solution of these difficulties, upon the glorious fact, that Christ hath
deserved all these saving gifts for His people?   To him who
believes an unconditional election, there is no difficulty here;
because he believes that these saving gifts are all pledged to the
believing sinner, not only before he fulfills any instrumental conditions, but before he is born.   There is no difficulty in it all to
God; because all is of grace.

The relations of faith and repentance *inter se*, as to the
order of production, are important to an
4. Which Precedes; understanding of conversion.   Both these
Faith or Repentance? graces are the exercises of a regenerate heart
alone; they presuppose the new birth.   Now, Calvin, with perhaps the current of Calvinistic divines, says, that "repentance
not only immediately follows faith, but is produced by it."
Again: "When we speak of faith as the origin of repentance,
we dream not of any space of time which it employs in producing it; but we intend to signify that a man cannot truly devote
himself to repentance, unless he knows himself to be of God."

And this, he adds, only becomes known by appropriating faith. The view usually urged is, that the convicted sinner cannot exercise that tender and affectionate sorrow for sin, which involves a true love to God, until he entertains some hope that God loves him, in Christ.. They quote such passages as Ps. cxxx: 4; 1 Jno. iv: 19. Before hope of mercy dawns, they argue there can be nothing but stubborn remorse and despair, after the example of Jer. xviii: 12. Now there is a fair sense in which all this is true; and that, no doubt, the sense in which it commended itself to the minds of those great and good men. But there is also a great danger of holding it in an erroneous and mischievous sense. In what we have to say, guarding these views, let us premise that we make no priority of time in the order of repentance and faith; and no gap of duration between the birth of the one or the other. Either implies the other, in that sense. Nor do we dream of the existence of such a thing as a penitent unbeliever, nor suppose that there is any other means of producing repentance than the preaching of the gospel. Repentance can exist nowhere except where God works it. In rational adults He works it only by means, and that means is the gospel revelation; none other. Nor do we retract one word of what we said as to the prime efficiency of the doctrine of the cross, and of the hope, gratitude, love, tenderness, and humiliation, which faith draws therefrom, as means for cultivating repentance. But in our view it is erroneous to represent faith as existing irrespective of penitence, in its very first acting, and as begetting penitence through the medium of hope. On the contrary, we believe that the very first acting of faith implies some repentance, as the prompter thereof. True, the two twin graces ever after stimulate each other reciprocally; but the man begins to believe because he has also begun to repent.

The reasons are: first, that the other view gives a degrading and mercenary character to repentance; as though the sinner selfishly conditioned his willingness to feel aright concerning his sin, on the previous assurance of impunity. It is as though the condemned felon should say: "Let me go free, and I will sincerely avow that I have done very wrong. But if I am to swing for it, I will neither acknowledge guilt, nor say, "God bless my country." Is this ingenuous repentance? Is this the experience of the contrite heart? No; its language always is: (Ps. li, pt. 1, v. 5:)

Argument.

> "Should sudden vengeance seize my breath,
> I must pronounce Thee just in death;
> And if my soul is sent to hell,
> Thy righteous law approves it well."

Second. Godly sorrow for sin must be presupposed or implied in the first actings of faith, because faith embraces Christ as a. Saviour from sin. See Cat., que. 86, last clause especially.

42*

Surely the Scriptures do not present Christ to our faith only, or even mainly, as a way of impunity.   See Matt. i : 21 ; Acts iii : 26; Titus ii : 14.   As we have pointed out, the most characteristic defect of a dead faith, is, that it would quite heartily embrace Christ as God's provision for immunity in sin : but God offers Him to faith for a very different purpose, viz : for restoration to holiness, including immunity from wrath as one of the secondary consequences thereof.   (Hence, we must demur at Owen's declaration, that the special object of saving faith is only Christ in His priestly, and not in His kingly and prophetic offices.)   But now, a man does not flee from an evil, except as a consequence of feeling it an evil.   Hence, there can be no embracing of Christ with the heart, as a whole present Saviour, unless sin be felt to be in itself a present evil ; and there be a genuine desire to avoid it as well as its penalty. But does not such a desire imply a renewal of the will ?   This view has appeared so unavoidable to many who go with Calvin, that they have admitted, " Legal repentance precedes, but Evangelical repentance follows faith and hope."   (See above pp. 653, 654.)   But does not such a legal repentance imply the new birth ?   Does any man thus justify and revere the very law which condemns him, and regard the Divine character, while devoid, as he supposes, of hope in its favour, with new and adoring approbation, while yet his carnal mind is enmity against God ?   Surely not.   The error of their argument is in supposing that this legal repentance was the exercise of an unrenewed heart.

Third : Some passages of Scripture imply the order I have assigned ; and I am not aware of any which contradict it.   See Mark i : 15 ; Acts ii : 38 ; v : 31 ; xx : 21 ; 2 Tim. ii : 25, especially the last.

In a word, Repentance and Faith are twin graces, both implicitly contained in the gift of the new heart ; and they cannot but co-exist. Repentance is the right sense and volition which the renewed heart has of its sin ; faith is the turning of that heart from its sin to Christ.   Repentance feels the disease, faith embraces the remedy.   But when we inquire for the first conscious acting of faith or repentance after the instant of the new birth, the result is decided by the object to which the soul happens to be first directed.   If the object of its first regenerate look be its own ungodliness, the first conscious exercise will be one of repentance ; but just so surely as the volition is, potentially, in the preponderating motive, so surely does that soul look from its ungodliness to Christ, the remedy of it ; it may be unconsciously at first, but in due time, consciously. Or if Christ be the first object to which the new-born soul looks, its first act may be one of trust and joy in Him.   Yet that trust

They are Twin Graces.

implies a sense of the evil of sin, as the thing for deliverance from which Christ is trusted.

The exercise of repentance, while absolutely necessary in all who are saved, creates no atoning merit;

5. Repentance not Atoning. and constitutes no ground whatever in justice, why the penitent should have remission of his sins. See Conf., xv: 3. The carnal mind here labours under an obstinate delusion; and how often are pastors told, even by those who desire to profess themselves Christians, "That they hope their sins are pardoned, because they have repented?" Hence, importance.

A moral fitness which demands that no impenitent person shall be pardoned, is here mistaken for

Argument. another thing. Now, the ground of that moral fitness is this: that, pardon having otherwise been made just, God's holiness and majesty may have some practical assurance, in the state of the sinner's own feelings, against his repetition of his sins. But this end does not express the whole intent of God's law; if it did, the law would be a mere expediency, unworthy of God. Its true object is, to express and sustain His immutable holiness. It demands perfect and perpetual obedience. Repentance is not obedience. This leads,

Second, to the remark, that repentance is no reparation whatever for past disobedience. It cannot place the sinner, in the eye of the law, in the position of Him who has never sinned. It has in itself no relevancy to repairing the mischiefs the sin has inflicted. Thus men judge. To the man who had injured you, you would say: Your repentance is very proper; but it cannot recall the past, or undo that which is done.

Third: Indeed, what is a repentance but a feeling of ill-desert, and consequent guilt? Confession is its language. Now, can a man pay a just debt by his acknowledgments of its justice? It is a contradiction, which would lead us to this absurdity; that the more thoroughly unworthy a man felt, the more worthy he would thereby become.

Fourth: Repentance after transgression is a work. Acts xvii: 30. So that justification by repentance would be a justification by works; and all the principles of Luke xvii: 10; Rom. iii: 28, apply to it.

But last: Repentance is as much a gift of God (Acts v: 31), as the remission which it is supposed to purchase. This settles the matter. While, therefore, the impenitent cannot be justified, yet the sole ground of justification is the righteousness of Christ imputed to us, and received by faith alone.

The Scriptures command us to "bring forth fruits meet for repentance." These fruits will, in gen-

6. Fruits Meet for Repentance. eral, include all holy living; for repentance is a "turning unto God from sin, with full purpose of, and endeavour after, new obedience." But there are certain acts which are essentially dictated by repentance and which proceed immediately from the attitude of penitence.

1. Sincere penitence must lead to confession. "Out of the abundance of the heart the mouth speaketh." See Prov. xxviii: 13. The highest form of this duty is the confession of all our sins to God, in secret prayer. True repentance will always thus utter itself to Him. Then, if our sins have scandalized the Church, we must also make public confession of the particular sins which have produced this result. Again, if our sin is immediately aimed at our fellow-man, and known to him, repentance must lead to confession to him.

2. The next consequence of repentance will be, to prompt us to make reparation of our sin, wherever it is practicable. He who truly repents, wishes his sin undone. But if he truly wishes it undone, he will, of course, undo it if in his power.

3. The next fruit of repentance must be holy watchfulness against its recurrence. This is too obvious to need proof. See 2 Cor. vii :11, as admirably expounded by Calvin, Institutes, Bk. 3, ch. 3, § 15.

The worthless distinction of Rome between attrition and contrition, and the assigning of a religious value to the former, are sufficiently refuted by what precedes. Nor does the duty of auricular confession, so called, find any Scriptural support plausible enough to demand discussion. As to her ascetical exercises of penitence, they are the inventions of fanaticism and spiritual pride. The mortification which Scripture enjoins, is that of the sins, and not of the unreasoning members.

LECTURE LVI.

SANCTIFICATION AND GOOD WORKS.

SYLLABUS.

1. State the usages and meanings of original words rendered "sanctify," and the nature and extent of sanctification.
    Shorter Cat., Qu. 35. Conf. of Faith, ch. 13, 16. Lexicons. Turrettin, Loc. xvii, ch. 1. Hodge, Theol., pt. iii, ch. 18, § 1, 2, 3. Dick, Lect. 74.
2. How is sanctification distinguished from, and how related to justification and regeneration?
    Turrettin, Qu. 1, § 9 to end. Dick as above. Hill, bk. v, ch. 4, § 2. Knapp, § 116, 126. Ridgley, Qu. 78.
3. Who is the Agent, and what the means of sanctification?
    Dick, Lect. 75. Ridgley. Qu. 75.
4. Is sanctification ever perfect in this life? Consider views of Pelagians, Socinians, Wesleyans and recent advocates of "Higher Life."
    Turrettin as above, Qu. 2. Hodge, Theol. as above, § 7, 8. Dick. Lect. 74. Hill, bk. v, ch. 4, § 3. Ridgley, Qu. 78. Watson's Theo. Inst., ch. 29.

IN discussing this subject, we turn again to Scripture to settle the meaning of the word. In the Old Testament we find

1. Sanctify: Definition of. the word קָדַשׁ used in the piel and hiphil, to express sanctification. In its lowest sense, it seems to mean simply separation to a particular purpose, and that purpose not sacred, as Jer. xxii : 7. More frequently it is used in the sense of consecrate, or dedicate as priests, utensils, the Sabbath day, where the idea is that of setting apart to a holy use. See Exod. xxviii : 41 ; xxix : 36 ; Deut. v : 12. But in its proper sense, it means to cleanse away ceremonial, and, especially, moral pollution. 2 Sam xi : 4 ; Num. xv : 40. Kindred to this is the sense where God is said to sanctify Himself, or to be sanctified by His people— i. e., declaratively. Ezek. xxxviii : 23.

Use of Word in New Testament. In the Greek Scriptures ἁγιάζω is used clearly in all the above senses, to separate, to consecrate, to purify morally, and to declare God's holiness. There is a use of this verb, of which the clearest instances are seen in the Epistle to the Hebrews, especially ii : 11 ; x : 10, 14 ; xiii : 12, compared with i : 3. Dr. Sampson here renders the word popularly by " redeem." Sin carries two consequences—guilt and pollution—(nearly associated in the mind of a Hebrew). From the former, Christ's blood cleanses, from the latter, His Spirit. When Christ is said to " sanctify" us by His blood, His sacrifice, &c., it is the former element, cleansing away of guilt, which is intended prominently. This is evident from the fact that the verb is used by the Septuagint as the rendering for כָּפַר, which is strengthened by the fact that the kindred word καθαρίζω is used for propitiation ; e. g., 1 Jno. i : 7. See Sampson on Hebrews, i : 3 ; and ii : 11.

Sanctification is of the Soul. Proofs. Sanctification, in the gospel sense, means then, not only cleansing from guilt, though it presupposes this, nor only consecration, though it includes this, nor only reformation of morals and life, though it produces this ; but, essentially, the moral purification of the soul. This is the great idea to which all the ceremonial sanctity of the typical dispensation pointed ; (see Ps. li : 6, 7 ; xxiv : 4, &c.,) and it is yet more emphatically and prominently expressed in the New Testament word ἁγιάζω. In our discussions with Pelagians, we have already shown that their idea is erroneous, viz: that holiness can only be acted by man. We have proved that there must be a previous spring in the principles of the soul, and the dispositions which dictate volitions ; otherwise volitions materially right can have no true holiness. Outward reformation cannot, then, be sanctification ; because the former can only be the consequence thereof ; as is well stated in Turrettin, and is clearly implied by Matt. xii : 33, 34, &c. This important practical truth may be farther supported by considering, (b) that holiness in man must be conceived as the counterpart of sin. (The Pelagian admits this). But sin ᴉ𝔰 both original and actual. Sin of heart is the fountain of the sin of life. Hence, it is fair to infer, as our Saviour does, in fact, in the places cited, that sanctification has its seat in the heart. (c) This appears also by the fact, which none will deny, that infants may be subjects of sanctification. They cannot act a sanctification. (d) Again, the synonymous phrases all speak of "a clean heart," of "circumcising the heart," &c. And last, the Scriptures are emphatic in their assertions. I Thess. v : 23 ; Eph. iv : 23, 24 ; Gal. v : 24 ; Titus iii : 5 ; Luke xvii : 21 ; Rom. xiv : 17.

When we inquire after the extent of sanctification, or the parts of the human person affected by it, the Catechism answers, that we are renewed "in the whole man." In I Thess. v : 23, the Apostle expresses the same idea of completeness, by employing the three comprehensive terms of the Platonic anthropology current in his day, (not meaning to endorse that scheme). Now, when we analyse that element of human character and of human action, in which moral quality resides, we are compelled to say that, strictly speaking, it is only in the state and actings of man's active powers. If there is neither emotional activity nor choice involved in any human act, that act has no moral character. Hence, in strictness of speech, the true seat of sanctification is the will: the human soul in that class of its actings expressed in Scripture by the word heart. But the Apostle is writing popularly, and not scientifically. The emotional and voluntary capacity of the soul is not a different member, or department of it, from the intellectual. It is the one indivisible unit, acting in different modes.

Sanctification is of the Whole Person. In What Sense of Other Parts than the Heart?

It is the soul which is sanctified, and not a faculty thereof. True, that sanctification is only a moral change of the soul, in its essence ; but in its results, it modifies every acting of the soul, whether through intellect, appetite, or corporeal volition. Every one would consider that he was speaking with sufficient accuracy in using the words "a wicked thought." Now, in the same sense in which a thought can be wicked, in that sense the power of thinking can be sanctified. What is that sense ? A thought is wicked, not because the faculty of thinking, or pure intellection, is the seat of moral quality, abstractly considered ; but because the soul that thinks, gives to that thought, by the concurrence of its active or emotional, or voluntary power, a complex character, in which complex there is a wrong moral element. To sanctify the intellect, then, is to sanctify the soul in such a way that in its complex acts, the moral element shall be right instead of wrong. So we speak, with entire propriety, of a "wicked blow." The bones, skin, and muscles, which corporeally inflicted it, are the unreasoning and passive imple-

The Soul has no Parts.

ment of the soul that emitted the volition to strike. But our members are sanctified, when the volitions which move them are holy; and when the impressions of sense and appetite, of which they are the inlets, become the occasions of no wrong feelings or volitions.

The sanctification of our bodies consists, therefore, not in the ascetic mortification of our nerves, mus-
Sanctification of the Body not Asceticism? cles, glands, &c., but in the employment of the members as the implements of none but holy volitions, and in such management and regulations of the senses, that they shall be the inlets of no objective, or occasional causes of wrong feeling. This will imply, of course, strict temperance, continence, and avoidance of temptation to the sinful awakening of appetite, as well as the preservation of muscular vigour, and healthy activity, by self denial and bodily hardihood. See 1 Cor. ix : 27; 2 Pet. ii : 14; Jas. iii : 2. But the whole theory of asceticism is refuted by the simple fact, that the soul is the seat of holiness; and that the body is only indirectly holy or unholy, as it is the tool of the soul. The whole delusion, so far as it has sought a Scriptural support, rests on the mistake of the meaning of the word "flesh," "*caro*," "σάρξ," which the sacred writers use to mean depraved human nature; not the body. What those fleshly members are, which sanctification mortifies, may be seen in Col. iii : 5; Gal. v : 19–21.

Sanctification only matures what regeneration began.
2. Relation of Sanctification to New Birth and Justification. The latter sprouted the seed of grace, the former continues its growth, until there appears first the blade, then the ear, then the full corn in the ear. The agent and influences are therefore the same.

In the order of production, justification precedes sanctification; for one of the benefits received by the justified believer, in virtue of his acceptance, is sanctifying grace. While the two graces are practically inseparable, still their discrimination is of the highest importance; for it is by confounding the two that Rome has re-introduced her theory of justification, by self-righteousness. Hence, let the student remember, that the results of the two graces are different. Justification removes the guilt of sin, sanctification its pollution. Justification changes only our legal relations, sanctification our actual moral condition. Justification is an act, sanctification is a process; the one is instantaneous and complete in all, the other is imperfect in its degree in all, unequal in different Christians, and is increased throughout life. Justification takes place in God's court, sanctification in the sinner's own breast.

The necessary and uniform connection between the two has been argued substantially in the last lec-
Sanctification Essential to Salvation. ture on Justification, and to that the student

is referred. But the proposition is of such prime importance, that it will not be amiss, in closing this head, to state the points of our argument in somewhat different order.

(a.) The Covenant of Grace embraces both. Jer. xxxi : 33; Rom. viii : 30.

(b.) The sanctity of the divine nature requires it. 1 Pet. i : 15, 16.

(c.) The connection appears inevitable from the offices of Christ; for He is King, as well as Priest, to all His people. Rom. viii : 29; vi : 11; Titus ii : 14; Rom. viii : 1, 2.

(d.) The office of the Holy Ghost shows this connection; for His influences are a part of Christ's purchase. But He is the Spirit of Holiness. Rom. viii : 9.

(e.) The sacraments symbolize cleansing from pollution as well as from guilt. Col. ii : 11, 12; Titus iii : 5.

(f.) Redemption would be a mockery without sanctification; for sin itself, and not the external wrath of God, is the cause of misery here, and eternal death hereafter. Hence, to deliver the fallen son of Adam from his guilt, and leave him under the power of corruption, would be no salvation.

Last: The chief ultimate end of redemption, which is God's glory (Rom. xi : 36; Is. lxi : 3; Eph. i : 6), would be utterly disappointed, were believers not required to depart from all sin. For God's holiness, His consummate attribute, would be tarnished by taking to His favour polluted creatures. This point suggests, also, the second, where God points to His own perfect holiness as the reason for the purification of His people. No argument could be plainer. An unholy creature has no place in the favour and bosom of a holy God. As I have argued in another place, God's holy law is as immutable as His nature; and no change of relation whatever, can abrogate it as a rule of right action.

To return a moment to the third point, I would add on it a remark which I omitted, in order to avoid interrupting the outline. The selfishness and guilty conscience of man prompt him powerfully to look to the Saviour exclusively as a remedy for guilt, even when awakened by the Spirit. The first and most urgent want of the soul, convicted of its guilt and danger, is impunity. Hence, the undue prevalence, even in preaching, of that view of Christ which holds Him up as expiation only. We have seen that even an Owen could be guilty of what I regard as the dangerous statement, that the true believer, in embracing Christ, first receives Him only in His priestly office! The faith which does no more than this, is but partial, and can bear but spurious fruits. Is not this the explanation of much of that defective and spurious religion with which the Church is cursed? The man who is savingly wrought upon by the Holy Ghost, is made to feel that his bondage under corruption is an evil as inexora-

Faith Embraces Christ in all His Offices.

ble and dreadful as the penal curse of the law. He needs and
desires Christ in His prophetic and kingly offices, as much as in
His priestly. His faith "receives Him as He is offered to us
in the gospel;" that is, as a "Saviour of His people from
their sins."

The Scriptures attribute sanctification so often to God, as
in 1 Thess. v : 23, that it is hardly necessary
to set about collecting proofs. The sense in
which He is the Author of the grace has
been indicated, when we said that sanctifica-
tion is but the continuance of the process of which regeneration
is the initiation. If regeneration is supernatural, and by a mysterious, but real and almighty operation, more than the moral
suasion of the truth, then sanctification is the result of the same
kind of agency. The proper and immediate Agent is the Holy
Ghost, as appears from Ps. li : 11 ; Jno. xvi : 8, 9 ; 2 Thess. ii :
13, &c., &c. This work is also attributed to the Son, in 1 Cor.
i : 30, &c.; and this not merely in the sense of the Epistle to
the Hebrews, because His righteousness is there mentioned
distinctly. Now, Christ is our Sanctifier, because He procures
the benefit for us by His justifying righteousness; because He
is now the God of Providence, and Dispenser of means to His
people; and because, by His perpetual intercession, He procures and dispenses the influences of the Holy Ghost to us, who
proceedeth from the Father and the Son. The Father is also
spoken of as our Sanctifier ; e. g., Jno xvii : 17, because He
stands in the Covenant of Grace as the Representative of the
whole Trinity, and is the Deviser of the whole gracious means,
and the Sender of the Son and Holy Ghost.

*3. Agent of Sanctifi-
cation in one Sense the
Father, and the Son,
but specially the Spirit.*

While the agency in sanctification is supernatural, and the
inscrutable indwelling and operation of the
Holy Ghost are required, not only to initiate,
but to continue growth in grace, yet He operates through means
usually. And these means may be said comprehensively to be
God's truth, His ordinances, and His providence. Such passages as Ps. xix : 1-7, plainly show that not only God's revealed
word, but His truth seen through the works of nature, may
sanctify the believer. But there is no reason to suppose that
these truths of Natural Theology have any sanctifying agency,
where they are not confirmed and enlarged by revelation.
While truth has no adequate efficiency to sanctify by itself; yet
it has a natural adaptation to be the means of sanctification in
the hand of the Holy Ghost. For it is religious truth which
presents all the objective conditions of holy exercises and acts.
That man's active powers may be holily exercised, an object of
acting is needed, as well as a power of acting. Thus in natural
vision. Now, religious truth presents that whole body of theological facts, of examples, of inducements, of external motives,
by which the soul is incited to act. By the ordinances, we mean

The Means Three.

God's worship and sacraments ; for the preaching of the word comes more properly under the former head.   Worship is a sanctifying means, because the petitions there offered are the appointed medium for receiving grace ; and because all the parts of worship give expression and exercise, and thus growth, to holy principles.   The sacraments are means whereby God symbolizes and seals to us the same truths expressed verbally in Revelation.   They are, therefore, a kind of acted instead of spoken word, bringing to the soul, in a still more lively manner, those views of truth, which the Holy Ghost makes the occasion, or objective of holy exercises.

Last, God's providences, both prosperous and adverse, are powerful means of sanctification, because they impress religious truth, and force it home, by operating with the word and Holy Ghost, on our natural emotions.   See Ps. cxix : 71 ; Heb. xii : 10; Rom. ii : 4.   But it should be remarked, that two things must concur for the sanctifying effect of Providences—the light of the word on the Providences to interpret them and give them their meaning, and the agency of the Holy Ghost inclining the heart to embrace the truths they serve to impress.   Mere suffering has no holiness in it.

Looking back, we now see that there is a sense in which But the Word is the the Revealed Word is the uniform means of Means in the other In- sanctification.   It gives fulness and authority struments. to Natural Theology.   It guides, authorizes, and instructs our worship.   It is symbolized in the sacraments. And it shines through the Providences, which do but illustrate it.   So that the Word is the means, after all, in all other means, Jno. xvii : 17.   Where the Word is not, there is no holiness.

Now, there are two graces, by whose intervention the efficacy of all these means of sanctification is Repentance and always mediated to the soul.   In other words, Faith Mother-Graces. these two graces are the *media* through which all other means come in efficacious contact with the soul.   They may, therefore, be called the mother graces of all the others. They are Repentance and Faith.   It is only when an object is apprehended by a full and active belief, that it becomes the occasion of any act of the soul.   A hundred illustrations are at hand, which show that this is universally true, and as true in man's carnal, as in his spiritual life.   Belief is the instigator of action.   But in order that belief may instigate action, the object believed must be so related to the affections of the mind, that there shall be appetency and repulsion.   In the case of saving faith, that relation is repentance—i. e., the active affections of the regenerate soul as to holiness and sin, and the means for attaining the one and shunning the other.   The student may now understand why God gives these graces such prominence in practical religion.   They are the *media* for the exercise of all others.   It follows, obviously, that repentance

and faith must be in perpetual exercise during the whole progress of sanctification.

It has been a question long mooted between Evangelical
Christians, and Pelagians, Socinians, Jesuits,
and Wesleyans, whether sanctification is ever
perfect in this life. The Pelagians and So-
cinians had an interest to assert that it may be; because such
an opinion is necessary to establish their doctrine of justification
by works; the Jesuits in order to uphold the possibility of
"merits of supererogation;" and the Wesleyans, to sustain their
theory of free-will and the type of religion which they foster.
As we have, practically, most to do with Wesleyans, on this
point, and they reproduce the arguments of the others, let us
address ourselves to their views. They assert that it is scriptural to expect some cases of perfect sanctification in this life;
because, 1. The means provided by God are confessedly adequate to this complete result, should He please to bless them;
and that it seems derogatory to His holy character when He
assures us that "this is the will of God, even our sanctification,"
to suppose He will not hear and answer prayers for a blessing
on those means, to any extent to which the faith of His children may urge those prayers. And 2. He has actually commanded us to pray for entire sanctification. Ps. cxix : 5, 6.
Surely, He does not cause the seed of Jacob to seek Him in
vain? 3. Not only has He thus encouraged, but commanded
us to seek perfection. See Matt. v : 48. Unless obedience
were possible, the command would be unjust. And 4. Perfect
sanctification is nowhere connected with the death of the body
by explicit texts. Indeed, the opinion that it must be, savours
of Gnosticism, by representing that the seat of ungodliness is
in the corporeal part, whereas, we know that the body is but
the passive tool of the responsible spirit. As to the involuntary
imperfections which every man, not insanely vain, must acknowledge, they are not properly sin; for God does not hold man
guilty for those infirmities which are the inevitable results of
his feeble and limited nature. Here, the Wesleyan very manifestly implies a resort to the two Pelagian principles; that man
is not responsible for his volitions unless they are free not only
from co-action, but from certainty; and that moral quality
resides only in acts of choice; so that a volition which is prevalently good is wholly good. Hence, those imperfections in
saints, into which they fall through mere inattention, or sudden
gust of temptation, contrary to their sincere bent and preference, incur no guilt whatever. Last: They claim actual cases
in Scripture, as of Noah, Gen. vi : 9 ; Ps. cxix : 1 ; Job i : 1
and 8 ; David, Ps. xxxvii : 37 ; Zechariah ; Luke i : 6 ; 1
Jno. iii : 9.

We reply : Perfection is only predicated of these saints, to

4. Wesleyan Doctrine of Sinless Perfection.

show that they had Christian sincerity; that
they had all the graces essential to the Christian character in actual exercise. As if to
refute the idea of their sinless perfection, Scripture in every
case records of them some fault, drunkenness of Noah, lying of
Abraham, adultery and murder of David, unbelief of Zechariah, Luke i : 20, while Job concludes by saying, "I abhor
myself, and repent in dust and ashes."

No Bible Saint Per-
fect.

The most objectionable trait about this theory of perfect
sanctification, is its affinities to Jesuitism and
Pelagianism. These are several ways mani-
fest. We saw that the old Pelagians, admitting that a complete
obedience is requisite for a justification by works, claimed that
the obedience which is materially in strict accordance with the
statute, and prevalently right in purpose, is perfectly right. We
saw, also, how they defended this view in consistency with
their false ethicks. For they place the moral quality of acts in
the volition, denying any certain efficiency to subjective (as to
objective) motive. Now, volition is, of course, an entire and
single act. The motives of a single volition may be complex ;
but the volition has a perfect unicity. Hence, if the morality
of the act is wholly in the volition, and not in those complex
motives, if the purpose is right, it is wholly right. But say,
with us, that the volition derives its moral quality from the subjective motives, (which is the doctrine of common sense and
the Bible,) and it follows that a volition may have a complex
moral character; it may be prevalently right, and yet not perfectly right. For, while volition is single, motive is complex.
I showed you, that the least complex motive must involve a
judgment and an appetency, and that no objective thing is
ever inducement to volition, until it stands, in the soul's view, in
the category of the true and the good, (the natural good, at
least). In the sense of this discussion, we should include in
the "subjective motive" of a given volition, all the precedaneous
states of judgment and appetency in the soul, which have causative influence in the rise of that volition. Then, many elements may enter into the subjective motive of a single volition ;
elements intellective, and elements conative. Every one of
these elements which has a moral quality, i. e. which arises
under the regulative power of subjective, moral disposition, may
contribute of its moral character to the resultant volition. Now,
then, it is the plainest thing in the world, that these elements
may be, some unholy, and some holy. Hence, the volition,
while possessed of an absolute singleness as a psychological
function, may have mixed moral character,—because, simply, it
has morally mixed subjective springs in the agent's soul. This
solution is simple ; and in several problems it is vital. Let it
explain itself in an instance. A good Christian man is met in
public by a destitute person, who asks alms. With deliberate

Pelagian Features.

consideration the relief is bestowed. The things which were present in the Christian's consciousness were these : The rush of instinctive or animal sympathy (morally negative while merely animal): A rational movement of ἀγάπη, or love (morally good): Recollection of, and desire for Christ's glory as displayed in the succour of His creature, (morally good): The thought of, and pleasure in, his own applause as a philanthropist (morally negative at least, and if inordinate, criminal): Selfish appetency to retain the money needed by the destitute person, for his own gratification, (morally evil). And last, a judgment of conscience. Now, the nature of that Christian's process of soul, during the instant he stood deliberating, was an adjusting of these concurring and competing elements of motive. The result was, that the better ones preponderated over the selfish reluctance, and the alms were given voluntarily and deliberately. Let us credit the Christian with giving the preponderant weight to Christian love, zeal for Christ's honour, and the conscientious judgment of obligation. Then these elements of motive have constituted the concrete act a prevalently godly one. But there ought to have been no selfish reluctance ! Then the very fact, that this evil element was there and was felt, and even needed suppressing, was an element of moral defect. There again, was the personal craving for applause, which was enough felt, to cause at least a partial disregard of our Saviour's rule, Matt. vi : 3, at the time of giving the alms, or afterward. Then, this also detracts from the perfectness of the action. Yet it was a prevalently godly action. So, an act may be socially virtuous, while prevalently ungodly ; or an act may be wholly godless and vicious. Only those, in whom concupiscence has been finally extinguished, perform perfectly godly acts. Such, we repeat, is the analysis of common-sense, and of the Bible. But the Wesleyan, acknowledging remainders of concupiscence in his "complete" saint, and yet asserting that his prevalently godly acts are perfect acts, has unconsciously adopted the false Pelagian philosophy, in two points : that "concupiscence is not itself sinful ;" and that the "moral quality resides exclusively in the act of soul." Again : when the Wesleyan says that an act, to which the good man is hurried by a gust of temptation so sudden and violent as to prevent deliberation ; an act which is against his prevalent bent and purpose, and which is at once deplored, is an infirmity, but not a sin; he is pelagianizing. He has virtually made the distinction between mortal and venial sins, which Rome borrows from Pelagius, and he is founding on that heretic's false dogmas, that responsibility ends when the will is no longer in *equilibrio*. (In this case it is the sudden gust of temptation which suspends the equilibrium).

There is also a dangerous affinity between these principles, and those horrible deductions from Pelagianism, made by the Jesuits, under the name of the art of "directing the attention," and venial sins. The origin is in the same speculations of those early heretics. The student may see an account and refutation in the unrivalled " Provincial Letters " of Blaise Pascal. The general doctrine is: that if, in perpetrating a crime, the direction of the intention is to a right end, this makes the act right, because the act which is prevalently right is wholly right. The abominations to which this Pelagian dogma led, in Jesuits' hands, were such, that they contributed to their suppression. It is not charged that Wesleyans countenance any of these immoral and loathesome conclusions: but their premises are dangerous, as appears from these results.

To proceed: it is true that the Bible does not say, in so many words, that the soul's connection with the present body is what makes for sanctification's incompleteness. But it asserts the equivalent truth; as when it teaches us, that at death the saints are made perfect in holiness. It is no Gnosticism, but Scripture and common sense, to attribute some obstacles to entire sanctification to the continuance of the animal appetites in man. While God's omnipotence could overcome those obstacles, yet it is according to His manner of working, that He has seen fit to connect the final completeness of His work of grace in the soul, with this last change. Hence, when the Scriptures show that this is His plan, we are prepared to believe it so.

God commands us, says the Wesleyan, to "be perfect, even as our Father in heaven is perfect," whence its possibility must follow. I reply. True; God cannot require of us a physical impossibility. But our inability to keep God's whole law perfectly is not physical. It began in man's sin. By that sin we lost none of those faculties which, when Adam's will was right, enabled him to keep God's command without sin. Our impotency is an "inability of will." Hence, it ought not to alter the demands of God's justice on His creatures. It is right in God to require perfection of us, and instruct us to seek it, because His own perfect nature can accept no less. Did God allow an inability of will to reduce His just claims on the creature, then the more sinful he became, the less guilt would attach to his shortcomings. A creature need only render himself utterly depraved to become completely irresponsible!

But we argue, affirmatively, that sanctification is never complete in this life. (a). Because the Scripture says expressly that remains of sin exist in all living men. See, for instance, I Jno. i: 8; Jas. iii: 2; I Kings viii: 46: Prov. xx: 9. How can such assertions be evaded?

(b.) I argue it, also from the perpetual warfare which the Scriptures say is going on between the flesh and the Spirit of God. See Rom. vii: 14, to end; Gal. v: 17, etc. This warfare, says

the Bible, constitutes the Christian life. And it is of no avail
for the Wesleyan to attempt evading this picture of Rom. vii:
as the language of Paul convicted but not yet converted; for
other similar passages remain, as Rom. viii: 7; Gal. v: 17;
Phil. iii: 13: 1 Tim. vi: 12, etc., etc. Now, as long as the contest lasts, there must be an enemy. (c). The impossibility of a
perfect obedience by ransomed men is clearly asserted in Scripture. Ps. cxix: 96; Acts xv: 10. It is true, that in the latter
place the ceremonial law is more immediately in Peter's view;
bnt the whole law is included, as is obvious from his scope ; and
if either could be perfectly kept, surely the ceremonial would
be the easier. Last: The Lord's Prayer teaches all Christians
to pray for the pardon of sin; a command which would not be
universally appropriate if this doctrine were true. And if
human experience can settle such a point, it is wholly on our
side ; for those who are obviously most advanced in sanctification, both among inspired and uninspired saints, are most
emphatic in their confessions of shortcoming; while those who
arrogantly claim perfect sanctification, usually discredit their
pretentions sooner or later, by shameful falls. It is well that
the Arminians have coupled the doctrine of falling from grace
with this. Otherwise their own professors of complete sanctification would have refuted it with a regularity that would have
been almost a fatality.

Now. the Almighty Spirit could subdue all sin, in a living
saint, if He chose. Bible truths certainly present sufficient
inducements to act as the angels, were our wills completely
rectified. Why God does not choose, in any case, to work this
complete result in this life, we cannot tell. "Even so, Father;
for so it seemed good in Thy sight."

The Wesleyans are accustomed to claim a more stimulat-
ing influence toward the pursuit of holiness,
for their doctrine, and to reproach ours with
paralyzing results. They say, that with a
rational agent, hope is a necessary element in the incentives to
exertion ; and that it is unnatural and impossible a man should
attempt, in good earnest, what he thinks impossible to be
achieved. But tell him that success, though arduous,is possible,
and he will strain every nerve, and at least make great progress.
They say that Calvinists practically teach their converts not to
aim high, and to make up their minds to low attainments in holiness, And hence the feeble and crippled character of the most
of the religion exhibited in their churches. We reply, that this
calculation misrepresents the facts, and leaves out one of the
most important of them. We do not forbid hope. We teach
our people to hope for constant advances in holiness, by which
they approach perfection continually, without actually reaching
it in this life. The essential fact left out of the estimate is the
invincible opposition of the new nature to all sin. The man

renewed by God is incapable of contenting himself with any degree of sin. Here is the safeguard against the cessation of the struggle under the discouraging belief that victory is only after death. If the indwelling enemy is thus as long-lived as the body, and immortal as long as the body lives, yet truce is impossible because the hostility of the new-born soul to it is unquenchable. Does it follow from this view, that the life must be a life-long battle ? I reply, even so ; this is just what the Bible represents it to be.

We can retort on the Wesleyan, a juster objection to the working of his theory. By giving a false definition of what perfection is, it incurs a much greater risk of inciting false pride, and dragging the conscience into a tolerance of what it calls guiltless, or venial infirmities. The Bible-Christian, the more he is conformed to God, advances just so much the more in tenderness aud perspicacity of conscience. Sin grows more odious, just as holiness grows more attractive. Thus, when there is, in God's view, less indwelling sin to extirpate in the heart, it is nerved by its contrition to a more determined war against what remains. Thus an ever progressive sanctification is provided for, conformably to the rational and free nature of man. But our question is : If the Christian be taught that what remains of indwelling sin, after a distinctive and decisive reign of grace begins in the soul, " is infirmity but not sin," do we not run a terrible risque of encouraging him to rest on the laurels of past attainments ; do we not drug his conscience, and do we not thus prepare the way for just those backslidings, by which these high pretenders have so frequently signalized their scheme ? Wesleyans sometimes say, that their doctrine of perfect sanctification, as defined by them, amounts to precisely the same with our statement concerning those better Christians, who, with Caleb and Joshua, (Numb. xiv: 24), "followed the Lord fully," and who enjoy an assurance of their own grace and salvation. Our objection is, that a dangerous and deluding statement is thus made of a scriptural truth. All Christians should be urged to these higher spiritual attainments ; but they should not be taught to call that "perfection," which is not really perfect, nor to depreciate their remaining sins into mere " infirmities."

A form of virtual perfectionism has become current recently, among Christians whose antecedents were not Arminian, but Reformed. They call themselves advocates of the " Higher Christian Life." This stage, they say, is reached by those who were before Christians, by a species of second conversion. The person gains his own full consent to undertake, in reliance on Christ, a life entirely above sin ; a life which shall tolerate no form or grade of shortcoming. As soon as this full resolve is entertained, and is pleaded before God with an entire faith, the believer receives the corresponding grace and strength.

in accordance with the promise; "Ask and ye shall receive." This attainment is often accompanied with a new "baptism of the Spirit," bestowing this full victory over sin, with a perfect assurance of acceptance; which baptism is immediately and infallibly recognized by the recipient, and in some cases, is even perceptible to bystanders, by infallible signs. Thencefoward, the recipient "walks in the light," enjoys perfect peace, and lives above all sin. It is pleaded by the advocates of this claim; that there is no limit to the gospel promises, nor to the merits of Christ, nor to the paternal grace of God; that the only reason we do not get fuller grace is, that we do not believingly ask it: and that no scriptural limit may be put upon this last proposition, this side of a perfect victory over sin. If, say they, men had a perfect faith to ask, they would receive of Christ's fulness a perfect answer. They quote such promises as these; "Open thy mouth wide, and I will fill it," Ps. lxxxi: 10. "Ask and ye shall receive," Matt. vii: 8. "This is the will of God, even your sanctification." 1 Thess. iv: 3.

That the promises of God in Christ hold out indefinite encouragement to believers, is a precious truth. That it is the duty of all to press forward to the mark, is indisputable. But when men say, that a perfect faith would receive a perfect answer, they are but uttering a valueless truism. The man who had a perfect faith would be a perfect man. He would need no more sanctification. Unfortunately for this theory, the indwelling sin which creates the need for farther sanctification, inevitably involves some imperfection and weakness of the faith. We shall always have to raise the disciples' cry; "Lord increase our faith," as long as we cry for increase of grace. So, if a believer's heart were finally, immutably, and perfectly united, through every moment, in the resolve to live, by Christ's strength, absolutely above sin, he would doubtless meet with no rebuff in any petition for strength, at Christ's throne of grace. But in order to have such a state of purpose, there must be no indwelling sin in that heart. This scheme, stripped of its robes, comes therefore to this truism: "Were a man absolutely perfect, he would be absolutely perfect?" The picture of the Christian's militant life, which we ever see portrayed in Scripture, is that of an imperfect, but progressive faith uniting him to his Saviour, always finding Him faithful to His promises, and always deriving from Him measures of grace corresponding to the vigour of its exercise, yet always leaving room for farther advances. There is an exceedingly broad and conclusive argument against all forms of perfectionism in this fact: That the provisions of grace described in the Bible are all provisions for imperfect and sinning men. The gospel is a religion for sinners, not for glorified saints. This is the only conception of it which appears in any part of scripture.

Only a little experience and scriptural knowledge are nec-

43*

essary, to make us view the claims of the spiritual baptism advanced above, with suspicion.   The immediate visitation of the Holy Ghost should attest itself by miraculous "signs," by "tongues," or "gifts of healings;" as it did in apostolic days. If these be lacking, we have no other test of its presence, than the fruits of holy living; and for these we should wait.   The Christian who, instead of waiting for this attestation, presumes on an intuitive and infallible consciousness of the endowment, can never scripturally know but that the impulse he mistakes for the Spirit's baptism is natural fanaticism, or the temptation of him, who is able to transform himself into an angel of light.

LECTURE LVII.

SANCTIFICATION AND GOOD WORKS. —
Concluded.

SYLLABUS.

5. What is the Subject of Sanctification; man's fallen Nature, or something else? And are Sanctification and mortification of sin progressive?
" Notes on Genesis," by C. H. M. of Dublin, p. 200, &c.   " Waymarks in the Wilderness," by Jas. Inglis, Vol i, p. 10; Vol. iii, pp. 75–332; Vol. v, pp. 29, 37, &c., Dr. Jno. Owen, on Indwelling Sin.
6. What constitutes an Evangelical Good Work?   Are any works of the natural man godly works?
Turrettin, Loc. xvii, Qu. 4.   Dick, Lect. 76.   Hill, bk. v, ch. 4.   Hodge's Theol. pt. iii, ch. 18, § 4.
7. Can man merit of God, by works?   What the Doctrine of Rome concerning congruous and condign Merit?
Turrettin, Qu. 5.   Hill, as above § 2.   Knapp, § 108, 125.   Hodge as above.
8. State and refute the Popish Doctrine of *Concilia Perfectionis*, and Supererogation.
Th. Aquinas, *Pars Prima Secundæ*, Qu. 108.   Suppl, Qu. 13.   Turrettin, Loc. xi, Qu. 4.   Knapp, § 125.   Hill as above.   Hodge as above.
9. What the standard for our sanctification?   Show the value and relation of Christ's example thereto.
Dick. Lect. 75.   Knapp, 117.   Chalmer's Theol, Inst. Vol. ii, ch. 10.

THE relation between regeneration and sanctification has been stated: The first implants a life which the second nourishes and develops.   It is the heart of
Sanctification is Progressive.
man, or his soul, which is the seat of the first.   It is, of course, the same heart, which is the seat of the second.   The latter is defined in our Catechism (Qu. 35), as a "work of God's free grace, whereby we are renewed in the whole man after the image of God, and are enabled more and more to die unto sin, and live unto righteousness."   See also Larger Catech., Qu. 75, and Conf. of Faith, ch. 13, § 1.   We regard sanctification then as advancing that renovation of man's heart, which regeneration begins.   The process of sanctification and that of the mortification of sin are counterparts.   The more we live unto righteousness, the more

we die unto sin. Grace and indwelling sin are complementary quantities, if a material illustration may be borrowed, such that the increase of the one is the corresponding decrease of the other. But in opposition to this established view of the Reformed Churches, the Plymouth Brethren's theology asserts that both the ideas of the mortification of the "old man" and of progressive sanctification are false. They ascribe the same completeness to sanctification from its inception, as to justification; if they do not quite combine them. Thus: ("Waymarks in the Wilderness," vol. iii, pp. 342, 343), regeneration is defined: "It is a new birth, the imparting of a new life, the implantation of a new nature, the formation of a new man. The old nature remains in all its distinctness; and the new nature is introduced in all its distinctness. This new nature has its own desires, its own habits, its own tendencies, its own affections. All these are spiritual, heavenly, divine. Its aspirations are all upward. It is ever breathing after the heavenly source from which it emanated. Regeneration is to the soul what the birth of Isaac was to the household of Abraham. Ishmael remained the same Ishmael, but Isaac was introduced." On p. 80th, "Be warned that the old nature is unchanged. The hope of transforming that into holiness is vain as the dream of a philosopher's stone, which was to change the dross of earth into gold." . . . . "On the other hand, never be discouraged by new proof, that that which is born of the flesh is flesh. It is there; but it is condemned and crucified with its affections and lusts. Reckon it so, and that therefore you are no longer to serve it. It is just as true, that that which is born of the Spirit is spirit, and remains uncontaminated by that with which it maintains a ceaseless conflict." So. vol. v, p. 302. "Thus, two men there are in the Christian: so hath he evil; and so hath he not evil. If therefore he purge out the evil, it is his new man purging out his old man. Now these two men, within the control of the personality of the Christian, are real men, having each his own will, his own energy, and his own enjoyment."

Plymouth Doctrine.

In answer to this exaggerated view, we assert, first, that while the Apostle, Rom. vii : 23, speaks of "another law in his members, warring against the law of his mind," the Scriptures nowhere say that regeneration implants a "new nature; or that the Christian has in him "two natures;" much less, two "real men." Shall I be reminded of Gal. v : 17, where the "Spirit" and "flesh" lust against each other? The "Spirit" is the Holy Ghost. So judges Calvin; and so the scope of Paul's context, in verses 16th and 18th, decides. So, in that chapter, it is a violence to the Apostle's meaning, to represent the "works of the flesh," verse 19th, &c., and the "fruits of the Spirit," verse 23d, as occupying the same man, in full force,

The New Nature What?

cotemporaneously.   The 24th verse shows, that the latter extrude and succeed the former; and that this result is the evidence of a state of grace.   Our popular language sometimes uses the word "nature" in the sense of moral *Habitus;* and we speak of grace as "changing the nature," or "producing a new nature."   But in strictness, the language is neither philosophical, nor scriptural.   A "nature" is the *essentia*, the aggregate of essential attributes with which the creature was *natus*. Were this changed, the personal identity would be gone, and the whole responsibility dissolved.   The fall did not change man's *essentia;* nor does the new creation; each changed the moral *habitus* of man's powers : the fall to depravity, the new creation back towards holiness.   The notion of two personalities also, in one man, is preposterous.   Here the appeal to consciousness is decisive.   If there were either two "natures" or two "real men," every Christian must have a dual consciousness.   But I need not dwell on the truth which every man knows, that, while there is a vital change, consciousness is as much one, as in the unrenewed state.   The explanation given in the last lecture solves this whole confusion.   While the will is one, motives are complex.   Regeneration works a prevalent, but not absolute revolution, in the moral disposition regulative of the Christian's motives.   Amidst the complex of subjective states which leads to any one volition, some elements may be spiritual and some carnal.   As regeneration established a new and prevalent (though not exclusive) law of disposition, so sanctification confirms and extends that new law in introducing more and more of the right elements, and more and more extruding the wrong elements.

Let us, second, bring the matter to the test of Scripture. The thing which is renewed is the sinful soul. Eph. iv : 23: ii : 1–5; I Cor. vi : 11 ; Col. i : 21, 22.   Both the sanctification of the soul, and the mortification of sin are expressly declared to be progressive processes. Let the student consult the following references : 2 Cor. i : 22; v : 5 ; Acts xx : 32; 2 Cor. iii : 18 ; Eph. iv : 11–16 ; Phil. iii : 13–15 ; I Thess. v : 23; 2 Cor. vii: 1 , Heb. vi: 1 ; I Peter, ii : 2; 2 Peter, iii : 18; Rom. viii : 13 ; Col. iii : 5.   So, the Bible compares the saint to living and growing things; as the vine, the fruit tree, the plant of corn, the infant; all of which exhibit their lives in growth.   Grace is also compared to the " morning light, waxing brighter and brighter to the perfect day ;" and to the leaven, spreading through the whole vessel of meal : and to the mustard-seed, the smallest sown by the Jewish husbandman, but gradually growing to the largest of herbs. Is not the rhetoric of the Word just?   Then we must suppose the analogy exists ; and that spiritual life, like vegetable and animal, regularly displays its power by growth.   These innovators borrow the Popish plea, that " the new-creation, being God's

(margin note) Scripture Argument.

work, must be perfect." I reply; The infant is also a work of God's power and skill; but he is designed to grow to an adult.

We find this idea incompatible, in the third place, with the laws of a finite rational creature. These ordain, that every faculty, affection, and habit must grow by their exercise, or be enervated by their disuse and suppression. Depravity grows in sinners, (2 Tim. iii : 13) as long as it is unchecked. So, holiness must grow by its exercise. Even the pagan Horace understood this,—*Crescentem sequitur cura pecuniam, majorumque fames.* This being the law of man's mutable nature, it must follow, that, as exercise increases the principles of holiness, so the denial of self and flesh must enervate and diminish the principles of sin.

All Principles are Progressive.

I object, in the last place, to the antinomian tendencies which are, at least latently, involved in this scheme. If one believes that he has two "real men," or "two natures" in him, he will be tempted to argue that the new man is in no way responsible for the perversity of the old. Here is a perilous deduction. But the next is worse, as it is more obvious. If the new nature is complete at first; and the old nature never loses any of its strength until death; then the presence, and even the flagrancy of indwelling sin need suggest to the believer no doubts whatever, whether his faith is spurious. How can it be denied that there is here terrible danger of carnal security in sin? How different this from the Bible which says Jas. ii : 18, "Show me thy faith without thy works ; and I will show thee my faith by my works." If then any professed believer finds the "old man" in undiminished strength, this is proof that he has never "put on the new man." If the flesh is reviving, spiritual life is just to that extent receding; and just in degree as that recession proceeds, has he scriptural ground to suspect that his faith is (and always was) dead.

Tendencies of Dual Doctrine Antinomian.

There is a gospel sense, in which the Scriptures speak of the acts and affections of Christians as good works. By this, it is not meant that they are perfect, that they could stand the strictness of the divine judgment, or that they are such as would receive the reward of eternal life under the Covenant of Works. Yet they are essentially different in moral quality from the actions of the unrenewed; and they do express a new and holy nature, as the principle from which they spring. There is also a certain sense in which God approves and rewards them. How are these evangelical actions of the soul defined? We conceive that the Scripture characterizes them thus: 1. They must be the actions of a regenerate soul; because no other can have the dispositions to prompt such actions, and feel such motives as must concur. See Matt. xii : 33, or vii : 17, 18. 2. The

6. A Good Work, What ?

action must be, in matter, regulated by the revealed will of God; for He allows no other rule of right and wrong for the creature. No act of obedience to rules of mere human or ecclesiastical device can claim to be a good work; it is more probably an offence unto God. See Deut. iv : 2; Is. i ; 12; xxix : 13; Matt. xv : 9. As God's will is to us practically the fountain of authority and obligation, it is obviously unreasonable that the debtor should decide for the creditor, how much or what the former sees fit to pay. And moreover, such is the distance between God and man, and the darkness of the sinful mind of man, we are no suitable judges of what service is proper to render God. Man's duty is simply what God requires of him. Can we err in defining good works as the right performance of duty ? 3. In order for that performance to be a good work its prevalent motive or motives must be holy : and among these, especially, must be a respectful, righteous, and filial regard, either habitual or express, to the will of God commanding the act. See 1 Cor. x : 31; Rom. xi : 36, and xii : 1. No principle of common sense is plainer, than that the quality of the act depends on the quality of the intention. An act not intended to please God is, of course, not pleasing in His sight, no matter how conformed in outward shape to His precepts.

Such works are not perfectly, but prevalently holy. I have A Work not per- more than once remarked, that the motive of fectly Holy may be most of our volitions is a complex of several prevalently so. appetencies. Now, this habitual, or present filial regard to God's authority may be the prevalent motive of a given act ; and yet it may be short of that fulness and strength which the perfect rectitude and goodness of the heavenly Father deserve. It may also be associated with other lower motives. Of these, some may be personal, and yet legitimate ; as a reasonable subordinate regard to our own proper welfare. (The presence of such a motive in the complex would not make the volition sinful.) But other motives may, and nearly always do, mix with our regard for God, which are not only personal, but sinful: either because inordinate, or impure, as a craving for applause, or a desire to gratify a spiteful emulation. Remembering the views established in the last lecture, you will perceive that in such a case, the volition would be on the whole, right and pious, and still short of perfect rightness, or even involving, with its holiness, a taint of sin.

But the best natural virtues of the heathen, and of all un- No True Good converted persons, come short of being gos- Works done by Un- pel good works. See, for instance, Gen. vi : converted or Heathen. 5, and Rom. viii : 8. This truth recalls the assertion made of the total depravity of the race, and its grounds. It will be remembered that we did not deny the secular sincerity of the social virtues, which many pagans and unrenewed men possess. Nor did we represent that their virtues

were equal to the vices of the wicked.   But what we mean is,
that while nearer right than the open vices, they are still short
of right; because they lack the essential motive, regard to
God's revealed will and the claims of His love.   " God is not in
all their thoughts."   Now, as our relation to God is the nearest
and most supreme, an act which ignores this, however right it
may be in other motives, still remains prevalently wrong in the
sight of God.   It does not reach the level of Bible holiness at
all, though it may rise much nearer towards it than the sins of
the reprobate.   We do not, then, represent God as judging the
amiable and decent transgressor equal to a monster of crime,
nor condemning all secular virtues as spurious and worthless
between man and man.

The proposition, that even the good works of believers do
not earn eternal life by their intrinsic merit,
7. Merit. Rome's has been found very repugnant to human
Distinction into Con-
gruous and Condign. pride.   Rome consequently seeks to evade
the omission of it, by her distinction of congruous and condign
merit.   (*Meritum de congruo de condigno.*)   The former she
makes only a qualified kind of merit.   It is that favourable
quality which attaches to the good works done by the unrenewed man before conversion, which properly moves God to
bestow on him the help of His grace.   The condign merit is
that which attaches to evangelical good works done after conversion, by the help of grace, which, by its proper value and
force, entitles the believer to eternal life.   True, Bellarmine and
the Council of Trent, with the most of Romanists, say that eternal
life comes to the obedient believer partly by the merit of his own
works, and partly by virtue of Christ's promise and purchase;
so that. were there no Saviour, human merit would come short
of earning heaven.   But they hold this essentially erroneous
idea, that, in the gracious works of the justified man, there is a
real and intrinsic merit of reward.

To clear up this matter, let us observe that the word merit
is used in two senses, the one strict or proper,
Merit, strictly the other loose.   Strictly speaking, a merito-
What? Three sorts. rious work is that to which, on on account of
its own intrinsic value and dignity, the reward is justly due from
commutative justice.   But when men use the word loosely, they
include works deserving of approval, and works to which a reward is anyhow attached as a consequence.   Now, in these latter senses, no one denies that the works of the regenerate are
meritorious.   They are praiseworthy, in a sense.   They are followed by a recompense.   But in the strict sense, of righteously
bringing God in the doer's debt, by their own intrinsic moral
value, no human works are meritorious.   The chief confusion
of thought, then, which is to be cleared away, is that between
the approvable and the meritorious.   An act is not meritorious,
only because it is morally approvable.

Note further, that it is wholly another thing to do works
which may fall within the terms of some cov-
Hypothetical Merit.   enant of promise, which God may have graciously bestowed. If the king is pleased, in his undeserved
kindness, to promise the inheritance for the doing of some little
service utterly inadequate to the reward, and if any creature
complies with the terms exactly, then the king is, of course,
bound to give what he has engaged. But he is bound by fidelity to himself, not by commutative justice to the service rendered ; for that, intrinsically, is inadequate.

In the strict sense, then, no work of man brings God in the
doer's debt, to reward him. The work which
Strictly, no Creature   is worthy of this must have the following
can Merit.   traits . It must be one which was not already
owed to God.   See Luke xvii : 10. It must be done in the
man's own strength; for if he only does it by the strength of
Christ, he cannot take to himself the credit of it. " It is not he
that liveth, but Christ that liveth in him." It must be perfectly
and completely right; for if stained with defect, it cannot merit.
Last, it must be of sufficient importance to bear some equitable
ratio to the amount of reward. One would not expect a large
sum of money as wages for the momentary act of handing a
draught of water, however cheerfully done. Now, it is plain
at the first glance, that no work of man to God can bring Him,
by its own intrinsic merit, under an obligation to reward. All
our works are owed to God ; if all were done, we should only
" have done what was our duty to do." No right work is done
in our own mere strength. None are perfect. There is no
equality between the service of a fleeting life and an inheritance
of eternal glory.

We may argue, farther, that the congruous merit of the
Papist is imaginary, because nothing the un-
Natural Works have believer does can please God :   " Without
no Merit of Congruity. faith it is impossible to please Him."   " They
that are in the flesh cannot please God," Every man is under
condemnation, until he believes on Christ with living faith. But
if the person is under condemnation, none of his acts can merit.
Second : There is an irreconcilable contrast between grace and
works. See Rom. xi : 6. The two are mutually exclusive, and
cannot be combined. Grace is undeserved bestowal ; merit
purchases by its desert. This being so, it is vain for the Papist
to attempt to excuse his error of a congruous merit subordinated
to, and dependent on, free grace, by any false analogies of first
and second causes. The human affection or act springing out
of grace, may have approvableness, but no sort of merit. The
practical remark should be made here, that when the awakened
sinner is thus encouraged to claim saving graces as due to the
congruous merit of his strivings, tears, reformations, or sacraments, he is put in the greatest peril of mistaking the way of

salvation, grieving the Spirit, and falling into a fatal self-righteousness. What more insolent and deadly mistake can be made,
than this telling of God, on the part of a miserable sinner, pen-
sioner on His mere mercy, that the wretch's carnal, selfish strivings, or expedients, have brought the Almighty in his debt, in a
sense, to bestow saving helps? Third; The whole Scripture
holds forth the truth, that Christ bestows saving graces, not
because of any form of merit, but in spite of utter demerit.
We receive them "without money and without price." It
was "when we were enemies, that we were reconciled to
God by the death of His Son." Even the saint seeking grace
always, in the Scripture seeks it purely of grace. Much more
must the sinner. See Ps. li : 1-4; Dan. ix : 18; 1 Tim. i : 12-
16. In conclusion of this point, it will be instructive to notice
the close connection between this claim of "congruous merit,"
and the value attached by those Protestants who are syner-
gists, to those expedients which they devise, to prepare the
way for faith. Awakened sinners are encouraged to use them,
and to look to them, not indeed as justifying; but as somehow leading on to more saving graces. Yet, there is a certain relationship of sequence, between the exercisings and
strivings of carnal conviction and saving converson. "They that
be whole need not a physician, but they that be sick." The
pangs of the sick man have a certain instrumentality in prompting him to send for the physician who cures him. In this sense
they may be viewed as useful. But, *per se*, they are not in the
least degree curative they are but parts of the disease, whose
only tendency is death.

That no merit of condignity attaches even to the good
works of saints, is clear from the conditions

No Condign merit in
Works of Regenerate.
we have shown to be requisite. (See page
680). The most conclusive passages are
such as these : Luke xvii : 9, 10; Rom. vi : 23; v : 15–18 ;
Eph. ii : 8–10 , 2 Tim. i : 9 ; Titus iii : 5, and such like. The
first gives an argument by analogy, founded on the Judean
husbandman's relation to his bondsman (his δουλος not his hire-
ling). The master had legitimate property in his labour and
industry—not in his moral personality, which belonged inalien-
ably to God. Hence, when the bondsman rendered that service, the master did not for a moment think that he was thereby
pecuniarily indebted to him for a labour which was already his
own property : however he might regard the docility and
fidelity of the bondsman highly approvable, he never dreamed
that he owed him wages therefor. So we are God's property.
He has, at the outset of our transacting with Him, ownership
in all our service. Hence, if we even served Him perfectly,
(which we never do,) we could not claim that we had paid God
any overplus of our dues, or brought Him into our debt. He
might approve our fidelity, but He would owe us no wages. In

Rom. vi : 23, the Apostle actually breaks the symmetry of his antithesis, in order to teach that we merit nothing of God's commutative justice. Death is the wages which sin earns : but eternal life is the gift of God, and not wages earned by the Christian. The remaining passages teach the same.

Turrettin sustains this view farther, by showing that the gracious acts, for which Romanists claim merit of condignity, and the eternal life attached to them, are always spoken of as the Father's gifts; that they are always spoken of as the Redeemer's purchase; that the Christians who do them are represented in the Bible as acknowledging themselves "unprofitable servants;" and that they always confess the unworthiness of their best works, especially in view of the everlasting reward. The Scriptures which might be collected under these heads would present an overwhelming array of proof.

But carnal men strongly resent this conclusion; and urge, It does not Follow as though it were a self-evident refutation, that because Sin Merits, that as sin and good works are in antithesis, our Works Do. we cannot hold that man's sin carries a true and essential desert of punishment, and deny that his good work carries an equal desert of reward. To affix the one and refuse the other, they exclaim, would be a flagrant injustice. I reply: Between human rulers and ruled, it would. But they forget here the prime fact, that God is the Maker and sovereign Proprietor of men. The property may be delinquent towards its sovereign Owner, but it cannot make the Owner delinquent to it. If it fails in due service, it injures the rights of its Owner: if it renders the service, it only satisfies those rights; nothing more. But here a certain concession should be made. While a creature's perfect obedience is not meritorious of any claim of reward upon his Lord, in the strict sense, there is a relation of moral propriety between such obedience and reward. We saw that it appeared unreasonable to claim everlasting reward for temporal service. But does not a perfect temporal service deserve of God temporal reward? I would say, in a eertain sense, Yes; supposing the creature in a state of innocency and harmony with his Lord. That is, it would be inconsistent with God's rectitude and benevolence, to begin to visit on this innocent creature the evils due to sin, before he transgressed. God would not infringe, by any suffering or wrath, that natural blessedness, with which His own holiness and goodness always leads Him to endow the state of innocency. But here the obligation is to God's own perfections, rather than to the creature's merit.

Some have supposed these views to be inconsistent with Did Adam and Elect the terms of the Covenant of Works between Angels Merit under God and the elect angels, and God and Adam. Covenant of Works? They say that Paul, Rom. iv : 4, 5, and xi : 6, in drawing the contrast already cited between works and g₊ace, assigns condign merit to a perfect service done under a Covenant of Works. "To him that worketh is the reward reckoned not of grace, but of debt." I reply: this of course, is true of works done under a covenant of works: but to overthrow the Reformed argument, they must show that it would be true also of works done under the natural relation to God, as Lord before any covenant of promise. When once God has gratuitously condescended to promise, a claim of right for the perfect service rendered does emerge: of course. It emerges out of God's fidelity; not out of commutative justice. And when the creature, as Gabriel for instance, complies with the covenanted terms perfectly, and in his own strength, he gets his reward on different terms from those of the pardoned sinner. There is, in a sense, an earning under compact; such as the sinner can never boast; and this, we presume, is all the Apostle ever meant.

It only remains, on this head, to explain the relation between the good works of the justified believer and his heavenly reward. It is explained by the distinction between an intrinsic and original merit of reward, and the hypothetical merit granted by promise. If the slave fulfills his master's orders, he does not bring the latter in his debt. "He is an unprofitable servant; he has only done what was his duty to do." But if the master chooses, in mere generosity, to promise freedom and an inheritance of a thousand talents for some slight service, cheerfully performed, then the service must be followed by the reward. The master owes it not to the intrinsic value of the slave's acts, (the actual pecuniary addition made thereby to the master's wealth may be little or nothing,) but to his own word. Now, in this sense, the blessings of heaven bear the relation of a "free reward" to the believer's service. It contributes nothing essential to earning the inheritance; in that point of view it is as wholly gratuitous to the believer, as though he had been all the time asleep. The essential merit that earned it is Christ's. Yet it is related to the loving obedience of the believer, as appointed consequence. Thus it appears how all the defects in his evangelical obedience (defects which, were he under a legal covenant, would procure the curse, and not blessing,) are covered by the Saviour's righteousness; so that, through Him, the inadequate works receive a recompense. Moreover, it is clearly taught that God has seen fit, in apportioning degrees of blessedness to different justified persons, to measure them by the amount of their good works. See Matt. xvi : 27 ; 1 Cor. iii : 8, of which Turrettin remarks, that the reward is "according to," but not "on account of" the works. See also, 2 Cor. ix : 6 ; Luke xix : 17, 18. Not only the sovereignty, but the wisdom and righteousness of a gracious God are seen in this arrangement. Thus a rational motive is applied to educe dili-

In what Sense are Believer's Works Rewarded?

gent obedience. Thus it is evinced that the gospel is not a ministration of indolence or disobedience; and God's verdicts in Christ not inconsistent with natural justice. It is thus, because the grace given on earth is a preparation of the soul for more grace in heaven. And last, good works are the only practical and valid test of the genuineness of that faith, by which believers receive the perfect merits of Christ. This last fact, especially, makes it proper that the "free reward" shall be bestowed "according to their works;" and explains a multitude of passages, which Papists suppose make the reward depend on the works.

It may be said that the Romish Church is indebted to the age of Thomas Aquinas, and most probably to him, for the final theory of "works of supererogation." He found among the Fathers, the distinction between Christ's *praecepta* and *consilia*. This distinction pretending to find its grounds in certain texts of the New Testament, more probably had its origin in a desire to imitate the exoteric and the esoteric, higher and lower, morals of the New Platonists. The instances of *Concilia* usually quoted are those of Matt. xix: 12 and 21: 1 Cor. vii: 38–40; Acts xxi: 23, 24, and they are usually grouped by them under the three virtues of voluntary poverty, perpetual chastity, and regular obedience. The Church had long held, that while every one must strive to obey all the precepts of Christ, on pain of damnation, he is not expressly bound to comply with the "councils of perfection." If he sees fit to omit them, he incurs no wrath. They are but recommendations. Yet, if his devoted spirit impels him to keep them for the glory of God, he thereby earns supererogatory merit, superfluous to his own justification. Aquinas now proceeds to build on this foundation thus: One man can work a righteousness, either penal or supererogatory, so that its imputation to his brother may take place. What else, he argues, is the meaning of Gal. vi: 2; "Bear ye one another's burdens," etc.? And among men, one man's generous efforts are permitted in a thousand ways to avail for another, as in suretyships. "But with God, love avails for more than with men." Yea, a less penance is a satisfaction for a brother's guilt than would be requisite for one's own, in the case of an equal sin. Because the purer disinterestedness, displayed in atoning for the penitential guilt of a brother, renders it more amiable in the sight of God, and so, more expiatory. If a sinning believer hits himself twenty blows with his whip on his bare shoulders, it may be that a selfish fear of purgatory is a large part of his motive; and God will subtract from the merit of the act accordingly. But when he does it for his brother's sin, it is pure disinterested love and zeal for God's honor, the twenty blows will count for more.

The philosopher then resorts to the doctrine of the unity

Imputation of Super-
erogatory Merit, and
Indulgence Thereby
of Penitential Guilt.
of the Church, and the communion of saints in each other's graces and sufferings, to show that the merit of these supererogatory services and sufferings is imputed to others. There is, in the holy Catholic Church then, a treasury to which all this spare merit flows. As the priesthood hold the power of the keys, they of course are the proper persons to dispense and apply it. But as the unity of the Church is especially represented in its earthly head, the Pope, he especially is the proper person to have charge of the treasury.   And this is the way *indulgentia* is procured ; the Pope imputes some of this supererogatory merit of works and penance out of the Church treasure ; whence the remission to the culprit of the penitential and purgatorial satisfaction due from him for sin. But his confession, absolution, and contrition are necessary ; otherwise indulgence does no good, because without these exercises the man's own personal penance would have done no good.   Last, this indulgence may properly be given by the Church, in return for money, provided it be directed to a holy use, as repairing churches, building monasteries, etc. (He forgot our Saviour's words :   " Freely ye have received, freely give.")

The overthrow of all this artificial structure is very easy for

Distinctions of Coun-
sels of Perfection Re-
futed.
the Protestant.   We utterly deny the distinction of the pretended " counsels of perfection," from the precepts, as wicked and senseless.   It is impossible that it can hold: because we are told that the precepts go to this extent, viz : requiring us to love God with all the soul and heart and mind, and strength. If, then, any Christian has indeed found out that his circumstances are such, the refraining from a given act, before and elsewhere indifferent, has become necessary to Christ's highest glory; then for him it is obligatory, and no longer optional.   " To him that knoweth to do good, and doeth it not, to him it is sin." Rome's own instance refutes her.   In Matt. xix : 23, 24, the rich ruler incurs, by rejecting our Saviour's counsel, not the loss of supererogatory merit, but the loss of heaven ! Again : how can he have superfluity who lacks enough for himself?   But all lack righteousness for their own justification ; for " in many things we offend all."   So, the Scriptures utterly repudiate the notion that the righteousness of one man is imputable to another.   Christian fellowship carries no such result. It was necessary (for reasons unfolded in the discussion of the Mediator), that God should effectuate the miracle of the hypostatic union, in order to make a Person, whose merit was imputable.   "None of them can by any means redeem his brother, or give to God a ransom for him."   Nor does the Protestant recognize the existence of that penitential guilt, which is professed to be remitted by the indulgence.

The standard set for the believer's sanctification is the

9. Standard of Sanc-
tification, Law, and
Jesus' Example.
character of God as expressed in His preceptive law. This rule is perfect, and should be
sufficient for our guidance. But God, in
condescension to our weak and corporeal nature, has also given
us an example in the life of the Redeemer. And this was a sub-
sidiary, yet important object of His mission. See 1 Pet. ii: 21.
(We recognize in its proper place, this prophetic function of the
Mediator, which the Socinian makes the sole one.) The advantage of having the holy law teaching by example is obvious.
Man is notoriously an imitative creature. God would fain
avail Himself of this powerful lever of education for his moral
culture. Example is also superior in perspicuity and interest,
possessing all the advantage over precept, which illustration
has over abstract statement. If we inspect the example of
Christ, we shall find that it has been adjusted to its purpose
with a skill and wisdom only inferior to that displayed in His
atoning offices. Examining first the conditions of an effective
example, we find that they all concur in Christ. It is desirable
that our examplar be human; for though holiness in God and in
angels is, in principle, identical with man's, yet in detail it is too
different to be a guide. Yet while it is so desirable that the
example be human, it must be perfect; for fallible man would be
too sure to imitate defects, on an exaggerated scale. Man is
naturally out of harmony with holiness, too far to be allured by
its example; he would rather be alienated and angered by it.
Hence, the exemplar must begin by putting forth a regenerating
and reconciling agency. Last: it is exceedingly desirous that
the examplar should also be an object of warm affection;
because we notice that the imitative instinct always acts far
most strongly towards one beloved. But Christ is made by His
work the prime object of the believer's love.

The value of Christ's example may be also illustrated in
Value of Christ's
Example.
the following particulars: It verifies for us
the conception of holiness, as generally displayed in God. That conception must
lack definiteness, until we see it embodied in this "Image of the
invisible God," who is "the brightness of His glory, and the
express image of His person." See Lect. vii: end. Next,
Christ has illustrated the duties of all ages and stations; for the
divine wisdom collected into His brief life all grades, making
Him show us a perfect child, youth, man, son, friend, teacher,
subject, ruler, king, hero, and sufferer. Again, Christ teaches
us how common duties are exalted when performed from an
elevated motive; for He was earning for His Church infinite
blessedness, and for His Father eternal glory, when fulfilling the
humble tasks of a peasant and mechanic. And last, in His
death especially, He illustrated those duties which are at once
hardest aud most essential, because attaching to the most critical emergencies of our being, the duties of forgiveness under

wrong, patience and fortitude under anguish, and faith and courage in the hour of death. Consult, Rom. xv: 3; Phil. ii: 5; Heb.xii: 2, 3; 1 Jno. iii: 16; Eph. iv: 13; Jno. xiii: 15; 1 Cor. xi: 1.

Some have endeavoured to object, that we must not imitate even an incarnate Christ, because He is God and man, and His mediatorial sphere of action above ours. I reply: of course we do not presume to imitate His divine acts. But was He not made under our law? One end of this was that He might show us a human perfection, adapted for our imitation.

LECTURE LVIII.

PERSEVERANCE OF THE SAINTS.

SYLLABUS.

I. State the Doctrines of Calvinists, Pelagians, Papists and Arminians hereon.

Conf. of Faith, ch. xvii. Turrettin, Loc. xv, Qu. 16. § 1-8. Witsius, bk. iii, ch. 13, § 1-11.

II. Prove the doctrine from: 1. The immutability of election;   2. The freedom of God's electing love;   3. Christ's merit and intercession;   4. The indwelling of the Holy Spirit;   5. The Covenant of redemption.

Turrettin as above, § 9-28. Dick, Lect. 79. Ridgley, Qu. 79. Witsius, as above, § 12-37.

III. Present other Scriptural proofs.

Turrettin as above, Qu. 16, § 25-28. Ridgley. Qu. 79.

IV. Reconcile objections; and especially those founded on Scripture-passages, as Ezek. xviii : 24; Heb. vi : 4, &c.; x : 29, 38; iii : 12. 1 Cor. ix : 27; 2 Peter, ii : 20; Rom. xiv : 15. &c.

Turrettin, as above, Qu. 16, § 29-end. Dick, Lect. 79. Ridgley, Qu. 79, § 4. Sampson on Hebrews. Watson's Theol. Inst. ch. 25.

V. What is the moral Tendency of the Doctrine?

Witsius as above, § 39-46.

SCRIPTURE and experience concur in imputing to man, in his natural state, an obduracy and deadness of heart, which would leave the preacher of the gospel to labor in despair, were it not for his dependence on the sovereign grace of God. But when he believes firmly in the eternal covenant of grace, whereby God has promised His Son a chosen seed, not for any merit which He sees in sinners, and to call and perfect this seed by His efficacious grace, there is ground laid for cheerful exertions. The laborious Christian then looks upon his own efforts for sinners, as one of the preordained steps in this plan of mercy, upon his prayers as taught him by the Holy Ghost, and therefore surely destined to an answer; and upon the visible success of his labours, as the evidence that God, whose plans are immutable, and who always perfects what He undertakes, is working. He is joyfully hopeful concerning the final triumph

This Doctrine Encouraging to Preacher.

of those who are born unto God by his instrumentality, because he sees an eternal purpose and unchangeable love engaged for their upholding. He can cheerfully leave them, though surrounded with the snares of the world; because he leaves the Chief Shepherd with them, who will easily raise up other instruments and provide other means for their guidance.

In this spirit the Apostle says, Phil. i:6, that from the first

St. Paul Found it so.

day of their conversion till now, his prayers for his Philippian converts had always been offered in joy, because he was confident that the Redeemer, who had begun the blessed work in them, by their regeneration, faith, and repentance, would continue that work of sanctification, till it was perfected at the second coming of Jesus Christ, in the resurrection of their bodies, and their complete glorification. This work was begun in them by God, not by their own free choice, independent of grace; for that choice always would have been, most freely and heartily, to choose sin. It must have been begun by God from deliberate design; for God worketh all things after the counsel of His own will. That design and purpose of mercy was not founded on anything good in them, but on God's unchangeable mercy; and therefore it would not be changed by any of their faults, but the unchanging God would carry it out to perfection.

We have here the Apostle's plain expression of his belief

Doctrine to be Discussed Fairly.

in the perseverance of the truly regenerate, in a state of repentance, unto the end. In attempting the discussion of this doctrine, let us exercise the spirit of humility and candor, laying aside prejudice, avoiding all abuses or perversions of God's truth, and striving to apprehend it just as He has presented it. I would at the outset guard the truth from abuse, and from opposition by defining:

I. That this perseverance in a state of grace is not innate and

Perseverance Defined.

necessary, with the new-born nature, but gracious. It does not proceed from anything in the interior state of the regenerate soul, but wholly from God's purpose of mercy towards that soul. Security from fall is the attribute of none but God, Adam in Paradise was capable of apostasy. Holy angels were capable of apostasy; for many of them fell; and doubtless the angels and glorified saints in heaven owe their infallibility, not to their own strength, but to God's unchanging grace working in them. Much more would the Christian, in his imperfection, be liable to fall.

This perseverance does not imply that a man may be living

Not Compatible with Sin.

in habitual and purposed sin, and yet be in a justified state, because he who is once justified cannot come into condemnation. We heartily join in everything which can be said against so odious a doctrine. It is impossible, because the living in such a state of sin proves that the man never was, and is not now, in a justified state, whatever may be his names and boasts.

Our doctrine does not teach that many will not be finally lost, who are connected with the visible Church outwardly, and whom the Scriptures may call believers in a certain sense, because they have a temporary or historical faith, like that of Simon Magus. But those who have once had in them the true principle of spiritual life, never lose it.

Nor do we teach that all Christians have equal spiritual vitality at all times; but they may fall into partial errors of doctrine, coldness and sin, which may for a time wholly interrupt their comfort in religion, and overcloud their evidence of a gracious state. Yet is the root of the matter there.

It is simply this; that "They whom God hath accepted in His Beloved, and effectually called and sanctified by His Spirit, can neither totally nor finally fall away from the state of grace; but shall certainly persevere therein to the end, and be eternally saved."

Definition of Westminister Assembly.

As I have taken the definition of the doctrine from the Confession of Faith, I cannot do better than to take my method of discussion from the same source. Under each head many Scriptures will come in, more naturally and easily, so that the support they give to the doctrine will be more manifest, and more clearly understood.

Before proceeding, however, the competing opinions should be stated. Pelagians, Papists, and Arminians teach, in common, that the truly regenerate believer may totally and finally fall away, and be lost. Some Weslyans, in view of Heb. vi:6, teach that apostasy from a true state of grace is possible, but that the reconversion of the man thus fallen never occurs. The premise by which this denial of the saints' perseverance is dictated, is their favourite definition of free agency, as involving necessarily the contingency of the will. They are consistent with their false philosophy; for the will of the saint who certainly perseveres is obviously not in a contingent state. Hence, in their view, his gracious acts would not be free nor responsible. Some of the Reformed have modified the doctrine to this extent. They suppose that an elect man may totally fall away; but that God's purpose of grace towards him is always effectuated by his reconversion, before he dies. Thus; they would suppose that at the time of David's shocking crimes, faith and spiritual life had utterly died in him. But God's faithful purpose called him back to true repentance in due time. The motive of this statement is pious; they think it safer to teach thus, than to say that there was even a spark of true life in David's soul while he was acting so criminally; because the latter view may tempt men

Opposite Opinions.

44*

living in gross sin to flatter themselves with a false hope. Yet their view, however well-intended, is not scriptural, and is obnoxious to a part of the arguments we shall use. It is inconsistent with that vitality of the seed of godliness asserted in the gospel.

II. The Doctrine Proved.

1. This is proved by the immutability of the decree of election. When anyone is born again of the Holy Ghost and justified in Christ, it is because God had formed, from eternity, the unchangeable purpose to save that soul. The work of grace in it is the mere carrying out of that unchangeable purpose. As the plan is unchangeable, so must be its execution, when that execution is in the hands of the Almighty. How can argument be more direct? Heb. vi : 17, 18. God, willing more abundantly to show unto the heirs of promise the immutability of His counsel, confirmed it by an oath, &c. See also Matt. xxiv : 24 ; 2 Tim. ii : 19 ; Rom. viii : 29 ; viii : 33, &c.

And even though this unchangeable election were con-

Might be Argued from Certain Foreknowledge. ditional, and made in foresight of the believer's faith and obedience, yet if it has any certainty, it must imply that the believer shall certainly be kept from finally falling away. If it even rose no higher than simple foreknowledge, yet a foreknowledge which means anything, must be certain. If God does not certainly know whether a given event shall take place or not, then He does not foreknow it at all. But if He certainly knows that it shall occur, the occurrence of that event must be without failure ; otherwise God's foreknowledge would be false ! So that unless we impiously strip God of His foreknowledge, (to say nothing of His having an all-wise, almighty, and immutable plan), we must suppose that the perseverance in a gracious state, of all those whom He foresees will be finally saved, is so far necessary that they cannot finally fall away.

" The perseverance of believers follows from the free and

2. Argued from Freedom of Electing Love. No Unforeseen Provocation of God Arises. unchangeable love of God the Father," which was the ground of their being chosen unto salvation. The Scriptures make it plain that the reason why God ever determined to save any man was not His seeing in him anything good, attractive or extenuating, but something without, known to His wisdom, which was to God a good and wise reason to bestow His eternal love on that particular sinner. Rom. ix : 11 and 16. This sovereign and unmerited love is the cause of the believer's effectual calling. Jer. xxxi : 3 ; Rom. viii : 30. Now, as the cause is unchangeable, the effect will be unchangeable. That effect is, the constant communication of grace to the believer in whom God hath begun a good work. God was not induced to bestow His renewing grace in the first instance, by anything which He saw, meritorious or attractive, in the repenting sinner ; and therefore the subsequent absence of everything good in him would be no new motive to God for withdrawing His grace. When He first bestowed that grace, He knew that the sinner on whom He bestowed it was totally depraved, and wholly and only hateful in himself to the divine holiness; and therefore no new instance of ingratitude or unfaithfulness, of which the sinner may become guilty after his conversion, can be any provocation to God, to change His mind, and wholly withdraw His sustaining grace. God knew all this ingratitude before. He will chastise it, by temporarily withdrawing His Holy Ghost, or His providential mercies; but if He had not intended from the first to bear with it, and to forgive it in Christ, He would not have called the sinner by His grace at first. In a word, the causes for which God determined to bestow His electing love on the sinner are wholly in God, and not at all in the believer; and hence, nothing in the believer's heart or conduct can finally change that purpose of love. Is. liv : 10; Rom. xi : 29. Compare carefully Rom. v : 8–10; viii : 32, with whole scope of Rom. viii : 28–end. This illustrious passage is but an argument for our proposition: "What shall separate us from the love of Christ?"

This doctrine depends "upon the efficacy of the merit and intercession of Jesus Christ." As all Christians agree, the sole ground of the acceptance of believers is the justifying righteousness of Jesus Christ. The objects of God's eternal love were "chosen in Christ, before the foundation of the world," "accepted in the beloved," and made the recipients of saving blessings, on account of what Christ does in their stead. Now, this ground of justification, this atonement for sin, this motive for the bestowal of divine love, is perfect. Christ's atonement surmounts the demerit of all possible sin or ingratitude. His righteousness is a complete price to purchase the sinner's pardon and acceptance. See Heb. ix : 12; x : 12 and 14; Jno. v : 24. See with what splendid assurance and boldness Paul argues from this ground. Rom. viii : 33 and 34. Can one who has been fully justified in Christ, whose sins have been all blotted out, irrespective of their heinousness, by the perfect and efficacious price paid by Jesus Christ, become again unjustified, and fall under condemnation without a dishonour done to Christ's righteousness?

3. Argued from Christ's Merit.

So likewise the prevalent and perpetual intercession of Christ, founded on the perfect merit of His work, ensures the salvation of all for whom He has once undertaken. We are assured that the Father heareth Him always, when He speaks as the Mediator of His people. Jno. xi : 42; Heb. vii : 25. Now, after He has uttered for His believing people—for all who should believe Him through the gospel of His apostles—such prayers as those of Jno. xvii : 20, &c., 24, must not the answer

From Christ's Intercession.

of this request, or, in other words, the certain final redemption
of all who ever shared His intercession, be as sure as the truth
of God? But if any man is ever justified, that man has shared
the intercession of Christ; for it was only through this that He
was first accepted.

The perseverance of the saints proceeds "from the abiding of the Spirit, and of the seed of God

4. Argued from the within them." Every Christian, at the hour
Indwelling of the Holy he believes, is so united to Christ, that he
Ghost.
partakes of His indwelling Spirit. This union is a permanent
one. The moving cause for instituting it, God's free and eternal love, is a permanent and unchangeable cause. The indwelling of the Spirit promised to believers is a permanent and
abiding gift. 1 Jno. ii : 27.

His regenerating operations are spoken of as a "seal,"
and an "earnest" of our redemption. Eph.

From the Seal and i : 13, 14; 2 Cor. i : 22. The use of a seal is
Earnest. to ratify a covenant, and make the fulfilment
of it certain to both parties. An "earnest" ($\dot{a}\rho\rho\ddot{a}\beta\dot{\omega}\nu$) is a
small portion of the thing covenanted, given in advance, as a
pledge of the certain intention to bestow the whole, at the
promised time. Thus, he who promised to give a sum of
money for some possession, at some appointed future day, gave
a small sum in advance, when the covenant was formed, as a
pledge for the rest. So the renewing of the Holy Ghost is, to
every believer who has enjoyed it, a seal, impressing the image
of Christ on the wax of his softened heart, closing and certifying the engagement of God's love, to redeem the soul. It is
the earnest, or advance, made to the soul, to engage God to
the final bestowal of complete holiness and glory. Unless the
final perseverance of believers is certain, it could be no pledge
nor seal. The inference is as simple and as strong as words
can express, that he who has once enjoyed this seal and earnest
is thereby certified that God will continue to give the Holy
Ghost until the end.

It is a most low and unworthy estimate of the wisdom of
the Holy Ghost and of His work in the

Work of Holy Ghost heart, to suppose that He will begin the work
not Fickle. now, and presently desert it; that the vital
spark of heavenly birth is an *ignis fatuus*, burning for a short
season, and then expiring in utter darkness; that the spiritual
life communicated in the new birth, is a sort of spasmodic or
galvanic vitality, giving the outward appearance of life in the
dead soul, and then dying. Not such is the seed of God within
us. Jno. v : 24. "Verily, verily I say unto you: He that
heareth My word, and believeth on Him that sent Me, hath
everlasting life." John iii : 15; vi : 54. The principle then
implanted, is a never-dying principle. In every believer an
eternal spiritual life is begun. If all did not persevere in holi-

ness, there would be some in whom there was a true spiritual life, but not everlasting. The promise would not be true. See also 1 John iii : 9 ; 1 Pet. i : 23.

Our doctrine follows, also, "from the nature of the Covenant of Grace." God did, from eternity, make with His Son a gracious covenant, engaging, in return for the Son's humiliation, to give Him the souls of all who were chosen in Him before the foundation of the world, "that they should be holy and without blame before Him in love." This covenant is an everlasting one. Jer. xxxii : 40. It is an unchangeable covenant. Ps. lxxxix : 34, (spoken of the second David). The sole condition of the covenant is Christ's work for His chosen people. Heb. x : 14. Now, the administration of such a covenant most plainly requires that there shall be no uncertainty in its results. If one of those, whose sins Christ bore, ever fell into final condemnation, the contract would be proved temporary, changeable and false. To derive the full force of this argument, we must again distinguish between the Covenant of Grace and the Covenant of Redemption. We argue from the latter. The Son (not believers) is the "party of the second part." Because he is omnipotent, holy and faithful, the compact cannot fail. Again ; in this covenant, the only procuring condition is one that has been already fulfilled, Christ's work and sacrifice. Hence the contract is closed and irrevocable. Hence it must ensure the redemption of its beneficiaries.

5. Argued from the Covenant of Redemption.

On the eternal certainty of this covenant is founded the faithfulness of the gospel offer, pledging God to every sinner who believes and repents, that he shall through Christ receive saving grace ; and among those gracious influences thus pledged with eternal truth to the believer, from the moment he truly believes, is persevering grace. Jer. xxxii : 40; (proved to be the gospel pledge by Heb. viii : 10); Is. liv : 10 ; Hos. ii : 19 and 20 ; 1 Thess. v : 23, 24 ; Jno. x : 27 ; 1 Pet. i : 5 ; Rom. viii : end. These are a few from the multitude of promises, assuring us of our final safety from every possible influence, when once they are truly in Christ.

This Covenant Pledges Grace to Persevere.

I am well aware that the force of these and all similar passages has been met, by asserting that in all gospel promises there is a condition implied, viz : That they shall be fulfilled, provided the believer does not backslide, on his part, from his gospel privileges. But is this all which these seemingly precious words mean ? Then they mean nothing. To him who knows his own heart, what is that promise of security worth, which offers him no certainty to secure him against his own weakness ? All "his sufficiency is of God." See also Rom. vii : 21. If his enjoyment of the promised grace is suspended upon his own perse-

Evasions.

verance in cleaving to it, then his apostasy is not a thing possible, or probable, but certain. There is no hope in the gospel. And when such a condition is thrust into such a promise as that of Jno. x : 27 : " None shall pluck them out of My hand," provided they do not choose to let themselves be plucked away; are we to suppose that Christ did not know that common Bible truth, that the only way any spiritual danger can assail any soul successfully, is by persuasion : that unless the adversary can get the consent of the believer's free will, he cannot harm him ? Was it not thus that Adam was ruined ? Is there any other way by which a soul can be plucked away from God ? Surely Jesus knew this; and if this supposed condition is to be understood, then this precious promise would be but a worthless and pompous truism. " Your souls shall never be destroyed, unless in a given way," and that way, the only and the common way, in which souls are ever destroyed. " You shall never fall, as long as you stand up."

But to thoroughly close the whole argument, we have only to remark, that the promise in Jer. xxxii : 40, which is most absolutely proved by Heb. viii : 10, &c., to be the gospel covenant, most expressly engages God to preserve believers from this very thing—their own backsliding. Not only does He engage that He will not depart from them, but " He will put His fear in their hearts, so that they shall not depart from Him."

Jer. xxxii : 40 Conclusive.

Other arguments exist, from independent assertions of Scriptures. It used to be common with the Calvinistic divines to advance the joy of the angels over repenting sinners, as a proof of their perseverance. The idea was, that if their state in grace were mutable, these wise and grand creatures would not have attached so much importance to it. To me this reasoning always appeared inconclusive. We have seen good Christians sometimes rejoicing very sincerely over what turned out to be a spurious conversion, because they supposed it to be genuine. Now, it does not appear that the angels are always infallible in their judgments of appearances, any more than we : although far wiser. Besides, if some true converts did fall from grace, the angels would still know that those who finally reach heaven must be sought among the sinners who experience conversion on earth. A much more conclusive argument may be drawn from those passages, which explain the apostasy of seeming converts, in consistency with the perseverance of true saints. One of these is found in 2 Pet. ii : 22. Here the apostate professor is an unclean animal, only outwardly cleansed; a " sow that was washed; " its nature is not turned into a lamb ; and this is the explanation of its return to the mire. A still stronger one is 1 Jno. ii : 19. Here the departure of apostates is explained by the fact, that their union to Christ and His peo-

III. Independent Arguments for Perseverance.

ple never was real; because had it been real they "no doubt would have continued with us;" and their apostasy was permissively designed by God to "manifest" the fact that they never had been true believers.

Another proof presents itself in the parable of the sower. Matt. xiii : 6 and 21. The stony-ground-hearer withers, because he "hath no root in himself." Still another may be found in 2 Tim. ii : 19. There the Apostle, referring to such temporary professors as Hymenæus and Philetus, explains that their apostasy implied no uncertainty as to the constitution of the body of Christ's redeemed: because God knew all the time who were truly His; and the foundation of His purpose concerning their salvation stood immovable amidst all the changes and apostasies which startle blind men.

With reference to all objections founded on the cases of Solomon, David, Peter, Judas and such like, I reply briefly, that the explanation is either that of John's first Epistle 2 : 19, that they never had true grace to lose, or else, the history contains proof that their apostasy was neither total nor final, though grievous. In Peter's case, Christ says, Luke xxii: 32, that "Satan desired to sift him like wheat, but He prayed for him that his faith should not fail." Peter's faith, therefore, did not fail, though his duty did. So the prayer of David, Ps. li : 11, 12, shows that he was a true saint before and after his sin. That the principle of true grace can exist, and can be for a time so foully obscured, as in David's case, is indeed a startling and alarming truth. Yet does not the experience of society and of our own hearts substantiate the view?

Backslidings Explained.

Here let us return to notice the view of those who deem it safer to say, that David's grace was all extinct when he committed these crimes; lest the opposite doctrine should encourage carnal security. We have seen that several of our scriptural proofs refute the idea of a complete extinction and subsequent restoration of spiritual life. It is inconsistent with the permanency of that principle, and with the nature of the Spirit's indwelling, seal, and earnest. But the licentious result feared is effectually warded off by a proper knowledge of the Scriptures. The true believer's hope of personal acceptance is always obscured, just in proportion to the extent of his backslidings. Hence, if he listens to the Scriptures, he cannot both indulge his backslidings and a carnal security. For he is expressly told in the Bible, that there is a counterfeit faith and repentance; and that the fruits of consistent holiness are the only criterion by which the professor himself, or anybody else, except the Omniscient one, can know an apparent faith to be genuine. Hence to the backslider, the hypothesis that his previous graces, however plausible, were spurious and counterfeit is always more reasonable than the other hypothesis, that true faith could go so far astray. And if when sinning grievously, He could be capable of making David's case an argument of carnal security in sin ; this would complete the proof of his deadness . David's case is an encouragement to the backslider to return, provided he has David's deep contrition. See Ps. xxxii, and li.

Your commentaries and other text books will give you those detailed explanations which you need, of the texts advanced by Arminians against our doctrine. I may say that the two *loca palmaria* on which they rely chiefly care Heb. vi : 4–6, and Ezek. xviii : 24–29. The solution of these meets all the rest.

IV. Texts Advanced in Objection.

Of the first we may briefly remark, that it does not appear the spiritual endowments there described of the apostate, amount to a true state of grace. A detailed criticism and comparison of the traits " being enlightened," &c., will show that according to the usage of the Scriptures, they describe, not a regenerate state, but one of deep conviction and concern, great privilege, with perhaps charisms of tongues or healings. The exemplars are to be found in such men as Balaam, Simon Magus, and Demas. And this is most consistent with the Apostle's scope. The terms here, if meant to describe ordinary saving conversion, would at least be most singular and unusual. They are evidently vague, and intentionally so : because God does not care to enable us to decide exactly how near we may go to the impassable line of grieving His Spirit, and yet be forgiven.

Heb. vi. : 4.

With reference to the passage from Ezekiel, it could only be claimed by Arminians, in virtue of great inattention to the prophet's object in the passage. Ezekiel's mission was to call Israel (especially the people in captivity in Mesopotamia) to repentance. He points to their calamities and the destruction of the larger part of their nation, as proof of their great guilt. They attempt to evad his charge, by pleading that "their teeth were set on edge, because their fathers had eaten sour grapes." God answers, in the early part of the chapter, that this explanation of their calamities is untenable ; because (while much of His providence over men does visit the father's sins upon sinful children) the guilt of sinful fathers is never, in His theocracy, and according to the covenant of Horeb, visited on righteous children. He then goes farther, and reminds them that not only did He always restore prosperity, in the theocracy, as soon as an obedient generation succeeded a rebellious one ; but even more, as soon as a rebellious man truly repented, he was forgiven ; just as when a righteous man apostatizes, he is punished. It would appear, therefore, that the thing of which the prophet is speaking is not a state of grace at all ; but the outward, formal, and civic decency of a citizen of the theocracy ; and that the punishments into which

Ezek. xviii : 24 &c.

such a man fell on lapsing into rebellion, were temporal calamities. But farther, the whole passage is hypothetical. It merely supposes a pair of cases. If the transgressor repents, he shall be forgiven. Does the prophet mean to teach that any do savingly repent, in whom God does not purpose to work repentance? Let ch. xxxvi: 26, 27, and xxxvii: 1-10, answer. So, does He mean to teach that any actually fall into rebellion, who share the grace of God? Let ch. xxxvi: 27, &c., again answer.

There is one general element of objection in all these texts; *General Answer.* that when God warns the righteous, the believer, &c., against the dangers of apostasy; or when He stimulates him to zeal in holy living by the thought of those dangers, God thereby clearly implies that believers may apostatise. The answer is: Naturally speaking, so he may. The certainty that he will not, arises, not from the strength of a regenerated heart, but from God's secret, unchangeable purpose concerning the believer; which purpose He executes towards, and in him, by moral means consistent with the creature's free agency. Among these appropriate motives are these very warnings of dangers and wholesome fears about apostasy. Therefore, God's application of these motives to the regenerate free agent, proves not at all that it is God's secret purpose to let him apostatise. They are a part of that plan by which God intends to ensure that he shall not. Compare carefully Acts xxvii: 22, 23, 24, 25, with 31.

In conclusion, we believe that all the supposed licentious results of the doctrine of perseverance result *V. Practical Results Sanctifying.* from misapprehension; and that its true tendencies are eminently encouraging and sanctifying. (a.) How can the intelligent Bible Christian be encouraged to sin, by a doctrine which assures him of a perseverance in holiness, if he is a true believer? (b.) So far as a rational self-love is a proper motive for a sanctified mind, this doctrine leaves it in full force; because when the Arminian would be led by a backsliding, to fear he had fallen from grace, the Calvinist would be led, just as much, to fear he never had had any grace; a fear much more wholesome and searching than the erring Arminian's. For this alarmed Calvinist would see, that, while he had been flattering himself he was advancing heavenward, he was, in fact, all the time in the high road to hell; and so now, if he would not be damned, he must make a new beginning, and lay better foundations than his old ones (not like the alarmed Arminian, merely set about repairing the same old ones). (c.) Certainty of success, condition on honest efforts, is the very best stimulus to active exertion. Witness the skilful general encouraging his army. (d.) Last: Such a gift of redemption as the Calvinist represents is far nobler and more gracious, and hence elicits more love and **gratitude**, which are the noblest motives, the strongest and best.

Just so far as the Calvinist is enabled scripturally to hope
that he is now born again, he is, to that ex-
Comfort of the Doc- tent, entitled to hope that his triumph is sure;
trine.
that death and hell are disarmed, and that
his heaven is awaiting his efforts. To him who knows the
weakness of the human heart, and the power of our spiritual
enemies, the Arminian's adoption, beset by the constant liability
to fall, would bring little consolation indeed. It is love and
confidence, not selfish fear, which most effectually stimulates
Christian effort. Let the student see how St. Paul puts this in
1 Cor. xv : 58.

LECTURE LIX.

THE ASSURANCE OF GRACE AND SALVATION.

SYLLABUS.

1. What is the distinction made by the Westminster Assembly, between this
grace, and the assurance of Faith?
    Conf. of Faith, ch. 18.   Ridgley, Qu. 80, § 1. Turrettin, Loc. xv, Qu. 17,
§ 3–10.
2. State the Doctrine of Rome, concerning assurance of grace and Salvation,
and her motives herein : Of early Reformers ; and of our Standards.
    Council of Trent. Sess. 6, ch. 9, and Canones, 13, 14. Bellarmine, de Justif.
bk. iii, chs. 6, 8. Calvin, Inst. bk. iii, ch. 2. Com. on Rom. iv : 16 ; viii : 34.
Genevan Cat. p. 137. Niemyer. Augsburg Conf. § 5, and 20, Dorner's
Hist. Prot. Theol., Vol, i, § 1, ch. 4, § a. Louis Le Blanc against Bossuet.
Turrettin, as above. Hill. bk. v. ch. 2. Conf. § 3.
3. Is the assurance of grace and salvation of the essence of Saving Faith?
    See Calvin, Turrettin and Conf. as above. Ridgley, Qu. 81. Dick, Lect. 68.
So. Presb. Rev. Jan. 1872., Art. i. Theol. of Plym. Brethren. Hill, as above.
Sir W. Hamilton, on Unconscious Modifications of the Mind.
4. Prove that this assurance is attainable ; and should be the aim of every
Believer.
    Turrettin, as above. Ridgley, Qu. 80.
5. By what means is it to be sought?
    See Rom. vii : 16, with Calv., Scott, Hodge, &c., in Loco. Watson's
Theol. Inst. ch. 22, § 2. Hill, as above. J. Newton's Sermon, 20. H.
Born's "Way of Peace," pp. 23, 24, 39, 262. Waymarks in Wilderness,
Vol. xi, pp. 245, 263. Theol. of Plym. Brethren, as above. Chalmers'
Theol. Inst. Vol. ii, ch. 10.
6. Reply to objections; and especially to the fear of its fostering Carnal
Security.
    Same authorities, and Turrettin, Loc. iv, Qu. 13. Dick, Lect. 78.

"THE Assurance of Grace and Salvation" is "an infallible
     assurance of faith," that the subject is in a state of grace,
and will be saved. The saving faith which
1. Definitions. our Confession discriminates from this, is the
direct action of a full and cordial belief in the Gospel promise,
with a receiving and resting on Christ from the heart. The latter, every true believer has, except when confused temporarily
by the extreme buffetings of temptation; the former is the
complementary attainment of mature and vigorous faith. Some

works present us the same distinction by the phrases: " Assurance of Hope;" "Assurance of Faith." Others of the Reformed divines object much to this nomenclature, as being of a Jesuit origin. They argue, also, that assurance of hope must always accompany assurance of faith, because there must always be some hope, where there is any belief of the heart. They ask: How is hope defined? As desire, with expectation. Now, if a man has any belief of the heart, he desires. So, hope and faith, and the assurance of each, must be inseparable. This reasoning is employed, both against the pair of terms as a nomenclature; and (by others) against the very discrimination, which our Confession asserts. See here, say they, proof, that the Westminster Confession was wrong, and Calvin right: and that there is is no faith where there are not both kinds of $\pi\lambda\eta\rho o$-$\varphi o\rho ia$. But the solution is extremely easy. No supporter of the Westminster view denies, that even the weakest true faith is attended with an element of hope, more or less consciously felt; all we assert is: that there may be saving faith, and yet not a $\pi\lambda\eta\rho o\varphi o\rho ia$ $\varepsilon\lambda\pi ido\varsigma$. Others, as we intimated, seem shy of this nomenclature, because of its Jesuit origin. They indeed, used, as they invented it *mala fide*: They represented the assurance of hope as grounded partly on the believer's own pious disposition, which they always assert to be mutable. Such an affection would not deserve to be called an assurance. But let us represent to ourselves an assurance of hope grounded " upon the divine truth of the promises of salvation, the inward evidence of the graces unto which these promises are made, and the testimony of the Spirit of adoption witnessing with our spirits that we are the children of God;" and I see not why the phraseology should be rejected. It is, indeed, entirely scriptural. See Owen on Heb. vi : 11, and Poole's Synopsis on Col. ii : 2; Heb. xi : 1. Here we have the $\pi\lambda\eta\rho o\varphi o\rho ia$ $\tau\eta\varsigma$ $\sigma\upsilon\nu\varepsilon\sigma\varepsilon\omega\varsigma$, and the $\pi\lambda\eta\rho o\varphi o\rho ia$ $\varepsilon\lambda\pi ido\varsigma$. Does not the apostle distinguish between the assurance of the understanding and the assurance of hope? Again, it is objected, that since the faith and the hope have the same object, the blessings of redemption and the same warrant, the promises of God, they must be inseparable. I have admitted, that some degree of hope, perhaps scarcely conscious hope, is involved in all true faith. But the answer is in this fact. The promises are always practically conditioned on an instrumental condition; whence the assured expectation of enjoying them, the essential element of the $\pi\lambda\eta\rho o\varphi o\rho ia$ $\varepsilon\lambda\pi ido\varsigma$, must be practically suspended on the consciousness that the terms are fulfilled. The promises are assuredly mine, provided I have genuine faith. (This expresses the $\pi\lambda\eta\rho o\varphi o\rho ia$ $\varepsilon\lambda\pi ido\varsigma$.) But I know that there is a spurious faith. Hence, although I have some $\varepsilon\lambda\pi\iota\varsigma$ from the moment I embrace that truth, I do not have the $\pi\lambda\eta\rho o\varphi o\rho ia$ $\varepsilon\lambda\pi ido\varsigma$, until I have eliminated the doubt whether my faith is, possibly, of the spurious kind.

Many quibbles have been offered by Papists and rationalists, to show that neither of these (and
especially not the assurance of hope) can
rise so high as to deserve the name of an in-
fallible assurance. If the latter did, it is urged, it should give
a certainty of heaven equal to the certainty of our own existence, a certainty admitting of no degrees, and no increase by
additions of subsequent evidence. But what sober believer can
honestly claim this? Now, the answer to all this is easily found
in an appeal to common sense. What does a man mean when
he says he is sure of a thing? That he clearly sees some evidence of its truth, which mounts above even the highest probability, to demonstration. Any valid portion of such evidence is
proper ground of certain conviction. Does this imply that the
evidence cannot be increased, so that the certainty shall have a
wider basis? By no means. So, although it was certainty
before, it now becomes a more satisfactory certainty. Again:
Assurance of faith, and still more, assurance of hope, embrace
as elements of evidence, the state of the soul's own moral affections. The latter, for instance, is based upon a consciousness
of the exercise of trust, love, penitence, submission, and peace.
Hence, to every one who knows human nature, it is manifest
that, however demonstrative may be such evidence in its very
highest and purest examples, the certainty based upon it will
be much more felt and conscious, at some times than at others,
because the actings of those holy emotions, and the soul's attention to and consciousness of their actings, are more lively at
times, than at others. Will not the soul, after it is actually in
heaven, have more lively attention to, and consciousness of, its
present blessedness at some times than at others? Does not
the bereaved widow, who knows her loss only too well at all
times, feel it far more sensibly at some times than at others?
Third: it is a most incorrect analysis which either banishes the
will from among the causes of belief, in cases of moral truths
and evidences presented to the mind, or which denies that the
certainty arising of such moral truths can be intellectually correct; because there is a voluntary element in it. In the case of
all moral objects of belief, conviction is far from being a bare
intellectual result; the state of the will powerfully modifies it.
(See my analysis of Saving Faith). So obvious is this, that
Des Cartes actually places belief among the emotional states
of the soul. And yet, the rectitude of the state of will, which
concurs in producing a given moral conviction of mind, may
itself be the object of the mind's certain cognition. So that
the mind, while aware that this mental conviction has been produced in part by a state of will, as well as by a light of evidence, shall also be certain that the will acted aright in that
case; and hence, the given belief, though in part a result of the
affections, will be felt to be intellectually as valid as though

*Cavils against Possi-
bility of Assurance.*

it were a cold truth of abstract mathematics. If the student will remember, that the belief of this proposition, " I am now in a state of grace," or " I am not," is just one of those moral propositions, concerning which the state of will is most influential, he will see the application of these principles. It will appear why the intellectual belief of such propositions should vary in its felt strength ; viz : because the active and voluntary part of its elements vary. And it will appear that this degree of fluctuation (so to speak) is not at all incompatible with certainty, and a proper intellectual basis of evidence. To dispute this, is as though one should say that, because the waters of the sea do not bear up the boat with the same immobility with which a stone pedestal bears its statue, therefore the waters do not sustain the boat. The assurance of hope, in the breast of the true and eminent saint, is a certainty at its lowest ebbs ; at its higher floods, it is both solid and joyful.

That the saint ought to know he is a saint as clearly as he knows that he breathes, is simply playing with words. Who does not know that sensational consciousness has a palpable element about it, which belongs to no intellectual belief, not even that of the exact sciences ? The scholar knows that " the square of the hypothenuse is equal," &c. ; but he does not feel it, as he feels his existence.

Assurance a Moral Conviction, not a Sense Perception.

Romanists deny that a certain assurance of hope can be attained, except in the case of those eminent saints and ascetics, to whom God gives it by special revelation—as to Stephen and Paul. In other cases, they judge it not attainable, not to be sought after, and not beneficial, even if attainable. Their motive is, obviously, to retain that power of priestcraft over souls, by which they may make gain of their absolutions, masses, indulgences, &c. The soul completely and finally justified in Christ, and assured thereof by grace, would be independent. 2 Cor. iii : 17.

2. Romish Doctrine Touching Assurance.

The earlier Reformers, having learned to abhor this trafficking in the peace of immortal souls, felt impelled to teach that assurance is of the essence of saving faith, (though compelled to modify their assertion, in order to include even Bible saints). Thus, Calvin, Institutes, Bk. iii, ch. 2, § 7 : " Faith is a steady and certain knowledge of the divine benevolence towards us," &c. Com. on Rom. viii : 16. " *Stat itaque Sententia, Neminem posse nomenari filium Dei, qui non se talem agnoscat.*" Of this, more anon.

Reformers' Doctrine,

The earlier Arminians (of Holland) taught that certain assurance of final salvation is not attainable in this life ; and that to doubt thereof is salutary, and conducive to humility. So far as assurance is predicated of our final perseverance, and our election, the later

Arminian Doctrine.

Arminians of Wesley's school must of course concur. But they teach, as one of their most distinctive points, that an assurance of present conversion (followed by some hope of final salvation) is not only possible, but essential to every true believer. And this is the immediate teaching of the Holy Ghost to the heart, without the Word or self-examination. Yet assurance of hope is not made by them of the essence of faith. First, say they, come repentance and faith, then justification, then regeneration, then this inwrought consciousness of adoption—faith itself being defined as a believing and embracing of the gospel. Here we have the mystico-scholastic notion of a revealed and immediate witness, borrowed from Rome through a Moravian medium by Wesley, and asserted as the privilege and attainment of every true convert. A still more direct historical channel may be found for the transmission of this doctrine into the Wesleyan System from the scholastic theology of the Romish monks. Wesley was a great admirer of Thomas a Kempis, of whose work he published an edition. Here, in the experience of this mystical scholastic, the idea appears in full form.

The Calvinistic world has now generally settled down upon the doctrine of the Westminster Assembly, that assurance of hope is not of the essence of saving faith; so that many believers may be justified though not having the former: and may remain long without it; but yet an infallible assurance, founded on a comparison of their hearts and lives with Scripture, and the teaching and light of the Holy Ghost, through and in the Word, is the privilege, and should be the aim of every true believer. Yet, this assurance, while both scriptural, reasonable and spiritual, and thus solid, may be more sensibly felt at sometimes, and may even be temporarily lost through sin, according to the remarks of our section I.

Doctrine of West-minster Assembly.

Before proceeding to argue this, let us briefly show (see Lect. on Faith,) what we have again asserted; that assurance of hope is not of the essence of saving faith. First: not only do some, yea many, who give other excellent evidences by their fruits, in our days lack this assurance; but some Bible saints lacked it at times. See Ps. xxxi : 22; lxxvii 2, 5; Is. l : 10, &c. These men did not therefore cease to be believers? The proof is so obvious that Calvin is obliged to modify the assertions of which we have seen specimens, to include these cases, until he has virtually retracted his doctrine.

3. Assurance not of the essence of Faith, proved (a) by experience.

(b.) Second: this doctrine really adds to the proposition which is the object of saving faith. That proposition is : "whosoever believeth shall be saved;" and according to its very nature, it must follow that the moment it is believed,

The Opposite Would Place Another Proposition as Object of Faith.

the sinner is saved, whether he sees any other truth or not.   To
teach the view of the first Reformers, instead of exalting Christ,
as they, with their modern imitators boastfully claim, really
calls the soul away from Christ, and bids him look at another
proposition touching the state and actings of his own soul,
before he is permitted to trust in Christ.   Our view scripturally
directs him to find salvation by looking wholly out of himself
to Christ.   Indeed, if we adhere strictly to the terms of the
gospel, we shall see that the exercise of such a faith as Calvin
describes is an impossibility, without a new and direct revelation in every case.   Thus, "no man is saved in Christ till
he has come to believe that Christ has saved him."   But it
is only by believing that he is saved in Christ; so that this
definition of faith requires the effect to precede its own cause.
The sinner must therefore find out the "benevolence of Christ
towards himself," not from the gospel promise, but from the
Holy Ghost directly, without the gospel.   But are we ready
for this?   Do we surrender the great truth, that Christ is the
object, to which the Holy Ghost points the believing soul?
And is Christ revealed anywhere but in the Word?   I repeat:
the Word nowhere says that A. B. shall be saved; but that
"whosoever believeth shall be saved."   How then is A. B. to
know scripturally, that he is actually saved?   Only by the
rational deduction from the pair of premises, of which one is
given by the Word, and the other by his regenerated consciousness: thus, "whosoever truly believes is saved."   But
I am conscious of truly believing; therefore I am saved."
Now, my point is: that the mind cannot know the conclusion
before it knows the minor premise thereof.   On the contrary,
it can only know the conclusion by first knowing both the
premises.   The student may see the rational and scriptural
order copiously discussed by Turrettin, Loc. xiv. qu. 14, § 45
to 52.   The attempt may be made to escape this argument by
saying that since faith is a divine and supernatural grace inwrought
by the almighty Spirit, it can proceed independent of this rational
order.   But I answer: Does not the Holy Ghost always act on
the soul according to its rational laws?   Are not those laws of
God's making?   Does the assistance of the Spirit of all Truth
result in the soul's acting abnormally, and against its proper laws?
Unless then, there is a direct, immediate revelation to A. B. of
his personal share in Christ, which no Calvinist asserts, there is
no escape from my argument.

     Third : if faith were such an exercise as this, when once
Finally Lost, Could the finally impenitent reach hell, it will no
not be Convicted for longer be fair to punish them for not believ-
Unbelief.   ing unto salvation; for it will then be manifest that had they believed in Christ's electing love towards
themselves, it would not have been true.   So that in refusing
to believe, they acted so far properly: the Holy Ghost never

gave them a warrant to believe.   But the premise which leads
to this conclusion cannot be right; for we know that God commands all men, everywhere, to repent and believe.

The scriptural argument against this exaggerated doctrine
may be much strengthened by recalling the
passages where self-examination is enjoined
on professed believers; and that, not only as
to the general propriety of their lives, but as to the very point,
whether their state of grace is genuine.   Here may be consulted Rom. v : 4; 1 Cor. xi : 28; 2 Cor. xiii : 5; 2 Pet. i : 10.
Marks or signs are also laid down, by which one may try
whether he has true or spurious faith.   Jno. xv : 14; 1 Epist. of
John iii : 14, 19. This apostle tells his people, that he wrote
the epistle in order to enable them to know that they had
eternal life.   Our argument is : that had the assurance of our
own grace and salvation been an essential part of faith, believers could not have been reasonably commanded to examine
and settle the question : the simple fact that it needed examination would have shown them no believers at all.

Scripture Enjoins Self-Examination.

The scriptural argument advanced by Calvin for his
extreme view of faith amounts mainly to
this : that the Apostles generally address
believers and speak of them as persons
assured in their hope, e. g., 2 Cor. xiii : 5; v : 1; 1 Peter i : 8
and 9; 1 Jno. v : 19, &c.   But the first of these passages, when
properly construed, only says that men are reprobates unless
they have Christ formed in them, not unless they recognize
Him in them.   And to all of them, we reply, that when the
sacred writers thus address a whole Church of professed
believers in terms appropriate only to the best, they only use
the language of Christian hope, charity and courtesy.   The
proof is indisputable : for those very Corinthians are sharply
rebuked by Paul, and exhorted to examine themselves jeal-
ously; and John says that one object he had in writing his
epistle, was to enable the people to come to an assurance of
hope.   2 Pet. i : 10; 1 Jno. iii : 9, 10.   The "we" which these
apostles use are often no others than the apostles themselves,
with any Christians of like attainments.   But there is also some
justice in the surmise, that assurance of hope was more generally given in those primitive days, because the Church was
called to testify, and to suffer more.   So that if it should even
appear that it was the common attainment of believers then,
this would not prove it of the essence of faith.

Scriptures Quoted Against Us.

Those who revive the doctrine of Calvin here, also argue,
that doubt and faith are opposites; so that where there is
doubt, there cannot be hearty faith : that my conception of
faith is really no faith at all; because it directs the inquirer to
repose his trust, not upon the word and faithfulness of Christ,
but upon certain affections which he supposes he sees in him-

self: and that, since consciousness attends all the operations of the soul, no man can believe without being conscious he believes. They insist much on the immediate and intuitive nature of consciousness in this concern, and even represent it as a species of sense-instinct. It is compared to "the animal sense of departed pain and present ease."

The reply to the first of these points is, that the weak believer does not doubt Christ at all; but only himself. It is not on the major, but on the minor premise of the believer's syllogism, that his consciousness is obscure. He can always say, with emphasis, that, were he only sure his deceitful heart was not deluding him with a dead faith, his assurance would be perfect. Now, mistrust of Christ is inconsistent with faith; but we are yet to learn that self-mistrust is incompatible with that grace. The second point receives its solution from the same syllogism. What would the minor premise be worth to establish a conclusion, without the major? But the weak believer takes that proposition: "Whosoever believeth is saved," solely on the authority of God. When that same God tells him that there are two kinds of believing, only one of which fulfils the term of that proposition, and that the deceitfulness of the heart often causes the false kind to ape the true; and when the humble soul inspects his own faith to make sure that it meets the terms of God's promise, prompted to do so by mistrust of self, it passes common wit to see, wherein that process is a "trusting in self, instead of God's word." To the argument from consciousness, there are two replies. One is: that distinct consciousness does not attend all the actions of the soul. There are, unquestionably, unconscious modifications of the mind. But it is more to our purpose to remark, that when the mind is confused by great haste, or the agitation of vivid emotions, or when the mental states are very complex, the remembered consciousness is obscured, or even lost. This well known truth evinces, that there may be a soul exercising a true though immature faith, and not distinctly conscious of it. But the other reply is still shorter: There is a spurious, as well as a genuine faith. If the man thinks he believes aright, he is conscious of exercising what he thinks is a right faith. This is the correct statement. Now, if the faith needs a discrimination to distinguish it from the dead faith, just to the same extent will the consciousness about it need the same discrimination.

When the reasonings of these theologians are analysed, they evidently disclose this basis, viz: Because the testimony of consciousness is immediate and intuitive, they have obviously slidden into the idea that it is supra-rational. But the truth is, that consciousness is a rational faculty, just as truly as is the logical faculty. The only difference is, that its acts are

Answers.

True Account of Consciousness.

45*

primary acts of the reason, while the deductive and comparative are secondary. Hence, there is the most perfect consistency in our representing, as Scripture does, such consciousness as cohering with, and assisted by, the deductions of the reason. And when Scripture gives the premises for such deductions, and the illumination of the Spirit guides them, it is hard to see why they should be held so unworthy to be compared with the primary intuitions; seeing especially that these, if not guided by the same Spirit, must infallibly reflect whatever counterfeit affection the deceitfulness of indwelling sin may have injected. How short and plain this statement: that our whole salvation is by the instrumentality of the truth? But truth only acts on man's intelligence; whence the whole process of salvation must be as truly rational as it is spiritual.

4. Assurance Attainable. We argue that the assurance of hope is attainable, and should be sought by all believers; first, presumptively:

Because such a state of the case seems necessarily implied in the duty of seeking Christ. God makes **Because it is Our Duty to be in Christ.** it our duty to use means to place ourselves in union with Christ. Must there not be some way for us to know whether we have obeyed and do obey this command? It will not avail to say, that God makes it our duty to keep on striving just the same, to establish this union with Christ, to the end of life. True, He commands us to repeat our acts of faith and repentance all the time. But if we are not in Christ we have never believed aright, so that the thing we should be counselled to is, not to repeat those same abortive efforts, but to set about a new kind of efforts. See Rev. iii : 17, 18.

Second: The Scripture is full of commands, prayers, and **Promises Imply it.** promises for assurance of hope. 1 Cor. xi : 28 ; 2 Cor. xiii : 5 ; 1 Cor. ii : 12 ; John xiv : 20; Heb. vi : 18 ; 2 Pet. i : 10 ; 1 Jno. ii : 3 ; v : 13 ; iii : 14, &c. ; Rev. ii : 17. It is true that God commands us to be " perfect," as He is perfect, and to pray for entire conformity to Christ; while yet Calvinists do not believe that this perfection is attainable in this life, by any. But here are commands of a more definite sort. e. g., 1 Cor. xi : 28 ; 2 Cor. xiii : 5, commands to use an immediate means, self-examination, for the attainment of an end immediately connected therewith, namely, assurance. Here are promises given, Jno. xiv : 20, &c.; of the enjoyment of assurance. These things make out a different case.

Third: Both in Bible times and since, there have been **Has Actually Been Attained.** instances of assurance actually enjoyed through God's blessing on the ordinary means of grace. Since the days of inspiration, saints of the greatest sobriety and truthfulness have professed such assurance, and have been encouraged by it to brave the most fearful trials. Such cases are widely distinguished from the multitudes of fanatical self-deceivers. In Bible days we find a number of other cases. Ps. ciii : 2 ; xvi : 8–10 ; Rom. v : 1 ; Gal. v : 22 ; 1 Thess. v : 9 ; 2 Tim. i : 12 ; 1 Pet. i : 8 ; 1 Jno. ii : 3 ; Phil. iv : 6, 7, &c.

To these it has been objected, that they were inspired cases. Note, e. g., in 1 Pet. i : 8, the Apostle was inspired but not the Christians to whom he wrote ! Moreover, there are very few cases in Scripture where we see any individual receive a revealed assurance directly of his own interest in redemption. An examination will impress us how remarkably chary God has been of such helps ; and how generally peculiar spiritual charisms were bestowed for the benefit of the Church, and not of the individual.

Fourth : The nature of the graces in exercise in the Christian heart would show, that the true believer ought to be able, with due care, to come to a certain knowledge whether he has them. In other things, men can usually interpret their own consciousness with confidence; they can certainly tell whether they love or hate, or believe in a fellow-man. Villains usually have a lurking consciousness that they are villains ; and efforts at self-deception are usually conscious. But Christian principles are described as peculiar, and as the very strongest principles of the soul. Why then should not the love, joy, peace, trust, submission, penitence, of a renewed heart become palpable to it, with due self-examination ? We should remember also, that God, by His providential trials, calls to duty and sacrifice for His sake and bereavements, speedily gives most believers excellent tests of genuine religious principles. It is objected, that " the heart is deceitful above all things and desperately wicked. Who can know it ?" I reply, that the believer is not required to know everything about this deceitful heart, (an impossibility for him) in order to know his own conversion ; but only to know some things, And moreover, in knowing these, he is promised the aids of the Holy Ghost. And this leads us.

Consciousness of Graces Should Give it.

Last : To argue from the witnessing of the Holy Ghost. His testimony with our spirits is promised, in various places and forms ; and surely this pledges God to make assurance a practicable attainment. See Rom. viii : 16; Eph. i : 13 ; iv : 30; 2 Cor. i : 22 ; 1 Jno. ii : 27.

Holy Ghost Promises it by His Witness.

Comparing sections 3 and 4, we may see that although the dogma of the Reformers was erroneous, their practical feeling concerning the importance of assurance was much more correct than ours. The saints of that age did not, like so many now, sit year after year, in sinful indolence, complaining of the want of

We Should Never Tolerate its Absence.

assurance, and yet indifferent to its cultivation. To them it was as the vital breath, to be either enjoyed perpetually, or else, if not enjoyed, to be sought with intense exertion. Now, we say, that while Faith may subsist without assurance of hope, every believer can and ought to attain in due time to the latter. And though it may be absent from a true Christian, yet no true Christian can be satisfied with its absence. If he feels the reality of heaven, he will wish to know whether it is to be his. If he truly believes there is a hell, he must earnestly long to be certified that he shall avoid it. He cannot be content to plod on, not knowing whether or not his feet are on the blood of the Redeemer, whom he loves, whether the viper, sin, which he hates, still enfolds his heart ; whether he is to spend the approaching eternity bathing his weary soul in seas of heavenly rest, or buffeting the fiery billows of wrath. A willingness to be ignorant of these things is proof of indifference. The chief reason why so many live on without assurance is, that they have no true faith.

The means for attaining this assurance of hope are indi-
5. Means of Assu- cated by comparing the Confession, chap.
rance. Self-examina- xviii, § 1, 2, 3. In the first place, he who
tion, etc. would seek it successfully, must be a true
believer, (not clearly known to himself as such, for then there would be nothing farther to seek, but known as such to God). Hence he who seeks long, without attaining, should probably do his first works again. In the next place, he should endeavor to live, in heart and life, in a consistent manner, exercising those principles and that conduct which the Scriptures ascribe to true children of God. For, in the third place, one means of assurance is the comparison which the believer makes between the Bible description and his own heart and life. But the experience of Christians, I am persuaded, finds this process of self-examination and comparison rather an indirect than a direct means of assurance. For a faithful self-inspection usually reveals so much that is defective, that its first result is rather the discouragement than the encouragement of hope. But this leads the humbled Christian to look away from himself to the Redeemer ; and thus assurance, which is the reflex act of faith, is strengthened by strengthening the direct actings of faith itself. Now, if there is nothing, or little, in himself which can be compared favorably with the Bible-measuring rule, of course assurance cannot properly result. This comparison, then is to be made in the work of self-examination, which must be honestly, thoroughly, and prayerfully performed. We say, prayerfully, for man's heart is deceitful ; self-love, self-righteousness, spiritual pride, hope, and fear, are nearly interested in the decision, and the understanding of man is too feeble and uncertain an instrument, at best, to be trusted with the everlasting and irreparable issues of this question, when unaided.

But here, we are again compelled to defend our Confession against the charge: that by directing the believer to seek assurance of his gracious state from the discovery in himself of supposed graces, we are encouraging him to build on a self-righteous foundation. It is strange that these writers do not remember the fact, that the Bible commands Christians (see p. 704,) to do the very thing they denounce. And to a plain mind, it seems a most perverse charge, that it is self-righteous to infer from his possession of certain qualities in oneself that God is reconciled to him; when the very premise of his inference is, that he could never have wrought these qualities in himself; but if they are in him, they were wrought by sovereign grace. The question to be settled for our assurance is: Is God reconciled to us? The process is: "Yes, God is reconciled" (conclusion) "because we find in ourselves changes which He alone can work;" (premise) "and which only unbought love prompted Him to work." Where is the self-righteousness of this? How does it lead to boasting, or vain confidence? Let us, for illustration, compare the process by which our opponents suppose the immediate consciousness of believing ministers the assurance of salvation to every believer immediately. If that process holds, it yet involves thus much of an illation: "My consciousness of faith assures me I am saved, because God works faith in none but the saved." Now why is not the parallel process equally valid for any other grace, which only God works? He assures us, that "love, joy, peace, long-suffering, goodness, meekness, temperance" are as truly "fruits of the Spirit," as faith is. (Gal. v : 22). The only difference is, that faith is related to the other graces as a seminal principle: and that it is the organ of our justification: but this does not change the case. Why is it self-confidence and self-righteousness to infer God's favour from other effects which He alone works, and works only in His own people: and yet so scriptural to infer our safety from the faith which God works in us? And since there is a spurious faith, which is discriminated from the genuine by the lack of right fruits, it is too obvious to be disputed, that we should examine those fruits, in order to assure ourselves. So evident is this, that we find even Calvin, (Bk. iii : Ch. ii : § 7,) in view of the existence of a dead faith simulating the living, concede the doctrine. "In the meantime, the faithful are taught to examine themselves with solicitude and humility, lest carnal security insinuate itself, instead of the assurance of faith." And Luther, as Dorner assures us, sometimes speaks more scripturally than Calvin, distinguishing between "an assuring faith" (the fuller attainment) and "a receiving faith," which he regards as true faith, and justifying. Nor "did he shrink from treating the new life of love, which is forming, as an evidence of faith."

It may be argued, that unless the inward marks are infal-

Self-Examination Justified.

Spiritual Discernment lible, no assurance of our salvation can be
Necessary on Either founded on them; but their scheme offers
View. directly the infallible promise of God, as the
exclusive basis of the assurance. I answer by referring the
student to the fact, that the same quickening grace which
bestows faith, also bestows spiritual discernment. How else did
the sinner, blind by nature, see " the glory of God in the face
of Jesus Christ?" This spiritual discernment is promised to
direct the believer in his examination.

When arguing for these scriptural means, we should not
forget that the habit of introspection may be
Introspection Diffi- abused, to divert the eyes of the soul too
cult. much from Christ. Dr. Chalmers, in the
place cited, has admirably illustrated a law of the mind, which
should caution us against that abuse. The essential condition
for the conscious flow of any affection is the presence of its
object, at. least in thought, before the mind. Thus, Christ
must be directly before the thought, in order for love to Christ
to flow forth consciously to Him. But when we begin to
inspect our love for Him, we substitute another object. Hence
the current of our love subsides as soon as we attempt to measure it. This explains a difficulty which has embarrassed
many Christians : and it presents another ground for asserting
the necessity of the Spirits' witness, that we may safely interpret our own feelings.

This witnessing, saith the Confession, is without extraordinary revelation. His agencies here, are
The Witness What? doubtless what they are, as to their degree
and nature, in His other sanctifying operations through the
Word; neither more nor less inscrutable, and just to the same
extent supernatural. Thus, it is His to illuminate the soul,
giving to the understanding spiritual apprehensions of Truth.
It is His to shine upon His own work in our hearts, both bright-
ening it, and aiding us in the comparison of it. It is His to
stimulate our righteousness, caution, and impartiality, by renewing and sanctifying the dispositions, and quickening our apprehensions of the Divine Judge, and of the stake at issue. Thus
the comparison between our graces and the Bible standard, is
made under His superintendence and light; so that while He
communicates no new revealed fact, contributes nothing new, so
to speak, to the material of the comparison, or of the measuring
rule, the result of the measurement is trustworthy. If such a
soul finds in itself the evident actings of such graces as the Bible
calls for, then it has an assurance which is both scriptural and
reasonable and spiritual. It is according to the rule of Scripture. It is reached according to the laws of the human understanding, intelligently and solidly. But best of all, it is also
formed under the superintendence of the Holy Ghost, and
He enables the humble, prayerful inquirer, to repose on it

with "a hope inexpressible and full of glory." Such an assurance may well be called infallible. It may be aped indeed, so far as human judgment can distinguish, by false security; but the difference is known to God, and to the believer, conscious as he is of thorough candour, humility and submission; and the judgment day will reveal the difference.

Now the ideas of the Wesleyan concerning this witness of the Holy Ghost, are far different. He makes it indeed an independent revelation, by which the Holy Ghost reveals immediately to the convert's mind, without a mediate process of self-examination and comparison, that he is now reconciled. All the arguments on which they rely to establish this view, against ours, may be reduced to two: that two witnesses are said (Rom. viii: 16), to concur, whereas our view seems to make no other testimony than that of our own spirits (assisted indeed by the Holy Ghost), and that the assurance cannot proceed mediately from the believer's consciousness of Christian affections within; because those affections are only evoked by the assurance of our adoption. 1 Jno. iv: 19. To the first of these I reply, their view excludes the witnessing of the believer's spirit at least as much as ours seems to exclude that of God's.

Wesleyan Doctrine of the Witness.

But, how can this concurrence of two witnesses be better described than in such a case as we have supposed? We protest that our view does most fully and fairly avow the concurrence of God's Holy Ghost in the witnessing. He witnesseth along with our spirits. To the second argument, we reply that is worthless to all except a Synergist. It is simply absurd, in our view, to assert that the believer can never have any regenerate exercises characteristic of the new life, until after he has an assurance of his adoption: when we believe, and have proved, that faith itself is a regenerate exercise, as well as repentance. Second: it is false that the renewed soul has no regenerate exercises till they are evoked by an assurance of its acceptance. This is not the sense of Jno. iv: 19. The first love of the new-born soul is not thus mercenary; it cannot help loving, and repenting, and adoring, though unconscious of hope. And last: surely the exhibition of the goodness, grace, truth and love of God made to all sinners in Jno. iii: 16, is enough to evoke the first actings of love on the new-born sinner's part, while he is still unconscious of a personal hope. To say that a regenerate soul could look at this lovely exhibition of God's mercy towards "whosoever will receive it," and feel no love, because forsooth not yet assured of its own personal interest in it, is to say that that soul is still in the gall of bitterness.

Replies.

This idea of an immediate witness we disprove, 1st, by the fact that self-examination is commanded, which would be superfluous to him already

Refutation, Farther.

assured by a revelation.   2nd. Because revelations have
ceased, and Christians are now remanded to Scripture as the
whole and sole source of all the religious informations needed
to carry the soul to heaven. Jno. v : 39 ; 1 Cor. xiii : 8; 2 Tim. iii : 15
–17.   3rd. It contradicts the experience of the very best converts
[tried by their fruits], who often exhibit good marks of penitence, submission, love : when their souls are so absorbed by
the sense of God's holiness and majesty, and their own vileness,
that they dare not rejoice in their acceptance.   And it equally
contradicts the experience of maturer converts, who usually
have their assurance dawn slightly, and grow gradually, as their
experience and graces grow. See Is. xlii : 16; Rom. v ; 4. 4th.
It opens the doors for untold self-deceptions, mistaking the
whispers of self-love, carnal security, spiritual pride, fanaticism,
or Satan, for this super-scriptural witness.   The most biting
argument against it is in the history of Wesleyan revivals,
with their spurious conversions.   John Wesley was himself so
sensible of this objection, that he appeals to the other concurrent witnessing, that of the Christian's consciousness compared
with Scripture, to show him that the previous witness is the
Holy Ghost, not a delusion. This virtually surrenders his dogma:.
for this witness of the believer's spirit, although mentioned last,
is in reality precedent in order. As the ambasador's credentials
must precede his recognition, so this witnessing of the concious
graces in the heart must give credence to the immediate impression !

   Assurance of hope, scripturally founded, will result in
advantage only.   It increases spiritual joy.
6. Effects of Assur- Thus it promotes usefulness, Nehemiah viii :
ance Holy. 10.   It unseals the heart to praise God.   It
stimulates evangelical labours.   1 Cor. xv : 58.   It nerves us for
self-denial.   It lifts us above carnal temptations.   Phil. iv : 7.

   Some have thought the assurance of hope arrogant,
as though it were modest and seemly to be in suspense concerning our salvation.   I answer : If we expected to save ourselves, so it would be.   To be in suspense whether Christ is
able, and willing, and faithful, surely is no mark of our humility; but, on the contrary, it is a dishonor to Him.

   The main objection, however, is, that assurance, coupled
with the doctrine of perseverance of saints, will become the
sure occasion of spiritual indolence and carnal security.
We reply, that if an unrenewed man should persuade himself unscripturally that he is in Christ, this result would surely
follow.   But how can it follow to that man who scripturally
founds his hope on the existence in himself of a disposition to
flee from sin, strive after holiness, and fight the good fight of
faith ? He hopes he is a Christian, only because he sees re· son
to hope that he shall strive to the end. The perception in himself of the depraving consequence charged above, would at

once vitiate the evidence that he was, or ever had been, a child of God, just in proportion as it was realized. The watchful garrison are confident that they shall not fall victims to a surprise, because they intend to watch. Such assurance only stimulates effort. The drunken rioters go to sleep flattering themselves they shall not be surprised; but this is presumption, not assurance. In the actual experiences of Christians, he who enjoys the grace of assurance ever walks most carefully and tenderly before his God, lest the precious elixir be lost through negligence, See Ps. cxxxix: 21, 24; 2 Cor. v:6–9; Heb. vi:9–12.

LECTURE LX.

PRAYER.

SYLLABUS.

1. What is the definition, and what the parts of **prayer**?
Conf. of Faith, ch. xxi. Shorter Cat. Qu. 98 to end. **Directory of Worship,** chs. 5, 15, Dick, Lect. 93. Ridgley, Qu. 178.
2. Who is the proper object of prayer?
Dick, Lect. 93. Ridgley, Qu. 179.
3. What are the proper grounds by which the duty of prayer is sustained and enforced?
Pictet, bk. viii, ch. 10. Dick, Lect. 93. Hill, bk. v, § 3. Knapp, § 133, Appendix.
4. Refute the objections to the reasonableness of prayer, drawn from God's omniscience, immutability, independence, decrees; and from the stability of Nature.
So. Presb. Rev., Jan. 1870. Art. i, Dr. Girardeau. Chalmers' Nat, Theol. bk. v, ch. 3. Dick, Lect. 93. McCosh, Div. Gov. bk. ii, ch. 2, § 5, 6. Duke of Argyll, "Reign of Law," ch. 2. Sensualistic Phil. of 19th Cent. ch. 13.
5. What is the rule of prayer, and what the qualities of acceptable prayer?
Dick, as above. and Lect. 94. Pictet, as above. Ridgley, Qu. 185, 186.
6. What model is given for our prayers?
Dick, Lect. 95. See on the Whole, Magee on Atonement, dissertation 8th; and Dr. Leonard Wood's Lectures, 95 to 99.
7. What is the nature and extent of the warrant given us to expect answers?
See e. g., Matt. vii : 7, 8; Mark, xi : 24. Dick, Lect. 94. Pictet as above. Dr. Leonard Wood's Lectures, 95-99. So. Presb. Rev., Jan. 1872, Art. i. Theol. of Plym. Br. Life of Trust, or Biography of the Rev. Geo. Muller of Bristol.
8. Show that prayer should be both secret, social, ejaculatory, and stated.
Dick, Lect. 94.

"**P**RAYER is an offering up of our desires unto God for things agreeable to His will, in the name of Christ, with confession of our sins, and thankful acknowledgement of His mercies."

1. Definition.

Its several parts are stated, in the Directory for Worship, to be adoration, thanksgiving, confession, petition, intercession and pleading. See Directory. Ch. v:§ 2.

God alone is the proper object of religious worship. Matt.

2. God the Only Proper Object. iv: 10. The general reason for this is, that He alone possesses the attributes which are implied in the offer of religious worship. The Being who is to be worshipped by all the Church must be omniscient. Otherwise our prayers would never reach His ears. And if conveyed to Him, they would utterly confound and overwhelm any finite understanding, in the attempt to distinguish, comprehend, and judge concerning them. Then, moreover, the being to whom we resort in prayer, must be all-wise, in order to know infallibly what is best for us, and how to procure it. Such omniscience as we have above described implies, of course, omnipresence. Second. This Lord must be infinitely good, otherwise we should have no sufficient warrant to carry Him our wants, and His benevolence would be overtaxed by such constant and innumerable appeals. Third. He must be almighty, else He is no adequate refuge and dependence for our souls, in all exigencies. Some most urgent wants and dangers might arise, which only omnipotence could meet.

Prayer May be to the Persons of Trinity. For these reasons the offering of prayer is a virtual ascription of divinity to its object; and we reject all such appeals to saints and angels as idolatrous. For us sinners, the door of prayer is only opened by the Covenant of Grace. (Why?) Now we have seen that God the Father stands economically as the representative of the whole Trinity, on the part of the Godhead, as Christ the Son stands as sinner's representative in that transaction. Hence prayer is usually addressed to the Father through the Son, and by the Spirit. Eph. ii: 18. But we must not imagine that one person is more properly the object of prayer than another. All are made alike objects of worship, in the apostolic benediction, 2 Cor. xiii: 14, in the formula of baptism, and in Rev. i: 4. But more: we find Jesus Christ, so to speak, the separate object of worship, in Gen. xviii: 23; Josh. v: 14; Acts vii: 59; Rev. i: 17: v; 8; Heb. i: 6, etc. These examples authorize us to address a distinct petition to either of the Persons.

3. Proper grounds of Prayer: (a) God's command.— Reasonable. The duty of prayer reposes immediately on God's command, who "wills that men pray everywhere." I Tim. ii: 8. But this is a precept which most eminently commends itself to every man's conscience in the sight of God, because so clearly founded in nature. That is there are numerous and powerful reasons proceeding out of our very relations to God, for the duty of prayer. That this is true is obviously suggested by the strength of the instinct of devotion in every rational breast. The immediate prompting of the sense of want or sin, in the creature, is to make him say : " Lead me to the Rock that is higher than I." Ps. lxi: 2. And to pray, is mentioned of Saul as the characteristic evidence that he had learned to fear God. Acts ix: 11. Wherever there is religion, true or false, there is prayer. Even the speculative atheist, when pressed by danger, has been known to belie his pretended creed, by calling in anguish upon the God whom he had denied. This natural instinct of prayer reposes for its ground on God's perfections, and man's dependence and wants. And so long as these two facts remain what they are, man must be a praying creature. Let the student remember, also, that man, while finite and dependent, is also an essentially active creature. Emotion, and the expression of emotion. are the unavoidable, because natural outgoings of his powers. He cannot but put forth his activity in efforts tending to the objects of his desires; he must cease first to be man; and prayer is the inevitable, the natural effort of the dependent creature, in view of exegencies above his own power. To tell him who believes in a God, not to pray, is to command him to cease to be a man.

Prayer is the natural homage due from the creature to his heavenly Father. God being Himself all blessed, and the sole Source and Giver of blessedness, can receive no recompense from any creature. But is no form of homage therefore due? To say this, would be to say that the creature owes God nothing, because God bestows so much! It would extirpate religion practically from the universe. Now, I assert, in opposition to the Rationalistic Deists, who say that the only reasonable homage is a virtuous life, and the cultivation of right emotions; that prayer also is more directly, and still more naturally, that reasonable homage. God must bestow on man all the good he receives; then man ought to ask for all that good. It is the homage to God's beneficent power, appropriate to a creature dependent, yet intelligent and active. Man ought to thank God for all good; it is the natural homage due from receiver to Giver. Man ought to confess all his sin and guilt; it is the natural homage due from sinfulness to sovereign holiness. Man ought to deprecate God's anger; it is the appropriate homage due from conscious guilt to power and righteousness. Man ought to praise God's perfections. Thus only can the moral intelligence God has created, pay to Him its tribute of intellectual service. I should like to see the reasoning analyzed, by which these skeptics are led to admit that the creature does owe to God the homage of a virtuous life and affections. I will pledge myself to show that the same reasoning equally proves he owes the homage of prayer. Conceive of God as bestowing all the forms of good on man which his dependent nature needs, without requiring any homage of prayer from man as the means of its bestowal; and you will immediately have, man being such as he is (an active being), a system of practical atheism. Religion, relation between man and God will be at an end.

(b) Is God's Due.

True, God would be related to man, but not man to God!
Anomalous and guilty condition! No feeling of dependence,
reverence, gratitude, wholesome fear, would find expression
from the creature.

This leads us, third, to the important remark, that prayer
is the natural means of grace appropriate to
(c) Is Means of the creature. Prayer is not intended to pro-
Grace, *Per se.*
duce a change in God, but in us. Rev.
Rowland Hill explained to sailors: " The man in the skiff at
the stern of a man-of war, does not pull the ship to himself, in
hauling at the line, but pulls the skiff to the ship. This line is
prayer. Prayer does not draw God down to us, but draws us
up to God, and thus establishes the connection." Now, as we
have seen, man being an essentially active creature, the exercise
of all those right affections which constitute gracious character necessitates their expression. And again,to refuse expression
to an affection chokes it; to give it its appropriate expression
fosters and strengthens it. See examples. We see at once,
therefore, how prayer is a natural and necessary means for all
gracious growth. Let us exemplify in detail. Faith is a mother
grace to all others; but prayer is the natural and necessary
expression of faith; it is its language, its vital breath. In
spiritual desire the life of religion may be said to consist. Desire
is implied in faith itself, for a man does not trust for what he
does not want, and it is yet more manifest in hope. For hope
is but desire, encouraged by the prospect of obtaining the
desired object. Repentance includes a desire for deliverance
from sin and attainment of holiness. Love of God includes a
desire for communion with Him, and for His favour. So that it
would not be very inaccurate to say that practical religion consists in the exercise of holy desires. But what is prayer, except
"the offering up of our desires to God?" Prayer is the vital
breath of religion in the soul. Again, it cultivates our sense of
dependence and of God's sovereignty. By confessing our
sins, the sense of sin is deepened. By rendering thanks, gratitude is enlivened. By adoring the divine perfections, we are
changed into the same image, from glory to glory. From all
this it is apparent that prayer is the Christian's vital breath. If
God had not required it, the Christian would be compelled to
offer it by his own irrepressible promptings. If he were taught
to believe that it was not only useless, but wrong, he would
doubtless offer it in his heart in spite of himself, even though
he were obliged to accompany it with a petition that God
would forgive the offering. To have no prayer is, for man, to
have no religion.

But last, and chiefly, prayer is a means of grace, because
God has appointed it as the instrument of
Chiefly; is Ordained
in God's Promises.   man's receiving His Spiritual influences. It is
enough for the Christian to know that all his

growth in grace is dependent, and that God hath ordained: "he that asketh receiveth."

Thus we see the high and essential grounds on which the duty of prayer rests, grounds laid in the very natures of God and of man, and in the relations between the two.

But it is from the nature of God that the rationalistic objections are drawn against the reasonable-ness of the duty. It is said, "Since God is omniscient, there is no meaning in our telling Him our wants, for He knows them already, better than we do. Since He is good, He already feels every proper impulse to make us happy, and to relieve our pains; and does not need any persuading on our part, to incline Him to mercy. And since He is immutable, and has already determined from eternity, every act of His future agency, by an unchangeable decree, to hope to change God by our importunity, is worse than useless; it is a reproach to Him. Hence there is nothing for the wise man to do, but to receive His allotments with calm submission, and to honour Him by imitating His moral perfections."

4. Reasonableness of Prayer Objected to.

We reply: to him who had any reverence for the Scripture these assertions of God's wisdom and goodness would be arguments to prove, instead of disproving, the propriety of prayer. For has not this wise and good being commanded prayer? Has He not seen fit to appoint prayer as the instrument for receiving His purposed blessings? Then, to the humble mind, there is the best proof that prayer is reasonable. But farther, we have already remarked that, so far as prayer is intended to produce any change, it is not a change in God, but in us. He does not command it because He needs to be informed of our wants, or to be made willing to help. He commands it because He has seen fit to ordain it as the appointed means for reception of His blessings. And we have seen abundant reasons why it is a suitable means to be thus ordained: a wise means, a right means. It is a necessary and instinctive outgoing of the rightly feeling soul. It is the proper homage for man to render God. It is an influence wholesome for man's soul itself. And now, God having seen these good reasons (doubtless with others) for ordaining prayer as the means of receiving His favour; there is nothing in His wisdom, goodness, or immutability, inconsistent with His regular enforcement of the rule, "ask, and ye shall receive."

General Reply.

Not in His goodness: For if any one should take such a view of the Divine benevolence as to suppose that it will in every case bestow on the creature such blessings as God's nature and purpose permit, without requiring to be persuaded by the creature's use of means, the whole course of His providence

God's Benevolence No Objection.

would refute it. God is benevolent in bestowing on multitudes of farmers the fruits of the earth. If any one trusts to His immutable goodness, without plowing and sowing his field, he will certainly be disappointed. The truth is just here : that God is infinitely benevolent, but still, it is a benevolence exercised always in harmony with His wisdom, and with all His other attributes. The question then is : Have God's wisdom, sovereignty, and other attributes, impelled Him to decide that He cannot consistently give some particular gifts except to those that ask? If so, it is vain to argue from His infinite goodness.

Nor do God's decree and unchangeableness show that it is inconsistent in Him to answer prayer. His immutability does not consist in acting with a mechanical sameness, irrespective of change of circumstances. It is an immutability of principles. The sameness of principle dictates a change of conduct when outward circumstances change. To refuse to change in such cases would often be mutability. And the familiar old answer here applies, that God's decree embraces the means as much as the end. Wherever it was His eternal purpose that any one should receive certain graces, it was His purpose equally that he should ask. In a word, these objections are just the same with those of the vulgar fatalist, who objects that, because " what is to be, will be," therefore it is of no use to make any effort. There is no difference whatever in the refinement or wisdom of the objectors. To be consistent, these rationalists who refuse to pray should also refuse to plow, to sow, to cultivate, to take medicine when sick, to watch against danger, &c.

His Immutability no Objection.

The difficulty, however, which is now thought most formidable, and is most frequently advanced by Rationalists, is that drawn from the stability of nature. The argument of the objection is, that except where God acts supernaturally, as in regeneration and the resurrection, He acts only through second causes ; that the tie between cause and effect is efficient, and the result regular; so that each effect is potentially in its antecedent cause, which is, very probably, an event that has already occurred, and is therefore irrevocable. Hence, it is impossible but that the effect must follow, pray as we may against it; unless God will miraculously break the ties of natural causation ; but that, we know, He will not do.

Objection from Stability of Nature.

Now, this is either an argument *ad ignorantiam*, or it is atheistic. The simple, popular (and sufficient) view which refutes it is : That God governs this world in every natural event through His special providence ; and the regular laws of nature are only the uniform modes of those second causes, which He employs to do so. Now, the objection is simply this : that God has constructed a machine, which is so perfect, and so completely His, that He

General Reply.

cannot modify its action without breaking it! That is, His success has been so complete, in constructing this machine of nature to work His intended ends, that He has shut Himself out of His own handiwork! Such is the absurdity which the matter must wear in the hands of a theist. Nature is a machine which God made and now uses to effect a set of ends, all of which were foreseen and purposed; and among which were all the destined answers to the acceptable prayers foreseen to be uttered. Of course God has not so made it as to exclude Himself and His own purposes. How does He manage the machine to make it work those purposes? We may not know how; but this is no evidence that He does not. The inference from His general wisdom and promise is proof enough that He can and does. A very good illustration may be taken from a railroad train. It is propelled, not by an animal which has senses to hear command, but by a steam engine. The mechanical force exerted is irresistible by man. The conditions of its movement are the most rigidly methodical; only up and down one track, within certain times. But there is a Conductor; and his personal will can arrest it at the request of the feeblest child.

But to be more exact: The objector urges that the general laws of nature are stable. Grant it. What *Prayer a Part of the General Law.* is nature? It is a universe of matter and mind related, and not of matter only. Now only postulate that desire, prayer, and the answers to prayer are among those general laws, which, as a complex whole, have been assigned to regulate nature, and the uniformity of nature only confirms the hope of answers to prayers. Has the philosopher explored all the ties of natural causation made by God? He does not pretend so. Then it may be that among the unexplored ties are some subtle and unexplained bonds which connect prayers with their answers as natural causes and effects. And all that we have said, in showing how natural prayer is to creatures, makes the postulate probable.

Again. Does natural law govern the universe? Or, does *God Rules by His Laws of Nature as He Pleases.* God govern it by natural law? Men perpetually cheat themselves with the idea that law is a power, whereas it is simply the method of a power. Whence the power of the natural second cause? Originally from God; and its working is maintained and regulated by God. Hence it is utterly improbable (whether we can comprehend or not) that God should have so arranged His own power communicated to His works as to obstruct His own personal will. Remember that God is personal, and not a mere *anima mundi.* He is a sovereign moral Person.

Last, recurring to the views given in explanation of God's *His Providence in all Second Causes.* providence (Lect. xxv), you will be reminded, that power in second causes only acts when the suitable relations are established between them and those things which are to be the recipients of the effects: that among all possible relations, many might be fruitful of no effects, and others of very different effects: That hence, there is here, room for the perpetual, present manipulation of the invisible Hand in providence. Thus, God always has resources to modify the acting of natural causes, they still acting according to their natures. As I remarked: All God's providence is special; and the supernatural is always with the natural; else the latter could not be.

The proposal has been made by modern Materialists, to test the efficacy of prayer by a physical test, such as is applied to try the efficacy of material causes. The absurdity, as well as impiety of this proposal appears from two remarks. One is, that the physical answers to prayer; or in other words, those effects which confer physical change and benefit, belong to that class of things which, as we shall show anon, God has never bound Himself, by any categorical promise, to bestow. We are encouraged to pray for them; but God holds the answer contingent to us, deciding to give or withhold according as He sees best in His secret sovereignty. Hence, in the only cases where a physical test could possibly apply, there is no definite promise to be tested. The other remark is: that unless the atheist's theory be demonstrated, it will remain at least possible that we shall find a personal will dispensing the answer to prayer. This proposal then requires this venerable Person to submit Himself to an additional test of His fidelity, after He has given His promise; and that on a demand which may always appear to Him petulant and insolent. So that, unless the proposed test is guilty of the sophism of begging the very question to be ascertained, it is always presumable, that this majestic Person may choose to refuse all response to the proposed test, and may deem this refusal necessary to His self-respect. In the parallel case, there is every probability that anyone of these Materialists would be silent, and stand on his dignity. If there is a God, (the thing to be ascertained in this inquiry) shall He not consult His self-respect? The proposed method of inquiry is then worthless.

The proper rule of prayer is the whole Word of God. Not only are its instances of inspired devotion our exemplars, and its promises our warrant; its precepts are the measure of our petitions, and its threatenings the stimulants. There is no part of Scripture which may not minister to the guidance of the Christian's prayers. But further, the Word of God is the rule of our prayers also in this sense, that all which it does not authorize, is excluded. Prayer being a homage to God, it is for Him to say what worship He will accept; all else is not homage, but presumption. Again, both man's blindness and corruption, and God's infinitude for-

Physical Test of Prayer.

5. Rule of Prayer.

bid that we should undertake to devise acts of worship, of our
own motion. They will be too apt to partake of some of our
depravity, or else to lead in some way, unforeseen to us, to
developments of depravity. And God's nature is too inscrutable to our feeble minds, for us to undertake to infer from it,
except as we are guided by the light of the Word. Hence, the
strict Protestant eschews "will worship" as a breach of the
decalogue.

When we examine the inspired rule of prayer, we find that,
to be acceptable, it must be sincere and hearty;
Qualities of Accept-
able Prayer. it must be addressed to God with faith in
Christ; it must be for objects agreeable to
God's will; it must be prompted by the Holy Ghost; it must
be accompanied with genuine repentance and gratitude. See
Ps. lxii : 8 ; Jer. xxix : 13 ; Jno. xiv : 6 ; 1 Jno. v : 14, 15 ;
Rom. viii : 26 ; Phil. iv : 6, 7 ; 1 Jno. iii : 22 ; Ps. lxvi : 18 ;
Heb. xi : 6, &c.

6. The more immediate model which God has given for our
prayer, is the Lord's prayer. That it was not intended for a
liturgy to be servilely followed, our authors have shown, in their
discussions of liturgies. But that it was intended both as a
general guide in the structure of our own petitions, and as a
form whose very words are to be employed by us on proper
occasions, is manifest. cf. Matt. vi : 9; Luke xi : 2. The
most plausible objection to it, as a model for Christians is, that
it contains no express reference to a Mediator, and answer
through His merit and intercession. The answer is, that it is
an Old Testament prayer : is intended as such, because that
dispensation was still standing. When it was about to close,
Christ completed this feature of it, by enjoining the use of His
name. See John xiv : 13 ; xv : 16 ; xvi : 23, 24.

We apprehend that there is much vagueness in the views
of Christians concerning the nature and ex-
7. Extent of War-
rant for Answer. tent of the warrant which they have to expect
an answer to their prayers. Some err by de-
fect, forming no definite view of the ground on which their
faith is entitled to rest; and consequently, approaching the
throne of Grace with no lively hopes whatever. Others err by
excess, holding the promises in a sense God did not intend them
to bear ; and consequently their hopes are fanatical and superstitious. Now, in order that our faith may be firm, it must be
correct and intelligent. The consequence of these erroneous
views ultimately is disappointment, and hence, either self-accusation, or skepticism.

The warrant for prayer is of course to be sought, immediately, in the promises. Of these some seem
Extreme View De-
scribed and Refuted. very emphatic : e. g., Matt. vii : 7 ; Mark xi :
24. On promises of the latter class especi-
ally, some have built a theory of prayer, thus : that the only

46*

reason any prayer of one in a state of grace, and actuated in the main by pious motives, is not specifically and infallibly answered, is, that it was not offered in faith, and that wherever such a saint fully believes that he shall receive that which he asks, he will receive it, as surely as inspiration. And such prayer it was the fashion to dignify with the title, "the prayer of faith," among some religioinists. In opposition, I would urge: First. Common sense refutes it; and shows that practically there is a limitation to these general promises of answer to prayer. Who believes that he can, provided his motives are in the main pious, pray away a spell of illness, or raise up a sick friend, or convert an individual sinner, with infallible certainty? But may they not put in a saving clause by saying: "Such prayers are dictated by the Holy Ghost? This makes all right." Ans.: The Christian has no mode of distinguishing the specific cases of spiritual impulse in his own heart; because the Holy Ghost operates in and through his natural capacities. Hence, to the Christian, the universal warrant is practically lacking. It is manifestly incompetent to the Christian to say, in advance of the answer: The Spirit dictates this prayer beyond doubt. Second: Scripture refutes it; for there are clear cases of petitions of Bible saints, made in faith, piety, urgency, and not specifically answered. See 2 Sam. xii: 16, 19; 2 Cor. xii: 8–10: and above all, Matt. xxvi: 39. And third: We can hardly suppose that God would abdicate His omniscience in His dealings towards the very objects of His redeeming love, and make their misguided, though pious desires the absolute rule of His conduct towards them. This would be the literal result, were He absolutely pledged to do for shortsighted Christians exactly what they, with pious motives, ask of Him. We may add fourth, that such an assumption is refuted by God's claim to chastise believers for their profit. They of course pray, and innocently pray for exemption. ("Remove Thy stroke from me; for I am consumed by the blow of Thine hand.") If God were under bond to hear every prayer of faith, He would have to lay down the rod in each case, as soon as it was taken up.

There is then, of course, some practical limitation in these general promises. What is it? I answer, Scriptural Limitations to Warrant. it is to be found in the whole tenour of Scripture. And generally in the language of 1 Jno. v: 14. All our prayers shall be specifically answered in God's time and way, but with literal and absolute accuracy, if they are believing and pious prayers, and for things according to God's will. Now there are only two ways to find out what things are such; one is by special revelation, as in the case of faith of miracles, and petitions for them; the other is by the Bible. Here the explanation of that erroneous view of the warrant of prayer, above described, is made easy and plain. It is said that if the Christian prays with right motives, and with an assured belief that he shall obtain, he will obtain ; no matter what he asks, (unless it be something unlawful). Yes, but what warrant has he for the belief that he shall obtain? Faith, without an intelligible warrant, is sheer presumption. Suppose, for instance, the object of petition is the recovery of a sick friend ; where does the applicant read God's pledge of a specific answer to that prayer? Certainly not in Scripture. Does he pretend a direct spiritual communication? Hardly. He has no specific warrant at all ; and if he works himself up into a notion that he is assured of the answer, it is but a baseless fantasy, rather insulting than honourable to God. I know that pious biography is full of supposed instances of this kind, as when Luther is said to have prayed for the recovery of Melancthon. These are the follies of good men ; and yet God's abounding mercy may in some cases answer prayers thus blemished.

We return then to Scripture, and ask again, what is the extent of the warrant there found? The answer is, that God, both by promise and example, clearly holds out two classes of objects for which Christians pray. One is the class of which an instance has just been cited — objects naturally desirable, and in themselves innocent, which yet are not essential to redemption ; such as recovery from sickness, recovery of friends, good name, daily bread, deliverance from persecution, conversion of particular sinners, &c., &c. It is right to pray for such things ; it is even commanded : and we have ground, in the benevolence, love, and power of God, and tender sympathy of the Mediator, to hope for the specific answer. But still the truest believer will offer those prayers with doubts of receiving the specific answer; for the simple reason that God has nowhere specifically promised to bestow it. The enlightened believer urges such petitions, perhaps warmly : but still all are conditioned on an " if it be possible," " if it be consistent with God's secret will." And he does not know whether he shall receive or not, just because that will is still secret. But such prayers, offered with this general trust in God's power, benevolence and better wisdom, and offered in pious motives, are accepted, even though not answered. cf. 2 Cor. xii : 8, with vs.' 9 ; Matt. xxvi : 39; with Heb. v : 7. God does not give the very thing sought, though innocent in itself ; He had never promised it : but He " makes all things work together for good to the petitioner." This should be enough to satisfy every saint.

Two Classes of Good. The Warrant for First Only is Absolute.

The other class of objects of prayer is, the benefits accompanying redemption ; all the gifts which make up, in the elect, growth in grace, perseverance, pardon, sanctification, complete redemption. For these we pray with full assurance of a specific answer, because God has told us, that it is His purpose specifically to bestow them in answer to all true prayer. See

Ps. lxxxiv : 11 ; Luke xi : 13: 1 Thess. iv : 3 ; Luke xii : 32; John xv : 8. So, we have a warrant to pray in faith, for the grace to do the things which God's word makes it our duty to do. In all such cases, our expectation of an answer is entitled to be as definite as was that of Apostles, when inspired with the faith of miracles. God may not give it in the shape or channel we expected ; He may choose to try our faith by unexpected delays, but the answer is sure, because definitely promised, in His own time and way. Here we may say, Habak. ii: 3, "For the vision is yet for an appointed time, but at the end it shall speak, and not lie; though it tarry, wait for it; because it will surely come, it will not tarry."

In addition to the promises, our expectation of an answer
Promises Confirmed. to prayer is strengthened by the following precious considerations. (a) When we pray for things agreeable to God's will, we virtually pray for what will promote His glory and good pleasure. We are like the industrious servant petitioning to a wise master, for a new tool or implement in order to work better for him. (b) Such prayers are prompted by the Holy Ghost, and therefore (Rom. viii: 27), are surely destined to be answered, because the good and truthful God would not evoke such desires only in order to repulse them. (c) Our union to Christ confirms this; because we know that the sap of spiritual affections circulates in us from Him our Root: so that the way we come to have a good desire is, by His having it first. Now, if He desires that thing too, we shall be like to get it. (d) Christ's intercession, so tender and generous, so prevalent, and perpetual, presents the most glorious ground of hope. He rejects no pious applicant. He ever liveth to intercede. The Farther heareth Him always. Hence, Heb. iv : 15, 16.

We are commanded to "pray always," "without ceasing."
8. Prayer Should be That is, the temper of prayer should be
Social and Secret,
Stated and Ejacula- always prevalent: and ejaculatory prayer
tory. should be habitual, and frequent as our spiritual exigencies. But it is also our duty to pray statedly : the morning and evening, at least, being obviously proper stated seasons for secret, and the Lord's day, at least, for social and public prayer. The reason is, that man, a finite creature, controlled so greatly by habit, cannot well perform any continuous duty, without a season appropriated to it; and that, a stated season. He needs all the aids of opportunity and leisure. Nor is there any incompatibility of such stated seasons, with our dependence on the Holy Ghost for ability to offer acceptable prayer. Some Christians seem to be infected with the Quaker idea, that because all true prayer is prompted by the Spirit, it is best not to attempt the duty at the stated hour, if His *afflatus* is not felt. The folly of this appears from our Saviour's words: "Behold I stand at the door and knock."

The Spirit is always waiting to prompt prayer. His command is, to pray always. If, at the appointed hour, an indisposition to pray is experienced, it is our duty to regard this as a marked symptom of spiritual want; and to make it a plea for the petition, " Lord, teach us to pray."

Again: Man must join in acts of social and public worship, because he is a social being; and hence he derives important aids in the difficult work of keeping alive the spirit of prayer within him. It is also his duty to glorify God before his fellow-creatures, by these public acts of homage, and to seek to benefit his fellows by the example of them. Yet the duty of public worship does not exclude that of secret. See Matt. vi : 6. Every soul is bound to pray statedly in secret, because of the example of Christ and the saints; because the relation between God and the soul is direct and personal, admitting no daysman but Christ: because secret prayer is the best test and cultivation of the spirit of true devotion : because each soul has special sins, mercies, wants, of which he should speak confidentially to his God; and because there is in secret prayer the most childllke and unrestrained intercourse between God and the soul. So important are these facts, that we may usually say, that he who has no habit of secret prayer has no spirit of prayer at all.

LECTURE LXI.

THE SACRAMENTS.

THE doctrine of the sacraments is closely dependent on that of the Church; and is treated by many authorities,
as strictly consequent thereon; as by Turrettin. It may also be remarked, that the doctrine of the Church is a head of the theology of redemption ; and may be treated as such, as well as a source for practical rules of church-order. But as that doctrine is ably treated in another department of this Seminary, I shall assume its main principles, and use them as foundations for the discussion of the sacraments, without intruding into that circle of inquiry.

Doctrine of Church and Sacraments Dependent.

Let us remember then, that the true Church of Christ is invisible, and consists of the whole body of the effectually called : That the same name is given, by accommodation, in the Scriptures, to a visible body, consisting of all those throughout the world, who make a credible profession of the true religion, together with their children : That the essential properties of unity, holiness, indefectibility, catholicity, belong to the invisible, and not the visible Church : That God has defined the visible Church catholic, by giving it, in all its parts, a ministry, the Word, the sacraments and other ordinances, and some measure of His sanctifying Spirit: That this visible Church is traced back at least to the family of Abraham, where it was organized by God's own authority on a gospel and ecclesiastical cov-

Definition of Church and its Attributes.

726

enant : That this visible Church is substantially the same
under both dispensations, retaining under the New, the same
membership and nature, though with a suitable change of circumstances, which it had under the Old Dispensation; and that
out of this visible Church catholic there is no ordinary possibility of salvation. In this visible Church, the sacraments are
both badges of membership, and sealing ordinances. They
also represent, apply, and seal, the chief truths of redemption.
Hence, the importance of their discussion. They will be found
to bear a close relation to our whole system, both of doctrine
and church-order.

When one examines the Scriptures, and sees the brief and
simple statements there given concerning the
1. Bible Ideas of Sa- sacraments, he will be very apt to feel that
crament Simple. the place assigned them in many Protestant,
and all Romish systems of divinity, is inordinately large. This
is an evidence of the strong tendency of mankind to formalism.
In our treatment of the subject, much of the length assigned it
will arise from our attempts to rebut these formal and superstitious tendencies, and reduce the sacraments to their Scriptural simplicity.

According to the definition of the Confession of Faith, ch.
27, § 1, 2, there are four things which concur
Constituted of Four to constitute a sacrament. (a.) A visible ma-
Things. material element. (b.) A covenanted grace
or graces, aptly symbolized and represented to the senses by
the element. (c.) A mutual pledge and seal of this covenant
between God and the soul. (d.) And an express divine institution. The usual patristic definition was, "a sacrament is a sensible sign of an invisible grace." But this is too indefinite, and
leaves out the federal feature. All ceremonies are not sacraments because they are of divine appointment; for they may
not have this material element as symbol of a spiritual grace;
nor are all symbols of divine appointment therefore sacraments;
because they may not be seals of a covenant.

One of the most important features is the express divine
appointment. Sacraments are acts of wor-
God's Appointment ship. All worship not instituted by God is
Most Essential. will-worship, and therefore offensive, because
He is infinite and inscrutable to finite minds, as well as our absolute Sovereign; so that it is presumption in man to devise ways
to please Him any farther than the appointment of His word
bears us out, and because the devices of depraved and short-
sighted man are always liable to be depraved and depraving.
These reasons, of course, apply in greater force to sacraments of
human device. But there is an additional one. A sacrament is
God's pledge of some covenanted grace to the true participant.
Now, by the same reason that nobody can put my sign and seal
to my bond save myself, no other than God can institute a

sacrament. It is the most aggravated form of will-worship.
The remarks of Dick and Hill concerning the etymology and
usage of the word, *sacramentum*, have been
sufficient; (as meaning first, a suitor's money
placed in pledge; second, a soldier's oath of
enlistment; third, some holy secret, the usual vulgate translation of μυστήριον.) It has been plausibly suggested, that the
latter is the sense primarily attached to it by the Latin Fathers,
when they used it in our technical sense; as μυστήριον is the
word usually employed therefor by the Greeks. This is reasonable: yet the other idea of oath of enlistment to Christ was,
we know, early attached to it. For in the earliest literature of
the martys, e. g., Tertullian, and thenceforward generally, we
find the ideas enlarged on, that the Christian is a soldier enlisted
and sworn, in the Lord's Supper, to die for Jesus.

Etymology and Meaning.

Much of the remainder of this Lecture will consist of an
attempt to substantiate the parts of our definition of a sacrament. The Socinians (and
as Lutherans and Papists charged, the Zwing-
lians), being outraged by the unscriptural and absurd doctrine
of Rome, concerning the intrinsic efficacy of sacraments, *ex
opere operato*, adopted this view, that a sacrament is but an instructive and commemorative symbol of certain facts and truths,
and a badge of profession. This we hold to be true so far as
it goes, but to be insufficient. They are also pledges and seals
on God's part of covenanted gospel blessings, as well as pledges
of service and fidelity on our part (which is implied in their
being badges of profession). And here we oppose the Papists
also, because they also repudiate the sphragistic nature of the
sacraments, in making them actually confer and work, instead of
signing and sealing, the appropriate graces.

2. Sacraments are Seals as well as Signs.

The arguments for our view are the following: It is expressly said, Rom. iv : 11, that circumcision,
one of the sacraments of the Old Testament,
was to Abraham a sign and "seal of the
righteousness of faith, which he had while yet uncircumcised."
It must have been equally a seal to all other genuine believers
of Israel; for the ground of its application to them was no
other than their coming under the very covenant then instituted
with Abraham, and inheriting the same promises. But baptism
is the circumcision of the New Testament, the initial sign of
the same covenant; and baptized believers are children of Abraham's promises by faith. Matt. xxviii : 19; Acts ii : 38, 39;
Rom. iv : 11, 16, &c. It seems very obvious therefore, that
Baptism is as much a seal as circumsion was. So the passover,
at its first institution, was a pledge (as well as sign) of a covenanted immunity. See Exod. xii ; 13, 23. When we establish
a similar identity between the Passover and the Supper, the
same argument will appear, that the latter also is a seal.

(a.) Because Circumsion was a Seal.

But second. The pledge contained in the sacraments is (b.) The Sacraments plainly indicated in the outward or ecclesias-Confer Outward Privi-tical privileges, into which they immediately lege. induct the partaker. He who received the sign, was thereby at once entitled to the enjoyment of certain privileges, the signs and means of saving graces. How can the idea of pledging be avoided here? And the sacramental union expressed in the Bible language implies the same. In Gen. xvii : 10, 13, circumsion is called the covenant. In Jno. iii : 5; Tit. iii : 5; baptism is called regeneration; and in Acts xxii : 16, remission of sins. In Exod. xii, *et passim*, the lamb is called the passover. In 1 Cor. xi : 24, 25, the bread and wine are called the body and blood. Now, this intimate union, implied in such language, must be either *opus operatum* (which we shall disprove), or a sealing pledge. For illustration, by what usage of human language could that symbolical act in a feudal investiture, hand-ing to the tenant a green sod cut from the manor conveyed, be called "Livery of seizin;" unless it was understood to represent the conveying and guaranteeing of possession in the land?

And third. When we remember that a sacrament symbolizes not any kind of fact or truth, but one peculiar (c) A Federal **Sign** sort, viz: a covenant; we see that in making is necessarily a **Seal.** a sacrament a symbol and badge, we make it a seal and pledge. For the latter idea is necessarily involved in a federal symbol, which is just the idea of the sacrament. When I shake hands as an indication only of general good will, the act may be merely symbolical; but when I give my hand on a bargain, the symbol inevitably conveys a sealing mean-ing.

Both the Popish and Protestant Scholastics have defined 3. Matter of the Sa-the sacraments as consisting in matter, and crament what? Natu-form. This proceeds upon the Peripatetic ral Foundation for it. analysis, adopted by the scholastic divines. They supposed that the most accurate definition of every ob-ject was made by stating, first the matter, $\ddot{\upsilon}\lambda\eta$, constitutive of the object, and then the form, $\sigma\chi\tilde{\eta}\mu\alpha$ which, when superinduced, dis-criminated that object from every other that was constituted of the same $\ddot{\upsilon}\lambda\eta$. This answers quite correctly, for a concrete ob-ject. Thus: a sword may be defined. Its matter is steel. But any steel is not a sword; there may be steel in a plough-share, or in an ingot, or in a bar. Add the special shape and fashion of the weapon, the form; and we have the idea of a sword. The student will see, that the attempt to extend this mode of definition to spiritual and ecclesiastical concepts is very ques-tionable : such, however, is the point of view, on which this de-finition turns. But here the student must note that, by form is not meant the shape of a material thing, or the formulary, or mode of observance outward; but (the idea of a sacrament be-ing complex) that trait which, when superinduced on the transaction, distinguishes it as a sacrament.   Both agree that the matter of the sacrament consists of a sensible symbol, and of a federal truth of religion symbolized.   The trait of human nature to which the institution of sacraments is accommodated is evidently this : that man being a sensuous being, suggestions prompted by a sensible object, are much more vivid and permanent than those prompted by mental conceptions merely, whether the associated suggestion be of thought, or emotion.   Society offers many illustrations of this mental law, and of useful social formalities founded on it.   What else is the meaning and use of friends, shaking hands?   Of civic ceremonials?   Of the symbolical acts in forming matrimonial vows?   Of commemorative monuments, painting and statues?   On this principle rest also the attractiveness of pilgrimages, the ties of all local associations, and the sacredness attached to the graves of the dust of those we love.

Hence, it is obvious that there will be in every sacrament, some material element, palpable to the senses, and especially to our eye-sight. This element should also be not merely an arbitrary, but a natural sign of the grace signified; that is, it should have some natural analogy to suggest the related grace.   By arbitrary agreement, soldiers have bargained that a certain blast of the trumpet shall signify advance, and algebraists, that a certain mark (+) shall represent addition.   There is no previous analogy.   But in circumcision, the removal of the *preputium* aptly and naturally represents putting away carnality; and results in a hidden, yet indelible mark, graphically signifying the inward renewal of the heart.   In baptism, water, which is the detergent element in nature, as aptly signifies cleansing of guilt and carnality.   In the passover, the sprinkled blood represented the atonement: and the eating of the sacrificed body of the lamb, faith's receptive act, in embracing Jesus Christ for the life of the soul. In the Lord's Supper, the same symbols almost, are retained; i. e., eating something that nourishes; but not in this case animal food, because the typical nature of the passover, contained in "the life which maketh atonement for our sin," had already terminated on Christ the antitype.   But it must be added, that a mere natural analogy does not constitute a sacrament.   The analogy must be selected, and consecrated by the express institution of God.

Hence, a Sacrament has, first, a Significant Material Part.

The Protestant scholastics very properly (if the extremely artificial analysis of the Peripatetics is to be retained at all) declared that the form which constitutes the element and theological truth a sacrament, is the instituted signification.   The Papists make the form of sacrament to consist in the words of institution.   Those words are indeed, in each case, expressive of the appointed signification; whence it may be supposed, that the difference of definition is unimpor-

The Form What?

tant.   But we shall see that the Papists are thereby smoothing
the way for their idea of the sacramental union, involving an
efficiency by *opus operatum*, and the power of the canonical
priest to constitute the ceremonial a sacrament or not, at his
will.

Our Confession declares, c. 27, § 2, that "there is, in every
sacrament, a spiritual relation, or sacramental
4. Sacramental
Union What? union, between the sign and the thing signified ; whence it comes to pass that the names
and effects of the one are attributed to the other."   Instances of
this sacramental language have been already given, (p. 729.)
Others may be found, where the grace is named by the sign,
in Matt. xxvi: 27, 28 ; 1 Pet. iii ; 21 ; Rom. vi: 4 ; Col. ii: 11,
12, &c.   This sacramental union is defined by the Confession
as " spiritual relation," and by Turretin, as a " relative and
moral union."   The latter repudiates the proposition, that it is
a " spiritual union;" but he repudiates it in the sense in which it
is asserted by Papists, who mean by it a literal connection of
the spiritual benefit with the material element, such that it is
conferred wherever the element is *ex opere operato*.   Turretin's
" moral relation "means the same with our Confession's " spiritual relation."   Both, of course, imply that this relation only is
real in those cases in which the recipient partakes with proper
state of heart.   In such cases (only), the elements are the
means and channels of gracious benefits, not in virtue of a physical union of the grace to the elements, but of their adaptation
and God's appointment and purpose, and the Holy Ghost's
influence.

Should any one assert a different union from that of the
Confession, he would be refuted by common
The Union not sense, which pronounces the absurdity of the
Physical. whole notion of the conveyance of spiritual
benefits by a physical power through a physical union.   It is
nothing better than an instance of a religious jugglery.   He is
opposed by the Old Testament, which declares its sacraments
to be only signs and seals of grace embraced through faith.
He is contradicted by the general tenour of the New Testament, which always conditions our participation of saving blessings on our state of heart.   And he is inconsistent with himself ;
for if the tie connecting the grace with the element were a
physical tie, the grace ought to go wherever the element goes.
It is so with the tie between substance and attributes, in every
other case.   If it is the nature of fire to burn, then fire surely
burns him whom it touches, whether it be conveyed to him
by friend or foe, by design or chance, in anger or in friendship.
Then, the intention of the priest, and the state of mortal sin in
the recipient ought to make no difference whatever as to the
gracious efficacy.   In placing these limitations, the Papist has
really given up his position ; he has virtually admitted that the

sacramental union is only a relation of instituted moral influence. But if it is such, then its efficacy must be tested just like other moral influence exerted by the Holy Ghost. Are any of them exerted, can they be exerted, any otherwise than through the intelligent embracing and acting upon the truth by the soul of the subject? The same topic will be more fully discussed when we consider the claim of *opus operatum*.

5. But two New Testament Sacraments. Rome has Seven. All Protestants are agreed that among the religious rites instituted by God for the New Testament Churches, there are but two, which meet the definition of a sacrament: Baptism and the Lord's supper. As they obviously present all the requisites, and as there is no dispute concerning their claim, we shall not argue it, but proceed to consider the pretensions of the five other so-called sacraments of the Romish Church: confirmation, penance, orders, matrimony, and extreme unction. To prove that the sacraments are seven, the Roman Catechism seems to rely chiefly on this argument: As there are seven things in physical life which are essential to the propagation and well-being of man and of society, that men be born, grow, be nourished, be healed when sick, be strengthened when weak, have rulers to govern them, and rear children lawfully; so in the analagous life of the Spirit, there are seven essential wants, to each of which a sacrament answers. In baptism the soul is born unto Christ, by confirmation we grow, in the eucharist we are fed with heavenly nourishment, in penance the soul is medicined for the returns of the diseases of sin, in extreme unction it is strengthened for its contest with the last enemy, in orders the spiritual magistracy is instituted, and in matrimony the production of legitimate offspring is secured. The answer to all this trifling is obvious, that by the same argument it would be as easy to make a dozen sacraments as seven: one to answer to man's home and shelter, one to his raiment to cover him, one to his fire to warm him, &c., &c., for these also are necessaries. But to proceed to details.

Confirmation no Sacrament. 1.   Confirmation is not a sacrament of the New Testament, because it utterly lacks the divine institution. The imposition of hands practiced in Acts viii: 17, and xix: 6, and mentioned in Heb. vi: 2, was a rite intended to confer the miraculous charisms of the Holy Ghost, and therefore peculiar to the apostolic age, and purely temporary. The evidences of this fact are presented in the exposition of Acts.* Let Rome or Canterbury so confer the Holy Ghost, by their imposition of hands, that they shall make men prophesy and speak with tongues (Acts xix: 6), and we will believe. Again: It is the sheerest blunder to pretend to find this rite of confirmation in any of those pass-

---

* See a crucial investigation of this point in my essay, "Prelacy a Blunder."— *Southern Presbyterian Review.* January 1876.

ages where apostles are said to "confirm" (Acts xiv : 22, στηρίζων) the churches, or the souls of the brethren. The context, dispassionately viewed, will show that this was merely the instructions and encouragements addressed to them by the apostles' prayers and preachings. For these reasons, and because the Scriptures direct us to expect in baptism and the Lord's Supper all the increments of grace which Christians receive through any sacramental channel, we do not hold modern confirmation to be a scriptural rite at all. But if it were, it could not be a sacrament, for two fatal reasons: that it has no material element (for the oil or chrism is of purely human addition, without one syllable of scriptural authority); and it has nc promise of grace attached to it by any divine institution. It seals no pledge God has given.

2. Papists profess to find the matter of the sacrament of
Penance No Sacrament. penance in the penitent's three exercises of contrition, confession and satisfaction; and its form in the priest's absolution. Now, in the case of sins which scandalize the Church openly, a confession to man is required by the New Testament, and a profession of contrition. And when such profession is credible, it is proper for the minister to pronounce the acquittal of the offending brother from Church censure. And this is the only case in which anything like confession and absolution is enjoined as an ecclesiastical rite in the New Testament. The only plausible case cited by Rome, that of Jas. v : 16, is non-ecclesiastical, because it is mutual confession, and its object is mutual prayers for each other's forgiveness. That would be a queer sacrament in which recipient should turn the tables on administrator, giving him the elements and conferring the grace! Having limited scriptural confession and absolution to the single case defined above, we find overwhelming reasons why, in that case, they cannot compose a sacrament. There is no element to symbolize the grace promised; for by what title can a set of feelings and acts in the penitent be called a material element? If this be waived, there is no analogy between this pretended element, and a symbolized grace; for contrition and confession do not represent, they are themselves graces, if genuine. There is no divine warrant, in words of institution, authorizing the minister to announce a divine grace; for all he is authorized to announce is acquittal from Church discipline. "Who can forgive sins but God only?" And last: It is the nature of a sacrament to be partaken by all alike who are within the covenant. But scriptural penance is appropriate only to the exceptional cases of those communicants who have scandalized their profession. The additions which the Papists have made, of auricular confession and satisfaction, greatly aggravate the objections.

3. The formulary for extreme unction may be found de-

Extreme Unction
No Sacrament.

scribed in Turrettin and others. **The only** places of Scripture cited in its support are Mark vi : 13, and Jas. v : 14. These cases so obviously fail to bear out the Popish sacrament that many of their own writers confess it. The objects were different; the apostles annointed to heal the bodies; the priests do it to prepare them for dying. The apostles anointed all sick persons who called on them, baptized, unbaptized, those in mortal sin; sacraments are properly only for Church members. The effect in the apostles' case was miraculous : can Rome claim this? And there can be no sacrament, because the priest has no divine institution and promise on which to proceed.

Orders No Sacrament.

4. Orders cannot be a sacrament, although when stripped of its superstitious additions, a New Testament rite. For it has no element. The imposition of hands with prayer (chrism, &c., is all extra-scriptural) is but an action, not an element. It has no saving grace connected with it, by any promise or word of institution. As has been shown by my colleague, in his course, ordination confers no grace, but only recognizes its possession. According to Rome, the action which she preposterously elevates into a matter, is not uniform ; but as there are seven orders of clergy, there are several different ceremonials enjoined in the different cases. And last: only one Christian out of a number is ordained to any office: whereas a sacrament is for all equally, who are in the covenant.

5. For the sacramental character of matrimony, the only showing of scriptural defence is the vulgate translation of Eph. v : 32 : " *Hoc est sacramentum magnum.*" Surely a mistranslation of a bad version is a bad foundation on which to build a Bible-claim ! And then, as has been well remarked, the great μυστήριον on which Paul remarks, is not the marriage relation at all, but the mystical union of Christ to His people. In matrimony there is no sacramental element at all, no divine warrant for sacramental institution, no grace of redemption signed and sealed to the recipients. And to crown the absurdity, the rite is not limited to God's people, but is equally valid among Pagans ! Indeed, marriage is a civil contract, and not an ecclesiastical one. Yet Rome has found it to her interest to lay her hand on the rite, and thus to elevate the question of divorce into an ecclesiastical one, and a *causa major.*

6. Sacraments of Old Testament Two. Sacrifices Not Sacraments, and Why.

As to the number of sacraments under the Old Testament dispensation Calvinistic divines are not agreed Some seem inclined to regard any or every symbolical rite there found as a sacrament. Others, far more correctly, as I conceive, limit them to two : circumcision and the passover. The claim of these two to be sacraments need hardly be much argued, inasmuch as it is not disputed. They are symbols

instituted by God; they have each their elements, bearing a
significant relation to the grace represented : the thing represented was in each case federal, so that they not only signified,
but sealed or pledged the benefits of a covenant.

But the various typical sacrifices of the Hebrews cannot
be properly regarded as sacraments, for the very reason that
they were mere types. (The passover also was a type, in that
it was a sacrifice proper, but it was also more than a type, a
commemorative and sealing ordinance). For a type points forward to an antitype to come. A sacrament points back to a
covenant already concluded. The type does not actually confer the good symbolized, but holds the soul in suspense, waiting
for it. The sacrament seals a present possession to the worthy
receiver. This was as true of the two Old Testament sacraments as of the New. See Rom. iv : 11 ; Exod. xii : 13. To
the obedient and observant Hebrew, the passover was, on the
night of its institution, the sign and seal of the remission of
death, bodily and spiritual death, the proper penalty of sin,
visited that night on a part of the Egyptians ; and doubtless, in
all subsequent ages, the truly believing Hebrew found it the
consoling pledge of a present and actual (not typical) remission
and spiritual life, through the merit of the " Lamb of God."
Again, a sacrament is a holy ordinance, to be observed alike by
all who are within the covenant. But many of the sacrifices
were adapted only to exceptional cases : as the Nazarites, the
trespass offering, the sacrifice for the purification of women, &c.

The question whether the sacraments of the Old and New
Sacraments of Both Testaments are the same substantially in
Testaments Same in their signification and efficacy will be found
Signification. in the sequel one of prime importance. The
grounds on which we assert their substantial identity are these.

(a.) Presumptively : The covenant of grace is the same
under the two testaments, offering the same blessing, redemption ; through the same agencies, justification and sanctification through the work of Christ and the Holy Ghost. Hence,
it is natural to suppose that sacraments, especially when sealing
the same covenant graces, should operate in substantially the
same way. (b.) The identity of the covenant, and of the
means of sealing it, is strongly implied by Paul, 1 Cor. x: 1-4,
when he says there was a sense in which the Hebrew Church
possessed baptism and the Lord's supper. Turrettin very
strangely argues from this, and deals with objections, as though
he understood the Apostle to teach that the Hebrews of the
Exodus had literally and formally a real sacrament of baptism,
and the supper, in the passage of the Red Sea, and the eating
and drinking of the Manna and water of Massah. This seems
to me to obscure the argument; and it would certainly have
this effect : that we must teach thet Israel had four sacraments
instead of two. The scope of the Apostle is, to show that par-

ticipation in sealing ordinances and ecclesiastical privileges does not ensure salvation. For Israel all shared these wondrous sealings to God, yet many of them perished. And to strengthen the analogy he compares them to the New Testament sacraments. Now, if Israel's consecration to God in this Exodus was virtually a baptizing and a Eucharist, we infer that the spirit of the Israelitish ordinances was not essentially different from that of the New Testament. The scope of the Apostle necessitates this view. His design was, to stimulate to watchfulness, by showing that sacraments alone do not guarantee our salvation. This premise he proves, from the case of the Israelites who, though enjoying their sacraments, perished by unbelief. If the New Testament sacraments differed from the Old in possessing *opus operatum* power, as Rome claims they do, then the logic of the Apostle would be shameful sophism. (c.) The supper is called by the name of the passover. I Cor. v: 7, 8. And the baptism is declared to be, Col. ii: 11, 12, the New Testament circumcision. (d.) The supper came in the room of the passover, as is manifest from the circumstances of its institution, and the baptism came in the room of circumcision; compare Gen. xvii: 11, with Matt. xxviii: 19. See Acts ii: 38, 39. And, last, circumcision and baptism signify and seal the same graces. This will be manifest from a comparison of Gen. xvii: 13, 14, with Acts ii: 41; Deut. x: 16, or xxx: 6, with Jno. iii: 5, or with Titus iii: 5, and Eph. v; 26; Acts vii: 8, with Rom. vi: 3, 4; Rom. iv: 11, with Acts ii: 38, and xxii: 16. We here learn that each sacrament signified entrance into the visible Church, remission of sin, regeneration, and the engagement to be the Lord's. So the passover and the supper signify substantially the same. In our passover, the Lamb of God is represented as slain, the blood as sprinkled, our souls feed upon Him by faith, and the consequence is that God's wrath passeth over us, and our souls live.

LECTURE LXII.

THE SACRAMENTS. — Continued.

THE Council of Trent asserts (Ses. 7 canon 11), that the
intention of doing at least what the Church proposes to do,

7. Rome's Doc-
trine of Intention.

is necessary in the administrator, to make
the sacraments valid. Some popish divines
are so accommodating as to teach, that if this
intention is habitual or virtual, though not present, because of
inattention, in the mind of the administrator at the moment of
pronouncing the words of institution, it is still valid ; and some
even say, that though the officiating person have heretical
notions of the efficacy of the Sacrament, e. g., the Presbyterian notion, and honestly intends a Sacrament, as he understands it, it is valid. Now, there is obviously a sense, in which
the validity of sacramental acts, depends on the intention of the
parties. If, for instance, a frivolous or profane clergyman
should, in a moment of levity, use the proper elements, and pronounce the proper words of institution, for purposes of mockery
or sinful sport, it would certainly not be a sacrament. But this
is a lack of intention, of a far different kind from the popish.
There would be neither the proper place, time, nor circumstances of a divine rite. The profanity of purpose would be
manifest and overt : and all parties would be guilty of it. The
participation on both sides, would be a high act of profanity.
But where the proper places, times and attendant circumstances
exist, so far as the honest worshipper can judge ; and all the
divine institution essential to the validity of the right is regularly performed with an appearance of religious sincerity and
solemnity, there we deny that the sincere participant can be

*47

deprived of the sacramental benefit, by the clergyman's secret lack of intention. And this: because

(a.) It is the opinion of all the Protestant divines, even

Refutation. including Calvin (Inst. Bk. iv: ch. 14), that the gracious efficacy of the sacraments is generally like that of the word. The sacraments are but an acted word, and a promise in symbol. They effect their gracious result through the Holy Ghost cultivating intelligent faith, etc. The efficacy of the word is not wholly dependent on the motives of him who conveys it. God sometimes saves a soul by a message delivered through a wicked man. Why may not it be thus with a sacrament ?

(b.) If the clergyman lack the right intention, that is simply his personal sin. It is preposterous to represent God as suspending the fate of a soul, or its edification, absolutely upon the good conduct of another fellow-sinner, whose secret fault that soul can neither prevent, nor even detect till too late. This is not Scripture. Prov. ix: 12; Rom. xiv: 4. This objection to Rome's doctrine is peculiarly forcible against her, because she represents the valid enjoyment of sacraments, as essential to salvation : and because she herself teaches that the validity of the sacraments is not dependent on the personal character of the clergyman, not even though he be in mortal sin. Why should this one sin, which is precisely a personal sin of the officiator, no more, no less, be an exception ?

(c.) The possible consequences of the doctrine, as pointed out by Turrettin, Dick, etc., are such as amount to a *reductio ad absurdum*. If it were true, it would bring in question the validity of any sacrament, of every priest's baptism and ordination, the validity of the Apostolic Succession at every link, and of every mass : so that the worshipper would never know, while worshipping the wafer, whether he were guilty of idolatry or not, even on Popish principles. According to the Canon Law, all orders conferred on unbaptized persons are null. Hence, if there is any uncertainty that the priest baptizing the Pope had the intention, there is the same uncertainty whether every grade of ordination he received, from the deaconship up to the papal, is not void ; and every clerical act he ever performed therefore invalid. Papists endeavour to evade this terrible consequence by saying that we have the moral evidence of human testimony, that the priests giving us the sacraments had the intention; and this is all the Protestant can have of his own baptism in infancy, because he was too young to know; and had to take the fact on the assertion of his parents or others. I reply : there are two vital differences: The Protestant does not believe water baptism essential to his redemption; an unconscious mistake in the fact would not be fatal. Water baptism is an overt act, cognizable by the senses, and a proper subject of authentic and complete testimony, by concurrent witnesses; but intention is a secret act of soul, not cognizable by any other than the priest, and impossible to be verified by any concurrent testimony.

Last: This doctrine is totally devoid of Bible support.

But these tremendous difficulties have not *Motive for the Dogma.* prevented Rome from asserting the doctrine.

Her purpose is to hold the laity in the most absolute and terrible dependence on the priesthood. She tells them that without valid sacraments it is impossible to be saved; and that even where they have the canonical form of a sacrament, they may utterly fail of getting the sacrament itself, through the priest's secret will; and may never find it out till they wake in hell, and find themselves damned for the want of it. What power could be more portentous?

In the scholastic jargon of Rome, means of grace naturally divide themselves into two classes— **8. Doctrine of Efficacy *ex Opere Operato*.** those which do good *ex opere operato*, and those which only do good *ex opere operantis.* The former do good by the simple performance of the proper ceremonial, without any act or movement of soul in the recipients, accommodating themselves intelligently to the grace signified. The latter only do good when the recipient exercises the appropriate acts of soul; and the good done is dependent on those exercises, as well as on the outward means. Of the latter kind of means is preaching, &c.; but Rome holds that the sacraments all belong to the former. Her meaning, then, is that the mere administration of the sacrament does the appointed good to the recipient, provided he is not in a state of mortal sin, whether he exercises suitable frames or not. So Council of Trent, Sess. 7, Canon, 6–8. But Romish Theologians are far from being of one mind, as to the nature of this immediate and absolute efficacy.

Their views may be grouped with tolerable accuracy under *Phases of it.* two classes. One class, embracing the Jesuit and more Popish Papists, regard the *opus operatum* efficacy as a proper and literal effect of the sacramental element and words of institution, by their own immediate causation. They do not, and cannot explain the nature of this causation, unless it be literally physical; and then it is absurd. The other class, including Jansenists, and the more spiritual, regard the sacramental efficacy as spiritual—i. e., as the almighty redeeming influence of Christ and the Holy Ghost, purchased for sinners by Christ; which spiritual influence they suppose God has been pleased in His mercy to tie by a constant purpose, and gracious promise, to the sacraments of the Church canonically administered, by a tie gracious and positive, yet absolute and unconditioned, so that the sacramental efficacy goes to every human being to whom the elements go with the proper word of institution, whether the recipient exercise faith or not. That is, God has been pleased, in His sovereign mercy to the Church, to make her sacraments the essential and unfailing channels of His spiritual grace. The opinion of the Prelatic Fathers seems to have been intermediate—that no one got saving grace except through the sacramental channel, (excepting the doubtful case of the uncovenanted mercies) out that in order to get grace through that channel, faith and repentance were also necessary. (See Augustine, in Calvin's *ubi supra*). And such is probably the real opinion of High Church Episcopalians, and of Campbellites, as to the grace of remission.

Now, Protestants believe that the sacraments, under proper Protestant View. circumstances, are not a hollow shell, devoid of gracious efficacy. Nor is their use that of a mere badge. But they are not the channels or vehicles for acquiring the saving grace first; inasmuch as the possession of those graces is a necessary prerequisite to proper participation in adults. The efficacy of the sacrament, therefore, is in no case more than to strengthen and nourish saving graces. And that efficacy they carry only as moral means of spiritual influences; so that the whole benefit depends on an intelligent, believing and penitent reception. And every believer has the graces of redemption in such degree as to save his soul, if a a true believer, whether he has any sacraments or not. See Confession of Faith, ch. xxvii : § 3. In this sense we deny the *opus operat.*

(a) Because that doctrine is contradicted by the analogy Proved. By Analo- of the mode in which the Word operates. gous Operation of As we have stated, Protestant divines admit Word. no generic difference between the mode in which the Holy Ghost works in the Word, and in the sacraments. The form of a sacrament is the instituted significance of it. But that significance is only learned in the Scriptures, and the word of institution is to be found, as well as its explanation, in the same place. The sacrament, without the intelligent signification, is dumb: it is naught. Scripture alone gives it its significance. Sacraments are but the word symbolized; the covenant before expressed in promissory language, now expressed in sphragistic symbols. But now, what is more clear, than that the word depends for its efficacy, on the believing and active reception of the sinner's soul? See 2 Cor. iii : 6; Heb. iv : 2, *et passim.* The same thing is true of the sacraments.

(b) The sacraments are defined in the Scriptures as signs and By Sphragistic seals, Rom. iv : 11; Gen. xvii : 10. Now to Character. signify and to promise a thing is different from doing it. Where the effect is present, the sign and pledge thereof is superseded. When the money is paid, the bond that engaged for its payment is done with. To make the sacraments effect redemption *ex opere operato*, therefore destroys their sacramental nature. But more: They are seals of a covenant. That Covenant, as far as man is a party (and in the sacrament, the recipient is one party), was suspended on an instrumental condition, a penitent and obedient faith. How can the seal have a more immediate and absolute efficiency than the covenant of which it is a seal. That covenant gives it all its force. It is to evade this fatal argument, that Bellarmine labours, with his and our enemies, the Socinians, to prove that sacraments are not seals.

(c) The sacraments cannot confer redeeming grace *ex* *opere operato*, because, in every adult, proper participation presupposes saving grace in exercise. See Rom. iv : 11, last clause, Acts viii ; 35, 36, 37; ix : 11 with 18; x : 34 with 47; Mark xvi : 16; 1 Peter iii : 21; Heb. xi : 6; 1 Cor. xi : 28, 29; v : 7, 8. Hence:

By Grace Presupposed.

(d) Several in Scripture were saved without any sacraments, as the thief on the cross. Cornelius, we have seen, and Abraham, were already in a state of redemption, before their participation in the sacraments. Now, inasmuch as we have proved that a true believer once in a state of grace can never fall totally away, we may say that Abraham and Cornelius were already redeemed. Jno. iii : 36; v : 24. And the overwhelming proof that the sacraments have no intrinsic efficacy, is in this glaring fact, that multitudes partake them, with what Rome calls canonical regularity, who never exhibit in their lives or death, one mark of Christian character. Nor will it avail for Rome to say, that they afterward lost the grace by committing mortal sin: for the Scriptures say that the redeemed soul cannot fall away into mortal sin: and multitudes exhibit their total depravity, not after a subsequent backsliding, but from the hour they leave the sacramental altar, by an unbroken life of sin.

By Instances of Salvation Without Sacraments.

(e) The claim of uniform and absolute efficiency, in its grosser form, is absolute absurdity. How can physical, material elements, with a word of institution pronounced over them (which of itself can go no farther into the hearer, than the tympanum of his ear), effect a moral and spiritual change? It is vile jugglery: degrading to Christianity, and reducing the holy sacraments to a pagan incantation. But the Jesuit pleads, that we see ten thousand cases, where the external physical world produces mental and moral effects, through sensation. We reply that this is not true in the sense necessary to support their doctrine. Sensation is not the efficient, but only the occasional cause of moral feeling, volition, &c. The efficient cause is in the mind's own dispositions and free agency. The confusion of thought in this plea is the same with that made by the sensualistic psychologist, when he mistakes inducement for motive.

De Absurdis.

But the sophism points us to the cause of a great fact in Church History. That fact is, that somehow, the *opus operatum* doctrine of the sacraments tends to accompany Pelagian views of human nature and grace. One has only to recall the semi-Pelagian tendencies of the Greek Church, of the Latin Church, notwithstanding its strong Augustinian impulse in its earlier ages, of the English and American Ritualists, and last, of the community founded by Alex. Campbell. These facts are too uniform for chance: they betray a causation. From the point of view just gained, we can easily detect it. The sacraments are external ordinances in this: that they present truth (in symbol) objectively. Hence it is impossible for a rational man to persuade himself that means, which common sense can only apprehend as didactic, if not fetiches, can of themselves cause spiritual acts of soul, (graces) on any other view of the will, than that of the Pelagian. If volitions and emotions are decisively regulated by dispositions, then the *a priori* revolution of the disposition, by the Holy Spirit, must be in order to the wholesome influence of any objective. But that is the Protestant view of a sacrament. If the sacrament occasions spiritual states and acts *ex opere operato*, it can only be on condition of the will's self-determination. Thus, every consistent Ritualist becomes a Pelagian. What is regeneration by moral suasion, except an *opus operatum* effect of the Word?

But if the other view of the *opus operatum* be urged: that the efficiency is spiritual, and results, not from the direct causation of the rite itself, but from the power of God graciously and sovereignly connected therewith; we demand the revealed warrant. Where is the promise to the Church from God, that this connection shall be absolute? The Scriptures are silent, when properly interpreted. The burden of proof must rest on the assertors. They have no text which meets the demand. Indeed, in many places the Scriptures explicitly declare the contrary See, for example, Deut. x : 16 ; Jer. iv : 4 ; Luke xiii : 26, 27 ; 1 Cor. xi : 29 ; Rom. ii : 25th to end. It may be urged that some of these places, and especially the last, speak of the sacraments of the old dispensation. It is in the vain hope of breaking the force of these unanswerable texts, that Rome asserts an essential difference between the sacraments of the old and the new dispensation, saying that the former only symbolize, while the latter work, saving graces. The student can now see the polemic interest Rome has in widening the differences between the Old Testament and the New, as much as possible, and in recognizing the least of gospel features in the Old. But I have proved that the same gospel is in both Testaments, and that there is no generic difference in the way the sacraments of the two exhibit grace. Here, in part, is the importance of that argument. Especially do I take my stand on 1 Cor. x : 1–10, and prove thence that the sacraments of the

New Testament were viewed by the Apostle, as no more effective, *ex opere operato*, than those of the Old. Thus, all the demonstrations of the inefficacy of circumcision without repentance and faith, apply against the Ritualist and Papist.

The whole strain of Scripture must strike every candid mind, as opposed to this theory of sacra-

Whole Tenour of Promises against it. mental grace. God portrays his gospel as a spiritual religion, the contrast of a formalistic one. He everywhere heaps scorn on mere formalism. As the man thinketh in his heart, so is he. To teach that a man becomes a Christian by the force of any ceremony, is totally opposite to all this. The argument may be placed in an exceedingly definite light thus. Let them deny the sphragistic nature of the sacraments as they may, it cannot be concealed. Least of all, can the emblematic relation between gospel promises and sacraments be denied. Now the emblem always means just what it is appointed didactically to emblematize: no more. The seal binds only to what is written above in the bond to which it is appended. In every contest as to the intent of a seal, this solution is so obvious, that any other is ridiculous: "Look into the bond, and see what is written above." The Bible is the bond. When we read there, we universally find redemption promised to faith and repentance. The seal appended beneath cannot contradict the body of the instrument.

Alien as the doctrine we refute is, from the whole letter and

Motive of Doctrine. spirit of Scripture; it has an element of popularity, which will always secure numerous votaries, until grace undeceives them. It chimes in with the superstition natural to a soul dead in sin. It is delightful to the soul which hates true repentance, and loves its spiritual laziness, and abhors thorough-going heart religion, and yet dreads hell, to be taught that it can be equipped for heaven, without these arduous means, by an easy piece of ecclesiastical legerdemain.

(f) But Papists and Prelatists quote a class of passages,

Scriptures Reconciled. which they claim to give an immediate efficiency to the rite itself. See Jno. iii : 5 ; Acts ii : 38 ; xxii : 16 ; Eph. v : 26 ; 1 Cor. x : 17 ; Rom. vi : 3 ; Luke xxii : 19, 20, &c. Protestants explain these passages in consistency with their views, by saying that they are all expressions based on the sacramental union, and to be explained in consistency with it : e. g., in Jno. iii : 5, the birth of the water means the birth by that which the water represents, the Holy Ghost. Nicodemus' great error was, that he had put too much dependence on water. He had relied too much on his "divers baptisms" and hand-washings. Christ says to him, that he must have a cleansing more efficacious than that by water, the cleansing of the Spirit. That He does not mean to assert for water baptism an equal effect and necessity with regeneration, is plain from the fact that in all the subsequent verses, he omits the water wholly. The propriety of this interpretation of all the similar places is defended, first by the analogous case of the hypostatic union in Christ's person, where God is in one place spoken of as having blood, and the Prince of Life as dying. Papists agree with us, that in virtue of the union of the two natures in one person, the person, even when denominated by the one nature, is represented as doing what, in strictness of speech, the other alone could do. So, in the sacraments, there are suggested two things—the rite, and the grace signified by the rite. How natural, then, that a Hebrew should atrribute to the rite, by figure, what the answering grace really effects? In the second place, this probability is greatly strengthened by noticing the way, natural to Hebrew mind, of speaking concerning all other symbols, as types, &c. The symbol is almost uniformly said to be the thing symbolized; when the meaning is, that it represents it. Third: our interpretation of these passages is adopted by Scripture itself, in one of the very strongest instances, thus authorizing our view of the exegesis of the whole class. See 1 Pet. iii; 21. Here, first baptism is said to save us, as the ark saved Noah. What expression could be stronger? But yet the Apostle explains himself by saying, it is not the putting away of the filth of the flesh which effects it, but the answer ($\dot{\epsilon}\pi\epsilon\rho\dot{\omega}\tau\eta\mu\alpha$) of a good conscience towards God. These words ascribe the efficacy of the sacrament to the honesty of the participant's confession; and this whether with Turrettin and Winer we translate "request to God," or with Neander and Robinson, "Sponsio." Fourth. If men will persist in making the above Scriptures teach the *opus operatum*, the only result will be that the Scripture will be made to contradict itself; for it is impossible to explain away all the proof-texts we have arrayed.

This difference between us and Rome is fundamental; because she teaches men to depend essentially on the wrong trust for salvation. The result must be ruin of souls.

The question of the necessity of the sacraments in order to salvation, is nearly connected with the pre-

9. Sacraments, in What Sense Necessary.

vious one. This is indicated by the fact that the same persons usually hold their essential necessity, and their efficacy *ex opere operato*. And this consistently; for if the sacraments have that marvellous virtue, it can hardly be supposed that man can safely lack them.

Now, there is a sense in which the neglect of the sacraments would destroy the soul. To observe them is God's command. He who willingly disobeys this command, and perseveres, will thereby destroy his soul, just for the same reason that any wilful disobedience will. But then, it is not the lack of the sacraments. but the impenitent state of the soul, which is the true cause of ruin. Turrettin; "*Eorum non privatio, sed con-*

temptus damnat." The command to observe them is not of perpetual and original, but only of positive institution; and owes its force over our consciences to the mere precept of God. Hence they should be regarded from the same general point of view with other positive rites. We sustain this:

(a) By reference to the free and spiritual character of the

Arguments.

gospel plan as indicated throughout Scripture. God has not tied His grace to forms, places, or sacerdotal orders. All men alike have access to His redeeming mercy, provided their hearts desire it, and under all outward circumstances. Jno. iv : 21, 23 ; Luke xviii : 14, &c.

(b). We infer the same thing from the numerous and exceedingly explicit passages which promise the immediate bestowal of redeeming grace, and mention no other term than believing. Some of them do it in terms which hardly admit of evasion. E. g., Jno. v : 24; vi : 29. Does not this seem to say that believing alone puts the soul in possession of redemption ? True the Papist may say that one passage of Scripture should be completed by another; and that in other places (e. g., Jno. iii : 5 ; Mark xvi : 16) the observance of the sacrament is coupled with the believing grace, as a term of salvation. But when those passages are well understood, it is seen that the importance of the outward sacrament depends wholly on the sacramental union. We repeat, that the places in which faith alone is mentioned as the instrumental condition, are so numerous, so explicit, and some of them professed answers to questions so distinct as (Acts xvi : 31), that it is simply incredible the Holy Ghost would have so omitted the mention of the sacraments if they were essential.

(c). But their nature shows they are not. They are sensible signs of an inward grace. The reception of them therefore implies the possession of grace ; a sufficient proof it does not originate it.

(d). This leads us to add, that many have actually been saved without any sacraments. Abraham and Cornelius were both in a state of grace before they partook of any sacrament. The penitent thief went to paradise without ever partaking Circumcision could not be administered till the eighth day of the Hebrew infant's life : and doubtless many died uncircumcised in the first week of their life. Were these all lost ? This Popish doctrine gives a frightful view of the condition of the infants of Pagans : that forsooth, because they are debarred from the sacrament of baptism, among the millions who die without actual transgression, there is not one elect infant ! Are all these lost ?

Last, the Scriptures everywhere hold out the truth, that the Word is the great means of redemption; and it is plainly indicated that it is the only essential means. See Rom. x : 14 : 2 Tim. iii : 15.

The traditions and usages of the Church as to lay admin-
10. Sacraments   istration of sacraments have been in the
Should be Adminis-   main very uniform.   It has always been con-
tered Only by Minis-   demned. The inordinate importance attached
ters.
to baptism did indeed lead the Romish
Church, (and after her, the English), to decide that the baptism
of a layman, and even of a woman, was valid, though irregular,
if the child was *in extremis*, and no priest at hand.   Even this,
most Presbyterians would condemn as utterly invalid.   The
German antiquaries (e. g., Mosheim) sometimes assert that in
the primitive Church any person who made a convert felt authorized to baptize him.   This appears to me very doubtful.
Ignatius, for instance, who is, if genuine, one of the earliest
Apostolic Fathers, says that the Eucharist which the Bishop
celebrates should alone be considered a valid one; and that no
one should presume to baptize, except the Bishop, or one commissioned by him.   This is certainly the language of uniform
antiquity, expressed in Councils and Fathers.   Nor is it merely
the result of clerical ambition and exclusiveness.   Since the sacraments are a solemn and formal representation of Gospel truth
by symbols, a sort of pantomimic Word, it seems most reasonable that the exhibition of them should be reserved to the same
class to whom is committed the authoritative preaching of the
Word.   And it may be urged, with yet more force, that since
the presbyters, and especially the pastor of the Church, are the
guardians of the sealing ordinances, responsible for their defence against abuse and profanation, it is reasonable, yea, necessary, that they should have the control of their administration.
This consideration seems to me to have the force of a just and
necessary inference.   Again the great commission (Matt. xxviii;
19; Mark xvi: 15) seems evidently to give the duties of preaching and baptizing to the same persons.   The persons primarily
addressed were the apostles; but the apostles as representative
of the whole Church.   To deny this would be to deny to all but
apostles authority to preach, and a share in the gracious promise
of Christ's presence which accompanies the commission; and
this again would compel us to admit that the right to preach,
and the promise of Christ's blessing, have been lost to the
whole Church for nearly 1800 years, or else to accept the Episcopal conclusion that the apostolic office still continues. Hence,
the argument from the commission gives only probable proof.
This, however, is strengthened by the fact that there is no instance in Scripture of any sacraments administered by any except men who were ministers of the gospel, either by charism,
or by ordination.   Perhaps the most practical argument against
lay administration of sacraments is, from the intolerable disorders and divisions, which have always arisen, and must ever
arise, from such a usage.   The sacraments have this use among
others, to be badges and pledges of Church membership.   The

control of them cannot therefore be given to others than the appointed rulers of the Church: to do so is utter disorganization.

The Council of Trent teaches that the three sacraments of baptism, confirmation and orders, can never be repeated, because they imprint on the recipient an indelible character. They have not, indeed, been able to decide what this character is, nor on what part of man it is imprinted. It cannot be the graces of redemption; because Rome teaches that they may all be lost by the true believer, through backsliding, while this character can never be lost, to whatever apostasy the man may sink: and because she teaches that the recipient in a state of mortal sin receives no graces through the sacrament, yet he would receive the "character." And again, all the sacraments confer grace, whereas only these three confer "character" indelibly. Nor can it be any other sort of qualification for office (in ordination, for instance), for men lose all qualification through infirmity, dotage, or heresy; yet they never lose the "character." Nor can they decide on what it is imprinted, whether on the body, mind, conscience, or affections. This uncertainty, together with the utter silence of the Scriptures, is the sufficient refutation of the absurdity. If you seek for the motive of Rome in endorsing such a doctrine, you will find it in her lust of power. By every baptism she acquires a subject of her ghostly empire, and every ordination, while it confers on the clergyman a ghostly eminence, also binds him in the tenfold bonds of the iron despotism of the canon law. Now, it suits the grasping and despotic temper of Rome to teach that these bonds of allegiance are inexorable: that when they are once incurred, no apostasy, no act of the subject's choice or will, can ever make him less a subject, or enable him to evade the tyrannical hand of his mistress.

11. Indelible Character Refuted.

As to confirmation and orders, we do not feel bound to solve any questions concerning their sacramental character, because we do not believe them to be sacraments. As to baptism, we assign this reason why it is never to be repeated to the same subject like the Lord's supper: It is the initiating sacrament, like circumcision. The man who is in the house needs no repeated introduction into the house. It "signifies our ingrafting into Christ." He who is grafted in once is virtually united, and requires no new union to be constituted.

APPENDIX.

The scriptural doctrine of the sacraments is so vital, so widely corrupted, and so involved in the claims of Prelacy and Apostolic Succession, that it is important for the student to gain a firm grasp of the relation.   Hence I desire, before proceeding to the specific discussion of the two sacraments, to clear up that connection.

Two theories of redemption prevail in Christendom, which are, in fact, essentially opposite.   If one is the gospel of God, the other cannot be ; and it must be condemned as " another gospel," whose teachers ought to be "Anathema, Maranatha." The one of these plans of salvation may be decribed as the high-prelatic ; it is held by the Roman and Greek Churches, and the Episcopalian Ritualists.   It is often called the theory of " sacramental grace ;" not because true Protestants deny all grace through sacraments, but because that theory endeavors to make sacraments essential to grace.   The dogma of tactual succession through prelates from the Apostles, is a corner-stone ; for it teaches that the Apostles transmitted their peculiar office, by ordination, to prelates, and with it, a peculiar χάρισμα of the Holy Ghost, making every " priest " through this laying on of hands, a depository of the spiritual energy, and every " bishop," or Apostle, a " proxy" of the Saviour Himself, endued with the redemptive gifts in the same sense in which He was endued with them by His Father.   Thus, for instance, prelacy interprets Jno. xx : 21.   "As my Father hath sent me, even so send I you."   The theory, then, amounts to this : that Christ's provision for applying redemption to man consisted simply in His instituting on earth a successive, prelatic hierarchy, as His " proxies," empowered to work, through His sacraments, the salvation of submissive participants, by a supernatural power precisely analogous to that by which He enabled Peter to speak in an unknown tongue, and by which Peter and John enabled the lame man to walk.   Let the student grasp distinctly what prelacy means here.   It is, that the " Bishop" (who is literally Apostle,) in ordaining a " priest," does the identical thing which Paul did, Acts xix : 6, to the first Ephesian converts : " when he laid his hands upon them, the Holy Ghost came on them, and they spake with tongues and prophesied ;" and that when this priest baptizes an infant, for instance, he supernaturally removes the disease of original sin by the water and the chrism, as the man whom an Apostle had endued with the χάρισμα of miracle-working healed epilepsy by his touch.   It follows of course, that the agency of these men, divinely endued with the χάρισμα of spiritual healing, and of the sacraments they use, are essential to the reception of redemptive grace.   So, the priestly efficiency, through the sacrament is " ex opere operato," and does its work on all souls to which it is applied, independent of their subjective exercises of receptive knowledge, faith and penitence; provided the obstacle of "mortal sin" be not interposed.

Now, if our, rival theory is true, it is perfectly obvious this scheme of "sacramental grace" is a profane dream, and is related to the Gospel precisely as a fetich, or a Pagan incantation. It is an attempt to cleanse the soul by an act of ecclesiastical jugglery. This enormous profanity is not charged upon every misguided votary of prelacy. As in so many other cases, so here, grace may render men's inward faith better than their dogma; the Holy Spirit may mercifully turn the soul's eye aside from the soul-destroying falsehood of the scheme, to the didactic truths so beautifully taught in the scriptural sacraments and the Word. But the godliness of such semi-prelatists is in spite of, and not because of, the scheme, which is essentially Pagan and not Christian. What a bait this dogma offers to the ambition of one like Simon Magus, greedy of the power of priestcraft, need not be explained. It is not charged that every prelatist adopts the delusion from this damnable motive; many doubtless lean to it from the unconscious prompting of self-importance. It is a fine thing, when a poor mortal can persuade himself that he is the essential channel of eternal life to his fellow, the "proxy" of the Son of God and king of heaven. The major part of the nominal Christian world has gone astray after this baptized paganism, from motives which are natural to sinful beings. They are instinctive superstition—one of the regular consequences of man's fall and apostasy—his unbelieving, sensuous nature, craving, like all other forms of idolatry, the palpable and material as the object of its exercises, and the intense longing of the sinful soul, remorseful and still enamoured of its sin, for some palpable mode of reconciliation without hearty, inward repentance and mortification of sin. As long as men are wicked, superstitious, conscious of guilt and in love with sin, the prelatic scheme will continue to have abundance of followers.

The rival doctrine of the application of redemption is summed up in the words of our Saviour, "Sanctify them through thy truth: Thy word is truth." Or, of the Apostle: "It pleased God, by the foolishness of preaching to save them that believe." (1 Cor. i : 20). "So then, faith cometh by hearing, and hearing by the word of God." (Rom. x : 4–17). Or, of the Evangelist, (Jno. i : 12) "To as many as received Him, to them gave He power (ἐξουσία) to become the sons of God; even to them which believed on His name." Or, of Eph. iii : 17. "Christ dwells in your hearts by faith." Or, of 1 Jno. v : 11, 12. "This is the record, that God hath given to us eternal life, and this life is in His Son. He that hath (ἔχει holds to) the Son, hath the life, and he that hath not the Son of God hath not the life." We learn by the previous chapters, that the "holding" of the

Son is simply faith. To exhaust the Bible-proofs of this view would be to repeat a large part of both Testaments. Ps. xix : 7–10 ; cxix : 9, 93, 98, 104, 130 ; Prov. iv : 13 ; Isaiah xxxiii : 6 ; liii : 11 ; Jer. iii : 15 ; Hos. iv : 6 ; Hab. ii : 14 ; 1 Jno. v : 1 ; 1 Pet. 1 : 23 ; Luke viii : 11 ; 1 Cor. iv : 15 ; Jno. viii : 32 ; v : 24 ; xv : 3 ; Jas. i : 18 ; Acts xiii : 26 ; xx : 32. The prelatic view of sacramental grace conflicts with the whole tenour of Scripture. This constantly teaches, that the purchased redemption is applied by the Holy Ghost, through Gospel truth intelligently believed and embraced, without other conditions or *media :* that hence, all preachers, even inspired Apostles, are only "ministers by whom we believed:" that Christ is the only priest in the universe : that the sacraments are only " means of grace" doing good generally like sound preaching : and that Christ reserves the administering of them to the ministers, not on any hierarchical or sacerdotal ground, but simply on grounds of εὐταξία and didactic propriety.

Now our refutation takes this form : First, that the whole prelatic structure rests on the assumption that whatever is said about the laying on of the Apostles' hands to confer the Holy Ghost, relates to ordination to clerical office. Second : that this reference is a mere blunder, an utter perversion of the Scriptures.

1. As a matter of fact, this unwarranted confusion does present the sole scriptural basis to which prelacy pretends. This we prove by the Romish standards. Rom. Cat. pt. 2, ch. vii, qu. 25, asserting that the administration of the "sacrament of orders" belongs to the bishop, cites Acts vi: 5, 6 ; xiv: 22. 2 Tim. i: 6. An examination of these texts (in the proper place) will show that the very blunder charged is made—Council of Trent, Sess. 23d, *De Ordine.* "The Sacred Scriptures. show—that the power of consecrating, sacrificing and distributing His body and blood, and also of remitting sins, has been delivered to the apostles and their successors in the priesthood." § iii. "Grace is conferred in holy orders." Canon iv. "If anybody says that the Holy Ghost is not given by holy orders, and that accordingly the bishops have no ground to say (to the recipient) " Receive ye the Holy Ghost ; " or that the character is not impressed through this sacrament, etc. let him be accursed." That the grace supposed to be received in orders is not that of sanctification and redemption, is clear from Rome's assertion, that the Canonical priest may, like Judas, wholly lack this. The grace in orders must then be the other ; the miracle working χάρισμα.

The Anglican Church bases its claim, so far as it is sacramentarian, on the same confusion, abusing the same texts. In the form for ordination, the prelate, in laying on hands, says; "Receive ye the Holy Ghost, for the office and work of a bishop in the Church of God, now committed unto thee by the imposition of our hands," &c. So, the Scripture here alluded to, John xx :21, is the one directed to be read before the consecration; and the words which follow are precisely those of 2 Tim. i : 6. The Anglican Church has learned her lessons from Rome well. The prelatic expositors disclose the same foundation for the sacramentarian doctrine. Theophylect, on 2 Tim. i : 6, gives, as the equivalent of the words, διὰ τῆς ἐπιθέςεως τῶν χειρῶν μου, this gloss : Τοῦτ' ἔστι ὅτε σε ἐχειροτόνουν ἐπίσχοπον—thus confounding the appointment to clerical office, with an apostle's bestowal of spiritual gifts. Chrysostom, on Acts vi :8, says : "This man (Stephen) derived a larger grace. But before his ordination he wrought no signs, but only after he was manifested. This was designed to teach them, that grace alone was not sufficient; but that ordination is requisite, in order that the access of the spirit may take place." Dr. Hammond (*Parainesis, Quere.* 5th) "χειροθεσία is answerable to that imposition of hands in ordination, so often mentioned in the New Testament—as generally, when by that laying on of hands, it is said they received the Holy Ghost : where the Holy Ghost contains all the χαρίσματα required for the pastoral function, and also signifies power from on high," &c. Hear him again : "Of this "ceremony thus used" (meaning ordination to the clerical office), several mentions there are. First, Acts viii : 17, where, after Philip the deacon had preached and baptized in Samaria, Peter and John the Apostles came from Jerusalem to perfect the work, and laid hands on them [not on all that were baptized, but on some special person whom they thought meet] and they received the Holy Ghost." Dr. Hammond was high authority with prelatists.

Another evidence of the fatal confusion, which is the basis of their whole scheme, involving the whole body of prelatists, is their own invention of the word, "Simony," to describe the procurement of "orders" by money. This term is confessedly taken from Simon Magus, of Acts viii : and of course it is meant to describe the sin which he proposed to commit, verses 18, 19. Note that the thing Simon craved was not the ability to speak with tongues, or work some such miraculous sign. Possibly he had already received this : as a reprobate Judas had. He desired the ability to confer this power on others. And this criminal proposal, so perfectly defined by Simon's own words, is precisely the thing selected by Rome and the Anglican Church, to denominate the sin of procuring clerical orders by money. The disclosure is complete. Prelacy deems that the thing Peter and John had been doing in Samaria, and the thing Simon wished to do, was transmitting the Apostolic succession by ordination.

It is thus proved, that the sole basis of Scripture which prelacy has to offer is the mistaken notion, that the "laying on of hands ' by which "the Holy Ghost was given," was prelatic ordination. The theory is, that the bishop (Apostle) thus confers a supernatural charism on the priest; by virtue of which the latter works the real presence in the eucharist and the "sacrifice of the altar," remits sin, and cleanses the infant's soul with baptismal water, precisely in the same generic mode in which the primitive disciple, endued with a χάρισμα, wrought a miracle.

II. But we complete the utter destruction of the scheme by proving that their conception of this χειροθεσία is a blunder, and a baseless folly. To effect this, we first describe the true understanding, and then establish it. We assert that this laying on of hands to confer the Holy Ghost was not ordination at all, and did not introduce its recipients into a clerical order, or make them less laymen than before. It was the bestowal of an extraordinary power, for a purely temporal purpose; to demonstrate to unbelievers the divine claim of the new dispensation. See 1 Cor. xiv : 22, with 14, 19; Mark xvi : 15–18; Acts iv : 29, 30; v : 12; Heb. ii : 4, and such like texts. The fact of Christ's resurrection is the corner-stone of the Gospel-evidence. This fact was to be established by the witness of twelve men. An unbelieving world was invited to commit its spiritual destiny to the "say-so" of twelve men, strangers and obscure. It was absolutely essential that God should sustain their witness by some supernatural attestations. See again, Mark xvi : 18; Acts ii : 32, 33. But twelve men could not preach everywhere : whence it was at first equally important that others should be armed with these divine "signs." Through what channel might these other evangelists best receive the power to emit them? The answer displays clearly the consistency of our exposition : It was most suitable that the power in others should come through the twelve witnesses; because thus the "signs" exhibited, reflected back an immediate attestation on their truth. Thus, let us represent to ourselves a child of Cornelius the Centurion, exercising gifts unquestionably supernatural before pagans in Cæsarea. This proves that God has here intervened. But for what end? That boy can be no eye-witness to Christ's resurrection; and he does not claim to be : for he did not see it, and he was not acquainted with Jesus' person and features. But he can say, that he derived his power from the witness, Peter; and, Peter assured him, direct from a risen Christ. Just so far, then, as spectators verify the supernatural character of that boy's performances, they are a divine attestation to Peter's word concerning the resurrection. So Timothy's χαρίσματα were related to the witnessing of Paul, who conferred them. In brief: it was proper that others' ability to exhibit "signs" should proceed visibly from the Apostles, because the use of the signs was to sustain the testimony of the twelve. Hence the rule in the Apostolic day, which the acute Simon so clearly perceived; that it was "through laying on of the Apostles' hands the Holy Ghost was given." And I assert that there is not a case in the New Testament, where any other than an Apostle's hand was employed to confer the Holy Ghost, if any human agency was employed. Search and see. Hence it follows, that since the death of the original twelve, there has never been a human being in the Church who was able to give this gift.

For, the necessity was temporary. After the death of the Apostles, the civilized world was dotted over with churches. The Canon of Scripture was complete. The unbelieving world was furnished with another adequate line of evidence (which has been deepening to our day) in souls sanctified and pagan society purified. The charismatic signs ceased because they were no longer essential. See Luke xvi : 31. The world is now in such relation to the Scripture testimony, as was the Jew of Christ's day.

Now, we claim a powerful and a sufficient proof of the correctness of this theory, in its satisfying consistency. It reconciles everything in the Scripture teachings and history. We claim that it tallies exactly with Paul's prediction of the cessation of the charismatic powers, in 1 Cor. xiii : 8. It explains exactly the date and mode of the cessation of genuine miracles out of the Church. Church historians know how anxiously miracles were claimed by the Fathers down to the 4th (and indeed the present) century, and the obscurity in which the facts in the 2nd and 3rd centuries are involved. Well: on our view, real miracles might have continued just one generation after the Twelve. John, the aged, might have conferred the power on some young evangelist, the year of the former's death. The Church would be naturally reluctant to surrender the splendid endowment. The discrimination between surprising, and truly supernatural events, was crude. The age of "pious frauds" was at hand. Thus, as the genuine miracles faded out, the spurious had their day.

Again: that this laying on of hands was not ordination and did not confer orders at all, and had nothing to do with an apostolic succession, is proved beyond all question, by these points. Paul ordains that a "neophyte" must not be permitted to receive orders. But this endowment was bestowed immediately after baptism; as in Acts viii : 15, 16 ; x : 44, 45 ; xix :6. Soundness in the faith was an absolute requisite to ordination. 1 Tim. ch. iii. These charisms were exercised by unbelievers. 1 Cor. ch. xiii. Again, apostles forbade women to receive orders : these powers were enjoyed by women, and by children. Acts. xxi : 9 : x : 44

Once more : that these endowments were not wrought by ordination is proved by the scriptural rule of election of all deacons and ministers, by the brotherhood, in order to their ordination. This usage proves that the ceremony of orders

48*

did not confer qualification, but only recognized its possession by the candidates; because its prior possession by them furnished to the brotherhood the sole criterion by which they were to judge the candidates suitable persons to vote for. It is on this principle, that the instructions of Acts vi : 2–6; 1 Tim. iii., and Titus i : 5–9, are given. Let this point be pondered.

But when we proceed to the examination of the places claimed by the Prelatists, and the bestowal of the Holy Ghost by putting on of apostles' hands, it can be proved exegetically that each place falls under our theory. We have seen that the main place, perverted by Rome and the Anglican Church, is Jno. xx : 21, 22. To the Protestant, these words are plain enough. Christ is God-man, Redeemer, High Priest, Sacrifice, Advocate and King to believers. These offices He devolves on nobody, but holds them always. He condesends, however, to be "sent" of His Father, in the humble office of preacher in the Church. This office He now devolves on the Twelve. They, as His ministers, are to teach men the terms of pardon : for " who can forgive sin but God only ?" But as they were to be inspired, their teachings of the terms would be authoritative and binding. This needed inspiration had been already promised. Jno. xvi : 13 ; and so had the miraculous attestations which would be requisite. Acts i : 4, 5. But the time was now so near at hand, that Christ renews the promise in the significant act of Jno. xx : 22. This gift of the Holy Ghost was no other than that realized at Pentecost. Acts ii : 4. The proofs are, 1. That Christ already recognized the Eleven as endued with that form of the Holy Ghost's power which works faith, repentance, and salvation. See and compare Matt. xxvi : 75 ; Luke xxii : 31, 32 ; Jno. xxi : 15. Hence, the form promised in that place must have been the only other known in Scripture; that namely, which wrought "signs." 2. Our Lord's words Acts i : 4, 5, prove it. " Wait," saith He, "for the promise of the Father which ye have heard of me." Heard of Him, where ? Evidently in John xx : 21, 22. The fulfilment was to be "not many days hence." This fixes it as the spiritual effusion of Pentecost. But now the anti-prelatic demonstration is perfect; for notoriously, the thing the Holy Ghost enabled the apostles to do at Pentecost was not " the consecration of priests," or the transmitting of an apostolic succession ; but the exhibition of miracles to attest the resurrection.

Peter's own explanation of the Pentecostal endowment gives us another demonstration against the prelatic theory. He tells the multitude (Acts ii : 14–36. See especially his main proposition in verse 36th). This is the New Dispensation of the Messiah. (Proposition) Proved by two signs ; (a.) The spiritual effusions promised in Joel and such like places. (b.) The resurrection of the sacrificed Messiah. Now the structure of this inspired argument is ruinous to the Prelatist in (at least) two points. 1. v. 33. The spiritual results were to be palpable to the senses "this which ye now see and hear." But no Prelatist pretends that the "grace in holy orders" is visible and audible. The bestowal was one of visible, sensible "signs," the very one, and the only one relevant to the demonstration. 2. Verses 17, 18. The spiritual endowment was one which would fall on children and females. But neither of these, according to scripture, can receive ordination. So that the prelatic theory is again absolutely excluded.

Let us now proceed to Acts vi: 3–8, because this is one of the places, on which Prelacy builds chiefly. It has been proved that Stephen's and Philip's possession of the χάρισμα of Miracles was the prerequisite, not the consequence, of their election and ordination to diaconal office. But in 1 Tim. iii: 8, to end, where this office is expressly defined, we hear of no such qualification or function. It is not a part of the regular, permanent diaconal endowment. But the Pentecostal Church in Jerusalem was adorned with many instances doubtless among its laymen, women and children (Acts ii: 17, 18), of this gift of "signs," as well as among its ministers. The juncture demanding the separate development of the diaconal office, was critical. The spirit of faction was already awake between the Christians of Hebrew and of Hellenistic blood. The duty was going to be a nice and delicate one. Hence the Apostles' advise that the men first chosen for it be not only commended to the whole brotherhood by their moral character, but by the seal of this splendid gift. We repeat: this endowment was the prerequisite to their appointment, not the consequence of it. It was, expressly an appointment to "serve tables." And it cannot be argued that still Stephen and Philip had received this χάρισμα of the Spirit, if at some previous time, yet by some ordaining act to a lower clerical grade; because the diaconal was then the lowest grade known to the Church. Thus their argument is fatally hedged out at every point.

In Acts viii: 15, etc., "Simon saw that through laying on of the Apostles' hands, the Holy Ghost was given." The endowment was, then, a visible one. But according to Prelatists, the grace in "holy orders" is invisible (so invisible indeed, to the sober senses of Protestants, as to be wholly imaginary!) Hence, this case was not one of ordination at all, or of apostolic succession. So, when the Holy Ghost was poured out on the Gentiles, in Cornelius' house (Acts x: 46), they of the circumcision "heard them speak with tongues." So, when Paul laid hands on the Ephesian converts, Acts xix: 6, "the Holy Ghost came on them, and they spake with tongues and prophesied." Here again the result was palpable. And that this was not a case of ordination at all, is proved also by the fact, that the endowment was given to all the little company, which was so small that it included but twelve males. (Verse 7.)

In 1 Cor. Chaps. xii. to xiv., the discussion of this χάρισμα is so explicit and full, as to leave nothing to be desired. The Apostle speaks of it, not as a clerical endowment, but a popular. He expressly says that its object is to be a sign to unbelievers. He expressly foretells its utter vanishing out of the Church after a time, which our experience has long verified. But ordination and the ministry are permanent.

Let us proceed, now, to the case of Timothy, 1 Tim. iv: 14; and 2 Tim. i: 6; because Prelatists suppose that here we have the clearest instance of an ordination conferring the Holy Spirit. But let us see: If these references are only to Timothy's ordination, then it was a presbyterial ordination ("by the laying on of the hands of the Presbytery"), and thus the prelatic scheme is ruined. But if the two texts do not describe one and the same transaction, then the proof is gone that ordination by prelate imparted the Holy Ghost to Timothy; because, if two transactions are alluded to, the Holy Ghost may have been imparted by the other. And 2. This was doubtless the case. The "presbytery" ordained Timothy to the ministry, the Holy Spirit having moved some prophetic person to advise it, as in the case of Barnabas and Saul. Acts xiii: 2. But the Apostle ("who was also a presbyter." See 1 Pet. v: 1,) acting by his apostolic power, added some χάρισμα of "signs," to assist his "beloved son in the ministry" in convincing unbelievers. This is our solution: it is evinced by its perfect correspondence with the history in Acts xvi. On this solution, Timothy's χάρισμα was derived, not from his ordination, but from a distinct action. Let the Prelatist reject this, and he inevitably falls back into the doctrine of presbyterial ordination abhorred by him. 3. Timothy's qualification for the ministry was not conferred by the ordaining act, but recognized in it as pre-existing in him. For Paul himself ascribes much of this qualification to the instructions of his mother and grandmother, 2 Tim. i: 5; iii: 14-17; and the whole of it, instrumentally, to the inspired Scriptures. He here declares that by the instructions of the Scriptures, the minister of the gospel is "qualified and thoroughly equipped," (ἄρτιος ἐξερτισμένος) for his work. This leaves nothing for the prelate's hands to do! From this fatal answer the Prelatist has no escape, except to attempt to render the term "man of God," believer, instead of minister. But this is absurd, being totally against the old Testament usage, against Paul's usage, who has always his own distinctive terms, πιστός, ἅγιος, ἀδελφός, for believers; and against his express precedent in the First Epistle, to Tim. vi: 11; where "man of God" unquestionably means minister.

We have thus dealt with the cases on which the Prelatist chiefly builds, and have wrested them from him. The student can examine for himself all the other cases of χειροθεσία in the New Testament, in the same way. It is thus evinced that the whole basis of this scheme, of Apostolic Succession and sacramental grace, is a blunder and a confusion.

Other heads of argument against this figment might be expanded; but they would lead us aside from the doctrine of the sacrament, which is our present object.   There can be no apostolic succession, because there could not be an Apostle in the earth, since the death of John.   It is impossible that any one but a cotemporary of Jesus, personally acquainted with His features, and personally cognizant of His resurrection, should be an Apostle.   There cannot be any apostolic succession, again, because there is nothing to succeed to.   Every Prelatist who understands himself says, the thing succeeded to is priesthood. But there has not been any priesthood on earth, and could not be any, for eighteen hundred years.   The figment has been refuted again, by showing that Prelacy has no continuous succession of any kind in its ministry.   It has been broken fatally a hundred times, by heresy, or atheism, or impiety, or simony. or anarchy.   Last: the whole scheme is refuted by the substantial identity which Scripture asserts between the redemption of the new dispensation, and the old.   Under the old, redemption was certainly not applied by sacramental grace. Rom. ii: 26-29; iv: 11, 12.   But the argument of 1 Cor. ch. x., teaches that it is no more so under the New Testament. (The student may find these views expanded, in the *Southern Presbyterian Review*, January 1876 p. i.)

The high prelatic scheme of sacramental efficiency is essentially involved in that of the apostolic succession and the "grace of orders."   Hence, the doctrine of the sacraments cannot be effectually cleared up here, without an understanding of the latter.   Its discussion verges towards another department of sacred science, that of Church government.   But the introduction of this argument will be excused on account of the insoluble connection.

LECTURE LXIII.

BAPTISM.

SYLLABUS.

1. Is water Baptism, by God's appointment, a permanent ordinance in the Church?

Turrettin, Loc. xix, Qu. 12. Hill, bk. v, ch. 6, § 1, 2.

2. What are the signification and effects of Baptism? Consider the doctrine of baptismal regeneration. Does Baptism represent, as Immersionists say, the burial and resurrection of Christ?

Turrettin, Qu. 19, § 1–16. Armstrong on Baptism, pt. ii, ch. 2, pt. i, chs. 8, 9. Dick, Lect. 89.

3. What formulary of words should accompany baptism? and what their signification? Are any other formalities admissible? or sponsors?

Turrettin, Qu. 17. Dick, Lects. 88, 89. Knapp, § 139.

4. Was John's Baptism the Christian sacrament of the new dispensation? For what signification was Christ baptized by him?

Turrettin, Qu. 16. Armstrong, pt i, ch. 9. Dick, Lect. 88. Calvin's Inst. bk. iv. ch. 15, § 7, 18.

5. State the classic, and then the scriptural meanings ot the words βαπτω and βαπτιζω and their usage when applied in the Septuagint and New Testament to Levitical washings.

Armstrong, pt. i, chs. 3, 4, 5. Rice & Campbell's Debate, Prop. 1. Da e's Classic Bap. Dale's Judaic Bap. Carson on Bap.

6. Show that a change of meaning and mode takes place in the word βαπτιζω, in passing from a secular to a sacred use.

Armstrong, pt. i, ch. 1, &c. On whole, Conf. of Faith, ch. 28.

THE general remarks made concerning the sacraments, and applied to baptism, will not be repeated. The earlier Socinians disputed the perpetual obligation of water-baptism, as the Quakers now do of both the sacraments, and on similar grounds. They plead that the new is intended to be a spiritual dispensation; that salvation is always in the New Testament conditioned essentially on the state of heart: that Paul (1 Cor. i: 17) says, "Christ sent me not to baptize, but to preach the gospel:" and that the water-baptism administered by the apostles was only a temporary badge to separate the Church from Jews and Pagans at its outset. Quakers suppose that the only sacraments to be observed in our day are those of the heart, the baptism of the Holy Ghost, and the feeding on Christ by faith. The answers are: That the Old Testament, with its numerous types and two sacraments, was also a spiritual dispensation, and saving benefits were then, just as much as now, conditioned on the state of the heart; that the commission to baptize men was evidently co-extensive with that to disciple and teach them, as is proved by the accompanying promise of grace; that the commission to baptize lasts at least till all nations are converted, which is not yet accomplished; that it was after the most glorious experiences of the true spiritual baptism, at Pentecost, that the water-baptism was most industriously adminis-

1. Water Baptism Perpetual.

tered; and that Paul only expresses the inferior importance of baptising to preaching, and his thankfulness at having baptized only three persons at Corinth, in view of the unpleasant fact that that Church was ranking itself in parties according to the ministers who introduced them to membership.

The folly and falsehood of baptismal regeneration have been already pointed out in the former lec-

2. Meaning of Baptism. ture. All the arguments there aimed against the *opus operatum* apply here. The error most probably grew as superstition increased in the primitive Church, out of the ungarded use of the sacramental language by the early fathers, whose doctrine on this point was sounder. We know that baptism, in supposed imitation of Titus iii:5, was currently called regeneration as early as Justin Martyr and Irenæus. It is easy to see how, as men's ideas of sacred subjects became more gross, this figurative use of the word introduced the real error.

According to the Shorter Catechism (Qu. 94) baptism "doth signify and seal our ingrafting into Christ and partaking of the benefits of the covenant of grace, and our engagements to be the Lord's." And in the Confession, chapter 28, those benefits of the Covenant of Grace are farther explained to be remission of sins and regeneration. Each part of this definition we can abundantly substantiate from scripture. See Gal. iii: 27; Rom. vi: 5; Jno. iii: 5; Titus iii: 5; Col. ii: 11, 12, &c.; Acts ii: 38; Mark i: 4; Acts xxii: 16, &c.; Rom. vi: 3, 4; 1 Cor. xii: 13: Matt. xxviii: 19; Rom. vi: 11, 12.

One of the most remarkable things about Baptism, to the

Derived from Jewish Purifications. attentive reader of Scripture, is the absence of all set explanations of its meaning in the New Testament, and at the same time, of all appearance of surprise at its novelty. Not so with the other sacrament although that was a continuation of the familiar Passover. These things, among others, convince me that Baptism was no novelty to the Jews, either in its form or signification. It was the thing symbolized by the Hebrews' purifications $\varkappa\alpha\vartheta\alpha\varrho\iota\sigma\mu\omicron\iota$. The idea of the purification included both cleansing and consecration; and the formalities represented both the removal of impurity from the person, in order that it might be adapted to the service of a holy God, and the consequent dedication to Him. Now, the main idea of Baptism is purification: and the element applied, the detergent element of nature, symbolizes the two-fold application of Christ's satisfaction (called His blood) and the Holy Ghost, cleansing from guilt and depravity, and thus also consecrating the cleansed person to the service of a holy God. Here then, we have involved the ideas of regeneration and remission, and also of engrafting and covenanting into Christ's service. This view will be farther susbtstantiated in treating the words $\beta\alpha\pi\tau\iota\sigma\mu\omicron\varsigma$ &c.

Now the Immersionists, (for what purpose we shall see),
Does Baptism Commemorate Christ's Burial and Resurrection? have departed from the uniform faith of Christendom, on this point: and while they do not wholly discard the purification, make baptism primarily symbolical of Christ's burial and resurrection. They teach that, as the supper commemorates His death, so baptism commemorates His burial and rising again. True, the believer, in commemorating His death in the supper, receives also a symbol of the benefits purchased for us therein. So, in commemorating His burial and resurrection, there is a symbolizing of our burial to sin, and living again unto holiness. But the main meaning is, to set forth Christ's burial and resurrection. Only three texts can be quoted for this view. Rom. vi: 3–5; Col. ii: 12, and 1 Cor. xv: 29, and especially the first.

Now our first objection to this view is its lack of all Bible
Disproved. No Scripture Proof. support. He would be a hardy man, who would base any theory on the exposition of a passage so obscure as 1 Cor. xv: 29. The most probable explanation is, that the Apostle here refers to the Levitical rule of Numb. xix: 14–19. Were there no resurrection, a corpse would be like any other clod; and there would be no reason for treating it as a symbol of moral defilement, or for bestowing on it, so religiously, the rites of sepulture. But this exposition presents not a particle of reason for regarding Christian baptism as a commemoration of Christ's burial. The other two passages are substantially identical: and, under the figure of a death and rising again, they obviously represent a regeneration. Compare especially Col. ii: 11, 12; Rom. vi: 4. So likewise the figures of circumcision, planting, and crucifixion, all represent the same, regeneration. This the immersionist himself cannot deny. The baptism here spoken of is, then, not directly a water baptism at all: but the spiritual baptism thereby represented. Col. ii: 11. It is the circumcision "made without hands." Rom. vi: 3, 4. It is a baptism not into water, but into death, i. e., a death to carnality. Therefore it is clear the symbolism here points to the grace of regeneration, and not to any supposed grace in Christ's burial. His burial and resurrection are themselves used here as symbols, to represent regeneration. As justly might the immersionist say that baptism commemorates a crucifixion, a planting, a building, a change of a stone into flesh, a putting off dirty garments; because these are all Scripture figures of regeneration, of which baptism is a figure. Nor is there in these famous passages any reference to the mode of baptism, because first the Apostle's scope in Rom. vi, forbids it: and second, the same mode of interpretation would compel us to find an analogy in the mode of baptism, to a planting and a crucifixion. See Scott in loco.

But second: by making baptism the commemoration of

No Proper Sacramental Analogy.

Christ's burial, and resurrection, the sacramental analogy (as well as the warrant) is totally lost. This analogy is not in the element to the grace; for in that aspect, there can be no resemblance. Water is not like a tomb, nor like the Holy Ghost, nor like Christ's atoning righteousness. Nor is bread like a man's body, nor wine like his blood. The selection of the sacramental element is not founded on a resemblance, but on an analogy. Distinguish. The bread and wine are elements, not because they are like a body and blood, in their qualities: but because there is a parallel in their uses, to nourish and cheer. So the water is an element of a sacrament, because there is a parallel in its uses, to the thing symbolized. The use of water is to cleanse. Where now is any analogy to Christ's burial? Nor is there even a resemblance in the action, not even when the immersionist's mode is granted. Water is not like a Hebrew tomb. The temporary demission of a man into the former, to be instantly raised out of it, is not like a burial.

Christ's Burial Not Vital.

Third: If we may judge by the two sacraments of the old dispensation, and by the supper, sacraments (always few) are only adopted by God to be commemorative of the most cardinal transactions of redemption. Christ's burial was not such. Christ's burial is nowhere proposed to us as an essential object of faith. His death and the Spirit's work are. His death and resurrection are; the former already commemorated in the other sacrament. And besides; it would seem strange that the essential work of the Holy Ghost should be symbolized by no sacrament, while that of Christ is commemorated by two! In the old dispensation the altar and the laver stood side by side. And here would be a two-fold covenant, with two seals to one of its promises, and none to the other!

And last: The Immersionist is involved by his theory in intense confusions. In the gospel history, Christ's death preceded His burial and resurrection: so the commemoration of the death ought to precede. But the Immersionist makes it follow, with peculiar rigidity. Again: the Supper was only practised either when the death was already accomplished, or immediately at hand; so that its commemorative intent was at once obvious. But the baptism was instituted long before the burial. Did it then point forward to it? Are sacraments types? And this difficulty presses peculiarly on the Immersionist, who makes John's baptism identical with Christian. What then did John's baptism signify to Jews, before Christ was either dead or buried, and before these events were foreknown by them?

3. Baptism in Whose Name?

In Matt. xxviii : 19 the formulary of words to be employed is given by Christ explicitly, ἐις τὸ ὄνομα, &c., and this preposition is retained in every case but one. Had our Saviour said that baptism should be ἐν τῳ ὀνοματι (dative), &c., His meaning would have appeared to be that the rite was applied by the authority of that name, i. e., hebraice, of that person.   The one case in which this formulary occurs (Acts x : 48) is probably to be explained in this way ; but the uniform observance of the other formulary, in all the other cases (especially see 1 Cor. i : 13 and x : 2), indicates clearly that the meaning of the rite is, that it purifies and dedicates us unto the Trinity, bringing us into a covenant relation to Him.   Here we see an additional argument for the definition given in § 2, of the meaning of baptism, and against the Immersionist idea.

Cases are not unfrequent (e. g., in Acts viii : 16 ; x : 48 ; xix : 5) in which no name is mentioned but that of Christ.   But I think we are by no means to infer hence that the apostles ever omitted any of the formulary enjoined by Christ.   Jews would have no objection to a baptism to God the Father. (John's was such, and exceedingly popular).   They were used to them. But Christ Jesus was the stumbling-block; and hence when the historian would indicate that a Hebrew had made a thorough submission to the new dispensation, he would think it enough to say that he had assumed Christ's name.   The rest was then easy to believe and was therefore left to be inferred.

The Church of Rome accompanied baptism with a number of superstitious rites, of which she still retains the most, and the Church of England, a part.   They were, blessing the water in the font, exorcism, renouncing the Devil, anointing in the form of a cross, anointing the eye-lids and ears with spittle, breathing on the candidate, washing the whole body *in puris naturalibus*, the baptism proper, tasting salt and honey, putting on the white robe, or at least, taking hold of a white cloth, and an imposition of hands.   The last, now separated from baptism, constitutes the sacrament of confirmation.   We repudiate all these, for two reasons : that they are unauthorized by Scripture, and, worse than this, that their use is suggestive of positive error and superstition.

The use of sponsors, who are now always other than the proper parents (when any sponsors are used), in the Episcopal and Romish Churches, has grown from gradual additions.   In the early Church the sponsors were always the natural parents of the infant, except in cases of orphanage and slavery : and then they were either the master, or some deacon or deaconess. (See Bingham, p. 523, &c.)   When an adult was *in extremis,* and even speechless, or maniacal, or insensible, if it could be proved that he had desired baptism, he was permitted to receive it, and some one stood sponsor for him.   If he recovered, this sponsor was expected to watch over his religious life and instruction.   And in the case of Catechumens, the sponsor was at first some clergy-

ιnan or deaconess, who undertook his religious guidance. It
was a universal rule that no one was allowed to be sponsor unless he undertook this *bona fide*. How perverted is this usage
now! Our great objection to the appearance of any one but
the natural parents, where there are any, or in other cases, of
him who is *in loco parentis*, as sponsors, is this: that no other
human has the right to dedicate the child. and no other has the
opportunity and authority to train it for God. To take these
vows in any other sense is mockery.

The Reformers strenuously identify John's baptism with
the Christian, arguing that his mission was a

4. Nature of John's sort of dawn of the new dispensation, that it
Baptism.
was the baptism of repentance, an evangeli-
cal grace, and that it is also stated (Luke iii : 3) to be for the
remission of sins. But later Calvinists hold, against them and
the Immersionists, that it was a baptism for a different purpose,
and therefore not the same sacramentally, however it may have
resembled as to mode, that of the Christian Church. Their
reasons are: 1st. That it was not administered in the name of the
Trinity, and did not bring the parties into covenant with Christ.
2nd. It was not the initiatory rite into the Church, and did not
signify our ingrafting into Christ, for the old dispensation still
subsisted, and those who received the rite were already in the
Church of that dispensation, whereas Christ's was not yet
opened, and therefore could not receive formal adherents. But,
3d, Paul seems clearly (Acts xix : 5) to have repeated Christian
baptism on those who already had John's. Calvin and Turrettin indeed evade this fact by making verse 5 the words of
Paul (not of Luke), reciting the fact that these brethren had
already (when they heard John) received baptism. But this
gloss is proved erroneous, not only by the whole drift of the
passage (why had they not received charisms?), by the force of
the μεν and δε, but above all by this: that if this verse 5 means
John's baptism, then John baptized in the name of Jesus. But
see Jno. i: 33; Matt. xi : 3. John's baptism was therefore not
the sacrament of the new dispensation, but one of those purifications, preparing the way of the Messiah about to come,
with which, we believe, the Jewish mind was familiar.

The interesting question arises: With what intent and
meaning did Christ submit to it? He could

Intent of Christ's not repent, and needed no remission. We
Baptism.
think it clear He could not have taken it in
these senses. Says Turrettin: He took it vicariously, doing
for His people, all that any one of them owed, to fulfill the law
in their stead ; and He refers, for support, to the fact that He
punctually conformed to all the Levitical ritual,—was circumcised, attended sacrifices, &c. But the cases are not parallel.
Christ as a Jew, (according to His humanity), would properly
render obedience to all the rules of the dispensation under

which He came vicariously; but it is not therefore proper that He should comply with the rules of a dispensation to be wholly founded on Him as Mediator, and which rules were all legislated by Him. This for those, who assert that John's baptism was the Christian Sacrament. There is no evidence that Christ partook of His other sacrament. See Luke xxii : 17. And while His vicarious attitude would make a ceremonial purification from guilt appropriate, it would not make a rite significant of repentance appropriate. Christ did not repent for imputed guilt, which did not stain His character. Nor would the other part of the signification apply to Him: for this imputed guilt was not pardoned to Him : He paid the debt to the full.

There seems then, to be no explanation; except that Christ's baptism was His priestly inauguration. John, himself an Aaronic priest, might naturally administer it. His age confirms it; compare Luke iii : 23, with Numb. iv : 3. A purification by water was a part of the original consecration of the Aaronic family. See Levit. viii : 6; or better, Exod. xxx : 17–21, &c. The unction Christ received immediately after, by the descent of the Holy Ghost. And last, John's language confirms it, together with the immediate opening of Christ's official work.

It was His Consecration to Priesthood.

We now approach the vexed question of the mode of baptism. The difference between us and immersionists is only this: whether the entire immersion of the body in water is essential to valid baptism. For we admit any application of water, by an ordained ministry, in the name of the Trinity, to be valid baptism. The question concerning the mode is of course one of meaning and usage of the words descriptive of the ordinance. But this preliminary question arises: of what usage? that of the classic, or of Hellenistic Greek? We answer, chiefly the latter; for the obvious reason that this was the idiom to which the writers of the New Testament were accustomed, especially when speaking Greek on a sacred subject. And this, enlightened immersionists scarcely dispute. Another preliminary question arises: should it be found that the usage of the words βαπτιζω, &c., when applied to common and secular washings, gives them one uniform meaning, would that be evidence enough that its meaning was precisely the same, in passing to a sacred ritual, and assuming a technical, sacred sense? I reply, by no means. There is scarcely a word, which has been borrowed from secular into sacred language, which does not undergo a necessary modification of meaning. Is ἐκκλησία the same word in the Scriptures, which it is in common secular Greek? Πρεσβύτερος means an elderly person, an embassador, a magistrate. Is this the precise meaning of the Church presbyter of the New Testament? He might be a young man. Above all is this change marked

5. Real Question as to Mode. Neither Etymology nor Secular Use Defines it.

in the word for the other sacrament, δεῖπνον. This word in secular, social use, whether in or out of Scripture, means the evening meal; and usually a full one, often a banquet, in which the bodily appetite was liberally fed. The Lord's Supper is usually not in the evening; it is not a meal; and by its design has no reference to satisfying the stomach, or nourishing the body. See 1 Cor. xi. Indeed, it is impossible to adopt a secular and known word, as the name cf this peculiar institution, a Christian Sacrament, without, in the very act of adopting it, superinducing upon it some shade of meaning different from its secular. Even if the favorite word of the Immersionists, immersion, were adopted, as the established name in English, of the sacrament; it would *ipso facto* receive an immediate modification of meaning as a sacramental word. Not any immersion whatever would constitute a sacrament. So that this very specific word would then require some specification. Thus we see that the assertion of the Immersionist, that βαπτίζω is a purely specific word, and, as a name of a sacrament, admits of no definition as to mode, would be untrue, even if it were perfectly specific in its common secular meaning, both in and out of Scripture. We might grant, then, that βαπτίζω, whenever non-ritual, is nothing but plunge, dip under, and still sustain our cause.

But we grant no such thing. Let it be borne in mind that
Immersionist Postulate as to Usage of Words. the thing the Immersionist must prove is no less than this: that βαπτίζω, &c., never can mean, in secular uses, whether in or out of the Scriptures, anything but dip under, plunge; for nothing less will prove that nothing but dipping wholly under is valid baptism. If the words mean frequently plunging, but sometimes wetting or washing without plunging, their cause is lost. For then it is no longer absolutely specific of mode. Let us then examine first the non-ritual or secular usage of the words, both in Hellenistic (Sept. Josephus) Greek, and in the New Testament. We freely admit that βάπτω very often means to dip, and βαπτίζω still more often, nay, usually, but not exclusively.

And first, the trick of Carson is to be exposed, by which
The Root βαπτω to be Examined. he endeavors to evade the examination of the shorter form, βάπτω, on the plea that βαπτίζω and its derivatives are the only ones ever used in relation to the sacrament of baptism. True; but by what process shall we more properly discover the meaning of βαπτίζω than by going to that of its root, βάπτω, from which it is formed by the simple addition of ίζω, meaning verbal activity, (the making of anything to be βαπτ). Well, we find the lexicons all defining βάπτω, dip, wash, stain. Suidas, πλύνω, to wash clothes. These definitions are sustained by the well known case, from the classics, of Homer's lake, βεβαμμένον, tinged with the blood of a dying mouse, which Carson himself

gives up. But among the instances from Hellenistic Greek, the more important to our purpose, consult the following: Rev. xix : 13, a vesture stained with blood, βεβαμμενον; Luke xvi : 24; Ex. xii : 22; 1 Sam. xiv : 27; Levit. iv : 6, 7; Dan. iv : 33. So there are cases of the secular use of the word βαπτιζω, where immersion is not expressed. See the lexicons quoted by Drs. Owen and Rice, in which it is defined, not only to immerse, but also to wash, substantiated by the cases of "the blister baptized with breast milk," in classic Greek, and of the altar, wood and victim of Elijah baptized by pouring on water in Origen. Hence, the common and secular usage is not uniformly in favor of dipping.

But if it were, the question would still be an open one; for it may well be, that when transferred to religious ritual, the word will undergo some such modification as we saw uniformly occurs in all other words transferred thus. We proceed, then, one step nearer, and examine the meaning of the word in the Septuagint and New Testament, when applied to religious rituals, other than the Christian sacrament itself; that is, to Jewish purifications. And here we find that the specific idea of the Jewish religious baptism was not dipping, but an act symbolical of purification, of which the actual mode was, in most cases, by affusion. In 2 Kings v: 14; Naaman baptized himself (εβαπτιζατο) seven times in the Jordan. This may have been dipping, but taking into account the Jewish mode of purification, was more probably by affusion. Eccl. xxxiv: 25; the Septuagint says: "He that baptizeth himself (βαπτιζεται) after he toucheth a dead body, if he touch it again, what availeth his washings?" How this baptism was performed, the reader may see in Numb. xxxi: 19, 24, and xix : 13-20. In Judith xii: 7, this chaste maiden is said to have baptized herself at a fountain of water by a vast camp! In Josephus Antiq. Bk. 4, ch. iv., the ashes of the red heifer used in purifying are said to be baptized in spring water.

In the New Testament there are four instances where the Jewish ritual purifications are described by the term baptize; and in all four cases it was undoubtedly by affusion. Mark vii: 4; Luke xi: 38; John ii: 6; Heb. ix: 10; vi: 2. (The last may possibly be Christian baptism, though its use in the plural would rather show that it included the Jewish.) Now that all these purifications called here βαπτισμοι and καθαρισμοι were by affusion, we learn, 1. From the Levitical law, which describes various washings and sprinklings, but not one immersion of a man's person for purification. 2. From well known antique habits still prevalent in the East, which limited the washings to the hands and feet, and performed them by affusion. Compare 2 Kings iii: 11; Exod. xxx: 21. 3. From

Marginal notes:

6. Βαπτιζω not Always Dip.

New Testament Use of the Verb Not Always Dip.

comparison of the two passages, Mark vii : 4, and Luke xi : 38 ; with Jno. ii : 6. These water pots were too narrow at the mouth, and too small (holding about two bushels) to receive a person's body, and were such as were borne on the shoulders of female servants. 4. From the great improbability that Jews would usually immerse all over so often, or that they could. 5. From the fact that they are declared to have practised, not only these baptisms of their persons, but of their utensils and massive couches. Numb. xix : 17, 18. It is simply preposterous that these should have been immersed as often as ceremonially defiled. Last the Levitical law, which these Jews professed to observe with such strictness, rendered an immersion impossible anywhere but in a deep running stream, or living pit of a fountain. For if anything ceremonially unclean went into a vessel of standing water, no matter whether large or small, the water was thereby defiled, and the vessel and all other water put into that vessel, and all persons who got into it. See Levit. xi : 32 to 36 ; Num. xix : 22.

It is true that Immersionists pretend to quote Talmudists (of whom I, and probably they, know nothing), saying that these purifications were by immersion ; and that Solomon's "sea" was for the priests to swim in. But the Talmud is 700 years A. D., and excessively absurd.

Now, if the religious baptisms of the Jews were not by dipping, but by affusion ; if their specific idea
Inference.
was that of religious purification, and not dipping ; and if Christian baptism is borrowed from the Jewish, and called by the same name, without explanation, can any one believe that dipping is its specific and essential form ? Immersionists acknowledge the justice of our inference, by attempting to dispute all the premises. Hard task !

LECTURE LXIV.

BAPTISM. — Continued.

A CONSIDERATION of some probable weight may be drawn from the fact that Christianity is intended to be a universal religion. Remember that it is characterized by fewness and simplicity of rites, that it is rather spiritual than ritual, that its purpose was to make those rites the reverse of burdensome, and that the elements of the other sacraments were chosen from articles common, cheap, and near at hand. Now, in many extensive countries, water is too scarce to make it convenient to accumulate enough for an immersion; in other regions all waters are frozen over during half the year. In many cases infirmity of body renders immersion highly inconvenient and even dangerous. It seems not very probable that, under these circumstances, a dispensation so little formalistic as the Christian, would have made immersion essential to the validity of baptism, for a universal Church, amidst all climes and habits.

7. Dipping Impracticable Sometimes.

But we derive an argument of far more importance, from the obviously correct analogy between the act of affusion and the graces signified and sealed in baptism. It is this which Immer

8. Grace Symbolized is Always Shed Forth.

768

sionists seek to evade when they endeavor, contrary to Scripture, to make baptism signify and commemorate primarily Christ's burial and resurrection. (Hence the importance of refuting that dream). The student will remember, that the selection of the element is founded, not upon the resemblance of its nature (for of this there can be none, between the material and spiritual), but on the analogy of its use to the graces symbolized. Water is the detergent element of nature. The great meaning of baptism is our cleansing from guilt by expiation (blood), and our cleansing from the depravity of heart, by the Holy Ghost. Now, in all Bible language, without a single exception, expiation is symbolized as sprinkled, or affused, or put on; and the renewing Spirit, as descending, or poured, or falling. See all the Jewish usages, and the whole tenour of the promises. Levit. xiv : 7, 51 ; xvi : 14 ; Numb. viii : 7 ; xix : 18 ; Heb. ix : 19–22, especially last verse; ix : 14 ; x : 22 ; Levit vii ; 14 ; Exod. xxix : 16, 21, &c.; Ps. xlv : 2 ; Is. xliv : 3 ; Ps. lxxii : 6 ; Is. xxxii : 15 ; Joel ii : 28, 29, quoted in Acts ii.

Nor is the force of this analogy a mere surmise of ours. See Is. lii : 15, where it is declared that the Redeemer, by His mediatorial, and especially His suffering work, "shall sprinkle many nations." The immediate reference here doubtless is not to water baptism, but to that which it signifies. But when God chooses in His own Word to call those baptismal graces a sprinkling, surely it gives no little authority to the belief that water baptism is by sprinkling ! Immersionists feel this so acutely that they have even availed themselves of the infidel glosses of the German Rationalists, who to get rid of the Messianic features of this glorious prophecy, render יַזֶּה—"to cause to start up," "to startle." The only plea they bring for this unscrupulous departure from established usage of the word is, that in all the other places this verb has as its regimen the element sprinkled, and not the object. This objection Dr. J. A. Alexander pronounces frivolous, and denies any Hebrew or Arabic support to the substituted translation. Again: In Ezek. xxxvi : 25, are promises which, although addressed primarily to the Jews of the Captivity, are evidently evangelical ; and there the sprinkling of clean water symbolizes the gospel blessings of regeneration, remission, and spiritual indwelling. The language is so strikingly favourable to us, that it seems hardly an overstraining of it to suppose it a prediction of the very sacrament of baptism. But this we do not claim.

Isaiah, and other Old Testament Instances.

Our argument is greatly strengthened when we proceed to the New Testament. Collate Matt. iii : 11 ; Acts i : 5 ; ii : 2–4 ; ii : 15–18 ; ii : 33 ; x : 44, 45, 48 ; xi : 16, 17. Here our argument

New Testament Examples of Grace by Affusion.

49*

is two-fold. First: that both John and Christ baptize with water, not in water. This language is wholly appropriate to the application of water to the person, wholly inappropriate to the application of the person to the water. No Immersionist would speak of dipping with water. They do indeed reclaim that the preposition is ἐν here translated "with," and should in all fidelity be rendered "in," according to its admitted use in the large majority of New Testament cases. This we utterly deny; first, because in the mouth of a Hebraistic Greek, ἐν being the established equivalent and translation of בְּ may naturally and frequently mean "with;" but second and chiefly because the parallel locutions of Luke iii : 16 ; Acts i : 5 ; xi : 16 ; Eph. v : 26 ; Heb. x : 22, identify the ἐν ὕδατι, &c., with the instrument. And from the same passages we argue farther, that the mode of the baptism with the Holy Ghost and fire, is fixed most indisputably by the description of the event in Acts ii :· 2 to 4. The long promised baptism occurred. And what was it ? It was the sitting of tongues of fire on each Apostle, and the "descent," the fall, the "pouring out," the "shedding forth," of the spiritual influences. To make the case still stronger, if possible, when the spiritual affusion on Cornelius and his house occurred, which made Peter feel that he was justified in authorizing their water-baptism, he informs his disapproving brethren in Jerusalem (Acts xi : 15, 16) that the "falling of the Holy Ghost on them as on us at the beginning," caused him "to re member" the great promise of a baptism, not with water only, but with the Holy Ghost and with fire. If baptism is never an affusion, how could such a suggestion ever arise ?

This reasoning is so cogent, that Immersionists feel the necessity of an evasion. Their Coryphæus, Carson, suggests two. No element, nor mode of applying an element, he says, can properly symbolize the essence of the Holy Ghost. It is immense, immaterial, unique. All men are at all times immersed in it. To suppose any analogy between water affused, and this infinite, spiritual essence, is gross materialism. Very true; yet here is some sort and sense in which a baptism with the Holy Ghost occurred ; and if it is gross anthropo-morphism to liken His ubiquitous essence to water affused, it is equally so to liken it to water for plunging. If there is no sense in which the analogy between the influences of the baptismal element and the influences of the Holy Ghost can be asserted, then it is God's Word which is in fault; for He has called the outpouring of those influences a baptism. The truth is, that here, just as when God is said to come, to go, to lift up His hand, it is not the divine essence which changes its place, but its sensible influences.

The other evasion is, to say that because this baptism is wholly figurative, and not a proper and literal baptism at all,

Evasions Answered.

therefore it can contain no reference whatever to mode. We deny both premise and conclusion : the conclusion, because Immersionists infer mode, with great positiveness, from a merely figurative baptism, in Rom. vi : 4 ; and the premise, because the baptism of Pentecost was in the best sense real, the most real baptism that ever was in the world. It was, indeed, not material : but if its literal reality be denied, then the inspiration of the Apostles is denied, and the whole New Testament Dispensation falls.

Our argument, then, is summed up thus : Here was a spiritual transaction, which Christ was pleased to call His baptism, in the peculiar sense. In this baptism the outward element descended upon the persons of the recipients, and the influences of the Holy Ghost, symbolized thereby, are spoken of as falling. Water baptism, which is intended, like the fire, to symbolize the spiritual baptism, should therefore be also applied by affusion.

This Argument Summed Up.

While we deny that these memorable events formed only a figurative baptism, yet the word baptism is used in Scripture in a sense more properly figurative, and wholly non-sacramental. Immersionists profess to find in all these an allusion to dipping ; but we shall show that in every case such allusion is uncertain, or impossible.

9. Argument from Figurative Baptisms.

The first instance is that of Christ's baptism in His sufferings at His death. Matt. xx : 20, 23 ; Mark x : 38, 39 ; Luke xii : 50. Although Luke refers to a different conversation, yet the allusion to His dying sufferings is undoubtedly the same. Now, it is common to say that these sufferings were called a baptism, because Christ was to be then covered with anguish as with an overwhelming flood. Even granting this, it must be remembered the Scriptures always speak of God's wrath as being poured out, and however copious the shower, an effusion from above bears a very questionable resemblance to an immersion of the person into a body of liquid beneath. Some (as Dr. Armstrong) find in this figure no reference to the mode of baptism, but suppose that the idea is one of consecration simply. Christ is supposed to call His dying sufferings a baptism, because by them He was inducted into His kingly office. But this is not wholly satisfactory. The true explanation is obviously that of the Greek fathers. As is well known to students of sacred history, the martyr's sufferings were considered his baptism. And so literal was the notion expressed by this, that the Fathers gravely argue that by martyrdom the unbaptized catechumen, who witnesses a good confession, becomes a baptized Christian, and has no reason whatever to regret his lack of water baptism, supposed by them to be, in other cases.

Christ's Baptism in Sorrow.

essential.   To the question why martyrdom is called by them a baptism, they answer with one voice, because Christ was pleased to call His own martyrdom a baptism, and to apply the same to the pious sufferings of James and John.   And they say farther, quoting the same texts, that the reason Christ calls His dying sufferings a baptism is, because they cleansed away sin, as the water of baptism symbolically does.   Here, then, is no reference to mode of water baptism, and these Greek fathers, if they in any case press the figure to a signification of mode, speak of Christ's body as baptized, or stained with His own blood, a baptism by affusion.   And the baptism of martyrdom is explained as a baptism of blood and fire.

1 Cor. x : 2 represents the Israelites as baptized unto Moses in the cloud and in the sea, in passing the Red sea.   Immersionists foolishly attempt to strain a reference to immersion here, by saying that the Israelites were surrounded with water, having the sea as a wall on the either hand, and the cloud overhead. But unfortunately for this far-fetched idea, it is expressly said that Israel went over dry-shod.   And the cloud was not over them, but behind them.   Nor is there any proof that it was an aqueous cloud (it was fire by night and luminous); and the allegorizing Greek Fathers currently understand it as representing, not the water of baptism, but God's Holy Ghost.   Nor have we any proof that even aqueous vapor can be substituted for the sacramental element.   There was an immersion in the case, but it was that of Pharaoh and his hosts.   The lost were immersed, the saved were baptized unto Moses!   The sense of the passage obviously is, that by this event Israel were dedicated, separated unto that religious service of which Moses was the teacher.   The word baptize here carries no reference to mode, but has its proper sense of religious separation.

Israel's Baptism to Moses.

The same is its meaning in 1 Cor. xii : 13; Gal. iii : 27; Eph. iv : 5, and 1 Pet. iii : 21.   When the believer is said to be baptized into (or unto) Christ, or into His one body, and thus to have put on Christ, there can be no allusion to mode, because then it would be the preposterous idea of immersing into Christ, or into His mystical body, instead of into water. The exact idea expressed is that of a consecrating separation. Baptism is here conceived by the Apostle as our separation from the ruined mass of mankind and annexation to the Saviour in our mystical union.   So in 1 Pet. iii : 21, baptism is called a figure like ($\dot{\alpha}\nu\tau\acute{\iota}\tau\upsilon\pi o\nu$) to the salvation of Noah's family in the ark.   This saving was from water, not by water, and it was effected in the ark.   Here again there is no modal reference to immersion, for the parties saved were not dipped, and all who were dipped were lost.   The baptism of Noah's family was therefore their separation from a sinful world, effected by

Believer's Baptism Into Christ.

the waters of the flood. If baptism in its most naked, spiritual meaning, carries to Hebrews the idea of a religious separation, it is very evident what mode it would suggest, should they permit their minds to advert to mode. Their separations were by sprinklings. The remaining passage (Eph. iv : 5) could only have been supposed to teach the essential necessity of observing water baptism in only one mode, by a mind insensible to the elevation and sacredness of the passage. It is the glorious spiritual unity between Christians and their Divine Head, resulting from the separating consecration which baptism represents.

The identification of baptism with the purification of the Jews, in Jno. iii : 25, 26, throws some light upon its mode. The question about purifying, agitated between the Jews and some of the Baptist's disciples, (v. 25), is evidently the question which they propound to John himself (in v. 26), viz: What was the meaning of Christ's baptizing. The whole tenour of John's answer proves this, for it is all addressed to the explanation of this point: why Christ, baptized by him, and thus seemingly his disciple, should administer a baptism independent of him. Any other explanation leaves an absurd chasm between verses 25 and 26. Baptism, then, is καθαρισμός, a striking testimony to the correctness of our account of its signification, a matter which we found to bear, in so important a way, upon its mode. But farther: Let anyone consider the Septuagint use of this word, and he cannot easily remain in doubt as to the mode in which a Jew would naturally administer it.

10. Baptism is Purification.

My time will not permit me to go into a full discussion of the actual mode indicated by the sacred historian in each case of baptism in the New Testament. Such detail is, indeed, not necessary, inasmuch as you may find the work well done in several of your authors, and especially in Armstrong, Part II, ch. 3, 4. The result of a thorough examination was well stated by a divine of our Church thus: Rule three columns on your blank paper; mark the first, 'Certainly by immersion; the second, 'Probably by immersion; the third, 'Certainly not by immersion.' Then, after the careful study of the Greek Testament, enter each case where it properly belongs. Under the first head there will be not a single instance; under the second, there may be a few; while the larger number will be under the third. Immersionists, when they read that John was baptizing in Jordan, and again at Ænon, "because there was much water there," conclude that he certainly immersed his penitents. But when we note that the language may as well be construed 'at' Jordan, and that the 'many waters' of Ænon were only a cluster of springs; considering also the unlikeliness of one man's performing such a multitude of immersions, and the uninspired

11. Mode of New Testament Baptism.

testimony of the early Church as to the method of our Saviour's baptism, the probabilities are all turned the other way. So, the improbability of sufficient access to water, at l'entecost, and the impossibility of twelve men's immersing three thousand in one afternoon, make the immersion of the Pentecostal converts out of the question. This is the conclusion of the learned Dr. Edward Robinson, after an inquiry on the spot. In like manner, the Eunuch's baptism may possibly have been by dipping, but was more probably by affusion; while the cases of Paul, Cornelius, and the jailer, were certainly in the latter mode.

The odious ecclesiastical consequences of the Immersionist dogma should be pressed; because 12. The Dogma Un- they form a most potent and just argument churches all. against it. All parties are agreed, that baptism is the initiatory rite which gives membership in the visible Church of Christ. The great commission was: Go ye, and disciple all nations, baptizing them into the Trinity. Baptism recognizes and constitutes the outward discipleship. Least of all, can any immersionist dispute this ground. Now, if all other forms of baptism than immersion are not only irregular, but null and void, all unimmersed persons are out of the visible Church. But if each and every member of a pædobaptist visible Church is thus unchurched: of course the whole body is unchurched. All pædobaptist societies, then, are guilty of an intrusive error, when they pretend to the character of a visible Church of Christ. Consequently, they can have no ministry; and this for several reasons. Surely no valid office can exist in an association whose claim to be an ecclesiastical commonwealth is utterly invalid. When the temple is non-existent, there can be no actual pillars to that temple. How can an unauthorized herd of unbaptized persons, to whom Christ concedes no church authority, confer any valid office? Again: it is preposterous that a man should receive and hold office in a commonwealth where he himself has no citizenship; but this unimmersed pædobaptist minister, so-called, is no member of any visible Church. There are no real ministers in the world, except the Immersionist preachers! The pretensions of all others, therefore, to act as ministers, and to administer the sacraments, are sinful intrusions. It is hard to see how any intelligent and conscientious Immersionist can do any act, which countenances or sanctions this profane intrusion. They should not allow any weak inclinations of fraternity and peace to sway their consciences in this point of high principle. They are bound, then, not only to practise close communion, but to refuse all ministerial recognition and communion to these intruders. The sacraments cannot go beyond the pale of the visible Church. Hence, the same stern denunciations ought to be hurled at the Lord's Supper in pædobaptist societies, and at all their prayers and preachings in public, as at the iniquity of "baby-sprinkling." The enlightened immersionist should treat all these societies, just as he does that ' Synagogue of Satan,' the Papal Church: there may be many good, misguided believers in them; but no church character, ministry, nor sacraments whatever.

But let the student now look at the enormity of this conclusion. Here are bodies of ministers adorned by the Lord with as many gifts and graces as any Immersionists; actually doing the largest part of all that is done on earth, to win the world to its divine Master. Here are four-fifths of Protestant Christendom, exhibiting as many of the solid fruits of grace as any body of men in the world, doing nearly all that is done for man's redemption, and sending up to heaven a constant harvest of ransomed souls. Yet are they not churches or ministers, at all: Why? Only because they have not used quite enough water in the outward form of an ordinance! What greater outrage on common sense, Christian charity, and the spirituality of Christ's visible Church was ever committed by the bigotry of prelacy or popery? The just mind replies to such a dogma, not only with a firm negative, but with the righteous indignation of an "*incredulus odi.*" When we remember, that this extreme high-churchism is enacted by a sect, which calls itself eminently spiritual, free and Protestant, the solecism becomes more repulsive. Only a part of the Immersionists have the nerve to assert this consequence. But their dogma involves it; and it is justly pressed on all.

Your acquaintance with Church history has taught you the tenour of the usual representations of the antiquaries, touching the mode of baptism in the patristic Churches. The usual version is, that in the second and third centuries the commonest mode of baptism was by a trine immersion, accompanied with a number of superstitious rites, of crossing, anointing, laying on hands, tasting honey and salt, clothing in a white garment, exorcism, &c. There are several reasons why we do not consider this testimony of any importance.

13. Patristic Modes.

First, the New Testament mode was evidently different, in most cases at least; and we do not feel bound by mere human authority (even though within a hundred and fifty years of the Apostles; a lapse of time within which great apostasies have often been matured). Second, we do not see how Immersionists can consistently claim this patristic precedent for dipping, as of authority, and refuse authority to all their other precedents for the human fooleries which so uniformly attended their baptisms. And farther, the many other corruptions of doctrine and government which were at the same time spread in the Church, prove the fathers to be wretched examples of the New Testament religion. Third, the usage was not as uniformly by immersion, as the antiquaries usually say. Thus, Cyprian teaches us (among many others) that clinic baptism was usually by pouring or sprinkling, in the third century; yet it was never regarded as therefore less valid; and that father speaks, with a tone nigh akin to contempt of the notion that its virtue was any less, because less water was used. Again, Dr. Robinson teaches us, that the early baptisms could not have uniformly been by immersion; because some baptismal urns of stone are still preserved, entirely too small to receive the applicant's whole person. And several monumental remains of great authenticity and antiquity show us baptisms actually by affusion, as that of the Emperor Constantine. Again, Mr. Taylor, in his Apostolic baptism, shows us very strong reasons to believe that the immersion of the whole body was not the sacrament of baptism, but a human addition and preliminary thereto. For instance, the connection of deaconesses with the baptizing of women, mentioned by not a few, is thus explained : That an immersion and actual washing *in puris naturalibus,* being supposed essential before baptism; the young women to be baptized were taken into the part of the baptistery where the pool was, and there, with closed doors, washed by the deaconesses ; for no male clergyman could assist here, compatibly with decency. And that after this, the candidates, dressed in their white garments, were presented to the presbyter, at the door of the Church, and received the actual baptism, by affusion, from him. This view of the distinction between the washing and the sacrament is also supported by what modern travelers observe, concerning the rite among some of the old, petrified, Oriental Churches.

These remarks are designed not for a full discussion : but to suggest the topics for your examination.

In conclusion of the subject of the Mode of Baptism, Recapitulation. let us review the positions successively established in a somewhat complicated discussion.

I. Having pointed out the superior importance of Hebraistic Greek usage, over the Classic, in determining this question, we separate the usage of the family of words expressing baptism into two questions; their meaning when expressive of common, secular washings, in either Classic or Hebraistic Greek, and their meaning when expressive of religious, or ritual washings.

II. We show that all common words applied to describe religious rituals, *ipso facto,* undergo some modification of signification. And hence, even if it could be shown that the family of words always mean nothing but dip, in common secular washings, it would not be therefore proved of baptism. But

III. The family of words do not always mean exclusive dipping, either in Classic or Hebraistic Greek, when expressive of common washings.

IV. Nor do they mean exclusive dipping, when applied to describe religious rituals other than the sacrament of Baptism, either in the Old Testament Greek, or in Josephus, or in the New Testament.

V. Nor, to come still nearer, is its proper sacramental meaning in the New Testament exclusive dipping; as we prove, by its symbolical meaning: From the analogy of figurative baptisms: From the actual attendant circumstances of the instances of the sacrament in the New Testament; And from the absurd consequences of the dogma. I commend Fairchild on Baptism, as a manual of this discussion remarkably compact, perspicuous, and comprehensive. I regard it as eminently adapted to circulation among our pastoral charges.

LECTURE LXV.

SUBJECTS OF BAPTISM.

SYLLABUS.

1. Who are proper subjects of Christian Baptism, and on what terms ?
Jo. Edwards. Qualific. for Communion. Mason on the Church, Essay i and v. Neander. Ch. Hist. on the Novatian and Donatist Schisms.
2. Meet the objection, that the nature of Baptism renders it necessarily inappropriate to infants, because they cannot believe. Review of Th. Ernest.
Dr. L. Woods' Lect. 111, 117, or Woods on Infant Baptism. Fairchild on Baptism. Armstrong on Baptism, pt. iii, ch. 3, Ridgley, Qu. 165. Note. Calv. bk. iv, ch. 16.
3. Argue infant-baptism from infant church-membership.
Mason on the Church, Essays ii, iv. Woods' Lect. 111, 112. Armstrong, pt. iii, ch. 4, 5. Calvin, bk. iv, ch. 16. Turrettin, Loc. xix, Qu. 20. Ridgley, Qu. 166.
4. What would have been the natural objections raised by the Jews, to Christianity had it excluded infants ?
Mason on the Church, Essay v.
5. State the argument from infant-baptism from the Great Commission. Matt. xxviii : 19, 20; Mark xvi : 15, 16 ; Luke xxiv : 47, &c.
Armstrong, pt. iii, chs. 2, 6. Woods' Lect. 113, &c. See on whole, Rev. of Theo. Ernest, chs. 4-6.

ALL adults who make an intelligent and credible profession of faith on Jesus Christ are to be baptized on their own application; and no other adults. The evidence of the last assertion is in Acts ii:41, 47; x : 47, with xi : 15, 16, and viii : 12, 37. The genuineness of the last text is indeed grievously questioned by the critical editors, except Knapp ; but even if spurious, its early and general introduction gives us an information of the clear conviction of the Church on this subject. Last: the truths signified by baptism, are such that it is obviously inappropriate to all adults but those who are true believers, in the judgment of charity.

1. Believing Adults to be Baptized.

We add that baptism is also to be administered to "the infants of one or both believing parents." (Conf. 28, § 4). The great question here raised will be the main subject of this and a

What Children May be Baptized ?

subsequent lecture. But a related question is still agitated among Pædobaptists themselves, whether one or both of the parents must be believers, or only decent baptized members of the Church. Papists baptize the children of all persons, and Episcopalians, Methodists, and not a few of the Presbyterian family of Churches, baptize those of all decent baptized persons. They plead the Church-membership of the parents, the example of the Jewish Church as to circumcision, and a kindly, liberal policy as to parents and infants. We object: First. The express language of our Standards, Conf. of Faith xxviii : 4; Larger Cat. Qu. 166. "Infants of one or both believing parents," "professing faith in Christ, and obedience to Him." Second: The language of 1 Cor. vii : 14, where it is not the baptized, but the "believing" parent, who sanctifies the unbelieving. Third: Those baptized, but unbelieving parents are Church members, subject to its guardianship and discipline; but they are not full members. They are ecclesiastical minors, cut off by their own guilty lack of spiritual qualification from all the spiritual privileges, and sealing ordinances. Fourth: Chiefly because it is preposterous that those who make no consecration of their own souls to Christ, and do not pretend to govern themselves by His laws, should profess to consecrate the souls of their children, and rear them to God. If then, it be urged that the children ought not to be deprived of their ecclesiastial privilege, because of the impenitence of the parents; I reply. Perfectly true: There is a great and cruel wrong committed on the little ones. But it is their own parents who commit it: not the Church authorities. They cannot repair that wrong, by giving them the shell of a sacrament which their parents' unbelief makes perfectly empty. This is no remedy; and it only violates Scripture, and introduces disorder. This will be greatly strengthened, when we show that Infant Baptism is a sacrament to the parents also.

Under the old Covenant the children of all circumcised persons were circumcised? True. But St. Paul has changed it; because, as we surmise, ours is a more spiritual dispensation, no State-Church separation exists from the world: and all unbelievers are spiritually "aliens."

Under the Jewish Church the children of mixed marriages were out of the Church, until they came in through the gate of proselytism. Neh. xiii : 23–28. But under the New Testament, if one parent is a credible believer, the child is within the Covenant. Our grounds are 1 Cor. vii : 14, and the circumcision and baptism of Timothy. Acts xvi : 3.

Before we proceed to the main point of debate, it will be well to remove out of the way the objection on which Immersionists place the main reliance. They urge that since infants cannot exercise the graces signified and sealed in baptism, (See Cate-

2, Immersionists Object; Infants Cannot Believe.

chism, Qu. 94), it is useless and preposterous to administer it to babies. Take, say they, Mark xvi : 15, 16, as a specimen of the many passages in which it is categorically said, or clearly implied, that one must believe, before it is proper to baptize him. Hence the administration of the rite to infants is a practical falsehood, and if unauthorized by God, even profane. What, they ask, can all your inferential arguments for infant Church-membership be worth, when the express words of Scripture prove that infants cannot have the necessary qualifications for baptism ?

We reply, this plausible statement proceeds on the usual fallacy of taking the speaker's words in a sense in which he did not mean them to be applied. In Mark xvi : 16, for instance, Christ was not speaking either of the terms of infant salvation, or of the terms on which they could become Church-members. Let the reader remember that the temporary commission to the apostles and seventy (Matt. x : 5) had already made them familiar with the fact that Christ's dispensation was to be preached to Jews. But now, in Mark xvi : 15, it is extended "to all the world," and to "every creature." These were the features of the new commission prominent to our Saviour's mind, and the disciples' attention. The terms on which Jewish families should be admitted were already familiar. The question was, how shall those be admitted who are now aliens? Why; on their faith. The evidence that infants were not here intended to be excluded from baptism by our Saviour's scope is absolutely demonstrative : for the Immersionist interpretation would equally make the passage prove that infants can neither be baptized, nor be saved, because they are incapable of faith; and it would equally make it prove that the salvation of infants is dependent on their baptism ! We may find many other illustrations of the absurdity of such interpretations ; as, for instance, in 2 Thess. iii : 10 : "If any one (εἴ τις) will not work, neither shall he eat." A similar reasoning would prove that infants should be starved.

Further : it does not follow that because infants cannot exercise intelligent graces, therefore there is no sense nor reason in administering to them sacraments significant thereof. Infants are capable of redemption. Glorious truth! Why, then, should it appear a thing incredible that they should partake of the sacraments of redemption? Baptism signifies God's covenant with souls, as well as their covenant with Him. Can there be no meaning in a pledge of God's covenant-favour applied to an infant, because the infant does not yet apprehend it? No sense at all; because it has no sense to him? Strange reasoning! But human suppositions are a bad test of what God may or may not think reasonable. To the Word and the Testimony! There we find two cases in which religious ordinances were applied to "unconscious babies." In Matt. xix : 14, Mark x : 14; Luke xviii : 16, our Saviour took up little children (βρέφη) into His arms, and blessed them, because they were Church members. Did they comprehend the blessing? The other case is that of circumcision, and it is peculiarly strong, because it was emblematic of the same spiritual exercises and graces, now signified by baptism. See Rom. ii : 28, 29; iv : 11; Col. ii : 11; Deut. xxx : 6; ix : 16; Phil, iii : 3. Yet circumcision was, by God's command, applied to all the infant males of God's people! Let the Immersionist, therefore, go and turn all the confident denunciation of "baby-sprinkling," against this parallel ordinance of God. We entrench ourselves behind it.

Once more: So far as the child himself is concerned, there is no absurdity in giving him the seal in advance of his fulfillment of the conditions. Are not seals often appended to promissory covenants? Yea, every covenant is in its nature promissory, including something to be done, as a condition of the bestowment. This is so of adult baptism. But, they say, the adult can be a party; infants not. I answer: parents are, and the efficacy of the parental relation, properly sanctified, is regular enough to justify this arrangement. Where, then, is the practical objection, so far as the infant's own subsequent edification is concerned, of his receiving the seal beforehand, so that he may ever after have the knowledge of that fact, with all its solemn meaning, and see it re-enacted in every infant baptism he afterward witnesses? But, above all, remember that the infant is not the only party, on man's side, to the sacrament. Infant baptism is a sacrament to the parent, as well as the child. It consecrates the relation of filiation, or parentage, and thus touches both the parties to the relation equally. The parent has momentous duties to perform, for God's glory; and momentous religious responsibilities, as to the soul of the child, which duties are also represented and pledged in this sacrament, as well as God's promised aid and blessing in their performance. Infant baptism is a sacrament to the parent as much as to the child. Now, whatever of warning, instruction, comfort, edification, the sacrament was intended to convey to the parent, to fit him better for his charge as the educator of the child for eternity: when should the parent receive that equipment? When does the moral education of the infant's soul begin? It begins just so soon as the formation of habit begins; so soon as petulance, anger, selfishness, can be exhibited by an infant; so soon as it can apprehend the light of a mother's smile beaming upon it as it hangs upon her breast; as soon as it can know to tremble at her frown. Here, then, is the great practical reason, which makes God's wisdom clear even to man's reason, in instituting the seal of Church membership at the dawn of life.

The Sacrament Embraces the Parents.

We proceed now to advance the positive evidences for infant baptism. Of these, the most solid and comprehensive is that from infant Church-membership in the New Testament Church. The major premise of our argument is, that baptism is, in all cases, the proper rite by which to recognize membership in the visible Church. The minor premise is, the infants of believing parents are members of the visible Church of Christ. Hence, the conclusion: such infants are proper subjects of baptism.

3. Argument from Infant Membership in Old Testament and New. Major Premise.

On the major premise there will probably be little dispute between us and Immersionists. In the great commission, we are taught that discipleship is formally constituted by baptism (Matt. xxviii : 19). In Acts ii : 41, language is used which plainly shows that the baptism of the three thousand was equivalent to their being added to the Church. In I Cor. xii : 13, the spiritual engrafting of true believers by the Holy Ghost into the spiritual body of Christ, the invisible Church, is called a baptism; in evident allusion to the effect of that rite in introducing to the visible Church.

The minor premise leads us to consider the origin and constitution of the Church. Having found in the Old Testament a visible Church-State, called קָהֵל and עֵדָה, and characterized by every mark of a Church, we trace that society up the stream of sacred history, until we find its institution (or re-institution) in the family of Abraham, and in that gospel and ecclesiastical covenant ratified with him in Genesis, ch. xvii. The patriarchal form was most naturally superinduced on this Church then; because it was the only organized form, with which man had hitherto been familiar, and the one best suited to that state of the world. The society there organized was set apart to the service and worship of God. It was organized under ecclesiastical rulers. It had the Word and gospel of God. It had its sacrament and other sacred rites. No one will dispute the continuity of this society under Moses and his successors; for the covenant of Horeb manifestly developed, it did not destroy, the body.

Minor Premise. Church Formed Under Abraham.

But can the same thing be said of the visible Church catholic which has existed since Christ, under the organization given it by the Apostles? The Reformed Churches answer, Yes. This is substantially the same with the Church of the Old Testament. The change of dispensation is the change of outward form, not of its substance or nature. This is proved. (a) By the fact that the repeal of God's Church-covenant with Abraham and his family is nowhere stated. The abrogation of the Mosaic economy does not destroy the old body, because that economy

The Same Under New Testament.

did not introduce it. The law, which was four hundred and thirty years after, could not disannul the covenant made with Abraham. Gal. iii : 17.

(b) The Apostles and Christ, by their acts and sayings, recognize the existence of a visible Church, which they do not abolish, but reform, and increase. Observe in how many instances particular churches were but synagogues Christianized. Consider also, how those traits of order and ritual which are distinctive of the new dispensation, were made to overlap those which marked the old. The substitution of the former for the latter was gradual. St. Paul observed the passover after he began to keep the Lord's Supper; he circumcised Timothy after he began to baptize Gentiles. There is no sudden cutting off of the old, but a gradual " splicing." of the new on it.

Apostles Develop, not Destroy it.

(c) The Apostle expressly teaches that Gentile converts, coming to Christ by faith, are under the terms of the Abrahamic covenant. Therefore that covenant is not abolished. They are "the seed;" they are the "children of Abraham." They are "the true Israel." Rom. iv : 12–17; Matt. iii : 9; Gal. iii : 7. Indeed, the " seed," to whom the promises were made, never was, at any time, strictly coincident with the lineal descendants of Abraham. Ishmael, Keturah's children, Esau, though circumcised, were no part of it. Every heathen proselyte was. See Gen. xvii : 12, 13; Exod. xii : 48; Deut. xxiii : 8. Gentiles were always, as truly (not as numerously) as now, a part of this seed.

Gentiles Formed it.

(d) The correlative promises that "all nations should be blessed in Abraham," and that he should be "Father of many nations," were only fulfilled as the Gentiles were made members of the Abrahamic body. See Rom. iv : 16, 17. It cannot be said that Abraham's paternity of the twelve tribes exhausted that promise, for Israel was but one nation. If, then, the Abrahamic Church expired before the Gentiles were brought in, this promise was never fulfilled. It will not help the cause to say that Abraham was father of these believers, in the sense of being their first exemplar. He was not. Noah, Enoch, Abel, probably Adam, were before him. The relationship is that of the head and founder of an organization, to the subsequent members of it. Nor will it be said, that the Gentiles becoming "Abraham's seed" only means their admission into the invisible Church, into which Abraham's faith admitted him. This is, indeed, a higher sequel to the privilege, as to all true believers, but not the whole of it. We have proved that the covenant was not purely spiritual, but also an ecclesiastical, visible Church covenant. Therefore the seed, or children of the covenant (see Acts iii : 25) are also thereby brought into the visible Church relationship.

Promises to it Only Fulfilled Under New Testament.

(e) The number of Old Testament promises to the visible Church, some of which were unfulfilled at the end of the old dispensation, must imply that the community is still in existence to receive their fulfillment. Otherwise God has failed. See, then, Isa. ii : 2, 3; liv : 1–5, xlix : 14–23; Ps. ii : 6, 8. It cannot be said that the invisible Church is the sole object of these promises.

(f) Last. The figure of Rom. xi : 17 to 24, plainly implies that the Old Testament visible Church is continued under the new dispensation. The good olive tree was not uprooted, but pruned, and new branches grafted in. And at last, the exscinded branches are to be regrafted "into their own olive tree." The argument is too clear and strong to need many words.

Rom. xi : 17, &c.

Thus, our minor premise is established. The ecclesiastical covenant made with Abraham still subsists unrepealed, and all Christians are brought under it. As children were members of that covenant, the inference is irresistible that they are members still, unless their positive exclusion can be pointed out in the New Testament. This inference is also greatly fortified, by showing, First: All God's general dispensations toward the human family have embraced the children along with the parents. In the Covenant of Works with Adam: in the curse for its breach: in the covenant with Noah: in the curse on Sodom: in the doom of the Canaanites and Amelekites: in the constitution of society and course of Providence in all ages: in the political commonwealths ordained by Him: in all these, the infant children go with the parents. Were the visible Church different, it would be a strange anomaly.

Inference. Confirmed by all Providences.

Second: Malachi tells us (ii : 15) that God's object in constituting the marriage relation and family as it is, was "to seek a godly seed;" i. e., to provide for the Christian rearing of the offspring. Now, this is the Church's object. Would it not be strange if the visible Church failed to embrace and consecrate the family institution as a subdivision of itself? Third: The affection, authority, and influence of parents are so unique, that when we properly consider them, it seems incredible God would have omitted them as parts of His Church instrumentalities, subject to the sanctifying rules of His house. Parental love is the strongest of the instinctive affections, and the most godlike in its permanence, forbearance, and disinterestedness. Parental authority is the most remarkable and absolute one delegated by God to man over his fellow man. Consider: it authorizes the parent to govern the child for a fourth of his life as a slave; to decide virtually his intelligence, culture, and social destiny, and even to elect for him a character and religious creed; thus seeming almost to infringe the inalienable responsibilities and liberties of the immortal soul! And last: the parental influence is so efficacious, especially in things moral and religious, that it does more than all others to decide the child's everlasting fate.   Can it be that God would omit such a lever as this, in constructing His Church, as the organism for man's moral and religious welfare ?   Fourth : The Church-membership of children seems to be implied in that duty which all right-minded Christians instinctively exercise, of caring for the welfare and salvation of the children of the brotherhood. Fifth : It follows from the declared identity of circumcision and baptism, and from many express Scriptures. See Col. ii : 11, 12, 13 ; Matt. xix : 13–15 ; Acts ii : 38, 39 ; 1 Cor. vii : 14.   The Church membership of infants having been thus established, the propriety of their baptism follows.   Indeed, immersionists virtually admit that if the second premise is true, the conclusion must follow, by denying the Church-membership of infants under the New Testament.

Many evasions of this argument are attempted.   Immer-
Visible Church in Old sionists deny that there was any visible
Testament Denied by Church-State appointed for saints in the
Immersionists. Answer. Old Testament !   This is a striking, and at once a mournful, proof of the stringency of my argument, that a body of evangelical Christians claiming especial scripturalness and orthodoxy, should be forced, in resisting it, to adopt one of the most monstrous assertions of those flagrant heretics and fanatics, the Anabaptists and Socinians.   You have only to notice how expressly it contradicts the Scriptures, Acts vii : 38 ; Rom. xi : 24 ; Heb. iii : 5, 6 : How it defies the plainest facts of the Old Testament history, which shows us God giving His people every possible feature of a visible Church-State ; gospel, ministry, sacraments, other ordinances, Sabbath, discipline, sanctuaries, &c. : How utterly it confounds all relations between the old and new dispensations : And how preposterously it represents Christ's own personal life, observances, and obedience, including especially His baptism by John, an Old Testament prophet, administering his rite in this Old Testament No-Church ; which rite is, according to immersionists, still the Christian sacrament !

Some of them assert that the argument, if good for any-
Objected that the thing, would equally make all adult unbeliev-
Argument Proves Too ing children of believing parents, and all un-
Much. Answer. believing domestic slaves, Church members.
Is no force to be allowed to the passing away of the patriarchal state, with the almost absolute authority of the father? None to the growing spirituality of the New Covenant? None to the express change in these features by apostolic authority, as is manifested in their precedents ?   Still, all that could be made of this argument would be to prove, not that the reasoning of Pedobaptists is unsound, but that their conduct may be inconsistent.

Sometimes it is objected that if infants were really made members of the visible Church, then, as they grow up, they must be admitted, without question, to all the privileges of membership, to suffrage, to office, to the Lord's supper. I reply that there is no commonwealth on earth, where mere citizenship entitles to all the higher franchises. In the State, all citizens are entitled to protection, and subject to jurisdiction. But all cannot vote and bear office. Christ's ecclesiastical commonwealth is a school, a place for teaching and training. To be a member of the school does not at once imply that one must share all its powers and privileges. The scholars are promoted according to their qualifications.

It is objected by some: If Peter and his brethren were in the visible Church, how comes it that Christ says to them: "I have chosen you out of the world?" Jno. xv: 19. I answer: Cannot that which is worldly, in the true sense, be in the visible Church? The objection begs the question. The very point in debate is, whether the Anabaptist definition of the visible Church, as a body containing only regenerate persons, is true. The Bible says that it is not: that Peter was yet worldly, while regularly in the visible Church, and was, out of that state chosen by Christ to the apostleship, and to effectual calling.

Peter, &c., "Chosen out of the World."

One more objection may be noted: If the visible Church of the Old and New Testaments is one, then circumcision and baptism are alike the initiatory rites. How came it then, that Jews, already regularly in it, were re-admitted by baptism? I reply first. It is not so certain that they were. Note, that we do not believe John's baptism to have been the Christian sacrament. But who can prove that the Twelve, and the Seventy were ever baptized again? As for the Jews after Pentecost, who certainly did receive Christian baptism, they were now, (after Christ's definite rejection, crucifixion, and ascension) "broken off for their unbelief;" and needed re-admittance on their repentance. But second, where is the anomaly of re-administering the initiatory rite to members already in the Society, at the season of the marked change of outward form, when it was receiving a large class of new members? I see nothing strange in the fact, that the old citizens took their oath of allegiance over again, along with the new.

Why were Jews Baptized if in the Church?

Immersionists delight to urge, that as baptism is a positive institution, no Protestant should administer it to infants, because the New Testament contains no explicit warrant for doing so. I shall show that the tables can be turned on this point.

4. No New Testament Warrant Required.

When a society undergoes important modifications, its sub-

stantial identity yet remaining, the fair presumption is, that all those things are intended
to remain unchanged, about the change of
which nothing is said.   We may illustrate from citizenship in a
Commonwealth, changing its constitution.   So, if there were
not one word in all the New Testament, indicating the continuance of infant Church-membership, the silence of Scripture
constitutes no disproof; and the burden of proof would rest on
the Immersionist.   And this burden he would have to assume
against every antecedent probability.   True, the cessation of
the Mosaic dispensation was accompanied with great changes ;
but infant membership and circumcision never were merely
Mosaic.   We may say of them, as of the Covenant to which
they belonged, as St. Paul says in Gal. iii : 17.   All that was
typical, passed away, because of the coming of the Antitype :
circumcision and infant membership never were types.   Again,
infant membership was esteemed by Jews a privilege.   We
understand that the new dispensation is an extension of the old
one, more liberal in its provisions, and its grace : and embracing
the whole human family.   It would be a strange thing indeed,
if this era of new liberality and breadth were the occasion for
a new and vast restriction, excluding a large class of the human
family, in whom the pious heart is most tenderly interested.
Consider this in the light of the Apostle's language : e. g., in
Rom. xi : 20 ; Acts iii : 23.   In these and similar passages, the
Jews are warned that unbelief of Christ, the great closing
Prophet of the line, (like resistance of previous Theocratic Messengers,) will be accompanied with loss of their church membership.   According to Immersionists, the meaning of this warning
would be: " Oh, Jew ; if you believe not on Jesus Christ, you
(and your children) forfeit your much valued visible Church
membership.   But if you believe on Him, then your innocent
children shall be punished for your obedience, by losing their
privileges !"

Burden of Disproof on the Immersionists.

Further, no Immersionist is consistent, in demanding an
express New Testament warrant in words,
for all his ordinances.   There is not an intelligent Protestant in the world, who does not
hold that what follows from the express Word, " by good and
necessary consequence," is binding, as well as the Word itself.
What other warrant have Immersionists for observing the
Lord's day as a Christian Sabbath, and neglecting the seventh
day ?   What warrant for admitting females to the Lord's
table ?   What warrant for their favourite usage of strict communion ?   This, pre-eminently, is only a deduction.

What New Testament Warrant for Close Com- munion, &c.

The presumption against the Immersionist is greatly
strengthened again, in my view, by the extreme improbability, that the sweeping revolution against infant Church membership

No Clamour, such as Must have Arisen at Ex- clusion of Infants.

could have been established by the Apostles, without some such clamour as would have been mentioned in the New Testament. We must remember that all Hebrews greatly prized their ecclesiastical birth. See Matt. iii : 9 ; Jno. viii : 33. To be cut off from among his people, was to the Jew, a shameful and dreaded degradation. The uncircumcised was a dog to him, unclean and despised. We have evidence enough that the believing Hebrews shared these feelings. Hence, when we saw that even believers among them were so suspicious, and the unbelievers full of rampant jealousy, and eager to object and revile the Nazarenes, how is it possible that this great abrogation of privilege could be established, while we hear none of that clamour which, the New Testament tells us, was provoked by the cessation of sacrifice, purifications, and circumcision?

But the Immersionist may rejoin : such a clamour may have existed, and it may be omitted in the sacred history, because the history is brief, and the purposes of inspiration may not have required its notice. One is not entitled to argue from the absence of proof. *De omni ignoto quasi de non existentibus.*

That no Such Clamour Argued.

I reply : we are not arguing herein from the mere absence of proof; for we give high probable evidence to show that if the fact had ever occurred, the traces of it must have been preserved. First : Not only is there a dead silence in the brief narrative of Scripture concerning any objection of Jews, such as must have been made had infant membership been abrogated; but there seems to be an equal silence in the Rabbinical literature against Christianity, and in the voluminous polemical works, from the days of Justin Martyr—*adversus Tryphonem*, down. Second : The objections, restiveness, and attacks growing out of the revolutionizing of other things, less important than infant membership, required and received full notice in the New Testament. Look for instance, at the Epistle to the Hebrews, written practically with this main object; to obviate the restiveness and tendency to revolt produced among Jewish Christians, by the abrogation of cherished customs. The main line of argument is to show that these innovations are justifiable, and scriptural; yet there is not one word to excuse this momentous innovation against infant membership! Third : The sacred narrative in Acts xvth approaches so near the topic of this innovation, that it is simply incredible an allusion to it should have been avoided, had the revolution been attempted. The question which agitated the whole Christian community to its core was : shall Gentile converts, entering the Church under the new dispensation, be required to be circumcised, and keep the ceremonial law? The very arguments by which this question was debated are given. Now, how inevitable would it have been, had the change in membership been made, which the Immersionist supposes, to say : " Whether you circumcise adult Gentile converts, or not; you cannot circumcise their children; because Jewish children and Gentile, are no longer admitted with their parents." But there is no whisper of this point raised. I cannot believe the innovation had been attempted. But if it had not been made at that stage, it was never made at all by divine authority; for the Immersionist professes to find it in Christ's commission at His ascension.

Pædobaptist writers are accustomed to attach importance to that great Commission. See Matt. xxviii: 19, 20; Mark xvi: 15, 16; Luke xxiv: 47–49. As we have already considered the supposed evidence for exclusive believer's baptism in Mark xvi: 16, we may take the language of Matthew as most explicit and full, of the three places. We consider that the Apostles would naturally have understood such a commission to include infants, for the following reasons:

5. Great Commission Implies Pædo-Baptism.

The first thing told them is to go, and "teach" more properly, "disciple" (μαθητεύσατε) all nations. Here, says the Immersionist, is strong evidence that only believer's baptism is enjoined, because they are to be taught first, and then baptized; whereas infants cannot be taught. The argument is unfortunately founded only on a failure to examine the original. For this turns it against the Immersionist. The term "disciple," is eminently appropriate to the conception of a school of Christ, which is one of the Bible conceptions of the Church. See Gen. xviii: 19; Deut. vi: 7; Is. ii: 3, &c. The young child is entered or enrolled at this school, before his religious education begins, in order that he may learn afterwards. Matt. xxviii: 20.

Second: what would a mind free from immersionist preconceptions naturally understand by the command to "disciple all nations?" Does not this include the infant children, as a part thereof? But we must remember, that the minds of the disciples were not only free from these prejudices, but accustomed to the Church-membership of infants. They had known nothing else but a Church-State in which the children went along with their parents. It seems then, that they would almost inevitably understand such a command, as including the authority to baptize infants, unless instructed to the contrary. Nor is this all: these disciples were accustomed to see cases of discipleship to Judaism occurring from time to time. Proselytes were not unusual. See Matt. xxiii: 15; Acts vi: 5; ii: 10; xiii: 43, and the uniform custom was to circumcise the children and receive them into the Jewish community, on the profession of the father. So that, if we set aside for the present, the question whether proselyte baptism was as yet practiced, it is clear the Apostles must be led by all they had been accustomed to witness, to suppose that their converts were to bring in their children along with them; unless the notion were contradicted by Christ. Where is the contradiction of it?

LECTURE LXVI.
SUBJECTS OF BAPTISM. — Concluded.

IT has been fashionable of late years for learned Pædobaptists (e. g., Dr. J. A. Alexander) to doubt whether the Jews prac-

6. Argument from Proselyte Baptism of Jews. ticed proselyte family baptism as early as the Christian era ; because, they say, it was first asserted in the Talmud (of 6th century) and these writers are unscrupulous. I see not why we may not in this case believe, because they are supported thus : (see Dr. Woods). They uniformly assert the antiquity of the usage. The usage is naturally deducible from Levitical purifications. It accounts for John's baptism being received with such facility, while neither in the New Testament, nor in Josephus, is any surprise expressed at his baptizing as a novelty. Jews certainly did practise proselyte baptism at a later day, and it can hardly be supposed that they borrowed it from the hated Christians. If they even did, it proves a prevalence of usage before they borrowed. Last : it does not seem very likely that such a pretence, if first invented in the Talmud, would have escaped denial by some earlier Christian or Jewish Christian.

Now, if apostles were accustomed to see families baptized into Judaism, it was very likely that they would understand the command to go and proselyte all peoples to Christianity and baptize them, as including whole families.

Had the English version been accurate in the employment of the words house οἶχος household οἰχία,

7. Argument From Baptism of Houses. our argument on this point would appear in it more just. According to the definition of

789

Aristotle, and well-defined classic and Hebraistic usage, the word οἶκος means literally, the apartments inhabited by the parents and children, and οἰκία, literally, the curtilage. Figuratively, the former, the family; the latter, the houshold. And the idea which constitutes the former a house is lineage. It is by birth of infants the house is built up; so that the word may more naturally mean young children distingûished from parents than *vice versa*. A house is a cluster of one lineage, receiving accretion by birth and growth of children. So that when it is said in the New Testament that the οἶκος was baptized (never the οἰκία), the presence of children is forcibly implied. This distinction in usage is always carefully observed in the New Testament as to the figurative sense of the two words, often as to the literal. E. g., Acts xvi: 31–34 (Greek); 1 Cor. i: 16, with xvi: 15; Phil. iv: 22. The argument is miserably obscured in the English version. Now, while eight individuals are spoken of by name, in the New Testament, as baptized, the houses of four of these are mentioned as baptized along with them. Cornelius', Acts x: 2, 44, 48; Lydia's, xvi: 15; the Philippian jailor's xvi: 33; Stephanas', 1 Cor. i: 16. Now, on the fact that, among the very few separate individual baptisms mentioned in the New Testament, four were of families, is ground of two-fold probability: that there were young children in some of them, who were baptized on their parents' faith, and that this sacramental recognition of the parental and family relation, looks like Pedobaptism amazingly. Immersionists do not use such language, so that even if it could be proved there probably were no young unconverted children, the argument remains.

They say they can prove in each case there were none: Cornelius' by verses 2, 44. But see Gen. xviii: 19; 2 Chron. xx: 13; Ezra viii: 21; Matt. xxi: 15, 16. That Lydia's house were all believing adult children, or servants, or apprentices, they argue from Acts xvi: 40, "brethren." But see verses 14, 15, nobody's faith is mentioned but Lydia's; and doubtless Paul had many other converts out of Lydia's house. The proof is, that the whole context shows the meeting in verse 40 was a public one, not a family one; and the Philippian church, a flourishing body was now planted.

These Houses Included Children.

That the jailor's family all believed is argued from verse 34. But the original places the πανοικί with rejoiced. That Stephanas' family were all baptized and believers, is argued from 1 Cor. xvi: 15. Answer: It was his οἰκία not his οἶκος which engaged in ministrations of Christian hospitality.

8. Infants are Addressed as Church-members.

An argument of equal, or perhaps greater importance is to be derived from the addressing of the titles of Church-members to little children in the New Testament. That the words Ἅγιοι,

:ιστός, or πιστεύων and 'Αδελφός are the current words employed to denote professed Christians, will not be denied. " Christians " is only used two or three times. The address of epistles to these titles is equivalent to their address to professed Church-members. Now in these cases we find children addressed in the epistles. Eph. vi : 1–4; Col. iii : 20; 1 John ii : 12, 13, τεκνία, παιδία. First, these were not adult children,

Further, in Titus i : 6, they are expressly called τέκνα πιστά.

The Bishop's Children Must be Members. Compare for illustration, in 1 Tim. vi : 2, Πιστοὺς δεσπότας, and 1 Tim. iii : 4, parallel passage where the Bishop's children being πιστά and ἐν ὑποταγῇ, is equivalent to being well ruled, and in subjection. If the alternative be taken that Titus' τέκνα πιστά mean adult children who are professors, on their own behalf, of godliness, we are led into absurdities; for what must be decided of the man whose children are yet small; and who being therefore in the prime of manhood, is fit to serve the Church ? Shall he wait, though otherwise fit, till it be seen whether his children will be converted ? Or if the children be already come to ages of intelligence, and not converted, in spite of the Father's good rearing, must he be refused ordination ? This would have excluded Legh Richmond, and many ministers blessed of God. The obvious sense is, the bishop's children must be consecrated and reared accordingly.

As the historical evidence for the early and constant prevalence of infant baptism is so well unfolded in Coleman, Woods, Bingham and Wall, and as your Church History enters fully into it, I shall not again detail the witnesses; but add some remarks to sum up. And first, Bingham and Wall, between them, mention nine fathers, of the first and second centuries, who seem pretty clearly to allude to infant baptism; some briefly and singly, others clearly and more than once. Now Mosheim's list of the genuine Fathers who wrote before A. D. 200, is only about 12 (Clement, Ignatius, Polycarp, Pseudo Barnabas, Pastor of Hermas, Ep. to Diognetus, (probably Justin's), Justin Martyr, Irenæus, Athenagoras, Theophilus of Antioch, Clem. Alexandrinus, Tertullian), if we omit 12 or 15 more, whose names and works are only made known to us by other Fathers who speak of them. And his list is nearly exhaustive. Now seeing that few of these works are voluminous, and that some are mere fragments; and seeing that if our theory of Pedobaptism is correct, it was a subject which did not need much agitation, as being undisputed and of ancient establishment; here is fully as much notice of it as was reasonably to be expected. After A. D. 200, the notices are abundant.

9. Authorities on Patristic Baptism. Remarks. 1st. Infant Baptism Early Mentioned.

The enumerations of heresies, and refutations of them

2d. Denial of it Not Mentioned of Any Heretics. drawn up by Irenæus, Epiphanius, Philastrius, Augustine, Theodoret, (Epiphanius, for instance; against 80 heresies), contain no reference to any heretics who denied infant baptism, except those (as some Gnostic sects) who denied all baptism. And Peter de Bruys is said to be the first sectary who ever denied it.

3d. Not Refused even by Pelagians, Under the Strongest Inducement. In the controversy between Augustine and Pelagians, the latter were much pressed with the argument: "If infants have neither depravity nor guilt, why baptize them?" Their answer was, to gain for them heaven, instead of eternal life. They would have gladly given the more satisfactory answer, if it had been true, that infant baptism was an innovation. But they do not. Celestius, it is stated, repudiated the insinuation that his doctrine would lead to the denial of infant baptism, saying, he had never known any sect wicked enough˙ for this. He and Pelagius were learned and traveled.

4th. Evidence in the Caticombs. In the Roman Catacombs, among the many interesting remains, are inscriptions over the graves of infants and young children, who are said to be baptized, and called "faithful," "believers," "brothers," while they are said to be of ages varying from 18 months to 12 years.

5th. Infant Communion. Infant communion, which Immersionists love to class as an equal and similar superstition to infant baptism, is a clear proof of the earlier prevalence of the latter. For the primitive Church never gave the Lord's Supper before baptism.

But Tradition no Authority to us. But we do not rely on the patristic testimony as our decisive argument, but on Scripture. The Church early became superstitious; and many of their superstitions, as baptismal regeneration and infant communion, they profess to base on Scripture. But where they do so, we can usually trace and expose their misunderstanding of it. This current and early testimony is relied on, not as proving by itself that we are warranted to baptize infants, but as raising a strong probability that it was an apostolic usage, and thus supporting our scriptural argument.

10. Does Infant Baptism Corrupt the Church. Immersionists object vehemently to infant baptism and membership, that it floods the spirituality of Christ's Church with a multitude of worldly, nominal Christians. One of them has written a book on "the evils of infant baptism." They point to the lamentable state of religion in Europe, in the Papacy, and in the Oriental Churches, as the legitimate result. They urge: If our Confession and Government are correct in saying, 'all baptized persons are members of the Church,' &c., (Bk. Disc. Ch. I, § 6), consistency would lead us, of course, to admit them, without saving change, to suffrage, to office, and to sealing ordinances; we should baptize their children in turn (as Methodists, Episcopalians, Papists do), and thus the whole world would be brought unsanctified into the Church, obliterating its spirituality. But Christ intended it to be composed only of His converted followers. The only reason why Presbyterian and other Churches in America, do not exhibit these abominable results is, that they do not act out their creeds, and practically regard the unconverted baptized as no members. I reply:

The notion that Christ would organize His religious kingdom on earth in contrast to human society, admitting none but pure members, is plausible and pretty. Yea, the unthinking may reason, that as He is autocrat, heart-searching, almighty, His voluntary embracing of any impure material would look like a voluntary connivance at sin, and indifference to that sanctity which the Church was formed to promote. But it is a utopian and unscriptural dream. See Matt. xiii : 24 and 47. Christ has not even formed the hearts of His own people thus; but permits evil to mix with them. A Church to be administered by human hands must be mixed; anything else is but a dishonest pretense, even among Immersionists. Christ permits a mixed body, not because He likes it, but because His wisdom sees it best under the circumstances.

1st. Mixture in the Church Foreseen by Christ.

It is not fair to argue from the abuse, but from proper use of an institution. Note: God's arrangement under the old dispensation was liable to the same evils, for infant Church-membership abused certainly was followed by horrid corruptions. The wide corruptions of Popish and other European Churches are not traceable to proper use of infant baptism, but to other manifest causes: neglect of youthful training, State establishments, Paganism infused, hierarchical institutions, &c. If infant membership were the great corrupter, and its absence the great safeguard, immersed Churches ought to be uniformly pure. How is this? It is an invidious task to make the inquiry; but it is their own test. Look, then, at Ironsides, Dunkers, Mormons, African Churches in America. We shall not be so uncharitable as to charge all this on immersion.

2nd. Mediæval Churches Corrupted Otherwise.

Enough for us to answer for our own principles, not those of Papists, Episcopalians, Methodists. We stated our limitations on infant baptism. Where they are observed, and the duties pledged in the sacrament are tolerably performed, it results in high benefit. When we teach that all baptized persons "should perform all the duties of Church-members," it is not meant with unconverted hearts. The Church states the great Bible doctrine that in baptism renewing graces are promised and sealed; and if the

3rd. Safeguards.

adult does not get them, it is his fault. Our doctrine does not break down the distinction made between spiritual and carnal by sealing ordinances one whit, or give to the baptized member one particle of power to corrupt the suffrage or government of the Church.

11. The remaining cavils are best answered by stating the Scriptural view of the relation of unregenerate baptized children to the Church, and the benefits thence inuring.

When our standards say, "All baptized persons are mem bers of the Church," this by no means im plies their title to all sealing ordinances, suffrage, and office. They are minor citizens in the ecclesiastical commonwealth, under tutelage, training, and instruction, and government; heirs, if they will exercise the graces obligatory on them, of all the ultimate franchises of the Church, but not allowed to enjoy them until qualified. Yet they are, justly, under ecclesiastical government. The reasonableness of this position is well illustrated by that of minors under the civil commonwealth. These owe allegiance and obedience, and are under the government; they are made to pay taxes, to testify in court, and, after a time, even to do military service and labour on the highway. They can be tried for crimes, and even capitally punished. But they may neither sit as judges in a jury, bear office, nor vote for officers, until a full age is supposed to confer the necessary qualification. Such must be the regulations of any organized society which embraces (on any theory) families within it. And if the family is conceived as the integer of which the society is constituted, this status of minor members of families is yet more proper, yea, unavoidable. But such is precisely the conception of the Scriptures, concerning the integers of which both the State and Church are constituted. Now, the visible Church is an organized human society, constituted of Christian families as integers, for spiritual ends—religious instruction, sanctification, holy living and glorification of its members. Hence, it seems most reasonable that unregenerate members of its families shall be, on the one hand, included under its government; and, on the other, not endowed with its higher franchises. The State, whose purposes are secular, fixed the young citizen's majority when, by full age, he is presumed to have that bodily and mental growth of the adult, which fits him for his duties. The Church recognizes the majority of its minor citizens when they show that spiritual qualification—a new heart—necessary for handling its spiritual concernments. The Church visible is also a school of Christ. Schools, notoriously, must include untaught children. That is what they exist for. But they do not allow these children to teach and govern ; they are there to be taught and restrained. The analogy is most instructive.

Baptized Persons in What Sense? Illustrated by Minors in Commonwealth.

The Immersionist says that our communion is only saved
from utter corruption by our own inconsist-
This Relation Nat-
ural. ency; that while our constitution calls our
children Church members, we fortunately
treat them, as they do, as not Church members. Whereas the
Immersionist charges us with a wicked inconsistency, I will
retort upon him the charge of a pious one: Those of them who
are truly good people, while they say their children are not
Church members, fortunately treat them as though they were.
They diligently bring them under the instructions, restraints,
and prayers of the Church and pastor. Happily, the instincts
and influences of the Christian family are so deeply founded
and so powerful, that a perverse and unscriptural theory cannot
arrest them. These Christians discard the Bible conception of
the visible Church, as an organized body whose integers are
Christian "houses," and adopt the unscriptural and impracticable theory of a visible Church organized of regenerate individuals. But, blessed be God! the light and love of a sanctified parent's heart are too strong to be wholly perverted by this
theory; they still bring the family, as a whole, virtually within
the Church. And this is the reason that true religion is perpetuated among them.

But a more definite answer may be desired to the inquiry:
Discipline Consists What are the precise shape and extent of
in Instruction and Re- this instruction and government, which constraint. stitute the Church's "discipline" over its
unregenerate members? To give a clear answer, let us distinguish the instruction from the restraint; the two together
make up the idea of discipline. As to the former, the teaching
of church-presbyters and catechists is by no means to supersede that of the parents, but only to assist and re-enforce it.
Into the sacred relation of parent and child no other human
authority, not even that which Christ Himself has appointed in
His Church, may intrude. None can sufficiently replace it.
But all these baptized members are the "charge" of the pastor
and session; and it is the duty of these "overseers" to provide
for them, and to see that they enjoy the public and social instructions of the gospel. And pastors and elders should,
moreover, extend to them that advice in temptation, and those
efforts to comfort them in affliction, and to secure the sanctification of their trials, which they extend to communing members.

As to the ecclesiastical control or restraint over these
Restraint Applied, unregenerate members, I remark, first, that
First, Through Pa- the rule of morals should be the same as that
rents. The Rule of imposed on communicating members, save
Living. that the former are not to be forced, nor
even permitted, without spiritual qualification, to take part in
sealing ordinances, and church-powers. [But as to their neg-
ect of these, they should be constantly taught that their dis-

qualification is their fault, and not their misfortune merely; a sinful exercise of their free-agency, a subject for personal and present repentance; a voluntary neglect and rejection of saving graces, the sincere offer whereof was sealed to them in their baptism. And for this, their sin of heart, the Church utters a continuous, a sad and affectionate, yet a righteous censure, in keeping them in the state of minor members.] The propriety of exacting the same rule of living, in other respects, appears thus: Christ has but one law for man; these baptized members are consecrated and separated to Christ's service in the Church as truly as the communicating members; they owe the same debt of devotion for the mercies of redemption; which are their offered heritage. Hence, it should be constantly taught them that questionable worldly amusements, for instance, are as inconsistent in them as in other Church members. In a word, the end of this Church authority, under which Providence has placed them, is to constrain them to live Christian lives, in order that thereby they may come unto the Christian graces in the heart.

Second, as to the means of enforcement of that rule, I would answer; that in the case of all baptized members of immature age, and especially of such as are still in the houses, and under the government, of parents, the Church-Session ought mainly to restrain them through their parents. That is, the authority of these rulers should be applied to the parents, to cause them, by their domestic authority, to lead outward Christian lives, and attend upon the means of grace. And the refusal or neglect of parents to do this duty, may doubtless subject them to just Church censure. Perhaps we may safely say, that the Session should reach this class of baptized members only through their parents, except in the case where the parents themselves refer the child's contumacy to the eldership. In this case the eldership may undoubtedly proceed to censure the recusant child. See an analogous case in the theocracy, Deut. xxi : 18, &c.

If these baptized, unregenerate members are fully adult, and passed from parental control, then the Church-Session must apply their restraint directly to them. The mere continuance of their unregeneracy, unfitting them for communion, will of course be no suitable ground for judicial prosecution. For the Church is already uttering her standing censure against this, in their exclusion from the Lord's table. If they become wayward in outward conduct, then the Session, in addition to their constant and affectionate admonitions against their impenitence, should administer paternal cautions, advice, and entreaty, looking towards a reformation. But if they persist in flagrant and indecent sins, such as the persistent neglect of all ordinances, sensuality, blasphemy, or dishonesty,

If Adult, the Restraint is Direct. It May Proceed to Excommunicate.

(such sins as would bring on a communing member excommunication), then nothing remains but that the Session shall proceed, by judicial prosecution, to cut the reprobate member off from the Church.

Not only the Scriptures, but common sense, justify this view. Are they "members of the Church?" (in the minor sense). Then natural justice teaches that they cannot be stripped of the privileges of that membership, be they what they may, without a fair opportunity for defence, and confronting the accusing witnesses. To judge a man without formal hearing is iniquity On the other hand, are they, in any sense, "members of the Church?" Then, to that degree, the Church is responsible for their discredit, and subject to the scandal of their irregularities. Common sense says, then, that there must be a fair way for the Church to obtain a formal severance of the membership, and publicly cleanse herself of the scandal of this contumacious member. That way can be none other than judicial prosecution. Finally, when a member is so thoroughly reprobate that, to human apprehension, there is no chance of his receiving any of the ends of a Church connection, there ought to be a way to terminate it; it has become objectless. Three objections are urged against the judicial prosecution of such members. 1. That its extremest sentence could only place them where they already are; self-excluded from full communion. I answer, this is clearly an oversight. This form of discipline will, of course, only be applied in cases of flagrant immorality; and then, it will do an entirely different thing from this self-exclusion : it will sever the minor membership, and rid the Church, until the culprit repents, of the scandal of his connection. It is argued, second, that judicial discipline is utterly inappropriate, where there is not even the profession of spiritual life. "It is like tieing a corpse to a whipping-post." That this is erroneous, is proved by every case of excommunication; for this extreme measure is always justified by the plea, that the man discloses himself to be unregenerate. Third : It is argued that judicial discipline is irrelevant to baptized members; because they are not the essential, but the accidental constituents of a visible Church. The fact is admitted ; but it is irrelevant. There could be a commonweath without minor citizens, but if there are minor citizens they must be judged as to their right to their lesser franchise, as other citizens are. No youth of sixteen years in Virginia would think it just to be hung or banished without trial, because he was not "of age ;" nor would the commonwealth deem that a sufficient reason to let him rob and murder with impunity. In fine, the practice of at least some of the Reformed Churches once illustrated the benefits of this position.

On this statement of the matter, it is obvious that the

Some Fair Way Must be Provided to Cut Off the Reprobate.

Our Usage Delin-
quent.
usage in our churches has fallen exceedingly far from the Bible rule, and that the taunts of the Immersionists are to a great degree well founded : that we are not consistent in our pædobaptism. And it may be, that the leavening of men's minds, in this country, with the unscriptural ideas of the Immersionists may have produced a license of feeling among youths, which greatly increases the difficulty of Church Sessions' doing their whole duty.   It may, indeed, be almost impossible for any single Session to do it among us, in the face of this unfortunate corruption of society. and of the obstinate neglect of all sister Church Sessions around them.   But the question for the honest mind is : Should a corrupt practice continue to preclude a right principle ?   Or should the correct principle amend the vicious practice ?   And the happy example of many of the Reformed Churches teaches us that this discipline of baptized members is feasible, reasonable, and most profitable.   The Presbyterian Church of Holland, for instance, in its better days ; and the Evangelical Church of Holland now, uniformly governs their children on the Scriptural principles above described.

Benefits of the Bible Plan—Children of the Church its Hope.
The benefits of infant baptism, and of this form of membership for the children of God's believing people, are great.   Some of them are very forcibly set forth by Dr. John M. Mason, in his invaluable treatise on the Church.   Borrowing in part from him, I would remark, that this relation to the Church, and this discipline, are, first, in exact harmony with the great fact of experience, that the children of God's people are the great hope of the Church's increase.   This being a fact, it is obviously wisdom to organize the Church with reference to it, so as to provide every proper means of training for working up this the most hopeful material for Zion's increase.   To neglect this obvious policy seems, indeed, little short of madness.   As we have seen, Immersionists' communions only enjoy true prosperity, in virtue of their virtual employment of the principle of infant Church-membership ; grace and love being in them fortunately, stronger than a bad theory.

The Bible Plan Agrees with Nature and Grace. Prov. xxii : 6.
Second : This Bible plan is in strict conformity with those doctrines of grace, and principles of human nature, which God employs for the sanctification of His people.   Our theory assumes that God's covenant is with His people and their seed. (Acts ii : 39).   That their seed are heirs of the promises made to the fathers (Acts iii : 25) : that the cause which excludes any such from saving interest in redemption is voluntary and criminal, viz., unbelief and impenitence—a cause which they are all bound to correct at once, if they are arrived at the years of discretion: that the continuance of this cause, however just a reason for the eldership's excluding them from certain priv:-

leges and functions, is no justification whatever for their neglecting them. And, above all, does our plan found itself on the
great rule of experience, common sense, and Scripture, that if
you would form a soul to the hearty embracing of right principles, you must make him observe the conduct which those
principles dictate. Every faithful parent in the world acts on
this rule in rearing his children. If the child is untruthful,
unsympathizing, unforgiving, indolent, he compels him, while
young, to observe a course of truth, charity, forgiveness and
industry. Why? Because the parent considers that the outward observance of these virtues will be either permanent or
praiseworthy if, when the child becomes a man, he only observes
them from fear or hypocrisy? Not at all; but because the
parent knows, that human nature is moulded by habits; that
the practice of a principle always strengthens it; that this use
of his parental authority is the most natural and hopeful means
to teach the child heartily to prefer and adopt the right principle, when he becomes his own man; that it would be the
merest folly to pretend didactically to teach the child the right,
and leave all-powerful HABIT to teach him the wrong, and to let
the child spend his youth in riveting the bonds of bad habit,
which, if he is ever to adopt and love the right principle, he
must break. Will not our heavenly Father act on the same rule
of good sense toward His children? Is not the professed principle of the Immersionist just the folly we have described?
Happily, Scripture agrees with all experience and practical
wisdom, in saying that if you wish a child to adopt and love the
principles of a Church-member when he is grown, you must
make him behave as a Church-member while he is growing.

Third: Many collateral advantages are gained by this
minor citizenship of the baptized in the
Collateral Advantages. Church. They are retained under wholesome restraints. Their carnal opposition to the truth is greatly
disarmed by early association. The numerical and pecuniary
basis of the Church's operations is widened. And where the
sealing ordinances are properly guarded, these advantages are
gained without any compromise of the Church's spirituality.
Pædobaptist communities which are scripturally conducted present as high a grade of purity, even including their baptized
members, as any others. For, on this corrupt earth, the best
communion is far from being what it ought to be. Where the
duties represented in the sacrament of baptism are properly
followed up, the actual regeneration of children is the ordinary
result.

LECTURE LXVII.

THE LORD'S SUPPER.

SYLLABUS.

See Conf. of Faith, ch. 29 with Catechisms.

1. Give a definition of this sacrament, with the Scriptural account of its institution, names, and ceremonial.

See Matt. xxvi : 26–29; Mark xiv : 22–26; Luke xxii : 15–21; 1 Cor. x : 16, 17; xi : 17 to end. Dick, Lect. 92. Turrettin, Loc. xix, Qu. 21.

2. What are the elements, in what manner to be prepared and set apart, and what their sacramental significance?

Turrettin, Qu. 22, 23, 24. Hill, bk. v, ch. 7. Dick, Lect. 92.

3. State and refute the doctrine of the real presence by a Transubstantiation, with the elevation and worship of the host.

Council of Trent, Sess. 13, especially ch. 4, and Canons Cat. Rom. pt. ii, ch. 4, Qu. 17–41. Turrettin, Qu. 26, 27. Calvin's Inst., bk. iv, ch. 18. Hill, as above. Archbishop Tillottson and Bishop Stillingfleet against Transubstantiation. Dick, Lect. 90.

4. State and refute the doctrine of Consubstantiation.

Turrettin, Qu. 26, 28. Augsb. Confession, and other Lutheran symbols. Hill, as above. Dick, Lect. 91.

THE only sacrament which Protestants recognize, besides baptism, is that called by them, in imitation of Paul (1 Cor. xi : 20), "The Lord's Supper" (Δεῖπνον κυριακὸν). The only other Scriptural names which seem clearly established are the breaking of bread (κλάσις τοῦ ἄρτου, Acts ii : 42–46; xx : 7), and possibly κοινωνία (1 Cor. x : 16). The cup is called ποτήριον τῆς εὐλογίας (1 Cor. x : 16), but this is evidently not a name for the whole ordinance. And in verse 21, communicating is called partaking of the Lord's Table (τράπεζα). This hardly amounts to a calling of the ordinance by the name of "table;" but it is instructive, as showing no favour whatever to the notion of altars and sacrifice, as connected with the Lord's Supper.

1. Scriptural Names.

Among the fathers it was called often εὐχαριστία, sometimes συνάξις or λειτουργία; more often θυσία, or μυστήριον; or among the Latins, *missa*. The use of the word θυσία was at first only rhetorical and figurative; and thus the error of considering the Lord's Supper an actual sacrifice had its way prepared. While the Romanists sometimes endeavor to trace the word *missa* to other etynoms (as to מַס tribute; מִשְׁתֶּה, banquet; or to μύησις, initiation),

Patristic Names.

its derivation is undoubtedly from the formulary with which the spectators and catechumens were dismissed before the celebration of the Lord's Supper: *missa est* (viz., congregatio).

The definition which Presbyterians hold, is that of our Catechisms, e. g., Shorter, Qu. 96: "The Lord's supper is a sacrament wherein, by

Definition and Nature.

800

giving and receiving bread and wine, according to Christ's appointment, His death is showed forth; and the worthy receivers are not after a corporal and carnal manner, but by faith made partakers of His body and blood, with all His benefits, to their spiritual nourishment and growth in grace." This is obviously no more than a correct digest of the views stated or implied in the sundry passages where the ordinance is described. Its institution was evidently simple and free from mystery; and had not the strange career of superstition been run on this subject by the Christian Church, the dispassionate reader would have derived no conceptions from the sacred narrative but the simple ones of a commemorative seal. And these natural, popular views of the sacrament are doubtless best adapted for edification.

I hold that our Saviour undoubtedly held His last passover on the regular passover evening, and that History of Institution. this ordinance, intended by Him to supersede and replace the passover (1 Cor. v : 7), was very quietly introduced at its close. To do this, He took up the bread (doubtless the unleavened bread of the occasion), and the cup of wine (after Jewish fashion mingled with water), provided for the occasion, and introduced them to their new use by an act of solemn thanksgiving to God. Then He brake the bread and distributed it, and, after the bread, the wine—partaking of neither Himself—saying: "This do in remembrance of Me; eat, drink ye all of it, to show forth the Lord's death till He come." These mandatory words were accompanied also with certain explicatory words, conveying the nature of the symbol and pledge; stating that the bread represented His body, and the cup the covenant made in His blood—the body lacerated and killed, and the blood shed, for redemption. The sacramental acts, therefore, warranted by Christ are, the taking, breaking, and distributing the elements, on the administrator's part, and their manual reception, and eating or drinking, on the recipient's part. The sacramental words are the thanksgiving, the explicatory and promissory, and the mandatory. The whole is then appropriately concluded with another act of praise (not sacramental, but an appendage thereto), either by praying, or singing, or both. And to add anything else is superstition.

To continue this subject: The elements are bread and wine. The Greek Church says the bread 2. Elements. must be leavened, the Latin unleavened, making this a point of serious importance. We believe that the bread used was paschal. But it was not Christ's intention to give ritually a paschal character to the new sacrament; and bread is employed as the material element of nutrition, the one most familiar and universal. Hence, we regard all the disputes as to leaven, and the other *minutiæ* made essential by the Romish

51*

ιubrick (wheaten, mingled with proper water, not worm-eaten, &c.,) as non-essential. Probably the wine was also mingled with water on the first occasion; but, on the same grounds, we regard it as selected simply as the most common and familiar refreshment of the human race; and the presence of water is therefore non-essential. Indeed, modern chemistry has shown that, in all wine, water is the solvent, and the largest constituent.

According to all Christians, these elements are conceived as undergoing some kind of consecration. Rome places this in the pronunciation of the words of institution, "This is My body," and teaches that it results in a total change of the substance of the bread and wine into the body and blood of Christ. But the only change which Protestants admit in a consecration of the elements, is the simple change of their use, from a common, to a sacred and sacramental one. And this consecration we believe to be wrought, not by pronouncing the words, "This is My body," but by the eucharistic act of worship which introduces the sacrament. For the natural language of consecration is that of worship; not that of a didactic and promissory sentence. Witness the cases of grace over our food, and all the consecrations of the Old Testament, e. g., Deut. xxvi : 5–10. When Christ says, "This is My Body," were the consecration what Papists suppose, these words would imply that it is already made. And last, the words, supposed by them to be words of consecration, are too variant in the different histories of the sacrament in sacred Scripture.

Their Consecration What?

The breaking of the bread is plainly one of the sacramental acts, and should never be done beforehand, by others, nor ommitted by the minister. The words εἰς ἄρτος (1 Cor. x : 17) are not correctly represented in the English version. The proper force of the word, as may be seen in Jno. vi : 9, is loaf, or more properly, cake; and the Apostle's idea is, that the oneness of the mass of bread, and of the cup, partaken by all, signifies their unity in one spiritual body. It would be better that the bread should be taken by the officiator in one mass, and broken before the people, after the prayer. The proper significancy of the sacrament requires it; for the Christ we commemorate is the Christ lacerated and slain. Further; Christ brake the bread in distributing it; and commanded us to imitate Him, saying: "This do," &c. Third; the Apostles undoubtedly made the breaking one of the sacramental acts; for Paul says, 1 Cor. x : 16, "The bread which we break," &c. Last, when the sacrament itself is more often called "the breaking of bread," than by any other one name, it can hardly be supposed that the breaking is not a proper part of the ceremonial.

Breaking of the Bread Significant.

There is also a significancy in the taking of the wine after
Pouring of the Wine, after the Bread, Significant. the bread, in a distinct act of reception;
because it is the blood as separated from the
body by death, that we commemorate.
Hence the soaking of the bread in the cup is improper, as well
as the plea by which Rome justifies communion in one kind;
that as the blood is in the body, the bread conveys alone a
complete sacrament. As we should commemorate it, the blood
is not in the body, but poured out.

The acts on the Communicant's part, also, are sacramental
and significant, viz: the taking and eating.
Significant Acts of Communicants. These acts symbolize generally, Faith, as the
soul's receptive act; just as the elements
distributed by God's institution signify that which is the object
of faith, Christ slain for our redemption. But the Confession
29, § 1, states, in greater detail, and with strict scriptural propriety, that these acts commemorate Christ's death, constitute a
profession and engagement to serve Him, show the reception
of a covenanted redemption thus sealed to us, and indicate our
communion with each other and Christ, our Head, in one spiritual body. The first idea is plainly set forth in 1 Cor. xi : 24,
last clause, as well as parallel passages, and in verses 25 and
26. The second is implied in the first, in the individnal character of the act, in 1 Cor. xi : 25, "covenant," and in the
nature of faith, which embraces Christ as our Saviour from sin
unto holiness. The third idea is plainly implied in the significancy of the elements themselves, which are the materials of
nutrition and refreshment; as well as in Jno. vi : 50–55. For
though we strenuously dispute, against Rome, that the language of this passage is descriptive of the Lord's Supper, it is
manifest that the Supper was afterward's devised upon the analogy which furnished the metaphor of the passage. And the
didactic and promissory language, "This is My body," "This
is My blood," sacramentally understood, obviously convey the
idea of nutrition offered to the soul. The last idea is very
clearly set forth in 1 Cor. x : 16, 17. And this is the feature
of the sacrament from which it has received its popular name,
of Communion of the Lord's Supper.

The parties who may properly partake of the Lord's Sup-
Who May Partake? per are so clearly defined, 1 Cor. xi : 27–30,
as to leave no room for debate. It is those
who have examined themselves successfully "of their knowledge to discern the Lord's body, and faith to feed on Him,
repentance, love, and, new obedience." Shorter Catechism,
question 97. See, also, Larger Catechism, question 171–175.
That this sacrament is to be given only to credible professors,
does not indeed follow necessarily from the fact that it symbolizes saving grace; for baptism does this; but from the express
limitation of Paul, and from the different graces symbolized.

Baptism symbolizes those graces which initiate the Christian life : The Supper, those also which continue it. Hence, while the former is once applied to infants born within the covenant, to ratify their outward membership, in the dependence on the gracious promise that they shall be brought to commence the Christian life afterwards; it would be wrong to grant the second sacrament to any who have not given some indication of an actual progress in spiritual life.

Thus far, all has been intelligible, reasonable, and adapted to nourish and comfort the faith of the plain believer. But the well-informed are aware that this ordinance, so quietly and simply introduced by our Saviour, and so simply explained, has met the strange fortune of becoming the especial subject of superstitious amplification; until, in the Romish Church, it has become nearly the whole of worship. It would be interesting to trace the history of this growth; but time only allows us to remark, that two unscriptural ideas became early associated with it; in consequence of a pagan grossness of perception, and a false exposition of Scripture. One of these was that of a literal or real corporeal presence; the other that of a true sacrifice for sin. Still, those more superstitious Christians who held these two ideas, did not, for a long time, define the manner in which they were supposed to be true. At length two theories developed themselves, that of Paschasius Radbert, transubstantiation; and that of Berengar, consubstantiation. The former of these triumphed in the Lateran Council 1215 ; the latter was condemned as heretical, till Luther revived it, though stripped of the sacrificial feature.

3. The Supper soon Perverted by two Errors.

According to Rome, when the priest canonically, and with proper intention, pronounces the words in the mass : " *Hoc est corpus meum,*" the bread and wine are changed into the very body and blood of the living Christ, including, of course, His soul and divinity ; which mediatorial person, the priest does then truly and literally break and offer again, as a proper sacrifice for the sins of the living and the dead ; and he and the people eat Him. True ; the accidents, or material qualities of bread and wine remain, but in and under them, the substance of bread is gone, and the substance really existing is Christ's person. But in this condition of things, it exists without the customary material attributes of locality, extension, and divisibility ; for He is none the less in heaven, and in all the ' hosts,' all over the world at once ; and into however small parts they may be divided, each is a perfect Christ ! Hence, to elevate, and carry this host in procession, and to worship it with Λατρεῖα is perfectly proper. Whether such a batch of absurdities is really believed by any reflecting mind, it is not for us to decide.

Transubstantiation.

The scriptural basis for this monstrous superstr cture is

very narrow, while the papal is wide enough.
Rome depends chiefly in Scripture on the
language of Jno. vi : 50, &c., and on the as-
sertion of the absolutely literal interpretation of the words of
institution in the parallel passages cited by us at the beginning.
We easily set aside the argument from Jno. vi : 50, &c., by the
remark, that it applies not to the Lord's Supper, but to the spiritual actings of faith on Christ figuratively described. For the
Lord's Supper was not yet instituted; and it is absurd to suppose that our Saviour would use language necessarily unintelligible to all His followers, the subject never having been divulged
to them. On the contrary, in verse 35, we find that the coming
and eating is defined as the actings of faith. If the chapter be
forced into an application to the Supper, then verses 53 and 54
explicitly teach that every one who eats the Supper goes to
heaven, and that no one who fails to eat it does; neither of
which Rome admits : And in verse 63, our Saviour fixes a figurative and spiritual interpretation of His words, beyond all
question.

Scriptural Arguments for.

When we proceed to the words of institution, we assert
that the obvious meaning is tropical; and is
equivalent to " This represents my body."
The evidences of this are manifold. First,
we cite the frequency of similar locutions in Hebrew, and Hebraistic Greek. Consult Gen. xli : 26, 27; Ezek. xxxvii : 11;
Dan. vii : 24; Exod. xii : 11; Matt. xiii : 38, 39; Rev. i : 20;
xvii : 9, 12, 18, *et passim.* Yea, we find Christ saying of Himself: " I am the way, the truth, the life," Jno. xiv : 6; "the vine,"
Jno. xv : 1; "the door," Jno. x : 9. Why is a tropical exposition
more reasonable or neccessary here? Yet, without it we make
absolute nonsense.

Words of Institution Properly Explained.

But even if we had no usage to illustrate our Saviour'
sense, it would be manifest from the text and
context alone, that His sense is tropical. The
τοῦτο must be demonstrative of bread, and
equivalent to, this bread (is my body); because bread is the
nearest antecedent, the whole series of the narrative shows it ;
in the parallel case of the wine, cup is, in one narrative, expressed:
and the allusion of Paul, 1 Cor. x : 16, " The bread which we
break," shows it. So, the σῶμα means evidently the body dead
(corpse), as is proved by the expression "broken for you," and
by the fact that the blood is separated from it: as well as by
current usage of narratives. Now paraphrase the sentence :
" This bread is my dead body," and any other than a tropical
sense is impossible. For (a.) The predication is self-contradictory; if it is bread, it is not body; if body, it is not bread, subject or predicate is out of joint. (b.) The body was not yet
dead, by many hours. (c.) Incompatibles cannot be predicated of each other. A given substance A. cannot be changed

True Meaning of Props.

into a substance B. which was pre-existent before the change, because the change must bring B. into existence.

Again: all will admit that the proper sense is that in which the disciples comprehended the words as first spoken. It is impossible that they should have understood the bread as truly the body: because they saw the body handling the bread! The body would have been wholly in its own hand!

So the Disciples must have Apprehended it.

Scripture calls it bread still after it is said, by Papists, to be transubstantiated. 1 Cor. x : 17. "All partakers of that one bread." See also, 1 Cor. xi : 26, 27, 28.

There are variations of language which are utterly incompatible with a strictly literal sense. In the gospels it is said: "He took the cup . . . and said This is my blood," &c. There must be here a metonomy of the cup for that which it contains—at least. But in 1 Cor. xi : 25, the words are " This cup is the new covenant of my blood," &c., where, if literalness is retained, we get the impossible and most unpopish idea, that the cup was the covenant.

But passing from the exegetical, to the general argument, a literal transubstantiation is impossible, because it violates our senses. They all tell us it is still bread and wine, by touch, taste, smell, sight. The senses are the only inlets of information as to external facts; if we may not believe their deliberate testimony, there is an end of all acquired knowledge. This may be fairly stated in a stronger form: it is impossible that my mind can be validly taught the fact of such a transubstantiation; for the only channel by which I can be taught it is the senses; and transubstantiation, if true, would teach me that my senses do not convey truth. It is just as likely that I do not hear Rome saying, "Transubstantiation is true," when I seem to hear her, as that I do not see a wafer, but a Christ, when I seem to see it. Nor is it any answer to say : the senses deceive us. This is only when hurried; and the sensible medium imperfect, or senses diseased. Here all the four senses of all men, in health unanimously perceive only bread and wine.

Transubstantiation Absurd. (a.) Because it Violates our Senses.

In the second place, it is impossible to be true ; because it violates our understanding. Our mental intuitions compel us to recognize substance by its sensible attributes. Those attributes inhere only in the substance, and can only be present by its presence. It is impossible to avoid this reference. An attribute or accident is relative to its substance ; to attempt to conceive of it as separate destroys it. Again : it is impossible for us to abstract from matter, the attributes of locality, dimension, and divisibility. But transubstantiation requires us to conceive of Christ's body without all these. Again : it is impossible for matter to be ubiquitous; but Christ's body must be so, if this

(b.) It violates Reason. No Plea to call it a Miracle.

doctrine be true. And it is vain to attempt an evasion of these two arguments from sense and reason, by pleading a great and mysterious miracle. For God's omnipotence does not work the impossible and the natural contradiction. And whatever miracle has ever taken place, has necessarily been just as dependent on human senses, for man's cognizance of its occurrence, as any common event. So that if the fundamental law of the senses is outraged, man is as incapable of knowing a miracle as any other thing.

Once more the doctrine of transubstantiation contradicts the analogy of faith. It is incompatible with our Saviour's professed attitude and intention, which was then to institute a sacrament. But Rome herself defines a sacrament as an outward sign of an invisible grace. Hence Christ's attitude and intention naturally lead us to regard the elements as only signs. This is true of all the sacraments of Old and New Testaments, unless this be an exception: and especially of the passover, on which the Supper was engrafted.

(c.) It violates the Analogy of Faith.

Transubstantiation would utterly destroy the nature of a sacrament; because, if the symbols are changed into the Christ, there is no sign.

It contradicts also the doctrine of Christ's ascension and second advent. For these teach us, that He is at the Father's right hand now, and will only come thence at the final consummation.

It contradicts the doctrine of atonement, substituting a loathsome form of sacred (literal) cannibalism, for that faith of the soul, which receives the legal effects of Christ's atoning sufferings as its justification.

Transubstantiation being disproved, all elevation and worship of the host, as well as kneeling at the sacrament, are disproved. The Episcopal reasons for the latter are, that while no change of the bread and wine is admitted, and no worship of them designed, yet the reverence, contrition and homage of the believer for his crucified Saviour prompt him to kneel to Christ. We reply, that the worship of Christ is of course proper at all proper times. But the attitude of kneeling is not proper at the moment when Christ expressly commands us to do something else than kneel. Had the paralytic, for instance, of Matt. ix: 5, 6. when he received the order, "Arise, take up thy bed and go," insisted on kneeling just then, it would have been disobedience, and not reverence. So, when Christ calls us to a communion in eating together His sacramental supper, the proper posture is that of a guest, for the time. If any Christian desires to show his homage by coming to the table from his knees, and returning from it to them, very well. But let him not kneel, in the very act in which Christ commands him to feast.

Therefore, Host not to be Worshipped.

Consubstantiation teaches that there is no literal change of the elements, but that they remain simple bread and wine. Yet, in a mysterious and miraculous manner, there is a real presence, in, under, and along with them, of the whole person of Christ, which is literally, though invisibly, eaten along with them. Unworthy communicants also receive it, to their own damnation. While this doctrine is not attended with the impious results of transubstantiation, it is liable to nearly all the exegetical, sensible, rational, and doctrinal objections. Indeed, in one sense, the exegetical objections are stronger; because if literalness must needs be retained in the words of institution, it is a less violation of language to make them mean the bread is the body, than that the bread accompanies the body. The Lutheran exegesis, while boasting of its faithful preservation of our Saviour's language, really neither makes it literal, nor interprets it by any allowable trope. It does not outrage the understanding so much, by requiring us to believe that substance can be separate from all its accidents; for it professes to leave the substance of the bread untouched. Nor is it so obnoxious to the last head of objections raised against transubstantiation, in that it does not destroy the sacramental sign. But the rest of my arguments apply against it, and need not be recapitulated.

4, Consubstantiation Equally Erroneous, but not so Impious.

LECTURE LXVIII.

THE LORD'S SUPPER. — Concluded.

THERE is a sense, in which all evangelical Christians would admit a real presence in the Lord's Supper. The second Person of the Trinity being very God, immense and ubiquitous, is of course present wherever the bread and wine are distributed.

5. Reformed View of Real Presence.

Likewise, His operations are present, through the power of the Holy Ghost employing the elements as means of grace, with all true believers communicating. (Matt. xviii : 20). But this is the only sort of presence admitted by us.

Zwinglian View of Supper.

Zwinglius, seemingly the most emancipated of all the Reformers from superstition and prejudice, taught that the sacrament is only a commemorative seal, and that the human part of Christ's person is not present in the sacrament, except to the faith of the intelligent believer. This he sustains irrefragably by the many passages in which we are taught that Christ's humanity is ascended into the heavens, thence to return no more till the end of all things. That this humanity, however glorified, has its *ubi*, just as strictly as any human body; that if there is any literal humanity fed upon for redemption by the believing communicant, it must be his passible and suffering humanity, while Christ's proper humanity is now glorified; (which would necessitate giving Christ a double humanity); and that the sacramental language is tropical, as is evinced by a sound exegesis and the testimony of the better Fathers. The defect of the Zwinglian view is, that while it hints, it does not

809

distinctly enough assert, the sealing nature of the sacraments. Both Romanist and Lutheran minds, accustomed to regard the Eucharist from points of view intensely mystical, received the Zwinglian with loud clamour, as being odiously bald and rationalistic. Calvin, therefore, being perhaps somewhat influenced by personal attachments to Melancthon, and by a desire to heal the lamentable dissensions of Reformed and Lutherans, propounded (in his Inst. and elsewhere) an intermediate view. This is, that the humanity, as well as the divinity of Christ, in a word, his whole person, is spiritually, yet really present, not to the bodily mouth, but to the souls of true communicants, so that though the humanity be in heaven only, it is still fed on in some ineffable, yet real and literal way, by the souls of believers. The ingenious and acute defence of this strange opinion, contained in the Inst. Bk. iv : Ch. 17, proceeds upon this postulate, which I regard as correct, and as eminently illustrative of the true nature of the sacramental efficiency; that the Lord's Supper represents and applies the vital, mystical union of the Lord with believers. Such therefore as the vital union is, such must be our view of the sacrament of the Supper. Is the vital union then, only a secret relationship between Christ and the soul, instituted when faith is first exercised, and constituted by the indwelling and operation of the Holy Ghost : or, is it a mysterious, yet substantial conjunction, of the spiritual substance, soul, to the whole substance of the mediatorial Person, including especially the humanity? In a word, does the spiritual vitality propagate itself in a mode strictly analogous to that, in which vegetable vitality is propagated from the stock into the graft, by actual conjunction of substance? Now Calvin answers, emphatically : the union is of the latter kind. His view seems to be, that not only the mediatorial Person, but especially the corporeal part thereof, has been established by the incarnation, as a sort of duct through which the inherent spiritual life of God, the fountain is transmitted to believers, through the mystical union. His arguments are, that the body of Christ is asserted to be our life, in places so numerous and emphatic (Jno. i : 1, 14 ; vi : 27, 33, 51–59 ; Eph. v : 30 ; 1 Cor. vi : 15 ; Eph. iv : 16) that exegetical fidelity requires of us to understand by it more than a participation in spiritual indwelling and influences purchased for believers by His death ; that the incomprehensibility of a spiritual, though true and literal, substantial conjunction of our souls with Christ's flesh in heaven, should not lead us to reject the word of our God ; and that faith cannot be the whole amount of the vital union of believers to Christ, inasmuch as it is said to be by faith. The union must be more than the means which constitutes it.

Now, it is this view of Calvin, which we find Hill asserting,

Calvin's View. Properly Grounded on Vital Union to Christ; yet Overstrains it.

Is Calvin's the West-minster Doctrine? and Dick and Cunningham denying, as the established doctrine of the Anglican and Scotch Churches, and of the Westminster Assembly. A careful examination of Ch. xxix : § 7, the decisive passage of our Confession, will show, I think, that it was the intention of the Westminster Assembly, while not repudiating Calvin's views or phraseology in a marked and individual manner, yet to modify all that was untenable and unscriptural in it. It is declared that worthy communicants " do really and indeed, yet not carnally and corporeally, but spiritually, receive and feed upon Christ crucified and all the benefits of his death: the body and blood of Christ being then not corporeally or carnally in, with, or under the bread and wine ; yet as really, but spiritually, present to the faith of believers," as the elements themselves to their senses. Note first : that they say believers receive and feed spiritually upon Christ crucified and the benefits of His death ; not with Calvin, on His literal flesh and blood. Next, the presence which grounds this receiving, is only a presence to our faith, of Christ's body and blood ! Hence we construe the Confession we think fairly, to mean by the receiving and feeding, precisely the spiritual actings of faith in Christ as our Redeemer, and on His body slain, and blood poured out, as the steps of His atoning work ; so that the thing which the soul actually embraces, is not the corporeal substance of His slain body and shed blood, but their Redeeming virtue. The discriminating remarks of Turrettin, Qu. 28, (Introduc.) are doubtless correct : and are doubtless the expression of the very view the Assembly intended to embody. The human person of Christ cannot be said to be present in the sense of substantive proximity or contact ; but only in this sense ; that we say a thing is present, when it is under the cognizance of the faculty naturally adapted for its apprehension. Thus the sun is called present in day, absent at night. He is no farther distant in fact ; but his beams do not operate on our visual organ. The blind man is said to be without light ; although the rays may touch his sightless balls. So a mental or spiritual presence, is that which places the object before the cognizance of the appropriate mental faculty. In this sense only, the sacrament brings Christ before us ; that it places Him, in faith, before the cognizance of the sanctified understanding and heart.

We reject the view of Calvin concerning the real presence, [recognizing our obligation to meet and account for the Scriptures he quotes, in a believing, and not in a rationalistic spirit] ; first, because it is not only incomprehensible, but impossible. Calvin's Proposition Impossible. Does it not require us to admit, in admitting the literal (though spiritual) reception of Christ's corporeal part, it in a distant heaven, and we on earth ; that matter may exist without its essential attributes of locality and dimension ? Have not our souls their *ubi?* They are limited, substantively, to some spot within the superficies of our bodies, just as really as though they were material. Has not Christ's flesh its *ubi,* though glorified, and as much more brilliant than ours, as a diamond is than carbon? To my mind, therefore, there is as real a violation of my intuitive reason, in this doctrine; as when transubstantiation requires me to believe that the flesh of Christ is present, indivisible and unextended, in each crumb or drop of the elements. Both are contrary to the laws of extension. And that Christ's glorified body dwells on high, no more to return actually to earth till the final consummation is asserted too plainly and frequently to be disputed. (Matt. xxvi : 11 ; Jno. xvi : 28; xvii : 11; xvi : 7; Luke xxiv : 51; Acts iii : 21 ; i : 11.

Second. The bread broken and wine poured out symbolize the body broken and slain, and blood

If any Body Present, it is the Body Dead. shed, by death. Now, according to Calvin, it is a mystical union which is sealed and applied in the Lord's Supper, so as to propagate spiritual life; and throughout John vi, where His life-giving flesh is so much spoken of, it is not the Lord's Supper, but the believers' union to Christ, which is described. Well, how unreasonable it is to suppose spiritual life communicated through the actual, corporeal substance of Christ's body, at the very stage at which the body is itself lifeless?

Third. While the Old Testament believers had not the

Old Testament Saints could not Share it. identical sacraments which we have, they had the same kind of spiritual life, nourished in the same way. (See Rom. iv : 5 ; Heb. xi, and especially 1 Cor. x : 1-4). Here the very same figure is employed—that of eating and drinking. How could this be an eating of His flesh, when that flesh was not yet in existence?

This remark brings that theory of the mystical union, on which the Romish, the Lutheran, and the patristic doctrines of the "real presence rest," to a decisive test. Were Old Testament saints saved in the same gospel way with us? Yes. Then that theory which makes the theanthropic Person the corporeal duct of spiritual life, is not true: for when they were saved, there was no theanthropic Person.

Fourth. The sixth chapter of John contains many internal marks, by which the feeding on Christ is

The Conjunction is Simply Believing. identified with faith, and His flesh is shown to be only a figure for the benefits of His redemption. The occasion—the miracle of feeding the thousands with five loaves and two fishes, and the consequent pursuit of Christ by the multitude, made it very natural that Christ should adopt the figure of an eating of food, to represent receiving Him. Verse 29 shows that eating is simply believing; for had Calvin's sense been true, our Saviour would not have said so emphatically, that believing was the work of God. In verse 35, again, it is implied that the eating is but coming, i. e., believing. So, verses 40, 47 with 50. In verse 53, we have language which is as destructive of a spiritual feeding on the literal body in the sacraments, as of a corporeal; for in either case it would be made to teach the unscriptural doctrine, that a soul cannot be saved without the sacraments. In verses 63, our Saviour plainly interprets His own meaning. Christ's omniscience having shown Him that the hearers were misconcieving His words, as of a literal and corporeal eating; He here proceeds to correct that mistake. His scope may be thus paraphrased: "Are your minds so gross as to suppose that salvation is to be attained by a literal eating of the Saviour's material flesh? No wonder you are scandalized by so gross an idea! Is it not a sufficient proof of its erroneousness, that in a few months you are to see the Redeemer's person (divine and corporeal) ascend to the heavens from which the eternal Word descended? Of course, that utter seclusion of His material body from the militant Church sufficiently explodes every idea of a material presence and literal eating. But besides: all such notions misconceive the true nature of redemption. This is a spiritual work; no material flesh can have any profitable agency to promote it, as it is a propagation of life in the soul; the agency must be spiritual; not physical. And the vehicle of that agency is the gospel word, not any material flesh, however connected with the redeeming Person. The thing you lack, is not any such literal eating (a thing as useless as impossible) but true, living faith on Christ." (Verses 60–64). The best proof of the justice of this exposition is its perfect coherency with the context. Calvin (*Com. in loco*) labours hard, but unsuccessfully, to make the passage bear another sense, which would not be fatal to the peculiar feature of his theory. And the whole tenour of Scripture (e. g. Matt. xv : 17, 18), is unfavourable to the conception of the moral condition of the soul's being made dependent on a reception of corporeal substance.

Last. (See 1 Cor. xi : 27, 29). The destructive effects of unworthy communicating are here described in terms which plainly make this mischief the counterpart of the benefit which the true believer derives, by proper communicating. Now, if this latter is an access of spiritual life through a substantial (though spiritual) reception of Christ's Person, the former must be a propagation of spiritual death, through the poisonous effects of this same Person, substantively present to the soul. But, says Calvin, with obvious correctness, the unbelieving communicant does not get the Person of Christ into contact with his soul at all! The thing he guiltily does, is the keeping of Christ away from his soul totally, by his unbelief.

Calvin Inconsistent with Results of Unworthy Eating.

Here we may appropriately answer the tenth question. We hold that the Lord's Supper is a means of grace; and the scriptural conception of this phrase explains the manner in which the sacrament is efficacious to worthy communicants.

6. True Nature of Sacramental Efficiency.

It sets forth the central truths of redemption, in a manner admirably adapted to our nature sanctified; and these truths, applied by the Holy Ghost, are the instruments of sanctification and spiritual life, in a manner generically the same with, though in degree more energetic, than the written and spoken word. So, the guilt of the unbelieving communicant is not one inevitably damning; but it is the guilt of Christ's rejection; it is the guilt of doing despite to the crucified Saviour by whom he should have been redeemed; and this under circumstances of peculiar profanity. But the profanation varies according to the decree of conscious hypocrisy, and the motive of the act.

In conclusion of this head, I would remark that all these objections to that modified form of the real presence which Calvin held, apply *a fortiori*, to the grosser doctrines of the Lutheran and Romanist. The intelligent student can go over the application himself.

Rome asserts most emphatically that the Lord's Supper is a proper and literal sacrifice; in which the elements, having become the very body blood, human spirit, and divinity of Christ, are again offered to God upon the altar; and the transaction is thus a repetition of the very sacrifice of the cross, and avails to atone for the sins of the living, and of the dead in purgatory. And all this is dependent on the priest's intention. After the authority of Church Fathers and councils, which we set aside with a simple denial, Rome argues from Scripture, that Christ was a priest after the order of Melchizedek; but He presented as priest, bread and wine as an oblation to God, and then made Abraham communicate in it: That Christ is a "priest forever," and therefore must have a perpetually recurring sacrifice to present: That Malachi (i : 11), predicts the continuance of a Christian sacrifice among the Gentiles, under the New Testament. That the words of institution: "This is My body which is broken for you," when taken literally, as they ought to be, imply a sacrifice, because the bread, having become the veritable body, must be whatever the body is; but the body is there a sacrifice. And that Paul (1 Cor. x : 21), contrasts the Lord's table with that of devils (i. e., idols). But the latter was confessedly a table of sacrifice, whence the former must be so. But the true argument with Rome for teaching this doctrine, is that of Acts xix : 25; they "know that by this craft they have their wealth." The great necessity of the human soul, awakened by remorse, or by the convincing Spirit of God, is atonement. By making this horrible and impious invention, Rome has brought the guilty consciences of miserable sinners under her dominion, in order to make merchandise of their sin and fear. While nothing can transcend the unscripturalness of the doctriue of Transubstantiation, I regard this of the sacrifice of the Mass as the most impious and mischievous of all the heresies of Rome.

In answer to her pretended scriptural arguments: There is not one word of evidence that the bread and wine of Melchizedek, if even an oblation, were a sacrifice. Does Rome mean to represent the sacrament of the Lord's Supper as in exercise 1400 years before Christ had any body to commemorate? Christ's priesthood is perpetual; but it is perpetuated, according to Hebrews, in His function of intercession, which He continually performs in the heavenly Sanctuary. And besides: it is a queer way to perpetuate His priestly functions, by having a line of other priests offer Him as the victim of their sacrifices! Rome replies, that her priest, in offering, acts in Christ's room, and speaks in His name. Such impiety is not strange on the part of Rome. We set aside the whole dream by demanding, where is the evidence that Christ has ever called one of His ministers a priest, or deputized to him this function? The prediction of Malachi is obviously to be explained by the remark, that he foretells the prevalence of Christian institutions among the Gentiles, in terms and imagery borrowed from Jewish rites. The same bungling interpretation which Rome makes here, would equally prove from Is. ii : 1, 4, that the great annual feasts at Jerusalem are to be personally attended by all the people of Europe, Australia, America, &c.; and from Is. lvi : 7, that not only the "unbloody offering of the Mass," but literal burnt offerings shall be presented under the New Testament by the Gentiles. By disproving the transubstantiation of the bread, we have already overthrown the argument founded on it. And last: it is evidently an overstraining of the Apostle's words, to infer from 1 Cor. x : 21, that the thing literally eaten at the Lord's table must be a literal sacrifice. Since the elements eaten are the symbols of the divine sacrifice, there is in this an abundant ground for the Apostle's parallel. And moreover, when the Pagans met after the sacrifice, to eat of the body of the victim, the table was not an altar, nor was the act a sacrificial one.

The direct refutation of this dogma has been so well executed by Calvin, Turrettin, and other Protestants, that nothing more remains, than to collect and state in their proper order the more important arguments. The silence of the Scripture is a just objection to it; because the burden of proof properly lies on those who assert the doctrine. The circumstances of the first administration of the Supper exclude all sacrificial character. No one will deny that this sacrament must bear the same meaning and character in all subsequent repetitions, which

Christ gave it at first.   But on that night, it could not be a sacrifice, because His sacrifice was not yet made.   Christ was as
yet unslain.   Nothing was offered to God; but on the contrary,
Christ gave the elements to man: whereas, in a proper sacrifice, it is man that offers to God.   Not one of the proper traits
or characteristics of a true sacrifice is present.   There is no victim, shedding His blood; and "without the shedding of blood
is no remission."   There is no sacrificial act whatever; and this
is especially fatal to Romanists; because the only oblation to
God, which can by any pretext be found in the history of the
institution in Scripture, is that of the eucharistic prayer.   But,
say they, the transubstantiation does not take place till after
this, in the pronouncing of the words of institution.   There
is no death and consumption of a victim by fire; for the only
thing like a killing is the breaking of the bread: but according
to Romanists, this occurred in our Saviour's institution, before
the transubstantiation.   Again: The mere fact that the Supper
is a sacrament is incompatible with its being a sacrifice; for the
nature of the two is dissimilar.   True, the passover was both,
but this was at different stages.   But we object with yet more
emphasis, that the doctrine is impiously derogatory to Christ's
one priesthood and sacrifice, and to the sufficiency thereof, as
asserted in Scripture.   Christ is sole priest.   (1 Tim. ii : 5;
Heb. vii : 24; ix : 12), and He offers one sacrifice, which neither
needs nor admits repetition.   (Heb. vii : 27; ix : 25; x : 1, 2,
10, 12, 14 and 26 with ix : 12–14).

Protestants deny the propriety of private communions.
8. Private Commun- because they deny that the Supper is a sac-
ion Rejected. Why? rifice.   It is a commemoration of Christ's
death, and shows forth His death.   There
should therefore be fellow communicants to whom to show it
forth, or at least spectators.   It is a communion, representing
our membership in the common body of Christ.   Hence to celebrate it when no members are present to participate is an
abuse.   The motive for desiring private communion is usually
superstitious, and therefore our Church does wisely in refusing it.

The grounds on which Rome withholds the cup from the
9. Laity Entitled to laity may be seen stated in the Council of
the Cup. Trent, and cited in Dick.   They are too
trivial to need refutation.   It is enough to
say that the assertion that the bread by itself is a whole sacrament, because the blood is in the body, is false.   For it is the
very nature of the Lord's Supper to signify, that the blood is
not in the body, having been poured out from it in death.   We
might justly ask: Why is not the bread alone sufficient for the
priests also, if it is a whole sacrament?   The outrage upon
Christ's institute is peculiarly glaring, because the injunction to
give the cup to the communicants is as clear and positive as to
observe the sacrament at all.   And our Saviour, as though

foreseeing the abuse, in Mark xiv : 23, and Matt xxvi : 27, has emphatically declared that all who eat are also to drink. This innovation of Rome is comparatively modern ; being not more against the Word of God, than against the voice and usage of Christian antiquity. It presents one of the strongest examples of her insolent arrogance both towards her people and God. The true motive, doubtless, is, to exalt the priesthood into a superior caste.

10. For the answer to this, see Lectures on the Sacraments in General. Qu. 10.

LECTURE LXIX.
DEATH OF BELIEVERS.

SYLLABUS.

1. Why does Death befall Justified persons?
   Dick, Lect. 80. Ridgley, Qu. 84. Knapp, Theol. § 147.
2. Death a means of glory to saint, unmixed curse to sinner.
3. What benefits do believers receive at Death? Is entire sanctification one of them?
   Dick, Lect. 81. Ridgley, Qu. 86. Knapp, as above.
4. Review the Arguments for the Immortality of the soul.
   Butler's Analogy. pt. i. Turrettin, Loc. v, Qu. 14. Dick as above.
   Ridgley, Qu. 86. Breckinridge's Theol., Vol. i. bk. i, ch. 6.
5. Are any Souls detained in any other place (as a Hades, &c.) than Heaven and Hell?
   Turrettin, Loc. xii, Qu. 11. Hodge, pt. iv, ch. i § 1, 3. Knapp, as above,
6. Is the Soul Conscious and Active, between Death and the Resurrection?
   Hodge, as above § 2. Dick, Lect. 81. Ridgley, Qu. 86. Dr. Jno. Miller,
   Questions raised by the Bible, pt. i. "Last Things," by Dr. Gardiner Spring.

DEATH is undoutedly a penal evil; and not merely a natural law, as Socinians and Pelagians teach. This we

1. Death is a Penal Evil. Why Then Inflicted on the Justified? have already shown by the Bible, (Gen. ii : 17; iii : 17-19; v : 3; Rom. v : 12, 14), and by the obvious reasoning, that the benevolence and righteousness, with the infinite power of God, would combine to prevent any suffering to His moral creatures while free from guilt. Man enters life now, subject to the whole penalty of death, including temporal physical evils, spiritual death, and bodily death; and this is the consequence of Adam's fall through our federal connection with him. From spiritual death, all believers are delivered at their regeneration. Physical evils and bodily death remain; and inasmuch as the latter was a most distinctive and emphatic retribution for sin, the question is, how it comes to be inflicted on those who are absolutely justified in Christ. On the one hand, bodily death was a penal infliction. On the other hand, we have taught that believers are justified from all guilt, and are required to render no penal satisfaction whatever.   (Rom. v : 1 ; Heb. x : 14, &c.)   Yet all believers die ?

Now this question is very inadequately met by such views as these : That this anomaly is no greater than many others in the divine dealings ; e. g., the continuance of imperfection and indwelling sin so many years in believers, or their subjection to the malice of evil men and demons.   That the destruction of the body is necessary to a perfect sanctification ; a thing shown to be untrue in the cases of Enoch, Elijah, the human soul of Christ, and all the believers who shall be on earth at the last consummation; or, that the natural law of mortality, and the rule of God's kingdom, that men must " walk by faith, not by sight," would both be violated, if so visible a difference were placed between saints and sinners, as the entire exemption of the former from bodily death.   These are partial explanations. The true answer is, that although believers are fully justified, yet according to that plan of grace which God has seen fit to adopt, bodily death is a necessary and wholesome chastisement for the good of the believer's soul.   If this postulate can be shown to be correct, the occurrence of death to the justified man will fall into the same class with all other paternal chas tisements, and will receive the same explanation.

False and True An-swers.

Let us then recall some principles which were established in our defence of our view of the Atone- ment against Romanists, &c.   First. A chas- tisement, while God's motive in it is only benevolent, does not cease to be, to the believer, a natural evil. We may call it a blessing in disguise ; but the Christian smart- ing under it feels, that if this language means that it is not a real evil, it is a mere play upon words.   The accurate statement is, that God wisely and kindly exercises in chastisements His divine prerogative of bringing good out of evil.   Bodily death does not cease to be to the believer a real natural evil in itself, and to be feared and felt as such.   Second. Hence, chastise- ment is a means of spiritual benefit appropriate only to sinning children of God.   It would not be just, for instance, that God should adopt chastisements as a means to advance Gabriel, who never had any guilt, to some higher stage of sanctified capaci- ties and blessedness ; because where there is no guilt there is no suffering.   Third. Still, God's motive in chastising the believer is not at all retributive, but wholly beneficent ; whereas His retributions of the guilty are intended, not primarily to benefit them, but to satisfy righteousness.   Here then is the distinctive difference between Rome and us : that we hold, while the sufferings endured in chastisements have a reference to our sin- ful and guilty condition, in the believer's case they are neither paid by him, nor received by God, as any penal satisfaction whatever for guilt : that satisfaction is wholly paid by our surety.

Ground and Nature of Chastisements.

Heb. xii : 6–10 ; Rom. viii : 18–28 ; 2 Cor. iv : 17 : with Rom. viii : 33 ; Ps. ciii : 12 ; Micah vii : 19. Whereas, Rome teaches that penitential sufferings of believers go to complete the actual penal satisfaction for the *reatum pœnæ*, left incomplete by Christ.

Fourth. The use of such means of sanctification is compatible with divine justice, although an infinite vicarious satisfaction is made for our guilt by our surety; because, as we saw, a vicarious satisfaction is not a commercial equivalent for our guilt; a legal tender such as brings our Divine Creditor under a righteous obligation to cancel our whole indebtedness. But His acceptance of it as a legal satisfaction was, on His part, an act of pure grace; and therefore the acceptance acquits us just so far as, and no farther than, God is pleased to allow it. And we learn from His word, that He has been pleased to accept it just thus far; that the believer shall be required to pay no more penal satisfaction to the broken law; yet shall be liable to such suffering of chastisements as shall be wholesome for his own improvement, and appropriate to his sinning condition.

How Compatible with Satisfaction for Sin.

Now then, does bodily death subserve the purposes of a wholesome and sanctifying chastisement? I answer, most eminently. The prospect of it serves, from the earliest day when it begins to stir the sinner's conscience to a wholesome seriousness, through all his convictions, conversion, Christian warfare, to humble the proud soul, to mortify carnality, to check pride, to foster spiritual mindedness. It is the fact that sicknesses are premonitions of death, which make them active means of sanctification. Bereavements through the death of friends form another valuable class of disciplinary sufferings. Now that death may be actually in prospect, death must actually occur. And when the closing scene approaches, no doubt in every case where the believer is conscious, the pains of its approach, the solemn thoughts and emotions it suggests, are all used by the Holy Ghost as powerful means of sanctification to ripen the soul rapidly for Heaven. I doubt not, that when we take into view the whole moral influences of the life-long prospect of our own deaths, the prospect and occurrence of bereavement by death of friends, the pungent efficiency given to sickness by its connection with death, as well as the actual influences of the closing scene, we shall see that all other chastisements put together, are far less efficacious in checking inordinate affection and sanctifying the soul: yea, that without this, there would be no efficacious chastisement at all left in the world. A race of sinners must be a race of mortals; Death is the only check (of the nature of means) potent enough to prevent depravity from breaking out with a power which would make the state of the world perfectly intolerable! Another reason for inflicting death

Bodily Death an Edifying Chastisement.

on justified believers may be found in 1 Peter iv : 12, 13. It is the supreme test of the power of faith. Death is the greatest of temporal and natural evils, abhorrent to the strongest instincts of man's nature, and involving the maximum of natural losses and privations. If faith and grace can overcome this enemy, and extract his sting, then indeed have we a manifestation of their virtue, which is transcendent. As Christ, our Captain of salvation, gave that supreme evidence of His love and devotion, so it is most appropriate that His people should present the like evidence of the power of His Spirit and principles in them. It is thus we become " partakers of His sufferings," and assist in signalizing His victory over death.

Yet, as the afflictions of the righteous differ much from the torments of the wicked, this is peculiarly true of their deaths. To the impenitent man, death is full of the sting of sin. In the case of the saint, this sting is extracted by redemption. There may not be the abounding triumphs of spiritual joy ; but if the believer is conscious, he usually enjoys a peace, which controls and calms the agitations of the natural feelings recoiling from death. In the case of the sinner, the horror of dying is made up of two sets of feelings, the instinctive love of life, with the natural affections which tie him to the earth ; and evil conscience with dread of future retributions. And the latter is often predominant in the sinner's anguish. But in the case of the saint it is removed ; and death is only an evil in the apprehension of the former feelings. Second : to the sinner, death is the beginning of his utter misery ; to the saint it is the usher, (a dreaded one indeed) into his real blessedness. By it the death in sins and bondage of depravity are fixed upon the sinner irrevocably : but the saint is delivered by it from all his indwelling sins. Death removes the sinner forever from God, from partial gospel privileges and communions. But to the saint, it is the means of breaking down the veil, and introducing him into the full fruition and vision of God.

2. Death a Means of Glory to Saint, Unmixed Curse to Sinner.

See Shorter Cat. Qu. 37. Three benefits are here mentioned as received from Christ at the believer's death : perfect sanctification, immediate entrance into glory, and the prospect of a bodily resurrection.

3. Benefits Received by Saint at Death—1. Complete Sanctification.

We take up here, the first, postponing the others for separate discussion ; and assuming for the time, the implied truth of the immortality of the soul. The complete sanctification of believers at death would hardly be denied by any, who admitted that their souls entered at once into the place of our Saviour's glorified residence, and of God's visible throne. It is those who teach a separate state, a transmigration, or Hades, or purgatory, or sleep in the grave, who deny the immediate sanctification of souls. For, the attributes of God and heaven are

such as obviously to require perfect purity of all who dwell
there. Let the student bear this in mind, and have in view the
truth to be hereafter established, that the souls of believers
" do immediately pass into glory." The place is holy, and
debars the approach of all moral impurity. (Rev. xxi : 27).
The inhabitants, the holy angels are pure, and could not appropriately admit the companionship of one tainted with indwelling
sin. True ; they now fly forth to "minister to them who shall
be the heirs of salvation ;" but this is not a companionship. The
King of that world is too pure to receive sinners to His bosom.
He does indeed condescend, by His Holy Ghost, into the polluted breasts of sinners on earth ; but this is a far different
thing from a public, full and final admission of sin into the place
of His holiness. See I Peter i : 15, 16 ; Ps. v : 4 : xv : 2 ; Is.
vi : 5. The blessedness of the redeemed is incompatible with
any remaining imperfection (Rev. xxi : 4). For wherever there
is sin, there must be suffering. And last, this glorious truth is
plainly asserted in the word of God. Heb. xii : 23 ; Eph. v :
27 ; I John iii : 2.

How this sanctification is wrought, we may not tell. Recall
the remark made when sanctification was dis-
Made Feasible by cussed ; that it is not mysticism, nor gnosti-
Body's Death. cism, nor asceticism, to ascribe its completion
to our release from the body, as a convenient occasion. Bodily
appetites are the occasions of the larger part of most men's
sins : as the bodily members are the instruments of all their
overt sins. How natural, then, that when these are removed,
God should finally remove sin ? The agent of this work is still,
no doubt, the Holy Spirit.

I have already remarked that all these views presuppose
that immortality which is brought to light
Old and New Testa- in the gospel. It has always seemed to me
ments teach Immortality. that the Bible treats the question of man's
immortality, as it does that of God's existence ; assumes it as
an undisputed postulate. Hence the debate urged by Warburton and his opposers, whether Moses taught a future existence, seems to me preposterous. To dispute that he did, flies
into the very teeth of Scripture. (Matt. xxii : 32 ; Heb. ii :
16, 26 ; and in Pentateuch, Gen. v : 22, 24 ; Gen. xv : 15 ; xxv :
8 ; xxxv : 29 ; xxxvii : 35 ; Jude : 14, 15 ; Numb. xx : 24 ;
xxvii : 13. All religion and even all morality imply a future
existence. But our Saviour, whose purpose it was to reaffirm
the truths of Old Testament Revelation, and of natural Religion,
which had been obscured by the perverse skepticism of men,
does teach man's immortality with peculiar distinctness and
fullness. The reader may consult for instance, Matt. x : 28 ;
Luke xvi : 26 ; Matt. xx : 33 ; xxv : to the end ; Jno. v : 24 ;
viii : 51 : xi : 25 ; xii : 25 ; 2 Cor. v : 1–10 ; I Cor. xv : &c.
This may perhaps be a part of the Apostle's meaning, when he

says, (2 Tim. i : 10) that Christ "hath brought life and immortality to light in the gospel." But it would certainly be a great abuse of his meaning, to understand from him that Christ was the first adequately to teach that there is an immortal existence. Paul speaks rather, as the context clearly shows, ("hath abolished death,") of spiritual life and a happy immortality which Christianity procures. And it is the glory of the religion of the Bible to have clearly made this known to man.

It may be well to note that the immortality of the Bible is that of the whole man, body and soul ; and herein God's word transcends entirely all the guesses of natural reason. And this future existence implies the continuance of our consciousness, memory, mental, and personal identity; of the same soul in the same body, (after the resurrection). There must be also the essential and characteristic exercises of our reasonable and moral nature, with an unbroken continuity. For if the being who is to live, and be affected with weal or woe by my conduct here, is not the *I*, who now act, and hope, and fear, that future existence is of small moment to me.

Which is that of Soul and Body.

It may not be amiss here, to review the amount of light which natural reason has been able to collect concerning man's future existence. Since the resurrection of the body is purely a doctrine of revelation, of which reason could not have any surmise (witness the Pagan philosophies), the question must be discussed rationally as a question concerning the immortality of the soul only. All that natural experience ever sees of the body is its death, dissolution, and seemingly irreparable destruction. But since the soul is the true seat of sensation, knowledge, emotion, merit, and will, the assertion of its immortality is far the most important doctrine of man's future existence. The various opinions of men on this subject, who had no revelation, may be seen stated in Knapp's Theol. § 149, viz : materialism (Epicurus,) transmigrations, (Brahmins Pythagoras, and some Jews,) reabsorption into the πᾶν (Stoic Pantheists), and separate disembodied immortality (Plato, &c). Among the many reasonings advanced by ancients and moderns, these following seem to me to have probable weight.

4. Rational Arguments Reviewed.

(a) The *consensus populorum*, especially when we consider how naturally man's sensuous nature and evil conscience might incline him to neglect the truth.

(b) The analogy of the fact, that man and all other living things obviously experience several stages ; first the *fœtus*, then infant, then adult. It is natural to expect other stages. (Butler).

(c) A present existence raises a presumption of continued existence, (as the sun's rising, that it will rise again) unless there is something in the body's dissolution to destroy the probability. But is there ? No. For body sleeps while soul wakes. Body may waste, fatten, be amputated, undergo flux of particles, loss of sensible organs, while soul remains identical. In sensation, the soul only uses the organs of sense, as one might feel with a stick, or see through a glass. The more essential operations of spirit, conception, memory, comparison, reasoning, &c., are only related to bodily functions, if at all; as causes to effects: whence we conclude that the essential subsistence of the soul is independent of the body. (Butler)

(d) The soul is simple, a *monad*, as is proved by consciousness. But there is not a particle of analogy, in the universe, to show that it is probable God will annihilate any substance He has created. The only instances of destruction we see, are those of disorganization of the complex. (Butler: Brown).

(e) The soul has higher powers than any of God's terrestrial works; strange that the brute, earth, and even elephants, eagles, and geese should be more long-lived! It has a capacity for mental and moral development beyond any which it attains in this life. God has ordained that all things else should fulfill the ends of their existence. It can know and glorify God: strange that God, making all things for His own glory, should make His rational servants such that the honour derived from them must utterly terminate.

(f) Conscience points directly to a superior moral Ruler, and a future existence, with its retributions.

(g) The unequal distribution of retributions here on earth, coupled with our confidence in the righteousness of God, compels a belief in a future existence, where all shall be equalized.

We have asserted it, as the doctrine of the Bible, that the souls of believers do pass immediately into glory. In opposition to this, there are some, among the professed believers in the Bible, who hold some kind of intermediate state, in which the souls of all, saints and sinners, are detained. The opinions of this kind may be ranked under three heads: 1. That of the Romish Purgatory, which has been already discussed. 2. That of the Jewish Hades, held by some Rabbins and Prelatists, early and modern; and 3d. That of the ancient Socinians and modern Thomasites, who hold that the soul will sleep unconscious until the body's resurrection. The second of these opinions will be the subject of the present section; and the the third, of the sixth and last.

5. Is there an Intermediate Place?

The Jewish doctrine seems to have been, that the souls of departed men do not pass at once into their ultimate abode; but into the invisible world, *Ἀιδης* שְׁאוֹל where they await their final doom, until the final consummation, in a state of partial and negative blessedness or misery, respectively. This Hades has two departments, that of the blessed, Paradise, or the Bosom of Abraham, and that of

Jewish Doctrine.

the lost, Tartarus.   But this Paradise is far short of the heavens proper in blessedness, as well as different in locality, and this Tartarus far less intolerable than Gehenna, or hell proper.   The following passages were supposed by them to favor this opinion : Gen. xxxvii : 35 ; xlii : 38 ; "Go down to Hades ;" 1 Samuel xxviii : 11, 14 and 19 : "An old man cometh up," "Be with me to-morrow :" Zech. ix : 11 ; where it is supposed the souls are in a place like a dry pit : Ps. vi ; 5 ; lxxxviii : 10 ; cxv : 17; cxliii : 3 ; where the state of the dead is described seemingly as a senseless and negative one.   And some Papists have supposed that their kindred notion of a *Limbus patrum* found support in Luke xvi : 23 ; in that Dives and Lazarus seem to be near enough to each other, to converse.   This, they suppose, proves that both are in the same "under-world."   They quote also Eccles. ix : 5, 6, and similar passages, which seem to teach the state of the dead to be one of inactivity and negation.

　　The reply to this Jewish and patristic notion must proceed on the postulate, that they both misunderstand the Scriptures ; the Fathers and Prelatists following the errors of the Rabbins.

Intermediate State Discussed.

One general remark to be made is, that when the Old Testament seems to speak of the spirit-world, as a place of darkness and inaction, it evidently speaks "*ad sensum*."   It is thus that the dead appear to us : As to terrestrial interests, their activities and knowledge are ended.   These passages are not to be strained to deny that souls enter upon new, spiritual activities, beyond the sphere of human experience.

　　(1)   The general drift of Scriptures certainly teaches, that at death man's probation ends.   "As the tree falleth, so it shall lie."   See also, Rev. xxii : 11.   Now, why should the future career and destiny of souls be thus held in abeyance and suspense, so many ages after probation ends ?   The intrinsic activity of the soul, as well as the propriety of the result, makes it probable that the reward, either for good or evil, will begin as soon as it is completely secured.   See 2 Cor. v : 10.

　　(2)   The death of believers is, in both Testaments, represented as an entrance upon their rest.   See, for instance, Is. lvii : 1, 2.   So the death of sinners is the beginning of their judgment.   Heb. ix : 27.

　　(3)   To this agree the expectations of the Apostle Paul, 2 Cor. v : 4, 8 ; Phil. i : 21–24.   To be "absent from the body is to be present with the Lord."   He anticipates no interval. Again : while to live is Christ to him ; "to die is gain."   Were the Rabbinical doctrine true, death, as compared with a Christian and fruitful life, would be comparative loss.   Especially would it have been impossible for the apostle to be "in a strait," betwixt the desires of living and dying, if he had supposed that the choice was between the active life of an apostle, yielding constant good to men and glory to God, as well as

rich enjoyment, amidst his tribulations, of spiritual happiness;
and the empty, silent, useless, expectant existence of a melancholy ghost in the Hades of the fanciful Jews.

(4 This is expressly confirmed by the history of the dead
saints which is given us in Scripture. On the mount of trans-
figuration, Moses and Elijah are seen already in glory. Of
Moses, at least it may be said, that he died a real corporeal
death. Again: in Luke xvi : 22 to end. Lazarus is " in
Abraham's bosom," he " is comforted ; " while Dives is in the
fire of " torment," in the actual receipt of his penal retribution.
When we compare Matt. viii : 11, we see that Abraham is in
"the kingdom of heaven" which here, evidently means heaven.
Again : Christ promises the converted robber: " This day shalt
thou be with Me in Paradise." That Paradise is the heaven of
bliss, and not some limbus in a Jewish Hades, is clear from 2
Cor. xii : 2–4, and Rev. ii : 7. It is the same as the " third
heaven." It is the place where Christ abides in glory, and the
tree of life is found. So in Rev. xiv : 13. Those who die in
the Lord are blessed from the date of their death (for such is
the only tenable rendering of the " from henceforth," $\dot{\alpha}\pi'$ $\ddot{\alpha}\rho\tau\iota$.).
So Heb. xii : 23, the spirits of the just were already made per-
fect, and denizens, with the angels, of "the city of the living
God, the heavenly Jerusalem," when that Epistle was written.

The consistent exposition of the much criticized passage,
1 Peter, iii : 19, 20, may be seen, Lect. 38.

The other unscriptural theory which we promised to
notice is, that the soul sleeps, or remains
6. Theories of   without consciousness; or at least, without
Sleep of the Soul.   external activities, from death to the resurrection. This is held in several forms. The early followers of
Socinus, while not denying to the human spirit all consciousness during its disembodied state, taught that, without its sense-
organs, it could have no intercourse with any being out of itself.
Thus, they supposed it spent the interval in a state of fruitless
insulation. Again, there have been many, who while asserting
fully the substantive existence of spirit as distinct from matter,
supposed that it could not exist or act separate from matter.
They taught that finite spirit cannot be related to space, or be
possessed of any consciousness, save through its incorporation.
Hence they must either hold that spirit, immediately upon the
death of the body, is united to an etherial, but still, an organized investment; as Swedenborg, (who also taught that the soul
never receives, by any farther resurrection, any other incorporation) or they hold that all spiritual functions must remain in
abeyance, until the bodily organism is reconstructed. To this
view, even Isaac Taylor and Archbishop Whately seem to have
leaned. Others, again, are materialists: They regard spirit
not as a substance, but only as a function. If this be all, then
of course, when the material structure shall be dissolved, spirit

will cease, as truly as sound when the harp-string is burned. The modern speculations of the Evolutionists, who are also materialists, seek to remove the just odium attaching to their doctrine, by elevating the matter with which they have identified our spirits into something immaterial. Having denied the substantiality of spirit, they proceed also to deny the substantiality of matter : and reduce both to forms of energy proceeding (if they be theists) as they say, from God; or, (if they be atheists) merely different modifications of one eternal, self-existent Force. The doctrine of this school is : that the earliest "dust of the earth is a divine efficiency; and then life another ; and then thought another ; and then conscience more ; all bred of God, and yet dependent back the one upon the other." This obviously, if it is not atheism, is pantheism ; for the only personality recognized, if any be

Replies.

recognized, is God's ? Those who attempt to reconcile these speculations with Scripture, although they flout the immortality of the soul, yet promise us a personal, or incorporate immortality, through a bodily resurrection guaranteed by God, and omnipotently wrought at Christ's final advent. Such an expectation is obviously an excrescence on their system, so heterogeneous to it, that we may very confidently anticipate its final rejection by those who now hold it. The logical and natural sequel to be drawn from their scheme is annihilation. Once teach men there is no substantive spirit, by whose mental identity the continuity of our being is preserved, while the body is scattered in dust ; and the promise of a resurrection becomes to them meaningless and absurd. The whole basis for future rewards and penalties is gone. There is no more real identity between the mind that sinned here, and the new mind that arises there, than there is between the weed of this year bred of the vegetable mould which resulted from the rotting of the weed of last year. It is not one weed but two.

I shall not consume time by repeating the evidences of man's substantive spirituality; inasmuch as they have been twice briefly stated in this course, and more fully and impregnably established in my Discussion of the Sensualistic Philosophy of the Nineteenth Century. There are those, however, who admitting that spirit is a distinct substance, hold that, from the necessity of its nature, it must be either infinite, or incorporate in some organism, either carnal or ethereal. Says Isaac Taylor : it is impossible to assign spirit its *ubi*, without connecting it with a body; because locality is itself a mode of extension; and thus, in ascribing a *ubi* to pure spirit, we are ascribing extension to it. We might justly ask : if the last assertion were true, how would the matter be helped by assigning this spirit its *ubi* in a body occupying a finite portion of space ? The extended body is more certainly burdened with the attributes of extension, than the finite portion of space it occupies; so that, were there any real difficulty in the point, it would be more difficult for us to believe the unextended spirit localized in the extended body, than in the vacant, finite portion of space occupied thereby. But Taylor's whole difficulty has arisen from the oversight of a distinction which Turrettin has long ago given. Finite spirit of course does not occupy space circumscriptively; as the measure of corn fills the bushel-measure, and assumes its cylindrical shape: But spirit may be in space definitively. The mathematical point has neither length, breadth, nor thickness: yet surely none will deny to it position in space; since the point is the first rudiment of the whole science of dimensions!

No man has ever had experience of cognitions and consciousness apart from his sense-organs. Of course, then, no man can picture to himself how these mental functions are to proceed in the disembodied state. But this is wholly another thing from proving either consciousness, or even objective perceptions, impossible for a mind not incorporate. Is intelligence the faculty of the sense-organs; or of the mind which uses them? Surely of the latter! Then the *a priori* probability is wholly in favour of the mind's exercising its own faculty (in some new way) when deprived of these instruments. If my sense of touch is able, through the intervention of a stick, to cognize a solid resisting object a yard distant, does anybody suppose that I will have any more difficulty in ascertaining its resistance to my tactual sense, without the stick, by my hand alone? So, it is obviously possible, that my intelligence may only get the nearer to its object, by the removal of its present instrument, the sense-organ.

It is too plain to need any elaboration that those who philosophize as do all our opponents, must deny the whole teaching of the Scriptures concerning the angels. If they are pure spirits, their existence, cognitions, and activities contradict every assertion these writers advance.

The sleep of the soul is inferred from such Scriptures as these: Death is called a sleep. The resurrection promised is frequently that of the man, and not of his body merely. In the famous chapter, 1 Cor. xv, the apostle argues for the resurrection, as though it were the Christian's only alternative hope against annihilation. See verses 18, 19, 29–32. This implies, they plead; that the ressurection is to be the recall of both soul and body out of the grave. For, were the doctrine of the soul's separate immortality true, the apostle would have seen in that a substantial ground for hope beyond the grave, whether the body be raised or not.

Scriptural Arguments for the Sleep of the Soul.

I reply, that the phenomena of death, the absolute quies-

These Perversions of cence of the corpse, the withdrawal of the
Scripture Answered. soul from all known and experienced activities of this life, and its entrance upon its
heavenly rest, are abundantly sufficient to justify the calling of
a Christian death "a sleep," consistently with the Bible-doc-
trine of the separate activity of the soul. This is evidently
what the Scriptures mean by the figure. That the man, and
not the body, is so often spoken of as resurrected, is easily explained by that natural figure, by which sensuous beings, as we
all are, speak of a corpse as "a man." But all doubt is cleared
away, by such passages as Phil. iii : 21. There, the resurrection is declared to be a "changing of our vile body, and fashioning of it like unto His glorious body." 1 Cor. xv : 42.
That which "is sown in corruption," is "raised in incorruption."
What can this be, but the body? In verse 42. "We have
borne the image of the earthy." Wherein ? In that we have
animal and perishable bodies. Then the *ego* and the body
which it "has borne," are distinct. The ingenious cavil from
verses 18, 19, and 29 to 32, is easily solved by the following
facts : The final immortality which the Bible teaches is, as we
have distinctly stated, not that of souls disembodied, but of
incorporate men. Hence it was altogether natural for the
apostle to speak of our prospect for an immortality as identical with that of a resurrection. But again, (what is far more
important), the apostle's argument was proceeding upon these
truths : that the reality of Christ's resurrection, on one hand,
was vital to all hope of a redeemed immortality for us in any
form. See verses 12 to 18. But on the other hand, the fact
of Christ's resurrection involves the truth, that we also shall
rise as He did. Under this state of the argument, it is
thoroughly consistent with our doctrine, that the apostle should
argue as he did. The apostle does argue, that practically, the
believer's resurrection is his only alternative hope against
"perishing," but he does not argue that it is his only alternative
hope against annihilation. The latter idea is nowhere entertained as an alternative.

In proof that ransomed souls are not detained in uncon-
Positive Scripture- sciousness in the grave, we advance posi-
proofs. tively all those texts which show us such
souls already in heaven. Here all the pas-
sages quoted under the former head apply : We need not consume time in repeating them. We add, that the protomartyr,
Stephen, when dying said, with the full light of inspiration in
his mind : "Lord Jesus, receive my spirit." He certainly expected an immediate glorification with Christ. See Acts vii : 59.
So, in Matt. x : 28, the distinction of spirit and body is indisputably made ; and those who truly fear God are taught that
though the persecutor may kill the body, the soul is happy in
Christ. In Rev. iv : 4, 6, with v : 9, John sees the redeemed

already amidst the raptures of heaven, in the persons of the twenty-four elders, and the four living creatures. So, in Rev. vi : 9 to 11, the souls of the martyrs were seen under (or below) the altar, in the full possession of their intelligence and activity, and adorned with their white robes. All this was before the resurrection.

It is the glory of the gospel, that it gives a victory over death. Over the true man, the being who feels, and hopes and fears, it has no dominion. The body alone falls under its stroke; but when it does so, it is unconscious of that stroke. Whatever there may be in the grave, with its gloom and worm, that is repulsive to man; with all that the true *Ego* has no part. While the worms destroy the unconscious flesh, the conscious spirit has soared away to the light and rest of its Saviour's bosom.

The True Ego Never feels Death.

LECTURE LXX.
THE RESURRECTION.

SYLLABUS.

1. What were the opinions of the ancient Heathens, and what of the Jews, on this subject? Does nature furnish any analogy in favor of it?
  Dr. Christian Knapp, § 151. Hodge Theol., pt. iv, § 1, 2. Dick, Lect. 82.
2. State the precise meaning of the Scripture doctine. What will be the qualities of our resurrection bodies?
  Turrettin, Loc. xx, Qu. 1, 2, 9. Knapp, § 152, 153. Dick, Lect. 82.
3. Will the resurrection bodies be the same which men have now? In what sense the same? Discuss objections.
  Turrettin Qu. 2. Dick, Lect. 82. Watson's Theol. Inst., ch. 29.
4. Prove the doctrine of the Resurrection, from the Old Testament; from the New.
  Turrettin, Qu. 1. Dick, Lect. 82.
5. How is the resurrection of the Saints, and how is that of sinners, related to the resurrection of Christ?
  Dick, Lect. 82. Breckinridge Theol., Vol. i, bk, i, ch. 6.
6. What will be the time? Will there be a double resurrection?
  Turrettin, Qu. 3. Dick. Lect. 82. Scott, Com. on Rev., ch. 20. Brown's Second Advent. Knapp, § 154. Hodge, as above, chs. 3, 4. See on whole, Ridgley, Qu. 87. Geo. Bush on the Resurrection. Davies' Sermons. Young's Last Day.

THE definite philosophic speculations among the ancient heathen all discarded the doctrine of a proper resurrection; so that the Bible stands alone in acknowledging the share of the body in man's immortality. It is true that the poet (Hesiod, Homer, Virgil) expressing the popular and traditionary belief, (in this case, as in that of the soul's immortality, less incorrect than the philosopher's speculations), speak of the

1. Pagan Theories Embrace no Resurrection.

future life as a bodily one, of members, food, labours, &c., in Tartarus and Elysium. But it is difficult to say how far these sensuous representations of the future existence were due to mere inaccuracy and grossness of conception, or how far to perspicuous ideas of a bodily existence conjoined with the spiritual. The Brahmins speak of many transmigrations and incarnations, of their deified men; but none of them are resurrections proper. The Pythagoreans and Platonists dreamed of an ὄχημα, an etherial, semi-spiritual investment, which the glorified spirit, after its metempsychoses are finished, develops for itself. The pantheistic sects, whether Buddhists or Stoics, of course utterly rejected the idea of a bodily existence after death, when they denied even a personal existence of the soul.

But the Jews, with the exception of the Sadducees and
What Jews Believed   Essenses, seem to have held firmly to the
it.   doctrine. Nor can I see any evidence, except the prejudice of hypothesis and fancy, for the notion of Knapp, and many Germans, that their belief in this doctrine dated only from the time of the Babylonish captivity. There is no historical evidence. If the proof-texts of the earlier Hebrew Scriptures are perversely explained away, and those of the Maccabees, &c., admitted, there is some show of plausibility. But it is far better reasoning to say that this unquestioning belief in the doctrine by the Jews, is evidence that they understood their earlier as well as their later Scriptures to teach it. The evidence of the state of opinion among them, and especially among the Pharisees, is found in their uninspired writings: 2 Mac. vii : 9, &c., xii : 43, 45 ; Josephus and Philo, and in New Testament allusions to their ideas. See Matt. xxii ; Luke xx ; John xi : 24 ; Acts xxiii : 6, 8 ; Heb. xi : 35. But the doctrine was a subject of mocking skepticism to most of the speculative Pagans ; as the interlocutor in Minutius Felix' Octavius, Pliny, jr., Lucian, Celsus, &c. See Acts xvii : 32 ; xxvi : 8, 24.

Hence, we may infer that the doctrine of the resurrection
No Natural Proofs   is purely one of revelation. Analogies and
of it.   probable arguments have been sought in favor of it, as by the early fathers and later writers ; but while some rise in dignity above the fable of the Phœnix, none of them can claim to be demonstrations. The fact that all nature moves in cycles, restoring a state of things again which had passed away ; that the trees bud after the sterility and mimic death of winter ; that moons wax again after they have waned ; that sun and stars, after setting in the west, rise again in the east ; that seeds germinate and reproduce their ird ; can scarcely be called a proper analogy ; for in all these cases, there is no proper destruction, by a disorganization of atoms, but a mere return of the same complex body, without a moment's breach of its organic unity, into the same state in

which it had previously been, If we were perfectly honest, we should rather admit that the proper analogies of nature are against the doctrine ; for when a seed germinates that particular seed is produced no more ; there is, in what comes from it, only a generic, not a numerical identity. When the tree really perishes, its mould and moisture and gases are never reconstructed into that same tree, but pass irrevocably into other vegetable forms. Dick supposes that the argument said to have been stated B. C. 450, by Phocylides, the Milesian, is more plausible ; that inasmuch as God's wisdom led Him to introduce a *genus* of rational beings, of body and spirit combined, the same wisdom will always lead him to perpetuate that kind. But if, after the soul's departure, the body were never reanimated, man would become simply an inferior angel, and the *genus* would be obliterated. To this, also, we may reply ; that this argument is not valid until it is also shown that the wisdom, which called this *genus* of complex beings into existence, will not be satisfied by its temporary continuance as a separate *genus.* But this we can never prove by mere reason. For instance : the same reasoning would prove equally well, both an immortality and a bodily resurrection, for any of the *genera* of brutes ! Another argument is presented by Turrettin from the justice of God, which, if possessed of feeble weight by itself, at least has the advantage of harmonizing with Bible representations. It is, that the justice of God is more appropriately satisfied, by punishing and rewarding souls in the very bodies, and with the whole personal identity, with which they sinned (Comp. 2 Cor. v : 10) or obeyed.

In Scripture the image of a resurrection, ἀνάστασις, is undoubtedly used sometimes in a figurative sense, to describe regeneration, (John v : 25 ; Eph. v : 14,) and sometimes, restoration from calamity and captivity to prosperity and joy. (Ezek. xxxvii : 12 : Is. xxvi : 19). But it is equally certain that the words are intended to be used in a literal sense, of the restoration of the same body that dies to life, by its reunion to the soul. This then is the doctrine. For when the resurrection of the dead, (νεκρῶν) of those that are in their graves, of those that sleep in the dust of the earth, is declared, the sense is unequivocal. Without at this time particularizing Scripture proofs, we assert that they mean to describe a bodily existence as literally as when they speak of man's soul in this life, as residing in a body ; and this, though wonderfully changed in qualities, the same body, in the proper, honest sense of the word same, which the soul laid down at death. This resurrection will embrace all the individuals of the human race, good and bad, except those whose bodies have already passed into heaven, and those of the last generation, who will be alive on the earth at the last trump. But on the bodies of these the resurrection change will pass,

2. True Meaning of Resurrection.

though they do not die. The signal of this resurrection is to be the "last trump," an expression probably taken from the transactions at Sinai; (Exod. xix : 16, 19 ; cf. Heb. xii : 26), which may, very possibly, be some literal, audible summons, sounded through the whole atmosphere of the world. But the agent will be Christ, by His direct and almighty power, with the Holy Ghost.

The qualities of the resurrection bodies of the saints are described in 1 Cor. xv : 42, 50, with as much particularity, probably, as we can comprehend. Whereas the body is buried in a state of dissolution; it is raised indissoluble, no longer liable to disorganization, by separation of particles, either because protected therefrom by the special power of God, or by the absence of assailing chemical forces. It is buried, disfigured and loathsome. It will be raised beautiful. Since it is a literal material body that is raised, it is far the most natural to suppose that the glory predicated of it, is literal, material beauty. As to its kind, see Matt. xiii : 43 ; Phil. iii : 21, with Rev. i : 13, 14. Some may think that it is unworthy of God's redemption to suppose it conferring an advantage so trivial and sensuous as personal beauty. But is not this a remnant of that Gnostic or Neo-Platonic asceticism, which cast off the body itself as too worthless to be an object of redeeming power? We know that sanctified affections now always beautify and ennoble the countenance. See Exod. xxxiv : 29, 30. And if God did not deem it too trivial for His attention, to clothe the landscape with verdure, to cast every form of nature in lines of grace, to dye the skies with purest azure, and to paint the sun and stars with splendour, in order to gratify the eyes of His children here, we may assume that He will condescend to beautify even the bodies of His saints, in that world where all is made perfect. Next, the body is buried in weakness ; it has just given the crowning evidence of feebleness, by yielding to death. It will be raised in immortal vigour, so as to perform its functions with perfect facility, and without fatigue.

And last ; it is buried an animal body ; i. e., this is the character it has hitherto had. The σῶμα ψυχικὸν is unfortunately translated " natural body" in the English version. The Apostle here evidently avails himself of the popular Greek distinction, growing out of the currency of Pythagorean and Platonic philosophy, to express his distinction, without meaning to endorse their anthropology. The σῶμα ψυχικὸν is evidently the body as characterized chiefly by its animal functions. What these are, there can be little doubt, if we keep in mind the established Greek sense of the ψυχή, viz : the functions of the appetite and sense. Then the σῶμα πνευματικόν must mean not a body now material, as the Swedenborgians, &c., claim (a positive contra-

Qualities of Resurrection Bodies.

"Natural Body" and "Spiritual Body;" What?

diction and impossibility), but a body actuated only by processes of intellection and moral affection; for these, Paul's readers supposed were the proper processes of the πνεῦμα or νοῦς. But the Apostle vs. 44, 50, defines his own meaning. To show that "there is an animal body, and a spiritual body;" that it is no fancy nor impossibility, he points to the fact that such have already existed, in the case of Adam and his natural seed, and of Christ. And as we were federally connected, first with Adam, and then with Christ, we bear first the animal body, (Adam's) and then the spiritual (Christ's). And Christ's humanity also, during His humiliation, passed through that first stage, to the second; because he assumed all the innocent weaknesses and affections of a literal man. Our σῶμα πνευμα-τικόν, then, is defined to be what Christ's glorified body now in Heaven is. Complete this definition by what we find in Matt. xxii : 30. The spiritual body then, is one occupied and actuated only by the spiritual processes of a sanctified soul; but which neither smarts with pain, nor feels fatigue, nor has appetites, nor takes any literal, material supplies therefor.

It seems every way reasonable to suppose that while the bodies of the wicked will be raised without the glory or splendour of the saints, they also will be no longer animal bodies, and will be endued with immortal vigour to endure.

Resurrection Bodies of Sinners.

The Scriptures plainly teach that our resurrection bodies will be the bodies we now have, only modified; that is, that they will be substantially identical. This follows from the divine justice, so far as it prompts God to work a resurrection. For if we have not the very body in which we sinned, when called to judgment, that "every man may receive the things done in the body," there will be no relevancy in the punishment, so far as it falls on the body. The same truth follows from the believer's union to Christ. If He redeemed our bodies, must they not be the very ones we have here? (1 Cor. iii : 16; vi : 15). It appears evidently, from Christ's resurrection, which is the earnest, exemplar, and pledge of ours. For in His case, the body that was raised was the very one that died and was buried. But if, in our case, the body that dies is finally dissipated, and another is reconstructed, there is small resemblance indeed to our Saviour's resurrection. This leads us to remark, fourth, that the very words ἀνίστημι, ἀνάσ-τασις plainly imply the rearing of the same thing that fell; otherwise there is an abuse of language in applying them to a proper creation. Last, the language of Scripture in Dan. xii ; 2 ; John v : 28, 29 : 1 Cor. xv : 21, 53, 54 ; 1 Thess. iv : 16 ; it is that which is "in the dust of the earth," "in the μνήμεια," the νέκροι ; corpses, which is raised. It is "this mortal" which "puts on immortality." From the days of the Latin Fathers, and their speculative Pagan opposers, certain objections have

3. Identity of the Bodies Raised, Proofs.

53*

been pompously raised against such a resurrection, as though it were intrinsically absurd. They may be found reproduced by Geo. Bush on the Resurrection.

The general objection is from the incredible greatness of the work; that since the particles that composed human bodies are scattered asunder by almost every conceivable agency, fire, winds, waters, birds and beasts of prey, mingled with the soil of the fields, and dissolved in the waters of the ocean, it is unreasonable to expect they will be assembled again. We reply, (reserving the question whether a proper corporeal identity implies the presence of all the constituent particles; of which more anon), that this objection is founded only on a denial of God's omnipotence, omniscience, and almighty power. The work of the resurrection does indeed present a most wondrous and glorious display of divine power. But to God all things are easy. We may briefly reply, that to all who believe in a special Providence, there is a standing and triumphant answer visible to our eyes. It is in the existence of our present bodies. Are they not formed by God? Are they not also formed from "the dust of the earth?" And it is not any one hundred and fifty pounds of earth, which God moulds into a body of that weight; but there is a most wonderful, extensive, and nice selection of particles, where a million of atoms are assorted over and rejected, for one that is selected; and that from thousands of miles. In my body there are atoms, probably, that came from Java (in coffee), and from Cuba or Manilla (in sugar), and from the western prairies (in pork), and from the savannahs of Carolina (in rice), and from the green hills of Western Virginia (in beef and butter), and from our own fields (in fruits). Do you say, the selection and aggregation have been accomplished gradually, by sundry natural laws of vegetation and nutrition? Yea, but what are natural laws? Only regular modes of God's working through matter, which He has in His wisdom proposed to Himself? If God actually does this thing now, why may He not do another thing just like it, only more quickly?

But an objection supposed to be still more formidable, is derived from the supposed flux of particles in the human body, and the cases in which particles which belonged to one man at his death, become parts of the structure of another man's body, through cannibalism, or the derivation by beasts from the mould enriched with human dust, which beasts are in turn consumed by men, &c., &c. Now, since one material atom cannot be in two places at the same time, the resurrection of the same bodies, say they, is a physical impossibility. And if the flux of particles be admitted, which shall the man claim, as composing his bodily identity; those he had first, or those he had last: or all he ever had? To the first of these questions, we reply, that there is no evidence that a particle of matter composing a portion of a human corpse, has ever been assimilated by another human body. It is only assumed that it may be so. But now, inasmuch as the truth of Scripture has been demonstrated by an independent course of moral evidences, and it asserts the same body shall be raised, if there is, indeed, any difficulty about this question of the atoms, the burden of proof lies upon the objector; and he must demonstrate that the difficulty exists, and is insuperable. It is not sufficient merely to surmise that it may exist. Now, I repeat, a surmise is good enough to meet a surmise. Let me assume this hypothesis, that it may be a physiological law, that a molecule, once assimilated and vitalized by a man (or other animal), undergoes an influence which renders it afterwards incapable of assimilation by another being of the same species. This, indeed, is not without plausible evidence from analogy: witness, for instance, the fertility of a soil to another crop, when a proper rotation is pursued, which had become barren as to the first crop too long repeated. But, if there is any such law, the case supposed by the objector against the resurrection, never occurs. But, second: in answer to both objections, it can never be shown that the numerical identity of all the constituent atoms is necessary to that bodily sameness, which is asserted by the Bible of our resurrection bodies. We are under no forensic obligation whatever, to define precisely in what that sameness consists, but take our stand here, that the Bible, being written in popular language, when it says our resurrection bodies will be the same, it means precisely what popular consciousness and common language apprehend, when it is said my body at forty is the same body grown stronger, which I had at fifteen. Let that meaning be whatever it may be, if this doctrine of the flux of particles, and this possibility of a particle that once belonged to one man becoming a part of another, prove that our resurrection bodies cannot be the same that died, they equally prove that my body cannot now be the body I had some years ago, for that flux, if there is any truth in it, has already occurred; and there is just as much probability that I have been nourished with a few particles from a potatoe, manured with the hair of some man who is still living, as that two men will both claim the same particles at the resurrection. But my consciousness tells me (the most demonstrative of all proof), that I have had the same body all the time, so that, if these famous objections disprove a resurrection, they equally contradict consciousness. You will notice that I propound no theory as to what constitutes precisely our consciousness of bodily identity, as it is wholly unnecessary to our argument that I should; and that I do not undertake to define precisely how the resurrection body will be constituted in this particular; and this is most proper for me, because the Bible propounds no theory on this point. But if curiosity leads you to enquire, I answer that it appears to me our consciousness of bodily identity (as to a limb, or member, or organ of sense, for instance) does not include an apprehension of the numerical identy of all the constituent atoms all the while, but that it consists of an apprehension of a continued relation of the organism of the limb or organ to our mental consciousness all the time, implying also that there is no suden change of a majority, or even any large fraction of the constituent atoms thereof at any one time.

Bodily Identity During Life, What?

In presenting the Bible-proof, nothing more will be done, than to cite the passages, with such word of explanation as may be necessary to show their application. If we believe our Saviour, implications of this doctrine appear at a very early stage of the Old Testament Scriptures; for indeed the sort of immortality implied all along, is the immortality of man, body and soul. (See then Exod. iii : 6, as explained in Matt. xxii : 31, 32; Mark xii : 26, 27). The next passage is Job xix : 26, which I claim *quicunque vult*, as containing a clear assertion of a resurrection. In Ps. xvi : 9, 11, (expounded Acts ii : 29, 32; xiii : 36, 37) David is made by the Holy Ghost to foretell Christ's resurrection. Doubtless, the Psalmist. if he distinctly knew that he was personating Christ in this language, apprehended his own resurrection as a corollary of Christ's. Ps. xvii : 15 probably alludes also to a resurrection in the phrase : "awake in thy likeness;" for what awakes, except the body? Nothing else sleeps. So Is. xxv : 8, may be seen interpreted in 1 Cor. xv : 54; Dan. xii : 2. Both teach the same doctrine.

4. Proofs That Bodies Will Rise.

In the New Testament the proofs of bodily resurrection are still more **numerous** and explicit. The following are the chief; Matt. xxii : 31, &c.; Mark xii : 26, 27 ; John v : 21, 29; vi : 39, 40 ; xi : 24 ; Acts as above; 1 Cor. xv; 1 Thess. iv : 13 to end; 2 Tim. ii : 8; Phil. iii : 21 ; Heb. vi : 2 ; xi : 35.

Other strong Scriptural proofs are urged by the Reformed divines, which need little more than a mere statement here. The resurrection of Christ is both the example and proof of ours. 1 Cor. xv : 20; 1 Peter i : 3. First, it demonstrates that the work is feasible for God. Second, it demonstrates the sufficiency and acceptance of Christ's satisfaction for His people's guilt: but bodily death is a part of our penalty therefor: and must be repaired when we are fully invested with the avails of that purchase. Third: Scripture shows such a union between Christ, the Head, and His members; that our glorification must result as His does. 1 Cor. vi : 15.

The exposition given of the Covenant of Grace, by our Saviour Himself in Matt. xxii : 31, &c., shows that it includes a resurrection for the body. This covenant, Christ there teaches ıs, is first, perpetual: death does not sever it. But second, it was a covenant not between God and angels or ghosts; but between Him and the incorporate men, Abraham, Isaac, and Jacob. Then, its consummation must restore them to their incorporate state.

The inhabitation of our bodies by the Holy Ghost implies the redemption of the body also. Although not the primary seat of sanctification, the body, thus closely dedicated to the Spirit's indwelling, will not be left in the dust. Rom. viii : 11.

Last, we have seen Turrettin unfold the reasonableness of men's being judged in the bodies in which they have lived. The rewards and penalties cannot, in any other way, be so appropriate, as when God makes the bodily members which were abused or consecrated, the inlets of the deserved penalties, or the free rewards. See 1 Cor. v : 10.

Some divines, as e. g. Breckinridge, say that the resurrection of both saints and sinners is of **5. Reprobate not raised in Christ, but by Christ.** Christ's purchase, quoting 1 Cor. xv : 22, making the "all" mean the whole human race. But we teach, that while Christ, as King in Zion, commands the resurrection of both, it is in different relations. The resurrection of His people being a gift of His purchase, is effectuated in them by the union to Him, and is one result of the indwelling of the Holy Ghost. The resurrection of the evil is an act of pure dominion, effected in them by His avenging sovereignty. The other idea would represent the wicked also, as vitally connected with Christ, by a mystical union. But if so, why does not that union sanctify and save? Are we authorized to say that, had Christ not come, there would have been no resurrection unto damnation for Adam's fallen race at all? Moreover, that opinion puts an unauthorized and dangerous sense upon 1 Cor. xv : 22, *et sim.*

The wisdom and modesty of the Westminster Assembly are displayed in the caution with which they **6. Millennium and Second Advent.** speak on these difficult subjects. Their full discussion would lead into a thorough investigation of that vast and intricate subject, unfulfilled prophecy. Nothing more can be attempted here, than a brief statement of competing schemes. They each embrace, and attempt to adjust, the following points: The millennium, or thousand years' reign of Christ on earth: Christ's second advent: The destruction of the Kingdom of Satan among men: The resurrection of the righteous and the wicked: and the general judgment and final consummation. That doctrine which we hold, and which we assert to be the Apostolic and Church doctrine, teaches, just as much as the pre-Adventists, the literal and personal second advent of Christ, and we hold, with the Apostolic Christians, that it is, next to heaven, the dearest and most glorious of the believer's hopes: as bringing the epoch of his full deliverance from death, and full introduction into the society of his adored Saviour. This hope of a literal second advent we base on such Scriptures as these: Acts i : 11 : iii : 20, 21 ; Heb. ix : 28 ; 1 Thess. iv : 15, 16 ; Phil. iii : 20 ; Matt. xxvi : 64, &c., &c. Before this second advent, the following events must have occurred. The development and secular overthrow of Antichrist, (2 Thess. ii : 3 to 9 ; Dan. vii : 24–26 ; Rev. xvii, xviii :) which is the Papacy. The proclamation of the Gospel to all nations, and the general triumph of Christianity over all false religions, in all nations. (Ps. lxxii: 8–11 ; Is. ii : 2–4 ; Dan. ii : 44, 45 ; vii: 14 ; Matt. xxviii : 19, 20 ; Rom. xi : 12, 15, 25 ; Mark xiii: 10; Matt. xxiv: 14). The general and national return of the Jews to the Christian Church. (Rom. xi : 25, 26). And then a partial relapse from this state of high prosperity, into unbelief and sin. (Rev. xx : 7, 8). During this partial decline, at a time unexpected to formal Christians and the profane, and not to be expressly foreknown by any true saint on earth, the second Advent of Christ will take place, in the manner described in 1 Thess. It will be immediately followed by the resurrection of all the dead, the redeemed dead taking the precedence. Then the generation of men living at the time will be changed (without dying) into their immortal bodies, the world will undergo its great change by fire, the general judgment will be held; and last, the saved and the lost will severally depart to their final abodes, the former to be forever with the Lord, the the latter with Satan and his angels.

It is not easy to state the scheme of the pre-Adventists, because they are so inconsistent with each other, that a part of their company will disclaim some points of any statement which is made for them. The following propositions, however, are held by the most of pre-Adventists. The present dispensation of the Gospel is neither sufficient nor designed for the general conversion of the world. Missionary efforts can only prepare the way for Christ's coming, by gathering out of the doomed mass the elect scattered among them. For, Christ's advent may be at any time, before any general evangelization of either Jews or Gentiles; and when He comes, the wicked will be destroyed by it, and not converted. At this advent, the saints, or the more illustrious of them, at least, will be raised from the dead. The converted Jews will return to Canaan, the temple will be rebuilt and its service restored ; and the incarnate Messiah will reign a thousand years, (or a long cycle symbolized by a thousand years,) on earth, with the risen saints. This will be the millennium of Rev. xxth. At the end of this time, the general resurrection of the wicked will take place, and be followed by the general judgment and final consummation.

The boast is: that they are the only faithful party in expounding prophecy according to its literal meaning : and that the daily expectation of this advent is exceedingly promo-

tive of faith and holy living. I can attempt no more than to set
down for you a few leading remarks.

Of these the first is : that though it is now the fashion for
these pre-Adventists to claim the special
honours of orthodoxy, their system is distinctly against that of the Westminster Confession. Not only does that standard ignore it totally : it
expressly asserts the contrary : Ch. viii : § 4. "Christ shall
return to judge men and angels at the end of the world." (Ch.
xxxii : § 2). "At the last day . . . all the dead shall be
raised up." (Chap. xxxiii : § 3). "So will He have that day
unknown to men," &c. (Larger Cat. Qu. 56). "Christ shall
come again at the last day," &c., Qu. 86, 87. "The members
of the invisible Church . . . wait for the full redemption
of their bodies . . . till at the last day they be again
united to their souls." "We are to believe that at the last
day there shall be a general resurrection of the dead, both of
the just and unjust."

*Their Scheme Hete-
rodox, by Confession.*

2nd. To me it appears that the temper which secretly prompts
this scheme is one of unbelief. Overweening
and egotistical hopes of the early evangeli-
zing of the whole world, fostered by partial
considerations, meet with disappointment. Hence results a
feeling of skepticism; and they are heard pronouncing the
present agencies committed to the Church, as manifestly inadequate. But the temper which Christ enjoins on us is one of
humble, faithful, believing diligence in the use of those agencies, relying on His faithfulness and power to make them do
their glorious work. He commands us also to remember how
much they have already accomplished, when energized by His
grace, and to take courage. The tendencies of the pre-Advent
scheme are unwholesome, though it has been held by some
spiritually minded men.

*The Scheme Sug-
gested by Mistrust.*

Its advocates boast that they alone interpret the symbols of
prophecy faithfully. But when we examine,
we find that they make no nearer approach
to an exact system of exposition; and that
they can take as wild figurative licenses when it suits their purposes, as any others. The new interpretations are usually but
violations of the familiar and well-established canon, that the
prophets represent the evangelical blessings under the tropes of
the Jewish usages known to themselves.

*Their Exegesis no
more Faithful.*

3d. The pre-Advent scheme disparages the present, the dispensation of the Holy Ghost, and the means committed to the
Church for the conversion of sinners. It thus tends to dis-
courage faith and missionary effort. Whereas Christ represents
the presence of the Holy Ghost, and this His dispensation, as
so desirable, that it was expedient for Him to go away that the
Paraclete might come. John xvi : 7. Pre-Adventism repre-

sents it as so undesirable that every saint ought to pray for its immediate abrogation. Incredulity as to the conversion of the world by the "means of grace," is hotly, and even scornfully, inferred from visible results and experiences, in a temper which we confess appears to us the same with that of unbelievers in 2 Peter iii : 4 : "Where is the promise of his coming?" &c. They seem to us to "judge the Lord by feeble sense," instead of "trusting Him for His grace." Thus it is unfavorable to a faithful performance of ecclesiastical duties. If no visible Church, however orthodox, is to be Christ's instrument for over-throwing Satan's kingdom here—if Christ is to sweep the best of them away as so much rubbish, along with all "world-pow-ers," at His Advent—if it is our duty to expect and desire this catastrophe daily; who does not see that we shall feel very slight value for ecclesiastical ties and duties? And should we differ unpleasantly from our Church courts, we shall be tempted to feel that it is pious to spurn them. Are we not daily pray-ing for an event which will render them useless lumber?

4th. Their scheme is obnoxious to fatal Scriptural objections: That Christ comes but twice, to atone and to judge; (Heb. ix : 28). That the heavens must receive Christ until the times of the restitution of all things. (Acts iii : 21). That the blessedness of the saints is always placed by Scripture in "those new heavens and new earth," which succeed the judgment. That on this scheme the date of the world's end will be known long before it comes; whereas the Scripture represents it as wholly unexpected to all when it comes : That only one resurrection is anywhere mentioned in the most express didactic passages; so that it behooves us to explain the symbolical passage in Rev. xx : 4 to 6, in consistency with them : That the Scriptures say, (e. g., 1 Cor. xv : 23; 2 Thess. i : 10; 1 Thess. iii : 13), that the whole Church will be complete at Christ's next coming. And that then the sacraments, and other "means of grace," will cease finally. The opinion is also beset by insuperable difficul-ties, such as these : whether these resurrected martyrs will die again; whether they will enjoy innocent corporeal pleasures; whether (if the affirmative be taken) their children will be born with original sin; if not, whence those apostate men are to come, who make the final brief falling away just before the second resurrection, &c. On all these points the pre-Adventists make the wildest and most contradictory surmises.

Collides with Scrip-tural Facts.

5th. Thus, the scheme tends towards the Rabbinical view of the present state of departed saints. All admit, that their condi-tion is not equal in blessedness and glory, to that upon which they will enter after the resurrection of the body. In the view of the pre-Adventist, it must be also lower than the millennial state; because they hold that Christs advent, and the "first resurrection," is a promotion much to be desired by them.

But pre-Adventists confess, with us, that the final state, after "the marriage supper of the Lamb," will be highest of all. Then the present condition of the sainted dead is, according to this doctrine, lower than another mid-way state, which in turn, is lower than the highest. May not the present state then, be quite low indeed? May it not be almost as irksome as that of souls in the Rabbinical Hades? So some pre-Adventists do not stickle to intimate.

6th. Pre-Adventists usually claim that their expectation of the Lord's coming is peculiarly promotive of spiritual-mindedness, strong faith, and close walking with God. A Christian who had not adopted their scheme, is represented as exclaiming, when it was unfolded: "If I believed so, I must live near my Saviour indeed!" If he did, he exclaimed foolishly. For first, did not God give one and the same system of sanctification to us and to primitive Christians? But these could not have cherished the expectation of seeing the "personal advent" before death; for stubborn facts have proved that it was not less than 1800 years distant. Second, every Christian, even if he is a pre-Adventist, must know that it is far more probable his body will die before the "advent," than that he will live to see it. All admit that in a few years the body must die. Then the season of repentance will be done, the spiritual state of our souls decided forever, and our spirits reunited to a glorified Redeemer in a better world than this. Now, if there is faith, these certainties contain more wholesome stimulus for it, than can possibly be presented in the surmises of any pre-Adventist theory. The only reason the latter is to any persons more exciting, is the romance attaching to it; the same reason which enabled the false prophet, Miller, to drive multitudes into wild alarm by the dream of approaching judgment, who were unmoved by the sober certainty of approaching death. The hope of us common Christians is to meet our glorified Lord very certainly and very soon (when our bodies die) in the other world. It passes our wits to see how a less certain hope of meeting Him in this world (a worse one) can evince more "love for His appearing."

LECTURE LXXI.

THE GENERAL JUDGMENT AND ETERNAL LIFE.

IT might seem that the purposes of God's righteousness and government might, at first view, be sufficiently satisfied by a final distribution of rewards and punishments, to men, as they successively passed out of this life. But His declarative glory requires not only this, but a more formal, forensic act, by which His righteous, holy, and merciful dealing shall be collectively displayed before the Universe. For His creatures, both angels and men, are finite, and would remain forever in ignorance of a great part of His righteous dispensation, unless they received this formal publication. By bringing all His subjects (at least of this province of His Universe) together, and displaying to all, the conduct and doom of all, He will silence every cavil, and compel every one to justify Him in all His dealings.

1. Objects of General Judgment.

But more than this : man is, during all his probationary state, a sensuous being. So that he certainly, if not angels, is powerfully actuated by many motives arising out of a judgment, to shun sin, and seek after righteousness. The strict account, the prompt and irrevocable sentence pronounced upon it, the publication of his sins, secret and open, to all the world, the accessories of grandeur and awe which will attend the last award, all appeal to his nature, as a social and corporeal creature, arousing conscience, fear, hope, shame of exposure, affection for fellow-men, and giving substance and reality to the doctrine of future rewards, in a way which could not be felt, if there were no judgment day. But, as was remarked concerning the death

It Stimulates Conscience.

842

of the saints; if any benefit is to be realized from the certain prospect of an event, the event must be certain.

Several arguments have been announced by theologians to show that reason might anticipate a general judgment. (a). From the necessity of some means to readjust the inequalities between men's fates in this life and their merits. (b). From the terrors of man's own guilty conscience. (c). From the pagan myths concerning future Judges, *Rhamnusia, Æacus, Minos, Rhadamanthus.* But these are rather evidences of future rewards and punishments, than of their distribution in the particular forensic form of a general judgment. Reason can offer no more than a probable evidence of the latter; and this evidence is best seen from the objects which God secures by a judgment, when considered in the light of these convictions. So far as God Himself is concerned in the satisfaction of the attributes of justice in His own breast, it would be enough that He should see for Himself, each man's whole conduct and merits, and assign each one, at such time and place as He please, the adequate rewards. But reason and conscience make a judgment probable, because they obviously indicate the above valuable ends to be subserved by it. For it enables God, not only to right all the inequalities of His temporal providence, and to sanction the verdicts of man's conscience, but to show all this to His kingdom, to the glory of His grace and holiness; to unmask secret sin when He punishes it; to stop the mouths of the accusers of His people while He reveals and rewards their secret graces and virtues; and to apply to the soul, while on earth, the most pungent *stimuli* to obedience.

But this is more clearly the doctrine of Revelation. It would indeed be inaccurate to apply to a general judgment every thing which is said in the Bible about God's judgment: as is done to too great an extent by some writers. For this word is sometimes used for God's government in general (John v : 22) for a command or precept, (Ps. xix : 9 ;) sometimes for God's chastisements (1 Pet. iv : 17,) sometimes for His vengeance, (Ps. cxlix : 9 ;) sometimes for the attribute of righteousness, (Ps. lxxii : 2, or lxxxix : 14 ;) sometimes for a special sentence pronounced. But the following passages may be said to have more or less of a proper application to the general judgment, and from them it will be learned that this has been the doctrine of the Church from the earliest ages, viz; Jude 14 ; Eccles. xii : 14 ; Ps. 1 ; 3–6, 21 ; possibly Ps. xcvi : 13 ; Dan. vii : 10 ; Matt. xii : 36 ; xiii : 41 ; xvi : 27 ; and most notably xxv : 31–46 ; Acts xvii : 31 ; 2 Cor. v : 10 ; 2 Thess. i : 7–10 ; 2 Tim. iv : 1 ; Rev. xx : 12. Other passages which will be quoted to show who are the Judge, and parties judged, and what the subjects of judgment, also apply fairly to this point. They need not be anticpiated here.

Rational Arguments Invalid, Though Probable.

Revelation Teaches it.

Some laxer theologians, especially of the German school,
have taught that all these passages do not
teach a literal, universal, forensic act, but
merely a state, to which God will successively
bring all His creatures according to their respective merits; in
short that the whole representation is merely figurative of certain principles of retribution. The answer is, to point to the
previous arguments, which show that not only equal retributions,
but a public formal declaration thereof, are called for by the
purposes of God's government, and the system of doctrines;
and to show that the strong terms of the Scriptures cannot
be satisfied by such an explanation. There are figures; but
those figures must be literalized according to fair exegetical
laws; and they plainly describe the judgment as something that
precedes the execution of the retribution.

The Judgment not merely Metaphorical.

The time of this great transaction, absolutely speaking, is,
and is intended to be, utterly unknown to the
whole human race, in order that its uncertainty may cause all to fear; 1 Thess. v : 2 ; 2 Pet.
iii : 10 ; Matt. xxiv : 36, &c. Hence we may see the unscripturalness of those who endeavor to fix approximately a day, which
God intends to conceal, by their interpretations of unfulfilled
prophecy. If the beginning of the millennium can be definitely fixed by an event so marked as the personal advent of
Christ; if its continuance can be marked off by one thousand
literal, solar years; and if the short apostasy which is to follow
is to last only a few years, then God's people will foreknow
pretty accurately when to expect the last day. Again: the
Jewish Christians, among many vague expectations concerning
Christ's kingdom, evidently expected that the final consummation would come at the end of one generation from Christ's
ascension. This erroneous idea was a very natural deduction
from the Jewish belief, that their temple and ritual were to subsist till the final consummation, when coupled with Christ's
declaration, in Matt. xxiv : that Jerusalem should be destroyed
in the day of some then living. See this misconception betrayed, Matt. xxiv : 3 ; Acts i : 7. So they doubtless misunderstood Matt. xvi ; 28. Now, it has ever been a favorite charge
against the inspiration of the Apostles, in the mouths of infidels,
that they evidently shared in this mistake. E. g. in James v :
8 ; 2 Peter iii : 12 ; Phil. iv : 5, &c. But this charge is founded
only in the ignorance of the Apostles' various meanings when
they speak of the " coming," or "presence," of Christ. Oftentimes they mean the believer's death ; for that is practically His
coming and the end of the world, to that believer; and the
space between that and the general judgment is to him no
space practically : because nothing can be done in it to redeem
the soul. Their misunderstanding is clearly enough evinced by
Paul in 2 Thess. ii : 1–3, &c., with 1 Thess. iv : 15, 17. For the

2. Time of the Judgment. Did Apostles Miscalculate.

latter place contains language than which none would be more
liable to these skeptical perversions.   Yet in the former citation
we see Paul explicitly correcting the mistake.

But while, absolutely, the time of the judgment is unknown,
It Follows Resurrec- relatively it is distinctly fixed.   It will be
tion. How Long Pro- immediately after the general resurrection,
tracted? and just coincident with, or just after the
final destruction of the globe by fire.   The good and evil men
do, live after them.   Hence, that measure of merit and demerit,
which is taken from consequences, is not completely visible to
creatures until time is completed.   St. Paul is still doing good:
Simon Magus is still doing mischief.   "They being dead, yet
speak."   We thus perceive a reason why God's declarative
judgment of men, meant as it is for the instruction of the creatures and practical vindication of His justice, should be postponed
until men's conduct has borne its full earthly fruits.   Hence
it is that the great assize is placed immediately after the resurrection.   See Rev. xx : 10 to end ; 2 Thess. i : 7 to 10, and
similar passages.   The duration of the judgment is commonly
called a day ; Act xvii : 31.   Some, conceiving that the work
of the judgment will include the intelligible revealing of the
whole secret life of every creature, to every other creature, suppose that the period will vastly exceed one solar day in length,
stretching possibly to thousands of years.   If all this is to be
done, they may well suppose the time will be long.   But to me,
it seems far from certain that this universal revealing of every
creature to every other, is either possible or necessary. Can any
but an infinite mind comprehend all this immense number of
particulars ?   Is it necessary, in order that any one creature
may have all defective and erroneous ideas about God's government corrected, which he has contracted in this life, to be introduced to the knowledge of parts of His dealings utterly unknown
to, and unconnected with him ?   Hence I would say, that of
the actual duration of the august scene, we know nothing.   But
we are told that its accessories will be vast and majestic.   The
terrors of the resurrection will have just occurred, the earth
will be just consigned to destruction.   Jesus Christ will appear
on the scene with ineffable pomp, attended with all the redeemed
and the angels ; Acts i : 11.   The souls of the blessed will be
reunited to their bodies, and then they will be assorted out from
the risen crowd of humanity, and their acquittal and glorification
declared to the whole assemblage ; while the unbelievers will
receive their sentence of eternal condemnation.

The place of this transaction has also been subject of in-
Place. quiry.   To me it appears indubitable that it
will occupy a place in the literal sense of the
word.   To say nothing of the fact that disembodied souls are
not ubiquitous, the actors in this transaction will be, many of
them, clothed with literal bodies, which, although glorified or

damned, will occupy space just as really as here on earth.   All
that Scripture says about the place is, I Thess. iv : 17, that we
" shall be caught up   .   .   .   into the clouds, to meet the Lord
in the air."   Some, as Davies, have supposed that the upper
regions of our atmosphere will be the place where the vast
assembly will be held; while they will behold the world beneath
them, either just before, or during the grand assize, wrapped in
the universal fires.   But see 2 Peter iii : 10.   It would seem
most obvious from our notions of combustion, as well as from
this passage, that however that conflagration may be produced,
our atmosphere, the great supporter of combustion, will be involved in it.   This may serve as a specimen of the ill-success
which usually meets us when we attempt to be " wise above
that which is written" on these high subjects.   The place is not
revealed to, and cannot be surmised by us.

The Judge will unquestionably be Jesus Christ, in His
mediatorial person.   See Matt. xxv : 31, 32;
xxviii : 18; John v : 27; Acts x : 42 : xvii :
31; Rom. xiv : 10; Phil. ii : 10; 2 Tim. iv : 1.
These passages are indisputable.   Nor have the Scriptures left
us ignorant entirely, of the grounds of this arrangement.   The
honor and prerogative of judging " the quick and the dead," is
plainly declared, in Phil. ii : 9, 10, to be a part of Christ's mediatorial exaltation, and a just consequence of His humiliation.
It was right that when the Lord of all condescended, in His
unspeakable mercy, to assume the form of a servant, and endure the extremest indignities of His enemies, He should enjoy
this highest triumph over them, in the very form and nature of
His humiliation.   Indeed, in this aspect, His judging the world
is but the crowning honor of His kingship; so that whatever
views explain His kingly office, explain this function of it.   But
more than this: His saints have an interest in it.   Then only is
their redemption completed, justification proclaimed finally,
and the last consequences of sin obliterated.   By the same
reason that it was necessary they should have a " merciful and
faithful High Priest," in all the previous exigencies of their
redemption, it is desirable that they should have their Mediator
for their judge in this last crisis.   Otherwise they would sink in
despair before the terrible bar.   They would be unable to answer a word to the accuser of the brethren, or to present any
excuse for their sins.   But when they see their Almighty
Friend in the judgment seat, their souls are re-assured.   This
may be the meaning of the words " because He is the Son of
man."   John v : 27.

There seems to be a sense, in which the saints will sit and
judge with Christ.   Ps. cxlix : 6–9; 1 Cor.
vi : 2, 3; Rev. xx : 4.   We suppose no one
will understand from these passages, that
Christians can, or will, exercise those incommunicable functions

[side note:] 3. The Judge Christ. Why?

[side note:] The Saints Assess-ors.

of searching hearts, apportioning infinite penalties to infinite demerits, and executing the sentence with almighty power. There are two lower meanings in which it may be said that saints shall judge sinners. Thus, in Matt. xii : 41, 42, the contrast of Nineveh's penitence is a sort of practical rebuke and condemnation to those who persist in the opposite conduct. But this does not express the whole truth. The saints are adopted sons of God; "heirs of God, and joint heirs with Christ; if so be we suffer with Him, that we may be also glorified together." Rom. viii : 17. They also are "kings and priests unto God." In this sense, they share, by a sort of reflected dignity, the exaltation of their elder brother; and in this, the culminating point of His mediatorial royalty, they are graciously exalted to share with Him, according to their lower measure. Having had their own acquittal and adoption first declared, they are placed in the post of honour, represented as Christ's right hand, and there concur as assessors with Christ, in the remainder of the transaction.

The persons to be judged will embrace all wicked angels and all the race of man. The evidence of the former part of this proposition is explicit. See Matt. viii : 29; 1 Cor. vi : 3; 2 Pet. ii : 4; Jude 6. And that every individual of the human race will be present is evident from Eccles. xii : 14; Ps. 1:4; 2 Cor. v : 10; Rom. xiv : 10; Matt. xii : 36, 37 ; xxv : 32; Rev. xx : 12.

4. Who Will be Judged ?

Some have endeavored to limit this judgment, (as the Pelagians), to those men alone who have enjoyed gospel privileges. But if there are any principles in God's government, calling for a general judgment of those subject to it, and if pagans are subject to it, then they also should be judged. And if the passages above cited do not assert an actual universality of the judgment, it is hard to see how any language could. It will be noticed that men will be judged, and doubtless, the wicked angels likewise, for all their thoughts, words and deeds. This is obviously just, and is called for by the purposes of a judgment. For if there was any class of moral acts which had not this prospect of a judgment awaiting them, men would think they could indulge in these with impunity. Upon the question whether the sins of the righteous, already pardoned in Christ, will receive publicity in that day, Dick states the respective arguments. To me it appears that we must admit they will be, unless we can prove that the places where men are warned that they must be judged "for every idle word," for "every secret thing," were not addressed to Christians at all, but only to sinners. The disposition to deny that pardoned sins will be published in the day of judgment, doubtless arises from the feeling that it would produce a shame and compunction incompatible with the blessedness of their state. But will the saints not publish their sins themselves, in their confessions? And is it not the sweetest type of spiritual joy, that which proceeds from contrition for sin ?

It may be further noticed, that the Scriptures are utterly silent as to the judging of the holy angels. It is therefore our duty to refrain from asserting anything about it. Some have surmised that though they are not mentioned, they will be judged, because they have some connection through their ministry of love, with the men who will be judged. But, on the other hand, it may be remarked, there is significance in the fact, that all the creatures spoken of as standing at Christ's judgment are sinful ones. The holy angels never sinned ; they have been long ago justified through a method totally inapplicable to fallen beings, the Covenant of Works, and this may constitute a valid reason why they should not bear a share in this judgment of sinning beings, who are either justified by free grace or condemned.

Will Elect Angels be Judged?

So far as the judgment is a display of God's attributes to the creature, it is doubtless to those creatures who are conversant with this scene of earthly struggle. The holy angels are concerned in it as interested and loving spectators ; the wicked angels as causes and promoters of all the mischief; man, as the victim and agent of earthly sin. If God has other orders of intelligent creatures, connected with the countless worlds of which astronomy professes to inform us, who are not included in these three classes ; it is not necessary to suppose that they will share in this scene, because we have no evidence that they are cognizant of the sins and grace which lead to it. But here all is only dim surmise.

The Spectators.

The rule by which sinners and saints will be judged, will be the will of God made known to them. The Gentiles will be judged by that natural law written on their hearts ; the Jews of the Old Testament by that, and the Old Testament alone ; but those who have enjoyed the Gospel in addition to the others, shall be judged by all three. (See Rom. ii : 12 ; Jno. xii : 48 ; Luke xii : 47 ; Jno. xv : 22). God will judge justly, and render to every man his due. In Dan. vii : 10 ; Rev. xx : 12 ; the same phrase is employed : " The judgment was set, and the books opened." Perhaps the mode of understanding this, most accordant with the mind of the Spirit, would be to attempt to apply the phrase, book, to nothing in particular, in the judgments of man; but to regard it as a mere carrying out of the august figure; a grand judicial trial. But if a more particular explanation must be had, we may perhaps concur in the belief, that one of these books is the Word of God, which is the statute-book, under which the cases must be decided ; another, the book of God's remembrance, from which the evidence of conduct will be read : and still another, the book of God's decrees, where the names of men were recorded before the foundation of the world.

5. The Rule.

In Matt. xxv, the reprobate are condemned because they
Relation of Works have not performed to God's suffering chil-
of Charity to Judg- dren acts of beneficence and charity, and the
ment. righteous acquitted because they have. It
may be briefly remarked here, that while sinners will be condemned strictly on the merit of their own conduct, saints will
be acquitted solely on the merit of Christ.   They are rewarded
according to, not because of the deeds done in the flesh.   The
evidence of this may be seen, where we refuted the doctrine
of justification by works, and these very passsges were brought
into review.   But the purpose of God in the judgment is to
evince the holiness, justice, love, and mercy of His dealings to
all His subjects.   But as they cannot read the secret faith, love
and penitence of the heart, the sentence must be regulated
according to some external and visible conduct, which is cognizable by creatures, and is a proper test of regenerate character.
It is very noticeable that not all righteous conduct, but only
one kind, is mentioned as the test ; these works of charity.
And this is most appropriate, not only because they are accurate tests of true holiness, but because it was most proper that
in a judgment where the accquittal can in no case occur, except through divine grace and pardon, a disposition to mercy
should be required of those who hope for acceptance. (See
Jas. ii : 13 ; Matt. x : 12, xviii : 28, &c.

The sentence of the righteous is everlasting blessedness ;
that of the wicked, everlasting misery.   The
6. The Sentences. discussion of the latter must be the subject
of another lecture.   The nature of eternal life I shall now endeavor to state.   Far be it from us, to presume to be wise above
that which is written ; let us modestly collect those traits of the
saint's everlasting rest, which the Bible, in its great reserve on
this subject, has seen fit to reveal.

The place of this eternal life is usually called heaven.   It
is undoubtedly a place proper, and not
The Place of Reward. merely a state.   For there are now, the
material bodies of Christ, and of Enoch and Elijah, if not of
others.   There will be a multitude of bodies.   The finite glorified spirits there also have a *ubi*. It is vain for us to surmise, in
what part of the Universe Christ's glorified humanity now holds
its court.   The phrases " up," " above," " ascend," &c., teach
nothing ; for what is above to us, is beneath to our antipodes,
in whose places we shall be in twelve hours.

But it is not place, but character, which confers essential
The Saints' Blessed- happiness.   We are taught indeed that occa-
ness. (a) In Exemp- sion for this spiritual blessedness will be
tion. (b) In Holiness. secured to the saints by their perfect exemption from all natural evils, such as unsatisfied wants, pain, grief,
sickness, violence, and death.   (See Job iii : 17 ; Is. xxv : 8 ;
Rev. vii : 16, 17 ; xxi : 4.)   But the most important fact is, that

54*

the blessedness of the life everlasting is simply the perfection of
that state which is begun here by the new birth and sanctification. As saith M. Henry, " Grace is glory begun, and glory
is but grace consummated." (See Jno. v : 24 ; vi : 47 ; Gal. vi :
7). On entering heaven, the soul is made perfectly holy ; and
thus every root of misery is removed. When we inquire for
the objective sources of the saints' bliss, we find them subordi-
nately in the society of fellow-saints, but chiefly in God Himself, and especially in the Redeemer. (Ps. lxxiii : 25 ; Rev.
xxi : 23). That the saints' happiness will be social, is plain
from the Bible representations ; and I believe that those who
have known and loved each other here, will recognize each
other there. (See 1 Thess. ii : 19 ; 2 Sam. xii : 23). And it
appears very unreasonable that the love, and other social graces
which are there perfected in their glorified humanity, should
then have no objects. But the Holy Trinity will ever be the
central and chief object, from which the believer's bliss will be
derived.

This happiness will consist in the satisfaction of both mind
and heart. Curiosity is one of the keenest
Elements of this Hap-
piness Intellective. and most uncloying sources of interest and
pleasure to the healthy mind. Then "we
shall know even as we are known ;" and our minds will find
perpetual delight in learning the things of God and His providence. Here will be matter of study ample enough to fill
eternity.

Again : To love is to be happy : saith the Apostle John,
" He that dwelleth in love, dwelleth in God,
Moral. and God in him." Our terrestrial objects of
affection have taught us, that if the heart could always be exercising its affection towards some worthy object, this would constitute happiness. But the object being earthly, we are constantly liable to be separated from it by distance, or to have it
torn from us by death, when our affection becomes our torment.
Or, being imperfect, it may wound us by infidelity or injustice.
Or else, corporeal wants drive us from it to labour. But now
let us suppose the soul, endowed with an object of love wholly
worthy and suitable, never separated by distance, nor torn
away by death, incapable of infidelity, or unkindness ; is it not
plain that in the possession and love of this object, there would
be perpetual blessedness ; external evils being fenced off ?
Such an object is God, and such is the blessedness of heaven,
springing from the perpetual indulgence of a love that never
cloys, that is never interrupted, and never wounded, and that
expresses its happiness in untiring praises.

The answer to the question, where shall be the place of
the saints' final abode, is not vital. Where
7. Probable Place of
the Final Glory. holiness, rest and Christ are, is heaven. But
the doctrine that this earth is to be recon-

structed after its purgation by fire, and is to become the dwelling place of redeemed men and the God-Man, in their resurrection bodies, is beautifully illustrative of some other truths; and it seems strongly supported by the Scriptures.   First, that destruction which awaits the world by fire (2 Peter iii : 7 ; 2 Thess. i : 8,) is not to be an annihilation.   There is no evidence that any atom of substance is annihilated ; and we know that combustion annihilates no part of the fuel we burn.   Words equally as strong (Gen. vi : 13 ; Heb. ii : 14 ; 2 Peter iii : 6), are used concerning the flood, and the judgment of Satan and the wicked, where there was no annihilation.   But if the earth is to exist after the final consummation, for what end will God use it ?   Second : many Scriptures speak of this earth as a permanent structure, and as given to man for his home.   See Ps. lxxviii : 69 ; xc : 2 ; cxv : 16 ; xxxvii : 29 ; viii : 5, 6 ; Matt. v : 5.   The promise of the last three can scarcely be understood of any other than the renovated earth, because, as long as the Church is in its militant state, the righteous and the meek are forewarned that " in this world they shall have tribulation." Third ; the striking analogy between our bodies' resurrection, and this παλιγγενεσια of our earth, gives probability to the doctrine.   Man was created an incorporate, but holy and immortal creature.   By his sin he corrupted his body with death.   Redemption does not propose to cast off this polluted body and save him as a new species of disembodied spirit: No, redemption proposes to restore both parts of man's nature, spirit and body, and in spite of sin and Satan, to realize in eternal perfection God's original conception of a holy, glorious and immortal, incorporate creature.   So, by analogy, we naturally expect that when the earth, man's heritage and home, is cursed for his sin and usurped by Satan, it is not to be surrendered to the usurpation, but to be redeemed and purged for its original destination, the eternal home of a glorified human race.   This, fourth: agrees exactly with Rom. viii : 19 to 23 ; and with Eph. i : 14.   The material creation is here represented, by a vivid impersonation, as interested in our redemption, and destined to share it : and there is no other idea which answers so well to that of a purchased possession to be redeemed for us hereafter, as this.

Fifth : when we pass to the New Testament prophecies, the evidence is clearer.   Rev. v : 10, the representatives of the ransomed Church sing to the Lamb : " Thou hast made us to our God kings and priests : and we shall reign on the earth !"   This is a privilege which is to follow their present state of expectant glory.   So 2 Peter iii : 13, tells us that believers are entitled to "look for new heavens and a new earth, wherein dwelleth righteousness."   This promise is given in connection with the previous renovation of the earth by fire.   In Rev. xxi · 1, 2, the apostle sees " a new heaven and a new earth "   .   .   .   " and the holy city, new Jerusalem, coming down from God out of heaven." In verse 3d he hears a great voice out of heaven, saying: "Behold the tabernacle of God is with men, and He will dwell with them." The crowning formula of the Covenant of Grace then follows, showing that this descent of God's tabernacle to earth is the final consummation of the redemption of men.

This conclusion gives us a noble view of the immutability of God's purpose of grace, and the glory of His victory over sin and Satan. This planet was fashioned to be man's heritage; and a part of it, at least, adorned with the beauties of a paradise, for his home. Satan sought to mar the divine plan, by the seduction of our first parents. For long ages he has seemed to triumph, and has filled His usurped dominion with crime and misery. But his insolent invasion is not to be destined to obstruct the Almighty's beneficent design. The intrusion will be in vain. God's purpose shall be executed. Messiah will come and re-establish His throne in the midst of His scarred and ravaged realm; He will cleanse away every stain of sin and death, and make this earth bloom forever with more than its pristine splendour; so that the very plan which was initiated when "the morning stars sang together and the sons of God shouted for joy," will stand to everlasting ages.

LECTURE LXXII.

NATURE AND DURATION OF HELL-TORMENTS.

SYLLABUS.

1. In what will the torments of the wicked consist?
Turrettin, Loc. xx, Qu. 7.   Ridgley, Qu. 89.   Knapp, § 156.
2. State the various opinions which have prevailed as to the duration of these pains.   Which now most prevalent among Universalists?
Turrettin as above.   Knapp, § 156-158.   Debate between Rice and Pingree.
3. State and refute the usual objections against everlasting punishments, from God's wisdom, mercy, benevolence, &c.
Knapp as above.   Rice and Pingree.   M. Stuart: "Letters on Future Punishment."
4. What is the proper force in the Scriptures of the original words which state the duration of these torments?
Knapp, § 157.   De Quincey's Essays.
5. Prove the everlasting duration of these torments from the sinner's perpetual sinfulness; from the Scriptural terms, redemption, pardon, salvation, &c.; from Universal relation in Providence between conduct and destiny; from the existence of condemned angels; from the Resurrection; from temporal judgments of God on the wicked, as Sodom, &c.; from the justice of God and the unequal distribution of rewards here.
Same authorities.   Shedd: "Doctrine of Endless Punishment."

THE just reward of ill-desert is suffering. The Judgment results in a curse upon the impenitent, which dooms them,

1. Natural Penalties.   as none doubt, to some form of suffering. Theologians divide the pains which are thus

adjudged to the condemned, into natural, and positive. The
former are those which proceed from the natural working of
their own evil principles, of themselves, and according to natural law; such pains as are foreshadowed in Is. iii : 11 ; Gal.
vi : 8 ; Jas. i : 15. These natural penalties consist of the loss
or privation of eternal happiness, which only faith, repentance,
and holiness can procure ; of the remorse, self-accusation, and
despair, which the soul will inflict on itself for its own folly and
sin ; of all the disorders, inward and social, of inordinate and
malignant emotions ; and as is most probable, at least, of the
stings of carnal, sensual, and sinful desires deprived of all their
earthly *pabulum*. As to this last, it appears most consistent to
limit what is said, (1 Cor. xv : 45—end) of the spirituality and
blessedness of the resurrection body, to the saints. The reprobate will rise again; but as they never were savingly united
to Christ, they will never "bear the image of the heavenly "Adam.
Hence, we naturally and reasonably anticipate, that their bodies, while immortal, will not share the glory and purification of
the bodies of the Redeemed, but will still be animal bodies,
having the appetites and wants of such. But earthly supplies
therefor will be forever lacking. Hence, they will be a prey to
perpetual cravings unsatisfied.

The positive penalties of sin will be such as God will Himself add, by new dispensations of His power,
Positive Penalties.   to inflict anguish on His enemies. The
Scriptures always represent Him as arising to avenge Himself,
as "pouring out His wrath" upon His enemies ; and in such
like, and a multitude of other expressions, whatever may be
their figurative character, we cannot fail to see this truth, that
God puts forth new and direct power, to inflict pain. The stupidity and obstinacy of many sinners, obviously, would be
restrained by nothing less than the fear of these positive penalties. The mere natural penalties would appear to them wholly
illusory, or trivial. Indeed, most sinners are so well pleased
with their carnal affections, that they would rather declare
themselves glad to accept, and even cherish, their merely natural fruits.

These positive penalties undoubtedly will include, when
the body is raised, some corporeal pains, and
Will They Afflict   perhaps, consist chiefly in them ; else, why
the Body!   need the body be raised? And there is too
obvious a propriety in God's punishing sinners through those
members which they have perverted into " members of unrighteousness," for us to imagine for a moment, that He will omit it.
Once more; the imagery by which the punishments of the
wicked are represented, however interpreted, is so uniform, as
to make it impossible to suppose the bodies of the wicked are
exempted. But whether their bodies will be burned with literal fire and sulphur, does not appear so certain. In Matt. xxv,

the fire into which they depart is said to have been prepared from the foundation of the world, for the Devil and
his angels.   They are, and will always remain, incorporeal
beings; and it does not seem probable that literal fire is the
instrument which God has devised expressly for their torment.
Some weight may also be given to this thought ; that other adjuncts, as the darkness, the gnawing worm, the brimstone, the
smoke, &c., seem to be images adopted from human tortures
and earthly scenes of anguish.   Hence the conclusion to
which Turrettin comes; that this is all imagery.   But, however
that may be, the images must be interpreted according to plain
rules of right rhetoric.   Interpret it as we may, we cannot get
anything less from it than this : that sin will be punished with
extreme and terrible bodily torments, as well as with natural
pains.

Those who deny the eternity of future punishments may
be divided into three classes.   First are

**2. Eternal Punish-
ments denied. 1. By
Annihilationists. 2.
Restorationists. 3. Uni-
versalists.**

those who resolve the punishment of the
wicked into annihilation. They believe accordingly, that only the redeemed enjoy a resurrection.   Second are the ancient and modern
Restorationists, who hold to future punishments, longer or
shorter, according to men's guilt; but who suppose that each
man's repentance will be accepted after his penal debt is paid ;
so that at length, perhaps after a long interval, all will be saved.
It is said that the Originists believed that Satan and his angels
would also be at last saved.   The third opinion is that which is
now widely prevalent among modern Universalists.   This supposes, that the external and internal sufferings which each soul
experiences during this life, and *in articulo mortis*, will satisfy
all the essential demands of the divine justice against its sins :
and that there will, accordingly, be no future punishments.
At death, they suppose, those not already penitent and holy,
will be summarily sanctified by God, in His universal mercy
through Christ, and at once received into heaven forever.   This
scheme is the baldest and most extreme of all the forms of
Universalism, and stands in most complete opposition to Scripture.   My arguments will therefore have a special reference to it.

To clear the way, the Annihilationist may be easily refuted,
by all those passages which speak of future

First Class Refuted.

punishment, even though we grant it not eternal.   Such are Mark ix: 48; Matt. xxv, &c.   The resurrection extends to the wicked, as well as the righteous (Dan.
xii : 2; John v : 28, 29).   Nor does the quibble avail, that the
phrase, "everlasting destruction," or such-like, implies annihilation.   If this consisted in reducing the sinner forever to nothing, it would be instant destruction, not everlasting.   How can
punishment continue, when the subject of it has ceased to exist?

But it may be well to clear away obstructions, by refuting

3. God's Love Consists With Eternal Punishments.

the general grounds on which the eternity of future punishments is denied. The most common of these is that construction of the text, " God is Love," which makes Him pure benevolence, denying to Him all other moral attributes, and resolving them into phases of benevolence. But we reply; other texts say, "God is Light ;" "Our God is a consuming Fire." Is He nothing but pure intelligence ? Is He nothing but punitive justice? We see the absurd contradictions into which such a mode of interpretation would lead us. Infinite benevolence, intelligence, justice, and truth are co-ordinate and consistent attributes, acting harmoniously. That God is not benevolent in such a sense as to exclude punitive justice, is proved thus : "It is a fearful thing to fall into the hands of the Living God" (Heb. x : 31. See also, 2 Cor. v : 11 ; Ps. lxvi : 5. Again ; God is not too benevolent to punish devils, once His holy children, eternally (See Rev. xx : 10). Nor can this ruinous fact be evaded by denying the personality of the devils ; the usual resort of the Universalists. The marks of the real personality of devils are as clear as for Judas Iscariot's.

It is equally vain to appeal to the paternal benevolence of a father, claiming that God is more tender, and to ask whether any earthly parent is capable of tormenting his own child, however erring, with endless fire. The answer is in such passages as Ps. l : 21. "Thou thoughtest that I was altogether such an one as thyself, but I will rebuke thee," (Is. lv : 8,) and by the stubborn fact, that this "God of Love" does punish a sinful world, under our eyes, with continual woes, many of them gigantic. How are these dealings to be reconciled with God's benevolence ? By the sufferer's guilt. Then, if the guilt of any is endless, the benevolence of God may permit them to suffer endlessly. Even if we accept the erroneous parallel to a human parent as exact, we may ask : Would a benevolent, wise, and just parent so spare an incorrigibly wicked son, as to sacrifice the order of his house, and the rights of the good children to his impunity ? This argument is sometimes put in this form : "We are commanded to be like God. We are also commanded to forgive and love our enemies. But if we were like the Calvinists' God, we must hate and damn our enemies." The replies are, that God is also a magistrate ; and that human magistrates are strictly required to condemn the wicked ; that we are under no circumstances required to pardon and love enemies, at the expense of justice and truth ; that we are only required to restore the injurious enemy to our confidence and esteem, when he repents ; the one great reason why we are enjoined not to revenge ourselves, is that "vengeance is God's ; He will repay ;" and that God does exhibit an infinite forbearance towards His enemies, by giving His own Son to die for their reconciliation

God not to be Measured by Men.

on the terms of faith and repentance; the only terms consistent with His perfections.

The attempt to argue, that God's wisdom would forbid *God's Wisdom Con-* Him to create immortal beings, and then *sists with Eternal Pun-* permit them to forfeit the ends of their exist- *ishments.* ence, is exceedingly weak and presumptuous. Before the argument can apply, it must be determined what is God's secret purpose as to the ultimate end of their existence. He must suppose himself omniscient, who imagines himself competent to decide.

One would think that the declarations of the Scriptures about eternal punishments were clear enough *4. Scriptural Terms* to decide the debate. But you are aware *Considered.* that the words used in the Scriptures for everlasting, eternal, &c., are said to mean also an "age," a "dispensation," a finite duration; and that we hear of the ever- lasting hills, and the covenant with David's house as eternal as the sun; whereas we are told elsewhere, that the hills shall melt, and the sun be darkened, as David's dynasty has perished.

But these words are as strong as any the Greek language affords. (Aristotle, αἰώνιος from ἀεὶ ὤν). They are the same words which are used to express the eternity of God. If they have a secondary and limited meaning in some applications, the subject and context should be appealed to, in order to settle the sense, Now, when these words are used to describe a state, they always express one as long as the nature of the subject to which they are applied can permit. When, e. g., the hills are called everlasting, it is evidently meant, that they will endure as long as the earth on which they rest. Now if "everlasting tor- ment" is said to be the state of a sinful soul, those who believe the soul immortal are bound to understand by it a duration of the punishment coeval with that of the sufferer's being. See thus Rev. xiv : 11 ; xx : 10 ; with xxii : 5 ; 2 Thess. i : 9; Mark iii : 29 ; Matt. xviii : 8. The conclusive fact is, that in Matt. xxv : 46, the same word describes the duration of the saint's bliss and the sinner's penalty. If the latter is not properly un- ending, the former is not.

But more than this: Many texts convey the idea that the torments of sinners will never end, in terms *Eternal Torments* and modes to which this quibble cannot *taught in other Terms.* attach. Thus, the state of men after death is changeless; and when the state of it is fixed at death, nothing more can be done to modify it: Eccles. ix : 10 ; John ix : 4 ; Eccles. xi : 3. Then it is asserted that "their worm dieth not." "The fire is not quenched." Mark ix: 43-48; John iii: 3 and 36 ; Luke xvi : 26 ; Rev. xxi : 8. Compared with verses 1 and 4, Rev. xxii : 11, 12.

But the strength of our argument is, that to teach the

5. Universalists Contradict whole Scripture; as Satan's Personality.— Man's Probation. limited duration of the punishment of sin, Universalists and Restorationists have to contradict nearly every fact and doctrine of of the Bible. We have seen how they are compelled by their dogma to deny the personality of Satan. The Scriptures bear upon their very face this truth, that man must fulfill some condition in order to secure his destiny. Let that faith on which salvation turns be what it may, it is a something the doing or not doing of which decides the soul's state in different ways. See e. g., Mark xvi : 16, as one of a thousand places. But if the Universalist is true, he who believes and he who believes not, will fare precisely alike. And here I may add that powerful analogical argument; that under the observed course of God's providence, men are never treated alike irrespective of their doings and exertions ; conduct always influences destiny. But if the Universalist is true, the other world will be in contradiction to this.

Again : if either the Universalist or Restorationist is true, **There is no Pardon, &c., nor Satisfaction by Christ.** there is no grace, no pardon, no redemption, and no salvation. For according to both, all the guilt men contract is paid for; according to the one party, in temporal sufferings on earth ; according to the other, in temporary sufferings beyond the grave. Now that which is paid for by the sinner himself is not remitted to him. There is no pardon or mercy. Nor can it be said that there is any salvation. For the only evils to which the sinner is at any time liable, he meets and endures to the full. None are escaped ; there is no deliverance ; no salvation. So we may charge, that their doctrines are inconsistent with that of Christ's satisfaction or atonement. For of course, if each sinner bears his own guilt, there is no need of a substitute to bear it. Hence we find the advocates of these schemes explaining away the vicarious satisfaction of Christ.

Indeed, it may justly be added, that the tendency of their **Universalists Skeptical.** system is to depreciate the authority of the Word, to deny its plenary inspiration, to question its teachings with irreverent license, and to disclose much closer affinities with infidelity than with humble faith. This charge is fully sustained by the history of Universalist churches (so called) and of their teachers and councils. Finally, passing over for the time, the unanswerable argument, that sin has infinite ill desert, as committed against an excellent, perfect and universal law, and an infinite lawgiver, I may argue that even though the desert of a temporary season of sinning were only temporary penalties, yet if man continues in hell to sin forever, he will continue to suffer forever. While he was paying off a previous debt of guilt he would contract an additional one, and so be forever subject to penalty.

An attempt is made to argue universal salvation from a

Their Proof-texts Considered. few passages represented by Rom. v : 18, and 1 Cor. xv : 22, in which the word " all," is used.   I reply, 1st, that those who use this argument do not believe that "all," or any "come into condemnation" by Adam's sin, or " die in Adam ;" and they have no right to argue thence that they will be saved in Christ. They cannot contradict me when I charge them with flatly denying the imputation of Adam's guilt to any of his posterity. I reply, 2d, that the word "all" is, notoriously, used often in the Scripture when it does not mean actual universality; but only all of a certain class; Matt. iii : 5 ; Mark i : 37. So, in these texts, the meaning obviously is, that as in Adam all are condemned, all die, who are federally connected with him, so, in Christ, all savingly connected with Him are made alive. See the context. The very chapter which says, " The free gift came upon all," &c., begins by saying that being "justified by faith," we have peace with God. It must be then that the free gift comes upon " all " that believe. So 1 Cor. xv : 22, is immediately followed by these words : " But every man in his own order, Christ the first fruits; afterwards they that are Christ's at His coming." Obviously, it is " all " who are Christ's, who are made alive in Him. But let the Scripture tell us who are Christ's. " If any man have not the spirit of Christ, he is none of His." There is this answer also, to the Universalist, quoting 1 Cor. xv : 22, that, apply it to whom we will, it teaches after all, not future blessedness, but the resurrection of the body.

This doctrine of the Resurrection also suggests an argument against Universalism, because it is most clearly taught that there are two resurrections; one for the just and one for the unjust; one desirable, and one dreadful; one for which holy men of old strove, and one which they shunned. But if all at the resurrection were renewed and saved, there would be but one resurrection. The passage quoted from Jno. v : 29, settles that point. For it cannot be evaded by the figment of a metaphorical resurrection, i. e., a conversion in this life, because of this Christ had thus been speaking in verses 25 to 27. It is in contrast with this, that He then sets the real, material resurrection before us, in verses 28, &c. Moreover, if the resurrection be made a metaphorical one, then in verse 29, we should have the good, in common with the wicked, coming out of that state of depravity and ruin, represented by the " graves " of verses 25, 26. (See also, Phil. iii : 11 ; Heb. xi : 35).

If the modern Universalist scheme is true, then the only thing which prevents this life from being an unmingled curse, and death a natural good, is the pain of parting and dissolution. If these were evaded by a quick and easy death, it would be an immeasurable benefit; a step to an assured blissful state, from one both

The Doctrine of Two Resurrections.

Death Would Not be a Judgment to Sinners.

sinful and unhappy. The most fortunate life here is almost worthless, compared with heaven. Hence, when one is suddenly taken from this life, it is not a penalty, but a favour. We must contradict all that the Scriptures teach, of sudden deaths being a judgment of God against sinners. The antediluvians were gloriously distinguished from Noah, by being illustriously rewarded for their sins by a sudden and summary introduction to holiness and happiness; while he was punished for his piety, by being condemned to many hundreds of years of suffering, including all the horrors of his watery imprisonment. So, the Sodomites were rewarded for their sins, while Lot was punished by his piety. The cruel Egyptians were swept into glory on the waters of the Red Sea, while Moses was punished for his obedience by a tiresome pilgrimage of forty years.

Again: the assertion that each man's temporal sufferings in this life, and in *articulo mortis*, are a just recompense for his sins, is false. Scripture and observation deny it; the former in Ps. lxxii : 2, 14; Luke xvi : 25, and similiar passages; the latter in the numerous instances seen by every experienced person, where the humble, pure, retired, prayerful Christian spends years in pain, sickness, and poverty; while the sturdy rake or covetous man revels in the sensual joys or gains which he prefers, and then dies a painless and sudden death. In short, the facts are so plainly against this theory, that the notorious inequality of deserts and rewards in this life has furnished to every reflecting mind, both pagan and Christian, one of the strongest evidences in favour of future rewards and punishments.

Sins Are Not Adequately Requited here.

In this connection I would argue also, that on the modern Universal scheme, God would often be odiously unjust. But see Ps. lxxxix : 14; Gen. xviii : 25; Rom. ii : 6, &c. Now our adversaries stoutly deny that any guilt is imputed to Christ and punished in Him. Hence, the flagrant inequality remains, according to them, forever uncompensated. The vilest and the purest would receive the same rewards, nay, in many cases, the advantage would be against the good ; Providence would often reward vice and punish virtue. For, if the monster of sin is at death renewed and carried immediately to heaven, just as is the saint, thenceforward they are equal; but before the sinner had the advantage. While holy Paul was wearing out a painful life in efforts to do good, many a sensualist, like his persecutor Nero, was floating in his preferred enjoyments. Both died violent and sudden deaths ; and then, as they met in the world of spirits, the monster receives the same destiny with the saint. So every one of even a short experience, can recall instances somewhat similar, which have fallen under his own observation. I can recall a pair of such persons, whose history may

God Would Therefore be Partial.

Instances.   illustrate both my last arguments. Their lives and deaths were nearly cotemporary, and I was acquainted with the history of both. The one was a Christian female, in whom a refined and noble disposition, sanctified by grace, presented one of the most beautiful examp es of virtue which this world can often see.   She united early and long-tried piety, moral courage, generosity, self-devotion, with the most feminine refinement of tastes, charity and tenderness.   There was a high frame of devotion without a shade of austerity ; there was the courage of a martyr, without a tinge of harshness.   She combined the most rigid economy towards herself with the most liberal benefactions.   For many years, she denied herself the indulgence of her elegant tastes, except such as nature offered without expense in the beauties of flower, and forest, and landscape, in order that she might husband the proceeds of a moderate competency for the needy, for the suffering, and for God.   Her days were passed in a pure retirement, far from the strifes and corruptions of the world.   Her house was the unfailing refuge of the sick and the unfortunate among her kindred and the poor ; her life was little else than a long and painful ministration to their calamities; and more than once she had flown, with a moral heroism which astonished her friends, into the midst of pestilence, to be the ministering angel at the solitary couch of her suffering relatives.   Never did neglect cause her devotion to flag, and never did reproach or injury wring from her a word or deed of retaliation, although she received not a little of both, even from those whom she strove to bless.   Such was her life to the last.

And now let us look at her earthly reward.   Her whole life was spent in uncertain, or in feeble health.   It was often her lot to have her kindness misunderstood, and her sensitive affections lacerated.   She scarcely tasted earthly luxuries or ease; for she lived for others.   At length, three years before her death, she was overtaken by that most agonizing and incurable of all the scourges which afflict humanity, cancer.   For three long years her sufferings grew, and with them her patience.   The most painful remedies were endured in vain.   The last weeks of her life were spent in utter prostration, and unceasing agony, so strong that her nurses declared themselves amazed and affrighted to see a nature so frail as man's bearing such a load of anguish.   A peculiarity of constitution deprived her even of that poor resource of suffering, the insensibility of opiates. Up to the very last hour of death, there was no respite ; without one moment of relaxation in the agony, to commend her soul to her Saviour; maddened by unbearable pangs; crying like her dying Redeemer, " My God, my God, why hast thou forsaken me," she approached the river of death, and its waters were not assuaged to ease her passage.

Now for the contrast.   During nearly the same period, and

in an adjoining county, there lived a man, who embodied as many repulsive qualities as it has ever been my lot to see in one human breast. His dark, suspicious eye, and malignant countenance gave fit expression to the soul within. Licentious, a drunkard, devoid of natural affection, dishonest, quarrelsome, litigious, a terror to his neighbors, he was soiled with dark suspicion of murder. He revelled in robust health; and as far as human eye could see, his soul was steeped in ignorance and sensuality, and his conscience seared as with heated iron. He was successful in escaping the clutches of the law, and seemed to live in the enjoyment of his preferred indulgences. At length this man, at the monthly court of his county, retired to a chamber in the second story of the tavern, drunk, as was his wont, and lay down to sleep. The next morning, he was found under the window, stone dead, and with a broken neck. Whether he had walked in his sleep, or the hand of revenge had thrust him out, was never known. In all probability he never knew what killed him, and went into the other world without tasting a single pang, either in body or soul, of the sorrows of dissolution.

Now let us suppose that these two persons, appearing so nearly at the same time in the presence of God, were together introduced into the same heaven. Where is the equality between their deserts and their rewards? On the whole, the providential difference was in favour of the most guilty. If this is God's justice, then is He more fearful than blind chance, than the Prince of Darkness himself. To believe our everlasting destiny is in the hand of such unprincipled omnipotence, is more horrible than to dwell on the deceitful crust of a volcano. And if heaven consists in dwelling in His presence, it can have no attractions for the righteous soul.

Can Justice Make These Equal?

.In conclusion; whether Universalism be true or false, it is absurdity to teach it. If it turns out true, no one will have lost his soul for not learning it. If it turns out false, every one who has embraced it thereby will incur an immense and irreparable evil. Hence, though the probabilities of its truth were as a million to one, it would be madness and cruelty to teach it.

Universalism has no Motive for Propagating it.

But, apart from all argument, what should a right-minded man infer from the fact, that of all intelligent and honest students of the Scriptures, scarcely one in a million has found the doctrine of universal salvation in them.

The chief practical argument in favor of Universalism is, doubtless, the sinful callousness of Christians towards this tremendous destiny of their sinful fellow-creatures. Can we contemplate the exposure of our friends, neighbours, and children to a fate so terrible, and feel so little sensibility, and make efforts so few

Its Chief Pretext is Insensibility of Believers.

and weak for their deliverance! And yet, we profess to have faith! How can our unbelieving friends be made to credit the sincerity of our convictions? Here, doubtless, is the best argument of Satan, for their skepticism. And the best refutation of this heresy is the exhibition by God's people of a holy, tender, humble, yet burning zeal to pluck men as brands from the burning.

LECTURE LXXIII.

THE CIVIL MAGISTRATE.

SYLLABUS.

1. State the two theories of the origin of civil government out of a "social contract," and out of the ordinance of God. Establish the true one.
2. What is civil liberty? What its limits?
3. What are the proper objects of the powers of the Civil Magistrate? What their limits? What the limits to the obedience of a Christian man to the Civil Magistrate? When and how far is the Christian entitled to plead a 'higher law?'
4. Is the citizen bound always to passive obedience? If not, when does the right of forcible resistance to an unjust government begin?

See Confession of Faith, ch. 23. Blackstone's Com. bk. i. Introduc. ₰ 2. Paley's Moral Phil. bk. vi, ch. 1-5, *Montesquieu Esprit des Loix*, bk. i. ch. 11. *Burlemaqui*, Vol. iv, pt. i. Locke's Treatise of Civil Gov., bk. ii. Princeton Review, Jan., 1851. Bledsoe on Liberty and Slavery, ch. 1, So. Rev. Art. 'Civil Liberty.' Defence of Virginia and the South, ch. 7, ₰ 3.

THE duty of the Christian citizen to civil society is so extensive and important, and so many questions arise as to its limits and nature, the propriety of holding
Examined in its Christian Aspects Only. office, the powers exercised by the magistrate, &c., that the teacher of the Church should be well grounded in the true doctrine of the nature of the commonwealth. Hence, our Confession has very properly placed this doctrine in its 23d chapter. It is emphatically a doctrine of Scripture.

Two opposing theories have prevailed, among nominally Christian philosophers, as to the origin and
1. Theories of Government Origin. extent of the Civil Magistrate's powers. The one traces them to a supposed social contract. Men are to be at first apprehended, they say, as insulated individuals, separate human integers, all naturally equal, and each by nature absolutely free, having a natural liberty to exercise his whole will, as a " Lord of Creation." But the experience of the exposure, inconveniences, and mutual violences of so many independent wills, led them, in time, to be willing to surrender a part of their independence, in order to secure the enjoyment of the rest of their rights. To do this, they are supposed to have conferred, and to have entered

into a compact with each other, binding themselves to each other to submit to certain rules and restraints upon their natural rights, and to obey certain ones selected to rule, in order that the power thus delegated to their hands might be used for the protection of the remaining rights of all. Subsequent citizens entering the society, by birth or immigration, are supposed to have given an assent, express or implied, to this compact. The terms of it form the organic law, or constitution of the commonwealth. And the reason why men are bound to obey the legitimate commands of the magistrate is, that they have thus bargained with their fellow-citizens to obey, for the sake of mutual benefits.

Many writers, as Blackstone and Burlemaqui, are too sensible not to see that this theory is false to Social Contract Theory the facts of the case; but they still urge, Modified. that although individual men never existed, in fact, in the insulated state supposed, and did not actually pass out of that state into a commonwealth state, by a formal social contract; yet such a contract must be assumed as implied, and as offering the virtual source of political power and obligation. Thus Blackstone, *ubi supra*, p. 47 : " But though society had not its formal beginning from any convention of individuals, actuated by their wants and their fears; yet it is the sense of their weakness and imperfection which keeps mankind together; that demonstrates the necessity of this union; and that therefore is the solid and natural foundation, as well as the cement of civil society." To us it appears, that if the compact never occurred in fact, but is only a supposititious one, a legal fiction it is no basis for any theory, and no source for practical rights and duties.

The other theory may be called the Christian. It traces civil government to the will and providence Christian Theory. of God, who, from the first, created man with social instincts and placed him under social relations (when men were few, the patriarchal, as they increased, the commonwealth). It teaches that some form of social government is as original as man himself. If asked, whence the obligation to obey the civil magistrate, it answers: from the will of God, which is the great source of all obligation. The fact that such obedience is greatly promotive of human convenience, well-being and order, confirms and illustrates the obligation, but did not originate it. Hence, civil government is an ordinance of God; magistrates rule by His providence and by His command, and are His agents or ministers. Obedience to them, in the Lord, is a religious duty, and rebellion against them is not only injustice to our fellow-men, but disobedience to God. This is the theory plainly asserted by Paul, Rom. xiii : 1–7, and 1 Peter ii : 13–18 It may be illustrated by the parental state.

This account of the matter has been also pushed to a most

Theory of Divine Right. vicious extreme, by the party known as Legitimatists, or advocates of the Divine right of royalty. The Bible here teaches us, they assert, that the power the civil magistrate holds, is in no sense delegated from the people, but wholly from God; that the people have no option to select or change their form of government, any more than a child has to choose its parent, or a soul the deity it will worship; that no matter how oppressive or unjust the government may be, the citizen has no duty nor right but passive submission, and that the divinely selected form is hereditary monarchy—the form first instituted in the hand of Adam, continued in ʰhe patriarchal institution, re-affirmed in the New Testament, and never departed from except by heaven-defying republicans, &c.

Refutation. This servile theory we easily retute by many facts: 1st. Men in society do not bear to rulers the relation of children to parents, either in their greater weakness, inferiority of knowledge or virtue, or in the natural affection felt for them, but are, in the general, the natural equals of their rulers. Hence, the argument from the family to the commonwealth to prove that it is monarchical, utterly fails. 2d. The chosen form given by God to the Hebrew Commonwealth was not monarchical, but republican. And when He reluctantly gave them a king, the succession was not hereditary, but virtually elective, as witness the cases of David, Jeroboam, Jehu, &c. 3d. The New Testament does not limit its teachings to the religious obligation ·to obey kings, but says generally! "the Powers that be are ordained of God." "There is no power but of God": thus giving the religious source, equally to the authority of kings and constables, and giving it to any form of government which providentially existed *de facto*. The thing then, which God ordains, is not a particular form of government, but that men shall maintain some form of government. Last, it is peculiarly fatal to the Legitimatist theory that the actual government of Rome, which the New Testament immediately enjoined Christians to obey, was not a legitimate, nor a hereditary monarchy, but one very lately formed in the usurpation of Octavius Cæsar, and not in a single instance transmitted by descent, so far as Paul's day.

The Ruler for the People. On the contrary, while we emphatically ascribe the fact of civil government and the obligation to obey it, to the will of God, we also assert that in the secondary sense, the government is, potentially, the people. The original source of the power, the authority and the obligation to obey it, is God, the human source is not an irresponsible Ruler, but the body of the ruled themselves, that ıs, the sovereignty, so far as it is human, resides in the people, and is held by the rulers, by delegation from them. It is, indeed, the ordinance of the supreme God, that such delegation should be made, and the power so delegated be obeyed, by each individual; but still the power, so far as it is human, is the people's power, and not the ruler's. This is proved by two facts. All the citizens have a general native equality; they possess a common title, in the general, to the benefits of existence, as being all human beings and children of a common Creator. They are all alike under the golden rule, which is God's great charter of a general equality. Hence the second fact, that the government is for the governed, not for the especial benefit of the governors. The object of the institution, which God had in view, was the good of the community. The people are not for the rulers, but the rulers for the people. This is expressly stated by Paul, Rom. xiii : 3, 4. Now, as before stated, the rulers have no monopoly of sense, virtue, experience, natural right, over their fellow-citizens, and hence the power of selecting rulers should be in the citizens.

Having thus cleared the Scriptural theory from the odious *Social Contract Re-* perversions of the advocates of "legitimacy," *futed. 1st. Not Found-* I proceed to affirm it against the vain dream *ed on Facts.* of a social contract, and the theory of obligation based upon it. 1st. It is notoriously false to the actual facts. Civil government is not only a theory, but a fact; the origin of it can therefore be only found in a fact, not in a legal fiction. The fact is, that men never rightfully existed for one moment in the state of independent insulation, out of which they are supposed to have passed, by their own option, into a state of society. God never gave them such independency. Their responsibility to Him, and their civic relations to fellow-men, as ordained by God, are as native as their existence is. They do not choose their civic obligations, but are born under them; just as a child is born to his filial obligations. And the simple, practical proof is, that if one man were now to claim this option to assume civic relations and obligations, or to decline them, and so forego the advantages of civic life, any civilized government on earth would laugh his claim to scorn, and would immediately compel his allegiance by force. The mere assumption of such an attitude as that imagined for the normal one of man, and of the act in which it is supposed government legitimately originates, would constitute him an outlaw; a being whom every civil society claims a natural right to destroy; the right of self-preservation.

The theory is atheistic, utterly ignoring man's relation to *2d. Atheistic.* his Creator, the right of that Creator to determine under what obligations man shall live; and the great Bible fact, that God has determined he shall live under civic obligations.

It is utterly unphilosophical, in that, while the ethics of *3d. Not Inductive.* government should be an inductive science, this theory is, and by its very nature must be,

55*

utterly devoid of experimental evidence! Hence it has no claims to be even entertained for discussion, *in foro scientiæ*.

If the authority of laws and constitutions and magistrates originates in the social contract, then certain most inconvenient and preposterous conse-
4th. Inconvenient.
quences would logically follow. One is, that however inconvenient and even ruinous, the institutions of the country might become, by reason of the changes of time and circumstance, no majority could ever righteously change them, against the will of any minority; for the reason that the inconveniences of a bargain which a man has voluntarily made, are no justification for his breaking it. The righteous man must not change, though he has "sworn to his own hurt." Another inconvenience would be, that it could never be settled what were the terms agreed upon in the original social contract; and what part of the existing laws were the accretions of time and of unwarranted power, save where the original constitution was in writing. A worse consequence would be, that if the compact originated the obligation to obey the civil magistrate, then any one unconstitutional or unjust act of the ruler would break that compact. But when broken by one side, it is broken for both; and allegiance would be wholly voided.

Last : The civil magistrate is armed with some powers, which could not have been created by a social contract alone ; because they did not belong to the contracting parties, viz : individual men cannot give, for instance, the right of life and death. No man's life belongs to him, but to God alone. He cannot transfer what does not belong to him ; nor can one say, that although the individual may not have the right to delegate away a power over his own life which he does not possess, yet the community may be justified in assuming it, by the law of self-preservation. For there is no community as yet, until this theory of its derivation from a social contract is established. There is only a number of individual, unrelated, independent men.

To elucidate and establish these ideas farther, let us inquire what is the true difference between man's natural liberty and his civil liberty. The advocates of the theory of a social compact seem to consider, as indeed some of them define, men's natural liberty to be a freedom to do what they please. They all say that Government limits or restrains it somewhat, the individual surrendering a part in order to have the rest better protected. Hence it follows, that all government, even the republican, being of the nature of restraint, is in itself a natural evil, and a natural infringement on right, to be endured only as an expedient for avoiding the greater evil of anarchy ! Well might such theorists deduce the consequence, that there is no ethical ground for obedience to government. except the implied assent of the individual; the question would be, whether it is not a surrender of duty to come under such an obligation? They also, of course, confound a man's natural rights and natural liberties together; they would be still more consistent, if, with their great inventor, Hobbes, they denied that there was any such thing as rights, distinct from might, until they were factitiously created by the restraints of civil government.

This view I consider, although embraced in part by the current of Christian moralists, is only worthy of an atheist, who denies the existence of any original relations between the Creator and creature, and of any original moral distinctions. It ignores the great fact, that man's will never was his proper law; it simply passes over, in the insane pride of human perfectionism, the great fact of original sin, by which every man's will is more or less inclined to do unrighteousness. It falsely supposes a state of nature, in which man's might makes his right; whereas no man is righteously entitled to exist in that state for one instant. But if you would see how simple and impregnable is the Bible theory of natural and civil liberty, take these facts, undisputed by any Christian. The rule of action is moral: moral obligations are as original (as natural) as man himself. The practical source and measure of them is God's will. That will, *ab initio*, binds upon man certain relations and duties which he owes to God and to his fellow man; and also defines his right, i. e., those things which it is the duty of other beings to allow him to have and to do. Man enters existence with those moral relations resting, by God's will, upon him. And a part of that will, as taught by His law and providence is, that man shall be a member of, and obey, civil government, Hence, government is as natural as man is. What then is man's natural liberty? I answer: it is freedom to do whatever he has a moral right to do. Freedom to do whatever a man is physically able to do, is not a liberty of nature or law, but a natural license, a natural iniquity. What is civil liberty then? I reply still, it is (under a just government) freedom to do whatever a man has a moral right to do. Perhaps no government is perfectly just. Some withhold more, some fewer of the citizen's moral rights: none withhold them all. Under all governments there are some rights left; and so, some liberty. A fair and just government would be one that would leave to each subject of it, in the general, (excepting exceptional cases of incidental hardship,) freedom to do whatever he had a moral right to do, and take away all other, so far as secular and civic acts are concerned. Such a government, then, would not restrain the natural liberty of the citizens at all. Their natural would be identical with their civic liberty. Government then does not originate our rights, neither can it take them away. Good government does

Radical Theory False. True Stated.

originate our liberty in a practical sense, i. e., it secures the exercise of it to us.

The instance most commonly cited, as one of a natural right surrendered to civil society, is the right of self-defence. We accept the instance, and assert that it fully confirms our view.

No Natural Right Sacrificed to Just Government.

For if it means the liberty of forcible defence at the time the unprovoked aggression is made, that is not surrendered; it is allowed under all enlightened governments fully. If it mean the privilege of a savage's retaliation, I deny that any human ever had such a right by nature. "Vengeance is mine, saith the Lord." If it mean the privilege to attach the righteous temporal penalty, and execute it ourselves, on the aggressor, so as to deter him and others from similar assaults, I deny that this is naturally a personal right; for nothing is more unnatural than for a man to be judge in his own case. Other instances of supposed loss of natural rights are alleged with more plausibility; as when a citizen is restrained by law from selling his corn out of the country, (a thing naturally moral *per se*) from some economic motive of public good; and yet the righteous citizen feels bound to obey. I reply : if the restriction of the government is not unjust, then there exists such a state of circumstances among the fellow citizens, that the sale of the corn out of the country, under those circumstances, would have been a natural breach of the law of righteousness and love towards them. So that, under the particular state of the case, the man's natural right to sell his corn had terminated. Natural rights may change with circumstances.

Here we may understand, in what sense "all men are by nature free and equal." Obviously no man is by nature free, in the sense of being born in possession of that vile license to do whatever he has will and physical ability to do, which the infidel moralists understand by the sacred name of liberty. For every man is born under obligation to God, to his parents, and to such form of government as may providentially be over his parents. (I may add the obligation to ecclesiastical government is also native). But all men have a native title to that liberty which I have defined, viz : freedom to do what they have a moral right to do. But as rights differ, the amount of this freedom to which given men have a natural title, varies in different cases. But all men are alike in this; that they all have the same general right by nature, to enjoy their own natural *quantum* of freedom, be it what it may. Again : are all men naturally equal in strength, in virtue, in capacity, or in rights? The thought is preposterous. The same man does not even continue to have the same natural rights all the time. The female child is born with a different set of rights in part, from the male child of the same parents; because born to different native capacities and

Natural Equality what? Golden Rule.

natural relations and duties. In what then are men naturally equal? I answer, first: in their common title to the several *quantums* of liberty appropriate to each, differing as they do in different men; second, they are equal in their common humanity, and their common share in the obligations and benefits of the golden rule. All men are reciprocally bound to love their neighbors as themselves; and to do unto others, as they would that others should do to them. See Job xxxi : 13–15. Here inspiration defines that equality as in full force between master and slave; and as entirely compatible with that relation. Here is the great charter of Bible republicanism. Men have by nature, a general equality in this; not a specific one. Hence, the general equality of nature will by no means produce a literal and universal equality of civil condition; for the simple reason that the different classes of citizens have very different specific rights; and this grows out of their differences of sex, virtue, intelligence, civilization, &c., and the demands of the common welfare. Thus, if the low grade of intelligence, virtue and civilization of the African in America, disqualified him for being his own guardian, and if his own true welfare (taking the "general run" of cases) and that of the community, would be plainly marred by this freedom ; then the law decided correctly, that the African here has no natural right to his self-control, as to his own labour and locomotion. Hence, his natural liberty is only that which remains after that privilege is retrenched. Still he has natural rights, (to marriage, to a livelihood from his own labour, to the Sabbath, and to the service of God, and immortality, &c., &c). Freedom to enjoy all these constitutes his natural liberty, and if the laws violate any of it causelessly, they are unjust.

3. Proper Sphere of Civil Government. The two remaining questions are more practical, and may be discussed more briefly. We discard the theocratic conception of civil government. The proper object of it is, in general, to secure to man his life, liberty, and property, i. e., his secular rights. Man's intellectual and spiritual concerns belong to different jurisdictions; the parental and the ecclesiastical. The evidence is, that the parental, and the ecclesiastical departments of duty and right are separately recognized by Scripture and distinctly fenced off, as independent circles. (See also Jno. xviii : 35, 36; Luke xii : 14 ; 2 Cor. x : 4 ; Matt. xxii : 21). The powers of the civil magistrate then, are limited by righteousness, (not always by facts) to these general functions, regulating and adjudicating all secular rights, and protecting all members of civil society in their enjoyment of their several proper shares thereof. This general function implies a number of others; prominently, these three : taxation, punishment, including capital for capital crimes, and defensive war. For the first, (see Matt. xxii : 21 ; Rom. xiii : 6, 7 ;) for the second, (see Gen. ix :

5, 6; Num. xxxv : 33 ; Rom. xiii : 1–5 ;) for the third, (Ex. xvii : 9, and *passim* in Old Testament ; Luke iii : 14, 15 ; Acts x : 1, 2). The same thing follows from the power of capital punishment. Aggressive war is wholesale murder. The magistrate who is charged with the sword, to avenge and prevent domestic murder, is *a fortiori* charged to punish and prevent the foreign murderer.

But, few governments are strictly just; and the inquiry Duty of Christians therefore arises : How shall the Christian to Unjust Civil Gov- citizen act, under an oppressive command of ernment. the civil magistrate ? I reply, if the act which he requires is not positively a sin *per se*, it must be obeyed, although in obeying we surrender a clear, moral right of our own. The proof is the example of the Bible saints— the fact that the very government to which Paul and Peter challenged obedience as a Christian duty, was far from being an equitable one; and the truth that a harsh and unjust government is a far less evil than the absence of all government. The duty of obedience, does not, as we have seen, spring out of our assent, nor from the government's being the one of our choice, but from the providence of God which placed us under it, coupled with the fact that government is His ordinance. If the thing commanded by the civil magistrate is positively sinful, then the Christian citizen must refuse obedience, but yield submission to the penalty therefor. Of course, he is entitled, while submitting either in this or the former case, to seek the peaceable repeal of the sinful law or command ; but that he is bound to disobey it in the latter case, is clear from the example of the apostles and martyrs: Acts iv : 19 ; v ; 29 ; and from the obvious consideration, that since the civil magistrate is but God's minister, it is preposterous God's power committed to him should be used to pull down God's authority. But does not the duty of disobeying imply that there ought to be an immunity from penalty for so doing? I reply, of course, in strict justice, there ought ; but this is one of those rights which the private Christian may not defend by violence, against the civil magistrate. The magistrate is magistrate still, and his authority in all things, not carrying necessary guilt in the compliance, is still binding, notwithstanding his unrighteous command. To suffer is not sin *per se :* hence, although when he commanded you to sin, you refused, when he commands you to suffer for that refusal, you acquiesce. It should be again remembered, that an unjust government is far better than none at all. It is God's will that such a government, even, should be obeyed by individuals, rather than have anarchy. If a man holds office under a government, and the official function enjoined upon him is positive sin, it is his duty to resign, giving up his office and its emoluments, along with its responsibilities, and then he has no more concern with the unrighteous law than any other private citizen. That concern is simply to seek its repeal by constitutional means. If the majority, or other controlling force in the constitution make that appeal unattainable for him, then the private citizen is clear of the sin, and has no concern with the sinful law. He is neither bound, nor permitted to resist it by force. But for an official of government to hold office, promise official obedience, and draw his compensation therefor, and yet undertake to refuse to perform the official duties of his place, on the ground that his conscience tells him the acts are morally wrong; this is but a disgusting compound of pharisaism, avarice and perjury. Thus we have, in a nutshell, the true doctrine of a "higher law," as distinguished from the spurious.

One more question remains: Who is to be the judge when the act required of the citizen by law is morally wrong? I reply, the citizen himself, in the last resort. This is the great Protestant and Scriptural doctrine of private judgment. We sustain it by the obvious fact, that when the issue is thus made between the government and its citizen, if that is to be absolute judge in its own case, there is an end of personal independence and liberty. But the government's judgment being thus set aside, there remains no other human umpire. 2d. Every intelligent being lies under moral relations to God, which are immediate and inevitable. No creature in the universe can answer for him, in a case of conscience, or step between him and his guilt. Hence, it is the most monstrous and unnatural injustice that any power should dictate to his conscience, except His divine Judge. See Prov. ix : 12 ; Rom. xiv : 4. The clear example of Bible saints sustains this, as cited above ; for while they clearly recognized the legitimacy of the magistrate's authority, they claim the privilege of private judgment in disobeying their commands to sin. If it be said that this doctrine is in danger of introducing disorder and insubordination, I answer, no; not under any government that at all deserves to stand ; for when the right of private judgment is thus exercised, as an appeal to God's judgment, and with the fact before our faces, that if we feel bound to disobey the law, we shall be still bound to submit meekly to the penalty, none of us will be apt to exercise the privilege too lightly.

Right of Private Judgment Asserted.

Thus far, we have considered the individual action of the citizen towards an unrighteous government, and have shown that, even when constrained to disobey an unrighteous law, he must submit to the penalty. Do we then inculcate the slavish doctrine of passive obedience, which asserts the divine and irresponsible right of kings, so that even though they so abuse their powers that the proper ends of government are lost, God forbids resistance? By no means. To Americans, whose national existence and glory are all founded on the "right of revolution," slight

4. Right of Revolution Discussed.

arguments would probably be needed to support it. But, it is
the duty of thinking men to have some better support for their
opinions, than the popularity of them.

The argument for passive obedience, from Romans 13, is
Argument for Pas- at first view, plausible, but will not bear
sive Obedience Re- inquiry. Note that the thing which is there
futed.   declared to be of divine authority, is not a
particular form of government, but submission to the government, whatever it is. God has not ordained what government
mankind shall live under, but only that they shall live under a
government. The end of government is not the gratification
of the rulers, but the good of the ruled. When a form of government entirely ceases, as a whole, to subserve its proper end,
is it still to subsist forever? This is preposterous. Who then
is to change it? The submissionists say, Providence alone.
But Providence works by means. Shall those means be external force or internal force? These are the only alternatives;
for of course corrupt abuses will not correct themselves, when
their whole interest is, to be perpetuated. External force is
unauthorized; for nothing is clearer than that a nation should
not interfere, uncalled, in the affairs of another. Again: we
have seen that the sovereignty is in the people rather than the
rulers; and that the power the rulers hold is delegated. May
the people never resume their own, when it is wholly abused to
their injury? There may be obviously a point then where
"resistance to tyrants is obedience to God." The meaning of
the apostle is, that this resistance must be the act, not of the
individual, but of the people. The insubordination which he
condemns, is that which arrays against a government, bad like
that of the Cæsars perhaps, the worse anarchy of the individual
will. But the body of the citizens is the commonwealth; and
when the commonwealth arises and supersedes the abused
authority of her public servants, the allegiance of the individual
is due to her, just as before to her servants. But it may be
asked, How can the commonwealth move to do this, except by
the personal movement of individuals against the "powers that
be?" I answer, (and this explains the true nature of the right
of revolution): true: but if the individual moves, when he is
not inspired by the movement of the popular heart; when his
motion is not the exponent, as well as the occasion, of theirs,
he has made a mistake—he has done wrong—he must bear his
guilt. It is usually said, as by Paley, that a revolution is only
justifiable when the evils of the government are worse than the
probable evils of the convulsive change; and when there is a
reasonable prospect of success. The latter point is doubtful.
Some of the noblest revolutions, as that of the Swiss, were
rather the result of indignation at intolerable wrong, and a generous despair, than of this calculation of chances of success.

LECTURE LXXIV.
RELIGIOUS LIBERTY AND CHURCH AND STATE.

YOU may suppose it superfluous to lecture on a subject so well understood, and universally admitted, as this is among us; but you will be mistaken. Our ancestors understood it, because they had studied it, with all the earnestness of persecuted men, who had to contend with sword and pen. We hold their correct theory; but, it is to be feared, only by prescription and prejudice. Consequence. that when temptation comes, and the theory of religious liberty seems awkward just at a particular juncture, we shall be carried about with any wind of doctrine. This is ever the course; for fundamental truths to be practically learned by one generation, handed down to the next, held by prejudice for a few generations, (the words used and sense dropped) and at last lost in practice.

I. The Question not Obsolete.

Again, many, even of statesmen, do not defend Religious Liberty on sound and rational grounds. Even Brougham and Macaulay (see his History of England) seem not to have found out that the proposition, "man is not responsible for his belief," is not the same with that of Religious Liberty.

Augustine First Advocate of Persecution.

The arguments by which Augustine induced persecution of the Donatists have ever been the staple ones of the Roman Church, for intolerance. They are so wretched and flimsy, as to be unworthy of a separate discussion. Their answer will be apparent in the sequel. But it should be observed, that the doctrines of intolerance are consistent with the claims of the Romish Church to infallibility, and supremacy. A man ought not to have liberty to destroy his own soul by refusing the infallible teachings of God, on earth. This claim of infallibility puts the relations between the unbeliever and Church, on the same footing as those between the unbeliever and his God. To both he is guilty. But is the claim of infallibility to be implicitly admitted? The answer to this question shows that a

873

denial of the right of private judgment, is essential to the Romanists' intolerance. For if the infallibility is to be brought into question, then the basis of the right to enforce absolute conformity is melted away.

A far more plausible argument for the right to enforce religious conformity has been glanced at by later Romish writers. It is hard to answer by many a Protestant, who inconsiderately holds to Religious Liberty. Man is responsible for his belief. His religious error is not simply his misfortune, but his crime. Bad volitions are at the bottom. Truth is discoverable, certain. This crime has a very certain, though indirect evil influence; not only on men's religious, but secular conducts and interests. The heretic injures the public morals, health, order, wealth, the value of real estate, &c., &c. He may be doing mischief on a far larger scale than the bandit. Now, if his religious belief is of a moral quality, voluntary and criminal; and is also mischievous—highly so; and that, to the interests both Church and State protect, why not punishable? Why does it claim to be exempted from the list of offences amenable to law? The cruel abuses of the power of punishing heretics, by ignorant or savage rulers, are no argument against its use, any more than the Draconian penalties conclude against moderate power in the magistrate, of repressing secular crimes." Answer.

Heresy is Criminal.

Every thing which is moral evil, and is detrimental to the interests of society, is not, therefore, properly punishable by society (e. g. prodigality, indolence, gluttony, drunkenness). The thing must be, moreover, shown to be brought within the scope of the penalties, by the objects and purposes of Government; and the relevancy of corporeal pains and penalties to be a useful corrective; and the directness of the concern of society in its bad consequences. Society may not infringe directly a natural right of one of its members, to protect itself from an indirect injury which may or may not occur. It only has a right to stand on the defensive, and wait for the overt aggression. It is not the business of society to keep a man from injuring himself, but from injuring others. As to his personal interests he is his own master. Now, that religious error, though moral evil, voluntary and guilty, does not come within the above conditions, we will show, and at the same time will adduce arguments of a positive weight.

But Force Not the Remedy.

1. Premise. Church and State are distinct institutions, since theocratic institutions are done away; they have distinct objects. The Church is to teach men the way to heaven, and to help them thither. The State is to protect each citizen in the enjoyment of temporal rights. The Church has no civil pains and penalties at command; because Christ has given her none; and

State and Church Have Different Objects.

because they have no relevancy whatever to produce her object
—the hearty belief of saving truth (see John xviii : 36, 2 Cor.
x : 4, &c.). The main weapon of the Civil Government is civil
pains and penalties (Rom. xiii : 4).

2. Premise. In the State, the good of the governed being
the object, (in temporal interests) the governed are the earthly sources of sovereignty.
Rulers have only a delegated power, and are
the agents of the community, who depute to them, for the general good, so much of power as is necessary.

State Has Only Delegated Powers.

Now, for the direct argument, observe: The Church's bearing penal power, and being armed with civil
pains, is utterly inconsistent with her spiritual character, her objects, and the laws of
Christ. Rome herself did not claim it. When the Church persecutes, it is through the commonwealth. This lends its corporeal power to the Church. When Romish Priests persecute,
they bear a twofold capacity, magisterial and clerical.

Spiritual Judge Has no Civil Penalties.

But, by what power shall the magistrate persecute his own
Sovereign? Whence delegated? All the
power he has is delegated. Now a citizen
cannot delegate to another the right of judg-
ing for him what is right, because to do so is a self-contradiction, and unutterable absurdity; and because to do so would be
a crime. For the merit of all my religious belief and acting
depends on my free, conscientious convictions; and God has
made me responsible for them, so that I cannot give away the
responsibility.

1. Magistrate has no Spiritual Jurisdiction.

By the same general fact, it appears that when intolerance
commands me to surrender my private judg-
ment in religion, it is to the Magistrate I surrender it; i. e., a man not sacred, nor even
clerical, an officer purely secular, and even upon Romish
teachings, no more entitled than me, to judge in religion. But,
it is said, "the Magistrate persecutes not for himself, but on
behalf of a Church infallible and divinely authorized, to which
he has dutifully bowed, and lent his secular power, as he ought;
so that it is to this infallible Church we are compelled by the
Magistrate's sword to surrender our private judgment." No;
how did the Magistrate find out that this Church is infallible?
Suppose I, the subject, choose to dispute it? who shall decide
between us? Not the Church in question; because the very
question in debate between us is, whether the Church ought to
be allowed a supreme authority over my, or his conscience. It
is to the civil Magistrate's judgment, after all, that I am compelled to yield my private judgment, and that, in a thing purely
religious.

2. Nor Right to Arrest my Private Judgment.

The civil authority of the magistrate is not due to his Chris-

3. Magistrates Not Even Christians. tianity, but to his official character. This follows from the entire distinctness of the Church and State in their objects and characters. It is proved by Scripture asserting the civil authority of Pagan magistrates; Matt. xxii : 21; Rom. xiii ; 1 Peter ii : 13. If we were citizens of a Mohammedan or pagan country, we should owe obedience to their civil rulers in things temporal. And this shows that the authority is not dependent on the magistrate's christianity, even where he happens to be a Christian, Now what an absurdity is it, for that which is not Christian at all to choose my Christianity for me ? To see this, only suppose a case where the magistrate is actually infidel. The Greeks and Protestants in Constantinople struggle with each other. The Turk, more sensible than intolerant Christians, merely stands by and derides both. But suppose one of them should manage to get him on their side, and use his temporal power to persecute their brethren? Can a Turkish infidel, who has nothing to do with Christianity, confer on one sect a power to persecute another? Confer what he has not? Outrageous. But the reason of the thing is the same in any other country; because the civil authority of the magistrate is no more due to his Christianity than that of the Grand Turk in Turkey, who has no Christianity.

But suppose the persecuting Church repudiates the aid of **4. Which Religion Shall Coerce ?** the magistrate, and claims that she herself, as a spiritual power, is entitled to wield both swords, temporal and spiritual, for suppression of error, in person, as Rome does in some of her more imperious moods. Then all the absurdities are incurred which arise from confounding the two opposite societies of Church and State and their objects; and all the Scriptures above quoted must be defied. But other arguments, still more unanswerable, apply. Among competing religious communions, which shall have the right to coerce the other? Of course, the orthodox one. This is ever the ground of the claim. "I am right and you are wrong; therefore, I must compel you to think as I do." But each communion is orthodox in its own eyes. Every one is erroneous to its rivals. If Rome says, there are evidences of our being the apostolic infallible Church, so clear, that no one can resist them without obstinate guilt, Geneva says to Rome just the same. Whatsoever any Church believes, it believes to be true. There is no umpire under God; shall the magistrate decide? He has no right. He is not religious. There is no umpire. Each one's claim to persecute is equally good. The strongest rules. Might makes right.

But again : The Church cannot use persecution to gain her **5. Coercion Not a Means to Faith.** end, which is the belief of religious truth; because penalties have no relevancy whatever to beget belief. **Evidence** begets con-

viction; not fear and pain. While we do not think that belief
or unbelief of moral truth is of no moral character, with
Brougham, we do know that it must be the voluntary, spontaneous result of evidence, and that it must be rational. That
a spiritual society, whose object is to produce moral beliefs, and
acts determined thereby, should do it by civil pains, is an infinite absurdity. This is enhanced by the other fact: that the
virtue and efficacy of religious belief and acts before God depend wholly on their heartiness and sincerity. Feigned belief,
unwilling service, are no graces, but sins: do not save, but
damn. . . . Nor do persecutions have any preparing effect
to open the mind to the rational and moral means which the
Church is afterwards to use. This the Augustinian plea. To
punish, imprison, impoverish, torment, burn a man, because he
does not see your arguments as strong as you think them, is
surely a strange way of making him favorable thereto! To
give him the strongest cause to hate the reasoner, is a strange
way to make him like the reasonings! The most likely possible
way is taken to give him an ill opinion of that communion he
is wished to join. These measures have some natural tendency,
on weak natures, to make hypocrites; but none to make sincere believers.

Under this head, too, notice the outrageous impolicy of
persecuting measures. Supposing the doc-
Persecution Prejudi- trines persecuted to be erroneous, the very
ces Truth. way is taken to make them popular, by array-
ing on their side the sentiments of injured right, virtuous indignation, sympathy with the oppressed, and in general, all the
noblest principles, and to make the opposing truth unpopular,
by associating it with high handed oppression, cruelty, &c.
The history is, that no communion ever persecuted which did
not cut its own throat thereby unless it persecuted so as to
crush and brutify wholly, and trample out all active religious
life *pro* or *con* to itself. The persecuting communion dies,
either by the hand of the outraged and irresistible reaction it
produces; or if the persecution is thorough, by the *syncope*
and atrophy of a spiritual stagnation, that leaves it a religious
communion only in name. Of the former, the examples are
the Episcopacy of Laud, in Scotland and England, Colonial
Church of Virginia against Baptists, &c. Of the latter, the
Popish Church of France, Spain, Italy. "The blood of the
martyrs is the seed of the Church."

All acts of religious intolerance are inconsistent with the
relations which God has established between
6. Intrudes into God's Himself and rational souls. Here is the
Province. main point. God holds every soul directly
responsible to Himself. That responsibility necessarily implies
that no one shall step in between him and his God. No one
can relieve him of his responsibility, answer for him to God, and

bear his punishment, if he has betrayed his duty. Therefore no one should interfere to hinder his judging for himself. "What hast thou to do, to judge another man's servant?" Here it is plain how essential the claim of infallibility is to a plausible theory of persecution. For a man who acknowledges himself fallible, to intrude his leadership by force on his fellow-man, who is no more fallible than himself, when it is possible he may thereby ruin his soul, is a position as satanic as impudent. But where the persecutor can say, " I know infallibly that my way is right, and if he will come into it he will certainly be saved," there is a little plausibility. But if infallibility is disproved, that little is gone. And more : Each man is directly bound to his God to render a belief and service hearty ; proceeding primarily from a regard to God's will, not man's. Else it is sin. Now, how impious is he, who, professing to contend for God, thus thrusts himself between God and His creature ? Substitutes fear of him for fear of God? Thrusts himself into God's place? He that does it is an anti-Christ. Man's belief is a thing sacred, inviolable.

7. Let it be added, also, that persecutions ruin that cause which they profess to promote, the cause of God, by demoralizing the persecuting community. They tend to confound and corrupt all moral ideas in the populace, who see moral, merciful, peaceful men punished with the pains due to the most atrocious crimes, because they do not take certain arguments in a certain way. They beget on the one hand subserviency, hypocrisy, cunning, falsehood and deceit, the weapons of oppressed weakness ; and on the other, cruelty, unmercifulness, rapacity, injustice. Ages of persecution have always been ages of deep moral corruption ; and where persecution has been successful, it has plunged the nations into an abyss of vice and relaxed morals.

Again: we have hinted at the tendency of intolerance to disappoint its own ends. All history is a commentary on this. More persecution, the more sects, (except where it is so extreme as to produce a religious paralysis, and there there are no sects, because there is no belief, but only stupid apathy or secret atheism). Rome tried it to the full. And under her *regime*, christendom was more and more full of sectaries, who increased till the freedom of the Reformation extinguished them : Waldenses, Albigenses, Cathari, Paulicians, Beghards, Fratricelli, Turlupins, Brethren of Free Spirit, Wickliffeites, Hussites, &c., &c. There have always been wider divergences of doctrinal opinion, within the bosom of the Romish Church itself, than there are now, between all the evangelical branches of the Protestant family, with all their freedom. And the effect of the Reformation, (most in freest countries), has been to kill off, or render perfectly impotent, all more extravagant and hurtful

8. Persecution Aggravates Divisions.

sects. Where are any Turlupins, or mystical Pantheists like those of Germany of the 14th Century? Where any Schwestriones? Manichæans?

9. Religious sects are nearly harmless to the State, when they are no longer persecuted. It is wholly to their oppression that their supposed factiousness is due; cease to oppress, and they become mild and loyal. This is just the absurd and treacherous trick of persecutors, to say, " conventicles are secret," when it is their oppression which makes them secret. They would gladly be open, if they might have leave. " Conventicles are factious ;" it is injustice which makes them factious. Let the State treat all sectaries justly and mildly, and they at once have the strongest motive to be true to the State; indeed, the same which the majority has; that of strongest self-interest.

Persecution for conscience' sake is always supremely false and hypocritical, as appears by this fact. The motive assigned by persecuting religionists is, that the souls of men may be saved from the ruinous effects of error; of the heretic himself, if he can be reclaimed; of others whom he might corrupt, at any rate. But while they have been imprisoning, tormenting, burning men of innocent morals, because they held some forbidden tenets, have they not always tolerated the grossest vices in those who would submit to the Church? Adultery, profanity, violence, ignorance, drunkenness, gluttony? Was it not so during all the Inquisition in Spain and Italy, Laud's persecutions in England, James' in Scotland? But a bad life is the worst heresy. Surely this destroys souls and corrupts communities. Why do not these men then, who so vehemently love the souls of their neighbours, that they must burn their bodies to ashes, love the vicious enough to restrain their vices? Persecution for opinion's sake is wholly a political measure cloaked under religion. Its true object always is, to secure domination, not to save souls.

10. Coercion Hypocritical.

This, therefore, is the only safe theory. The ends of the State are for time and earth; those of the Church are for eternity. The weapon of the State is corporeal, that of the Church is spiritual. The two cannot be combined, without confounding heaven and earth. The only means that can be used to produce religious belief are moral. No man is to be visited with any civil penalty for his belief, as long as he does not directly infringe upon the purpose of the government, which is the protection of the temporal rights of his fellow-citizens. The State is bound to see that every man enjoys his religious freedom untouched, because the right to this religious freedom is a secular, or political right.

Conclusion.

The doctrine of religious liberty was not evolved at the Reformation: Protestants held it a right and duty to persecute heretics. " Rome's guilt was that she persecuted those nearer

right than herself, and did it cruelly and unjustly." The first
treatise taking the true ground, as far as I know, was written by
Brown (founder of sect of Brownists). Dr. Jno. Owen wrote
for the same cause. Dr. Jeremy Taylor wrote his plea for
liberty of prophesying. Milton and Locke are well known.
Roger Williams, of Rhode Island, perhaps deserves the credit
of being the first Ruler in the world, who granted absolute freedom to all sects, having power to do otherwise.

The separation and independence of Church and State was
not only not the doctrine of the Refor-
.11. Church and State.
The Protestant Churches mation. No Christian nation holds it to
all Established. this day, except ours. In 17th and 18th
centuries some Independents and others in England, and Seceders in Scotland, advocated such separation, but were branded
as outrageous radicals. All the Reformation Churches, Lutheran and Reformed, held it as an axiom, that the State had,
under God, the supreme care of religion. " *Cujus Regio, ejus
Religio.*" Dissenters of England now usually hold our views.
(as well as Seceders in Scotland), called there voluntaryism.
The Free Church, at the head of whom was Dr. Chalmers, held
to establishments. Ours is the first fair trial.

Two theories of Church establishments prevail among
II. Establishments nominal Protestants. The higher is that
Justified by two squinted at briefly in Vattel, bk. 1, ch. 12,
Theories. The Pre- § 129, and more fully developed by Glad-
latic.
stone, Church and State, Chap. 2. That the government is
instituted for the highest good of the whole in every concern,
and is bound to do all it has in its reach for this object, in every
department. That a commonwealth is a moral person, having
a personality, judgment, conscience, responsibility, and is therefore bound, as a body, to recognize and obey the true religion.
Hence the State must have its religion, as a State. This is a
necessary duty of its corporate or individual nature. Hence it
must profess this, by State acts. It must of course have a
religious test for office, because otherwise the religious character of the State would be lost; and it must use its State
power to propagate this State religion.

Let us discuss the abstract grounds of this theory first;
then take up the second, or freer theory of Church establishments, and conclude with some general historical views applicable to both theories.

Says Vattel: "If all men are bound to serve God, the
entire nation in her national capacity is
Vattel's View. doubtless bound to serve and honour Him.
This is based on a general principle; that all men are everywhere bound by laws of nature; and therefore the entire
nation, whose common will is but the united wills of all the
members, must be bound by these natural laws; because the
accident of association cannot release men from bonds that are

universal." (See § 5). This is true in a sense, but not the sense necessary to prove a state religion obligatory. So far as any acts of any associated body of men have any moral or religious character, they should conform to the same moral and religious rules, by which the individuals are bound. But (a) the obligation is nothing else but the individual obligation of all the members, and nothing more is needed to defend or sanction it than their individual morality and religiousness. And (b) there are associations whose objects are not directly religious, but secular. How can they appropriately have a corporate religious character, when their corporate character has no direct reference to religion.

Gladstone puts the same argument substantially, calling it his ethical argument. "A State is a corpo-

Gladstone's View.

ration. It has personality, judgment, reason, foresight. Its acts have moral character. The only safe and sufficient basis of morals is Christianity; therefore they should have Christian character. All things we do have religious relations and responsibilities; therefore the acts of rulers as such, should have a Christian character. In a word, a State is a moral person, corporately regarded, and like any other person, must have its personal Christian character. Else it is anti-Christian, and atheistic." Mr. Macaulay, (Ed. Review, 1839), so terribly damaged this argument, by pointing out that, by this reasoning, it was made the duty of armies, Banking, Insurance, Gas, Railroad, Stage Coach companies, Art Union, incorporate clubs, &c., &c., to have a corporate religion (consider the absurdities), that in his second edition, the author modified and fortified it. "These corporations are trivial, partial. Everybody not bound to belong to one; their operations not far reaching, not of divine appointment, temporary. But there are two natural associations of men, alike in these three fundamental traits. They are of divine appointment; they are perpetual, they embrace everybody, i. e., every human being is bound to belong to them; they are the family and the State. All good men admit that the family ought to have a family religion. The State, a similar institution, a larger family, ought to have a State-religion."

This is the only ingenious and plausible thing in his book. The nature of the reasoning compels us to discuss the fundamental questions as to the constitution and objects of civil society. For our answer must take this shape. The family association is wholly dissimilar from the commonwealth; because its direct objects are not the same. The source and nature of the authority are not the same. There is not the same inferiority in the governed to the governors; and there is not the same affection and interest.

(Remember, however, the fact that all men are bound to be members of some family and State, has no relevancy to

56*

prove that these associations must have religious corporate character, unlike all other partial societies. Nor does the fact that they are not voluntary, but of divine appointment ; because under certain circumstances, it may be of divine appointment that men should belong to an army ; and this does not prove that an army ought to profess a religion as such).

The object of the family as to children, is to promote their
III. State and whole welfare. The object of civil govern-
Church have Different ment is simply the protection of temporal
Ends.   rights against aggression, foreign or domestic.
But this is just the view which all claimants for high powers in governments deny. Like Mr. Gladstone, they claim that the proper view of government is, that it is an association intended to take in hand all the interests and welfare of human beings, of every kind ; everything in which man is interested, and in which combination can aid in success, is the proper end o. human government. It is το Παν : The total human association. Now, the plain answers to this are three : the Bible says the con- trary. Rom. xiii : 4. It is utterly impracticable ; for, by the necessary imperfection of human nature, an agency which is best adapted to one function must be worst adapted to others ; and an association which should do every thing, would be sure to do all in the worst possible manner. But last, and chiefly ; if this is true ; then there cannot be any other association of human beings, except as it is a part and creature of the State. There is no Church. The State is the Church, and ecclesi- astical persons and assemblies are but magistrates engaged in one part of their functions. There is no such thing as the family, an independent, original institution of divine appoint- ment. The parent is but the delegate of the government, and when he applies the birch to the child, it is in fact, by State authority ! All combinations, to trade, to do banking business, to teach, to preach, to navigate, to buy pictures, to nurse the sick, to mine, &c., &c., are parts and creatures of the State ! Or if it be said that the State, though it has the right to do every thing, is not bound to do every thing, unless she finds it convenient and advantageous, then the ethical argument is relinquished ; and the ground of expediency assumed, on which we will remark presently. But the ethical argument fails, also.

(a) In this : That it makes the right and duty of the Sultan to establish Mohammedanism ; the King of Spain, Popery ; Queen Victoria, Prelacy ; the Emperor of China, Boodhism, &c. Julian was right in ousting Christians ; Theodosius, Platonists, Constanti::, Athanasians ; Jovian, Arians. For if the State is a moral person, bound to have and promote its religion, the Sovereign must choose his religion conscientiously. The one he believes right, he must enforce. This is admitted by the advo- cates. Now, of all the potentates on earth, there is but one, that would conscientiously advocate what these men think the

right religion—Prelacy.   How sensible is that theory which, in
the present state of the world, would ensure the teaching of
errors, by all the authority of the governments over all the
world, except in one kingdom ?

(b) If strictly carried out, it would ensure the worst governing, and the worst preaching, possible.   An
organization intended for a particular end,
should choose agents best adapted to sub-

*Hence, Agencies of
one Unfit for Other.*

serve that end, irrespective of other things.   Otherwise, it will
be miserably inefficient.   And if it is best organized for that
end, it must, for that very reason, be ill adapted to a different
end.   Hence, there should be no jumbling of functions; but
each institution should be left to subserve its own objects.   Suppose the British Government act out this theory.   It must say
to the skillful and honest financier: " You shall not help in my
treasury, because you do not believe in Apostolic Succession ;"
to the Presbyterian General: " I will have none of your courage
and skill to release my armies from probable destruction, because
you listen to a preacher who never had a Prelate's hand on his
head;" to the faithful pilot: " You shall not steer one of my
ships off a lee shore, because you take the communion sitting,"
&c.   How absurd; and how utter the failure of a government
thus conducted !

(c) By the same reason that it is the duty of the State to
use a part of its power to propagate its religion, it is its duty to
use all; and the doctrine of persecution for opinion's sake is the
necessary inference.   For the State has power to fine, imprison, kill.

(Before we proceed to the more plausible and liberal theory
advanced by Vattel, Warburton, Chalmers,
&c., let us notice a point urged by the first
mentioned, in § 139, &c. : That there must

*2. State Needs not to
Control the Ministry.*

be a connection between Church and State, in order that the
Sovereign may have control over ecclesiastics and religion.   If
men wielding such immense spiritual influences, are not held in
official subordination to the Chief Ruler, he cannot govern the
country.   It would be a sufficient reply to say that Vattel knew
Church officers, chiefly as Papists.   Take away their power of
the keys, their exemption from civil jurisdiction, and their
ecclesiastical dependence on a foreign Pope, and the difficulty
is gone.   The minister of religion should be a citizen, subject
to all laws, liable to be punished for any overt crime committed
or prompted by him.   This is subordination enough.   As for
the power still left him to inculcate doctrines of dangerous tendency, unchecked by the State, the proper defence is free discussion.   The medicine of error is not violent repression, but
light.   Let the Ruler content himself with protecting and diffusing free discussion.   And again, Vattel's argument may,
with equal justice, be extended to political teachers; and then
the freedom of the press and of speech is gone).

But we come now to what we may call the Chalmerian
theory. "The proper object of civil government is man's secular well-being. But the
right to prosecute this, implies the right to perform all those
functions which are essential to the main end—yea, the duty.
Public morals are essential to the public welfare. The only
source of public morals is Christianity. Christianity will not be
sufficiently diffused, unless the State lends its aid and means to
do it. Therefore it is right, yea, binding, that the State shall
enter into an alliance with Christianity (in that form or forms
best adapted to the end), to teach its citizens religion and morals, as a necessary means for the public good. To fail to do so,
is for the State to betray its charge."

Chalmers' View.

The contested point here, is in these propositions: That
" voluntaryism " will usually fail to diffuse a sufficient degree of
public morals; and that a State-endowed Church, or Churches,
of good character and spiritual independence will do it far better. And on this point, all the divisions of " Dissent," splitting
up of small communities until the congregations are all too
small to sustain themselves, the insufficiency of funds furnished
by voluntary contribution, are urged, &c., &c.

Now, here we join issue, and assert; in the first place, that
an endowed Church, on this plan, will usually
effect less for true religion and public morals,
than voluntary Churches, notwithstanding
these difficulties. For remember that the State is, in fact, and
must usually be, non-religious; i. e., the Rulers themselves will
usually have a personal character irreligious, carnal, anti-
evangelical. What is the fact? How is the composition of
governments determined? By the sword, or by intrigue, by
party tactics, by political and forensic skill, by the demands of
secular interests and measures, by bribery, by riches and family,
by everything else than grace. It must be so; for the assumed
necessity for a State endowment and alliance is in the fact that
the community is yet prevalently irreligious, and needs to be
made religious. Now, all just government is representative.
It must reflect the national character. To disfranchise, and
shut out of office, citizens, because carnally minded, would be
an absurd and impracticable injustice in the present state of
communities. Now remember (Rom. viii : 7) : This enmity is
innate, instinctive, spontaneous. If the State selects preachers,
some individual officers of the State select them ; and the least
evangelical will most frequently be selected. Natural affinities
of feeling will operate. Here, then, is one usual result of a
Church establishment; that of the men who are nominal members of the Church endowed, the least evangelical and useful
will receive the best share of all that influence, power and
money which the State bestows. Exceptions may occur : this
is the general rule. What says History? Arians under Roman

*Voluntaryism Most
Efficient.*

Empire; under Teuton Princes, High Church Arminians; worldly men; semi-Papists in England; Arminians in Holland; Moderates in Scotland.

Again: The pecuniary support will be liberal and certain. Its tenure will be the favor of the Rulers; not of God's people. Hence carnally minded men will infallibly be attracted into the ministry by mercenary motives: and the most mercenary will be the most pushing. Hence a progressive deterioration of the endowed ministry, as in English and all Popish and Lutheran Churches. Shall we be pointed to large infusion of excellent men in English and Scotch establishments? We answer, that their continuance is mainly due to the wholesome competition of Dissent. (Just the contrary of the plea, that the Establishment is worth its cost, by its wholesome influence in curbing Dissent). And the proof is, that wherever Dissent has been thoroughly extinguished, the leaden weight of State patronage has in every case, brought down the endowed clergy to the basest depths of mercenary character, and most utter inefficiency for all good. E. g., Spain, France, Italy, Austria, Russia.

Clergy Tempted by Ease.

Again: Just as soon as any Church is endowed, it is put in an oppressive attitude towards all that part of the community who do not belong to it, so that prejudice will prevent much of usefulness in its ministrations to them, and perpetually stimulate secession. That I should be taxed to pay for the preaching of doctrines which I do not believe or approve, is of the nature of an oppression. That my minister should have no lot nor part in the manse and salary provided at the common expense, but monopolized by another man who is willing to endorse some doctrine which I think erroneous, is an odious distinction. Indeed, it might be urged, as an independent argument against the mildest form of Church Establishment, that it implies some degree of oppression for opinion's sake; it makes the State a judge, where it has no business to judge, and exercises partiality, where there should be equality. Nor will it at all answer to attempt to elude this difficulty, as in the colonial government of Massachusetts; because this would enlist the State in the diffusion of error and truth alike; a thing wicked; and it gives to the worst forms of nominal Christianity a strength they would not otherwise have, because all the "Nothingarians," being compelled to support some Church, elect the one that has least religion.

Endowment Unfair and Oppressive.

And once more: The only fair experiment of full religious liberty, without Church and State, that of our country, proves, so far, that the voluntary system is more efficient than the endowed, in adequately supplying the growing wants of a nation. Let all denominations enjoy complete freedom and equality, and their differences become practically less, they approximate to a virtual unity and peace on an evangelic ground, and their emulation and zeal do far more than the State could do. The fact is, that this day, notwithstanding our heterogeneous people, and immense growth, we have more gospel, in proportion to our wants, than any except Scotland. And in England and Scotland almost all the enterprise, which has kept up with growth and evangelized new districts, has been either dissenting, or a sort of voluntaryism among Established Church people ; as in getting up the *Quoad Sacra* chapels in Scotland. Our success is the grand argument against State Churches.

But, second, and more conclusive. This union, on this theory, between Church and State, necessitates the surrender of the Church's spiritual independence. It can no longer preserve its allegiance to Jesus Christ perfect. The necessity of this allegiance we will not stop to prove. If the State employs a denomination to teach its subjects religion and morals, it is bound to have them well taught. The magistrate owes it to his constituents to see that the public money is well spent in teaching what shall be for the public good. And whether the doctrine taught is so or not, the magistrate must be the sovereign judge under God. In other words, the preachers of this State Church are, in their ministerial functions, State officials, and, of course, should be subordinate, as to those functions, to the State. Responsibility must bind back to the source whence the office comes. But now where is this minsters's allegiance to Christ ? Whenever it happens that the magistrate differs from his conscience, he can only retain his fidelity to his Master by dissolving his State connection.

This was completely verified in the disruption of the Scotch Establishment. The British government claimed jurisdiction over spiritual affairs, which they supported by their salaries. The faithful men of the Free Church found that the only way to retain their allegiance to Christ was to relinquish their connection with the State. When the secession Churches now exclaimed : " Here is an illustration of the incompatibility of spiritual independence and Church establishments," the Free Church men answered : " No. We admit that the jurisdiction of the State and its courts is just as to the temporal emoluments of a parish, but deny it as to the care of souls, or fitness for that care." But does not a suit about pay for value received necessarily bring into court the nature of the value received ? Must not the magistrate who decides on the *quid*, decide on the *pro quo* ? The right of the State is to present to the Parish, and not to the salary of the Parish, only. The State has the same right to see the parochial duties performed by whom she pleases, as the salary enjoyed by whom she pleases.

In the incipiency of the English Establishment, the grand

3. Christian State no Theocracy. appeal of its advocates was to the example of the Israelitish kingdom, where State and Church were united so intimately. Hence were drawn all the arguments, nearly, for the King's headship over the Church. Hence Calvin's idea of State and Church. Nor is the argument yet given up. But the answer is, that a theocratic State is no rule for a State not theocratic. When a State can be shown, where there is but one denomination to choose, and that immediately organized by God Himself just then; where there is an assurance of a succession of inspired prophets to keep this denomination on the right track; where the king who is to be at the head of this State Church is supernaturally nominated by God, and guided in his action by an oracle, then we will admit the application of the case.

In conclusion : The application for such an alliance does not always come from the side of the Church. Commonwealths have sometimes been fonder of leaning on the Church than the Church on Commonwealths. Do not suppose that this question will never again be practical.

INDEX.

J.

S.

W.

Z.